THE ROUGH GUIDE TO

Tanzania

Written, researched and updated by

Jens Finke

**ROUGH
GUIDES**

roughguides.com

Contents

Introduction to

Tanzania

Lying just south of the equator, Tanzania, East Africa's largest country, is an endlessly fascinating place to visit. Filling the brochures are several world-famous attractions: Zanzibar, with its idyllic palm-fringed Indian Ocean beaches, pristine coral reefs and historic Stone Town; the almost six-kilometre-high Mount Kilimanjaro, Africa's highest peak, which can be climbed in a week; and a glorious spread of wildlife sanctuaries that cover one third of the country, and include Ngorongoro Crater, and the dusty Serengeti plains – the classic Africa of elephants, antelopes, lions, leopards and cheetahs. Add to this Tanzania's rich ethnic diversity, rainforest hikes, and arguably the continent's best diving and snorkelling, and you have a holiday of a lifetime.

For all these headline grabbers, Tanzania's richest asset is its **people**. Welcoming, unassuming and relaxed, they'll treat you with uncommon warmth and courtesy. Unusually for Africa, Tanzanians have a strong and peaceful sense of *dual* identity: as proud of their nation as they are of their tribe. Although most ditched their traditional modes of life decades ago, a handful resist, the most famous of which are the **Maasai** – whose fiercely proud, red-robed spear-carrying warriors are a leitmotif for East Africa. Yet there are almost 130 other tribes, all with rich traditions, histories, customs, beliefs and music – some of which you'll be able to experience first-hand via Tanzania's award-winning cultural-tourism programmes.

Where to go

Most visitors make a beeline for the national parks and reserves of Northern Tanzania, which includes the **Serengeti**, whose annual migration of over 2.5 million wildebeest, zebra and antelope – trailed by lions and hyenas, and picked off by crocodiles at river crossings – is an awesome spectacle. Another highlight is **Ngorongoro Crater** next door, an enormous volcanic caldera providing a year-round haven for rhinos, and plentiful

ABOVE STONE TOWN, ZANZIBAR; **OPPOSITE** ELEPHANTS IN THE WILD

predators. Ngorongoro is also the starting point for a wild hike to Tanzania's only active volcano, **Ol Doinyo Lengai**, and on to **Lake Natron**, an immense salt lake appealing to flamingos and desert fanatics alike. Less well-known parks include **Tarangire**, fantastic for elephants, whose size is amply complemented by forests of gigantic baobabs; **Lake Manyara**, in a particularly spectacular section of the Rift Valley; and **Arusha National Park**, which contains the country's second-highest mountain, **Mount Meru**. The main base for Northern Circuit safaris is **Arusha**, which also has a clutch of **cultural tourism programmes**. East of here is snow-capped **Mount Kilimanjaro**, the week-long ascent of which is an exhausting but fulfilling challenge, while to the south are the ancient formations of the **Pare** and **Usambara mountains**, repositories of some of the world's most biologically diverse rainforests, especially at **Amani Nature Reserve** near the coast, which well deserves its nickname of "the Galápagos of Africa".

Much of Central Tanzania is dry and semi-arid woodland, at the centre of which – almost a desert – is **Dodoma**, Tanzania's administrative capital. It's mainly useful as a springboard for seeing the fabulous **prehistoric**

FACT FILE

• Tanzania was **created in 1964** through the union of Tanganyika and Zanzibar.

• Covering **945,203 square kilometres**, Tanzania is four times bigger than the UK, and twice the size of California. The population is 49 million.

• Tanzania is a **multi-party democracy** governed by a President. Zanzibar is semi-autonomous and has its own President and legislature.

• Tanzania is among the world's poorest countries, with an average salary of $60–100 a month, and a third of the population subsisting on under a **two dollars a day**, but its economy is growing fast, currently seven percent a year.

• Tanzania is among the four most **naturally diverse** nations on earth, and thirty percent of the country is protected natural habitat.

• With 128 officially recognized tribes, Tanzania is second only to Congo for **ethnic diversity** in Africa. Unlike Congo, Tanzania's ethnic melange is admirably peaceful, helped along by Kiswahili as a common **language**.

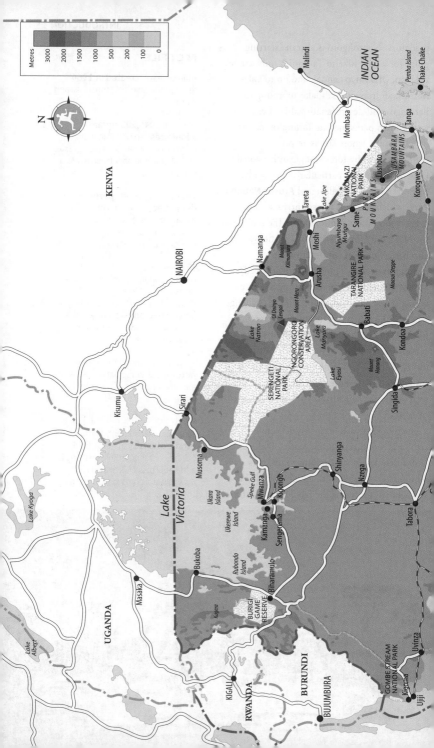

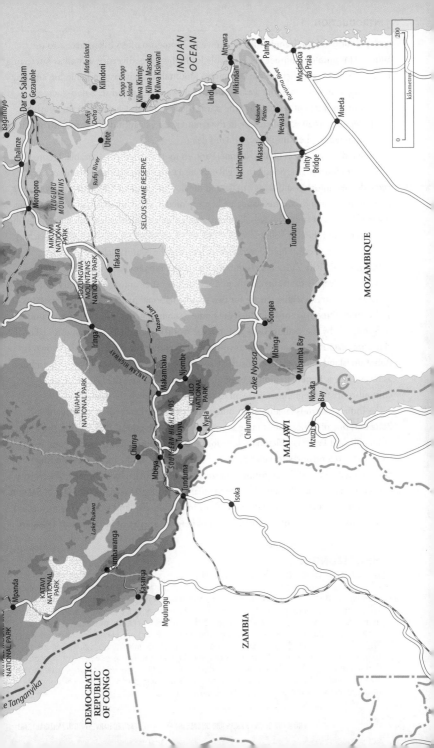

rock paintings of the Irangi Hills. The town of Morogoro offers hikers access to the **Uluguru Mountains**, another place notable for high species diversity, as well as interesting local culture. Even richer are the **Udzungwa Mountains**: their eastern flanks are amazing for seeing primates, while the western side is birdwatching paradise. Safari-goers are catered for by a trio of sanctuaries: the star is the vast **Selous Game Reserve**, housing more elephants than anywhere else in the country. It's a beautiful place, too, the northern sector watered by the Rufiji River's inland delta.

Also good for wildlife is **Ruaha National Park**, en route to southern Tanzania. Ignored by mainstream tourism, the Southern Highlands are a walkers' wonderland of volcanic crater lakes, dense rainforests and craggy peaks and the flower-bedecked **Kitulo Plateau**, with over fifty species of orchid. The highlands are best explored in the company of a guide from the town of Mbeya, or from Tukuyu – Tanzania's wettest place. Further south is **Lake Nyasa**, the southernmost of the Rift Valley lakes and home to hundreds of species of colourful cichlid fish; a port-hopping trip on the weekly ferry is one of the country's classic journeys.

The other big Rift Valley lake is the immense **Lake Tanganyika** – the world's longest and second-deepest freshwater body, and scene of another unforgettable ferry ride. The lakeshore is also the scenic setting for two remote national parks – **Mahale Mountains** and **Gombe Stream** – both of which are home to **chimpanzees**. Northwestern Tanzania is dominated by the shallow **Lake Victoria**, the world's second-largest freshwater lake. The views are magnificent, and the lake's southwestern corner contains the little-known **Rubondo Island National Park**, positively swarming with birds. Equally remote, and just as rewarding, is **Kagera Region** between Uganda, Rwanda and the lake, where a cultural-tourism programme gets you to places few tourists have seen.

The Indian Ocean is an altogether different experience. Especially recommended is **Zanzibar**, one of Africa's most famous and enticing destinations. It comprises the islands of Unguja and Pemba, which have languorous **beaches** and multicoloured coral reefs (perfect for **diving and snorkelling**), ancient ruins, and – in the form of **Stone Town** – a fascinating Arabian-style labyrinth of narrow alleyways packed with nineteenth-century mansions, palaces and bazaars. On the mainland, the biggest settlement is **Dar es Salaam**, the country's former capital and still its most important city, and worth hanging around in to sample its exuberant nightlife. North of here are a series of beach resorts (**Pangani** is

---

HEY, MZUNGU!

Mzungu (plural *wazungu*) is a word white travellers will hear all over East Africa – children, especially, take great delight in chanting it whenever you're around. Strictly speaking, a *mzungu* is a white European, although Afro-Europeans and Afro-Americans need not feel left out, being known as *mzungu mwafrikano* (Asian travellers will have to content themselves with *mchina*, and Indians *mhindi*). The term was first reported by nineteenth-century missionaries and explorers, who flattered themselves to think that it meant wondrous, clever or extraordinary. The real meaning of the word is perhaps more appropriate. Stemming from *zungua*, it means to go round, to turn, to wander, to travel, or just to be tiresome. However weary you may grow of the *mzungu* tag, you should at least be grateful that the Maasai word for Europeans didn't stick: inspired by the sight of the trouser-wearing invaders from the north, they christened the newcomers *iloridaa enjekat* – those who confine their farts.

Author picks

Fifteen years of bouncing around Tanzania's highways and byways has conjured up a lot of magical experiences for your author. Here are a few of his personal highlights.

Staying at home No, not your home, but with a Tanzanian family, most easily done as part of a cultural tourism programme. Part of the proceeds fund school libraries, clinics, or other community projects. See p.65

Lake Natron This author's African baptism was a solo bicycle ride across the Sahara aged 18, since when he's jumped at any excuse to go wandering around desolate wildernesses. Caustic Lake Natron is just such a place. See p.349

Neema Crafts It's not often your author gets all dewy-eyed about something, but this extraordinary self-help project for disabled people in Iringa is one of them, breaking down centuries-old cultural taboos. See p.419

Mango Garden It's not a garden, and it doesn't have mango trees, but it is one of Dar es Salaam's best loved venues for old-time Congolese-style jazz bands, attracting fans of all ages. See p.111

Snorkelling Don a mask and snorkel, strap on some flippers, take a deep breath and say hello to life under the waves on any of the coral reefs fringing the Tanzanian coastline. See p.68

Maasai singing The Maasai are among Africa's most conservative tribes. Tending their precious cattle are young morani warriors whose boastful shindigs feature competitive dances accompanied by guttural, buzzing throat singing. See p.529

Kilimanjaro Region It was on spotting an entire village jovially dancing above the roadside here, the women's colourful kangas a maelstrom of colour in the evening sun, that this author knew that Tanzania was going to be a love affair. See p.232

Mambo and Mtae The vertiginous viewpoints at Mambo and Mtae in the northwest Usambara Mountains are truly awe-inspiring, with spectacular vistas. p.269

> Our author recommendations don't end here. We've flagged up our favourite places – a perfectly sited hotel, an atmospheric café, a special restaurant – throughout the guide, highlighted with the ★ symbol.

FROM TOP MAASAI WOMEN; LAKE NATRON (P.349)

best), the coastal **Saadani National Park**, and several towns involved in the nineteenth-century **slave trade** – most infamously **Bagamoyo**. Tanzania's south coast is wilder: historical colour is provided by the ruins of the medieval island-state of **Kilwa**, in its heyday one of the wealthiest and most important cities in all of Africa. Offshore, the **Mafia archipelago** has its own fair share of historical ruins, plus stunning reefs.

When to go

Being tropical, Tanzania lacks the four seasons of temperate zones, and instead has two rainy and two dry seasons, mostly dictated by the western Indian Ocean's monsoon winds and currents. The **long rains** (*masika*) should fall from March to May (almost certainly in April and May), but the lighter **short rains** (*mvuli*) are impossible to predict with certainty: they should, depending on the location, fall for about a month sometime between October and December, but in southern Tanzania they tend to merge with the long rains, giving just one dry season, being May or June to November. **Coastal and lakeside regions** are hot and almost always humid, making the air feel even hotter than it really is. Temperatures drop by about 6°C (11°F) for every 1000m you climb, making for very pleasant conditions in **highland regions**, although it can get chilly in June and July.

In general, **dry-season travel** – particularly June to September – is best: it's not as humid, wildlife is easier to see, and even the roughest unsurfaced roads are drivable, which isn't always the case in the rains. Try to avoid the coast (including Zanzibar) during the rains, when the heavy humidity and insects can be intolerable. Also not the best time for Zanzibar, but with not much impact on the mainland, is the month of **Ramadan** (see p.79), when most restaurants are closed, and the daytime mood, in Stone Town particularly, isn't at its brightest.

AVERAGE MONTHLY TEMPERATURES AND RAINFALL

	Jan	Feb	Mar	Apr	May	Jun	Jul	Aug	Sep	Oct	Nov	Dec
ARUSHA (ALTITUDE 1400M)												
Max/min (°C)	28/14	29/14	28/15	25/16	23/15	22/13	22/12	23/13	25/12	27/14	27/15	27/14
Rainfall (mm)	70	75	140	225	85	15	10	6	10	25	125	100
DAR ES SALAAM (SEA LEVEL)												
Max/min (°C)	32/23	32/23	32/23	31/22	30/21	29/19	29/18	29/18	30/18	31/20	31/21	32/23
Rainfall (mm)	80	60	130	265	180	40	30	25	25	60	120	110
KIGOMA (ALTITUDE 781M)												
Max/min (°C)	28/19	28/19	28/19	28/20	29/19	29/17	29/16	30/17	30/19	29/20	28/19	28/19
Rainfall (mm)	75	75	60	100	20	0	0	10	20	70	120	155
MBEYA (ALTITUDE 1700M)												
Max/min (°C)	23/14	24/14	24/13	23/12	22/9	22/5	22/5	23/6	25/9	27/12	26/13	24/13
Rainfall (mm)	200	170	170	110	20	1	0	0	5	15	65	180
ZANZIBAR (SEA LEVEL)												
Max/min (°C)	32/22	32/24	32/25	30/25	28/23	28/23	27/22	28/22	28/22	30/22	31/23	31/24
Rainfall (mm)	75	60	150	350	280	55	45	40	50	90	170	145

15

things not to miss

It's not possible to see everything that Tanzania has to offer in one visit, and we don't suggest you try. What follows is a selective taste of the country's highlights – dramatic landscapes, idyllic beaches and awe-inspiring wildlife. All highlights have a page reference to take you straight into the guide, where you can find out more.

1

1 SERENGETI
Page 338

The legendary Serengeti is home to Africa's highest density of plains game and the backdrop to one of the greatest wildlife spectacles on earth, when over 2.5 million animals set off on their annual migration.

2 LAKE FERRIES
Pages 377, 387 & 442

Each of Tanzania's great lakes has ferry services, including two classic overnight journeys: down Lake Tanganyika aboard the venerable MV Liemba, or alongside the uplifting Livingstone Mountains on Lake Nyasa.

3 SEAFOOD, ZANZIBAR
Pages 467 & 489

Seafood features prominently in Swahili cooking, especially in Zanzibar, where fish, prawns, squid and lobster are served with subtle spices and blended with sauces.

4 CHIMPANZEES AT GOMBE STREAM AND MAHALE MOUNTAINS
Pages 393 & 398

Studies of wild chimp populations at Mahale Mountains and Gombe Stream national parks have shed light on many fascinating aspects of chimp life.

5 STONE TOWN
Page 452

Stone Town's labyrinthine network of narrow streets is magically atmospheric, with opulent nineteenth-century palaces and poignant reminders of the slave trade at every turn.

6 TARANGIRE NATIONAL PARK
Page 314

In the dry season, Tarangire is the best place in all of Africa for seeing elephants – though even these mighty beasts are dwarfed by the park's huge baobab trees, many of them over a thousand years old.

7 INDIAN OCEAN FLIGHTS
Page 48

Any flight from the mainland to Zanzibar or Mafia Island offers an unforgettable bird's-eye panorama of the coral reefs of the Indian Ocean.

8 HIKING IN THE USAMBARA AND UDZUNGWA MOUNTAINS
Pages 210 & 260

Ancient rainforests, rare plant and animal species, and eyeball-to-eyeball encounters with primates; hiking in the Usambara and Udzungwa mountains is one of Tanzania's foremost pleasures.

9 KONDOA-IRANGI ROCK PAINTINGS
Page 221

The Irangi Hills of central Tanzania are home to a remarkable complex of painted rock shelters, the oldest dating back some 18,000 years.

10 CULTURAL TOURISM
Page 65

Often tacked on to the end of a trip as an afterthought, Tanzania's cultural-tourism programmes end up being the highlight of many a holiday.

16

11 MOUNT KILIMANJARO
Page 244

Africa's highest mountain and the world's tallest free-standing volcano, Kilimanjaro draws hikers from all over the world – although only two thirds of them get to Uhuru Peak at the very top.

12 SCUBA DIVING
Page 67

The coral reefs off Tanzania's coast at Zanzibar and Mafia Island offer some of the world's finest scuba diving.

13 KILWA KISIWANI
Page 163

The spectacular ruins of the island city-state of Kilwa Kisiwani are testimony to the immense riches that were made first from gold, then from ivory and slaves.

14 BEACHES, ZANZIBAR
Page 450

There's no better place to relax after a hot and dusty safari than on Zanzibar's beaches.

15 NGORONGORO CONSERVATION AREA
Page 332

An enormous caldera of an extinct volcano provides the spectacular setting for Ngorongoro's abundant plains game and their predators – close-up encounters with lions, buffaloes and rhinos are virtually guaranteed.

11

12

13

Itineraries

The following itineraries cover Tanzania's wildlife parks, cultural tourism, and quality time on and off the Indian Ocean's limpid shores. The classic holiday is a "beach and bush" combo of wildlife safari followed by sea and sand, with a bit of cultural tourism thrown in too. Two weeks is enough to experience all three, but the more time you have, the merrier you'll be.

THE NORTHERN CIRCUIT

You've heard of the Serengeti, Kilimanjaro, and the Maasai… now get to see them for real.

❶ **Usambara and Pare Mountains** Distinct granite massifs whose isolation has created some of the world's most biodiverse forests. **See p.253 & 261**

❷ **Mkomazi National Park** Huddled around the back of the Pare Mountains: great scenery, tons of animals, and only a few Homo sapiens. **See p.259**

❸ **Kilimanjaro** The roof of Africa is a gigantic dormant volcano, whose 5892m peak can be scaled in a week, but be prepared: no pain, no gain! **See p.244**

❹ **Arusha and around** The Northern Safari Circuit's capital is also a major base for cultural tourism, some run by Maasai. **See p.276**

❺ **Tarangire** Need elephants? Look no further. Equally imposing are the baobab trees. **See p.314**

❻ **Babati & Kondoa** Tours of prehistoric rock art, story tellers and encounters with a fascinating mix of tribes, some with Ethiopian ancestry. **See p.219 & 222**

❼ **Lake Manyara** Flamingoes à gogo, night game drives, and lions up in trees. **See p.325**

❽ **Ngorongoro** The gigantic and spectacular volcanic crater at Ngorongoro's heart is home to almost every species you came to see. **See p.328**

❾ **Serengeti** The archetypal African savanna, home to the greatest, grandest, and goriest wildlife migration on earth. **See p.338**

THE WILD WEST

Western Tanzania is dominated by three enormous lakes: Victoria, Tanganyika and Nyasa, but even with improved roads, distances are long, so take your time.

❶ **Lake Victoria** The Nile's principal source offers several attractions, among them Ukerewe Island **(see p.367)**, the nearby Kagera Region **(see p.373)** and Rubondo Island **(see p.379)**

❷ **Lake Tanganyika** Come for Chimpanzee tracking at Gombe Stream and the Mahale Mountains, the spot where Stanley famously exclaimed, "Dr Livingstone, I presume?", and the centenarian MV Liemba ferry **(see p.384)**

❸ **Katavi National Park** Enticingly remote, its rivers and floodplains stuffed with hippos, crocs and buffalo. **See p.409**

❹ **The Southern Highlands** The volcanic scenery is the main attraction here: crater lakes, lavastone bridges, and the botanical wonderland of Kitulo Plateau. **See p.430**

❺ **Lake Nyasa** A dreamy ferry ride, some dreamy beaches, and even snorkelling, in search of colourful and always weird fishy evolutionary marvels called cichlids. **See p.441**

❻ **Ruaha National Park** A huge wilderness

ABOVE WILDEBEEST AT SUNRISE

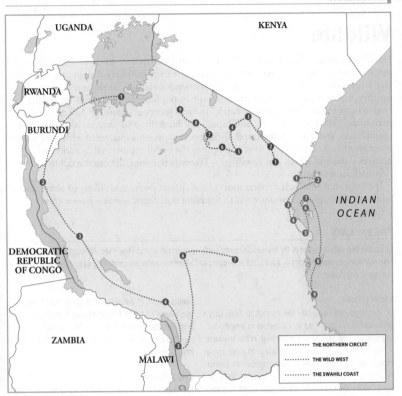

containing many species not found elsewhere. Great birding, too. **See p.425**

⓿ Udzungwa Mountains Nirvana for monkeys and hikers, and with a pristine forest canopy. **See p.210**

THE SWAHILI COAST

Blissful beaches, teeming underwater life, and a rich history and culture

❶ Tanga Elegant colonial architecture; bat-filled caves, hot water springs, medieval ruins, and a mysterious island. **See p.130**

❷ Pemba Island Some of the best scuba diving this side of the Indian Ocean, plus a primeval forest and ancient ruins. **See p.498**

❸ Saadani Beach and bush in one handy package. And a river, full of crocs, birds, hippos and monkeys. **See p.127**

❹ Bagamoyo Rub shoulders with the ghosts of nineteenth-century explorers, missionaries and slavers in what was East Africa's biggest slave mart. **See p.116**

❺ Dar es Salaam Africa's most genteel big city, with fine restaurants, exuberant nightlife and a good museum, plus beaches, snorkelling, boat trips and even cultural tourism. **See p.82**

❻ Stone Town An Arabian-style labyrinth stuffed with palaces and haunting reminders of the slave trade. The restaurants are an epicurean delight, and there are lots of excursions. **See p.452**

❼ Zanzibar's beaches Lilting palm trees, powdery sands, ineffable shades of turquoise… Nungwi and Kendwa appeal to hedonists **(see p.492 & p.497)**, Matemwe is more somnolent **(see p.492)** and the southeast is more village oriented **(see pp.480–489)**

❽ Mafia Archipelago Mafia has always been off the radar, but divers know it for superlative reefs. **See p.150**

❾ Kilwa A major player in the western Indian Ocean before the Portuguese. Their fortress, and the ruins of the city it subjugated, can still be seen. **See p.163**

Wildlife

"Hic Svnt Leones" ("Here be lions") read the medieval maps – to cover their gaps – and not without reason. Tanzania contains more lions than anywhere else on earth. But big lazy felines are just the start of it. Despite tremendous habitat losses over the last century, due to a twenty-fold increase in human population, Tanzania is one of the twelve most biodiverse nations on earth. The species counts don't lie: 320 types of mammals, 1200 kinds of birds, 1400 species of butterfly, 380 varieties of reptiles and amphibians, and over ten thousand distinct plant species, a quarter of which are found nowhere else. And with over thirty percent of the country protected as parks and reserves – most of which can be visited – Tanzania is among the finest wildlife destinations on earth.

The following field guide covers most of the species you're most likely to come across while on safari, plus a few more worth winkling out. *Safari njema* – have a great journey!

THE BIG CATS

Tanzania's **big cats** are some of the most exciting and easily recognizable animals you'll see. Although often portrayed as fearsome hunters, many species do a fair bit of scavenging and all are content to eat smaller fry when conditions dictate or the opportunity arises.

LION (SIMBA)

Of the large cats, lions are the easiest to find. Lazy, gregarious and large – up to 1.8 metres in length, not counting the tail, and up to a metre high at the shoulder – they rarely make much effort to hide or to move away, except on occasions when a large number of tourist vehicles intrude, or if elephants are passing through. They can be seen in nearly all the parks and reserves. Especially good photo opportunities are in the Serengeti, where they form particularly large prides; at Ngorongoro, Mikumi and Ruaha you may well also see them hunting. Normally, it's females which do the hunting (often co-operatively and at night). Surprisingly, their success rate is only about one in three attacks, so they tend to target young, old or sick animals. When they don't kill their own prey, they'll happily steal the kills of other predators.

LEOPARD (CHUI)

Intensely secretive, alert and wary, leopards are stealth hunters, and live all across the country except in the most treeless zones. Their unmistakable call, likened to a big saw being pulled back and forth, is unforgettable. Solitary and mainly active at night, you may see them by day resting up in trees. They also sometimes survive on the outskirts of towns and villages, carefully preying on different domestic animals to avoid a routine. They tolerate nearby human habitation and rarely kill people unless provoked. For the most part, leopards live off any small animals that come their way, including small mammals, primates and birds,

pouncing from an ambush and dragging the kill up into a tree where it may be consumed over several days, away from the attentions of scavengers. The spots on a leopard vary from individual to individual, but are always in the form of rosettes.

CHEETAH (DUMA)

The world's fastest mammal and the most elegant hunter, commonly seen in the Serengeti, is the cheetah. Often confused with leopards because of their spots, once you get to know them they're easy to identify: slender, more finely spotted, and with small heads, long legs and distinctive "tears" under their eyes. Cheetahs prefer open ground where they can hunt… at speeds clocked at up to seventy miles per hour (112km/h). As they hunt by day, cheetahs are easily spooked by humans: keep your distance and be quiet.

SERVAL (MONDO)

The part-spotted, part-striped serval is found in most of the parks, though its nocturnal nature means it's usually seen scavenging around lodges at night. Up to a metre long including the tail, it uses its large ears to locate and approach prey – game birds, bustards, rodents, hares, snakes or frogs – before pouncing.

CARACAL (SIMBA MANGU)

Also nocturnal but much rarer than the African civet is the aggressive, tuft-eared caracal, a kind of lynx that favours drier zones such as Mkomazi and Tarangire.

1 LEOPARD; **2** CHEETAH; **3** LION; **4** SERVAL; **5** CARACAL >

SMALLER CARNIVORES

HONEY BADGER (NYEGERE)

The unusual honey badger or ratel is related to the European badger and has a reputation for defending itself extremely fiercely. Primarily an omnivorous forager, it will tear open beehives (to which it is led by a small bird, the honey-guide), its thick, loose hide rendering it impervious to their stings.

MONGOOSE (NGUCHIRO)

Most species of mongoose, attractive animals with elongated bodies and long tails, are also tolerant of humans and, even when disturbed out in the bush, can usually be observed for some time before disappearing. Their snake-fighting reputation is greatly overplayed: in practice they are mostly social foragers, fanning out through the bush, rooting for anything edible – mostly invertebrates, eggs, lizards and frogs. The most common are the dwarf, banded and black-tipped (also called slender mongoose), this last often seen darting across tracks as you approach. Rarer are the marsh mongoose (frequent at Gombe) and white-tailed mongoose (also at Gombe, and Serengeti).

GENET (KANU)

The solitary and nocturnal genets are reminiscent of slender, elongated black-and-white cats, with spotted coats and ringed tails. They were once domesticated around the Mediterranean, but cats proved better mouse-hunters, and in fact genets are related to mongooses. They're frequently seen after dark around national park lodges.

SPOTTED HYENA (FISI MADOA)

History hasn't had a good word to say about the hyena, but it's a fascinating creature. The spotted hyena is the biggest carnivore after the lion. Although considered a scavenger *par excellence*, the spotted hyena – with its distinctive sloping back, limping gait and short, broad muzzle – is also a formidable hunter, most often found where antelopes and zebras are present. In fact, their success rate at hunting, in packs and at speeds up to 50km/h, is twice that of some specialized predators. Exceptionally efficient consumers, with strong teeth and jaws, spotted hyenas eat virtually every part of their prey in a matter of minutes, including bones and hide. Although they can be seen by day, they are most often active at night, when they issue their unnerving, whooping cries. Socially, hyenas form territorial groups of up to eighty animals. These so-called clans are dominated by females, which are larger than males and compete with each other for rank. Underscoring the dominance of females are their enlarged clitorises, which make them hard to distinguish from males. In view of all their attributes, the hyena is a key figure in mythology and folklore, usually as a limping, heartless bad guy, or as a symbol of duplicitous cunning.

STRIPED HYENA (FISI MIRABA)

In comparison with the spotted hyena, you're not very likely to see a striped hyena. A usually solitary animal, it's slighter and much rarer than its spotted relative, though occasionally glimpsed very early in the morning. You have reasonable odds of seeing them at Tarangire, and at Ruaha, which marks their southernmost extent.

AFRICAN HUNTING DOG (MBWA MWITU)

The unusual and rather magnificent African hunting dogs, also called wild dogs or "painted wolves" (after their Latin name, *Lycaon pictus*), have disappeared from much of their historical range in Africa. Their remaining strongholds are at Mikumi, Selous and Ruaha, and there are smaller and more endangered populations at Mkomazi and Tarangire. Canine distemper and rabies have played as big a role in their decline as human predation and habitat disruption. They are efficient pack hunters, running their prey in relays to exhaustion before tearing it apart, and live in groups of up to forty animals, with ranges of almost eight hundred square kilometres.

JACKAL (BWEHA)

The commonest members of the dog family in Tanzania are the jackals, one of the few mammalian species in which mating couples stay together for life. The black-backed or silver-backed jackal and the similar side-striped jackal can be seen just about anywhere, usually in pairs. While all three will scavenge, in the main their meals are hunted birds, small mammals and insects.

BAT-EARED FOX (MBWEHA MASIKIO)

Bat-eared foxes live in burrows in the plains, and while not uncommon, they are rarely seen as they're most active at dawn and dusk; you stand a better chance of sighting them the further south you go. Their large ears, which make them unmistakeable, serve two functions: to lose excess heat, and to hear their prey – not an easy task, as they're insectivorous. The other oddity is that, unlike other canids, it's the males who look after the little 'uns once they're done with their mothers' milk, usually at the age of 14 or 15 weeks.

1 HONEY BADGER; **2** MONGOOSE **3** GENET; **4** SPOTTED HYENA; **5** STRIPED HYENA; **6** AFRICAN HUNTING DOG; **7** JACKAL; **8** BAT-EARED FOX >

THE GIANTS

Tanzania has long been a land of giants, starting with the 150-million-year-old twelve-metre-tall fossilized Brachiosaurus found at Tendaguru in southern Tanzania. The giants these days are black rhino, hippo, elephant and buffalo.

AFRICAN ELEPHANT (TEMBO OR NDOVU)

Larger than their Asian cousins and rarely domesticated, African elephants are found in most Tanzanian parks and reserves. They're even bigger than you would imagine – you'll need little persuasion from those flapping, warning ears to back off if you're too close. By and large, they're surprisingly quiet, at least to our ears: researchers have discovered that vibrations from stamping elephant feet can be picked up 50km away, and are almost certainly a form of communication, complementing their equally remarkable language of very low-frequency rumbles. Like us, elephants lead complex, interdependent social lives, growing from helpless infancy, through self-conscious adolescence, to adulthood. Babies are born after a 22-month gestation, and suckle for two to three years. The basic family units are composed of a group of related females, tightly protecting their babies and young and led by a venerable matriarch. Old animals die in their seventies or eighties, when their last set of teeth wears out and they can no longer feed, but it's rare to see an elephant so old; most fall to ivory poachers, who – after a pause following the international ban on the ivory trade in 1989 – are once again massacring Africa's herds. Selous Game Reserve alone has lost eighty percent of its elephant population over the last six years, representing half of Tanzania's total. The best place to see them is in the better protected Tarangire National Park.

HIPPO (KIBOKO)

Hippos are among the most impressive of Africa's creatures – lugubrious pink monsters weighing up to three tons and measuring up to four metres from whiskered chin to stubby tail. Despite their ungainly appearance they're highly adaptable and found wherever rivers or freshwater lakes and pools are deep enough for them to submerge. They're supremely adapted to long periods in water, a necessity as they need to protect their hairless skin from dehydration; their pinkish colour is a natural secretion that acts as a sunblock. In the water, their clumsy feet become supple paddles, and they can remain completely submerged for six minutes, and for hours on end with just their nostrils, eyes and ears protruding. They communicate underwater with clicks, pulses, croaks and whines, and at the surface with grunts, snorts and aggressive displays of fearsome dentition – their jaws are capable of applying over a ton of pressure per inch. After dark, and sometimes on wet and overcast days, hippos leave the water to spend the whole night grazing, their stumpy legs carrying them up to 10km in one session. Beware: what looks like an idle yawn is actually a warning, and you should know that hippos are responsible for more human deaths in Africa that any animal other than the malarial mosquito. So, don't get yourself between a hippo and its pool or river, keep your distance when they're with calves, and be especially wary when canoeing. The best place to see them is Katavi National Park, whose rivers at times contain more hippos than water.

BLACK RHINOCEROS (KIFARU)

The rhino is one of the world's oldest mammalian species, having appeared some fifty to sixty million years ago, shortly after the demise of the dinosaurs. There are five species worldwide, the Tanzanian one being the hook-lipped or black rhinoceros. The name is a misnomer, having been given in counterpoint to the white rhino, where "white" was a mistranslation of the Afrikaans for "wide", referring to its lip: the white rhino's broad lip is suitable for grazing, whereas the black rhino's is adapted for browsing. Both species are actually grey. Their gestation lasts up to 18 months, and calves remain dependent on their mothers until the age of five, when the next one comes along. This slow reproductive cycle, coupled with the commercial value of their horns in Arabia and the Far East, makes them one of the most critically endangered big mammals, as a result of catastrophic poaching for their valuable horns. The location and size of most surviving populations in Tanzania is, understandably, a closely guarded secret, so the only rhinos that can readily be seen by tourists are at Ngorongoro Crater.

AFRICAN OR CAPE BUFFALO (NYATI OR MBOGO)

The big, bad boy of the cattle world, the fearsome African or Cape buffalo weighs close to a tonne and has an unpredictable temper. With its massive flattened horns and eight-hundred-kilogram bulk, it's a common and much-photographed animal, closely related to the domestic cow. They live in herds of several hundred, which can swell to over a thousand in times of drought. Though untroubled by close contact with humans or vehicles, they are one of Africa's most dangerous animals when alone, when their behaviour is unpredictable. Try to be understanding: their eyesight is bad, and as their calves make easy prey, adults will charge anything that looks or even smells vaguely like a threat. Their preferred habitat is swamp and marsh, though they have also adapted to life in highland forests. Buffaloes are often accompanied by oxpeckers and cattle egrets, which hitch rides on the backs of buffalo and other game. They have a symbiotic relationship with their hosts, feeding off parasites such as ticks and blood-sucking flies. The oxpeckers also have an alarm call that warns their hosts of danger like lurking predators.

1 AFRICAN ELEPHANT; 2 HIPPO; 3 BLACK RHINOCEROS; 4 AFRICAN BUFFALO >

PLAINS GAME

BURCHELL'S ZEBRA (PUNDA MILIA)

Zebras are closely related to horses and, together with wild asses, form the equid family. Burchell's zebra is the only Tanzanian species, and is found throughout the country. In Serengeti and Tarangire, zebras gather in migrating herds up to several hundred thousand strong, along with wildebeest and other grazers. Socially, they're organized into family groups of up to fifteen individuals led by a stallion. The stripes appear to be a defence mechanism for confusing predators: bunched up in a jostling herd, the confusion of stripes makes it very difficult to single out an individual to chase; the stripes are also said to confuse tsetse flies. Predators generally treat them with caution; a kick from the hind legs of an adult can be fatal.

MAASAI GIRAFFE (TWIGA)

Tanzania's national symbol, and the world's tallest mammal (up to five metres), is the giraffe, found wherever there are trees. Evolution stretched their necks to let them browse the upper branches of acacias without having to compete with other species; but surprisingly their necks are supported by seven vertebrae, just like ours. The species in Tanzania is the irregularly patterned Maasai giraffe. Both sexes have horns, but can be distinguished by the shorter height of the females, and by the tufts of hair over their horns. Daylight hours are spent browsing on the leaves of trees too high for other species; acacia and combretum are favourites. Non-territorial, they gather in loose leaderless herds, with bulls testing their strength while in bachelor herds. When a female comes into oestrus, which can happen at any time of year, the dominant male mates with her. She will give birth after a gestation of approximately fourteen months. Over half of all young fall prey to lions or hyenas, though.

WILDEBEEST (NYUMBU)

Also called gnus, wildebeest are fast food for predators. Large herds of white-bearded wildebeest or gnu are particularly associated with the Serengeti; half a million calves are born in the Serengeti at the start of the year, coinciding with the lush grazing afforded by the long rains, before they begin an epic migration to Kenya's Maasai Mara. There's security in numbers: the larger the herd, the better the chances of newborns surviving. The blue wildebeest (or brindled gnu) of central and southern Tanzania lack beards and are paler in colour. The strong shoulders and comparatively puny hindquarters of both species lend them an ungainly appearance, but the light rear end is useful for their wild and erratic bucking when attacked. Calves begin walking within minutes – a necessity when predators are always on the lookout.

GAZELLE (SWALA TOMI/SWALA GRANTI)

Gazelles are every predator's favourite repast, but catching them takes work. Their top speed isn't far off a cheetah's and, to confound chasers, herds will scatter when startled. They are extremely agile leapers, turning 180 degrees in little more than a stride. Thomson's gazelles ("Tommies") can survive extremely arid conditions – along with the larger Grant's gazelle, it's often seen at roadsides.

IMPALA (SWALA PALA)

Almost as common as gazelles is the impala, seen either in breeding herds of females, calves and one male, or in bachelor herds. They're seldom far from cover and, when panicked, the herd "explodes" in all directions, confusing predators. Only males have horns.

ELAND (MPOFU OR MBUNGU)

The huge, cow-like eland weighs six hundred to nine hundred kilograms and has a distinctive dewlap. Females are reddish, males are grey, and both have corkscrew-like horns.

FRINGE-EARED ORYX (CHOROA)

The imposing fringe-eared oryx is present in small numbers throughout the country but best seen at Tarangire – their long straight horns may explain the unicorn myth. They live in herds of up to forty animals, and are migratory.

GERENUK (SWALA TWIGA)

The elegant gerenuk is an unusual browsing gazelle able to nibble from bushes standing on its hind legs (its name is Somali for "giraffe-necked"); in Tanzania, its range is restricted to the semi-arid north, around Lake Natron, Longido and Mkomazi, with a few in Tarangire.

THE GREAT MIGRATION

The Serengeti owes its hallowed place in our imagination to the annual 800km migration of over 2.5 million animals, the largest mammalian migration on earth. A continuous, milling and unsettled mass, over half of which are wildebeest, the migration offers visitors one of nature's most staggering displays, one in which the predators play vital roles. River crossings are the biggest obstacles, namely the Grumeti in Serengeti, and the Mara along the Kenyan border. Both can be the scene of true carnage as panicked herds struggle across the raging flows in a writhing mass of bodies, while the weak, injured or careless are picked off by crocodiles and lions. The hazards of the migration are such that only one in three newborns survive.

---

1 BURCHELL'S ZEBRA; **2** MAASAI GIRAFFE; **3** WILDEBEEST; **4** GAZELLE; **5** IMPALA; **6** ELAND; **7** FRINGE-EARED ORYX; **8** GERENUK >

WOODLAND ANTELOPES

HARTEBEEST (KONGONI)

The rather ungainly, long-faced hartebeest family, with its distinctive S-shaped horns, has three representatives in Tanzania: the reddish Liechtenstein's hartebeest is the most common, especially in *miombo* and acacia woodland (Saadani is a good place to spot them); the paler Coke's hartebeest, with a longer, narrower head, is rarely found in the north.

KUDU (TANDALA)

The striped kudu are very localized, and their preference for dense bush makes them hard to see; your best chance is at dawn or dusk. There are two species, both browsers: greater kudu (tandala mkubwa), with eight to ten lateral stripes, are best seen at Selous, Mikumi and Saadani; the smaller lesser kudu (tandala mdogo), which has more stripes, can be seen in Mkomazi and Tarangire. Both can be seen at Ruaha. The spiralled horns of the male greater kudus can grow up to 180cm, and have long been used by local people for making musical instruments.

SABLE ANTELOPE (PALAHALA)

Related to the roan antelope are the sable antelope, which have handsome curved and swept-back horns. Males are black with white bellies and face markings; females are all brown. They thrive in *miombo* woodland, making them regular sightings at Mikumi, Selous, Ruaha, Mahale and Katavi. There's also a lighter and smaller subspecies at Saadani on the coast.

KIRK'S DIKDIK (DIGIDIGI OR DIKA)

Top marks for Bambi-like looks goes to Kirk's dikdik, a miniature antelope found all over the country. Measuring no more than 40cm in height (4kg in weight), they're most active in the morning and evening. Usually seen in monogamous pairs (the males are horned, the females are slightly larger), their territories are marked by piles of droppings and secretions deposited on grass stems. Their name mimics their whistling alarm call when fleeing.

SUNI (SUNI)

The forest-loving suni is even daintier than Kirk's dikdik, measuring up to 32cm in height, but rare and with a scattered distribution: you have very good odds on seeing them on Prison Island in Zanzibar, and a reasonable chance at Zanzibar's Jozani Forest, in the Udzungwa Mountains and on Rubondo Island where they've been introduced.

DUIKER

The duikers (Dutch for "diver", referring to their plunging into the bush) are larger – the common duiker (*Nysa*) is around 60cm high – though they appear smaller because of their shorter forelimbs. It's found throughout the country in many habitats, but most duikers are more choosy and prefer plenty of dense cover and thicket. Their isolation from other communities means that they've evolved into several subspecies which still confuse taxonomists: the most common family is that of the blue duiker (*Paa*), and related Abbot's duiker (*Mindi*), which ranges from Mount Rungwe in the south to the world's largest population in the forests of Kilimanjaro. Rarer subspecies include the tiny Ader's duiker in Zanzibar (*Paa nunga*); the Pemba blue duiker (*Chesi* or *Paa wa Pemba*), in Ngezi Forest; red duikers (*Funo* or *Kiduku*), found at Kilimanjaro and Udzungwa and grey duikers (*Paa*), in Gombe and Kilimanjaro.

KLIPSPRINGER (MBUZI MAWE)

The grey and shaggy klipspringer (Afrikaans for "stone jumper") has wonderfully adapted hooves for scaling near-vertical cliffs. Klipspringers can easily be seen in Ruaha, Tarangire and Manyara, and sometimes in Udzungwa. Like dikdiks, they're monogamous, and have just one offspring each year.

PRIMATES

Closest to us on the evolutionary ladder, primates are easy animals to relate to. They are found all over Tanzania; to spoil yourself, have a gander through the forests of the Udzungwa Mountains.

CHIMPANZEE (SOKWE)

Chimpanzees live right across Africa's tropical rainforest belt, from The Gambia to Lake Tanganyika in western Tanzania, where there are several communities at both Gombe Stream and Mahale Mountains national parks. Chimpanzees are our closest living relatives, sharing between 94 and 99 percent of our genes, and irresistibly fascinating. Like us, they're intelligent and complex (and sometimes temperamental) social creatures which feel and share emotions, and are able to adapt to different environments and foods, pass on knowledge learned from experience and make and use simple tools, like probes for fishing ants and termites from their nests. They also hunt in a human way, use plants medicinally, raid each other's communities and sometimes descend into states of war. Their communities consist of fifteen to eighty individuals, headed by "alpha males", whose dominance depends not so much on physical strength as an ability to form and keep strategic alliances with other males. Chimps are endangered, their global population having dropped from two million a century ago to under 300,000, a figure that's expected to halve over the next three chimpanzee generations. The main threats are ongoing habitat loss, subsistence hunting and the killing of mothers to capture infants for the pet trade, entertainment industry and – notoriously – biomedical research.

VERVET MONKEY (NGEDERE)

These small and slender fellows can be seen almost anywhere with a few trees, and have effortlessly adapted to humans, and their food. Away from us, they forage for fruits, leaves, insects and just about anything else small and tasty. Their main predators are leopards and large birds such as the crowned eagle, hence the vervet's constant and nervous skyward glances. Males are distinguished by a natty set of blue genitalia; the more vibrant the colour, the higher the individual's rank.

BABOON (NYANI)

Like chimpanzees, baboons are hierarchical, but you'll see them all over the place. Tanzania has two species: yellow baboons in the centre and south, and the larger olive baboons in the north. Baboons live in complex and highly territorial troops led by dominant males, in which social ties are reinforced by mutual grooming. Large males are quite capable of mauling humans, so treat them with respect – and never feed or tease baboons, or tempt them with food.

BLUE AND RED-TAILED MONKEYS (NYABU)

Almost as common as baboons in certain areas, notably on the coast and in lowland rainforests, are agile blue monkeys, whose predilection for agricultural crops makes them a pest (and has given rise to all sorts of unlikely tales, including their sure aim when hurling back rocks that were thrown at them by farmers). Blue monkeys are genetically almost identical to red-tailed monkeys (whose tails are actually orange), from whom they diverged only recently. Male blue monkeys who fail to gather their own "harem" can be accepted into a troop of red tails, and hybrids of the two species are known.

COLOBUS MONKEY (MBEGA)

The most arboreal of Tanzania's primates, and found all over the country, is the acrobatic black-and-white colobus monkey, which rarely descends to the ground, and can be distinguished by its lack of thumbs. Rare offshoots include various species of red colobus monkey, notably in the Udzungwa Mountains, in Zanzibar's Jozani Forest, in northwestern Selous, and at both Gombe and Mahale.

BUSHBABY (KOMBA)

Another common primate, which you're likely to see or at least hear if you stay in a game lodge, is the diminutive bushbaby (galago). There are two species: the cat-sized greater galago, and the kitten-sized lesser galago. Both are very cute, with sensitive, inquisitive fingers and large eyes and ears to aid their hunt for insects and small animals. Impressive, especially given its small size, is its jump: bushbabies store energy in their tendons on landing, which, on release, can catapult them upwards by two metres. They also have ear-splitting cries (hence the name), something that may well wake you with a jolt at night.

1 CHIMPANZEE; **2** VERVET MONKEY; **3** BABOON; **4** BLUE AND RED-TAILED MONKEYS; **5** COLOBUS MONKEY; **6** BLACK AND WHITE COLOBUS MONKEY; **7** BUSHBABY >

OTHER MAMMALS

AARDVARK (MHANGA)

That much-loved dictionary leader, the aardvark, is one of Africa's strangest mammals, a solitary termite-eater weighing up to 70kg. Its name, Afrikaans for "earth pig", is an apt description, as it holes up during the day in large burrows, excavated with remarkable speed and energy, and emerges at night to visit termite mounds within a radius of 5km. It's most likely to be common in bush country well scattered with tall termite spires.

GROUND PANGOLIN (KAKAKUONA)

Ground pangolins are equally unusual – nocturnal, scale-covered mammals, resembling armadillos and feeding on ants and termites. Under attack, they roll into a ball.

WARTHOG (KURO)

The commonest wild pig in Tanzania is the comical warthog. Quick of movement and nervous, warthogs are notoriously hard to photograph as they're generally on the run through the bush, often with the young in single file, tails erect like antennae, though you can catch them browsing in a kneeling position. They shelter in holes in the ground, usually old aardvark burrows, and live in family groups generally consisting of a mother and her litter of two to four piglets, or occasionally two or three females and their young. Boars join the group only to mate, and are distinguishable from sows by their longer tusks, and the warts below their eyes, which are thought to be defensive pads to protect their heads during often violent fights.

BATS (POPO)

Tanzania's many bats will usually be a mere flicker over a waterhole at twilight, or sometimes a flash across headlights. The only bats you can normally observe in any decent way are fruit bats hanging from their roosting sites by day; there are visitable roosts on Chole Island in the Mafia Archipelago, at Misali and Makoongwe islands off Pemba Island and in Pemba Island's Ngezi Forest (the endemic Pemba flying fox or Mega Bat). For more "traditional" bat viewing, visit the incredible colonies of the Amboni Caves near Tanga.

THE ELEPHANTS' LITTLE SIBLINGS...

The science of genetics has uncovered many secrets over its short lifetime, perhaps none more bizarre than the discovery of two most unlikely but real cousins of the elephant.

ELEPHANT SHREW (SENGI)

With the exception of the giant sengi (see p.211), unknown until a decade ago, the average elephant shrew is no bigger than a small squirrel, and, with the help of amply proportioned hind feet, prefers leaping to scurrying. The name refers to their trunk-like snout, but weirdest of all is the discovery that, far from being shrews, they are in fact much more closely related to elephants. They're extremely adaptable, as their habitat ranges from the semi-desert around Lake Natron to the lush forests of Amani, Gombe, Jozani and Udzungwa.

HYRAXES (PIMBI)

Small, furry, bucktoothed and cute: you're certain to see hyraxes sunning themselves around the lodges of the Serengeti. They look like rodents, but are in fact ungulates (hoofed mammals), and form a classificatory level entirely their own. Incredibly, their closest living relatives are elephants. Present-day hyraxes are pygmies compared with their prehistoric ancestors, some of which were as big as bears. Rock hyraxes live in busy, vocal colonies of twenty or thirty females and young, plus a male. Away from the lodges, they're timid in the extreme – not surprising in view of the wide range of predators targeting them.

REPTILES AND AMPHIBIANS

NILE CROCODILE (MAMBA)

The Nile crocodile can reach six metres or more in length. You'll see them, log-like, on the sandy shores of most of Tanzania's rivers and lakes. Although they mostly live off fish, they are also dangerous opportunists, seizing the unwary with disconcerting speed. Once caught, either by the mouth or after being tossed into the water by a flick of their powerful tails, the victim is spun underwater to drown it, before massive jaws make short work of the carcass.

SNAKES (NYOKA)

Tanzania has many species of snakes, some of them quite common, but your chances of seeing a wild specimen are remote. In Tanzania, as all over Africa, snakes are both revered and reviled, and while they frequently have symbolic significance for local people that is quite often forgotten in the rush to hack them to bits when found. All in all, snakes have a very hard time surviving in Tanzania: their turnover is high but their speed of exit from the scene when humans show up is remarkable. If you want to see them, wear boots and walk softly. If you want to avoid them completely, tread firmly and they'll flee on detecting your vibrations. The exception is the puff adder, which relies on camouflage to get within striking distance of prey, but will only bite when threatened (or stood on); around ten percent of its bites are fatal. Other common poisonous species include black mambas (fast, agile and arboreal; properly called black-mouthed mambas), the boomslang, the spitting cobra and blotched forest cobra, night adder, bush snake and bush viper. Common non-poisonous snakes include the constricting African python (a favoured partner of the Sukuma tribe's dance societies; see p.362), the egg-eating snake and the sand boa.

TORTOISES (KOBE)

Tortoises are quite frequently encountered on park roads in the morning or late afternoon. Some, like the leopard tortoise, can be quite large, up to 50cm in length, while the hinged tortoise (which not only retreats inside its shell but shuts the door, too) is much smaller – up to 30cm. In rocky areas, look out for the unusual pancake tortoise, a flexible-shelled species that can put on quite a turn of speed but, when cornered in its fissure in the rocks, will inflate to wedge itself inextricably to avoid capture.

LIZARDS (MJUSI)

Lizards are common everywhere, harmless, often colourful and always amusing to watch. The commonest are rock agamas (*mjusi kafiri*), the males often seen in courting "plumage", with brilliant orange heads and blue bodies, ducking and bobbing at each other. They live in loose colonies often near human habitation; one hotel may have hundreds, its neighbours none. The biggest lizards, Nile monitors (*kenge*), grow to nearly two metres in length and are often seen near water. From a distance, as they race off, they look like speeding baby crocodiles. A large, docile lizard you may come across is the plated lizard (*guruguru*), an intelligent, mild-mannered reptile often found around coastal hotels, looking for scraps from the kitchen or pool terrace. At night on the coast, the translucent little aliens on the ceiling are geckos (*mjusi*), catching moths and other insects. Their gravity-defying agility is due to countless microscopic hairs on their padded toes, whose adhesiveness functions at an atomic level. By day, their minuscule relatives the day geckos (velvet grey and yellow), patrol coastal walls. In the highlands you may come across prehistoric-looking three-horned Jackson's chameleons creeping through the foliage, and there are several other species, most also in the highlands.

FROGS AND TOADS (CHURA)

Night is usually the best time for spotting amphibians, though unless you make an effort to track down the perpetrators of the frog chorus down by the lodge water pump, you'll probably only come across the odd toad. There are, however, dozens of species of frogs and tree frogs, including the diminutive and unique Kihansi spray toad, whose discovery in the spray at the bottom of a waterfall in 1996 scuppered the profitability of a hydroelectric dam in the Southern Highlands, which now has to divert part of its flow to keep the toads moist.

BIRDS

Tanzania's wide variety of habitats and altitudinal ranges gives it one of Africa's highest counts of **bird species**, with around 1200 recorded so far, representing 75 families. Nearly eighty percent are thought to breed in the country. Of the **migratory species**, most arrive towards the end of the year, coinciding with the northern hemisphere's winter. Many are familiar British summer visitors, such as swallows, nightingales and whitethroats, which have to negotiate or skirt the inhospitable Sahara. The scale of the migration is mind-boggling: around six *billion* birds annually. The following section details some of the more frequently seen and easily identified species.

OSTRICH (MBUNI)

Several species of large, terrestrial (or partly terrestrial) birds are regularly seen on safari. The flightless ostrich is found in dry, open plains and semi-desert in the far north, namely Tarangire, Ngorongoro, Serengeti, and around Lake Natron. At up to 2.5m high, it's the world's biggest bird, and one of the fastest runners when needs be. The females are neutral in colour, but courting males wow the dames with their hairless pink necks and thighs. Contrary to popular belief, they don't bury their heads in the sand, but do hide them in their plumage while resting.

SECRETARY BIRD (KARANI TAMBA)

The large, long-tailed secretary bird is easily identified, and gets its name from its head quills, which resemble pens propped behind ears, although its "bestockinged" legs and sashaying gait are suggestive, too. It's often seen in dry, open bush and wooded country, usually in pairs, and feeds on beetles, grasshoppers, reptiles and rodents.

KORI BUSTARD (TANDAWALA MKUBWA)

Also commonly seen is the world's heaviest flying bird, albeit one that prefers spending its time on the ground: the greyish-brown Kori bustard, whose males average 12kg (though the heaviest top 20kg).

GUINEAFOWL (KANGA)

These gregarious ground birds, similar in size and apparent intelligence to chickens, have brightly coloured heads and a luxurious covering of royal blue feathers, often spotted white – which explains how their Kiswahili name became attached to the traditional cotton wraps used by women (the first ones imported, several hundred years ago, evidently had a similar polka-dot style). They're often seen in flocks on drivable tracks inside national parks and, rather than scatter as you advance, will run down the track ahead of you; only in extremis will they take flight.

FLAMINGO (HEROE)

Many visitors are astounded by their first sight of flamingos – a sea of pink on a soda-encrusted Rift Valley lake (Natron and Manyara are the best places). There are two species in Tanzania: the greater flamingo, and the much more common lesser flamingo, which can be seen in flocks of tens and sometimes hundreds of thousands. The lesser flamingo is smaller, pinker and with a darker bill than its greater relative. The Rift Valley population – which only nests at Lake Natron – numbers several million, and is one of only three groups in Africa. Flocks can leave or arrive at an area in a very short period of time, the movements depending on all sorts of factors including the water's alkalinity and the presence of algal blooms, so sighting big flocks is impossible to predict. Lesser flamingos feed by filtering suspended aquatic food, mainly blue-green diatom algae that occur in huge concentrations on the shallow soda lakes of the Rift Valley. Greater flamingos may occur in their thousands but are considerably fewer in number than the lesser, and are bottom feeders, filtering small invertebrates as well as algae. Although greaters tend to be less nomadic than their relatives, they are more likely to move away from the Rift Valley lakes to smaller water bodies and even the coast.

IBIS (KWARARA)

The most widely distributed ibis species (stork-like birds with down-curved bills) is the sacred ibis, which occurs near water and human settlements. It has a white body with a black head and neck, and black tips to the wings. Also frequently encountered is the hadada ibis, a bird of wooded streams, cultivated areas and parks in northern Tanzania. It's brown with a green-bronze sheen to the wings, and calls noisily in flight.

HERON (KOIKOI)

The commonest large heron is the black-headed species, which can sometimes be found far from water. Mainly grey with a black head and legs, the black heron can be seen "umbrella-fishing" along coastal creeks and marsh shores: it cloaks its head with its wings while fishing, which is thought to cut down surface reflection from the water, allowing the bird to see its prey more easily.

HAMERKOP (MSINGWE)

The hamerkop or hammer-headed stork is a brown, heron-like bird with a sturdy bill and mane of brown feathers, which gives it a top-heavy, slightly prehistoric appearance in flight, like a miniature pterodactyl. Hamerkops are widespread near water and build large, conspicuous nests that are often taken over by other animals, including owls, geese, ducks, monitor lizards or snakes.

1 OSTRICH; **2** SECRETARY BIRD; **3** KORI BUSTARD; **4** GUINEAFOWL; **5** IBIS; **6** FLAMINGO; **7** HERON; **8** HAMERKOP >

MARABOU STORK (KORONGO)

The marabou stork is easy to spot – large and exceptionally ugly, up to 1.2m in height and with a bald head, long pointed funnel-like beak and dangling, pink throat pouch. The marabou flies with its head and neck retracted (unlike other storks) and is often seen in dry areas, including towns, where it feeds on small animals, carrion and refuse. If you're lucky, you'll see them roosting in trees.

AFRICAN FISH EAGLE (FURUKOMBE)

The most elegant of Tanzania's eagles is the black-and-white African fish eagle, which, true to its name, is a formidable catcher of fish. It's usually seen perched in trees overlooking water, waiting. Once it spies a fish close to the surface, it swoops, and in a single swipe grabs the prey in its claws.

VULTURE (TUMBUSI)

Six species of vulture range over the plains and bushlands of Tanzania and are often seen soaring in search of a carcass. All the species can occur together, and birds may travel vast distances to feed. The main differences are in feeding behaviour: the lappet-faced vulture, for example, pulls open carcasses; the African white-backed feeds mainly on internal organs; and the hooded vulture picks the bones.

GO-AWAY BIRDS AND TURACOS (GOWEE)

These distinctive, related families are found only in Africa. Medium-sized and with long tails, most go-away birds and turacos have short rounded wings. They are not excellent fliers, but are very agile in their movements along branches and through vegetation. Many species are colourful and display a crest. Turacos are generally green or violet in colour, and all are confined to thickly wooded and forest areas. Open-country species, such as the widely distributed and common white-bellied go-away bird (go-aways are named after their call), are white or grey in colour.

HORNBILL (FILIMBI)

Named for their long, heavy bills, surmounted by a casque or bony helmet, hornbills generally have black and white plumage. Their flight consists of a series of alternate flaps and glides. When in flight, hornbills may be heard before they are seen, the beaten wings making a "whooshing" noise as air rushes through the flight feathers. Many species have bare areas of skin on the face and throat and

around the eyes, with the bill and the casque often brightly coloured, their colours changing with the age of the bird. Most hornbills are omnivorous, but tend largely to eat fruit. Several species are common open-country birds, including the silvery-cheeked and red-billed hornbills. Hornbills have interesting breeding habits: the male generally incarcerates the female in a hollow tree, leaving a hole through which he feeds her while she incubates the eggs and rears the young. The unusual ground hornbill lives in open country and is the largest hornbill by far, black with red face and wattles, bearing a distinct resemblance to a turkey. They nest among rocks or in tree stumps, and the Maasai say their calls resemble humans talking.

KINGFISHER (MDIRIA OR MTILILI)

There are around a dozen species of colourful kingfishers found in Tanzania, ranging in size from the tiny African pygmy kingfisher, which feeds on insects and is generally found near water, to the giant kingfisher, a shy fish-eating species of wooded streams in the west of the country. Several species eat insects rather than fish and they can often be seen perched high in trees or on open posts in the bush where they wait to pounce on passing prey. One of the more common is the malachite kingfisher, which stays true to its roots by catching small fish: it swallows its prey head first after killing it by whacking it against branches.

SUPERB STARLING (KWENZI)

The iridescent blue, green and orange superb starling is found everywhere from remote national parks to gardens in Arusha, so long as there are acacia nearby, and is often seen feeding on the ground. It's quite tame, so easy enough to photograph up close.

WEAVER (KWERA)

Weavers are among Tanzania's most widespread birds. Males tend to be easy to spot, as most have bright yellow or yellow-and-black plumage, but females are sparrow-like. The various species are distinguished by range, preferred habitat, and by the shape and size of their extraordinary woven nests, which, as weavers live in colonies, can completely change the appearance of a tree. Rare species popular with birders include the unique Kilombero weaver in central Tanzania's Kilombero floodplain; the Usambara weaver in the Usambara Mountains; and the rufous-tailed weaver, for which the best odds are in Tarangire.

LIFE BENEATH THE WAVES

Tanzania's beaches are spectacular, but there's more to the coast than blissful sands: a short dip or boat trip away are some of Africa's richest coral reefs, explorable with a mask and snorkel, or scuba gear. At the heart of the ecosystems are microscopic animals called polyps, whose exoskeletons grow at the pace of fingernails, to eventually form reefs: perfect habitats for a bewildering array of marine life.

MORAY EEL (MKUNGA CHUI)
Even though the giant moray measures 1.5m, the most you're likely to see of it is its fearsome head gawping out from a crevice in the coral. They're ambush predators, snatching anything that swims within striking distance – including overly inquisitive fingers. To swallow prey, morays have a second set of mobile jaws that drag the fish into their guts.

NUDIBRANCH (KOJOJO)
Sea slugs to you and me, nudibranchs are the (toxic) Christmas tree baubles of the deep: vividly coloured, bizarrely patterned and weirdly shaped. In fact, everything about them is weird, including sex – nudibranchs are hermaphrodites. A favourite with scuba divers, the Spanish dancer is named after its fetching red "skirt".

SEA TURTLE (KASA)
Tanzania is home to five of the world's seven species of sea turtle (green, hawksbill, loggerhead, leatherback and olive ridley). Green turtles are believed to migrate from Australia just to lay eggs on Africa's shores. The exercise serves them well: they tend to live longer than humans, and turtles have changed little over the last 110 million years. All sea turtle species are endangered, but at least in Tanzania, many of their nesting beaches are protected. On Mafia Island and Saadani National Park, you could even coincide with a hatch-out.

DUGONG OR MANATEE (NGUVA)
On the brink of extinction in East Africa, where they used to be hunted for their meat and are still caught accidentally in shark nets, the dugong is a seal-like mammal related to dolphins and whales, and an unlikely inspiration for sailors' tales of mermaids. The legends may have had something to do with the dugong's habit of floating around on its back, letting a pair of bobbing, ample breasts work their magic on the mariners of yore. Their favoured habitat is seagrass beds, which in Tanzania corresponds to the section of coastline between the mainland and the Mafia Archipelago.

OCTOPUS (PWEZA)
The master of the art of camouflage, the octopus cannot only instantly change its colour to match its surroundings, but its texture, too, making it difficult to spot unless on the move. Octopuses are also clever, capable not only of predicting the result of World Cup fixtures, but of unscrewing the tops of discarded jars in order to use them as homes.

DOLPHIN (POMBOO)
Tanzania's most common marine mammal is the gregarious dolphin, especially the Indo-Pacific bottlenose and Indo-Pacific humpback. Dolphins communicate using sound, including squeaks, whistles and body language noises such as slapping their tails on the water. They're most easily seen off southern Unguja, Zanzibar.

MANTA RAY (KARWE)
With a "wing" span topping seven metres, a gliding manta ray (from the Portuguese for "cloak") is an awe-inspiring sight, and may be seen by scuba divers off Pemba Island. Mantas rid themselves of parasites by scrubbing themselves against coral reefs, and are often accompanied by remora – hitch-hiking fish that hold on using sucker-shaped fins.

1 MORAY EEL; **2** NUDIBRANCH; **3** SEA TURTLE; **4** DUGONG OR MANATEE; **5** DOLPHIN; **6** OCTOPUS; **7** MANTA RAY >

MAASAI, MTO WA MBU

Basics

Getting there

Flying is the only practical way to reach Tanzania from outside East Africa, with direct or one-stop flights from Europe, and flights with one or more stops from elsewhere. Tanzania's international airports are Dar es Salaam (DAR), Kilimanjaro (JRO), which is between Moshi and Arusha and well placed for the main national parks, and Zanzibar (ZNZ). Flights to Zanzibar can be very expensive, so consider flying to Dar es Salaam and changing there for a local flight, or taking a ferry. For the best airfares, buy well in advance, even six months before travel, and shop around, as the cost of the same seat can vary greatly. Departure taxes are in included the price of international flights.

Flights from the UK and Ireland

There are no direct flights to Tanzania **from the British Isles**. The cheapest one-stop returns in high season are currently with Turkish Airlines from Gatwick or Dublin via Istanbul (13–14hr: Dar £350/€490, Kilimanjaro £550/€790), though they arrive in Tanzania after midnight. The Kenya Airways (plus codeshare) flights are better timed, arriving in the morning (Dar £620/€850, 11–14hr; Kilimanjaro £750/€1100, 13–14hr; Zanzibar £730/$1100, 12–14hr). Other good options from London, all travelling via their home hubs and arriving in the afternoon, are Emirates (Dar £480, 16hr), Ethiopian Airlines (Dar £580, 15hr; Kilimanjaro £650, 14hr 30min) and Oman Air (Zanzibar £620, 16hr).

Flights from the US and Canada

Consistently the best option **from North America** is on KLM via Amsterdam, combining short flight times with prices only little more expensive than longer multi-stop routings. The main points of departure are JFK (Dar $1350, 19hr; Kilimanjaro

$1800, 21hr) and Toronto (Dar Can$2100, 21hr; Kilimanjaro Can$2300, 20hr). From Montreal, Kenya Airways' flight via Nairobi is a good bet (Dar Can$2000, 18hr; Kilimanjaro Can$2000, 20hr). All prices quoted are high season returns.

Flights from Australia, New Zealand and South Africa

Flying from the Antipodes involves at least one stop in Asia or South Africa. Currently, the best option **from Australia** is the South African Airways flight from Sydney to Dar es Salaam (Aus$1800, 27hr 30min); for Kilimanjaro, online booking sites offer a plethora of two-stop 30-hour-plus routings from Aus$2300. The cheapest flight **from New Zealand** (Auckland) to Dar is on Emirates via Dubai (NZ$2400, 31hr), though a quicker, and not unreasonably priced, option is the Air New Zealand/Qatar Airways codeshare (Dar NZ$3000, 27hr; Kilimanjaro NZ$3000, 30hr). **From South Africa**, budget airline Fastjet can be as cheap as R3000 for a Johannesburg–Dar return, arriving 4am (sunrise is around 6am); of the more traditional carriers, South African Airways is best, but make sure the flight arrives in the afternoon (R5500, 3hr 30min). For Kilimanjaro, Kenya Airways via Nairobi is cheapest (R6500), and has a couple of routings: 6hr is the fastest, but lands at night; the 8hr one arrives in the morning. Flights from Cape Town cost an additional K2000–3000.

RTW tickets

Tanzania seldom features as an option on **Round the World (RTW) tickets**, but Kenya's capital, Nairobi, does, and it's just a few hours away by bus. Prices range from £1500 to £2500/$2500 to $4000. The classic African RTW option is to arrive in Nairobi and make your way overland to Johannesburg or Cape Town for the onward flight. Recommended **RTW specialists** include UK-based Ⓦ roundtheworldflights.com, and US-based Ⓦ airtreks.com. The major airline alliances also offer RTW tickets (Ⓦ rtw.oneworld.com and Ⓦ staralliance.com/en/fares/round-the-world-fare); the latter also offers an "Africa

---

A BETTER KIND OF TRAVEL

At Rough Guides we are passionately committed to travel. We believe it helps us understand the world we live in and the people we share it with – and of course tourism is vital to many developing economies. But the scale of modern tourism has also damaged some places irreparably, and climate change is accelerated by most forms of transport, especially flying. All Rough Guides' flights are carbon-offset, and every year we donate money to a variety of environmental charities.

Airpass" that includes Dar es Salaam (W staralliance .com/en/fares/airpasses/africa-airpass).

AIRLINES

Air New Zealand W airnewzealand.com.
Emirates W emirates.com.
Ethiopian Airlines W ethiopianairlines.com.
Fastjet W fastjet.com.
Kenya Airways W kenya-airways.com.
KLM W klm.com.
Oman Air W omanair.com.
Qatar Airways W qatarairways.com.
Turkish Airlines W turkishairlines.com.
South African Airways W flysaa.com.

TRAVEL AGENTS

North South Travel UK ☎ 01245 608 291, W northsouthtravel .co.uk. Friendly, competitive travel agency, offering discounted fares worldwide. Profits are used to support projects in the developing world, especially the promotion of sustainable tourism.

STA Travel UK ☎ 0333 321 0099, US ☎ 1800 781 4040, Australia ☎ 134 782, New Zealand ☎ 0800 474 400, South Africa ☎ 0861 781 781; W statravel.com. Worldwide specialists in independent travel; also student IDs, travel insurance, car rental, rail passes, and more. Good discounts for students and under-26s.

Trailfinders UK ☎ 020 7368 1200, Ireland ☎ 021 464 8800; W trailfinders.com. One of the best-informed and most efficient agents for independent travellers, offering student and under-26 discounts.

Travel CUTS Canada ☎ 1800 667 2887, US ☎ 1800 592 2887, W travelcuts.com. Canadian youth and student travel firm.

USIT Ireland ☎ 01 602 1906, Australia ☎ 1800 092 499; W usit.ie. Ireland's main student and youth travel specialist.

Overland travel

The only useful **buses into Tanzania** are from Kenya (Nairobi to Mwanza, Arusha or Dar es Salaam; Mombasa to Tanga or Dar es Salaam) and Uganda (Kampala to Bukoba). There are also cross-border buses from Malawi and Zambia, but border formalities for an entire bus load can take up to 24 hours, so for those two countries, and Tanzania's other neighbours, you're better off catching a vehicle to the border, walking through immigration, then catching another vehicle on the other side. There's a weekly **ferry** from Malawi's Nkhata Bay to Mbamba Bay, and a fortnightly one from Mpulungu in Zambia to Kigoma (in theory, though the latter is often broken down). There's no cross-border **train**, but there are connecting services either side of the Zambian border if you're on the TAZARA Railway.

Overlanding from South Africa is perfectly feasible, whether by road (sealed all the way), or by train via Zambia. Travelling overland from Egypt, however, is only feasible via northern Sudan and Ethiopia and is not for the faint hearted, as several stretches are known for banditry.

Overland truck tours

The young at heart can consider an **overland truck tour** in a converted lorry, taking three to twelve weeks from Cape Town to Tanzania (and on to Kenya), or vice versa. Given the wealth of things to see and do along the way, they can be rather hurried affairs, and are often dominated by party animals who could be on Mars for all they cared, but the trips do provide an easy way of getting a feel for a large swathe of Africa. The classic trans-Africa trip used to go from the UK to Cape Town via Morocco or Egypt, but conflict in the Sahara and Sudan (the latter currently at an ebb) means that most tours only cover Kenya to South Africa, usually via Tanzania. Costs vary depending on how much time you spend inside the national parks: expect to pay £50–100 per day, including your contribution to the "kitty".

TRUCK TOUR OPERATORS

Absolute Africa UK ☎ 020 8742 0226, W absoluteafrica.com.
African Trails UK ☎ 01524 419909, W africantrails.co.uk.
Drifters South Africa ☎ 011 888 1160, W drifters.co.za.
Exodus UK ☎ 0845 805 0358, Ireland ☎ 01 804 7153, US ☎ 1 844 227 9087, Canada ☎ 1 800 267 3347, Australia ☎ 1300 131 564, New Zealand ☎ 0800 238 368, South Africa ☎ 011 408 8000; W exodus.co.uk.

Package tours

As far as Tanzania is concerned, the typical **package tour** is a "beach and bush" combination of wildlife safari followed by Zanzibar or, less commonly, the Mafia Archipelago. While there are hundreds of overseas operators offering such packages, very few run the trips themselves (and then only through subsidiaries). The rest piece together their offerings using (hopefully) carefully selected hotels, lodges and safari companies. Of course, you could do the same thing using the information in this book, but you won't get the often hefty discounts on accommodation available to agents, some of which may be passed on to you. It's also much easier to deal with just one company and pay just one overall price.

While many companies offer **pre-packaged tours** with set departure dates, all claim to specialize in **tailor-made** trips. What this means is that you either take a sample itinerary and send it back marked with your preferences, or – better, but time-consuming – work out exactly what you want beforehand in terms of so many nights here or there and in what kind of accommodation, then fire it off to several operators and see what comes back. Incidentally, tours offered by UK operators can also be booked by people outside the UK, and vice versa, so don't limit yourself to companies in your own country.

The following are the cream of the more reasonably priced overseas **specialist tour operators** for Tanzania. Most demand full payment up to three months before departure. Offering the same services are **Tanzanian safari operators**, the best of them in Arusha (see pp.288–289) and Dar es Salaam (see p.103).

PACKAGE TOUR OPERATORS

Africa Travel Resource UK ☎ 01306 880770, US & Canada ☎ 1 888 487 5418, South Africa ☎ 21 876 4913; ⓦ africatravelresource .com. An outfit with a solid reputation for mid- to upper-range safaris, built on a comprehensive and impartial website. Staff don't actually run the trips, but their knowledge of the various options, especially accommodation, is unrivalled.

African Portfolio US ☎ 1 800 700 3677, ⓦ onsafari.com. Highly regarded US–Zimbabwean outfit offering a range of packages, including birding.

Aim 4 Africa UK ☎ 0845 408 4541, ⓦ aim4africa.com. Responsible agent for all manner of trips and in all price ranges, including a dollop of cultural interaction and offbeat activities.

Awaken to Africa US ☎ 1 888 271 8269, ⓦ awakentoafrica.com. A Tanzanian–American company (registered in Tanzania, too), with excellent service and guides, responsible involvement, and a preference for smaller and more intimate lodges and camps, as well as cultural side trips.

Baobab Travel UK ☎ 0121 314 6011, South Africa ☎ 021 788 9628; ⓦ baobabtravel.com. Responsible and ethical agent offering tailor-made packages all over the country; Tanzanian-owned operators are preferred.

Exodus UK ☎ 0845 805 0358, Ireland ☎ 01 804 7153, US ☎ 1 844 227 9087, Canada ☎ 1 800 267 3347, Australia ☎ 1300 131 564, New Zealand ☎ 0800 238 368, South Africa ☎ 011 408 8000; ⓦ exodus.co.uk. Originally just focused on overlanding, Exodus now offers adventures worldwide. It has set departures for Tanzania up to mid-range level, and pays more than lip service to responsible tourism.

Gane & Marshall UK ☎ 01822 600 600, ⓦ ganeandmarshall.com. A long-established agent using ethically and environmentally sound local companies. Also offers walking and cycling in the Rift Valley, and various options in western Tanzania.

IntoAfrica UK ☎ 0114 255 5610, ⓦ intoafrica.co.uk. A Tanzanian–British outfit gleaning tons of highly deserved recommendations, particularly useful for veering off the beaten track. It runs its own trips (the Tanzanian arm is Maasai Wanderings, ⓦ maasaiwanderings.com), and fully lives up to its fair-trade, ethical promise.

Naipenda Safaris US ☎ 1 888 404 4499, ⓦ naipendasafaris.com. More a Tanzanian company with US representation, this affordable set-up offers an unusual array of custom-made trips including on tribal culture, volunteering, art, and even cooking.

Tanzania Odyssey UK ☎ 0208 704 1216, US ☎ 1 866 356 4691, Australia ☎ 1 800 025068; ⓦ tanzaniaodyssey.com. Long-established and knowledgeable specialist whose trump card is tailor-made safaris at cost, so its profit lies in commissions (which you'd be paying anyway if booking direct).

Tribes UK ☎ 01473 890499, ⓦ tribes.co.uk. A wide choice of luxurious yet adventurous trips away from the crowds, with some community involvement, inevitably with the Maasai.

Getting around

Chaotic and uncomfortably packed it may be, but Tanzania's public transport will get you to most destinations in the country within the same day. Buses and minibuses are the usual way to travel and Tanzania's main roads are now mostly tarmac, with work under way to pave much of what remains. Other roads are unsurfaced, making them either dusty or muddy, and potentially impassable in the rains. There are also two very slow railway lines, plus ferry services across lakes Tanganyika, Victoria and Nyasa, and from Dar to Zanzibar. Local airlines, most operating light aircraft, cover the entire country, including the national parks. Plane fares can be relatively affordable on short or well-travelled routes, but are extremely expensive otherwise.

Buses, minibuses and pick-ups

For most Tanzanians and independent tourists, buses, minibuses (called "daladalas") or pick-ups are the usual way of getting around: sometimes driven with breathtaking lack of road sense, they do reach pretty much every corner of the country, and can actually be an enjoyable way of getting around, throwing you into close contact with the locals. That said, on **unsurfaced roads** especially you should be prepared for a degree of physical discomfort: vehicles tend to be stuffed full with passengers and their bags, boxes, chickens or even goats, and rough roads aren't kind to bottoms, either, nor to heads if you're sitting on a "catapult seat" near the rear axle – hitting bumps at full speed can literally bounce you off the ceiling. Only a handful of buses have **toilets**. Instead, vehicles stop every few hours for passengers to scurry into the bush, women on one side, men on the other. You won't need to bring **food** as there's plenty available

SAFARI NJEMA…HAVE A SAFE JOURNEY!

Tanzania has an appalling **road safety record**, and it's getting worse as more and more roads are paved, making them faster. Driving standards are abysmal, with speeding and reckless overtaking the primary culprits. Therefore the "Arrival and departure" sections throughout this guide contain recommendations for the **safer companies**, and warn against the most dangerous. Nonetheless, things do change, so always seek advice from several people before choosing, and be clear when asking: for some, "the best bus" means the fastest, and the English word "safe" is confusingly similar to *safi*, meaning clean, which could be taken to mean the newest bus, not necessarily the safest. If you're really worried, you can minimize the statistical risk of injury by sitting in the middle of the vehicle away from windows.

from hawkers along the way, and on long trips you'll stop for lunch at a roadside restaurant.

Buses cover all the main routes, asphalted or not, and are the primary means of transport. On unpaved roads, the buses are very old, battered and uncomfortable, and break down frequently (for which reason they carry their own mechanics). On the main highways, you're more likely to end up in a modern Chinese import with reclining seats, and music videos or Bollywood films on the TV. Minibus **daladalas** (also called "Hiace") are invariably falling apart: they, and the larger **Coaster** minibuses (also called DCM), are safe enough for urban journeys, but rarely recommendable for longer runs, when they're driven by maniacs – exceptions are noted in the guide. West of Arusha, complementing these services are Toyota minivans known by their brand name, **Noah**. In remote areas with particularly bad roads, transport will be by **pick-up**, often a Land Rover ("One Ten"), or an open-backed truck.

Departure times tend to be reliable (it's the arrival times that vary), being a fairly standard 6am or "twelve o'clock" in Swahili time (see p.80 for an explanation): departure at other times are noted throughout the guide. Buses usually leave from a central **bus stand** (bus station), where you'll find the ticket offices. For any long distance route, buy your ticket at least a day before: you'll not only be sure of a seat, but can choose it, too. The least uncomfortable place to sit is in the front of the vehicle away from the rear axle. Consider which side will be shadier, remembering that in the southern hemisphere the sun travels in the northern half of the sky. Public transport is prohibited from travelling between midnight and 4am, so if you're on a long-distance bus that gets delayed, expect to spend the night in your seat. **Fares** are paid in shillings, and are usually around Tsh2000 ($1.10) for an hour's travel. As a tourist you may be overcharged a little, but no more than a local who doesn't know the price either. Baggage charges shouldn't be levied unless you're transporting commercial goods.

Urban transport

Daladalas are the standard way of getting around large towns; fares for most journeys are Tsh400 ($0.25). The vehicles run along pre-determined routes, often colour-coded; their destination is usually painted on the front. Daladalas have the advantage of being plentiful and quick; the downside is that they can get amazingly crowded – 25 people in a vehicle with just twelve seats is common. When boarding a vehicle at a daladala stand, choose one that's full and about to leave, so you don't have to wait.

More comfortable are **taxis**, which are also the only safe way of getting around at night. They lack meters, so agree a fare before getting in. A ride around town averages Tsh5000, but drivers will invariably try for more – haggle hard and, if you get nowhere, try another. **Motorized rickshaws** (*bajaj*), which take their name from the Indian manufacturer, Bajaj Auto, cost less than half the price of a taxi. These tiny three-wheelers have space for two passengers, and can be found in most towns. Even cheaper are **motorbike taxis**, variously called **bodaboda** or **pikipiki**, which are not recommended – especially in cities – as their safety record is very poor.

Hitching

Hitchhiking is generally not recommended, especially for lone females, but may be unavoidable in very remote areas – in which case the risks are considerably less. Beckon the driver to stop with your whole arm, and be prepared to pay.

Car rental

For freedom of movement, it's hard to match a **private vehicle**, though very few car rental companies let tourists self-drive in national parks. Instead, a **driver** is included in the deal, and the price should include his accommodation and meals. It's actually no bad thing to have a driver along: he's fluent in Kiswahili, obviously, and will likely double as a wildlife guide.

The other constraint is that **4WD** (necessary for entering most national parks) doesn't come cheap unless you can share the cost. The classic safari vehicles are Land Rovers or Land Cruisers, **prices** for which average $200 per day (with driver or self-drive), including 120km but excluding fuel; additional kilometres cost around $1. Cheaper are Rav 4 vehicles, which are smaller and have lower clearance but are rugged enough for most conditions. For one of these, you'll pay $100–150 per day self-drive, with each kilometre above 120km charged at $0.80 or so. Rates are always cheaper by the week, and many firms are prepared to negotiate, but be wary of VAT (twenty percent, not always included in quotes), and check whether the driver's allowance is included. Expect to pay a hefty deposit or even the full amount upfront; that, or a credit card. Most **car rental companies** are in Dar, Arusha, Mwanza and Stone Town; we've noted the best ones in those city and town accounts. As with safari companies, car rentals need a valid TALA licence to enter national parks (see p.63).

Self-drive saloon cars, for paved roads only, cost $80–120 a day, excluding fuel. With a driver, add $20 or so. Less hassle, if you just need an ordinary car, is to **rent a taxi**, though it'll cost about the same unless you have your bargaining hat on straight.

Self-drive rules and regulations

Self-drive is no cheaper than going with a company driver, as you'll have to pay insurance premiums instead. Before signing on the dotted line, check the small print for **insurance** arrangements, and always pay the daily collision damage waiver (CDW), else even a small bump could be costly. Theft protection waiver (TPW) should also be taken. Even with these, however, you'll still be up for **excess liability** (anything from $300 to $3000) if you total the car. Some companies are distinctly cagey about these matters – as a rule of thumb, excess liability over $1000 is the trademark of outfits secretly hoping their punters crash for cash.

Drivers must be between 25 and 70 years old and have held a licence for at least two years. Zanzibar additionally requires an **International Driving Permit** (available from motoring organizations), which must be endorsed by the police on arrival. If you don't have one, a temporary fifteen-day permit can be obtained on production of your national licence and $15. Car rental companies can arrange all this.

Fuel is available almost everywhere except along remote roads or in the smallest villages. Out of the way, it won't be delivered by pump but in plastic bottles. Fill up wherever you can. You'll get 10–14km per litre out of a Land Rover TDI, less from a Land Cruiser. Fuel is priced in shillings (currently about Tsh 2200/litre); the dollar-equivalent hovers around $1.25 a litre.

Trains

Tanzania has two passenger-carrying railways, both comfortable enough if you travel in a sleeper, though delays are frequent, so don't count on arriving at the scheduled time. All trains have a dining car (which doubles as a bar), but food can also be ordered from a roving waiter, and on long journeys the train stops at trackside villages whose inhabitants sell some of the best "street" food in the country. For news and up-to-date schedules, see the excellent website Ⓦseat61.com.

Twice a week, the dilapidated **Central Line** runs 1254km between Dar es Salaam and Kigoma on Lake Tanganyika, with branches to Mwanza (Lake Victoria) and Mpanda. The main stretch was laid by the Germans just before World War I; the Mwanza branch was completed in 1928, and the Mpanda branch in 1950. It takes over 38 hours from Dar to Kigoma or Mwanza.

The **TAZARA Line** (Ⓦtazarasite.com) runs 1992km from Dar es Salaam to New Kapiri Mposhi in Zambia, via Mbeya. In both countries the trains terminate at Nakonde, on the border, with timetables synchronized to allow a reasonable onward connection. A trip from Dar to New Kapiri Mposhi takes around 49–51 hours, including the change at the border: it's about half that to Mbeya. There are two trains a week in either direction, including the gloriously misnamed "Kilimanjaro Express". Southbound services are relatively reliable: the northbound services less so.

The line was constructed by Chinese engineers in the 1960s to provide an outlet for Zambian copper exports without going through the racist regimes of Southern Rhodesia (Zimbabwe), South-West Africa (Namibia) and South Africa, or through the war-torn Portuguese colonies of Angola and Mozambique. The route passes through some especially beautiful landscapes, including part of Selous Game Reserve, where, by day, you might see antelopes, buffaloes or giraffes. If the train leaves in the morning, it's a very nice way of getting to the Udzungwa Mountains, too (get off at Mang'ula).

Tickets

There are four kinds of ticket. **First class** on the Central Line is in compartments with just two bunks each, ideal for couples. On the TAZARA Line they have four bunks. **Second class** is in compartments with six bunks each, segregated by sex unless you book and pay for six people. Both first- and second-class have washbasins, bed linen and blankets. Both kinds should be reserved in advance; ticket offices take bookings up to three months ahead. **Second-class seating** is also in compartments and can be booked. **Third class**, which is seating in open carriages, can be uncomfortably crowded with plenty of suitcases, boxes, baskets, chickens and, of course, people.

Fares are priced in shillings; slipping exchange rates mean that dollar equivalents have remained stable over the last decade. For Dar to Kigoma, current fares are Tsh75,500 ($43) in first class, Tsh55,400 ($32) in a second-class bunk, and Tsh27,700 ($16) in third class.

Safety

Overnight trains are obvious targets for **thieves**. If you have a compartment, keep the door and windows locked when you're asleep or outside, or ensure that there's always someone there to look after bags (Tanzanian travellers are just as wary). Be especially careful when the train pulls in at main stations, especially Dodoma and Tabora on the Central Line. You should also be wary of people looking for a spare seat in second class (genuine passengers always have numbered tickets corresponding to a particular compartment) and of passengers without bags – they may leave with yours. If you get suspicious, stay awake until the ticket inspector comes round. In third class you'll probably have to stay awake all night or else stash your valuables out of reach (in a bag under your seat hemmed in by other people's bags, for example). All this is not to say that you should be paranoid – just don't drop your guard.

Flights

Tanzania has a number of **domestic airlines** and it's well worth seeing the country from above at least once: the flight from Dar es Salaam or Stone Town to Pemba, over spice and coconut plantations, reefs, sandbanks and creeks, is especially beautiful. Large planes are operated by Fastjet (Airbus), Precisionair and Air Tanzania (both twin-engine turboprops), but other companies rely on **light aircraft**, frequently single-engine. Don't fret: unlike buses, Tanzanian planes are generally well

maintained. On light aircraft, the **baggage limit** is usually 15kg, and bags should be soft; additional weight can be carried at the pilot's discretion (and at extra cost: usually $3/kg).

Ticket prices on Fastjet are quoted in shillings, and vary according to availability: factoring in taxes and baggage charges, one-way from Dar to Mbeya starts at around Tsh100,000 ($60). Other local airlines quote dollar fares for tourists ("non-residents"), which can be paid in the shilling equivalent. If you've been around a while, you may be able to wangle cheaper "resident" fares on less touristy routes – it all depends on the person serving you, as resident status is not checked at the airports. Some sample non-resident one-way fares, including taxes are: Arusha–Dar $275; Arusha–Mwanza $330; Dar–Zanzibar $80; Dar–Selous $165–195. **Taxes** (airport $8, safety $1) are not included in the published fares, but are included in the final price paid. Precisionair is the exception, so be sure you have some dollars to pay at the airport.

TANZANIAN AIRLINES

Air Excel Ⓦ airexcelonline.com
Air Tanzania Ⓦ airtanzania.co.tz
Auric Air Ⓦ auricair.com
Coastal Aviation Ⓦ coastal.co.tz
Fastjet Ⓦ fastjet.com
Precisionair Ⓦ precisionairtz.com
Regional Air Ⓦ regionaltanzania.com
Safari Airlink Ⓦ safariaviation.info
Tropical Air Ⓦ tropicalair.co.tz
ZanAir Ⓦ zanair.com

Ferries

There are several daily ferries between Dar es Salaam and **Zanzibar** (Stone Town), and a few each week to Pemba. There are currently no ferries from Tanga to Pemba, but this may change. On **Lake Victoria**, steamers sail several times a week from Mwanza to Bukoba (see p.377), and daily to Ukerewe Island. On **Lake Tanganyika**, the marvellous MV *Liemba*, a pre-World War I relic (see p.387), connects Kigoma to Mpulungu in northern Zambia every fortnight, though it is often out of service for repair. Slightly more reliable is the weekly ferry on **Lake Nyasa**, between Itungi Port and Mbamba Bay, from where another ferry crosses over to Malawi (see p.442).

Dhows

Dhow-hopping along the Tanzanian coastline, or between the mainland and Zanzibar, is an undeniably romantic prospect, though the reality is rather different. For a start, it's potentially dangerous, and officials won't necessarily be angling for bribes when they try to discourage you: dhows do capsize, and there's little chance of being rescued should that happen. You should also be prepared for cramped conditions, diesel-fume-laced air, choppy seas, the language barrier, and rudimentary toilet facilities slung over the vessel's side (it's always best to clear your bowels beforehand). Any useful route takes at least five or six hours, and considerably longer if there are problems with motors or the weather, so bring food and water with you. In addition, it's rumoured to be illegal for tourists to catch non-motorized dhows for long-distance trips.

If all that doesn't put off, the best places to try for dhows on the mainland are **Pangani** (on the north coast) for Mkokotoni and Nungwi on Zanzibar, **Kisiju** (90km south of Dar) for Mafia Island, and **Kilwa Kivinje** (on the south coast) for Lindi or Songo Songo, and from there on to Mafia Island. To arrange a dhow, first enquire locally about the latest situation, then pay a visit to the **harbour master** or **dhow registrar** (whose offices are usually inside the harbour or close by) to find out what ships are heading your way. Then agree a fare with the captain – anything up to $30 per person for tourists. Once settled, the dhow registrar will inscribe your name on the manifest and collect a **harbour tax** (Tsh5000 at most). In theory, that's all that's needed if you're not leaving the country, but you may have to inform the **immigration and customs** departments too – check with the harbour master whether this is necessary.

Lastly, catching a dhow to or from Zanzibar can be impossible during the clove harvests (Sept to Nov and around Feb), when smuggling is common and the routes are tightly controlled. It's also wise to avoid going by dhow at times of political turmoil on Zanzibar – basically the months before and after elections; the next bout is due at the end of 2015. If you're heading south to Mozambique, make sure you get your visa in Dar before heading off, as you can't buy Mozambican visas on arrival.

Cycling

Tanzania's climate, hilly terrain, and reckless drivers aren't exactly perfect for **cyclists**, but with plenty of time, some decent life insurance, and a rear-view mirror bolted on to your handlebars, you can reach parts of the country that would be virtually impossible to visit by other means except walking. Pedal-powered foreigners are also still a novelty, so you'll be the star attraction wherever you turn up. Bringing your own bicycle is not straightforward (contact your airline for conditions, fees and packing requirements), and it's much easier is to **buy a bike** on arrival: basic mountain bikes can be bought in most towns for around $100.

Obviously, you'll need to be extremely cautious when **cycling on main roads**, and be ready to leave the road if necessary, even if it means ending up in a ditch – local cyclists wisely scatter like chickens at the approach of a bus.

Accommodation

Tanzania's accommodation ranges from humble guesthouses charging under $10 a night to luxurious beach resorts and bush camps priced in the thousands. Irrespective of the price range, single travellers get a rough deal, rarely paying less than eighty percent of the price of a double, as cheaper hotels tend to charge per room, while upmarket places slap on hefty "single supplements". Note that en-suite rooms are also known as "self-contained". In many places, including inside national parks and nature reserves, the cheapest – and often most enchanting – way of staying is in your own tent, though camping is illegal on Zanzibar. Kiswahili terms for accommodation are listed on pp.538–539.

Booking ahead is essential if staying in upmarket hotels, particularly in peak season (generally July–Sept, and from mid-Dec to Feb). Bookings are also necessary in Zanzibar, Stone Town in particular, at festival times: February for Sauti za Busara, and July for ZIFF. Given that a fifty percent **deposit** is usually required to confirm reservations, and full payment due ten to twelve weeks before arriving, you should rightly expect perfection. Unfortunately, price is not always a reliable guide, so before making a reservation or letting a tour operator arrange things for you, read some recent client **reviews online**. Best for this is ⓦtripadvisor.com, though look out for fake posts; also useful are ⓦvirtualtourist.com, ⓦexpertafrica .com, and travellers' forums (see p.80). In cheaper hotels and guesthouses reservations are not usually required, but if a place appeals, there's no harm in trying. You'll rarely be expected to pay a deposit, but there are no guarantees of your reservation actually being honoured: bringing along print-outs of any email correspondence might help.

ACCOMMODATION PRICES

Unless otherwise stated, accommodation prices in this guide are for a **standard double or twin room** in high season, based on walk-in or "rack" rates – you may get the same room for less via a travel agent, safari company or online booking service. Abbreviations used are: BB (bed and breakfast); HB (half board); FB (full board). Where no abbreviation is given, the hotel's rates are bed-only. For **dormitory accommodation** and **campsites**, prices are given per person.

Most mid-range hotels, almost all upmarket accommodation, and all hotels on Zanzibar have two tariffs: one for **non-residents** (tourists) priced in US dollars but also payable in shillings, albeit at bad rates; the other for **residents** (East Africans and sometimes also expats), usually quoted in shillings and invariably much cheaper; rates at such places vary according to the season. We've quoted non-resident rates.

Tourist seasons mainly affect prices in upmarket hotels. **High season** can be almost the entire year, with **low season** (disingenuously dubbed "green season") restricted to April and May, and perhaps a month either side, coinciding with the long rains. More reasonable hoteliers consider high season to be August, and from mid-December to January or February. Peak season supplements are charged for Christmas, New Year and Easter.

Security

In the cheapest places, don't take **security** for granted, especially in cities. Obviously, the more an establishment relies on its bar or on "short time" guests for income, the less secure it will be. While all hotels disclaim responsibility for thefts, **leaving valuables in rooms** is usually safe enough, but don't leave stuff lying around temptingly, and if you get a bad vibe, try to take the key with you when you go out. Actually, **keys** themselves are good indicators: some are so simple that they'd open every other door in the country. If you leave valuables in your room, bury them in the bottom of your bag and use padlocks or other devices to deter temptation. You might also consider hiding stuff between a mattress and the bed frame – usually safe enough, judging by the amount of accumulated grime.

If you decide to leave things with the management, exercise caution, and ensure you get an **itemized receipt** (signed by the manager or owner, not the receptionist), including banknote serial numbers.

Hostels and guesthouses

Nearly every town in Tanzania has at least one clean and comfortable **guesthouse**, usually a two- or three-storey building, sometimes with a bar and restaurant too. Guesthouses are often fairly quiet themselves, but street noise, mosques, nearby bars or discos, or bus stations might keep you awake or wake you earlier than you might wish. The less reputable guesthouses, often close to markets or bus terminals, maximize their potential by admitting couples on "short time", though they're rarely too tawdry. The more puritanical display belligerent signs forbidding "women of immoral turpitude". Virtually all guesthouses have **security guards** (*askaris*) at night, whom you'll need to wake if you're staggering home after the doors or gates are locked. Similar in standards to guesthouses, but with a cloying atmosphere and often with overly narrow beds are **church-run hostels**. These have no membership- or faith-based requirements, but night owls should look elsewhere. There are no internationally affiliated youth hostels in Tanzania.

At a decent guesthouse, you should get running water, toilet seats and intact nets, with **room rates** around Tsh20,000–40,000 ($11–22) per night for a double room with a bathroom, or half that for shared bathrooms. Comparable singles are rarely less than eighty percent of the cost of a double. Guesthouses in Dar es Salaam and on Zanzibar are usually priced in dollars and are more expensive, with the cheapest doubles starting at $30, though you should be able to bargain in low season or if you're staying a few days. **Before signing in**, test the lights and fans (and electric socket if you need it), running water, toilets and the size and condition of the mosquito nets. Toilet paper, soap and towels are provided in all but the humblest places, but it's a good idea to bring your own (towels aren't always clean), as well as pillow cases and two thin cotton sheets (a *kanga* or *kitenge* will do) to replace the ubiquitous nylon ones, many of which are too small for the beds. **Hot water** is sometimes available from the tap, but more common is a heater attached to the shower head,

MOSQUITO NETS AND BUG SPRAY

Mosquitoes, and hence malaria, are prevalent in most parts of Tanzania. Virtually every guesthouse and hotel room comes with **mosquito nets** for its beds, so you don't need to bring your own. Some rooms also have wire-mesh window screens, but they don't offer one hundred percent protection on their own (mosquitoes can simply follow you in). Before signing in to a hotel, always check nets and screens for size and holes. A stapler or duct tape can be useful for quick repairs.

We've made a distinction in our hotel reviews between **round nets**, hung from a single point, and **box nets**, which are hung from four points or from a wooden frame. The latter are preferable as they give you more room to move about in at night without touching the net. Less than perfect are the large "walk-in" nets preferred by posher places, and the box nets with "entrance flaps" popular on Zanzibar, few of which close properly; for those, you'll need to check whether it's possible to tuck them in under the mattress, or be sure that nets reaching the floor really do touch the floor all the way around. Also potentially problematic are Zanzibar's four-poster *semadari* beds, as the fancy carved ends can leave plenty of gaps for mosquitoes if the net is hung outside rather than inside the frame.

Some mid-range and upmarket hotels prefer the **bug spray** approach: not wonderful, either, even ignoring potential toxicity, as the effect only lasts a few hours, and, in humid areas, the spray's perfume becomes a mangy stench over time.

which gives instant hot water, providing the electricity is working and the pressure isn't too bad. If there's neither, you'll be brought hot water in a bucket on request.

Hotels

For mid-range and upmarket travellers, the mainstay in **towns** are **hotels** as opposed to guesthouses, where you'll get a room with private bathroom and hot water, plus satellite or cable TV, air conditioning, and breakfast included. Prices are almost always in dollars, though you can pay in shillings, albeit at bad exchange rates. For $150–200 a night and upwards, you should be getting facilities and standards of service equivalent to four- or five-star hotels worldwide. In more modest places, the majority charging between $40 and $80, price isn't always a reliable guide: some are bristlingly smart and efficient, but others can be bland, or even boozy, if there's a bar attached.

With the exception of the resorts just north of Dar es Salaam, and Kiwengwa on Zanzibar, Tanzania's **beach hotels** are almost all low-key and low-rise. Rooms are usually in **bungalows**, either individual, or containing two or more guest rooms perhaps sharing the same veranda or balcony. It's worth spending a little more to be sure of a sea view, if there is one, and for air conditioning, especially between November and March when the heat and humidity are sapping. **Costs** can be surprisingly reasonable: from $40–60 or so per night for two people on Zanzibar, though some "boutique" hotels charge over $600.

Wildlife lodges and luxury tented camps

At the top of the scale are the lodges and luxury tented camps in and around Tanzania's **national parks and game reserves**, which can charge pretty much what they like as demand far outstrips availability: indeed, when reserving rooms, you need a degree of flexibility regarding dates even if you book half a year in advance. The more remote of these places tend to be closed in April and May during the long rains.

The **lodges** are the mainstay of mid-range and "cheaper" upmarket safaris, and are essentially large four- and five-star hotels transported into the bush. The better ones can feel quite intimate, but by and large this is package-tour land, and they lack any wilderness feeling you might be hankering for. For that, either camp (if you're on a budget), or drain your bank account (upwards of $450 for a couple) and stay at one of an ever-growing number of **luxury tented camps** (or "tented lodges"). Accommodation in these is usually in large, walk-in tents pitched on raised wooden platforms, with a bathroom plumbed in at the back. There's invariably also a thatched restaurant, bar and lounge area, and an atmosphere that tends to be neo-colonial, dominated by "white hunter"-type wildlife guides, tall tales around evening camp fires, and minimal if any local involvement beyond the employment of menial staff and perhaps a Maasai warrior or two to lend some tribal colour. Bush walks are often possible, and should be – together with game drives – included in "all inclusive" prices.

ECO-TOURISM: MYTH AND REALITY

Most wildlife lodges and camps like to vaunt themselves as "ecofriendly", but few really are. For a start, their very existence in "unspoiled" areas takes a toll on the **environment**, no matter how many safeguards are in place. Indeed, many establishments seem to equate "ecological" with their extensive use of natural materials, when in fact the opposite is the case. Tropical hardwoods, mangrove poles, and wood for firing limewash are all exploited in wholly unsustainable and usually illegal ways. In short, don't believe the hype.

On the positive side, an encouraging trend outside national parks has been to involve **local communities**, not just as staff but sometimes as part-owners and managers. In our reviews for accommodation and safari companies, we've tried, as far as possible, to keep environmental and ethical matters in sight, and have excluded obvious offenders (with the exception of lodges around Ngorongoro Crater, all of them environmental blights but which cannot practically be excluded due to the huge number of tourists staying there). We've also excluded companies known for **other abuses**, including racism, physical violence towards staff, miserly contributions to local communities, and involvement in the corruption-riddled world of trophy hunting. Of course, it's not possible to guarantee that all companies featured in this book are ethical: if you know better, please let us know – your feedback is very welcome.

Camping

Camping is illegal on Zanzibar, but mainland Tanzania has enough **campsites** to make bringing a tent worthwhile. The advantages are the low cost (usually no more than $10 per person), and often gorgeous locations. In rural areas, hotel may also let you camp in their grounds. During the dry seasons you'll rarely have trouble finding wood for a fire, so a stove is optional, but don't burn more fuel than you need, and take care to put out embers completely before leaving. A torch is also useful, and a foam sleeping mat is essential.

The public campsites in Tanzania's **national parks** ($30 per person plus entrance fees) are the cheapest way of staying over, and don't require booking. Most but not all have toilets and showers: details are given throughout this guide. The parks' "special campsites" ($50 per person) do require reservations, and as far ahead as possible as they're often block-booked by upmarket tour companies. They're generally miles away from the crowds and have no facilities at all, but can be reserved for your exclusive use: contact TANAPA in Arusha (see p.287), or the park headquarters (contacts are given throughout this guide). Collecting **firewood** is not permitted in the parks; some provide it for a small fee, others insist you use gas canisters (available in Arusha and Dar es Salaam).

Unless you're with someone who knows the area well, **camping rough** is not recommended, although a decent dose of common sense should keep you safe. Wherever you are, before pitching a tent seek permission from the headman or an elder (*jumbe*) in the nearest village – or else a worried delegation armed with *pangas* may turn up to see who you are. Obviously, don't pitch beside roads, in dry riverbeds or near animal trails. **Areas to be wary of** include: Loliondo district north of the Serengeti (wildlife risk, and bandits were present until a few years ago); Mara district north of Musoma (clashes between Kuria clans); the fringes of Maasai territory (cattle rustling); areas bordering Burundi and Rwanda; anywhere around Selous Game Reserve including between Masasi and Songea (lions); and between Dodoma and Kondoa (also lions). In addition, camping on any but the most deserted of beaches could be an invitation to robbers.

Food and drink

On the Tanzanian mainland, culinary traditions are necessarily humble, but that's not to say that the food isn't tasty: venturing beyond the realm of fast food (chicken, chips and various snacks), your taste buds are in for a treat, as the relatively limited selection of ingredients in each area has fostered plenty of innovation. The classic Tanzanian meal – eaten with your hands, although as a tourist you'll usually be given cutlery – consists of several stews based on vegetables, beans or even plantain, into which you dip a small ball of rice or thick cornmeal porridge (*ugali*). Where Tanzanian cuisine really comes into its own, however, is on Zanzibar, where you'll find an eclectic and delicious gastronomic tradition. Its cuisine is

distinctive, subtle and tasty, making inspired use of the island's famous spices and fruits: fish, octopus or squid simmered in coconut sauce is a classic.

Restaurants

Upmarket restaurants are two a penny in Arusha, Dar and Zanzibar, though Tanzanian cuisine is rare here, and menus play it safe with international "classics", accompanied by pretentious trimmings, hovering waiters, starched tablecloths and polished silverware. In these places you can easily blow upwards of Tsh30,000 ($17) on a main course, never mind a starter, drinks or dessert. Although they are undoubtedly sophisticated, you only rarely get real ambience, or much of an inkling that you are in Africa.

Tanzanian cuisine begins to make an appearance in **mid-range restaurants**, especially in the form of "Swahili-style" seafood (spiced lightly, if at all, and cooked in coconut sauce). They also serve international fare, from burgers and pizzas to 1970s recipes, such as pepper steaks, beef stroganoff and long lists of Indian, Chinese and Italian dishes. Meals here coast around Tsh15,000–25,000 ($8.50–14) a plate.

Cheap restaurants can be found almost everywhere: in a **hoteli** (a restaurant, not a hotel) or a **mgahawa** (even more basic), where dishes are intended to fill you up as cheaply as possible, often for under Tsh3500 ($2). In the most popular places, your meal arrives on a metal platter containing several hollows, one for each dish (various stews, ugali or rice, vegetables, and meat or fish), so you can mix things as you wish. Salads are rarely offered: where they are, they'll often be fresher in local dives, where they're made to order, than in touristic establishments.

Lunch is typically served from noon to 2pm, with dinner no later than 8pm, but many restaurants are open all day: we've given opening times throughout this book. **Reservations** are rarely necessary: more touristy places have heaps of space, while local establishments find the very concept of reserving tables bizarre.

Street food and snacks

A fun and cheap alternative to restaurants is **street food**, which you'll find in or around most transport terminals and markets. Most vendors – known as mama/baba lisha (feeding women/men) offer just one or two snacks, but some provide full (and often wholesome) meals, eaten at makeshift tables – and which, at night, in the flickering light of charcoal braziers and oil lamps, can be very memorable experiences. Zanzibar has an especially regal choice of seafood. The majority of vendors, however, rely on **standard favourites**, including kuku choma (fried chicken, which is often coated in bright orange masala spices), mishkaki (skewers of grilled meat), chipsi mayai (Spanish-style omelettes made with chips) and mahindi (grilled corncobs) or muhogo (cassava). The latter can be mouth-drying, but at its best is deliciously moist, especially when doused with a lemony chilli sauce.

Wherever you are, ask for local or seasonal **specialities**, as the street is often the only place you'll find such things other than in someone's home. On Pemba, for instance, you could try cockles (cooked in a tomato- and onion-based broth with potatoes) or stewed octopus. Around the great lakes, try dagaa, which are tiny freshwater sardines, fried and eaten whole, while in semi-arid Dodoma, some of the critters that make farmers' lives hell end up on hawkers' platters: field mice, say (whenever there's an invasion), or deep fried bite-sized birds.

Less squeamish **snacks**, which you'll also find in modest mgahawa restaurants, include samosas (sometimes vegetarian), chapatis (which, when

VEGETARIANS

The **vegetarian** ideology is a strange concept for most Tanzanians. Although the majority consume little meat, that's mostly a consequence of income: given the choice – as can be seen in nyama choma bars – most people would jump at the chance of meat-centred meals. So, as a vegetarian, you need to tread softly in some areas. If you're strict about your diet (no fish), the main problem is getting enough protein. In modest restaurants, beans are almost certain to feature, but in more expensive places it can be difficult avoiding omelettes (again). Indian restaurants, which you'll find in most large towns and on Zanzibar, are a good bet (various pulses and cooked cheeses), as are Chinese restaurants (bean sprouts, cashews, even tofu).

For your own supplies, supermarkets in Arusha, Moshi and Dar es Salaam stock a good range of **dairy produce**, much of it pasteurized; Tanzania's best cheese (excellent at that) is produced in the Usambara Mountains.

stuffed in any of several dozen of ways, are called *mantabali* or "Zanzibari pizza"), *kitumbua* (rice cakes), *kababu* (meat balls) and *katlesi* (chops), which can be all sorts of fried things but are usually either minced meat or a whole egg wrapped in mashed potato and batter.

Breakfast

Most mainland hotels, and virtually every hotel on Zanzibar, include **breakfast** in their rates, not that it's always worth getting up for (a slice or two of stale white bread, a smudge of plastic-tasting Blue Band margarine, another smear of jam, and a cup of weak tea or instant coffee). The better guesthouses include eggs and a good dose of seasonal fruit. For something different, local *mgahawa* restaurants are sure to have **andazi** – sweet, puffy, deep-fried doughnuts that are best accompanied by sweet milky *chai* (tea), which is particularly refreshing when laced with ginger (*chai tangawizi*). Bars can also be good for breakfast, and not just for dipsomaniacs: many open at dawn, and most will offer **supu**, a light broth made from bony or gristly pieces of meat, chicken or fish, or indeed boiled hooves (*supu ya makongoro*) or intestines (*supu ya utumbo*) – infinitely nicer than it sounds. Commonly accompanied by chapati, *supu* is also a matchless hangover cure (being salty, and laced with lemon, pepper, and sometimes chilli pepper). Other good and filling traditional breakfasts, often provided by street food vendors, include *uji* millet gruel, and – from Arusha westwards – a plantain stew called **mtori**.

Upmarket, **luxury hotels** and lodges lay on lavish expanses of hot and cold buffets that you can't possibly do justice to; if you're staying elsewhere, expect to pay $12–20 for the pleasure. Dropping down a few notches, most **mid-priced hotels** offer full English-style breakfasts – sausages (beef, not pork), eggs and baked beans.

Lunch and dinner

Tanzania's main **staples** are *ugali* (a thick cornmeal porridge, which can either be stodgy, or soft and deliciously aromatic), rice, cassava, over a hundred varieties of bananas or plantain, and – especially in the form of chips – potatoes. Less common but more traditional staples are sorghum and eleusine millet. Unfortunately, giving specific names to dishes is often quite impossible, as most meals go by the names of their main ingredient(s).

The classic Tanzanian meal consists of one of the staples served with two or more **stews**, often including beans, vegetables, and perhaps a small amount of fish or meat. The vegetable stews, in particular, are worth seeking out, as they often make use of local varieties with distinct tastes, especially spinach. You may also discover vegetables you never know existed, such as *nyanya chungu* ("bitter tomato"), a small yellow-green aubergine that makes wonderful sauces. Other meals are all-in-one stews: the marriage of potatoes, plantain and chicken innards is especially felicitous, as is the green and gloopy mess made from cassava leaves, cassava flour and cornmeal, known simply as *kisamvu* ("cassava leaves").

Eating out isn't a tradition among Tanzanians, but there's one exception; a feast of **nyama choma** (grilled beef or goat), which you'll find in most bars, along with grilled bananas or *ugali*. After roasting (order by weight), the meat is brought to your table on a wooden platter and chopped into bite-size pieces. The better places bring you a small bowl of home-made **chilli sauce** – at its best laced with tomato, onion and lemon or vinegar, where the subtlety and freshness seems to caress the kick. More humble places simply chop up a scotch bonnet chilli, varying in potency from hot to incendiary.

Over on Zanzibar, so-called **Swahili cooking** is the product of centuries of contact across the Indian Ocean, resulting in a wonderful blend of African and Asian, Indian and Arabian flavours and aromas. Drawing on ample maritime resources – prawns, octopus, squid, and dozens of varieties of fish – it can taste like heaven even at its simplest, when grilled. But where the Swahili really shine is in their brilliant use of herbs, spices, coconut milk, and even fruit (tamarind with seafood? genius). The classic dishes are fish or octopus simmered in coconut sauce (*samaki na nazi* and *pweza na nazi*), and fish encrusted in mango compote (often spelled on menus as "fish mango combat"). **Pilau**, which you'll also find in Dar, is another enduring favourite: rice flavoured with cloves, cinnamon and fresh peppercorns, and perhaps also coriander, cumin, fenugreek or aniseed.

Fruit and nuts

Fruit is always a delight. Bananas and papayas provide year-round pleasure. Seasonal fruits include mango and pineapple, citrus fruits, plum, melon and jackfruit, the latter banned from some local guesthouses on account of the smell. Also look out for passion fruit (the sweeter and less acidic yellow ones are quite something), tree tomatoes, custard apples (sweetsops) and guavas – all distinctive and delicious.

BEING INVITED TO EAT AT HOME

If you're invited for **a meal at someone's home**, do accept – it's an honour, for the people whose home you visit as well as for you – and the food is likely to be way better than in a restaurant. That said, it can be galling to know that the family slaughtered their last chicken just to honour you, so at the very least bring some gifts (see pp.71–72).

Make sure you are hungry before coming – your hosts will probably make a huge play out of the fact that you're not eating enough, even if you've just gobbled up twice what anyone else has. Before eating, one of the girls or women will appear with a bowl, some soap, and a jug of hot water for you to **wash your hands**. Traditionally, food is eaten with the right hand from a communal bowl or plate. Never use your left hand to take or give food, as it's destined for ablutions and is considered unclean, no matter how much you've washed it.

Eating techniques vary between regions, but in general you take a small handful of *ugali* or rice and roll it in your palm to make a small ball (the messy part), which is dipped in one of the sauces before being popped into your mouth. Don't worry about making a mess: as a foreigner, you're almost expected to – and it'll give the kids something to laugh about for many moons to come!

You may also find local fruits with no English names; rarely very sweet, they're worth trying at least once.

On the coast, roasted **cashew nuts** are popular, especially in the south where they're grown and processed, while **coconuts** are filling and nutritious, going through several satisfying changes of condition (all edible) before becoming the familiar hairy brown nuts.

Non-alcoholic drinks

A legacy of colonization, East Africa's national beverage is **tea** (*chai*). Drunk mainly in the morning, it's a hyper-sweet variant on the classic British brew (lots of milk), and very reviving. Variants laced with ginger (*chai tangawizi*) or other spices (*chai masala*) are even better. Ironically for a major coffee-producer, **coffee** is often limited to a tin of instant Africafé, although the commercial acumen of Mbeya's Utengule Estate, among others, is changing things for the better: in touristy areas, posher hotels, cafés and restaurants are now likely to offer brews made from real beans. The best coffee, though, is from Moshi: if purple has a taste, Kilimanjaro's Arabica is it. For a cup of coffee on the hoof, in larger towns and cities and especially on Zanzibar, look or ask for a coffee vendor, who will charge little more than Tsh200 for a small Turkish-style cupful; double your money and you'll get some *kashata*, too: sugared cashews, peanuts, coconut or pistachios.

Sodas are cheap, and crates of Coke and Fanta find their way to the wildest corners of the country. Local varieties include Krest bitter lemon, and the supremely punchy Stoney Tangawizi ginger ale. Fresh **juice** is available in towns, especially on the coast. Passion fruit is excellent, but may just be watered-down concentrate. You might also find orange, pineapple, sugar cane (sometimes laced with ginger or lime), watermelon, mango, the sublimely refreshing tamarind (always mixed with water, and sometimes laced with cardamom), or the delightful bungo, which tastes like a cross between mango and peach. It comes from the strychnine tree: don't worry, it's the bark and seeds that are toxic, not the pulp.

Bottled water can be bought everywhere but is expensive at around Tsh1200 ($0.70) for 1.5 litres, and most brands are merely purified tap water. The best **real mineral water**, almost sweet in taste, is from southern Tanzania – either *Ndanda*, available in the southeast, or *Rungwe Peak*, in the southwest. **Tap water**, unless cloudy, is often drinkable if you're up to date with inoculations (typhoid being particularly important), but heed local advice.

Alcoholic drinks

Mainland Tanzania has a vibrant drinking culture, and you should attract plenty of (mostly pleasant) attention in the country's bars. There are bars on Muslim Zanzibar, too, almost all of them aimed at tourists. When leaving a bar, don't take your bottle unless you've paid the deposit.

Beer and cider

Tanzania's **beer** is good stuff as far as lagers go. A bottle costs Tsh2200 ($1.25) in local dives, and up to Tsh6000 ($3.40) in hotel bars, or on Zanzibar. The main brands are Safari, Kilimanjaro, Tusker and Serengeti. The latter matches the requirements of the German *Reinheitsgebot* "beer purity law" (malt, water, hops, and nothing else), and has even won international accolades. You can also find some

Pilsner-style beers, and a couple more distinctive brews: Ndovu ("Elephant"), with a very sweet aroma, and the infamously strong The Kick (seven percent alcohol). If you're around Lake Victoria, look out for some local speciality beers, including Senator and Eagle that are made from sorghum. **Imported beers**, or brands brewed under licence, include Namibia's Windhoek, South Africa's Castle, the Czech Pilsner Urquell (superb), and Miller, Carlsberg and Heineken. There are also two **stouts**: a head-thumping "Export" version of Guinness which, at 7.5 percent, owes more to soya sauce than pure genius (connoisseurs mix it with Coca-Cola to soften the blow); and Castle Milk Stout (six percent), milder and far more palatable. Alternatively, try a **fake cider**: Savanna, 49er or Redds Cool, all sickly-sweet concoctions that have never been near real apples.

In rural locations, and especially if you're invited to a celebration, you may come across home brew generally known as **pombe**. Often frothy and deceptively strong, *pombe* is as varied in taste and colour as its ingredients, which may include fermented sugar cane (*boha*), maize and honey (*kangara*), bananas and sorghum (*rubisi*), cashew fruit (*gongo*), bamboo juice (*ulanzi*), and barley and/or millet (*busa*). Herbs and roots may also be added, for flavouring or to initiate fermentation.

Wine, spirits and liqueurs

Wine is sold at posher restaurants and bars, but is expensive at $25 and up for a bottle. South Africa's output travels best, but if you're up for adventure, track down a bottle of Tanzanian wine: the best is Sakharani Usambara, made by the Benedictine Fathers in the Usambara Mountains, and the output of CetaWico winery in Dodoma (see p.218). More widely distributed is wine under the "Dodoma" brand, which is just about palatable. In Moshi, Arusha and Lushoto, look for bottles of **banana wine**. On the coast, lopping off a shoot at the top of a coconut palm produces a sweet and very drinkable sap which, when left to ferment (a day suffices), becomes **palm wine** (*tembo*). Despite the dominance of Islam in coastal areas, the drink is popular (headless palm trees bearing witness), even if *tembo* drinking sessions have a furtive discretion about them. When indulging, keep a Kiswahili proverb in mind: "If the maker of *tembo* is praised for his wine, he adds water to it" (*mgema akisifiwa tembo hulitia maji*).

Spirits are nothing to write home about, unless you're a Scotsman aghast at the local take on "whisky" (usually sold in plastic sachets called *kiroba*, as is "vodka"). You'll find plenty of imported spirits, though, and the home-grown gin-like **Konyagi**.

Originally made from papaya, it's now a blend of imported spirits and mysterious "Konyagi flavour", which may be papaya, or cashew nut, or just sugar cane. It's drinkable neat, but is usually mixed with bitter lemon (Konyagi Ice being the same in bottles). Stay away from illegally distilled spirits collectively known as **chang'aa**: often deliberately contaminated with gasoline, acetone or worse (to give a kick), this routinely kills drinking parties en masse.

Liqueurs, where you can find them, are international brands. A couple less common ones you might find are Ghana's chocolate and coconut Afrikoko, and South Africa's Amarula, made from the eponymous fruit much loved by elephants.

Health

With up-to-date inoculations, anti-malarials (and safe sex, if you will), Tanzania is unlikely to afflict you with more than an upset stomach, sunburn or heatstroke. Just as well, given the scarcity of well-equipped hospitals and clinics. The best of them, privately run, are in Arusha, Dar es Salaam and Dodoma, contacts for which are given in the guide.

At least three weeks before leaving home, visit a doctor or travel clinic for advice, prescriptions and **vaccinations**. A course of malaria prophylaxis is essential, and jabs or boosters are recommended for typhoid, tetanus, polio and hepatitis A. The one for rabies is not strictly necessary, unless you'll be handling a lot of animals. Officially, a **yellow fever** certificate is only needed if arriving directly from an endemic zone (all Tanzania's neighbours, except Malawi and Mozambique). You won't need one if you transited through an endemic zone but didn't leave the airport. Immigration officials, however, can be officious, especially on Zanzibar, so get the jab to avoid one on arrival ($50; and yes, they use clean needles).

MEDICAL RESOURCES

The following maintain lists of travel clinics, and provide general advice:

Australia & New Zealand The Travel Doctor – TMVC ⓦ traveldoctor.com.au.

Canada Canadian Society for International Health ☎ 613 241 5785, ⓦ csih.org.

Ireland Tropical Medical Bureau ☎ 1850 487 674, ⓦ tmb.ie. Also lists centres in the UK and elsewhere.

South Africa Travel Doctor ☎ 0861 300 911, ⓦ traveldoctor.co.za.

UK National Health Travel Network ☎ 020 3447 5943 or ☎ 0141 300 1100 (Scotland), ⓦ nathnac.org.

US CDC ☎ (800)232 4636, TTY ☎ (888)232 6348, ⓦ cdc.gov/travel.

General precautions

In the hot and humid tropics, take more care than usual over minor **cuts and scrapes**, which can become throbbing infections should you ignore them. Tropical conditions also favour **fungal infections**, which flourish well in groins, between toes, or under thick hair. Rarely more than itchy inconveniences, fungal infections can be difficult to get rid of once firmly established, so shy away from using soap or damp or dirty towels that are not your own. After washing, dry yourself thoroughly, and, if you sweat profusely, use medicated talc to dust yourself off with. In bedrooms and bathrooms, it's best to wear (your own) sandals: you never know what fungus has taken a liking to the floor, or to the flip-flops provided by guesthouses.

Other reasons for not walking barefoot (except on sandy beaches) are **jiggers**: fly pupae that like to burrow into your toes. Less horrible than they sound, jiggers are easily disposed of by physically removing the bugs with a pin or a pair of tweezers, and repeatedly dousing the cavities with iodine or some other disinfectant until the holes close up, a few days later.

In cheap hotels, check bedsheets for tiny brown spots (**fleas** are messy eaters). Move elsewhere if you find them, as fleas can also carry diseases. That said, out of the hundreds of guesthouses sampled by the author so far, only four had fleas…

Solar protection

Tanzania lies just south of the equator, so for much of the day the sun hangs near its zenith. This means that skin that is normally vertical is less likely to get **sunburn** than in, say, Spain or Miami, but it makes the sun a bigger hazard for shoulders, noses, tops of balding heads, even feet – in short, anything horizontal. The solution, obviously, is to use high-factor sunblock on exposed limbs and lip salve, and to wear a hat. If you're dipping underwater, however, it's best to replace sunblock with clothing: Tanzania's amazing marine life doesn't thrive on sun cream. Failing prevention, a great **sunburn remedy** is yoghurt or curdled milk (ask for *mtindi* or *maziwa mgando*), spread generously on affected areas, or use aloe vera, available in some local supermarkets.

Your eyes also need protection: shiny white beaches can strain and even "snow-blind" your eyes. UV-shielded **sunglasses** minimize the risks, but raise psychological barriers against people (no eye contact), so use them only when you really need to.

The intensity of the equatorial sun (fewer atmospheric kilometres to burn through) can also stoke **heatstroke**, a potentially dangerous condition where you stop sweating while still hot. Subsequent symptoms include fever, cramps, rapid pulse and/or vomiting, followed by mental confusion or hallucinations. Victims should be removed to as cool a place as possible, covered in wet towels or have their clothes soaked in water, and be given rehydration mix (see p.59). More common but not dangerous are **skin rashes**, especially between November and March when the weather's particularly sultry. Oddly enough, a warm shower helps (it opens the pores), as does wearing loose cotton clothes. Lastly, if you tend to **sweat** a lot, you should keep cooler than most other people, but you'll need to eat more salt to compensate.

Malaria

East Africa's **malaria** strain, *Plasmodium falciparum*, is transmitted by the bite of female *Anopheles*

MEDICINE BAG

Common medicines are widely available in Tanzania, so your **medical kit** only needs to tide you over until you reach a clinic or pharmacy: a day at most unless you're way off the beaten track, meaning you can dispense with antibiotics. Apart from **malarial prophylactics**, **solar protection** and perhaps **insect repellent**, the following are useful to have around:

Anti-diarrhoeal tablets Imodium (Loperamide) does the trick; for emergency use only.
Antihistamine cream For insect bites. Alternatively, smear bites with toothpaste: you heard it here first…
Antiseptic More versatile than creams are alcohol, tea tree oil or iodine (also useful for purifying water).
Pain relief Aspirin also relieves inflammations.
Tweezers Included in Swiss Army knives.
Wound dressing Fabric plasters adhere best and let wounds breathe. If you'll be indulging in physically dangerous activities (such as mountaineering), also pack gauze, surgical tape and wound-closures.

mosquitoes, and can be fatal if untreated. The disease is present throughout Tanzania, and peaks during and after the rains, though the risk decreases with altitude: negligible above 1400m, absent over 1800m. The disease is most prevalent along the coast (including Zanzibar), around lakes, and anywhere with still or stagnant water, including banana groves, as the plants hold pools of water. **Prevention** is better than cure: start a course of prophylactics before leaving home, and take precautions against bites once you arrive. Don't worry yourself sick about malaria: it's treatable if properly diagnosed. The symptoms appear anything from a few days to several weeks after infection, so if you feel poorly after returning home, tell your doctor where you've been.

Prophylactics

Most **anti-malarial tablets** contain synthetic quinine. A doctor or travel clinic can provide personalized recommendations – especially important for children, pregnant women and those with medical conditions. The main drugs are:

Malarone Taken daily. A combination of Atovaquone and Proguanil hydrochloride, this is very effective, with few side effects so long as your liver and kidneys are OK. In Europe, it's only prescribed for trips up to three weeks duration.

Mefloquine Taken weekly. Better known by the brand name Lariam, this is very cheap ($3 a tablet in Tanzania), and can be taken over several months, but is beset by potential side effects – most commonly mild depression, dizziness or sleep disturbances – and is specifically warned against for scuba divers. Some travellers report minimizing side effects by taking half a tablet at four-day intervals; start two weeks before leaving home to test your reaction.

Doxycycline Taken daily. An antibiotic useful for those allergic to quinine. The major side effect is exaggerated sensitivity to sunlight (skin and eyes), so cover up.

Avoiding bites

The best way to avoid malaria is to avoid getting bitten. *Anopheles* mosquitoes like to bite in the evening and at night; you can minimize the chance of being bitten by sleeping under **mosquito nets**, provided by virtually every hotel and guesthouse in the country, and by burning **mosquito coils**, available locally. At dusk and at night, keep your limbs covered, and consider using **insect repellent**. Most contain diethyltoluamide ("DEET"), an oily substance that corrodes many artificial materials, including plastic. If you're bringing a net, it's worth impregnating it with insecticide as well. If you don't like synthetic protection, note that **natural alternatives** based on pyrethrum flowers or citronella (lemon grass) are also effective.

Symptoms and treatment

Common **symptoms** include waves of flu-like fever, shivering, headaches or joint pain. Some people also get diarrhoea. If you suspect malaria, get a **blood test** as quickly as possible. **Treatment** essentially consists of stuffing yourself with quinine: anything but the prophylaxis you were taking. Locals use an effective brew made from the extremely bitter leaves of the neem tree (known as the *muarbaini*, or "forty tree", owing to its many uses).

Sleeping sickness

Potentially fatal **sleeping sickness**, *trypanosomiasis*, is transmitted by the tsetse fly, which is present in heavily wooded areas, particularly in and around Ruaha National Park, Selous Game Reserve, Tarangire (Lake Burunge and southwards) and southern Serengeti. There are no tsetse flies in urban areas, and those on Zanzibar do not carry the disease. The flies are active by day. Less than one hundred cases are reported annually in Tanzania, most afflicting villagers living beside wildlife areas.

The blood-sucking **tsetse flies** are extremely persistent, and have evolved amazing resilience – DEET doesn't seem to work, and you need to put some gumption into your swipes to stop them. One trick worth trying is to wear **light-coloured clothes**, as the flies are attracted by dark hues (especially blue, but not red). Though being bitten is painful, the bites don't linger and aren't venomous, but try to resist the urge to scratch them. When driving, roll up the windows when in a tsetse fly zone, and if you have a/c, use it – it slows them down.

One or two bites are unlikely to give you sleeping sickness, but if you get feasted on, seek local advice about the presence of the disease. See a **doctor** immediately if your neck lymph nodes swell up or an irregular fever develops – the quicker the disease is diagnosed, the better the chances of treating it successfully.

Water and stomach bugs

In some towns, locals are quite happy quaffing **tap water**, but most tourists give it, and ice, a wide berth. On short trips, **bottled water** (sold throughout Tanzania) is the popular choice. More environmentally sound (no bottles) is **purifying water** yourself: if the water is cloudy, filter it first through fine muslin, then boil or add iodine tincture (four drops per litre), shake and wait twenty minutes. Chlorine tablets do the same but impart a vile taste.

On longer trips, **travellers' diarrhoea** – a catch-all for all sorts of minor bugs caught from badly washed or spoiled food or contaminated water – is best weathered rather than blasted with antibiotics (which don't work on viruses anyway). The important thing is to stay hydrated. A typical **rehydration mix** consists of four heaped teaspoons of sugar and half a teaspoon of salt in a litre of water; commercial rehydration remedies are much the same. Avoid coffee, strong fruit juice and alcohol. Most upsets resolve themselves after a couple of days. If you have to travel a long way and have diarrhoea, note that **anti-diarrhoea tablets** are available in Tanzania: most merely slow your digestive tract, so shouldn't be overused.

Outbreaks of **cholera** (scary but actually easily treated) are rare, and tend to be limited to highly populated urban areas that lack adequate sanitation, occurring when the water supply is contaminated during periods of flooding. Also contracted through contaminated water, more frequently too, is **giardiasis**, which just makes you feel terrible while blessing you with horrendously smelly burps and farts. It normally clears up after three days; the definitive treatment, and for **amoebic dysentery**, is metronidazole.

Terrestrial animals

Tanzania knows its animals, and their value: "man-eaters", those critters you pay lots of money to see, are largely confined to national parks and reserves. That said, fences are few and far between, and **lions** do sporadically terrorize some districts, especially between Dodoma and Babati, and the whole region around Selous Game Reserve, most notoriously Tunduru. Still, there's no reason to be terrified unless you're a farmer (for whom elephants are also a threat) or like camping rough, in which case you should always seek local advice. Actually, far more dangerous are **hippos** (never get between them and their water), and solitary male **buffaloes**, which may well help you reveal tree climbing skills you never knew you had. Heading down the scale, **dogs** – rarely seen, and often despised – are usually sad and skulking, posing little threat. Troops of **baboons**, however, should be treated with caution: keep food out of sight,

and ideally in airtight containers.

Snakes are mostly harmless, and to see one at all you'd need to search stealthily; walk heavily and most species obligingly disappear. In bushy or wooded areas, wear boots and long trousers to minimize the risk of scratched "bites". If someone *is* bitten, apply a tourniquet, but open it every fifteen minutes. Victims should be hospitalized as quickly as possible (even toxic bites are survivable if treated in time). Above all, **don't panic** – shock can be just as fatal. Also, don't try to suck out the poison like you see in films: that technique was discredited years ago. If you're really worried, any market should have **jiwe ya punju** ("snake bite medicine stone"), which looks like a small piece of charcoal, and is applied to a wound immediately after a bite: it might actually work, as it sucks up liquid via capillary action.

Lastly, don't worry about spiders (quite harmless), and while **scorpions** abound, they're hardly ever seen unless you deliberately turn over rocks or logs (something baboons do purposely; scorpions are tasty snacks). While the stings are painful, they're almost never fatal: clean the wound and pack with ice to slow the spread of the venom.

Aquatic hazards

Dar es Salaam suffered a short but deadly spate of **shark attacks** in 2000, the first in Tanzanian waters in recorded memory. There have been no attacks since, so the "freak migration from southern Africa" theory proffered at the time fits convincingly, and you can safely forget about a rerun of *Jaws*. Rather more likely is the painful annoyance of stepping on a **sea urchin**: spreading papaya pulp helps extract the spines, and dousing the wound in 50°C water reduces the pain. You might also be stung by jellyfish, for which vinegar is the miracle cure. Much more serious, but only likely to afflict incautious scuba divers, are neuro-toxic darts delivered by **cone shells**: apply a non-constrictive compress and seek urgent medical attention.

Swimming in lakes and rivers poses far greater risks: hippos and crocodiles, obviously, but also **bilharzia** (schistosomiasis), a dangerous but curable disease caused by tiny flukes living in freshwater snails. As part of their life cycle, they leave their hosts to multiply in mammals. The standard advice is never swim in, wash with, or even touch lake water that cannot be vouched for. The risks are higher close to river inlets and in turbid or slow-moving water, especially around vegetation. Well-maintained swimming pools are fine.

The media

Tanzania is a nation absorbed in its press, with many lively and outspoken newspapers and magazines, mostly in Kiswahili. Local TV is rather staid but very popular: you'll find sets in even the most modest bars and restaurants. Radio is best for swotting up on the latest music craze.

Newspapers and magazines

The leading **English-language daily** is *The Guardian*, whose independence relies on the financial clout of tycoon Reginald Mengi. The government-owned *Daily News* is strong on eastern and southern African affairs, but is spoiled by slavish bias toward the ruling CCM party, and its habit of copying things from the internet. Both have good coverage of the main global stories. *The Citizen* is independent and has improved since its cut-and-paste early days.

Best of the **weeklies** is *The East African*, whose relatively weighty, conservatively styled round-up of regional affairs is shot through with an admirable measure of cynicism. It also carries syndicated articles from European and American broadsheets, but concentrates on financial matters. Better for social and political news is *The Guardian on Sunday*, with incisive columnists. Less substantial but equally impartial is *The African*, combining a combative and occasionally scurrilous editorial line with syndicated articles from Britain's *Guardian* newspaper. *The Express* is more downmarket but still entertaining.

Tanzanian magazines in English are limited to touristic themes. Easiest to find are the **free listings booklets** available in Arusha, Dar and Zanzibar. The main ones, with good articles, are the *Dar Guide* and *What's Happening in Dar es Salaam*, and, on Zanzibar, *Swahili Coast* (Ⓦswahilicoast.com). For wildlife, *Tanzania Wildlife* (an insert in the Kiswahili *Kakakuona*) carries good articles on ecology, people and conservation. If you can read a bit of Kiswahili, there are tons more to choose from, from smutty cartoons to music and Christian fundamentalist propaganda.

Of the **foreign press**, The *Daily Telegraph*, *USA Today* and *International Herald Tribune* get to all sorts of expatriate bastions a day or two late: availability largely depends on what passengers left on the plane. The UK's *The Times*, *Express*, *Daily Mail* and, occasionally, *The Guardian* can sometimes be found in Arusha or Dar. **International magazines** often available include *Time*, *The Economist*, *Newsweek*, and the BBC's *Focus on Africa*.

CURRENT AFFAIRS WEBSITES

Ⓦ **afrika.no/NewsUpdate** Daily summaries from Africa's press; free email news service.

Ⓦ **allafrica.com/tanzania** Collation from many sources; searchable archive.

Ⓦ **dailynews.co.tz** Digital edition of Tanzania's *Daily News*.

Ⓦ **ippmedia.com** Digital edition of Tanzania's *The Guardian*.

Ⓦ **theeastafrican.co.ke** Digital edition and archive of the leading weekly.

Ⓦ **theexpress.com** Digital edition of the English-language weekly.

Ⓦ **theguardian.com/world/tanzania** Archive of Tanzanian stories that made international news.

Radio

The government-run **Radio Tanzania** broadcasts mainly in Kiswahili but is good for getting to know traditional music. The station competes with several **independent networks**, most of them on a diet of imported soul and home-grown "Bongo Flava". For a taste, check out the online streams listed at Ⓦstreema.com/radios/country/Tanzania.

Television

Founded in 2000, the government-run **TBC1** is the country's most popular TV station, thanks to its preference for Kiswahili, and a popular blend of political propaganda, religious material (Muslim on Friday, Christian on Sunday), interviews, local as well as Nigerian ("Nollywood") soaps, and Tanzanian music. Its main competitor is **ITV**. Both channels carry newsfeeds from CNN, the BBC and – way better for in-depth coverage – Al Jazeera. On Zanzibar, TVZ is a particularly noxious example of state control when it comes to political coverage. There are also some none too memorable regional stations. **Satellite** (commonly a selection of channels delivered via cable by the commercial **DStv** service) is ubiquitous in bars, restaurants and hotels: it pipes up to sixty different channels, ranging from BBC World and Discovery to Iranian stations featuring sombre Saudi clerics, and a ton of Bollywood flicks.

Festivals

Compared with West Africa, East Africa is quiet for celebrations, but Tanzania still has a handful of traditional events well

worth catching, and a growing number of contemporary festivals that rival Africa's finest.

The best areas for **traditional celebrations** are the country's remotest corners, including much of the south and west, plus mountainous zones, and the semi-arid and arid lands in the north. The celebrations mark virtually every stage of life, from the birth of a child and its being named (sometimes years later) to circumcision and passage into adulthood, marriage, a woman's first child, the life-giving seasons, and death… There's rarely a clear distinction between performer and spectator, so if you do chance upon an event, do join in.

Also traditional are **Islamic celebrations**, whose dates shift forward by ten or eleven days each year (see p.79 for the next few years). Like their Christian counterparts, they're national holidays, and are best experienced if you can stay with a local family. Zanzibar is the main place, though there are also sizeable Muslim communities on the mainland, especially along the coast. The big dates, other than the month-long fast of Ramadan (not the best time to be on Zanzibar, when many restaurants are closed), are **Idd al-Fitr** (or *Idd al-Fitri*), being a two-to four-day holiday immediately after Ramadan (much feasting, merrymaking, gleeful kids, and firecrackers), and **Maulidi** (or *Maulid an-Nabi*), the Prophet Muhammad's birthday. The other big event, but a more private affair, is **Idd al-Haj** (or *Idd al-Adha*; the one-day feast of the sacrifice). At all these times hotels fill up quickly, so arrive a few days early or book ahead.

The following events are worth changing your travel plans to coincide with:

FEBRUARY

Sauti za Busara Festival Stone Town (see p.470), Ⓦ busaramusic .org. One of Africa's best music festivals, focused on both contemporary and traditional genres from East Africa.

JUNE

Bulabo Bujora Mwanza (see p.362). A traditional music contest (*mashindano*) of the Sukuma tribe, coinciding with Corpus Christi, pitting rival dance societies against each another in gladiatorial-style displays of crowd-pulling prowess.

JULY

Mwaka Kogwa Makunduchi Zanzibar (see p.481). Weirdly wonderful thousand-year-old celebrations to see out the Zoroastrian Year, Persian-style.

Zanzibar International Film Festival Unguja (see p.470), Ⓦ ziff .or.tz. A major cinematic event, also with musicians from around the Indian Ocean.

AUGUST

MaKuYa Festival Mtwara, Ⓦ makuyafestival.blogspot.com (see p.178). Traditional music and dance from the Makonde, Makua and Yao tribes of southern Tanzania. Sometimes held in October.

SEPTEMBER

Bagamoyo International Festival of Arts and Culture Bagamoyo, Ⓦ tasuba.ac.tz (see p.124). A bit of everything; disorganized but fun. Usually held late September or early October.

OCTOBER

Visa 2 Dance Dar es Salaam, Ⓦ visa2dance.com (see p.111). Dance, mostly contemporary but also traditional.

NOVEMBER

East African Art Biennale Dar es Salaam, Ⓦ eastafab.com (see p.111). Contemporary East African art; held in odd-numbered years.

DECEMBER

Kizimkazi Cultural Music Festival Zanzibar, Ⓦ kizinoor.org (see p.480). A Rasta-run shindig covering all of the isles' musical style.

Bullfighting Pemba Island (see p.504). A very enjoyable example of Zanzibar's multicultural compote. The fights were introduced during Portuguese rule in the seventeenth century, and, as in the original, the bulls aren't killed but merely annoyed. The fights run from December through to February and are at their most traditional in February, just before the long rains.

Safaris

Tanzania has more designated wildlife areas than any other country on earth, with one-third of its surface area given over to national parks, game and forest reserves and other valuable protected spaces.

Central to the country's wildlife crown are its sixteen **national parks**: unfenced wildlife sanctuaries with no settlements other than facilities for tourists and researchers. None have asphalt roads, and consumptive utilization of natural resources is prohibited. The classic parks such as Serengeti mostly occupy plains, and are where you'll get to see the animals you probably came to Tanzania for, albeit from inside a **vehicle** – although some parks now allow limited hiking in designated areas, usually arranged as part of an organized tour. Getting around the more forested parks of Udzungwa Mountains, Mahale Mountains, Gombe Stream and Kitulo is done **on foot**, usually in the company of an official guide or ranger. Acting as ecological buffers around the parks are over sixty **game reserves**, which allow limited human settlement and resource use; in some, wildlife viewing can be as good as inside the parks, especially if they include land visited during annual migrations. Forest reserves, some of which are now officially nature reserves, are usually in mountainous areas, and are rarely visited, as few have any facilities, and getting the required permit can be awkward, too; we've given details where appropriate.

Organized safaris

The easiest and often the cheapest way to get to know Tanzania's wild side is on an **organized safari** arranged through a safari company in Tanzania (see p.103 for Dar, pp.288–289 for Arusha), or via an overseas tour operator (see pp.44–45). For mid-range and upmarket trips, **booking ahead** by months rather than weeks is essential to be sure of getting the dates and accommodation you want, but at the budget level, where quality is a mercurial beast, it's fine to arrange things once you arrive, which gives you the chance to check out the company in person.

Safari vehicles tend to be Land Rovers or Land Cruisers, sometimes with roof hatches (handy for taking pictures). On a normal driving safari, you can keep costs down by sharing with other travellers; in a group of four or five, you might pay half what you would have paid in a couple. **Minibuses** are not normally recommended due to bigger group sizes: ensure at least that it has a pop-up roof or roof hatch, and that a window seat is guaranteed. When on safari, don't take too passive an attitude. Although some of the **itinerary** may be fixed, some aspects may be **flexible**, and daily routines can be altered to suit you and your fellow travellers – if you want to go on an early game drive, for example, don't be afraid to suggest you skip breakfast, or take sandwiches. As long as the staff know there are reasonable tips awaiting them at the end, most will go out of their way to help.

Types of safari

The **type of safari** you take is largely determined by your budget, with accommodation being the main factor, but it's never cheap. And be aware that in safari-speak, a "three-day safari" actually means two nights, and that most of the first and last days will likely be spent getting to and from the wildlife areas if you're not flying. For this reason we'd recommend at least three nights unless you're starting close by. **Prices** should include everything except alcoholic drinks and tips.

Budget safaris (camping)

At the lower end are so-called "budget" or "adventure" camping safaris. These are touted for a little as $150 per person per day, but a trip with a reliable operator costs **$200–300 per person per day**, depending on the group size, the duration of the safari, exactly where you'll be going, and whether you're sharing the trip with other travellers. Nights are usually spent in small tents, either in public campsites inside the parks, or in cheaper ones outside. Expect to muck in with the crew for some of the work, like pitching tents and washing up, and be prepared for a degree of discomfort: thin mattresses and sleeping bags, not having a shower every night, and basic food. More expensive camping trips ($275–350) get you better tents, camp-beds with linen, portable (chemical) toilets, and tend to use wilder "special" campsites as opposed to the public ones.

Mid-range safaris (lodges and tented camps)

For **$350–500 per person per day**, you get to stay in wildlife lodges or at the more basic tented camps,

---

PARK REGULATIONS AND GUIDELINES

Driving Most national parks and game reserves have a speed limit of 50kph, with 25kph recommended to avoid throwing up too much dust or scaring animals; driving is only permitted in daylight. Keep to authorized tracks and roads: off-road driving is illegal and causes irreparable damage to fragile ecosystems via erosion-fuelled chain reactions.

Do not disturb So much is made of seeing the "Big Five" – elephant, lion, leopard, cheetah (or buffalo) and rhino – that at times you'll find up to a dozen vehicles converging on the same pride or pissed-off leopard up in a tree. For some species, this is just an annoyance, but for cheetahs, it's a serious problem: they only hunt by day, and it's difficult to be stealthy when surrounded by gaggles of tourists. So, let the driver know your preference. Also, be quiet while game-viewing, switch off the engine, and keep a distance of 25m.

Do not feed animals This leads to dependence on humans; you can see the effect on baboons and vervet monkeys, which can be brazen, and even violent.

Leave no trace Don't pick or damage plants, and take care putting out campfires and cigarettes.

which have proper rooms (or walk-in tents that are much the same), restaurants, bars and often also swimming pools. Some can be wonderfully intimate, but most are large (eighty rooms or so), overrun by package tours, and lack any wilderness feeling. Before booking, find out what kind of vehicle will be used, if you're on a shared safari, and establish the maximum group size. Be aware that group sizes may become irrelevant if you end up being ferried around in convoys, as frequently happens with the larger operators dealing with (mostly US) package tours.

Upmarket safaris (tented camps)

Spending **$500–900** per person a day gets you a private "tailor-made" safari including **flights** – dispensing with the dusty discomfort and time wasted getting to places by road. On such jaunts, the guiding and service should be top-notch, as should the **tented camps** you'll be staying in, some of them amazingly luxurious affairs straight out of the pages of *Condé Nast*. Pulling out all the stops, for a blistering **$1500 a day** and up or thereabouts you can treat yourself to a Hemingwayesque "**mobile camping safari**", with fly-camps set up in the bush before your arrival each evening, champagne break-fasts (actually sparkling wine), and a rifle-toting expat as your wildlife guide. The main disadvantage to such capers is the almost total exclusion of Tanzanians from the safari and its profits – most of these outfits are owned by Europeans or South Africans.

Choosing a reliable safari operator

Given the considerable cost of safaris, and the hefty **deposit** required when booking ahead (anything from thirty percent to the full amount upfront), the importance of taking your time in choosing a reliable and trustworthy safari company cannot be stressed highly enough. We've been extremely careful with our selections, and they should be among the most responsible, ethical, and – within reason – best priced. Most of them are based in Arusha (see pp.288–289) or Dar es Salaam (see p.103), but there are also some in Mwanza (see p.364), Iringa (see p.423), and – specializing in Kilimanjaro climbs – in and around Moshi (see pp.252–253). The better overseas tour operators (see pp.44–45) have their own Tanzanian operations, too. Standards can and do change, however, so always check up on companies you're interested in beforehand online.

Before you go

In order to enter national parks with clients, safari companies need a **TALA licence**, valid for one year

starting July 1. The licence comes in several types, the most common being "Safari operator" or "Tour operator", which costs the company a minimum of $2000 and should (but doesn't, in practice) guarantee that the company owns at least five vehicles. The "mountaineering" version is only valid for climbing Kilimanjaro or Mount Meru, and lets the company use its own guides. PDFs listing licensees are posted at ⓦtanzaniaparks.com and ⓦtanzaniatouristboard.com. Most but not all reputable safari companies also belong to the **Tanzania Association of Tour Operators** (list on ⓦtatotz.org). There are no quality checks, but membership does at least guarantee that companies aren't bad enough to be expelled.

There are several good **travellers' forums** where you can search for answers and ask advice (see p.80), but don't believe everything you read on the internet, especially multiple recommendations in bad English for previously unheard-of companies. Similarly, just because a company has a flashy website it doesn't guarantee quality, but if the blurb goes into passionate detail about non-standard options (birding off the beaten track, say, or rock art or village tourism), they're more likely to be credible.

Many safari and tour companies, including overseas "specialists", don't run their own trips at all, but subcontract them to **local companies** ("ground handlers"). Get the local company's name before booking, so you can check them out. On shared safaris, simple economics mean that most companies will farm out clients to other operators if they can't fill enough seats to make a trip worth-while. You should be informed of this at the very least, and be given a chance to back out.

In Tanzania

The **tourist board offices** in Arusha and Dar es Salaam each maintain a **blacklist** of particularly noxious companies (in reality just a collection of tattered business cards). Hardly comprehensive and often very old, the list is at least useful for comparing PO box numbers of your choice (if not on the TALA list) against known bad eggs – such companies will change their names and phone numbers, but tend to stick to the same address. Incidentally, don't necessarily believe recommendations from the tourist offices, or the ads on their walls. If a company claims to have a **TALA licence** but you can't find them on the official list (see above), demand to see their original licence – not a photocopy – and be sure the date and company name are correct.

Never book with **flycatchers**: these are young men who approach tourists with offers of cheap

TANZANIA'S WILDLIFE AREAS AT A GLANCE

Amani (see pp.272–275). The ancient rainforests of the East Usambara Mountains, nicknamed "Galapagos of Africa" on account of their immense biodiversity, are a delight for hikers, with many unique plant and animal species, including bright orange land crabs.

Arusha (see pp.297–301). This encloses most of Mount Meru, a dormant 4566m volcano looming over Arusha city. Hike to the top in three days, or drive or walk around the mountain's base in search of plains game. Canoeing is also possible. Wildlife includes buffaloes, elephants, monkeys and plains game.

Gombe Stream (see pp.393–398). A forested hillside rising from Lake Tanganyika's northern shore, made famous by Jane Goodall's long-term study of its chimpanzees.

Katavi (see pp.409–412). A remote floodplain in western Tanzania filled with hippos, buffaloes and crocodiles, among which you're welcome to walk – safe in the company of an armed ranger.

Kilimanjaro (see pp.244–253). Africa's tallest mountain, and the world's highest free-standing massif, presents sturdy legs with a 5892m ice-capped challenge, best tackled over six or seven days.

Kitulo (see pp.436–438). Best visited during the rains, this highland plateau, locally dubbed "God's Garden", is a wonderland of wild flowers, especially orchids, and is also home to the extremely rare Kipunji monkey, only discovered in 2004. Driving is allowed, but hiking is far better.

Lake Manyara (see pp.325–328). At the base of a Rift Valley escarpment, Manyara's tangled shoreline is home to many species, including tree-climbing lions. The lake itself has hippos and vast flocks of pink flamingoes, drawn by algae that thrive off alkaline springs.

Mahale Mountains (see pp.398–400). Halfway down Lake Tanganyika, this contains even more chimpanzees than Gombe – and they're the reason to come.

Mikumi (see pp.200–204). Within easy reach of Dar es Salaam and Morogoro, this has heaps of classic plains game, including sometimes sizeable packs of endangered African hunting dogs.

Mkomazi (see pp.259–260). A picturesque savanna park between the Pare Mountains and Kenya's border Tsavo West National Park, with a range of predators, and few, if any, tourists.

Ngorongoro (see pp.332–338). The world's densest population of predators is to be found in the volcanic caldera at the heart of this conservation area, which is also the only place in Tanzania to virtually guarantee sightings of black rhino. Most visitors come on game drives, but an exciting alternative is to explore the Ngorongoro's northern highlands on foot, in the company of an armed ranger.

Ruaha (see pp.425–429). The southernmost of the Rift Valley parks, watered on and off by the Great Ruaha River. All the plains game of northern Tanzania plus elephants, the usual predators and rich birdlife, but with far fewer crowds.

Rubondo Island (see pp.379–381). An isolated bird-rich haven in Lake Victoria's southwest corner, but awkward (or expensive) access means it's one for dedicated twitchers only.

Saadani (see pp.127–130). Bush, beach, mangroves, forest and river: Saadani's variety of habitats draws a rich selection of animals, though a recent history of poaching means that many are skittish. Activities are game drives, boat trips, snorkelling and bush walks.

Selous (see pp.204–210). Africa's second-largest animal sanctuary. Plenty of birds but mammals can be elusive. Activities include game drives, boat safaris and bush walks.

Serengeti (see pp.338–347). The famous "endless plains" are centre-stage for the world's biggest mammalian migration, with millions of animals including wildebeest, zebra and ever-attentive lions. Game drives are the usual way around, though lodges can arrange short hikes, and you float over the lot in a hot-air balloon.

Tarangire (see pp.314–322). Like the Serengeti, Tarangire bushland is the turntable for a wildlife migration. A perennial river ensures good animal spotting year-round, especially of elephants. The park's other giants are baobab trees. Birding is big, too, and you can go hiking in the adjacent conservation area.

Udzungwa Mountains (see pp.210–214). Several types of pristine rainforest cover a wide range of elevations here, all of them rich in often unique species, including primates and birds. There are plenty of waterfalls, too, making it ideal hiking territory.

safaris, usually for disreputable companies. Any outfit that values its name shouldn't need to tout for business. Likewise, be wary of companies offering free rides in from the airport, no matter how slick their patter.

Driving off-road in national parks is illegal and destructive. Plenty of companies do it, though, even some of the big ones (excluded from this book). Test a company's moral resolve by innocently asking whether it would be possible to drive off-road for that perfect shot of a lion or leopard.

Even the worst companies will show you **comments books** overflowing with praise, but as no company asks dissatisfied punters to pen their opinions, they're not much use. Here's a trick that works though: ask the company what kind of complaints they receive. There isn't a single safari outfit, in any price range, that doesn't receive complaints from time to time, so if they say they never receive complaints, they're lying.

Any finally, although fellow travellers can be a great source of **up-to-date advice**, remain wary of recommendations: good companies can turn bad very quickly, while even the most consistently bad company can occasionally come up trumps.

Complaints

First off, you've only yourself to blame if a $150-a-day safari bought off the street turns sour. Also, be understanding about things outside a company's control – like bad weather, lack of animals (unless they explicitly promised sightings), and breakdowns caused by things like broken fuel-injection pumps, which even the best mechanics cannot predict. For justified complaints, operators should at least offer a partial refund or replacement trip. Should the operator not be forthcoming, there's little you can do to force redress, but you can make things difficult for them in future. The national parks authority, TANAPA (🌐 tanzaniaparks.com), takes complaints seriously, and has a hand in the issuing of TALA licences – contacting the tourist board can result in them blacklisting an operator (see p.289). You could also contact TATO (see p.63) which has the power to expel errant members (though it rarely does). Posting your experiences online also helps (but be reasonable!), and you can write to the guidebooks (we're at 🌐 roughguides.com).

Arranging your own safari

Arranging your own trip has the advantage of **flexibility** and being able to choose your companions, but isn't necessarily cheaper than going through a company if you're going to need a vehicle, unless you can fill all the seats (usually five or seven). You'll also be paying full "rack rates" on mid-range and upmarket accommodation, which might otherwise be discounted if booked through a safari company.

Parks and reserves that can be entered **without vehicles** are Gombe Stream, Kilimanjaro (requiring prepayment in Arusha), Kitulo, Mahale Mountains, Rubondo Island and Udzungwa Mountains. At a few others, you can get to a nearby village or town on **public transport** and arrange things there. These are Katavi (at Sitalike), Lake Manyara (Mto wa Mbu); Mikumi (Mikumi village or, more expensive, Morogoro); Ngorongoro (Karatu or Mto wa Mbu); Ruaha (Iringa or Tungamalenga) and Selous (Mloka). For all other parks you'll need to rent a **4WD vehicle** (see pp.46–47).

The basic **daily costs** are park fees (these vary enormously; details are given for each individual park), car rental ($180–250 a day excluding fuel but including the driver and his costs), meals, maps, guidebooks, tips, a guide or ranger (sometimes optional; $20) and accommodation. The cheapest stays inside the parks are camping or using park-run *bandas* (both $30 per person), though you'll need to take all your supplies with you.

Entry fees are paid on arrival, and are made electronically by Visa or MasterCard, or, if you don't have one, via a prepaid TANAPA card that can be obtained at TANAPA headquarters in Arusha (see p.287).

Activities

Tanzania boasts plenty of wholesome outdoor activities, and not just wildlife safaris: take your pick from diving or snorkelling, boating, canoeing or hiking. Alternatively, you can go birdwatching, or sample some of the country's pioneering cultural tourism projects.

Cultural tourism

Most tourists come to Tanzania for a beach-and-bush experience, and perhaps also to climb Kilimanjaro, but an increasing number find that mixing with the locals is the real highlight of their stay.

Tanzania's pioneering **Cultural Tourism Programme** (🌐 tanzaniaculturaltourism.com) was set up in 1995 by SNV, a Dutch NGO, in response to a request from Longido's Maasai community for help establishing tourism that would benefit them directly. The programme is now ably coordinated by the tourist board in Arusha (see p.287), and offers intimate hands-on experiences in **over sixty locations**, most of them accessible by public transport. The concept is as simple as it is effective: visitors get to know locals, their way of life, history and environment in intimate, respectful and invariably memorable ways; in turn, villagers benefit directly from receipts (for guides, food, accommodation, entrance fees), and through "development fees" funding community-managed projects such as irrigation, dispensaries and schools.

The various "modules" range from two hours to over a week, and **costs** are reasonable, especially if you book direct or via the tourist board in Arusha (see p.287) – typically no more than $30 or $40 for a full day and night. You'll pay a premium if going through a safari company as part of a safari, but there are no ethical worries as the basic costs mentioned above stay with the community. A **warning**: only book at the offices or places mentioned in this book or on the project's website, as the project's success has in some places attracted scammers and dupers. A **list** of the country's cultural tourism options reviewed in this book is included under "Cultural tourism" in the index.

Hiking

Hiking gives you unparalleled contact with nature as well as locals, and that delicious feeling of being at one with the world, something you'd never get by just driving around. For a sheer challenge, it's hard to beat a six- or seven-day climb up and down Africa's highest peak, the 5892m **Mount Kilimanjaro**. It's a distinctly masochistic undertaking, for your wallet as well as you, as you won't get much change out of $1500. Cheaper and a little easier, but equally invigorating, is a two- or three-day ascent of **Mount Meru** (4566m), the beautiful hulk that looms up over Arusha. Other climbable peaks include the 3417m **Mount Hanang** near Babati, and the carbonate-spewing **Ol Doinyo Lengai** (2889m, at least before its last eruption in 2008), between Ngorongoro and the wild desert around Lake Natron. Climbs up Mount Hanang are arranged locally; the others can be organized through safari companies (also overseas) or with specialist hiking companies based in or around Moshi. None of the climbs needs special skills, but you do need to be in good shape, and both Kilimanjaro and Meru require some preparations (see p.248).

Getting to the top of mountains is one thing. Just as rewarding can be exploring the rainforests on their flanks, for which there are few places better in Africa than the ancient **Eastern Arc mountains**, a disparate chain of isolated ranges that include North and South Pare, West and East Usambara (including the "Galapagos of Africa", Amani Nature Reserve), the Ulugurus and Udzungwa Mountains National Park, all of which are easily explored on foot. The rewards are many: enchanting liana-draped forest scenery, hidden brooks and waterfalls in which to refresh tired limbs, and some of the most biodiverse terrain on earth, with hundreds of unique species of plants and flowers, birds and bugs (including butterflies), and primates. Further south, Tanzania's **southern highlands** beckon, a land studded with crater lakes, hot springs, and the dormant 2960m Mount Rungwe volcano, which can be climbed in a day or, better, over three. The jewel of this area is **Kitulo National Park**: dubbed "God's Garden" by locals, the highland plateau is home to over fifty species of orchid as well as the newly discovered Kipunji monkey and, for now, receives virtually no tourists whatsoever.

Equally wild for walking, but for a few hours rather than days, are wildlife parks and reserves, where a **bush walk** – in the company of an armed ranger or guide – can get you face-to-face with elephants, buffalo, antelopes and other beasts. The walks are best arranged through a safari company or lodge, as you can't just turn up at the gate and start marching. Particularly good are: Arusha National Park to explore the lower inclines of Mount Meru; Gombe Stream and Mahale on the shore of Lake Tanganyika for tracking chimpanzees; Ruaha for classic savanna wildlife; Ngorongoro for the "Crater Highlands", a trek of several days; Katavi for unimaginable quantities of hippos and crocs; and Selous, simply because it's beautiful.

Birding

Tanzania boasts around 1200 **bird species**, including dozens of endangered "Red Book" endemics found only in particular forests or mountain ranges. The best time for birding is from November to March, when residents are joined by Eurasian and Palearctic migrants. It's impossible to recommend one area over another, as every place has something special, but highlights include: Tarangire National Park and its adjacent Conservation Area, which contain over 550 recorded species; Lake Natron for immense flocks of flamingos and rare raptors; Lake Manyara, also for flamingos and almost four hundred other species; and Rubondo Island in Lake Victoria, paradise for water birds. For endemics, the rainforest at Amani Nature Reserve in East Usambara is the place to head to, while other Eastern Arc mountain ranges – including Uluguru and Udzungwa – also contain rare endemics.

A few **safari companies** offer specialized birding trips. Especially recommended are Dar's Wild Things Safaris (see p.103), Arusha's East African Safari and Touring Company (see p.289) and Birding & Beyond (Ⓦtanzaniabirding.com), US-based Wings Birding Tours (Ⓦwingsbirds.com), whose Tanzanian twitcher is based in Arusha, and South Africa's Rockjumper Birding (Ⓦrockjumperbirding.com). Useful **websites**, which include checklists, are Ⓦtanzaniabirdatlas.com and Ⓦafricanbirdclub.org, though it can also pay to get hold of a dedicated birding **guidebook** (see p.526–527).

Diving and snorkelling

Caressed and nourished by the warm South Equatorial Current, Tanzania's fringing coral reefs offer exhilarating **scuba diving and snorkelling**, with an abundance of colourful and sometimes heart-stopping marine life to be seen within a short boat ride of most beaches. For snorkellers, the best areas – with plenty of shallow reefs and a myriad corals and creatures – are Mafia Island and the east coast of Zanzibar's Unguja Island. For scuba divers, the choice is more a matter of personal preference, though both Mafia and Pemba come in for heaps of praise.

Scuba diving

Tanzania is as good a place as any to learn how to dive: there are dozens of locations with **dive centres**, almost all of them offering PADI-accredited courses. On any dive you can expect to see a profusion of colourful tropical fish in extensive **coral gardens**, together with larger open-water (pelagic) species such as giant groupers, Napoleon wrasse, barracuda, kingfish, tuna and wahoo – enormous, super-fast versions of mackerel. **Dolphins and turtles** are also seen, and year-round too, but you'll need luck (and the right season) for whale-sharks or **whales**, which migrate up the coast from southern Africa in the latter half of the year to nurse their offspring in East Africa's warm waters. Depending on the location, experienced divers can also enjoy drift dives, wreck dives, and **night dives** (great for colourful sea slugs, properly called nudibranchs).

Arguably Tanzania's most spectacular diving location, certainly with the clearest water, is **Pemba**, whose vertiginous drop-offs are stuffed with a stupendous variety of life; Misali Island is a particular gem. However, the strong currents that add spice to many a dive here are also potentially dangerous – hence, novices should learn the ropes around Zanzibar's **Unguja Island** instead, whose eastern shore is bounded by a sheltering barrier reef. Often forgotten, but also good, are the handful of islands – protected as a marine reserve – off the coast **north of Dar**, though some of the reefs have been badly damaged by dynamite fishing. Also worth exploring are the coral gardens around the tidal Maziwe Island near Pangani, in the north. South of Dar, the reefs around **Mafia Island** rival Pemba's for beauty, and have more big fish, too. Further south, you can also dive off **Kilwa Masoko** (steep drop-offs), and in the barely known but pristine **Mnazi Bay–Ruvuma Estuary Marine Park**, on the border with Mozambique.

The **best months** for diving should be November and March, when the water is clearest and conditions calm, but as the seasons have gone haywire of late, you might find October or February better, as there's a chance of strong wind from November to January. June to September, the time of the *kusi* monsoon, is also windy, and the choppy seas and strong currents will restrict you to sites within lagoons or bays.

Safety

Proportionally, scuba diving claims more fatalities than any other sport, so **safety**, not cost, should be your primary concern when choosing a dive centre. At the time of writing, the ones reviewed in this book were accredited by **PADI** (Professional Association of Diving Instructors), which unfortunately doesn't mean as much as it should do, as PADI neither visit nor vet dive centres, basing their certifications instead on the centre's throughput. Nonetheless, we'd strongly recommend you avoid companies not reviewed in this book, and even for those we list, try to interview them beforehand to get a feel for how serious they are about your safety. One thing to ask is whether they use **marker buoys**: life-savers where drifts or strong currents are normal, such as around Pemba. Have a look at the equipment, too: a messy storage area, or battered tanks and regulators, are not a good sign. The boats can tell a tale, as well: the best are state-of-the-art inflatables equipped with oxygen, HF radio and powerful engines; others are converted dhows; while many are just normal boats with outboards. All should have life-jackets, and ideally two engines. Recommended dive centres and reefs are described in boxed sections throughout this book: look under "diving" in the index. You could also post a query on Ⓦscubaboard.com.

RESPONSIBLE DIVING AND SNORKELLING

Despite their apparent solidity, **coral reefs** are among the most fragile ecosystems on earth, with even minor environmental changes wreaking disastrous results. In places, the 1997–98 El Niño event, which raised the water temperature by one measly degree for just a few months, killed over ninety percent of corals, and some of Tanzania's reefs have yet to recover fully. Minimize your own impact by following these rules:

Swim carefully. Coral polyps die if covered with silt or sand, commonly stirred up by careless swipes of fins (flippers). Be aware of where your feet are, and when you're close to something, use your hands to swim. If you haven't dived for a while, take a refresher course and practise buoyancy control in a swimming pool.

No feeding. Some irresponsible companies encourage their clients to feed fish, but this risks screwing up feeding and mating patterns.

No touching. Leave corals, shellfish and other critters alone: you might damage them, or they might damage you – many are poisonous or otherwise bad for your health. Also, resist the temptation to collect shells on the beach, or to buy them from hawkers: the export of many species is illegal, both in Tanzania and internationally.

Courses, costs and equipment

In theory, a **medical certificate** is necessary for beginners, but it's rarely asked for. Novices can try a one-day **Discover scuba course** ($70–150), or jump straight in with the standard four or five day **Open Water certification** (around $500, including the obligatory manual), completion of which gives you the right to dive to 18m with any qualified diver worldwide. Details of these and other courses are given on ⓦpadi.com.

For already qualified divers (bring your card), costs average $50 per dive, plus $30–60 a day if a longer boat trip is required. You don't need to bring equipment, but pack **specialist gear** like dive computers or waterproof cameras as renting locally can be expensive. Tanzania's only **recompression chamber** is at Matemwe on Unguja: your insurance should cover use of this, and the better dive centres should provide insurance anyway.

Snorkelling

Snorkelling is a rewarding and cheap way of dipping beneath the ocean surface, and as most diving reefs have shallower ones nearby, snorkellers can often get there on diving boats, which cuts costs. The most accessible reefs are in Mafia's Chole Bay, and off the eastern side of Unguja, where a barrier reef encloses a series of shallow and sheltered tidal lagoons. One really special reef accessible to snorkellers but not to divers is **Chumbe Island**, southwest of Unguja, which has among the densest coral growth and diversity in Africa (over two hundred species), and provides shelter for ninety percent of East Africa's varieties of fish. For something completely different, go freshwater snorkelling at the north end of **Lake Nyasa**

near Matema, remarkable for its extraordinary number of colourful cichlids.

Bring your own **equipment** if you plan to do much snorkelling, since the daily cost of renting a mask, flippers and snorkel (up to Tsh10,000) soon adds up. Buying a set in Dar or Stone Town costs around Tsh40,000. The price of **renting a boat** varies: some fishermen will happily take you out for Tsh10,000 per person or Tsh20,000 per boat, but some dive centres and beach hotels will charge ten times as much.

Boating

The classic way to mess about on East Africa's waters is on a **dhow trip**. If arranged specially for tourists, these are usually day-trips (see p.48–49 for dhow-hopping along the coast), and can involve snorkelling, exploring mangroves and islands, or cruising lazily up a river in search of birds, monkeys, crocodiles and hippo.

The main places for dhow trips are Pangani and Saadani on the north coast (both with rivers, mangroves and snorkelling), Mafia Island in the south (various islands, snorkelling and mangroves), the Ruvuma River (wildlife and snorkelling in the marine park, most easily arranged in Mikindani), Kilwa Masoko (mainly for visiting Kilwa Kisiwani and other ancient ruins), Stone Town (sunset cruises and snorkelling trips), Nungwi and Pemba (boozy sunset cruises), Pemba (snorkelling deserted islands and mangroves), and almost anywhere on Unguja's eastern seaboard (more snorkelling and mangroves).

As Tanzania has few rivers navigable for more than a few dozen kilometres, boat trips inland – beside ferry journeys on the lakes – are limited to wildlife **cruises** on the Rufiji in Selous, and for getting to

Gombe, Mahale and Rubondo Island national parks. **Dugouts** are useful for exploring Lake Babati and Lake Nyasa (from Matema), but take care as they're inherently unstable: you don't want to become someone's next meal. You can also **canoe** at two places near Arusha: the Momela Lakes in Arusha National Park, and Lake Duluti (a crater lake) nearby.

Crime and personal safety

Tanzania is generally a safe and peaceful country to travel around, with the biggest threat to your personal safety being on the road. Insane drivers aside, if you stick to the following mostly common-sense advice, you're unlikely to run into trouble.

Robbery and theft

Your chances of being **robbed** in Tanzania are slim but you should nonetheless be conscious of your belongings, and never leave anything unguarded. In addition, be careful where you walk, at least until you've settled in somewhere; known trouble spots are mentioned throughout the guide. Be especially alert in bus and ferry terminals, and if you can't help walking around with valuables and are in town for more than a couple of days, vary your route and schedule. For advice on keeping things safe in a hotel, see p.50.

The best way to avoid being **mugged** is not to walk around at night unless you're sure the area is safe, and not to carry unnecessary valuables, especially anything visible. It should go without saying that you shouldn't wear dangling earrings or any kind of chain or necklace, expensive-looking sunglasses or wristwatches. Not so obvious is that certain brands of sports shoes (sneakers) can also be tempting, but which brands is impossible to say,

as it depends on fashion. Similarly, try to avoid carrying valuables in shoulder bags or even small rucksacks, as these provide visible temptation. Old plastic bags are a much less conspicuous way of carrying cameras. If you clearly have nothing on you, you're unlikely to feel, or be, threatened.

If you do get mugged, **don't resist**, since knives and guns are occasionally carried. It will be over in an instant and you're unlikely to be hurt. You can usually forget about enlisting the police to try and get your stuff back. In fact, their lackadaisical attitude, and that of the courts, favours **mob justice**. So, as angry as you may feel about being robbed, if you shout "Mwizi!" ("Thief!" in Kiswahili) **be ready to intercede** should a crowd manage to turn up the thief, as he might otherwise be killed.

Driving hazards

Don't leave **valuables** in an unlocked or unguarded vehicle. In towns, find an *askari* (security guard) to keep an eye on it: Tsh2000 is enough for a few hours. If you can, **avoid driving at night**: armed hold-ups in remote areas are sporadically reported, and in cities you risk grab-and-run robberies if your doors are unlocked or the windows open. Don't worry too much about car-jackers though: they tend to shun the typical (ie slightly battered) Land Rover or Land Cruiser you'll likely be driving.

Police, bribes and politics

Though you might sometimes hear stories of extraordinary kindness and amazing bursts of efficiency, **Tanzanian police** are notoriously corrupt, and it's best to steer clear. If you need to deal with them, patience and politeness, smiles and handshakes always help, and treat even the most offensively corrupt cop with respect (greeting him with "Shikamoo, Mzee" for starters). Having said this, in unofficial dealings the police can go out of their way to help you with food, transport or accommo-

---

CARRYING MONEY SAFELY

The safest place for banknotes, passports and credit cards is a flat **money belt**, strapped around your waist under your clothes. Avoid nylon belts as these can irritate your skin. If you sweat a lot, wrap your things in a plastic bag before putting them away. Although the belts are effectively invisible, it still makes sense to stash some emergency money and perhaps a spare credit card elsewhere, perhaps in the lining of a suitcase or rucksack. The voluminous "**bum bags**" (also called "fanny packs") should definitely be avoided, and not just for linguistic reasons, as even if worn back to front, they're one short step away from announcing your stash with flashing neon lights. Equally dumb are pouches hung around your neck, and ordinary wallets are a pickpocket's dream.

Place daily **spending money** in a pocket or somewhere else accessible: you don't want to be rooting around your groin every time you have to pay for something, and you'll feel safer with at least some money to hand, as few muggers will believe you have nothing on you whatsoever.

SCAMS

Most scams are confidence tricks. There's no reason to be overly paranoid about new friends (indeed, one or two scams are a play on paranoia), but a healthy sense of cynicism is always useful. Here are some of the most popular tricks:

Ticket scams A tout sells you a ticket for a non-existent ferry, or you buy a ticket at cheaper "resident" rates, only to be pulled over by the inspector to pay the full fare plus a fine. Solution: don't buy anything from touts, and if there are "non-resident" rates, just pay them.

Greedy victim scams Should a stranger, finding a wad of cash, wish to share it with you – say, down a convenient alley – well, at least the resulting robbery would vindicate Darwin.

Money changers Changing money on the street doesn't get you better rates than in a bank or an exchange bureau, and anyone promising the contrary is bent on swindling you. You should also know that you're not obliged to buy Tanzanian shillings on arriving in the country – despite what you may be told to the contrary.

Drugging on public transport One we've not heard reported from Tanzania, but nasty, so worth being wary of: a stranger strikes up a friendship, and gives you food, drink or even a cigarette. When you come to, your new friend, and all your stuff, has vanished.

Fake sponsorship Children or "students" approach you with a sponsorship form. It may be true, but schooling is now free, so most requests are just cons.

dation, especially in remote outposts. Try to reciprocate. Police salaries are low and aren't always paid on time, so they rely on unofficial channels to get by.

Unless you're driving a car, police are rarely out to solicit **bribes** from tourists, although on Zanzibar robberies at fake police roadblocks (possibly manned by real police) have been reported. If you *have* done something wrong, it really is better to pay the full fine (with receipt) than to go for the cheaper bribe. Still, if a bribe it is (in which case there'll be no receipt), wait for it to be hinted at, then haggle as you would over a purchase; Tsh5000 is enough to oil small wheels, but traffic police will expect something more substantial from tourists. Bribery is, of course, illegal – if you've done nothing wrong and are not in a rush, refusing a bribe will only cost a short delay until the cop gives up and tries someone else. Insisting on seeing his ID may help, too. If the officer persists in his pursuit, insist on going to the police station to sort things out, where you'll be able to kick up a fuss with his superior, or threaten legal action, demand legal assistance and so on – a time-consuming charade that hopefully won't be worth the corrupt cop's time, or his job.

Drugs

Tourists are occasionally offered **marijuana**. Grass (*bangi*) is widely smoked and remarkably cheap, but it is illegal, so if you're going to indulge, be discreet, and be careful who you buy from, or get high with. Never buy on the street – you're guaranteed to be conned or, worse, shopped to the police. If you're caught, you'll be hit with a heavy fine, and possibly imprisoned or deported, depending on the quantity.

Anything harder than marijuana (increasingly a problem on Zanzibar) will land you in serious trouble.

Culture and etiquette

Tanzanians are known for their tactfulness and courtesy, qualities that are highly valued right across the social spectrum. The desire to maintain healthy relationships with both neighbours and strangers epitomizes the peaceful and non-tribalistic nature of Tanzanian society, and expresses itself in the warm welcome given to visitors. As such, you'll be treated as an honoured guest by many people, and if you make the effort, you'll be welcomed to a side of Tanzania that too few tourists see.

There are few hard-and-fast rules about public behaviour. In **Islamic areas** you should obviously avoid dress that might be deemed indecent or displays of sexual intimacy (although holding hands is fine), and non-Muslims shouldn't enter mosques without permission. During Ramadan, it's also polite not to be seen eating, drinking or smoking in public by day.

Elsewhere, only a few things are considered offensive; these include both verbal and material **immodesty** (so don't flaunt your wealth), and **bad temper or impatience**, though there are exceptions to this – if you're a woman being pestered by a man, an angry outburst should result in embarrassed bystanders coming to your rescue. Also, it's not cool to take **photographs of people** without their permission. Always ask first, and cough up (or refrain) if they ask for money in return. You should also ask permission if you want to **smoke** in an enclosed public space such as a bar or restaurant.

Tipping is only really expected on safari or when climbing Mount Meru or Kilimanjaro. In bars, restaurants and taxis, tips are appreciated but not required.

Religious beliefs

The majority of mainland Tanzanians are **Christians** – if sometimes only in name. Varieties of Catholicism and Protestantism dominate: there are several thousand flavours in all, often based around the teachings of local preachers. On the coast and Zanzibar, **Sunni Islam** dominates, and is in the ascendant throughout the country. The Aga Khan's moderate **Ismaïli** sect is also influential, with powerful business interests, the profits from which are often used in (secular) development projects. Unless you're given permission, **mosques** should only be entered by Muslims. **Hindu** and **Sikh** temples are found in most large towns, and there are adherents of **Jainism** and **Bahai** faith, too.

An ever decreasing minority still hold **traditional beliefs**, which are not so much religions as worldviews or cosmologies. These are mostly based on the idea that so long as deceased **ancestors** are remembered and honoured by the living, frequently via offerings of food or drink, they remain alive in the spirit world, where they're able to influence God in matters of weather, disease and other things beyond human control. Sadly, these beliefs, together with much collective wisdom, traditional music and modes of life, are gradually being destroyed by the expansion of Christianity, even among conservative peoples such as the Maasai and Barbaig, so traditional beliefs are now confined to remote areas.

Appearance

Tanzanians make an effort to appear well dressed, and so should you. The simple rule is to wear comfortable and decent **clothes** (you'll feel cooler in loose cotton); they should also be clean, within reason.

Although Islamic moral strictures tend to be generously interpreted, in Muslim majority areas – mainly the coast and all of Zanzibar – visitors should **cover up** when not on a beach frequented by tourists. This means wearing long trousers and any kind of shirt for men, and a long dress, skirt, *kanga* or trousers for women. Uncovered shoulders

are fine, and there's no need for headgear either, but don't show cleavage or any other part of your torso. Although people are far too polite to admonish strangers, tourists who ignore the dress code – which is posted in pretty much every hotel on Zanzibar – are viewed with considerable scorn.

The other reason for covering up, other than minimizing the risk of Caucasians turning lobster-red, is that you'll attract less **hassle** in the main tourist centres of Arusha, Moshi, Dar es Salaam, Stone Town, and the more popular Zanzibari beaches. While it's impossible not to look like a tourist (expats are known by all), you can dress down and look like you've been travelling for months, so that hustlers will assume you're streetwise. Avoid wearing anything brand new, especially white, and make sure your shoes aren't too shiny. Some tourists swear by sunglasses to avoid making unwanted eye-contact; while this usually works in fending off hasslers, it also cuts you off from everyone else… the same people who make Tanzania so special.

Greetings

Lengthy greetings – preferably in Kiswahili – are important, and people will value your efforts to master them. Elderly men and women are invariably treated with great deference. The word for greeting anyone older than you is *Shikamoo*, best followed by an honorific title. If you're addressed with "Shikamoo" – usually by children in rural areas – do respond with the requisite "Marahaba" (pulling a silly face goes down a storm, too). There's more information on these and other **common greetings** in the "Language" section at the end of the guide (see pp.535–536).

As well as the verbal greeting, younger women make a slight **curtsy** when greeting elders, while men invariably shake hands both at meeting and parting. It's especially polite to clasp your right forearm or wrist with your left hand as you do so. Younger people have a number of more elaborate and ever-changing handshakes that anyone will be happy to teach you. Incidentally, if someone's hands are wet or dirty when you meet, they'll offer their wrist instead. You should always use your right hand to shake, or to give or receive anything.

Gifts

When invited into someone's home, bring small **presents** for the family. Elderly men often appreciate tobacco, whether "raw" (a piece of a thick, pungent coil that you can buy in markets everywhere; ask for *tumbako*) or a couple of packets of filterless "sharp cigarettes" or *sigara kali* (also nicknamed *sigara ya babu* "grandfather's cigarettes"). Women appreciate anything that helps keep down household expenses, be it soap, sugar, tea, meat, or a few loaves of bread. Kids, of course, adore sweets – but give them to the mother to hand out or you'll end up getting mobbed.

If you're **staying longer**, slightly more elaborate presents are in order. Increase the number of practical things you bring, and perhaps buy a *kanga* or *kitenge* for the mother and grandmother (see p.74). Ballpoint pens and notepads will always find use, and kids will like books (Tanzania's literacy rate, though down from a peak of ninety percent-plus in the 1980s, is still high by African standards, and getting better – currently around eighty percent of 15–24 year olds). Most bookshops sell gorgeously illustrated children's books in Kiswahili. For other gift ideas, ask your host before coming – and insist beyond their polite insistence that the only presents you need to bring is your own presence.

Lastly, **do not give gifts to children** if you don't know them already: it encourages begging, as proved in touristic areas by the chirpy choruses of "Mzungu give me money/pen/sweet…" If you really want to give something, hand it to an adult to share out, or make a donation to the local school. If you'll be travelling or staying for some time and really want to prepare, get a large batch of photos of you and your family with your address on the back. You'll get lots of mail.

Sexuality

Sexual mores in Tanzania are generally quite open. The price is the prevalence of sexually transmitted diseases. At least one in twenty Tanzanians aged 15–49 carries **HIV**, so it goes without saying that casual sex without a condom is a deadly gamble and you should assume any sexual contact to be HIV-positive. **Condoms** are openly sold in pharmacies and supermarkets; a reliable brand is Salama, but check the expiry date and don't buy ones whose boxes have been bleached by sunshine.

Despite the risks, **female prostitution** flourishes openly in urban areas, particularly in bars and nightclubs frequented by better-off Tanzanians and foreigners. On Zanzibar, **male gigolos** abound, with enough female tourists indulging in sexual adventures to make flirtatious pestering a fairly constant feature, but don't kid yourself: your cute dreadlocked potential lover probably romances for a living. The attention can of course be irritating as

well as amusing, but fortunately really obnoxious individuals are usually on their own. A useful trick for women travelling unaccompanied by men is to wear a "wedding" ring (silver ones are less likely to attract robbers), though for this to be really credible it helps to take along a picture of a burly male friend with a suitably husband-like message written on the back as "proof".

Male **homosexuality** is officially illegal. Although men holding hands is normal, up to a point (ie if someone's leading you by the arm), public displays of affection are guaranteed to offend, and may even get you up to 25 years in the slammer. In contrast, there are no overtly gay or lesbian venues in Tanzania, and few hotels will let two men share a room. Women sharing a room should be fine. *Shoga* is the word for gay man; *msagaji* is a lesbian.

Hassle

Most Tanzanians will go well out of their way to help visitors, but in touristic areas it's possible to fall prey to misunderstandings with young men – generally known as **flycatchers** or, on Zanzibar, *papasi*, meaning "ticks" – offering anything you might conceivably want, from safaris and hotel rooms to drugs and souvenirs, and themselves as guides, helpers or even lovers. You shouldn't assume anything they do is out of simple kindness. It may well be, but if not, you're expected to pay. If you're being bugged by someone whose "help" you don't need, just let them know you can't pay for their trouble. It may not make you a friend, but it's better than a row later on.

Far less likely to harangue you are **beggars** – common in Arusha, Dar es Salaam and Dodoma, but rare elsewhere. Most are visibly destitute. Some are cripples, lepers or blind; others are homeless mothers with children. A Tsh100 coin suffices; Tsh500 will delight. More common, especially in Arusha, are **street children**. Some may be AIDS orphans or may have escaped physical abuse; others may be begging on an adult's behalf; some are lost to the world on glue; all are persistent. Western sensibilities make them hard to ignore, especially when they trail you around murmuring pitifully until you cough up. If you want to help, it's probably best giving food, or getting in touch with an orphanage.

Shopping

There are heaps of attractive souvenirs you could bring home with you from

Tanzania, from well-crafted woodwork to colourful kangas and kitenges. While many items are portable, others – like life-size statues of Maasai warriors – require the services of a shipping agent, which the seller should be able to arrange. Rooting around markets for groceries is fun too: coffee and honey make great souvenirs, as do essentials oils from Zanzibar.

For basic goods and services used by the majority of Tanzanians, which includes food, the prices are known by all, so even an ignorant foreigner isn't likely to be overcharged by much. Where you will get ripped off – unless your haggling hat is on straight – is when buying souvenirs, where the opening "special price, my friend" can be ten times what the vendor is really prepared to accept. Once you get into bargaining, though, you'll rarely end up paying more than double the going rate, but don't take it to extremes and start quibbling over a few hundred shillings for a few lemons.

Woodwork

Woodwork souvenirs are ubiquitous, most famously from Southern Tanzania's **Makonde tribe** (see p.184), who have literally carved a global reputation for themselves. Their best-known works are the "tree of life" or "people pole" carvings in the **Ujamaa style**: intricately carved columns of interlocking human figures representing unity, continuity, and communal strength or power known as *dimoongo* in Kimakonde. In the carvings, the central figure is a mother surrounded by clinging children, supporting (both literally and symbolically) later

generations, on top. Lively and full of movement, rhythm and balance, these are the works that justly brought the Makonde their fame. Less well known is the naturalistic **Binadamu style**, which represents traditional modes of life such as old men smoking pipes, and the more abstract **Shetani style**, depicting folkloric spirits in distorted and often fantastically grotesque ways. Though the tradition's roots allude to the birth of the Makonde themselves (see p.184), the modern carvings are mostly made with an eye to the tastes of tourists and collectors. They're not always by Makonde either, prompting some to decry their output as mere "airport art". But don't listen to the snobs: even mass-produced carvings possess a grace and elegance that easily endures repeated viewing.

Also worth buying are **bao boards**. Known elsewhere in Africa as *mancala* and by a host of local names, *bao* is the quintessential African board game, and you'll see it being played throughout Tanzania. The board, either carved or just a series of depressions scratched into the ground, typically has four rows with eight holes each. The basic idea is for two players to take turns in distributing counters (seeds, beans or stones) from one of the holes on the row closest to them into adjacent holes, clockwise or anticlockwise, one seed per hole. The objective is to clear your opponent's inner row by capturing their seeds. The permutations are mind-boggling and, as with chess, the best players ruminate over many moves in advance. Like chess, too, *bao* has ancient roots: wooden game boards survive from the sixth century, and there are much older "boards" etched into rocks at various Stone Age sites, possibly including Matombo near Morogoro (see pp.199–200).

Other woodwork items include walking sticks,

TIPS AND TRICKS FOR HAGGLING

Know your limit If buying souvenirs, visit a gift shop in a large hotel first to get an idea of the maximum price. For other things, ask disinterested locals about the real price beforehand. The bottom line though is that if you're happy with a price, then it's a good price, irrespective of what locals might have paid.

Bargain only for what you want Don't start haggling for something you'll never buy.

Dress down Put that camera away, brush up on your Kiswahili, and definitely don't wear swimming trunks or a bikini while shopping. The less you look like a tourist, the lower the price.

Feign disinterest If a seller knows you're hooked on something, the price is going to stick. Insouciance is what you need.

Bluff Bargaining is basically just bluffing, so don't be shy of making a big scene (it's all part of the fun). If things really aren't going your way, say it's too much, thank the seller for his time, get up and start to walk away. That's often all that's needed to elicit a better offer.

Buy in bulk Striking a good deal is easier if you have more items to play with.

Show your money Once you're close to finalizing, pull out the cash: the sight of impending riches may encourage the seller to squeeze the price down just that little bit more. Or not, if you time it badly…

Maasai spears (you can't take these in your hand luggage), combs, animal figures, and rather excellent "goat boards" (*kibao cha mbuzi*), which are foldable stools with an attached metal grater for gouging out the contents of coconuts. With the notable exception of motorbike-style "helmet masks" from the Makonde, called *mapiko*, **masks** are notably absent: what you can find, other than rather ugly stylized warrior heads, are reproductions of central African designs. Beware: almost all of them are fake, no matter how much congealed cow dung appears to fill the crevices.

Tingatinga paintings

Apart from Makonde carvings, Southern Tanzania's other great "airport art" tradition is **Tingatinga paintings** – vibrantly colourful tableaux of cartoon-like people and animals daubed in bicycle paint and sold virtually everywhere. The style takes its name from Eduardo Saidi Tingatinga, born in 1937 to a rural Makua family. He moved to Tanga when he was 16, and when not working on building sites, made paintings and signboards for shops. In the mid-1960s, he began selling his paintings from the **Morogoro Stores** in Dar es Salaam, and quickly garnered a reputation as Tanzania's foremost artist. In particular, it was his use of *shetani* ("spirit") imagery that caught the eye – often amusingly grotesque beings gobbling their feet or those of other figures, and which apparently inspired the Makonde's Shetani style of woodcarving. Tingatinga was shot dead in 1972, when police mistook him for a criminal.

His style lives on, but the subjects of most modern versions are typically touristic scenes depicting wildlife, baobabs and Kilimanjaro. That's not to dismiss them, however – they make singularly cheerful and attractive souvenirs, and are portable too. **Prices** are generally very reasonable, with a large A3-sized painting costing no more than Tsh25,000 if you're adept at bargaining.

Kangas and kitenges

The colourful printed cotton wraps worn by many Tanzanian women are called **kangas** ("guinea fowl", alluding to early polka dot designs imported by Portuguese merchants). Two *kangas* joined together are called **doti**, and are often cut in two by the buyer, one part being worn around the body, the other around the head or shoulders. *Kanga* designs always include the words of a **proverb or riddle** (*neno* – statements): a way of making public sentiments that would be taboo in another form. So, a wife wishing to reprimand her husband for infidelity or neglect might buy a *kanga* for herself with the proverb, "The gratitude of a donkey is a kick" (*Fadhila ya punda ni mateke*), while one reading "A heart deep in love has no patience" (*Moyo wa kupenda hauna subira*) might be bought for a woman by her lover, expressing his desire to get married.

Similar to a *kanga*, but without the proverb or riddle, is a **kitenge**, made of thicker cloth and as a double-pane; their size makes them ideal for bedlinen. **Prices** for simple *kangas* range from Tsh5000 to Tsh8000 depending on the design and where you buy it, while *doti* and *kitenges* go for Tsh7000–10,000. Women will be happy to show you some ways of tying it. For more ideas, check out Tanzania's bookshops for *Kangas: 101 Uses* by Jeanette Hanby and David Bygott, or *The Krazy Book of Kangas* by Pascal Bogaert.

Other souvenirs

The country's distinctive **toys** make good souvenirs: most worthwhile are beautifully fashioned buses, cars, lorries and even motorbikes made out of wire and cans. Also recycled are small **oil lanterns** called *kibatari*. **Batiks** are common but rarely outstanding; reams of them will be shoved under your nose in Arusha by hawkers. Other frequently seen items include a huge variety of **sisal baskets**, jewellery

---

WHAT NOT TO BUY

The purchase or export of most items sourced from wildlife is illegal, internationally and in Tanzania, not that you'd ever guess it looking at the products for sale in touristic areas. This includes **ivory**, **turtleshell** (often miscalled "tortoiseshell"), **seahorses**, **coral**, and many species of **seashells**. If caught with any of these, you risk a heavy fine or imprisonment. Similarly off-limits are **animal skins and game trophies** lacking the requisite paperwork, and even with the right papers, possession of them may still be illegal in other countries. Finally, when buying carvings, if you must go for **ebony** (*mpingo* in Kiswahili), consider making a donation to the African Blackwood Conservation Project (🕸 blackwoodconservation.org), which strives to avoid the exhaustion of this fast-diminishing resource.

(especially iconic is colourful Maasai **beadwork**), and **soapstone carvings** imported from Kisii in Kenya.

Imitations of **traditional crafts**, often smaller and more portable in scale than the originals, include weapons, shields, drums, musical instruments, stools and headrests. There's also some really nice **pottery** about, especially in West Usambara, and on the north shore of Lake Nyasa, but little that's easily portable. Much more pocketable are some unusual **cures**, such as *jiwe ya punju*, a little stone for treating snake bites, and small clay cylinders (the names differ locally) stuffed with minerals that are useful during pregnancies. On Zanzibar, root around for **essential oils** (*mafuta*), which are a great way of being reminded of Africa's "spice islands" long after you've returned home. Clove oil is the main one, but also worth seeking out is lemongrass. You can also find aromatherapy oils, which use coconut oil for their base.

Lastly, if you're in Dar or Bagamoyo, have a look at some **contemporary art**: paintings often display an eye for movement and colour (not necessary gaudy, like Tingatinga paintings) that has long been absent from Western art.

Travelling with children

Assuming you can keep your child healthy, Tanzania is a great country for kids, especially of school age. Most Tanzanians are mad about children, who should make friends easily, thereby helping you to get to know Tanzanians outside the touristic context.

You won't have any trouble finding people to look after children should you need a break, and **breast-feeding** in public is perfectly acceptable, even on Zanzibar (with the help of a well-placed *kanga*). Tinned baby milk can be bought in supermarkets in larger towns and cities, together with disposable nappies, though these are rarely used locally (it's cheaper and more ecological to wash and reuse cloths).

The big worry, however, is **malaria**. This is a particular concern as none of the drugs used for adult prophylaxis are recommended for young children. Instead, you'll need to rely on bug spray, repellent and mosquito nets (buy a cot-covering tent for babies). Your family doctor should be your first point of contact, who will also advise you about inoculations (see p.56). The other concern is protecting children from the **sun**: keep them smothered in sunblock, insist on hats, and also T-shirts when swimming.

Sunglasses are also a good idea, even for babies: you can always find little novelty ones to fit. And of course, make sure they drink plenty of water.

For a family with under-5s, **going on safari**, especially a shared one, probably isn't a great idea: young children aren't overly excited about seeing animals from a distance, and the long drives can be tedious. Hiring a car with a driver is feasible, however, and gives you the flexibility and privacy you need for changing nappies, toilet stops and shouting at each other. Few cars in Tanzania have working (or even fitted) seat belts, however, so you will be taking a risk, even if you bring a detachable baby seat. The most child-friendly parks, needing only short drives, are Arusha National Park and, if your kids can cope with a two- or three-hour drive, Ngorongoro and Tarangire (which has lots of elephants – a big favourite). Many lodges and hotels "discourage" children, often under-6s, sometimes under-12s, either because wildlife tends to wander through the grounds, or just to avoid having noisy kids tearing around.

Much more fun for kids are the **beaches**. We'd recommend staying in Jambiani on Zanzibar, which has a really pleasant village feeling, and shallow sheltered waters that retreat at low tide exposing all sorts of interesting critters in coral pools. Larger hotels should be able to provide babysitters given a few hours' notice, and a handful – mentioned in our reviews – offer a full range of children's activities.

Travel essentials

Costs

For tourists, Tanzania is not cheap unless you're content with cultural tourism as your main activity: safaris, Kilimanjaro climbs, scuba diving, chimp tracking, and anything involving rented cars will all blow a hole in your budget. Having a **student card** (**W** isiccard.com) may get you reductions on international flights, but nothing in Tanzania itself. With the exception of food, most costs are **negotiable**, so it's worth honing your bargaining skills; see p.73. One thing you can't bargain is your status: foreigners pay **"non-resident" rates** for touristic services, which are usually priced in dollars and always more than the "resident" rates paid by locals. It's a rip-off, definitely, albeit legally sanctioned and, if you think about it, justifiable: why should people who earn thirty times Tanzania's average salary pay the same as locals?

For **basic costs**, excluding activities but including two simple meals and a couple of drinks, solo travellers can get by comfortably on $20 a day (roughly £13, €16 or Tsh36,000), or double that on Zanzibar, but if you're unfussy and don't drink alcohol, this can drop to $15 on the mainland, or $30 on Zanzibar. To this add transport: bus fares average Tsh2000 ($1.10) an hour. Couples sharing a room will end up paying less per person: from $15 each on the mainland, and $25 on Zanzibar, including a couple of drinks. Factor in **activities** and costs begin to spiral – expect to pay from $1600 for a six-day ascent of Kilimanjaro, $180 a day for a wildlife safari, and $500 for an Open Water scuba-diving course. Snorkelling or cultural tourism are more affordable, rarely costing more than $30 a day.

On **mid-range** trips, costs vary enormously, depending on where you eat and sleep, and how you travel around. Minimum costs for two people sharing a decent three-star standard hotel room, eating in good but not overly expensive restaurants with a couple of drinks each, and travelling by taxi in towns, are $120, or $80 if travelling alone; doubling those costs would give you far greater choice of accommodation. To this add on **activities**: from $1400 for a four- or five-day wildlife safari, and up to $2500 for a seven-day ascent of Kilimanjaro. If you want to travel by rental car instead of public transport, add on $180–250 per day for the vehicle. Travelling **upmarket**, the sky's the limit. Most travellers in that range come on package holidays, with prices starting at around $400 a day (excluding international flights but including a safari, transport and full board), but they can easily be double or triple that.

Electricity

Tanzania uses British-style square **three-pin plugs** – theoretically 220V, but in practice the range fluctuates between 160V and 260V. Power cuts, surges, spikes, drop-offs and rationing are very frequent, especially in Dar, and particularly at the end of dry spells, when reservoirs are too low to run hydroelectric stations. Most rural areas are not connected to the national grid: electricity in those places, if any, is provided by local oil-fired power stations. The result is that many businesses, including hotels, have their own generators.

Entry requirements

Visitors to Tanzania need a passport valid for six months beyond the end of the stay; possibly a yellow fever **vaccination certificate** if travelling from elsewhere in Africa (see p.56); and a visa, which can be bought without fuss at airports and land borders. The standard three-month **tourist visa** costs $50 (cash only), except for US and Irish nationals, who pay $100. You can also pay in Euros and sterling, but will still be charged fifty of them, so dollars are cheaper. A **multiple-entry visa** is next to impossible to obtain, even though it appears as an option on the form. Contrary to what you might read on the internet, tourist visas are *not* valid for the rest of East Africa. Visa **extensions** can be obtained at immigration offices in Tanzania, and cost $100. Alternatively, spend a few days in a neighbouring country and get a new visa when you return.

Customs officials are unlikely to show much interest unless you're carrying a mountain of specialist gear. Items that are obviously for personal use (binoculars, cameras, laptops) pose no problem, particularly if they aren't in their original packaging: at worst you'll have to sign (and pay) a bond, redeemable when leaving the country. If you're taking expensive presents, however, you'll have to pay duty.

Insurance

The most important component of a travel insurance policy is **medical cover**, which should include evacuation and hospital expenses. You'll have to pay an extra premium for potentially **dangerous activities**, including travelling by *pikipiki* (motorbike), safaris (even by car), snorkelling, scuba diving, and any kind of hiking. If you need to make a claim for stolen possessions, obtain an official statement from the police, who invariably demand an unofficial "fee" for the favour (more than Tsh10,000 would be excessive)

Internet

Most Tanzanian towns are blessed with satellite-based broadband, and a handful of **internet cafés**. Most post offices also have access. Prices average Tsh1500 an hour (under a dollar). Many hotels popular with tourists or businessmen, even at the budget end, provide wi-fi – at least around the reception area if not from bedrooms – usually at no extra charge. Unless you're technically confident, avoid internet banking or making payments from public computers, as most are infested with viruses. For the same reason, be careful when using USB flash drives, as these can become infected, in turn infecting your own device.

If you want to use your phone but need a **modem** (3G USB), these cost Tsh50,000–75,000 including some prepaid time. Access costs around Tsh10,000 for 250MB. More time can be bought at phone company payshops, which you can find all over: M-Pesa (Vodacom), Tigo-Pesa, Airtel Money and EzyPesa (Zantel).

Laundry

There are no laundromats in Tanzania. When washing your own clothes, beware of the popular but all-dissolving New Blue Omo soap powder. Except in the rains on the coast, including Zanzibar, when everything is damp, clothes dry fast if you can hang them outside. Most bigger hotels have expensive laundry services; in more humble places, staff are happy supplementing their wages with a bit of washing and ironing. Tsh2000 for a modest bundle should be gladly received.

Mail

Tanzania's **postal service** is slow but things do eventually arrive: airmail should take about five days to Europe, ten to North America or Australasia. For something more urgent, the post office's EMS service is reliable, and cheaper than an **international courier**, though the latter are better for sending valuables; DHL has branches throughout Tanzania (W dhl.co.tz).

Couriers are also useful for **parcels** but, if you're not in a rush, surface parcel post (taking up to four months) is cheaper: $100 for 20kg to the UK, Canada and New Zealand; $80 to the US; $60 to Ireland; $65 to Australia; and $40 to South Africa.

To receive mail, **poste restante** works for major towns: ask correspondents to underline and capitalize your surname. Smaller post offices also hold mail, but your correspondent should mark the letter "To Be Collected". If you're expecting a parcel, you'll probably have to pay import duty: having the sender mark packages "Contents to be re-exported from Tanzania" can be helpful. There's no home delivery in Tanzania: **addresses** are always box numbers (PO box or SLP, its Kiswahili equivalent) or, out in the sticks, "Private Bag" with no number.

Maps

The best **general map of Tanzania** is Reise Know-How's waterproof *Tanzania, Rwanda, Burundi* (1:1,200,000; W reise-know-how.de), frequently updated, packed with detail, and with relief shown as both contours and colouring. Almost as detailed, just as accurate, but updated less frequently, is harms-ic-verlag's *Tanzania, Rwanda and Burundi* (1:1,400,000; W harms-ic-verlag.de). Nelles Verlag's *Tanzania, Rwanda, Burundi* (1:1,500,000, W nelles -verlag.de) is also good, and up to date.

The prettiest maps of the **Northern Safari Circuit**, one for each park, are Giovanni Tombazzi's painted plans (W gtmaps.com), last published over a decade ago, so not too accurate, but still useful. All are double-sided: the wildlife ones come with a dry-season version on one side and wet-season on the other (showing the changes of vegetation and illustrating commonly seen plants and trees). The most accurate map of **Ngorongoro** is harms-ic-verlag's *Ngorongoro Conservation Area* (1:230,000).

For **Zanzibar**, the best is harms-ic-verlag's *Zanzibar*, with Unguja (1:100,000), plus insets of Pemba and Stone Town. Zanzibar's dive sites are presented on Giovanni Tombazzi's *Zanzibar at Sea*, an attractive compilation of painted plans.

For **off-the-beaten-track hiking**, you need 1:50,000 topographical sheets available at the Government's Mapping & Surveys Division in Dar es Salaam (Kivukoni Front; Mon–Fri 8am–3.30pm; T 022 212 4575), which cover the whole country. They've run out of the popular sheets, but it may be possible to buy photocopies. A caveat: most were produced between 1959 and 1962, so while the topographical detail remains more or less accurate

---

ROUGH GUIDES TRAVEL INSURANCE

Rough Guides has teamed up with **WorldNomads.com** to offer great travel insurance deals. Policies are available to residents of over 150 countries, with cover for a wide range of adventure sports, 24hr emergency assistance, high levels of medical and evacuation cover, and a stream of travel safety information. **Roughguides.com** users can take advantage of their policies online 24/7, from anywhere in the world – even if you're already travelling. And since plans often change when you're on the road, you can extend your policy and even claim online. Roughguides.com users who buy travel insurance with WorldNomads.com can also leave a positive footprint and donate to a community development project. For more information, go to W roughguides.com/shop.

(though don't expect the forest cover to be anywhere near as extensive), things like roads and villages will have changed.

Money

Tanzania's **currency** is the shilling ("Tsh"), which floats freely against major hard currencies. **Exchange rates** at the time of writing were US$1/Tsh1700, €1/Tsh2100, £1/Tsh2700, Can$1/Tsh1500, Aus$/Tsh1450, NZ$/Tsh1350 and ZAR10/Tsh1550. Rates on Zanzibar are typically ten percent less. ⓦoanda.com shows the latest rates, though, surprisingly, local kiosk rates can be better. You can **change money** safely at banks and foreign exchange bureaux ("forexes"); the former have better rates but may charge high commission (ask first), and queues can be long.

The most widely accepted **foreign currency** is the **US dollar**; indeed, many tourist services are priced in dollars, and some can only be paid in dollars cash (including the ferries to Zanzibar, and on lakes Tanganyika and Nyasa), so it's wise to take a few hundred dollars with you, including a spread of $1, $5 and $10 bills. When changing cash, $100 bills attract better rates than smaller denominations, but $500 notes are rarely accepted. Avoid dollar notes printed before 2006, which are rarely accepted because of the risk of forgery. If you need more dollars, Tanzanian forexes oblige, though your currency will be changed into shillings first, then dollars, so you'll pay the commission twice. When changing money into shillings, ask for a spread of notes, not just Tsh10,000 ones, which are awkward to change in non-touristic areas. Never carry more cash with you than you're prepared to lose.

Cards and ATMs

Using **credit cards and debit cards** to withdraw cash from ATMs is the easiest way to access money in Tanzania. Visa and MasterCard are accepted in all but one network (NMB). All **ATMs** dole out shillings, and the transaction limit is Tsh400,000. There are machines all over Tanzania, including in small towns, with most ATMs in cubicles watched over by security guards; if you're worried about security, get a friend to cover your back. ATMs and their networks can be unreliable, of course, so bring several cards, and try to withdraw cash a day or two before you really need it. Cards with **six-digit PINs** may work using only the first four digits, but check with your issuing company first. Before leaving home, let your card issuer know you'll be in Tanzania, to avoid your account being blocked, and

if you're away for more than two months, set up a standing order to cover the monthly minimum fee.

Direct payments with cards are rarely possible for anything other than upmarket accommodation and services (flights, safaris and car rental), and attract premiums of five to ten percent on Visa or MasterCard, and up to twenty percent on American Express, if it's accepted at all.

A **prepaid debit card** that works in most ATMs can be useful: you load up your account with funds, and can top up the card online (though don't trust Tanzania's internet cafés for that). There are several to chose from: easiest to find is Travelex's "Cash Passport" (ⓦcashpassport.com), which can be bought at various banks, high street retailers, travel agents and exchange bureaux in the UK, Ireland, US, Canada, Australia, New Zealand and South Africa.

As a last resort, you can **wire funds** via Western Union (ⓦwesternunion.com) or MoneyGram (ⓦmoneygram.com). Both have agents throughout the country.

Opening hours and public holidays

Most **shops** are open Monday to Friday from 8.30am to 5pm, sometimes to 7pm, and sometimes with a lunch break; they're also open Saturday mornings until around noon. Supermarkets, and stores and kiosks in residential or rural areas, may be open later. **Government offices** have slightly variable times, but you'll always find them open Monday to Friday from 8am to 2.30pm. Other opening times: **post offices** Mon–Fri 8am–4.30pm, Sat 9am–noon; **banks** Mon–Fri 8.30am–4pm, Sat 8.30am–1pm (rural branches close at 12.30pm weekdays, 10.30am Sat); **forex bureaux** variable, but often Mon–Fri 9am–4.30pm, Sat 9am–noon.

Government offices, banks, post offices and other official establishments are closed on **public holidays**, including Christian and Muslim celebrations (except Ramadan). If a holiday falls on a weekend, the following Monday is the day off. Holidays with **fixed dates** are: January 1 (New Year); January 12 (Zanzibar Revolution Day); April 7 (Karume Day); April 26 (Union Day between Zanzibar and Tanganyika); May 1 (Workers' Day); July 7 (Industrial Day); August 8 (Farmers' Day); October 14 (Nyerere Day); December 9 (Independence Day); December 25 (Christmas); December 26 (Boxing Day). Holidays with **variable dates** are Easter (Good Friday and Easter Monday) and the four Muslim celebrations, whose dates are approximate as they depend on moon sightings:

Maulidi Dec 24, 2015; Dec 12, 2016; Dec 1, 2017; Nov 21, 2018; Nov 10, 2019.

Start of Ramadan June 18, 2015; June 6, 2016; May 27, 2017; May 16, 2018; May 6, 2019.

Idd al-Fitri July 17, 2015; July 5, 2016; June 25, 2017; June 15, 2018; June 5, 2019.

Idd al-Haj (Idd al-Adha) Sep 23, 2015; Sep 11, 2016; Sep 1, 2017; Aug 22, 2018; Aug 12, 2019.

Phones

TTCL operates Tanzania's terrestrial network; reliability is improving, but is still smitten by power cuts and the theft of copper wires. As such, Tanzanians have embraced **mobile phones** with gusto. Tanzania's networks are GSM 900/1800, with 3G internet. Local "phone mechanics" (*fundi simu*) can unlock most handsets for no more than $10, so that you can use a Tanzanian SIM card (Tsh1000/$0.60) in your phone. Alternatively, buy a handset on arrival ($25 for something basic). **International calls** can be as cheap as $0.50 a minute; sending an SMS averages $0.15, or is free. Phones are **topped up** with a scratch card (a *vocha*, voucher), available absolutely everywhere (as are SIM cards – just look for a phone company logo) in denominations up to Tsh10,000/$6. The phone companies are Vodacom, Airtel, Tigo and Zantel; Zantel is best for Zanzibar, and is partnered with Vodacom on the mainland. Coverage is pretty good, and includes most of the national parks. Given the low cost of SIM cards, many people have several cards, swapping between them when needed.

With no mobile, you can call from a hotel (usually extortionate), or use **public phones**. These include a cumbersome "operator-assisted" procedure inside TTCL offices; coin- or card-operated phones outside TTCL offices, at bus stations, and in some bars and hotels; and informal "assisted call" centres, often around bus stations. Costs are rarely less than $0.80 a minute for international calls. Cheaper are VoIP phone services such as Skype offered by a handful of internet cafés (strictly speaking, illegally), mostly in Arusha and Stone Town. **Collect calls** (reverse charge) cannot be made from Tanzania.

Photography

Digital photography is ideal for taking pictures in equatorial climates – the light here can be tricky, as can dark skin on bright backgrounds, so instant feedback is invaluable. Make sure you protect your camera from **dust** (zip-lock freezer bags are ideal). Bring **spare batteries**, and plenty of memory cards, plus a USB memory card reader to transfer or send photos online at internet cafés, or make backups.

When **photographing people**, never take pictures without asking permission first, and pay for the right if asked: the Maasai have made quite a business of it. Blithely aiming at strangers may well get you into trouble, and remember that in Islamic areas popular belief equates the act of taking a picture with stealing a piece of someone's soul.

It's also a bad idea to snap things that could even vaguely be construed as **strategic targets**, including police stations, prisons, airports, harbours, bridges, and the president. It depends who sees you, of course – but protesting your innocence won't appease small-minded officials with big shoulder chips.

Responsible tourism

The most active organization concerned with **responsible tourism** is Tourism Concern (Ⓦtour ismconcern.org.uk), whose website contains heaps of practical advice and lists of recommended tour operators; it also publishes the *Ethical Travel Guide* (free to members), reviewing community-based tourism initiatives throughout Africa, and elsewhere. You can also download a couple of related **ebooks**, both unfortunately outdated: the *Responsible Travel Handbook* (2006; Ⓦtransitionsa broad.com), and *The Rough Guide To A Better World* (2004; Ⓦroughguide-betterworld.com).

PHONE NUMBERS AND CALLING HOME

Most **land lines** have seven-digit subscriber numbers plus a three-digit area code (022 to 028), which can be omitted when calling locally; **mobile phones** have four-digit operator codes beginning "07" which must be always be dialled. The initial "0" should be omitted when calling from outside Tanzania. Tanzania's **country code** is 255, but from Kenya or Uganda dial ☎004 instead.

Calling from Tanzania, dial ☎000 followed by the country code and phone number, omitting any initial "0". The exceptions are Kenya (☎005 followed by the area and subscriber number) and Uganda (☎006). Some **country codes**: Australia 61, Canada 1, Ireland 353, New Zealand 64, South Africa 27, UK 44, US 1.

Time

Tanzania is **three hours ahead** of GMT year-round, meaning two hours ahead of Britain in summer, three in winter. It's seven or eight hours ahead of US Eastern Standard Time; one hour ahead of South Africa; and seven hours behind Australia (Sydney).

Tanzanians – and their transport timetables – begin counting the day's hours at 6am (roughly sunrise) and 6pm (roughly sunset), so that six o'clock (*saa sita*) in "Swahili time" equates to noon or midnight as you know it. In other words, just add or subtract six hours.

Tipping

When **tipping**, bear in mind that the average Tanzanian salary is less than $100 a month. In local hotels, bars and restaurants, tipping is not customary, but if you wish to do so, the gesture is appreciated. In tourist-class establishments, on safari, and when climbing Kilimanjaro, staff generally will expect tips, not just because you're "rich", but because they may not be paid at all, tips being their only source of income.

For small services, Tsh1000 is fine, with Tsh2000 reasonable for portering a lot of luggage. **On safari**, expectations vary widely, but anything less than $10 a day from each safari-goer to each member of staff would be mean, so count on $30 per day in all. If service is excellent, by all means tip more. On the other hand if the driving was dangerous or the guiding awful, tip less or not at all – but do explain why. Lack of wildlife is no reason to tip less, however – animals don't keep to schedules.

Toilets

Tanzania's few **public toilets** are not places you want to mess with: usually reeking long-drops covered by two slabs of concrete for positioning the feet, with no guarantee of water, and certainly no paper. Better would be to find a mid-range hotel or restaurant and ask politely. These tend to have Western-style toilets with flushes, and should have toilet paper to hand. In lowlier places, such toilets may lack seats, and be flushed with a bucket. Asian-style "squats", often in the same cubicle as showers, are mostly quite hygienic, and may also have flushing mechanisms. Locals rarely if ever use toilet paper, and there's a reason: in the tropical heat, rinsing your nether regions with water (using your *left* hand) is much cleaner than wiping with tissue, so long as you wash your hands afterwards. There's invariably a tap to hand, with a bucket for flushing and a plastic jug for rinsing. If you can't or won't adapt, you can find toilet paper in towns.

Tourist information

The **Tanzania Tourist Board** (TTB) has no offices overseas, but does maintain a quartet of tourist information offices in Tanzania: the main ones are in Arusha and Dar, neither of which are particularly clued up, with two much more helpful branches, in Mwanza and Iringa. Apart from these, and a handful of privately run information centres mentioned in this guide, information on the ground is difficult to find without being half-fluent in Kiswahili. The best source of information (other than guidebooks), then, is the internet.

USEFUL WEBSITES

Ⓦ **fodors.com/community** A busy forum mainly patronized by upmarket travellers.

Ⓦ **tanzaniaculturaltourism.go.tz** Home of the award-winning cultural tourism programme.

Ⓦ **tanzaniaparks.com** Official national parks site; informative and nicely illustrated.

Ⓦ **tanzaniatouristboard.com** The official tourism portal, and stuffed with information.

Ⓦ **travbuddy.com** A great collection of blogs.

Ⓦ **tripadvisor.com** Candid client reviews of mostly upmarket lodges, plus a forum.

Ⓦ **zanzibar.net** A good portal for the isles.

GOVERNMENT ADVICE

The following websites are where governments post official advice and warnings to their citizens about travelling to other countries. They always err on the side of caution, especially as regards terrorism, so read them with a pinch of salt.

Australia Ⓦ smartraveller.gov.au.

Canada Ⓦ travel.gc.ca.

Ireland Ⓦ dfa.ie.

New Zealand Ⓦ safetravel.govt.nz.

UK Ⓦ fco.gov.uk.

US Ⓦ travel.state.gov.

Travellers with disabilities

Tanzanian **attitudes** towards disabled people are schizophrenic. There's little official support, as you'll see from the polio- or leprosy-afflicted beggars in Arusha, Dar and Dodoma, while lingering superstitions in some areas keep physically and mentally handicapped people out of sight. But overall things are improving, sometimes quite spectacularly, such as the *Neema Crafts* project (see p.419).

In the company of a helper, a Tanzanian holiday for physically disabled people is quite feasible, although you should expect physical knocks, just like everyone else, while **on safari**, even with a mollycoddling driver, as the roads are often awful. The most comfortable national parks to access by road are (from Arusha) Lake Manyara, Tarangire, Ngorongoro and Serengeti (also from Mwanza) and, from Dar es Salaam, Mikumi. For other parks, **flying** is recommended, though on some planes there's simply no room for movement, or a wheelchair, so check beforehand.

Semi-accessible **accommodation** can be found virtually everywhere, if only because most hotels have ground-floor rooms. A number on the coast and larger hotels in Arusha and Dar have ramped access to public areas, while some in Stone Town have elevators. With help, many wildlife lodges and camps are also just about accessible. Almost any **safari companies** touting "tailor-made" tours should be able to provide suitable itineraries. Alternatively, there are two **specialist operators**: the highly recommended Go Africa Safaris in Kenya (Ⓦ go-africa-safaris.com), and Eco-Adventure International in the US (Ⓦ accessibleworldadventures .com).

Navigating **towns** can actually be more challenging: pavements are invariably pot-holed or blocked by parked cars and hawkers, there are few if any ramps, and taxis are small, but with a little perseverance you should be able to find a minibus taxi (which are the norm on Zanzibar). **Public road transport** is not disabled-friendly (it's not exactly "abled-friendly" either); catching a **train** is possible, though you'd have to be carried aboard, and possibly also to the toilets, as the corridors are narrow.

For more information and inspiration, get a second-hand copy of Gordon Rattray's *Access Africa* **guidebook** (Bradt Guides, 2009), which, despite being out of date, provides plenty of practical advice and inspiration for Tanzania, one of six countries covered. Useful **websites** include Ⓦ gimponthego.com and Ⓦ tourismforall.org.uk.

Volunteering

A great way of getting to know Tanzania is through **voluntary work**. Some projects accept anyone, but most require **specialist skills**, such as teaching, biology, IT or accounting. You can arrange things directly with an organization in Tanzania or, easier, via an agency. Ⓦ studyabroad.com and Ⓦ worldvolunteerweb.org have useful listings.

Volunteers usually pay for their own upkeep, but if you're expected to pay a substantial amount, take care as the voluntary sector is infested with **get-rich-quick schemes**. The internet is your friend here: check whether the ideals of an NGO as espoused in their blurb has ever translated into something concrete (and whether your payment can reasonably be squared with the results). You should also check whether they're really registered as charities or non-profits, but be aware that there are few controls over who can register an NGO in Tanzania. Ask on travel forums for up-to-date feedback on volunteer projects, as even those with a good reputation can go downhill fast if circumstances change or a key person leaves.

TANZANIAN DIPLOMATIC MISSIONS

Visas for volunteering or work need to be arranged beforehand in your home country at an embassy or high commission:

Australia Melbourne ☎ 03 9846 6996, Ⓦ tanzaniaconsul.org; Perth ☎ 08 9221 0033, Ⓦ tanzaniaconsul.com

Canada Ottawa ☎ 613 232 1509, Ⓦ tzrepottawa.ca

New Zealand Christchurch (honorary consul) ☎ 03 359 9218, Ⓔ stuartbatty@e3.net.nz, or contact the embassy in Tokyo Ⓦ tanzaniaembassy.or.jp

South Africa Pretoria ☎ 012 342 4371, Ⓦ tanzania.org.za

UK & Ireland London ☎ 020 7569 1470, Ⓦ tanzaniahighcommission.co.uk

US Washington ☎ 202 884 1080, Ⓦ tanzaniaembassy-us.org

VOLUNTEER ORGANIZATIONS

Genuine international organizations involved in Tanzania include:

Gap Medics UK ☎ 0191 603 1111, US ☎ 1844 340-4576, Australia ☎ 1800 351 691; Ⓦ gapmedics.com. Gap year premedic placements in Iringa, central Tanzania.

Peace Corps US only ☎ 1 800 424 8580, Ⓦ peacecorps.gov. Places Americans with specialist skills in 27-month postings, mostly in education or AIDS awareness.

Voluntary Service Overseas (VSO) UK ☎ 020 8780 7500, Ⓦ vso .org.uk; Ireland ☎ 01 640 1060, Ⓦ vso.ie; Canada ☎ 1 888 434 2876, Ⓦ cusointernational.org; Australia ☎ 1800 331 292, Ⓦ australianvolunteers.com; New Zealand ☎ 04 499 2208, Ⓦ vsa .org.nz. Government-funded agencies for placing skilled volunteers.

Dar es Salaam

TRAFFIC AT CORNER OF AZIKIWE AND INDIA
STREETS, DAR ES SALAAM

1

Dar es Salaam

If you like cities, you'll love Dar es Salaam. From a moribund settlement of just three thousand people at the end of the nineteenth century, Dar has blossomed into a metropolis of over four million. The residents' nickname for their city is "Bongo" – "brains" or "wits" – which is what's needed to survive there. For most travellers, Dar is merely a stepping-stone to Zanzibar or southern Tanzania, but it warrants a longer stay, especially if music or nightlife are your thing – the city's nocturnal scene is the envy of East Africa. But even sound sleepers have plenty to inspire them: colourful markets, sandy beaches, a modest but well thought-out national museum, and an exhuberant arts scene. You can also explore the outlying attractions, including some islands (for picnics, snorkelling and scuba diving), a cluster of medieval ruins at Kunduchi, and community-based tourism at the fishing village of Gezaulole.

Although the city lost its status as Tanzania's official capital in 1973, it's the nation's **de facto capital**, and, fuelled by a booming economy, has changed enormously over the last decade. Shiny high-rise buildings have sprouted everywhere, even in suburbs such as Kariakoo which, until recently, consisted almost entirely of single-storey family compounds, complete with chicken and goats. The rate of change is still increasing, but despite the realities of urban poverty, it's a likeable place, friendly and (aside from cursing gridlocked drivers) easy going: wooden dhows bob alongside freighters and oil tankers in the harbour; buzzing markets and colonial architectural gems huddle in the shadows of blue-glass skyscrapers; while gluttonous 4WDs share the pot-holed streets with smoke-belching daladalas and hand-cranked tricycles ridden by polio victims. Dar is very much a **melting pot**, having absorbed immigrants from all over the nation, and beyond, without alienating them, or their cultures. On the pot-holed pavements, Omani women shrouded in black burkas and Indians in lurid sarees rub shoulders with Catholic nuns, Swahili ladies donning the latest colourful *kangas*, and red-robed Maasai medicine men patiently awaiting their clients. In short, it's a scruffy but voluptuous maelstrom for the senses, one in which the entire cultural gamut of the western Indian Ocean can be experienced.

Brief history

Dar es Salaam dates from 1862, when Zanzibar's **Sultan Seyyid Majid** chose the Zaramo fishing village of **Mzizima**, on the mainland, as the site for his new summer palace, which he hoped would eventually replace Stone Town as capital of the Busaïdi dynasty. The location was ideal: its fine natural harbour was perfectly placed to exploit the flourishing trade in **ivory and slaves**; and, unlike Bagamoyo and Kilwa Kivinje, whose caravans were routinely pillaged and disrupted, Dar was untroubled by warlike neighbours. Sultan Majid named the place **Bandar es Salaam** – the "Peaceful Harbour".

By 1867, Majid's palace was sufficiently complete to host a lavish banquet in honour of European and American consuls, whose economic and military might the Sultan unwisely courted. Hadhramaut Arabs from Yemen were invited to develop coconut

MARKET, DAR ES SALAAM

Highlights

❶ National Museum Nothing fancy, but covers every angle on Tanzanian culture and history, from Nutcracker Man and prehistoric fish to wooden bicycles and xylophones. **See p.90**

❷ Kariakoo Market Crowded, hectic, bewildering, exhilarating… a pungent feast for the senses. **See p.93**

❸ Wonder Workshop Some of the weirdest and most gratifying metalwork you've ever seen, made from scrap by an inspirational collective of 42 disabled artists. **See p.94**

❹ Bongoyo and Mbudya Islands A couple of blissful sandy islands surrounded by reefs provide a perfect setting for soaking up the sun, or snorkelling – and are just a thirty-minute boat ride from the city. **See p.95**

❺ Food Dar is a cosmopolitan city, as is deliciously reflected in its restaurants, which can be as fancy or wholesome as you like. **See p.109**

❻ Nightlife With bars, nightclubs and dance-halls galore, Dar is the driving force behind the Bongo Flava's musical conquest of East Africa, and heaven for night owls. **See p.109**

HIGHLIGHTS ARE MARKED ON THE MAP ON P. 86

1

plantations in the hinterland, and, with the arrival of Indian merchants, the fledgling city seemed set to flourish. The sultan, however, died before his plans could be realized (ironically, breaking his neck in his new palace), and his successor, **Sultan Barghash**, showed no interest in the project whatsoever, particularly after the British forced him to ban the sea-borne slave trade in 1873, and the mainland slave trade three years later.

German rule

With little economic *raison d'être* left, the dhows and caravans returned to Kilwa and Bagamoyo, and Dar became a fishing village once more. So it remained until 1887, when the **Deutsch-Ostafrikanische Gesellschaft** – the commercial front for Germany's colonial effort – established a station here, and swiftly asserted its authority by torching Majid's palace. In 1891, with the German conquest in full and bloody swing, the capital of German East Africa was transferred from troublesome Bagamoyo to Dar, and the construction of the city began in earnest. Benedictine and Lutheran missionaries were among the first on the scene, their churches serving as bases for the spiritual conquest of the natives. Dar es Salaam's economic importance was sealed by the **Mittelland Bahn** – now the Central Line railway – which facilitated commerce with Central Africa via Lake Tanganyika and, after World War I, via Lake Victoria too.

British rule

Following the war, the British took over Tanganyika. Retaining Dar as their commercial and administrative centre, they divided it into three racially segregated zones. **Uzunguni**, in the east, was for Europeans, and benefited from tree-lined avenues, stone buildings, a hospital, a botanical garden inherited from the Germans, and other amenities. The more compact **Uhindini** area in the centre was reserved for Asian "coolies" brought in by the British to construct the new colony; the shops and businesses of their descendants still form the city's commercial heart. Lastly, **Uswahilini**, to the west (now Kariakoo), was left to Africans, who were deprived of even the most

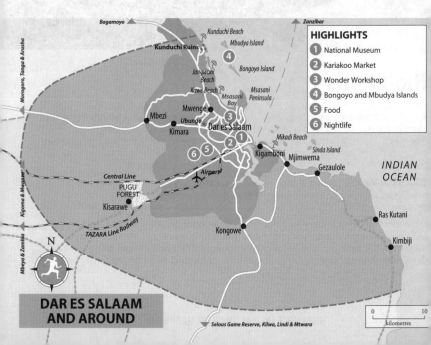

HIGHLIGHTS

1. National Museum
2. Kariakoo Market
3. Wonder Workshop
4. Bongoyo and Mbudya Islands
5. Food
6. Nightlife

DAR ES SALAAM AND AROUND

Bagamoyo
Zanzibar
Kunduchi Beach
Kunduchi Ruins
Mbudya Island
Bongoyo Island
Jangwani Beach
Kawe Beach
Msasani Bay
Msasani Peninsula
Mwenge
Mbezi
Ubungo
Kimara
Dar es Salaam
Mikadi Beach
Sinda Island
Kigamboni
Mjimwema
Gezaulole
Airport
INDIAN OCEAN
Morogoro, Tanga & Arusha
Kigoma & Mwanza
Central Line
PUGU FOREST
Kisarawe
TAZARA Line Railway
Kongowe
Mbeya & Zambia
Ras Kutani
Kimbiji
N
Selous Game Reserve, Kilwa, Lindi & Mtwara
0   10
kilometres

basic facilities. Although the names are no longer in use, the racial stamp is still apparent in the architecture and feel of each zone.

Independence

As the city and its population grew, so did social and political awareness. The **Tanganyika African Association**, an ethnically diverse welfare agency and social club, was founded in Dar in 1927 to advocate the betterment of the African lot. Spreading to rural communities, it eventually merged with the Tanganyika African National Union (TANU) to become the driving force behind the push for independence. Throughout this period, the city expanded relentlessly, and following **independence** in 1961 became the capital of Tanganyika and, subsequently, Tanzania.

Alas, President Nyerere's well-meant but economically disastrous **Ujamaa** policy (see p.520) effectively bankrupted the city, which also lost its status as capital to Dodoma in 1973. Two decades of stagnation followed before the effects of economic liberalization finally kicked in. These days, with the economy booming, Dar es Salaam is undergoing the biggest building spree in its history, with blue-glass high-rise buildings shooting up all over the place, even in the poorest districts. But for all the construction work and shiny new motors choking the streets, **poverty** remains a daily reality for the great majority, and with more people migrating to the city each year, the challenges are enormous. It may take ten, twenty or thirty years for the economic benefits of current policies to filter through, but if history be a guide, Dar's resilient sense of community will continue to hold everything together. Especially with a generous dose of *bongo*…

Kivukoni

With much of Dar es Salaam sinking under a sea of concrete, steel and glass, the city's best-preserved colonial district is the former European area Uzunguni, now called **Kivukoni**, which spreads east of Maktaba and Azikiwe streets to the shore. With its broad tree-lined avenues and gardens, imposing yet delicate colonial-era structures, including some lovely wood-balconied buildings, a hint of sea breeze, and not all that many people, Kivukoni makes a pleasant contrast to the rest of the city. It's Dar's administrative centre, and includes **State House**, home to the Tanzanian president; although the house is not open to the public, you can peer through the fence to see eland and peacocks in its garden. The **beach** starts just north of the ferry terminal to Kigamboni, on the south side of the harbour entrance, but the water here is polluted,

---

ORIENTATION

Dar es Salaam's historical heart is the **Ilala district** north of the harbour, which is divided into wards that correspond to the racial British colonial divisions. Fronting the Indian Ocean is **Kivukoni** ("Uzunguni" in colonial times), an area of tree-lined avenues housing the President's and Prime Minister's residences, some embassies, NGOs and banks, the National Museum and Botanical Gardens, a golf course, and a handful of mostly upmarket hotels.

West of here, the city's commercial heart is in **Kisutu and Mchafukoge** (the British "Uhindini", or Asian area), and is where you'll find most shops, restaurants and cheaper accommodation, but not too many bars – the area is still predominantly Asian, especially Muslim. Adjoining Mchafukoge is **Kariakoo** (the former "Uswahilini" or African quarter), centred around an extraordinary market, and presently undergoing a Chinese-style building boom.

These days, most embassies, upmarket restaurants and bars have shifted north to the **Msasani Peninsula**, comprising Msasani and Namanga at its neck, with Oyster Bay and Masaki further along – here, you'll find a handful of beach (or at least ocean-side) hotels. Beyond the peninsula is a string of densely populated areas that play host to some great live music venues, some of them on the beach.

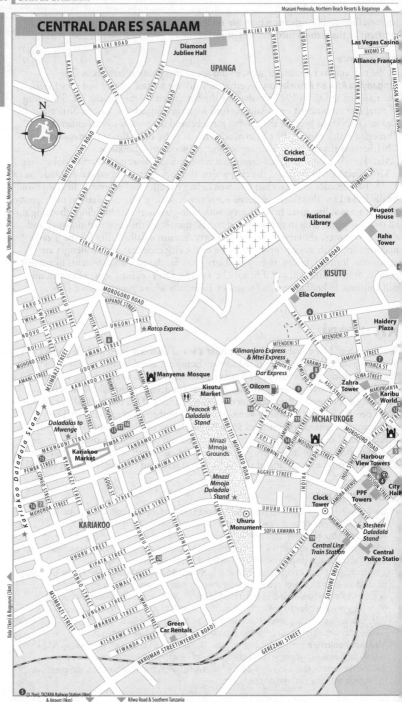

CENTRAL DAR ES SALAAM

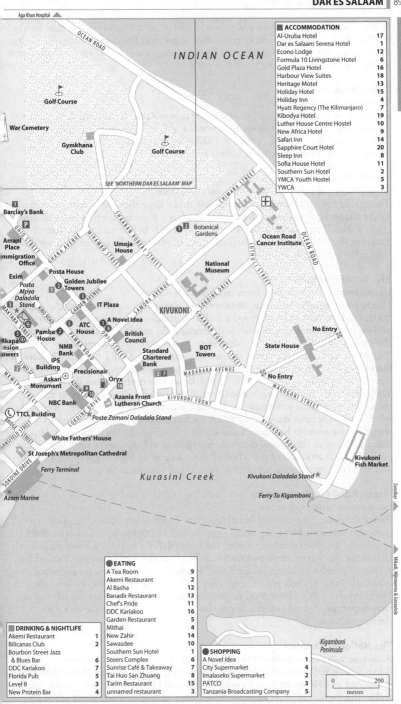

INDIAN OCEAN

Golf Course

War Cemetery

Gymkhana Club

Golf Course

SEE 'NORTHERN DAR ES SALAAM' MAP

Aga Khan Hospital

OCEAN ROAD

ACCOMMODATION
Al-Uruba Hotel	17
Dar es Salaam Serena Hotel	1
Econo Lodge	12
Formula 10 Livingstone Hotel	6
Gold Plaza Hotel	16
Harbour View Suites	18
Heritage Motel	13
Holiday Hotel	15
Holiday Inn	4
Hyatt Regency (The Kilimanjaro)	7
Kibodya Hotel	19
Luther House Centre Hostel	10
New Africa Hotel	9
Safari Inn	14
Sapphire Court Hotel	20
Sleep Inn	8
Sofia House Hotel	11
Southern Sun Hotel	2
YMCA Youth Hostel	5
YWCA	3

Barclay's Bank
Amani Place
Immigration Office
Exim
Posta House
Golden Jubilee Towers
IT Plaza
Umoja House
Botanical Gardens
National Museum
Ocean Road Cancer Institute
A Novel Idea
ATC House
Pamba House
NMB Bank
IPS Building
Precisionair
Askari Monument
NBC Bank
British Council
Standard Chartered Bank
BOT Towers
State House
No Entry
No Entry
TTCL Building
Azania Front Lutheran Church
Posta Zamani Daladala Stand
White Fathers' House
St Joseph's Metropolitan Cathedral
Ferry Terminal
Azam Marine
Kurasini Creek
Kivukoni Daladala Stand
Ferry To Kigamboni
Kivukoni Fish Market
KIVUKONI
Posta Mpya Daladala Stand

SHAABAN ROBERT STREET, MIRAMBO STREET, GHANA AVENUE, OHIO STREET, MAKTABA STREET, KIBO ROAD, GARDEN AVENUE, SAMORA AVENUE, LUTHULI STREET, OCEAN ROAD, SOKOINE DRIVE, SHAABAN ROBERT STREET, MADARAKA AVENUE, MAGOGONI STREET, KIVUKONI FRONT, MKWEPU STREET, BRIDGE STREET, MANSFIELD STREET, SOKOINE DRIVE, PAMBA ROAD, AJINWEZI, SIMU STREET, CHIMARA STREET

Kigamboni Peninsula

Zanzibar

Mikadi, Mjimwema & Gezaulole

DRINKING & NIGHTLIFE
Akemi Restaurant	1
Bilicanas Club	2
Bourbon Street Jazz & Blues Bar	6
DDC Kariakoo	7
Florida Pub	5
Level 8	3
New Protein Bar	4

EATING
A Tea Room	9
Akemi Restaurant	2
Al Basha	12
Banadir Restaurant	13
Chef's Pride	11
DDC Kariakoo	16
Garden Restaurant	5
Mithai	
New Zahir	14
Sawasdee	10
Southern Sun Hotel	1
Steers Complex	6
Sunrise Café & Takeaway	7
Tai Huo San Zhuang	8
Tarim Restaurant	15
unnamed restaurant	3

SHOPPING
A Novel Idea	1
City Supermarket	4
Imalaseko Supermarket	2
PATCO	3
Tanzania Broadcasting Company	5

0 — 200 metres

1

so most people just sit around and enjoy the breeze, sip coconuts bought from nearby vendors, or stroll out onto the extensive flats at low tide. For cleaner water, the nearest stretches are Mikadi and Mjimwema a few kilometres south (see p.98), or Coco Beach on Msasani Peninsula, in the north (see p.95).

Askari Monument
Corner of Azikiwe St and Samora Ave

Designed by James Alexander Stevenson, the bronze **Askari Monument** depicts an African *askari* advancing, rifle ready, in honour of Carrier Corps porters who lost their lives in World War I. It was erected in 1927 to replace a statue of Hermann von Wissmann, the German explorer, soldier and governor.

Azania Front Lutheran Church
Junction of Sokoine St and Kivukoni Front • Services (in Kiswahili) at 7am & 9.30am

The start of the harbour-side avenue leading to the Kigamboni ferry terminal is marked by the **Azania Front Lutheran Church**. With its fancy Rhineland-style tower and tiled roofs, it took three years to build, from 1898 to 1901. In line with the austere Lutheran doctrine, there's little decoration inside other than its stained glass windows, shipped in from Germany.

Kivukoni Fish Market
East end of Kivukoni Front • Daily 6.30am–6pm, though some foodstalls open a little later

Heading east along the harbour, **Kivukoni Front** leads past a number of graceful German buildings, most adorned with wooden Indian-style balconies, which are nowadays occupied by government ministries and offices. At the eastern end of Kivukoni Front, in the shadow of a modern marine traffic control tower, is the ferry terminal for Kigamboni and, almost opposite, the new terminal for the DART fast bus. **Kivukoni Fish Market** is a few dozen metres further on, on the ocean side of road – not that you need directions to get there as the smell is unmistakable. Unsurprisingly, it's the best place in Dar to buy and eat ultra-fresh seafood, with a number of stalls and tables set up inside the southern entrance to the market. The stalls are very basic (and pungent, should the wind be blowing from the north, through the fish market), with plastic seating or roughly hewn wooden benches around simple tables, right by the *mama lisha* ("feeding ladies") who work their magic over wide frying pans, or huge pots of *ugali* and cassava porridge. Hunt around and you'll find all sorts of delights, from red snapper, kingfish and barracuda, to octopus, squid, crab, prawns and sometimes lobster.

Ocean Road Cancer Institute
East end of Samora Ave • Not open to the public

Facing the ocean, just north of State House (the President's residence; no photography) is another substantial building from German times, the **Ocean Road Cancer Institute,** a world-class oncological research centre and hospital. Built in 1886 as a malaria research laboratory, this was where **Robert Koch** developed the standard laboratory method for preparing pure bacterial strains, the Koch Method. It was also where he discovered tuberculin (wrongly believed to be the cure for TB), for which he was awarded the Nobel Prize in 1905. He went on to discover, correctly this time, that flea-infested rats were responsible for the bubonic plague, and that the tsetse fly was the vector for sleeping sickness.

The National Museum
Shaaban Robert St • Daily 9.30am–6pm • Tsh6500 • Photography permitted • ☎ 022 213 0112, ⊕ houseofculture.or.tz

A five-minute walk southwest from the Cancer Hospital is Tanzania's **National Museum**, established in 1940 as the King George V Memorial Museum. It's patchy in the quality and instructiveness of its displays: some are clearly in need of work, while others are quite superb and capable of grabbing your complete attention. Despite the flaws, the museum is well worth a visit, particularly for the overview it gives of most aspects of Tanzanian life, culture, history and prehistory, and – less convincingly – wildlife, ecology and art. To round off your visit, there's a **gift shop** (not run by the museum) containing the usual tourist souvenirs and books, and a **restaurant**-cum-café (which you can visit without paying the museum entrance fee) with seats in the museum garden.

The Biology Hall

Behind the modern building at the front, the original museum building is a pretty Orientalist construction with keyhole arches, which contains two large rooms. On the left is the **Biology Hall**, which is, lamentably for such a biodiverse nation, by far the museum's poorest collection. Among the jumbled hotchpotch of items here, drawn from marine and terrestrial environments, are some corals, a trio of dull fish tanks, model dhows, ant and bird nests, a few stuffed game trophies, and – pretty much the only genuinely impressive exhibit in the hall – an enormous elephant skull.

Ethnographic Hall

Far more interesting is the rather dusty collection in the **Ethnographic Hall**, which includes some fascinating objects, with rich and informative descriptions in both English and Kiswahili, that give an insight into Tanzania's many and varied cultures. Even if ethnography per se leaves you indifferent, you'll find some quirky exhibits here, such as a fully functional wooden bicycle (still occasionally seen in rural areas), a gorgeously resonant Zaramo xylophone, a canoe made of sewn leather, plus some grotesque clay figurines traditionally used in initiation ceremonies and for sexual education.

Hall of Man

The big hall on the ground floor of the newer part of the museum houses temporary exhibitions, while the permanent displays, arranged by theme, are on the first floor. Well labelled and extensively explained, the **Hall of Man** exhibit traces human evolution, from our first tentative attempts at walking on two legs some 4.2 million years ago, to the present day. Highlights include a cast of Ngorongoro's "Laetoli footprints", which proved that our ancestors walked upright way before anyone had imagined, plus fossilized skulls from Oldupai Gorge and elsewhere, including the 1,750,000-year-old partial skull of *Australopithecus boisei*, whose impressive jaw led to him being dubbed "Nutcracker Man". For a while this gentleman was believed to have been our ancestor, until other finds packed him off into an evolutionary dead-end.

Rock Art exhibit

The **Rock Art exhibit** consists mostly of photographs of rock art, accompanied by extensive texts that are well worth reading. There's also a mock-up of two rock faces painted with designs from all over Africa. The exhibit was made by the Trust for African Rock Art (TARA; ⓦ africanrockart.org), which was founded in Nairobi in 1996 by the photographer David Coulson, and has been tireless in its work to protect the continent's astounding wealth of prehistoric and proto-historic rock paintings and engravings, including those at Kolo in Tanzania.

History Room

The **History Room** contains a pleasant hotchpotch of artefacts. The medieval mercantile Swahili civilization is amply represented by Indian trading beads, Chinese porcelain prised off grave pillars, and coins minted in fifteenth-century Kilwa – all proof of the vitality of Indian Ocean trade prior to the Portuguese conquest. There's little on display from the Portuguese period, though the arrival of English and German explorers in the nineteenth century coincided with the advent of photography, of which the exhibits make excellent use. You might not be surprised at the snaps of Burton and Speke,

1

bewhiskered in typical Victorian style, but the profile of Hans Meyer – first to reach the summit of Kilimanjaro, in 1889 – is remarkable for just how young and modern he looks. The displays continue with insights into the duplicity and brutality of the German conquest, then British rule, and finally reach the most riveting part: Tanzanian Independence, achieved on December 9, 1961. The numerous photos of the leader of the struggle for independence from Britain, and subsequently the first President of Tanzania, Julius Nyerere, are remarkable – he was a small, dapper and elegant man, with intense and expressive eyes. During his lifetime he was known by the honorific title of Mwalimu (Teacher) – and it is in large part thanks to his consistently egalitarian (if economically disastrous) policies that Tanzania has suffered none of the divisive tribalism that bedevils five of its seven neighbours (Malawi and Zambia are the exceptions).

Gallery of Contemporary Art

The last room on the first floor houses a mixed bag of **contemporary art**, from the 1950s to the present day, interspersed with a few traditional works. The quality is variable, but among the more humdrum paintings and portraits – "naive" or otherwise – are quite a few gems, including the obligatory Makonde blackwood carvings (with some suitably grotesque *shetani* sculptures of imaginary demons), and a two-headed Zaramo drum hollowed out of a tree trunk , with the surprising addition of a pair of breast and a pregnant belly carved out of its base.

The Botanical Gardens

Adjacent to the National Museum, entrances on Samora and Garden aves • Daily sunrise–sunset • Free

The **Botanical Gardens** are ever more modest, having recently lost a chunk to a tourism training college, but what's left is still a shady and peaceful oasis. Established in 1893 as a testing ground for cash crops, the gardens still contain a few species of palm trees, some primeval fern-like cycads, and a raucous population of wing-clipped peacocks. The gardener's office may have copies of an explanatory leaflet.

Kisutu and Mchafukoge

Historically, the city's commercial heart – a square kilometre bounded by Bibi Titi Mohamed Road, Samora Avenue and Maktaba/Azikiwe Street – Uhindini was the area reserved by the British for Indian labourers shipped in to construct the city. Nowadays split into **Kisutu and Mchafukoge**, it remains a hive of activity, one whose stores stock almost anything you might need, from motor spares to gold jewellery, together with tea rooms, restaurants, sweet shops, and dozens of temples and mosques. Sadly, much of Mchafukoge's considerable architectural heritage has fallen victim to the bull-dozers, though Kisutu, further east, still preserves some very fine Art Deco and Indo–Swahili–European buildings. There's no real centre to either district, nor any specific sights – the pleasure lies in the details, such as men selling beautifully arranged flower petals outside temples, or women spying on the streets from intricate wooden latticework balconies up above, so keep your eyes open as you wander around.

White Fathers' House

Sokoine Drive • No fixed times • Free

Down by the harbour, in the shadow of a trio of huge skyscrapers, are a handful of buildings surviving from Sultan Majid's rule in the 1860s, including the **White Fathers' House** (also known as Atiman House). This served as the Sultan's harem before it was put to holier use in 1921 by the Society of Missionaries of Africa (the streetfront veranda is an addition from that time). The mission still occupies the building, together with their archives, and a small exhibit of German-era photographs. The building's alternative name honours Adrien Atiman, who was freed from slavery by the Society's

1

missionaries, then spent almost seven decades working as a doctor on Lake Tanganyika (see p.401). The larger building on left, on the corner of Bridge St, is Forodhani School; dating from German times, it was built by Benedictine missionaries to serve a school, clinic and orphanage.

St Joseph's Metropolitan Cathedral

Sokoine Drive facing the ferry terminal • Daily 6am–5.30pm • Sunday Mass (in Kiswahili) at 7am, 10am & 4.30pm; (in English) at 8.30am & 11.45am

The bay-front **St Joseph's Metropolitan Cathedral**, consecrated in 1897 and completed in 1902, is a major city landmark and a good place to experience Dar's church music (*kwaya*), best heard during Sunday Mass. The cathedral, built by the Bavarian Benedictine Order of St Ottilien, is notable for its twin confessionals, one in Baroque style, the other Gothic – the leading German architectural styles at the time.

Kisutu Street

Kisutu Street (also called Pramukh Swami Street) is at the heart of Dar's Asian quarter, and retains a mostly Indian population. You are welcome to look round the Hindu and Jain temples here, which are the centre of community life. The street is also a great place to sample **Indian sweets** – try *Mithai* at the west end of the street (see p.108) – and **paan**, one of India's stranger cultural exports which is essentially a mildly narcotic dessert. To try it, first choose from a range of sweet spices, chopped nuts and bits of vegetable, which are then mixed with syrup, white lime and *katu* gum, and wrapped in a betel leaf (*tambuu*). Pop the triangular parcel in your mouth, munch, and spit out the pith when you're finished.

Kisutu Market

Bibi Titi Mohamed Rd • Daily 7am–6pm

Don't miss the atmospheric if insalubrious little **Kisutu Market**, a gentler introduction to African market life than Kariakoo further west. Among the stalls selling fruit and vegetables, honey, beans and pulses are others peddling baskets of squawking chickens, dried fish, and some gorgeously pungent herbs.

Kariakoo district

West of Kisutu and Mchafukoge, beyond the grassy Mnazi Mmoja Grounds, lies **Kariakoo**, the heart of what the British called Uswahilini ("Swahili area"). Chaotic, potentially disorienting and definitely dangerous to walk around in at night, it's by far the city centre's liveliest and most stimulating district, and exudes a solid sense of community that manages to combine both tribal and religious identities.

Kariakoo got its name from the barracks of the hated British Carrier Corps, into which thousands of Tanzanians were conscripted during World War I to serve as porters. After the war, Kariakoo and Ilala, further west, were abandoned to the African population – no amenities were provided, and some parts still lack the most basic facilities today, though things are changing fast. Barely a decade ago, the district's characteristic mud-walled "Swahili houses" were touted as an attraction by the tourist board, while today Kariakoo is transforming, at an ever-accelerating pace, into a jungle of high-rise buildings.

Kariakoo Market

Between Mkunguni, Tandamuti, Nyamwezi and Swahili st • Daily sunrise–sunset

In many ways, Kariakoo is a microcosm of the country, so it's fitting that it plays host to **Kariakoo Market**, which occupies the site of the Carrier Corps barracks, beneath a bizarre roof resembling a forest of upturned parasols that was designed to collect rainwater. In it, and in the maze of shops and stalls surrounding it, you can buy everything from sea, land or factory – exotic fruit and vegetables, blocks of compacted tamarind paste (resembling hashish), and all manner of meat, fresh and abuzz with flies, cooked, or still bleating. There are also aromatic spices, herbs, Kilimanjaro coffee, handicrafts, textiles, local brews (*pombe*), and children's toys made from wire and recycled tin cans. You'll see Maasai selling medicinal herbs, potions and powders in little bottles salvaged from hospitals, as well as bundles of tree bark, dried lizards and seashells with curative properties, while, elsewhere, you might be offered tart baobab seeds, snuff tobacco or dodgy imported electronics branded with deliberate misspellings such as "Soni".

What's also striking is the care with which everything is displayed – look out for pieces of cloth rolled into tight cones and propped up on the ground, little pyramids of oranges and other fruits, and fresh flowers inserted between mounds of coconuts. Take precautions against pickpockets, and don't walk around here after dusk – at least not without a trustworthy escort. For a breather, join the locals at Tanzania's oldest African bar, the famous *DDC Kariakoo Social Hall* on Muhonda Street, two blocks south (see p.109).

Msasani and the north coast

Some five kilometres north of the city centre, **MSASANI PENINSULA** is the address of choice for diplomats, civil servants, NGOs, and the otherwise rich, privileged or corrupt. There are several posh hotels here (see pp.105–106), some right on the shore, an ever-changing scattering of snazzy international restaurants (see p.109), and similarly expensive nightspots (see pp.110–111), all of which are popular with expats and well-to-do Tanzanians. Frequented by the same crowd are a trio of shopping centres stuffed with craft and souvenir shops, themed restaurants, cafés, ice-cream parlours and the like, the best of which is *The Slipway* (see p.112), as it's right on the shore.

Dar's main beach resorts are at **Jangwani and Kunduchi beaches**, some 20km north of the city, with resort-style hotels and activities such as boat trips, snorkelling, and diving around the islands of Dar es Salaam Marine Reserve. The downside is a series of ugly breakwaters designed to hinder erosion, so if you're looking for more than just a brief break, you're better off heading to the beaches on the south coast (see p.98).

Wonder Workshop

5km north of the city centre on Karume Rd, Namanga, at the start of Msasani Peninsula • ☎ 0754 051417, ⓦ wonderwelders.org • Mon–Fri 8.30am–6pm, Sat 10am–6pm • Free • Catch a Posta–Masaki daladala to "TTCL" on Haile Selassie Rd, then walk 600m left along Karume Rd

The much-admired **Wonder Workshop** (Wonder Welders) is a collective of 42 mostly disabled artists, many of them polio victims, who create some of Tanzania's most inspired – and inspiring – souvenirs. They started in 2005 producing sculptures and masks from scrap metal, but soon branched out into other areas of recycled art: glass jewellery, handmade paper, soaps and candles, and baby-friendly wooden toys (which are interesting enough to please older kids, too). But it's the metalwork that's utterly captivating, and, given the raw materials, unique.

The Village Museum

7km along Ali Hassan Mwinyi Rd (Bagamoyo Rd), Kijitonyama • ☎ 022 270 0437 or ☎ 022 270 0193, ✉ utamadunikijijini@gmail.com • Daily 9.30am–6pm • Tsh6500 • Get there on a Posta–Mwenge daladala, dropping off at "Makumbusho"

The open-air **Village Museum** (Kijiji cha Makumbusho) was founded in 1966 to preserve some of Tanzania's architectural and material traditions. Spread out over the site are houses built in the styles of sixteen tribes, each furnished with typical household items and utensils, and surrounded by small plots of local crops and animal pens. Traditional arts and crafts, including carving, weaving and pottery, are demonstrated by resident "villagers", and a blacksmith explains the intricacies of an art that has existed in East Africa for at least two millennia. The finished products are sold in the museum shop, which also stocks books and souvenirs. There's a small café serving drinks and Tanzanian food, plus performances of **traditional dance** (officially Tues–Sun 2–6pm, but more likely Sat & Sun 4–6pm), followed by one of a medley of events: cinema, comedy, theatre and, on Saturday, the ever-popular FM Academia band (Tsh10,000).

Although laudable, the aims of the museum became grimly ironic in the years following its establishment, when President Nyerere embarked on his economically disastrous *Ujamaa* policy, in which the majority of rural Tanzanians were forcibly moved into collective villages, ultimately wrecking the very traditions the museum undertook to preserve.

Coco Beach (Oyster Bay Beach)

5km north of the city centre on Touré Drive, on the eastern side of the Msasani Peninsula • Free • Posta–Masaki daladalas pass by

While most of the Msasani Peninsula is a preserve of the wealthy, **Coco Beach** has long been a favoured weekend spot for ordinary Tanzanians. The sand here is mixed with coral ragstone, but the water is clean enough for swimming at high tide, and there's often a bit of a breeze, too. At weekends, you'll find informal street-food, coconut and beer sellers opposite Oyster Bay Shopping Centre, but the best part of the beach is a little further up by *Coco Beach Bar* (see p.110). If you're carrying valuables, be wary of the quieter stretches, but walking along the road is fine.

Kawe Beach

10km north of the city centre • Catch a Posta–Kawe or Kariakoo–Kawe daladala (marked "via A.H. Mwinyi Rd")

Msasani's beaches have rather coarse sands – for something finer underfoot head to **Kawe Beach**, stretching 4km north of Msasani Peninsula. There are several good beach bars scattered along the shore (see pp.110–111), which, like Coco Beach, are popular with Tanzanians at weekends. A good place to aim for is *Msasani Beach Club* (see p.110), with live music on Sunday from 3pm. **Swimming** at Kawe, as at Coco Beach, is only possible at high tide.

Bongoyo and Mbudya Islands

Bongoyo Island, 4km off the Msasani Peninsula, and Mbudya Island, 3km off Kundachi Beach • ⓦ marineparks.go.tz • Motorized dhows to both islands are run by Tanzaquatic (☏ 0772 011202 or ☏ 0756 504987, ⓦ facebook.com/Tanzaquatic) and leave from The Slipway shopping centre on Msasani Peninsula. Boats to Bongoyo leave daily at 9.30am, 11.30am and 1.30pm, returning at 12.30pm, 2.30pm and 5pm, and cost $30 per person, including $10 marine park entry fee; snorkelling equipment $5 extra. Boats to Mbudya leave at 10am on Sat & sun, returning at 4pm, and cost $40 per person • Trips to Mbudya can also be arranged from hotels at Jambiani and Kunduchi beaches, and Tanzaquatic also offers shorter excursions by glass-bottomed boat

The islands of Bongoyo and Mbudya are both protected **marine reserves**, as are the nearby Pangavini Islet and Fungu Yasini Reef. All offer great snorkelling, and with lovely beaches they make for a fantastic and satisfyingly cheap day out from the city. Popular with picnickers at weekends, **Bongoyo Island** has some nature trails, though snorkelling conditions are best around **Mbudya Island**, 3km off Kunduchi Beach, which has shady casuarinas, baobabs and palms, and a population of endangered coconut crabs. Underwater, you might see butterfly fish, sweet lips, giant clams, octopus and, with luck, either hawksbill or green turtles. On both islands, enterprising locals sell delicious barbecued fish and chips (for Tsh8000 or so), sodas, and sometimes beer, as well as renting out deckchairs and *bandas*.

Kunduchi Wet 'n' Wild Water Park

21km north of the city centre, 3.2km off Bagamoyo Rd at Kunduchi • Daily 9.30am–6pm • Mon–Fri Tsh12,000, Sat & Sun Tsh14,000, or Tsh18,000–25,000 with a meal • ☏ 022 265 0050 or ☏ 0688 138773, ⓦ wetnwild.co.tz • Mwenge–Kunduchi daladalas stop right by the entrance; taxis charge at least Tsh40,000 from the city centre

East Africa's largest water park, **Kundachi Wet 'n' Wild** boasts more than twenty water slides and tubes, plus seven swimming pools, and reams of other activities (at additional cost) including kite-surfing, jet-skiing, beach buggies, slot machines and even a go-kart track. The downside is the food, which is mostly fried, and served with fries. No cotton shorts allowed.

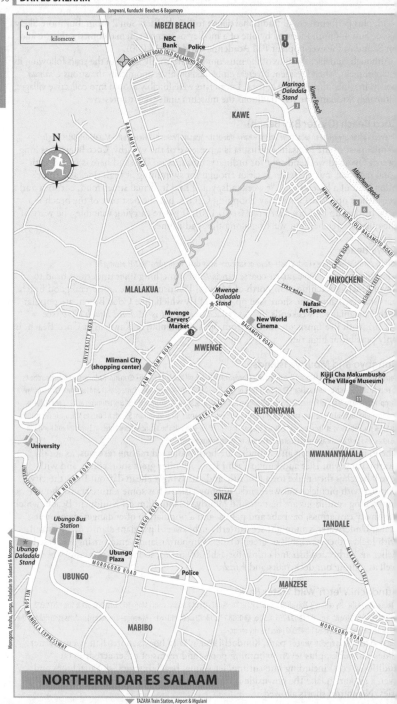

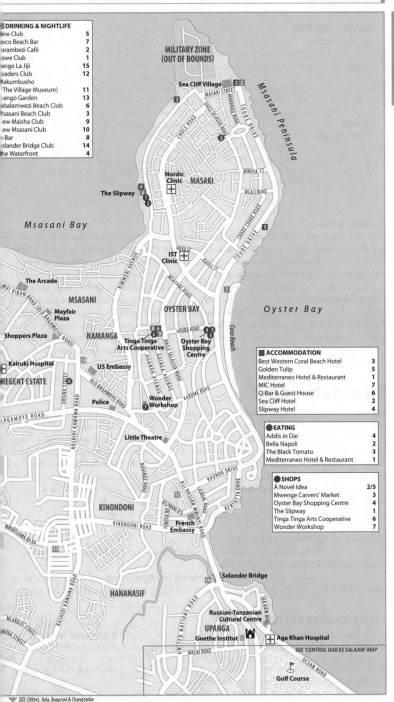

MILITARY ZONE
(OUT OF BOUNDS)

Sea Cliff Village

Msasani Peninsula

MASAKI STREET
MAHANGO ROAD
TOURE DRIVE

CHOLE ROAD

HAILE SELASSIE ROAD

MWAYA ST.

MLALI ROAD

Nordic
Clinic

MASAKI

CHAKE CHAKE ROAD

TOURE DRIVE

The Slipway

Msasani Bay

IST
Clinic

RUVU ST.

KAOLE ST.

MSASANI ROAD

KIMWERI AVENUE

The Arcade

WAI KIBAN ROAD (OLD BAGAMOYO ROAD)

MSASANI

Mayfair
Plaza

OYSTER BAY

Oyster Bay

Shoppers Plaza

NAMANGA

Tinga Tinga
Arts Cooperative

GHUBA ROAD

Oyster Bay
Shopping
Centre

Goco Beach

Kairuki Hospital

HAILE SELASSIE ROAD

ALGANDA AVENUE

GUINEA AVENUE

US Embassy

REGENT ESTATE

URSINO STREET

OLD BAGAMOYO ROAD

Wonder
Workshop

KARUME ROAD

AGAMOYO ROAD

RASHIDI KAWAWA ROAD

Police

Little Theatre

KAUNDA DRIVE

BUHINDE ROAD

KINONDONI

KILIMANI RD.

ALI HASSAN MWINYI ROAD

LIBYA RD.

KENYATTA DRIVE

French
Embassy

KINONDONI ROAD

MWINYIJUMA ROAD

Selander Bridge

RASHIDI KAWAWA ROAD

HANANASIF

UNITED NATIONS ROAD

SEA VIEW ROAD

Russian-Tanzanian
Cultural Centre

MLANDIZI STREET

UPANGA

Goethe Institut

Aga Khan Hospital

NDOA STREET

MALIKI ROAD

OCEAN ROAD

SEE 'CENTRAL DAR ES SALAAM' MAP

Golf Course

(300m), Ilala, Buguruni & Chang'ombe

1

SCUBA DIVING

The **coral reefs** of Dar es Salaam's marine reserves are in mixed condition, having suffered from dynamite fishing in the 1990s before the reserve was created. The three-kilometre-long **Fungu Yasini Reef**, 6km north of Kundachi, is the closest scuba-diving reef to shore, and has a wide variety of corals (down to 40m), which house oddities such as crocodile fish, lionfish and pufferfish, a surprising variety of colourful nudibranchs (sea slugs), as well as a lot of coral-devouring crown-of-thorns starfish. **Big T Reef** (Mbudya Patches), further out, is in better shape, so you're more likely to see large pelagic species, including kingfish and tuna, or perhaps bull sharks and white-tipped reef sharks. Whales have even been sighted, or heard. **Wreck divers** can explore the *Schlammerstadt*, scuttled in Oyster Bay in 1908 following a fire.

The area's only PADI-accredited **dive centre**, safety conscious and with good equipment, is Sea Breeze Marine, based at The Slipway on Msasani Peninsula (daily 8am–7pm; ☎0754 783241, ⓦseabreezemarine.org). It runs an Open Water course for $475, while ten-dive packages cost $600, including equipment.

Kunduchi ruins

21.5km north of the city centre, 3.7km off Bagamoyo Rd (signposted to Kunduchi Beach Hotel) • Tsh10,000 • Mwenge–Kunduchi daladala go as far as Kunduchi Wet 'n' Wild Water Park. The ruins are just 500m walk north of here, but it's best to do this last bit by *bajaj* (Tsh2000 return from the Kunduchi Beach Hotel), if you're carrying any valuables with you, as there has been a spate of muggings in the past

The little-visited **Kunduchi ruins** (*magofu*, "ruins") comprise a sixteenth-century mosque and various other remains set in a grove of baobabs and bushes, together with graves dating from the eighteenth and nineteenth centuries. The gravestones are of particular interest: many bear distinctive obelisk-like pillars; others are ornately carved from coral ragstone, and inset with blue-and-white Chinese porcelain bowls – it's one of the few sites where the bowls are still in their original setting. Their presence is a reminder of the scope of the Indian Ocean's monsoon-driven dhow trading network, now long gone.

The south coast

Beyond the suburb of **Kigamboni**, on the south side of Dar es Salaam's harbour, stretches a string of small fishing villages set amid thick coconut, banana and mango plantations and far removed from the hectic pace of city life. Here, you'll find a couple of low-key beaches at **Mikadi** and **Mjimwema**, and a cultural tourism programme in the village of **Gezaulole**. However, all this is set to change with a new bridge over the south side of the harbour nearing completion, and plans afoot for a huge development project, which will transform the area into an ultra modern satellite city. The new bridge will be accessible from Nelson Mandela Road, off Kilwa Road, roughly 7km south of the city centre, and will certainly have daladalas running along it.

Mikadi and Mjimwema beaches

Mikadi is 2.5km east of the Kigamboni ferry jetty, Mjimwema is 5km beyond • Daladalas from the ferry charge Tsh400 to either place; a *bajaj* costs about Tsh2000 to Mikadi, and Tsh6000 to Mjimwema

Dar's nicest beaches lie south of the city at **Mikadi** and **Mjimwema** – they are peaceful and quiet, with activities largely limited to eating, drinking, swimming and simply lounging

THE KIGAMBONI FERRY

The most interesting approach to Dar's southern beaches is on the **Kigamboni ferry**, which leaves from the east end of Kivukoni Front. It runs day and night, making the eight-minute journey to Kigamboni every thirty minutes or so, and costs just Tsh200 for pedestrians. There are daladalas and *bajaj* at the ferry terminal. Watch your bags and pockets and don't try to walk from the ferry to the beaches, as there are thieves about.

around. So far, both have eluded a tidal wave of development, and – provided you don't arrive at the same time as the overland trucks – can offer quite a meditative experience. Access to the beach is usually through a hotel (see p.107), and day-trippers are welcome. *Mikadi Beach Camp*'s entry fee (Tsh5000) includes use of its swimming pool, while *Sunrise Beach Resort*'s makes a similar charge, which is refunded against meals.

Gezaulole

Some 15km from the Kigamboni ferry, the coastal settlement of **GEZAULOLE** (also called Mbwamaji) is a cosmopolitan little place thanks to its having been a "collective village" during President Nyerere's *Ujamaa* experiment (see p.520). Earlier, it was an entrepôt for ivory and slaves, and the ruins of a slave-holding house can still be seen, as can a restored seventeenth-century mosque. Gezaulole's first inhabitants were Zaramo fishermen, who used the site as a temporary camp. After a while they decided to settle permanently and so – according to legend – asked their soothsayer for advice. He ordered a young virgin be buried alive here, and added, "then *gezaulole* (try and see) whether you can stay here". Today, the inhabitants survive on agriculture, fishing and some seaweed harvesting, but it looks like the old days are numbered: developers have already built an upmarket housing estate here, with more likely to follow.

Kali Mata Ki Jai! cultural tourism

Signposted from Mwembe Mgambo daladala stand • ☎ 0784 976984 or ☎ 0784 314040, ⓦ vrouwen.net/kalimata • Daladalas from the Kigamboni ferry cost Tsh750 (every 30min 7am–7pm); taxis charge Tsh15,000 and *bajaj* Tsh5000–7000

Gezaulole's **cultural tourism programme** is run by **Kali Mata Ki Jai!** women's group. Since 1990, Kali Mata has promoted a number of small-scale development projects among the village's women, most successfully the export of henna to Europe. For tourists, they run various **guided walks** to meet farmers, crafters, potters and fishermen, and to visit the grave of the unfortunate virgin who was buried live here (see above). They offer **lessons in local skills**, such as hair plaiting, henna painting, cooking, or music and dance, plus dhow trips to Sinda Island (see box below). There's also a basic, but welcoming and very cheap, guesthouse on site (Tsh9000).

Zionzuri Art and Culture Village

Signposted from Mwembe Mgambo daladala stand • Daladalas from Kigamboni ferry cost Tsh750 (every 30min 7am–7pm) • ☎ 0714 794086 or ☎ 0713 635771, ⓦ zionzuri.blogspot.com

The offbeat and distinctly chilled out **Zionzuri Art and Culture Village** focuses principally on arts and music with a Rastafarian flavour and is very much family oriented. It's not your average tourist destination, but more of a "muck in share our dream" kind of place, where you're welcome to try your hand at woodcarving, clay modelling and pottery, batik design and making clothes, drawing and painting, farming or cooking in the Jamaican Rastafarian Ital (vegan) tradition.

You're welcome to **stay** overnight for around Tsh15,000 per person: they have rooms in an eclectic variety of "tribal" houses constructed from local materials, ranging from mud huts amid a patch of thick vegetation, to a rickety but charming three-storey construction, its ground floor made of clay, its upper floors of wood. If music's your thing, the best days to visit are Fri–Sun.

SINDA ISLAND

Some five kilometres offshore, the uninhabited **Sinda Island** has a superb beach, and surrounding reefs that are great for **snorkelling**. Kali Mata Ki Jai! Cultural Tourism (see above) can arrange sailing and snorkelling trips here on a **dhow** (bring your own equipment). Prices are very reasonable: a guide for half a day costs around Tsh20,000, and the boat to Sinda Island and back is Tsh40,000. Alternatively, Dekeza Dhows (☎0787 217040 or ☎0754 276178), based at Kipepeo (see p.107), runs snorkelling trips here for $35 per person for a few hours, and **kayaking** trips for $25 per person.

1

ARRIVAL AND DEPARTURE

BY PLANE

Julius Nyerere International Airport Dar es Salaam's airport is 11km southwest of the city along Nyerere Rd, though traffic jams mean that this short journey can take up to two hours, so allow plenty of time. Domestic flights on light aircraft use Terminal 1; facilities here are limited to a snack bar, toilet and charter airline offices. International flights and domestic flights on bigger aircraft (Air Tanzania and some Precisionair routes) use Terminal 2, which has a car-rental agency, an ATM, and an exchange bureau with bad rates. Avoid the safari operators here, unless we've reviewed the companies (see p.103), and be wary of touts.

Taxis to and from the airport You can book taxis from the airport at a desk outside each arrivals hall, though they are expensive: it costs Tsh35,000 to the city centre, Tsh45,000 to Msasani Peninsula, and Tsh60,000 to the northern beaches. Haggling might get you Tsh5000 off, but given that you'll likely be hot, tired and sweaty, you might as well resign yourself to paying full whack.

Daladalas to and from the airport If you're feeling fresh and don't have a mountain of luggage, you can catch a daladala on Nyerere Rd, 400m from Terminal 1, 1250m from Terminal 2 (Tsh400 to the city centre). The most useful are to Posta in the city centre; avoid ones to Kariakoo unless you know the area, as you'll likely be dropped on or just off Msimbazi Street, chaotic even at the best of times. For Msasani, catch one for Masaki. Going to the airport from the centre, catch a daladala from Posta, Kariakoo or Mnazi Mmoja to U/Ndege, P/Kajiungeni or Vingunguti; coming from Ubungo or Msasani Peninsula, get one for G/Uboto (Gonga la Uboto). The Kiswahili for airport is "uwanja wa ndege".

Airlines Domestic flights can be booked online (see p.48), or through a travel agent (see p.113). Tanzanian airlines with offices in Dar are: Air Tanzania, ATC House, corner of Ohio St and Garden Ave (☎022 211 4688); Auric Air, 1st floor, Haidery Plaza, east end of Kisutu St (☎0688 937166 or ☎0765 540382); Coastal Aviation, The Slipway, Msasani (☎022 260 2430 or ☎0787 232747); Fastjet, Samora Ave facing Pamba Rd (☎0686 680533); Flightlink, Seacliff Village, Msasani and Airport Terminal 1 (☎022 213 7885 or ☎0783 354448); Precisionair, Pamba Rd (☎022 216 8000 or ☎0787 888417); Safari Air Link, no office (☎022 550 438 or ☎0783 397235).

Destinations Arusha (8 daily; 1hr 15min–2hr 30min) Dodoma (2 daily; 1hr 40min); Kigoma (1–2 daily; 3hr 10min Kilimanjaro (6 daily; 1hr–1hr 15min); Kilwa (1 daily; 1hr 10min); Mafia (2 daily; 30min); Manyara (daily; 4hr); Mikumi (daily; 30min); Mtwara (1–2 daily; 1hr); Musoma (4 weekly 2hr 10min); Mwanza (4–5 daily; 1hr 30min–3hr); Ngorongoro (daily; 4hr 15min); Pangani (daily; 40min); Pemba (3–4 daily; 1hr–1hr 30min); Ruaha (2 daily; 2hr 30min); Saadani (3 daily 20min); Selous (4 daily; 45min); Serengeti (2 daily; 3hr 30min–6hr); Tabora (1–2 daily; 2–3hr); Tanga (daily; 1hr 35min); Zanzibar (hourly; 20–25min).

BY BUS

Dar es Salaam has direct connections to almost everywhere in the country, although a journey to the far west may involve an overnight stop. The tourist office in Dar has timetables and contacts for all companies. Safety should be your first consideration when choosing a bus, but as reputations change from year to year, ask as many people as possible beforehand which companies they recommend, and take it from there. Recommended companies are also mentioned in the "Arrival and departure" sections for many destinations.

BUSES TO/FROM BAGAMOYO

Buses to Bagamoyo (hourly; 1hr) leave from and drop off at Mwenge daladala stand, 9km northwest of the centre along Bagamoyo Rd (the continuation of Ali Hassan Mwinyi Rd), which has plenty of daladalas in all directions.

BUSES TO/FROM KILWA

Buses to Kilwa (3–4 daily; 5–6hr) start at Rangi Tatu in Mbagala, 13km south of the city along Kilwa Rd. Most buses leave at 6am, but to avoid the need to catch a pre-dawn taxi (upwards of Tsh20,000), you should opt for the Swahili Bus service, which leaves at 1pm and is run by the safest operator. To be sure of getting a seat, go to Rangi Tatu a few days before to buy your ticket: daladalas marked

---

SECURITY IN DAR

Arriving in Dar es Salaam is disorienting if there are hustlers or touts about. Keep your guard up, and if you're at all unsure, invest in a taxi ride into town. Although Dar is relatively safe for an African city of its size, do keep your *bongo* (wits) about you, especially if you're new to Tanzania, and heed basic advice on avoiding trouble (see p.69). It's worth repeating that you should be on your guard for **thieves** in crowded markets and transport terminals, and don't go **walking at night** unless you're absolutely sure the area is safe (the general rule is the more people, traffic and lights there are, the less the risk). **Walking by day**, even in crowded suburbs, poses no problem so long as you're not visibly nervous, or carrying anything that looks valuable. The exceptions are the beach running alongside **Ocean Road** and parts of **Coco Beach**, where you should take care if there aren't many people around.

'Rangi/3' from Posta, Stesheni and Kariakoo stands drop you beside the bus terminal and the ticket offices.

BUSES TO OTHER DESTINATIONS
Other than Kilwa and Bagamoyo services, all long-distance buses leave from the enormous Ubungo bus station, 8km west of the city along Morogoro Rd (see map p.96) – getting here in time for a usual 6am departure involves an expensive taxi ride (from Tsh20,000 at that time). For later departures, catch a DART bus along Morogoro Rd (see p.102). At any time of day or night, stay on your toes, as the bus station and its environs is known for thieves, con artists and pushy touts. As ever, to be sure of a seat, buy your ticket a day or two before. Most bus companies have offices at Ubungo, but some also have central offices, including four of the following recommended companies:

Dar Express Cnr Morogoro Rd and Libya St, Kisutu ☎ 0654 517509. Currently enjoying the safest reputation for Moshi, Arusha and Karatu (on Ngorongoro's doorstep), and to Nairobi.

Kilimanjaro Express Cnr Morogoro Rd and Libya St, Kisutu ☎ 0784 555208. For Moshi and Arusha, with the advantage of two buses (5am and 6am, before the traffic snarls up) leaving from the office, so you don't need to go to Ubungo.

Mtei Express Cnr Morogoro Rd and Libya St, Kisutu ☎ 0655 361221 or ☎ 0715 066113. Old and sometimes unreliable buses, but slower and thus relatively safe, for Moshi, Arusha and Babati.

Ratco Express Amani St, just off Lumumba St, Kariakoo ☎ 0716 268850. Reliable, well-driven and comfortable luxury buses to Tanga, throughout the day.

Shabiby Line Ubungo bus station ☎ 0719 777779. One of the safer operators for Morogoro and Dodoma, with buses continuing on to Singida.

Sumry Ubungo bus station ☎ 0715 777127 or ☎ 0715 777215. A mixed bag of buses, some better than others, but it's one of the more reliable companies for southern and western Tanzania.

Destinations Most bus services peter out by noon or early afternoon (with the notable exception of Morogoro and Tanga), so "hourly" below refers to services up to that time: Arusha (20 daily; 9hr); Dodoma (hourly; 8hr); Ifakara (3 daily; 7hr); Iringa (hourly; 6–7hr); Kampala (2–3 daily; 26hr); Karatu (2 daily; 12hr); Kyela (4 daily; 13hr); Lindi (6–7 daily; 8hr); Lushoto (3–5 daily; 5hr); Mahenge (2 daily; 12hr); Mang'ula (2 daily; 6hr); Masasi (3–4 daily; 11–12hr); Mbeya (10 daily; 11–12hr); Mombasa (3 daily; 9–11hr); Morogoro (1–2 hourly; 2hr 45min); Moshi (20 daily; 8–9hr); Mtwara (8–10 daily; 9hr); Musoma via Kenya (2 daily; 21–24hr); Mwanza via Kenya (2 daily; 24–27hr); Mwanza via Singida (4 daily; 32–34hr); Nairobi (4 daily; 12–14hr); Newala (daily; 11–12hr); Njombe (5 daily; 9hr); Singida (2 daily; 13–16hr); Songea (3 daily; 9–11hr); Tanga (6–8 daily; 6hr).

BY TRAIN
Two passenger railways start in Dar, from different stations: the TAZARA Line to Mbeya and the Zambian border, from where a connecting service continues on to New Kapiri Mposhi; and the Central Line, to Kigoma via Morogoro, Dodoma and Tabora, with branches to Mpanda and Mwanza. More information is given in Basics (see p.47).

THE TAZARA LINE
The TAZARA Line station lies 5km west along Nyerere Rd (ticket office Mon–Fri 7.30am–12.30pm & 2–4.30pm, Sat 9am–12.30pm; ☎ 0753 783 444, ⊛ tazarasite.com). It's on several dalada routes between Posta or Kariakoo and U/ Ndege, Vingunguti or Buguruni (Tsh400); taxis charge around Tsh12,000 to/from the city centre, and a DART bus service is planned. There are two trains a week: "Ordinary" (Fri at 10.30pm), and the scarcely faster "Kilimanjaro Express" (Tues at 10.10am). Both finish at Nakonde on the Zambian border, from where another train (the "Mukuba Express") continues on to New Kapiri Mposhi.

Destinations Kisaki, for Selous (2 weekly; 3hr 15min–5hr 10min); Mang'ula, for Udzungwa (2 weekly; 6hr 20min–7hr 30min); Mbeya (2 weekly; 21hr 20min–24hr 30min); Nakonde (2 weekly; 26hr 30min–30hr); New Kapiri Mposhi, Zambia on connecting train from Nakonde (2 weekly; 48hr 20min–51hr 10min).

THE CENTRAL LINE
The Central Line station is in the city centre just off Sokoine Drive at the corner of Railway and Gerezani streets (ticket office Mon–Fri 8am–1pm & 2–5pm, Sat & Sun 8am–1pm, and from two hours prior to departure; ☎ 022 213 3428, ☎ 0713 280751 or ☎ 0713 236296). Stesheni dalada stand is behind the buildings facing the station entrance. There are two trains a week (Tues & Fri at 5pm) for Kigoma and Mwanza, splitting at Tabora, from where there's also connection for Mpanda.

Destinations Dodoma (2 weekly; 15hr); Kigoma (2 weekly; 38hr 25min); Morogoro (2 weekly; 7hr); Mpanda via Tabora (2 weekly; 41hr 30min); Mwanza (2 weekly; 38hr 25min); Tabora (2 weekly; 25hr 25min).

BY FERRY
The dock for ferries to and from Zanzibar and Pemba is on Sokoine Drive, at the end of Morogoro Rd in the city centre. You can catch a DART bus from outside the port along Morogoro Rd, while daladalas to most of the city leave from the Posta Zamani dalada stand, two blocks east, until around 9pm. Azam Marine's new air-conditioned, tout-free terminal means that buying tickets here is a relatively hassle-free experience (☎ 022 212 3324 or ☎ 0774 707172, ⊛ azammarine.com). As a tourist, you'll have to pay non-resident fares – don't try to swing a residents' ticket, as that will just set you up for trouble. The best boats are Azam

Marine's (also called Kilimanjaro Ferries and Coastal Fast Ferries); they cost $30–40 to Zanzibar (7am–3.45pm 5–9 daily; 2–5hr) and $70–80 to Pemba (at least 2 weekly at 7am on Wed and Sat; 6hr), including harbour tax, and as their prices are only a little more expensive than the competition, we recommend you stick with them.

INFORMATION

Tourist office Dar's tourist office (Mon–Fri 8am–4pm, Sat 8.30am–12.30pm; ☎022 213 1555 or ☎022 212 0373, ⓦtanzaniatouristboard.com) is on the ground floor of Matasalamat Mansions on Samora Avenue, four blocks southwest of the Askari Monument. Nowadays, the website is more informative than the office itself, but staff still dispense glossy brochures, and maintain useful lists of licensed safari operators (see p.103), plus bus, rail and ferry contacts and schedules.

Listings booklets For listings and forthcoming events (of an expat/upmarket nature), pick up a monthly listings booklet: the glossy *Dar Guide*, the similar *What's Happening in Dar es Salaam*, or – for classifieds and day-by-day listings – the weekly *Advertising in Dar*. All are free and are sporadically distributed to the tourist office, major travel agents, hotels, restaurants and bookshops.

GETTING AROUND

By taxi Taxis can be found almost everywhere, especially outside hotels, clubs, restaurants and bars, and at major road junctions. Licensed cabs are white with a green band around them, and a yellow taxi sign on top; others risk being pulled up by the police, at your inconvenience. Fares for point-to-point trips within the city shouldn't top Tsh5000; journeys to the inner suburbs cost Tsh8000, and Tsh10,000–15,000 would be fair for a ride from the centre to Msasani Peninsula or Mwenge. These, and other fares quoted in this chapter, are the usual tourist rates; if you're an able bargainer, you might pay twenty percent less. Hourly or daily rates can be negotiated; starting prices are around Tsh80,000 per day excluding fuel.

By rapid bus (DART or BRT) Intended to alleviate chronic traffic congestion, Phase 1 of the Dar Rapid Transit system (ⓦdart.go.tz) should be up and running by the time you read this. It's a series of kerbed-off central lanes for the system's buses, which are boarded from stations with raised platforms, and will eventually feature on all main roads into the city. Phase 1 follows Morogoro Road,

---

USEFUL DALADALA TERMINALS

Daladala terminals are called *stendi* (stands). Throughout this chapter, we've noted useful daladala **routes**; if just the route is given (eg "Posta–Mwenge") with no further directions, you can assume the vehicle passes right by the entrance.

CENTRAL TERMINALS

Kariakoo Various stops along and off Msimbazi Street, between Mkunguni Street and Uhuru Street, 3km west of the city centre. Daladalas that start on Msimbazi Street itself head all over the city. Vehicles to Mwenge and Msasani congregate at the north end of Kariakoo market on Mkunguni Street. One block west are daladalas to Tegeta, close to the northern beaches.

Kivukoni East end of Kivukoni Front. Mainly for getting to and from Kigamboni ferry, for the southern beaches. Has services to/from Posta Zamani, Stesheni, and further west and south.

Mnazi Mmoja Uhuru Street as it crosses Mnazi Mmoja Grounds. Westbound services to Ilala, TAZARA and the airport, most of which pass via Kariakoo.

Peacock Bibi Titi Mohamed Road, facing *Peacock Hotel*. Posta–Ubungo and Posta–Mwenge daladalas pass here.

Posta Comprises two places: "Posta Mpya" (New Post Office) along Maktaba Street (mainly for dropping off), and, at the street's southern end along the harbour, "Posta Zamani" (Old Post Office), serving most destinations.

Stesheni One block east of Central Line Train Station. Mainly southbound, including Kilwa Road (Mgulani) and Temeke.

TERMINALS OUT OF TOWN

There are plenty of daladalas from Posta, Kariakoo and Peacock to the following:

Mwenge 9km northwest at the junction of Bagamoyo and Sam Nujoma roads. For services further north, including Jangwani and Kunduchi (though you'll need a taxi for the last bit). Also to the university (Chuo Kikuu) and Bagamoyo (Chapter 2).

Ubungo A few hundred metres west of the main bus terminal on Morogoro Road. For the western outskirts, Mwenge, and the university (Chuo Kikuu).

from Kimara, 20km west, via Ubungo bus station, to the Zanzibar ferry port, then along the bay to Kivukoni, facing the ferry for Kigamboni. Phase 2, which is currently being built, runs along Kilwa Road, to the south. Phase 3 is Nyerere Road, to the southwest (useful for the airport and TAZARA train station), and Phase 4 is Bagamoyo Road, to the north. Use of the system will require a prepaid card (available at the stations; Tsh500 plus whatever you charge it with); fares are slated to be Tsh700.

By daladala Despite periodic complaints in the press about dangerous driving, dirty uniforms and unsociably loud music (all true), Dar es Salaam's daladalas are surprisingly efficient and will get you almost anywhere within a twenty-kilometre radius of the city for only a few hundred shillings (currently Tsh400 for most journeys).

Most services run from 5am to 9pm. Routes are colour-coded (a thick band around the vehicle), with destinations clearly marked on the front. The only potential hassle is at major terminals (see box, p.100), where you'll have to contend with touts competing to get you in their vehicles; the fullest ones are most likely to leave first.

By car The following car rental companies are reliable and have the requisite TALA licences for national parks, but read our advice first (see p.46): Green Car Rentals, Nkrumah St (☎022 218 3718 or ☎0713 227788, ⓦgreencarstz.com); Sam's Car Rental, Bagamoyo Rd (☎022 262 7747 or ☎0784 437283, ⓦsamscarental.com); Skylink Rent A Car (Avis), *Hyatt Regency*, Kivukoni Front, and at the airport (☎022 212 1061, ⓦfirstcarrental.co.tz); Xpress Rent-A-Car (no self-drive), Senegal St, Upanga (☎022 212 8356, ⓦxpresstours.org).

TOURS AND SAFARIS

Dar es Salaam is the main base for the **Southern Safari Circuit**, comprising Mikumi and Ruaha national parks, and Selous Game Reserve. Trips to the first two can be arranged more cheaply on site (see p.202 & p.428), so you'll only really need a safari operator from Dar to visit Selous. Avoid Dar's lower end operators, most of which are clustered in Kisutu near the cheaper tourist hotels, as few are licensed or recommendable. Udzungwa Mountains National Park needs no safari company, as it's directly accessible by bus from Dar (to Mang'ula, en route to Ifakara), and can be explored on foot, alone, or in the company of a park ranger. For safaris further afield, the following mid-range and upmarket companies are worth considering; many also offer flying safaris, which let you tack on Katavi, Gombe Stream or Mahale Mountains national parks, the last two famous for their chimpanzees, as well as Mafia Island and Zanzibar.

Authentic Tanzania Senga Road, Mikocheni ☎0786 019965, ⓦauthentictanzania.com. A responsible and reliable operator offering innovative itineraries throughout southern and western Tanzania, plus Zanzibar and Mafia. Choose from tailor-made flying safaris, extended road trips, mid-range fly-camping trips, or unusual activities for Tanzania such as horseriding, mountain biking or ornithology. Great guides, too, and not snobbish either.

Coastal Travels The Slipway, Msasani Peninsula ☎022 260 2430 or ☎0752 627 825, ⓦcoastal.co.tz. With its own airline (Coastal Aviation), Coastal was the pioneer of Tanzania's "flying safaris", and offers good-value trips all over the country, including tailor-made trips, but is best for southern and western Tanzania: it has its own camps in Selous and Ruaha, and on Mafia and Zanzibar.

Foxes African Safaris TAZARA Railway Station, Nyerere Rd ☎0754 237422 (UK: ☎01452 862288), ⓦtanzaniasafaris.info. A long-established, highly regarded and ethically run English family affair offering luxurious but keenly priced off-the-beaten-track forays, often using flights on its Safari Airlink airline. Nights are usually spent in their own lodges in Mikumi, Selous, Ruaha and Katavi and, away from the animals, at *Lazy Lagoon Island Lodge* near Bagamoyo, and *Mufindi Highlands Lodge* in the south.

Hippo Tours ☎0733 128662 or ☎0754 267706, ⓦhippotours.com. One of the most reliable mid-range operators for southern circuit trips, including the coast, all tailor-made but not necessarily pricey: they're happy to offer Selous with overnights outside the reserve, for instance.

Leopard Tours Dar es Salaam Serena Hotel, Ohio St ☎022 211 9754, ⓦleopard-tours.com. Huge yet efficient mid-market operator, often dealing with package tours (towing luggage in trailers is a clever idea), and reasonably priced for the quality – though in high season you risk travelling in convoy.

Tent with a View Safaris Zahra Tower, corner of Zanaki and Makunganya st ☎022 211 0507 or ☎0713 323318, ⓦtentwithaview.com. A reliable, enthusiastic and relatively affordable outfit with its own lodges in Selous (*Sable Mountain Lodge*) and Saadani (*A Tent With a View Safari Lodge*).

Wild Things Safaris ☎022 261 7166 or ☎0773 503502, ⓦwildthingsafaris.com. An enthusiastic and efficient British-run company committed to sustainable tourism, and the only tour operator specializing in the otherwise unknown Kilombero Valley, a birding paradise south of the Udzungwa Mountains – trips here are run in conjunction with local communities. Its also operates temporary mobile camps in Mikumi and Ruaha. The guides are second to none (including for birds), and the company also offers trekking and cultural tours.

1

ACCOMMODATION

Dar es Salaam has a decent spread of accommodation. Rooms in the cheaper hotels can be exceedingly hot from October to February, so make sure they have good fans and ventilation, or a/c. Most of central Dar's leading hotels, along with their plush, pricey bars and restaurants, are in the leafy former European quarter of Kivukoni, or you may prefer to base yourself just outside the city at one of an ever-growing number of beach hotels. The nearest campsites are at Mikadi and Mjimwema beaches (see p.107).

KIVUKONI

Dar es Salaam Serena Hotel Ohio St ☎022 211 2416, ⓦserenahotels.com; map pp.88–89. Dar's leading five-star hotel enjoys stringent security, with concrete bollards up front, checks of the undersides of cars, and x-ray machines. Behind all this is a very calm and plush hotel that pips the *Hyatt Regency* for class. Accommodation is in two adjoining cream-coloured eight-storey wings with vaguely Arabian styling, with the best rooms ("superior"; $403) at the back overlooking the golf course and the ocean some distance beyond. Facilities include a couple of restaurants, two bars that also have food, a patisserie and coffee shop, an open-air swimming pool, safari shops and an exchange bureau. BB $373

Holiday Inn Cnr Upanga Rd and Maktaba St ☎022 213 9250, ⓦholidayinn.co.tz; map pp.88–89. A slick and soulless blue-glass tower aimed at the corporate market. The rooms are on the small side but have good views over the city or the ocean, as does the eleventh-floor rooftop bar and restaurant. There are more eating and drinking places on the ground floor, and an internet café and gym, but no swimming pool. BB $189

Hyatt Regency Dar es Salaam (The Kilimanjaro) Kivukoni Front ☎0764 701234 or ☎0783 670695, ⓦdaressalaam.kilimanjaro.hyatt.com; map pp.88–89. It took more than a lick of paint to transform this once sombre 1960s monolith into an airy five-star hotel. The best thing going for it is the harbour view from its front sea-facing rooms ($388), but the "city view" rooms at the back may have to put up with noise from the Bank of Tanzania's generators if there's a power cut, and are therefore overpriced – as is the usually empty restaurant. Also has a gym and rooftop pool. BB $363

Luther House Centre Hostel Sokoine Drive ☎022 212 6247 or ☎022 212 0734, ⓔluthercentre@yahoo.com; map pp.88–89. An adequate but pricey and never very welcoming Christian-run backpackers' haunt – yet it's often fully booked. All rooms have a/c (not always working), and the back rooms have glimpses of the harbour. The restaurant is poor. BB twin $60, double $65

New Africa Hotel Azikiwe St ☎022 211 7050, ⓦnewafricahotel.com; map pp.88–89. Once Dar's leading hotel, this lacks the space of the *Hyatt Regency* and *Serena*, and the rooms are blander, too, but it's a good deal cheaper than either, and for a mere $10 extra you get a harbour view. There's also a casino, bar, two restaurants, including the superb *Sawasdee* (see p.107), and a swimming pool. BB $223

Southern Sun Garden Ave ☎022 213 7575 or ☎0757 700000, ⓦsouthernsuntz.com; map pp.88–89. A five-storey hotel beside the Botanical Gardens, and the only one of the biggies whose architecture – a take on British Raj – fits the area's heritage. Overall it feels a little cramped, though it does manage to squeeze in a swimming pool. BB $251

YMCA Youth Hostel Upanga Rd ☎022 213 5457, ⓔymcahosteldsm@gmail.com; map pp.88–89. A bit of a dump, with all the charm of an army barracks (only half-finished, at that), but it is very cheap for the location; it has a bar as well as a restaurant, a quiet courtyard garden and an internet café. The bedrooms, all sharing bathrooms, are ragged but clean, and have nets and fans. BB Tsh28,000

YWCA Ghana Ave ☎0713 622707; map pp.88–89. Best budget choice in the area, this also admits men and couples, and is friendly if the matriarchs take a shine to you. A renovation is in the offing. For now, the rooms, sharing bathrooms (here, "en suite" just means a sink) are a little scruffy, but they have nets and fans, and there's a better restaurant. Rooms with bathrooms are in self-catering flats (two-bed flat Tsh30,000; three-bed flat Tsh45,000). The *askari* will let you in after the curfew. Reservations advisable. BB Tsh25,000,

KISUTU AND MCHAFUKOGE

The Asian district retains much of its original character, and contains Dar's main backpacker hostels (all with signs forbidding "women of immoral turpitude"), a handful of safari companies, and a small contingent of mostly harmless safari touts. The area has some good cheap restaurants, and used to have a few amusing boozers, too, but Dar's current building spree has flattened most of them, and what remains isn't very appealing. Walking at night between local restaurants and hotels is generally safe (there are *askaris*), but ask for local advice, especially if venturing further afield.

Econo Lodge Off Libya Street ☎022 211 6048, ⓔeconolodge@raha.com; map pp.88–89. Uninspiring this budget hotel may be, but it's usefully located, calm, safe, and perfectly adequate for the price. Its rooms, all twins or doubles, are on several floors; ones higher up are airier and therefore preferable. A/c rooms cost Tsh10,000 extra. Free wi-fi in the reception. BB Tsh35,000

★Harbour View Suites Harbour View Towers, Samora Ave ☎022 212 4040, ⓦharbourview-suites .com; map pp.88–89. Occupying the 9th–14th floors of a building that, not even a decade old, has already been dwarfed by skyscrapers on its eastern and western sides, this is aimed primarily at business executives but is very value good value for its huge rooms; get a south-facing one for views over the bay. All the rooms are well appointed, with a/c, fully equipped kitchens, plasma screen TVs and wi-fi, and the suites ($150) have balconies. There are also a swimming pool, gym, and an expensive Cajun-style rooftop bar and restaurant. Safe parking. BB **$125**

Heritage Motel Cnr Katuta and Bridge st ☎ 022 211 7471, ⊕ heritagemotel.co.tz; map pp.88–89. A modern six-storey hotel with lift access and bright, well-kept rooms with a/c, TV and internet, and the Al Basha Lebanese restaurant downstairs. It's a good option for now but is gradually being crowded out by taller buildings. Street parking. BB **$80**

Holiday Hotel Jamhuri St ☎ 022 211 2246, ✉ yasinmjuma@hotmail.com; map pp.88–89. A secure backpackers' choice in a 1930s building. The doubles are perfectly acceptable, especially those with street-facing balconies, and some have bathrooms, but the singles are tiny and stuffy. **Tsh30,000**

Kibodya Hotel Nkrumah St ☎ 0767 537119, ⊕ kibodyahotel6.com; map pp.88–89. Above a branch of Barclays, this is suitably secure, but with a dark and unappetizing entrance. The rooms themselves, doubles or twins, are tatty but reasonably priced, and have TVs. A/c rooms cost Tsh10,000 extra. **Tsh25,000**

Safari Inn Band St ☎ 022 213 8101 or ☎ 0754 485013, ⊕ safariinn.co.tz; map pp.88–89. Another backpackers' haunt, with small but bright, clean and airy en-suite rooms with big double beds, fans and nets, and some with a/c (Tsh10,000 extra). The bathrooms can be smelly, but it's decent nonetheless, and the staff are helpful. Internet café and cheap restaurant. BB **Tsh35,000**

Sleep Inn Jamhuri St ☎ 022 212 7340 or ☎ 0754 362866, ⊕ sleepinnhoteltz.com; map pp.88–89. A new centrally located highrise with very decent and decently priced modern rooms with shiny ceramic floors. They're either doubles or twins, all with cable TV, a/c (so no nets), street views, and – at the front – balconies. No alcohol allowed. **$75**

Sofia House Hotel Bibi Titi Mohamed Rd ☎ 022 211 2521, ⊕ sophiahouse.com; map pp.88–89. Unexciting but well-priced mid-range option, all rooms with TVs, fans and a/c, but smelling of bug spray. The better rooms (twins) face Mnazi Mmoja Grounds. Wi-fi. Safe parking. BB **$50**

KARIAKOO

Over the last decade, the former mud-and-thatch district of Kariakoo, sprawling westwards from Mnazi Mmoja Grounds, has been transformed by mushrooming high-rises. There are now two or three hotels on almost every street, most of them modern, despite which many are dingy and overpriced. The better ones are reviewed below, but do check the rooms first, as new buildings sprouting next door can turn bright and breezy rooms into dark hot cells. Kariakoo is not safe for

walking at night, or by day with valuables.

★**Al-Uruba Hotel** Mkunguni St ☎ 022 218 0133 or ☎ 0688 607938, ✉ lmaonac@gmail.com; map pp.88–89. The once brilliant views in this long-established Somali-run hotel have mostly been lost to adjacent buildings, but rooms facing west still get plenty of light, and are excellent value for money (plus, it doesn't hurt having one of Dar es Salaam's best and busiest budget restaurants, the Banadir, downstairs). The staff are unfailingly friendly, and the well-kept rooms have bathrooms, desk and chair, window nets, hot water, ceiling fan, TV and (old) a/c units. Couples need proof of marriage. **Tsh20,000**

Formula 10 Livingstone Hotel Cnr Amani and Livingstone st ☎ 022 218 1462, ⊕ livingstone-tz.com; map pp.88–89. On eight floors, this is almost budget in price but business class in its standards. All rooms have a/c, cable TV and wi-fi, but there's no restaurant. BB **$45**

Gold Plaza Hotel Mkunguni St ☎ 022 218 2306; map pp.88–89. The reception area in this nine-storey block is unpromising, but the rooms themselves – singles, doubles or twins – are in excellent shape and pretty good value, with a/c, fans and TVs. Lift access (after five steps). Couples require proof of marriage. BB **$35**

Sapphire Court Hotel Cnr Sikukuu and Lindi st ☎ 022 218 1834, ⊕ sapphirecourthotel.com; map pp.88–89. A new nine-storey tower with 64 unexciting but decent rooms (ones on top are best), all with a/c, cable TV (with huge screens) and wi-fi – in the lobby, at least. Staff are friendly, and everything's clean. There's also lift access and a back-up generator. BB **Tsh45,000**

MSASANI PENINSULA AND KAWE BEACH

The plush suburbs on Msasani Peninsula, 6km north of the centre, contain mostly upmarket hotels, and similarly well-to-do restaurants, bars and clubs. Taxis charge Tsh10,000–15,000 from the city centre, or Tsh45,000 from the airport. Posta–Masaki daladalas pass by Q-Bar and the Golden Tulip to finish at the Sea Cliff. Some hotels have ocean views, though much of the shoreline is rocky – for a proper beach, head to Kawe Beach, 10–11km from the centre: take a daladala from Posta or Kariakoo to "Maringo" at Kawe (there's a big roundabout), then walk 600m to Kawe Club, or 1.5km to the Mediterraneo Hotel, both on the beach.

Best Western Coral Beach Hotel Close to Sea Cliff Village, Msasani Peninsula ☎ 022 260 1928, ⊕ coralbeach-tz.com; map pp.96–97. Seen from the outside, this is an uninspired stab at a beach resort, hampered by rather too many buildings for the available space, and a lack of beach (it's on a low headland). That said, the rooms are very well equipped, and those in the new wing – all sea-facing ($210) – are positively regal. The fine swimming pool, restaurant and bar also have sea views, and there's also a gym. Safe parking. Wi-fi in public areas only. BB **$180**

Golden Tulip Touré Drive, Msasani Peninsula ☎ 022 260

1

0288, ⓦ goldentulipdaressalaam.com; map pp.96–97. Despite the Arabian styling, this huge resort-style hotel remains impersonal (more for conferences than holidays), but is amply endowed, including a massive swimming pool, and most rooms have sea-view balconies. Safe parking. BB $190

Mediterraneo Hotel & Restaurant 1.5km north of "Maringo" daladala stop, Kawe Beach ⓣ 0754 812567 or ⓣ 0777 812569, ⓦ mediterraneotanzania.com; map pp.96–97. A cluster of low, colourfully kitted out Mediterranean-style buildings in gardens set back from the beach. Amenities include a beach bar and seafront Italian restaurant, a decently sized swimming pool, and a boat for island trips. Safe parking. BB $140

★**Q-Bar & Guest House** Off Haile Selassie Rd, Msasani Peninsula ⓣ 0754 282474, ⓦ qbardar.com; map pp.96–97. The noise here can be extreme on Wed and Fri, thanks to the lively courtyard bar downstairs, and the equally popular *New Maisha Club* behind. But if you're intending to indulge nocturnal pleasures, it's a good place because of its very cheap eight-bed backpacker room, with a/c. Other rooms differ widely (cheaper ones share bathrooms), but all have satellite TV, a/c, fridge and free wi-fi. Parking is on the street, guarded by *askari*. Dorm per person $15, double (BB) $50

Sea Cliff Hotel Touré Drive, Msasani Peninsula ⓣ 0764 700600, ⓦ hotelseacliff.com; map pp.96–97. With over one hundred rooms in a three-storey thatched monolith and in the adjacent Sea Cliff Village shopping centre (no sea views; $220), this hotel is stylish inside, and if you get a bright sea-facing room, the views – from the cliff at peninsula's tip (no beach) – are spectacular. There's a mass of facilities, too, including internet access, several restaurants, cafés and bars, a swimming pool, health spa, gym, casino, and even a bowling alley. Safe parking. BB $360

Slipway Hotel The Slipway, Msasani Peninsula ⓣ 022 260 0893 or ⓣ 0713 888301, ⓦ slipway.net; map pp.96–97. Modern creature comforts wrapped in Arabian style, on three floors. The rooms have limited if any sea views, though you do get a good vista from the swimming pool. The spacious rooms and apartments have a/c and satellite TV, and The Slipway's restaurants and bars are at your feet. Safe parking. BB $130

UBUNGO BUS STATION

MIC Hotel Outside the eastern boundary of the bus station ⓣ 022 245 1469 or ⓣ 0754 232323, ⓦ mic-hotel .com; map pp.96–97. Clean, secure and reliable, and with a restaurant. To get here from the bus station, leave through either of its two exits and turn left along Morogoro Rd: passing the end of the bus station, take the first left (70m from the station's easternmost exit), and the hotel is 160m along on the right. Even though the bus station is only a few minutes' walk, if you have an early morning departure, pay the hotel *askari* to escort you there. BB $50

JANGWANI AND KUNDUCHI BEACHES

Dar's main beach strip starts 20km north of the city in the form of Jangwani and Kunduchi beaches, separated by a short but swampy inlet and a 10km drive. All hotels can also arrange trips to Mbudya Island for snorkelling (see p.95). Walking unaccompanied on the access roads away from the hotels, or on the beach beyond the hotels, isn't safe, as muggers have long been drawn to the area. For Jangwani beach, turn right off Bagamoyo Rd on to Africana Rd, some 18km north of Dar; for Kunduchi beach, continue along Bagamoyo Rd for another 3km before turning right. There are direct daladalas from Mwenge to Kunduchi; for Jangwani's hotels, get a daladala from Posta or Kariakoo for Tegeta but get off at the start of Africana Rd, where you can catch a *bajaj* (Tsh3000–5000).

Beachcomber Hotel & Resort Jangwani Beach, 4.4km along Africana Rd ⓣ 022 264 7772, ⓦ beachcomber.co.tz. An informal package-tour place with an airy and cheerful design, and colourfully decorated rooms, though the beach is a little ragged, and most of the sea views from the rooms are side-on. Among the ample amenities are a huge pool, a decent restaurant and children's activities, making it good value for money. BB $132

Jangwani Sea Breeze Resort Jangwani Beach, 3.6km along Africana Rd ⓣ 022 264 7215 or ⓣ 0786 800870, ⓦ jangwaniseabreezeresort.com. An unpretentious resort perfect for families, with a great beach complete with thatched parasols, bright rooms decked in primary colours, and a welter of amenities, including three swimming pools, a jacuzzi, massage, all manner of arcade and console games, a shisha lounge and Fri and Sat night discos. Good value for the location and facilities, and the airport transfer is also reasonable at $35 per vehicle. BB $155

Kunduchi Beach Hotel & Resort Kunduchi Beach, 3km from Bagamoyo Rd ⓣ 022 265 0050, ⓦ kunduchi.com. Bounded by a creek and the Wet 'n' Wild water park (see p.95), this is a huge, well-managed, swish resort, with a sandy beach whose lack of breakwaters makes it by far the area's nicest, complete with loungers and parasols. Facilities include countless watersports, several restaurants and bars, and a huge free-form swimming pool. Most of the 138 rooms and apartments have sea-facing balconies, and there's plenty for kids, including a crèche. Grown-ups have live bands weekends, and ocean views from the bar. Mwenge–Kunduchi daladalas drop you at the entrance. BB $145

Silver Sands Hotel Kunduchi Beach, 4.3km from Bayamoyo Rd ⓣ 022 265 0567 or ⓣ 0784 835006. Owned by the University, this is the oldest of the north coast hotels. It's a little run down (not in a disagreeable way, mind), but very good value. As well as rooms (all a/c, some with TV), there are four-bed dorms with nets and shared bathrooms. Facilities include a bar and beachside restaurant, swimming pool, 400m of beach cut by breakwaters, a snorkelling centre, and excursions to the Kunduchi ruins.

There's also an adequately secured campsite. Camping per person $\overline{\underline{5}}$, dorm per person $\overline{\underline{15}}$, BB $\overline{\underline{50}}$

White Sands Hotel Jangwani Beach, 4km along Africana Rd ☎0784 467150 or ☎0758 818698, ⓦhotelwhitesands.com. On the beach, this has 146 spacious and well-equipped rooms with sea-view verandas (some views are obscured by trees though, so ask for one on top and away from the main building). There's a large octagonal pool, several bars and restaurants, theme nights, and a great Sunday lunch at the beach café with spit-roast lamb, live music and acrobats. Also has a flashy nightclub (Fri & Sat). Transfer from Dar included. BB $\overline{\underline{180}}$

MIKADI AND MJIMWEMA BEACHES

Mikadi Beach, just south of the city, is a popular stop for truck tours, and staying overnight can be a lot of fun if you're happy slipping into road-trip mentality. There are fewer dazed tourists at Mjimwema, 5km further on, which is calmer and more intimate. Camping is possible at all three places reviewed below. Access is on the Kigamboni ferry followed by daladala, taxi or *bajaj* (see p.98).

★**Kipepeo** Mjimwema: 7.5km east of Kigamboni, then 700m along a dirt road ☎0713 757515, ⓦkipepeobeach.com. Spread out along a huge sandy beach, intimate *Kipepeo* ("butterfly") is recommended whatever your budget: *Kipepeo Beach Camp* has fourteen simple but comfortable thatched twin-bed beach *bandas* with large nets, fans and lights; while the more expensive *Kipepeo Village* has a row of twenty cosy, locally styled chalets on stilts in the bush behind

the beach, all en suite, with hot water and power. The food's good (also weekend barbecues), as is the *Swimming Cow Pub* (their beach bar). Camping per person $\overline{\underline{9.50}}$, beach *bandas* $\overline{\underline{28}}$, chalets BB $\overline{\underline{85}}$

★**Mikadi Beach Camp** Mikadi Beach, 2.4km east of Kigamboni ☎0754 370269 or ☎0758 782330, ⓦmikadibeach.com. A long-standing favourite with overlanders, this has now been refurbished, and sports a dashing swimming pool, and an open-sided thatched beach bar and restaurant (great home-made burgers). Most people camp (the campsite has plenty of shade), but there are also seventeen thatched *bandas* on stilts facing the beach, each with two beds, big nets, fans and lockable door: two have their own bathrooms (Tsh70,000). Internet access costs Tsh4500/200MB. Camping per person $\overline{\text{Tsh12,000}}$, *banda* $\overline{\text{Tsh45,000}}$

Sunrise Beach Resort Mjimwema, 7.5km east of Kigamboni, then 400m along a dirt road ☎0755 400 900, ⓦsunrisebeachresort.co.tz. A quirky Indian-run place, with good if tightly spaced rooms in cottages and two-storey rondavels; all have TV, fridge and Zanzibari four-posters. The beach is a peach, and has recliners and parasols. Add a swimming pool, a restaurant serving expensive but very good Indian food, as well as flambées, two bars (one on the beach), children's activities, camel and horse rides, boat trips to Sinda Island (see p.99), and you have great value for money. However, it's often noisy (either guests, or motorized watersports), and service is sometimes lackadaisical. Camping per person $\overline{\underline{10}}$, double $\overline{\underline{30}}$

EATING

Dar es Salaam has enough high-quality places to eat, in all price ranges, to stimulate all palates. Most of the city's flashier restaurants specialize in one or two international cuisines rather than Tanzanian, and are located in and around Msasani Peninsula, north of the centre – though fickle foodie fashion ensures only few of them stick around more than a few years, so ring ahead before going. The cheapest eats are in Kariakoo, just west of the centre, and at street food stalls (see p.108). Most bars and clubs also sell food (see pp.109–111), as do the posher hotels, albeit at painful prices.

KIVUKONI

★**Akemi Restaurant** 21st Floor, Golden Jubilee Towers, Ohio St ☎0687 360360, ⓦakemidining.com; map pp.88–89. Perched on top of a skyscraper and revolving slowly through 360°, this restaurant serves a "Swahili fusion" of nouvelle cuisine with Zanzibari spices (cumin, coriander, cloves) and less common ingredients, such as sweet potato leaves (*matembele*), and sweet *ugali*, butternut squash and smoked fish. You pay for the gob-smacking panorama, though – an evening meal including drinks can cost Tsh80,000, which makes the Tsh30,000 weekday buffet a bargain (noon–3pm), and the regal Sunday brunch buffet isn't bad value either (Tsh45,000; noon–4pm). There's a live band on Thurs and Fri from 6pm, and Sun from noon, and you're also welcome just for drinks. Reservations recommended. Daily 11am–11pm.

Garden Restaurant Cnr Garden Ave and Pamba Rd; map pp.88–89. The heavily shaded outdoor location is one reason to dine here. Another is its lunchtime buffet (Mon–Sat; Tsh18,000), against which à la carte (around Tsh12,000 a plate) can feel a bit pricey, but the food's good, especially the fish – try the *changu* (bream) or kingfish. They also own the bakery and patisserie next door, so serve good bread, cakes and coffee. Daily: snacks all day, full meals 6–10.30am, noon–4pm & 6–10pm.

★**Sawasdee** New Africa Hotel, Azikiwe St ☎022 211 7050; map pp.88–89. Perched on the ninth floor, this long-established restaurant offers fabulous à la carte Thai food, and enchanting night-time views of the harbour. The classic Tom Yam Goong soup goes for Tsh10,500, and it's good for fish – try the hot-pan prawns, or seafood stir-fry – with main courses around Tsh20,000. Reservations recommended. Daily 7–11pm.

1

STREET FOOD

You can find tasty and often dirt-cheap street food around markets and transport terminals, along much of **Zanaki St**, and at the junction of Morogoro Rd with **Jamhuri St**. For seafood, go to **Kivukoni Fish Market**, whose *mama lisha* ("feeding ladies") dish up some of the finest grilled fish in Tanzania, as well as snacks (try the chicken kebabs wrapped in chapatis), plus full meals along the lines of rice, *ugali* or bananas (sometimes cooked in coconut milk) accompanied by stews.

In the morning look out for **coffee vendors**, especially in Kisutu and Kariakoo, and at daladala stands, who dole out their brew in tiny porcelain cups. You can also find **fruit**, including finely peeled oranges and chunks of sugar cane, and **ice cream**, sold by vendors on tricycles, who announce their presence by a rendition of *O Sole Mio* (Presley's *It's Now or Never*).

Southern Sun Hotel Garden Ave ☎ 022 213 7575; map pp.88–89. Both dining rooms here (the *Baraza* and *Kivulini*) have swish service but unexceptional surroundings; it's best to eat outside. Recommended for grills and Swahili-style seafood cooked in coconut milk (around Tsh18,000), plus well-priced lunchtime buffets (Tsh24,000). Daily noon–10pm.

Steers Complex Cnr Samora Ave and Ohio St; map pp.88–89. Burgers, pizzas, stir fries and other fast food faves in various restaurants owned by a South African chain. The food's nothing special, but it's handy for a quick bite in an otherwise expensive area, and there's the bonus of a pleasant street corner terrace with parasols. No alcohol. Daily 8am–10pm.

Unnamed restaurant Ohio St; map pp.88–89. Evicted from its former premises to make way for yet another high-rise, this moved up the street, losing its shipping-container kitchen in the process, but not its charm. It's what a garden restaurant should be – friendly, relaxed and breezy, with talkative Indian crows in the trees, scrawny cats at your feet, and proper Tanzanian meals (*ugali*, rice or *pilau* with great stews) for under Tsh5000. Daily 8am–5pm.

KISUTU AND MCHAFUKOGE

Al Basha Heritage Motel, Cnr Katuta and Bridge st; map pp.88–89. Fine if pricey Lebanese food in an elegant but plain a/c dining room on the ground floor. Vegetarians will have a ball – the tart *labneh* (strained yoghurt, served with pitta bread; Tsh8000) is wonderful, as is the *warak enab* (vine leaves stuffed with rice, onion, tomato and mint; Tsh9500). A selection of *mezzeh* costs Tsh19,000. Daily midday–1pm.

Chef's Pride Chagga St; map pp.88–89. A split-level place popular with backpackers, this has an embarrassment of choice, most of it freshly cooked, whether birianis, or Zanzibari-style fish in coconut, or tender roast chicken. It also dishes up fast-food favourites, pizzas, snacks and breakfast combos, but it's getting pricey (mains around Tsh10,000), and standards are not always up to scratch. No alcohol. Closed during Ramadan. Daily 7am–8pm.

Mithai Kisutu St; map pp.88–89. Best known for its colourful selection of Indian sweets (*mithai*), including sinful *katli* (cashew fudge, also with strawberry), and – on Sun – super-sweet *jalebi* (deep-fried fermented flour and yoghurt, soaked in syrup). It also has good savoury snacks (*farsan* and *vasas*), and full South Indian meals, for around Tsh15,000 including soft drinks and sweets. The *dhosa* (crepes made from lentils) are especially tasty. Daily 7am–11pm.

New Zahir Mosque St; map pp.88–89. Run-down in appearance, this is nonetheless popular with locals, attracted by affordable and often excellent cooking. The curries, birianis and chicken *masala* (none costing more than Tsh5000) are delicious, but you'll also find *mishkaki*, chips and friends. Get there early or be patient, especially if you want a table on the streetside terrace. No alcohol. Closed Ramadan daytimes. Daily 7am–8pm.

Sunrise Café & Takeaway Jamhuri St; map pp.88–89. Under a canvas roof on top of a low building, with street views, and a menu daubed up on a whiteboard – nothing over Tsh5000. Expect plantain, rice or *ugali* with various meat stews, tilapia or liver (with cinnamon), accompanied by fresh juices such as tamarind laced with cardamom (Tsh1000). Mon–Sat 5am–4pm.

Tai Huo San Zhuang Jamhuri St; map pp.88–89. Inside this cold dining room resembling a Victorian powder room, is one of Dar's better Chinese restaurants. It's well priced at around Tsh12,000 for main courses with rice (try the prawn dumplings, *wonton*), a little less for noodles or vegetarian (including a sizzling *hong shao tofu* cooked with rice wine, soya sauce, star anise and sugar). Impatient service, well-stocked bar. Daily 10am–11.30pm.

A Tea Room Cnr Jamhuri St and Morogoro Rd; map pp.88–89. The best of several unfussy "tea rooms" around here, serving a wide range of traditional but expensive snacks (potato and meat balls, samosas, *kababu*, doughnuts and so on) to accompany classic *chai masala* (spiced milky tea). They also have filling chicken *pilau* at lunchtime, which is good value at Tsh4000, and a chicken or mutton biriani Sun lunch (Tsh4500–5000). No alcohol. Daily 6am–9pm.

KARIAKOO

★ **Banadir Restaurant** Al-Uruba Hotel, Mkunguni St;

map pp.88–89. You'd think a hundred-odd chairs would be enough, but this Somali-run restaurant is so consistently good that you might have to wait anyway. It's worth it: at the back of the dining room you can see everything prepared that day, usually a score of stews that can be mixed and matched, including good vegetarian options, and ingredients otherwise little seen in restaurants, such as *nyanya chungu* (bitter tomato), and various types of spinach and leaves. It's a great place to experiment with new flavours, and you'll rarely pay more than Tsh6000 to get stuffed. Also has fresh juices and fruit. No alcohol. Closed Ramadan daytimes. Daily 6am–10pm.

DDC Kariakoo Social Hall Muhonda St; map pp.88–89. Dar's longest-running bar and live music venue is also one of the best places for a really cheap eat, with metal platters of cheap and tasty Tanzanian dishes – *pilau*, beans and stews for under Tsh4000. It also has great *supu* for breakfast. On Tues and Sat evenings plus Sun afternoons, it turns into one of Dar's best-loved live music venues. Daily 6am–late.

Tarim Restaurant Cnr Mkunguni and Congo st; map pp.88–89. A great local canteen-style place, perfect for breakfast, whether you fancy bites like *sambusas*, classic *supu* broth with chapatis, or full-on cooked meals such as stews with grilled bananas. There's even more choice at lunchtime, like red masala chicken, *pilau*, liver, goat or beef. Most mains cost Tsh2500, though chicken (Tsh4000) is the exception. No alcohol. Closed Ramadan daytimes. Daily 5am–8pm.

MSASANI PENINSULA AND KAWE BEACH

★ **Addis in Dar** 35 Ursino St, off Bagamoyo Rd, Regent Estate ☏ 0713 266299; map pp.96–97. Long-established north Ethiopian place, with traditional decor and wafting incense. The basic staple is *injera*, a huge sour dough pancake that you share with your partner, using it to mop up a variety of highly spiced sauces and stews (under Tsh17,000). Good coffee. Posta–Mwenge daladalas to Rashidi Kawawa Rd, then walk 500m. Mon–Sat noon–10.30pm.

Bella Napoli 530 Haile Selassie Rd, Msasani Peninsula ☏ 022 260 0326, ⊛ bellanapolitz.com; map pp.96–97. Arguably Dar's best Italian, and definitely so for children, thanks to a brilliant playground. The food's good, too, with great pasta and proper pizzas (crispy and thin; Tsh15,000–20,000), gluten-free versions of the same, a wide vegetarian selection, and home-made ice cream (Tsh4500 a scoop). Tues–Fri 6–10.30pm, Sat–Sun noon–10.30pm.

The Black Tomato Oyster Bay Shopping Centre ☏ 0787 866286; map pp.96–97. Serves fantastic sandwiches on excellent bread, including ciabatta-style, with an inspired use of tropical fruits (under Tsh10,000). Also has veggie burgers, inventive salads, rice bowls, tapas, a good wine (and whisky) list, real coffee, wicked buns, fine *chai tangawizi* (ginger-laced tea), and frequent musical and artistic events in the evening. Light meals cost around Tsh15,000. Free wi-fi. Posta–Masaki daladalas. Mon–Sat 8am–6pm, later for special events.

Mediterraneo Hotel & Restaurant 1.5km north of "Maringo" daladala stop, Kawe Beach ☏ 0754 812567 or 0777 812569, ⊛ mediterraneotanzania.com; map pp.96–97. An open-sided, stylishly rustic ocean-front restaurant serving Mediterranean dishes, including wood-baked pizzas, home-made pasta and seafood (Tsh20,000 and up), plus a Japanese selection in the "Buddha Dar" above. Daily 11.45am–11pm.

DRINKING AND NIGHTLIFE

Central Dar has a handful of trendy venues doubling as restaurants or clubs, and bars salted away in the city's upmarket hotels, some of which have good views. To make a proper night of things, however, head out to the suburbs, where the bars, clubs and live music venues brim over with people. Upmarket areas like Msasani Peninsula have their fair share of places too, glitzy, brash or downright expensive, though many also attract prostitutes on the prowl. Entrance fees for discos and concerts are a fairly standard Tsh5000–10,000 for most venues, up to Tsh20,000 in posher places. Use taxis after dark; there are cabs outside most bars and venues even at the most unsociable hours.

BARS

CITY CENTRE

Akemi Restaurant 21st Floor, Golden Jubilee Towers, Ohio St ☏ 0687 360360, ⊛ facebook.com/akemidining; map pp.88–89. You don't have to dine to enjoy the spectacular views from this revolving restaurant and bar, but bring enough cash for drinks (beers from Tsh6500). The entry fee for events such as live bands, DJs, theme nights or beauty contests (currently Thurs–Sat from 6.30pm) can be as high as Tsh50,000. Daily 11am–late; special events from around 6.30pm.

Bourbon Street Jazz & Blues Bar 9th floor, Harbour View Towers, Samora Ave; map pp.88–89. The rooftop harbour view is the real draw at this otherwise overpriced Louisiana-themed bar and restaurant (Tsh5000 for a beer; Tsh18,000 for a cocktail), complete with wrought-iron balustrades, but muzak instead of jazz or blues. Daily 11am–11pm.

DDC Kariakoo Social Hall Muhonda St, Kariakoo; map pp.88–89. Tucked under a vaulted roof, this is Dar's oldest bar, and home on Sun (from 5pm) to the famous DDC Mlimani Park Orchestra. Modern Taarab music features on Tues and Sat. Daily 7am–late.

Florida Pub Mansfield St; map pp.88–89. Dark and pricey a/c bar with haughty barmaids, but the only one in the area. There's Castle lager on tap, a mute

TV, two pool tables, and reasonable food. Mon–Fri 11am–11pm.

Level 8 Hyatt Regency, Kivukoni Front ☏ 0764 701234; map pp.88–89. The expensive drinks are worth it for the harbour views, either from inside through big plate glass windows, or from a breezy terrace. Mon–Sat 5pm–midnight, Sun 5–11pm.

New Protein Bar Jamhuri St, facing *Holiday Hotel*; map pp.88–89. An ability to humour dipsomaniacs would be an asset at this dingy but, shall we say, characterful bar, which would scarcely be worth a mention were it not the only surviving local drinking hole east of Kariakoo. It's friendly enough, and can make for an eclectic and even enjoyable evening. Also has cheap food. Daily noon–10pm.

NORTH OF THE CENTRE

Cine Club Mikocheni Beach, 8.5km north of the centre, off Mwai Kibaki Rd (Old Bagamoyo Rd) ☏ 0754 374436 or ☏ 0715 374436; map pp.96–97. Essentially an outdoor restaurant and beer garden with access to a swoonsome beach, this is popular with locals, including families, at the weekend, especially on Sun when there's a live band from 4–9pm. Bands also play most Thurs and Sat evenings. Posta–Kawe daladalas pass by. Daily 10am–late.

Coco Beach Bar Touré Drive, Msasani Peninsula, 6km north; map pp.96–97. The peninsula's most popular daytime bar, thanks to its great beachfront location. Beers are cheap by Msasani's standards, there are pool tables, and a wide range of food is served, with *nyama choma* the star. It keeps hold of its clientele on Sat night with a disco; there are also discos on Thurs and Fri, and karaoke on Wed. Posta–Masaki daladalas pass by. Daily 10am–late.

Karambezi Café *Sea Cliff Hotel*, Touré Drive, Msasani Peninsula, 9km north ☏ 022 260 0380, ⓦ karambezicafe.com; map pp.96–97. Very expensive light meals (burgers from Tsh23,500) and drinks, but boasting east-facing ocean views from the tip of the peninsula, which you can can also enjoy from a deck outside. Posta–Masaki daladalas pass by. Daily 6am–11pm.

Kawe Club Off Mwai Kibaki Rd (Old Bagamoyo Rd), Kawe Beach, 11km north; map pp.96–97. A breezy beach club established in 1952 by the Tanganyika Packers (lapsed purveyors of corned beef), with a more dishevelled local vibe than other places in the area, a nice beach, and good food (especially grilled fish). May have live music weekends. Posta–Kawe daladalas to Maringo, 800m away. Daily noon–late.

Mbalamwezi Beach Club Off Mwai Kibaki Rd (Old Bagamoyo Rd), Mikocheni Beach, 8.5km north ☏ 0713 228272, ⓦ mbalamwezibeach.com; map pp.96–97. Flash and brash with hiked-up food prices, this place gets packed for Full Moon parties, and its weekly events: Thurs Karaoke, Fri & Sat DJs, Sun live band from 4pm to 9.30pm. Although it's getting run down, the beach is a peach, and there's also a swimming pool, children's playground, and even life guards. Posta–Kawe daladalas pass by. Daily 11am–late

Msasani Beach Club Kawe Beach: 10km north of the centre, off Mwai Kibaki Rd (Old Bagamoyo Rd) ☏ 0713 216129; map pp.96–97. A cavernous, army-owned place with a scrubby beach-front garden, tables under parasols, and swimming at high tide. Food is the usual *chipsi* and *nyama choma*, but you can also bring a picnic. Sun is the big day, featuring live music by Congolese-style Akudo Impact band from 3pm onwards (kids are welcome). Posta–Kawe daladalas pass by. Daily 10am–late.

Q-Bar Off Haile Selassie Rd, Msasani Peninsula, 5.5km north ☏ 0754 282474, ⓦ qbardar.com; map pp.96–97. A courtyard bar and night venue popular with locals, expatriates and well-dressed prostitutes. It's particularly lively on Thurs & Fri (live bands), Sat (disco), and on European football nights. Also has good food, pool tables, and TVs screening sports. Posta–Masaki daladalas. Daily noon–late.

The Waterfront The Slipway, Msasani Peninsula, 7.5km north ☏ 0762 883321; map pp.96–97. A

LIVE MUSIC

The mainstay of Dar's effervescent live music scene is **muziki wa dansi**: the older bands play brassy, guitar-rich sounds popular with all ages; newer ones favour Congo's raunchier rhythms and butt-shaking style (see p.530), while **Modern Taarab** bands are also easy enough to track down.

Most live music **venues** are open-air and double as normal bars, with a dancefloor between the tables and the band. Things generally heat up after 10pm, except on Sundays, when the proceedings often kick off around 4pm. Sundays can be great for families, especially at beachside venues (Kawe Beach has several). Finding out which bands are playing when and where is best done online: ⓦ bongotutoke.com has up-to-date **listings** for over forty venues. Taxi drivers also know about popular nightspots, and the Saturday edition of the *Nipashe* newspaper sometimes prints listings on its inside back page. More upmarket events are mentioned in Dar's listings booklets (see p.102).

restaurant/café/bar in this upmarket shopping centre, with a sweeping westward view of Msasani Bay, both from its terrace and a row of tables beside the beach itself. Catch a Posta–Masaki to "The Slipway" stand on Chole Rd, 250m away. Daily 10am–midnight.

CLUBS AND LIVE MUSIC

Bilicanas Club Cnr Mkwepu and Makunganya streets, entrance on Simu St ☎022 212 0605; map pp.88–89. Central Dar's most popular disco, with good lighting and sound over two floors and seven bars; also has theme nights, live bands, and oodles of prostitutes. The main nights are Wed & Fri–Sun. Daily 8pm–late.

Lango La Jiji Mikumi St, off Mpiji St, Magomeni, 3km along Morogoro Rd ☎0754 912070; map pp.96–97. Jahazi Modern Taarab's big rivals, East African Melody, play here on Mon. Gusa Gusa Band, exponents of a strange but popular cross between Modern Taarab and Bongo Flava, woo the crowds on Wed & Sat. Any daladala to Magomeni gets close. Live music Mon, Wed & Sat from 8pm.

Leaders Club Dahomey Rd, off Kilimani Rd, Kinondoni, 3km north ☎0657 141371; map pp.96–97. A large club run by the ruling CCM political party, best known for its "Bonanza" events on Sun afternoon, invariably featuring one or more big-name bands, such as Twanga Pepeta. Fri night and Sat afternoon can also be lively. Posta–Mwenge daladalas to the French embassy ("Ubalozi wa Ufaransa"), 400m away. Live music Fri from 8pm, Sat & Sun from 2pm.

Mango Garden Mwinyijuma Rd, off Rashidi Kawawa Rd, Kinondoni, 5km northwest ☎0657 969337; map pp.96–97. One of the oldest and best loved live music clubs, with FM Academia on Tues or Wed, Modern Taarab on Thurs, Twanga Pepeta on Sat, and usually also something on Fri. Catch a Posta–Mwananyamala or Posta–Makumbusho daladala and get off at Vijana. Live music Tues–Sat from 9pm.

New Maisha Club Off Haile Selassie Rd (behind Q-Bar), Msasani Peninsula, 5.5km north ☎022 276 1439; map pp.96–97. This modern two-floor club appeals to well-to-do locals, including plenty of prostitutes, attracted to gangsta-posturing rap and Bongo Flava, and sometimes live rap on Fri. Mon & Tues 7am–11pm, Wed–Sun 7am–7am, busiest Wed, Fri & Sun.

New Msasani Club Mwai Kibaki Rd (Old Bagamoyo Rd), Namanga, 5.5km north ☎0713 613799 or ☎0757 113347; map pp.96–97. A huge, and on weekdays largely empty, outdoor plot fills up to the seams at the weekend, with a rare hip-hop session ("Hip Hop Kilinge") on Sat, and *dansi* stalwarts FM Academia on Sun. Posta–Kawe daladalas, or Kariakoo–Kawe marked "via A.H. Mwinyi Rd"; get off at Ubalozi. Live music Sat from 8pm, Sun from 2pm.

Selander Bridge Club Cnr Ali Hassan Mwinyi and United Nations roads, just before Selander Bridge, 1.6km north; map pp.96–97. The former Italian Club, founded in 1956, hosts the equally venerable Kilimanjaro Band ("Wananjenje", now in its fifth decade) every Sat from 10pm. Live music Sat from 10pm.

FILM, THEATRE AND THE ARTS

Neither film nor theatre have much prominence in Dar, and dance is largely limited to the **Visa 2 Dance festival** of contemporary dance in October (Ⓦvisa2dance.com). The fine arts fare better, with the output of contemporary Tanzanian artists presented in a number of galleries, and the acclaimed **East Africa Art Biennale** (EASTAFAB; November in odd-numbered years; Ⓦeastafab.com; free entry) showcasing works by over a hundred painters, sculptors, photographers and cartoonists. For **information** on what's happening and where, see the monthly listings booklets (see p.102).

FILM AND THEATRE

Century Cinemax Mlimani City, Sam Nujoma Rd ☎0715 246362; map pp.96–97. The latest from Hollywood, sometimes even in 3D. Posta–Mwenge daladalas, then one towards Ubungo.

New World Cinema Bagamoyo Rd ☎022 277 1409; map pp.96–97. The best of Bollywood. Posta–Mwenge daladalas, alighting at "TV".

The Little Theatre Off Haile Selassie Rd near Ali Hassan Mwinyi Rd (Bagamoyo Rd) ☎0765 706282; map pp.96–97. Monthly English-language plays, musicals (and pantos at Christmas) put on by the Dar es Salaam Players, founded in 1947. Details in *Advertising in Dar* (see p.102).

GALLERIES AND CULTURAL CENTRES

★**Alliance Française** Off Ali Hassan Mwinyi Rd, 600m north of *Dar es Salaam Serena Hotel* ☎022 213 1406,

Ⓦafdar.com; map pp.88–90. By far the most energetic and relevant of the foreign cultural centres, with changing monthly exhibitions, arty gatherings, and music, theatre and even acrobats on their outdoor stage, often combining Francophone African with Tanzanian artists or performers. Also has a first-floor terrace bar and restaurant. Mon–Fri 9am–6pm, Sat 9am–1pm, plus evenings for special events (usually from 7.30pm).

Goethe Institut Alykhan Rd, 1km north of the Serena hotel just off Ali Hassan Mwinyi Rd ☎022 213 4800, Ⓦgoethe.de/tanzania; map pp.96–97. Art-house film screenings every Thurs evening, plus a handful of concerts and poetry or literature events every month. Variable times (depends on the event).

Nafasi Art Space Eyasi Rd, Mikocheni ☎0717 072399 or ☎0754 26381, Ⓦnafasiartspace.org; map pp.96–97. Tanzania's leading contemporary visual arts centre, with over a dozen artists in residence, month-long exhibitions of high-quality work, art workshops every Sat afternoon (followed by live music; free entry), and film

SHOPPING

BOOKSHOPS

Most English-language **Tanzanian works** on history and culture (including proverbs, short stories and traditional tales) were published in the 1970s and 1980s, and a few can still be found at a handful of bookstores: Dar es Salaam Bookshop and School Text Books, both at the east end of Makunganya St; General Publishing House, south end of Mkwepu St; and the University Bookshop, at the University (all open Mon–Fri 9am–5pm). The best store for **English-language works** is A Novel Idea (w anovelideatz.com), which sells mostly imported novels, coffee-table tomes, academic works, guidebooks and maps, and has three branches in the city: on Ohio St, beside Steers (daily 10am–6pm), in The Slipway shopping centre (daily 9am–7pm), and in the Oyster Bay Shopping Centre (Mon–Sat 9am–7pm). Also worth a rummage are the **second-hand bookstalls** along the southern part of Pamba Rd.

MARKETS

As the nation's commercial capital, you can buy almost anything in Dar, with markets such as Kisutu (see p.93), Kariakoo (see p.93) and Kivukoni (see p.90) having the best prices for fresh produce. Probably Tanzania's largest, the daily **Ilala Market** (daily sunrise–sunset) is a massive sprawl along Uhuru Street west of Kariakoo (most daladalas to Buguruni, leaving from Kariakoo, Posta and Kivukoni, pass by the entrance). It's particularly good for fabrics and clothes, whether new or secondhand.

SOUVENIRS

Apart from those listed below, there are a couple of souvenir shops in the departure lounge of the airport's international terminal. Art galleries (see p.111) are also a good source, as is the Village Museum (see p.94) and the Wonder Workshop, for its captivating metalwork and recycled art (see p.94). For *kitenges* and *kangas*, rummage around the shops on Uhuru Street between the clock-tower and Bibi Titi Mohamed Road, or those on Nyamwezi Street south of Kariakoo Market.

Karibu Art Gallery Bagamoyo Rd, 15km north of the city near Mbezi Beach ☎0718 711993. A great choice at reasonable prices, with an especially wide selection of wood carvings, including Makonde *mapiko* ("helmet masks"). There's a bar and restaurant at the back. Mwenge–Tegeta daladalas. Mon–Fri 10am–11pm, Sat–Sun 10am–midnight.

Mwenge Carvers' Market Sam Nujoma Rd, Mwenge, 9.5km north of the city centre; map pp.96–97. Almost a hundred stalls in this long-established, makeshift market represent not just the Makonde tradition (whose carvers

screenings on the third Tues of each month (7.30pm; neither Hollywood nor Bollywood). Tues–Sat 10am–5pm; closes later for special events.

you can see at work) but other woodcarving traditions as well, including Zaramo (figurines), Zanzibari (pirate-style chests), masks, bao games, coconut shredders, and even Ethiopian-style idols. You'll also find other souvenirs. Posta–Mwenge or Kariakoo–Mwenge daladalas, then walk 400m. Daily 8am–6pm.

The Slipway Yacht Club Rd, Msasani Peninsula, 7.5km north of the city centre w slipway.net; map pp.96–97. As well as cafés and restaurants, this upmarket oceanside mall contains over a dozen ever-changing crafts shops and galleries, and – in a warehouse beside it – lots of locally run stalls, which are packed to the rafters with batiks, Makonde carvings and other crafts. Catch a Posta–Masaki to "The Slipway" stop on Chole Rd, 250m away. Shops' opening hours vary, but usually daily 8am–6pm.

Tanzania Broadcasting Company Nyerere Rd, just before the TAZARA train station, 4.5km southwest of the city centre ✉info@tbc.go.tz. This houses the priceless archives of Radio Tanzania Dar es Salaam (RTD), which started recording the nation's music in the 1960s. The shop sells cassettes (*kanda*) of almost a hundred recordings of traditional music (*ngoma ya kiasili*), and even more of popular Tanzanian music (*muziki ya jazzi*), from the heady days of "Twist" to the present day. The tapes cost Tsh3000 each, and the quality is generally good. If you want something on CD (Tsh10,000), you'll have to wait for it to be burned in real time. Some recommendations: any *ngoma ya kiasili* from the Gogo, Haya, Kuria or Luguru tribes. For information about a project aiming to preserve the lot on CD, see w tanzaniaheritageproject.org. Daily 6am–4pm.

Tinga Tinga Arts Cooperative Off Haile Selassie Rd (behind Q-Bar), Msasani Peninsula, 5.5km from the city centre ☎0654 574808 or ☎0715 266156, w tingatinga .org; map pp.96–97. It was here that Eduardo Tingatinga (see p.74) first sold his work, and it's here you should head to buy, or simply admire, paintings made in his pioneering style, together with a welter of other crafts sold in a cluster of stalls in and around the old Morogoro Stores. Catch a Posta–Masaki daladala to Morogoro Stores. Daily 8am–6pm.

SUPERMARKETS

The most central supermarkets are City Supermarket, Harbour View Towers, Samora Ave (daily 9am–7.30pm); Imalaseko, Pamba House, corner of Garden Ave and Pamba Rd (Mon–Fri 9am–7pm, Sat–Sun 10am–4pm); and PATCO, 1st floor, Mkapa Pension Towers, Maktaba St (Mon–Sat 8am–8pm). There's also a supermarket at The Slipway shopping centre on the Msasani Peninsula (Mon–Sat 9–8pm, Sun 9–4pm).

DIRECTORY

Embassies and consulates Australia, 431 Mahando St, Msasani Peninsula ☎ 022 260 2584, ✉ australianconsulatetz @gmail.com; Burundi, 1007 Lugalo Rd, Upanga ☎ 022 211 7615, ✉ burundemb@raha.com; Canada, 38 Mirambo St ☎ 022 216 3300, ⊕ tanzania.gc.ca; Ireland, 353 Touré Drive, Masaki ☎ 022 260 2355, ⊕ embassyofireland.or.tz; Kenya, Harambee Plaza, Corner of Ali Hassan Mwinyi Rd and Kaunda Drive, Kinondoni ☎ 022 266 8285, ⊕ kenyahighcomtz.org; Malawi, Rose Garden Area, Mikocheni B ☎ 022 212 4623, ✉ mhc@cats-net.com; Mozambique, 25 Garden Ave ☎ 022 211 6502, ✉ embamoc.tanzania@minec.gov.mz; Rwanda, 452 Haile Selasie Rd, Msasani Peninsula, near IST ☎ 022 260 0500, ⊕ tanzania.embassy.gov.rw; South Africa, 1338 Mwaya Rd, Msasani Peninsula ☎ 022 260 1800, ⊕ dfa.gov.za /foreign/sa_abroad/sat.htm; Uganda, 25 Msasani Rd, Msasani Peninsula ☎ 022 266 7391, ✉ info@ughc.co.tz; UK, Umoja House, cnr Garden Ave and Mirambo St ☎ 022 229 0000, ⊕ ukintanzania.fco.gov.uk; USA, Mwai Kibaki Rd (Old Bagamoyo Rd), Namanga ☎ 022 229 4000, ⊕ tanzania .usembassy.gov; Zambia, Cnr Ohio and Sokoine st ☎ 022 212 5529, ✉ zhcd@raha.com.

Football Dar has three top-flight teams: long-time rivals Simba (⊕ simbasportsclub.co.tz) and Young Africans ("Yanga"; ⊕ youngafricans.co.tz), both at the world-class National Stadium off Nelson Mandela Expressway in Mgulani, 5km south of the centre; and current champions Azam FC (⊕ azamfc.co.tz), at Chamazi Stadium in Mbagala, 22km south of the centre. Tickets can be bought on match days, and fixtures are announced on ⊕ tff.or.tz/fixtures.

Health There are basic pharmacies all over the city, most open Mon–Fri 9am–6pm & Sat 9am–noon, but in populous districts such as Kariakoo many are open all day Sat & Sun too. The pharmacy inside Ebrahim Haji Health Centre, Asia St (☎ 022 211 4995, ⊕ ebrahimhaji.com) is open 24hrs a day. For emergencies requiring hospitalization, the best choice is Aga Khan Hospital, Ocean Rd (☎ 022 211 5151, ⊕ agakhanhospitals.org/dar). Equally competent is Kairuki Hospital, Mwai Kibaki Rd (Old Bagamoyo Rd), Mikocheni (☎ 022 270 0021, ⊕ kairukihospital.org). For non-urgent treatment, best is the Dutch-run IST Clinic, International School of Tanganyika Campus, Ruvu St, Masaki (☎ 0754 783393 or ☎ 022 260 1307, ⊕ istclinic.com). Private ambulances include Knight Support (☎ 0754 777100 or ☎ 0784 555911), available 24hrs a day.

Immigration ⊕ immigration.go.tz. For visa extensions, start at the immigration office (Huduma za Uhamiaji) at the Cnr Ohio St and Ghana Ave (☎ 022 211 8637), but be prepared to then go to the headquarters on Engaruka St, off Loliondo St in Kurasini, 6km south, just east of Kilwa Rd (☎ 022 285 0575).

Internet access Most hotels, including cheaper ones, now offer free wi-fi, even if only close to reception. The most reliable internet cafés are *Hotspot*, Harbour View Towers, Samora Ave (Mon–Fri 6.30am–8pm, Sat 9am–8pm, Sun 9am–5pm; Tsh2500/hr); *Digital City*, 1st floor, Mkapa Pension Towers, Maktaba St (Mon–Fri 8am–7pm, Sat 8am–3pm; Tsh3000/hr); and the post office, also on Maktaba St (Mon–Fri 8am–4.30pm, Sat 9am–noon).

Language courses Tanzania Swahili Language School, The Arcade, Mwai Kibaki Rd (Old Bagamoyo Rd), Mikocheni (☎ 022 277 2234 or ☎ 0784 924723, ⊕ tanzaniaswahili.or.tz) is well established, friendly and fun, and offers three-week beginners' courses, plus tailor-made crash courses.

Money 24hr ATMs for Visa and MasterCard can be found at banks all over town, including in Kariakoo; to minimize the risk of robbery, use ones inside shopping centres, or in the calmer Kivukoni area east of Maktaba and Azikiwe streets, where there are more security guards and less people. To change cash, there are several exchange bureaux on Samora Ave near the tourist office, and nearby at Crown Forex, Corner of India and Zanaki streets. To change cash on Sundays, try Karafuu, ground floor, Mkapa Pension Towers, Maktaba St, or – at bad rates – Equity, at the *Serena Hotel* (10am–1pm).

Police Emergencies ☎ 112. To report theft and deal with insurance paperwork, Central Police Station, Sokoine Drive ☎ 022 211 7362.

Post and couriers The main post office, with international parcel and the EMS courier services, is on Maktaba St. DHL has two central offices: J. M. Mall (Harbour View Towers), Samora Ave (☎ 0713 57193), and Peugeot House, corner of Bibi Titi Mohamed and Upanga rds (☎ 022 211 3171).

Swimming None of the central hotels let non-residents use their pools, so day-trippers should head to one of the hotels on the south coast (see p.107), on the north coast (see pp.106–107), or the *Golden Tulip Hotel* on Msasani Peninsula (see p.105): all charge Tsh10,000 a day. There's also the Wet 'n' Wild water park at Kunduchi Beach (see p.95). The sea north of Kivukoni is tempting at high tide, but at low tide you'll see exactly what lies beneath the surface, including what seem to be sewerage pipes, and anything left lying on the beach here will surely disappear.

Travel agents Kearsley Travel & Tours, Zanaki St (☎ 022 213 7713, ⊕ kearsleys.com); Rickshaw Travels, at the *Dar es Salaam Serena Hotel* (☎ 022 213 7275, ⊕ rickshawtz.com) and at the *Hyatt Regency* (☎ 022 212 7734); Karibu World (Walji's Travel), cnr Zanaki and Makunganya st (☎ 022 266 8838, ⊕ karibuworld.com).

The north coast

WOMAN ON THE BEACH AT PANGANI

The north coast

North of Dar es Salaam the beach resorts give way to a string of little-visited fishing villages interspersed by mangrove forests and sweeping sandy beaches that have been largely overlooked by tourism: the Sirenic charms of Zanzibar, just offshore, have seen to that. But there is plenty to enjoy, and not just beaches. Bagamoyo, the first major settlement north from Dar, is a hugely atmospheric town. In the nineteenth century it was East Africa's foremost slaving port, from which time there are many picturesque reminders, and German colonial remains, too. Heading back further in time, the nearby ruins of Kaole hint at the luxuries of coastal life almost eight centuries ago.

North of Bagamoyo, **Saadani National Park** combines the pleasures of beaches with wildlife: game drives, bush walks and river cruises are all possible. The coastline north of the park is a string of near-deserted sandy **beaches** with good snorkelling and diving reefs just offshore. A series of attractive, small-scale hotels here, especially at **Ushongo**, offer mainland Tanzania's most convincing alternative to Zanzibar as a beach destination. For culture, you need look no further than **Pangani**, a small, chilled-out fishing town at the mouth of its eponymous river, with a scatter of ruins related to slavery and colonialism, and a cultural tourism programme that can also organize river tours, and snorkelling offshore. Closer to Kenya, the harbour town of **Tanga** has been in gradual decline for more than half a century, and has even – so far – been bypassed by Tanzania's unprecedented economic boom of the last few years. Which, although locals may disagree, may turn out to have been a blessing in disguise: the lack of building development has left its colonial centre largely intact, making it one of Tanzania's prettiest towns, and one of the more relaxing for simply wandering about in. It's also a handy base for visiting Amani Nature Reserve (chapter 5) and, closer in, the Amboni **cave complex**, and extensive **Shirazi ruins** at Tongoni.

Bagamoyo and around

Set on a beautiful mangrove-fringed bay 72km north of Dar, the tumbledown nineteenth-century slaving town of **BAGAMOYO** positively wallows in its sordid past. It's an attractive day-trip from Dar, and has enough of interest to reward longer stays, too, including a vibrant **arts scene**, and some unusual possible excursions, including birdwatching or hippo-spotting on the **Ruvu River**, and the medieval ruins of **Kaole** nearby.

Bagamoyo's historic centre, Mji Mkongwe, or "Old Town", contains a wealth of buildings from **slaving times**, often achingly poignant, and always photogenic, especially when framed by slender coconut palms and glimpses of the ocean. They're

RUINS OF THE OLD CUSTOMS HOUSE, BAGAMOYO

Highlights

❶ **Bagamoyo** A major slaving port in the nineteenth century, its name meaning "lay down my heart". Atmospheric and poignant, it's now the heart of a lively arts scene. **See p.116**

❷ **Kaole** The ruins of a medieval trading town that blossomed during the heyday of the Shirazi trading civilization before the arrival of the Portuguese. Much of the site was long ago reclaimed by the sea, but what remains is nonetheless impressive. **See p.125**

❸ **Saadani National Park** A beach holiday and wildlife safari rolled into one; this coastal wilderness, with several comfortable beach lodges, combines marine, savannah, forest and riverine environments. **See p.127**

❹ **Tanga** Once an important port, Tanga has been out of sorts since the 1960s, but a welcome side-effect of its economic stagnation is a lovely hotchpotch of elegant buildings and its welcoming, laidback feeling. **See p.130**

❺ **Amboni Caves** Winding passageways, dripping stalactites, colonies of bats, an assortment of unlikely legends and a nearby forest and hot-water springs make for a great day-trip from Tanga. **See p.139**

❻ **Pangani** Like Bagamoyo, a former slave-trading town, and delightfully somnolent and decrepit. It has superb beaches, a disappeared desert island perfect for snorkelling and a good cultural tourism programme too. **See p.141**

HIGHLIGHTS ARE MARKED ON THE MAP ON P.118

very gradually being restored (too slowly for some, alas, which have already collapsed), but the town is not, as often claimed, a World Heritage Site – corruption and bureaucracy have kept it firmly on UNESCO's "tentative" list, and now, with construction under way a few kilometres to the south on what will be by far the **largest container port in East Africa**, Bagamoyo is looking at radical change, one in which tourism will take a back seat. Not that **beach holidays** have ever really been its strength: the predominance of mangroves, and the proximity of the town itself, makes for murkier waters than you might desire, and there's no swimming in any case at low tide, when the ocean retreats by up to a kilometre. Much better are the stretches of sand at Pangani to the north, and on Zanzibar, with the result that most of Bagamoyo's beach hotels concentrate on corporate shindigs and conferences.

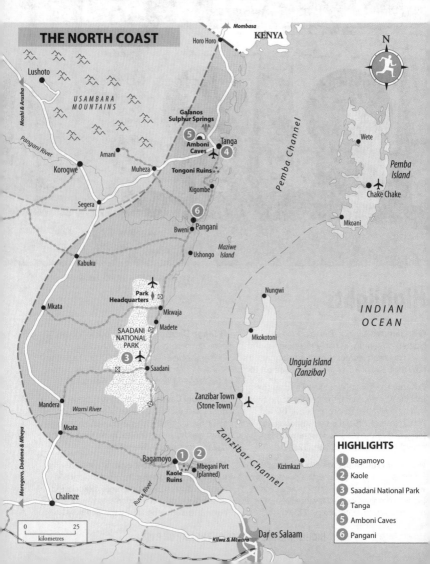

THE NORTH COAST

HIGHLIGHTS

1. Bagamoyo
2. Kaole
3. Saadani National Park
4. Tanga
5. Amboni Caves
6. Pangani

> ## BAGAMOYO: LAY DOWN MY HEART
>
> The name "**Bagamoyo**" derives from *bwaga* (to put down) and *moyo* (heart). As exact meaning in Kiswahili depends upon the context in which it is spoken, so there are two theories behind the name. The first contends the words were uttered by slaves on reaching the coast, where the impending sea voyage to Zanzibar crushed any lingering hopes of escape. For them, Bagamoyo meant "crush your heart". More likely, however, is that the words were spoken by caravan porters on arriving from the interior. For them, *bwaga moyo* was a place to "lay down the burden of your heart" – an expression of relief.

2

Brief history

Bagamoyo's proximity to Zanzibar, 42km offshore, is key to the town's historical importance. During the eighteenth and nineteenth centuries, trade in the western Indian Ocean was controlled by Zanzibar's Busaïdi Sultanate, which became one of the wealthiest dynasties Africa has ever seen. Their riches stemmed from the export of goods from the mainland, especially **slaves and ivory**, which were exchanged for cotton, beads and other manufactured goods. An estimated 769,000 slaves were transported from the East African coast during the nineteenth century, most of whom passed through Bagamoyo, which served as the major caravan terminus for routes from Lake Tanganyika and Lake Victoria, both more than 1000km away. Countless more died, uncounted, along the caravan routes long before reaching the ocean.

Given its trading links, Bagamoyo was a logical starting or ending point for many a European foray into the "dark continent". Stanley, Burton, Speke and Grant all passed through, as did a number of Christian missionaries and, most famously, the body of David Livingstone.

In the 1880s, following the groundwork laid by explorers and missionaries, the European **colonization** of East Africa began in earnest, and for the Germans – who had been accorded the territories now comprising Tanganyika, Burundi and Rwanda – Bagamoyo was an obvious choice for the capital of German East Africa. It was a status it enjoyed for less than a decade, as the **Abushiri War** of 1888–89 (see box, p.121) prompted the Germans to shift their capital to Dar es Salaam. Bagamoyo continued as provincial capital, but with the slave and ivory trades at an end, and with Bagamoyo's shallow harbour eclipsed by new facilities at Dar es Salaam, Tanga and Mombasa, the town entered a long period of economic decline from which, until a few years ago, it had never really escaped. How things change: construction of a gigantic $11-billion Chinese-built **container port** at Mbegani, a few kilometres beyond Kaole, to the south, promises to change the face of Bagamoyo forever. When complete, supposedly in 2017, it will be by far the largest port in East Africa, bigger than Dar es Salaam and Mombasa combined.

Holy Ghost Mission

Off Ocean Rd • Museum open daily 10am–5pm • Tsh2500

At the north end of town in what used to be a slave-worked coconut plantation, the Catholic **Holy Ghost Mission** occupies a series of whitewashed buildings whose plain appearance belies their historical importance. Also called **Freedom Village**, the mission was founded in 1868 by French missionaries instructed to spend as much as they could on buying slaves their freedom. Although the immediate impact was limited to a few hundred souls, the boost in morale it gave the Abolitionary movement may well have heralded the beginning of the end for the East African slave trade. In 1873, Sultan Barghash, under pressure from the British, abolished the slave trade between Zanzibar and the mainland, although the trade continued illicitly for several decades more.

2

The Roman Catholic Mission Museum

The story of the mission and its fight against the slave trade is told by the **Roman Catholic Mission Museum**, housed in the Sisters' House of 1876. There's a small collection of woodcarvings, books and booklets for sale, and plenty of material documenting not only the arrival and progress of Christianity, but also Bagamoyo's pre-history, with extensive explanations in English. Other items include

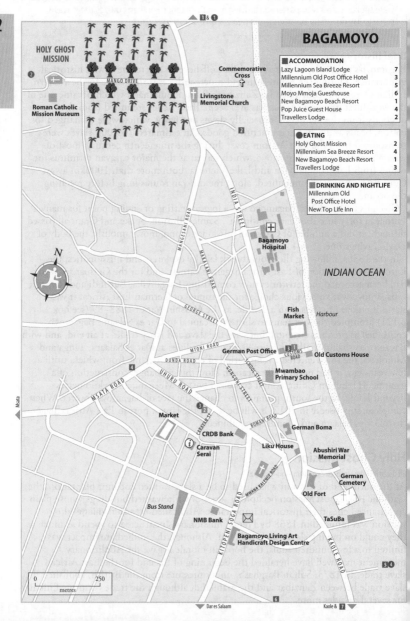

BAGAMOYO

ACCOMMODATION
Lazy Lagoon Island Lodge	7
Millennium Old Post Office Hotel	3
Millennium Sea Breeze Resort	5
Moyo Mmoja Guesthouse	6
New Bagamoyo Beach Resort	1
Pop Juice Guest House	4
Travellers Lodge	2

EATING
Holy Ghost Mission	2
Millennium Sea Breeze Resort	4
New Bagamoyo Beach Resort	1
Travellers Lodge	3

DRINKING AND NIGHTLIFE
Millennium Old Post Office Hotel	1
New Top Life Inn	2

HOLY GHOST MISSION

MANGO DRIVE

Commemorative Cross

Livingstone Memorial Church

Roman Catholic Mission Museum

N

INDIA STREET

MANGESANI ROAD

MAKILENI ROAD

Bagamoyo Hospital

INDIAN OCEAN

GEORGE STREET

Fish Market

Harbour

MTONI ROAD

DUNDA ROAD

German Post Office

CUSTOMS ROAD

Old Customs House

UHURU ROAD

MSATA ROAD

GOROGNI STREET

CHOLE STREET

Mwambao Primary School

Mvata

Market

CARAVAN ST

CRDB Bank

BOMANI ROAD

German Boma

Caravan Serai

Liku House

Abushiri War Memorial

MWINA RAENGE ROAD

German Cemetery

Old Fort

Bus Stand

KITOPENI SOGA ROAD

NMB Bank

Bagamoyo Living Art Handicraft Design Centre

TaSuBa

KAOLE ROAD

0   250
metres

Dar es Salaam

Kaole & 7

2

THE ABUSHIRI WAR

Before the European conquest, northern Tanganyika's coastal strip was ostensibly ruled by Zanzibar. In reality, though, only in **Bagamoyo** – the most important slaving port – was Zanzibari dominion assured, thanks to a much-feared garrison of **Baluch mercenaries** from Oman. So when the British forced Zanzibar's Sultan Barghash to ban the sea-borne slave trade in 1873, it was Bagamoyo that took the hit. For Bagamoyo's more independently minded rivals, **Pangani** and **Saadani**, the following fifteen years proved to be immensely profitable.

Saadani's leader was **Bwana Heri**, a slave trader from the Zigua tribe whose influence stretched as far as Unyamwezi (Tabora). A missionary writing in 1877 described slave caravans passing daily into Saadani, each with a hundred children in chains. With the profits, Bwana Heri bought arms with which to tighten his grip on power. He would need them. In November 1884, **Karl Peters**, charged with securing German interests in Tanganyika (part of Germany's spoils from the "scramble for Africa"), set off from Saadani to strike a series of bogus treaties with tribal chiefs, effectively grabbing their land. Bit by bit, Bwana Heri's influence over the interior was usurped, but it was not until 1888 that he and other slaving magnates, notably **Abushiri ibn Salim al-Harthi**, a wealthy Arab trader in Pangani, began to see their political and economic might directly threatened, when Zanzibar's sultan granted Germany the right to extract customs duties on the mainland.

With local passions already inflamed by the desecration of a Pangani mosque by German soldiers and dogs, and various other instances of perceived arrogance, Saadani and Pangani erupted in **popular rebellion**, and by September 1888 the Germans had been expelled from all but two enclaves – Dar and Bagamoyo. The German response took time to arrive, but was brutal. In April 1889, **Major Hermann von Wissmann** and an army comprised mostly of Sudanese Nubians and South African Zulus began the first major assault of the **Abushiri War**. Saadani was bombarded and taken in June and Pangani followed in July. Fleeing inland, Bwana Heri built a series of forts, each destroyed by the pursuing Germans, until he surrendered in April 1890. Abushiri, for his part, lost control of the rebellion in November 1888, half a year before the German attack, and began a futile six-month siege of Germany's colonial capital, Bagamoyo. He was captured in December 1889 and hanged at Pangani. His **grave** site is unknown.

Indian and Arab door frames, and shackles, chains and whips, though even these are not as disturbing as the photographs of slaves tied together with chains around their necks.

Madame Chevalier's baobab

The baobab tree outside the mission office was planted in 1868. Poking out of its trunk is a short piece of metal **chain**. The story goes that sometime after 1895 a certain Madame Chevalier, who had been running a dispensary in Zanzibar, arrived as a volunteer. She fastened a chain around the tree in order to tie her donkey to it, and eventually forgot all about it. Since then, the tree's circumference has swelled by more than seven metres, engulfing all but a foot or so of the chain.

The Church

The church itself, built in the midst of the 1872 cholera epidemic, is East Africa's oldest Catholic building. Its squat tower – the so-called **Livingstone Tower**, topped with a combination of arches and pinnacles resembling a mitre – is named after the explorer-cum-missionary (see p.390), whose body was laid out here for a night on February 24, 1874, having been carried on an epic eleven-month journey from Chitambo, in present-day Zambia, by his extraordinarily devoted servants Abdullah Susi and James Chuma. The following morning his body was taken to Zanzibar aboard the wryly named MS *Vulture*, and thence to England, for burial in London's Westminster Abbey.

The Fathers' House

The colonnaded **Fathers' House** facing the church was completed in 1873, and in 1876 a small chapel (also called the Grotto) was dedicated to Our Lady of Lourdes, who'd made her miraculous appearance in France in 1858. Over the following years, especially during a second cholera outbreak during the Abushiri War, Freedom Village's population increased as people sought refuge, and it's from them that many of Bagamoyo's present-day inhabitants descend.

2

Livingstone Memorial Church

Ocean Rd, at the start of the driveway to the Holy Ghost Mission

At the junction of the Catholic mission's driveway and Ocean Road are a cluster of pushy woodcarvers, and the small **Anglican church**. A sign reads, "Through this door David Livingstone passed", which is a very fine example of linguistic sophistry: Livingstone did indeed pass through it, but at the time the door was 1200km away on the shore of Lake Tanganyika. It was donated by an Anglican parish in 1974 following the construction of the present church, which is thought to occupy the site of the tree under which Livingstone's body was laid while awaiting the high tide to carry him to Zanzibar. Set in a small garden by the shore is a **commemorative cross**, not without its own touch of spin: inscribed "First Cross of the RC Church in East Africa planted 17.6.1868", it's made of concrete.

Mji Mkongwe ("Old Town")

In theory, to enter the old town – a kilometre-long coastal strip bounded by India St – you need to pay a Tsh20,000 entry fee, either at the Caravan Serai, or at the Old Fort. If you're just passing through, however (en route to a beach hotel, say, or to the fish market), it would be churlish but not impossible for someone to hassle you about not having the ticket – if you're going to be stopping and taking snaps, it's best to cough up and be done with it

The heart of old Bagamoyo is known as **Mji Mkongwe** ("Old Town") and occupies the length of **India Street** (sometimes also called Ocean Road), running parallel to the coast about 150 metres inland. This is where you'll find most of Bagamoyo's historical and architectural monuments. Not so long ago, India Street was unsurfaced, but it is now graced by modern cobbles, which seems to be the Antiquities Department's way of marking its realm, and thus the area you need the entrance ticket for.

Bagamoyo Hospital

India St • No admission (unless you need treatment!)

Walking down from the mission or the beach hotels along Ocean Road, the first major building you reach, on your left, is **Bagamoyo Hospital**. Built in 1895, it's one of several public works from **Sewa Haji**, a Pakistani trader whose condition for financing the hospital was that it would admit people of any race or religion. The Ismaïli branch of Shiite Islam to which Sewa Haji belonged has long enjoyed a tradition of trans-religious altruism, most visible these days under the patronage of the Aga Khan Foundation. Sewa Haji's own unstinting philanthropy was rewarded with a knighthood from Queen Victoria.

The harbour and fish market

Customs Rd

Half a kilometre along India Street from either end are a handful of very practical German buildings clustered around what was, and still is, the focal point of Bagamoyo's much diminished harbour. The first, at the corner of Customs Road, is the 1890s **German Post Office**, which housed East Africa's first telegraphic office, but was originally built by Sewa Haji to serve as a tailor's shop. It now houses part of the

Millennium Old Post Office Hotel, whose modern accommodation block next to it has blighted what had previously been an entirely nineteenth-century skyline. Beyond this, at the end of Customs Road on the right, is the **Old Customs House**, dating from 1895, which still sports an elegant sequence of keyhole arches. Facing it is a tumbledown storehouse dating from 1888. Behind the storehouse is the **fish market**, which some say once functioned as a slave mart. It's busiest, and most fun to visit (but don't take valuables), in the afternoon when the fishing dhows return.

Mwambao Primary School
School St

Set back a touch from India Street is another of Sewa Haji's gifts: the three-storey **Mwambao Primary School**. Built in 1896, it was donated to the colonial government on condition that it remained multiracial. Restored in 2006 with German funding, its most famous pupil is Tanzania's incumbent president (until the end of 2015), Jakaya Kikwete, who signed off on Bagamoyo's container port project.

German Boma
India St

Once the seat of German colonial might, Bagamoyo's most striking and imposing edifice, the **German Boma**, has been reduced to a most pitiful sight. Built in 1897 to replace Liku House as the seat of the German regional administration, it's flanked by twin crenellated towers similar to the single-towered Boma at Mikindani on Tanzania's south coast. Long neglected, its roof collapsed after the 1997 El Niño rains, and the building's guts – including a gorgeous arabesque gallery – spilled out a few years later, to be carted off by locals for building something more useful. It currently sports a corrugated metal roof and is very slowly being restored. Admission may be possible once this is complete, but for now only bats have access.

Liku House
South end of India St

Between the Boma and the Old Fort, and currently housing the immigration department, is **Liku House**, built in 1885 as the headquarters of the Deutsch-Ostafrikanische Gesellschaft (German East Africa Company). The building is linked to **Emin Pasha**, originally a German Silesian Jew called Eduard Schnitzer, who adopted a Turkish name and Muslim way of life while serving as Ottoman governor of northern Albania. In 1878 he was appointed Pasha of Sudan's Equatorial Province by **General Charles George Gordon**, whose mission was to extend Anglo–Egyptian rule over the Sudan. The resulting Mahdist Uprising cost Gordon his life (and gave him heroic status in Victorian Britain). Emin Pasha, however, felt his position was secure enough, and had to be reluctantly "rescued" from the "furious hordes" by **Henry Morton Stanley**. Evidently in need of another scoop to cap his meeting with Livingstone, Stanley subsequently published *In Darkest Africa, or The Quest, Rescue and Retreat of Emin, Governor of Equatoria*. Together with their sizeable entourage (albeit reduced to 196 from an original 708), Stanley and Emin Pasha arrived in Bagamoyo in December 1889. To celebrate their safe passage, the Germans threw a lavish party at Liku House, at which Emin Pasha, "supremely gay and happy" in the words of Stanley, but also short-sighted, tumbled fourteen feet off the balcony and fractured his skull. He did recover, but was murdered two years later by Arab slavers in the Congo.

The Old Fort
South end of India St • Daily 9am–6pm • Tsh20,000 entrance fee includes the rest of Mji Mkongwe, and the Caravan Serai

Just south of Liku House is the **Old Fort** (or Arab Fort), large, whitewashed and unadorned. The original structure dates from 1856, but was totally remodelled and fortified in the 1870s during Sultan Barghash's reign. Its serene location, set amid coconut palms overlooking the ocean, is grimly ironic thanks to its (legendary, at least) nineteenth-century role as a holding place for slaves. Held in small, dark and overcrowded cells, it's said that the slaves were led blindfolded through the courtyard and up a treacherously steep flight of stairs to the upper level of the fort, from where they were led back down along another stairway and out to the waiting dhows – a disorienting procedure intended to foil last-minute escapes. The fort subsequently served as a German military camp, a British prison, a customs office and police headquarters.

The German Cemetery and gallows

East off the south end of India St

A short walk east of the fort are a couple of reminders of the 1888–89 Abushiri War (p.121). The **German Cemetery**, down a path beside the former BADECO Hotel (now government offices), contains the graves of about twenty soldiers killed during the uprising, and over the following years when the *Schutztruppe* was almost constantly engaged in quelling resistance. The African dead, of which there were thousands, are commemorated by a small plinth just inside the former hotel's gate, marking the **gallows** (not a "hanging tree" as often claimed) where Abushiri's supporters were executed in December 1889.

The Caravan Serai

Caravan Rd, one block from the bus station • Daily 9am–6pm • Tsh20,000 entrance fee includes all of Mji Mkongwe and the Old Fort

About 800m west of the Old Fort, and one block north of the bus station, is the **Caravan Serai**, once the assembly and arrival point for caravans, complete with temporary rooms for porters, a slave camp on its western side (possibly where the covered market is now), and pens for pack animals. The present building, from German times, is a large rectangular enclosure, symbolically rather than architecturally important, and contains a modest **museum** covering the slave and ivory trade and German colonization, mostly in photos, and the town's tourist information office.

ARTS AND CRAFTS IN BAGAMOYO

Bagamoyo is a major arts centre, with an arts college, sculpture school, and several artists' collectives and studios to its name. The latter crop up but also disappear frequently enough, and while most are aimed squarely at tourists, hunt around and you'll find some truly extraordinary stuff, such as the delightfully surreal life-sized busts. The annual **Bagamoyo International Festival of Arts and Culture** (September or early October; ⓦ bagamoyo.com or ⓦ tasuba.ac.tz should have the dates; Tsh5000 admission per event/performance) showcases fine arts and performing arts, including theatre, dance, acrobatics, music and even comedy, from college students and abroad.

TaSUBa (formerly Bagamoyo College of Arts)
Kaole Rd ☎ 023 244 0032, ⓦ tasuba.ac.tz. The Institute of Arts and Culture Bagamoyo, known by its Kiswahili acronym, is Tanzania's oldest arts college, teaching drama, fine arts, handicrafts, music and dance, and even acrobatics, and now has a spanking new 2000-seat auditorium. You're welcome to watch performances and art classes (and buy the students' work). For personal tuition, say on traditional musical instruments, you'll pay $10 an hour. Mon–Sat 8am–3pm.

Bagamoyo Living Art Handicraft Design Centre
Facing the post office ⓦ jamani.nl/site/BLACC.html. An NGO training disadvantaged women in handicraft and business skills; their showroom sells pottery and ceramics, textiles, embroidery, basketry and clothes. You're welcome to visit the women at work. Mon–Sat 9am–4.30pm.

The Kaole ruins

5km south of Bagamoyo, 1km beyond Kaole village • Daily 8am–5.30pm • Tsh20,000 – this is not the same as Bagamoyo's Mji Kongwe ticket; tip appreciated for the optional guide • There's no public transport from Bagamoyo, and walking carries a risk of mugging, so go by bike (around Tsh8000 a day) or taxi (Tsh15,000 return is fair)

The atmospheric ruins of the once prosperous trading town of **KAOLE**, 5km south of Bagamoyo, include what may be the oldest mosque on the East African mainland, and are among Tanzania's most impressive remains from Shirazi times.

The town went into decline following the arrival of the Portuguese in the 1500s, and by the time the Omanis gained control of Bagamoyo in the eighteenth century, Kaole's harbour had silted up and was abandoned. Kaole's original name was Pumbuji, but it was renamed "Kalole" by the Zaramo after the town's desertion, meaning "go and see" what had been left behind. Much of the town has now been reclaimed by sea and mangroves.

As well as the thirteenth-century **mosque**, which includes a well-preserved *mihrab*, and another mosque from the fifteenth century, Kaole contains **twenty-two tombs**, which are of particular interest for the pillars rising from their headstones. Such "pillar tombs" are unique to the East African coast, and appear to have their roots in pre-Islamic fertility rites: the twelfth-century Iberian geographer Al-Idrisi reported the "worship" of fish-oil-anointed megaliths (menhirs) in Somalia. Kaole's earliest pillar tombs are from the fourteenth century, the latest – with a legible inscription – from 1854 (1270 in the Muslim calendar). That pillar's five depressions formerly held Chinese porcelain bowls: three were stolen, the other two are in Dar's National Museum. Also unusual is the double "**Love Grave**", said to house the remains of a couple drowned at sea, and "**Sharifa's grave**", a "hut tomb" of a holy woman still venerated by women today, who pray to her for help and leave modest offerings in a small metal bowl inside the tomb. The admission fee also includes entry to a small but interesting **museum** containing pottery shards, oil lamps and other artefacts, some of them Chinese.

Just before entering Kaole village, look for the two glaringly phallic **pillar tombs** on your right, quite different from the pillar tombs found in the archeological site, but likely stemming from the same tradition.

The Ruvu River

The road to Msata, west of Bagamoyo on the Dar to Tanga/Arusha highway, was the last leg of the old slaving route, passing through the beautifully verdant if swampy **Ruvu River valley**, whose diminutive villages consist of tiny houses perched on stilts. The area positively pullulates with colourful **birds**, and if you're determined you'll also see monkeys and, in the river, **hippos**. For more than a fleeting glimpse from a daladala, hire a bicycle in town (it's a 30min ride), but to explore the river itself you'll need to arrange a **boat trip** in Bagamoyo, either with fishermen, or through a hotel or the tourist office ($150 for two people for a full day).

ARRIVAL AND DEPARTURE · BAGAMOYO AND AROUND

To and from Dar Bagamoyo's bus station is on the same road as NMB Bank. The town is 72km north of Dar es Salaam on a good sealed road; private cars take about an hour, daladalas and Coasters – throughout the day from Dar's Mwenge terminal – about twice that (Tsh3000).

To and from Msata There are two approaches from the north: quickest is from Msata on the Tanga highway (anything going to Dar from Tanga, Arusha, Moshi or Lushoto passes by), from where there are hourly daladalas to and from Bagamoyo, taking 2–3 hours.

To and from Pangani A slower, more expensive and (for now) far more adventurous option from the north is to follow the bumpy coastal road down from Pangani: by bus or Coaster to Pangani itself, then over the river by ferry, by bus to Mkwaja, then 32km by informal transport such as motorbike (*pikipiki*) to Saadani village (before which you'll have to pay the national park entrance fee of $30), and finally by daladala from there to Bagamoyo (3hrs). That said, the route is only possible at present due to a temporary bridge over the Wami River, the condition of which you should ask about before setting off.

2

INFORMATION AND TOURS

Tourist information Bagamoyo's tourist office, run by Tanzania's Department of Antiquities, is at the Caravan Serai, one block northeast of the bus station on Caravan Road (daily 9am–6pm). This is where you'll part with Tsh20,000 for the entry fee to Mji Mkongwe (see p.122). The Roman Catholic Mission Museum (see p.119) is well informed about historical matters, and has several good books and booklets for sale. The best website for historical coverage and useful but infrequently updated practical information is ⓦ bagamoyo.com.

Staying safe Bagamoyo's chronic unemployment explains the pilfering of carved doors and stones from historic buildings, but also the town's sorry reputation for muggers and touts. The local police don't give a monkey's, so the onus is on you: catch a taxi or *bajaj* from the bus station to your hotel (no more than Tsh5000 or

Tsh2500 respectively), and when going out carry only what you'll need. Other than not walking unaccompanied to Kaole, or almost anywhere at night, there are no areas to avoid if you're not carrying valuables or wearing fancy clothes, but you should nevertheless be wary on beaches away from hotels, places near mangroves, at the bus station, and in the fish market in the afternoons.

Tours The offices at the Caravan Serai and in the Old Fort, and most hotels, can fit you up with a decent guide – it's expensive for short walks, but better value for half- or full-day trips (minimum two people) which could include some cultural tourism and visits to a traditional healer, and shouldn't cost more than $35 per person unless you need wheels. Bicycle hire, for around $10 a day, can be arranged informally at most hotels.

ACCOMMODATION

Most **beach hotels** garner their business from conferences, which means they're either full of paunchy execs on expense accounts, or resoundingly empty. There are some nice exceptions, though, and plenty of basic **guesthouses** in town, especially at the west end of Uhuru Road and around, close to the bus station. At all places, check the **mosquito nets** before moving in, as the critters abound, especially during and shortly after the rains. **Camping** is possible at *Travellers Lodge*, *New Bagamoyo Beach Resort* and *Moyo Mmoja Guesthouse*.

★ **Lazy Lagoon Island Lodge** 6km south of Bagamoyo (10km by road) ☎ 0754 237422 or ☎ 0784 237422, ⓦ lazylagoonisland.com. Snug as a bug on its own island-like peninsula, replete with bushbabies, wild pigs, genets, baboons, duiker and suni antelopes, this British-run place oozes opulence – and, though expensive, is excellent value. The main building is a spectacular vaulted affair; bedrooms are in twelve wood-and-thatch sea-facing cottages with hammocks and lofts (great for kids). The wonderfully designed restaurant and bar have panoramic views, and there's a swimming pool, not that you need one with all that beach around. The price includes kayaking, sailing and snorkelling, but change is in the offing: that $11-billion container port is coming to life just 2km away on the mainland. FB $350

Millennium Old Post Office Hotel Customs Rd ☎ 023 244 0201, ⓦ millennium.co.tz. This hotel signals the end of Bagamoyo's aspirations of attaining World Heritage Site status: while the original conversion of the German Post Office was sensitively done (it's now the hotel entrance and bar-cum-restaurant, with a few rooms on top), the new five-storey accommodation block next to it is, despite its superficial Swahili styling, an eyesore for anyone not staying there. That said, the rooms themselves are well appointed if uninspiring, and have interesting views the higher you go, including over the fish market north. The lack of a beach is not compensated for by its large swimming pool, which is walled in. BB $140

Millennium Sea Breeze Resort 200m south of TaSUBa ☎ 023 244 0201, ⓦ millennium.co.tz. The best of the conference-style places, on a great stretch of sand (shared with locals, except – if the guards remain vigilant – hustlers). The business-oriented atmosphere extends to the uninspiring modern decor of its otherwise well-equipped rooms, which are in a cluster of well-spaced, two-storey rondavels, the better ones with (shared) sea-view balconies, all with a/c. There's a good beachside restaurant, swimming pool, a couple of bars, disco and wi-fi. BB $140

Moyo Mmoja Guesthouse 400m southeast of the post office (signposted) ☎ 023 244 0277 or ☎ 0754 978628, ⓦ moyommoja-guesthouse.com. Ten minutes from the beach, this is the best lower-mid-range choice, with a nicely homely feel. There's a big garden, a fully equipped kitchen (they can provide meals) and six rooms, most sharing bathrooms: three in the main house and three more in a couple of cosy tribal-style garden huts. All are cheerfully decorated, have box nets and fans or, for Tsh10,000 more, a/c. Profits fund programmes for orphans and vulnerable children. Book ahead. Camping negotiable (Tsh15,000 per person with their tent). Hut Tsh40,000, room Tsh45,000

New Bagamoyo Beach Resort North beach, 600m beyond the Anglican church ☎ 023 244 0083 or ☎ 0783 261655, ⓦ facebook.com/NewBagamoyoBeachResort. French-run and with friendly staff, this has various types of room, eighteen – most of them renovated – set well back from the beach but with large box nets, comfy beds, big patios and a/c. Much more basic, but cheaper and more memorable, are its three beach *bandas* sharing bathrooms, but do check the mosquito nets first. Amenities include a swimming pool, bar and well-priced restaurant, wi-fi, boat trips, sailing and even kite-surfing. Camping negotiable. BB *bandas* **$30**, rooms **$90**

Pop Juice Guest House Town centre, Msata Rd ☎ 0784 595112. One of at least a dozen cheap and mostly cheerful guesthouses in this area, this one is perfectly decent, with basic but clean rooms with or without bathrooms (squat toilets). It can be noisy though. **Tsh9000**

Travellers Lodge North beach, before the Anglican church ☎ 023 244 0077 or ☎ 0754 855485, ⓦ travellers -lodge.com. A pleasant mid-range place consisting of 26 simple but attractively designed en-suite cottages scattered around lush gardens (with an improbable but true 131 species of palm), and gently sloping sandy beach. All cottages have verandas and a/c; the garden cottages can be rather dark due to the vegetation, so get one closer to the beach, for better views too, but check bathrooms before settling in. The bar and restaurant (great breakfasts) have some mind-blowing Makonde-style carvings; there's also a wild playground. Book ahead. Camping per person **$12**. BB **$90**

EATING, DRINKING AND NIGHTLIFE

The beach hotels offer a good range of **seafood**, including prawns, and both Italian and Indian favourites. There's cheaper and more basic fare in town, and street food around the market in the evening. If you're into **live music**, traditional or modern, ask at the arts college.

Holy Ghost Mission Off Ocean Rd. The small area with thatched *bandas* at the rear of the mission buildings is good for cheap lunches (*ugali* or rice with fish) for less than Tsh7000 and soft drinks. Daily noon–2.30pm.

Millennium Old Post Office Hotel Customs Rd. Recommended not so much its food but for the view from rooftop bar and restaurant, for which you'll need to buy a drink. Daily 11am–10pm.

Millennium Sea Breeze Resort 200m south of Bagamoyo College of Arts. The beachfront restaurant here enjoys a fine reputation, albeit for filling rather than fancy food – the waiter won't bat an eyelid if you ask for chips along with your red snapper à la coconut sauce (Tsh12,000). Also has lunchtime buffets, and a swimming pool. Daily 11am–10pm.

New Bagamoyo Beach Resort North beach, 600m beyond the Anglican church. Another good and

well-priced place for seafood, but don't come in a hurry. Recommended is the fisherman's platter (from Tsh15,000). Daily noon–9pm.

New Top Life Inn Cnr Uhuru Rd and Caravan St. The most popular local bar in town, and has been for decades. It also serves up simple but good dishes such as *ugali* or rice with *mishkaki*, stewed goat, fish or roast chicken, with a full plate unlikely to top Tsh5000. Also has a streetside patio. Daily 8am–late.

Travellers Lodge North beach, before the Anglican church. The open-air restaurant and bar here enjoy a fabulous location, and their astonishing Makonde-style woodcarvings are worth a visit in their own right. The food isn't bad either: the Swahili-styled seafood is particularly prized, including superb prawns, but isn't cheap at around Tsh20,000 a plate. Daily 7.30am–9pm.

DIRECTORY

Health The Holy Ghost Mission's St Elizabeth's dispensary (☎ 023 244 0253) does reliable malaria tests and is useful for minor emergencies.

Internet access The most reliable internet access is inside the post office. There are several internet cafés in the area around *New Top Life Inn*, and at the arts college. Most hotels offer free wi-fi for their guests.

Money CRDB on Uhuru Rd at the top of the road in from Dar has a 24hr ATM for Visa and MasterCard. NMB, on the same road as the bus station, changes cash.

Police Kaole Rd (☎ 023 244 0026) but rarely helpful.

Swimming pools Using hotel pools largely depends on who's at reception and how much you're willing to pay.

Saadani National Park

The rarely visited 1062-square-kilometre **SAADANI NATIONAL PARK**, 45km north of Bagamoyo, is unique in combining marine, terrestrial and riverine environments. Bush walks are the thing here, sometimes hair-raising, always fascinating, and there's fantastic birding throughout (see box, p.128). But even though you are unlikely to see big game on the beach (as is sometimes touted), the plains and swamps behind the shore are home to thirty-odd species of large mammals. A history of poaching means many are both rare and shy, so don't come expecting a wealth of photo-ops. That said, the animals' very elusiveness makes spotting them all the more thrilling. Denizens include warthog, elephants (most likely in the north), buffalo, zebra and giraffe, and a host of antelopes: Liechtenstein's hartebeest, wildebeest, waterbuck, bushbuck, dikdik, eland, kudu, oryx and the rare Roosevelt and Roan sables. The most numerous **predators** are leopards, though lions are more visible.

The **best time to visit** is June to October, when animals converge on the river. January and February, after the short rains, are visually rewarding, when the park is painted green.

2

The beach

The **beach**, of course, is an attraction in itself. As for shoreline wildlife, baboons and sometimes waterbuck are all you'll likely see, and perhaps mongooses at night, out hunting crabs. While snorkelling or on a boat, look for bottle-nosed **dolphins**, which are common off the southern shore, as are small **sharks** – which prefer prawns to humans. Saadani's nesting sites for endangered **green turtles** can be visited through *A Tent with a View Safari Lodge*, which also maintains an egg incubation and hatching centre. Time things right (contact them beforehand) and you might catch a "hatch out" (year-round), when the hatchlings make their D-Day dash into the ocean.

The northern sector

The park's **northern sector** sustains some fifty **elephants**, but their memories of poaching are fresh (in Saadani's days as a game reserve, rangers knew the area as Kosovo), so take care as they're less predictable than elsewhere. Two **rare antelope species** are the greater kudu, well camouflaged and hard to see (they spend much of the day under bushes), and sable antelope, mainly southwest of Mkwaja. These are smaller and lighter in colour than the common sable, and have shorter horns, which for a time led zoologists to class them as a separate species. While you're in the area, pay your respects to the lugubrious hippos along the seasonal Madete River.

The southern sector

The **Wami River** marks the park's southern boundary: there's fabulous birdlife all along (including flamingoes in the estuary), plus **hippos and crocs**, and, in the flanking forest, black-and-white **colobus monkeys**, given away by the crashing of branches as they flee. In swampy areas, Eastern Bohor **reedbuck** can be seen in reed beds, but bushbuck, while common, hide out in dense riverside bush. In the southwest, low hills are covered with rare remnants of coastal woodland, of which **Zaraninge Forest** is the jewel, with several primates including black-and-white colobus and blue monkeys, and yet more birds.

BIRDLIFE IN SAADANI

With its mix of habitats, Saadani's **birdlife** is rich and varied, whether along the Wami River, in acacia woodland, in Zaraninge Forest, or along the shore. **Waders** include the woolly-necked stork, yellow-billed stork, open-billed stork, common sandpiper and grey heron. The dense **acacia woodland** in the south also has spectacular birding: colourful lilac-breasted rollers, fork-tailed drongos, grey hornbills, bee-eaters, flocks of Meyer's parrots and red-cheeked cordonbleus can all be seen. **Birds of prey** include palmnut and white-backed vultures, yellow-billed kites and various eagles, including the eye-catching African fish eagle, which perches in trees awaiting prey carried up on the high tide.

ESSENTIALS

SAADANI NATIONAL PARK

Park headquarters The park headquarters are 8km northwest of Mkwaja village in the park's northern sector, 6km west of the road in from Pangani (daily 7.30am–5.30pm; ☎0689 062346, ☎0767 536133 or ☎0713 340776, ✉saadani@tanzaniaparks.com).

Entrance fees Entrance fees are levied at gates on the access roads into the park, or – if you're flying in – at the park headquarters, and are $30 per person, plus Tsh20,000 per vehicle (both for 24hrs), payable with Visa or MasterCard, but not cash.

Information The best guidebook is TANAPA's colourful *Saadani and Bagamoyo*, available at the park headquarters, and in Dar's and Arusha's better bookshops. The park's official website is ⓦ saadanipark.org.

ARRIVAL AND DEPARTURE

Saadani's access roads are much better than they once were, particularly coming from the south, but independent travellers serious about wildlife will have a hard time exploring the park beyond its coastal strip without wheels, making an organized safari much the preferable option. Driving times (up to two hours from Bweni, south of Pangani; three hours from Dar) mean that day-trips are only recommended if you're coming from Bagamoyo. Although Saadani village itself technically lies outside the park, you'll still have to pay park entrance fees for the time you're there.

Organized safaris Access is easiest on an organized safari combining overnights at one of the park's lodges with one or two daily activities, with road transfer from Dar, or flights from Dar, Zanzibar or elsewhere: we've recommended reliable safari companies (see p.103) or you can contact the lodges directly (see p.130). Safaris can also be arranged semi-formally in Pangani and Bagamoyo, but as costs there are based on extremely pricey car hire (upwards of $250 a day, plus park fees, guide, lunch etc), you won't save any money.

Self-drive 4WD is obligatory for game drives, and the park's internal road network, especially in the south, can be waterlogged during and after rains. To make the most of the experience, hire a guide at one of the gates. Whichever route you take, arrive before 6pm or you won't be admitted.

By plane Saadani's two airstrips are inside the national park, so park entrance fees apply. Scheduled flights to Saadani are operated by Coast Aviation (ⓦcoastal.co.tz), Safari Airlink (ⓦsafariaviation.info) and ZanAir (ⓦzanair .com) from Dar (approximately $140) and Zanzibar ($75), with connections from Arusha and the southern national parks of Mikumi, Ruaha and Selous.

Destinations Dar (3 daily; 1hr); Zanzibar (3 daily; 15min), with connections elsewhere.

By bus and pick-up The easiest approach is by daladala from Bagamoyo to Saadani village, which currently operate until mid-afternoon. Coming from Pangani (actually from Bweni, facing it), there's an unreliable midday bus to Mkwaja village, where there's a basic guesthouse. For the remaining 32km between there and Saadani village you'll probably find yourself riding pillion on the back of a *pikipiki* (motorbike), and will need to pay your park fees at Madete Gate, a third of the way along. From Tanga, either get yourself to Pangani and follow the directions above, or catch a bus towards Dar and get off at Mandera, from where daladalas continue to Saadani village. From Dar, there's a daily 1pm bus to Saadani village from Ubungo Maji, 300m west of the Ubungo daladala stand on Morogoro Rd.

By boat An enjoyable alternative approach is by boat from Bagamoyo, a service offered by *Sanctuary Saadani Safari Lodge* for upwards of $220 per boat (3 passengers).

ACTIVITIES

The upmarket lodges have heaps of activities for guests (included in "game package" rates, otherwise at additional cost), and possibly for others, too, but only if arranged in advance. *A Tent with a View Safari Lodge* for one are happy to oblige so long as they're not too busy, and you give them at least 24 hours' notice: assuming a minimum of two people, they charge $50 per half-day activity (ie 4hr or so), plus park fees. If you're travelling independently, you might get lucky and find a park ranger in Saadani village to take you on a bush walk, but you're unlikely to find a suitable car there for a game drive, nor is there any guarantee of arranging a boat safari at Wami Gate in the south. The following are the "standard" activities; cultural tours (usually around Saadani village) are also possible.

Game drives Game drives, in open-sided vehicles, are best up north where the park headquarters are (and where you can hire a guide; $20–25 depending on the length of the drive). Outside the park, Kisampa Camp offers spotlit night-time drives: lots of glowing eyes.

Bush walks In the company of an armed ranger (available in theory if not always in practice at the park headquarters; $70 per person including entry fee), these are an often heart-stopping way of eyeballing Saadani's denizens, and getting to see Zaraninge Forest.

Boat cruises Cruises on the Wami River are nirvana for birders, with countless specimens in and around the flanking forest, but don't rock the boat: those floating logs are crocodiles, and there be hippos, too.

ACCOMMODATION

Campsites Three locations; bookings not necessary; pay at the park gates. The national park itself has three official campsites. One is on the beach beside *Saadani Guest House*. The other two require a vehicle; one at Kinyonga on the Wami River in the south, the other more central at Tengwe, 8km northwest of Saadani village. Per person **$30**, plus park fees.

★**Kisampa Camp** Outside the park's southwestern boundary ☎0769 204159 or ☎0754 642232, ⊛afrikaafrikasafaris.com. Set on a ridge in a conservation area also comprising grasslands, hills, riverine forest and oxbow lakes, *Kisampa* is run in partnership with five villages, and is one of Tanzania's best examples of responsible tourism. On the menu, beside the usual activities, are butterfly walks and birding, visits to a bee-keeping project and school funded by the camp's activities, village visits, and wobbling around in dugouts on the nearby Wami River. Accommodation is in six large, open-sided thatched *bandas*; "rustic simplicity" means no electricity in the *bandas*, and bucket showers (hung from trees). To change scenery, you can camp in the bush, or on the beach – they have a patch north of Madete. Children welcome (and under-12s are free). FB including activities outside the park $360

Saadani Guest House 1.5km north of Saadani village; book through the park headquarters, and pay at the park gates ⊛saadanipark.org. This simple, recently renovated park-run hostel, with ten pleasant twin-bed rooms, is worth trying to book ahead, as it's right on the beach (there's a great terrace). It has running water, and electricity provided by solar panels. Per person $30

★**Sanctuary Saadani Safari Lodge** 1km north of Saadani village ⊛sanctuaryretreats.com. The most traditional of the lodges, with fifteen extremely stylish cottages (one of them with its own swimming pool), strung along the beach – all large and airy, with wooden floors, big Zanzibari four-posters, lots of draperies and ocean-view verandas. There's also a treehouse overlooking a waterhole, a swimming pool, bar and library, and a superb restaurant (especially for seafood). Special activities include forest walks and snorkelling. No children under 12. Game package (including park fees and one activity a day) from $756

★**A Tent with a View Safari Lodge** 7km south of Mkwaja, outside the park ☎0713 323318 or ☎022 211 0507 (in Dar), ⊛saadani.com. On the beach in a former coconut plantation, this is stylish without being frilly, and has maintained the same high standards for years. Special activities include birding by canoe along the mangrove-lined Mafue River (there's also good birding in the immediate vicinity, which you're free to explore), and admiring newly hatched turtles. Accommodation is in ten comfortable solar-powered *bandas* (eight of them on stilts) pitched along the blissful beach, all with large ocean-view balconies (and hammocks), and making nicely inventive use of driftwood in their decor. Honeymooners have three secluded suites, and the rickety Heath Robinson-like wood-and-thatch "Roof of Saadani" tower to stay in, twenty metres above ground, which comes with its own chef and waiter. The restaurant also has sea views and there's a hide overlooking a waterhole. Children welcome. Game packages cost an extra $100 per person. FB *bandas* $550, suites $750, "Roof of Saadani" $1000

Tanga

Located on a large mangrove-lined bay 200km due north of Dar es Salaam (350km along the highway), **TANGA** is Tanzania's second-busiest port and the country's third largest town, with 250,000 inhabitants. Not that it feels anything like that big: most of the population lives on the outskirts, giving the city centre an extraordinarily somnolent feel that is really quite charming. And yes, it is a good place to hunker down in for a few days: outlying attractions include the **Amboni Caves**, **Galanos Sulphur Springs**, the medieval **Tongoni ruins**, and yet more ruins, as well as mangroves on **Toten Island** in the bay. The **seafood** can be good, too, and the **nightlife** surprisingly lively. The only thing missing is a proper paradisical Indian Ocean beach, but that little irk has been remedied by the introduction of snorkelling trips to a sandbank in the north (and you can always head off to nearby Pangani if you're dreaming of sand).

Nowadays, Tanga is actually two places. The colourful crowded streets and haphazard structures of the dusty (or muddy) grid-like **Ngamiani district**, inland, is where the bulk of the population live and work, and is fun to explore. In the old **colonial district**, between the railway and the harbour, economic decline has had the felicitous side effect, so far, of keeping blue-glass, high-rise development firmly away.

As a result, the town's **colonial heart** is remarkably well preserved, and there's little to dispel its gently mouldering atmosphere, with a wealth of gorgeous old buildings – many of them with an Indian flavour – slowly wilting away in the humidity and heat, despite the sterling efforts of the **Tanga Heritage Project** to rescue the more impressive ones. But they're a resilient bunch, Tanga's buildings: no matter how dilapidated they look, they still stand – it might have something to do with the quality of the cement (which, along with sisal, is Tanga's main export). There's no real focus to this part of town, but any walk is rewarding, as most streets contain a least a handful of photogenic old buildings, many of them colonnaded, or with beautifully carved wooden balconies.

2

Brief history

Tanga was founded in the fourteenth century by Persian traders, but all that remains of their presence are graves and ruins on Toten Island in the bay, and the town's seafaring name: *tanga* is a woven sail, as in "tweka tanga" – to set sail. In 1498, Vasco da Gama dropped by at nearby Tongoni en route to India, when one of his three ships, the *São Raphael*, temporarily beached on a shoal. The Portuguese maintained cordial relations with Tanga until evicted from East Africa by Omani Arabs, who sailed into Tanga's harbour in the eighteenth century. Under Omani tutelage the port become a major entrepôt for Zanzibar-bound **ivory**, and in the 1830s the town received its first Indian immigrants, and subsequently a Baluchi garrison, to collect taxes on the Sultan of Zanzibar's behalf. The Indian presence, unbroken ever since, has left an especially profound mark on the town's so characteristic architecture. Inevitably, Tanga's trading links attracted European interest, and by the 1880s the town had become a major focus for the **German conquest** of the interior. As their regional headquarters, Tanga looked set to prosper, especially when construction began on a railway to Moshi. The real driving force was **sisal** (see box, p.135) but when the market collapsed after World War II (synthetics having edged out natural fibres), Tanga entered a period of decline from which it's still struggling to emerge. The railway, like the town, is now rusting away, and what was once the country's second most powerful economic region now limps along in sixteenth place.

THE "BATTLE OF THE BEES"

From the British point view, **World War I** in East Africa was a disaster from the start, when, on November 2, 1914, General Arthur Aitken ordered: "Tanga is to be taken tonight." It was not to be. The 48-hour delay in landing troops gave the Germans plenty of time to organize their defences, and when confrontation finally came, the eight thousand Allied troops, mostly Indian reserves, found themselves facing **Paul Emil von Lettow-Vorbeck**'s well-trained, thousand-strong force of mostly African *askaris*, lying in wait on the far side of the railway cutting at the neck of **Raskazone** peninsula. Although some Allied forces fought their way into the town centre, others were ambushed at the railway, got lost in rubber and sisal plantations, or were famously stung by **bees** enraged at having had their hives pierced by stray bullets, hence the battle's name. The inept nature of the assault was typified by the story of 25 **cattle** stolen by the British to feed their beleaguered troops. The following night, the African cattle herders snuck in behind British lines and took them back, without anyone even noticing. After three days and 795 casualties, the British retreated to Mombasa, leaving behind 16 machine guns, 455 rifles and 600,000 rounds of ammunition – enough for a year's fighting. Lettow-Vorbeck went on to harry British forces throughout the war, and was undefeated when the 1918 Armistice forced his surrender.

The northern section of Tanga's **European cemetery**, east of the centre, includes the graves of 48 African and 16 German soldiers who died in the battle. One of them contains **Tom von Prince**, commander of the German army's bitter 1894–98 campaign against Chief Mkwawa of the Hehe (see p.422), but his and many other gravestones, or their inscriptions, are sadly missing. The cemetery also contains British graves.

2

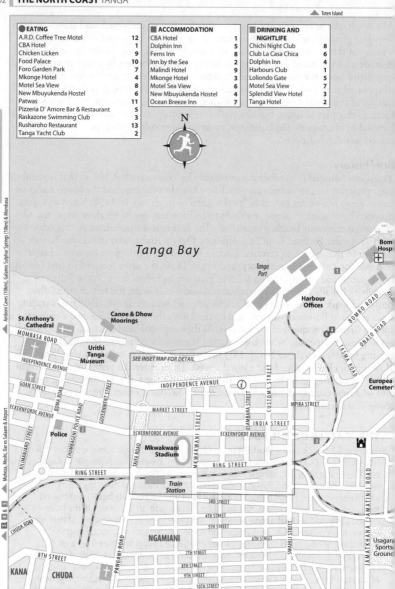

● EATING		■ ACCOMMODATION		■ DRINKING AND	
A.R.D. Coffee Tree Motel	12	CBA Hotel	1	NIGHTLIFE	
CBA Hotel	1	Dolphin Inn	5	Chichi Night Club	8
Chicken Licken	9	Ferns Inn	8	Club La Casa Chica	6
Food Palace	10	Inn by the Sea	2	Dolphin Inn	4
Foro Garden Park	7	Malindi Hotel	9	Harbours Club	1
Mkonge Hotel	4	Mkonge Hotel	3	Loliondo Gate	5
Motel Sea View	8	Motel Sea View	6	Motel Sea View	7
New Mbuyukenda Hostel	6	New Mbuyukenda Hostel	4	Splendid View Hotel	3
Patwas	11	Ocean Breeze Inn	7	Tanga Hotel	2
Pizzeria D' Amore Bar & Restaurant	5				
Raskazone Swimming Club	3				
Rusharoho Restaurant	13				
Tanga Yacht Club	2				

Urithi Tanga Museum

Independence Ave • Mon–Sat 9am–5pm, Sun 10am–2pm • Tsh2000 • ☏ 0784 440068

The town's main draw is its architecture, of which beautiful examples are scattered all over the colonial centre. To gain an insight into the details, and an overview of the whole, head west along Independence Avenue to the **Urithi Tanga Museum**. Occupying the so-called second German Boma, this is itself an architectural gem; a fine example of the deliberately imposing German colonial architecture at the start

2

of their rule which, for defence against locals as well as the climate, retained some characteristics of fortresses, especially the thick walls and stocky yet still elegant pillars. The Boma, together with its now ruined forerunner 50m away, was built in 1890 after the end of the Abushiri War (see box, p.121), and served as the office of the District Commissioner until after Independence. After a period of neglect, it was restored by the **Tanga Heritage Project** to house the present museum, opened in 2009.

The collection is rather scant, occupying the ground floor only, but there are dreams of fleshing it out properly. For now, the most interesting and informative display is a series of captioned photographs depicting Tanga's most emblematic buildings, organized in terms of their style, which will open your eyes when you wander around town afterwards. Note details such as the pillars supporting the first floor *baraza* balconies, and the changing style of roofs, reflecting various attempts at achieving adequate ventilation: the ideal design, on paper, was eventually abandoned in practice when mischievous monkeys also found them ideal to live in.

Tanga Library

Independence Ave • Mon–Fri 9am–6pm, Sat 9am–2pm • Tsh3000 daily membership

The fluted Islamic-style arches fronting the airy 1940s **Tanga Library**, still bearing its original moniker of George V Memorial Library, are a nice example of a simple but effective adaptation of "local" architecture, in this case Arabic, for a specific purpose: the preservation of books, which, in Tanga's humid atmosphere, is not the easiest thing. The design facilitates ventilation, and lets in plenty of light. The library itself is well stocked, and often full of students.

Jamhuri Gardens

Independence Ave

Students taking a break from their studies in the library have the adjacent **Jamhuri Gardens** to lounge around in, and so do you – with its grassy lawns, sea views and breezes, and not one but two children's playgrounds, one at either end, it's a lovely place to catch your breath in. There's basic food available from a round building in the centre (see p.137). On the east side of the gardens is a grandiose **obelisk** commemorating German marines who died in the **Abushiri War**. The explanation was originally on a brass plaque, but that was stolen more than a decade ago, presumably for sale as scrap. Another reminder of German rule is the clock tower nearby, erected in 1901; as with the obelisk's plaque, the clock itself has now also disappeared.

Usambara Court House

Usambara St

Apart from the Boma, the German period is best represented by the beautifully restored neo-Gothic **Usambara Court House** on Usambara Street, which was formerly the German governor's house. The town's tourist office, at the side on Independence Avenue, occupies a small round building (a *msonge*) from the same period, whose original use is not recorded.

The train station

Ring St

The British took control of Tanganyika after World War I under a League of Nations mandate. As such, it was never really considered a British colony, and the British invested comparatively little on infrastructure. The exception, in Tanga, was the **train station**, which, despite the deactivation of the railway itself, is still standing, and is a very pretty green-and-white gabled affair. The station is normally closed, as are the shunting yards behind it which house a number of rusty steam locos and carriages, but if you can track down the stationmaster-cum-caretaker, he may be amenable to the pleadings of ardent train buffs.

2

SISAL

Tanga Region was once the world's biggest producer of **sisal** (*katani*), the fibre extracted from aloe-like plants (*mkonge*) used for making ropes and sacks. The plants, originally from the Yucatan, Mexico, were introduced to Tanganyika in 1892 by the German botanist Richard Hindorf. Despite only 62 of the thousand plants surviving the journey, sisal proved to be spectacularly well adapted – by 1908 there were more than ten million sisal plants in Tanganyika, and at its height the region was producing 250,000 tonnes of fibre a year. The plantations, which stretch westwards from Tanga along much of the plains edging the Usambara Mountains, still constitute the region's major cash crop, and the new millennium has brought some reason for hope: a greener global consciousness and rising interest in bio-fuels are reviving the once moribund sisal market – from an all-time low of 20,000 tonnes exported in 2000, Tanga Region now exports more than 40,000 tonnes a year, and counting.

German war cemetery

Cnr Swahili and Mpira sts

The tragically farcical British attempt to take Tanga at the start of the first World War (see p.131) caused German and Tanzanian casualties too, whose graves you'll find in the **German war cemetery** on the north side of Tanga's European cemetery, just east of the old colonial centre. Forty-eight African soldiers and porters, and sixteen German soldiers, lie here, including **Tom von Prince**, who had commanded the German army's bitter 1894–98 campaign against Chief Mkwawa of the Hehe (see p.422). There are few remaining legible headstones, which, as you might have guessed, have been appropriated for more practical use elsewhere.

ARRIVAL AND DEPARTURE   TANGA

By plane The airport is 4km southwest of town; taxis cost Tsh6000 from the town centre, or Tsh10,000 from Raskazone. Two Tanzanian airlines land here: Auric Air (☎0783 491496 or ☎0757 466648, ⓦauricair.com), bookable at TATONA's tourist office (see p.136), which flies Dar–Zanzibar–Pemba–Tanga and back again every morning, and Coastal Aviation (no office; ☎0752 627825, ⓦcoastal.co.tz) covering much the same route, plus Arusha, with connections elsewhere. Indirect flights cost more, so check out both companies for the cheapest ticket. At the time of writing, a flight to or from Zanzibar costs $110–120.

Destinations Arusha (2 daily; 1hr 15min); Dar (3 daily; 1hr 35min); Pemba (2 daily; 25min); Zanzibar (3 daily; 1hr 5min).

By bus Tanga's bus stand is 10min walk from the centre along Pangani Rd, from where all but Ratco Express operate. Take care of your bags and pockets on arrival, and be wary of touts – offers to show you to a hotel may be conditioned by whoever pays them commission. When leaving, buy your ticket the day before, unrestrained by luggage or time. Ratco Express operates from its own petrol station on Ring St facing the stadium (☎0655 555682 or ☎0766 974239), and is by far the safest and most comfortable company for Dar es Salaam. It runs at least six buses a day, the first leaving at 6.30am, the last at 5pm. There's currently no "luxury" service for Arusha (but ask around). Mombasa is served by two Kenyan companies, both "luxury" – Smart (whose drivers are anything but) and the much safer Modern. The road is now asphalt all the way, so it's just a 2hr drive plus however long it takes to get non-East Africans through immigration. For Dodoma and Morogoro, ask around beforehand as to the safest services. The wildest route from Tanga is across the Maasai Steppe to Kondoa in central Tanzania: Mwambao Bus and Coastal Bus have been covering this twice a week in the dry season for more than a decade, and take more than 24hr (there's an overnight stop along the way). For Amani Nature Reserve, get yourself to Muheza: any southbound bus or Coaster with the exception of ones to Pangani pass by. Lushoto is covered by Coaster minibuses throughout the day, most of them sanely driven.

Destinations Arusha (6 daily; 6hr); Dar (hourly; 6hr); Kondoa (2 weekly, dry weather only; 26hr); Korogwe (hourly; 1hr 30min); Lushoto (hourly; 3hr); Mombasa (4 daily; 3hr); Mombo (hourly; 2hr); Morogoro (4 daily; 5–6hr); Moshi (3–4 daily; 5hr); Muheza (frequent; 45min); Pangani (5 daily; 2–3hr).

By boat In the wake of the sinking of the MV *Spice Islander* in September 2011, there have only been sporadic ferry connections from Tanga, but there's talk of resuming a weekly service to Pemba (6hrs) using the government-owned MV *Maendeleo*. The romantic-sounding alternative of catching a dhow is almost certain to run aground on a shoal of bureaucracy at the port. It's easier to arrange such a trip in Pangani.

GETTING AROUND

By taxi Short taxi rides within town cost Tsh3000–4000.

By bicycle Bicycles are a popular way to get around: you can rent one via the tour operators, or ask at the tourist office: a no-frills bike costs Tsh3000–5000 for the day, but expect to pay up to Tsh10,000 for a mountain bike.

On foot Walking by day is safe (but pay attention in and around the bus station), and the colonial part of town should be safe at night, too, as there are plenty of *askaris* about, but do seek local advice.

INFORMATION AND TOURS

Tourist information Tanga's tourist office is operated by TATONA, the Tanga Tourism Network Association. It's in the round building at the corner of Independence Ave and Usambara St (Mon–Fri 8am–5pm, Sat 8am–noon; ☎0768 971166, ⓦtangatourism.org), and is genuinely useful, including for queries relating to Pangani. They also have copies of the *Tanga Tourism Guide*, which can also be downloaded from their website.

Tour operators A number of local tour operators, some much better than others, offer day-trips around Tanga,

including the now-classic combination of the Amboni Caves with the Galanos Hot Springs, and day-long snorkelling trips off a sandbank north of Tanga. Reliable operators with reasonable prices are: Ilya Tours, at the *Ocean Breeze Inn* (Mon–Sat 9am–7pm, Sun variable; ☎0713 560569 or ☎0784 660569, ⓦilyatours.com), and Tangawonders, Zanetti Building, Independence Ave, just east of *Club La Casa Chica* (Mon–Sat 8am–6pm, Sun variable; ☎0715 335403 or ☎0787 335403, ⓦtangawonders.com).

ACCOMMODATION

Tanga has plenty of accommodation in all ranges. Solo budget travellers may feel short-changed, as only more upmarket hotels have single room rates. There's no campsite at present.

TOWN CENTRE

Dolphin Inn Chuda area, 1km west of the bus stand ☎027 264 5005, ⓔdolphinhotel2000@yahoo.com. Chuda area lies south and east of the old railway tracks and has more than a dozen bars and clubs, and as many guesthouses, most of them very decent, so useful if you're saving pennies. This one's a long-standing favourite, efficiently run, with thirteen rooms with nets, fans, tiled bathrooms, big beds and cotton sheets. There's also a lively bar. BB Tsh12,000

Ferns Inn Usambara St ☎027 264 6947 or ☎0713 481608. Run by a sweet Goan and his son, this has clean en-suite rooms with fans and (round) nets, and three with a/c (and double beds). All have cable TV. There's a small, friendly bar, and decent food. BB fan Tsh18,000, a/c Tsh35,000

Malindi Hotel Ring St ☎0757 488310. A four-storey affair (with a pool table at the entrance) offering good value for money, and clean cotton sheets. The atmosphere is a mite tawdry, however, and it all feels rather dark. Cheaper rooms share bathrooms, and more expensive ones have a/c. BB Tsh15,000, a/c Tsh20,000

Motel Sea View Independence Ave ☎0713 383868, ⓔmotelseaviewtanga@hotmail.com. After an on-off restoration that took almost a decade (to 2009), this is fading once again, with cracking ceilings and scabrous paintwork all too evident, but it remains, by a long shot, one of Tanga's most atmospheric abodes, especially if you get one of the four front rooms on the first floor whose private balconies have spectacular harbour views. All rooms are large, have old a/c units (no fans), TV and wi-fi,

and mosquito nets are available on request. The downstairs bar has a lovely streetside terrace, where you can also take meals. BB $35

Ocean Breeze Inn Clock Tower St ☎027 264 4545. If you're not fussy (really, *not* fussy), this is the best central budget choice, especially if you get a top floor room with north-facing balcony, for views of Tanga Bay between the trees. The rooms, all en suite and with TVs (local stations only), are large and fine so long as the mosquito net isn't too damaged, but both the plumbing and wiring is astonishingly bad, and some of the a/c units prefer rattle to hum, if they work at all. There's a bar downstairs, with tables in the adjacent courtyard, and good food. Tsh15,000

RASKAZONE

The verdant (and humid) Raskazone peninsula has an almost rural feel. Unfortunately there's no real beach to speak of other than a handful of clearings cut from the mangroves years ago, and now occupied by swimming clubs, *Tanga Yacht Club* and *Inn by the Sea*. Frequent daladalas run up and down Bombo Road (Tsh400).

CBA Hotel 30m beyond Tanga Yacht Club ☎0689 444000, ⓦcbahotel.com. A welcoming, low-key conference-style place in a large grassy plot, with smallish but comfortable and, unusually for Tanga, very well kept rooms, all with a/c, cable TV and wi-fi. There's also a bar, restaurant and plenty of shaded tables outside. The only thing missing is sea views, but the two swimming clubs and *Tanga Yacht Club* are just outside. BB Tsh55,000

Inn by the Sea 1.5km along Bombo Rd ☎027 264 4614 or ☎0713 588002. Perched on a low cliff among lush bougainvillea hedges, this very basic and somewhat narcoleptic place sees little trade, but has the peninsula's best location (and you can swim, too), and is thus the best budget place for an actual holiday. The rooms, in two rows plus a few more in the main building, are perfectly acceptable if run down. Great bay views from the back rooms, and from an open-sided terrace and lounge. No food, and alcohol is not allowed (this may change), but there's *Raskazone Swimming Club* next door under the same ownership. BB Tsh25,000

Mkonge Hotel 1.25km along Bombo Rd ☏ 027 264 3440, ⊛ mkongehotel.com. Tanga's leading abode, set in a baobab-studded lawn by the bay. The fringing mangroves mean no swimming, but a swimming pool compensates. The main building, containing the bar, restaurant and internet café, is a sensitively restored hulk dating from the happier days of the sisal industry; less enticing is the 1970s accommodation block accessed along a long dark corridor, although its large rooms – with polished parquet – are cheerfully furnished and equipped with a/c (no nets), satellite TV, spotless bathrooms and small terraces. The better ones have fine bay views, albeit through trees and a fence; best from the top floor. BB garden view $90, sea view $100

New Mbuyukenda Hostel 400m along Bombo Rd ☏ 027 266 0027 or ☏ 0717 363935, ✉ mbuyukenda hostel@elct-ned.org. A former German mission station, this is still run by the Lutheran Church, and has a few prim and proper cottages (containing twelve en-suite rooms in all) set in delightful mature gardens with hugely impressive trees, making it an excellent choice for families (no shoreline though). Also has a sleepy restaurant. BB Tsh30,000

EATING

Street food in the town centre is restricted to a handful of fruit stalls, coconut-juice vendors and peanut and cashew pedlars rhythmically marking their presence with seed rattles. The area around the bus station has more choice, and the narrow beach beside the canoe and dhow moorings just east of St Anthony's Cathedral is the best place for fried fish. As for **restaurants**, there's not a huge selection, but what there is can be unusually good (the big speciality is prawns). You can also find (rather average) *nyama choma* and *chipsi mayai* in some bars, and (much better) *supu* in the morning.

A.R.D. Coffee Tree Motel Cnr Usambara and India sts. A nice sleepy local bar for an afternoon tot that also dishes up filling Tanzanian fare like *ugali* with fish, or meat and banana stew (all around Tsh3000), and with tables on a veranda outside. There's also a pool table. Daily noon–10pm or later.

CBA Hotel 20m beyond Tanga Yacht Club, Raskazone. This lacks the *Tanga Yacht Club*'s views but has friendlier vibe, and plenty of tables under parasols in the grassy garden. The food is good, but isn't much cheaper than the *Club*. They're especially proud of their pan-fried kingfish fillet (Tsh10,000). Also has a well-stocked bar. Daily noon–11pm.

Chicken Licken Cnr Customs and Arab sts. A branch of the South African fast food chain, which doesn't look like much from the outside, but has gained a reputation for really tasty pizzas, reasonably priced at Tsh5000–8000 depending on size. The pasta is good too, and as the name suggests they also do chicken, including chicken burgers. Home deliveries. Daily noon–10pm.

Food Palace Market St. Ever popular with expats and Tanzanian Indians, the menu isn't extensive but the food is reliably good, and includes pizzas, Gujarati dishes, evening barbecues (Fri–Sun) and excellent snacks (good for breakfast). Main courses with all the trimmings for around Tsh7000. The streetside veranda has a few tables. Mon–Thurs 7.30am–3.30pm, Fri–Sun 7.30am–3.30pm & 7–10.30pm.

Foro Garden Park Jamhuri Gardens, Independence Ave. The eastern half of Jamhuri Gardens has dozens of tables and even a TV strapped to a tree, for customers of the two eateries based in the round building facing *Motel Sea View*. The main one has substandard streetfood (chips, *chipsi mayai*, *mishkaki*, etc) and more interesting fried octopus, squid and, occasionally, one or two proper dishes, but check the prices before ordering. To its left you can regale yourself with clean, freshly cut fruits and juices. Daily 8am–8pm.

Mkonge Hotel 1.25km along Bombo Rd. A surprisingly affordable restaurant given the plush surroundings, with two menus, one for Indian cuisine, the other for everything else, including Chinese. As you might expect, there's plenty of seafood, whether fish or prawns, probably best savoured grilled with few trimmings. Most mains cost Tsh12,000, so expect to part with Tsh20,000 for a full meal. It also has cheaper but rather boring vegetarian options. Eat in the garden for bay views (through a wire fence). Daily noon–10pm.

★**Motel Sea View** Independence Ave. Delicious seafood with an Indian twist, including octopus, prawns, kingfish and curry rice, which you can eat on the hotel's lovely streetside terrace. Almost everything costs less than Tsh10,000, including a creamy Bengali-style fish curry; the exception is grilled jumbo prawns with garlic naan, for Tsh14,000. Daily 7–10pm or later.

New Mbuyukenda Hostel 400m along Bombo Rd. Hugely ambitious menus are not normally a good sign, but most of the stuff on this one is easy enough to make: excellent sandwiches and omelettes (both under Tsh3500), full-on breakfasts (Tsh5000) and decent if a little bland meals for Tsh7000 or less, including a good *pilau*. Extra brownie points for its glorious garden; eat under one of two enormous mango trees. No alcohol, and don't come if you're in a rush. Daily 7am–9.30pm.

2

Patwas Mkwakwani St. Occupying a bright and sometimes breezy former factory, this has ambled along for almost half a century, dispensing very good juices and milkshakes, snacks (be sure they're fresh, as some sit around) and full meals, including curries (around Tsh6000). No alcohol. Mon–Sat 8am–8pm.

Pizzeria D' Amore Bar & Restaurant Majuba's Bed & Breakfast, Bombo Rd. The location doesn't have much going for it, but if you're craving pizza or a decent salad, or are pining for other European fare (there's nothing Tanzanian here), this refined little place has a very good reputation. Pizzas cost around Tsh12,000, prawns Tsh16,000, and you can finish with a home-made sorbet (Tsh3500). Tues–Sun 11.30am–3pm & 6.30–10pm

Raskazone Swimming Club 1.6km along Bombo Rd. Scattered along a steep and thickly vegetated slope over the bay, and with direct access for swimming, this is the better of the two swimming clubs, and serves alcohol as well as meals under the name "Mumbai Darbar" – a wide and possibly over-ambitious selection of mostly Asian cuisine emphasizing masala-spiced dishes, including prawns and fish; for something more locally flavoured, try the *changu* (bream) fish soup, which is actually a stew and a meal in itself. Most dishes cost Tsh9000. The Tsh2000 admission is only charged if you're just going to swim, not eat or drink. Daily 11am–midnight.

★**Rusharoho Restaurant** Mkwakwani St. No burgers, pizzas or pasta here, just classic Swahili cuisine, and delicious at that, to be eaten in modern Swahili-style dining rooms, or on a streetside veranda. There's no menu: instead, see what they've been cooking and choose – main courses cost around Tsh5000. Particularly good are its stews (vegetarian also, including ones based on bananas or coconut), and they make a very aromatic *pilau* rice. Also has fresh juices (try the tamarind with cardamom), but the coffee is instant, and its snacks are pricey, which bumps up the cost of breakfast. Daily 6.30am–9pm.

★**Tanga Yacht Club** 2.3km along Bombo Rd. If you're okay with the expat vibe and sometimes surly service, this very sophisticated place comes recommended for great bayside views and excellent meals, including grilled king prawns (Tsh12,000). Other dishes cost less than Tsh10,000, making it a bargain even counting the Tsh2000 admission fee and Tsh5000 minimum spend on drinks. Also has a small beach (and showers), and a pool table. Daily 10am–11pm or later; meals Mon–Fri 10am–2.30pm & 5.30–10pm, Sat & Sun 10am–10pm.

DRINKING AND NIGHTLIFE

Tanga is famous for nightlife: there are **drinking** holes all over town, with things getting lively after 8pm. Other than places mentioned below, the nocturnal focus is a cluster of lively bars and clubs in Chuda district: try the *Loliondo Gate* or *Dolphin Inn*, both on Chuda Road.

Chichi Night Club Independence Ave, beside Motel Sea View. Partly outdoor bar and discotheque, sleepy by day, lively weekend nights and sometimes also on Thurs, and stuffed with prostitutes. Thurs & Fri–Sun from 9pm.

Club La Casa Chica Top floor, Sachak House, Independence Ave. A popular Western-style disco, often with live music too, but with the appearance of a fire trap. Tsh5000–7000 admission. Wed & Fri–Sun from 9pm.

Harbours Club Off Bombo Rd ☎027 264 2341. A bayside venue that's lively when they host visiting bands, often Taarab or *muziki wa dansi* (usually Fri; around Tsh5000 entrance). Upcoming events are announced on posters around town.

Motel Sea View Independence Ave. The covered colonial-style streetside veranda here is a delicious place to chill out in on a sultry afternoon. They also do fresh juices, and good food in the evenings. Daily noon–10pm or later.

Splendid View Hotel Eckernforde Ave ☎027 264 4356. Live music venue, including big-name bands from Dar (most likely on Sat).

Tanga Hotel Cnr Eckernforde Ave and Chumbageni Police Rd. One of the most popular town-centre bars, large and not too noisy, with as many women as men thanks to the friendly atmosphere (and police station around the corner). There's also passable *nyama choma*, a restaurant, satellite TV, dartboard and pool table. Good chance of live bands on Wed, Sat & Sun (Tsh4000). Daily noon–late.

DIRECTORY

Health Bombo Hospital, Bombo Rd ☎027 264 2997. Private clinics: Fazal Memorial Hospital, Independence Ave ☎027 264 6895; Tanga Medicare Centre Hospital, Independence Ave ☎027 264 6920, also with a dentist. There's are several pharmacies in town, and one just before Bombo Hospital (Tangaraha); most are open Mon–Fri 9am–12.30pm & 2–6pm, and Sat–Sun 9am–12.30pm,

Internet access Currently reliable is Click On Line, Customs Rd (Mon–Sat 9am–6pm; Tsh1000 an hour, or Tsh1500 if they're using their generator).

Money All banks have 24hr ATMs. Barclays and Exim are at he east end of Independence Ave, and there's a CRDB beside *Ocean Breeze Hotel*. To change cash, try NBC, cnr ank St and Sokoine Ave, but be patient.

Police Off Independence Ave near Tanga Library ☎ 027 264 4519.

Shopping Woodcarvers sell their work in stalls at the west end of the central market, between Market St and Independence Ave. Facing it is S.D. Vasant Supermarket (Mon–Sat 9am–6pm). The city's main market lies south in the streets behind the bus station.

Around Tanga

Except for Toten Island, the following places can be reached by bicycle, taxi or daladala (followed by a short walk). If you want a guide – recommended if you're not on a strictly shoestring budget – contact one of Tanga's tour operators (see p.136). Prices are negotiable, depending on group size, mode of transport, and your perceived wealth, but even starting prices are not unreasonable at $25–50 according to where you're going.

The Amboni Caves

Kiomoni, 10km north of Tanga • Daily 9am–4pm • Tsh20,000 entrance fee • A guided bicycle trip from Tanga takes about 3hrs, or 5hrs if combined with the Galanos Sulphur Springs (see p.140); the combined trip shouldn't cost more than $35–40per person including the entrance fee. Without a guide, cycle or catch a daladala 8km along the Mombasa road, then turn off 2km to Kiomoni

With their winding passageways and galleries, dripping stalactites, suggestive stalagmites and unlikely legends, the limestone **Amboni Caves** ("Mapango ya Amboni") are among the region's highlights. Thought to have formed during the Bathonian Period (176–169 million years ago), the caves cover 15 sq km, making them the most extensive known in East Africa. They contain at least ten networks of caverns and passageways, two of which – 3a and 3b – can be visited. There's no light, and even with your guide's torch it takes a few minutes for your eyes to adjust, so the first thing you'll notice is the soft ground, and the smell. Both are the product of **bats** (*popo*), living in colonies numbering tens of thousands. For most of the day they hang around upside down in enormous bunches, but if you hang around the entrance at sunset, you'll see clouds of them flitting out to feed – an amazing sight in itself. After your visit, go see the patch of **riverine forest** above and around the caves, which affords good bird- and butterfly-watching, and chance encounters with black-and-white colobus monkeys.

The Mombasa Road Cavern

Inside are various **chambers**, most with nicknames, some of which allude to their stalagmites: among them are a miniature Mount Kilimanjaro, a doppelgänger Virgin Mary, and the Statue of Liberty. Others reflect tall tales. The **Mombasa Road Cavern**, for instance, is said to go all the way to the Kenyan port. Another passage is rumoured to lead to Kilimanjaro, a story that started after World War II, when two Europeans exploring the caves apparently disappeared without trace. Their dog was found dead a few months later outside another cave 400km away, near Kilimanjaro. Sadly, the fun was scotched by a German–Turkish survey in 1994, which concluded that the longest of the caves extended no further than 900m from the entrance.

The Chamber of the Spirits

Of more genuine significance is Mzimuni, the **Chamber of the Spirits**, which locals believe is inhabited by a snake-like force, Mabavu, capable of granting fertility to childless women. They come here to pray and leave offerings; the chamber floor is littered with bottles, flags, charcoal and the remains of food.

The Lake of No Return

Another cavern, containing the chillingly named **Lake of No Return** (not always included in tours), is said to have been the place where the Digo tribe threw albino babies, which were believed to be bad omens. **Albinos** have a hard time of it in Tanzania: a spate of grisly murders and dismemberments since 2007 (apparently because of a belief that albino body parts have magical or at least medicinal properties) has made international headlines, and prompted a high-profile and ongoing campaign by the government and NGOs to educate people about the reality of the albino condition.

Galanos Sulphur Springs

3km east of the Amboni caves • No fixed price or hours • Usually visited on a guided 5hr+ bicycle tour from Tanga to the Amboni Caves (see p.139); $35–40per person for the tour

Named after a Greek sisal planter, the **Galanos Sulphur Springs** are rarely visited and the small spa beside them has been derelict for years, but it is possible to bathe in the hot, green and stinky water – particularly beneficial, it is said, for arthritis and skin ailments. Coming from Amboni, you'll have to cross the **Sigi River** by dugout (your guide will arrange this): look out for crocodiles and, needless to say, don't swim.

Tongoni ruins

20km south of Tanga towards Pangani • Daily 9am–4pm • Tsh10,000 entrance fee levied by Antiquities Department (paid to caretaker; tip appreciated) • The ruins lie close to the beach, 10min on foot from the Pangani Rd: access is simplest and cheapest by bicycle from Tanga; alternatively, taxis charge a negotiable Tsh35,000 for the round trip. Tanga's tourist offices ask a negotiable $20 per person if cycling with a guide, or $30–35 if travelling by car. You can also get here on any Pangani-bound bus or daladala (Tsh1000), but to be able to get back to Tanga (or carry on to Pangani), don't leave too late, as it's wise not to rely on the last bus back (for either direction), supposedly passing Tongoni around 5pm

The first European to visit **TONGONI**, a now ruined town beside a village of the same name, was **Vasco da Gama** in 1498, when, en route to opening the sea route to India, one of his three ships, the São Raphael, ran aground on Mtangata shoal nearby. Likely founded in the thirteenth century, the original Tongoni was long ago reclaimed by the ocean: a ruined mosque and a jumble of graves are all that remain of the evidently once-prosperous town, but the site remains evocative and atmospheric. The **mosque** measures 12m by 13m, large for its time, though you'll need a lively imagination to picture what it might have looked like: its roof disappeared long ago, leaving only pillars, ragged walls and a finely arched *mihrab*.

Surrounding the mosque on three sides is East Africa's largest collection of **Shirazi tombs**, more than forty in all, with doubtless many more having succumbed to the creeping ocean. About half date from the fourteenth century, when the Shirazi–Swahili civilization was at its height. Their curious **pillars** are characteristic of Shirazi tombs in East Africa: some are square, others octagonal, but at Tongoni only one of the latter still stands erect. As with Kunduchi near Dar, and Kaole, the recesses in some of these pillars originally held Chinese or Islamic ceramic bowls, of which no trace remains. Other tombs bear marks of fine relief work, all testifying to the town's former riches; the extent of Tongoni's trading links were shown by one tomb which bore an imported glazed tile with a Persian inscription – the only such example ever found in East Africa – and which has since rather scandalously been "lost". More recent tombs, crude in comparison, date from Tongoni's brief revival in the eighteenth and nineteenth centuries, when it was occupied by **Kilwan migrants** who marvellously named the place *Sitahabu*, meaning "better than there".

Toten Island

1km offshore in Tanga Bay • Independent visits not encouraged as the island is controlled by the Tanzanian Navy and requires special permission, but access is possible via tour operators such as Ilya Tours and Tangawonders (a negotiable $40–60per person by dhow or motorboat depending on group size)

Should Tongoni have woken the sleeping archeologist in you, the mangrove-cloaked

Toten Island harbours another cluster of ruins, and over a dozen graves, both Shirazi and (from World War I) German. Assuming your guide actually knows the place, once you've trudged ashore through the mangroves, finding the graves and the overgrown mosque remains (seventeenth century, if not earlier) is simple enough, but a quest for the other mosque surveyed in the 1960s will likely end in an impassable tangle of undergrowth.

Pangani and around

Located at the mouth of the Pangani, Tanzania's second-longest river, the small and very friendly town of **PANGANI** served in the nineteenth century as a **slaving port**, before becoming a focus for the Abushiri uprising against the German presence. There are more than a dozen atmospherically decayed **buildings** from those times, some with lovely carved doors. Historical interest aside, the coastline either side of Pangani – especially at **Ushongo**, to the south – has some of the country's best **beaches**, each with an ever-growing string of intimate beach hotels. Cap this with a very clued up **cultural tourism programme**, dhow trips, snorkelling and a **scuba diving centre** to the south, and you have a perfect place for a few days, or even weeks, of pure languor.

Pangani is small enough to be walked around in an hour or so, but its sombre past is best explored on the cultural tourism programme's **historical walk** (see pp.144–145). Whether or not you're with a guide, a walk is always a pleasure – there are picturesque tumbledown buildings all over the place, and kids are invariably ecstatic to greet visitors (as are adults, for that matter).

The Boma and around

At the west end of town is Pangani's oldest building, the **Boma**, with particularly fine carved doors. Built in 1810 by an Omani slave trader, who is said to have buried a live slave in each of its corners to ensure strong foundations (a belief that was also current in Zanzibar). The Germans made it their district office, a function it retains today. Behind it is the "**slave prison**", also from German times: despite the abolition of the

North Coast Beach Hotels, Tanga & Muheza

ACCOMMODATION

River View Inn	3
Seaside Community Centre Hostel	1
Stopover Guest	2

EATING AND DRINKING

Central Bar	2
Pangadeco Bar	3
Safari Lodge	1

German Cemetery

Hospital

Boma

Slave Prison

Memorial Garden

Market

Bus Stand

Cultural Tourism Programme

TANGA ROAD

Police

NMB Bank

Maulidi Gardens

Uhuru Gardens

JAMHURI STREET

Slave Depot

Customs House

Buses to Tanga & Muheza

Ferry to Bweni

BUKINDO STREET

MAZIWE STREET

MARKET STREET

Saba Saba Grounds

Funguni Beach

Kiwanjani Coconut-husking Ground

Pangani River

N

0 200 metres

PANGANI TOWN

BWENI

South Coast Beach Hotels & Saadani National Park

2

PANGANI AND RHAPTA

According to some, Pangani's origins – or possibly those of Bweni village on the south bank – can be traced back almost two millennia to a trading "metropolis" called **Rhapta**, mentioned in the *Periplus of the Erythraean Sea* (c.130–140 AD), an anonymous account of the considerable trade that flourished along the coast at that time. A fuller account, describing the journey of a Greek merchant named Diogenes, was given by the Egyptian geographer **Ptolemy** a century or so later, beyond which, he wrote, dwelled the *anthropophagoi* – cannibals.

The identification of Pangani with Rhapta is given credence by Diogenes' claim to have "travelled for a twenty-five days journey [from Rhapta] and reached a place in the vicinity of the two great lakes and the snowy mountains from where the Nile draws its sources". Although doubted by those who consider 25 days too short a time to reach Lake Victoria (700km distant), never mind the Ruwenzori Mountains, there's nowhere else on the coast that's closer, and the mountains could be Kilimanjaro and Mount Kenya. In any case, the account proves that European knowledge of the interior was a great deal more advanced in those times than it was in the middle of the nineteenth century when the first explorers started bumbling around.

slave trade, slavery itself continued well into the British period. Subsequently, the building served as the district hospital, and it presently houses government offices and, once more, some cells. Two hundred metres northwest of here is the **German cemetery**. Some of its graves apparently date from the Abushiri War, others possibly contain the remains of seventeenth-century Portuguese mariners, but as all have lost their inscriptions, no one's really sure. A handful were excavated a couple of decades ago, not by archeologists, but by locals believing the Germans had left treasure.

The riverfront

Heading to the shore, the small **memorial garden** by the ferry slipway contains a crumbling "pillar" commemorating the handful of Germans who died in the Abushiri War (surprisingly, no memorial exists to the thousands of African victims). Walking east along the riverfront, you'll see the imposing **Customs House**, which took four years to build, opening in 1916 just before the Germans were ejected. It's used to store coconuts, most of them from plantations across the river – a legacy of the slave trade when cheap labour was plentiful. In the 1930s, **Shaaban Robert**, Tanzania's foremost poet, worked here as a customs official: his broken and rusty typewriter sits in the office. Almost next door, the **Slave Depot**, derelict and close to collapse, used to have a whipping platform where slaves were punished, and a tunnel which led to the river for ferrying blindfolded slaves to the dhows. A particularly gruesome story concerning the building tells of a slave-owner's wife's request to see an unborn child, for which a pregnant slave had her stomach sliced open while still alive.

The market

The **market**, up the street beside the Slave Depot, makes an enjoyable detour. Look for an *mbuzi* – not a goat (though those are available too), but a coconut shredder. Properly called a *kibao cha mbuzi* ("goat board"), it resembles a small bookstand or foldable wooden chair, from one end of which – resembling a goat's tail – protrudes a serrated metal spatula. You sit on the chair part and then grate off the flesh of half a coconut on the blade.

Uhindini Street

One street east of the market is the road in from Tanga, whose southern continuation is **Uhindini Street** (Indian St), the place for tailors, many of whose businesses and buildings date from the 1870s when Calcutta linen was the economic mainstay of Pangani's Indian immigrants.

Kiwanjani

Back on the river, the area between Uhindini Street and the river mouth is called **Kiwanjani** ("fallow land"). This is where some fifty workers de-husk giant mounds of **coconuts** with sharp iron crowbars, leaving behind a surreal debris of tens of thousands of coconut husks that are carried out to sea whenever the river floods. Pangani District's vast coconut plantations constitute about half of Tanzania's production.

Funguni Beach

Beyond the husking ground, either follow the shore itself as it curls north into **Funguni Beach** and the ocean proper, or continue along the road past *Seaside Community Centre Hostel*, which also has beach access. Although the water doesn't look too enticing (the brown colour comes from the silt gathered along the river's 400km journey), it's apparently safe to bathe here so long as you stay to the left, away from the river, but **be careful** of currents: the river pushes its waters out a good few kilometres before losing itself in the ocean. At low tide you can walk almost 1km out to sea over the sand flats, but keep an eye on the tide. It's fine to walk up the beach to Mkoma Bay (4km) if you're not carrying valuables.

BEACHES AROUND PANGANI

● EATING AND DRINKING

The Beach Crab Resort	3
Mkoma Bay Tented Lodge	1
The Tides Lodge	2

■ ACCOMMODATION

The Beach Crab Resort	7
Capricorn Beach Cottages	2
Emayani Beach Lodge	5
Mkoma Bay Tented Lodge	3
Peponi Beach Resort	1
Tembo Kijani	8
The Tides Lodge	6
YMCA Hostel	4

ARRIVAL AND DEPARTURE   PANGANI

Apart from the road up from Saadani National Park (the ferry across the Pangani River, linking the town with Bweni village, operates between 6am and 6pm), there are two approaches, one from Tanga, the other from Muheza. Neither is surfaced, and they may require 4WD in the rains if they haven't recently been graded, especially the Muheza road which passes over easily waterlogged soil. Pangani is hassle-free, so there's no problem wandering around with your bags on arrival.

By plane Pangani's airstrip, sometimes called Mashado, is south of the river, and is primarily used by guests of the Ushongo's beach hotels. Safari Aviation (ⓦ safariaviation.info)

flies into Pangani twice a day to and from Dar, Zanzibar and Saadani; Coastal Aviation (ⓦ coastal.co.tz) also drops by twice a day on more complicated routings linking Arusha, Moshi, Dar and Zanzibar.

Destinations Arusha (2 daily; 2hr); Dar (3 daily; 50min); Zanzibar (2 daily; 20min), with connections for various national parks in central and northern Tanzania.

By daladala or bus Coming from Tanga (47km), five buses and a few daladalas lurch along the bumpy road each day (roughly 7.30am–5pm). Buy tickets early to be sure of a seat. The road winds through sparsely populated marshland (look for herons and other waders) and a sisal estate, then passes farming communities surrounded by ragged coconut groves. If you're staying at one of the beach hotels north of Pangani, ask to be dropped at the appropriate turning. From Muheza, there's at least one daily bus during the dry season (2–3hr), plus a few battered Land Rovers and daladalas, which leave Muheza between 10am and 3pm – get there early to be sure of a ride. The Muheza road joins the Tanga road 3km north of Pangani. The first buses and daladalas, for Tanga and Muheza, leave between 6am and 6.30am. You should definitely catch one of these if you're heading on to Amani Nature Reserve or Dar, and buy your onward ticket as soon as you arrive. The last guaranteed vehicle to Muheza leaves at 8am. The last bus to Tanga departs at 4.30pm. If you're driving, there's an adventurous and infrequently travelled route south of Pangani into Saadani National Park (see p.127).

Destinations Muheza (2 daily; 2–3hr); Tanga (5 daily; 2–3hr).

By taxi Taxis from Tanga charge at least Tsh60,000 to Pangani town, or Tsh40,000 to Kigombe for the *Peponi Beach Resort* and *Capricorn Beach Cottages*.

By boat In contrast to Tanga, getting passage from Pangani on a dhow to Zanzibar (either to Mkokotoni or, more usually, Kendwa or Nungwi at the northern end of Unguja Island) is relatively straightforward – although read our advice first (see p.48). There are at least two motorized dhows each week, taking four hours if things run smoothly (the cost is $30–60 per person depending on the number of passengers) – ask at the cultural tourism office, who can also arrange a boat specially for the trip for a minimum of $150, or $40 per person for larger groups. There's currently also a scheduled speedboat for tourists (with all requisite safety gear) operated by Kasa Divers in Ushongo (see below) to either Kendwa (Unguja) or Mkoani (Pemba), who charge around $300 for the boat.

INFORMATION

Cultural tourism Pangani's cultural tourism programme, whose tourist information office faces the market and main bus stand (Mon–Sat 8.30am–8pm, Sun 10am–4.30pm; ☎0784 489129 or ☎0784 539141, ⓦenvaya.org/PCCTP), is among Tanzania's oldest, and most affordable (the more expensive cultural tours

---

MAZIWE ISLAND MARINE RESERVE

Maziwe Island Marine Reserve, 13km southeast of Pangani, was established after the island's fringing corals were badly damaged by dynamite fishing and careless anchoring. It protects one of the north coast's best reefs for **snorkelling and diving**, with some especially beautiful coral heads ("bommies") and sea fans providing food and shelter for hundreds of tropical fish species, including moray eels, poison-barbed lionfish, butterfly fish, leaf fish, clownfish, starfish and octopus. Keep your eyes peeled on the way out, as bottlenose **dolphins** are frequently seen. Divers may also get to see green turtles and blue-spotted rays.

The island itself has a **strange history**. Nowadays merely a sandbank, until the 1960s it was wooded with casuarina trees, fringed with mangroves, and its beaches served as East Africa's most important nesting ground for three species of turtle. By 1976, the last casuarina had been felled, and the final blow came during the 1978–79 war with Idi Amin's Uganda, when, it is said (not entirely plausibly), the remaining mangroves were cleared away for security reasons. The mangroves never returned, and the ensuing erosion – coupled with rising sea levels – causes the island to be completely submerged at high tide.

PRACTICALITIES

On **snorkelling trips**, costs are $30–60 per person including equipment, according to group size, boat used (motorboat or *ngalawa* outrigger), and where you arrange things: hotels are more expensive, cheaper is the cultural tourism programme. Outriggers take ninety minutes, motorboats about half that. A modest marine park fee donation to the Friends of Maziwe (an association of hoteliers, boat owners and fishermen, the reserve's effective custodians; ⓦfriendsofmaziwe.com) should be included in the cost. Sailing out from Pangani, notice the German fort (1916) on the river's south bank, half-hidden by vegetation.

Ideally placed for divers wishing to explore Maziwe is the PADI-accredited Kasa Divers **scuba diving centre** at *Emayani Lodge* on Ushongo Beach, 16km south of town (☎0786 427645 or ☎0784 134056, ⓦkasa-divers.com), who also offer the usual array of courses. It's best to stay at one of the south coast hotels if you'll be diving, as bus times don't really fit.

offered by Pangani's beach hotels are much the same thing). First of all, get to grips with Pangani's history with a two-hour guided walk around town ($10). Longer trips tend to involve cycling, and include poking around the 200–300-million-year-old dinosaur fossils at Mkoma Bay (3hr; $20 per person), hippo-spotting near Saadani (full day; $35 per person excluding lunch), and a sisal-themed tour on the south side of the river. There are also options for messing about on (and under) the water: a trip with local fishermen aboard a dhow ($20 per person), sunset river cruises where you might spot colobus monkeys (3hr;

$15–30 depending on group size), and, best of all, dhow trips for snorkelling at Maziwe island (see box, p.142; 7hrs; $90 for the boat, or $40 per person for four people of more, including marine park fees and snorkelling equipment).

Bicycle hire If you want to explore alone, most hotels, and the cultural tourism programme, can fix you up; use of a mountain bike shouldn't cost more than Tsh10,000 a day.

Money The ATM at Pangani's bank, NMB, only accepts local cards only, and while you can change cash there, it's best to change money before coming.

ACCOMMODATION

With one exception, Pangani's central hotels are quite basic; way better, and not always bank-breaking, are a string of intimate beach hotels either side of town. Alternatively, talk to the cultural tourism programme about homestays ($10 per person plus meals and anything else consumed, like henna, for a temporary tattoo), where you may well be pampered silly, and, assuming you hit it off with your hosts, will open up an entirely new facet of life for you. Pangani's water supply comes from badly maintained boreholes; purify tap water if you're going to drink it (that is, if the supply is flowing at all). Camping is currently restricted to two options, both way out of town: *Peponi Beach Resort*, 17km north, and *The Beach Crab Resort*, 18km south.

CENTRAL PANGANI

At all the following, check mosquito nets for size and holes before settling in.

River View Inn Jamhuri St ☎0784 530371. For those counting pennies, this isn't bad at all, despite a certain shabbiness that it never seems to lose. Most of the nine rooms, all large, share bathrooms. The bar has soft drinks only; meals available. Tsh8000

★**Seaside Community Centre Hostel** Funguni Beach ☎0755 276422, ✉alcposs.spiritualcentre @yahoo.com. Nicknamed "Masista", this quiet and homely place fronting a beautiful beach is easily the most comfortable abode in central Pangani. It's run by Catholic sisters, who also dish up good food. Obviously, if you're planning on sampling the town's nightlife, it would be more polite to stay elsewhere. BB $30

Stopover Guest House Funguni Beach ☎0784 498458. A reasonable second choice should the nearby hostel be full, with well-kept en-suite rooms, and simple meals available, but of course it's not on the beach. Tsh10,000

NORTH COAST

These hotels are signposted off the Tanga road. All but *Capricorn* and *Peponi* are astride low headlands, with the beaches below disappearing at high tide. The farther north you go, the clearer the water.

Capricorn Beach Cottages Kigombe, 17km north of Pangani, 30km south of Tanga ☎0784 632529, ⓦcapricornbeachcottages.com. Relaxed and friendly, this has just three secluded and well-furnished self-catering cottages, with lovely ocean views, framed by baobabs, from their verandas. Each cottage has a kitchen,

bathroom, big beds with box nets and fans. The barbecue area is perfect for seafood bought from local fishermen, and the lodge stocks smoked fish, bread, cheese, wine and other treats. Snorkelling and dhow trips can be arranged. Internet access. BB $114

Mkoma Bay Tented Lodge Mkoma Bay, 5km north of Pangani ☎0784 283565 or ☎0786 434001, ⓦmkomabay.com. This pleasingly idiosyncratic place is a stylish blend of traditional architecture and modern quirkiness. The cheaper rooms are in a self-catering "Swahili House" with four bedrooms, but most visitors swoon at the safari-style tents on platforms under *makuti* roofs, each with a small veranda (no sea views however), Zanzibari beds, box nets and bathroom. Facilities include a small swimming pool, a very good restaurant (with great sea views) and wi-fi. Rates include bicycles and kayaks; cruises and snorkelling trips are extra. BB room $180, tent $220

★**Peponi Beach Resort** Kigombe, 17km north of Pangani, 30km south of Tanga ☎0784 202962 or ☎0713 540139, ⓦpeponiresort.com. Welcoming, well run and extremely good value, with eight comfortable two- to six-bed cottages set back from the beach in grassy gardens. Each is made from mangrove poles, coconut leaves, fibre and sisal, and has a bathroom, fans and box nets. The food is delicious and reasonably priced (à la carte or set menus), but ring ahead if you're not staying overnight. The sandy beach is a peach, there are mangroves nearby, and the hotel has its own dhow for birding and snorkelling. There's a sea-view swimming pool, too. "Peponi" means paradise – can't argue with that unless being miles from anywhere is somehow irksome. Camping per person $5; HB $95; FB $112

2

YMCA Hostel Mkoma Bay, 5km north of Pangani ☎ 0787 525592 or ☎ 0736 204762. This place has been run-down for nigh on two decades yet remains open for what little business it gets, and at the price – unchanged for years – is now a bargain. The six large rooms are acceptable, some en suite, with twin beds, and verandas with ocean views. Simple food is available if ordered well in advance. BB T̲s̲h̲2̲8̲,̲0̲0̲0̲

SOUTH COAST: USHONGO AND BEYOND

Most of the hotels south of Pangani are at Ushongo, the turning to which is 11km south of Bweni. Unfortunately, with only very occasional exceptions, the two or three buses stick to the road 5km inland, leaving you with a 5–7km walk to the hotels. Better to arrange a transfer (usually $30) or, for day-trips, a bicycle.

★**The Beach Crab Resort** 18km south of Pangani ☎ 0784 543700 or ☎ 0767 543700, ⓦ thebeachcrab .com. German-run, this is the cheapest place on Ushongo (and has fair rates for solo travellers, too), with eight "beach huts" which are actually safari tents pitched under thatched shelters (each with double bed, box net and electricity) sharing bathrooms, and some very nice, spacious, en-suite "coconut bungalows" made of mangrove poles and palm weave, well furnished and with verandas. Activities (not included in the price) include kayaking, snorkelling, surfing, biking and scuba diving with Kasa Divers (see box, p.144), and there's an excellent multilevel beach bar and restaurant (see p.147). Camping per person $̲6̲. BB beach hut $̲3̲6̲, bungalow $̲1̲0̲0̲

★**Emayani Beach Lodge** 16km south of Pangani ☎ 027 264 0755 or ☎ 0782 457668, ⓦ emayanilodge .com. An intimate, relaxed and breezy Dutch-run place set in a coconut grove on an area of the beach with tidal pools, with plenty of activities including snorkelling,

birdwatching (in nearby mangroves), river trips, windsurfing and sailing. The twelve cool and spacious thatched en-suite bungalows, nicely irregular, are decked out in castaway style, and have beach-facing verandas with jaw-dropping views. Breakfasts are lavish, meals are reasonably priced, and there's a well-stocked bar, too. Activities (extra cost) include snorkelling, sailing, birding, sunset cruises and diving with Kasa Divers, which is are based here. HB $̲1̲8̲0̲

★**Tembo Kijani** 40km south of Pangani ☎ 0687 027454, ⓦ tembokijani.com. Neither here nor there isn't a bad thing if you want to get away from it all, and has worked wonders for this highly praised eco-lodge, halfway between Pangani and Saadani and, for now, the only one in the area. This means that wildlife, including gazelle and monkeys, still abound, and that you and your fellow guests (there are only seven rooms) will have the deserted beach all for yourselves. Choose between wood-and-thatch bush *bandas* on stilts, or larger stone-floor beach bungalows; both are comfortable and even elegant. The food has an equally felicitous reputation. Safaris into Saadani (€200 per person) and boat trips can be arranged. Reservations required. FB *bandas* €̲1̲1̲0̲, beach bungalows €̲1̲6̲0̲

The Tides Lodge 17km south of Pangani ☎ 0784 225812, ⓦ thetideslodge.com. An intimate British-owned place, classy yet rustic and unostentatious, in a lovely beachfront location among palm trees. There are seven individually styled thatch-roofed chalets (all very attractive), a couple of suites and a family house, plus a beachside bar, swimming pool and one of Tanzania's best seafood restaurants, perfect for romantic candlelit dinners (see p.147). Activities include snorkelling around Maziwe Island, dhow trips, kayaking and guided walks around Ushongo village (free). They also arrange trips to Saadani National Park. Internet access. HB $̲3̲2̲3̲

EATING AND DRINKING

Some of Tanzania's best seafood restaurants, and with equally delicious ocean views, are in the **beach hotels** at Ushongo, south of town. Most of them happily receive day-trippers for lunch, but ring beforehand as they may be busy with their own guests. Eating out in Pangani itself is the antithesis of fine dining, so unless you're content with chips/rice with fried chicken/fish, order early. The cheapest eats, including stewed or grilled octopus, are at the **foodstalls** along Jamhuri St near the ferry. Given that Pangani is mainly Muslim, the ever-growing battalion of **bars** is quite a surprise (if you're uncertain about delving into the local night scene, the cultural tourism programme can supply a guide-cum-chaperone). The nocturnal revelry is a source of considerable exasperation for the **muezzin** of the main mosque, famed for his unusually blunt early morning exhortations to the not-so-faithful, starting with a strident series of loudspeakered "*Amka!*" ("Wake up!"), followed by a litany of colourful curses, which invariably include the line, "If you sleep now, your bed shall be your bier and your sheets your shroud!"

CENTRAL PANGANI

Central Bar Halfway between the river and the market. For good, cheap and filling portions of *nyama choma* (evenings, Tsh5000 per half kilo), grilled chicken and *chipsi mayai*, this is definitely the place to be, and it stays

open late. There are tables on the street corner veranda, a dartboard, cheerful music and satellite TV. Daily 10am–10pm or later.

Pangadeco Bar Funguni Beach. Having started life as a hotel, then a restaurant and bar, then a tawdry discotheque and bar, and back to being a bar again, this has finally fallen silent, but the unbeatable beachfront location makes it well worth asking about, just in case.

Safari Lodge 200m north of the ferry. Functions mainly as an (often loud) bar. The food is reasonably priced, though, with most dishes around Tsh6000, complete with fresh salad. Daily 11am–8pm (for food).

NORTH AND SOUTH COAST

★ **The Beach Crab Resort** 18km south at Ushongo ⊕0784 543700 or ⊕0767 543700. The enchanting multilevel beach bar and restaurant here has a great reputation for making inspired use of local ingredients, whether home-made seafood ravioli, marinated octopus or vegetable stews, and equally inventive desserts (how about *mokka* ice with orange cashew nut crunch?). Also bakes its own German-style bread. Light lunches cost Tsh9000, the main course for dinner Tsh13,000, and three-courses for Tsh25,000. Daily breakfast, lunch and dinner.

Mkoma Bay Tented Lodge 5km north at Mkoma Bay ⊕0784 283565 or ⊕0786 434001. Great seafood and fantastic ocean views, a snappy menu (lobster?!) including light lunches, and the bonus of genuine espresso and a good wine list. À la carte starts at around $15, a seafood barbecue at $30. Diners may also be able to use the swimming pool. Daily lunch and dinner, book ahead.

★ **The Tides Lodge** 17km south at Ushongo, ⊕0784 225812. Some people have been known to fly in just to have lunch at this elegant open-sided restaurant. Understated sophistication is the thing, and quite spectacular seafood – including a $30 platter you can share. Main courses, like prawns in garlic and herb butter, average $12–15. Daily lunch and dinner.

2

The south coast

DHOW , MAFIA ISLAND

The south coast

Formerly Tanzania's forgotten quarter, the south coast now has vastly improved road access, and the region's economic fortunes look set to improve dramatically over the new few years thanks to the vast natural gas reserves that have been discovered here. For now, however, the coast retains a backwater feeling, and its attractions are simple – great beaches, fantastic snorkelling and scuba diving, and a wealth of historical sites, from the earliest days of the Persian landfall over a thousand years ago, through medieval times, to the slave trade and the German conquest.

Combining many of these attractions is the **Mafia archipelago**, whose coral reefs are highly rated by scuba divers and snorkellers alike, and where you can also explore old Swahili ruins, or just swan around by dhow exploring mangroves. The other big pull is **Kilwa**, beyond the swampy Rufiji River delta, which is actually three towns: tumbledown Kilwa Kivinje, steeped in the history of slavery and German colonialism; Kilwa Masoko, the main base for visitors with a handful of beach hotels; and Kilwa Kisiwani, the impressive ruins of the medieval island-state which controlled much of East Africa's commerce with Arabia, India, Indonesia and China.

The main ports in the region, **Lindi and Mtwara**, are not much of a draw in themselves, but do have access to some nice beaches. Without a beach, but arguably more interesting, is the former slave-trading town of **Mikindani**, with a palpable sense of history, one of southern Tanzania's most atmospheric hotels, and an NGO offering a variety of excursions. In addition, the town has an excellent **scuba-diving** centre, whose speciality is the rarely visited **Mnazi Bay–Ruvuma Estuary Marine Park**, along the border with Mozambique. Heading inland, your options are limited to Selous Game Reserve (covered in chapter 4), or, from Mtwara or Lindi, a wild route over to Lake Nyasa, which skirts the **Makonde Plateau**, home of the famous woodcarving tribe.

The Mafia archipelago

Just 25km offshore from the Rufiji delta, and 130km south of Dar, the **Mafia Archipelago** comprises Mafia Island, the much smaller islands of Chole, Juani and Jibondo, plus a host of minor atolls. Much of the archipelago is protected by **Mafia Island Marine Park**, an area rich in aquatic life that is home to more than four hundred species of fish, over sixty types of corals, 140 forms of sponge, seven mangrove species, 134 species of marine algae, and a seagrass area inhabited by the locally near-extinct **dugong**. The archipelago is also an important nesting site for **hawksbill and green turtles**, and is an extended stopover on the annual migration route of the world's biggest fish, docile **whale sharks**, which you can swim with.

MAKUA TRIBE DANCERS AT THE MAKUYA FESTIVAL

Highlights

❶ Mafia archipelago Superb scuba diving, equally good snorkelling, plenty of messing about in dhows, heaps of historical interest, and some very nice beaches. **See p.150**

❷ Kilwa Kisiwani The ruins of this medieval island state, in its time the wealthiest metropolis in East Africa, are among the country's most impressive and evocative historical sites. **See p.163**

❸ Kilwa Kivinje A picturesque and very tumbledown nineteenth-century slaving harbour, whose rise signalled the demise of Kilwa Kisiwani. **See p.168**

❹ Mikindani Another old slaving port with plenty of ruins, a pleasantly laid-back atmosphere and one of Tanzania's nicest hotels. See p.173

❺ MaKuYa It's just once a year, but Mtwara's festival of traditional Makonde, Makua and Yao music is reason enough to head south. **See p.178**

❻ Mnazi Bay–Ruvuma Estuary Marine Park Superb beaches, snorkelling and scuba diving along the border with Mozambique, and virtually no other visitors. **See p.182**

HIGHLIGHTS ARE MARKED ON THE MAP ON P.152

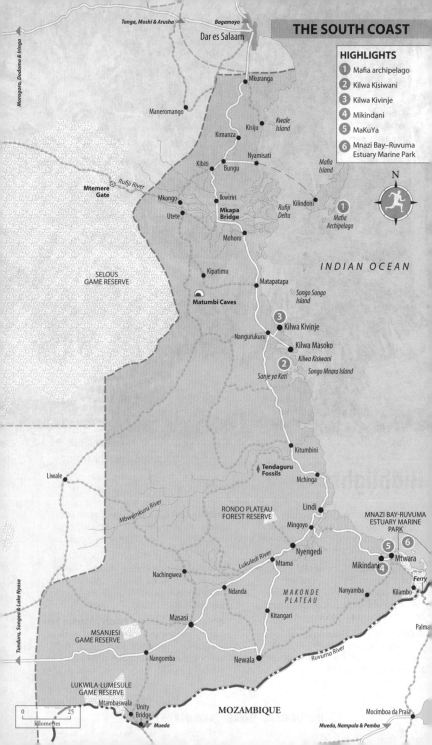

Most of the archipelago's shoreline is fronted by mangroves, but there are also some nice **beaches**, especially on Mafia Island's west coast. Other attractions include a series of overgrown **ruins** from medieval and colonial times, remnants of **coastal forest** (where you might see duikers, monkeys, wild pigs, bushbabies, or black and rufous elephant shrews), good birdwatching (with 130 recorded species), and even some "dwarf" **hippos**, which dwell in a couple of marshy inlet systems on Mafia Island's west coast.

Brief history

The discovery of ancient Egyptian, Greco–Roman and Indian pottery and Syrian glass in a cave on Juani Island proves that the archipelago was well embedded in the western Indian Ocean's trading network by 600 BC. Whether the first inhabitants here were Africans or immigrants is open to debate, but Iron Age forges show that an agricultural people had crossed over from the mainland no later than 200 AD. Around that time, the mainland trading port of **Rhapta** – possibly in the Rufiji delta, or at Pangani (see p.142) – was, according to the *Periplus of the Erythraean Sea*, ruled by the Yemeni state of Ma'afir, whose name may have stuck. Alternatively, "Mafia" may derive from the Arabic *morfiya*, meaning group, and so, by extension, archipelago.

In its heyday, Mafia was trading as far afield as Ming-dynasty China, though its fortunes nose-dived following the arrival of the bellicose **Portuguese** in 1508; this culminated in the destruction of Kua, the island's main town, by cannibalistic Madagascan visitors, the Sakalava, in 1829. The archipelago's fortunes revived briefly after 1840 under the control of Zanzibar's **Busaïdi dynasty**, but the days of the slave trade were numbered. When, in 1890, Zanzibar became a British "protectorate", its sultan was forced to sell Mafia to Germany for four million marks. The British seized Mafia in 1915 for use as a base in their hunt for the cruiser **Königsberg**, which had taken refuge in the Rufiji delta – a cat and mouse affair that tied down British troops and resources for over eleven months. Once the cruiser was located (and sunk by the Germans, who escaped with the ship's guns), Mafia became the backwater it is today.

This eclectic history is reflected in the archipelago's **inhabitants**. Apart from the Mbwera, believed to be related to Mafia's first African inhabitants, there are Shirazis, Hadhramaut Arabs, Omanis, Indians, Pakistani Baluch, and Madagascan and Comoran traders. But the majority descend from slaves, including northern Kenya's Pokomo tribe. The most recent immigrants are Makonde, who settled in Utende in 1991, having fled Mozambique's civil war.

Mafia Island

The largest by far of the archipelago's islands is **Mafia Island**, spanning 55km from northeast to southwest, much of it covered by coconut plantations. It is where most of the archipleago's accommodation and facilities are sited, though the historical attractions are on the smaller islands, accessed from Chole Bay, on Mafia Island's east coast. Snorkelling and diving is also best off Chole Bay, though the beaches and whale-watching are better on the island's west coast, north of the archipelago's capital Kilindoni.

Kilindoni

Mafia Island's main town and only port is **Kilindoni**, a scruffy, dozy little place (especially during the rains), but endowed with a nice beach, an attractively poky market and an animated harbour. Try to coincide your visit with a **full moon**, when an age-old ritual procession brings the place alive. Starting in the evening, the milling crowd is headed by women singing to the rhythms of a brass band and drummers, as kids dash around in an excitable frenzy. The music resembles Taarab, not only in rhythm and melody, but because it's women who dictate the words and therefore the

3

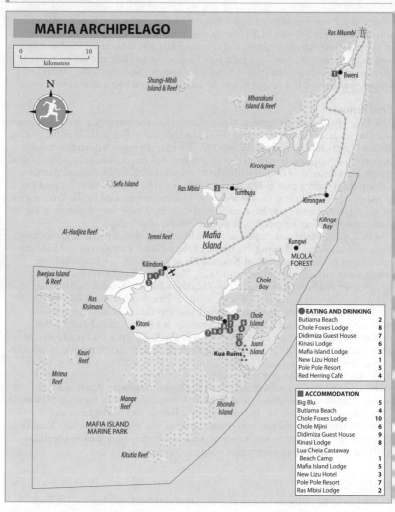

MAFIA ARCHIPELAGO

Ras Mkumbi

Bweni 1

Shungi-Mbili
Island & Reef

Mbarakuni
Island & Reef

Kirongwe

Sefu Island

Ras Mbisi 2 Tumbuju

Kirongwe

Kifinge
Bay

Al-Hadjira Reef   Tereni Reef   Mafia
Island

Kungwi

MLOLA
FOREST

Bwejuu Island
& Reef

Kilindoni

Chole
Bay

Ras
Kisimani

Kitoni

Utende 5 3 Chole
Island
4 6
7 9 8 10
8 Juani
Island

Kauri
Reef

Kua Ruins

Mrima
Reef

Mange
Reef

Jibondo
Island

MAFIA ISLAND
MARINE PARK

Kitutia Reef

● EATING AND DRINKING	
Butiama Beach	2
Chole Foxes Lodge	8
Didimiza Guest House	7
Kinasi Lodge	6
Mafia Island Lodge	3
New Lizu Hotel	1
Pole Pole Resort	5
Red Herring Café	4

■ ACCOMMODATION	
Big Blu	5
Butiama Beach	4
Chole Foxes Lodge	10
Chole Mjini	6
Didimiza Guest House	9
Kinasi Lodge	8
Lua Cheia Castaway Beach Camp	1
Mafia Island Lodge	5
New Lizu Hotel	3
Pole Pole Resort	7
Ras Mbisi Lodge	2

0   10
kilometres

mood. Although the new moon is important in Islam, marking the months of the Hegira calendar, the significance of the full moon is rooted in pre-Islamic times. Respect for more orthodox Islam is evident when the procession falls silent as it moves past the Friday Mosque (only to pick up with more verve on the other side).

Chole Bay

Daladalas run throughout the day from Kilindoni; taxis charge up to Tsh40,000 ($25)

Some 14km southeast of Kilindoni, the shallow and sheltered **Chole Bay** (just beyond the village of Utende) is home to variety of birdlife including waders, falcons and fish eagles, lilac-breasted rollers, black kites and crab plovers. It's also where most of Mafia Island's tourist hotels and scuba-diving companies are located, and where most dhow trips and snorkelling excursions leave from (see p.155). For a day-trip from Kilindoni, both *Big Blu* and *Mafia Island Lodge* have decent beaches, with swimming at high tide: both can also organize snorkelling, meals and drinks.

SNORKELLING, DIVING AND WHALE SHARKS

SCUBA DIVING

The Mafia archipelago has some of the best scuba diving in East Africa, although visibility isn't always great. Conditions are best in November and February, but strong winds between June and September, and sometimes in December and January, may confine you to Chole Bay. **Kinasi Wall** is always good – a glorious drift dive, whose dense coral formations are home to huge groupers, large shoals of snappers, stingrays and ribbontail rays, plus occasional "heavyweights" such as white-tipped reef and tiger sharks, barracuda and turtles. Also good is **Chole Wall**, inside Chole Bay, which has fewer big fish but pristine corals, and a good chance of seeing turtles.

Mafia has two PADI-accredited **dive centres** that are open to walk-ins, both at Chole Bay (see below). Three hotels also have diving operations for overnight guests only – *Lua Cheia Castaway Beach Camp*, *Chole Mjini* and *Kinasi Lodge*. All offer dive packages with discounted accommodation. For general information on scuba diving in Tanzania, see p.67.

Big Blu ☎0787 474108 or ☎0654 089659, 🌐bigblumafia.com. Pleasingly informal dive outfit yet solid in standards. Ten dives cost $330 plus $25/day for equipment. Night dives cost $45, and the four-day Open Water course is $505.

Mafia Island Diving Mafia Island Lodge, Chole Bay ☎0688 218569, 🌐mafiadiving.com. Long-established, well-regarded PADI five star centre. Ten dives cost $390 plus $20/day for equipment and an extra $20 for night dives. The Open Water course costs $495. Underwater camera hire $40–60/day.

SNORKELLING

The best snorkelling is inside **Chole Bay**, whose shallow coral outcrops are teeming with life, including lionfish, damselfish, angelfish, sponges, sea cucumbers and all sorts of crustaceans. Other good areas are Okuta Reef off **Jibondo Island**, the "Blue Lagoon" south of **Juani Island**, and **Kifinge Bay** on the northeastern side of Mafia Island, which is also a nesting site for green turtles. With more time, **Kitutia Reef** to the south of Mafia Island is also recommended, and has a lovely sand bank on which, tides permitting, you could have lunch.

Access to the reefs is by *mashua* dhow or *ngalawa* outrigger, which can be rented informally with fishermen on the beach facing *Mafia Island Lodge* ($30 per person including equipment). It's best to arrange things the day before, and you'll need some luck with tides and winds. More reliable are motorboats (minimum four or six people) operated by the lodges and dive centres; you'll pay $55–80 for a full day's snorkelling, including lunch.

SWIMMING WITH WHALE SHARKS

Mafia's most famous denizens are its **whale sharks**, averaging ten metres in length, and nicknamed "dominoes" on account of their characteristic spots. They feed on plankton and small fish, and are completely docile, a characteristic that has permitted a minor "swim with the whale sharks" industry to develop. Kilindoni's hustlers tout these experiences all year round, but the sharks spend half the year in deep water, and the time to see them is between October and March, when they feed near the surface. The two main operators are the locally run Afro Whale Shark Safari, based in Kilindoni (☎0653 962524 or ☎0757 610162, 🌐afrowhalesharksafari. blogspot.com), and the more professional Kitu Kiblu, affiliated with Chole Island's *Chole Mjiji Lodge* (☎0784 520799, 🌐kitukiblu.com). A half-day-trip costs $60 to $100 per person.

Chole Island

1km east of Chole Bay, inside the marine park • Outriggers leave Chole Bay from the beach facing *Mafia Island Lodge* (10min; Tsh1000) • Chole Bay's hotels offer half-day-trips for $15–20 per person

The tiny, lushly vegetated **Chole Island** is the archipelago's oldest continuously inhabited settlement, having taken over Kua's mantle as capital when the latter was sacked in 1829 (see p.157). Under Zanzibari rule, Chole gained notoriety as a major slave-trading centre, so much so that the larger Mafia Island was for a time known as "Chole's Farm", as its coconut plantations were owned by slavers from Chole. Now all that remains of the once-wealthy nineteenth-century town is a picturesque collection of overgrown ruins embraced by the twisted roots of strangling fig trees.

Boats land in the island's northwest corner, next to the community-run *Red Herring Café*, where you can buy high-quality **woven mats** made from the fronds of *mikindu* phoenix palms. These colourful, naturally dyed mats have been made for centuries and come in two forms: large, rectangular floor mats (*majamvi*), or oval prayer mats (*misala*).

The ruins

Behind the *Red Herring Café*, in the lee of some frangipani trees, is the impressive coral ragstone façade of the two-storey **Old Boma**, which is currently being rebuilt and converted into suites for *Chole Mjini* lodge (see p.159). It served as first the Omani and then the German headquarters, until, in 1913, the island's capital was moved to Kilindoni. The old **prison**, almost next door, also dates from Omani times. It has eight small and now roofless cells, each said to have held up to fifty inmates – presumably slaves, working Mafia Island's extensive plantations.

Further along the broad Market Street, a series of rectangular stumps within a low wall are said to have been the tethering pillars of the **slave market**, although it may just have been a warehouse. The ruins of a **Hindu temple** further on have, like the prison, acquired an impressive encrustation of fig-tree roots, which appear to be the only things keeping the walls standing. A **mosque**, wells and other stone houses can also be seen.

The bat trail

Among Chole's curiosities are colonies of giant **Comoros fruit bats** (also called "flying foxes", and *popo* in Kiswahili), which roost by day in big mango trees and baobabs and – unlike their cave-dwelling cousins – rely on eyesight rather than sonar to navigate. You can visit the colonies on a **bat trail**, whose winding pathways provide an ideal way of acquainting yourself with the island's lush vegetation. Leaflets detailing the trail and other walks can be picked up at the island's two hotels (see p.159), or at the *Red Herring Café*.

Juani Island

East of Chole Island, inside the marine park • Chole Bay's hotels can arrange dhow trips here for around $40 per person for a few hours

Separated from Chole Island by the narrow mangrove-lined Kua Channel, **Juani** is the archipelago's second largest island, supporting a number of monkeys, feral pigs (introduced by the Portuguese), and diminutive blue duiker **antelopes**. The island is also the main nesting site for **turtles**; the best time to see hatchlings is from May to September. Amateur archeologists can visit a limestone **cave** in which excavations have unearthed Mediterranean and Lower Egyptian sherds dating to the start of the first millennium BC, and Indian sherds from over two thousand years ago: evidence of the scope of western Indian Ocean trade.

Kua

Juani's main attraction is the ruins of **Kua**. According to legend, the town was founded early in the eleventh century by Bashat, son of the Shirazi founder of Kilwa, on the mainland. Believed by locals to be haunted, the old town languishes almost forgotten on the west side of the island amid a dense tangle of baobab-studded undergrowth. Excavations in 1955 unearthed a grid of streets, along with Chinese and Indian coins from the thirteenth and fourteenth centuries. Kua appears to have covered about one and a half square kilometres, and its **ruins** include a palace dating from the eighteenth century, two graveyards, fifteen houses and seven mosques, the oldest from the fourteenth century. Exactly what you see depends on the state of the vegetation.

Jibondo Island

10km south of Chole Bay, inside the marine park • Chole Bay hotels can arrange dhow and snorkelling trips here for $40–50 per person

The most traditional of the archipelago's settlements, **Jibondo Island** has around two

KUA, KISIMANI AND CANNIBALS

Mafia's strategic location made it a coveted base for traders, and it created plenty of **rivalries**, too; initially between Persian and Arab immigrants, then between the archipelago's main towns of **Kua** (on Juani Island), and **Kisimani** (on Mafia Island), which were allied to Kilwa and Zanzibar respectively.

Legend tells the dark tale of a large *jahazi* **dhow** that was to be launched at Kisimani. The people of Kua were invited over for the celebrations, but on arriving, their children were bound, laid in front of the dhow and then crushed as the dhow was launched. **Revenge** took time to come: after a few years, the people of Kua invited their rivals to a wedding. The people of Kisimani, assuming they'd been forgiven for killing the children, arrived unsuspecting. The wedding feast was held in a beautifully decorated underground chamber, from which, one by one, the people of Kua excused themselves, until only a very old man remained to entertain the guests. The chamber entrance was sealed off, and the scores were settled.

Historians still debate the **catastrophe** that subsequently overtook Kua. According to one story, a harsh queen ruled Kua at the start of the nineteenth century and some of her opponents travelled to Madagascar to seek help from the ruling **Sakalava**. The Sakalava people agreed to help overthrow the queen on condition that they be allowed to rule Kua, but when they arrived, in 1829, with a force of eighty canoes, they proceeded to sack the entire town, regardless of allegiance, allegedly eating many of its inhabitants in the process. A good proportion of the three thousand survivors were sold into slavery, and by 1840 the last inhabitants had deserted Kua to start new lives on Kome Island, halfway between Mafia and Kisiju on the mainland. Locals say that both Kua and Kisimani were destroyed for their wickedness, Kisimani having been erased from the map by a cyclone in 1872.

thousand inhabitants, most of whom make their living by shark fishing and octopus baiting, though seaweed farming also provides income. Traditionally, the islanders also caught **turtles**, but they and their nesting grounds are now protected by the marine park. Until recently, the islanders were also famed for their skill in **building dhows** without using iron, or even nails, a tradition going back almost two millennia. Sadly, the art is now obsolete, although ongoing repairs and small-scale construction of *mashua* dhows keep some of the craftsmen in business.

ARRIVAL AND DEPARTURE
MAFIA ARCHIPELAGO

By plane The archipelago is most easily reached by plane, which lands at the airport right in the middle of Kilindoni. The short flight from Dar ($110–130 one way) is impressive as it passes over a string of photogenic reefs, mangroves and islands. Several companies fly daily: Auric Air (**☎** 0783 233334, **⊗** auricair.com) from Dar; Tropical Air (**☎** 024 223 2511, **⊗** tropicalair.co.tz) on its Zanzibar–Dar–Mafia–Dar–Zanzibar–Pemba routing, connecting with Arusha; and Coastal Aviation (**☎** 0752 627825, **⊗** coastal.co.tz), which flies the same route plus Tanga and Kilwa if there are at least five passengers. The pricier Safari Airlink (**☎** 022 550 4384, **⊗** safariaviation.info) also sometimes flies to/from Mikumi, Selous and Ruaha.

Destinations Arusha (2 daily; 3hr 30min); Dar (4 daily; 30min); Kilwa (1 daily; 30min); Pemba (2 daily; 2hr 35min–3hr 30min); Tanga (1 daily; 3hr 10min); Zanzibar (3 daily; 1hr 35min–1hr 50min).

By boat Kilindoni sports a kilometre-long metal jetty. Although a regular ferry from Dar es Salaam has long been mooted, the only ferries that dock here at present – actually creaky, little cargo boats that also take passengers – are from Nyamisati, 160km by road from Dar (Tsh12,500). Their sailing times tend to be early morning or even pre-dawn, though some captains head off in the afternoon, making it possible – with luck – to get from Dar to Mafia the same day. To try, catch a 6am daladala from Dar to Rangi Tatu, 13km south (Tsh400), and change there for one to Nyamisati (Tsh6000; 3hr). If you get stuck in Nyamisati, its church (*kanisa*) has rooms (Tsh10,000 per person).

ESSENTIALS

Entrance fees Mafia Island Marine Park (**⊗** marineparks.go.tz) covers most of the east and all of the south coast of Mafia Island, including Chole Bay, plus the islands of Chole, Jibondi and Juani. To enter the park

– even if you won't be venturing on to the water – you have to pay an entrance fee of $20 per person per day, payable in cash at a road barrier in Utende, 14km southeast of Kilindoni at Chole Bay. The law says you can pay in shillings equivalent, but they prefer dollars, so change some money before coming. In addition, Bweni village, outside the park in the north, charges $5 entry to tourists, while Chole Island also charges a $5 community fee to be paid at the *Red Herring Café* (see p.160) on arrival.

Internet access *New Lizu Hotel* in Kilindoni has two networked computers and wi-fi (Tsh3000/hr; daily 8am–8pm), available to non-guests.

Money Kilindoni's branch of NMB Bank changes cash, but its ATM only takes Tanzanian cards. Some beach hotels accept credit cards.

GETTING AROUND

By bike Bicycles can be rented informally in Kilindoni (up to Tsh10,000 a day).

By taxi and bajaj Taxis will charge around Tsh40,000 (roughly $25) from Kildoni to the beach hotels, as they'll probably head back empty; a *bajaj* should cost no more than half that.

Hotel transfers Beach hotels offer transfers from Kilindoni for $30–50 per vehicle ($100 to *Lua Cheia*).

ACCOMMODATION AND EATING

The main concentration of **hotels** for all budgets is on Mafia Island at Chole Bay, 14km southeast of Kilindoni, which provides easy access to Chole, Juani and Jibondo islands, and is near all the best snorkelling and diving sites. Kilindoni town on the west coast of Mafia Island has some cheap but often quite dismal **guesthouses**: while staying here offers better beaches and sunsets, it's ill-placed for most activities other than seeing whale sharks. **Camping** is possible at *Chole Foxes Lodge* on Chole Island.

MAFIA ISLAND: KILINDONI AND THE WEST COAST

Butiama Beach Kilindoni, 2km southwest on the beach (3.5km by road) ☎0787 474084, ⓦbutiamabeach.com. A consistently recommended Italian/Tanzanian hotel within sight of Kilindoni harbour, its ten swanky *bandas* fashionably decked out in pastel ethno-rustic designs and boutique-style furnishings. The *bandas*, which are 70–90m back along the shore, are cosy and comfortable, and some have full-on sea views. The beach is great for swimming. FB $300

Lua Cheia Castaway Beach Camp Ras Bweni, 34km northeast of Kilindoni (50km by road) ☎0787 424588, ⓦluacheiabeach.com. The only hotel this far north, with 400m of beach and sandbanks to the south, and 2.5km of beach to the north, part of it backed by fishing villages. There are just six rooms, actually large buff-coloured safari tents with plumbed in bathrooms pitched on stone platforms next to the beach, complete with verandas perfect for sunsets. The theme is barefoot luxury: intimate, casual and expensive. Lots of activities (at extra cost), including an on-site diving operation. Closed April–May. FB $310

New Lizu Hotel Kilindoni, at the junction of the roads from the airport and the harbour, 500m from either ☎0783 323806 or ☎0653 416489, ⓦnewlizuhotel.blogspot.com. Athough past its prime, this is still the best budget choice in town, with ever-helpful owners. Each of the five rooms is en suite, with a double bed, adequately sized net, table, ceiling fan and electric sockets, and it's the only place in Kilindoni with wi-fi. Tsh20,000

★Ras Mbisi Lodge Ras Mbisi, 12.5km northeast of Kilindoni (19km by road) ☎0754 663739, ⓦrasmbisimafia.co.tz. On a six-kilometre beach surrounded by regimented coconut plantations, this British-owned place has an intimate vibe, friendly staff, fabulous food, and a pool, so is perfect for families and couples. Accommodation is in nine *bandas* 30–50m from the beach, all made from natural materials, including plenty of coconut wood and thatch. Activities (at extra cost) include snorkelling, diving, sunset cruises, canoeing and various land excursions. The location is relatively sheltered, so it's also a good choice for the windier months of June–Sept. FB $370

MAFIA ISLAND: CHOLE BAY

Big Blu Chole Bay, at the end of the road on the left ☎0787 474108 or ☎0654 089659, ⓦbigblumafia. com. Primarily a scuba diving operation (together with snorkelling, whale shark watching and other excursions), it also has nine rooms, three in *bandas*, and six in tents back from the shore. Simple yet comfortable, the beach *bandas* have attractive thatch and palm-wave exteriors, with sea views and optional a/c. The walk-in dome tents, pitched under thatched roofs, contain two beds each and little more (their bathrooms are shared). BB tent $30, *banda* $110

Didimiza Guest House Chole Bay, signposted on the right 1km before the park gate ☎0787 071543 or ☎0784 303554, ⓦdidimiza.com. A cheap family-run option 200m back from the mangrove-lined shore in a scruffy garden, with four bare but adequate en-suite bungalows with their own verandas: inside, big nets surround a double bed or two singles, plus ceiling fan (twin beds an extra $10). The low cost is one attraction; the other is the big-hearted Tanzanian family than runs it. BB $30

Kinasi Lodge Chole Bay ☎ 0787 424588, ✎ mafiaisland.com. A slightly strange place, halfway between classic holiday resort and boutique hideaway. It has a pool, dive centre, and plenty of facilities; it's certainly elegant, and supremely comfortable, but lacks charm. The guest rooms are in fourteen large and airy *makuti*-roofed bungalows set on a low hillside, six facing the sea ($40 extra). The open-plan lounge area is a delight, with a bar, satellite TV and superb reference library. Bicycles, kayaks and windsurf boards are provided free of charge. Closed April–May. FB $360

Mafia Island Lodge Chole Bay ☎ 022 260 1747 (Dar), ✎ mafialodge.com. A welcome transformation of a once-stark government-run hotel into an attractive, unpretentious and relatively affordable *makuti*-thatched resort. The 36 comfortable rooms are in long coral-stone blocks; all have a/c, hot water, fans and nets, and bay-view verandas. There's an excellent (and natural) beach. Facilities include a seafood restaurant and terrace bar, a dive centre, a full range of excursions (not included), plus internet access. HB $290

★ **Pole Pole Resort** Chole Bay ✎ polepole.com. An intimate and effortless stylish Italian-run lodge with a well-regarded dive centre, and a pool. Guests stay in one of seven exquisitely furnished ocean-facing bungalows on stilts with private verandas, including two for families. The lodge is run on sound ethical principles, with good local relations, and supports community development projects. Service and food are excellent. Rates include dhow trips and snorkelling. Closed April–May. FB €440

CHOLE ISLAND

★ **Chole Foxes Lodge** Chole Island, a 2km walk from where the boats drop you ☎ 0715 877393 or ☎ 0764 494938, ✎ cholefoxestz.com. Tanzanian owned and operated, this little gem is hidden away on the south end of the island, just behind a mangrove-lined shore. A clearing in the mangroves gives access to the sea and swimming at high tide, but there's no beach. It's secluded, relaxing, personal and friendly, with great sunsets, and a nightly show of stars and fireflies. Its four rooms are basic (bucket showers, and solar power only, so no fans or a/c), but the showers are strong. Snorkelling can be arranged, and locals are happy to guide you around the island (in search of fruit bats, say, or over to Juani Island at low tide). Camping per person $10; *bandas* BB $50, HB $70

Chole Mjini Chole Island, close to where the boats drop you ☎ 0784 520799 or ☎ 0787 712427, ✎ cholemjini .com. Run by a South African couple, this hotel has six very alluring Robinson-Crusoe-style tree houses built from wood, thatch and mangrove poles, each with two floors, a double bed, a bucket shower and composting toilet in a straw shelter at the base. There's also one ground-level room, and three suites are being built in the Old Boma nearby. The lack of electricity can be an attraction (gadgets can be charged from solar batteries), but the lack of beach isn't. Nonetheless, it charms pretty much everyone who stays here. Snorkelling and dhow trips are included in the rates, and they can also arrange diving for guests. Closed mid-March–mid-June. FB $440

EATING AND DRINKING

Many of the hotel **restaurants** at Chole Bay serve excellent if pricey seafood, but do drop by beforehand, to check them out, and to let them know you're coming, as the ingredients are usually bought in fresh the same morning. For lunch, most snorkelling or sandbank excursions ($30–50 per person) include a **picnic**, which can be very fancy if organized by one of the better hotels. In Kilindoni, try also the **food stalls** at the market, or near the harbour. For **drinks**, only *New Lizu Hotel* (Kilindoni), *Mafia Island Lodge* (Chole Bay) and *Red Herring Café* (Chole Island) are likely to welcome guests intent on boozing without dining.

MAFIA ISLAND

★ **Butiama Beach** Kilindoni, 2km southwest on the beach (3.5km by road) ☎ 0787 474084. Beautiful sunsets, castaway chic decor, and stylish food, delightfully presented. Snacks and light meals are served throughout the day, starting with a fine breakfast complete with muffins, yoghurt and pancakes ($10). The limited lunch menu is light fare, like seafood salad (or burgers and chips), and isn't overly spicy. Dinner (served at 7.30–8pm) is an ever-changing three-course affair (from $20). Reservations recommended. Daily 7am–8pm.

Didimiza Guest House Chole Bay, signposted on the right 1km before the park gate ☎ 0787 071543 or ☎ 0784 303554. Tanzanian-run, and very adept at seafood, which you and other guests eat with the family at

one big table. A great place to sample the classic Swahili fish in coconut sauce. Lunch is $10, dinner $15. Daily, but must be ordered in advance.

★ **Kinasi Lodge** Chole Bay ☎ 0787 424588. The menu here covers four main bases: Swahili, Barbecue, Indian and Oriental. The Swahili selection is exceptionally good, and one of the few to offer really fine meat dishes, too, such as chicken cooked in banana leaves with lemon grass. The luxurious buffet and grill costs $20, or $25 for the far more formal dinner. Great wine list. Closed April–May. Daily lunch served 12.30–1pm, dinner 7.30–8pm.

Mafia Island Lodge Chole Bay. The busiest and cheapest of the Chole Bay restaurants (lunch $15, dinner $20), but also the least personal and least consistent. Both the restaurant and bar have a sea-view terrace, and there's also

3

3

THE RUFIJI RIVER DELTA

The swampy, mosquito-infested **Rufiji River delta** spans almost 70km from north to south, starting some 100km south of Dar. Flanking its myriad streams, lakes, tidal marshes and sandbanks is East Africa's largest **mangrove forest** (around 439 square kilometres), which serves as a gigantic filter for Tanzania's biggest river, letting through micronutrients while retaining sediments that would otherwise suffocate the marvellous corals of the Mafia archipelago, just offshore.

During the long rains, the river jumps its banks by up to fifteen kilometres, fertilizing the surrounding land and feeding innumerable lakes and pools. The waters are important breeding grounds for prawns, shrimps and fish, and coupled with the largely intact riverine forest attract incredibly rich **birdlife** (the delta is a RAMSAR conservation site). The plain-backed sunbird, longbills, lovebirds and majestic African fish eagle are commonly seen, while rarer species include the African pitta, found north of the river, and Livingstone's flycatcher, to the south. There are moves afoot to establish community-based tourism in the delta (check ⓦfacebook.com/pages/Rufiji-Delta-Six-Islands/250178748486841 for the latest details), but for now the only practical approach is on a pricey **boat trip** from one of the Mafia Island lodges.

a beach bar for snacks such as salads and sandwiches. Daily 11am–8pm.

New Lizu Hotel Kilindoni, at the junction of the roads from the airport and the harbour. The restaurant attached to Kilindoni's oldest hotel provides filling, tasty and usually quite simple meals, along the lines of fish with *ugali* or rice (Tsh2500), but – with a few hours' notice – they can conjure up fancier items like *pilau* with prawns or octopus, which is a bargain at Tsh6500. They also sell alcohol. Daily 7.30–9am, lunch variable, dinner 7–9pm.

★**Pole Pole Resort** Chole Bay ⓦpolepole.com. Meals in the split-level dining room and bar are *always* excellent: at its best, an elegant fusion of African ingredients and Italian form and style (say, octopus salad or sautéed giant crab claws as the antipasto), and they also offer gluten-free dishes. Light lunches from $15, and superb four-course

dinners $30. Fine wine list. Reservations recommended. Closed April–May. Daily lunch served 12.30–1pm, dinner 7.30pm–8pm.

CHOLE ISLAND

★**Chole Foxes Lodge** Chole Island, a 2km walk from where the boats drop you ☏0715 877393. This blissfully located Tanzanian-owned place dishes up consistently good seafood, especially for its evening barbecues ($12) – though its location means that these are only available for overnight guests. Lunch is less lavish but just as tasty ($10). Daily, but must be ordered in advance.

Red Herring Café Chole Island, where the boats drop you. Set up by *Chole Mjiji* and locally staffed, this is a public bar and snack shop that serves simple meals like rice with fish for Tsh6000, accompanied by memorable sunsets over Mafia Island. Daily variable, but usually 10am–7pm.

The Kilwas

South of the Rufiji delta, the first place of note is the Kilwa peninsula, at the southern end of which sits the modest town of **Kilwa Masoko**. It has a couple of nice beaches, but the main reason to visit is for the ruins of **Kilwa Kisiwani**, 2km offshore. In medieval times, Kilwa was an immensely wealthy and powerful city-state, enjoying a monopoly over the gold trade from what is now Mozambique and Zimbabwe. The ruins are very well preserved (enough to have been declared a World Heritage Site), and it requires little effort to picture what the place must have been like during its heyday. Similar, smaller sites can be found on the nearby islands of **Songo Mnara** and **Sanje ya Kati**. At the top of the peninsula, **Kilwa Kivinje** was a major nineteenth-century slave-trading centre whose historical core is now in a woefully dilapidated but picturesque state.

Kilwa Masoko

The small town of **KILWA MASOKO** ("Kilwa of the Market") is the main base on the peninsula, and it is here that you are likely to stay. It has a couple of beaches: **Jimbiza**,

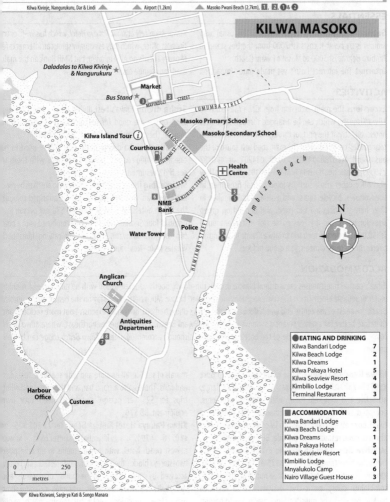

KILWA MASOKO

Kilwa Kivinje, Nangurukuru, Dar & Lindi ▲   ▲ Airport (1.2km)   ▲ Masoko Pwani Beach (2.7km), ❶, ❷, ❶ & ❷

Daladalas to Kilwa Kivinje & Nangurukuru

Market
Bus Stand ❸   MAPINDUZI   ❸ STREET
LUMUMBA STREET

Masoko Primary School
Kilwa Island Tour ⓘ   Masoko Secondary School
Courthouse

Health Centre

Jimbiza Beach

BANK STREET
NMB Bank ❻   NANJIRINJI STREET

Police
Water Tower

HAMJAMBO STREET

N

Anglican Church

Antiquities Department

EATING AND DRINKING
Kilwa Bandari Lodge	7
Kilwa Beach Lodge	2
Kilwa Dreams	1
Kilwa Pakaya Hotel	5
Kilwa Seaview Resort	4
Kimbilio Lodge	3
Terminal Restaurant	3

Harbour Office
Customs

0   250
metres

ACCOMMODATION
Kilwa Bandari Lodge	8
Kilwa Beach Lodge	2
Kilwa Dreams	1
Kilwa Pakaya Hotel	5
Kilwa Seaview Resort	4
Kimbilio Lodge	7
Mnyalukolo Camp	6
Nairo Village Guest House	3

Kilwa Kisiwani, Sanje ya Kati & Songo Manara ▼

in the middle of town, which harbours Kilwa's modest dhow fleet, and the more tide-dependent but secluded **Masoko Pwani**, four kilometres north. **Snorkelling** trips can be arranged from the town, as can day-trips to the nearby ruins at Kilwa Kisiwani.

ARRIVAL AND DEPARTURE

KILWA MASOKO

By bus Kilwa Masoko is served by direct buses and Coaster minibuses from Dar (3–4 daily; 5–6hr; Tsh12,000) and Lindi (hourly until midday; 3–4hr; Tsh7000). Coaster minibuses from Dar leave up to midday (see p.100), but all vehicles to Dar leave Kilwa around 5.30am. Coasters to Lindi run until around late morning. Choose your company carefully: the road is fast, and some drivers treat the road up the peninsula as little more than a race track. At the time of writing, the safest – relatively speaking – was Swahili Bus, which is also the most comfortable. Ticket offices are at the bus stand just off the main road by the market.

By plane Kilwa Masoko's airport (a grass strip and a wooden shed) is 2km north of town. Coastal Aviation flies here (no agent in Kilwa; ☎0752 627825, ⊛coastal.co.tz), but it needs a minimum of five passengers, and is expensive: $300 one-way from Zanzibar, $250 from Dar, or $190 from Mafia.

Destinations Dar (daily; 1hr 10min); Mafia (daily; 30min); Pemba (daily; 3hr); Zanzibar (daily; 2hr 15min).

3

3

ESSENTIALS

Getting around Other than walking, the usual way around is by *bajaj*: it costs Tsh2000 from the bus stand to Jimbiza Beach, Tsh5000 to Masoko Pwani Beach.

Internet The internet hasn't yet made much impact on Kilwa. Ask nicely at *Kilwa Pakaya Hotel*, which has wi-fi, or try the post office, which may eventually sprout an internet café

Money There's no ATM in town, but NMB Bank on the main road can change cash.

ACTIVITIES

Excursions The main excursion from Kilwa Masoko is to Kilwa Kisiwani, which can be arranged through the better hotels, directly at the port, or through Kilwa Islands Tour, a tour guides' cooperative on the main road just south of the bus stand (☎0788 719837, 0787 034201 or ☎0787 219099; erratic hours, usually Mon–Sat 10am–4pm). They also offer other trips, such as joining local fishermen in their dhows, bicycle tours, and visiting local families in their homes. Prices are not fixed, and depend on group sizes for boats, but are reasonable (for instance, around Tsh50,000 per person for a trip to Kilwa Kivinje including an overnight there, and meals, in a group of four).

Scuba diving Kilwa's best diving reefs – mostly steep drop-offs – are good for pelagics such as sharks, blue marlin (best Sept), and tuna (Dec), though there's currently no scuba diving outfit here. There used to be one at *Kimbilio Lodge* (see p.163) – check with them to see if it's resumed.

Snorkelling The best reefs for snorkelling are 4km beyond Masoko Pwani Beach. Trips here can be arranged through the beach hotels for a fairly standard $30 per person in a group of four. Snorkelling can also be combined with a boat trip to Kilwa Kisiwani. Look out for calving humpback whales (Aug–Nov), and turtles.

ACCOMMODATION

Kilwa's central guesthouses are a dismal bunch: usually run-down, poorly ventilated, and with no guarantee of running water or reliable electricity – the few exceptions are reviewed below. Much better is to stay on the beach: either Jimbiza Beach, just east of the centre and which doubles as the town's dhow harbour, or – more extensive but more secluded and therefore better for women wearing swimwear – Masoko Pwani Beach, a few kilometres northeast, where *Kilwa Beach Lodge* also offers camping. None of the hotels accept cards, although accommodation at *Kilwa Beach Lodge* can be paid online.

Kilwa Bandari Lodge On the main road close to port ☎0713 748309, ✉alimzinga@gmail.com. Six large, attractive and well-kept rooms with spotless bathrooms, equipped with Zanzibar-style *semadari* beds (double or twin), box nets and fans, and with TV or a/c in some. There's also a bar and restaurant at the side. BB **Tsh49,000**

★**Kilwa Beach Lodge** Masoko Pwani Beach, 3.5km from the bus stand ☎0774 423175 or ☎0685 411630, �🌐kilwa.co.tz. The best of the three hotels on this beach, combining classy rustic-chic design with a laidback backpacker vibe. The guest cottages are in a wild garden next to the coconut palm-fringed beach. The seven octagonal *bandas* are small but comfy, with rustic furniture, electricity, fans and nets, and great sea views (for en suite, you'll pay an extra $45). Much more expensive, and with less satisfying views, are a couple of two-storey Robinson-Crusoe-style cottages. Facing the beach is a great open-sided restaurant and bar. Snorkelling and dhow trips can be arranged. Closed mid-March–April. Camping per tent **Tsh30,000**, *banda* (BB) **$55**, cottages (BB) **$200–250**

Kilwa Dreams Masoko Pwani Beach, 3.6km from the bus stand ☎0784 585330, �🌐kilwadreams.com. This Tanzanian/Danish place is an affordable and quiet beach stay, occupying a wild plot dotted with palm trees and backed by a narrow saltwater creek. It has seven simple but well-maintained sea-facing bungalows painted with funky

murals of sea life, all en suite and with sea-view verandas, and fans. There's also a good bar, and they run snorkelling trips for $25 per person, but you'll need your own equipment. BB **$70**

Kilwa Pakaya Hotel Jimbiza Beach ☎023 201 3253 or ☎0776 570425, ⍉kilwapakayahotel.co.tz. Kilwa's newest beach hotel, with twenty rooms in an uninspired two-storey block: there's a bar and restaurant below, accessed by steep stairs, and a bunch of parasols and volleyball net on the beach itself. The rooms, including some twins, have surprisingly poky bathrooms, which might explain the musty smell in the rains. You also get a ceiling fan, TV, fridge and, supposedly, wi-fi, but no mosquito nets – the place relies on its a/c and bug spray. The hotel's main attraction, however, is the unimpeded ocean views from the wooden balconies attached to each bedroom. HB **$115**

Kilwa Seaview Resort Jimbiza Beach ☎023 201 3064 or ☎0784 613335, ⍉kilwa.net. A sleepy place atop a crumbling cliff at the north end of Jimbiza Beach – the nearest swimmable section is a few hundred metres west beyond the fishing boats. The concrete-walled, *makuti*-roofed cottages are decently fitted out, if slightly tatty. Rooms 1–4 have unimpeded sea views; others have vegetation in front, or are in a row of two-storey houses behind, the better rooms there being on top. There's an open-sided restaurant, a separate bar, and a murky

wimming pool. Excursions to Kilwa Kisiwani are $30 a
head; other dhow trips (say to Songo Mnara and Sanje ya
ati, or exploring mangroves) cost $150 per boat. Camping
er person $10; rooms **$110**

imbilio Lodge Jimbiza Beach ☎0656 022166 or
☎022 260 1747 (Dar), ⓦkimbiliolodges.com. This
alian-managed place has five pink rondavels and a family
anda, all with thatched roofs, on a scrubby lawn beside
he beach. The rooms are all spacious and stylishly
ecorated, with big beds, ceiling fans and washed cement
oors. There's also a great bar and restaurant, both with
ews. BB **$130**

Mnyalukolo Camp On the main road ☎0787 112055.
A messy hotchpotch between the road and the mangroves
to the west, with reasonable en-suite guest rooms at the
back, plus three cheaper ones in converted container crates
that are in an almost comical state of disrepair. There's also
a small bar with outdoor tables, a billiards table, and
decent meals. BB **Tsh15,000**

Nairo Village Guest House Mapinduzi St
☎0755 397688. One of few Kilwan budget-level lodgings
that isn't squalid, with several clean en-suite rooms, all
with big beds, ceiling fans, a/c and TVs (but no guarantee of
them working). The more expensive rooms are the same,
but larger. **Tsh10,000**

ATING AND DRINKING

ilwa's best **restaurants** are in the beach hotels, most of which offer a small selection of daily specials, such as prawns
nd octopus (grilled or stewed), as well as lobster, squid, meaty *kolekole* and dorado. For simple eats, try the **market**,
hich stays open well into the night. The area around the market, especially along the main road, is stuffed with foodstalls
nd bars (populated by a number of prostitutes), which can get lively at weekends. The beach hotels don't always accept
alk-ins, especially large groups, so contact them or drop in beforehand if you're thinking of drinking or dining. Walking
round town at night is considered safe until around 11pm.

ilwa Bandari Lodge On the main road close to port.
he roadside location isn't that special, but the food is, and
considerably cheaper than the beach hotels, too: fish of
he day with *ugali* costs Tsh7000, and the special Sunday
iriani Tsh5500. They also offer more modest repasts such
s *chipsi mayai* (Tsh3000), and serve alcohol. Daily
pm–midnight.

★ **Kilwa Beach Lodge** Masoko Pwani Beach, 3.5km
rom the bus stand ☎0774 423175 or ☎0685 411630.
peach of a beach, complete with waving coconut palms,
ome draped with swings, make this the perfect place to
while away a lazy afternoon. The bar and restaurant are a
arge open-sided *makuti*-thatched structure with sea
iews, furnished in ever-popular rustic chic style, complete
ith old dhows converted into shelves and tables. A
eafood lunch costs around Tsh16,000. Closed mid-March–
pril. Daily noon–2pm & 7–9pm.

ilwa Dreams Masoko Pwani Beach, 3.6km from the bus
tand ☎0784 585330. Informal and calm, with very good
ut pricey seafood, starting at Tsh20,000 for main courses –
he seafood platter including crab and lobster costs Tsh35,000
rder 4 hours before). Daily noon–3pm & 7–9pm.

ilwa Pakaya Hotel Jimbiza Beach ☎023 201 3253 or
☎0776 570425. This has a very pleasant indoor restaurant
nd bar (lots of dark wood, African decor and sea views),

where seafood is (unsurprisingly) the speciality. Lunch and
dinner are four-course set meals ($20), featuring dishes
like octopus with mashed potatoes. You're also welcome for
snacks, or just for drinks. Daily 10am–9pm.

Kilwa Seaview Resort Jimbiza Beach ☎023 201 3064
or ☎0784 613335. Above the beach on a low cliff, this has
great views and lovely sunsets, but average and rather
overpriced meals (lunch or dinner costs Tsh25,000, or
Tsh30,000 with prawns). There's also a well-stocked bar
around a baobab tree. Daily noon–9pm or 10pm.

Kimbilio Lodge Jimbiza Beach ☎0656 022166. One of
the more attractive hotel restaurants, open-sided and with
lots of wood and thatch, just above the beach's high-tide
mark. The Italian-inspired menu comprises half a dozen
dishes chalked up on a blackboard; lunch costs $10, with a
more substantial dinner $20. Seafood with an Italian slant
is the theme, but they're happy catering for vegetarians.
The bar is very well stocked but primarily for overnight
guests. Lunch served noon–1pm, dinner at 7.30pm.

★ **Terminal Restaurant** Mapinduzi St. An excellent
local restaurant serving very tasty breakfasts, including
supu as well as the usual snacks (*andazi, kababu, sambusa*),
and, from midday, full meals of *pilau* or rice with fish,
octopus, chicken or goat, all for a mere Tsh1500–2000. No
alcohol. Daily 6.30am–11pm.

Kilwa Kisiwani

ust 2km across the water from Kilwa Masoko's port are the spectacular ruins of **Kilwa
Kisiwani** ("Kilwa of the Island"), on the mangrove-rimmed island of the same name. At
ts height the island-state – known at the time as just Kilwa – was the most important
rading centre on the East African coast, and ruins include a fourteenth-century palace

that was the largest stone structure in sub-Saharan Africa. There are also several mosques, dozens of Shirazi graves set amid gigantic baobab trees, and a well-preserved Omani fortress.

The **ruins** – complete with walkways and signboards – are scattered in and around the present-day settlement of Kilwa Kisiwani, whose simple mud houses provide a stark contrast to the wealthy city Kilwa once was. The bulk of the ruins are in the northwest and cover little more than one square kilometre. Husuni Kubwa and Husuni Ndogo sit together 2km to the east, accessed by narrow footpaths wending between plots of irrigated farmland, cashew plantations, mango groves and acacia and baobab thickets where, with a keen eye, you may spot bee-eaters and bulbuls.

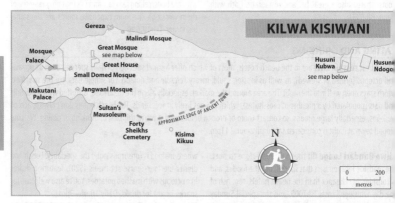

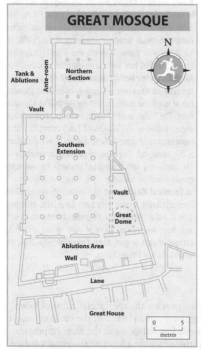

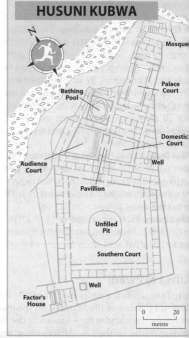

Adapted from John Sutton (1998), in Azania 33. Reproduced by permission of the British Institute in Eastern Africa

Brief history

According to legend (see p.513), Kilwa was founded in 975 AD by Hassan bin Ali, son of the king of Shiraz (now Iran). After being shipwrecked on the island, Ali bought it from a local chief in return for a quantity of cloth. The town reached its apogee in the fourteenth and fifteenth centuries, from which time the bulk of the surviving ruins date. Key to Kilwa's success was its control of maritime trade in the western Indian Ocean, in particular the port of **Sofala** in central Mozambique, which was the main conduit for **gold** produced by Zimbabwe's Monomotapa kingdom. At its height, Kilwa boasted sub-Saharan Africa's largest stone building, its largest mosque, and the very first mint. Its ruling class lived in stone houses with indoor plumbing, wore silk and fine cotton, and ate off Chinese porcelain. In 1332, **Ibn Battuta**, Morocco's celebrated globetrotter, described Kilwa as "amongst the most beautiful of cities and elegantly built".

The Portuguese and decline

Portugal's second India-bound fleet, commanded by **Pedro Álvares Cabral**, dropped anchor off Kilwa in 1500. They found a flourishing and powerful city, exporting gold, silver, precious stones, ivory, myrrh, animal skins, frankincense, ambergris and a few slaves, receiving spices and metal goods in return. Cabral ordered a cannon salvo to honour Kilwa's ruler, **Amir Ibrahim**, who, unfortunately, mistook the gesture for aggression, and refused to have any more dealings with the newcomers. In 1502, **Vasco da Gama** stormed into Kilwa threatening to burn the city and kill its inhabitants unless he was paid tribute. Wisely, the Amir coughed up.

In 1505 **Dom Francisco d'Almeida**, who was about to assume the post of viceroy of the newly conquered territories of India, declared "Kilwa, of all the places I know in the world, has the best port and the fairest land that can be", then promptly ransacked the town. By 1513, Portuguese aggression throughout the western Indian Ocean had destroyed the former trading networks, and so, with no further use for Kilwa, the Portuguese left. In 1587, forty percent of Kilwa's population was massacred, and some of them allegedly eaten, by the marauding **Zimba tribe**, who originated in northwestern Mozambique.

Kilwa's fortunes revived briefly in the eighteenth century when the **slave trade** supplanted gold as the coast's major commodity. But in 1842, Kilwa was captured by Omani Arabs from Zanzibar, who diverted the slave caravans to the new port of Kilwa Kivinje, 25km to the north. Kilwa Kisiwani was once again abandoned, and collapsed into the ruins you see today.

The Gereza fortress

The crenellated **Gereza** (also known as the fort or the prison) is Kilwa Kisiwani's most prominent building, and has commanding views over the waterway to Kilwa Masoko. Parts of the northern walls have crumbled into the sea, but the Gereza is otherwise in fine fettle. The first fortress on the site was erected by the **Portuguese** in, it's said, under three weeks, but when the **Omanis** gained control, in the early nineteenth century, they rebuilt the entire thing with the exception of the tower foundations – this is the building you see today.

There's only one entrance to the fortress, through a relatively modern door, above which is a slot for muskets; there are more slits along the parapet. Inside, the courtyard has a number of benches along the walls, and spy holes from the middle level of the surrounding three-storey edifice – you'll find the best-preserved rooms in the southeast corner, on your left as you enter.

The Great Mosque

The **Great Mosque** (or Friday Mosque) lies on the edge of the present-day village, in an area frequented by goats. In its time the largest mosque in East Africa, it was excavated between 1958 and 1960 by Neville Chittick, who reconstructed parts of it and also left behind a short length of railway and an upturned carriage, which had been used to clear debris. The mosque is a truly beautiful building, its architecture reflecting Kilwa's rising prosperity over the centuries.

The roofless **northern section** is the oldest part, built no later than the **twelfth century**, when the gold trade was in its infancy. Its flat, coral-concrete roof was supported by nine sixteen-sided wooden columns set in rows of three, on top of which three beams were laid. The wood, of course, rotted away long ago, leaving only the gaps in the masonry into which the beams and pillars fitted.

As Kilwa prospered, the mosque's **southern extension** was given an elaborately vaulted roof surmounted by 22 domes, supported by thin octagonal stone pillars, which were unable to bear the weight of the roof, and collapsed around 1350. The pillars were replaced with coral limestone blocks, most of which stand today; the original pillars lie discarded beside the eastern wall, and the domes' interiors are occupied by bats. At the southern end of the mosque, the **ablutions area** houses a bench, water trough, and a slab of round sandstone on which the faithful could wash their feet.

If you peer into the well beside the mosque, you'll see two **underground passages** leading off it about halfway down. The one on the eastern side is said to lead to the Gereza and may have been used for moving slaves, while the one to the west goes to Makutani Palace.

The Small Domed Mosque

The **Small Domed Mosque**, 150m southwest of the Great Mosque, is the best preserved and most attractive of Kilwa's medieval buildings, with more than half its original roof intact. It dates from the middle of the fifteenth century when Kilwa's prosperity was at its height. Inside, the mosque is an architectural gem. As with the Great Mosque, the African influence is visible in the overall form of the building, which is based on a rectangular prayer hall with a roof supported on numerous pillars, rather than on the contemporary Arabian "pavilion" style featuring arcaded courtyards. The central dome was inlaid with circles of green-glazed ceramic bowls, some of which can still be seen, and there's an elegant *mihrab* in the north wall. The **ablutions area** to the southwest contains a latrine and two water tanks, plus some circular foot-scrubbing stones.

The Makutani Palace

Close to the western shore is the **Makutani Palace**. Its name means "gathering place", suggesting a mode of rule that valued collective decisions, as was traditional among many Tanzanian tribes before the nineteenth century. With the exception of the perimeter walls, most of the fifteenth-century structure was demolished at the end of the eighteenth century to provide building material for the new palace, which is still largely intact, and surrounded by enormous defensive outer walls that open only to the shore.

The old palace consists of a **residential section** to the west and barracks or storerooms around a large **courtyard** to the east. The rusty cannon in the courtyard adds to the impression that defence was a prime concern, as does the water cistern – invaluable during a siege. Both wings of the palace had long, narrow rooms, their width limited by the length of the mangrove poles that supported the ceilings. The reception rooms and living quarters were on the upper two floors, the latter provided with toilets.

Jangwani Mosque

A few hundred metres southeast of the palace are the scant remains of **Jangwani Mosque**, of interest mainly to archeologists on account of the unique water jars set into its walls just inside the main entrance. Just south of the mosque, you can cut across the inlet at low tide to reach the so-called **Forty Sheikhs Cemetery**, part of which has been eroded by the sea. Like the vast majority of known Shirazi grave sites, the tombs nestle in groves of baobabs, including one of the biggest you're ever likely to see. Legend has it that when a ultan died, a pair of baobab saplings would be planted at either end of his grave; these would eventually grow together, effectively making the tomb part of the tree.

Husuni Kubwa

Built on a rocky spur high above the mangroves, 2km east of the Gereza, **Husuni Kubwa** ("Great Palace") was, in its time, the largest permanent building in sub-Saharan Africa, and remains one of its most enigmatic constructions. Acces is via a footpath from the Gereza and the village: once the undergrowth clears, you'll see a grey maze of courtyards, hallways, galleries, staircases and rooms up to three storeys high. Excavations suggest that the construction was never completed, nor lived in by more than three generations of sultans before the dynasty decamped to the Makutani Palace. No one knows why the building was abandoned, especially as the cliff-top location was ideal, benefiting from continuous sea breezes as well as commanding views.

A plaque found in the palace sings the praises of Sultan "al-Malik al-Mansur" ("the Conquering Ruler") al-Hasan ibn Sulaiman, dating the bulk of the palace's construction to the 1320s. The very size of the palace illustrates the wealth accrued from the gold trade at that time – if you've seen the display on Kilwa in the National Museum in Dar (see p.90), with its Chinese porcelain bowls, elaborate friezes, oil lamps, pottery and coins, it's not difficult to imagine the opulence that once existed here.

The palace

You approach the palace via the large **southern court**, enclosed by a double range of rooms. Near the centre of the courtyard is a large irregular pit, which was either used as a quarry or may have been intended to form a cistern. North of here is the **palace** itself, occupying the north- and west-facing tip of the headland. First, you pass through the **domestic court**, which is surrounded by terraces. To the west is the **pavilion** where the sultan received visitors and conducted public business. A short flight of steps below the pavilion leads to the **audience court**, flanked by wide terraces which may also have been used for receptions and dances, and which offer a fine view westwards over the coast and harbour.

Beyond the audience court is an octagonal **bathing pool**, set in an unroofed square enclosure; it holds some eighty thousand litres of water, which had to be hauled by hand from the well beside the Domestic Court. The sheer scale of palace fittings, like these, suggests why the site might have been abandoned prematurely – its upkeep may imply have been too expensive, even for Kilwa. North of the Bathing Pool and through the rectangular **palace court**, steps lead down to a landing creek in the mangroves, where most dhows collect passengers before returning to Kilwa Masoko.

Husuni Ndogo

Separated from Husuni Kubwa by a deep gully, **Husuni Ndogo**, or "Small Palace", is believed to have been constructed in the fifteenth century, though archeologists know little about the building. With the exception of its outer walls and turrets, it contains virtually no internal structures, and dense thorny shrubs render access difficult.

ARRIVAL AND INFORMATION   KILWA KISIWANI

Access to the site is by boat from Kilwa Masoko's port (see p.162). Boats usually drop you at the Gereza fortress, where the captain will locate a guide. You're then shown around the ruins, and finish up 2km east at Husuni Kubwa, where, with luck, your boatman will be waiting. You can either take a tour from one of the hotels, or you can arrange your own boat, in which case you'll also have to sort out your own visitor permit and guide, which won't work out much cheaper than taking an organized tour. Hiring a guide is optional but recommended, and will cost around Tsh15,000–20,000 per group.

Organized excursions All Kilwa Masoko's beach hotels offer trips to Kilwa Kisiwani. The total cost, including a boat there and back, permit and guide, is around $50 per person, though the Kilwa Islands Tour (see p.162) is

cheaper, charging around $35 per person (Tsh50,000).

By boat Locals get to and from the island on the aquatic equivalent of a daladala, being a sail powered *mashua* dhow. If there are other passengers (quite likely at 7am; get your permit the day before), it shouldn't cost more than Tsh1000 per person, but if you want the dhow to yourself – as the captain is likely to assume you do – you'll pay Tsh15,000–20,000 per boat for the return trip, or Tsh35,000 for one with a motor. You can double those prices for Sanje ya Kati or Songo Mnara.

Visitor permits Visitors to Kilwa Kisiwani, Songo Mnara an Sanje ya Kati (see below) need to buy a day permit (Tsh27,00C from the Antiquities Department in Kilwa Masoko, housed i the administrative block facing the post office (ask for "Ofisi y Mambo ya Kale"; Mon–Fri 7.30am–3.30pm; ☎ 0784 61951! ☎ 0787 882524 or ☎ 0715 282524).

ACCOMMODATION AND EATING

Antiquities Department Guesthouse In the village behind the Gereza; contact the Antiquities Department in Kilwa Masoko (see above). Kilwa Kiliwani's only lodging has been refurbished, and now sports large rooms,

fans, running water, and even a TV. The setup is still ver informal (no fixed prices), as the place is mainly used b visiting researchers. Basic supplies, including cold drink: can be bought in the village. **Tsh15,000**

Songo Mnara and Sanje ya Kati

To the south of Kilwa Kisiwani are several other islands with yet more ruins, including Sanje ya Kati, and, on the mainland, Songo Mnara. Those at **Songo Mnara** (15km from Kilwa Masoko by boat), also designated a World Heritage Site, are the most impressive Mostly dating from the fourteenth and fifteenth centuries, they comprise an extensive palace complex, at least four mosques, and dozens of graves and houses, all surrounded by a defensive wall. Diminutive **Sanje ya Kati**, formerly known as Shanga, lies 3km to the west and contains the foundations of oblong houses and a tenth-century mosque, although they're little more than rubble.

ARRIVAL AND INFORMATION

SONGO MNARA AND SANJE YA KAT

Organized excursions Both sites can be visited on trips organized by Kilwa Masoko's beach hotels, or though Kilwa Islands Tour (see p.162), which will include the visitor permit.
By boat If the cost of hiring a boat (see p.167) is prohibitive, note that Songo Mnara is also accessible by irregular *mashua* dhows (2–3hr; Tsh2000 for locals) sailing between Kilwa Masoko and Pande, further south; you'll

have to wade through the water to get ashore. Be sure t double-check arrangements for your pick-up on the retur trip, as there are no facilities on the island, though Song Mnara has a guide who may put you up for a night (and wi expect a tip for showing you around).
Visitor permits You need to buy a permit (Tsh27,00C from the Antiquities Department in Kilwa Masoko to vis both sites (see above for details).

Kilwa Kivinje

Facing the ocean at the top of Kilwa peninsula, 25km north of Kilwa Masoko, is the dilapidated, rarely visited but strangely charming and photogenic town of **KILWA KIVINJE**, "Kilwa of the Casuarina Trees". In the mid-nineteenth century, under Omani

---

MWEMBE KINYONGA

Kilwa put up strong resistance during the Abushiri War (see p.121), and was one of the last places to be "pacified" when, in November 1895, its leader **Hassan bin Omari Makunganya** was hanged from a mango tree. The site, known locally as *Mwembe Kinyonga* ("hangman's mango tree"), is on the road into town, 1.25km before the harbour. The tree is no more, but the site is marked by a wooden sculpture of an old man. He is **Kinjikitile Ngwale**, a soothsayer from the Matumbi Hills northwest of Kilwa, and the spark that ignited the **Maji Maji Uprising** of 1905–06. Kinjikitile claimed to have discovered a spring of water which, when sprinkled on a person, gave protection against bullets. Within months, word of the charm had spread and the entire south of the country rose up in arms against the Germans. Although missing its arms, the wooden figure has a gourd strapped to its waist, presumably containing the magic bullet-proof water. Kinjikitile was one of the first victims of the German reprisal, and was hanged from the same tree as Makunganya.

ule from Zanzibar, it usurped Kilwa Kisiwani as the major **slaving terminus** on the
oute from Lake Nyasa. Over twenty thousand slaves were shipped out from here in the
860s, either to the market in Zanzibar, or to the French colonies of Madagascar,
Réunion and Mauritius. Later it became a **German garrison** town and played a key role
n the suppression of the **Maji Maji Uprising**. Today, it's little more than a large sleepy
ishing village, and many of its historic buildings have collapsed, with others a whisker
way from doing the same.

Most of the survivors can be admired in the first three streets back from the harbour,
nd many still boast some beautiful **balconies and carved doors**. The most impressive
building is the ruined two-storey **German courthouse** facing the silty beach and fishing
harbour. At low tide the ocean recedes by almost a kilometre, making for fine walks
along the shore.

ARRIVAL AND DEPARTURE | **KILWA KIVINJE**

By daladala There are direct daladalas to Kilwa Kivinje
rom Kilwa Masoko. Alternatively, catch one for
Nangurukuru but get off at "Njia panda ya Kivinje", a
junction just under 4km away: from here you can catch
one of the frequent daladalas from Nangurukuru
(10min).

ACCOMMODATION AND EATING

Restaurants in Kilwa Kivinje vary in quality: more reliable are the ramshackle stalls on the beach in front of the ruined
German courthouse, where you'll find delicious grilled fish and squid, and seasonal fruit. Personal security isn't a problem
by day so long as you keep anything tempting hidden, but get someone reliable to escort you at night, as muggings have
been reported.

Savoye Guesthouse Beside the commercial harbour.
The most bearable of several cheap but very basic
guesthouses, if you don't mind doing without electricity
and a private bathroom. It has cleanish rooms with
mosquito nets, and friendly owners, who only speak
Kiswahili. Tsh8000

Lindi

Some 450km south of Dar, the Indian Ocean port of **LINDI** ("Deep Channel")
was founded in the eighteenth century as a caravan terminus on the slave and
ivory route from Lake Nyasa. It sits at the mouth of the Lukuledi River, and is
capital of one of Tanzania's most impoverished regions, having long suffered
from poor soil, the development of Mtwara (at Lindi's expense), and geographical
isolation. However, the discovery of vast offshore gas reserves and the
impending construction of a refinery and pumping terminal (due to come online
in 2020) are likely to completely transform the local economy, and appearance
of Lindi, too.

For now, the town's crumbling infrastructure makes it hard to imagine that Lindi was
once home to a thriving expatriate community. Most of them left after Independence
and only a handful remain, generally NGO workers and missionaries. Few people
speak English, but the locals are unfailingly friendly (if initially reserved) and the town
is enjoyable enough, with a number of attractive buildings dating from the first half of
the twentieth century. The location is lovely, too, flanked by hills on both its landward
and river sides, and by the ocean to the northeast, where dhows under sail are a
common sight.

Ocean Road

North of Lindi's commercial harbour, along Ocean Road, are a couple of colonial
survivors worth a look, including the **German Boma**. Once the colonial headquarters,
it's now so ruined that a veritable forest of fig trees has sprouted inside, and it's the trees

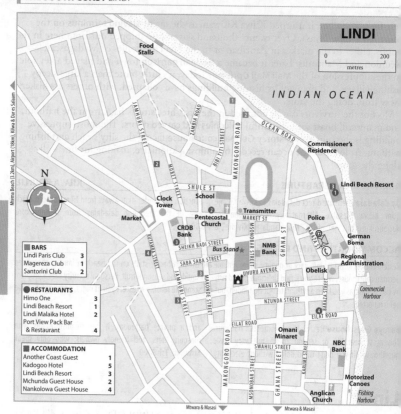

rather than mortar that's hold the place together. Further north, beyond *Lindi Beach Resort*, the marvellously dilapidated **Commissioner's Residence** still stands unaided, its flags and bunting replaced by festoons of ivy.

Around the fishing harbour

South of the commercial harbour, the small **fishing harbour** also has a small **market**, with stalls selling fresh grilled fish. Just behind is the **Anglican Church**, a clumsy stab at the formal proportions of Neoclassicism, not helped by battleship-grey cement. Along nearby Karume Street, Lindi's oldest construction is the battered and lopsided domed **Omani minaret** dating from the nineteenth century.

The beaches

The **town-centre beaches** are mainly used by fishing boats, and for the most part are lined with houses, so woman certainly shouldn't bathe here in swimwear. The beaches north of town provide more privacy, with the nearest decent stretch starting about 3.5km along the highway from the market. The beach curves away to a big headland, beyond which lies the beautiful kilometre-long **Mtema Beach** (accessed along a 300-metre dirt road from the highway, 4km from the market). Thieves have been reported here, however, so go in a group. Alternatively, the beautiful, sheltered, turquoise beach at **Kitunda** can be accessed by taking a motorized canoe (Tsh1000)

TANZANIA'S JURASSIC PARK

The **Tendaguru Hills**, northwest of Lindi, are famed among palaeontologists as Africa's richest deposit of late Jurassic **fossils**. Their similarity to the Morrison Formation in the western USA illustrates the existence, some 150 million years ago, of land bridges between the various continents. The site was discovered by a German mining engineer, Bernhard Sattler, in 1907, while searching for garnets. Locals were already familiar with the fossils, believing them to be the remains of a man-eating ogre whose toes had been slit open by warriors to release the people he had eaten. The excavation of Tendaguru began in 1909 under the auspices of Berlin's Museum für Naturkunde, which still houses the finds, including a twelve-metre-tall *Brachiosaurus brancai* – the Tanzanian Government has spent years trying to retrieve it, but with little success so far.

rom the fish market for the five-minute crossing across the estuary: from here it's a .5km walk northeast between the mangroves and the shore, or inland along the edges of small fields.

Kisiwa cha Popo

The wide river estuary contains a number of secluded beaches and creeks, mangroves, outlandish limestone formations, crocodiles, and the small island of **Kisiwa cha Popo** ("Bat Island"), which is a daytime roost for fruit bats. To explore the waterways and sland, you can rent a whole canoe, with its owner, from Lindi's market for around Tsh50,000 a day.

ARRIVAL AND DEPARTURE

LINDI

By bus Buses and from Dar, plus buses and Coasters to and from Mtwara, Masasi and Newala pull in and leave from Lindi's bus stand in the middle of town between Makongoro Rd and Msonobar St.

Destinations Dar (6–7 daily; 8hr); Kilwa Masoko (hourly until midday; 3–4hr); Masasi (4–6 daily; 2hr 30min); Mikindani (hourly; 1hr 15min); Mingoyo (hourly; 30min); Mtwara (hourly; 1hr 30min); Newala (2–3 daily; 4–5hr).

INFORMATION

Banks NBC, south of the harbour, and CRDB, by the clocktower, have 24hr ATMs for Visa and MasterCard.

Post office The post office is on Baraza St (Mon–Fri 8am–5pm, Sat 8am–1pm), and is the best place in town for internet access.

ACCOMMODATION

Another Coast Guest House Jamhuri St ☎0782 199922 or 0787 699703. Close to the town beach, its ocean view mostly obscured by buildings, this has nine clean en-suite singles (with beds big enough to be shared by married couples), with box nets and TVs. **Tsh15,000**

Kadogoo Hotel Jamhuri St, two blocks west of the bus stand ☎0754 875154. A business-class hotel with seventeen rooms on three floors, plus nine more in an adjacent annexe, all en suite, with flat-screen TV, box net and a/c (no fans): some have balconies (Tsh10,000 extra). Safe parking. Couples need marriage certificates to share rooms. BB **50,000**

Lindi Beach Resort Ocean Rd ☎0656 032044 or ☎023 220 2829. A large, inoffensive, comfortable conference-oriented hotel, behind the beach on the estuary. All rooms have a/c and wi-fi, and the "executive" ones have cable TV, though they also have carpets, which means they can get

musty. There's a swimming pool (not always clean), and a bar and restaurant with tables on a lawn. The whole thing is separated from the beach by a fence. Despite see-sawing standards (and loud music from the nearby *Police Mess* Fri and Sat nights), the price is fine for the location. BB **$65**

★**Mchunda Guest House** Jamhuri St ☎0682 498426. The best of the cheap guesthouses north of the centre, with very friendly staff, and twelve well-equipped rooms which, although small, are in good condition. All have big beds, box nets, fans, 16-channel TV, and clean showers and squat toilets – en-suite costs an extra Tsh5000. **Tsh10,000**

Nankolowa Guest House Rutamba St ☎0685 191045. Once the backpacker's mainstay, this has become ever more basic over the years, but is still a safe and exceptionally cheap option. There's a jumble of rooms, some en suite (Tsh2000 extra), with ceiling fans and big box nets. It can get smelly during the rains. **Tsh5000**

EATING AND DRINKING

Lindi has a handful of half-decent restaurants, but what's really recommended is the row of **street vendors** inside the bu
stand who every evening rustle up roast or fried chicken, eggs and chips for hungry travellers. There are chairs and table
arranged at the front, so you can sit under the stars and watch the world go by in the flickering light of *kibatari* oil lamps
Waitresses from nearby bars bring sodas and beers, and the atmosphere is very friendly, with kids dancing to music blarin
from surrounding stores. Street food, including king-size prawns, can also be sampled at the fishing harbour, and at foo
stalls further north facing the beach, where you'll find especially good grilled fish. Walking around at night is relativel
safe, but being escorted by a reliable local would be wise as there are no street lights.

RESTAURANTS

Himo One Jamhuri St. Charcoal-grilled chicken masala is the big thing to eat here (Tsh7000). They also serve a good biriani, very good juices, and quick traditional snacks (samosas and the like). Daily 7am–10pm.

Lindi Beach Resort Ocean Rd. The only proper restaurant by the shore, with tables on a beachside lawn. The food is mostly Indian but they also cater for other tastes, and serve up usually decent grilled chicken or fish (Tsh12,000–15,000). Daily noon–8pm.

Lindi Malaika Hotel Market Ave. Unfriendly service but still one of Lindi's sweeter restaurants, with great breakfasts and fresh juices. The portions are generous and prices low – Tsh4000 for *pilau* or banana and meat stew, Tsh5000 for biriani. Daily 8am–8.30pm.

Port View Pack Bar & Restaurant Baraza St. A large, more or less central restaurant/bar that becomes a club at night. It plays cheerful music throughout the day, when its

excellent *nyama choma* (Tsh10,000/kg) is the reason t come. Daily 10am–10pm or later.

BARS

Lindi Paris Club Cnr of Uhuru Ave and Makonde St Pleasantly quiet by day, this place gets busy for its weeken night discos; it may also host live bands. There are tables i a large covered courtyard, and unspeakable toilets. Dail noon–10pm or later.

Magereza Club North end of Makongoro Rd. Operate by the prison authority, this is popular in the evenings fo its coastal breezes. You can also drink in the overgrow garden facing the bar – a lovely daytime refuge, and there' the usual bar food too. Daily 11am–10pm.

Santorini Club On the coast at the top of Makongor Rd. Lindi's main nightspot, with heaving discos on weeken nights, and a gaggle of prostitutes. It's open during the day, too, but usually completely empty. Daily 10am–late.

Rondo Forest Reserve

Seventy kilometres west of Lindi on the flanks of the Rondo Plateau, rising to over 900m above sea level, is one of Tanzania's few remaining patches of indigenous coastal forest, part of which is ostensibly protected as **Rondo Forest Reserve**. Despite it being coastal forest, Rondo is not actually by the sea – the generic term refers to forests watered by cyclical monsoon rains, irrespective of their actual distance from the coast. Largely trashed by commercial logging and plantations during the British period, the eighteen square kilometres of surviving semi-deciduous forest are surprisingly **biodiverse**, and include dozens of unique plants, an almost endemic species of bushbaby (the Rondo dwarf galago, discovered in the 1990s), and some extremely **rare birds**, among them the East Coast akalat, spotted ground thrush, and Rondo green barbet. There are also some rock paintings, not that many people, even locals, know where they are.

As with other East African coastal forests, Rondo is under increasing threat from logging, charcoal production and fires, and the protection afforded by its Forest Reserve status hasn't been sufficient to safeguard it. It is hoped that a mooted upgrade to Nature Reserve may stem the steady erosion of its boundaries. For now, tourists are virtually unheard of, so any visit will have an adventurous flavour.

ARRIVAL AND DEPARTURE   RONDO FOREST RESERVE

By organized tour The best way to visit the forest is on a two-day tour organized via Mikindani's *The Old Boma Hotel* (see p.175). The trip costs Tsh100,000–200,000 per person depending on group size (roughly $60–120), and includes a night at a former plantation manager's residence (a

romantic place with oil lamps, serenading cicadas and frogs, but very run down).

By 4WD If you are determined to arrange things independently, first visit the Natural Resources office in Lindi, at the Regional Administration block near the commercial harbour (☎ 023 222 0501; ask for the *Afisa ya Maliasili*), to obtain the necessary forest permit – currently $10 per person per day. The officer should be able to suggest a suitable guide, and possibly even transport, ideally a 4WD with driver. If you have your own transport, head to Nyengedi, 52km west of Lindi on the highway towards Masasi (27km west of Mingoyo, at the junction with the highway to Mtwara), where the access road to Rondo begins. Rondo village, just outside the reserve's eastern boundary, is 26km north of Nyengedi along an unpaved road that becomes treacherously muddy during the rains. In dry weather, the drive takes three hours each way from Lindi. There's no longer any good guide in Rondo for the forest, as the charming old man who used to guide visitors passed away, without, it seems, transmitting his knowledge or enthusiasm to others.

Mikindani

Set inside an almost circular, mangrove-lined harbour some 11km by road before Mtwara, **MIKINDANI** is home to fifteen thousand people, for whom the ocean is their livelihood. The peaceful, almost languid atmosphere belies a brutal past, when the town was one of the coast's major seaports for ivory- and slave-carrying **caravans**. Mikindani's stone buildings, many in ruins, are eloquent and picturesque reminders of those darker but more prosperous times, while sandy beaches on the far side of the harbour, a wide choice of excursions, a scuba diving school, and one of southern Tanzania's most beautiful hotels make it a great place to get away from it all.

Mikindani is small and shady enough to walk around, with the main sights easy to find – if in doubt, just ask a passer-by to direct you. As you're wandering along the narrow, winding streets, look for the attractive first-floor wooden balconies (*uzio*) and the elaborately carved wooden doorways, both typical of Swahili coastal settlements. Most of the stone buildings date from the slaving era and are constructed of coral rock (ragstone) embedded in lime mortar. Much of the original lime stucco facing has disappeared, but where patches remain, the buildings make photogenic subjects.

Brief history

Mikindani's sheltered location offered an ideal base for early traders sailing up and down the coast, and the town – or rather Pemba village, on the northern spur of land guarding the harbour's entrance – was swiftly incorporated into the Indian Ocean trading network. The arrival of **Arabs** in the ninth century stimulated trade, and by the end of the fifteenth century – when Mikindani proper replaced Pemba as the main port – the town was trading inland as far as present-day Malawi, Zambia, Angola and Congo.

Decline set in with the arrival of the **Portuguese**, but the town's fortunes picked up once more in the eighteenth century, once the Portuguese had left. Towards the end of the nineteenth century, the reign of Zanzibari sultan **Seyyid Barghash** saw the consolidation of the town's importance and the construction of several fine buildings, notably the Friday Mosque. The legacy of the **slave trade** is reflected in the village's tribal make-up, which includes descendants of Yao, Makua and Mwera slaves, as well as Ngoni who first came as caravan porters working for the Arabs, and Makonde, some of whom had been slave traders themselves.

German rule was marked by the introduction of cash crops such as sisal, rubber, coconut and oil seed, but failed to reverse the decline in the town's fortunes that followed the abolition of the slave trade. Things changed little under **British rule** and by the 1950s Mikindani had also outlived its usefulness as a harbour, too shallow for the vessels of the day. Come Independence, most of the area's colonial plantations were abandoned, and the town's buildings began to crumble as Mikindani reverted to its original status as a humble fishing village.

3

The Friday Mosque

Notable among the buildings dating from the reign of Sultan Barghash is the **Friday Mosque** in the centre of town. The beautiful carved door was the work of an Ndonde slave called Gulum Dosa (the Ndonde are closely related to Makonde), who belonged to an Indian customs officer in the Zanzibari government. The three **stone graves** outside the mosque are believed to date from the fifteenth century, and face north towards Mecca. They're marked by baobab trees, which has led some to believe that they belong to sultans.

The Slave Market

When the Germans arrived, slaves were still the town's most valuable asset, and it took them a while to eliminate the trade. Indeed, according to some accounts, it was the Germans themselves who built Mikindani's "**Slave Market**", at the bottom of the grand cobbled roadway leading to the German Boma. Some confusion remains about whether the building really was used as a slave market, or if it was simply built on the site of an older one. The thick walls, up to 60cm in places, seem to point to the former, which would show that slavery was at least tolerated during the early years of German occupation. Sadly, renovation has completely destroyed the charm of the previously ruined building – its wonderful pastel-shaded arches and vaults now hidden by internal walls enclosing various offices and a modest restaurant.

The German Boma

On the hill behind the village, the **German Boma** has been sensitively restored and beautifully converted into the luxurious *Old Boma Hotel*. Built in 1895 as the seat of the German colonial administration, the single-towered limewashed building is the town's most distinctive and attractive landmark, combining German, Arab and Swahili architectural elements. Visitors are welcome to look around – on entering, check out the stunning door carvings, the work of Gulum Dosa, who also carved the mosque's doorway. Inside is a cool courtyard, with rooms arranged around it on two floors. One corner of the building has a three-storey tower with crenellated battlements, resembling an Andalusian minaret. The gardens surrounding the Boma are attractive too, with colourful frangipani and flame trees providing shade and shelter for blue monkeys.

Bismarck Hill

Just behind the Boma above the coconut groves stands **Bismarck Hill**, named after the first chancellor of unified Germany – it's worth the thirty-minute climb to the top, not only for the views but also for a curious piece of history. The hill is popularly known as Baobab Hill, because of the lone baobab (*mbuyu*) on its summit. These trees are traditionally thought to be inhabited by benevolent spirits, and so were considered safe places to bury things, like money, which gave rise to the common belief that the Germans buried treasure near baobabs when they left. In this case, the great big hole on top was made by a batty treasure-seeking *maganga* (traditional healer), who, sadly for him or her, failed to find anything.

Livingstone House

At the bottom of the hill leading to the Boma, **Livingstone House** is a rather bland two-storey construction with little decoration, dating from German times. It occupies the site of an earlier house in which David Livingstone supposedly stayed in 1866 while preparing for his fifth and final expedition to the Great Lakes, which was to become famous for his encounter with Stanley (see p.390). Although his journal isn't too clear about the matter, it's more likely that Livingstone actually stayed in Pemba village on the northern lip of the bay, first camping, and then in a house rented for four dollars a month. The building here has been recently renovated and plans for its final use have yet to be agreed – check ⓦfacebook.com/oldboma for the latest.

Around the bay

Mikindani's big drawback is its lack of beach: don't be tempted by the silty shore facing either hotel – this part of the bay functions as the town's latrine. Much cleaner, and largely out of sight, is a narrow stretch of sand by the **Yacht Club**, 1.5km towards Mtwara from the hotels. The club itself is almost defunct, with no facilities other than a few tables and, for now, free use of its toilet and shower.

More private, and definitely more romantic, is a small patch of sand on the bay's southern lip, to which dhow trips can be arranged (see below). On the bay's western lip is another good stretch of sand, **Naumbu Beach**, about 7km from Mikindani. To walk or cycle, head up the road towards Lindi and bear right before the bridge and past the boatyard. The track follows an old railway embankment between the bay and the electric fence of Mikindani Estate (watch out for snakes). If you stay on the track closest to the bay you'll eventually come to **Pemba**, which has the remains of an old Arab mosque (possibly from the ninth century), and some graves. The beach is on the ocean side of the village – ask for directions.

ARRIVAL AND INFORMATION

MIKINDANI

By daladala Mikindani is easily reached from Mtwara by daladala, which run throughout the day (Tsh500); buses and Coasters between Mtwara and either Masasi, Lindi or Dar also pass through, but if you're leaving Mikindani on anything but a daladala to Mtwara, buy your ticket beforehand in Mtwara to be sure of a seat (see p.180). The bus station is in the western part of town, but you can ask to be dropped at either of the hotels, a few hundred metres to the east.
Destinations Lindi (hourly; 1hr 30min); Mtwara (frequent daladalas; 20min).

Tourist information Mikindani's hotels are useful sources of information, especially *The Old Boma Hotel*, which has dozens of useful sheets covering attractions here and elsewhere in the region. Trade Aid, the British NGO running the hotel (ⓦtradeaiduk.org), is involved in education, and the preservation of the village's historic buildings, and has long-standing plans to turn Livingstone House into a tourist information office.

TOURS AND ACTIVITIES

The Old Boma Hotel (see p.176), and eco2 dive centre, two doors down from *Ten Degrees South* (☎0784 855833 or ☎0783 279446, ⓦeco2tz.com), are the best places to head if you want to hire local guides, rent bicycles, dugouts or outriggers, or a dhow with skipper. Prices vary according to whom they contact, and group size, but shouldn't be more than Tsh20,000–40,000 for half a day.

Day-trips *The Old Boma Hotel* arranges day-long excursions by road to the Mozambique border, stopping at the Ruvuma River for a spot of hippo watching, followed by a spell on Msimbati Beach, in Mnazi Bay (Tsh150,000–200,000 per person).

Dhow rental Old Boma Hotel and eco2 dive centre can organize dhow rental for Tsh100,000 for a half day.

Kayak rental eco2 dive centre rents out kayaks for Tsh15,000/hr, or Tsh50,000/day.

Night-fishing *The Old Boma Hotel* can organize nocturnal fishing trips by canoe for around Tsh20,000.

Painting, cookery and language lessons Crash courses in Tingatinga painting, cooking, or Kiswahili can be arranged at *The Old Boma Hotel*.

Scuba diving and snorkelling eco2 is the only PADI-accredited dive centre between Mafia and Mozambique, and specializes in the otherwise unknown Mnazi Bay-Ruvuma Estuary Marine Park, south of Mtwara (see p.182). It offers the full range of PADI dive courses, from Open Water ($485 including manuals) to Dive Master, plus a few marine biology courses of their own. Snorkellers are welcome to tag along ($30 per person).

Whale watching eco2 dive centre offers humpback whale-watching trips in Sept and Oct, when cetacean mothers-to-be return to East Africa's warm waters to calve, often in the company of a "midwife" ($40 per person; minimum four people; no guarantees).

ACCOMMODATION

★**The Old Boma Hotel** On the hill behind Livingstone House ☎0784 360110, ⓦmikindani .com. Set inside the beautifully restored German Boma above the village, this is southern Tanzania's best hotel by miles, with bags of atmosphere, outstanding accommodation, and a wide range of activities and excursions (see p.175). There's also a sophisticated restaurant and bar, wi-fi in the reception, and a swimming pool. The eight high-ceilinged rooms, some with balconies, have large timber beds and are decorated with local handicrafts, and no TVs! Two rooms have a/c; thick walls, sea breezes and ceiling fans keep things cool in the others. It's worth spending a little more for a view. No smoking inside. Credit cards accepted. BB **£100**

Ten Degrees South Facing the harbour at the east end of the village ☎0766 059380 or ☎0684 059381, ⓦtendegreessouth.com. A small, welcoming and informal place with links to the eco2 scuba diving centre two doors down. It has two types of room: four in an old, cool, thick-walled house, boasting solid Zanzibari beds, walk-in mosquito nets (with fans *inside* them), clean cotton sheets, and shared bathrooms; and four rooms in a new wing by the roadside, less atmospheric but with private bathrooms, hot water, and terraces at the front ($40 extra). In between the two is Mikindani's best bar, good food, and free wi-fi. BB **$20**

EATING AND DRINKING

CCM building Behind the bus stand. An empty courtyard where discos are held. No alcohol is sold – the dancing kings and queens fuel up first at *Muku's*, opposite. Tsh2000 admission. Mostly Fri & Sat 7pm–2am.

★**The Old Boma Hotel** On the hill behind Livingstone House. Consistently delicious and inventive cooking, always with a decent selection of vegetable soups (Tsh6000), unbeatably fresh salads and herbs from their own garden, and fresh seafood, including prawns (from Tsh18,000). Eat under parasols or trees, by the pool or on a private terrace. Diners can also use the pool (Tsh6000 if you're not eating). There's also a bar. Daily 7am–9pm.

Samaki Restaurant In the Slave Market. A simple but effective *mgahawa* that serves tea, snacks and very cheap meals (fish with rice costs around Tsh2000). It's handy for breakfasts too. Daily 7am–2pm.

★**Ten Degrees South Lodge** Big portions are the norm here: the mashed potato deserves a special mention, and seafood is always good, especially the Thai prawn curry (Tsh16,000) – ask for the special chilli sauce, packed with other spices, and ginger. The real attraction, however, is the bar – good music, cold drinks, some of Tanzania's cheapest wine (Tsh15,000 a bottle), satellite TV, and often lively conversation. Restaurant daily 7am–8pm; bar daily 10am until late.

SHOPPING

Mr Kichele's and Son's Fine Art Halfway up the driveway to The Old Boma Hotel ☎0756 332838. Workshop run by a father and son, who produce all manner of paintings. The prices are reasonable, and it's not just tourist guff. Daily 8am–6pm.

The Old Boma Hotel On the hill behind Livingstone House ☎0784 360110. The hotel shop sells a good selection of unusual arts and crafts that have been sourced from a variety of self-help projects in southern Tanzania. Daily 7am–10pm.

Mtwara

The south coast's largest town, **MTWARA** lies 560km south of Dar and some 82km south of Mingoyo, close to the border with Mozambique. Once dubbed "Siberia" by civil servants because of its isolation from the rest of Tanzania, this modern town is an anomaly, and testimony to the failure of the **Groundnut Scheme** – a grand plan for regional development put into action by the British colonial powers after World War II, which saw the establishment of Mtwara itself in 1947. Unfortunately, the British never once considered whether the soil was suitable for growing groundnuts (peanuts) – it was not – and the project collapsed amid colossal losses and bitter recriminations. The 211-kilometre railway from Mtwara to Nachingwea that had been built as part of the scheme was ripped up (there are now plans to re-lay it), leaving only the empty spaces that intersperse Mtwara's broad street layout to bear witness to the grandiose and short-sighted dreams of the past.

For a few decades, the town scraped by on the fickle proceeds of the cashew-nut industry instead, plus revenue from NGOs and aid organizations. Since 2010, however, when vast reserves of **offshore gas** were discovered, work has been under way to

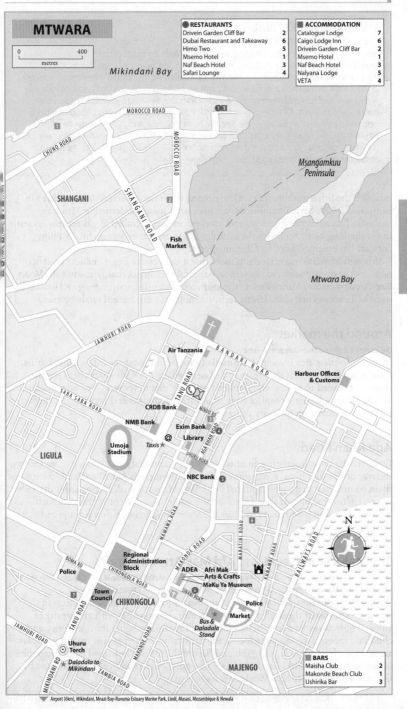

MTWARA

0	400
metres	

Mikindani Bay

Msangamkuu Peninsula

Mtwara Bay

● RESTAURANTS

Drivein Garden Cliff Bar	2
Dubai Restaurant and Takeaway	6
Himo Two	5
Msemo Hotel	1
Naf Beach Hotel	3
Safari Lounge	4

■ ACCOMMODATION

Catalogue Lodge	7
Caigo Lodge Inn	6
Drivein Garden Cliff Bar	2
Msemo Hotel	1
Naf Beach Hotel	3
Nalyana Lodge	5
VETA	4

MOROCCO ROAD

CHUNO ROAD

SHANGANI

SHANGANI ROAD

MOROCCO ROAD

Fish Market

JAMHURI ROAD

BANDARI ROAD

Air Tanzania

Harbour Offices & Customs

TANU ROAD

SABA SABA ROAD

MINDU RD

CRDB Bank

NMB Bank

Exim Bank

KSG WAMI ROAD

@

Library

Taxis ★

UHURU ROAD

Umoja Stadium

LIGULA

NBC Bank

MAKWAKWA ROAD

MAKONDE ROAD

MABATINI ROAD

KINANBI ROAD

RAILWAYS ROAD

N

BOMA RD

Police

CHIKONGOLA ROAD

Regional Administration Block

ADEA

Afri Mak Arts & Crafts

MaKu Ya Museum

SINANI ROAD

Town Council

CHIKONGOLA

TANU ROAD

Police

Market

Bus & Daladala Stand

JAMHURI ROAD

MIKINDANI RD

ZAMBIA ROAD

MAKONDE ROAD

Uhuru Torch

Daladala to Mikindani ★

MAJENGO

■ BARS

Maisha Club	2
Makonde Beach Club	1
Ushirika Bar	3

▼ Airport (6km), Mikindani, Mnazi Bay-Ruvuma Estuary Marine Park, Lindi, Masasi, Mozambique & Newala

3

THE MAKUYA FESTIVAL

First held in 2008, the **MaKuYa Festival** of traditional music was such a success that it has been repeated annually ever since, attracting ever larger crowds, almost all of them Tanzanians. The festival's name is a contraction of three major southern Tanzanian tribes, the Makonde, Makua (Kua) and Yao. All three tribes enjoy vivid **musical traditions**, including the Makonde's wonderful *sindimba* stilt dance, various masquerades capable of scattering children, and women's groups with powerful displays of drumming. The festival (W makuyafestival.blogspot.com) takes place over three days in mid-October or mid-August. It's usually hosted in Mtwara (though has been held twice in Masasi) and admission is free. The hugely popular annual festival was developed by the African Development through Economics and the Arts (ADEA) NGO, which was founded in 2003 to prioritize art as a means of development. The NGO is also responsible for the MaKuYa museum and the highly regarded crafts cooperative, Afri Mak (see below).

establish the infrastructure that will be needed when the gas starts to be pumped in earnest, in 2020. Several million dollars have been spent modernizing Mtwara's harbour, Tanzania's third busiest, and hotel prices have spiralled as gas companies settle in for the long haul. And with the asphalt road from Dar es Salaam finally built, Mtwara has emerged from its Siberian winter.

Although Mtwara's modern origins mean that it lacks even a single building or sight of note, it does sit on one of Tanzania's most beautiful stretches of coastline, while the **Mnazi Bay–Ruvuma Estuary Marine Park** to the south offers superlative swimming and snorkelling, some of Tanzania's best scuba-diving reefs, and miles of palm-fringed sandy beaches.

Around the market

One block east of the bus stand • Daily sunrise–sunset

Mtwara's liveliest area is around the **market** (Soko Kuu) near the bus station, but its most interesting sight is the area north of here, where the wide spaces between the roads – intended to have been populated by a city that never was – are now filled with almost village-like life, complete with small farms and plots and pecking chickens: really quite endearing for a city centre.

Aga Khan Road

Probably the most interesting architectural sight – and that's stretching it – are the two terraces of two-storey concrete stores facing one another on **Aga Khan Road**, the town's main commercial drag, where pirated Nigerian videos sell well. Dating from the 1950s to the 1970s, the pillared shop fronts are the modern equivalent of the traditional balconied Swahili townhouses you can still see in Mikindani, Kilwa Kivinje and elsewhere.

The MaKuYa Museum and Afri Mak Arts and Crafts

Sinani Rd • Free, but contributions welcome for the museum • W adeaafrica.org • **MaKuYa Museum** Mon–Sat 8.30am–5pm • ☎ 0784 491471 • **Afri Mak Arts and Crafts** Mon–Sat 8.30am–5.30pm, Sun 1–5.30pm • ☎ 0786 738900 or 0714 005657

The **MaKuYa Museum** displays many of the masks used by traditional dancers in previous editions of the MaKuYa Festival (see above), together with all manner of cultural objects sourced from across southern Tanzania, ranging from jewellery and children's toys to farming implements and musical instruments. The items on display are extensively captioned in English and Kiswahili, and accompanied by photographs of the items in use, and historical photos of similar objects and ceremonies made by German ethnographer Karl Weule over a century ago.

FROM TOP RUINS OF THE GREAT MOSQUE, KILWA KISIWANI (PP.165–166); HAIR BRAIDING IN MIKINDANI (P.173)

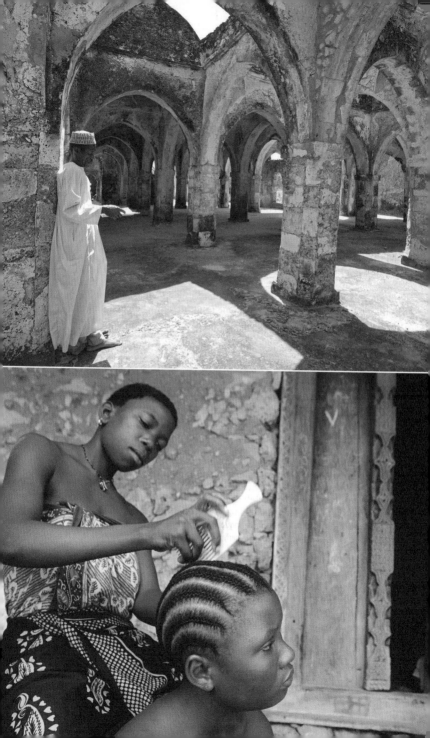

The same building houses the **Afri Mak Arts and Crafts** cooperative, where several dozen artists in residence produce highly inventive and elegant arts and crafts, such as Tingatinga paintings, Makonde carvings, batik work and tailoring. You're welcome to drop in for a chat, watch the artists at work, and buy some of their handicrafts.

Shangani beaches

2km north of town • There's no public transport so *bajajs* are best unless you're happy walking

The town's main beaches are in the NGO-colonized suburb of **Shangani**. The beach on the north side is quite rocky and has little sand, but the views (variegated blues and greens) are blissful, as is – for most of the year – the breeze. Swimming is only possible at high tide; at low tide, kids can rummage around the exposed coral pools in search of crabs and other critters. The water is quite clean, although the beaches can get covered in seaweed. Access to the shoreline is possible all the way along, so there are plenty of fine **picnic** sites to choose from.

Msangamkuu beaches

Across the harbour • The car-carrying MV *Mafanikio* makes the ten-minute journey throughout the day from the jetty beside the fish market • Tsh500

Msangamkuu – the "Big Sand" – is a giant spit of land, coral and sand across the harbour entrance where you'll find some really attractive beaches. There are ocean-facing beaches on either side of the ferry jerry: an ever-changing sand spit to the southwest, and a seemingly endless stretch to the northeast, whose first four kilometres – as far as Msangamkuu village – are virtually deserted. Don't bring valuables, but if you must, don't leave them unattended.

ARRIVAL AND DEPARTURE   MTWARA

Mtwara's expansive street layout isn't conducive to walking: the best way around is by *bajaj*, which can be found at the bus stand, at the Uhuru Torch roundabout, and at the corner of TANU and Uhuru roads. Taxis charge Tsh4000–5000 for most journeys within town, *bajajs* half that.

By bus The bus and daladala stand is beside the market. Safety is a problem, especially now that the road to Dar is paved, making it perilously fast. Maning Nice (☎ 0655 689789 in Dar) is considered safest (three a day, the last at 12.30pm), while Chatco, Machinga Transport and Southern Express are known for their speed. For Kilwa, catch a daladala or Coaster to Lindi, and change there (the last leave Lindi at around 2pm). Destinations Dar (8–10 daily; 9hr); Lindi (hourly; 1hr

30min); Masasi (4–5 daily; 4hr); Mikindani (frequent daladalas; 20min); Newala (1–2 daily; 4–5hr).
By plane The airport is 6km south of town. Flights to and from Dar es Salaam (1–2 daily; 1hr–1hr 15min) are operated by Precisionair, at the post office, TANU Rd (☎ 023 233 4116 or 0787 818442, ⊛ precisionairtz.com), and, much cheaper, Air Tanzania, Korosho House, TANU Rd (☎ 023 233 3417, ⊛ airtanzania.co.tz).

ACCOMMODATION

Mtwara's hotel prices have spiralled under demand from gas companies, but there are still some gems, including one right on the shore. Electricity is quite reliable by Tanzanian standards, but Mtwara's tap water can contain sediment, so is unsafe to drink.

Caigo Lodge Inn Off Mabatini Rd ☎ 0784 766580. One of the cheaper options, and okay for that, especially if you appreciate the bar at the side beneath a tree, which is quiet, but does attract boozers throughout the day. Just six rooms, all en suite, one with a fan (which costs half the price, the others with a/c. Safe parking. BB (a/c) <u>Tsh20,000</u>
Catalogue Lodge West of TANU Rd, near the police station ☎ 023 233 4713 or ☎ 0715 460405. A friendly place offering nine en-suite one-bed rooms (which can be

shared) with clean squat toilets, fans, a/c, wi-fi and local TV. The rooms behind the bar are small and quite basic despite their accessories; the more expensive ones at the side are bigger and in much better condition. BB <u>Tsh30,000</u>
Drivein Garden Cliff Bar 1.3km west of the end of Shangani Rd, Shangani ☎ 0784 503007. On the land side of the road next to the shore, this quirky place occupies a lushly vegetated former ragstone quarry. It started as a garden bar and campsite, but now also has a restaurant (see

below) and two rooms in a big rondavel, which is very well priced for the location (so book ahead), with box nets, fans and the inevitable bucket in the bathroom. BB Tsh20,000

★**Msemo Hotel** Shangani ☎0786 678283, ✉hotelmsemo@gmail.com. Currently Mtwara's only shore-side hotel, with some of the town's most comfortable and charming rooms. The best are in individual bungalows ($20 more), all large with high ceilings, tiled, with Zanzibar-style *semadari* four-poster beds, box nets, cable TV, fridge and kettle, a/c and fan, and – best of all – unimpeded sea views from their verandas. The standard rooms are fine, too, and most of them also have good sea views, though they are slightly less well kept, and with local TV rather than cable. The beach is mainly wild and strewn with jagged blocks of blackened coral, but there's a sandier section at one end. There's a Maasai-run souvenir emporium in the parking area, wi-fi at reception, and safe parking. BB $80

Naf Beach Hotel 1.6km west of the end of Shangani Rd, Shangani ☎023 233 4706, ⊕nafbeachhotels.com. Mtwara's newest business-class hotel on the land side of the road, with a stunning view, so spend a bit more ($30 extra) for a sea-facing room. Understated it is not: it's on

four storeys wrapped in blueish glass and gold panels, with lift shafts on the exterior, but the rooms themselves are surprisingly elegant, well kept, and well equipped (the a/c is necessary given the huge windows, which trap a lot of heat). All the rooms have wi-fi; there's also a tacky bar, and a dull restaurant. BB $100

Nalyana Lodge Off Mabatini Rd ☎0755 777715. A modern, calm, friendly Muslim-run place, with large, well-kept en-suite rooms, all with big double beds, a/c, fan, satellite TV, cotton sheets and box nets, and wi-fi throughout. Couples sharing rooms must be married. Secure parking. BB double Tsh40,000, twin Tsh50,000

VETA 1.8km west of the end of Shangani Rd, Shangani ☎023 233 4094, ✉vetasoutheast@yahoo.com. On the other side of the road from the beautiful beach, this walled-in hotel is attached to a training institute, and has eager-to-please staff and breezy, well-tended rooms equipped with cable TV – the front ones have nice views. "Singles" can be shared by couples; if you need more space, opt for a suite (Tsh25,000 extra). The reception has wi-fi, and the restaurant is decent. The beach here is shallow and rocky, so not much good for swimming, but the hotel has a pool. BB Tsh35,000

EATING AND DRINKING

RESTAURANTS

Drivein Garden Cliff Bar 1.3km west of the end of Shangani Rd, Shangani. A great excuse for a wander along Shangani's shoreline, the lush garden here comes complete with a tidal pond. A walkway over the pond leads to one of several gazebos scattered around, where you can eat or drink. The restaurant mainstays are half chicken and chips (Tsh10,000), prawns (Tsh12,000) and succulent pork chops (Tsh15,000). Daily noon–10pm.

Dubai Restaurant and Takeaway Sinani Rd. One of several cheap restaurants in this area, serving breakfast (including reasonable *supu*), snacks (the *katlesi* meat "chops" are excellent) and full meals (Tsh4000) in efficient cafeteria style. Avoid the stringy chicken, but the stews are excellent, as is the *pilau*. No alcohol. Daily 8am–10pm.

Himo 2 Makonde Rd. The best choice for meat, including a famed chicken masala, grilled on the pavement outside, though it's not so good for snacks, many of which get the microwave treatment, making them soggy. A full plate averages Tsh7000, including a mutton biriani Mon–Fri. It also serves jackfruit juice. No alcohol. Daily 7am–10pm.

★**Msemo Hotel** Shangani. The views from the breezy seaside terrace are beguiling in themselves, and the food's not bad either: grilled seafood costs Tsh15,000–18,000, but the rest of the menu is mostly continental, including steaks and pasta. There's also a well-stocked bar. Daily 11am–10.45pm

Naf Beach Hotel 1.6km west of the end of Shangani Rd, Shangani. Sometimes, unimaginative can be good, especially if you're craving a steak, which will set you back around Tsh15,000 any which way you want it, and with an

egg on top. Basic fish dishes are similarly priced, except the lobster (Tsh22,500), but most of the menu is Indian, plus sizzlers. Supposedly open 24hrs.

Safari Lounge Aga Khan Rd. This kitsch cocktail lounge comes with lots of stained burgundy velour, nasty 1970s furniture and mirror balls that wouldn't look out of place in a Vegas casino. By night, it's something of a pick-up joint, but by day it's an affordable restaurant (and bar), with wooden tables outside on the street-corner veranda. Most mains cost Tsh8000 (including fish fingers!), except the chicken, which is only Tsh6000. Daily 7am–midnight.

BARS

Maisha Club Morocco Rd, Shangani. A very fashionable outdoor club playing the latest cheesy Bongo Flava on a powerful sound rig. It's also known for its grilled octopus (Tsh10,000 for half, which is more than enough for one person). Ladies night is Thurs; otherwise entrance costs Tsh10,000–15,000. Wed–Sun 10pm–6am.

Makonde Beach Club Chuno Rd, 300m from Shangani St. Mtwara's main nightspot is a big, brash *makuti*-thatched club by the beach (but separated from it by a chicken wire fence). It makes a pleasant venue for an afternoon drink, but gets busy during the thrice-weekly discos (Tsh5000), which are in a two-storey building with padded walls, that feels like a firetrap. Food includes bar stalwarts like *nyama choma* and *chipsi mayai*, plus fish with *ugali* (Tsh10,000). Bar daily 8am–midnight, disco Wed, Fri & Sat 10pm–4am or 5am.

★**Msemo Hotel** Shangani Elegant and blissfully located

MNAZI BAY-RUVUMA
ESTUARY MARINE PARK

Mikindani Bay

Msangamkuu

MARINE PARK

Mongo
Island

INDIAN OCEAN

Kisima
Ndogo
Island

Mtwara
Bay

Sinde

Namponda
Island

Mtwara

Mnazi
Bay

Msimbati
Peninsula

Ruvula

Ruvula Sea Safari

Mangamba

✈ **Airport**

Ziwani

Natural gas
extraction

⊠ **Marine Park Gate**
Msimbati

Mngoji

Madimba

Litembe

MARINE PARK

Tangazo

N

Kitunguli

Ferry

Kilambo

MOZAMBIQUE

▼ Namoto & Mocimboa da Praia

over the rocks at the end of Shangani Beach, with a fantastic ocean view, and perfect sunsets. Drinks are reasonably priced, and they're happy to do cocktails, too. Daily 11am–10.45pm.

DIRECTORY

Internet Reliable internet cafés include *Info Solution*, CCM Building, Uhuru Rd (Mon–Fri 8.30am–9.30pm, Sat 8.30am–noon), and *Posta*, beside the post office (Mon–Fri 8am–4.30pm, Sat 9am–noon).

Money The following banks have 24hr ATMs that accept foreign cards: NBC, Uhuru Rd; CRDB, TANU Rd; and Exim, Aga Khan Rd.

Swimming pool VETA, 1.8km west of the end of Shangani Rd, Shangani (Tsh5000; closes at 6pm).

Mnazi Bay–Ruvuma Estuary Marine Park

Entrance fees of $20 per day (payable in shillings or dollars) are paid at the Marine Park Gate just beyond Msimbati village • ⓦ marineparks.go.tz

Established in 2000, **Mnazi Bay–Ruvuma Estuary Marine Park** covers a large part of the land and ocean southeast of Mtwara between Msangamkuu Peninsula and the mouth of the Ruvuma River on the Mozambique border, encompassing a network of estuarine, mangrove, tidal, peninsular, island and coral reef environments. The reefs offer superb snorkelling and diving, especially on **Ruvula Reef**, off the north end of Msimbati Peninsula, which slopes steeply right up to the shore, while the **beaches**

CROSSING THE MOZAMBIQUE BORDER

Tanzanian visas can be bought on arrival, but **Mozambican visas** cannot, so, if you don't have one, visit the Mozambican embassy in Dar before heading on (see p.113).

KILAMBO CROSSING

The main border crossing is across the Ruvuma River at Kilambo, 5km south of Kitunguli village, and 40km south of Mtwara. The 2km crossing is by landing craft (Tsh500 per person; Tsh30,000 for a car), but is subject to the whims of the river's ever-changing sand banks and tides. Pick-ups and daladalas from Mtwara tend to leave in time to coincide with anticipated crossings (high tide), but the service may not operate during and after heavy rains if the river is in spate. Once in Mozambique, *chapas* (daladalas) cover the 8km to the immigration post at Namoto.

UNITY BRIDGE CROSSING

The 720-metre **Unity Bridge** over the Ruvuma, inaugurated in 2010, was supposed to become the main border crossing, but for some incomprehensible reason was placed not at the coast where it would have been useful, or close to Newala, but in a tsetse-fly infested area far away from any town. Access on the Tanzanian side is easy enough, along 70km of unsurfaced but decent road from Nangomba, 40km west of Masasi, but on the Mozambican side you face 175km of unimproved dirt to Mueda, which becomes impassible in the rains. More accessible is the **Unity Bridge 2** crossing (see p.449), south of Songea towards the west.

BY BOAT

The only **ferries** to Mozambique are on Lake Nyasa via Malawi (see p.445). On the coast, you might find a commercial dhow or motorboat from Mtwara to either Mocímboa da Praia (at least 48hr; $15 or so) or Pemba (not the Zanzibar one!): enquire at Mtwara's harbour office in the main port complex (Mon–Fri 8am–5pm; ☏ 023 233 3243). You'll need to clear customs there, too, and immigration at the Regional Administration Block on TANU Rd in Mtwara. Be prepared to grovel at all these places, as service with a smile is not their style.

– with all the white sand, fringing palm trees and warm turquoise water you've dreamed of – are among Tanzania's most enthralling.

The easiest beach to access is just beyond **Msimbati** village and the park gate, though it's used by fishermen for peeling prawns and cleaning fish. Much nicer is the one after **Ruvula**, 6km northwest of Msimbati village on the tip of the peninsula, and backed by thick vegetation. Here, it's possible to arrange **dhow trips** with local fishermen to Namponda Island, 3km offshore; with more time, you could also explore Mongo Island and the diminutive Kisima Ndogo Island nearby. A word of caution when swimming: there's a **dangerous undertow** at Msimbati beach and possibly elsewhere at spring tide (new moon and full moon), so seek local advice.

ARRIVAL AND DEPARTURE MNAZI BAY–RUVUMA ESTUARY MARINE PARK

By daladala The heart of the park, Msimbati Peninsula, is a couple of hours from Mtwara by daladala, which go as far as Msimbati village, 2km short of Msimbati beach. To get to Ruvula, at the tip of the peninsula, either walk the remaining 8km along a sandy track, or hitch – you shouldn't have to wait long as there are plenty of workers travelling to and from the gas plant at the end of the peninsula.

By car Driving from Mtwara takes around an hour: head south from Uhuru Torch roundabout for 900m and turn left; after 3.7km, turn left again, off the tarmac, on to the wide

murram (clay and gravel) road for Kilambo. The turning for Msimbati is at Madimba, 17.5km along the *murram* road. The rest of the drive is deep sand.

By organized tour Day-long excursions combining hippo-spotting on the Ruvuma River with time at Msimbati Beach are run by *The Old Boma Hotel* in Mikindani (see p.175), while the eco2 dive centre, also in Mikindani (see p.175), runs snorkelling and scuba-diving trips in and around the marine park. If you're coming by boat on a diving or snorkelling trip, the dive centre will collect the park entrance fees.

ACCOMMODATION

Ruvula Sea Safari Lodge Ruvula beach ☏ 0784 367439. If you ignore the gas plant at the end of the

beach 2.5km southwest (which doesn't impinge on the sea views), this place is idyllically sited, on the

THE MAKONDE AND THEIR CARVINGS

The Makonde Plateau, as you might guess, is home to the **Makonde**, one of Tanzania's largest and most heterogeneous tribes, who have achieved worldwide fame for their woodcarvings (see p.73). They're also one of Tanzania's more traditional societies, having historically preferred to remain isolated from their neighbours, and wisely so: for much of the eighteenth and nineteenth centuries, southern Tanzania was lacerated by slave raids, but the steep-sided plateau was left largely untouched.

The birth of their celebrated woodcarving tradition is entwined with the **mythical origin** of the Makonde themselves, similar to the story of Adam and Eve. Instead of a rib, the lonely male forebear carved a female figure from a piece of wood, and placed it beside his dwelling. Presto, the following morning the figure had transformed into a beautiful woman. They conceived a child, but it died three days later, so they moved upriver, but their second child died as well. So, they moved up in to the highlands, where their third child was born and survived.

The myth alludes to the Makonde's **migration** away from the frequently flooded lowlands of northern Mozambique. Up on the plateau, their isolation from other tribes meant that they kept some **traditions** that were lost elsewhere, including matrilineal descent. Motherhood is also a quasi-sacred state of being, and such is the female domination of Makonde society that older men travelling alone may take a carved female figurine with them for protection.

Another traditional form of Makonde carving is **masks**, representing spirits or ancestors and commonly used in dances for initiation ceremonies and harvest celebrations. There are three main kinds: face masks, body masks (which cover the dancer's torso) and helmet masks (*mapiko*), worn over the head like helmets, and which represent a terrifying force: whether traditional spirits, turbaned slave traders, or even Europeans. The masks are made and kept in a secret bush location known as *mpolo*, which women are forbidden to approach. *Mapiko* dances and *sindimba* dances (in which the dancers perform on stilts called *machopila*) still take place every year when a new generation is initiated into adulthood. If you can time your visit with Mtwara's MaKuYa festival in August or October (see p.178), you're almost guaranteed to see this. For more on the Makonde, pictures and sound clips, visit ⓦ bluegecko.org/kenya/tribes/makonde.

west-facing tip of Msimbati Peninsula, with powdery soft white sandy beaches either side. The sparsely furnished stone *bandas* (sharing bathrooms) are rather run down and massively overpriced (but should be negotiable), but for camping it's perfect: the showers and toilets are simple but work, and good meals are available if pre-ordered. Self-catering is possible, as most of the basics, including fish, can be bought from locals, and firewood from the lodge. Boat trips can be arranged to the islands and for snorkelling, but bring your own equipment. Camping per person $12, rooms $45

The Makonde Plateau and westwards

Rising just north of the Ruvuma River, which marks the boundary between Tanzania and Mozambique, the **Makonde Plateau** is a river-gouged massif peaking at 900m and the region's main geographical feature. The plateau's abrupt southern edge is quite spectacular, but the plateau itself is pretty rather than beautiful, the main attraction being its deeply rural nature. The main town is **Newala**, on the plateau's southwestern edge and within walking distance of jaw-dropping views over the Ruvuma River and Mozambique. Dusty **Masasi**, in the lowlands to the west, is Tanzania's cashew-nut capital, with several climbable granite inselbergs nearby (outcrops, usually devoid of vegetation), two of which have **Neolithic rock paintings**. Beyond, the only settlement of note is **Tunduru**, a rough and ready gemstone mining town along the road to Songea.

Newala

A fine base for exploring the Makonde Plateau, the town of **NEWALA** is perched on the plateau's southwestern rim, and makes a pleasant stopover if you're taking the direct but unsurfaced road from Mtwara to Masasi. The views from the edge of town, where the plateau gives way to the valley of the Ruvuma River half a kilometre below, are invigorating. Equally refreshing is the town's relatively cool climate: considered glacial by locals, it should be just right for foreigners, though you'll still have to contend with mosquitoes. The town centre is at the junction of the roads from Mtwara and Masasi. The **market** (and post office) is 200m southwest of here at the start of the town's main street, a broad, tree-lined avenue of vibrant orange sand.

German Boma
1.3km southwest of the centre

Newala's oldest building is the squat **German Boma**, unusual for its sloping black walls. The Boma is occupied by the police, who, uniquely, are quite happy having tourists poke around; indeed, they have a guest book, and will likely give you a guided tour, too. Behind the Boma, which is built on a spur of land jutting out from the plateau rim, the land plunges away on three sides, giving fantastic **views** over a distance of nearly 100km, including the Ruvuma River (the beige band of sand), Mozambique, and the isolated peaks around Masasi in the far west.

Shimo la Mungu

A particularly vertiginous drop can be seen from **Shimo la Mungu** ("God's Hole"), just to the north of the German Boma. The easiest way there is to backtrack 400m along the avenue from the Boma, then turn left (north) along another tree-lined road. After 700m you cross the west end of the airstrip and the escarpment is just beyond it on your left. Alternatively, pay some local kids to show you the way.

3

ARRIVAL AND DEPARTURE   **NEWALA**

By bus Newala's bus stand is on the road in from Mtwara, 800m northeast of the town centre. Transport to and from Masasi runs until 4pm, but if you're heading to Mtwara, Lindi or Dar, it's best to start early: the first buses head off at 5am. Destinations Dar (daily; 11–12hr); Lindi (2–3 daily; 4–5hr); Masasi (hourly; 2hr 30min); Mtwara (1–2 daily;

4–5hr).
By car If you're driving from Mtwara during heavy rains, take the longer route via Mtama (on the paved Mingoyo–Masasi road), as the direct road via Nanyamba is prone to flooding and sections of it can be very muddy, though work has begun on paving it.

THE MAKUA

The **Makua**, like their neighbours the Makonde and Yao, were originally from what's now northern Mozambique, and settled in the region around Masasi most likely in the sixteenth century. They called their new home Machashi, describing the head of the wild millet plant, which was large and heavy with grain here. In the eighteenth and nineteenth centuries, Masasi – as the first properly productive land encountered by caravans arriving from the west – became an important stopping point for **slavers**, who picked up not just victuals but many of the inhabitants, who were scattered far and wide; some of their descendants include a community of over two hundred thousand hundred Makua in Madagascar.

The caravan road also attracted **missionaries**, including Masasi's first Anglican bishop, **William Vincent Lucas**, who made his mark by pioneering (in 1925) a Christian version of the traditional Jando **initiation ceremony** for boys. The combination of circumcision and Christian confirmation flew in the face of more orthodox Christian beliefs, and the new rite was accused of being "little better than an orgy". But Lucas's show of respect for local traditions – which he rather unfortunately once described as "a wonderful opportunity … for the Christian priest of getting into real personal touch with his boys" – won over the Makua. Another winsome Bishop who graced Masasi (1960–68) was **Trevor Huddlestone**, a long-standing opponent of southern Africa's apartheid regimes.

For a good overview of **Makua traditions**, which in many ways mirror those of other Tanzanian tribes, read *Excerpts of Makua Traditions* by Father Kubat and Brother Mpokasaye, at ⓦ sds-ch.ch/centre/artyk/articel/makua.htm.

ESSENTIALS

Banks Bring all the money you'll need, as Newala's bank, NMB, is in no hurry to change cash, and its ATM only take local plastic. The closest ATMs for foreign cards are in Masasi.

Bike rental You can rent bicycles at a stand facing the side of the post office at the edge of the market (just remember that what goes down has to be ridden or pushed back up).

Car rental For longer or lazier excursions, including down to the Ruvuma River, *Country Lodge* (see below) rents out a Land Cruiser with driver for about a dollar a km.

ACCOMMODATION AND EATING

There's a scatter of decent guesthouses on the road leading into town from the bus stand. For local bars, filled with young women and older men, try any of the places between *Country Lodge* and the town centre, and around the corner from the post office facing the market. Newala has water problems, so don't drink the tap water, and don't expect hotel showers to work. Also, don't count on electricity: if they receive more than a few hours' a day, the locals feel blessed.

Country Lodge 1.8km from the bus stand: walk 700m into the town centre, take the first major right, then right again on to the Masasi road – it's 900m on the right ☎ 023 241 0355. The town's oldest proper hotel, and still its most comfortable, with fine en-suite rooms, twin or double beds with matching nets, plus a sofa, chair and table, and local TV. The restaurant here is a large thatched affair, which serves uncommonly good seafood (Tsh8000, a little more for prawns), and doubles as a bar. BB **Tsh40,000**

Masasi

Sprawling along almost 5km of highway, the scruffy crossroads town of **MASASI** lies west of the Makonde Plateau, on the edge of a weird and wonderful landscape characterized by isolated inselbergs. Of interest mainly to cashew-nut (*korosho*) traders, the town itself lacks an obvious focus, though it does boast some interesting **rock art** at nearby Mtandi Hill. It also makes a reasonable stop for travellers heading on to Tunduru (for Songea and Lake Nyasa) or Mozambique.

Mtandi Hill rock art

From Masasi's western bus stand, follow the highway east towards Lindi for 3.5km, then take the left fork (signposted to the Anglican cathedral); the cathedral is 1km further on, where you can ask for a guide to show you the rock art on the inselberg just behind.

A trip to see Masasi's prehistoric **rock art** is as good an excuse as any to go poking around the inselbergs on the north side of town. Located in natural shelters, the red ochre paintings are abstract and geometric and, unlike Kondoa-Irangi's rock art (see p.223), include what are thought to be "sun symbols" (circles with radiating lines), as well as stylized axes. Visitors should avoid touching or getting the paintings wet, as this can cause damage.

TUNDURU'S MAN-EATERS

Tunduru District is known for its **man-eating lions**, so you should avoid camping wild, and, if you've broken down, stay close to your vehicle. The gruesome attacks, some even on the edge of Tunduru town, started in the 1980s, and continued until at least 2007, since when no attacks have been reported (though that's not to say that none have occurred). The most infamous attacks were in 1986, when a single lion claimed the lives of 42 inhabitants. The problem was given a surreal slant by superstitious locals, who have long feared the powerful reputation of Mozambique's **witch doctors**. The tale goes that a man had a quarrel with a neighbour, so crossed over the border to consult a witch, who gave him a rope that could be turned into a lion to attack his neighbour if he followed strict instructions. The man returned home and created the lion, but forgot the instructions and was promptly gobbled up, which is how the lion acquired its taste for humans. The more prosaic explanation is that Tunduru sits in the wildlife corridor between Tanzania's Selous Game Reserve and Mozambique's Reserva do Niassa, which wasn't a problem until Mozambique's brutal sixteen-year civil war wreaked havoc on the country's wildlife habitats, with the result that the big cats started looking elsewhere for their meals.

ARRIVAL AND DEPARTURE MASASI

By bus and minibus All the main roads to Masasi are tarred, so there's plenty of transport – usually daladalas or Coaster minibuses. Most buses and daladalas terminate at the main bus stand at the west end town, at the junction to Nachingwea, Newala and Tunduru. Vehicles coming from the east stop first at another stand 1.4km short of the junction, near the market and post office. Both stands are relatively calm. With the exception of buses to Dar, which run to schedule (6am departures), vehicles leave when full, which rarely entails having to wait more than an hour. The last services for Newala, Lindi and Mtwara head off in time to arrive around 6pm.

Destinations Dar (3–4 daily; 9hr); Lindi (4–6 daily; 2hr 30min); Mikindani (3–4 daily; 3hr 30min); Mtwara (4–5 daily; 4hr); Newala (hourly; 2hr 30min); Songea (1 daily; 13hr); Tunduru (hourly; 4–5hr).

Banks Both NBC, at the eastern bus stand, and CRDB bank, 400m southwest of the main bus stand along the road to Tunduru, have ATMs that accept international Visa and MasterCard.

ACCOMMODATION AND EATING

Most of Masasi's hotels, restaurants and bars are on the main road between the two bus stands. Many of the restaurants are primarily bars that also serve food, mainly the ubiquitous *ugali*, *nyama choma* and sometimes fried fish. You won't find much to write home about, though the local relish sold in the markets is worth searching out – ask for *kiungo cha embe* if you like mangoes, or *kiungo cha ndimo* for one made with lime. If you're feeling brave, seek out the local brew made from the distilled fermented juice of "cashew-apples" (*mabibo* or *makanju*) – the pulpy fruit that grows just above the nut.

Holiday Motel 70m east of the crossroads by the main (western) bus stand ☎0784 727911 or ☎0786 105487. Seven small, older but perfectly acceptable en-suite rooms with local TV, plus some swankier new rooms at twice the price. The former are often full, and the place has a solemn, almost institutional feel. **Tsh15,000**

Masasi Inn 200m east of the crossroads by the main (western) bus stand ☎0713 216342 or ☎023 251 0353.

Friendly, with six very well-kept modern rooms, all big-bedded "singles" (that can be shared by couples), fitted with good beds, a/c, TV, desk and fridge. The bar/restaurant is in a thatched two-storey building at the front, with TVs screening sports, and a menu that includes fish either fried or cooked in coconut sauce (mains around Tsh7000). Safe parking. Restaurant and bar daily 6am–10pm. BB **Tsh35,000**

Tunduru

The 196km tarred road between Masasi and Tunduru is an attractive one, ducking and swooping between huge eroded inselbergs before entering a forested area south of Selous Game Reserve. There's little reason to stop over in the rough mining town of **TUNDURU** unless gemstones are your thing – sapphires, rubies and alexandrite (trichroic, like tanzanite) are all mined here. Mining, so far entirely alluvial and thus dry-season only (mostly October and November), started here in the early 1990s, and has peaked several times since.

ARRIVAL AND DEPARTURE TUNDURU

By bus The Tunduru–Songea route has least two jam-packed buses a day in either direction, leaving both towns at 6am (2 daily; 7–8hr). In the rains, the buses are replaced by Land Rovers ("One Tens"), which also get packed to the seams and make the buses seem luxurious in comparison. The last bus for Masasi (hourly; 4–5hr) leaves at 2pm.

By 4WD Work is currently under way to pave the remaining 273km road west to Songea. Until it is fully tarred, the challenges for drivers are loose sand in the dry season, and mud in the rains, in which you're guaranteed to get stuck, so it's best to fill up with as many passengers as possible to provide muscle power when horse power fails. Alternatively, travel in a convoy. Needless to say, the route shouldn't be attempted by drivers not entirely confident in rough conditions, or not equipped with a reliable high-clearance 4WD, shovel, tow rope, spare oil, water and brake fluid.

ACCOMMODATION AND EATING

Mainland Hotel 300m from the bus stand towards Songea. Restaurant whose printed menu is wishful thinking, but you should be able to order, at least, their stock dish of rice with meat or beans. Mon–Fri 7am–8pm, Sat & Sun erratic hours.

Nyololo Lodge On the main road, 50m from the bus stand towards Masasi ☎025 268 0333. Recently refurbished, handily located, and therefore pick of the lot, with decent and clean en-suite rooms, complete with TVs. **Tsh15,000**

Central Tanzania

YELLOW-BILLED STORK, SELOUS GAME RESERVE

Central Tanzania

Tanzania's heartland is an amorphous region that has something for everyone: forest-cloaked mountains, unspoiled wildlife, swamps and meandering rivers, fascinating cultures, and art created back in the mists of time. First stop from Dar is the lively town of Morogoro, snug in the lee of the Uluguru Mountains, whose rich ecology and fascinating Luguru culture – one of Tanzania's few remaining matrilineal societies – provide an excellent reason to linger. Offering even better hiking for nature lovers are the rain-soaked Udzungwa Mountains, which, like Uluguru, are part of the ancient Eastern Arc mountain chain, and whose pristine rainforest is extraordinarily rich in primates, butterflies and birds.

For most visitors, though, central Tanzania boils down to a couple of more "traditional" national parks that form the backbone of the **Southern Safari Circuit**. For a chance to quickly spot most of the species you might want to see in Tanzania, including otherwise rare African hunting dogs, head to **Mikumi National Park**, close to Morogoro, which you can also see for free, if fleetingly, from any bus travelling along the Tanzam highway. Adjoining Mikumi's southern boundary is Africa's second-largest protected wildlife area, **Selous Game Reserve**, which you can explore on foot or by boat as well as on a game drive. The reserve's beautiful northern sector, watered by the **Rufiji River**, is a haven for animals (including birds, crocodiles and hippos), and heaven for safari-goers, though you'll need to be patient, as Selous' luxuriant vegetation can make animals difficult to spot. There are elephants, too, currently suffering industrial-scale poaching.

West of Mikumi and Selous, the very centre of Tanzania comes as quite a shock: unremittingly dry and dusty, and only sparsely vegetated, it's home to the hardy **Gogo tribe**, owners of one of Africa's most bewitching musical traditions. In the middle of their traditional terrain is **Dodoma**, the planned (but never quite completed) city that has served, in name at least, as Tanzania's capital since 1973. North of here the land rises sharply into the Irangi Hills, which contain some of the oldest and most beautiful **paleolithic rock paintings** on earth. The paintings can be visited via **cultural tourism** programmes, one centred on Kondoa but based in Arusha, the other in Babati, which also organizes climbs up **Mount Hanang** volcano, and intimate get-togethers with traditional **Barbaig** cattle-herders.

Morogoro

The bustling crossroads town of **MOROGORO**, 190km west of Dar es Salaam, has doubled its population over the last decade to more than 350,000, but retains a

Highlights

❶ Uluguru Mountains Waterfalls galore, forests and enjoyable encounters with the Luguru are some of the attractions when hiking (or biking) around these rugged old hills. **See p.197**

❷ Mikumi National Park Heaps of plains game within easy reach of Dar, including lions, elephants and even African hunting dogs. **See p.200**

❸ Selous Game Reserve Watered by the ever-photogenic Rufiji River, the inhabitants of Africa's second-largest wildlife sanctuary can be seen by boat, on foot, or on a game drive. **See p.204**

❹ Udzungwa Mountains Stretch your legs for an hour, or over five days, in Tanzania's most immaculate rainforest, which dozens of unique animal species call home. **See p.210**

❺ Kondoa-Irangi rock art Peek at the past through some of Africa's oldest and most beautiful prehistoric paintings, dating back 19,000 years, or more. **See p.221**

❻ Babati Climb Mount Hanang, dance with traditional Barbaig cattle-herders, or dodge hippos from a canoe on Lake Babati. **See p.222**

HIGHLIGHTS ARE MARKED ON THE MAP ON P.192

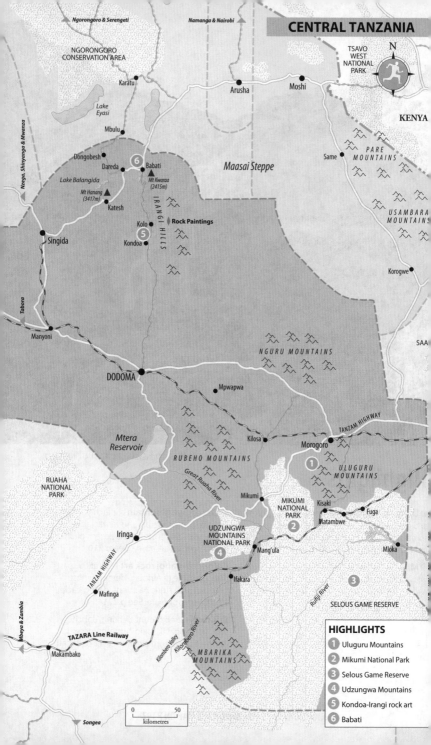

CENTRAL TANZANIA

Ngorongoro & Serengeti

Namanga & Nairobi

TSAVO WEST NATIONAL PARK

N

NGORONGORO CONSERVATION AREA

Karatu

Arusha

Moshi

KENYA

Lake Eyasi

Mbulu

Maasai Steppe

Same

PARE MOUNTAINS

Nzega, Shinyanga & Mwanza

Dongobesh

Dareda

⑥ Babati

Mt Kwaraa (2415m)

Lake Balangida

Mt Hanang (3417m)

Katesh

Kolo **Rock Paintings**

⑤

Kondoa

IRANGI HILLS

USAMBARA MOUNTAINS

Singida

Korogwe

Tabora

Manyoni

NGURU MOUNTAINS

SAA

DODOMA

Mpwapwa

RUBEHO MOUNTAINS

Kilosa

Morogoro ①

TANZAM HIGHWAY

ULUGURU MOUNTAINS

Mtera Reservoir

Great Ruaha River

RUAHA NATIONAL PARK

Mikumi

MIKUMI NATIONAL PARK

②

Kisaki

Fuga

Matambwe

Iringa

UDZUNGWA MOUNTAINS NATIONAL PARK

④

Mang'ula

Mloka

③

TANZAM HIGHWAY

Mafinga

Ifakara

Rufiji River

SELOUS GAME RESERVE

Mbeya & Zambia

TAZARA Line Railway

Makambako

Kilombero Valley

Kilombero River

MBARIKA MOUNTAINS

Songea

0   50
kilometres

HIGHLIGHTS

① Uluguru Mountains
② Mikumi National Park
③ Selous Game Reserve
④ Udzungwa Mountains
⑤ Kondoa-Irangi rock art
⑥ Babati

likeable small-town feel, and owes its prosperity to its fertile hinterland, watered by the rugged **Uluguru Mountains**, which can be explored on foot via a **cultural tourism** programme. Although seemingly nothing remains of Simbamwenni, the town's nineteenth-century precursor visited by Stanley, the legacy of that century's Muslim-dominated **caravan trade** lives on. In the town centre, the passage of time is marked by calls to prayer from the mosques, and Morogoro is one of few places outside Zanzibar where you'll see women wearing black burkas. The cultural compote is enhanced by a thriving Indian community, Maasai warriors in full tribal drag, and a dishevelled army of expats, including missionaries by the bushel.

Central Morogoro

Central Morogoro is pleasant but devoid of things to do other than visiting the main **market** off Madaraka Road (daily 6am–6pm), especially enjoyable on Saturday and Sunday when it also hosts vendors from villages in the Uluguru Mountains, purveyors of delicious fruit, delicately woven baskets, woodcarvings, copper bracelets, jewellery made from animal horn, clay *jikus* (stoves), coconut-wood chairs, and fine honey (around Tsh7000 a bottle). **Historical sights** are limited to the German-era train station, the *New Savoy Hotel* facing it (see box, p.196) and the pink German Boma, still housing the local administration, a few kilometres along Boma Road (no photography).

Rock Garden Resort

3km south of the centre along Rwagasore St • ☏ 0715 953 234, ⓦ facebook.com/RockGardenMorogoro • Daily 10am–6pm • Tsh2000

Popular with romantic locals, and perfect for a lazy afternoon, is **Rock Garden Resort** – a beautiful patch of natural, boulder-strewn forest flanking a wild stream that's deep enough in parts for a dip. There's also a bar, and, usually, bar food, including *nyama choma*. For something equally different, ask at Chilunga Cultural Tourism Programme about the school for disabled children, which offers **drum and dance lessons**.

ARRIVAL AND DEPARTURE   MOROGORO

By bus The bus station is 4km north of town at Msamvu roundabout on the Tanzam highway, at the turning for Dodoma; parking bays have destinations marked on the far side, away from the road. Try to buy your ticket a day or two before to be sure of a good seat, and a safe operator, especially if you're going to Dar; that highway is, along with Moshi–Arusha, Tanzania's most dangerous, and fatal bus crashes on it are reported with unnerving frequency. Obviously, reputations can and do change: be extremely careful in your choice of bus (ask multiple people their opinion beforehand). In 2014, the safest operators (a distinctly relative concept) were B.M. Bus (for Dar, Iringa and Mbeya) and Shabiby, covering Dar, Iringa, Mbeya, Kyela, Songea and Dodoma. Abood Bus is the biggest operator for Dar (office in town at the top of John Mahenge St), with buses every 30min or so until mid-afternoon, but has a patchy reputation, as does Hood. Arriving at the bus station you'll likely be greeted by a welter of taxi drivers frantically trying to grab your attention, or your bags. If it

feels too chaotic, catch your breath at one of the restaurants lining the bus stand. Daladalas into town charge Tsh400, taxis no more than Tsh5000, but be sure they're licensed (white number plates).

Destinations Arusha (daily; 8–10hr); Dar (1–2 hourly until 4pm; 3hr); Dodoma (1–2 hourly until noon; 3–4hr); Iringa (hourly; 4–5hr); Mang'ula (2 daily plus occasional Coasters; 3hr 30min–4hr); Mbeya (hourly; 11–12hr); Mikumi (hourly; 2–3hr).

By train The train station is 1.5km northeast of the centre; you'll arrive at night, but there are plenty of taxis, and several good hotels nearby. Eastbound trains to Dar es Salaam are very slow. More useful are those to Kigoma or Mwanza via Tabora, currently leaving around 2am on Wed and Sat. Buy your ticket in advance if you want a sleeper, and check the schedule.

Destinations Dar (2 weekly; 5hr 30min); Dodoma (2 weekly; 7hr); Kigoma (2 weekly; 30hr 30min); Mwanza (2 weekly; 30hr 30min); Tabora (2 weekly; 17hr 30min).

GETTING AROUND AND INFORMATION

By taxi Taxis around town cost Tsh4000–5000.
By bicycle The cultural tourism programme charges $2.50

an hour for mountain bikes; your hotel should be able to find you a basic bicycle for much less.

▲ 2 (2km) & Selous Game Reserve

MOROGORO

ACCOMMODATION
Hilux Hotel	5
Mama Pierina's	4
Morogoro Hotel	10
Nashera Hotel	8
New Acropol Hotel	6
New Savoy Hotel	1
Hotel Oasis	3
Rock Garden Resort	9
Sinai Guest House	2
Sofia Hotel	7

● DRINKING AND NIGHTLIFE
Chipukizi Club	6
King Tom Club	4
Maisha Club	1
New Acropol Hotel	5
New Savoy Hotel	3
Nyumbani Park	2

● EATING
Blue Room	7
Dragonaires	9
Hearts Snack Bar	6
King Tom Club	1
Lucky Star Café	5
Mama Pierina's	4
Nashera Hotel	10
New Acropol Hotel	4
Red Chilli Restaurant	2
Sofia Hotel	8

● SHOPPING
Masooma Supermarket	2
Murad's Supermarket	3
Pira's Cash & Carry	1

Train Station

KIPENGE STREET
BANDA STREET
KINGALU ROAD
RWAGASORE STREET
BOMA ROAD
MLAPAKOLO STREET
MAKONGORO STREET
UHURU STREET
KITOPE ROAD
OLD DAR ES SALAAM ROAD
STATION ROAD
NKOMO ROAD
KIKUNDI (MASIKAI) STREET
LUMUMBA STREET
JOHN MAHENGE ST
MADARAKA ROAD
KONGA STREET
NGOLO STREET

S.D.A. Church
St Patrick's Church
Hospital
Pamba House
NBC Bank
Chilunga Cultural Tourism
Clock Tower
Library
Police
Jamhuri Stadium
Valentine's
CRDB Bank
Ngerengere River
Barclays Bank
Exim Bank
Abood Bus Office
NMB Bank
Aga Khan Clinic
Daladala Stand
Market

◀ Tanzam Highway (Dar, Dodoma, Iringa), Msamvu Bus Station (3km), 1 & 2

◀ 8 & 10 (2.5km), German Boma & Morningside

▶ Sokoine University

0   metres   200

N

By car There's no official set up for car hire, but the cultural tourism programme, and *Hotel Oasis*, should be able to fix you up. It's never cheap: anything less than $250 a day would be exceptional. If you need a car for Mikumi National Park, it's cheaper to arrange things at Mikumi village.

Tourist information Chilunga Cultural Tourism Programme, Rwagasore Street (daily 7.30am–5.30pm; ☎0754 477582 or ☎023 261 3323, ⓦchilunga.or.tz), is happy to help out; its main purpose is organizing trips into the Uluguru mountains (see p.197).

ACCOMMODATION

Morogoro's mid-range hotels are a decent bunch, but at the budget end you'll have trouble finding anything salubrious for less than Tsh25,000. Camping is possible in the grounds of the *New Acropol*. Lastly, don't drink Morogoro's tap water without treating it first, as the city's pipework is contaminated with coliform bacteria, and has also seen outbreaks of typhoid in the past.

Hilux Hotel Old Dar es Salaam Rd ☎023 261 3946, ⓦsites.google.com/site/hiluxhotel. A sterile conference-heavy place with seventy-odd rooms crammed into two three-storey blocks, all with a/c, satellite TV, wi-fi, big box nets and spotless bathrooms. The better rooms are on the left side. Also has a reasonably priced restaurant with plenty of Tanzanian dishes (main courses Tsh8000–10,000), a couple of bars and safe parking, but it's hardly the place for a holiday. No single rates. BB **Tsh80,000**

Mama Pierina's Station Rd ☎0713 786913 or ☎0786 786913, ⓔdshatzis@hotmail.com. A quiet and friendly place offering a mixed bag of eleven rooms in a row at the back opening on to a scrubby garden. The rooms on the right have been renovated and are decent for the price but not cheap, but the rooms to the left, including three singles, are in need of work. There's a billiards table, and a pleasant restaurant and bar at the front with tables around the terrace. BB unrenovated (with fans) **Tsh35,000**, renovated (with a/c) **Tsh45,000**

Morogoro Hotel Rwagasore St ☎023 261 3270, ⓦmorogorohotel.com. A large cluster of 1970s buildings designed to look like traditional Luguru homesteads but which bear an uncanny resemblance to flying saucers. The bedrooms – smallish but with high ceilings and therefore cool – are in saucer segments, all with excellent bathrooms (and bathtubs in the suites), huge beds, box nets, a/c, fridge and satellite TV. Facilities include tennis courts, access to the golf course across the road, a large tree-studded garden with great views of the Ulugurus, internet access and a (hit-and-miss) restaurant and bar. Safe parking. BB **$75**

Nashera Hotel Old Boma Rd, 1.5km south of town ☎023 261 3932 or ☎0716 678233, ⓦnasherahotels.com. The town's newest, largest and smartest accommodation, aimed at conferences so rather bland, with fifty large, comfortable and very well-appointed rooms, some with views of Uluguru. The grounds are pleasant, and contain a swimming pool, and the restaurant is fine. BB **$135**

★ **New Acropol Hotel** Old Dar es Salaam Rd ☎0754 309410 or ☎0765 990198, ⓦnewacropolhotel.com. Morogoro's most stylish abode, Canadian-run, with nine spacious en-suite rooms and two suites (one with two bedrooms, ideal for families), all tastefully decorated and with big four-posters, a/c and fan, cable TV and fridge. There's also a bar and excellent restaurant (with great breakfasts), wi-fi, an adjoining massage room with a professional physio (Tsh10,000 for half an hour), and use of *Hotel Oasis'* swimming pool. Safe parking. Camping free, including toilets and showers, if you buy a few meals or drinks. BB **$65**

New Savoy Hotel Station Rd ☎0755 307166. This, in its first incarnation, was the *Bahnhof* (see box, p.196), and while it's hard to imagine it these days in colonial garb, you can still make out the original brickwork behind thick layers of paint. The place is adequately maintained (though water still comes in buckets), and makes up for its slightly tired rooms with a consistently warm welcome and positive vibe. The fifteen rooms, all en suite, are a potpourri, though all have clean cotton sheets and box nets, and some have TV, including the large "budget" rooms in the original building. The best rooms are the "standard" twins on the second floor of the newer building closest to the train station, which have fans. It also has a restaurant and bar, with live music some weekends (from 8.30pm). BB "budget" **Tsh25,000**, "standard". It also **Tsh35,000**

Hotel Oasis Station Rd ☎023 261 4178 or ☎0754 377602, ⓔhoteloasistz@morogoro.net. Set around a swimming pool (Tsh4000 if you're not staying here), this large and bland but well-run place attracts conferences and civil servants. The rooms are big and comfortable, some better than others, all with box nets, fridge, cable TV, fans, a/c, wi-fi, and tiled bathrooms. There's also a bar and a decent restaurant (most mains Tsh10,000 and up), and safe parking. BB **$60**

Sinai Guest House Kikundi (Masika) St ☎0787 524940. One of more than a dozen very similar single-storey guesthouses in this area, all relatively modern and with TVs in their rooms, and whose main difference is their state of repair, and whether they accept prostitutes. This one doesn't, and is clean and welcoming. BB **Tsh25,000**

Sofia Hotel John Mahenge St ☎0715 334425 or ☎0786 535555, ⓔmengi2@yahoo.com. This calm two-storey hotel has been ambling along for years, is used to tourists, and was recently renovated. The price remains much the same, making it the best budget option in the centre if you're okay with the unreliable water supply. All rooms are en suite, with a/c, cable TV, cotton sheets (a rarity even in more upmarket hotels) and large round nets. Also has a restaurant at the back. BB Tsh30,000

EATING

Morogoro's **street food** is very good: the stalls at the corner of Madaraka Rd and John Mahenge St get going towards dusk, when the air fills with aromatic plumes of smoke spiralling from dozens of charcoal stoves: grilled goat meat or chicken, roast bananas and maize cobs, chips and eggs are the staples. Other good spots for street food include Kitope Rd in front of the stadium (throughout the day), and, at night, the west end of Station Rd. For dessert, seek out someone with a mangle for sugar cane juice, one of Azam's ice-cream vendors (on tricycles), or a *dafu* coconut vendor. **Bar food** is also decent, with *supu*, *nyama choma* and pork (*kiti moto*) among the favourites.

Blue Room Makongoro St. Cheap snacks and no-fuss meals, including stews (less than Tsh4000; ignore the menu, just ask what they have) in a clean but dull interior, or at street-side tables, where there's also a grill. Also handy for breakfast. Daily 6.30am–8pm.

Dragonaires 2.5km along Old Dar es Salaam Rd ☎0787 600001. An expat hangout founded by white Zimbabweans that still pulls them in from Fri to Sun when American-style spare ribs and pizzas are the thing (around Tsh12,000; but really, *hot dog* pizza?) The tables, outside, have great mountain views, but let bug spray be your companion. There's also a pool table, a playground and a bar – sometimes with live music, other times country and western. Tues–Fri 3–11pm, Sat & Sun 11am–11pm.

Hearts Snack Bar One block north of the daladala stand. A big outdoor *nyama choma* bar, also with *mishkaki*, chicken and chips (Tsh4000) and proper meals. It's a nice place to watch the world – and the hawkers – go by. Daily noon–late.

★**King Tom Club** Station Rd. Once upon a time, this was a typical Tanzanian beer garden, but one whose reputation for good food (*nyama choma* at Tsh5000 per half kilo, grilled bananas, famously good pork, and – with luck – even duck) grew and grew. As a result, its garden has given way to a nonetheless agreeable sprawl of seats and chairs under thatched shelters and trees, between which lingers the ever-present smell of grilled meat. Daily 6am–late.

Lucky Star Café Behind Pira's Cash and Carry. Has a full range of fresh Tanzanian snacks, including egg chops, *katlesi* (balls of mashed potato and minced meat), *kababu* and *sambusa*, plus packaged ice cream and good juices. No alcohol. Daily 7am–6pm.

Mama Pierina's Station Rd. The menu here (mostly Tsh8000–10,000) pays respect to the family's Greek–Italian roots, occasionally including (ask nicely the day before) lasagne, moussaka, great pancakes, salads and *mezedes* – salami, cheese, olives and tomato (Tsh10,000). Eat inside or on the porch. You're welcome just for drinks, too. Daily 11am–10pm.

Nashera Hotel Old Boma Rd, 1.5km south of town. This big conference hotel (with lovely views of the Ulugurus from its ample grounds, and butterfly-shaped swimming pool) is the current darling for expats and families on lazy weekend afternoons. The snacks are OK, but the main menu fares much better with, in among predicable grills, burgers, pizzas, Indian and Chinese, some gems such as grilled tilapia served with grilled mango and avocado (Tsh9000). Daily noon–10pm.

★**New Acropol Hotel** Old Dar es Salaam Rd. You won't leave hungry here: arguably Morogoro's best restaurant, but definitely its quirkiest (the fake stuffed animal trophies help here), this dishes up huge portions of inventive international cuisine, and caters to all tastes and diets, including vegan and gluten-free – try the brown rice from Ifakara, or the superb home-made feta (in the Greek salad; Tsh8500). For carnivores, the pork selection is impressive: try the *piccata* (sautéed in butter and white wine, with capers; Tsh10,000). Also does sandwiches, burgers, nachos and good stir fries, and their Kilimanjaro *Arabica* is excellent. Daily 7am–11pm.

SCHMUTZ FOR SMUTS

World War I in Tanganyika was a cat-and-mouse affair, with the mouse very effectively played by a small but mobile force led by the German commander **Paul von Lettow-Vorbeck**. His tactic was simple: tie down Allied forces and resources by avoiding full-on confrontations. Having taken control of a string of towns south of Moshi, his pursuer, **General Jan Smuts**, believed that the Germans would make their last stand at the railway in Morogoro. He was mistaken. Before beating a hasty retreat in August 1916 (Lettow-Vorbeck was still running around in 1918 when the armistice forced his surrender), his troops left a coin-operated mechanical piano playing Deutschland über Alles in the *Bahnhof Hotel*, now the *New Savoy*, together with rather more earthy "presents" deposited on chairs and tables…

Red Chilli Restaurant Station Rd. A modest dining room or Indian cuisine, principally Mughlai, with most dishes – a *biryani*, say, or fiery *pilipili* chicken – costing around Tsh7000–9000, excluding rice or naan. Daily 10am–11pm.

Sofia Hotel John Mahenge St. Past the reception is a bland little dining room that serves basic but tasty meals of the meat/fish/chicken with *ugali*/chips/rice variety. Ask early if you want something a little fancier, such as braised ox liver (Tsh5000), or chicken curry (Tsh7000). No alcohol. Daily 7–10am, midday–2pm & 7–10pm.

DRINKING AND NIGHTLIFE

Morogoro is an excellent place for a tipple or five, but its most famous **dance bands** – Morogoro Jazz and Super Volcano – are long gone. A few other local bands fill the void, and you should enquire about visiting bands from Dar. The "in" **venues** change constantly, but – with the exception of *King Tom Club* – are likely to be on the Tanzam highway north of town near the bus station, where you'll also find a few discos: popular at the time of writing were *Nyumbani Park* (with live bands weekends) and *Maisha Club* (playing Bongo Flava; closed Mon, busiest Fri & Sat). The clubs get busy around 10pm, and stay so until 2am or later – don't even think of walking around that area after dusk.

Chipukizi Club Makongoro St. One of the largest, busiest and oldest local places, this street-corner bar sells a wide range of beers and good cheap food, and has a TV alternating between global channels and pirated videos (afternoons). At night, don't stumble into the cul-de-sac in front, which has a rough reputation. Daily 7am–late.

King Tom Club Station Rd ☎ 0716 648141. In his heart King Tom is a bar... one that keeps the punters pouring in for not just food (see p.196) but free live music, currently Tues, Thurs, Fri and Sun nights, either Mikumi Sound, or old-timers Levent Music. Daily 6am–late.

New Acropol Hotel Old Dar es Salaam Rd. With a spray of colonial antiques, walls adorned with fake game trophies, prints and paintings, and cats and dogs at your feet, what's not to like about this upmarket bar? Also has low tables facing the lush front garden, and great food. Daily 10am–10pm.

New Savoy Hotel Station Rd. Nights can be busy here from Friday to Sunday (from 8.30pm), when live bands pump out a mix of jazz oldies and newer Congolese-flavoured tunes. By day it's nicely quiet (unless a conference rolls in), and there's basic food. Daily noon–11pm.

DIRECTORY

Football Jamhuri Stadium hosts Premier League sides Polisi Morogoro and Mtibwa Sugar; Moro United are now based in Dar. Match tickets cost Tsh3000–8000.

Health For blood tests and emergencies, go to Aga Khan Clinic, Boma Rd ☎ 0788 538537. The government-run Regional Hospital is on Rwagasore St ☎ 023 232 3045.

Internet access Reliable places include the post office on Old Dar es Salaam Rd, and Valentine's by the stadium. *New Acropol Hotel* offers free wi-fi for drinkers or diners.

Money Most banks have 24hr ATMs: those at NBC (Old Dar es Salaam Rd) have armed guards.

Supermarkets Best-stocked, but without alcohol, is Murad's, just east of the bridge on Dar es Salaam Rd (daily 7.30am–8pm). For a different selection, plus alcohol, try Pira's Cash & Carry on Lumumba St (Mon–Sat 8.30am–6pm, Sun 8.30am–1pm). There's also Masooma Supermarket on John Mahenge St (daily 7.30am–9pm).

Swimming pools Hotel Oasis (Tsh4000); Nashera Hotel (Tsh5000).

The Uluguru Mountains

South and east of Morogoro and rising to more than 2600m, the spectacular **Uluguru Mountains** contain some of the most luxuriant – but sadly threatened – indigenous rainforest in the country. Spanning 100km north to south and 20km east to west, the range is one of several in the 25-million-year-old **Eastern Arc mountain chain** (see box, p.256). Their great age, coupled with a wide altitudinal range, high rainfall and stable climate over the ages, have favoured the development of some of the world's richest and most species-diverse **rainforests**. The Ulugurus contain eleven endemic reptilian and amphibian species and more than a hundred endemic plants, including African violets, busy lizzies and begonias. **Mammals** include yellow baboons, blue monkeys, black-and-white colobus monkeys, wild pigs and duiker antelopes. But where Uluguru really comes into its own is its **birdlife**, which includes fifteen rare or unique species. Notable among these are the Usambara eagle owl, which was found here in 1993 – only its third known habitat – and the endemic Uluguru bush-shrike, critically endangered thanks to ongoing deforestation on the lower slopes. The best time to visit is the dry season from July to September. The main rains fall between February and June, with the patchier – and these days most unpredictable – short rains coming sometime between October and January.

In the early 1960s, most of the mountains were still covered with forest, but a glance from Morogoro today tells a sorry tale of destruction, either deliberate – by timber extraction or clearance for cultivation – or accidental, by fire. While the ambitious **Uluguru Biodiversity Conservation Project** ran into a wall of intransigent bureaucracy, it survived for long enough to spawn a **cultural tourism programme**. This offers an exciting range of walks and hikes, combining natural attractions (forests, streams, waterfalls and beautiful views) with equally fascinating encounters with the Luguru tribe (see box, below). The main options are covered here. In addition, if you're around on a Saturday, ask for the fortnightly **Maasai market** (*mnada*), 30km along the Dodoma road.

Morningside

The views from the half-abandoned colonial settlement of **MORNINGSIDE**, a two- to three-hour walk south of Morogoro, are well worth braving the steep path for, and the cool mountain air makes for a bracing and welcome change from Morogoro's habitual swelter. Other than this, though, Morningside doesn't have much more to offer, and the old German building, which functioned as a hotel until the 1970s, is crumbling away. Energetic folk can continue an hour up a steep track or along the winding road to the boundary of the forested nature reserve, marked by an enormous eucalyptus tree planted in the 1960s, and finish at the transmitter-topped **Bondwa Peak**.

Start early for Morningside, as the lower part of the walk – through open farmland – gets hot. There's a shop halfway up with sodas, a waterfall nearby, and, further up, **Ruvuma village**. Although you could walk this route without a guide, there have been reports of unaccompanied tourists being mugged (especially on the way down), and Morningside itself can be hard to find when it's misty or cloudy.

THE LUGURU

The Uluguru Mountains are the traditional home of the 1.5-million-strong **Luguru tribe**, whose name means "people of the mountain" (*guru* being "mountain" or "high"). Although most now live in the lowlands, a hundred thousand or so live on the mountains' lower slopes, using self-composting ladder terraces and other tricks to eke the most out of the already very fertile soil and abundant rains.

Despite growing Christian and Islamic influence, Luguru society remains strongly **matrilineal**, and land is often the property of women. It passes from mother to daughter, either in their own name or in that of one of fifty clans to which all Luguru belong, which in turn are subdivided into around eight hundred **lineages** (essentially extended families). Although a man may inherit land from his mother, it reverts to his sister's children on his death, even if he has children of his own. This system gave Luguru women uncommon independence from their husbands, and those who displeased them were sent packing with nothing more than the clothes on their backs. Things are changing, however: the traditional system, coupled with the location along the road to Zambia (dubbed the "AIDS Highway") has brought with it the devastating spectre of HIV. Population pressure has also trashed the forests on the mountains' lower slopes, and with land now scarce, inheritance patterns are shifting.

Still, some things don't change, not least the so-called "**joking relationships**" (*utani*) between rival villages, and also between the Luguru and other tribes, which historically circumvented conflicts via an institutionalized form of friendship, neighbourly assistance and good humour. Villages in an *utani* relationship were (and still are) expected to share food with each other at times of hardship, in return for which donors were allowed to jibe at their neighbours' expense. But if you hear kids laughing their heads off on seeing you, well, there's probably another explanation…

Choma

The village of **CHOMA**, a three-hour walk east of Morogoro (8km), is the main place for cultural encounters, and has a number of activities for tourists, including a woman potter happy to explain her craft to visitors, and seeing mats and baskets being made from the fronds of the *mkindu* phoenix palm. The local women are also talented musicians, and for a small fee will introduce you to the delights of traditional Luguru **music and dance**; if you're in Dar, drop by the Tanzania Broadcasting Company (see p.112) to buy their two tapes of "Kiluguru" music, where you'll hear flutes blended with voices to mesmerizing effect. You can also see the production of "soil cake", a calcium-rich supplement used by pregnant women. Finish your visit with a **traditional lunch**, but take it easy with the various *pombe* home-brews unless you're staying over.

Madola

Huddled up against a bare rock face, the tiny hamlet of **MADOLA**, two to three hours on foot from Morogoro (6km), is known locally for its woodwork (including dolls and figurines), but was more famous for Bibi Maria, a remarkable **traditional healer** whose supernatural powers were revealed to her in a series of dreams when she was 6. She used dreams, and premonitions, to diagnose illness and determine the appropriate remedy – invariably a coupling of physical (medicinal plants) and spiritual (ritual). Bibi Maria has joined the spirit world, but her daughter continues her mother's craft, and is happy to receive inquisitive travellers, for a $25 fee. The track to Madola is steep and difficult to follow in places, but you're rewarded with beautiful views, patches of forest between fruit orchards and vegetable plots, and a small waterfall.

Lupanga peak

For that top-of-the-world feeling, set your sights on the 2150-metre **Lupanga Peak**, the closest to Morogoro, which takes upwards of nine hours to scale and descend. It's tough going, and inside the forest it be dangerously slippery in the rains, but you may be rewarded by glimpses of the rare Loveridge's sunbird or Fulleborn's black boubou, or by the more easily seen (or heard) Livingstone's turaco and silvery-cheeked hornbill. Costs are $40 per person, including the nature reserve permit, but excluding meals.

Bunduki and around

The area east of **BUNDUKI** village, a challenging three-hour drive south of Morogoro (turn left at Kipera and left again at Mgeta, where the Luguru first settled), offers some great hiking possibilities, including along the **Lukwangule Plateau** separating the mountains' northern and southern ranges. Just over an hour's walk east of the village are the impressive **Hululu Falls**, where water spills out of the forest over a rocky forty-metre drop: go with a local or a guide as the site is sacred. If you want to hike higher up, through Bunduki Forest Reserve, you'll need a forest reserve permit ($10); the extra cost is surely worth it for the superb east-facing views from the ridge, and, for keen birders, a chance of sighting the otherwise very rare **Mrs Moreau's warbler**. Bunduki's inhabitants are happy to rustle up food, swimming is possible in the river, and you're welcome to **camp**.

Matombo

On the eastern flank of the Ulugurus is **MATOMBO** village, straddling the unsurfaced road to Selous Game Reserve's Matambwe Gate (see p.207). You can get here by 4WD, or, for a bit of exercise, by bicycle (65km from Morogoro) or on foot from Bunduki (30km of very rough terrain, the whole thing best tackled over several days). The village is worth visiting for two very unusual attractions. The first is a **sacred cave** that contains a natural stone formation resembling a naked woman, and from which Matombo draws its name (it means "breasts"). The other attraction is in the river itself, at a place called **Usolo**: it's a curious rock (visible unless there's heavy rain) bearing rows

4

of evidently man-made, circular depressions. Although archeologists are at a loss to explain the significance of such "cup marks" (which are also found in Europe and Asia) locals know better. They say that a long time ago, two Luguru chiefs finally made peace after having quarrelled for many years. One of them, a certain Chief Hega, tapped his heel on the rock to magically create the depressions, then invited his erstwhile adversary to join him in a game of *usolo* – the local word for the traditional African board game of *bao* (see p.73). If you can, try to be in Matombo on a Friday or Saturday, which are its market days.

ESSENTIALS   THE ULUGURU MOUNTAINS

Access and costs Hiking or biking is best arranged in Morogoro through Chilunga Cultural Tourism Programme, Rwagasore Street (daily 7.30am–5.30pm; ☎0754 477582 or ☎023 261 3323, ⓦchilunga.or.tz), whose youthful guides are conscientious and knowledgeable. Costs are $25 per guide for a half-day walk (up to four tourists), $35–40 for a full day. To this, add meals, forest permits and any accommodation or transport.

Permits Uluguru's forests are either forest reserves or nature reserves, either of which need a $10 permit. The cultural tourism programme will obtain this for you, but not at weekends when the issuing office is closed, so

arrange things midweek, or send them a scan of your passport beforehand.

Equipment All routes are steep in places, so bring good walking boots or worn-in shoes with good tread, especially when it's raining. Take water, some food, suncream and – June to Sept – a fleece.

Websites A good academic website covering the Uluguru Mountains, with lots of documents to download, is ⓦeasternarc.or.tz/uluguru.

Accommodation Regular accommodation is limited to non-existent: Morogoro's cultural tourism programme can arrange homestays in Choma and elsewhere, and can also advise you about camping – tent hire costs $10 a day.

Mikumi, Selous and Udzungwa

The southern foothills of the Uluguru Mountains mark the start of an incredible ecosystem that covers a vast swathe of central and southern Tanzania, and includes the easily visited **Mikumi National Park**, and the untrammelled wilderness of **Selous Game Reserve**, visiting which requires a bit of planning if you've yet to win the lottery. The ecosystem's wealth in wildlife stems from both the perennial **Rufiji River**, and the dry **miombo woodland** that covers almost three-quarters of it. Unlike the scrubby savanna vegetation prevalent in northern Tanzania, *miombo* is dominated by deciduous *Brachystegia* trees. The leaves that are shed each year form the basis of a complex food chain, ultimately creating an ideal habitat for dozens if not hundreds of **large mammal species**. That humans haven't trashed the area is because *miombo* woodlands are the perfect habitat for **tsetse flies**, pernicious vectors of sleeping sickness. Wild mammals have acquired resistance, but domestic livestock and humans have not (but don't worry, your chances of contracting it are minute). The *miombo* woodlands are at their most beautiful in October and November, before and during the short rains, when they put out new leaves in all shades of red, copper, gold and orange, as well as green. For real forest, though, get yourself down to **Udzungwa Mountains National Park** south of Mikumi, a biological wonderland that offers possibly the most exhilarating walking in Tanzania, whether you're up for an adventurous hike over several days, or a quick saunter in search of monkeys, birds, butterflies and waterfalls.

Mikumi National Park

An hour's drive southwest of Morogoro, the 3230-square-kilometre **Mikumi National Park** is the first stop on most "Southern Circuit" safaris, and famed among photographers for its spine-tinglingly rich light. Framed by the Uluguru, Rubeho and Udzungwa mountains, and bounded by Selous Game Reserve to the south, Mikumi's grassy plains and thick *miombo* woodland are an oasis for wildlife. For those on really ight budgets, buses along the **Tanzam highway** pass straight through the park, giving you a good chance – best in the dry season – of seeing elephants, giraffes and antelopes. Mikumi actually owes its protection to the road, whose construction caused a massive increase in poaching, leading to the park's hasty creation in 1964. In spite of an 80kph speed limit and dozens of speed bumps, most drivers treat the highway as a race track. Smaller creatures like mongooses and, lamentably, African hunting dogs obviously aren't worth wearing out brake pads for, as the assortment of flattened roadkill bears witness.

Heading off the highway into the park itself, **plains game** is easily seen, including elephants and impala. Most guides should be able to locate a **lion** or three, but leopards are more elusive (your best chance is along watercourses). Black-backed jackals can sometimes be seen in the evenings, but the highlight is the **African hunting dog**, one of

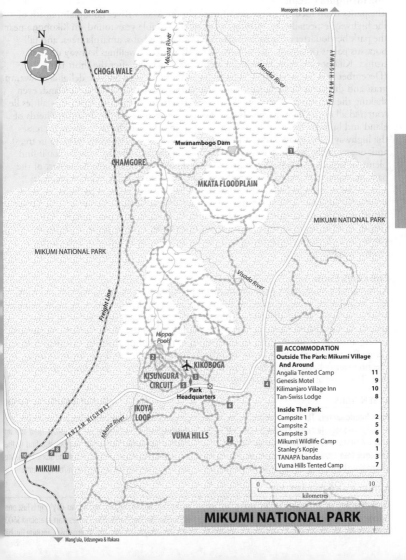

MIKUMI NATIONAL PARK

■ **ACCOMMODATION**

Outside The Park: Mikumi Village And Around

Angalia Tented Camp	11
Genesis Motel	9
Kilimanjaro Village Inn	10
Tan-Swiss Lodge	8

Inside The Park

Campsite 1	2
Campsite 2	5
Campsite 3	6
Mikumi Wildlife Camp	4
Stanley's Kopje	1
TANAPA bandas	3
Vuma Hills Tented Camp	7

0   10
kilometres

Africa's rarest mammals, which (a matter of luck) are sometimes seen in packs. **Birdlife** is profuse, with more than four hundred recorded species, including red-billed oxpeckers, marabou storks, pretty lilac-breasted rollers and malachite kingfishers, black-bellied bustards, and, between October and April, Eurasian migrants.

The **best times to go** are December to March, when wildlife numbers are their highest (and resident elephant herds are joined by their cousins from Selous and the Rubeho Mountains), or the dry season from mid-August to October, when animals are concentrated around water sources. Bad times are during the long rains, when most of the park's internal roads are impassable, and just before, when the landscape can be scarred by controlled fires.

The Kisingura Circuit

The park's main focus is a network of tracks in the Mkata River floodplain, north of the highway, especially the "**Kisingura Circuit**" (accessible year-round) in **Kikoboga** near the park headquarters. It's an area characterized by baobabs, amarula trees, and tall borassus palms (*mikumi*), which have strangely graceful swellings halfway up their trunks. Kikoboga is most famous for **elephants**, especially after the short rains (December and January), when they're drawn in by the gastronomic delights of swamp grass and the plum-like amarula fruit. Elephants gobble them by the thousand, even shaking the trees to get them to fall. Proof of the fruit's impressive laxative qualities lie scattered all over. **Other mammals** commonly seen around the floodplain are herds of eland and buffalo, Liechtenstein's hartebeest (often close to the river where it crosses the highway), and good odds on lions (sometimes in trees), leopards (also up in trees), and, occasionally, small packs of African hunting dogs. In the dry season, you'll find plenty of hippos and waterbirds around **waterholes**, especially 5km northwest of the park headquarters, and further north at Chamgore (also good for Bohor reedbuck), and at Mwanambogo Dam, which has the additional attraction of **pythons**, either at the water's edge or coiled up in trees. Take care: it may be non-venomous, but a body blow from this constrictor can topple an impala. You'll need a park ranger ($10) to venture further north to the picnic site at **Choga Wale**, a pretty glade of *Hyphaene* palms, acacias, strangling fig trees and pink jacarandas, the bark of which finds use against witchcraft.

The Ikoya Loop

Although the bulk of the park lies **south of the highway**, it's seldom visited, and only the "**Ikoya Loop**" is easy enough to follow without a guide (the park may insist you hire one in any case). In the dry season, hippos and other animals can be seen at Ikoya waterhole, but the best time is June to November, when the cassia thickets are covered in fragrant yellow flowers. The area beyond Ikoya, including the ridges close to Selous Game Reserve, is mostly *miombo* woodland, home to sable antelope, greater kudu, Liechtenstein's hartebeest, black-and-white colobus monkey… and clouds of tsetse flies. There are also hot water springs.

ESSENTIALS   MIKUMI NATIONAL PARK

Park headquarters The park headquarters are in the middle at Kikoboga, just off the highway (☎ 023 262 0487 or ☎ 0689 062334, ✉ mikumi@tanzaniaparks.com).

Entrance fees Entrance fees (not applicable if you're just passing along the highway) are $30 per person and Tsh20,000 per vehicle for 24 hours, payable by Visa or MasterCard.

Information The park headquarters sells a map and an excellent guidebook ($10), which you can also find in the lodges, and at bookstores in Arusha, Dar and Stone Town. The park's web page is ⊛ tanzaniaparks.com/mikumi.html.

ARRIVAL AND DEPARTURE

From Dar Any safari operator in Dar (see p.103) can arrange a trip to Mikumi, for which at least two days is recommended, ideally three, as it takes about four hours to drive the 286km to the park, and a "two-day" trip is just one night with two long game drives. Prices start at around $500 for a three-day safari from Dar. Alternatively, include Ruaha

National Park in your itinerary, or – if your operator is confident of its vehicles – try the east–west route through Selous Nature Reserve, for which you'll need a reliable 4WD.

From Morogoro Day-trips from Morogoro, a 1.5 hour drive away, are feasible, but expensive unless you have your own wheels: Morogoro's cultural tourism programme, for instance (see p.195), charges upwards of $350/day for a Land Cruiser, with driver, for six passengers (a saloon car costs around $250/day), to which you need to add park entrance fees.

From Mikumi village The cheapest approach, and one which leaves you free to tag on a hike at Udzungwa Mountains National Park (for which an organized safari is just money wasted), is to catch a bus to Mikumi village, a roadstead at the junction to Udzungwa just outside the park's western border, and hire a vehicle there, with or without a driver. Any bus heading along the Tanzam highway between Dar (5hr) or Morogoro (2hr) and Iringa (3hr) or Mbeya (8–9hr) passes by. Mikumi village's *Genesis Motel* asks $180 per person for a full day, $150 for half a day, including park fees and lunch. *Angalia Tented Camp* and *Tan-Swiss Lodge* charge $220/day for a vehicle ($150/half day), to which you add park fees and meals. The park headquarters can also organize game drives: ring them up first. An official guide ($20 plus tip for a few hours) can be hired at the park headquarters.

From Udzungwa *Hondo Hondo* (*Udzungwa Forest Camp*) at Mang'ula (see p.212) offers very reasonably priced trips to Mikumi from there, costing $220 per vehicle plus park fees and food.

Self-drive In theory, only 4WD vehicles are allowed in the park, but improvements to its internal road network mean that ordinary saloon cars are currently admitted, but this is not something you should rely on. There's no fuel inside the park.

By plane There's no point flying to Mikumi (usually from Dar or Zanzibar) unless you're pre-booked at a lodge. The main companies offering flying safaris, both with their own airlines, camps and lodges, are Foxes African Safaris (see p.103) and Coastal Travels (see p.103).

ACCOMMODATION, EATING AND DRINKING

The cheapest overnight inside the park is camping, or staying at the park-run *bandas*, although these are not well located. Standards at the three upmarket options have see-sawed considerably over the years, so find some recent online reviews before booking. None of them are fenced, so close encounters with animals are possible, be it elephants or, at night, civets, bushbabies and perhaps a honey badger. Mikumi village, outside the park, is basically an overgrown truckers' night stop, with plenty of tawdry guesthouses serving commercial drivers, but also some decent motel-style options, and, just outside the park, a beautiful tented camp.

OUTSIDE THE PARK: MIKUMI VILLAGE AND AROUND

In the following directions, "Udzungwa junction" is on the highway 6.8km west of Mikumi's western gate, at the start of the road to Mang'ula and Ifakara.

★ **Angalia Tented Camp** 6km east of Udzungwa junction (800m from the park gate), then 1.5km south ☏ 0787 518911 or ☏ 0652 999019, ⓦ angaliacamp.com. Spanish-run, this is a charming, romantic and very well-managed tented lodge, with large walk-in tents pitched on wooden platforms under thatched roofs, each with veranda and bathroom, that are comfortable and clean. The food, mostly Swahili and Mediterranean, is superb, there are evening camp fires, and the staff are great. There's also some wildlife. Electricity is from a generator in the evening. Vehicles for visiting the park itself cost $220 full day, $150 half day (plus park fees). BB **$210**, FB **$250**

Genesis Motel 4km east of Udzungwa junction ☏ 023 262 0461. Thirty comfortable en-suite twin-bed rooms, each with satellite TV, but erratic hot water. Also has an expensive restaurant and bar, a motley collection of live snakes and tortoises next door ($5 entry for non-guests), and a small campsite (per person $5). BB **$60**

Kilimanjaro Village Inn 1km east of Udzungwa junction ☏ 023 262 0429. Safe and clean, set in attractive gardens behind a wall, with a choice of rooms, some en suite, all with good beds, fans and nets. **Tsh10,000**, en suite **Tsh20,000**

★ **Tan-Swiss Lodge** 4.2km east of Udzungwa junction ☏ 0755 191827, ⓦ tan-swiss.com. Run by a charming Swiss–Tanzanian couple, this is a cheerful take on the classic US motel, complete with colourful murals. The comfortable rooms come with satellite TV and box nets, and the restaurant is well priced, its menu veering all over the place. Also has Mikumi's best bar (cocktails and South African wines), a playground and very reasonably priced Mikumi safaris. Camping per person **$7**, BB **$65**

INSIDE THE PARK

★ **Mikumi Wildlife Camp** Kikoboga ☏ 0684 886306 (Mikumi) or ☏ 022 260 0252 (Dar), ⓦ mikumiwildlifecamp.com. The best place for spotting wildlife from the comfort of an armchair, as two waterholes (one floodlit at night) attract elephant, buffalo, wildebeest and impala. Accommodation is in twelve spacious African-style *bandas* with drapes for windows and big verandas – get one at the far end. There's a swimming pool with sundeck and hot-tub, a look-out tower with 360° views and a bar. Meals can be taken around a campfire. Day-trippers are welcome for lunch (no entry fees apply if you arrive and leave between noon and 2pm). HB **$387**

4

Stanley's Kopje Mkata floodplain, 25km north of the park ☎0713 237422 or ☎0754 237422, ⓦstanleyskopje.com. Mikumi's classiest option, and the only one without views of buses on the distant highway. Set on a rocky kopje in prime game-viewing terrain (elephants are occasional visitors, attracted by Mwanambogo Dam), it boasts 360° views from its hilltop restaurant and bar. Accommodation is in twelve large and quirkily elegant en-suite tents on wooden platforms, their verandas with sweeping views. There's also a small swimming pool. Closed March–May. FB $400, game package $590

TANAPA bandas Kikoboga (book through the park headquarters, or TANAPA in Arusha; see p.287). Twelve modern cottages, clean, with big box nets, hot showers, a/c and even satellite TV – it looks like a bargain on paper, but the location, among the park's offices and workshops, has no wilderness feeling, so you might as well stay in Mikumi village. BB $100

TANAPA campsites Various locations (reservations not required; pay at the park gate or headquarters). The park itself has three public campsites: Campsite 1, near the park gate, with running water, pit latrines, shower, fireplace and firewood, but not much atmosphere; Campsite 2, along the Kisingura Circuit, under an old baobab with a toilet but no water; and Campsite 3, just south of the highway under a large fig tree, with just a toilet. Be wary of baboons while camping: don't eat in their presence, and keep food in sealed containers. Per person $30.

Vuma Hills Tented Camp 7km southeast of the park gate ☎0713 237422 or ☎0754 237422, ⓦvumahills .com. Welcoming, relaxed and luxurious, with good food and smart service, this is also suitable for families. There are sixteen spacious if rather closely spaced en-suite tents on raised wooden decks, with grassland vistas from their verandas, plus a small swimming pool and sundeck overlooked by the bar and restaurant, and a commendable library. FB $400, game package $590

Selous Game Reserve

Checking in at 54,600 square kilometres, **Selous Game Reserve** – a World Heritage Site – is Africa's second-largest wildlife sanctuary (after southern Africa's Great Limpopo Transfrontier Park), and the Southern Safari Circuit's undisputed highlight. Taken in combination with Mikumi and a number of adjoining reserves, Selous' rich and diverse ecosystem is home to an estimated 750,000 large mammals, including the world's largest populations of elephants, African hunting dogs, leopards, crocodiles, buffaloes and hippos.

Most of the reserve is set aside for hunting, but the small northern sector for "photographic tourism" is not just the reserve's but arguably one of the country's most beautiful places, its habitats ranging from grassy plains and rolling *miombo* woodland to dense patches of groundwater forest and the magnificent **Rufiji River**, best experienced from a boat. It's in Selous that the river – Tanzania's longest – is at its finest, its labyrinthine network of lagoons, channels, islets and swamps stuffed with hippos and crocs, and dressed in riverine forest a-chatter with **birds**: more than 450 species have been recorded inside the reserve.

Terrestrial wildlife isn't lacking, either, and can be seen either on a game drive or, more thrillingly, on a **bush walk**. Elephants are abundant, as are zebra, giraffe and all manner of antelopes, including wildebeest and impala, waterbuck, reedbuck, Roosevelt's sable and Liechtenstein's hartebeest. Smaller **nocturnal mammals** such as lesser bushbabies and small spotted genets are often seen or heard around camps at night, and mongooses are often seen scampering across tracks. The forests backing the waterways are good places for **primates**, including vervets, large troops of olive and yellow baboons, black-and-white colobus monkeys and, just as shy, blue monkeys. Rarer animals include Sharpe's grysbok, a tiny population of red colobus monkeys in the far northwest near the railway, and approximately 150 **black rhino**, the locations of which are closely guarded secrets.

Of the **predators**, lions – often in large prides – are the most visible; leopards, despite their considerable population, are more elusive. Cheetah and spotted hyena are also occasionally seen, but the real highlight is the **African hunting dog**, among the rarest of Africa's predators, which has found in Selous one of its last refuges: their population peaks in September and October.

For all these riches, don't count on being able to tick off species as you would in northern Tanzania, which is one of the reasons why tour operators recommend longer stays in the "hidden" Selous. The other reason is profit: factoring in entrance fees and activities, you won't find a double room inside the reserve for less than $940 a night. Should the prices scare you off, or the all-white, neo-colonial atmosphere prick your conscience, don't despair: with a tent, or simply staying just outside the reserve, the overall cost can actually be less than in northern Tanzania's more emblematic national parks.

The **best months** for large mammals are July to September/October, when the vegetation is lower and animals are clustered around the river and its lakes. The short dry spell in January and February is perfect for birds (including migrants), but terrestrial wildlife is more dispersed at that time, and the temperature can feel intense thanks to the gathering humidity. This culminates in the long rains (mid-March to late May), when most roads are cut off and the majority of lodges and camps inside the reserve are closed.

The Rufiji River

The magnificent **Rufiji River** is the heart and soul of Selous, and ineffably beautiful it is, too – its labyrinthine channels, lagoons, islets and their abundant wildlife making it easy to forget the ugly fibreglass-and-canvas boats used for cruises. **Birdlife** is plentiful throughout the wetlands: on the lagoons, look out for African skimmers, pink-backed and great white pelicans, ducks and Egyptian geese, giant kingfishers and white-fronted plovers, while the shallows and sandbanks are ideal for waders like herons and storks as well as kingfishers, African skimmers (again) and white-fronted bee-eaters. The groves of *mikumi* palms lining the shore in many parts are also rich twitching territory, including morning warblers, palmnut vultures, red-necked falcons, nesting African fish eagles, yellow-billed storks, ibises and palm swifts.

Lake Tagalala, actually a lagoon, is the main destination for boat safaris. The lake apparently contains the densest population of crocodiles on earth, presumably fed by

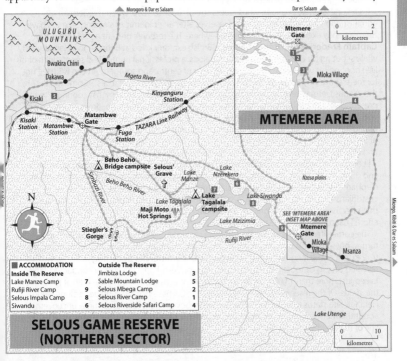

SELOUS GAME RESERVE (NORTHERN SECTOR)

MTEMERE AREA

■ ACCOMMODATION	Outside The Reserve	
Inside The Reserve	Jimbiza Lodge	3
Lake Manze Camp 7	Sable Mountain Lodge	5
Rufiji River Camp 9	Selous Mbega Camp	2
Selous Impala Camp 8	Selous River Camp	1
Siwandu 6	Selous Riverside Safari Camp	4

4

the profusion of wildlife that comes here to drink, and there are also plenty of hippos, though you shouldn't get too close as they will charge a boat if feeling threatened. Another good destination is **Stiegler's Gorge**, where the Great Ruaha River flows into the Rufiji. The gorge takes its name from a hunter who was killed here by an elephant in 1907, and offers a fair chance of spotting leopard.

The forest

The **riverine forest** is best visited on a **bush walk**, during which you might catch glimpses of black-and-white colobus monkeys, or hear the crashing of branches as they flee your approach. The walks are generally two- to three-hour affairs in the company of an armed ranger: necessary, as heart-stopping encounters with elephants, lions or buffalo are frequent enough. Bush walks are also good for spotting details you would otherwise miss, like the sticky secretions dik-diks deposit on top of grass stems to mark their territorial latrines, or the tracks and spoors left by animals whose bellowings kept you up the night before.

On a traditional **game drive**, your itinerary really depends on the state of the reserve's tracks, and what your guide reckons is best at the time, but there are a couple of places you could aim to include among all the bumping and sliding: the sulphurous **Maji Moto hot springs** on the eastern slope of Kipala Hill, near Lake

---

HUNTING, SHOOTING AND CONSERVATION?

One superlative that few brochures will tell you about is that Selous Game Reserve is the only place in Tanzania where the gentlemanly sport of **elephant hunting** is permitted, even if only a few dozen kills are legally made each year. In fact, all but three of the reserve's 45 "management blocks" are for hunting, the rationale being that plugging lead into animals provides eighty percent of the reserve's income.

It's an uneasy state of affairs, whose roots stretch back to 1896, when the German administration formed several hunting reserves after an epidemic of sleeping sickness gave them a handy excuse to shift the locals elsewhere. The reserve's present name comes from **Captain Frederick Courteney Selous**, a British explorer killed at Beho Beho in January 1917 while scouting for the 25th Royal Fusiliers. Selous, a professional hunter, had spent much of his life shooting his way through a colossal amount of central and southern African wildlife ("not for mere sport," he explained, "but also to gain the goodwill of the natives"). Come the British, the various German reserves were combined and expanded, a process that continues to the present day, with each enlargement having seen villagers evicted, sometimes by force. So it was that by the 1970s, resentful villagers relocated outside the reserve were only too willing to engage in commercial **poaching**. Between 1981 and 1989, they obliterated more than 75,000 of Selous' elephants (two-thirds of the original population, which numbered 110,000 in 1976) and all but a hundred of the reserve's three thousand black rhino.

Ecological disaster was only stemmed at the end of the decade when a **global ban** on ivory and rhino horn trading came into force. The effect was remarkable: within fifteen years, Selous' elephant population rebounded to more than 65,000, and it seemed that the reserve's custodians (the Ministry of Natural Resources and Tourism) had finally embraced the notion that effective conservation could only work, in Selous, by including local communities in the effort. That turned out to be a pipe dream.

The partial lifting of the global ban on ivory trade in 1999 brought fears – justified, as it turned out – that this would revive the then-moribund international market in ivory. But the true extent of the long-rumoured **resurgence of commercial poaching** in Selous was revealed only in October 2013, by the most rigorous elephant census ever conducted, which tallied just more than 13,000 elephants in the entire ecosystem – less even than at the end of the 1980s. Of the reserve's rhino, not a word. UNESCO has since downgraded Selous' World Heritage Site status to "in danger". The Tanzanian Government appears entirely unconcerned about the matter, which gives little hope that a final **catastrophe** in the Selous – the last in a line of many – can be averted.

Tagalala, which are cool enough in places for swimming (also visitable by boat); and **Captain Selous' grave**, at Beho Beho.

ESSENTIALS   SELOUS GAME RESERVE

Entrance fees Entry fees are paid at the reserve's gates: $75 per person for 24 hours, in cash, which includes a conservation fee. An armed ranger, doubling as a guide (obligatory if self-driving), costs $20 a day.

Information Indicative of the reserve's mismanagement is the lack of any official information about it: no website, no publications, no information centre, and any queries sink straight into the bureaucratic mire that is the Ministry of Natural Resources and Tourism (if you want to try: Ivory Room, Nyerere Rd, PO Box 1994, Dar es Salaam; ☎ 022 286 6064, ✉ sgrmp@raha.com). On arriving at the

reserve gate, however, you should be able to buy a copy of Rolf Baldus and Ludwig Siege's excellent *Selous Travel Guide* (Gallery Publications), and, with luck, the 1:500,000 *Visitor's Map of the Selous Game Reserve North of the Rufiji*, published by GTZ, showing relief, vegetation, accommodation, some walking trails and good places for spotting given species. The map is hard to find elsewhere, but the book can be bought in Arusha, Dar and Stone Town. The best website, with plenty of downloadable papers and articles in English and German, is ⓦ wildlife-baldus.com.

ARRIVAL AND DEPARTURE

Most visitors fly into Selous, but a handful of safari companies offer cheaper road trips; as you'll waste a full day getting here from Dar, and another back, it's best if you're on an extended trip.

By bus Leaving from Dar, you can get to the camps and lodges outside Selous' eastern boundary (see pp.208–210) in a day, where you can arrange safaris. The direct 5am bus from Dar's southern suburb of Temeke, and pick-ups from Kibiti on the Dar–Mtwara highway, which go via Mkongo (both with simple guesthouses), finish at Mloka village, 3.5km shy of Mtemere Gate. Heading back, the Dar bus leaves Mloka when full, which is any time between 4.30am and 7am.

By organized safari On a driving safari, lodges and campsites outside the reserve's eastern gate are the usual base. Access roads and roads within the reserve are rough, so don't pinch pennies when choosing an operator (see p.103): you'll need a reliable vehicle, competent driver and HF radio. For stays inside the reserve, the usual approach is by plane. Flying safaris are offered by lodges themselves, safari companies and travel agents. Coastal Travels (see p.103) offer alluring out-of-season deals for *Lake Manze Camp* and *Selous Impala Camp*, while Foxes African Safaris (see p.103) do the

same for *Rufiji River Camp*. ZanAir also offer packages.

By 4WD High-clearance 4WD, in excellent condition, is essential, but forget about driving here during the long rains (roughly mid-March to end– of May), when internal roads are impassable, and the reserve's lodges are closed. Even in dry weather, few rental companies will trust you self-driving in Selous, so you'll be provided with a driver. The reserve's gates close at 6pm, and no driving after 6.30pm. There are two main routes: 155km to Matambwe, in the northwest, from Morogoro, which is spectacular and completely off the beaten track (see below); and the Mtemere route (see map, p.152) – roughly 250km from Dar, 5hr in a perfect world, up to 8hr if not – with fast tarmac between Dar and Kibiti (170km), followed by *murram* to Mkongo and on to Mloka (77km), 3.5km before Mtemere Gate. Fill up on fuel at Morogoro, or at Kibiti if coming from Dar.

By train The TAZARA railway from Dar to Zambia dips tantalizingly into Selous' northwest corner, but a free safari

---

GETTING TO SELOUS VIA MATAMBWE

The scenic if finger-biting approach to Selous is by road from Morogoro to the reserve's northwestern **Matambwe Gate**. The unsurfaced 155km route – which is now covered by Coaster minibus from Morogoro – starts along Old Dar es Salaam Road (see map, p.192) and skirts the northern fringe of the Uluguru Mountains before turning south along the rugged eastern flank, passing a series of lively villages and almost jungly patches of forest interspersed with cracking views. The rocky and sometimes steep surface makes the first 80km slow going if passable, taking two-and-a-half to five hours depending on the road's state of repair. Leaving the Uluguru foothills, the road descends 45km towards the swampy north bank of the Mgeta River. If recently graded, this stretch is passable in most conditions, but if not it can get blocked after even moderate showers. The stretch beyond the river to **Kisaki village** and its train station, where the road crosses the Rudete and Msoro rivers before following the railway to Matambwe Gate, is fine. The only accommodation outside the park in this area is *Sable Mountain Lodge*.

isn't on the cards, as the trains (two a week in either direction) pass through at night – and are therefore only useful if you're staying at *Sable Mountain Lodge* (see p.210); someone will pick you up.

ACCOMMODATION

Camping is the cheapest way of staying in or around Selous (see box, below). **Inside the reserve**, an ever-expanding collection of luxury tented camps and lodges compete for your wallet, all soul-crushingly expensive, and whose style often recalls the good old days of Victorian and Edwardian supremacy, when rich white folk could do as they pleased… More affordable are a series of camps and lodges **outside the reserve** along the Rufiji's north bank, just before Mtemere Gate. Wildlife isn't as profuse here as inside the reserve, but the river is much the same. Inside or outside, all places offer game drives, boat trips and bush walks, and – outside the reserve – village walks. Such activities are included in **game packages**; otherwise, you'll pay (per person) roughly $15–30 for walks, $35–50 for short game drives or boat rides, or $80–100 for a full day, plus entry fees if you enter the reserve. Room rates exclude entry fees.

INSIDE THE RESERVE

Lake Manze Camp ☎ 022 260 1747 (Dar), ⊛ lakemanze .com. Twelve secluded tents amid doum palms and terminalia trees, all with lake views, and elephants trampling by in the morning. Quite plain but does the trick, and cheap by Selous' shocking standards. Children under 6 discouraged. FB $\overline{$600}$, game package $\overline{$900}$

★ **Rufiji River Camp** ☎ 0713 237422 or ☎ 0754 237422, ⊛ rufijirivercamp.com. Overlooking the river, this is unfussy, unpretentious and relaxed, with excellent guides for extended wildlife walks. The fourteen rustic tents are tucked away in the forest, each with a veranda for river and sunset views. There's also a shaded swimming pool, library and superb Tuscan-style cuisine. Children welcome. FB $\overline{$560}$, game package $\overline{$790}$

Selous Impala Camp ☎ 0753 115908 or ☎ 0787 817591 (both Dar), ⊛ adventurecampstz.com. Amid borassus palms and tamarinds on the Rufiji's north bank, between Mzizimia and Siwandu lakes, the accent is firmly on wildlife, including in the camp itself. The eight tents are rather plain (no colonial window-dressing here) and have river-view verandas, as does the bar, and a lovely open-sided two-storey main building made of wood and *makuti*. There's also a swimming pool. Children welcome. FB $\overline{$1190}$, game package $\overline{$1250}$

Siwandu ☎ 022 212 8485 (Dar), ⊛ selous.com. In a grove of lakeshore palms and *miombo* behind Lake Nzerekera, this is actually two locations, north and south, each with their own bar and dining area, lounges with wooden decks, and swimming pools. Understated elegance is the hallmark: luxurious octagonal tents under thatched roofs, personal butlers, sophisticated food, expert guides and great wildlife viewing even within the camp. No children under 8. Game package $\overline{$1700}$

OUTSIDE THE RESERVE

Jimbiza Lodge 3km from Mtemere Gate ☎ 022 261 8057 (Dar) or ☎ 0682 642012, ⊛ jimbizaselous.com. A nicely unfussy Tanzanian-run place with a spread of decent accommodation and a laidback vibe. The riverside *bandas* resemble guesthouse rooms and are nothing special at the price – better are the "riverside tents" (walk-in affairs under thatched shelters, with bathrooms and verandas), and

---

CAMPING IN AND AROUND SELOUS

The most exciting, hair-raising and potentially cheapest way of experiencing Selous – and the nocturnal concerts given by bush babies, bull frogs, lions, hippos and hyenas – is to camp. **Inside the reserve** are two public campsites: *Beho Beho Bridge* and *Lake Tagalala* ($30 per person, plus entry fees and $20 for an obligatory armed guard). Both have long-drop toilets and water (which needs purifying). Campfires are permitted if dead wood is used. **Outside the reserve**, you can pitch at *Selous River Camp* or *Jimbiza Lodge*.

LUXURY FLY-CAMPING

Some of Selous' upmarket camps and lodges offer optional **fly-camping excursions**, involving walks through bush and forest guided by white-hunter-type chaps, accompanied by armed rangers, and, for a gratuitous dab of colour, Maasai warriors. The camps are set up ahead of your arrival, and come with hot bucket showers hung from trees, long-drop or chemical toilets, evening banquets around campfires and champagne breakfasts. Prices start at a wallet-melting $1000 per person per day (minimum two nights) – rather rich given that you'll probably be sleeping on a camp bed in a small dome tent. More comfortable are the tents used by companies operating upmarket **seasonal tented camps** (also called "mobile camps" or "private camps"): Authentic Tanzania (⊛ authentictanzania.com) has a good reputation.

OPPOSITE WOMAN CARRYING A BASKET OF CARROTS, ULUGURU MOUNTAINS (P.198) >

similar "treetop rooms" (halfway up tree trunks), but the best deal is camping ($15 per person or $25 per person in their tent, to which add $15 a meal). FB $280–360

★**Sable Mountain Lodge** 10km from Kisaki village outside Matambwe Gate ☎022 211 0507 or ☎0713 323318 (both in Dar), ⓦselouslodge.com. Occupying three peaks of the Beho Beho Mountains above thick forest, with eight simple but stylish stone cottages and five luxury tented *bandas* facing the Uluguru Mountains, all secluded and with verandas and solar-powered light. The best – two "honeymoon *bandas*" – have private plunge pools and beautiful views down a valley towards a waterhole. A tree house nearby provides good game viewing; there's also a "snug" for star-gazing, two restaurants and bars, swimming pool, evening campfire and warm relations with local villages (who are paid a percentage of profits; good village tours). No children under 6. FB $350–590, game package (excluding reserve fees) $530–770

Selous Mbega Camp 1.4km from Mtemere Gate ☎022 265 0250 (Dar) or ☎0784 624664, ⓦselous-mbega -camp.com. Nestled amid lush riverine woodland (colobus monkeys – *mbega* – are sometimes seen), this has a dozen large, en-suite tents pitched on attractive wooden platforms, ten with river-facing verandas, and various more permanent

buildings in a mixture of European and African styles. Also ha‹ a restaurant enveloping a mahogany tree. FB $200

★**Selous River Camp** 1.2km from Mtemere Gate ☎0784 237525, ⓦselousrivercamp.com. An affordable self-catering place on the forested riverbank run by a charming Tanzanian–British couple. You can camp or stay in a walk-in tent, or – booking ahead – stay at delightful en-suite "mudhut" *bandas*, which have raised wooden verandas with wonderful views. The bar has similar vistas. Good food, but you can also self-cater (stock up on the basics in Mloka village): a cooking fire is provided. Children welcome. Camping $10 per person. FB *bandas* $285, tents $155

Selous Riverside Safari Camp 6km from Mtemere Gate, 2.5km southeast of Mloka ☎0715 278499 or ☎022 213 6770, ⓦselousriversidecamp.com. Several kilometres downstream from the other east-side options, this is, for now, nicely isolated and unpretentious, but pricey. It has ten large and attractively furnished tents (with mosquito screens) raised on wooden platforms under *makuti* shelters, with dense forest behind, all with river-view verandas. Meals are taken on a wooden deck beside a swimming pool, also with views. Tasty, mostly Tanzanian food, efficient staff and good guides. Game package from $550

Udzungwa Mountains National Park

Even with a thesaurus to hand, it's difficult to do justice to the wonder that is **Udzungwa Mountains National Park**, an immaculate forest-cloaked wilderness whose 1900 square kilometres are among the most biodiverse on earth. Protected as a national park in 1992, the driving rationale was to conserve the **catchments** of the Kilombero and Great Ruaha rivers, lifeblood of the Selous and of human populations elsewhere. The authorities of course also knew that the area they were protecting was rich in species, but just how rich continues to amaze. Forget about rare bugs and plants, new discoveries of which are two to a penny: Udzungwa still has the habit of turning up *mammals* hitherto unknown to science, the latest being the world's largest shrew (60cm from tip to toe), and not just a new species but an entirely new genus of monkey, which turned up at the same time it was also found at Kitulo National Park.

Like the Uluguru and Usambara mountains, the Udzungwas are part of the **Eastern Arc** (see box, p.256), a disjointed chain of ancient mountains whose great age and isolation, and a steady rain-soaked climate, has allowed its forests to evolve independently from each other, and quite spectacularly. But whereas most of the Eastern Arc's ranges have suffered major environmental damage over the last 150 years, Udzungwa is pristine, thanks both to its unusually steep terrain (limiting human intervention to the lowlands), and **taboos**. Locals around Udzungwa believe the mountain's forests are the abode of ancestral spirits (a belief that crops up elsewhere in Tanzania in places with long-established primate populations), so they restricted access to ceremonial purposes, and for burials. To disturb the spirits or the graves, people say, will bring great calamity, and should anyone dare cut down a *mitogo* tree, they're sure to become a lion's next meal… The result is the only place in East Africa with an unbroken virgin forest canopy from a low point of 250m above sea level to more than 2km high, covering *miombo* woodland, bamboo and lowland forest containing trees 50m tall, to montane rainforest up in the clouds.

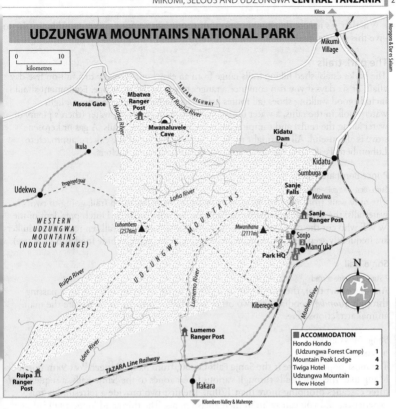

UDZUNGWA MOUNTAINS NATIONAL PARK

ACCOMMODATION	
Hondo Hondo (Udzungwa Forest Camp)	1
Mountain Peak Lodge	4
Twiga Hotel	2
Udzungwa Mountain View Hotel	3

Udzungwa's wildlife can be seen all year round, but as you'll be hiking the **best times to visit** are the dry months from June to October and December to February.

Biodiversity

Given its exceptionally well-preserved forest cover, Udzungwa's wildlife is rich, if not always easy to see. The park contains Tanzania's widest selection of **primates**, its twelve species including the recently discovered **kipunji** monkey, and four **endemics**: the Sanje crested mangabey, the Iringa (or Uhehe) red colobus, and two species of dwarf galago or bushbaby. Other primates include the thick-tailed galago, blue monkey and black-and-white colobus. The primates are concentrated in the east of the park, which is great news for hikers as this is where the main walking trails are located. Also frequently seen are **buffalo** (keep your distance), but the most you're likely to see of **elephants** is their droppings, or patches of vegetation flattened by portly backsides. **Rarer animals** include the red-legged sun squirrel, the recently rediscovered Lowe's servaline genet (previously seen seventy years ago), the red duiker, Abbot's duiker (also called blue duiker), Livingstone's suni, bush pig, bushbuck, spiny mice, the comical chequered elephant shrew (named after its trunk-like snout), and, also recently discovered, Philips' Congo shrew and the grey-faced sengi – a truly **giant elephant shrew** (whose wispy 700g somehow fill a 60cm-long frame). **Birders** are in for a treat, too, with possible sightings of rufous-winged sunbirds or Udzungwa partridges, both of them rare endemics. Other endemics include millipedes, a tree frog, more than seventy species of spider, a gecko, a skink, and the nattily named pygmy bearded chameleon.

Whether it's nature that turns you on, or you're just up for a yomp, you'd be insane to give this place a miss.

The park trails

The park's established **hiking trails** range from an easy hour's dawdle to a full-on five-day affair, or six days if you can convince a ranger to rise to the challenge. **Equipment** should include good walking shoes (all routes have steep and/or slippery sections), light waterproofs in the rains, a water bottle, something for purifying water (there's plenty of water along the trails) and camping equipment for overnight trails. A gas or kerosene stove is also useful. All overnight trails, with the exception of the eastern approach to Luhombero Peak, have **campsites** equipped with toilets and shelters.

Prince Bernhard Trail

1km • 40min • No guide needed

The only walk from the park headquarters is the **Prince Bernhard Trail**, going to two waterfalls: the small Prince Bernhard Falls, named after the then Dutch president of the WWF who cut the park's ribbon in 1992, and the Njokamoni Falls en route. Red duikers are frequently seen, as are habituated baboons and mangabeys (hide food and take care).

Sonjo Trail

2.5km • 2hr • Guide needed

Another short trail, the **Sonjo Trail**, starts 5km north of Mang'ula at Sonjo, passing through *miombo* woodland to two other waterfalls. Primates and birds are the main animal attractions here.

Sanje Falls Circuit

5km • 4hr • Guide needed

The most popular route is the **Sanje Falls Circuit**, from Sanje Ranger Post 9km north of Mang'ula. The trail heads through various forest zones to the Sanje Falls, a sequence of three cascades dropping more than 170m. The first two provide a refreshingly misty experience, and you can swim in their splash pools. The third and longest fall is difficult to see as you emerge from the dense forest right on top of it, though the hollows and undulating channels gouged into the rock by water are interesting. You can see the falls clearly on the way down to Sanje village, or on the bus from Mikumi for that matter. Primates are frequently seen, as are birds and butterflies.

Campsite 3 Circuit

13km • 10hr • Ranger or guide needed

The **Campsite 3 Circuit** is best for wildlife (or at least their dung), and also gives good odds on seeing bushbuck and duiker as well as primates, birds and butterflies. The trail starts at Campsite 3, 100m north of *Udzungwa Mountain View Hotel*, and ends 3km north of Mang'ula.

Mwanihana Trail

38km • Three days, two nights • Armed ranger needed

The **Mwanihana Trail** starts at Sonjo, 5km north of Mang'ula, and is the highlight of many a visit to Tanzania, taking you to Udzungwa's second-highest peak, Mwanihana (2111m). Be warned, however: the walk is exhausting (19km uphill, returning the same way) and you need to be sure-footed. The trail follows the Sonjo River for the most part, its steep and narrow valley necessitating at least fifteen crossings; in the dry season this just means wading across, but in the rains you'll be struggling through torrents while hanging on grimly to a guide rope, so unless you're covered by ample life insurance avoid this one from March to May. At other times you have the pleasure of passing through every one of the park's forest zones, before emerging onto the grassy plateau by the peak. The park blurb promises duiker, elephant and a herd of buffalo, but you'd be lucky to see any of them. More likely are glimpses of various monkeys. There are also lots of butterflies and birds.

Lumemo Trail

65km • Five days, four nights • Ranger needed

The park's newest walk is the **Lumemo Trail**, a clockwise circuit up the Lumemo (or Lumeno) River and down along the northern side of Mwanihana Peak. Access to the start of the trail is through Lumemo Ranger Post near Ifakara, around 50km south of Mang'ula. The cheapest way there is to arrange for the rangers to pick you from Ifakara train station, which you can reach by Coaster. If you're driving, turn right at the train station, and it's 12km along. A hike up to the park's highest point, **Luhombero Peak** (2576m; six days; armed ranger needed), is a serious and rarely attempted undertaking, as the trail is difficult to follow.

ESSENTIALS

Park headquarters The park headquarters are by the park gate in Mang'ula, 60km south of Mikumi village (☎ 023 262 0224, ☎ 0689 062291 or ☎ 0767 536131, ✉ udzungwa @gmail.com or ✉ udzungwa@tanzaniaparks.com).

Entrance fees The $30 entrance fee (valid 24hr, payable at the park headquarters by Visa or MasterCard) is for a single entry only.

Additional costs The only hiking trail starting at the park headquarters is the short Prince Bernhard Trail. All others require official guide or armed ranger ($20 per day), and transport to the starting point once you've paid your fees at

UDZUNGWA NATIONAL PARK

Mang'ula: you could catch a Coaster; alternatively, rent a Land Rover from the park, which charges approximately $30 per group for a lift to Sanje Ranger Post 9km north, or, for longer journeys, $150 for 100km. For long hikes you'll appreciate a porter, hired through the park. Suggested daily payments are Tsh15,000 for a 16–20kg load on the Sanje Falls Circuit, Tsh20,000 for Mwanihana Peak and Tsh25,000 for Luhombero Peak.

Information The park headquarters sells a map and a colourful guidebook. The park's website is ⓦ udzungwa .org.

ARRIVAL AND DEPARTURE

The western section of the park is more easily accessed from Iringa (see p.424).

By bus Mang'ula is on the road to Ifakara, to where there are daily buses and Coasters from Dar, Morogoro and Mikumi village. From the latter, the first vehicles leave around 10am (roughly hourly thereafter), but are often packed and badly driven, so it might be better waiting for Islam's Bus from Morogoro, which passes Mikumi at around 11am; leaving Mang'ula, buses for Dar also pass through at around 11am; Coaster minibuses to Mikumi and Morogoro are roughly hourly until 4pm.

Destinations (Mang'ula) Dar (2 daily; 7hr); Mikumi (2 daily plus hourly Coasters; 1hr 30min); Morogoro (2 daily plus occasional Coasters; 3hr 30min–4hr).

By 4WD Turning south off the Tanzam highway at Mikumi

village, you leave safari land behind and, after 40km or so, you leave the sealed road, too. The dirt road continues south, wending its bumpy and dusty way between the lime-green expanse of sugar cane plantations and rice paddies in the Msolwa Valley to the east, and the increasingly green and heavily forested Udzungwa Mountains to the west. The park headquarters, where you pay your entry fees, are 200m west of the road at Mang'ula, 60km from Mikumi village. If you're coming in your own vehicle, leave it at the park headquarters; they'll look after bags too.

By train Trains are not useful (once a week each from Dar and Mbeya, both arriving at night).

ACCOMMODATION, EATING AND DRINKING

Lying outside the park, but within 10min walk of the headquarters, are several **hotels** geared to hikers, including a fantastic lodge. There are basic guesthouses in Mang'ula village, 2km southeast: walk south along the main road past *Udzungwa Mountain View Hotel*, turn left at the post office and continue straight ahead. **Camping** is possible both inside the park, and outside.

★**Hondo Hondo (Udzungwa Forest Camp)** 100m north of the park headquarters ☎ 0758 844228, ⓦ udzungwaforestcamp.com. Run in collaboration with villagers by Wild Things Safaris (see p.103), this wonderful

place occupies what used to be farmland, since replanted with hundreds of trees, and has something for all budgets. At the lower end, the campsite has good bathrooms, a shop for snacks and essentials, tent hire ($6 per person), and four simple but comfortable mud-and-thatch *bandas* with double beds and nets, all with views over the valley. For something finer, the lodge tents are elegantly decked out, yet still rustic. But just as good are the huge number of activities offered, from short walks and bicycle rides (to village, for birding, or in a forest, each for around $15 per person), to rock climbing, canoeing, and multi-day treks inside the park, including the epic five-day Lumemo trail (approximately $200 per person per night). They also offer affordable safaris to Mikumi ($220 per vehicle plus park fees). Camping $6 per person ($16 with breakfast). BB (add $32 per person for FB) *bandas* $64, lodge tents $216

Mountain Peak Lodge Mang'ula village, 876m from the main road (so sayeth the sign) ☎ 0784 650392. Best of the local guesthouses, clean and with safe parking. Some of its rooms have bathrooms (squat toilets), all have fans and box nets, and there's a bar and restaurant (chicken or beef with chips or rice). Tsh12,000

TANAPA campsites Various locations; pay at the gate. The best of the park's three permanent campsites (with pit latrines but nothing else) is "number 2", in a beautiful patch of forest 2km inside the gate near a bubbling brook with swimmable rock pools. Per person $30 (plus park fees).

Twiga Hotel 1km east from the park headquarters (signposted), same contacts as the park headquarters. Set in shady gardens, this pleasantly rambling old place – recently renovated – is run by the park authority. It has plenty of simple but perfectly good twin-bed rooms, some with bathrooms, all with large nets, balconies and TV. Tasty food available (around Tsh10,000), and drinks. BB$60

Udzungwa Mountain View Hotel 600m south of the park headquarters ☎ 023 262 0218 or ☎ 0784 125111. Owned by Mikumi's *Genesis Motel*, this is similarly costly and also in need of renovation, but enjoys a nice location under a thick canopy of trees. It has twenty en-suite, twin-bed rooms, with a choice of fan or a/c. The restaurant charges upwards of Tsh15,000 a plate, but does have prawns and, somewhat worryingly, impala. There's also a bar with TV. Camping per person $5, BB $60

4 Dodoma

Tanzania's geographical centre – an arid plateau gouged by sand-filled gullies and studded with weathered granite outcrops – is inching ever closer to fully-blown desert. At its heart lies the planned city of **DODOMA**, Tanzania's political capital since 1973, and a reminder of a time when ideology and ideals carried more weight than common sense. The city has little of interest to tourists, but it's a pleasant stop nonetheless.

Dodoma is testimony to President Nyerere's idealistic plans for nation-building. Although he got it right most of the time, his choice of Dodoma was less felicitous. Straddling the Central Line railway, the site was chosen primarily on account of its location at the country's geographical heart, which, unfortunately, happens to be a disconsolately arid nowhere. Inspired by the artificial cities of Brasília (Brazil) and Abuja (Nigeria), Dodoma was supposed to be the centrepiece of Tanzania's multitribal identity, a kind of giant *Ujamaa* village. But the remote location, the billowing dust storms and the 40°C-plus temperatures were never going to facilitate things. The country's parliament has been there since 1996, but the government itself – well, every time it half-heartedly tries to shift itself from Dar es Salaam, twelve months later you'll find that the ministries and departments have snuck back to the coast.

DODOMA: THAT SINKING FEELING

Dodoma's name is a corruption of the Kigogo word *idodomia* or *yadodomela*, meaning "sinking" or "sunk". The prosaic explanation is that it was a metaphor for the fate of invaders unable to escape the spears and arrows of the brave Gogo defenders, but a taller tale refers to an elephant that came to drink in the Kikuyu River, got stuck and began to sink – to the delight of newspaper critics ever-fond of the old "white elephant" jibe. Another tale tells of Gogo warriors secretly lifting a herd of cattle from the Hehe, their southern neighbours. The Gogo feasted on the cattle, leaving only the tails, which they then stuck into the ground. When the Hehe came looking for their herd, the Gogo pointed to the tails and exclaimed, "Look, your cattle have sunk into the mud!"

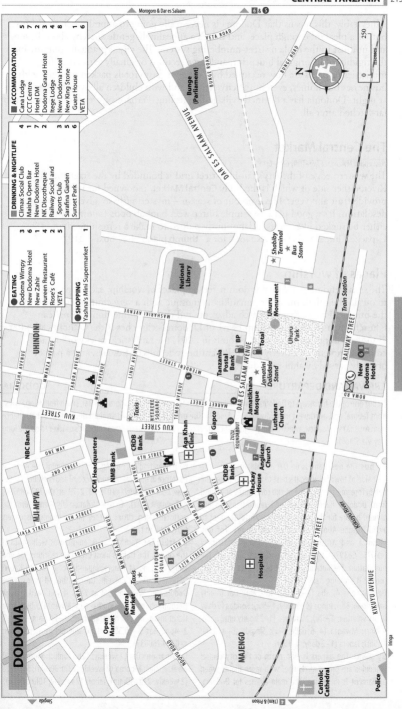

DODOMA

Morogoro & Dar es Salaam   6 & 5

■ ACCOMMODATION
Cana Lodge	5
CCT Centre	7
Hotel DM	2
Dodoma Grand Hotel	3
Itege Lodge	4
New Dodoma Hotel	8
New King Stone	1
Guest House	
VETA	6

■ DRINKING & NIGHTLIFE
Climax Social Club	4
Maisha Open Bar	1
New Dodoma Hotel	7
NK Discotheque	2
Railway Social and	3
Sports Club	
Sarafina Garden	5
Sunset Park	6

■ EATING
Dodoma Wimpy	3
New Dodoma Hotel	6
New Zahir	1
Nureen Restaurant	4
Rose's Café	2
VETA	5

■ SHOPPING
Yashna's Mini Supermarket	1

Singida

Iringa

Inevitably, this means that Dodoma is never really going to appeal much to visitors, but it's a pleasant enough place, and there's a appealingly gentle anarchy about it, too, and not just in the broken street-numbering system. The city is gradually outgrowing the rigidity of its original blueprint, and large sections originally earmarked for ministries or parks are now occupied by a maze of dusty roads packed not only with businesses but homes, even in the city centre, and with children all over the place, even at night, Dodoma has a distinctly village-like feeling. Perhaps Nyerere's dream wasn't so far-fetched after all.

The Central Market

West end of Mwangaza Ave • Daily 6am–6pm

The western edge of the city's fan-like street grid is bounded by the stagnant Kikuyu River, either side of which is the lively **Central Market**, renowned for its ability to provide fruit and vegetables even out of season – mysteriously so, given the region's desolation. It's a good place to sample bittersweet **baobab pods** (*ubuyu*), which can either be sucked like sweets or laboriously pulped to make a refreshing vitamin C-packed juice. You could also look for a "**thumb piano**" (see box, p.219).

Places of worship

The south end of Kuu Street is dominated by **places of worship**, each apparently vying to outdo the other: the brick Jamatikhana mosque with a very church-like clock tower, the minimalistic Lutheran church adjacent, and the Byzantine-domed Anglican Church opposite. The most impressive of Dodoma's churches is the **Catholic cathedral**, 2km west along Railway Street. Rebuilt in 2001, the fantastical brickwork facade comes complete with overly gilded Byzantine-style mosaic frescoes, and a pair of ornately carved Swahili-style doors.

ARRIVAL AND DEPARTURE   **DODOMA**

All but one of the highways to Dodoma have finally been tarred: east from Morogoro and Dar, south from Iringa, west from Tabora, and northwest from Mwanza via Singida. The exception is the road straight down from Babati (hence from Arusha) via Kondoa, which is still rough, but earmarked for asphalt – in the meantime, it's quicker to go the long way via Singida.

By bus The bus stand is on Dar es Salaam Ave on the east side of town; as ever, it's best to buy your ticket the day before you travel. None of the companies operating from Dodoma have unblemished reputations, so ask around before for the safest one on your route. Ones to avoid include Abood, Moro Best and Sumry. For Dar, Mwanza and Arusha, the best company is Shabiby (☏0755 683976), with its own enclosure adjoining the bus station. For Kondoa, the last bus leaves at midday (unless it's raining heavily).

Destinations Arusha (2–3 daily; 10–12hr); Dar (hourly until noon; 8hr); Iringa (4–6 daily; 4–5hr); Kondoa (5 daily in dry weather; 4–5hr); Morogoro (1–2 hourly until noon; 4–5hr); Mwanza (4–6 daily; 9hr); Singida (6–8 daily; 4–5hr); Tabora (1–2 daily; 8–10hr).

By plane The airport is 4km north of the city centre: schedules are prone to change, with more flights when parliament is in session. The main airlines for Dodoma,

both operating to and from Dar (1hr 40min), are Auric Air (no office in Dodoma; ⓦauricair.com) and Flightlink (at the *New Dodoma Hotel*; ☏0754 972173 or ☏0787 845200, ⓦflightlink.co.tz). Coastal Aviation fly here from the northern safari circuit if they have enough passengers (ⓦcoastal.co.tz).

By train The train station is ten minutes' walk south of the centre. The train is most useful for reaching Kigoma and, changing at Tabora, Mpanda for access to Katavi National Park. At present, the westbound trains leave Dodoma on Wed and Sat at 7am. If you need a bunk (recommended for Kigoma and Mwanza), buy your ticket in advance at the station (Mon–Fri 8am–noon & 2–4pm, Sat 8–10.30am, and 2hr before departures; ☏0714 260633).

Destinations Dar (2 weekly; 12hr 30min); Morogoro (2 weekly; 7hr); Kigoma (2 weekly; 23hr 30min); Mwanza (2 weekly; 23hr 30min); Tabora (2 weekly; 10hr 30min).

GETTING AROUND AND INFORMATION

By daladala Daladalas, locally nicknamed "Express", leave from Jamatini Stand on Dar es Salaam Ave, and cover the whole city (Tsh400 for most journeys).

By taxi Taxis congregate at transport terminals and outside the market; trips within the city cost Tsh4000–5000.

Advice Dodoma has plenty of (rarely pushy) beggars, often living with polio: you'll feel better with some coins or Tsh500 banknotes to hand. If the sun is wearying, invest in a colourful parasol, as many locals do.

ACCOMMODATION

Dodoma has an ever-growing selection of quite decent **accommodation**. A good thing too, as at times you'll have to visit three or four places before finding a free room. For many hoteliers, a "single" room means one with a double bed that can be shared by a couple. In the centre, the main concentration of hotels is in the fan-like grid of numbered streets west of Kuu Street; there are more mid-range choices in "Area C", a shadeless thirty-minute walk north from the centre, beyond the airstrip: catch a daladala from Jamatini stand towards Mnadani. Dodoma's **water** supply is unreliable and may be tainted by pesticides.

Cana Lodge 9th St **T** 0754 919996 or **T** 026 232 1199, **E** mwangason@yahoo.com. A reliable option if nothing special, and a little more expensive than similar places in this area, with well-kept en-suite rooms, all with cable TV, fans and nets, and very good showers. The better rooms are upstairs. There's also a modest restaurant and bar on the ground floor, and safe parking. BB **Tsh30,000**

CCT Centre Zuzu roundabout **T** 0754/473430, **E** cct_ctc@yahoo.com. Run by the Anglican Church, this has lots of bare rooms in polygonal clusters connected by open-sided corridors, mostly with shared bathrooms. Maintenance isn't divine – there are holey mosquito nets and window screens, and water problems – but the beds are clean, and there are also two- and three-bedroom units sharing sitting rooms, useful for families. Singles are cheap by local standards (Tsh12,000). Internet café and basic restaurant. Book ahead to avoid getting crowded out by a conference or workshop. BB **Tsh20,000**

Hotel DM Ndovu Rd **T** 0714 309230. Best-priced of the central options, near the market, with tatty but acceptable modern rooms, all with satellite TV, some with a/c, and others with massive double beds. There's a lively bar behind it with cheap meals (and a lot of noise weekend nights). BB **Tsh25,000**

Dodoma Grand Hotel Independence Sq **T** 026 232 3280 or **T** 0785 079777, **E** jackson.makundi@yahoo.com. A dependable but unexciting central option, with twenty rooms, all with cable TV and small ceiling fan, but no nets (rooms are sprayed if needed); the better rooms have balconies. First-floor restaurant. BB **Tsh40,000**

Itege Lodge 11th St **T** 0755 763574. A friendly and perfectly decent cheapie on several floors. All rooms with cable TV, box net and fan. **Tsh25,000**

New Dodoma Hotel Railway St **T** 026 232 1641, **W** newdodomahotel.com. Dodoma's former *Railway Hotel* is one of central Tanzania's best lodgings, with most of its 91 rooms, mostly twins and all with cable TV, wrapped around an attractive courtyard. The small standard ones have big beds (but small mosquito nets); better are the slightly larger deluxe rooms, some with a/c instead of fans, others with balconies. Service is as polished as the marble floors in the restaurants and bar, and there are plenty of tables in the courtyard next to an amusing pool and fake waterfall. There's also a proper if slightly murky swimming pool, a health "spa", internet café, wi-fi and forex. Safe parking. BB standard **$70**, deluxe **$95**

New King Stone Guest House 9th St **T** 026 232 3057. An excellent budget choice but often full, with small clean rooms, squat toilets (some rooms en suite), big box nets, cotton sheets, fan, even satellite TV. **Tsh15,000**

VETA VETA Rd, 2km east **T** 026 232 2931, **E** vetadom@do.ucc.co.tz. A training centre for chefs, waiters and hotel staff whose teachers know their stuff: rooms are clean and well kept, there's reliable hot water and service is excellent, making for a very pleasant stay. The 39 rooms have TVs: singles have round nets, twins (can be pushed together) have box nets; cheaper rooms share bathrooms. Good restaurant and bar (see p.218). Book ahead. BB **Tsh20,000–40,000**

EATING

Dodoma's selection of proper restaurants is surprisingly limited, and includes a number of decent if unexciting places in all but the cheapest hotels. You'll find street food and coffee vendors around the market, and along Dar es Salaam Ave.

Dodoma Wimpy Zuzu roundabout. No relation to the multinational, this popular outdoor meeting place serves fast-food snacks like samosas, fried chicken, chips and *kababu*; excellent *mishkaki*; plus coffee, tea and sodas; and

4

– for breakfast – *supu*. Also has full lunches (less than Tsh4000), but get there early for the full choice. No alcohol. Closed during Ramadan. Daily 6am–9pm.

★ **New Dodoma Hotel** Railway St ☎ 026 232 1641 or ☎ 0788 487668. Dodoma's plushest hotel contains three restaurants: *Ndigwa* for a mixture of cuisines "to please and tease"; the Italian *Cafe Massimo*, making good use of Tanzania's limited but excellent cheese production (try the risotto Gorgonzola for Tsh17,000); and *China Garden*, for genuine Cantonese, including *mapo* (tofu), sizzlers and fresh salads. You can also eat in the courtyard outside, which has a children's play area and *nyama choma* bar. Daily 10am–11pm.

New Zahir Mtendeni St. Down in the dumps but has been for years, this is still adequate for cheap full meals, including big portions of *pilau*, stews and birianis (all around Tsh4000), and real juice, including tamarind. No alcohol. Daily 7am–9pm.

Nureen Restaurant Dar es Salaam Ave. A down-at-heel Indian place, but their curries can be very good (unlike their snacks). Good *mishkaki* is sold on the street outside. No alcohol. Mon–Sat 11.30am–3pm.

Rose's Café 9th St, next to Cana Lodge. Cheap Tanzanian–Indian place, handy for snacks but full meals are much better value, featuring a small selection of curries, masalas and stews with rice or chapati, costing Tsh3500–5000. It also offers a very good lunchtime vegetarian *thali* (Tsh7000). Mon–Sat 9am–6pm.

VETA VETA Rd, 2km east ☎ 026 232 2931. Part of the training school (see p.217), the chef being the instructor, the staff his students: they're doing good work, as both food and service are excellent. There's a wide choice of tasty dishes (but nothing vegetarian) as well as pastries and, if you order a day early, a selection of set menus. Main courses cost Tsh6500 and up. Daily noon–3pm & 7–11pm.

DRINKING AND NIGHTLIFE

Dodoma has a good number of attractive outdoor **beer gardens**, all dishing up excellent *nyama choma*, grilled bananas, chicken and other snacks. The city's nocturnal scene is ever-changing, especially as regards venues for live bands. These tend to be in well-to-do outskirts, especially Area "D" district northeast of the airport. Posters announcing upcoming gigs are displayed throughout the city, and there are also banners strung over Independence Square near the market.

Climax Social Club 3km west of the centre beyond the prison ☎ 026 239 0252. Until Independence, this was Dodoma's main colonial hangout, and is still favoured by expats. As well as its bar and restaurant, there's a swimming pool. Daily membership Tsh2000. Daily noon–midnight.

Maisha Open Bar Ndovu Rd. In a courtyard behind *Hotel DM*, this is a sleepy bar and restaurant by day, but comes alive on weekend nights with impromptu discos and even, occasionally, live bands. Daily 10am–late.

New Dodoma Hotel Railway St. Expensive drinks in the hotel's peaceful courtyard, or at a rondavel perched over its fanciful "swimming" pool (there's a full-sized one at the back). Daily noon–10pm.

NK Discotheque Dar es Salaam Ave. Occupying a former cinema, this is Dodoma's only central disco, and sometimes also has live music. Wed, Fri & Sat 9pm–late, Sun from 3.30pm.

Railway Social and Sports Club East side of Uhuru Park, off Dar es Salaam Ave. A pleasant

---

DODOMA WINE

The noble craft of **winemaking** was introduced to Dodoma by Italian missionaries more than a century ago, and, until very recently indeed, had clearly lost something in translation, as the output from Dodoma's Tanganyika Vineyards company was quite possibly the world's worst plonk, imbibing which required a solid sense of humour (and stomach) to enjoy (the best was the Chenin Blanc, not for its cheesy bouquet, but for mercifully numbing your taste buds after the first sip).

Alas, for aficionados of comic tipples, something strange has happened, courtesy of a new generation of Italian vintners: Dodoma's wine is not just palatable these days, but is sometimes even good, particularly so an ever-widening offering of fortified wines made in the style of Port and Sherry. Of the normal wines, the most widely distributed in Tanzania is the unremarkable but nonetheless drinkable "Dodoma" (Dry Red/Dry White) by Tanzania Distillers, but the best, courtesy of the CetaWico winery (ⓦ cetawico.com), is "Presidential", made from Aglianico grapes.

To sample a selection *in situ*, head to the bar of the *New Dodoma Hotel*; to buy a bottle or five, *Yashna's Mini Supermarket* (see p.219) stocks the lot.

THE MUSIC OF THE GOGO

The Gogo are famous throughout Tanzania for their musical prowess, and one of their number, the late Hukwe Ubi Zawose, even made inroads on the World Music circuit. The ensemble of traditional Gogo music is called **sawosi** (in Kiswahili, *ngoma ya kigogo*), and is some of the most beautiful, haunting and subtle music you're ever likely to hear.

In common with the musical traditions of other "Nilotic-speaking" groups such as the Maasai, **multipart polyphony** is the thing: a subtle interweave of different rhythms, in which each musician plays or sings just a small part of one rhythm, which they're free to embellish within the greater scheme of things. This allows for a quasi-mathematical complexity.

While for the Maasai this is a purely vocal trick, for the Gogo the technique reaches its hypnotic apogee in an intricate interplay of voices with instruments: single-stringed **zeze** fiddles, and **marimba ya mkono** hand xylophones (or "thumb pianos"), also known by their Shona name, *mbira*. The marimbas are the Gogo's calling card: hand-held wooden sound boxes, either rectangular or rhomboidal, fitted with an array of metal forks which, nowadays, more often than not are metal shafts taken from screwdrivers.

Highly **recommended listening** are two tapes of Gogo recordings sold at the Tanzania Broadcasting Company in Dar (see p.112); CDs are rarely available in Tanzania (see p.533). If you're a dedicated music fanatic, the best time for *sawosi* (in Dodoma Region's villages, not in town) is the harvest and circumcision season from June to August, especially July, which features the *cidwanga* dance conducted by healers, in which ancestors are remembered and praised.

---

bar-cum-restaurant, somewhat in the shadow of the much busier (and shadier) *Sunset Park* next door, with a TV and good traditional Tanzanian food. Daily 8am–late.

Sarafina Garden Kuu St. Friendly outdoor place, but watch you don't come a cropper on the foot-snagging woodwork beside the bar, intended to stop people stealing the stools. Daily 8am–late.

Sunset Park East side of Uhuru Park. An oasis of shady trees and shrubs with plenty of secluded seating, this is very popular with workers at the end of their shifts (and yes, there *is* a sunset, over the bus stand). Good music, *nyama choma* and snacks. Daily 8am–late.

DIRECTORY

Health The best clinics are the Aga Khan Clinic, 6th St (☎026 232 2455), and Mackay House, west end of Dar es Salaam Ave (☎026 232 4299). A reasonable pharmacy is Central Tanganyika Chemist, Dar es Salaam Ave, west of Zuzu roundabout (☎026 232 4506).

Internet access Reliable places include *New Dodoma Hotel* (Mon–Sat 8am–6pm, Sun 8am–2.30pm; Tsh2000/hr), and the post office almost next door (daily 7.30am–8pm).

Money Quickest for changing cash is the *New Dodoma Hotel*, Railway St (daily 8am–9pm). The main banks are on Kuu St, all with ATMs.

Police Kikuyu Ave, on the way to Iringa ☎026 232 4266.

Supermarket Yashna's Mini Supermarket, 6th St, behind GAPCO near Zuzu roundabout (Mon–Sat 9am–6pm, Sun 10am–2.30pm), stocks expensive imported treats guaranteed to please, and most of Dodoma's wines.

Swimming pool *New Dodoma Hotel* charges non-guests Tsh5000.

Kondoa

Some 158km north of Dodoma along an infamously bad road is the small and dusty/muddy town of **KONDOA**, which can be a handy base for visiting the ancient **rock paintings** of the Irangi Hills. As the town's cultural tourism programme is now run out of Arusha, there's not a lot of reason to come here without having arranged things first, although if you're taking the direct road up from Dodoma, you may find yourself overnighting here in any case.

The town's **inhabitants** are mostly Rangi, but there are also Gogo and Sandawe, the latter having been hunter-gatherers until fifty years ago. Islam is the dominant religion: if you're awake at 5.30am, listen for hauntingly ethereal recitations of the 99 names of Allah. Perhaps because of its shared religion, the town has a strong if

THE RANGI

The main tribe in Kondoa and the Iringi Hills are the **Rangi** (also called Langi), an extraordinarily friendly and welcoming people. Wherever you go you'll be greeted with broad smiles, effusive greetings and handshakes, and gleeful kids going berserk as you pass by. Nowadays primarily agricultural, the Rangi's cattle-herding past is reflected in the saying "it is better to hit a person than his cattle", so if you're driving, take extra care. Originally plains-dwelling, the Rangi moved up into the hills a couple of centuries ago to avoid the inexorable advance of the warlike **Maasai**, and built their villages into wide natural hollows, rendering them almost invisible from the surrounding steppe. Nowadays, with no reason to hide, Rangi villages are notable for their use of **brickwork**, sometimes decorated with geometrical relief patterns similar to styles used in parts of Ethiopia and the Sahara. The Rangi's expertise in earthenware is even more artfully shown by their beautiful **black cooking pots**, which can be bought for a few thousand shillings at any of the region's markets (there's one every day somewhere in the hills – ask around). You'll see the pots perched on people's houses along with pumpkins – roofs are the only place where pots can be dried after washing without being smashed by the above-mentioned hyperactive children…

easy-going sense of identity, doubtlessly strengthened by the feeling that the government has ignored the region for too long – in spite of decades of promises, all roads leading to Kondoa remain unsurfaced, and are liable to be blocked in the rains. Unsurprisingly, the region is a stronghold of the opposition Civic United Front (CUF).

Kondoa itself has no real attractions, although the weird sight of gigantic baobabs growing in the town centre is memorable enough, and the town's **markets** are always fun; the main one adjoins the bus stand, and there's a tiny produce market a few blocks to the east beside a church, whose aged vendors are well worth the extra few shillings they'll winkle out of you. Few speak English, but no matter – people are eager to help out, and even the touts at the bus stand are uncommonly apologetic in their advances.

ARRIVAL AND DEPARTURE
KONDOA

By bus The bus stand is at the west end of town, one block south of the main road in. Most departures are at 6am. There are several daily buses and daladalas northwards to Babati and beyond, including Mtei Express (to Arusha) and Machame Bus (to Moshi via Arusha). Heading south, there are buses all the way to Dar, but to increase your chances of a safe ride beyond Dodoma (on devilishly fast tarmac), it's best to change in Dodoma, implying an overnight stop. For a wild run across the Maasai Steppe to Tanga via Korogwe, ask about Mwambao Bus and Coastal Bus, which leave at noon on Tuesday and Friday, stopping overnight at a guesthouse along the way, to arrive at 2pm the following afternoon.

Destinations Arusha (3–4 daily; 8–9hr); Babati (3–4 daily; 3–5hr); Dar (3 daily; 11hr); Dodoma (5 daily; 4–5hr); Kolo (5–6 daily; 1hr); Morogoro (3 daily; 8–9hr); Moshi (daily; 8–9hr); Pahi (daily; 2–3hr); Tanga (2 weekly; 24hr).

By 4WD Kondoa lies 3km west of the Babati–Dodoma road, slow-going on either side of Kondoa, and potentially treacherous in the rains, with the road from Dodoma, especially, likely to be blocked for days at a time between March and May.

INFORMATION

Cultural tourism programme The Kondoa Irangi Cultural Tourism programme is essentially a one-man operation run by Moshi Changai, who is now based in Arusha (☏0784 948858 or ☏0715 948858, ✉samoracha @yahoo.com, ⊕tanzaniaculturaltours.com). Don't let that put you off – although a locally based project would have been preferable, he's from Kondoa and knows the place backwards. Initial prices are relatively high on account of vehicle costs from Kondoa (or Arusha): for standard tours, a full day and night for two costs around $150 each, but you should get a substantial discount for cycling tours, or if you have your own vehicle. Activities include rock-painting tours, birding (and bird-trapping) with locals, honey-harvesting (best immediately after rains), traditional dances, consultations with a medicine woman, school visits, and a marvellous hike in the Sambwa Hills to

Ntomoko Falls where, myth has it, you might catch sight of Satu the snake, protector of the water source. Coming from Arusha, you might consider a seven-day round trip, which includes the Barbaig tribe, Lake Eyasi, and nights spent in

traditional flat-topped *tembe* houses (or camping). A women's co-operative provides meals.

Money NMB bank at the east end of town changes cash, but its ATM is for Tanzanian cards only.

ACCOMMODATION AND EATING

There's plenty of accommodation within a few hundred metres of the bus stand, and several more along Usandawe Rd (the road to Singida) which runs west from the south side of the bus stand. The bus stand is the focus for street food and coffee vendors.

New Planet Guest House 200m west of the bus stand along the continuation of the road in ☎ 0784 669322. Best of the lot, whose spotless rooms, some en suite, have large and comfortable beds, fans and TVs; they also cook tasty Tanzanian or continental dishes for under Tsh6000. BB **Tsh20,000**

Sunset Beach Guest House 800m along Usandawe Rd ☎ 0784 948858. Has a TV in its reception, some cheaper rooms sharing bathrooms, and food to order, but no alcohol. Or beach. **Tsh15,000**, en suite **Tsh20,000**

The Kondoa–Irangi rock paintings

The area between Singida and the Maasai Steppe to the east harbours one of the world's finest and most beautiful collections of rock art, collectively known as the **Kondoa–Irangi rock paintings** (or "Kolo rock paintings"), which give a vivid and fascinating insight into not just Tanzania's but humankind's earliest recorded history, and way of thinking. A World Heritage Site since 2006, the bulk of the paintings – an estimated 1600 spread around almost two hundred different locations – are in the **Irangi Hills** east of the Babati–Kondoa road. The most recent date from just a century or two ago, but the oldest may have been daubed an astonishing 28,000 years ago, placing them among the world's most ancient known examples of human artistic expression. There are fourteen major sites, each with an average of three painted shelters within a hundred metres or so of each other. The paintings are either on vertical rock faces with overhangs above, or on angled surfaces resembling cave entrances, both offering protection from millennia of rain, wind and sun. Most are located on the eastern edge of the Irangi Hills, giving striking views over the Maasai Steppe (and, more significantly, of the rising moon or sun).

Many of Tanzania's rock paintings have deteriorated at an alarming rate over the last few decades thanks to **vandalism**. Most obvious is the graffiti left by both Tanzanians and foreigners, which at two of Kondoa–Irangi's sites at least has defaced almost fifty percent of paintings that had hitherto survived thousands of years. Some panels have been disfigured by misguided "cleaning" efforts, while others have been damaged by attempts to enhance colours and contrast for photography by wetting the paintings, which dissolves the pigments. So, wherever you see rock art, please don't wet or touch the paintings (oil and acid in sweat has similar deleterious effects) or the surrounding rock. Depending on their orientation, the sites are best viewed and photographed in the morning or late evening, when the low sunlight enhances the paintings and lends a rich orange cast to the rock.

ARRIVAL AND INFORMATION   THE KONDOA–IRANGI ROCK PAINTINGS

The gateway to the Irangi Hills is Kolo village, 27km north of Kondoa, 82km south of Babati. Getting there in the rains is tricky, when the road from Babati can be extremely muddy, and the one from Kondoa possibly blocked, although it's due to be paved. With the exception of the "Kolo B" paintings, visitable on foot from Kolo (6km each way), access to the rock art sites is best by bike, using Kolo as your base (where you should be able to rent bicycles), or by 4WD, as the paintings are spread out over a 35km radius with limited public transport and accommodation.

By bus The 6am Machame Bus from Moshi to Kondoa and the 6am Mtei Express from Arusha to Kondoa pass through Kolo in the afternoon. There are also buses and daladalas from Babati, the last leaving around 10am. From Kondoa, catch any vehicle for Babati or Arusha, or wait for the midday bus to Pahi, deep in the Irangi Hills (it returns the next day at 4am).

On a tour The cultural tourism programmes in Kondoa (see p.220) and Babati (p.225) offer rock art tours, which – if you don't do any else with your time – amount to little more than car hire. At present, the most clued-up outfit for rock art tours

is Arusha's Finnish-run "Rock Art Information Centre", based at *Maasai Café* north of the AICC (☏ 0754 672256, ⊛ racctz.org) which offers a three-day trip from Arusha ($270 per person in a couple, $170 per person in a foursome): this includes one day with rock art, some cultural options, and two nights at their surprisingly classy *Amarula Campsite* near Kolo.

Permits Visitors to the rock art sites need a permit and a guide from the Antiquities Department on the main road in Kolo (☏ 0752 575096). The permit costs Tsh27,000, and a tip is appreciated.

ACCOMMODATION AND EATING

Accommodation for visitors is a rare thing in the Irangi Hills: the only guesthouses, neither of them entirely official, are in Pahi and Kolo. There are also a couple of campsites within an hour's walk. In the hills, camping gives you more freedom, but you'll need a guide who knows the area well. Eating out is limited to a handful of basic *mgahawa* joints in each village which are tiny restaurants dishing up tea, coffee and simple dishes like rice with beans. The weekly cycle of produce markets is good for roasted maize cobs, freshly grilled beef and goat meat (and beautiful Rangi cooking pots).

Amarula Campsite Mnenya village, 6km east of Kolo ☏ 0754 672256 (Arusha), ⊛ facebook.com /AmarulaCampsite. In a lovely setting shaded by acacias and amarula trees, you can camp in your own tent, or stay in one of three safari tents, each with two beds; bathrooms are shared. The communal areas are utterly gorgeous constructions made of clay and sustainably sourced wood, and include a lounge and cooking area (with gas stove and fridge), all lit by solar power. Safari tent per person $20, camping per person $10

Mary Leakey Campsite 4km east of Kolo (ask at the

Antiquities Department in Kolo). A riverside pitch close to "Kolo B" rock art site. There are no facilities, nor ever water in the dry season, and locals advise you only to use the site if you're in a large group (three or four tents at least), as there have been robberies in the past. Camping per person Tsh5,000

Silence Guest House Kolo, on the Babati–Kondoa road (ask at the Antiquities Department in Kolo). Basic but adequate rooms, lacking electricity, but with water and also able to rustle up tasty meals. Tsh8000

Babati and around

The small but fast-growing town of **BABATI**, 105km north of Kondoa and just four hours by bus from Arusha, is a nice place to hunker down in for a few days, as it enjoys not only a pretty location on the north shore of Lake Babati, but an excellent **cultural tourism programme**. As well as boat trips, this offers encounters with local **Gorowa** and **Barbaig** communities, and challenging hikes to the top of Tanzania's fourth-highest mountain, the solitary 3417-metre volcano, **Mount Hanang**.

Babati is capital of Manyara Region, but its *raison d'être* stems from its position at the crossroads between Arusha, Dodoma and the Great Lakes, which, in the good old days of unsurfaced roads (scarcely five years ago), made it a useful overnight stop for travellers. Now that the roads are surfaced, Babati is set to grow further, thanks to its fertile soil and a favourable climate, which has made it a major producer of maize and sunflower oil.

Lake Babati

2km south of the bus station • Walk down the Kondoa Rd, and take the track to your right that starts at an old mango tree facing the District Court • Guided walks and canoeing are offered by Babati's cultural tourism programme

A pleasant way to spend a day is to visit **Lake Babati**. The lake – one of few freshwater bodies of water in the Rift Valley – is a paradise for **birds**: more than three hundred species have been recorded so far, including flamingos.

Given the lack of a known outlet, the lake's level varies wildly according to the rains: during the 1997–98 El Niño rains, it rose so high that it flooded the Kondoa road in two

KONDOA–IRANGI ROCK PAINTINGS: HISTORY, STYLE AND MEANING

Kondoa–Irangi's rock paintings are remarkable not just for their quantity and quality, but for their astonishing timespan, the oldest possibly 28,000 (definitely 19,000) years old, the youngest mere centenarians left by ancestors of the present-day **Sandawe and Hadzabe**, both of them traditionally **hunter-gatherers**. The Sandawe, nowadays living west of the Irangi Hills, were forced to abandon their ancient way of life a few decades ago, but the Hadzabe, around Lake Eyasi further north, still persist, albeit against increasingly unfavourable odds. In the broader context the paintings are part of a stylistically similar chain of sites looping down from the Ethiopian Highlands to southern Africa, so it's no coincidence to find that the Hadzabe and Sandawe are the only Tanzanian tribes with languages characterized by clicks, similar to the languages of the Kalahari's "San" or "Bushmen", who were also prolific rock painters.

STYLE

The Kondoa–Irangi paintings vary greatly in style, subject, size and colour: the most common are depictions of animals and humans done in red or orange ochre (iron oxide bound with animal fat). Particularly remarkable are the fine **elongated human figures**, often with large heads or hairstyles, whose hands generally only have three fingers, the middle one being much longer than the other two. The large heads are intriguingly similar to a "round-head" style found in the Sahara's Tassili n'Ajjer Plateau, which has provoked all sorts of crackpot theories – including proof of helmet-wearing aliens.

At Kondoa–Irangi, the figures are depicted in a variety of **postures** and activities, some standing, others dancing, playing flutes, hunting and – in an exceptional painting at Kolo B1 dubbed "The Abduction" – showing a central female figure flanked by two pairs of males. The men on the right are wearing masks (the head of one clearly resembles a giraffe's) and are attempting to drag her off, while two unmasked men on the left attempt to hold her back. Animals are generally portrayed realistically, often with an amazing **sense of movement**, and include elephant, kudu, impala, zebra and giraffe, which occur in around seventy percent of central Tanzania's sites and which give their name to the so-called **giraffe phase**, tentatively dated to 28,000–7000 BC. The later **bubalus phase** (roughly 7000–4000 BC), generally in black (charcoal, ground bones, smoke or burnt fat), depicts buffalo, elephant and rhinoceros. Of these, the highly stylized herds of elephants at Pahi are uncannily similar to engravings found in Ethiopia. The more recent paintings of the **dirty-white phase**, from 2000 to 100 years ago, were made from kaolin, animal droppings or zinc oxide and generally feature more abstract and geometric forms such as concentric circles and symbols that in places resemble letters, eyes or anthropomorphs (stylized human figures).

MEANING

As to the meaning of the paintings, the once favoured "art for art's sake" explanation has been completely debunked, leaving us with plenty of theories but no certainties. Some hold that the paintings had a **magical-religious purpose**, whether shamanistic or as a form of sympathetic magic, the idea being to bring an animal's spirit to life by painting it, often from memory. This may have been to enable a successful hunt, or part of a more complex belief system which summoned the spirits of certain sacred animals to bring rain or fertility. The latter is evidenced by the practice of Kalahari shamans "becoming" elands when in a state of **hallucinogenic trance**. Another theory has it that rock shelters – as well as baobab trees – are **metaphors** for the "aboriginal womb" of creation. Indeed, the Sandawe *iyari* ritual surrounding the birth of twins once included rock painting, and, intriguingly, the Hadzabe were also in the habit, even in the last two decades, of retouching certain paintings for ritual purposes. For **further information**, the extraordinarily beautiful *African Rock Art: Paintings and Engravings on Stone*, by David Coulson and Alec Campbell (Harry N. Abrams Publishers, New York, 2001; ❿abramsbooks.com), features Kondoa–Irangi in its East Africa chapter.

laces – a boon for fishermen who made a tidy profit ferrying people across. Parts of the own itself were also flooded, and locals joke that all they had to do for their dinner was each out of a window to grab a fish. The event prompted an NGO to build an overflow ipeline from the lake to a river at lower altitude, which should prevent such flooding in future. The lake is said to be free of bilharzia, and kids are happy swimming in it, but not adults – the resident **hippos** are skittish and definitely dangerous, so swim or canoe at your own risk.

Although you don't really need a guide – you can follow the water's edge for most of the way, though a couple of swampy areas force you briefly back to the road – taking one from the cultural tourism programme is a good way to meet locals, and also gets you on a wobbly dugout in search of hippo (at your own risk) and chinwags with local fishermen. As **fishing** is not permitted during January to June, any fishermen you meet at that time may, like the hippos, also be rather skittish!

Mount Kwaraa

3km east of the centre · Guided walks are offered by Babati's cultural tourism programme (see p.225), whose staff will also arrange the required $10 Forest Reserve permit

The flat-topped mountain rising 3km east of Babati is **Mount Kwaraa**. Its 2415-metre peak is swathed in heavy forest and usually also in mist, so don't expect panoramic views if you climb it. What you will see is some fascinating and virtually untouched forest. The mountain is used by migratory herds of elephant and buffalo you almost certainly won't see them, but the presence of fresh dung and crushed undergrowth is enough to give most spines a tingle. The lower slopes, up to around 1750m, are mainly scrub, with dry montane forest and stunted woodland dominating the higher sections, which is part of the protected **Ufiome Forest Reserve**. The mountain can be climbed in a day, but two days (with a tent) is preferable as you'd have much more time to explore.

If you have the energy, **Bambaay Hill** – the southern part of Mount Kwaraa, roughly 8km south of Babati – can also be climbed, and, although below Kwaraa's peak, has views over the Maasai Steppe to the east, and north into Tarangire National Park. The cultural tourism programme combines Bambaay with the Gorowa village of Maisaka, whose elders are happy regaling guests with traditional tales and fables, and where you can also learn about local brickmaking techniques, and cow-powered biogas production.

Monthly markets

4km south of town on a hillside along the Kondoa Rd · Held on the 17th and 26th of each month, sunrise–sunset

The town's major cultural shindig is the grand twice **monthly market** (*mnada*), less than an hour's walk out of town. The event attracts thousands of people, many from outlying districts, and for some town-dwellers the market provides a perfect excuse to bunk off work and indulge in grilled beef, fresh sugar-cane juice and local brews at inflated prices (many are the tall stories of hung-over revellers waking up in the early hours to see packs of hyenas scavenging over the remains). The cattle auction is perhaps the day's highlight, and draws Maasai and Barbaig from all around. All in all, a great day out.

ARRIVAL AND DEPARTURE

By bus The bus stand is in the middle of town on the west side of the highway from Arusha. The highway continues to Singida, where it branches south for Dodoma, and west for Nzega and Mwanza – both routes are paved all the way. Arusha has frequent buses throughout the day, most of them reasonably well driven. For Mwanza and Dodoma, buy your ticket the day before, and for a bus that actually starts in Babati, not one passing through from Arusha or Moshi for which you won't have a choice of seating, if at all. For Dodoma buses currently take the long but surfaced road via Singida; the shorter route, south via Kondoa, is due to be paved: in the meantime, buses only go as far as Kondoa where you'll need to change. You can do this in the same day: Machame Bus sells through tickets. The main bus companies are Machame Bus (from Moshi), and the le reliable and slower but therefore slightly safer Mtei Express (from Arusha, and from Babati).

Destinations Arusha (hourly; 3–4hr); Dodoma via Singida (3 daily; 7–8hr); Karatu (daily; 8hr); Katesh (hourly; 1hr); Kondoa (3 daily; 3–5hr), with connections for Dodoma;

Mwanza (6–8 daily; 8–9hr); Singida (hourly; 2hr); Tabora (2–3 daily; 7–8hr); Tanga (daily; 10hr).

Money Three banks on the highway just south of the bus stand have ATMs that accept international Visa and MasterCard – NBC, Exim and CRDB.

INFORMATION

Cultural tourism programme The reason for the steady trickle of tourists to Babati is its long-established cultural tourism programme, whose office is at *Kahembe's Guest House*, one block north of the bus stand (☎0784 397477 or ☎0767 393477, ✆kahembeculturalsafaris.com). The shortest way is to leave the bus stand through its west side (furthest from the highway), and turn right – follow the road to its end, and you'll see the guesthouse opposite. Alternatively, turn left along the paved highway from the bus stand, and left again at a petrol station about 100m along – *Kahembe's* is 100m along on the right. Costs, including overnights at the guesthouse or outside Babati, currently average $55 per person for 24 hours, excluding transport ($5 for a bicycle, $5 per canoe), drinks and tips. Without

accommodation, the cost averages $35–40 per person per day. The programme offers a wide variety of flexible itineraries, including half-day dugout outings on Lake Babati in search of hippos, mornings spent being regaled by a centenarian Gorowa story-teller, mountain hiking up mounts Hanang (see p.226), Kwaraa and Bambaay, various cycling expeditions, walks over several days in the Mang'ati Plains to stay with the Barbaig (like the Maasai, whom they resemble, originally from the Nile Valley, and who may put on a mock fight to illustrate how they got their name; see p.227), rock art tours in the Irangi Hills (see p.221), and various options for short-term volunteers combining hands-on help with wildlife safaris.

ACCOMMODATION

4

There are almost two dozen guesthouses within a couple of blocks of the bus stand; most are quite basic but, as they're similarly priced, don't shy away from comparing a few – and the state of their beds, bathrooms and electric fittings. All of them are accessible on foot, or by *bajaj*.

Classic Guest House On the same road as the cultural tourism programme, 100m further west ☎0784 390940. The well-kept rooms here, all but one en suite, are very similar to *Kahembe's* and also have TVs, and are half the price, albeit without breakfast. Safe parking. Tsh10,000

Executive Lodge 200m west of the bus stand (across the football field, it's on your left 50m along the road heading up to a red-and-white phone mast) ☎0755 424666. Seven spanking new rooms, clean and tiled, all a/c, with flat screen TV, big beds with box nets, and everything works. Singles same price as doubles. Safe parking. BB Tsh30,000

Kahembe's Guest House Behind the cultural tourism programme office ☎0784 397477 or ☎0767 393477, ✆kahembeculturalsafaris.com. Eight small en-suite rooms set around a courtyard, with mosquito nets, hot showers, TV and full English breakfast, but pricey by Babati's standards if you're not taking a trip with the

cultural tourism programme run by the owner, Joas Kahembe. Campers can pitch a tent at the owner's farm (per person Tsh10,000). BB Tsh20,000

Royal Beach Hotel 1.5km off the highway on a finger of land jutting into Lake Babati. This is Babati's nicest location, right on the lake, but the self-contained *bandas* were uninhabitable at the time of writing, making this just a campsite at present. It's worth asking if its fortunes have revived. Camping per person Tsh12,000

Winners Hotel Two blocks east of the highway (cross it from the south side of the bus stand, and walk up 100m) ☎0754 670453 or ☎0684 182828, ✆winnershoteltz .com. Babati's best accommodation: twelve rooms, all well-kept and clean, decked out with large box nets, wi-fi, cable TV and a/c. The only difference between standard, executive and deluxe here is size. There's also a (quiet) bar and restaurant, and safe parking. Well priced. BB Tsh30,000

EATING, DRINKING AND ENTERTAINMENT

Babati has long been famous for fresh **fish**, usually tilapia but sometimes also catfish. The town's growth led to overfishing and often lengthy bans, but these have now settled into a permanent annual cycle, in which fishing – and thus fresh fish on your plate – is only permitted from July to Dec. For the rest of the year, settle for dried tilapia, either from here, or trucked in from Lake Victoria. Babati's **street food**, which includes full meals dished up by *mama lishas*, is good, and can be found all around the bus station and, on the other side of the highway, around the market. **Drinking** is the other big thing in Babati, which probably has more bars per square whatnot than anywhere else in the country; see whether you can find one stocking *komoni* (a traditional beer made from maize and finger millet), or the similar *busaa*.

Dolphin Bar 100m west of the cultural tourism office on the same road. This, under a steep *makuti*-thatched roof, has long been a favoured nightspot, thanks to its dance floor, which is liveliest weekend nights. It also has good bar food, including *nyama choma*, and goat meat *trupa* (a particularly tasty stew of pretty much everything). Daily 7am–late.

First and Last Bar On the highway two blocks north of the bus stand, on the left. With lots of tables on a large street corner veranda, this is one of the best bars at present, popular at night but still pleasant, and with good *nyama choma* too. Daily 7am–late.

Free Town Restaurant East side of the highway 70m north of the bus stand. A good place for a calm outdoor drink (it's set back from the highway behind some trees), or good cheap food, including fresh fish from Lake Babati (July–Dec; Tsh6000 with rice). Other dishes are cheaper (for Tsh4500 most meats, Tsh3000 just veg, with rice), and it has *supu* for breakfast. Daily 7.30am–10pm.

Paapaa Motel At the start of the first street south of the bus stand. Unlike the ultra cheap rooms here, which are seriously wilted, the bar and restaurant at the front (with a streetside veranda) hasn't changed one bit, and remains a lively and friendly venue for drinks, with excellent *nyama choma* (Tsh6000/kilo). Food daily 7.30am–10pm.

Winners Hotel Two blocks east of the highway (cross it from the south side of the bus stand, and walk up 100m) ☎ 0754 670453 or ☎ 0684 182828. A calm a/c restaurant, mostly functional, but the *trupa* can be memorable: a stew of chicken, beef or fish with beans, carrots, chickpeas, bananas, potatoes and other veg, a bargain at around Tsh5000. Daily 7am–9pm.

4 Mount Hanang

Heading west from Babati, the road – paved all the way to Mwanza and Dodoma – crosses the floodplain of Lake Babati, then twists up into the hills amid beautiful and ever-changing scenery before levelling out in a broad valley, with Mount Hanang to the south and the long barrier of the Rift Valley's Malbadow Escarpment to the west. The road forks at **Dareda** (Ndareda), 26km from Babati; here an unsurfaced road continues north to Karatu (see box, p.331).

Continuing straight at Dareda, the Babati–Singida road veers south towards Tanzania's fourth-highest mountain, **Mount Hanang**. An almost perfect volcanic cone, it rises up from the Mang'ati Plains to three summits, the highest at 3417m. Hanang is sacred to the Barbaig and Gorowa (or Fiome) tribes: it's tall enough to condense water vapour from clouds, making **Lake Balangida** one of the Rift Valley's most important watering points. The high water table also supports a surprisingly rich groundwater forest on the mountain's lower slopes. Higher up, this gives way to montane and upper montane forest, with trees up to 20m tall on the wetter southern, eastern and northern slopes, and dry montane forest on the western slopes. Above 2100m the forest gives way to grassland, thicket and bushland, while above 2700m moorland predominates.

Despite recurring problems with illegal logging, much of Hanang's forest has survived intact, apparently thanks to the Gorowa belief in **underground earth spirits** called Netlangw. The Netlangw are said to live under large trees where springs emerge, which makes Mount Hanang's girdling groundwater forest of prime importance. They are guardians of the water; if offended, say by forest clearance, they move away, taking the water with them. The logic is clear and unassailable: destroy trees and you destroy your water supply.

If you want to **climb** Hanang, it's easiest to arrange things at the cultural tourism programme in Babati (see p.225), whose staff are clued up on the practical side of things. First stop, after Babati, is the erstwhile village and now growing town of **Katesh**, on the south side of the mountain and 76km southwest of Babati, where the necessary Forest Reserve permits need to be acquired. The town is liveliest on the tenth and eleventh of each month during the *mnada* **market**, held 2km south of town along the Singida road.

THE BARBAIG

The **Mang'ati Plains**, an unremittingly dry expanse of savanna extending south from Mount Hanang, are at first sight a deeply inhospitable place. Yet they're home to some two hundred thousand people – the **Barbaig** (or Barabaig), a semi-nomadic, cattle-herding people distantly related to the Maasai. The key to their existence is the freshwater **Lake Balangida**, on the far side of Mount Hanang. The lake is fed by the mountain, which ensures that even when it's dry (an increasingly common occurrence), the deep wells that have been dug around its periphery still contain enough water for the Barbaig's cherished herds.

Tall, handsome and proud, the Barbaig are at first glance very similar to the Maasai. They dress alike, and cattle occupy a pivotal place in their culture. Like the Maasai, too, their society is organized into clans (*doshinga*) and age-sets (formalized generations of people of similar age, who undergo the various life stage ceremonies at the same time) that govern pasture and water rights. But for all their similarities, there's no love lost between the two. The Maasai have two names for the Barbaig. One is **Mbulu**, which means "unintelligent people". The other, reserved for the Barbaig alone, is **Il-Mang'ati**, meaning "the enemy", a simple tag which, coming from East Africa's most feared and warlike people, is almost a compliment. The name Barbaig itself comes from *bar* (to beat) and *baig* (sticks), alluding to a unique dance that is still performed today, in which fights are mimicked using sticks for weapons – all good training.

The Barbaig are one of nineteen tribes that originally made up a broader cluster of people called **Datooga** (or Tatoga). Like the Maasai and Kenya's Kalenjin, the Datooga are linguistically classed as Nilotic, meaning that they share a common origin, presumed to be in Sudan's Nile Valley. A fascinating relic from this time, which could also explain the extreme ritual importance of cattle in all Nilotic societies, is the Barbaig word for God, *Aseeta*, which is related to the Kalenjin word *Asiis*, which also means sun. Both words have their root in the name of the ancient Egyptian goddess **Isis**, who wore a solar disc and the horns of a cow and was the focus of a cattle and fertility cult throughout much of antiquity. According to Roman mythology – which adopted many Egyptian cults – the beautiful Isis, whom the Romans called Io, was kidnapped by an amorous Jupiter, but her mother, Juno, gave chase. Rather than give her back, Jupiter rather unfairly turned Io into a cow, and compounded the injustice by calling down a bumble bee from the heavens, which he commanded to sting the cow. Not terribly enchanted with this treatment, the miserable Io fled to Egypt, where she cried so much that her tears formed the Nile.

The Datooga's southward **migration** is believed to have started around three thousand years ago, possibly prompted by massive climate changes that coincided with the expansion of the Sahara. Around 1500 AD, the Datooga arrived at Mount Elgon on the Kenya–Uganda border, where they stayed until the eighteenth century, when they migrated south once more into Tanzania. The Datooga first settled at Ngorongoro before being pushed on by the Maasai, after which they separated into various tribes, many of which have now been assimilated by others. Lamentably, the Barbaig's southward migration continues even today. Loss of their ranges to commercial ranches, flower farms and seed-bean plantations, and encroachment by Maasai (who have themselves been pushed south by the creation of the Serengeti and Tarangire national parks) mean that the Barbaig are among Tanzania's poorest people. Child mortality rates are high, as is the incidence of cattle disease. The fact that none of this used to be the case supports the Barbaig claim that nothing other than the loss of their traditional land has caused these problems, but unfortunately the scattered nature of Barbaig society means that they have largely been absent from politics, and have consequently been marginalized. Their latest efforts to regain access to their land via a series of legal actions in the courts have stalled on the absurd grounds that they lack legally recognized title to the land.

For more information on the problems Barbaig culture faces, see *Passions Lost* by Charles Lane (Initiatives Publishers, Nairobi, 1996).

4

SSENTIALS

MOUNT HANANG

rrival (Katesh) When this book was first researched in 001, Katesh was a village, its road mud or dust, and its bus and a tree with Mtei Express' timetable nailed to its trunk.

Mtei Express still exists, but everything else has changed: the road is tarred, Katesh is a town, and there's a proper bus stand in place of the tree. Frequent daladalas and buses run from Babati (taking about two hours), and also from Arusha until early afternoon (any service that goes to Singida passes through).

Money Katesh does not (yet) have an ATM that accepts international cards, so change money before coming.

Climbing practicalities The combined ascent and descent takes at least one full day. You'll need a guide, and a $10 forest permit from Katesh's Forestry Department. There are no official guides or porters, so it's safest and easiest to arrange everything through Babati's cultural tourism programme (see p.225), which charges $125 per person, including transport to and from Katesh. This is for two days – the first to organize the practicalities (following by a bit of sight seeing), the second the climb

itself. Camping on the mountain is possible, but the extr equipment and porters involved can complicate things The hike can be combined over four days with a visit to Barbaig community. Altitude sickness isn't a major worry but don't underestimate the mountain: it gets pretty col at 3417m, so come suitably equipped. For general advic on mountaineering, read the Kilimanjaro section i Chapter 5 (see p.248 & pp.251–252).

Climbing routes The main ascent is the Katesh route from Katesh up the southwestern ridge: five to six hours t the summit, and a three- to four-hour descent. Longe alternatives are from Giting village on the northeast side c the mountain, and from Gendabi, 16km northwest o Katesh, but the latter is currently impassable.

ACCOMMODATION

There are plenty of guesthouses in Katesh on either side of the highway, most in the same area as the bus stand and market. Their prices don't differ much, but their standards do – generally, newer hotels will be better.

Bargish Guest House Two blocks north of the highway (the street starts to the right of Pick 'n Pay) ☎0786 276868. A quiet, modern and welcoming place with twelve spotless en-suite rooms, all with big box nets and TVs. Safe parking. **Tsh10,000**

Pick 'n Pay Guest House North side of the highway,

facing the bus stand ☎0784 467001. A safe choice, an easy to find, but getting tatty, and with pure nylon be sheets. The cheapest rooms, some without externa windows, share bathrooms; the en-suite ones have TVs; a have fans and box nets. Safe parking. Shared bathroor **Tsh7000**, en suite **Tsh15,000**

Singida

The town of **SINGIDA**, 178km southwest of Babati, lies at the northern end of a Centra Line railway branch from Dodoma, and is also an overnight stop for trucks plying between Lake Victoria and Arusha or Dodoma. Improvements in the roads (and new regulations letting buses roll on until midnight) mean that only a few buses now spend the night here, but if you do need a stop somewhere between Babati and Mwanza, Singida is the most attractive place for it, surrounded by a boulder-strewn, kopje-studded landscape and flanked by two **freshwater lakes**. Singida's main tribe is **Nyaturu** whose last chief, Senge Mghenyi, achieved fame during the military mutiny of 1964. To pledge his support to President Nyerere, he walked all the way from Singida to State House in Dar es Salaam, accompanied by a hyena – the traditional guardian of Nyaturu chiefs.

On the west side of town, 100m from Lake Singidani, **Singida Regional Museum** (Makumbusho ya Mkoa; Mon–Fri 9am–4.30pm; free, but tips appreciated; ☎026 250 2449) contains a small ethnographic collection. It's in the fenced Open University compound 200m beyond *Lake Hill Singida Motel*, on the right just before the roundabout.

ARRIVAL AND INFORMATION   SINGID/

By bus The bus stand is three blocks south of the TRA building and the highway. Singida is at the junction of all major routes heading west and northwest, so in addition to direct early-morning buses, you can also catch through buses later in the day.

Destinations Arusha (4–5 daily; 6–7hr); Babati (hourly; 2hr); Biharamulo (5 weekly; 8–9hr); Bukoba (5 weekly;

11–12hr); Dar (2 daily; 12–13hr); Dodoma (3–4 daily 4–5hr); Morogoro (2–3 daily; 8–9hr); Mwanza (2 daily 6–8hr); Tabora (1 daily; 6hr).

By train Singida is at the end of a branch line fron Dodoma, but there are no more passenger trains.

Money 24hr ATMs for international plastic are at CRD (TRA building), and at NBC, 300m west along the highway

ACCOMMODATION AND EATING

There are dozens of cheap and quite decent **hotels** in town for a quick stop – check the mosquito net before settling in. Much more memorable is to head out of town to stay at the lakeshore. For cheap fills, head to the stalls and bars around the bus stand. Singida is known for **chickens** (free-range, not battery farmed), which are sold as far away as Dar (hence the sorry spectacle of fowl stuffed into wicker baskets at the bus stand). The town's other speciality is **honey** (*asali*), sold in the market. In the directions below, the TRA building is three blocks north of the bus stand on the highway.

★ **KBH Hotel (Katala Beach Hotel)** Lake Singidani, 4km west from the TRA building: taxis charge Tsh7000, a *bajaj* Tsh5000 ☎ 0754 474791 or ☎ 0737 198562, ⓦ kbhsingida.com. Reason to linger: this modern three-storey hotel really is on the beach, with several kilometres of sands to explore, and as Singida's industrial area is just up the road, it doesn't impinge on the views – best from the second-floor rooms, most with balconies. Also has a bar, and restaurant (mains around Tsh10,000–15,000) featuring grills, and some Tanzanian dishes like *mchemsho* stew with either beef, chicken or goat. Free wi-fi. BB Tsh50,000

Lake Hill Singida Motel 900m west of the TRA building, past the hospital ☎ 0768 728007. Set in a large gardens visited by marabou storks and mongooses, this place survives off occasional conferences, and ambles on pleasantly in-between. Its rooms, all well kept and with TVs, are in four polygonal blocks, each enclosing a small garden. "Singles" can be shared; "doubles" are bigger, and have bathtubs (and hot water). The grounds also have slides and swings, a usually empty *nyama choma* bar, and

tables under parasols for drinks or meals. BB "single" Tsh25,000, "double" Tsh35,000

Lutheran Centre 200m west of the TRA building ☎ 0765 430234. Good if you're looking for something very cheap but still clean and safe (but uninspiring), with seven rooms, some twin-bedded; the en-suite ones have TVs and Western-style toilets and showers. Shared bathroom Tsh8000, en suite Tsh15,000

Singapoo Snack One block north of the bus stand (2nd road south of TRA building). Often packed, this simple restaurant dishes up superb filling meals for less than Tsh3000, including ravishingly good goat meat *supu* in the morning. Daily 7am–7pm.

Stanley Motel Sokoine Rd, one block northeast of the bus stand (or walk up to the TRA building on the highway, turn right, and right again) ☎ 026 250 2351 or ☎ 0754 476785, ⓦ stanleygroupofhotels.com. Ever-popular, with 21 decent rooms, most en suite, with hot water, fans, nets, cotton sheets and TVs. There's also a good restaurant. BB shared bathrooms Tsh15,000, en suite Tsh25,000

4

The northern highlands

WALKING TO MOSHI

5

The northern highlands

The lush and fertile northern highlands are among the most scenically dramatic areas in Tanzania, running inland from the coast through a series of mountain chains to culminate in the towering massif of Mount Kilimanjaro, Africa's highest peak. The region's attractions are manifold, ranging from the arduous trek to the summit of Kilimanjaro itself, Kibo, to less strenuous but hugely enjoyable hikes in the Usambara and Pare mountains, whose great age and climatic stability has resulted in the development of a unique and extraordinarily rich plant and animal life, of which the jewel is the montane rainforest of Amani Nature Reserve in the Eastern Usambaras.

Towering more than five kilometres above the surrounding plains, the massive volcanic hulk of **Mount Kilimanjaro** dominates much of the region named after it. At its base is the regional capital of **Moshi**, a bustling yet friendly town, and with – clear skies permitting – terrific views of Africa's most famous mountain. Although some forty thousand tourists are drawn to "Kili" every year by the challenge of trekking to the summit, only a few spend more than a couple of days in Moshi, or in the settlements at the start of its climbing routes. Since the 1990s, however, concerted efforts have been made to spread the economic benefits of tourism via the establishment of **cultural tourism programmes**. There are now ten such ventures in the northern highlands, including **Marangu and Machame**, at the start of Kilimanjaro's most popular hiking routes. Although most of them have lost their community-involving ethos along the way, they're still a great way to get to know the locals, and their often astoundingly beautiful world. Among the best are the cultural tourism programmes in the **Pare and Usambara mountain ranges** southeast of Kilimanjaro. Pare and Usambara are part of the Eastern Arc, a chain of granitic massifs whose primeval rainforests are among the most species-rich on earth, something that is especially true of **Amani Nature Reserve**. Take your time: the northern highlands are a vividly beautiful and hugely rewarding region to explore.

Moshi

An hour's drive east of Arusha, the busy commercial town of **MOSHI** is the capital of Kilimanjaro Region and beautifully located beneath the summit of the mountain. The views are unforgettable, especially when the blanket of cloud that clings to Kili by day dissipates – with luck – just before sunset, to reveal glimpses of Kibo and Mawenzi peaks, accompanied by the tweeting of thousands of wheeling swallows. The

FEMALE TWO-HORNED CHAMELEON, AMANI NATURE RESERVE

Highlights

❶ Coffee A brew of Kilimanjaro's heavenly Arabica at one of Moshi's coffee shops might just convince you to never go instant again. **See p.240**

❷ Mount Kilimanjaro The snowy top of Africa's highest mountain is an inspiring sight, and can be climbed by the hardy – or the foolhardy – over five to eight days. **See p.244**

❸ Pare Mountains Part of the ancient Eastern Arc mountain chain, these mountains contain patches of rich rainforest, highland meadows and the Pare tribe, renowned for their healers and witches. **See p.253**

❹ Mkomazi National Park This rarely trodden wilderness is the southern terminus of an annual migration of more than one thousand elephants from Kenya's Tsavo ecosystem. **See p.259**

❺ West Usambara Rising one kilometre above the plains, this Eastern Arc range is home to the welcoming Sambaa. Their culture and their home, including wonderful forests and breathtaking viewpoints, are best explored on foot. **See p.262**

❻ Amani Nature Reserve Dubbed "the Galapagos of Africa", this reserve is one of Tanzania's largest remnants of true primeval rainforest, and is also one of the oldest and most biodiverse on earth. **See p.272**

HIGHLIGHTS ARE MARKED ON THE MAP ON P.234

5

mountain's influence is pervasive. Meltwater streams permit year-round agriculture, especially of **coffee**, while the mountain is alluded to in the town's name: *moshi* in Kiswahili means "smoke", either from Kilimanjaro's last, minor eruption in the 1700s or because of the smoke-like cloud that often covers the mountain. The town itself is refreshingly open and spacious, with broad, tree-lined avenues and leafy suburbs, and – despite a population of more than 250,000 – is decidedly more laidback than Arusha. If you can cope with the persistent if generally friendly attentions of the flycatchers, especially around the clock tower and south from there along Mawenzi Road, Moshi is a relaxing place to wander around, although there are few actual sights as most of the town dates from the 1930s onwards. There are however plenty of good hotels, a few excellent restaurants and a good number of hiking companies, all in all making Moshi a great base for the climb up Kilimanjaro.

THE NORTHERN HIGHLANDS

HIGHLIGHTS

1 Coffee
2 Mount Kilimanjaro
3 Pare Mountains
4 Mkomazi National Park
5 West Usambara
6 Amani Nature Reserve

The central market

South of Chagga St • Mon–Sat 8am–4.30pm, Sun 8am–noon

Moshi's liveliest attraction is the bustling **central market**, a warren of narrow alleyways, where, in among a garish cornucopia of imported plastic and aluminium goods, you'll find locally produced coffee and cardamom, spices, fruits and vegetables, and some great souvenirs including drums, tapes of music (and CDs), all at a fraction of the price asked in souvenir shops. Keep an eye out for traditional **herbalists** in and around the market (usually old men sitting beside vast quantities of glass jars containing multicoloured powders). For other great souvenirs, head up to Guinea Street, one block north, for its **jua kali** (literally "sharp sun") craftsmen, who specialize in turning old tin cans into superb oil lamps, coffee pots, kettles and pans.

Roundabout monuments

Either end of Taifa Rd (Arusha Highway)

The monuments gracing the two roundabouts on the highway just north of the city centre are of little interest for their artistry, but provide a handy reminder of Tanzania's struggles, past and present. Coming from Arusha, the first roundabout is centred on a stylized torch, and commemorates the struggle for freedom (*uhuru*; see p.518). Further along the highway, the next roundabout is dominated by a painted statue of an African soldier (an *askari*), rifle at the ready, and commemorates the participation, often forced, of Tanzanians in both World Wars. Formerly known as the **Askari monument**, it's now better known after the newly painted inscription at its base: **Maji ni Uhai** ("water for life"), which is a call to arms against the deforestation of Kilimanjaro's lower slopes – the mountain provides the freshwater for most of Kilimanjaro and Tanga regions.

THE CHAGGA

Numbering more than a million, the **Chagga** occupy the southern and eastern slopes of Kilimanjaro and are among East Africa's wealthiest and most highly educated people. Their wealth stems from the fortunate conjunction of favourable climatic conditions and their own agricultural ingenuity. Watered by year-round snow and ice melt, the volcanic soils of Kilimanjaro's lower slopes are extremely fertile and are exploited by the Chagga using a sophisticated system of intensive irrigation and continuous fertilization with animal manure, permitting year-round cultivation that can support one of Tanzania's highest human population densities. *Arabica* coffee has been the Chagga's primary cash crop since colonial times, although maize and bananas remain staple foods. The cultivation of bananas is traditionally a man's work, as is that of eleusine seed (*ulezi*), which is boiled and mixed with mashed plantain to brew a local beer (*mbege*), still used as a form of payment to elders in their role as conflict arbiters.

In the past, the potential for such conflicts was great: even today there are some four hundred different Chagga clans – indeed it's barely a century since the Chagga finally coalesced into a distinct and unified tribe. Most are related to the Kamba of Kenya, who migrated northwards from Kilimanjaro a few centuries ago during a great drought. Other clans descend from the Taita, another Kenyan tribe, and others from the pastoral Maasai, whose influence is visible in the importance attached to cattle as bridewealth payments and in the grouping of men into age-sets analogous to the Maasai system. Today, the Chagga wield considerable political and financial clout, because of both their long contact with European models of education and Christianity (both of which dominate modern-day political and economic life) and their involvement in the coffee business, which remains the region's economic mainstay in spite of volatile world prices. Indeed, the Chagga are the one tribe you're almost guaranteed to meet in even the most obscure corners of Tanzania, working as traders, merchants, officials, teachers and doctors.

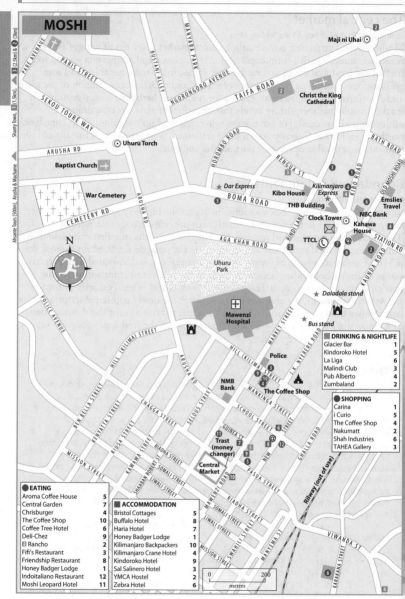

MOSHI

EATING
Aroma Coffee House	5
Central Garden	7
Chrisburger	4
The Coffee Shop	10
Coffee Tree Hotel	6
Deli-Chez	9
El Rancho	2
Fifi's Restaurant	3
Friendship Restaurant	8
Honey Badger Lodge	1
Indoitaliano Restaurant	12
Moshi Leopard Hotel	11

ACCOMMODATION
Bristol Cottages	5
Buffalo Hotel	8
Haria Hotel	7
Honey Badger Lodge	1
Kilimanjaro Backpackers	10
Kilimanjaro Crane Hotel	4
Kindoroko Hotel	9
Sal Salinero Hotel	3
YMCA Hostel	2
Zebra Hotel	6

DRINKING & NIGHTLIFE
Glacier Bar	1
Kindoroko Hotel	5
La Liga	6
Malindi Club	3
Pub Alberto	4
Zumbaland	2

SHOPPING
Carina	1
i Curio	5
The Coffee Shop	4
Nakumatt	2
Shah Industries	6
TAHEA Gallery	3

ARRIVAL AND DEPARTURE

MOSHI

Flycatchers touting for hotels and hiking companies are quick to spot new arrivals and, though harmless, can be persistent and intimidating. As ever, good humour is the best response, together with a reasonable sense of direction to get you from the bus station to a hotel: if you're undecided, the cluster of backpacker hotels four blocks south of the bus station is a good target. If you've arrived on Dar Express and it's not Sunday, you're in luck – you can seek refuge in the *Aroma Coffee House* across the road. Far more perilous than flycatchers is the Moshi–Arusha Highway, where the antics of the average driver are enough to induce visions of your life in flashback; the large Coaster minibuses, especially, crash with alarming – and fatal – frequency, and are best avoided. Of the proper buses, currently favoured along the Arusha–Dar highway are Dar Express and Kilimanjaro Express, but reputations can and do change, so ask around before buying a ticket. At the time of writing, companies to avoid completely along the Dar–Arusha highway include Abood, Airbus, Air Msae, Buffalo, Chakito and Hood.

By plane International flights land at Kilimanjaro International Airport, 34km west of Moshi and 6km south of the Arusha Highway (see pp.285–286). A taxi to the airport from Moshi officially costs $50 but should be bargainable, unlike the journey coming in. Cheaper, but possibly not useful for your flight, are the shuttle buses operated by Precisionair to meet theirs, and which accept other passengers too (Tsh10,000; office on Old Moshi Rd next to *Coffee Tree Hotel* ☎ 027 275 5205).

By bus Most public transport stops at the combined bus and daladala stand, south of the clock tower between Market St and Mawenzi Rd. There are ticket offices in the central building and clearly marked bays on either side: those on the north are for local daladalas, those on the south are for longer-distance Coasters and buses. The two currently favoured bus companies have their own terminals, well away from the bus station: Dar Express on Boma Road (☎ 0787 870766) and Kilimanjaro Express on Rengua Street (☎ 0767 213231 or ☎ 0715 213231).

Destinations Arusha (every 20min; 1hr 45min); Dar (hourly until 2pm; 8–9hr); Iringa (1–3 daily; 9–10hr); Karatu (3 daily; 5hr); Kisangara Chini (2 hourly; 1hr); Lushoto (3–4 daily; 4–5hr); Machame (hourly; 1hr); Marangu (hourly; 45min); Mbeya (1–3 daily; 15hr); Morogoro (3–4 daily; 6–7hr); Muheza (3–4 in the morning; 4hr); Mwanga (1–2 hourly; 1hr); Nairobi (6 daily; 8hr); Same (1–2 hourly; 2hr); Shinyanga (1 weekly; more than 24hr); Tanga (3–4 in the morning; 5–6hr); Taveta (hourly; 45min); Usangi (1 daily; 4–5hr).

By shuttle bus Getting to Nairobi is easy, with two companies operating daily shuttle buses via Arusha: Impala Shuttle on Kibo Rd beside *Chrisburger* (☎ 027 275 1786 or ☎ 0754 293119; 6.30am & 11.30am) and Riverside at the THB Building on Boma Road (☎ 027 275 0093; 11.30am). Either bus can pick you up at your hotel if you pre-book, and similarly can drop you at any central hotel. Kenyan visas, currently $50, can be bought on entry.

GETTING AROUND

Moshi's compact centre is easy to negotiate on foot and, unless you're carrying visibly tempting valuables, safety isn't much of an issue either. The exceptions are the Kuheshimo area, about a kilometre south of the central market, and the bus and daladala stand, which has pickpockets and bag snatchers. Shanty Town should be fine by day but if you're with your bags or other valuables, catch a cab.

By daladala The cheapest way to the suburbs is by daladala, nicknamed *vifordi* – alluding to the town's first-ever vehicle, a Model-T Ford. Most leave from the north side of the bus and daladala stand; journeys cost Tsh400. Daladalas heading along the Dar–Arusha highway can also be caught on Kibo Road.

By taxi Taxis park outside larger hotels, at major road junctions, around the bus and daladala stand, and on the west side of the Central Market on Market St. A journey

within town costs Tsh4000; rides to the outskirts shouldn't top Tsh5000 but expect to be asked for more.

By motorbike ("*bodaboda*") With or without a helmet, this is easily the most dangerous way around, and not recommended even though the asking price is half that of a taxi.

By bicycle Bicycles can be rented informally at most hotels; the cost should be no more than Tsh15,000 a day.

INFORMATION

Tourist information Moshi lacks a tourist office, so don't be misled by hiking companies displaying "tourist information" signboards. The best source of information used to be the *Moshi Guide* booklet, containing listings of pretty much everything you'd need, but it hasn't been

updated for years – ask at *The Coffee Shop* on Hill St. Also informative is ⊕ kiliweb.com. Moshi's main travellers' noticeboard is at *The Coffee Shop*, but be warned that not all the safari and hiking companies featured on it are reputable or licensed.

TOURS

A number of safari and hiking companies in Moshi, as well as individuals, offer short half- and full-day excursions. Possible **destinations** include hikes in Kilimanjaro Forest Reserve at Kibosho (15km north of town) and Rau Forest (10km northeast), swimming in hot water springs off the Arusha Highway, and visits to Lake Chala (beware of crocodiles) and Lake Jipe on the Kenyan border, both of which are good for birds, and – in July and Aug – may turn up a few migrating elephants. Also offered are cultural tours to Marangu (see p.241) or Machame (see p.244). For something more established, most of the cultural tourism programmes east of Arusha (see pp.301–303) can also be accessed from Moshi. The **price and quality** of these trips can vary considerably: the price depends on group size, mode of transport and your bargaining skills, but averages $35–70 per person per day. The quality is mostly dependent on the nous and knowledge of your guide. The following companies come recommended:

Nyange Adventures Contact them via The Coffee Shop ☎ 0717 385304, ⌨ nyangeadventures.com. This company started small but is expanding fast, and also offers properly licensed Kilimanjaro climbs.

Sacred Kilimanjaro Guides Ground floor, Kibo Tower, Boma Rd ☎ 0782 377804 or ☎ 0782 377699,

⌨ sacredkilimanjaroguides.com. In addition to the destinations listed above, this family-run Chagga/Sambaa company also offers great coffee tours in local *shambas* (small farms) that end with a cuppa made from coffee you roasted yourself, and are knowledgeable about the Usambara Mountains.

ACCOMMODATION

Town centre hotels are plentiful and generally good value, even at hiked-up "non-resident" (tourist) rates. A handful have rooftop "summit bars" for views of Kili; one or two also have rooms with views. Given Moshi's comparatively low altitude (810m), mosquitoes and malaria are prevalent: good-sized mosquito nets are preferable to window screens and/or bug spray.

Bristol Cottages Kilimanjaro Rindi Lane/Aga Khan Rd ☎ 027 275 5083, ⌨ bristolcottages.com. Clean and efficient, with a choice of cottages, or rooms in a three-storey block. The better rooms in the block have views of Kili (and a phone mast), and the top-floor suites are huge, and have TVs and bathtubs; they're cheaper, too, than the twin-bed cottage rooms, which don't have views but do have clunky old a/c units and TVs. There's also a restaurant with dining terrace, wi-fi and safe parking. BB **$80**

Buffalo Hotel New St ☎ 027 275 2775, ✉ buffalo hotel2000@yahoo.com. An affordable, clean and well-run three-storey hotel. The mostly en-suite rooms have fans, box nets and hot water; the better ones are larger, or have balconies facing Kilimanjaro. Wi-fi costs an additional Tsh1000/hr. There's also a decent restaurant, free luggage store and a couple of adjacent internet cafés. BB **$45**

Haria Hotel Guinea St ☎ 0752 328042. A modest and perfectly acceptable hotel aimed at backpackers, with nine rooms, all with box nets. The large en-suite doubles are a little musty; fresher and brighter are the three dorms sharing bathrooms. Free wi-fi, and a rooftop restaurant and bar with views of Kilimanjaro. BB dorm **$12**, double **$24**

★ **Honey Badger Lodge** Msaranga, 6km east of Moshi; daladalas to Kiboriloni or Mbwaruki pass by Msaranga junction, 1km away ☎ 0767 551190, ⌨ honeybadgerlodge.com. Tanzanian-run, this aims to provide everything you might need. While the on-site safari and mountaineering company (Milestone Safaris; correctly licensed) is rather expensive, especially for shorter excursions, the lodge's accommodation is great value: fourteen very comfortable en-suite rooms in *makuti*-thatched bungalows, all with high ceilings, funky decor, rustic Zanzibari-style furniture, and verandas. There's also a large swimming pool, children's playground, wi-fi, and a superb restaurant and bar. BB **$86**

Kilimanjaro Backpackers Mawenzi Rd ☎ 0713

377795. An attractive cheapie run by *Kindoroko Hotel*, with creaky floorboards, and a bar and restaurant (of variable quality) on the second floor with a street-view terrace. All rooms share bathrooms, and have fans and nets. Choose between the ultra-cheap dorms, four beds apiece, or twin-bedded doubles, but avoid the small and stuffy singles. Free wi-fi and luggage store. BB dorm **$6**, twin **$18**

Kilimanjaro Crane Hotel Kaunda Rd ☎ 027 275 1114, ⌨ kilimanjarocranehotel.com. A large, perfectly decent but unexciting and somewhat worn business-class hotel. The rooms, all en suite, have TV, fan or a/c, and smallish nets. Doubles and suites have massive beds (and bathtubs), and some have balconies. Facilities include a rooftop bar, two restaurants, swimming pool and safe parking. BB fans **$50**, a/c **$60**

Kindoroko Hotel Mawenzi Rd ☎ 027 275 4054, ⌨ kindorokohotels.com. A spotless and friendly four-storey hotel with spectacular views of Kili from the (roofed!) rooftop restaurant, reserved for guests only. Most doubles are decently sized, and there are a couple of twin-bed rooms too; all have satellite TV, fan and net, and wi-fi. Singles vary greatly in size, so ask to see a selection. There's a very nice bar and lounge downstairs open to the public, where you can also order food. Safe parking and free luggage store. BB **$30**

Sal Salinero Hotel Off Lema Rd, Shanty Town, 3.3km from Uhuru Torch roundabout ☎ 027 275 2240 or ☎ 0784 683605, ⌨ salsalinerohotel.com. Moshi's smartest address, a huge Italianate villa with polished wooden floors and 27 enormous, ornate en-suite rooms; packed with facilities, from TV to tea- and coffee-making facilities. Also boasts a gorgeous swimming pool, manicured grounds and a popular restaurant that screens English Premier League football every Saturday. BB **$150**

YMCA Hostel Junction of Taifa and Kilimanjaro rds ☎ 027 275 1754. Large institutional place where clean, bright rooms with nets, fans and good beds share bathrooms. The downside is the almost comically indolent service, yet it's all made good by a superb swimming pool with views of Kilimanjaro. There's also a poolside snack bar, good restaurant and curio shop. BB **$18**

Zebra Hotel New St ☎027 275 0611 ⓦzebrahotelstz

.com. A modern but bland eight-storey choice clearly intended to train tourists for Kili, as it has no lift, so prepare to scale the dizzying heights of the sixth floor for your breakfast, as that's where the restaurant is. The rooms are large, and have box nets and TV, and for now at least most things still work. Overpriced for singles. BB **$50**

EATING

Moshi has lots of **restaurants**, one or two of which are quite outstanding. Many of the better restaurants can be found in the misleadingly named Shanty Town, which is actually a leafy expat haven beginning 2km north of the centre, and is safe to walk to by day (without visible valuables, that is). Look out for regional speciality *mtori*, a thick mash of bananas usually served with meat. More ubiquitous, especially in bars, are *nyama choma*, *ndizi* and *chipsi mayai*: the busier the bar, the better the food. **Street food**, mainly roasted maize cobs, is found throughout town.

Aroma Coffee House Boma Rd. Facing the Dar Express bus stop and office, this isn't just a handy refuge from flycatchers, but a great place in its own right, with stylish decor, well-priced light lunches (less than Tsh5000) including veggie burgers, and snacks such as samosas, sandwiches, cakes and ice cream. The coffee is their own blend, which means it varies in taste and texture from good to outstanding. Also has tables outside facing the street. Mon–Sat 6.30am–8pm, Sun 6.30am–1pm.

Central Garden Facing the clock tower. Serves drinks, snacks or full meals in a lovely shady garden. The menu ranges from steaks and fast-food favourites to Indian dishes, all less than Tsh8000. Also has good juices and coffee. Daily 7.30am–6pm.

Chrisburger Kibo Rd. Handy for breakfast and cheap fast-food style lunches (less than Tsh4000), plus burgers and hot dogs and juices. Mon–Fri 8am–4.30pm, Sat 8am–2pm.

★**The Coffee Shop** Hill St ☎027 275 2707, ⓔcoffee _shop_moshi@yahoo.com. A superb place with a warmly decorated dining room, a garden at the back with tables and a few more on the shady street-front terrace. Serves a wide range of delicious meals and snacks, with little costing over Tsh5000, including a very filling *mtori* banana stew, spicy beef *pilau*, and – something of a fad in Moshi – Chinese. Snacks include soups and pies, mouthwatering cakes, samosas and ice cream, but best of all is its heavenly Kilimanjaro Arabica coffee. It's also a travellers' meeting place, has a noticeboard with ads for local artists and art centres, a crafts shop, book exchange and free wi-fi. Mon–Sat 7.30am–9.30pm.

Coffee Tree Hotel Off Old Moshi Rd. The guest rooms in this dilapidated four-storey monolith may have skipped a decade or three of tender loving care, but the top-floor restaurant and bar is still firmly embraced by a spectacular view of Kilimanjaro. The menu is short but nonetheless wishful thinking at times, so ask early for local specialities such as *mtori* (Tsh1000) or ox-tongue with bananas and veg (Tsh6000). Other dishes are humdrum but usually edible. Daily noon–10pm.

Deli-Chez Hill St. Halal Indian cooking leaning towards mild Bangladeshi cuisine, together with some Chinese and

continental dishes (for example, pepper steak), but nothing Tanzanian. Most mains cost around Tsh10,000. The main pull is the first floor terrace, but there's another on the streetside. Wed–Mon 9.30am–9.30pm.

El Rancho Ibra Line Rd, 200m off Lema Rd, Shanty Town, 3.2km from Uhuru Torch roundabout (walkable) – take the second right after the Impala Hotel ☎027 275 5115. This was once Moshi's go-to venue on Sunday afternoons, and still retains a friendly beer garden kind of feeling, with plenty of tables on its ample lawn at which to chow down on a variety of mostly north Indian but also Tanzanian and European dishes, with nothing costing more than Tsh13,500. Especially good is the chicken tikka, and the freshly cooked samosas. There's also a pool table and table football. Tues–Sun 12.30–11pm.

Fifi's Restaurant Rindi Lane. Classy international-standard coffee shop and restaurant, with comforting food for its largely *wazungu* clientele, including a good selection of meat and fish (around Tsh16,000, including pork chops), and vegetarian, say veggie burgers (Tsh8000). The snacks are great: muffins, brownies and cookies, shakes, ice creams, fresh juices and sandwiches, and the coffee rivals the best. Free wi-fi. Mon & Wed–Fri 7.30am–10pm, Sat & Sun 8.30am–10pm.

Friendship Restaurant Mawenzi Rd. Popular with locals throughout the day, dishing up good cheap food and drinks, including *nyama choma* (Tsh5000 for half a kilo). Daily 11am–late.

★**Honey Badger Lodge** Msaranga, 6km east of Moshi; daladalas to Kiboriloni or Mbwaruki pass by Msaranga junction, 1km away ☎0767 551190. This has excellent Tanzanian-flavoured international cuisine, including the "Badger Mmm'Buzi Burger" (goat meat, if you must know) with coleslaw for Tsh15,000, but it's most famous for its wood-fired pizzas (Tsh12,000) on Thurs and Fri evenings, and all-day weekends, when the place gets really busy. Also has great juices, including roselle (hibiscus; Tsh3000 for a big glass). Drinkers have a spacious outdoor bar, but to enjoy the swimming pool, either cough up Tsh10,000, or buy a Tsh25,000 "meal deal", giving you a

5

starter and main course as well. Food daily 7am–9pm, bar open later.

★**Indoitaliano Restaurant** New St, opposite Buffalo Hotel ☎027 275 2195. One of the nicest places in the evening, with a sunny streetside veranda, friendly service and – you'd never guess – both Indian and Italian food, including delicious pizzas, and particularly good vegetarian choices, whether aubergine parmigiana or lasagne or *dal punjabi*, black lentils stewed with tomatoes and onions. Mains cost around Tsh9000–12,000. Turn up before 8pm,

however, or you could well end up queuing on the street. Daily 6am–10pm.

Moshi Leopard Hotel Market St. This has possibly the cleanest kitchen in town (see for yourself – it's open plan), but it takes about an hour to deliver. As with most places in Moshi, the menu is extensive, which means that food can be average, but it is reasonably priced (for instance, chilli chicken for Tsh9000 and pizzas for less), and they boast a decent wine list. You can eat on an upstairs patio with views of Kilimanjaro. Daily noon–11pm.

DRINKING AND NIGHTLIFE

Moshi has lots of friendly local **bars** to keep your throat moist, few of which see many tourists, but the most popular places – especially at weekends, by day or at night – are two or three kilometres out of town along the highway in either direction; any self-respecting taxi driver should be able to show you the most popular. Walking around the city centre at night is generally safe, but if you're going more than a few blocks, it's wiser to catch a cab. Several **hotels** have "summit bars" with views of Kili.

Glacier's Inn Shanty Town, bottom of Lema Rd. Closed for renovation at the time of writing, this was a hugely popular reggae-heavy place that unfailingly pulled the crowds from Fri and Sun nights, with live music on Sat – worth asking what it's like now.

Kindoroko Hotel Mawenzi Rd. This has a great ground floor bar behind the reception area, the bamboo walls and wooden tables giving it a nicely warm feeling in the evening. A good place to meet up in without any hassle. Daily 11am–11pm.

La Liga Viwanda Rd, 500m beyond the railway tracks ☎0767 770022 or ☎0715 750076. The "Number 1 Nightclub in Tanzania" boast may be stretching the truth a little, but so long as you heed the dress code (the smarter the better, and no flip-flops), this is a fun place with a large dancefloor surrounded by viewing balcony, impressive lighting system, and even a free taxi to and from the centre of town. Tsh10,000 entry weekends, Tsh5000 otherwise.

Tues–Sun 6pm–late.

Malindi Club Rengua St. Entrance to Moshi's friendliest bar is through a set of giant concrete elephant legs. Once inside, you'll find a spacious, unpretentious place with televisions posted around the walls. Daily 10am–late.

Pub Alberto Kibo Rd. Moshi's brashest nightclub, with all the loud music, lasers and spinning mirrored globes you might want (or might not want if trying to sleep at the nearby *Coffee Tree Hotel*), and plenty of spangled prostitutes too. The music's pretty run of the mill but there's a pool table, and food is served throughout the night. Tues–Sun 6pm–4am.

Zumbaland Taifa Rd, next to the Cathedral. Moshi takes its weekend get-togethers pretty seriously: not content with the classic East African beer garden, this one's gone way better by blending it with an amusement park complete with rides, slides and even a pink light aircraft, resulting in one extremely strange and very enjoyable place to take the kids to on the weekend. Sat & Sun 11am–late.

COFFEE

The Kilimanjaro Region produces high-quality **Arabica coffee**, characterized by an exquisitely fresh flavour (with an aftertaste of mint), smooth texture and delicate aroma. Most of the coffee farms are smallholdings whose production is collected and marketed by the Kilimanjaro Native Coffee Union (KNCU), providing a guaranteed minimum income to farmers at times when world coffee prices slump, something that these days happens with alarming frequency.

Coffee bushes flower during the short rains (Oct–Nov), when they become covered in white blossom and give off a pervasive, jasmine-like scent. The best time to visit if you're interested in seeing how coffee is processed is between July and September, when the berries are harvested. Following harvesting, the beans' sweet, pulpy outer layer is mechanically removed, after which they're fermented in water and then dried in sunlight on long tables. After a few days, the outer casing (the "parchment") becomes brittle, and is easily removed at the coffee mill, after which the beans are graded for sale according to size and weight.

Several **coffee shops** in Moshi (see p.239) compete for the favours of aficionados: the longest-established, and still serving up a heavenly brew, is *The Coffee Shop*. The coffee-making process, from cultivation to roasting, can be seen on day-trips to working coffee farms (p.238), or as part of the cultural tourism programme at Tengeru near Arusha (see p.303).

SHOPPING

Moshi has far fewer **souvenir shops** than Arusha, but this is no bad thing – it's easier to choose, and a number of places stock stuff you won't find elsewhere. There are several more shops on Hill St and at the side of the *Kindoroko Hotel*.

The Coffee Shop Hill St ☎027 275 2707. This contains the Our Heritage crafts shop, but what really catches the eye are its edible and drinkable souvenirs, starting with that heavenly Kilimanjaro *Arabica*, at Tsh9000 for half a kilo. There's also good cheese from various locations, fine teas from Lutindi Mental Hospital south of the Usambara Mountains, and weird and wonderful jams and honey… just wrap it up well before committing it to airport baggage handlers. Mon–Sat 7.30am–9.30pm.

i Curio Pasua St, around the side of Kindoroko Hotel ☎0754 482723 or ☎0783 170486. Not the cheapest, nor the biggest selection, but benefits from fixed prices and a good eye for touristic tastes and fads. Particularly useful for T-shirts, carvings, Tingatinga paintings and coffee-table books. Daily 8am–6.30pm.

Shah Industries Karakana St ✉shahind@habari .co.tz. A crafts workshop occupying an old flour mill, many of whose forty employees are disabled. The main output is leatherwork, including "paintings" of safari scenes. These, and a huge choice of souvenirs made elsewhere, often unusual (eg decorated cow horns and pressed flowers), are available in the shop. Mon–Fri 8am–5pm, Sat 8am–1pm.

TAHEA Gallery Hill St, facing The Coffee Shop ☎0754 293171. Particularly nice jewellery from a vocational training programme for young people and women, plus passion fruit and mango juice concentrates. Mon–Fri 8am–6pm, Sat 8am–1pm.

DIRECTORY

Health KCMC (Kilimanjaro Christian Medical Centre), 6km north of town past Shanty Town (☎027 275 0748), is the best hospital in northern Tanzania but that's not saying much and you need to be referred by a doctor unless it's an emergency, or you are willing to pay a Tsh50,000 consultation fee. Blood tests can be done at Sima Hospital, Kenyatta St (☎027 275 1272; 24hr), and the dispensary there is open 24hr. Other pharmacies include Hapa Majengo Dispensary, near Majengo Block Supply (Mon–Fri 9am–4.30pm, Sat 9am–12.30pm; ☎027 275 0280); and Shanty Town Dispensary (Mon, Wed, Thurs & Fri 9am–1pm & 3–5pm, Tues 1.30–4pm, Sat 9am–1pm; ☎027 275 1418).

Immigration The Immigration Office is in Kibo House, Boma Rd, by the clock tower (Mon–Fri 7.30am–3pm; ☎027 275 1557).

Internet access Internet cafés usually charge Tsh1000/hr. Reliable ones include Easy.com, Kahawa House, by the clock tower (daily 8am–8.30pm), and a couple next to *Buffalo Hotel* (both daily 8am–10pm).

Money Most banks have 24hr ATMs for Visa and MasterCard (NMB is the exception, only accepting Tanzanian cards). Reliable forexes include Trast, cnr Mawenzi Rd and Chagga St (Mon–Sat 8am–4.30pm); and Chase, Subzali Building, Rindi Lane (Mon–Fri 8am–5pm, Sat 8am–2pm).

Police Market St ☎027 275 5055.

Sport The Kilimanjaro Marathon (and half marathon), which doesn't assault the mountain but follows roads at between 830m and 1150m above sea level, is held every Feb or March: register through ⊕kilimanjaro marathon.com.

Supermarkets Nakumatt, Kaunda Rd close to the clock tower (Mon–Sat 8am–10pm, Sun 10am–9.30pm); Carina, Kibo Rd near *Pub Alberto* (Mon–Sat 8am–6.30pm).

Swimming pools The best is the *YMCA Hostel*'s 25-metre pool (Tsh4000). Others are at the *Kilimanjaro Crane Hotel* on Kaunda Rd; *Sal Salinero* in Shanty Town, both charging Tsh5000; and *Honey Badger Lodge* 6km east of town at Msaranga (Tsh10,000).

Travel agent Emslies, Old Moshi Rd (☎027 275 2701 or ☎0689 772379, ⊕emsliesglobal.com).

Marangu and around

The base for most climbs up Kili is **MARANGU** village, an hour's drive northeast of Moshi. Marangu actually consists of two villages, both situated on the sealed road leading to the park gate: **Marangu-Arisi** is the section closest to the park, while **Marangu-Mtoni** is at the crossroads to Mamba and Rombo, 5.6km short of the park. There's more to Marangu than just a base for climbing the mountain, however. Marangu's hotels can arrange a number of **guided walks** in the area – the scenery is superb, especially close to the park, where you get unobstructed views of the Pare Mountains, Nyumba ya Mungu reservoir and Kibo (weather permitting), plus Kenya's Taita-Taveta plains and Lake Jipe.

5

You can get hassled a lot walking around Marangu: the persistent attention from young men wanting to take you to one of Marangu's waterfalls quickly becomes tedious. The basic problem is that although Marangu has a **cultural tourism programme**, the governing ethos here was every man for himself, which impeded the establishment of tourist office or other centre. The safest way to delve into local life is via the cultural trips offered by a hotel (see p.243). The tours are all easy half-day walks that can be combined into one- or two-day trips and include: excursions inside the park to **Mandara Huts** (including Maundi Crater and a waterfall); **Mamba village**, 3km east towards Rombo, for traditional blacksmiths and underground caves or tunnels, where villagers would hide themselves and their cattle during times of war; a 120-year-old Catholic mission church at **Kilema village**, its relics including what is purported to be a piece of Christ's cross, and in whose grounds Kilimanjaro's first coffee tree was planted; and a nature hike up **Ngangu Hill** on the west side of Marangu, for a great view and a cave containing the remains of a former chief.

The waterfalls

Seven **waterfalls** around Marangu can be visited: the closest, and therefore most commonly offered as short excursions, are the Kinukamori Falls, 1km north of Marangu-Mtoni; Ndoro Waterfalls, where you can swim in the splashpool, 2km west of Marangu-Mtoni past *Kibo Hotel*; and Kilasiya ("Endless") Waterfall, near the *Mountain Resort Hotel*. You can visit the waterfalls on your own, as they're signposted (admission fees average Tsh5000; don't expect anything official, or a receipt), but you'll probably be followed by a gaggle of wannabe guides. The **Cultural Temple** by Kinukamori Falls is less interesting and informative than the Chagga Live Museum, but is included in the entrance fee to the falls.

Chagga Live Museum

By Kilimanjaro Mountain Resort • Daily 10am–5pm • Tsh5000 or more (negotiable) including a usually enthusiastic guide

Also featuring on day-trips is the modest **Chagga Live Museum**, which presents the traditional material culture of the Chagga tribe, most of which was ditched long ago. There's a reconstruction of a traditional conical thatched house, which sometimes contains real cows, and all sorts of tools and implements, including items relating to the production of banana wine, and musical instruments, all labelled in English. Also on display, partly through photographs, is the history of the Chagga, more particularly that of Marangu's Marealle clan, which can be traced back over seventeen generations.

ARRIVAL AND INFORMATION

MARANGU AND AROUND

By daladala Daladalas from Moshi (roughly every 30min, 8am–6pm; Tsh2000) cover the 30km to Marangu-Mtoni. If you want to be dropped outside *Kibo Hotel* or *Kilimanjaro Mountain Resort*, make sure your daladala goes to Kilema. To be dropped at *Babylon Lodge*, you'll need one to Darakea unless you're fine walking the final kilometre. From Marangu-Mtoni to the park gate is a pleasant but steep 5km uphill walk; a shared taxi costs Tsh2000.

Cultural tourism Marangu's cultural tourism programme, founded in the late 1990s, was useful for establishing a series of local sights as low-key tourist attractions, but the cultural and community involvement

aspect of the project never took hold, so there's nothing official about any of the options, or guides. While trips can arranged with pushy touts on arrival, it's best to arrange things with a cooler head at one of Marangu's hotels, or as a day-trip from Moshi (see pp.237–238). The cost of a guide for a good half day shouldn't be more than $20 (*Kibo Hotel* can find you one for about half that); factoring in entrance fees, lunch and perhaps some local transport, you shouldn't be paying more than $40 per person per day. For a full day's walk inside the national park (to Mandera Huts, about four hours from the gate), *Babylon Lodge* is good value, charging $135 per person, including lunch, entrance fees, and transport to and from the gate.

ACCOMMODATION AND EATING

Marangu doesn't have a huge choice of hotels, but there's something decent for all pockets. Ensure your bed has adequate mosquito nets – Marangu's zillion banana plants favour the critters. All hotels have luggage stores for climbers. **Camping** is possible at several hotels.

★ **Babylon Lodge** 1km east of Marangu-Mtoni off the Rombo road ☎ 0762 016016 or ☎ 0757 997799, ⓦ babylonlodge.com. By far the most charming and bestvalue option in Marangu, this has 21 very characterful rooms (in a good sense) in a series of closely spaced cottages scattered along a hillside, with nicely designed gardens with plenty of shady nooks and crannies to chill out in. The rooms are colourfully decorated, have big beds with adequately sized box nets, and come with cable TV and wi-fi. There's also a good restaurant (see below), a very flash-looking bar, a fully licensed hiking operation and safe parking. Camping $7 per person. BB **$60**

Hotel Capricorn 2.7km from the park gate ☎ 0754 301140, ⓦ thecapricornhotels.com. A large, attractive option surrounded by lush gardens and dominated by a vast conical roof. Rooms in the old cottages have bathtubs; "new wing" rooms have showers, balconies, digital TV, fridge, phone and safe. Try to get a room facing south, as the others are very dark. Also has a nice restaurant (see p.244), an atmospheric bar and gift shop, but no pool. BB cottages **$120**, new wing **$200**

Coffee Tree Campsite 2km from the park gate ☎ 0754 691433, ⓦ coffeetreecampsite.com. The Spartan but clean dorm-like accommodation here, including some double rooms, is the closest to the park gate, and handy for a cheap night before a climb, and paradise when you return, thanks to its sauna ($10). The downside is no internet access, nor restaurant, but there is a cooking area. Camping $8 per person. Dorm **$12**, double **$30**

Kibo Hotel 1.4km west of Marangu-Mtoni ☎ 0754 038747, ⓦ kibohotel.com. One for those feeling nostalgic: a rambling old hotel from German times, imbued with charm and stuffed with mementoes of many a

glorious Kilimanjaro climb, but now – thanks to years of neglect (it bears little resemblance to the photos on the website) – crying out for some tender loving care. Until then, a handful of rooms, all large, are still maintained in a habitable state, and you can also camp in the slightly wild gardens. The swimming pool is empty. Also has a usually deserted bar and restaurant, the latter able to rustle up basic but unmemorable nosh (Tsh8000–12,000). Camping $5 per person. BB **$60**

Kilimanjaro Mountain Resort 1.5km west of Kibo Hotel ☎ 027 275 8950 or ☎ 0754 999755, ⓦ kilimountresort.com. More like a private mansion than a hotel, a mountain of money was used to build this vaguely Neoclassical place, and going by the pricing, it wants some of it back. So long as it maintains its standards, that's fine: the bedrooms, all large, are very well appointed, with shiny bathrooms (and big bathtubs), digital TV and fridge, and you get to enjoy a swimming pool, sauna, jacuzzi, internet café, kids' playground, a decent if pricey restaurant (main courses $15–20) and – no hotel should leave home without one – a duck pond. Camping $17 per person, or $30 in their tents. BB **$200**

Marangu Hotel 2km south of Marangu-Mtoni ☎ 0754 886092, ⓦ maranguhotel.com. Originally a coffee farm started by Czech immigrants in 1907, this became a guesthouse in the 1930s, and its unpretentious old colonial farm feeling remains true to that time. The rooms are darkish and very basic for the price, however, but the facilities include a good swimming pool, croquet lawn, bar, restaurant, safe parking, internet access and – probably the best reason to stay here, and it brings a discount – their hiking operation, which has long enjoyed an excellent reputation. Camping Tsh10,400 per person. HB **$160**

EATING AND DRINKING

Marangu's tourist-style restaurants are in its hotels; for cheaper eats, try any of the stalls at the junction in Marangu-Mtoni.

★ **Babylon Lodge** 1km east of Marangu-Mtoni off the Rombo road ☎ 0762 016016. Enjoying cheerful and even classy surroundings, with the option to take drinks or meals into the garden, this is the pick of the best at present. Its menu is suspiciously ambitious, but so long as the lodge remains popular, most of it should be available. Nonetheless, if something catches your eye, ask them in the morning to give them time to buy the ingredients. Choose from a wide selection of cheap snacks (less than Tsh1000), soups (including *mtori* for $2), or full meals including pork ribs, or tilapia with rice, chips or *ugali*, mostly less than $8 a plate.

The bar is Marangu's flashiest, and complete with projector for international sports. Daily noon–10pm.

Hotel Capricorn 2.7km from the park gate ☎ 0754 301140. An old-style lodge-like restaurant heavy on the wood, with one side open on its gardens. The menu is comfortingly short (a rare show of realism among Tanzania's ever-optimistic restaurateurs) and includes vegetarian dishes (around $7) but focuses on filling European-style meat courses such as pork escalope with mashed potatoes ($10). Well priced. Daily noon–8pm or later.

5

★**Marangu Hotel** 2km south of Marangu-Mtoni ☎0754 886092. Filling, tasty and very reasonably priced light lunches and snacks, including great samosas, burgers, fresh soups with wholemeal bread (and proper butter) and a rather famous lasagne (Tsh8000). Safe parking. Daily 10am–6pm (and dinner for overnight guests).

Machame and around

On the southwestern side of the mountain, **MACHAME** – the village at the start of Kilimanjaro's second most popular climbing route – is set in a beautiful area of steep valleys, thick forests, streams and fertile farmland, and has good views of the summit to boot. Most visitors only pass through en route to climbing the mountain (the Machame route is for ascent only), so there are no tourist facilities other than an infrequently visited **cultural tourism programme**, which offers a variety of guided walks and the chance to meet the locals. Among their hikes are the fascinating **Sienye-Ngira tour** (4–6hr) through Sienye rainforest to Masama village, southwest of Machame, and which can be extended over two days to include **Ng'uni**, upstream from Masama, with great views over the plains, where you can learn about constructing traditional *mbii* houses.

ARRIVAL AND INFORMATION   MACHAME AND AROUND

By daladala or bus Daladalas run hourly (7am–6pm) from Moshi's main bus stand, taking about an hour. Alternatively, catch a daladala or bus towards Arusha and get off at the signposted junction 12km west, where other daladalas connect with Machame – 14km to the north – every ten minutes or so from 8am to around 6pm. The park gate lies 4km beyond the village.

Cultural tourism programme Machame's cultural tourism programme is based at Kyalia near Foo village, about 1km beyond Machame (☎027 275 3885 or ☎0754 494924, ✉mushijonas@yahoo.com). Costs should be no more than $40 a day, all included. Make sure you arrange things through the office itself and not through someone on the street. They can also organize homestays for around Tsh10,000 per person. The official web page is ⊕tanzaniaculturaltourism.go.tz/machame.htm.

ACCOMMODATION

Protea Hotel Aishi Machame 6km north of the Moshi–Arusha highway ☎027 275 6948, ⊕proteahotels.com. Apart from homestays arranged through the cultural tourism programme, accommodation in Machame is limited to this hotel: thirty well-equipped rooms with TVs in a stylish three-storey block with tree-bark roof tiles, or in bungalows, all set in lush gardens with ponds, boardwalks and hundreds of banana plants. Facilities include a good restaurant (meals less than $20), solar-heated swimming pool, sauna and steam room. BB **$160**

Kilimanjaro National Park

As wide as all the world, great, high, and unbelievably white in the sun, was the square top of Kilimanjaro.
Ernest Hemingway, *The Snows of Kilimanjaro*

The ice-capped, dormant volcano that is **Mount Kilimanjaro** has exerted an irresistible fascination since it was "discovered" by Europeans in the mid-nineteenth century. Rising more than 5km from the surrounding plains to a peak of 5892m, Kilimanjaro is Africa's highest mountain, the world's tallest free-standing massif, and one of the world's largest volcanoes, covering some 3885 square kilometres. It is also an exceptionally beautiful mountain, from both afar and close up, and fills up brochures as easily as it does the horizon.

The mountain was formed during the most recent faulting of the Great Rift Valley two to three million years ago, an event that also produced Mount Meru and Mount Kenya. Kilimanjaro has three main peaks, together with parasitic volcanic cones and craters dotted around its sides. The youngest and highest peak is the distinctive snow-capped dome of **Kibo**, actually a large crater that was formed around 460,000 years ago during the last period of major volcanic activity. The pinnacle, Uhuru Peak, is

5892m high, but most maps mark it as 5895m – from the days before satellite surveys. The jagged, pimple-like **Mawenzi**, 11km to the east of Kibo (and is connected to it by a broad lava saddle), is all that remains of a volcanic cone that lost its eastern rim in a gigantic explosion; its highest point is Hans Meyer Peak (5149m). The oldest peak is the **Shira Ridge**, on the west side of the mountain.

For many visitors, the prospect of scaling the mountain, which can take anything from five to eight days, is as exciting as it is daunting. The fact that no technical climbing skills are required to reach the summit (it's said to be the world's highest non-technical climb) means that Kilimanjaro has acquired something of an easy reputation – a dangerous misconception, and one which you should ignore. The high altitude and the possibility of a quick ascent mean that an average of a dozen people lose their lives every year, usually as victims of **acute mountain sickness** (see p.248). In addition, almost everyone suffers with screaming headaches and utter exhaustion on summit day; of the forty thousand people who attempt the climb every year, only about two-thirds make it all the way to Uhuru Peak. Having said this, if you take your time and stay attentive to your body's needs, there's no reason why you shouldn't be able to make it to the top. The mountain also offers plenty of less strenuous alternatives for those for whom the prospect of summitting smacks of a mite too much masochism: a walk on the lower slopes, through rainforest and on to the edge of sub-alpine moorland, makes no extreme fitness demands, and can be done in a day.

Brief history

Non-Africans have known Kilimanjaro since at least the thirteenth century, when Chinese mariners reported a "great mountain" inland. Europe, however, remained ignorant of Kilimanjaro until 1848, when the German missionary **Johannes Rebmann**, having given up trying to convert coastal tribes to Christianity, headed inland to try his luck elsewhere. His report of a snow-capped mountain three degrees south of the Equator was met with scorn and ridicule back home, and it wasn't until 1861, when Kilimanjaro was scaled to a height of around 4300m by Dr Otto Kersten and Baron Karl Klaus von der Decken, that his report was accepted by the likes of the Royal Geographical Society. The first Europeans to reach the summit were the German geographer **Hans Meyer** and Austrian mountaineer **Ludwig Purtscheller**, who reached Kibo on October 6, 1889. Mawenzi was climbed in 1912.

The origin of the **mountain's name** is confusing. To some explorers it meant "that which cannot be conquered", to others it was the "mountain of greatness", or the "mountain of caravans". In both Kiswahili and Kichagga (the Chagga language), *mlima* means mountain, while *kilima* is a hill. The use of the diminutive could be affectionate, though Chagga place names are often preceded with *ki*. The second half of the name remains vague: *njaro* may be related to a Kichagga word for caravan, a throw-back to

MELTDOWN: THE END OF KILIMANJARO'S ICE CAP?

Incredible though it might seem, Kibo's emblematic white crown may soon be no more. Kilimanjaro is heating up, and its ice cap and glaciers are retreating at an alarming rate. In 1912, the ice cap covered just more than twelve square kilometres. By 2005, it had shrunk to under two square kilometres, having diminished by a full third over the previous fifteen years.

The primary cause is **global warming**, as worryingly proven by research using core samples of the ice cap as a weather archive. Hapless park and forest management has also done little to stop the ongoing **destruction of forest cover** on the mountain's lower slopes, through illegal logging and uncontrolled fires courtesy of honey-gatherers, poachers and careless farmers. Forests trap solar heat, so less forest means warmer ambient air, in turn hastening the big thaw.

Although some researchers posit 2021 or earlier for the demise of Kilimanjaro's ice cap, its last remnants are proving tenacious, and may yet survive until 2040 or so – some eleven thousand years after the peak last lost its snowy crown.

5

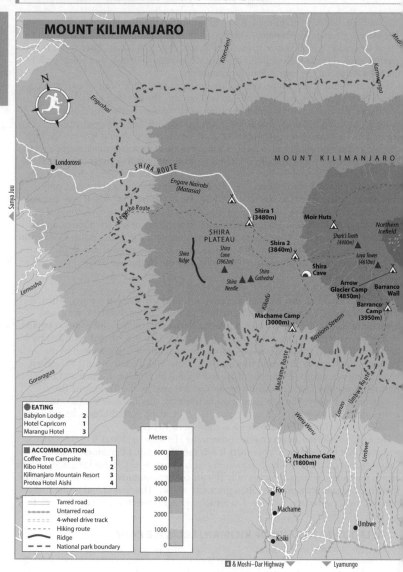

MOUNT KILIMANJARO

MOUNT KILIMANJARO

Londorossi

SHIRA ROUTE

Engare Nairobi (Matasia)

Shira 1 (3480m)

Moir Huts

Northern Icefield

Lemosho Route

SHIRA PLATEAU

Shira Cone (3962m)

Shira 2 (3840m)

Shark's Tooth (4400m)

Lava Tower (4610m)

Shira Cave

Shira Ridge

Shira Cathedral

Arrow Glacier Camp (4850m)

Barranco Wall

Shira Needle

Kilafu

Machame Camp (3000m)

Barranco Camp (3950m)

Bastions Stream

Gararagua

Machame Route

Weru Weru

Lonzo

Umbwe Route

Umbwe

Machame Gate (1800m)

Foo

Machame

Umbwe

Kisiki

EATING

Babylon Lodge	2
Hotel Capricorn	1
Marangu Hotel	3

ACCOMMODATION

Coffee Tree Campsite	1
Kibo Hotel	2
Kilimanjaro Mountain Resort	3
Protea Hotel Aishi	4

Metres

| 6000 |
| 5000 |
| 4000 |
| 3000 |
| 2000 |
| 1000 |
| 0 |

Tarred road
Untarred road
4-wheel drive track
Hiking route
Ridge
National park boundary

Engushai

Kitendeni

Kamwanga

Msa

Sanya Juu

Legosho Route

◄ & Moshi–Dar Highway ▼   ▼ Lyamungo

the slave and ivory trade, or to an old word for God, *kyaro*. An alternative meaning stems from the Maasai word *ngare*, meaning river – Kilimanjaro, of course, being the source of life for several of these.

The Chagga have a wonderful tale about the origin of Kilimanjaro's main peaks, **Kibo and Mawenzi**, who, they say, were sisters. Kibo was the wiser of the two, and was careful to store away food for times of hardship. Her sister, Mawenzi, however, had no such cares for the future, and fell into the habit of asking Kibo for help whenever times were bad. Eventually, Kibo became angry with her sister's begging, and hit her on the head with a spoon; hence Mawenzi's ragged and broken appearance. Another Chagga

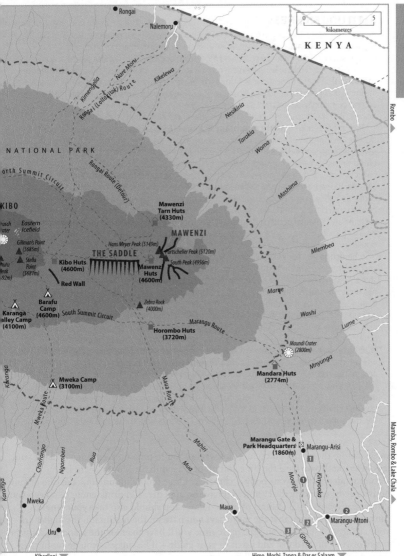

legend speaks of a great treasure on the mountain, one protected by powerful spirits who punished those foolhardy enough to dare climb it – extreme cold, exhaustion and altitude sickness are the very real modern forms of those spirits.

Climbing Kilimanjaro

Climbing Kilimanjaro is difficult and usually painful, so brace yourself for a big effort. Being adequately equipped and in good **physical condition** also helps, as does being mentally prepared. You don't have to be an athlete, but cut down on alcohol a few

5

ALTITUDE SICKNESS

Air gets thinner the higher you go; on the summit of Kilimanjaro, a lungful contains only half the oxygen you would inhale at sea level. Given enough time, the human body can adapt to an oxygen-scarce environment by producing more red blood cells. But, without weeks to acclimatize, almost everyone climbing Kili will experience the effects of high altitude, known as **altitude (or mountain)** sickness: these include shortness of breath, light-headedness, headaches, nausea, insomnia and, naturally enough, exhaustion. The symptoms appear towards the end of the second or third day. Staying hydrated is absolutely essential at high altitude and normal altitude sickness isn't much to worry about, although vomiting should be treated seriously.

Much more serious is **acute mountain sickness (AMS)**, the chronic form of altitude sickness. Symptoms of AMS include most of the above, plus one or more of the following: severe headache; shortness of breath at rest; flu-like symptoms; persistent dry cough; blood-tinged saliva or urine; unsteadiness or drowsiness; lack of mental clarity or hallucinations; and chest congestion. In these cases, **descend immediately** to a lower altitude. Be aware that mental fuzziness may convince the victim that he or she is fit to continue – they're not. A porter will usually accompany the victim, so the whole party won't have to turn back. Ignoring the symptoms of AMS can be fatal: complications like pulmonary oedema and cerebral oedema claim the lives of about a dozen climbers each year. Predicting who will get sick is impossible: AMS affects young and old alike, the fit and the not so fit, so don't deny the signs if you start feeling them, and heed your guide's advice.

Some **drugs** are claimed to eliminate such problems. **Diamox** (the trade name for acetazolamide) seems to be the most reliable and achieves the best results, however, opinion is sharply divided over their pros and cons, so consult a doctor before taking anything. The drug has two well-known short-term side effects: your fingers tingle, and it's an extremely efficient diuretic, so you'll be urinating every few hours day and night – drink lots of water to compensate. Some (unconfirmed) reports suggest that in rare cases the tingling or numbness in fingers may persist for several years. Nonetheless, most climbers do tend to have an easier time of things when on Diamox. As an alternative, some climbers swear by ginkgo biloba (120mg taken twice a day, starting a few days before the climb). Don't take it if you bleed easily.

Given the confusion over medication, **prevention** is a better approach: let your body acclimatize naturally by taking an extra day or two when climbing the mountain (at least six days, whichever route you're taking, ideally seven or eight – or else climb Mount Meru the preceding week to help you acclimatize); stay hydrated; climb slowly; and if you ascend a lot in one day, camp at a lower altitude, if possible. Lastly, don't go higher than the tree line (2700m) if you're suffering from fever, nosebleed, cold or influenza, sore throat or a respiratory infection.

weeks before the climb, go cycling and walk or jog to tune up your lungs and get your legs in shape. If you have the time and money, a climb up Mount Meru is recommended to help your body acclimatize. Once on the mountain, take care of your body's needs: eat properly, even if you have no appetite, and drink enough to keep your urine clear (generally 3–4 litres of water a day). You should also **take your time**. It cannot be said enough that the more days you have on the mountain, the higher are your chances of success – and the more time you'll have to enjoy the scenery. Lastly, be aware of your limitations, and listen to your guide – if he suggests you go no further, don't – as he knows what he's talking about.

The most popular **routes up the mountain** are the Marangu and Machame routes from the south, the Lemosho route from the west and the Rongai route from the north. Other routes may also be offered by hiking companies, but are not recommended for a first visit: the Umbwe route, from the south, is too short to acclimatize adequately, while the Western Breach (alternative to the Lemosho) is not just difficult but downright dangerous.

With the exception of the Marangu route, which has mountain huts for each overnight stop, night are spent at official campsites (often called huts on maps, as they do have huts… for park rangers only). Whichever route you take, the penultimate day is usually **summit day**. It's not a walk in the park, and isn't helped by a lack of sleep: hikers set off between 11pm and 1am, so the first six hours or so of your summit attempt are in the dark, with temperatures well below zero, and – if there's no moon – with only torches to light the way. The thin air forces frequent stops, and most climbers get lightheaded and nauseous, and suffer from headaches. Drink plenty of fluids, and when short of breath, inhale and exhale deeply and rapidly four or five times. If you manage to slog it out until sunrise, you should be within a stone's throw of the summit. **Descent** is usually along the Mweka or Marangu routes in the south, and can be split into two days. The greatest risk of injury is on the way down, so use a walking stick or ski pole, and resist the temptation to slide down the scree.

It's possible to **hike into the crater** if this is arranged in advance with your guide (at extra cost). Measuring 2km in diameter and 300m deep, the crater contains another, smaller crater named after Dr Richard Reusch, who in 1926 discovered the frozen leopard later made famous by Hemingway (see box p.250). In the centre of this is an ash pit, and there are some small but active steam fumaroles on its northern and eastern rim. Incidentally, it's not a good idea to spend a night on the summit (Furtwangler Camp, 5600m) unless you're taking at least nine days for the hike, as you'll need to be totally acclimatized to avoid coming down with AMS.

The Marangu route

The **Marangu route**, from the park headquarters near Marangu village in the southeast (see p.241), is the quickest, steepest and most popular way up, giving great views of craggy Mawenzi Peak once you're past the tangled rainforest above Marangu Gate (1800m). It's usually offered as a five-day trek, but an extra day considerably increases your chances of reaching the top – although even so the success rate is low compared with the Machame and Lemosho routes. Depending on the season (see p.251), the route can also be cloudy and muddy, and is often busy. You'll see litter left by dumb climbers (hence the trail's nickname, the "Coca-Cola route"), and graffiti adorning its **accommodation huts**: Mandara (2705m), Horombo (3714m) and Kibo (4713m). These are equipped with bunks, solar lighting, kitchens, toilets and rescue teams. Snacks and drinks, including beer, are available at all the huts – but wait until you descend to indulge in the booze. Bunks must be reserved through the park headquarters, or your hiking company.

The final push to the summit is from the east, along a trail that turns into a painful series of single-file zigzags up loose scree, for which a Zen-like mindset helps. At the top, a short rocky scramble gets you to within staggering distance of **Gillman's Point** (5685m) on the crater rim, where many climbers call it a day, to be consoled with the stupendous view and the sun rising from behind Mawenzi Peak. If you still have the oomph, it's ninety utterly exhausting minutes from Gillman's Point along an ice-covered trail to **Uhuru Peak** (5892m), and crowning glory.

The Machame route

Kilimanjaro's second-most popular route is the long, winding and dramatic **Machame route**, from Machame in the southwest (see p.244). The trek takes at least six days, but seven or eight are recommended to maximize your chances of success. The scenery is often extraordinary, ranging from dense and steamy rainforest alive with birdsong, to alpine tundra and the desolate volcanic wonderland of the Shira Plateau west of the summit, complete with ancient volcanic plugs and spectacular views of Kibo Peak as well as the mountain's fast retreating glaciers. While slower and more sedate than the Marangu route, it does have some very steep sections, including the Barranco Wall, which requires some hands-and-feet climbing.

The final ascent is from Barafu Camp, south of the summit crater, along an increasingly steep valley on the edge of scree fields, before passing between the

5

Rebmann and Ratzel glaciers to emerge at **Stella Point** (5672m) on the crater's southern rim, where you'll join those climbers on the Marangu and Rongai routes. **Uhuru Peak** is about an hour along.

The Lemosho route

The longest route up the mountain, and distinctly less-travelled than Marangu and Machame, is the **Lemosho route**. Eight or nine days are the normal completion time, which works in your favour as regards avoiding altitude sickness. The route approaches from the west, with the first day passing through forest once used as a migration route by elephants from Kenya's Amboseli National Park, though these days you'd be lucky to see much more than dung. The route joins the Machame route on the fourth day (see p.249), having crossed the Shira Plateau.

The Rongai route

The easiest of the four main paths to the summit, and the only one from the north, is the **Rongai route** (also called the Loitokitok or Nalemoru route). At first glance, it's also the least attractive: a drier climate than the southern and western flanks, coupled with deforestation on its lower slopes, means it lacks the lush rainforest that features on the first day of other routes, and scenically the first day's hike is rather dull. Things perk up considerably from the second day onwards, and as the descent is along the Marangu route, you get to see forest just before reaching the gate. A recommended detour, extending the hike to six or seven days, is to **Mawenzi Tarn**, a diminutive lake beside which you'll spend the night, in the shadow of Mawenzi Peak. The final section to the summit is the also same as the Marangu route (see p.249).

KILIMANJARO'S HIGH-ALTITUDE FLORA AND FAUNA

Kilimanjaro is covered by a series of distinctive habitat zones, determined by altitude. Above about 1800m, farmland ceases and forests take over. Up to around 2000m, much of the forest is secondary growth, but beyond here is dense primary **cloudforest**, containing more than 1800 species of flowering plants. In its lower reaches, the forest is dominated by ferns, podocarpus and camphor trees, and is home to three primate species: blue monkey, western black-and-white colobus, and bushbaby (galago). Leopards also live here (though you're most unlikely to see one), preying on mountain reedbuck and members of the world's largest population of Abbot's duiker.

Rainfall is less heavy at higher altitudes, so from around 2400m the forest becomes less dense. The tree line (2800–3000m) marks the start of the peculiar **afro-alpine moorland** (also called upland grassland) and the land of the giants – giant heather, giant groundsel (or tree senecio) and giant lobelia. The cabbages on stumps and the larger candelabra-like "trees" are two forms of the giant groundsel, which can have a sheaf of yellow flowers. The giant groundsel favours damp and sheltered locations such as stream beds; they're slow growers but, for such weedy-looking vegetables, they may be extraordinarily old – up to two hundred years. Higher up, in the alpine bogs, you'll see groundsel together with another strange plant, the tall and fluffy giant lobelia – the animal-like furriness insulates the delicate flowers. A number of mammals habitually pass into the moorland zone from the forests: grey duiker and eland are most commonly seen; bushbuck, red duiker and buffalo are more rare. There are few birds: the most common is the white-necked raven, often seen at campsites.

Above 4600m is the barren alpine desert zone. The sub-zero conditions here mean that few plants other than mosses and lichens are able to survive, although the daisy-like *Helichrysum newii* has been seen on Kibo's summit caldera at 5760m close to a fumarole. Even stranger was the mysterious leopard whose frozen body was found close to the summit in 1926 and which featured in Hemingway's *The Snows of Kilimanjaro*. No one knows what it was doing so far up the mountain.

ESSENTIALS

Park headquarters The park headquarters at Marangu Gate, 5.6km north of Marangu village (daily 8am–6pm; ☏0689 062309, ☏0767 536134 or ☏027 275 6605, ✉kinapa@tanzaniaparks.com) are useless for specialized queries, but the shop opposite the registration counter sells maps and books. The park's official page is ⊛tanzaniaparks .com/kili.html.

Guidebooks and maps The most comprehensive guidebook is *Kilimanjaro: The Trekking Guide to Africa's Highest Mountain* by Henry Stedman (Trailblazer); shorter and more personable is Jacquetta Megarry's *Explore Mount Kilimanjaro* (Rucksack Readers). Given that you'll be accompanied by a guide, a map isn't essential, but is good to have – a guide's conception of "not far" can differ radically from your own, and it's nice to put names to physical features. Easiest to find in Tanzania is Giovanni Tombazzi's hand-painted *New Map of Kilimanjaro*, with good inserts on flora. More accurate – and worth buying before you leave home – are Climbing Maps' *Kilimanjaro-Kibo* (1:80,000; ⊛climbing-map.com/en/maps/kilimanjaro.html), and ITMB's *Kilimanjaro Trekking Map* (1:62,500; ⊛itmb.ca), with 100m contours and tinting.

Websites There's lots of information on the internet, including hundreds of journey accounts, and recommendations for hiking companies, but be aware that the money associated with Kili climbs is such that fake reviews, and equally fake rumours and complaints about competitors, are rife. Best of the truly independent websites (not affiliated to hiking companies or other services), and up to date on the latest porter-related shenanigans, is Birgit Bradtke's ⊛mountkilimanjaroguide.com. Of the commercial ones, ⊛climbmountkilimanjaro.com is the most detailed.

COSTS

Climbing Kilimanjaro is an expensive business, even if you brave the hassle of arranging things yourself: "budget" seven-day climbs, with ethical and reliable hiking companies, start at $1600, while a climb with a mid-range company won't get you much change from $2500. Don't get excited if you're offered a hike for $1000 or less: some companies exclude park fees from their quoted rates. Prices depend on not just the quality of the company you climb but also the route you choose, with the Shira/Lemosho and Rongai routes tending to be costlier, as they take longer, and are also further away from Moshi and Arusha, so transport there and back adds on a bit more, too.

Entry fees The lion's share of the costs is taken up by park fees: $70 per person for 24hrs, plus $50 for a night's camping or $60 for hut space on the Marangu route. There's also a one-off $20 rescue fee. Then you need to pay for your crew: the obligatory guide as well as porters and a cook. Additional costs include food, equipment rental, and

KILIMANJARO NATIONAL PARK

transport to and from the park gates.

Tips Not included in the costs cited above are tips, which, even if theoretically optional, are expected (some hiking companies, including some of the largest, pay little or even nothing to the crew for that reason). How much to pay is a perennial headache, not helped by the sour mood of some climbers who fail to reach the top or by the constant and not-so-subtle hints from the guide and porters that can plague some trips. The best way to deal with it is to say you'll pay when you get down, but don't tie the promise of tips with a successful summit attempt: you'll be encouraging the guide to take risks, and success depends more on your body and attitude than on the guide and porters. A reasonable total gratuity is about a tenth of the overall cost of the trip; alternatively, something like $20 per day for the head guide, and $15 for each other crew member, also per day, split between the number of hikers, is fair. Leaving unneeded equipment with the guide and porters after the climb is welcome, but no substitute for a cash tip. Obviously, if the guide or porters were terrible, don't tip at all – but do explain to them why.

WHEN TO GO

The most popular climbing season is Dec to Feb, when the weather is generally clear. June to Sept is also good, though there's a chance of rain in June, and Sept can be devilishly cold. Kilimanjaro can be climbed during the intervening rainy seasons, but the lower slopes will be exceedingly muddy and there's no guarantee of clear skies higher up. The southeastern slopes receive most rain, so the Machame and Shira/Lemosho routes are generally drier than the Marangu route. It can snow on or near the summit all year round, though chances are highest during and shortly after the rainy seasons. Try to coincide with a full moon on summit day – it avoids the need for flashlights, and lends an eerie beauty to the scene.

WHAT TO TAKE

Porters will take your main backpack but tend to dash off ahead, so you'll need to bring a small daypack to carry stuff you'll need during the day, such as water bottles, snacks, camera, waterproofs, suncream and sunglasses. Don't pack too much weight, and ensure your pack is comfortable.

Clothing A good pair of boots and lots of warm clothes are the essentials for a Kilimanjaro climb. The important thing is to wear layers – several levels of clothing worn on top of one another provide better insulation than fewer but bulkier items. Thermal underwear and fleeces are essential, and as you won't have much chance to dry things out (open fires are no longer permitted), waterproofs are vital. Don't forget sunglasses and a sunhat, as well as a woolly hat and gloves (preferably a thinner inner layer and a thicker, waterproof outer glove) for the colder climates.

5

Camping equipment Your trekking agency will supply tents etc, though you will need to bring a warm (rated down to −10ºC) sleeping bag. Check to see if they will supply a ground mat or whether you need to bring this too. You don't need cooking equipment, as the porters bring this. There's a kiosk just inside the gate at the park headquarters at Marangu Gate that rents out some pretty good gear, from balaclavas to sleeping bags: as an idea of costs, hiring a sleeping bag with foam mat

costs $70 per climb.

Additional kit A headtorch, toilet paper, walking poles and water bottles (enough to carry three litres) are all pretty much essential. Plastic bags for keeping things dry, towel, sweets and money (for tips, and to buy drinks at the huts) are all useful too. High-altitude medication (see p.248), plasters, bandages and gauze, lip salve, and suncream (minimum factor 25) and rehydration powders/solutions should all be added to your standard medical kit (see p.57).

HIKING COMPANIES, GUIDES AND PORTERS

Any company directly organizing Kilimanjaro climbs needs a current **TALA Mountaineering Licence**: the national park offices at Marangu and Machame gates have lists of licensed companies, as do the tourist offices in Arusha and Dar es Salaam, and you'll also find them online at ⊛ tanzaniatourism.go.tz. Those reviewed here are among the more reputable, licensed outfits in Moshi and Marangu. We've also recommended Arusha-based companies (see pp.288–289). One company not reviewed here as it only deals with tour companies, but with an excellent reputation, is African Environments (⊛ africanenvironments.co.tz). Be wary of other companies not reviewed in this book – appearances are not everything. In addition, don't necessarily believe recommendations on the internet: several companies are adept at plugging themselves. And if a flycatcher claims to work for one of the following, ensure that you end up at the correct address – there have been cases of disreputable outfits "borrowing" the names of other companies to snare clients. Lastly, given that the cost of climbing is so much already, **don't scrimp** by going with a dodgy company: it's not worth the saving if you're going to end up with inexperienced guides, dud equipment and mistreated porters. Unfortunately, Moshi's trekking agencies have a bad reputation for the latter – a town-wide malaise with only few exceptions. The following companies are licensed, are members of TATO (see p.63), and were also KPAP partners before the project was shelved in 2014.

African Scenic Safaris ☏ 0783 080239, ⊛ africanscenicsafaris.com. A Tanzanian–Australian company genuinely committed to the ethical side of mountaineering, offering trips along all the main routes. A seven-day Machame climb costs $1600.

Ahsante Tours & Safaris Arusha Road, 850m west of Uhuru Torch roundabout, Moshi ☏ 027 275 0248, ⊛ ahsantetours.com. A helpful and friendly company that has long been the budget trekkers' agency of choice, offering one of the most reliable and best-value services on Kilimanjaro: six-day climbs start around $1600 per person in a group of four, with a nine-day Lemosho route climb costing around $2200, also in a group of four. It can also organize bicycle tours (including a fun if exhausting circum-Kilimanjaro jaunt), and is also fully licensed for wildlife safaris.

Marangu Hotel 2km south of Marangu-Mtoni ☏ 0754 886092, ⊛ maranguhotel.com. Long-established company with excellent guides and a reputation for thorough preparation. A fully equipped six-day Marangu hike costs around $1500 per person; an eight-day hike on another route starts from $2100 in group of four.

Summit Expeditions and Nomadic Experience (SENE) ☏ 027 275 3233, ⊛ nomadicexperience.com. Run by the irrepressible Simon Mtuy – holder of the record for the fastest combined ascent and descent of Kilimanjaro – SENE offers extremely well-prepared climbs on the Lemosho, Machame and Rongai routes, with each trek preceded by a couple of days relaxing on Simon's farm at Mbahe, in the foothills of the mountain, and another night there at the end. Not cheap, at

more than $3500 for a Machame or Rongai hike, but highly recommended by those who've sampled Simon's hospitality. For something completely different, ultra-marathonists have the Kilimanjaro Stage Run – an eight-day, 260km dash around the mountain, in October.

GUIDES

Your hiking company will provide you with guides and porters to help you up the mountain. Park regulations insist on one licensed guide to every two trekkers. Most of the guides are superb: many have climbed the mountain innumerable times, and they're usually fluent in English. That said, if you have a chance you should ask your company to meet your guide in advance, to see how you get on – after all, he's going to be your companion for the next week, and you are putting your life in his hands.

PORTERS

Your hiking company will also provide you with porters – usually about two or three per trekker, and sometimes also a cook – you'll be amazed at how good they are at rustling up some surprisingly delicious nosh. Porters are limited to carrying no more than 20kg each, plus 5kg of their own gear. Incidentally, porters don't scale the summit but instead stay at the last hut or campsite and meet up with you again on the way down. Though the amount they carry is now regulated, the porters still face one of the hardest jobs on the mountain, and many still perish in the course of doing their job. Unfortunately, although most companies pay lip service to this, the reality is somewhat different: there's a lot of money and politics behind the scenes, and some didn't take kindly to the establishment of the now largely defunct Kilimanjaro Porters Assistance Project (KPAP), whose website used to list "partner" trekking agencies who, in the opinion of porters themselves, treated them fairly (still online, but without the partner names, at ⓦ kiliporters.org). We've been careful in our recommendations but, as time goes on, you might conduct your own research as regards the treatment of porters: start with the websites we've reviewed (see p.251).

The Pare Mountains

To the southeast of Kilimanjaro rise the much older but equally beautiful **Pare Mountains**, a green, fertile and infrequently visited region divided into two distinct ranges – north and south. The practical business of getting around is not as difficult as it was, thanks to the establishment of three **cultural tourism programmes** (see p.65), two in the north at Usangi and Kisangara Chini, another at Mbaga in the south. Each programme offers a range of affordable activities based around guided walks in the mountains and their forests, and encounters with the rural culture of the **Pare** tribe, who have been living in the mountains for the last six hundred years.

The Pare is northeastern Tanzania's most traditional tribe. In the same way that the geologically separate Eastern Arc forests have developed an especially rich flora and fauna (see box, p.256), so the isolation of the Pare from other tribes has resulted in their strong and distinctive culture and sense of identity. Whereas traditional knowledge of plants and their uses is fast disappearing elsewhere, the Pare have kept much of their knowledge intact, and are famed throughout northern Tanzania for the power of their healers, and sometimes feared for witchcraft – witches, called *ndewa* in Kipare, are invariably associated with botanical knowledge garnered over many centuries. It's thanks to the continuity of Pare culture that many of the mountains' indigenous forests have been preserved, despite high human population densities, since the Pare consider the forests sacred places, guarded by the spirits of their ancestors. Add to all this the fact that the Pare, like their Sambaa cousins to the south (see box, p.260), are an unfailingly welcoming bunch, and you have an immensely rewarding place to visit.

In the plains between the mountains and the Kenyan border lies **Mkomazi National Park** (see p.259), which became the scene of controversy following the forced expulsion of Maasai cattle herders in 1988. It's a beautiful place, and still receives only few visitors, so is a fine alternative to the Northern Safari Circuit parks, even though its wildlife is not as prolific, nor as visible, and the park's much vaunted rhino sanctuary is off limits to most mere mortals.

North Pare

The **North Pare Mountains** are best visited through the cultural tourism programme at **Usangi**. Another programme, at **Kisangara Chini** on the Dar–Arusha highway, also offers walks into the mountains, but is better for trips to Nyumba ya Mungu reservoir in the plains to the west.

Usangi

The base for the North Pare Mountains' cultural tourism programme is **USANGI** village, 25km east of the highway in a beautiful location surrounded by no fewer than eleven peaks. Try to visit on a Monday or Thursday, when the village's **market** is held. The cultural tourism programme offers a range of **trips**; profits are currently used to help a local clinic. A guided half-day walk takes in farms on the lower slopes of the Pare Mountains before climbing to **Mangatu moorland** (1600m), near the sacred forest of the Mbale clan, with superb views of Kilimanjaro and Lake Jipe on the Kenyan border. A full-day trek can be arranged up North Pare's highest peak, **Mount Kindoroko** (2113m),

5

9km south of Usangi, for grand views of Kilimanjaro, Mount Meru, Lake Jipe and Nyumba ya Mungu reservoir. The walk goes through the surrounding rainforest, home to blue monkeys and birds, and you can also visit a women's pottery co-operative and a traditional healer, and listen to a storyteller. Another day-trip goes up **Mount Kamwala**, whose forests are sacred. Walks over several days can also be arranged; Ugweno village, near **Lake Jipe** on the Kenyan border, is a handy base both for walks and canoeing on Lake Jipe (watch out for the hippos and crocodiles), and has accommodation at the local school. You can also camp in the mountains, but will need to bring your own gear.

If you're not up for long hikes, there are several things to do in and around Usangi, including making visits to a brick-making co-operative and to other artisans producing pottery, clothes and traditional sugar-cane beer (*denge*).

ARRIVAL AND INFORMATION   USANGI

By bus Transport from Arusha or Moshi is on the daily Sahara Coach (10am from Arusha, passing Moshi around 11.30am, and leaving Usangi at 6am). Coming from Dar es Salaam, catch a bus for Moshi or Arusha and get off in the district capital, Mwanga, 50km southeast of Moshi, from where a handful of daily buses grind uphill along a good sandy road to Usangi (60min).

Cultural tourism programme The North Pare Cultural

Tourism Enterprise operates from Lomwe Secondary School in Usangi, where you should ask for the headmaster (☎0784 813787 or ☎027 275 7924, ✉lomwesec@gmail .com). Costs include a guide fee of Tsh20,000 (for a group of up to five people) per day (plus Tsh10,000 if you wish to camp overnight), and a Tsh5000 Village Development Fee. The official web page is ⊛tanzaniaculturaltourism.go.tz /northern_pare.htm.

ACCOMMODATION AND EATING

In Usangi, several families – most of them connected to the secondary school – offer accommodation (around Tsh10,000 per person) through the cultural tourism programme, and camping is also possible. The school itself also has a guesthouse, sleeping eight, and there's a guesthouse in the village near the mosque. Meals are provided by the Usangi Women's Group with dinner or lunch both Tsh6000.

Kisangara Chini

The easiest of Pare's cultural tourism programmes to visit is at **KISANGARA CHINI**, 12km south of Mwanga on the highway, sandwiched between vast sisal plantations in the shadow of Mount Kindoroko, North Pare's highest peak. Kisangara Chini's **market day** is Sunday, and there's a Maasai cattle market on Fridays at Mugagao.

The "must-do" is a hike up **Mount Kindoroko** (also offered by Usangi's cultural tourism programme), combined with visits to sites of ritual importance. The programme also arranges day-trips to **Nyumba ya Mungu** ("House of God") reservoir in the plains to the west, for bird-spotting, fishing excursions by canoe and encounters with local fishermen, some of whom emigrated here from Lake Victoria. Closer to Kisangara Chini, various **half-day walks** combine visits to carpentry workshops, brick and sisal factories, a traditional brewery producing beer from sugar cane or Lembeni Herbal Hospital, and crash courses in Pare cookery, storytelling and Kiswahili.

For all this, probably the most remarkable thing about Kisangara China is the **cultural tourism programme** itself. One of the very first to be established in Tanzania, in the mid-1990s, Kisangara Chini's had by far the most ambitious aim: to establish a boarding school for girls from rural families who were otherwise unable to pay for more than basic primary education for their daughters. While the cultural tours hardly made a dent in the projected costs, they did attract individuals working for what became the school's sponsors. With their help, the school was not only built, but expanded, and currently gives schooling and boarding to 180 girls.

ARRIVAL AND INFORMATION   KISANGARA CHINI

By bus Any bus running south of Moshi along the highway (to Dar, Tanga or Lushoto, and vice versa) passes through

Kisangara Chini; it's about an hour from Moshi – buses run until mid-afternoon.

CLOCKWISE FROM TOP MT KILIMANJARO (P.244); CHAGGA DANCE (P.235); COFFEE, MOSHI (P.240) >

5

Cultural tourism programme The programme is based at Msafiri English Medium Schools, 1.5km off the highway; the coordinator, Mama Grace Msafiri Mngara, asks that you contact her before coming (☎0754 487193, ✉gracemsafiri@yahoo.com). The official web page is ⓦtanzaniaculturaltourism.go.tz/kisangara.htm. The school is a 30min walk east of the village, and is not signposted, so keep asking for "Mama Grace" or "Shule ya Msafiri". The turning on the highway is at the sign for Shule ya Msingi Chanjale, 100m north of the Total filling station. You pass over a small stream after 70m. Go on, then turn right at the T-junction into a square with a huge tree. Keep left and exit the square. The compound is 1.5km further on, on the right as the road veers left (east) towards the mountain. The basic costs, excluding meals (Tsh15,000) and wheeled transport, are a one-off Village Development Fee of Tsh10,000 per person, and Tsh20,000 per day for a guide for groups of up to five people.

ACCOMMODATION AND EATING

There are a couple of simple guesthouses in the Kisangara Chini village, but the following are more comfortable.

Kindoroko Mountain Lodge On the highway behind the Total petrol station ☎027 275 8654, ⓦkindoroko .net. Easily the town's smartest option, a calm and reasonably well-tended place in pleasant gardens just back from the highway. Its tiled rooms, all en suite and with hot water, have large round mosquito nets (check them for holes first) and TVs, and are especially good value for singles (Tsh30,000). Food and drinks available, but only patchy internet access. BB Tsh60,000

Msafiri English Medium Schools ☎0754 487193, ✉gracemsafiri@yahoo.com. Mama Grace's dream incorporates the girls' school and a handful of large houses with kitchens for rent, and a campsite. Once you get past gate security (the girls are the guarded treasure), Mama Grace and her family are exceptionally welcoming, and, while it's certainly not cheap to stay here, at least you know where your money's going to. You're welcome to volunteer at the school, but for short periods only. Breakfast Tsh10,000, other meals Tsh15,000. Camping Tsh30,000 per pitch. Cottages Tsh50,000–200,000

South Pare

The district capital of the Pare region, **Same**, sits 52km south of Mwanga, at the western end of a lowland corridor separating North from South Pare. The mountains of **South Pare** are similar in many respects to their northern twin – just as beautiful, and with a superb cultural tourism programme at **Mbaga**, which may well entice you to stay longer than planned, and is also a good base for visiting Mkomazi National Park.

Same and around

Straddling the highway at the foot of the South Pare Mountains lies **SAME** (pronounced *sah-mé*). The main attraction is its **Sunday market**, drawing farmers from all over the

---

THE EASTERN ARC MOUNTAINS

The Pare Mountains are part of the Eastern Arc Mountains, an isolated range of ancient massifs that stretch from the Taita Hills in southeastern Kenya into Tanzania, where the range includes the Pare Mountains, East and West Usambara, the Ulugurus near Morogoro and the Udzungwa Mountains. Despite the proximity of the northern part of the Eastern Arc to the volcanic massifs of Mount Meru and Kilimanjaro, the steep crystalline ridges and peaks of the Eastern Arc are a much older and geologically separate formation. The current ranges began to take shape some 100 million years ago, and attained their present form at the start of the Miocene epoch, 25 million years ago.

The great age of the Eastern Arc Mountains, along with the physical isolation of the various ranges from one another, is one reason for their exceptional **biodiversity**. Another is the region's remarkable climatological stability over the last forty million years, thanks to the proximity of the Indian Ocean, whose monsoon system dictates weather patterns over much of the Eastern Arc, producing ample mist and rainfall from moisture-laden clouds coming in from the ocean. Together, these factors have fostered the evolution of the mountains' tremendously rich ecological systems, notably their forests, which contain literally thousands of plant and animal species found nowhere else on earth – not for nothing is the Eastern Arc often referred to as the "Galapagos of Africa".

mountains. A local speciality is honey (*asali*); the normal variety, called *msiku*, is from tended hives hung from trees; the sweeter and superior variety (the bee stings are also said to be more painful) is called *mpako*, and comes from wild beehives in the ground. Another item worth seeking out is the local **scorpion and snakebite cure**, called *nkulo*. Sold in powdered or stick form, it literally sucks venom out of wounds.

ARRIVAL AND INFORMATION   SAME

By bus Same is 116km southeast of Moshi and can be reached on any bus travelling between Dar or Tanga and Moshi or Arusha; the ride takes about 2hr from Moshi, with the last bus leaving mid-afternoon. Leaving Same, in addition to buses starting there, you can also catch a bus coming from elsewhere, most of which pass through between 7am and 3pm; currently recommended are Dar Express and Kilimanjaro Express. The bus stand is just off the eastern side of the highway.

Destinations (buses starting in Same) Arusha (2 daily;

3hr 30min); Mbaga (1 daily; 2hr 30min).

Information Same has a tourist information "office" close to the bus stand, run in collaboration with Mbaga's cultural tourism programme. Buses turn off the highway at a petrol station, from where a street heads uphill. The bus stop is 50m along on the left, but on the right is PADECO Safari Grill and, 20m beyond, the tourist office (there's a big sign), which is actually a clothes shop.

Exchange Change money at NMB, near the bus stand.

ACCOMMODATION, EATING AND DRINKING

There are a couple of very decent places to stay in Same either side of town on the highway, but the central options are a very basic bunch often doubling as brothels, and with little to recommend them other than the price, and the proximity of cheap restaurants and bars ("groceries").

Elephant Motel 1.4km south of the bus stand on the highway ☎027 275 8193 or ☎0754 839545, ⓦelephantmotel.com. Established years ago when hunting was still allowed in Mkomazi, this remains the most characterful place in Same. It has plenty of large and clean en-suite rooms, with box nets, but do check the TVs, plumbing and electric plugs if these are important to you (the free wi-fi is similarly unreliable). There's also decent restaurant (say, stuffed aubergine with melted cheese for Tsh7800), a pleasant outdoor bar with sports TV (it's not busy, so no worries about late-night noise), and you can camp in the verdant grounds ($10 per person). Safe parking. The affiliated tour company offers day-trips to Mkomazi, and a variety of other tours, but the latter are

expensive as the guide and driver (which most options need) cost $200 a day. BB $45

Nzoroko Hotel 2km north of the bus stand on the highway ☎0689 537601, ⓦnzorokohotel.com. A modern, somewhat bland but very well-kept and comfortable hotel, with spotless rooms complete with a/c and TV, a well-stocked bar, decent restaurant and safe parking. BB $40

Parrot Cafe In the centre, 10m along the side street behind PADECO Safari Grill. This has a pleasant shaded outdoor terrace and is as good a place as any to satiate your belly. The offering includes succulent *nyama choma* (Tsh4500 for half a kilo), and snacks such as samosas and rice cakes. Daily 7am–10pm.

Mbaga

South Pare's **cultural tourism programme** – one of Tanzania's best – is at **MBAGA** (or Manka), a former missionary station set in a lush area of terraced cultivation up in the mountains. It offers a wide variety of walks to various attractions and small villages that are little changed from centuries ago, and gives you a chance to experience local life and culture. Profits from the project have already paid for the construction of a pre-school building and dispensary, and now subsidize energy-efficient stoves, vocational scholarships and road maintenance. A good time to come is Wednesday, coinciding with the weekly **market**.

The cultural tourism programme offers a range of **walks** from easy half-day hikes to treks of three days or more; they can also arrange a day's safari in Mkomazi National Park (see p.259), though if you don't have wheels you'll need to wait a day or two for them to rent a vehicle in Same. One fascinating (and rather disturbing) half-day walk goes to the **Mghimbi Caves** and **Malameni Rock**. The caves provided shelter from slave raiders in the 1860s, while the rock, further up, was the site of child sacrifices until the practice was ended in the 1930s. The rock can be climbed,

5

but you need to be instructed on the appropriate behaviour by an elder first – your guide can arrange this.

Other good half-day destinations include **Mpepera Viewpoint**, giving views – on clear days – of Kilimanjaro and Mkomazi; and the hilltop **Red Reservoir** near the Tona Moorlands, frequently covered with water plants and good for birdwatching. A recommended full-day trip is to the tiny and beautiful agricultural village of **Ikongwe**, said to have been a gift from God, or to the 136-metre **Thornton Falls**, a ninety-minute walk from Gonja. Overnight stays in Ikongwe can be arranged with local families, and the trip can be combined with Mpepera Viewpoint.

ARRIVAL AND INFORMATION   MBAGA

By bus or daladala There are several Land Rovers and a couple of buses each day from Same to Mbaga (Tsh5000), taking two and a half to three hours. Quicker and more comfortable but five times the price is *Hill-Top Tona Lodge*'s vehicle (Tsh25,000 per person), which you should arrange beforehand, or via the tourist office in Same, but allow at least an hour and a half for the vehicle to arrive, and the same to get to Mbaga.

By 4WD There are two roads from Same to Mbaga: via the eastern flank of the Pare Mountains past Mkomazi National Park, then uphill from Kisimani village (treacherous even in dry weather; 4WD essential); or, much easier, up the western flank of the mountains via Mwembe village. The latter route is advisable if you're self-driving, taking just ninety minutes: the road starts 2km southeast of Same's *Elephant Motel* along the highway, at the signposted Kandoto Girls School.

Cultural tourism programme Transport stops outside *Hill-Top Tona Lodge*, the base for Mbaga's cultural tourism programme, coordinated by Mr Elly Kimbwereza (☏ 0754 852010, ⊛ tonalodge.org and ⊛ tanzaniaculturaltourism .go.tz/southern_pare.htm). Costs are very reasonable: $10 for a guide (maximum three tourists), $5 per person per day for the Village Development Fee and around $3 for meals, plus optional extras such as a consultation with a traditional healer (not as convincing as the sadly missed gentleman who used to offer this service), or a performance from the Tona Traditional Dancing Troupe ($10 plus tips). They can also arrange safaris into Mkomazi National Park. Camping away from Mbaga costs around $3, but you'll need your own tent. The lodge's main building was the residence of a German missionary named Jakob Dannholz, who wrote what are still the best works on Pare culture, including *Lute: The Curse and the Blessing* – an insightful and highly recommended read, translated from a German manuscript but now sadly out of print – the lodge used to sell copies, but still has one you can consult.

ACCOMMODATION AND EATING

★Hill-Top Tona Lodge Mbaga village ☏ 0754 852010, ⊛ tonalodge.org. Accommodation consists of several modest rooms in the main building, and several more in attractive brick cottages a few minutes away, each with electricity and bathroom with running water. Especially good value for singles. Camping is also possible in your own tent ($10 per person). Extraordinarily delicious traditional meals (Tsh5000) are available if ordered early; try *makande*, a light stew of maize and beans cooked with milk and vegetables, or anything with bananas. BB Rooms without bathrooms Per person $15, en-suite double $40

Chome village

Chome village, hidden in a lush green valley at the western base of Shengena Peak, is one of Pare's gems: a small, traditional and immensely friendly place, despite having suffered the mysterious abduction of dozens of villagers in 1929 – no one knows where they ended up. The village can be visited as part of Mbaga's cultural tourism programme (it's a day's walk along narrow footpaths), or through *Kisaka Villa Inn* in Chome itself. Apart from the hike up **Shengena Peak**, local attractions – most of which can be walked to in a few hours – include the Namoche Valley (scene of a victorious battle against the Maasai), warriors' graves, German ruins, local farms, waterfalls and viewpoints, and the **Kings' Stone**, once used for human sacrifices: victims were thrown off the top. It's a very steep and slippery climb through thick bush.

ARRIVAL AND DEPARTURE   CHOME VILLAGE

By bus Public transport from Same, 41km away, is limited to irregular Land Rovers and pick-ups, usually leaving Same in the afternoon.

By 4WD If you're driving, instead of turning left at

Mwembe for Mbaga, just keep going until you reach a signposted turning, leaving you with 26km to Chome. You might have to push your vehicle at the end, as the last part is very steep.

ACCOMMODATION

Kisaka Villa Inn Chome village ☎0754 288858, ✉kisakas@yahoo.co.uk. A large, modern two-storey alpine-style building with a rather religious atmosphere (no alcohol or smoking), and good but very pricey en-suite rooms. Camping $10 per person. HB **$130**

Mkomazi National Park

Much of the grey-green bushland behind the Pare and Usambara mountains is protected by the 3245 square kilometre **MKOMAZI NATIONAL PARK**, a wild and scenic stretch of semi-arid baobab-studded "nyika" savanna bounded by spectacular walls of rock: the Pare Mountains to the west, the Usambara Mountains to the south, and Kilimanjaro to the northwest. These natural barriers make Mkomazi the southernmost limit of the vast Tsavo ecosystem, offering a type of habitat that, while common enough in Kenya, is unique for Tanzania. The result is dozens of animal species that you won't find elsewhere in Tanzania. The park is home to more than 450 species of **birds** (including ostrich), and dozens of large mammalian species. Of these, antelopes, lesser kudu, dikdik, gazelle and impala are frequently seen, while migratory herds of elephant, buffalo, oryx and zebra are less common.

A rarity for Tanzania is the gerenuk, an agile antelope that gets up on its hind legs to browse trees. Of the **predators**, there are reasonable odds on hearing if not necessarily seeing lions, and the reserve's other carnivores – including leopards, cheetahs, and spotted and striped hyenas – are similarly elusive. Mkomazi's other two rare species, the **African hunting dog** and **black rhino**, have been reintroduced after having been wiped out in the 1980s. The dogs are occasionally seen around the park, but the rhino are being bred in the heavily guarded Mkomazi Rhino Project Sanctuary (off limits to visitors), which started with eight animals flown in from South Africa's Addo Elephant National Park. Mkomazi's current rhino population is undisclosed.

Mkomazi was only gazetted as a national park in 2008, and is – it must be said – a deeply controversial place, after Maasai pastoralists were forcibly evicted in 1988 on apparently spurious environmental grounds (it has never been shown that Maasai engaged in the commercial poaching of elephants and rhino that so ravaged Africa's wildlife areas in the 1980s; at the time, Mkomazi was officially a game reserve for trophy hunters…). The park is visitable as a day-trip from Same, Mbaga in the Pare Mountains, and Mambo in northwestern Usambara, and – for now – is a wild and indeed relatively cheap alternative to the far more travelled northern and southern safari circuits.

ESSENTIALS   MKOMAZI NATIONAL PARK

Park headquarters The park headquarters are at Zange Gate, 7km east of Same along the road to Kisiwani (daily 8am–4pm; ☎0689 062336 or ☎0767 536132, ✉mkomazi@tanzaniaparks.com).

Entrance fees Entrance fees are levied at gates on the access roads into the park, and are $30 per person, plus $20 for an obligatory guide, and Tsh20,000 per vehicle (all for 24hrs), payable with Visa or MasterCard, but not cash.

Activities Apart from game drives, guided bush walks in the company of armed rangers are possible: the rangers cost $20 a day, to which you need to add $20–25 per person for the walking permit. Advance booking is recommended for the bush walks.

When to go Migratory wildlife from Kenya's Tsavo West National Park, including around a thousand elephants, peaks during the long rains (from end-March to May), when the park's roads are liable to be impassable. Better for wildlife viewing, then, is late June to early September.

Websites The park's official website is ⓦmkomazi.com; more practical is the unofficial ⓦmkomazi.info, maintained by *Mambo View Point* (see p.271). Mkomazi Rhino Project is at ⓦsavetherhino.org.

5

ARRIVAL AND DEPARTURE

The park contains several airstrips but has no scheduled flights. The main entrance for vehicles is Zange Gate, 7km east of Same and the main highway, or 112km from Moshi. Without your own wheels, day-trips can easily be arranged in neighbouring towns, including at the *Elephant Motel* and tourist office in Same (see p.257), at Mbaga's *Hill-Top Tona Lodge* half a hour's drive away (see p.258) and at *Mambo View Point* in northwest Usambara, one and a half hour's drive away (see p.271). Costs are car rental plus park fees, guides and lunch: $150/day from *Elephant Motel* including fuel, excluding park fees; a negotiable Tsh2000 per kilometre from Mbaga, also excluding park fees; and $500 for two people from *Mambo View Point*, including park fees.

ACCOMMODATION

Accommodation inside the park is limited to one expensive semi-permanent tented camp, and a couple of park-run campsites.

Babu's Camp Close to Njiro Gate ☎027 254 8840 (Arusha) or ☎0784 402344 (direct), ✆anasasafari .com. Set amid acacia thorns and baobabs in the park's northern sector, this is a classic semi-permanent safari camp without the neo-colonial chintz that bedevils many such places elsewhere, which shines the spotlight firmly on the spectacular surroundings, and their wildlife. Accommodation is in five large fully furnished walk-in tents, each with attached bathroom (with hot water), veranda and generator-powered electricity;

meals are taken in a central mess tent that also doubles as a (well-stocked) library. FB excluding drinks, park fees and game drives $\overline{\underline{$568}}$

TANAPA campsites Several locations; bookings not necessary; pay at the park gates. The park's main campsite is at Ibaya, 15km from Zange Gate, which has water and toilets. Others, without facilities, include Kisima, 60km beyond, and Dindera Dam, which is great for spotting thirsty wildlife. Per person $30 ($50 at Dindera Dam), plus park fees.

THE LION KING OF USAMBARA

Unlike many East African tribes, for whom contact with the modern world came abruptly, traditional Sambaa culture had time to adapt to modern times rather than simply being swept away, thanks to the inaccessibility of its mountain terrain.

The Sambaa's agricultural way of life, and settled communities, favoured systems of leadership based around individuals rather than councils of elders. Their first great chief, a founding father of sorts, was **Mbega** (also spelled Mbegha), born in the late 1600s to a Zigua chief in Ngulu, down on the plains. Oral histories recount that Mbega was cheated of his inheritance and forced into exile. He wandered for many years, gaining a reputation as a skilled and generous hunter. At the time, the Sambaa were experiencing problems with an infestation of bush pigs, which were uprooting their crops, so they asked the famous hunter for assistance in ridding them of their problematic swine. Mbega set about his work, all the while distributing gifts of meat to the local people. Word of his skill, wisdom and fairness spread swiftly, and soon Mbega became sought after for his skills in settling disputes, too. So much so that the people of Vuga, near Soni in West Usambara, asked him to become their leader.

During his reign, which was characterized by intelligence and consideration, Mbega united the Sambaa clans into the **kingdom of Kilindi**, named after the place where Mbega had settled before coming to Usambara. Mbega himself became known as Simbawene, **the Lion King**. The Kilindi dynasty reached its height at the start of the nineteenth century, when the Sambaa ruled over not only Usambara, but also the Pare Mountains and much of the plains south and east. By the 1840s, however, the Zigua tribe from the plains were becoming dominant thanks to their involvement in the **slave trade**, which gave them access to firearms, and by the time the Germans arrived in the 1880s, the Sambaa's military weakness was such that they capitulated without a fight.

The Kilindi dynasty was granted limited power by the Germans, and by the British who followed, but their rule ended in 1962 when the Tanzanian government abolished tribal chiefdoms. Nonetheless, the lineal descendants of Mbega are still known by his title, the Lion King.

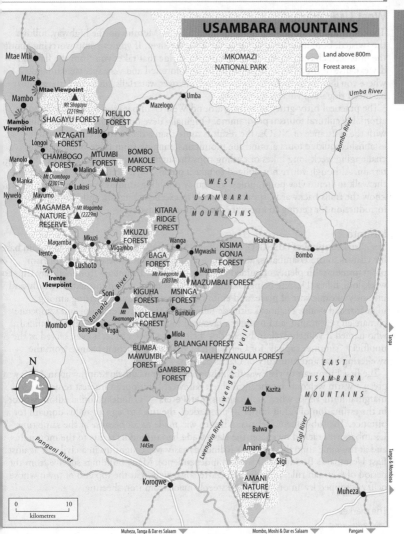

USAMBARA MOUNTAINS

Land above 800m

Forest areas

MKOMAZI NATIONAL PARK

Mtae Mtii

Mtae

Mtae Viewpoint

Mambo

Mt Shagayu (2219m)

Mambo Viewpoint

SHAGAYU FOREST

KIFILIO FOREST

Mazelogo

Umba

Umba River

Bombo River

Longoi

Mlalo

MZAGATI FOREST

Manolo

CHAMBOGO FOREST

Malindi

MTUMBI FOREST

BOMBO MAKOLE FOREST

Manka

Mt Chambogo (2301m)

Mt Makole

Lukosi

W E S T

Nywelo

Mavumo

MAGAMBA NATURE RESERVE

Mt Magamba (2229m)

U S A M B A R A

M O U N T A I N S

Magamba

Mkuzi

KITARA RIDGE FOREST

Msalaka

Irente

Migambo

MKUZU FOREST

Wanga

KISIMA GONJA FOREST

Bombo

Lushoto

BAGA FOREST

Mgwashi

Mazumbai

Irente Viewpoint

Mt Kwegoroto (2031m)

MAZUMBAI FOREST

Bangala River

Soni

KIGUHA FOREST

MSINGA FOREST

Mombo

Bangala

Vuga

Mt Kwamongo

NDELEMAI FOREST

Bumbuli

Mlola

BALANGAI FOREST

E A S T

BUMBA MAWUMBI FOREST

MAHENZANGULA FOREST

Lwengera Valley

GAMBERO FOREST

U S A M B A R A

M O U N T A I N S

Kazita

N

1253m

Lwengera River

Sigi River

Bulwa

1445m

Amani

Sigi

Pangani River

Korogwe

AMANI NATURE RESERVE

Muheza

0   10
kilometres

Tanga

Tanga & Mombasa

Muheza, Tanga & Dar es Salaam   Mombo, Moshi & Dar es Salaam   Pangani

The Usambara Mountains

Southeast of the Pare Mountains, and also belonging to the ancient Eastern Arc chain (see box, p.256), are the craggy and often mist-shrouded **Usambaras**, which rise with startling abruptness over a kilometre above the dusty plains below, forming two rocky, forest-cloaked ranges. The larger and more densely populated is **West Usambara**, home to the ever-friendly Sambaa people. It contains some of Tanzania's most spectacular hiking terrain, and plenty of swivel-eyed chameleons, too. The area is easily and most enjoyably explored via a cultural tourism programme. **East Usambara**, separated from the western range by the Lwengera valley, is equally alluring: the monsoon-fed rainforests of the Amani Nature Reserve, clinging to its vertiginous slopes, are the second-most biodiverse place in Africa.

5

West Usambara

The only paved road up into West Usambara, from Mombo on the highway, follows the twisted, boulder-strewn gorge of the **Bangala River**. If you can stop worrying about the unfenced chasm to your left, it's a dramatic ride that takes you from the flat and dry expanse of the Maasai Steppe into a lushly forested and very spectacular land, where you'll glimpse mountain peaks towering over waterfalls, and some precariously balanced ridge-top villages and farms.

The practical nitty-gritty of getting around West Usambara is a breeze thanks to an affordable **cultural tourism programme**. Originally developed in the 1990s by villagers with the assistance of NGOs, the result is more than a dozen different and well-established **guided tours** around the mountains, ranging from three-hour strolls to challenging week-long hikes or cycling trips through some of Tanzania's most inspiring terrain. Although you're not obliged to take a **guide**, you'll need one for anything but the walk to Irente viewpoint, unless you fancy rambling around in circles. Most guides know the trails backwards, speak reasonable to excellent English, and provide a great introduction for getting to know the locals more intimately.

Lushoto

The district capital of **LUSHOTO**, 34km from Mombo and the highway, is the main base for visitors to the Usambaras, and home to one of Tanzania's best cultural tourism programmes, with plenty of guided tours around West Usambara from half-day trips to week-long hikes. Despite being Usambara's biggest town, it's an intimate, friendly and instantly likeable sort of place, and enjoys an especially beautiful setting among high-forested peaks. Lushoto's altitude (almost 1400m) ensures a cool and temperate climate all year round, and made it a favoured mountain retreat for German officials, who named it **Wilhelmstal**, in honour of their Kaiser. For a time, it even served as the unofficial "summer capital" for German East Africa – a welcome change from the sweltering heat and humidity of Dar es Salaam.

The first European to visit was the missionary **Johann Ludwig Krapf**, who in 1849 was given a warm welcome by the local chief, Kimweri I. European interest remained marginal until 1886, when arch-colonist **Karl Peters** – "a model colonial administrator" in the estimation of Adolf Hitler – "persuaded" the ruler to sign away his domain for a pittance. The subsequent German advance was made easier because at the same time Usambara was racked by chaos: the **slave trade** had turned its sights to the mountains, and at the same time the Sambaa's Kilindi dynasty was caught up in a civil war against East Usambara's Bondei, who wanted independence. Many buildings survive from the period of German rule, including a bizarre construction at the top end of town whose belfry is topped by an onion-shaped steeple made from iron sheeting.

The market

Daily sunrise–sunset

Apart from the history, the scenery and cultural tourism, Lushoto's other attraction is its colourful **market**, which is liveliest on Thursday and Sunday when farmers descend from all around. Sunday is especially good for traditional pottery – either plain, or incised with geometric motifs inspired by plants. **Fruit** is another speciality, especially apples and pears (Easter), peaches and plums (Dec–Feb), jackfruit (Mar–Jun), tamarind (Nov–Jan), loquats (Jun & Jul), and berries all year round – all are amazingly cheap even by Tanzanian standards. Look out also for traditional medicinal herbs and bark (*madawa asili*, "ancestor medicine"), honey (*asali*) and *viungo vya chai* – powdered ginger (*tangawizi*) mixed with other spices for adding to tea. The best deals are made late, when vendors want to go home.

Irente Viewpoint

6km west of Lushoto (signposted) • Tsh2000 entrance fee is levied by Irente View Cliff Lodge, which gets you a soft drink • A guide is not needed, but a spate of muggings a few years ago means it's best to take one along: Lushoto's cultural tourism programmes charge around

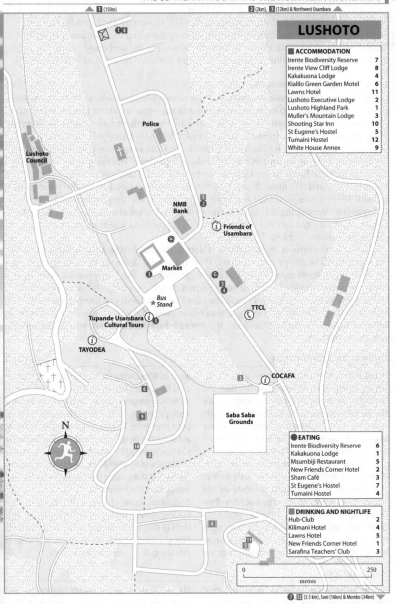

▲ **1** (150m)   **2** (2km), **3** (12km) & Northwest Usambara ▲

LUSHOTO

■ **ACCOMMODATION**
Irente Biodiversity Reserve	7
Irente View Cliff Lodge	8
Kakakuona Lodge	4
Kialilo Green Garden Motel	6
Lawns Hotel	11
Lushoto Executive Lodge	2
Lushoto Highland Park	1
Muller's Mountain Lodge	3
Shooting Star Inn	10
St Eugene's Hostel	5
Tumaini Hostel	12
White House Annex	9

● **EATING**
Irente Biodiversity Reserve	6
Kakakuona Lodge	1
Msumbiji Restaurant	5
New Friends Corner Hotel	2
Sham Café	3
St Eugene's Hostel	7
Tumaini Hostel	4

■ **DRINKING AND NIGHTLIFE**
Hub-Club	2
Kilimani Hotel	4
Lawns Hotel	5
New Friends Corner Hotel	1
Sarafina Teachers' Club	3

Police

Lushoto Council

NMB Bank

Friends of Usambara

Market

Bus Stand

Tupande Usambara Cultural Tours

TAYODEA

TTCL

COCAFA

Saba Saba Grounds

N

0	250
metres	

7, **12** (3.5 km), Soni (16km) & Mombo (34km) ▼

$25 per person, including lunch at *Irente Biodiversity Reserve*. Some tours include a performance of traditional drumming for a few dollars more. Alternatively, you could combine Irente Viewpoint with Magamba Forest, for which you do need a guide, which would flesh out the trip to a full day

The pleasant walk to and from **Irente Viewpoint** is the most popular short trip offered by the cultural tourism programmes, but is also the walk that can most easily be done without a guide, as the road is clearly signposted from town. Conscious of this, some of the cultural tourism programmes offer something you can't arrange yourself: a

5

performance of traditional drumming nearby. The viewpoint itself, perched on the southwestern edge of the Usambaras, offers a truly breathtaking panorama over the Maasai Steppe almost exactly one kilometre below. The isolated range facing you, with the knuckle-shaped outline, is Mount Mafi, and the settlement below is Mazinde.

Irente Biodiversity Reserve (Irente Farm)

4.3km west of Lushoto, 1.7km before Irente Viewpoint (signposted from Lushoto) • Daily sunrise–sunset (overnights possible; see p.265) • ☎ 0788 503002 or ☎ 0784 502935, ⊛ irentebiodiversityreserve.org • A taxi from Lushoto costs Tsh10,000, a motorbike under Tsh5000

On your return from Irente Viewpoint, stop by the Lutheran-run **Irente Biodiversity Reserve** (also known as Irente Farm), part of a 507-acre parcel of forest and farmland that's run by the Lutheran Church, and has long been popular as a picnic spot, with plenty of seating in colourful shaded gardens. The farm shop sells delicious **organic food**: heavy German-style rye bread, jams, pickles and other preserves, macadamia nuts, Arabica coffee, flavoured teas picked by the patients of Lutindi Mental Hospital near Korogwe at the base of the mountains, and – best of all – superb cheeses, including German-style Quark curd cheese, and one just like Tilziter. Contact the farm in advance (p.266) if you'd like them to prepare lunch, an extravagant picnic for just Tsh8000.

Adjacent to the farm is **Irente Children's Home**, also run by the church, around which the matron will be happy to escort you. Poverty and AIDS are the main problems, the latter having in some cases wiped out entire generations. The home houses more than twenty orphans, disabled children and children of parents with psychiatric disorders, and also trains older girls – who look after the little ones – in pre-nursing care and basic schooling. Nearby are two special-needs schools, also run by the church: **Irente Rainbow School** for autistic children, and **Irente School for the Blind**; you're welcome to visit either of them.

ARRIVAL AND DEPARTURE   LUSHOTO

By bus Lushoto is served by early morning buses (6am, 8am and sometimes 10am) from Arusha, Dar, Moshi and Tanga. Of the direct buses, Shambalai and Fasaha currently have the safer reputations, not that that's saying much; Chakito Bus is best avoided. From Tanga there are also daladalas and (safer and therefore preferable) large Coaster minibuses until mid-afternoon. Alternatively, catch any bus between Arusha/Moshi and Tanga/Dar and get off at Mombo at the start of the road up into West Usambara, from where there are frequent daladalas to Lushoto via Soni (1hr): you'll find them at the start of the road 100m off the highway. For transport within West Usambara, most useful are the daily buses between Lushoto and Mtae, which sometimes also pass Mombo. To get to Amani Nature Reserve in East Usambara, catch any vehicle for Tanga and

get off at Muheza, where you'll need to change for Amani. To get to Pangani, go all the way to Tanga and change there, as there's no guarantee of a connection along the shorter route starting in Muheza. Lastly, if you want to catch one of the better buses to Dar, Moshi or Arusha (currently Dar Express and Kilimanjaro Express), phone their offices in Arusha (see p.287) or Dar (see p.101) to book a seat, and tell them you'll board at *New Liverpool Hill Breeze*, a bar/restaurant/bus stop 1km north of Mombo along the highway where most long-distance buses take a short break.

Destinations Arusha (2 daily; 5–6hr); Dar (3–5 daily; 6–6.5hr); Mombo (daladalas every 30min until 5pm; 1hr); Moshi (2 daily; 4–5hr); Mtae (2 daily; 3–4hr); Muheza (3 daily plus daladalas until mid-afternoon; 2hr); Tanga (3 daily plus daladalas until mid-afternoon; 3hr).

INFORMATION

Tourist information Lushoto's competing cultural tourism programmes (see box p.268) also serve as unofficial tourist information offices. They're generally unbiased, except, of course, when it comes to recommending guides.

Bicycle rental Should you want to explore the surrounding area under your own power, mountain bikes can be rented through the cultural tourism programmes for Tsh10,000–15,000 a day.

Staying safe Given Lushoto's popularity with backpackers, there are sometimes aggressive touts in Lushoto or Mombo, and robberies are occasionally reported. So, take care of your bags on arrival (Lushoto's bus stand, though small, can be chaotic), and don't hire a guide on the street or on public transport, no matter how slick their patter or genuine their ID card appears to be; instead, arrange things at one of the cultural tourism programmes.

ACCOMMODATION

The cost of budget accommodation **in town** itself has shot up over the last few years, making its mid-range options all the more attractive. The cheapest hotels are a 5 or 10min walk southwest of the bus stand near a mosque, whose muezzin wakes all and sundry at 5am; places further north have the bells of the Catholic church to contend with. More worthy of a holiday are a handful of great places to stay at in the hills **around Lushoto**; in addition to these, the cultural tourism programmes can organize **homestays** as part of their hikes (no more than Tsh15,000 per person per night). **Camping** is possible at *Lawns Hotel*; further afield, you can pitch a tent at *Irente View Cliff Lodge*, 6km away at Irente Viewpoint (see below) or, just as atmospheric but without the dizzying views, at *Irente Biodiversity Reserve* (see below), 2km before the viewpoint.

IN TOWN

Kakakuona Lodge Behind the post office ☎0754 006969, ⊛kakakuonatz.com. This has a lovely calm and green location on a slope behind the post office, with a wide selection of modern self-contained rooms, all with TV and box nets, but slightly tatty. Also has an internet café, and a restaurant with tables outdoors. BB Tsh35,000

Kialilo Green Garden Motel ☎0786 809494, ✉kialilo24@yahoo.co.uk. A comfortable if strictly functional option in this area, this has seven clean and bright but narrow rooms with tiled bathrooms, hot water, TV, crisp linen and box nets, and food to order. Friendly staff and safe parking. BB Tsh30,000

Lawns Hotel ☎027 266 0005 or ☎027 266 0066, ⊛lawnshotel.com. This quirky old centenarian colonial pile has seen better days and is pricey for what you get, but it can still be a charmer, although the standards and style of its rooms, and service, vary considerably. More certain is its very pleasant location, tucked away on a lushly vegetated hillock on the south edge of town, but still within earshot of its bars, muezzins and pealing church bells. The better rooms have creaky floorboards, old fireplaces, heavy Art Deco beds and cast-iron baths. There's a quiet bar where you can catch wi-fi, but the food is uninspired and overpriced. Safe parking. Camping per person $12. BB $65

Lushoto Executive Lodge (Eddy's Lodge) 2.5km along the road to Magamba ☎027 260 0076, ⊛lushotoexecutivelodge.co.tz. Set in a hilly lawned garden with wonderful views, this is aimed at tourists as well as conferences. The main building is from German times, now with a modern extension; there are also a few new cottages. The rooms are needing a bit of attention but are still comfortable, with four-posters, box nets and satellite TV. It also has an average restaurant, a basic gym, massages, and golf putting course, all in all making it very good value. BB $65

Lushoto Highland Park At the top of the main road, 200m beyond the post office ☎0716 112132, ⊛highlandparktz.com. Aimed at business travellers, this is rather anodyne but comfortable nonetheless, and comes with TVs in its rooms, a restaurant and bar, and safe parking. BB $44

Shooting Star Inn ☎0782 734440. A reliably calm and welcoming Muslim-run place with better than average

en-suite rooms for this part of town, all "singles" (double beds) and with large box nets and TV. Food can be arranged, too. BB Tsh20,000

★**Tumaini Hostel** On the main road, 150m from the bus stand ☎027 266 0094, ⊛elct-ned.org. This Lutheran Church place is calm, decent and well priced, and thus often full despite having twenty rooms. These are bright and simple, all with box nets, and doubles with good bathrooms. Also has a decent restaurant (with seats in a cluttered garden), foreign exchange, internet café and safe parking. BB Tsh30,000

White House Annex ☎0719 346324 or ☎0754 299239. Among the cheapest acceptable options in town, with ten rooms, two of them sharing bathrooms (squat toilets). For twice the price you get a suite with TV. All have mosquito nets. There's also a popular bar with outside tables, and food available if you order early. Safe parking. Double Tsh15,000, suite Tsh30,000

OUT OF TOWN

Irente Biodiversity Reserve (Irente Farm) 4km southwest of Lushoto (signposted), 1.7km before Irente Viewpoint; a taxi from Lushoto costs Tsh10,000, a motorbike less than Tsh5000 ☎0788 503002 or ☎0784 502935, ⊛irentebiodiversityreserve.org. Most visitors get to see *Irente Farm* for lunch on the return leg of an Irente Viewpoint tour, but the lush location and ample birdlife may tempt you to stay longer. Accommodation is in a series of attractive buildings formerly used by staff, but the pleasure doesn't come cheaply, whether you stay in one of their three double rooms (not all self-contained), or manage to fill a self-catering house, of which "Mkuyu lodge" (Tsh175,000) sleeps six, and "Mshinga lodge" (Tsh200,000) four. Camping, on the other hand, is perfectly affordable (Tsh8000 per person), and explains the frequent visits by overland trucks. Breakfast is a superb spread of the farm's produce (see p.266). Guided walks and hikes can be arranged. HB Tsh66,000

Irente View Cliff Lodge 6km southwest of town, at Irente Viewpoint ☎0784 866877, ⊛irenteview.com. Perched right on the cliff edge, this outwardly ostentatious complex – a conference venue, really – has smothered the wild charm that Irente Viewpoint once had, and it doesn't even make good use of the vertiginous views it grabbed, as only the three "standard" rooms have vistas worth writing

5

home about, and those are from very narrow balconies as the bedroom windows themselves are covered by iron grilles. The "superior" rooms, larger and with bathtubs, are in two rows; those at the front have reasonable views, but the ones further back overlook a canyon and cliffs. All have satellite TV and wi-fi. The restaurant and bar in the main conical *makuti*-thatched building lack views. All in all a blot on the landscape, and wasted opportunity to boot. Camping $5 per person, or $10 in their tents. BB **$65**

Muller's Mountain Lodge 12km northeast of Lushoto at Mkuzi ☏027 266 0204 or ☏0782 315666, ⓦmullersmountainlodge.co.tz. Set in orchards and farmland between the Magamba and Mkuzu forests, this is a grand, two-storey 1935 farmhouse in the style of an English country manor (brick walls and steep, thatched gable roof), and blessed with a fittingly old-fashioned interior, including a cosy living room with a big fireplace and board games. The bedrooms, some en suite (including a two-bedroom cottage), are beginning to need attention but remain adequate. Amenities include a bar and restaurant, great walking guides and trips by car. To drive here, turn right at Magamba and right again after 5.3km at the signpost. Free lift from Lushoto if you stay two nights; taxis charge upwards of Tsh30,000. BB **$60**

St Eugene's Lodge 4km towards Soni, at Ubiri ☏027 266 0055 or ☏0784 523710, ⓦusambara-st-eugene.com. A source of funding for projects run by the Catholic Mission of the Montessori Sisters, this is a very well-run and tranquil option, in amid banana fields. The two-storey guesthouse – a starkly modern building whose green roof touches the ground – contains fourteen spotless and very comfortable guest rooms, all en suite, some with balconies. There's also a kitchen, breakfasts to rival those of *Irente Biodiversity Reserve*, and equally wonderful lunches and dinners. Walk, or catch a daladala. BB **$45**, FB **$72**

EATING

If you'll be staying overnight with locals as part of a cultural tour, see whether you can get someone to cook up **bada**, a Sambaa speciality consisting of a thick, greenish-brown porridge of pounded maize flour and dried fermented cassava, mixed with hot water and oil and served in aromatic banana leaves. It's exceedingly tasty, and is eaten, like *ugali*, dipped in sauces. *Bada* is usually served with chicken or meat, fried bananas or potatoes. The following are the pick of the town's better **restaurants**; try also the bars near the bus station, where you'll find good *nyama choma* (roughly Tsh4000 for half a kilo of beef), and several popular *mama lishe* ("feeding ladies") at the bus stand at night, who dish up basic but often delicious meals such as fish with rice, for under Tsh2000 a head.

IN TOWN

Kakakuona Lodge Behind the post office ☏0754 006969. This has a hit-and-miss reputation, sometimes excellent, other times not, but the pleasant grassy location and reasonable prices make it worth a try – Tsh5000 for snacks, around Tsh8500 for main courses such as lemon-laced chicken. Daily noon–8pm.

Msumbiji Restaurant Southwest corner of the bus stand. The closest thing in Lushoto to a typical Tanzanian beer garden, with tables under parasols in its scrubby garden, and decent *nyama choma* (Tsh5000 for half a kilo). Daily 11am–8pm.

New Friends Corner Hotel Behind NMB bank beside the Friends of Usambara office. Principally a bar, selling simple and tasty full meals of the meat/fish-with-*ugali*/rice/chips style, where you'll get stuffed for less than Tsh5000. At lunchtimes, they often do an exceptionally good *rost* (beans, rice and salad accompanying beef – with plenty of bone – cooked in foil). Daily 8am–late, best for lunch and dinner.

Sham Café Between the market and the bus stand. A great little place for cheap and unfussy meals, and they're happy to rustle up something special if you contact them beforehand. They also provide hot milk – a favourite with locals and just right on a cold day. Daily 6am–7pm.

Tumaini Hostel On the main road, 150m from the bus stand ☏027 266 0094. There are two dining areas here: indoors facing the street, and out the back in the garden. While the menu majors on standard tourist fodder such as burgers, pizza and vegetarian moussaka (Tsh6500), and a good range of meat and fish for a bit more, don't expect your choice to be available. It's pricey for snacks, but good value for more substantial dishes. Sometimes also has ice cream, juices and shakes. No alcohol. Daily 7am–8pm.

OUT OF TOWN

★**Irente Biodiversity Reserve (Irente Farm)** 4km southwest of Lushoto (signposted), 1.7km before Irente Viewpoint; a taxi from Lushoto costs Tsh10,000, a motorbike less than Tsh5000 ☏0788 503002 or ☏0784 502935, ⓦirentebiodiversityreserve.org. This bucolic place set in a lush colonial era farm is an epicurean delight, primarily on account of the food, be it rye bread, all sorts of cheeses, yoghurts, jams and juices. You can sample a good selection of these plus organic salad vegetables with the Farm's picnic lunch (Tsh8000). Also available is a small but appetizing selection of cooked dishes, including vegetarian, such as a lentil and tomato stew served with rye bread and cheese (Tsh8000). Daily, picnic lunch 9am–3.30pm, cooked lunch 12.30–3pm, dinner for overnight guests only.

St Eugene's Lodge 4km towards Soni, at Ubiri ☏027 266 0055 or ☏0784 523710, ⓦusambara-st-eugene.com. The

Catholic Montessori Sisters dish up some truly divine breakfasts: virtually everything here is home made, including the rye bread, butter, an array of cheeses, and famed "gooseberry" jam (which is actually cape gooseberry). They also sell the same, together with their very palatable "Dochi" banana wine. Other meals cost a very reasonable Tsh8000. Daily 6.30–9.30am, noon–2.30pm, 6–8pm: reservations required.

DRINKING AND NIGHTLIFE

The following are the best of the town's numerous **bars**. Many sell the local **sugar cane hooch**, *boha*, popular with both men and women – especially the latter during festivities such as "Kibwebwe", an all-night, women-only drumming celebration held after the birth of a mother's first child. At posher places, ask for the Montessori Sisters' surprisingly palatable "Dochi" **banana wine**. If you're still thirsty, the Benedictine Fathers in Sakharani, near Soni (❶ 027 266 0452), make one of Tanzania's best **grape wines**, a Chenin Blanc under the "Sakharani" label.

Hub-Club This has been here for decades, and has now been tarted up into a real nightclub, with lively discos on Friday and especially Saturday nights. Fri & Sat 7pm–3am.

Kilimani Hotel There are two bars here; the one worth mentioning is the beer garden, sometimes with discos on Friday or Saturday. There's also a wide choice of food, including hangover-quashing *supu*. Daily noon–late.

★**Lawns Hotel** This former colonial club contains Lushoto's nicest but priciest bar, very cosy and pub-like, its walls decorated with commemorative plates from around the globe, and many foreign coins and banknotes too. There's satellite TV in the room next door, and a dusty book swap library down the hall complete with creaky wooden floorboards. You can also drink in the garden. Daily 2pm–around midnight.

New Friends Corner Hotel Behind NMB bank beside the Friends of Usambara office. Apart from good food, this is a nice place for a drink, with a pleasant covered street-side veranda. Daily 8am–late.

Sarafina Teachers' Club A pleasant and laid-back place that also does good *nyama choma*. Daily noon–late.

DIRECTORY

Health The District Hospital is 1.5km back along the road to Soni (❶ 027 266 0098).

Internet access Hotels geared to foreign travellers are gradually installing wi-fi, and the Friends of Usambara (see p.268) offer it for free in their office. There is a handful of internet cafés: try the unnamed one facing NMB Bank, or ELCT beside *Tumaini Hostel* (both Mon–Sat 8am–6pm).

Money There's a foreign exchange facility at *Tumaini Hostel*, but better rates can be had without much fuss at NMB bank. A 24hr CRDB ATM for international Visa and MasterCard is outside the post office.

Magamba Nature Reserve

The physically demanding but rewarding walk through **Magamba Nature Reserve** takes you through one of the few remnants of indigenous rainforest that used to cover much of West Usambara. Along the way, you'll have a shot at spotting black-and-white colobus monkeys, horned chameleons, exotic birds such as the paradise flycatcher, plenty of butterflies and some weirdly extravagant fungi. It's usually done as a 5–6hr round trip from Lushoto, but can be extended to a full day by visiting the wild **Mkuzu Falls**, a narrow cascade in the thick of the forest off the road east of Magamba, and where you can swim. Alternatively, you can combine Magamba with Irente Biodiversity Reserve or Irente Viewpoint.

The standard tour begins with a stiff uphill hike along tracks to the east of the Lushoto–Magamba road, passing through the former colonial settlement of Jaegerstal and a camphorwood forest. Just north of Magamba village at the junction to Mkuzi, a track delves into the forest on your left. Emerging onto a forestry road, you continue uphill to a ridge giving expansive views over Lushoto and the Maasai Steppe. From the ridge, the track continues south to a rest house atop **Kiguu Hakwewa Hill**, whose name translates as "unclimbed by short leg", a delightful way of saying steep. There are 360-degree views and a toilet. If you (literally) stomp around here, you'll notice that the hill appears to be hollow, as indeed it is: it was excavated by German residents during World War I for use as a **bunker**. The bunker is said to contain almost one hundred rooms; it definitely contains bats. You're free to explore,

5

CULTURAL TOURISM IN WEST USAMBARA

West Usambara's cultural tourism programme, launched in 1996, is one of Tanzania's oldest. The price of success has been competition, with at least five Lushoto-based tour guide associations now vying for your business. The ones reviewed below are registered and licensed, so it no longer makes sense to refer to Friends of Usambara as "official" and the others as copycats, especially as many of the project's original guides have jumped ship. All offer the same basic hikes at similar prices, but differ in the details of their longer multi-day trips (the exact route taken, where you'll be overnighting, and perhaps what you'll be eating), and in the quality of their guides. Whichever you chose, way more important than scrimping is the character, personal interests, knowledge (and perhaps gender) of the guide you'll be hiking with, so ask to meet him or her beforehand to see whether you click – you might also email them a few specific questions tailored to your interests. Incidentally, while each group claims to directly benefit local communities, orphanages, schools and the like, take the more extravagant claims with a healthy dose of salt.

Costs vary according to the tour, group size and, sometimes, your perceived ability to pay. In 2014, a full day averaged $35–50 per person including lunch, or $40–60 with three meals and overnights. Obviously, exact costs depend on the mode of transport, what and where you'll be eating and sleeping, and how many times you need to enter gazetted nature reserves ($10 for each). Just remember that cheaper isn't always better.

COCAFA (Community Care and Friendship Association) 20m off the main road, 100m south of Tumaini Hostel ☎0756 796575, ⓦusambara adventures.com. Founded in 2009, this, like TAYODEA, isn't overly convincing as an organization, but they do have some good guides, especially for multi-day walks to Mtae, which use the same homestays as Friends of Usambara. Erratic hours, most likely 8–11am.

Friends of Usambara Behind NMB bank, signposted from the bus stand ☎027 266 0132 or ☎0787 094725, ⓦusambaratravels.com. This is what's left of the original cultural tourism programme which, over the years, has suffered plenty of rifts and defections. While it seems more of a commercial enterprise these days, and is more expensive than the competition, it remains a reliable choice, and is particularly enticing for some unique multi-day tours, including an epic 14-day hike from Mbaga in the Pare Mountains (see p.257) to Amani Nature Reserve in East Usambara (p.273), for around $70 per person per day. They also offer a shorter 6–7-day Lushoto to Amani hike, and can arrange homestays at Kwalei and Kwekanga in the eastern part of West Usambara, useful for an alternative approach to, or return from, Mtae and Mombo. Daily 7.30am–6.30pm.

TAYODEA In a bar next to Green Valley Annex, 100m southwest of the bus stand ☎0784 861969, ⓔyouthall2000@yahoo.com. This offshoot of a Tanga-based self-help group for unemployed youths was the second to plant roots in Lushoto, and maintains its original focus on employment rather than culture or development, and as such feels a little rough around the edges at times – a lot depends on the guide, on course. Mon–Sat 8am–6.30pm.

★**Tupande Usambara Cultural Tours** At the bus stand next to Msumbiji Restaurant ☎0783 908597 or ☎0766 976637, ⓦtupande-usambara. org. Established in 2011, this is by far the most credible outfit at present, for both the sraff's professionalism, and a real commitment to the community-based ethos of the original programme. It also has the benefit of several female guides. Among its more unusual offerings are a hands-on "kitchen tour", trips featuring Usambara's famed women potters (some of whose fantastic creations are sold at the office, together with other local crafts), cycling trips, an Irente trip combined with a performance of traditional drumming, and a historically themed tour to Vuga, capital of Usambara's Kilindi dynasty. Daily 8am–6pm.

Usambara Active Safaris At Kakakuona Lodge ☎0752 216258, ⓔjohngonnah30@gmail.com. This was being set up at the time of writing and, while making no pretence at not being a commercial venture, seemed decent enough.

but you'll need a torch, and watch out for snakes; the entrance is 100m downhill on the southeastern flank. From the hill, a steep and rocky path heads down through farmland to the royal village of **Kwembago**, one of the seats of the Kilindi dynasty, which has good views over Lushoto.

ARRIVAL AND DEPARTURE   MAGAMBA NATURE RESERVE

5

Magamba is visited on foot as a guided round-trip from Lushoto. If you're not feeling up for the whole walk, you can catch a local bus as far as the entrance gate. It's best not to try the walk unaccompanied, as there have been reports of robberies. A $10 nature reserve fee should be included in the cost, usually around $35–45, including lunch at *Irente Biodiversity Reserve*. You can also trek directly from *Irente Biodiversity Reserve* using their guides, for Tsh35,000 per person.

Mlalo

The straggling little town of **MLALO** lies on the southeastern slopes of Mount Shagayu, 50km north of Lushoto. The walk from Lushoto takes three or four days there and back, including some sections by bus, but is best combined with a visit to Mtae (see below) for an excellent six- or seven-day trip. The walk includes Magamba Rainforest, followed by a bus ride direct to Mlalo, or to Malindi, from where you walk. There are several good markets in the area. The one at **Kileti village** (also called Kwemieeti) is the main one, and also one of the best places for meeting female **potters**, for which you'll definitely need a guide who knows the area. The Sambaa liken the art of pottery to the creation of life in a mother's womb, so it's no surprise that pottery is traditionally a woman's occupation, with knowledge and rituals connected with the craft being passed from mother to daughter. Although men are allowed to collect clay, they are excluded from the pot-making process itself – it's believed that their presence may anger spirits, who might crack the pots during firing or, worse still, cause sterility.

ARRIVAL AND DEPARTURE   MLALO

Unless your Kiswahili is good, you won't get much out of Mlalo by visiting independently. The town is accessible via several daily minibuses from Lushoto (1.5 hrs), and by three buses a day from Arusha, which pass through Lushoto at around 2pm, but it's best reached as part of a multi-day guided walk from Lushoto to Mambo or Mtae along an anticlockwise route, parts of which can be covered by bus.

ACCOMMODATION

Silver Dollar Guest House The best of a trio of very basic guesthouses here, with clean rooms, shared bathrooms with long-drop toilets, and the boon of a good, cheap restaurant. Tsh8000

Mtae and around

The journey to **MTAE**, a village perched on the northwestern edge of the mountains, is the most popular long-distance hiking excursion from Lushoto, taking three to five days depending on how much you cheat by catching the bus. Although the trip can be done without a guide, you'll miss much of the context and contacts that make this walk so special. The views are simply gobsmacking, especially as you approach Mtae – look out for the unusual two-storey houses with intricately carved wooden balconies, accessed via external staircases, which are also found in the Pare Mountains.

The village of **Mtae** itself is utterly enchanting, and delights the eye with views you'll remember for the rest of your life. The location is everything: isolated on a spur that juts out from the northwestern edge of the mountains, in some places you have a plunging

---

THE GOAT AND THE LEOPARD

Mtae's motto is *Kesi ya mbuzi hakimu ni chui haki hakuna*, which means, if the leopard is the judge when a goat brings a court case against a lion, there will be no justice. The saying is illustrated by paintings hung up in some of the village's bars, and depicts a courtroom presided over by a leopard. The plaintiff is a lion, the defendant a goat. The saying alludes to colonial times, when there was little chance of justice from a German judge for an African accusing another German.

5

270-degree view over the plains almost a kilometre below, giving the impression you're flying. With clear skies, especially in the evenings, you can see the Taita Hills in Kenya to the north, and the Pare Mountains and sometimes even Kilimanjaro to the northwest – before the sun disappears in a kaleidoscope of colours and smoke from kitchens drifts into the air. In warm weather, night-time can be just as humbling, with the twinkling of fireflies seemingly reflecting that of the stars above. Don't sleep in, mind: during and just after the rains you might wake to the extraordinary sight of being above a blanket of clouds. If you want a room with view, head to the nearby village of **Mambo**, 3km southwest, which has two tourist lodges (and a campsite), all of which have wonderful vistas.

The Lutheran church
North end of Mtae

At any time of year, your alarm clock will be the drifting sound of crowing cocks and lowing cattle, followed by goats and children, while on Sundays the bells ring out from the **Lutheran church**, complete with its boisterous (if not always tuneful) brass band. The church was founded at the end of the nineteenth century on land that locals knew was haunted by spirits. The idea, at least if you believe the church's version of the story, had been to scare off the newcomers; but the church prospered, prompting many a local to convert to Christianity. Others remained true to their beliefs: the area around Mtae is renowned for the power of its traditional healers.

Mtae Mtii

A leisurely and recommended four-hour walk goes from Mtae to the small village of **MTAE MTII**, the last seat of the Kilindi dynasty in northwestern Usambara before chiefdoms were abolished in 1962 (the main seat was at Vuga near Soni), and you can do the return journey in a day. Mtae Mtii was also the site of a semi-mythical nineteenth-century battle between the Sambaa and the Maasai, who lived in the plains below. The story goes that the Maasai believed that the king of Usambara had the power to bring rain to the plains, so one day they went to ask him for rain. He refused, and the Maasai resolved to fight. Although the Maasai were better equipped, the Sambaa vanquished their attackers by rolling boulders down the steep inclines, killing most of them. As spoils, the Sambaa seized the Maasai's cattle. Locals say they are the ancestors of all the cows you'll see grazing contentedly in the mountains today.

The last king of Mtae Mtii died in the late 1990s. His **compound** can be visited as part of the cultural tourism programme and has a fantastic location on a crag overlooking the Mkomazi plains. Next to the surprisingly humble (and now abandoned) hut where the king lived is an enclosure made from branches, bushes and young trees.

Mambo

3km southwest from Mtae, 5km by road, and a hundred metres higher, is the village of **MAMBO**. Unlike Mtae, it's not well defined, but what *is* well defined is the vertiginous edge of the West Usambaras, which drops over a kilometre down to the valley that separates Usambara from South Pare – the lake in the middle is the reservoir created by Ndungu Dam. The main reason for coming to Mambo is to stay in one of two magnificently sited lodges, neither of them bank-breaking, and both with some of the most extraordinary views you might ever see.

ARRIVAL AND INFORMATION   **MTAE AND AROUND**

On foot Mtae is easily visited by bus from Lushoto, for which you don't need a guide, but it's much more rewarding to walk to Mtae over four to six days (you can cheat by doing bits by bus), and there's a variety of possible routes, so you could walk there and back from

Lushoto without retracing your steps. Hikers will need a guide from one of the cultural tourism programmes (see p.268).

By bus Getting to Mtae on public transport is easier than getting to Mambo, as the latter lies 2km off the graded road, and can be rough. There are several buses and daladalas from Lushoto throughout the day, taking about three hours. There are also buses from Arusha (9hr; Fasaha), Dar (8hr; Iberiki and Shambalai) and Tanga (7hr; Makadiri, Airbus and Tashrif, the latter two with reputations for dangerous driving), most of them departing at 6am. The buses head back from Mtae and around the same time. Many of these pass Mambo village (on the graded road, 2km from the lodges) but only rarely reach the lodges themselves – ⓦ mamboviewpoint.org has the latest.

By 4WD The roads north of Lushoto are unsurfaced, and vary in condition according to the severity of the last rains, and when they were last graded. For the latest on roads, and public transport, see ⓦ mamboviewpoint.org.

In your own 4WD, the adventurous approach – dry-season only, and even then not always passable – is up a series of steep unsurfaced hairpins from the plains in the northwest, also accessible from Mkomazi village on the Arusha–Dar highway. Far more reliable are the graded roads from Lushoto to Mtae, which are even traversable, in dry weather, by ordinary saloon cars (to Mtae, but not Mambo). There are several possible routes, as Usambara's roads tend to fork around mountain peaks, joining again on the other side. Mambo is 3km southwest of Mtae on foot, 5km by road.

By taxi A taxi from Lushoto takes about two hours, and should cost around Tsh80,000, but good luck convincing your driver to cover the last 2km to Mambo…

ACCOMMODATION AND EATING

Mtae has a handful of very cheap, very basic but perfectly acceptable guesthouses, within a few hundred metres of each other along the main road. Two of them have restaurants and bars. For a more luxurious stay, either of Mambo's lodges, 3km southwest (5km by road), come highly recommended, and offer a plethora of activities (at extra cost; cheaper at *Mambo Cliff Inn*) including guided or self-guided walks, and bicycle rides. You can also camp at either lodge.

IN MTAE

Kuna Maneno Guest House Mtae: by the bus stop ☎ 027 266 0200. The only establishment in the village with electricity, albeit powered by a none-too-reliable generator. There are eight doubles and one twin (shared bathrooms only) and reliable piped water, plus a large but usually empty bar. $6

Lutheran Mission Mtae: at the north end of the village ☎ 027 266 0102 (c/o ELCT in Lushoto). On a grassy rise, this has atmospheric and spacious rooms, all with high ceilings and creaking floorboards, in a wing adjacent to the church. Food is available if ordered in the morning for the evening. Camping per person Tsh4000–6000. Per person Tsh6000

Mwivano Guest House Mtae: two locations on the main road ☎ 0757 699389. This is actually two hotels on the main road. *Number 1* sits next to Mtae's best restaurant and has cell-like singles with clean, shared showers and toilets. *Number 2*, 200m back on the left, is much more appetizing for an overnight, with double rooms with clean shared bathrooms and stunning views through chicken-wire-covered windows over Mkomazi Game Reserve. Number 1 Tsh6000, Number 2 Tsh9000

IN MAMBO

★**Mambo Cliff Inn** ☎ 0784 734545 or ☎ 0719 181618,

ⓦ mambocliffinn.com. This is the backpacker's version of *Mambo View Point*, 500m away and 50m higher, and is owned and run by the latter's local manager. It offers one hell of a view from each of its five cottages, as well as from the bar and restaurant, which dishes up simple but filling meals (around Tsh6000–8000 for mains). The rooms, including a dorm and one for a family, are prettily decorated, and have box nets and showers. Camping Tsh30,000 for two people (Tsh40,000 with their tent). BB dorm per person Tsh25,000, Double Tsh60,000

★**Mambo View Point** ☎ 0785 272150 or ☎ 0769 522420, ⓦ mamboviewpoint.org. Owned by a charming Dutch couple genuinely committed to ethical tourism, this is how a lodge should be: properly ecofriendly, a benefit to the local community, and… oh, the views! These you can to savour from any of its dozen cottages and walk-in tents (the latter gradually being converted to cottages) scattered around the cliff buttress. The cottages are large, decked out in rustic style, and very comfortable, each with large windows and its own veranda, catching either sunrise or sunset. There are two similarly well-sited campsites (one for overland trucks), and self-catering is possible. Meals ($10–15) are simple but good, and there's reliable wi-fi in the lounge. BB $110

Soni and around

The busy little town of **SONI**, between Mombo and Lushoto, is famed for its twice-weekly **market** (Tuesdays and Fridays), where the entire array of West Usambara produce can be found. Fruits are especially good, including plums, passion fruit, mountain papaya (sweeter and more delicate than the lowland variety), coconuts and pineapples.

There are a number of good half- or full-day excursions in the area, which can be arranged through Lushoto's cultural tourism programmes. Apart from a quick visit to **Soni Falls** where the Mkuzu River becomes the Bangala (a swim is probably unwise

5

given Lushoto's position upstream), seek out the **"Growing Rock"** near Magila village, which seems to grow taller each year. In fact, it's the soil around the base that's disappearing, thanks to erosion. Then head to Mount Kwamongo, to take in good views and see lots of butterflies.

The best trip is a five-day hike (three if you drive back) to the **Mazumbai Rainforest**, West Usambara's best-preserved primary forest. It's a challenging trip, covering a variety of up-and-down terrain, and is particularly recommended for **birdwatchers**. Two of the birds will be on any birders' "must-see" list: the Usambara alakat (*Sheppardia montana*), and the endangered Usambara weaver (*Ploceus nicolli*).

ARRIVAL AND DEPARTURE SONI

Soni lies 18km from Lushoto along the road to Mombo, and is quickly and easily reached on daladalas running throughout the day from either town every half hour or so, the ride taking no more than 30min. The town can also be visited as part of a cultural tourism trip from Lushoto.

ACCOMMODATION

Maweni Lodge 2.5km east of Soni's main junction ☎ 0787 279371 or ☎ 0713 417858, ⓦ maweni.com. This is a lovely 1920s farmhouse snug in the lee of an imposing cliff, and is a great base for exploring the region around Soni and eastwards on foot (the lodge can arrange knowledgeable guides). There are thirteen well-kept rooms with box nets, most with bathrooms, plus four less attractive walk-in tents pitched on a concrete platform that overlook an ornamental pond. A wide variety of walks and bicycle rides can be arranged here. HB tent **$80,** double **$110**

East Usambara

Rising abruptly from the coastal lowlands a mere 40km from the ocean, the steep and lushly forested escarpments of the **East Usambara Mountains** level off about a kilometre above sea level onto a deeply furrowed plateau. The range is separated physically and biologically from West Usambara by the 4km-wide Lwengera Valley. With the exception of dry lowlands to the north, the climate is warm and humid, influenced by the proximity of the Indian Ocean. Rainfall averages 2000mm a year, which, together with the deeply weathered red loam soils, has created ideal conditions for the evolution of an astonishingly rich and complex **tropical rainforest ecosystem**.

The figures speak for themselves: of East Usambara's 230 tree species, sixteen are unique, while of the well over two thousand vascular plant species recorded so far,

---

CONSERVING AMANI

Up until the end of the nineteenth century, East Usambara was way more extensively covered by forest than it is now, and had only a small human population. The advent of colonialism, however, had catastrophic consequences, even if the initial impact was indirect. The expulsion of farmers outside the Usambaras, to make way for commercial ranches and plantations, pushed people up into the hills, where they set about clearing forests to make farmland. But it didn't take long for the colonists to turn their gaze upwards. For both the Germans and the British, forestry led to commercial exploitation, not conservation, and extensive forest clearance for commercial **tea plantations** was a major blow, as was large-scale **logging**. The figures are sobering – from an estimated 1000 square kilometres of prime forest cover in 1900, East Usambara now contains only 330, of which only a tenth remains relatively intact and undisturbed.

From the 1970s, the timber industry was actively supported by the Finnish government's development agency. Only in 1986 did the Finns realize just how grossly they had underestimated the ensuing ecological damage. Performing a perfect volte-face, commercial logging was terminated, and the Finns turned to conservation, spearheading the creation of **Amani Nature Reserve**. Although the forest's destruction has now been stemmed, many challenges remain, notably the provision of sustainable alternative sources of livelihood for communities living around the forests.

over a quarter are found nowhere else on earth. Most species of **African violet** originated in East Usambara, and are now the pride and joy of gardeners all over the world. Their genus, *Saintpaulia*, is named after Baron Walter von Saint Paul Illaire, the Tanga district commissioner of German East Africa. In 1892, he shipped a consignment of the small blue flowers to Berlin, starting a horticultural craze that continues to this day. The African violet's hidden genetic make-up tells of the forests' immense age: blue or violet in the wild, gardeners and botanists have managed to tease all sorts of colours from the plant's genes, from red and pink to white and even green – genetic diversity in evolution increases as time goes on.

The proportion of endemic **animal** species is just as astounding, ranging from ten to sixty percent depending on family and genera. Denizens include over thirty kinds of snakes and chameleons, among them the terrestrial pygmy leaf chameleon, the larger arboreal three-horned chameleon and a remarkable species of toad, *Nectophrynoides tornieri*, which gives birth to live offspring instead of eggs. There are also more than two hundred species of butterfly and close to 350 types of bird.

Amani Nature Reserve

The most accessible part of East Usambara is the **Amani Nature Reserve**, its name aptly meaning "peace". Established in 1997, this mountainous and heavily forested reserve is one of Tanzania's most attractive and least-visited destinations, offering beautiful scenery, weird and wonderful flora and fauna, a constant chorus of cicadas and tree frogs (joined by the screeching of bushbabies at night), one of Africa's largest botanical gardens, and enough hiking trails through primeval rainforest to keep you in raptures (or blister packs) for weeks. Even if your interest in things botanical is limited to the greens on your plate, the sight of the towering camphor trees festooned with vines, lianas or strangling fig trees that flank much of the drive up to the reserve is the stuff of dreams.

Birdwatchers will also be in heaven; despite difficult viewing conditions (the forest canopy conceals well), more than 335 species have been seen, including the endangered Amani sunbird, the long-billed apalis, and the banded green sunbird, which, although rare outside East Usambara, can sometimes be seen at Amani in flocks of up to sixty. Other rare species include the Usambara red-headed bluebill, long-billed tailorbird, Sokoke scops owl (named after Arabuko-Sokoke forest in Kenya), Usambara eagle owl, Tanzanian weaver and green-headed oriole.

There are few large **mammals** in the forest, which makes sighting them all the more rewarding, though all you're likely to see of the shy black-and-white colobus monkey is a flash of a tail in the canopy as it retreats deeper into the forest. Other primates include yellow baboons and blue monkeys, both pests for farmers – it's said that if you throw stones at blue monkeys to chase them off, they just pick them up and hurl them back, often with a surer eye. The Tanganyika mountain squirrel is the most common of the three squirrel species; and if you're really lucky, the rufous elephant shrew may put in a fleeting appearance on the forest paths.

There are eight **walking trails**, none longer than a day, some starting at Sigi Gate, others at Amani village, and others from elsewhere. In addition there are three "driving routes", actually better by **bicycle** (see p.274). The reserve headquarters can advise you about combining campsites with trails, giving you two or more days in the wild without having to return to Sigi or Amani village.

Walking trails

The rainforest is best seen along the **Amani–Sigi Mountain Trail** (3–5hr from Sigi Gate), a fairly tough and steep round trip that climbs 450m through primary and secondary lowland and submontane forest to the top of a ridge. The area has particularly tall trees

5

(many over 60m); on the lower stretches, you may see bright orange land crabs hiding under fallen leaves.

Another good trail, especially for getting between Sigi Gate and Amani village, goes through **Amani Botanical Garden**. Founded in 1902, the garden contains around three hundred tree species (indigenous and exotic), a large expanse of original forest, a spice garden, and a palmetum, whose indigenous cycads – an ancient and primitive species of palm – hint at the great age of the forests. The plants are not labelled, so take a guide if you want names.

Other trails detailed in the reserve's leaflets include visits to tea plantations (and a tea factory), waterfalls, villages and farms, viewpoints overlooking West Usambara, and cultural sites including sacred caves and the remains of a fortified Iron Age settlement. There's also a **butterfly-breeding project** with walk-in cages at Shebomeza, 2km from Amani village (Tsh2500; T 0784 802899 or T 0655 802899, W amanibutterflyproject.org).

For the more adventurous (a guide is essential), try scaling **Lutindi Peak** (1360m; one day with transport, three days entirely on foot) for jaw-dropping views over the Lwengera Valley, or a **five-day hike to West Usambara**, for which you'll need a tent, and a couple of days beforehand to arrange guides, food and other practicalities. The same route, in reverse, is much easier to arrange as it's one of the Friends of Usambara's offerings in Lushoto (see p.268), which also offers a mammoth fourteen-day trek from the Pare Mountains to Amani. Lastly, short **night walks** are also possible, and particularly recommended should tree frogs or chameleons turn you on.

ESSENTIALS — AMANI NATURE RESERVE

Entrance fees Unusually for Tanzania, Amani's entrance fees, paid at Sigi Gate or at the reserve headquarters, have no time limit: $10 per person, plus Tsh10,000 per vehicle, and you can pay in shillings. To this add $50 a day photography fee if you're going to be doing more than just taking snaps.

Visitor information The reserve headquarters are in Amani village (T 027 264 0313, W amaninature.org), where you can rent bicycles – an informal arrangement, usually $5/day. Sigi Gate's information centre provides leaflets detailing the various trails, which are also downloadable at W easternarc.or.tz, together with a heap of academic papers.

Guided walks Guided walks cost $15 per person per day (tips appreciated): well worth the modest cost for the guides' extensive botanical knowledge, and for not getting lost (easy enough, even with a map, as none of the trails are clearly marked). The guides can be hired at both Sigi Gate and at the reserve headquarters.

ARRIVAL AND DEPARTURE

Amani is accessed via **Muheza**, a messy little town on the highway 45km southwest of Tanga. The reserve's Sigi Gate is 26km west of Muheza along an all-weather murram road. The 9km between Sigi Gate and Amani village, much of it hairpin bends, is treacherously slippery in the rains, when a 4WD is recommended.

By bus and daladala Muheza's bus and daladala stand is just off the Tanga highway, and is served by frequent Coaster minibuses from Lushoto and Tanga, and by any bus going to or from Tanga, including Arusha, Dar, Dodoma and Morogoro. Get to Muheza in the morning if you can, as public transport into the reserve can be erratic. There should be at least two buses a day from the bus stand, leaving between 1 and 2pm. These continue

THE SIGI–TENGENI RAILWAY

Amani's information centre occupies the delicately restored wooden German Stationmaster's House, at the terminus of the short-lived **Sigi–Tengeni Railway**. Built between 1904 and 1910, the narrow-gauge line opened up 120 square kilometres of forest to timber exploitation, but fell into disuse after World War I, and was dismantled in the 1930s when the road from Muheza was opened. Apart from the Stationmaster's House, all that remains is a diminutive freight carriage and a square block in front of the house, which housed the station bell. There's also a giant cogwheel from a demolished sawmill.

on past Amani to Kwamkoro or Bulwa. There's also usually a pick-up or two, or a lorry or occasional daladala a little later, but rarely after 4pm. If you're feeling energetic, you could catch a vehicle to Kisiwani village, 3km short of Sigi Gate, for a very pleasant uphill walk through forest (watch out for snakes at night, though). Most transport from Amani to Muheza, including a bus from Kwamkoro and another from Bulwa, passes through Amani village between 6 and 6.30am, reaching Sigi Gate 30min later, and arriving in Muheza in time to catch onward transport to Pangani, Tanga, Dar or

Lushoto. A seat on Ratco Express, for Dar es Salaam (up to eight times a day), can be booked in Muheza at a kiosk on the highway a few metres north of the turning for the bus stand (☏ 0659 088410 or ☏ 0718 276672).

Destinations (Muheza) Amani (2 daily 1–2pm, plus irregular transport until 4pm; 1hr); Arusha (3–4 each morning; 5hr 30min); Dar (3 daily; 4–5hr); Lushoto (every 2hr until mid-afternoon; 2hr); Mombo (hourly; 1hr); Morogoro (every 2hr until 1pm; 4–5hr); Moshi (3–4 in the morning; 4hr); Pangani (2 daily except in the rains; 2–3hr); Tanga (every 30min; 45min).

ACCOMMODATION

There's accommodation at Sigi Gate and in Amani village, both of which are bases for walks. Camping along the various hiking trails costs $30 per person (or $40 including tent rental), but none of the sites, with the exception of Kiganga on the Kwamkoro trail, have any facilities at all.

Amani Conservation Centre Rest House Amani village, 9km from Sigi Gate (reservations through the reserve headquarters). Modern and comfortable, with nine large, triple-bed rooms with electricity, mosquito nets, hot showers and use of a kitchen. The rooms are treated as dorms ($10 per person), so if there are many visitors, you'll have to share. A small bar and restaurant sells cold sodas and beers, and rustles up great meals (Tsh6000). Per person Tsh15,000, or per person Tsh18,000 with breakfast

Amani Malaria Research Centre Rest House Amani

village, 9km from Sigi Gate ☏ 0719 978030. In a medical research complex established by the Germans in 1893, this place has several spacious and funky bedrooms, a cosy lounge with a huge fireplace and decent food. For drinks, try the *Welfare Club* nearby. FB per person $30

Sigi Rest House Sigi Gate (reservations through the reserve headquarters, or ☏ 0787 582467). This place is identical in every respect to *Amani Conservation Centre Rest House*. Per person Tsh15,000, or per person Tsh18,000 with breakfast

Arusha and around

MAASAI WOMEN IN FRONT OF MOUNT MERU

Arusha and around

Heading west from Moshi, the last major town before the rolling savanna of the Rift Valley kicks in is Arusha, Tanzania's booming safari capital and third-largest city. For most tourists, this is where you arrange a wildlife safari, and few stay longer than strictly necessary. Although the city itself has few traditional tourist attractions, there's loads to see and do in its immediate vicinity, be it hiking up the dormant Mount Meru volcano, or getting to know the locals, including Maasai, at one of more than a dozen cultural tourism programmes within an hour or two of the city. All offer hands-on cultural experiences, extendible over several days, that vie with safaris as the most memorable part of a Tanzanian holiday.

Overlooking Arusha is the near-perfect cone of **Mount Meru** – part of Arusha National Park – whose 4566m peak makes it Tanzania's second-highest mountain. It's achingly attractive, whether you want to scale it over three or four days, or nose around the crater lakes and wildlife-rich grasslands on its lower slopes, on foot or on a game drive. The mountain's rich volcanic soils account for the region's prosperity – every inch of the area seems to be taken up by *shambas* and settlements, producing half of the country's wheat and substantial amounts of coffee, seed-beans and flowers (including pyrethrum, a natural insecticide) for export, along with bananas, maize, millet and vegetables. Another climbable mountain close by is the mist-shrouded **Mount Longido**, which can be climbed as part of a Maasai-run **cultural tourism** programme. There are more such programmes in other rural locations, giving visitors the opportunity of combining meeting local people with hikes to unspoilt forests, rivers and waterfalls, and even camel-back safaris.

Arusha

Nestled among the lush foothills of Mount Meru, the booming city of **ARUSHA** is northern Tanzania's major commercial centre, and the country's undisputed safari capital. Arusha has changed enormously over the last two decades, during which time its population has doubled to more than half a million: its streets are now snarled with traffic, and its once modest skyline has given way to high-rise offices and hotels built, and still being built, on the back of tourism and tanzanite. It's not a promising first impression, but, once you get beyond your bewilderment, it's a welcoming, cosmopolitan and enjoyable place, with vibrant nightlife, some superb restaurants and, as you might expect from Tanzania's safari centre, some great souvenirs as well. Not forgetting the **Maasai**: the men in red or purple tartan *shukas* (cloth replaced leather towards the end of the nineteenth century), the women with shorn heads and huge disc-like necklaces (*esos*) sewn with hundreds of tiny beads. Some look bewildered in the metropolitan setting, but most are as nonchalant and at ease with themselves as they are in the savanna.

Highlights

❶ Safaris As the capital of Tanzania's "Northern Safari Circuit", most wildlife-spotting trips to the famed Serengeti plains and Ngorongoro Crater start in Arusha. **See p.288**

❷ Restaurants Arusha was a gastronomic wilderness not even two decades ago – it's now an oasis, offering some of the finest dining in East Africa, whether you're pining for pizza, nouvelle cuisine, or even sushi. **See pp.291–294.**

❸ Handicrafts With vivid and humorous Tingatinga paintings, Makonde carvings by the thousand, beaded Maasai jewellery and a whole

lot more, Arusha is a souvenir-hunter's paradise. **See p.295**

❹ Mount Meru Tanzania's second-highest peak can be climbed in three days, ideally four, and offers stunning scenery all the way, along with views of Kilimanjaro. **See p.298**

❺ Cultural tourism Arusha is the base for many of Tanzania's ground-breaking, community-run cultural tourism programmes, offering intimate encounters with local tribes, and dozens of walks to local attractions. **See pp.301–307**

HIGHLIGHTS ARE MARKED ON THE MAP ON P.280

Arusha's altitude, at around 1500m, ensures a temperate **climate** for most of the year, and also – apparently – prevents malaria; the cold season (mid-April to mid-Aug) requires nothing thicker than a sweater, though nights can be truly chilly in July. It gets fiercely hot in November before the short rains start.

Brief history

Arusha is the traditional home of two tribes: the Meru and the Il Larusa, hence the name Arusha. The **Meru** seem to be the original inhabitants of the foothills of the mountain that bears their name and are related to disappeared hunter-gatherer communities, whereas the **Il Larusa** are said to have migrated here about two centuries

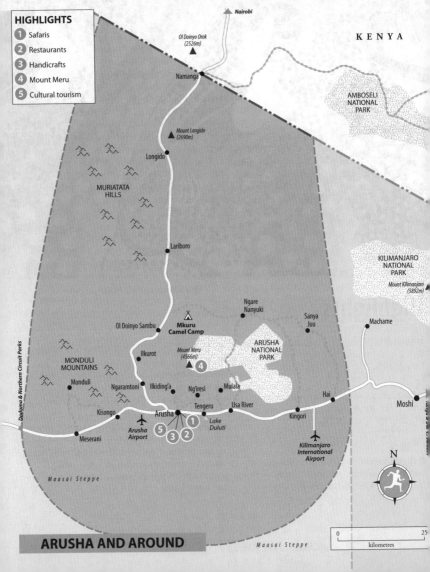

HIGHLIGHTS

1. Safaris
2. Restaurants
3. Handicrafts
4. Mount Meru
5. Cultural tourism

KENYA

Nairobi

Ol Doinyo Orok
(2526m) ▲

Namanga

AMBOSELI
NATIONAL
PARK

Mount Longido
(2690m) ▲

Longido

MURIATATA
HILLS

Lariboro

KILIMANJARO
NATIONAL
PARK

Mount Kilimanjaro
(5892m) ▲

Ngare
Nanyuki

Sanya
Juu

Machame

Ol Doinyo Sambu

Mkuru
Camel Camp

ARUSHA
NATIONAL
PARK

Ilkurot

Mount Meru
(4566m) ▲ ④

Dodoma & Northern Circuit Parks

MONDULI
MOUNTAINS

Monduli

Ngaramtoni

Ilkiding'a

Ng'iresi

Mulala

Hai

Moshi

Kisongo

Arusha
⑤ ③ ② ①

*Arusha
Airport*

Tengeru

Usa River

Kingori

Lake
Duluti

Meserani

*Kilimanjaro
International
Airport*

Maasai Steppe

N

ARUSHA AND AROUND

Maasai Steppe

0   25
kilometres

ago from south of Moshi. The reason for the migration is unclear: one theory holds that they were taken or captured by Maasai to dig wells and build irrigation furrows, and later intermarried. Their Maasai heritage is evidenced by their language, a dialect of Maa, and by the fact that Il Larusa practise horticulture rather than agriculture, dispensing with ploughs – a remnant of the Maasai taboo against breaking soil: cattle are sacred, and so too is the soil that nurtures the grass that feeds them.

The town of Arusha came into existence in the 1880s during **German colonial rule**. In 1886, a military garrison was established, and the settlement that grew up around it became the main market centre for the surrounding European-owned plantations. Later, it became a stopover for vehicles travelling down from Nairobi in Kenya on what became known as the **Great North Road**, which continued south into Zambia. Arusha's increasing importance was confirmed when it was made capital of Tanganyika's Northern Province. While under British rule, a 1929 brochure for the province, published to coincide with the opening of the railway from Moshi, enticed prospective settlers with the offer to recreate a little piece of England.

In some respects, the dream remained half-complete. The planned extension of the railway to Mwanza never happened, but Arusha's importance as a commercial and agricultural centre continued. Even so, the population remained surprisingly small, with the 1952 census putting it at just less than eight thousand, of which less than half were Africans. Since **Independence**, the pace of development has been dramatic, and the present population numbers well over half a million, many of them migrants seeking waged employment.

The clock tower

South end of Boma Rd

At the heart of the old colonial quarter is one of Arusha's more distinctive landmarks, the **clock tower**, where many of the city's flycatchers, second-hand newspaper vendors and "batik boys" hang out. A small plaque at the base states that Arusha is the halfway point between Cape Town and Cairo – but it's actually somewhere in the swamps of the Congo River basin. The story comes from the megalomaniacal ambitions of the British arch-colonialist Cecil Rhodes, who dreamt of seeing the entirety of eastern Africa painted red on the map. Had his vision of a projected "Cape to Cairo" railway ever come to fruition, Arusha may well have been the mid-point.

The German Boma

North end of Boma Rd • Museum daily 9am–5pm • Tsh8000 (students Tsh5000), photography $10

Heading up Boma Road past the tourist office brings you to a squat, white wall enclosing a number of defensive-looking whitewashed buildings. This is the **German Boma**, built in

---

ORIENTATION

Arusha has two distinct centres: the old **colonial quarter** between Goliondoi and Boma roads in the east, which contains most of the shops and offices you might need plus a few gemstone dealers; and the much larger central business district of shops (and hotels) around the **central market** and bus stand in the west. In the east, beyond the Themi River, is **Uzunguni** ("the place of Europeans"), a spread-out area of trees and guarded houses where the local elite live, along with a good many expats, which is where you'll find most of Arusha's upmarket restaurants; Njiro, southeast of there, is similarly upmarket. To the north and south are populous **residential suburbs** – areas such as Sanawari, Sekei and Sakina to the north, Unga Limited in the south, and Kijenge to the east. These suburbs are busy, bustling places, home to innumerable little stores and cottage industries, from batik designers to coffin makers, as well as most of the city's population.

6

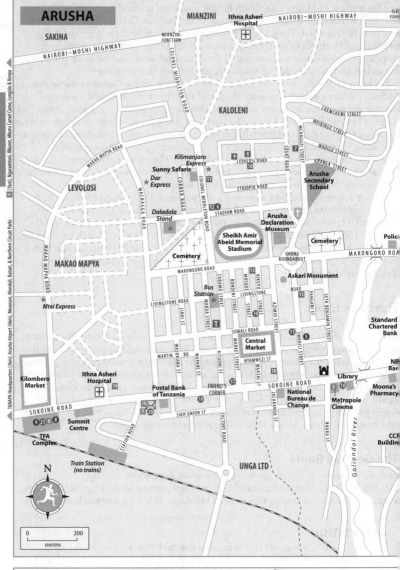

ARUSHA

1 (1km), Ngaramtoni, Illkurot, Mkuru Camel Camo, Longido & Kenya

TANAPA Headquarters (3km), Arusha Airport (6km), Meserani, Mondoli, Babati, & Northern Circuit Parks

MIANZINI

SAKINA

Ithna Asheri Hospital

NAIROBI–MOSHI HIGHWAY

ILE JUN

NAIROBI–MOSHI HIGHWAY

MIANZINI JUNCTION

COLONEL MIDDLETON ROAD

KALOLENI

CHEMCHEMI STREET

MVIBINGO STREET

WADIGO STREET

MCHAGUZI STREET

COURT ROAD

KIPANGA STREET

MAKAO MAPYA ROAD

Kilimanjaro Express

Sunny Safaris

Dar Express

LEVOLOSI

WACHAGGA ROAD

MAKAO MAPYA ROAD

CORNER ROAD

LEVOLOSI ROAD

COLONEL MIDDLETON ROAD

ETHIOPIA ROAD

Arusha Secondary School

STADIUM ROAD

Daladala Stand

Arusha Declaration Museum

Sheikh Amir Abeid Memorial Stadium

Cemetery

Cemetery

Police

MAKONGORO ROAD

MAKAO MAPYA

Mtei Express

MAKONGORO ROAD

UHURU ROUNDABOUT

Askari Monument

Kilombero Market

Ithna Asheri Hospital

Bus Station

LIVINGSTONE ROAD

LINDI ST

MAKUA ROAD

ZARAMO STREET

BONDENI STREET

MOSQUE STREET

LIVINGSTONE STREET

KIKUYU STREET

AZIMIO STREET

PANGANI ST

SETH BENJAMIN STREET

Standard Chartered Bank

SOMALI ROAD

WASUKUMA ST

MARTIN RD

WAPARE ST

KITUONI ST

MARKET STREET

Central Market

NYAMWEZI ST

SWAHILI STREET

MASSAI ST

NE Bar

Postal Bank of Tanzania

FRIEND'S CORNER

JACARANDA ST

SOKOINE ROAD

National Bureau de Change

Library

Metropole Cinema

Moona's Pharmacy

SOKOINE ROAD

SIKH UNION ST

FACTORY ROAD

NAURA ST

Goliondoi River

CCI Buildin

Summit Centre

STATION ROAD

TFA Complex

Train Station (no trains)

UNGA LTD

N

0   200
metres

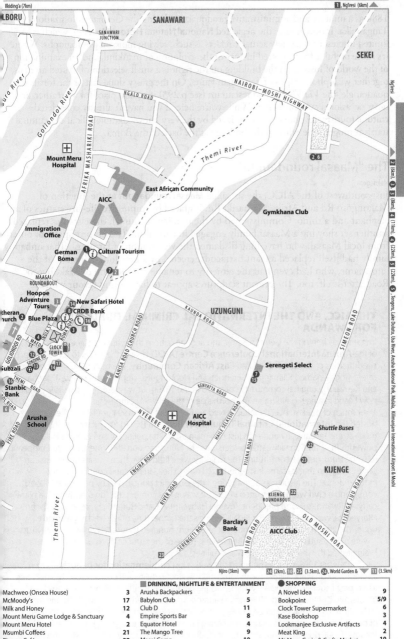

Ilkiding'a (7km) ◀

■ 1 Ng'iresi (6km) ▲

SANAWARI

SANAWARI
JUNCTION

SEKEI

NAIROBI–MOSHI HIGHWAY

6

LBORU

Aura River

Golliondoi River

NGALO ROAD

AFRIKA MASHARIKI ROAD

Themi River

❶

❷❻

Mount Meru Hospital

East African Community

Gymkhana Club

AICC

Immigration Office

German Boma

ⓘ Cultural Tourism

❼

MAASAI ROUNDABOUT

Hoopoe Adventure Tours

❸

heran urch

ⓘ ❷

New Safari Hotel

❶⓮ ⓘ

Blue Plaza

CRDB Bank

⓯ ⓰

❸ ❹

KAUNDA ROAD

UZUNGUNI

I MAEDA ST

BOMA ROAD

CLOCK TOWER

SOKOINE RD

ubzali

@

⓱

THEMI ROAD

Stanbic Bank

❻

FIRE ROAD

GOLLONDOI RD

Arusha School

Themi River

KANISA ROAD (CHURCH ROAD)

SIMEON ROAD

Serengeti Select

❼⓯

KENYATTA ROAD

NYERERE ROAD

✚ **AICC Hospital**

HALLE SELASSIE ROAD

VIJANA ROAD

★ **Shuttle Buses**

㉒

ENGIRA ROAD

❾

㉑

RIVER ROAD

KIJENGE

㉓

KIJENGE ROUNDABOUT

KIJENGE JUU ROAD

OLD MOSHI ROAD

Barclay's Bank

SERENGETI ROAD

NJIRO ROAD

AICC Club

㉓

		■ DRINKING, NIGHTLIFE & ENTERTAINMENT		● SHOPPING	
Machweo (Onsea House)	**3**	Arusha Backpackers	**7**	A Novel Idea	**9**
McMoody's	**17**	Babylon Club	**5**	Bookpoint	**5/9**
Milk and Honey	**12**	Club D	**11**	Clock Tower Supermarket	**6**
Mount Meru Game Lodge & Sanctuary	**4**	Empire Sports Bar	**8**	Kase Bookshop	**3**
Mount Meru Hotel	**2**	Equator Hotel	**4**	Lookmanjee Exclusive Artifacts	**4**
Msumbi Coffees	**21**	The Mango Tree	**9**	Meat King	**2**
Picasso Café	**22**	Masai Camp	**10**	Mt Meru Curio & Crafts Market	**10**
Quality Fast Food	**19**	Police Mess	**6**	Museum Arts Centre	**1**
Rivertrees Country Inn	**5**	Triple-A	**1**	Nakumatt	**8**
Shanghai Chinese	**20**	Via Via	**2**	Safari Care	**9**
Spices & Herbs	**23**	YMCA	**3**	Schwari	**7**
Via Via	**7**			TFA complex	**9**

1886 as a military and administrative headquarters during the German colonization of Tanganyika. It now houses the neglected **National Natural History Museum**, which is of limited interest as it has few actual artefacts as such, relying more on photographs. Where it's more useful is for its potted history of the evolution of mankind, and an examination of the world of insects. In the building on the right is a small selection of stuffed animals, together with photographs of Tanzanian fauna. On the grassy slope east of the fortified quadrangle, the *Via Via* bar and restaurant (see p.293) is a good place for a breather, and hosts occasional **cultural events**. While you're here, if you haven't already considered **cultural tourism**, let yourself be convinced by the very knowledgeable folk at the cultural tourism programme office in the building at the back of the Boma.

The "Maasai roundabout"

Makongoro Rd

Just southwest of the AICC, the so-called **Maasai roundabout** at the junction of Makongoro Rd and Afrika Mashariki Rd, is graced by impressive life-size statues of an elephant and a rhino. Commissioned by the municipal council, these statues replaced another set showing a Maasai family engaged in agriculture (which prompted an outcry from local Maasai, who have long disdained the very notion of farming). That unhappy family had itself replaced a giant barracuda, erected by a now long-gone bar of the same name, who had even had the temerity to rename that portion of Makongoro Road after itself, too. The present sculptures appear to have found favour with all.

THE AICC, AND THE INTERNATIONAL CRIMINAL TRIBUNAL FOR RWANDA

Immediately behind the German Boma, and accessible from there, are the three office blocks of the **Arusha International Conference Centre** (**AICC**), built in the 1960s to serve as the headquarters of the original, ill-fated **East African Community**. The triangular layout of the three wings – named Kilimanjaro, Serengeti and Ngorongoro – represent Tanzania, Uganda and Kenya. The original community collapsed in the 1970s but was resurrected in 1999, and is now based in a new building on the north side of the original complex.

For much of its existence, the AICC served as offices, but from 1994 until 2014, the complex hosted the **International Criminal Tribunal for Rwanda** (**ICTR**) (⦿ unictr.org). Unlike multi-ethnic Tanzania, Rwanda has just two main tribes: the politically and economically powerful Tutsi, traditionally cattle herders, and the Hutu, traditionally farmers. Prior to European rule, the Hutu, despite constituting the majority, were little more than vassals of the Tutsi, an unjust situation that became institutionalized during Belgian rule, and continued after independence. The result was a simmering ethnic conflict punctuated by periodical killings, coups, and a **civil war** that erupted in 1990. It was in this context that, on 6 April 1994, a plane carrying Rwanda's (Hutu) president, Juvénal Habyarimana, and Burundian president Cyprien Ntaryamira, was shot down near Kigali. This was the trigger for a hundred-day **genocide**: under the impotent gaze of UN troops, at least eight hundred thousand people – mainly Tutsi – were massacred by Hutu militia and civilians, some of the latter coerced or even brainwashed (by the hateful Radio Mille Collines).

In September 1998, the ICTR delivered the world's first **condemnation for genocide**, when former Rwandan Prime Minister Jean Kambanda was found guilty, and over the years has delivered a number of equally high-profile verdicts, including the conviction, in 2008, of the so-called "mastermind" of the genocide, Theoneste Bagosora, who had been a colonel in the Rwandan army.

Over its twenty-year existence, however, the tribunal was dogged by criticisms – accusations of overly lenient sentences, of bias in ignoring crimes committed by the (Tutsi) Rwandan Patriotic Front, now in power, and – naturally enough for a UN body – for its lavish and ineffectual **bureaucracy**: in all, the ICTR indited just 93 people (of whom 61 were condemned), for a total cost of more than 1.7 billion dollars. Nonetheless, the tribunal's very existence was a global landmark: the first time, other than during the Nuremberg Trials after World War II, that the crime of genocide was judged in an internationally recognized tribunal.

The Uhuru roundabout

Makongoro Rd

Heading west, Makongoro Road crosses the Goliondoi and Naura rivers before reaching, after 1km, another most impressive roundabout monument – two intersecting concrete arches surmounted by a tall pillar, on top of which is a metal sculpture of the **Uhuru Torch**. The original torch was placed atop Mount Kilimanjaro's Kibo peak on the eve of Tanzania's Independence, in December 1961, to – in the words of Nyerere – "shine beyond our borders, giving hope where there is despair, love where there is hate, and dignity where before there was only humiliation". At the time, Kenya – whose border skirts the north and east side of the mountain – was still under colonial rule, having only recently emerged from the bloody Mau Mau Rebellion. The "eternal" flame, below the arches, flickered out ages ago, but the relief panels in the sides of the monument have been repainted in colourful detail, and show mainly agricultural scenes.

6

Arusha Declaration Museum

Facing Uhuru Torch roundabout, entrance on Mchaguzi St • Daily 9am–5pm • Tsh8000 (students Tsh5000), photography $10 • ☎ 027 250 7800

If you've been to the National Museum in Dar es Salaam (see p.90), you won't miss much by skipping the **Arusha Declaration Museum**. The museum, founded in 1977 and little changed since, mostly contains rare documentary photographs, and tells Tanzania's history from just before colonial times to **Ujamaa** – President Nyerere's experiment in self-reliant rural socialism (see p.520). The policy was announced in Arusha in 1967, and stressed the importance of hard work and longer working hours as the key to Tanzania's future economic success, rather than dependence on foreign aid, loans and industrialization. Economically, the policy was an unmitigated disaster, but socially the project had the felicitous side-effect of helping to cement Tanzania's extraordinarily cohesive sense of identity among its 120-plus tribes, resulting in a rare oasis of peace in a continent otherwise riven by ethnic strife.

Central Market (Soko Kuu)

Between Somali Rd, Market St (Soko Kuu St), Nyamwezi St and Azimo St • Mon–Sat 7am–6pm, Sun 7am–2pm

The city's enjoyable **Central Market** is five minutes' walk southwest from the Arusha Declaration Museum, in the thick of the Muslim district. Don't be intimidated by the swarming mass of people (but do beware of pickpockets) – the market and the streets to the west of it offer a dazzling variety of produce, from fruit and vegetables, meat and fish (fresh or sun-dried) to herbs, spices, traditional medicine, cooking implements, colourful kangas, clothing and sandals made from truck tyres and traditional grass baskets, all displayed with geometric precision. A couple of other unusual things worth seeking out are pale pink baobab seeds that are used to make juice, or sucked like sweets; and fresh tamarind (at the end of the year), which is good for juices and sucking, and great for cooking with.

ARRIVAL AND DEPARTURE   ARUSHA

Arusha is northern Tanzania's transport hub, with several daily bus connections to all major towns in the north, east and centre of the country, and to Mombasa, Nairobi and Kampala. There are frequent flights to most national parks, northwestern towns, Dar, Nairobi and Zanzibar. A reliable travel agent for ticketing (and safaris) is Easy Travel & Tours, Boma Rd (☎ 0754 400141, ⓦ easytravel.co.tz).

BY PLANE
KILIMANJARO INTERNATIONAL AIRPORT
International flights land at Kilimanjaro International Airport (KIA, officially coded JRO), 46km east of Arusha, 6km south of the Moshi highway. Visas (see p.76), and a

yellow fever jabs (see p.76), can be bought without fuss on arrival. There's an ATM by the front entrance, and a forex that pays twenty percent less than ones in town. Flying out, you have access to gift shops, a restaurant and bar. The closest buses and daladalas are 6km away on the

6

highway. A taxi to Arusha or Moshi costs $50; much cheaper is a shuttle bus, to either town. Fastjet's shuttle bus is for their own passengers, but two others take anyone – Precisionair (Tsh10,000; office on Boma Rd; see below), and, meeting KLM's flights, Impala Shuttle (Tsh20,000; office at *Impala Hotel*, ☏0767 080460). KIA closes after the last flight, reopening at 6am, so you can't spend the night there.

ARUSHA AIRPORT

Arriving from elsewhere in Tanzania, most flights land at the small Arusha airport, 6km along the Dodoma road west of town, then 1.2km along its sliproad. Dadadalas between Arusha and Monduli pass the sliproad entrance every half hour or so (Tsh400). There are no buses or daladalas from the airport itself, so either walk those 1.2km, or catch a taxi, which shouldn't charge more than Tsh15,000 to or from Arusha.

DOMESTIC FLIGHTS

For airline websites, see Basics (p.48). Companies flying from Arusha and Kilimanjaro are: **AA** (Auric Air: TFA complex (west wing), Sokoine Rd ☏0688 723274); **AE** (Air Excel: Subzali Building (over Exim Bank), Goliondoi Rd ☏027 254 8429); **CA** (Coastal Aviation: Arusha airport ☏0785 500004); **FJ** (Fastjet: Blue Plaza, 2nd Floor, India St ☏0783 540540); **PA** (Precisionair: Boma Rd ☏027 250 8589); **RA** (Regional Air: Nairobi Rd, west of Kilombero Market ☏027 250 4164); **ZA** (ZanAir; no office). All destinations have at least one daily flight; airlines with faster or more frequent flights are listed first:

From Kilimanjaro Arusha (CA RA AE: 10min); Dar (FJ PA AE: 1–2hr); Manyara (RA: 1hr); Mwanza (PA: 1hr 20min–2hr); Serengeti (RA: 2–3hr); Zanzibar (PA AE: 1hr 30min–2hr 30min).

From Arusha Dar (PA CA AE ZA AA RA: 2hr–3hr 30min) Kilimanjaro (CA RA AE: 15min); Mafia (CA: 3hr 15min) Manyara (CA RA AE AA: 30min); Mwanza (CA: 3hr 45min) Ngorongoro (CA: 1hr); Pangani (CA: 2hr); Pemba (ZA CA: 2h 15min–3hr); Rubondo (CA: 4hr 30min); Saadani (CA: 4h 15min); Selous (CA: 3hr); Serengeti (RA AE CA AA ZA: 1hr–2h 45min); Tanga (CA: 1hr 5min); Tarangire (CA: 15min) Zanzibar (PA ZA AE CA AA RA: 1hr 10min–2hr 30min).

BY BUS

There are buses from Arusha to almost everywhere in Tanzania, but to avoid getting stuck on a bus overnight (o risk an insane driver trying to meet unrealistic schedules) the longest routes that can safely be covered in a day are clockwise, Tanga, Dar, Morogoro, Dodoma, Tabora and Mwanza. The bus station is centrally located betweer Zaramo and Makua sts, but some companies use their own terminals (see p.287). New arrivals will have to contenc with taxi and safari touts, who are pushy but rarely aggressive, but keep an eye on your belongings. Leaving Arusha, the first long-distance services leave at 5.30am and the last ones no later than mid-morning, so buy you ticket in advance.

BUS COMPANIES

Hundreds of buses and dozens of bus companies operate from Arusha, some with just one or two clapped out buses others with modern fleets. Before buying a ticket, ask around for impartial advice on the safest, as reputation change. Companies to avoid include Air Bus, Air Msae (indeed, *Air* anything), Buffalo, Burudani, Chakito, Hood Meridian, Osaka and Sai Baba. Also avoid, at all cost, the large "Coaster" minibuses to Moshi, which crash with alarming frequency. While there was no consistently good company at the time of writing, the best, covering most of the main routes, are the following:

SECURITY

Given the volume of tourists that pass through Arusha each year, don't be surprised if some people treat you as an easy source of income. That said, as long as you avoid booking with safari companies touted on the street by "flycatchers" (see p.72), there's little to worry about.

As to **theft and robbery**, you'd be extremely unlucky to have problems by day, but keep a close eye on your bags and pockets in bus and daladala stands and around markets. After dusk, taking a taxi is strongly advised, but women should not catch a taxi alone unless the driver can be vouched for (ask your hotel or wherever you're leaving from to call a reliable taxi for you). If you are walking, there are a number of **areas to avoid at dusk**. These include bridges, which attract thieves as they give the victim little room to escape; the ones over the Themi River along the Nairobi–Moshi Highway, Sokoine Road where it crosses the Goliondoi River, and Nyerere Road just east of the clock tower are notorious. Indeed, the entirety of **Nyerere Road** should be avoided at night. North of town, **Sanawari** is the roughest district, though serious incidents are rare. In the city centre, **Sokoine Road** – especially the junction with Factory Road known as Friend's Corner, and the western stretch towards Kilombero Market – is known for opportunistic bag-snatchers and pickpockets. If you're driving, roll up your windows.

Dar Express Wachagga Rd (☎0754 525361), for Dar es Salaam and Nairobi.

Fasaha at the main bus stand, for Lushoto direct (and beyond, to Mtae).

Ibra Line at the main bus stand, safest for Moshi.

Kilimanjaro Express Colonel Middleton Rd, two blocks north of the bus station (☎0767 344301 or ☎0715 144301), for Dar es Salaam.

Mtei Express Makao Mapya Rd (☎0754 875429), whose battered fleet covers much of western and central Tanzania via Babati, including Kondoa, Singida, Dodoma and Mwanza.

Shabiby at the main bus stand (☎0715 422222), safest for Morogoro and Dodoma via Chalinze (other buses go via Singida).

Destinations Babati (hourly; 3–4hr); Bukoba (2 daily; 13–15hr); Dar (28 daily; 9–11hr); Dodoma (5 daily 9hr; 11hr via Chalinze); Iringa (1 daily; 12–13hr); Karatu (3 daily plus daladalas; 3hr); Kigoma (2 daily; 18–20hr); Kondoa (3–4 daily; 8–9hr); Lushoto (3–4 daily; 6–7hr); Mbeya (2 daily; 16–18hr); Mombasa (3 daily; 6–7hr); Morogoro (3 daily plus buses continuing south; 8–10hr); Moshi (hourly plus buses continuing east; 1hr 20min); Musoma via Serengeti (1 daily; 10hr); Mwanza (6 daily; 13–14hr); Nairobi (12 daily; 4–6hr); Namanga (hourly daladalas and "Noah" minivans; 2hr); Same (8 daily plus buses continuing south; 3hr); Singida (7 daily plus buses continuing west; 6hr); Tabora (2–4 daily; 12hr); Tanga (8 daily; 6–7hr); Usangi (1 daily; 4hr).

SELF-DRIVE

All major routes from Arusha are paved, but the stretch up to Namanga on the Kenyan border is prone to flooding during heavy rains. The main hazard is reckless driving, especially between Arusha and Moshi. If you're driving, be on your guard when the road swoops down towards bridges, where high-speed crashes and collisions are common. When parking in central Arusha, look for a parking attendant (in an orange bib) – the fee is Tsh1000 a day.

GETTING AROUND

By daladala Daladalas (nicknamed *vifordi*) cover much of the town's outskirts; most trips cost Tsh400. Destinations are painted on the front of the vehicles. The main daladala stand is north of the bus station off Stadium Rd. Services heading east to Usa River and Tengeru (for Lake Duluti) are best caught at Sanawari junction, between Afrika Mashariki Rd and the Nairobi–Moshi Highway. Daladalas to the eastern suburbs of Kijenge and Njiro (including *Masai Camp*) can be boarded on Sokoine Rd between Swahili and Seth Benjamin sts.

By taxi Taxis – invariably white Toyota saloons – are found throughout town, and at night outside most bars, restaurants and clubs. Licensed taxis are white with a dark thin horizontal stripe, and white number plate. A ride within town as far as the Nairobi–Moshi Highway costs Tsh5000. Although taxis are usually safe (ignoring their parlous and often comical state of disrepair), avoid taking a cab if there's already a passenger inside.

By motorbike A motorbike (*bodaboda* or *toyo*) is less than half the price of a taxi – but is your life worth the saving? Even with a helmet and sensible rider (good luck with that), there's no guarantee about the talents of other road users.

INFORMATION

Tourist board The official information office is on Boma Rd (Mon–Fri 8am–4pm, Sat 8.30am–1pm; ☎027 250 3842, ✉ttb-info@habari.co.tz, ⓦtanzaniatouristboard .com), most useful for its lists of bus timetables, licensed safari operators and a sporadically updated blacklist of really bad ones. They also stock information about various cultural tourism programmes in the region.

Cultural tourism programme For the full run-down on cultural tourism, including practicalities, prices and bookings, visit the programme's headquarters at the German Boma (Mon–Fri 8am–4pm, Sat 8.30am–1pm; ☎027 250 0025, ✉ctp@tanzaniaculturaltourism.go.tz, ⓦtanzaniaculturaltourism.go.tz).

National parks The national park headquarters (TANAPA) are 5km along the Dodoma road (Mon–Fri 8am–4pm; ☎027 250 3471 or ☎027 250 4082, ⓦtanzaniaparks .com); catch a daladala towards Monduli and get off after the African Heritage souvenir centre (Tsh400). More convenient is the Ngorongoro Information Centre on Boma Rd, close to the tourist office (Mon–Fri 8am–5pm, Sat 8am–1pm; ☎027 254 4625, ⓦngorongorocrater.org), which also stocks national parks information.

ACCOMMODATION

Arusha's best hotels are a scatter of rural set-ups out of town, but there's plenty of decent accommodation in the centre as well. Power cuts are frequent (the better hotels have generators), so water supplies can be erratic as many hotels use pumps to fill their tanks.

CITY CENTRE

The main concentration of budget hotels is in Kaloleni district, north of the stadium; it's pretty safe, in spite of its dilapidated appearance, dirty unsurfaced streets and numerous boozers. The streets around the main bus station and central market are also lively and have some reasonable mid-range options. Other areas are distinctly quieter, even deserted at night. There's no central **campsite**; best of the ones further out are *Masai Camp* (see p.291) and *Meserani Snake Park* (see p.306).

African Tulip Serengeti Rd ☎027 254 3004 or ☎0783 714104, ⓦtheafricantulip.com. Welcoming and efficient, with 29 huge, individually designed en-suite rooms, each with TV, a/c, mini-bar, safe and wi-fi. Also has a swimming pool (for guests only), a plush wood-panelled bar and a reasonably priced restaurant featuring a floor-to-ceiling sculpture of a baobab trunk, and a metal ostrich. BB $230

Annex Arusha by Night (New Annex Hotel) Colonel Middleton Rd, entrance on Stadium Rd ☎0755 260975. Not everyone's glass of beer, this – its main *raison d'être* appears to be to sleep off the effects of the adjacent bar with or without company. There are more than thirty large and clean en-suite rooms off a dark corridor, all with cable TV. Some have their mosquito nets adorned with pink frills and the walls above the beds are mounted with green light bulbs (!), which mercifully you don't need to use as the ceiling lights are normal. All have hot showers, and there's also safe parking and a cheap restaurant. Can be noisy until midnight, and on the side facing the street. BB Tsh30,000

★ **Arusha Backpackers** Sokoine Rd ☎027 250 4474 or ☎0773 377795, ⓦarushabackpackers.co.tz. Safe, friendly and significantly cheaper than other options, this is

---

SAFARIS FROM ARUSHA

Arusha is the starting point for most **"northern circuit" safaris**, principally to Ngorongoro Conservation Area and Serengeti National Park, but also to the national parks of Arusha, Lake Manyara and Tarangire. The city hosts more than two hundred **safari companies**, including plenty of "budget" ones pushed by flycatchers, but standards at the lower end are extremely variable so we'd recommend you spend a little more and go with one of the companies reviewed here, most of which are located a short taxi ride away in the suburbs. Many companies also offer Crater Highlands walks to Lake Natron via Ol Doinyo Lengai, Mount Meru and Kilimanjaro climbs (be sure the company has a TALA "Mountaineering" licence for these), and can tack on cultural tourism (see pp.65–66). A safari of three days (one full day and two half-days) gives you time to enjoy game drives in Tarangire, Manyara and Ngorongoro. Over four days, the Serengeti is a possibility, but five or six days are recommended. For **self-drive**, contact Fortes Car Hire or Serengeti Select, both reviewed here. But before diving in, do read the "Safaris" section in Basics (see pp.61–65).

BUDGET (AND UP)

Duma Explorer PPF Oloirien Estate, 2km before Njiro complex 0787 079127, ⓦdumaexplorer.com. An American-owned, Tanzanian-run company licensed for both mountaineering (overpriced for Mount Meru) and wildlife parks, the latter best value over five nights or more, using a mix of public and private campsites.

Easy Travel & Tours New Safari Hotel, Boma Rd ☎0754 400141, ⓦeasytravel.co.tz. Large, reputable and well informed, with a wide range of trips, from budget camping to semi-luxury mobile camping expeditions. They also offer scheduled departures, Kilimanjaro climbs (for which they're licensed), and Zanzibar beach stays.

Fortes Car Hire Nairobi highway, Sakina ☎027 250 6094 or ☎027 254 4887, ⓦfortescarhire.com. Arusha's biggest car rental company, with a huge fleet of Land Rovers and Land Cruisers, for which you'll pay at least $250/day plus fuel for self-drive, or $300 for one with a driver.

Maasai Wanderings Block C, #11–15, Njiro (behind Abercrombie & Kent) ☎0755 984925 or ☎0753 984925, ⓦmaasaiwanderings.com. A Tanzanian/British outfit gleaning tons of highly deserved recommendations, particularly useful for veering off the beaten track, and which fully lives up to their fair-trade/ethical promise. Similarly good for Kilimanjaro, for which they're licensed.

Safari Makers 5km east of the clocktower at Moshono (after St Jude's Primary School) ☎0732 979195 or ☎0754 300817, ⓦsafarimakers.com. A Tanzanian/US outfit with good vehicles, a solid reputation, and flexible itineraries, from budget camping and Crater Highlands jaunts (up to ten days) to lodge-based trips. They're also licensed for Kilimanjaro and Mount Meru.

Serengeti Select Haile Selassie Rd ☎027 254 4222 or ☎0754 595410, ⓦserengetisafaris.com. A reliable and adaptable company offering tailor-made tours, in all price ranges, in well-maintained Land Rovers, and happy to cater for more unusual requests (and school groups), as well as self-drive: the latter costs $1/km (minimum 100km), plus $6 per person per day for everything you'll need for camping.

Sunny Safaris Colonel Middleton Rd ☎027 250 8184 or ☎0754 268475, ⓦsunnysafaris.com. A long-established, family-friendly and clued-up outfit offering a full gamut of trips, from shared safaris and

a proper backpackers. It also has a great open-sided bar and restaurant on top (see p.294) complete with wi-fi. The rooms, on the first and second floor, are small and bare (other than ceiling fans) and lack bathrooms, but are clean. The single rooms are scarcely bigger than their beds but most face the street so are bright and don't feel like cells (avoid ones without windows); the doubles and dorms have bunk beds. Booking ahead is wise. BB dorm $10, single $12, double $22

Arusha Centre Inn Off Swahili St ☎ 027 250 0421 or ☎ 0764 294384, ⓦ arushacenterinn.com. Eighteen small but well-kept en-suite rooms on three floors (no lift), with nets, cable TV and wi-fi (but neither fans nor a/c, not that you need it in Arusha), and some with views of Mount

Meru. At the restaurant downstairs, almost everything costs Tsh12,000. BB $35

Arusha Crown Hotel Makongoro Rd ☎ 027 250 8523, ⓦ arushacrownhotel.com. A well-run and oddly upmarket high-rise for the area, with lift access, and plenty of rooms, some with views of Mount Meru and the football stadium. All have cable TV and standing fans that double as radiators, and mosquito nets on request. There's also a reasonably priced restaurant. Streetside parking is guarded by askaris. BB $70

The Arusha Hotel By the clock tower ☎ 027 250 7777, ⓦ thearushahotel.com. This rambling 1920s hotel is among Arusha's most attractive. Extensively renovated and enlarged, its 86 rooms (some with a/c) come with safes, satellite TV, large box nets and bathtubs. An extra $50 gets

"adventure camping" (both budget) to luxury. Their 4WDs have pop-up roofs as well as roof hatches, and guaranteed window seats. They also offer birding, Crater Highlands treks, and Kilimanjaro climbs (for which they're licensed).

MID-RANGE

East African Safari & Touring Company Sakina, off the Nairobi Highway ☎ 0787 293727, ⓦ eastafricansafari.net A flexible and pleasingly offbeat Australian/Tanzanian outfit with an excellent reputation for off-the-beaten-track tours, priced to suit all budgets. Their speciality is Tarangire Conservation Area (where they own *Boundary Hill Lodge* and *Naitolia Camp*), the Crater Highlands and Lake Natron, and Tanzania's far northwest. Other offerings include birding, mountain biking, and a bumper 21-day "Tanzania Explorer".

Nature Discovery 5km west along the Nairobi Highway, Sakina ☎ 0732 971859, ⓦ nature discovery.com. An efficient, safety-conscious, ethical and keenly priced firm offering 4WD camping and lodge safaris, plus a number of interesting hiking options in the Crater Highlands, donkey trekking from Longido, birding, and walks along the eastern side of Lake Eyasi. Mountain climbing is another speciality – they're licensed and enjoy an outstanding reputation for Kilimanjaro, on which they carry oxygen and a portable altitude chamber.

Safari Care TFA complex (west wing), Sokoine Rd ☎ 027 254 8168 or ☎ 0787 999551, ⓦ safaricare. com. Tailor-made safaris for all pockets (including budget, tastes (cycling, hiking, luxury) or requirements (medical, disability), and reasonably priced, including a ten-day "Honeymoon Adventure" combining the northern circuit with Zanzibar.

Tropical Trails Masai Camp, Old Moshi Rd ☎ 027 250 0358, ⓦ tropicaltrails.com. A highly respected

firm offering affordable camping safaris as well as personalized trips (with a touch of New Age if you like, including yoga and beachside healing retreats), either by vehicle or on foot outside the parks (anything up to two weeks), with knowledgeable guides. They also offer Crater Highlands treks and walks in the Rift Valley with Maasai guides.

EXPENSIVE

Amazing Tanzania Based at Gibb's Farm in Karatu, 140km west of Arusha ☎ 0786 797078, ⓦ amazing tanzania.com. Attention to detail and personal service is the hallmark here. Most options are tailor-made and feature luxurious mobile camps; they also have plenty of experience with elderly clients.

Dorobo Safaris Olasiti, 6km along the Dodoma road, then 3km south ⓦ dorobosafaris.com. A very ethical and personable outfit run by three American brothers, who were first off the mark with cultural tours, in the early 1990s. The exclusive tailor-made trips feature an enjoyable and instructive blend of culture and wildlife in mostly little-travelled locations, and excel in rugged treks outside the national parks. If you have enough time and money, a two- or three-week trip is recommended to really get under the skin of rural Tanzania.

Firelight Safaris ☎ 027 250 8773, ⓦ tanzania firelightsafaris.com. Extremely upmarket flying safari operator distinguishing itself by its emphasis on western Tanzania – with luxury camps in Katavi National Park and on Lupita Island in Lake Tanganyika (combinable with chimp tracking at Mahale National Park), as well as in the Serengeti.

Hoopoe Adventure Tours India St ☎ 027 250 7011, ⓦ hoopoe.com. Specialists in off-the-beaten-track safaris, often staying in intimate luxury tented camps in Tarangire Conservation Area, their own concessions at Loliondo next to Serengeti, Ngorongoro and West Kilimanjaro, or in searingly expensive mobile camps.

you a balcony and slightly larger bed(s). Amenities include a swimming pool set in pleasant gardens, two bars, a terrace restaurant, gift shops, gym and safe parking. BB $\overline{\text{Tsh273}}$

Arusha Tourist Inn Sokoine Rd ☎ 027 254 7803 or ☎ 0754 583455, ⌨ atihoteltz.com. Situated behind the new overpriced *Meru House Inn*, under the same ownership, this puts its neighbour to shame. The 29 en-suite rooms are very well kept, come with all the facilities you'd expect (including cable TV and wi-fi), but being hemmed in by high-rises means they don't have views – the brightest are at the back on top. There's lift access, a decent restaurant and safe parking. BB $\overline{\text{Tsh60,000}}$

Coyote Guest House Azimio St ☎ 0784 600252. On the first floor above a small supermarket, the gloomy stairway promises little, but it's actually a friendly (and safe) hotel, if rather uninspiring, with eight large rooms, all with cable TV, ceiling fans (but no nets), and new bathrooms. Here, a "single" means a double, and a "double" is a twin-bed room. $\overline{\text{Tsh30,000}}$

Equator Hotel Boma Rd ☎ 027 250 8409, ⌨ equator -hotel.com. This large monolithic hotel has never really found its niche, alternating between trying to attract tourists, businessmen and conferences. This aside, so long as you get a room at the back (those at the front face a similar building inhabited by the Revenue Authority), you have a nice view of the hotel's gardens edging the Themi River. The rooms are large, and have absolutely gigantic mosquito nets, plus fans and TVs. Service is good, and there's a bar and restaurant (with tables in the garden), but light sleepers should avoid Fri nights, which feature live music until after midnight. BB $\overline{\text{$85}}$

Giraffe Motel Levolosi Rd ☎ 0754 817912. One of Kaloleni's smartest options: thirteen squeaky-clean tiled en-suite rooms, with big beds, TVs, and nothing else – mosquito nets on request. Small restaurant at the back. BB $\overline{\text{Tsh25,000}}$

Golden Rose Hotel Colonel Middleton Rd ☎ 027 250 7959 or ☎ 0713 510696, ⌨ goldenrosehoteltz.com. Two large adjacent buildings facing the road, with dozens of decent en-suite rooms, all with big beds and box nets, cable TV, and – at the front – balconies overlooking the street (which can be noisy at night). One of the buildings was undergoing renovation at the time of writing, which should hopefully fix problems with damp. Facilities include an internet café, forex and safe parking. BB $\overline{\text{$50}}$

The Impala Hotel Kijenge roundabout ☎ 027 254 3082, ⌨ impalahotel.com. Still popular and good value despite lackadaisical service, most of the 160 rooms are in a nine-storey block fitted with panoramic lifts running up the outside. Some have TV, others offer great views of Mount Meru; all have nets. Amenities include three restaurants, two bars, a small swimming pool and internet café. BB $\overline{\text{$130}}$

Monje's Guest House Levolosi Rd, Kaloleni ☎ 0769 206303 or ☎ 0782 999011, ⌨ monjestz.com. This is actually three guesthouses. "B" is best, with well-kept

en-suite rooms around a central courtyard, all with TV. "A" opposite, is more basic and not worth the slight drop i price. "C", actually on Court Rd at the end of Levolosi St, ha two storeys, the brighter ones on top (one with a view c Mount Meru), and a small bar in the courtyard (saf parking). It also has some cheaper single rooms sharin bathrooms (Tsh15,000). Both "B" and "C" have wate heaters attached to the showers; at "A", hot water arrives i a bucket. BB $\overline{\text{Tsh20,000–30,000}}$.

★**Mount Meru Hotel** Nairobi–Moshi Highway ☎ 02 254 5111, ⌨ mountmeruhotel.com. Once a charmles concrete block, this has been completely transformed int an extremely stylish upmarket option, with pleasant view from its south side over its lawns and the golf cours beyond, and, from the north side, spectacular vistas c Mount Meru beyond the highway. Unlike the *The Arush Hotel* with which it competes, it benefits from space, givin it a far more airy and uncluttered feel. All 178 rooms ar elegantly styled and comfortable, as are the thre restaurants and pool-side pizza parlour. There's also a fore and gift shops, and they can arrange access to the adjacen golf course. There's one room for disabled guests. BB $\overline{\text{$235}}$

The Outpost Serengeti Rd, off Nyerere Rd ☎ 027 25 8405 or ☎ 0754 318523, ⌨ outpost-lodge.com. A likeable choice in the gardens of a colonial-era house. Th old house contains a family room, plus bar and restaurant other rooms are in a modern two-storey L-shaped win and are comfortable if not memorable. Also has a gift shop internet café and a small swimming pool. BB $\overline{\text{$81}}$

Palace Hotel Makongoro Rd ☎ 027 254 5800, ⌨ palace hotelarusha.com. A brash blue-glass highrise on the outside this perks up inside, with comfortable rooms, good staff, anc full-on views of Mount Meru from most of its north-facing rooms, as well as from the sauna. The sub-par restaurant is the spoiler, but otherwise it's a decent choice. BB $\overline{\text{$145}}$

OUT OF TOWN

The advantage of staying outside town is the peaceful anc rural atmosphere. On clear days, many places also have views of Mount Meru (reviews of hotels in and around Arusha National Park are covered later in the chapter; see pp.300– 301), but take the "Kilimanjaro view" claims with a pinch of salt – it's in cloud for much of the year. For something completely different, consider staying at one of the cultural tourism programmes in the area (see pp.301–307), or – ar oasis for campers – at *Meserani Snake Park* (see p.306).

★**Karama Lodge & Spa** 1.5km off Old Moshi Rd from just beyond Masai Camp ☎ 0732 971823 or ☎ 0754 475188, ⌨ karama-lodge.com. This is a rare animal... a Tanzanian hotel without TV (but with wi-fi). Tranquil and very welcoming, it comprises 22 simple but comfortable wood-and-thatch cottages on stilts (all with verandas) scattered around a steep hillside, with forest above, and cultivated land and local houses below, but with enough trees to give the illusion of being in the wilds; certainly, the resident troop of vervet monkeys think so. The overall style is rustic, with plenty of rough-hewn wood and quirky decor, including carvings in pillars and door frames, and a fabulous wooden bicycle in the lounge. The "Spa" part is serious: apart from massages, you can indulge in other holistic treatments, or join a yoga class. You could also meditate on the food (see p.293). A small swimming pool rounds off the offering. BB $142, HB $189

★**Kigongoni Lodge** 11km towards Moshi at Tengeru ☎027 255 3087 or ☎0732 978876, ⊚ kigongoni.net. On a beautiful, partially-forested coffee estate with views of Mount Meru, this lodge funds the adjacent Sibusiso Foundation for mentally disabled children. The eighteen attractive cottages are rustic in style, with fireplaces, four-posters, and wooden verandas overlooking the forest and some jittery monkeys, duikers and dikdiks, and even bushbuck. There's a swimming pool with great views, free wi-fi, and guided walks through the estate's rose and coffee plantations, and to nearby forest, waterfalls and Lake Duluti. BB $220

★**L'Oasis Lodge & Restaurant** 800m north of the Nairobi–Moshi Highway at Sekei ☎027 250 7089 or ☎0755 866421, ⊚loasistanzania.com. Of the local districts north of the highway, Sekei is the most approachable (well, excepting the terrible road), thanks in part to many surviving small farms, mud houses and thick stands of banana plants. Set amid walled-in gardens, this place has a variety of cosy rooms, mostly in traditionally built rondavels, but also in large wooden houses on stilts. The cheaper "Backpackers' Annex" opposite is flanked by banana plants, and has twelve twin-bed rooms in a long house on stilts, each with a washbasin (shared bathrooms). There's also a comfy restaurant and bar, internet café and swimming pool. BB $100 (or $25 per person in the Backpackers' Annex)

Masai Camp Old Moshi Rd, 2.5km east of Kijenge ☎0754 488202, ⊚masai-camp.com. In a very green, tree-studded plot, the campsite here ($8 per person) is the usual haunt for overland trucks, but there are also some of Arusha's cheapest rooms, albeit at the cost of having to use taxis or daladalas to get between here and town, as walking unaccompanied is not wise. The Tropical Trails safari company is based here (see p.289), and there's also a children's playground and a restaurant-cum-bar that used to be a major nocturnal venue on Fri and Sat, when they had bands or discos: ring ahead to check, as such events went on until 5am. Room $25–50, dorm $10

Moivaro Lodge 6km towards Moshi at Moivaro, then 1.8km south ☎027 250 6315 or ☎0754 324193, ⊚moivaro.com. Understated farmhouse elegance is the theme at this pleasant coffee-estate getaway, in tended gardens dotted with venerable old trees (which you can get to know on a 2km walking circuit). There are forty brick cottages, each with a fireplace and small but private veranda. Amenities include a pool with views of Mount Meru, bar and restaurant, a kids' playground and wi-fi in public areas. BB $273

Onsea House 5km towards Moshi, then 700m south ☎0784 833207, ⊚onseahouse.com. This cosy, intimate and exclusive Afro-colonial place offers Arusha's most exclusive out-of-town accommodation; a secluded hideaway with just five rooms, with the benefit of gorgeous grounds, and quite superlative dining at *Machweo* restaurant (see p.293). There's also a swimming pool, and a hot tub with a view of Mount Meru and the Maasai Steppe. BB $378, HB $518

★**Rivertrees Country Inn** 22km towards Moshi at Usa River ☎0732 971667 or ☎0713 339873, ⊚rivertrees.com. An extremely stylish yet unpretentious hotel that started life as a three-room B&B. Now with 22, it's kept every bit of its homely charm, and preserves your privacy by scattering the rooms — in various low cottages and buildings decked out in Swahili style — across ten acres of mature gardens, as popular with children as they are with baboons. Amenities include a swimming pool, bar and great food (see p.294). Costing extra are Swedish-style massages, guided walks, canoeing on Lake Duluti and trips to Arusha National Park. Closed April–mid-May. BB $270

EATING

Some of Arusha's restaurants offer reason enough to visit the city (not that the rest of Tanzania is so badly endowed these days). Especially notable is an ever-expanding selection of top-notch locales in the outskirts, but even the centre conceals some treasures. As elsewhere in Tanzania, most **bars** rustle up cheap eats, be it grilled meat (Arusha is famous for beef), or – a local invention – *trupa* (or *trooper*), a very hearty stew of beef or chicken with bananas, potatoes and all manner of seasonal vegetables. Another speciality is a thick banana mash called *mashalali*. There's also **street food**: roast maize cobs, *mishkaki* meat skewers, fried cassava and sometimes even stir-fries can be bought from vendors along Swahili St near the market, as well as in Kaloleni district, and at various street corners in the western part of town.

CITY CENTRE

Africafe Boma Rd, by the tourist office. One of three central coffee shops, this one warmly decorated with wood, leather and a wonderfully pervasive aroma of coffee. Other than the excellent brews (also teas), the menu is distinctly non-Tanzanian: pancakes (with maple syrup, Tsh8000), shakes and smoothies (featuring imported fruit; Tsh6000), and "gourmet" burgers (upwards of Tsh12,000, or Tsh9000 vegetarian). Full meals include grilled Nile perch from Lake Victoria (Tsh18,000). Mon–Fri 7.30am–9pm, Sat & Sun 8am–9pm.

Annex Arusha by Night (New Annex Hotel) Colonel

6

Middleton Rd, entrance on Stadium Rd. The courtyard here gives access to a covered bar popular with prostitutes and their clients at night; by day, the courtyard has a few tables for cheap yet decent meals and snacks, with most meat dishes – including stews and grills, such as chicken masala, or grilled tilapia – costing Tsh7000. Also has soups, salads, ice creams and juices. Daily 7.30am–11pm.

The Arusha Hotel By the clock tower. Central Arusha's most elegant and expensive venue, but nice on a sultry day, when its garden-facing terrace is a welcome respite. The à la carte covers most bases, including Indian (from Tsh15,000 a plate), but more interesting are its refined versions of Tanzanian classics, such as Lake Victoria tilapia served with *ugali* and pickled onion salad (Tsh20,000). Also worth trying is the smoked trout (from Mount Meru's streams) with garlic toast and mustard (Tsh20,000). Daily 6am–10pm, snacks 24hrs.

★**Bigg Bites** Swahili St ☎0754 311474 or ☎0682 358679, ⊕facebook.com/BiggBites. The naff name and grimy street outside belie the exquisite Mughlai and tandoori cooking within, making this one of the finest Indian restaurants in East Africa, and very reasonably priced at that. Any of the *paneer* (cottage cheese) dishes are recommended (up to Tsh12,500), as are the *palak*, unbelievably succulent chicken or mutton cooked in spinach purée (Tsh11,000), and even simple dishes, such as buttered naan, are full of subtle flavours. Ask for the day's specials, too. Home deliveries are possible (one day, hopes the owner, even by quadcopter!). Reservations recommended. Wed–Mon noon–2.30pm & 6–9.30pm.

★**Blue Heron** Haile Selassie Rd ☎0785 555127, ⊕blue-heron-tanzania.com. A swish, German-run expat hangout in a pretty garden adorned with metal sculptures of animals, and dotted with capacious, comfy chairs – the ideal place for coffee and cake (say, lemon meringue), or ice cream – the same as *Ciao Gelati*'s (see below). Also good are the wood-fired pizzas (not least a gigantic one-metre-wide one for groups, for Tsh25,000), and snacks, including panninis and *shawarma*. Full meals, mostly less than Tsh20,000, are Italian – try the home-made ravioli, or seafood risotto. There's also a gift shop (see p.295), and wi-fi. Mon–Thurs 9am–5pm, Fri & Sat 9am–10pm.

Cafe Barrista Sokoine Rd near the clock tower. The smallest of the three coffee shops in this area, arguably with the best brew, and reasonably priced. Especially good are the pizzas (around Tsh12,000 for a ten-incher; try the Mawenzi, with minced meat, or the spicy vegetarian), and cheap burgers by Arusha's standards (up to Tsh7000). You'll also find the usual raft of light meals and snacks, including cakes, ice cream, fresh juices and shakes. There's an internet café at the back, and wi-fi for diners. Mon–Sat 7am–6.30pm, Sun 7am–4pm.

Ciao Gelati TFA complex (east wing), Sokoine Rd. A craving must be satiated, no matter the price – and this

place does it right, offering a wide range of *only* home made ices, either scoops (Tsh4000) or coupes (aroun Tsh15,000), fresh and fruity, or layer upon layer of ric chocolate and cakes. They also have a good choice of ho meals (most touching Tsh15,000) including risottos, pizza and pasta, and cheaper bites such as bruschettas, panninis soups and salads. Mon–Sat 8.30–5pm.

Equator Hotel Boma Rd. Best on a sunny day, when you can escape the cavernous dining room and bar and si outside in the garden, which drops down to the Them River. The menu is overambitious but reads well (fo example baked lamb casserole, pork stir-fry, or grilled kingfish; mostly Tsh10,000–12,000), so ask early i anything takes your fancy. Daily noon–9pm.

★**Fifi's Restaurant** Themi Rd. Modern, large, bright and airy coffee shop and restaurant, with coffee-related decoration, a comfortable lounge at the back with wi-fi and sockets for laptops, and as popular with Tanzanians as it is with tourists. The coffee is good, and it has a great selection of ice creams (sundaes Tsh7500), muffins and pastries, and a pleasingly inventive menu: from "traditional English" fish and chips (featuring red snapper; Tsh16,000), to genial juice blends such as beetroot with papaya and avocado (Tsh3000, Tsh4500 large). All fresh, and with plenty for vegetarians, and good bread too. Mon–Sat 7.30am–9pm, Sun 8.30am–9pm.

Green Hut Sokoine Rd. Handy for breakfast, with hamburgers, samosas, *kababu* and juices, and with cheap full meals too, including liver (Tsh4500 with rice or *ugali*). Daily 7.30am–8pm.

Khan's Barbeque Mosque St, just north of the central market. Car mechanic by day, pavement restaurant at night, serving famously good grills. So successful that they now print their own T-shirts. It's admittedly a bit of a tourist trap, but you can't knock the quality of the kebabs or chicken, nor some of the deliciously fiery sauces that accompany them. The mixed grill costs Tsh12,000, including naan and salad. Daily 6.30–11.45pm. Closed Mon–Thurs during Ramadan.

★**Maasai Café** Ngalo Rd, north of the AICC ⊕maasai-cafe.com. A fun and fashion-conscious pizza and pasta joint popular expats and well-heeled locals, in a house and walled-in garden close to forest-lined Themi River. Wood-fired pizzas (around Tsh10,000) are the mainstay, but there are also tapas, salads, steaks and even paella. The well-stocked bar can conjure up cocktails; there's also a health spa (massages, facials and other pampering), gift shop (featuring kangas, and clothes made from them), and kids' activities on Sat morning. Daily 10am–10pm.

McMoody's Sokoine Rd. This started many moons ago as a poor imitation of McDonald's, but has since found its own identity: a cool, calm, almost posh take on western junk-food, complete with table service. Has dozens of types of burger (from Tsh5500 for the veggie, Tsh6000 meat), but you'll pay at least Tsh12,000 with chips and a juice thrown

. Also has pizzas, various fishy things (including fingers), nd good shakes. No alcohol. Tues—Sun 10.30am—9.30pm.

Milk and Honey Sokoine Rd near the clock tower. Cheap no-frills fills in this busy little canteen. It's best to ask what's available given the mostly speculative menu, but you should certainly find some stews and curries (Tsh5000), as well as fried or grilled tilapia (Tsh7500), all with chips, rice, plantain or ugali. Mon—Sat 7am—7pm.

★**Mount Meru Hotel** Nairobi—Moshi Highway ☎027 254 5111. This classy yet relaxing five-star hotel has three restaurants sharing the same menu, and a fourth – a pizzeria – by the swimming pool. All are elegant and have outdoor seating overlooking the garden. The menu is refined, includes a smattering of Tanzanian dishes, and is not excessively priced for the location: for example, rack of lamb with rosemary sauce for Tsh22,000, or oxtail with ugali for Tsh17,500. Over by the pool (use of which, for non-guests, costs an extra Tsh15,000; Tsh10,000 for children), you'll find good pizzas and lasagne for Tsh11,500 and up. If the hotel is busy, they also offer buffet lunches for $25. Daily 6am—11pm.

★**Msumbi Coffees** TFA complex (east wing), Sokoine Rd. There's always something a bit odd about drinking or dining in African shopping centres (the predominantly expat and Indian punters, for a start), but this one – the best of several in this complex – is beautifully kitted out with plenty of rough-hewn wood and hessian, all imbued with the aroma of coffee, freshly baked muffins and rich chocolate cakes. The coffee is indeed good (if expensive to buy loose – up to Tsh42,000 a kilo), and is the only place in Arusha offering not only brews made from Kilimanjaro and Mbeya (Utengule) Arabica, but also Zanzibar's little known Robusta variety known as Liberica – all roasted on the premises. Mon—Sat 7.30am—7pm, Sun 7.30am—4pm.

Picasso Café Simeon Rd. A relaxing but expensive little place, with sofas inside, and dark wood furniture outside, and a good range of coffee and cakes (plus wi-fi). The main menus, for lunch and dinner (the latter around Tsh20,000 a plate) cover most bases, but most remarkable is the serious sushi (and sashimi), generous platters of which will set you back around Tsh30,000. Also good are its food-fired pizzas (Tsh11,000—17,000) and inventive salads. The only gripe is that a lot of the food is imported, including meat (from Kenya). Mon—Sat 9am—11pm, Sun 10am—5pm.

Quality Fast Food Sokoine Rd, just west of Friends Corner. Fast this courtyard eatery certainly is, and cheap too, and it's proper food, not junk – rice, pilau or ugali with stews, meat, fried fish or beans, mostly for Tsh3500 or under. Also has good bites for breakfast, and juices, including cardamom-laced tamarind. Mon—Sat 7am—8pm.

★**Shanghai Chinese** Behind Meru Post Office, Sokoine. Genuine Chinese cuisine with a sprinkle of Thai, like the spicy prawn and lemongrass soup (Tsh5000). The sizzling platters are especially renowned, say ginger crab with spring onion, honeyed chicken, or prawns cooked in

soya sauce and lemon paste, mostly for Tsh11,500 and up. Efficient service, and also does takeaways. Daily 11.30am—3pm & 6—10.30pm.

Spices & Herbs Simeon Rd. Excellent Ethiopian cuisine, also suitable for vegetarians, in a gradually crumbling colonial-era house, with some seats outside. Groups should try their siga beyayentu, a mix of spicy stews and pickles placed on the traditional Ethiopian bread-cum-plate of injera – a huge soft pancake (Tsh45,000 for four people). Note that there's also Western food if you don't like spices – Ethiopian food is hot. Most dishes are around Tsh15,000. Finish with home-made honey wine (tej; Tsh3000 a glass). Daily 7am—10.30pm.

Via Via German Boma, top end of Boma Rd (entrance to the right of the main gate). Sitting on the grassy bank of the Themi River, there's plenty of shaded seating here, and excellent food, from snacks such as pancakes, soups, burgers and salads, to substantial mains: try the spicy chicken in coconut sauce (Tsh12,000). It also does fresh juices, milk shakes and coffee. Mon—Sat 10am—10pm.

OUT OF TOWN

Most of the out-of-town hotels have perfectly good restaurants, but a handful are worth a special trip.

★**Karama Lodge & Spa** 1.5km off Old Moshi Rd from just beyond Masai Camp ☎0732 971823 or ☎0754 475188, ⓦ karama-lodge.com. The lush, partially forested location is a delight, as is the organic food, featuring more than a touch of Greek, and very well priced at around Tsh16,000 for a main course, whether seafood (even shrimps), or meat, such as cumin lamb steak. There's always a proper vegetarian option, also African (not necessarily Tanzanian), and special dietary needs are catered for. Reservations required for dinner: take the opportunity to ask about upcoming theme nights, which are events in their own right, extending to the decor. Daily: light meals all day, full meals 12.30—2.30pm & 7—9.30pm.

★**Machweo (Onsea House)** 5km towards Moshi, then 700m south ☎0787 112498, ⓦ machweo.com. Possibly the finest dining in East Africa, dreamed up by a Belgian chef experienced in Michelin-starred restaurants. The menus change daily: lunch ($35) is three courses, usually ending with coffee and Belgian chocolates, while the romantic candlelit dinner ($65, including wine) is a six-course extravaganza, from a trio of amuses-bouche at the start, to coffee and cake (served with rather wonderful sauces, like orange blossom), passing en route via ingredients such as Parma ham, fresh crab and wild mushrooms. Dine in the garden, or on a first floor balcony. Reservations required for dinner. Daily 12.30—2.30pm & 7—9.30pm.

Mount Meru Game Lodge & Sanctuary 22km towards Moshi at Usa River ☎0732 971771, ⓦ intimate-places.com. Founded in 1959 and styled on a colonial hunting lodge, the main draw here is the game sanctuary (daily 7am—5pm; Tsh1000), which started off as a zoo for ill or orphaned animals; there's also a pond with flamingos, pelicans and herons, and gardens grazed by eland and a lone zebra – perfect for a lazy Sunday afternoon with the kids, for whom there's a fun menu. The cuisine is good and well priced (Tsh12,000 for most mains), including home-made pasta, spinach quiche, or chicken *shawarma* (in a chapati roll). Good hearty soups, too (especially pumpkin or tomato; Tsh6000). To digest, take a walk through the estate, or, with a guide, to a village or a farm. Catch a daladala towards Usa River or Kikatiti. Daily noon–2.30pm & 7–10pm; light meals all day.

★**Rivertrees Country Inn** 22km towards Moshi at Us River ⊕0732 971667 or ⊕0713 339873, ⊕rivertree .com. The idyllic location, in ten acres of mature garden bounded by the Usa river, is one reason to come. The food i the other, including famously good wood-fired pizzas bake in a beehive-shaped oven, and a good selection of variation on English farmhouse classics, including succulent pork rib with mango sauce and mashed potato. These and other mai courses average Tsh15,000 a plate; you can also go for a se three-course lunch ($26), or four-course dinner ($30). Dail noon–9.30pm.

DRINKING AND NIGHTLIFE

Worth trying at least once is Meru **banana wine**, which comes in two varieties – sweet and dry. You'll find it in some loca bars, and in supermarkets. Arusha's liveliest **nightlife** is on the outskirts. The slew of bars along the Nairobi–Mosh Highway, from Sakina in the west to Sekei in the east, have always been popular, while Njiro, southeast of the centre attracts a more upmarket crowd. Unless you'll be in Arusha for a while, Njiro is the safer if more conservative bet, but it fashion-conscious clientele makes it impossible to predict which places will remain popular over the lifetime of this book taxi drivers should know the latest. For **live music**, *Triple-A* and *Via Via* are the likeliest spots. Don't walk at night; you' find taxis outside virtually every bar and club that's still open.

BARS

Arusha Backpackers Sokoine Rd. The open-sided top-floor bar and restaurant here, up a steep wooden staircase, is where you can watch the bustling street life below, gawp at Mount Meru, or just plug yourself into the wi-fi. There's comfy soft seating all around, a well-stocked bar, and a short but decent menu: poached fish with garlic sauce and veg, say (Tsh10,000), or plain old grilled pork chops (Tsh13,000). Daily 7am–11pm.

Babylon Club Sokoine Rd. Overlooking the street from the first floor balcony of the currently defunct Metropole cinema, this is a youthful and rather rough-looking place (you'll need to pass a metal detector first), but with the right frame of mind can be exhilarating, especially on Fri–Sun nights, when it gets packed. Music is played throughout the day, principally Bongo Flava, and there's food available in the courtyard downstairs. Daily 8am–late.

Empire Sports Bar TFA complex (east wing), Sokoine Rd ⊕0754 695670. Sports bars are the natural habitat of greater spotted red-necked expats, but this one attracts plenty of Tanzanians, too, particularly on Fri and Sat nights when a band (9pm–midnight) delivers a danceable mix of reggae, Bongo Flava and whatever's making waves in Kinshasa (currently Bolingo), followed by a disco. Also has pool table and karaoke on Wed night, and screens football and other sports throughout the day. The short but enticing menu features some Swahili classics as well as pizzas (Tsh10,000–13,000). Daily 9am–late; food to around 11pm.

Equator Hotel Boma Rd. On a good day, sit outside and enjoy drinks in the garden. On Fri, it turns into one of Arusha's top nightspots, with Lima Lima Band cheering the punters with danceable old-time *muziki ya jazzi* (from 7pm; free entry). Daily 10am–10pm (to around 1am on Fri).

The Mango Tree Nyerere Rd ⊕0786 021128 ⊕facebook.com/mangotree.arusha. Occupying an ol colonial building at the back of a tree-shaded garde facing the street, this is happily awkward to categorize: ba sports bar, restaurant or movie venue. Either way, it's foun favour with the clubbing crowd, both African and European Mon is movie night, but the really big nights are Thurs an Sat. By day, settle down in the garden for drinks, with o without a shisha, or a meal (say, spiced meat balls wit mashed potatoes, for Tsh8000). Has wi-fi. Daily noon–late.

Masai Camp ("Barafu") Old Moshi Rd, 2.5km east o Kijenge. Ask around about this bar-cum-restaurant befor heading out, as it was quiet at the last check. It used to hos live bands, and discos, on Fri and Sat nights, and wa especially enjoyable whenever overland tour trucks were i residence. Also has pool tables, darts and satellite TV.

Police Mess School Rd, off Sokoine Rd. A wonderfull relaxed old-style beer garden, with lots of tables unde trees and shelters, some secluded. In keeping wit tradition, staff dish up superb *nyama choma* (Tsh4000 fo half a kilo), and other cheap meals like rice with fish (Tsh4000). Daily 7am–11pm or later.

★**Via Via** German Boma, top end of Boma Rd (entrance to the right of the main gate). One of the nicest and friendliest bars in town, with great music, good food, competing TVs (one set to sports, the other soap operas), and grassy verges on which to chill out on. There's also at least one event each week. Thurs nights are wel established, with live music (sometimes hip-hop) followed by karaoke and disco (from 7pm; Tsh7000 admission); with luck, you'll also find traditional music on Sat (also from

7pm; currently free). Mon–Sat 10am–10pm (to 4am for special events).

YMCA India St. Nominally under the tutelage of the YMCA, this is essentially just a bar (with good food), and a few gloomy rooms at the side. The clientele are rarely rowdy, so it serves as a gentle introduction to local bars, which can otherwise feel a little intimidating at first. Busiest at lunchtime. Daily 11am–11pm.

CLUBS

Club D World Garden, Old Moshi Rd, 4km east of Kijenge ☎ 0715 837670. Arusha's flashiest disco, with full-on lighting and sound system, and prices and rules to keep out the riff-raff: Tsh10,000 admission (ladies free on Thurs); no shorts, no sandals or flip-flops, nor baseball caps. You can also have a massage in between dances, or chow-down on *nyama choma* outside. Thurs–Sat 9pm–5am.

Triple-A Nairobi–Moshi Highway, Sakina; opposite Nairobi Rd. Arusha's favourite disco, with a nicely mellow feel. Particularly popular on a Wed when ladies skip the Tsh5000 entry fee, but there's a disco every night of the week. Also hosts live bands (usually Fri & Sat), including rap and Bongo Flava, and music contests. Daily, busiest 10pm–late.

6

ENTERTAINMENT

Century Cinemax Njiro shopping mall, southeast of the centre. Hollywood versus Bollywood (the latter clearly the favourite), with screenings spooling-off at 2pm, and the last film starting at 10pm. Tickets Tsh5000–7000. Office opens 1pm; closed Mon.

★ **Via Via** German Boma, top end of Boma Rd (entrance to the right of the main gate). The main venue for performances, art exhibitions and even art-house film screenings, with an outdoor stage beside the Themi River. Apart from live music (see p.294), you can also take crash courses in Tanzanian cooking ($30 for three hours) or drumming lessons ($15/hour), or learn how to make a drum, or arrange a guide for various local trips, including city tours ($20, with a Maasai market on

the outskirts), and yomps around Mount Meru's foothills and waterfalls ($40). Mon–Sat 10am–10pm.

World Garden Old Moshi Rd, 4km east of Kijenge ☎ 0715 837670. One of Arusha's more bizarre attractions: a noisy blend of beer- and *nyama choma*-garden, funfair, upmarket shopping and nightclub, all dominated by an extraordinary building with four tall and very steep spikes forming its roof. By day, it's best for families, with several swimming pools (Tsh10,000; Tsh5000 children), and a "fantasy world" replete with rides and slides and even a bouncy castle (Tsh5000 admission, plus Tsh1000–2000 for rides needing electricity). At night, the focus switches to the sassy *Club D* (see above). Daily 10am–10pm.

SHOPPING

Arusha offers a vast selection of **souvenirs**, with arts and crafts from all over the country, as well as from Kenya (luridly coloured soapstone carvings), and reproduction tribal masks from central and western Africa. Typical items include Makonde woodcarvings, bright Tingatinga paintings, batiks, musical instruments (the metal-tongued "thumb pianos" of the Gogo, from around Dodoma, are great fun, as are the slender *zeze* fiddles) and Maasai bead jewellery. Prices are fixed in upmarket souvenir emporiums; elsewhere, dust off those bargaining skills (see p.73). **Coffee** also makes a good souvenir – all of the coffee shops sell attractive packages of beans or powder.

SOUVENIRS

Lookmanjee Exclusive Artifacts Joel Maeda St. One of the best selections in the city centre, especially for carvings, and keenly priced, too. They also stock carvings from Kenya's Kamba tribe, who make good figurines. Other stuff includes Congolese and Malian masks, and – occasionally – a circumcision mask from Tanzania's Luguru. Mon–Sat 8.30am–6pm, Sun 9am–1pm.

Mt Meru Curio & Crafts Market Fire Rd, 350m south of the clocktower. With more than a hundred stalls tightly packed along four or five narrow alleyways, there are more souvenirs here than you can shake a Maasai spear at. The fact that there are so many means that bargaining a decent price isn't as daunting as at first it sounds, as you can play them off against each other, and the sellers are not as pushy as at first they seem. On offer is virtually everything you could imagine, from xylophones, drums, imported or replica masks and life-size wooden statues, to a vast array

of beaded Maasai jewellery (some of them made in front of you), a forest of Makonde carvings, toys made from wire, or old tin cans, all sorts of pottery, soapstone carvings from Kenya and scary-looking daggers and spears that will need to go in your hold luggage on the way back. Daily 8.30am–6pm.

Museum Arts Centre German Boma. On the north side of the Boma complex, and also accessible from the AICC, are plenty of stalls where the artists themselves (painters and batik artists) make and sell their wares. Mon–Sat 8am–6.30pm.

Schwari At the Blue Heron, Haile Selassie Rd. Stuffed with unusual and very stylish gifts, many of them from self-help projects around the country. Particularly eye-catching are the scrap-metal sculptures, natural soaps, baby shoes, fabrics (including cushion covers embellished with Maasai bead designs) and glassware. Mon–Fri 9am–5pm, Sat 9am–12.30pm.

6

TFA complex West end of Sokoine Rd. For an unhurried but rather soulless shopping experience, this shopping centre contains almost a dozen souvenir shops, all with fixed prices. While there's nothing that really stands out, it's a handy place to get an idea of maximum prices. Mostly Mon–Fri 9am–5.30pm, Sat 9am–2pm.

BOOKS AND MAPS

A Novel Idea TFA complex (east wing), Sokoine Rd ☎027 254 7333. One of two Arusha branches of the Dar-based chain, and the best for English-language novels, self-help books and the like, sold at the published (sterling or dollar) price. They also have a great selection of coffee table books. Mon–Sat 9am–5.30pm, Sun 9am–2pm.

Bookpoint Two branches: Swahili St facing Bigg Bites, and at the TFA complex (west wing) ☎027 254 8272 or ☎0786 309095. Best by far for locally published titles, mostly in Kiswahili (great presents if you'll be visiting Tanzanians at home), plus some Tanzanian works in English, and a formidable section of imported africana, wildlife field guides, cookery and coffee-table books, mostly discounted from the published prices. Also has a full range of national parks maps. Mon–Fri 8am–5pm, Sat 8am–1.30pm.

Kase Bookshop Two stores in the centre: Boma Rd, and Joel Maeda St ☎027 250 2640 or ☎0765 401914.

Either of these stores, within two minutes' walk of each other, are worth a rummage, as you may yet find some old books of translated Tanzanian proverbs, riddles and traditional tales. Mon–Fri 9am–5.30pm, Sat 9am–2pm.

CAMPING EQUIPMENT

Safari Care TFA complex (west wing), Sokoine Rd ☎027 254 8168. Arusha's best-equipped camping store, but not cheap, and don't rely on it to have just what you want in your size (especially hiking boots). It is good for GPS systems, knives, water purifiers, batteries, hats and head torches. Mon–Sat 10am–5pm.

SUPERMARKETS AND GROCERIES

Clock Tower Supermarket South side of the clock tower. This handily located minimarket, recently expanded, probably has what you're looking for, but it's expensive. Mon–Fri 9am–5pm, Sat 9am–noon.

Meat King Goliondoi Rd. Favoured by expats for fresh meat as well as smoked hams, sausages, salami and cheese, perfect for picnics. Mon–Fri 9am–5pm, Sat 9am–noon.

Nakumatt TFA complex, Sokoine Rd. Arusha's largest supermarket, a branch of Kenya's leading chain. Mon–Fri 8am–7pm, Sat 8am–5pm, Sun 8am–1pm.

NOT EVERYTHING THAT GLITTERS IS... TANZANITE

Northern Tanzania – specifically the Mererani Hills between Arusha and Moshi – is the only known source of **tanzanite**, a precious transparent gemstone discovered in 1967. In its natural form, the stone is an irregular brownish lump, but when heated to 400–500°C it acquires a characteristic colour and brilliance, predominantly blue, with other shades ranging from violet to a dullish olive green depending on the angle its viewed at (the stone is trichroic). The facets are made by lapidaries.

Arusha is the main marketing (and smuggling) centre for tanzanite and other gemstones – ruby, green garnet (locally called tsavorite), green tourmaline, emerald and sapphire – some of them spirited in from Congo and Mozambique. The stones are classified into five main **grades**, from AAA (the finest) to C. The price depends on colour (deep and radiant is most expensive), size and inclusions; in 2014, cut AAA-grade stones retailed at around $300 per carat locally. Do your research before buying tanzanite: its many shades make **scamming** easy, such as passing off iolite (which costs $10 per carat) as tanzanite.

Even ignoring the wild rumours that al-Qaeda had a hand in the business, tanzanite mining has been beset by **controversy**. Local miners have gradually been pushed out by multinational enterprises whose heavy-handed tactics in dealing with "scavengers" – as they refer to artisanal miners – were frequently reported in the press. The mines themselves have a lamentable safety record, with several hundred reported deaths so far.

In a bid to polish the industry's tarnished image (and bolster the stone's price), the biggest multinational, TanzaniteOne, has established a series of expensive stores in Tanzania that it likes to call "**museums**", which illustrate the entire process, from geology and mining to cutting and grading. In Arusha, the main one is at Blue Plaza on India St (Mon–Fri 8am–5pm, Sat 9am–1pm; ☎027 250 5101, ⊛tanzaniteexperience.com). For a view from the other side, local miners have established the "Mirerani Tanzanite" **cultural tourism** programme, combining tours of the mines themselves with a variety of cultural encounters with the Maasai. For more information, see ⊛tanzaniaculturaltourism.go.tz/mirerani.htm.

DIRECTORY

Football Matches are held at Sheikh Amri Abeid Memorial Stadium; the local team is Arusha FC. Tickets at the gate on Makongoro Rd (Tsh3000–8000).

Health AICC Hospital, Nyerere Rd (☎ 027 254 4113) is the best for emergencies. For minor ailments, tests and dentistry, go to the Aga Khan Health Centre, Seth Benjamin St (Mon–Fri 9am–5pm, Sat 9am–2pm; ☎ 0757 231230 or ☎ 0655 231233). For pharmacies, try Moona's, Sokoine Rd, just west of NBC Bank (Mon–Fri 8.45am–5.30pm, Sat 8.45am–2pm; ☎ 027 250 9800), or Quas Pharmacy, Nanenane, Njiro (Mon–Sat 8am–10pm, Sun 10am–10pm; ☎ 0769 181852 or ☎ 0765 537616).

Immigration office Afrika Mashariki Rd (Mon–Fri 7.30am–3pm; ☎ 027 250 6565).

Internet access There's an internet café on virtually every street. Good connections and computers at the post office, facing the clock tower (Mon–Fri 8am–4.30pm, Sat 9am–noon). Also handy is Cafe Barrista, nearby on Sokoine Rd (Mon–Sat 7am–6.30pm, Sun 7am–4pm). It, and Fifi's

around the corner on Themi Rd (Mon–Sat 7.30am–9pm, Sun 8.30am–9pm), offer free wi-fi if you're eating there.

Money There are banks with 24hr ATMs throughout town (all but NMBs should work with Visa and MasterCard), and plenty of forexes. Those on Joel Maeda St near the clock tower have good rates.

Police Emergency ☎ 112. Report thefts for insurance paperwork at the station on the north side of Makongoro Rd ☎ 027 250 3641.

Post The main post office is on Boma Rd (Mon–Fri 8am–4.30pm, Sat 9am–noon), and has a stationery shop and philatelic bureau. To send international parcels, you need to arrive before 10am (Mon–Fri), when the customs officer is on duty.

Swimming pools Nicest is the outdoor pool at Mount Meru Hotel, but it's expensive at Tsh15,000 (Tsh10,000 for children). Cheaper and also nice is the one at The Arusha Hotel (Mon–Fri Tsh5000, Sat–Sun Tsh8000). Both are open daytime only.

Arusha National Park

In spite of its proximity to Arusha, **Arusha National Park** is little visited – which is good news for visitors who make it here, as they can enjoy the park's stunning volcanic scenery, expansive views (including of its giant neighbour, Kilimanjaro), hauntingly beautiful rainforest and plentiful wildlife in relative solitude. Dominating the park is the volcanic **Mount Meru** (4566m), Tanzania's second-highest mountain.

While Meru appears as an almost perfect cone when viewed from Arusha, from the east it shows the effects of the cataclysmic volcanic explosion which, a quarter of a million years ago, blew away the entire eastern side and top of the mountain – which was once taller than Kilimanjaro. The event unleashed a devastating flood of water, rocks, mud, ash and lava – boulders disgorged by the explosion have been found more than 70km away. Although the volcano is now classed as dormant, earth tremors still occur, and a series of minor eruptions were recorded in colonial times, the most recent in 1910.

The national park and its fringing forest reserve encloses much of the mountain, including the 3.5km-wide **Meru Crater** on the summit and the entire shattered eastern slope. Here you'll find **Ngurdoto Crater**, an unbroken three-kilometre-wide caldera whose wildlife has earned it the nickname "Little Ngorongoro", and the shallow, alkaline **Momela Lakes**, known for their birdlife, especially flamingos. **Wildlife** you're likely to see includes buffaloes (especially in forest glades), elephants, hippos, giraffes, warthogs, antelopes, zebras, black-and-white colobus and blue monkeys. Leopards and hyenas are present but rarely seen (there are no resident lions). Birders will be a-twitch with 575 species spotted so far, and butterfly fanatics should be in for a flutter, too.

Momela Lakes

The **Momela Lakes** in the northeast of the park comprise seven shallow lakes whose alkalinity is ideal for various forms of algae, which account for the lakes' opaque shades of emerald and turquoise and provide an ideal habitat for filter feeders such as flamingos. Other birds include pelicans, ducks and a host of migrants, especially between May and October. Glimpses of black-and-white colobus monkeys are virtually

6

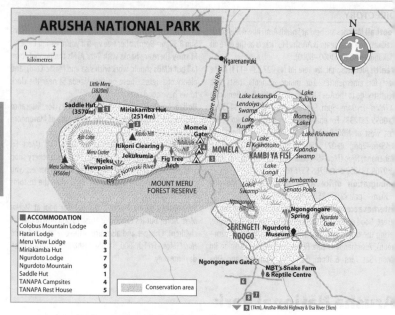

guaranteed in the forests around the lakes, and you may also catch sight of blue monkeys, bushbucks, buffaloes, hippos, giraffes and zebras.

Ngurdoto Crater and around

Three more lakes and Lokie Swamp flank the drivable road south from Momela Lakes to **Ngurdoto Crater**, an unbroken, 3km-wide, 400m-deep volcanic caldera (inevitably dubbed "Little Ngorongoro") produced when two volcanic cones merged and finally collapsed – you can walk along the crater's western and southern rims. Like Ngorongoro, Ngurdoto plays host to a rich variety of wildlife, including buffaloes, elephants and baboons and occasionally rhinos. To protect this little Eden, especially the highly endangered rhinos (which were hunted to the brink of extinction in the 1980s), visitors aren't allowed to descend to the crater floor. Instead, you can view the crater's denizens from a series of viewpoints on the south side of the rim, which also gives good views of Kilimanjaro, weather permitting. Heading back towards Momela, keep an eye out for wildlife in the diminutive patch of grassland to the right; dubbed **Serengeti Ndogo** ("Little Serengeti") it contains a variety of plains game, including a population of zebra introduced after the collapse of an export scheme.

Ngurdoto Museum

2km west of Ngurdoto Crater • Daily 6am–5pm • Free

The **Ngurdoto Museum** contains modest displays of butterflies, moths, insects, birds and – more worryingly – snares used by poachers. The most startling exhibit is a rhinoceros skull with a wire snare embedded several centimetres into it; the rhino survived several years before the wire finally killed it.

Mount Meru

Mount Meru is sometimes treated as an acclimatization trip before an attempt on Kilimanjaro, and although the summit is more than a kilometre lower, the climb can be just as rewarding, with spectacular scenery and dense forest. The mountain's **vegetational zones** are similar to Kilimanjaro's, though the high-altitude glaciers and ice fields are absent. Evergreen forest begins at around 1800m, which is moist, cool and thick at first, then thins as you rise. The higher forest, including giant bamboo thickets (up to 12m tall), offers an ideal habitat for small duiker antelopes and primates, notably blue monkeys and black-and-white colobus monkeys, which are often seen by climbers. The forest disappears at around 2900m, giving way to floral meadows where you might spot buffalo, giraffe or warthog. The meadows are followed by a zone of giant lobelia and groundsel (see p.250), and finally – above the last of the trees at 3400m – bleak alpine desert where the only sounds, apart from your breathing, are the wind and the cries of white-necked ravens.

The **best time to visit** depends on what you want to do. Mount Meru can be climbed throughout the year, but is best avoided during the long rains (March–May), when you can get very wet, cold and muddy. Skies are clearest in September (when the mountain is bitterly cold), and again from December to February (when the temperature is marginally more clement). Birdwatching is best between May and October, when migrants visit.

The ascent

Climbs of Mount Meru are usually organized through a safari company, though if you're suitably equipped (see pp.251–252), you can save a modest amount of money by arranging things yourself. The ascent starts at Momela Gate (1500m), where rangers, guides and porters can be hired. The trek is usually done over three days (two up, one down); those on a four-day climb will find that the extra day is spent on the descent (stopping for a second time at Miriakamba Hut) rather than on the ascent, so there is no advantage, acclimatization-wise, of taking the extra day. Although **altitude sickness** isn't as much of a problem on Mount Meru as on Kilimanjaro, symptoms should nonetheless be treated seriously. If you come down with the mild form of altitude sickness, Little Meru Peak, also on the crater rim but 750m lower than Meru Summit, is an easier target than Meru summit itself.

Day one

Day one (4–5hr) goes from Momela Gate to **Miriakamba Hut** (2514m). There are two routes; the steeper and more direct one heads up due west (and is mainly used by walkers when descending), and the longer and more picturesque route follows a drivable trail to the south which begins by hugging the boulder-strewn **Ngarenanyuki** (Red River); look for tawny eagles in the yellow-bark acacia trees here. The trail curves around **Tululusia Hill** (Sentinel Hill), in the lee of which stands an enormous strangling fig tree whose aerial roots have formed a natural arch; there's a waterfall on the Tululusia River near the tree. A kilometre beyond the tree is **Itikoni Clearing**, a popular grazing area for buffaloes (there is also a "special campsite" here), and 1km further on is Jekukumia, where a small diversion takes you to the confluence of Ngarenanyuki and **Jekukumia** rivers. At around 2000m both routes enter the rainforest, characterized by the African olive tree (rare elsewhere thanks to its useful timber), and bushbuck may be seen here. Buffalo and elephant droppings mean you should be careful when walking around Miriakamba Hut at night.

Day two and three

Day two heads on up to **Saddle Hut** (3570m) below the northern rim of the summit's horseshoe crater (2–3hr). If you have time and energy, a short detour to **Little Meru Peak** (3820m) is possible (5–6hr from Miriakamba Hut), though the symptoms of altitude sickness kick in on this day. **Day three** starts no later than 2am for the 4–5hr ascent to **Meru Summit** (4562.13m according to the sign at the top), following a very narrow ridge along the western rim of the crater, to arrive in time for sunrise over Kilimanjaro. Lunch is taken on the way down at Saddle Hut, and Momela Gate is reached by late afternoon. Alternatively, you could take it easy and spend an extra night at Miriakamba Hut, some four to five hours' walk from the summit.

6

ESSENTIALS

Park headquarters The park headquarters are Momela Gate on the park's northern side (daily 6.30am–6.30pm; ☎027 255 3995, ☎0689 062363 or ☎0767 536136, ✉arusha@tanzaniaparks.com).

Entrance fees Entrance fees are usually paid at Ngongongare Gate on the park's southern side, or at the headquarters if coming from the northwest. Entrance fees are $45 per person, plus Tsh20,000 per vehicle (both for 24hrs), payable with Visa or MasterCard, but not cash. The tickets are for a single entry only, so, unless you're sleeping inside the park, it's best to enter the park first thing in the morning. Climbers also pay a one-off $20 rescue fee if going beyond Miriakamba Hut.

Guides, rangers and porters Rangers, guides and porters are hired at the park headquarters. If you're driving, an official guide ($20) is optional. If you're hiking, an park ranger is obligatory ($15 per group per day; tips expected). Porters come from nearby villages; the set daily rate is around Tsh10,000 for carrying a maximum of 20kg, but

ARUSHA NATIONAL PARK

Tsh15,000 for a maximum of 15kg would be fairer.

Climbing Mount Meru The total cost for a self-arranged four-day ascent and descent of the mountain works out a $380 including ranger and hut fees but excluding transport food, porters and additional guides. A four-day hik arranged through a safari company in Arusha average $500 per person.

Canoeing Canoeing is possible on Little Momela Lake (up to 2.5hr), and can be arranged by any lodge, or direct with the operator, ✇wayoafrica.com. It costs $85 per person o top of park entrance fees and transport.

Information The beautifully illustrated Arusha guidebook ($10), published by TANAPA, contains lots of information about the park, and is especially recommended if butterflie are your thing. The only decent map is Giovanni Tombazzi painted version – ensure you get the "New" one – availabl at the park gates, Arusha's bookshops and the Ngorongor Conservation Authority office on Boma Rd. The park's web page is ✇tanzaniaparks.com/arusha.html.

ARRIVAL AND DEPARTURE

The park is usually approached from Usa River on the Arusha–Moshi highway, from where a 7.5km roa leads to Ngongongare Gate, on the park's southern boundary. The starting point for hikes up Mount Meru is Momel Gate, 17km further on, getting to which from Ngongongare Gate requires the payment of entrance fees, even if you're on a bus.

On an organized trip The Momela Lakes and Ngurdoto Crater can be visited on a day-trip from Arusha (see pp.288–289), or from the lodges outside the park (*Meru View Lodge* charges $165 per person in a couple, including park fees). For climbing Mount Meru, ensure your company has a TALA licence for mountaineering.

By bus or daladala From Arusha, the 1pm Urio Bus traverses the park from south to north, ending at

Ngarenanyuki, beyond Momela Gate, taking no more than ninety minutes. The bus passes back through Momela a 7am. The same route can be done by daladala: catch one to Usa River from Arusha or Moshi, and another toward Ngarenanyuki.

By car 2WD is sufficient for most roads in the east of the park during the dry season, but 4WD is advisable, and essential during or shortly after the rains.

ACCOMMODATION

Colobus Mountain Lodge Outside the park: 7.3km north of Usa River, 300m west of Ngongongare Gate ☎027 250 2813, ✇colobusmountain.lodge.com. This slightly scruffy eighteen-room hotel centres on a large *makuti*-thatched bar and restaurant, with its rooms – including triples, and some accessible to wheelchairs – in two-room thatch-roofed stone *bandas* with fireplaces and verandas. There's also a swimming pool and on/off wi-fi, but it's not particularly good value unless you're camping (they can provide the tents; $10 per person). HB $\underline{144}$

Hatari Lodge Outside the park, 1km north of Momela Gate (park fees apply if arriving via Ngongongare Gate) ☎0752 553456, ✇hatarilodge.com. Run by a former guidebook writer (there's hope for us yet), this is oddly decked out in funky 1960s and 1970s style. There are nine spacious rooms, all with fireplaces, plus a good bar

and library, delicious food, and a veranda for views o Meru and Kili. Immediate wildlife interest includes giraffe and bushbabies and genets at night, and a boardwall accesses a clearing where buffalo, waterbuck and eland may be seen. Walks and game drives are included. Game package $\underline{700}$

Meru View Lodge Outside the park: 6.5km north of Usa River on the right ☎0784 419232, ✇african-view .com. A quiet, well-priced option run by a Tanzanian–German couple. Surrounded by lawns, its fifteen bright comfortable cottages are divided into two en-suite rooms with big double beds and pine furniture. There's also a swimming pool, and various hikes can be arranged including a full-day coffee tour ($35–50 depending on group size) and day-trips into the national park are knowledgeable for longer hikes, too. The food is good, and doesn't shy away from Tanzanian dishes, or its wine... and they're happy to cater for unusual diets, too. Wi-fi in the garden. BB $\overline{\underline{Tsh140}}$, HB $\overline{\underline{Tsh173}}$

Ngurdoto Lodge Outside the park: 6.5km north of Usa River, then 600m east ☎0784 419232, ⊚african-view .com. Not to be confused with *Ngurdoto Mountain Lodge*, this is owned by *Meru View Lodge*, and is equally welcoming but more exclusive, with just nine rooms. The main building is a replica of a two-storey colonial-era coffee estate house, with elegant horizontal lines, wooden floors, and spacious rooms on the first floor; the other bedrooms are in red-painted bungalows shaped like the number 8. Also has a swimming pool. BB $\overline{\underline{Tsh280}}$, HB $\overline{\underline{Tsh323}}$

Ngurdoto Mountain Lodge Outside the park: 2.5km north of Usa River, then 1km east ☎027 254 2217 or ☎0713 224716, ⊚thengurdotomountainlodge.com. The area's best-appointed and biggest hotel (it's more like a resort), with rooms decked out in classic Africana, most with hot tubs. Its size, overly landscaped gardens and Disneylandish architecture detract from the experience, but it's good value, and has a pool, golf course and rooms for disabled guests. BB $\overline{\underline{Tsh270}}$

TANAPA campsites Inside the park: various locations; pay at the gate or park headquarters. Camping is possible outside Miriakamba Hut and Saddle Hut on the climbing route, and at three park-run pitches a kilometre or two southwest of Momela Gate. Per person $\overline{\underline{Tsh30}}$

TANAPA mountain huts (Miriakamba Hut & Saddle Hut) Inside the park: along the summit hiking route; pay at the park gate, or in advance via TANAPA in Arusha (see p.287). Summitting hikers can stay in two mountain huts, with facilities limited to bunk beds, toilets and cooking areas. Miriakamba Hut (2514m) has water, but at Saddle Hut (3570m) you may have to collect your own from the lower gorges. The huts are rarely full, but the park recommends booking ahead. Per person $\overline{\underline{Tsh30}}$

TANAPA rest house Inside the park: 1.3km south of Momela Gate; turn east at the signpost for "Halali"; book through TANAPA in Arusha (see p.287). Perfectly decent bunks and bathrooms. Per person $\overline{\underline{Tsh30}}$

Cultural tourism around Arusha

Arusha National Park only covers the summit and shattered eastern flank of Mount Meru. Its other slopes, and an increasing number of places beyond, can be visited through **cultural tourism programmes**, which combine beautiful views and intimate encounters with local communities (Maasai, Il Larusa or Arusha, and Meru), with walks (or, in some cases, camel rides) to local attractions such as waterfalls, viewpoints, hills, places of spiritual or legendary significance, traditional homesteads (*bomas*), farms, schools, and anything else that might plausibly be of interest to you. At most programmes, the various options can be combined over several days, with nights spent in local guesthouses, camping, or – more memorable – in homestays (any of which cost less than a cheap hotel in Arusha).

The programmes described below are supported by the Tanzania Tourist Board, whose cultural tourism department in Arusha's German Boma (see p.287) is unusually well managed, and is as knowledgeable as it is enthusiastic; they can fill you in on the latest practicalities and prices, and book many of them for you. **Costs** depend on group size and what options you choose, but average Tsh25,000–35,000 per person for half a day, Tsh35,000–60,000 for a full day, or Tsh50,000–80,000 for a day and night. The money you pay is put to good use, with some of it funding schools, healthcare programmes, and other beneficial things such as the purchase of energy-efficient stoves.

Ilkiding'a

On the southern slopes of Mount Meru, within walking distance of Arusha, is the Il Larusa village of **ILKIDING'A**, whose cultural tourism programme offers guided walks to farms, a *boma*, a healer and craftspeople, and to the school that benefits financially from your visit. You can also hike along **Njeche Canyon** (which has caves) and up **Leleto Hill**, for a bird's eye view of Arusha. A three-day hike, with nights spent camping or in family homes, also features forest reserves and the villages of Ilkurot (see p.304) and Ngaramtoni (see p.303).

WEEKLY MARKETS AROUND ARUSHA

Rural Tanzania's **markets** take the form of weekly fairs, where you can find absolutely anything a farmer or herder might need, from imported kitchenware and veritable fields of flip-flops and clothes, to veterinary medicine, agricultural tools, spirals of raw tobacco, and – no Maasai leaves home without one – mobile phones. The markets are held at several locations around Arusha, and are wonderfully colourful and fascinating events, crammed with buyers and vendors, and with separate livestock sections where you'll find hundreds of Maasai herders with their cattle and goats. Cooked food is available, as is local hooch (take care). Tourists are rare, but welcome, but please ask permission before taking photographs (and put your camera away when not using it).

Several markets are easily visited from Arusha by direct daladala. These include Tengeru, Kisongo and Longido on Wednesday; Ngaramtoni on Thursday; Kikatiti on Friday; Tengeru and Oldonyo Sambu on Saturday; and Ngaramtoni again on Sunday.

ESSENTIALS
ILKIDING'A

Location and access Ilkiding'a is 7km northwest of Arusha; the signposted turning is Mianzini junction on the Nairobi–Moshi highway, where taxis can be hired, but the road is bad – those 7km take 20min – so it can cost up to Tsh20,000 each way. Alternatively, one of the guides can meet you in Arusha.

Cultural tourism programme The project's contacts are ☎0713 520264 or ☎0732 978570, ✉info @ilkidinga.com, 🌐ilkidinga.com. Count on about Tsh30,000 for half a day.

Mulala

On the southeastern slopes of Mount Meru is the beautifully located Meru village of **MULALA**. Its cultural tourism programme is run by Agape Women's Group (a welcome change from the usual male guides), who will show you their cheese dairy, bakery, stores, farms, and perhaps a few nifty dance moves. You can also visit the school whose buildings are being patched up with the programme's profits. Various two-hour walks are offered, and can be combined into a full day: **Lemeka Hill** (via coffee and banana farms) for views and a traditional healer; the **Marisha River** whose thick tropical vegetation is alive with birds and monkeys; and **Ziwa la Mzungu** (Whiteman's Lake), where, legend says, a European fisherman disappeared after demonic sounds arose from the waters (a possible reference to volcanic activity). The only demons you'll see are fruit bats, who have colonized the trees around the lake.

ESSENTIALS
MULALA

Location and access Mulala is 34km east of Arusha: catch a daladala for Usa River (several an hour throughout the day; 40min) but get off 1km before at the signboard for *Dik Dik Hotel*. Here, catch a daladala, pick-up or motorbike to Ngani Cooperative Society, 9km north of the highway, and close to the coordinator's house (ask for Mama Anna).

Cultural tourism programme The programme coordinator is Anna Pallangyo (☎0784 499044 or ☎0784 747433, ✉agapetourism@yahoo.com, 🌐tanzaniacultural tourism.go.tz/mulala.htm). Costs are around Tsh30,000 for half a day.

Ng'iresi

The exceedingly lush southern slopes of Mount Meru north of Arusha are inhabited by Il Larusa, who have switched from cattle-herding and life in Maasai-style *bomas* to agriculture and permanent stone buildings. The cultural tourism programme at **NG'IRESI** offers several walks, from a few hours to a couple of days (you'll need camping equipment). Suitable destinations include the **waterfalls** of Songota and Navaru, a **viewpoint** on Lekimana Hill, and the **forests** of Kivesi Hill and Olgilai Forest Reserve, together with visits to farms, agricultural development projects, and a traditional healer. A women's group provides meals.

ESSENTIALS **NG'IRESI**

Location and access Ng'iresi is a pleasant 6km walk north of the Nairobi–Moshi Highway, along the road starting just east of *Mount Meru Hotel*. You'll have trouble convincing a taxi to take you (the road is bad once the tarmac ends).

Cultural tourism programme The coordinator is Mzee Loti Sareyo (T 0754 476079 or T 0754 320966, E lotisareyo@yahoo.com, W tanzaniaculturaltourism.go.tz/ngiresi.htm), but trips are usually arranged through the tourist office in Arusha. Count on about Tsh30,000 for half a day.

6

Tengeru and Lake Duluti

The fertile lands either side of the highway east of Arusha were among the first in Tanzania to be colonized by Europeans, who grew tobacco to barter with Maasai for livestock. **Coffee** soon took over, and remains the area's major crop. You can see the coffee-making process at the cultural tourism programme in **TENGERU.** The programme is mainly patronized by guests of upmarket lodges nearby, which, combined with Tengeru's colonial past, makes for a less "traditional" experience than one might hope for: instead of *bomas* and healers, you'll visit primary schools and an AIDS/HIV orphanage, and, more practically, get stuck in with some tree planting. Refresh yourself with a hike along the Malala River to **Mangalia waterfalls**. The best days to visit are Wednesday and Saturday, for Tengeru's all-day **market**.

Lake Duluti

Tengeru's other attraction is **Lake Duluti**, 2km south – one of several water-filled satellite craters associated with Mount Meru. Partially flanked by a thin slice of forest through which wends a nature trail, it's a pretty place, particularly at sunset, both for the sky-show and the many birds, but the ever-expanding suburb of Tengeru means that the upmarket *Lake Duluti Serena Hotel*(W serenahotels.com) advises its clients to take an *askari* as escort when leaving the hotel grounds. Swimming is not permitted, so the best way to see the lake is from a **canoe**.

ESSENTIALS **TENGERU AND LAKE DULUTI**

Location and access Tengeru is 12km east of Arusha along the Moshi highway. Loads of daladalas pass by throughout the day (the most frequent are those to Usa River and Kikatiti): ask to be dropped at the Natoil petrol station.

Cultural tourism programme Tengeru Cultural Tourism Programme is based at *Tengeru Campsite*, 1km north of the highway: take the road facing Natoil, turn right after 350m, and left at the signpost (T 0756 981602, W tengeruculturaltourism.org). Costs average $25 per person for half a day ($30 with lunch).

Canoeing A 90-minute canoe trip can be arranged via the cultural tourism programme, or any lodge in the area, such as *Rivertrees* ($25 per person plus $30 for a car). Alternatively, contact W wayoafrica.com, which charges $40 per person.

Ngaramtoni

Rounding the southwestern flank of Mount Meru, the first major settlement you come to is **NGARAMTONI**, 4km from which is the area's cultural tourism programme. Its name, *Osotwa*, means "good relations between people", and the project covers nine neighbouring villages. On offer are various walks accompanied by Il Larusa guides (who, here, appear to prefer being called Maasai) for visits to a *boma*, traditional healers, crafters, and a much-venerated sacred fig tree. Longer walks include a clamber up the 2200m **Sambasha Hill** to its crater and forest for great views, and to spot birds (you'll be provided with binoculars), butterflies and monkeys, both colobus and blue (4–5hr). You can also poke around the catchment forests of **Kitaakuu Hill** (6–7hr) on the western flank of Mount Meru, where the project is involved in soil and tree conservation. Come on Thursday or Sunday for **Ngaramtoni market**, where you'll find fantastic spherical pots at throwaway prices.

Location and access Ngaramtoni is 20km from Arusha along the Nairobi highway, served by twice-hourly daladalas from Arusha (30min; Tsh800).

Cultural tourism programme "Osotwa Cultural Tourism Initiatives" is signposted a walkable 4km east from Ngaramtoni at Olmotonyi, but a guide can accompany you

from Arusha if you wish (☎0754 960905 or ☎0756 346739, ✉osotwa_cbco@yahoo.com, ⊛tanzaniacultural tourism.go.tz/osotwa.htm). Costs should be no more than Tsh35,000 per person for half a day, plus $10 if visiting Kitaakuu Hill. Homestays and camping are possible, and there are tents.

Ilkurot

Whereas Ngaramtoni is largely inhabited by settled Il Larusa, the drier terrain further north is the domain of their cattle-herding cousins, the Maasai. A great place to get to know them is **ILKUROT**, whose long-running cultural tourism programme offers thoroughly recommended visits to Maasai *bomas*, herders, herbalists, warriors and women (through the now inevitable handicrafts group). Also offered are half-day hikes up **Ngorora Hill** for sweeping views, and full-day walks to the crater on **Kilimamoto ("hot hill")**. You can get around on foot, by camel or by bicycle, and the options can be combined over two or three days, with nights spent in a *boma*. Profits from the programme funded the expansion of a primary school; a secondary school is now the target.

Location and access Ilkurot is 28km from Arusha along the Nairobi highway, 8km beyond Ngaramtoni. Any daladala or Noah going to Longido or Namanga passes by (at least once an hour; 40min). Alternatively, catch one to Ngaramtoni, and change there for Oldonyo Sambu. Ask to be dropped at SITAU.

Cultural tourism programme The project's base is at a

campsite 400m west of the SITAU stop on the highway (☎0784 459296 or ☎0769 423966, ✉maasaitourism @yahoo.com, ⊛tanzaniaculturaltourism.go.tz/ilkurot .htm). Costs are no more than Tsh25,000 per person for half a day, Tsh35,000 for a full day. For overnights (at extra cost), stay in a *boma* or in a guesthouse, or camp.

Mkuru Camel Camp

The Maasai settlement of **MKURU**, 55km from Arusha on the north side of Mount Meru, is famed for its camels, which were introduced in the early 1990s, as they fare better in semi-arid conditions than cattle. By offering **camel rides**, Mkuru's cultural tourism programme hit on a winner, and is one of the most professionally run in Tanzania, offering short jaunts, but also, and much more memorable, expeditions of up to six days, with Lake Natron, Ol Doinyo Lengai or Mount Longido as the targets. En route, you'll indulge in wildlife-spotting and birding, and nights are spent camping with your Maasai guides.

THE NAMANGA BORDER CROSSING

The busiest of Tanzania's four border crossings with Kenya is Namanga, 120km north of Arusha. Looming over it is **Ol Doinyo Orok** (2526m), a mountain that's sacred to the Maasai.

Buses, daladalas and pick-ups to Namanga run once or twice an hour throughout the day from both Nairobi and Arusha; the trip from Arusha takes ninety minutes to two hours. Tourists have to complete formalities, which can take up to half an hour on each side. **Visas** ($50 for most nationalities) are usually paid in dollars cash. Don't be suckered into **changing money** on the street: there's a KCB bank on the Kenyan side, and an NBC in Tanzania within the customs area, both with **ATMs** accepting Visa and MasterCard (they spit out shillings).

The Kenyan side of the border is famed for its admirably tenacious Maasai women, who sell trinkets and pose for photos. The Tanzanian side is marginally calmer if you can avoid the red-eyed daladala touts, but watch your luggage on both sides. If you want or need to spend the night at Namanga, there's a slew of cheap **guesthouses** on either side.

ESSENTIALS **MKURU**

Location and access Mkuru Camel Camp is awkward to access without your own wheels. By public transport, catch a bus or Noah as far as the signposted turning for Mkuru, 1km beyond Oldonyo Sambu. From there, unless you can catch a lift, you face a 9km walk east, which is signposted.

Cultural tourism programme The programme can be contacted on T 0784 472475 or T 0784 724498, W mkurucamelsafari.com. The camel rides can also be booked as part of a wildlife safari (see pp.288–289). Costs average $80–100 for a full day and night.

Longido

Located 80km north of Arusha along the Nairobi Highway in the heart of Maasai land, **LONGIDO** is one of the more popular cultural tourism programmes around Arusha. Rising abruptly in the east, **Mount Longido**'s 2690-metre elevation makes for a dramatic change of vegetation, winding up through dense cloudforest before following a series of buffalo trails across drier montane forest and scrub. The climb is possible in a day (8–9hr return trip), but two days, with overnight camping at Kimokouwa (bring your own tent), is recommended. Good weather is most likely from May to October.

Other walks are possible in the plains around the mountain, including a half-day hike to Maasai *bomas* at Ol Tepesi, and a day-trip to Kimokouwa's "Valley of Wells" (the wells lead to an underground river); both of the hikes offer the chance of sighting gerenuk (common in southern Kenya but rare in Tanzania), lesser kudu and klipspringer, giraffe, zebra, gazelle and buffalo. The guides are young Maasai warriors, and most speak reasonable English. The best **day to visit** is Wednesday, for the weekly cattle market, where you can also buy *kiloriti*: a root taken as an infusion for its stimulating properties.

ESSENTIALS **LONGIDO**

Access Buses and Noah vans leave from Arusha's main daladala stand every hour or so, and take 1hr30min.

Cultural tourism programme The office is signposted a short distance from the highway in Longido (T 0787 855185 or T 0715 855185, E touryman1@yahoo.com, W tanzaniaculturaltourism.com/longido.htm). Costs supposedly depend on group size but often seem to include a measure of price gouging (contact them beforehand): you shouldn't pay more than Tsh50,000 for a half day, or Tsh80,000 for a climb up Mount Longido. There are three campsites connected to the tourism programme, a clean guesthouse in the village and several *hotelis* for food.

West of Arusha

Heading **west from Arusha** along the Dodoma road, towards the wildlife parks and central Tanzania, the landscape changes with startling abruptness from Mount Meru's lushly forested foothills, into a bleak and largely featureless expanse of savanna. Although it turns green in the rains, for much of the year it's unremittingly dry and unforgiving, and the disastrous effects of **overgrazing** are depressingly apparent. Floods have gouged deep, lunar gullies across the land, which in the dry season are the playground of spinning dust devils. Often seen as an indictment of the Maasai obsession with cattle, the massive erosion is actually more the result of the eviction of Maasai herders from their traditional ranges further west, which has created unnaturally high population densities elsewhere.

Meserani

The first major settlement after Kisongo, 16km from Arusha, is **MESERANI**, 14km beyond, which holds livestock auctions on Tuesdays (all day; mornings are best). Thanks to a fine campsite (and brilliant bar) at a snake park here, and the possibility of short camel rides, Meserani stars in many an overland truck itinerary.

Meserani Snake Park

On the highway at the west end of Meserani • Daily 7.30am–6pm (the bar and restaurant are open later) • Combined entrance to the snake park and Maasai Cultural Museum costs $10 ($5 children) • ☎ 0754 440800 or ☎ 0754 445911, ⊚ meseranisnakepark.com

Started by a South African family in 1993, **Meserani Snake Park** was almost wholly desert when they arrived, but the judicious planting of drought-resistant indigenous trees has created a veritable oasis. Most of the snakes are collected from local farms and villages; in return for not killing them, locals benefit from free anti-venom. Highlights include black and red spitting cobras and two black-mouthed mambas. There are also lizards and a crocodile pool, the fence serving mainly to keep out drunken overlanders.

Maasai Cultural Museum

Facing Meserani Snake Park • Combined entrance to the museum and snake park costs $10 ($5 children) • Daily 7.30am–6pm

Next to the snake park and run by the same people is an excellent **Maasai Cultural Museum**, containing dozens of dioramas of figures in various situations (daily life, dance, an *orpul* meat feast, circumcision, and "milking" blood from a cow, among others). The guide will explain anything that catches your eye. Behind the museum are some thickly thatched houses built by Maasai, who sell **handicrafts**; there's little hassle, so take your time. The Maasai outside the snake park can also arrange **camel rides** (Tsh2000 for a short jaunt; $12 for two hours), and guided walks through the village.

Souvenir shops

On the highway at the west end of Meserani • Daily 7.30am–6.30pm • Free admission

If you don't find something to your liking at the Maasai Cultural Museum, there's stacks more choice at a couple of **souvenir shops** on the opposite side of the highway: Tingatinga Art Gallery, and Oldoinyo Orok Arts and Gallery. Both have reasonable fixed prices (even counting the hefty commissions paid to safari drivers). Apart from an enormous selection of Makonde carvings and their ilk, you'll find good masks, sometimes strange musical instruments and a vast selection of tanzanite jewellery.

ARRIVAL AND DEPARTURE   MESERANI

By daladala Any daladala from Arusha to Monduli passes Meserani (roughly hourly; Tsh1200).

ACCOMMODATION AND EATING

The best option is camping at the snake park, but don't feel left out if you don't have a tent, as Meserani has a handful of cheap if basic guesthouses. All of them function primarily as bars, but the atmosphere isn't heavy, and their staff are genuinely surprised to see tourists.

Meserani Pub and Guest House West end of town, facing Tingatinga Art Gallery. Ten simple but decent rooms behind the bar, each containing just a good sized bed and mosquito net that fits. Bathrooms are shared – bucket showers are the norm. Tsh10,000

★ **Meserani Snake Park** West end of town ☎ 0754 440800 or ☎ 0754 445911, ⊚ meseranisnakepark .com. If you have a tent, use it here – one of East Africa's classic camp grounds, with very cheap touristy grub (burgers from Tsh3500), and one of the funkiest bars between the Cape and Cairo (cold beers, cool cocktails, warm atmosphere and zillions of flags), which becomes something of a riot whenever overland trucks roll in. If you just want to sample the bar and restaurant without seeing the snakes, you don't have to pay the $10 entrance fee. Camping per person $6.

Monduli

The **Monduli Mountains**, rising 40km west of Arusha, act as condensers for rainfall, and so are of obvious importance to the Maasai, providing year-round water and pasture. The area's main town, 42km from Arusha and 12km north of Meserani, is

MONDULI CHINI (Lower Monduli; usually just called Monduli), at the foot of the mountains. **MONDULI JUU** (Upper Monduli), 10km further into mountains, is actually a cluster of four villages: Emairete, Enguiki, Eluwai and Mfereji. Emairete is the main one, and occupies a crater that was once considered sacred. The **Maasai** are of course the main reason to visit, ideally via Monduli's **cultural tourism programme**.

The various tours, from half a day to four days or more, all feature visits to *bomas*. For half- or full-day walks, you could hike up **Kona Saba escarpment** for great views over the Rift Valley, or clamber up through **rainforest** to Kilete Peak. There are also excursions to small dams popular with birds, a herbal **doctor** and a small jewellery "factory". A two-day hiking trip gets you to **Olkarya**, where warriors collect the red ochre with which they adorn themselves. That trip includes an *orpul* (a "meat feast" in a camp traditionally reserved for warriors and their friends), and can be extended up to five days. Emairete's **weekly market** is on Saturday.

ESSENTIALS   MONDULI

Location and access There are roughly hourly buses from Arusha to both Monduli Chini and Monduli Juu, taking about 1.5hr (Tsh2000).

Cultural tourism programme Monduli's cultural tourism programme is not the best run, and has suffered from rifts and copycat projects in the past, some of which (sadly now defunct) were better. Ask about the latest situation at the cultural tourism programme office in Arusha (see p.287). The official page is ⓦtanzaniaculturaltourism.go.tz/monduli.htm; you'll find more information, but with out-dated practicalities at ⓦmonduli-juu.org and ⓦmonduliculturalandnature tourism.blogspot.com. Costs are unlikely to be less than $50–80 for a full day and night, excluding transport.

The Northern Safari Circuit

LIONS IN SERENGETI NATIONAL PARK

The Northern Safari Circuit

Head west out of Arusha and the land quickly turns to dry and dusty savanna, marking the start of traditional Maasai pastureland, and the journey to paradise for hundreds of thousands of safari-goers each year – eighty percent of Tanzania's visitors. The pride of the country's blossoming tourist industry is a quartet of wildlife areas between Arusha and Lake Victoria, collectively known as the Northern Safari Circuit. The most famous is Serengeti National Park, whose plains are the archetypal African grassland. If you time your visit right, they offer one of the most spectacular wildlife spectacles on earth: a massive annual migration of over 2.5 million wildebeest, zebra and other animals, from the Serengeti Plains north into Kenya's Maasai Mara Game Reserve and back down, following the life-giving rains.

7

The Northern Safari Circuit's other undeniable jewel is the **Ngorongoro Conservation Area**, the centrepiece of which is an enormous caldera (volcanic crater) – one of the world's largest – whose base, comprising grassland, swamp, forest and a shallow alkaline lake, contains an incredible density of plains game, and a full complement of predators. Ngorongoro is also one of few Tanzanian wildlife areas to tolerate human presence beyond tourism: the undulating grasslands around the crater belong to the cattle-herding **Maasai**, whose red-robed, spear-carrying warriors are likely to leave an indelible impression. To cynics, Ngorongoro's popularity makes it resemble little more than a zoo, with the presence of dozens of other safari vehicles all looking for that perfect photo opportunity. Nonetheless, Ngorongoro is the highlight of many a trip, and its popularity is a small price to pay for virtually guaranteed sightings of lion, buffalo, leopard, cheetah, and the highly endangered black rhino.

East of the Serengeti and Ngorongoro, in the **Great Rift Valley**, are two more national parks, less well known, but each with its own appeal. **Lake Manyara**, at the foot of the valley's western escarpment, is one of Tanzania's smallest national parks, despite which it attracts disproportionately dense wildlife populations, and its bushy terrain can make for heart-stopping encounters with animals. The lake itself is a popular feeding ground for large flocks of flamingos, and has a series of picturesque hot springs on its shore. Southeast of the lake, only two hours by road from Arusha, is **Tarangire National Park**, a likeably scruffy place where millenarian baobab trees dwarf even the park's substantial elephant population; in the dry season, this is probably the best place in all of Africa to see pachyderms.

But it's not all about wildlife. Three **cultural tourism programmes**, at Mto wa Mbu near Lake Manyara, at Engaruka along the road to Lake Natron, and at Karatu near Ngorongoro, offer intimate and enlightening encounters with local communities, and

MAASAI DANCING, NGORONGORO CONSERVATION AREA

Highlights

❶ Ngorongoro Crater When a volcano collapsed 2.5 million years ago, it left a huge crater, which now contains the world's biggest concentration of predators. **See p.332**

❷ Oldupai Gorge The archeological site that revealed the cranium of 1.75-million-year-old "Nutcracker Man", and many other hominid fossils and stone tools. **See p.334**

❸ The Maasai East Africa's emblematic tribe, and one of the most traditional. Aside from their imposing appearance, their singing is among the continent's most beautiful. **See pp.336–337**

❹ The Serengeti The name says it all. When the migration of 2.5 million wild animals is at home, the Serengeti Plains contain the world's largest concentration of mammals. **See p.338**

❺ Lake Natron A gigantic sump of soda and salt, much of it caked with crystals, and home to the world's largest breeding colony of flamingos. **See p.349**

❻ Ol Doinyo Lengai The Maasai's "Mountain of God", this near-perfect cone is East Africa's only active volcano, and can be climbed in a day, or as part of an extended "Crater Highlands" trek. **See p.351**

HIGHLIGHTS ARE MARKED ON THE MAP ON P.312

there are also a number of **archeological sites** worth visiting. **Engaruka** contains the ruins of seven villages and their irrigation network, while the Serengeti's weathered granite outcrops have rock paintings of shields and animals daubed by Maasai warriors, and an enigmatic **rock gong**, part of a huge boulder that was once used as a musical instrument. Ngorongoro, for its part, was where the **origin of mankind** first began to make sense, in the paleontological paradise of **Oldupai Gorge**.

Fans of really wild places also have a couple of destinations to head to. **Lake Natron**, in the desolate north, is an enormous soda sump, much of its surface covered by a thick crust of pinkish-white soda crystals. At its southern end rises the perfectly conical and supremely photogenic **Ol Doinyo Lengai**, the Maasai's "Mountain of God", which is East Africa's only active volcano. It can be climbed in a day, or as part of a longer hike from Ngorongoro's **Crater Highlands**.

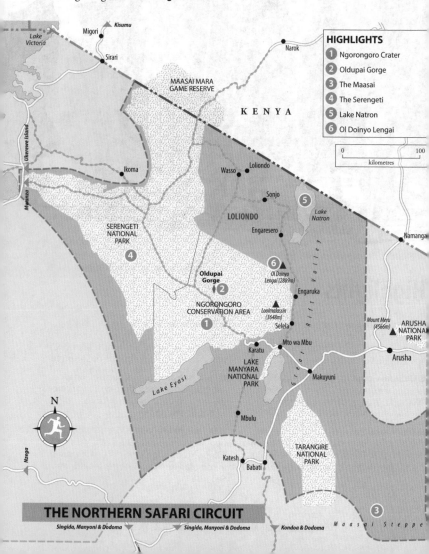

HIGHLIGHTS

1. Ngorongoro Crater
2. Oldupai Gorge
3. The Maasai
4. The Serengeti
5. Lake Natron
6. Ol Doinyo Lengai

THE NORTHERN SAFARI CIRCUIT

By organized safari Almost everyone visits on an organized safari from Arusha (see pp.288–289), but you can also arrange trips from Mwanza (see p.364) or Dar (see p.103), though you'll pay more due to the extra distance involved. For practical advice on arranging safaris and avoiding dodgy companies, plus information on what to expect, see Basics (pp.61–65).

By car Renting a car, preferably with a safari company's driver, is a great way of experiencing things at your own pace, and can be relatively cheap if you fill all the seats. There are car rental companies in Arusha (see p.288), Dar (see p.103) and Mwanza (see p.364); vehicles can also be rented in Mto wa Mbu, close to Lake Manyara, and in Karatu, close to Ngorongoro.

By public transport Buses, daladalas and "Noah" minivans can cut costs when visiting Lake Manyara (from Mto wa Mbu) or Ngorongoro (from Karatu). The only buses venturing into the parks are a daily bus from Arusha to the Ngorongoro Conservation Area headquarters, where you could try for a walking safari, and four to six buses a week (operated by Serengeti Liners, Coast Line or Kimotco) between Arusha and Musoma, which pass straight through Ngorongoro and Serengeti, but forget about this as a cheap safari: you still have to pay entrance fees ($120), on top of the Tsh35,000 bus fare.

By plane Accessing the parks by plane is mainly useful for guests of upmarket lodges and camps, whose "game package" rates include game drives and other activities.

7

The Great Rift Valley

The **Great Rift Valley**, which furrows its way clean through Tanzania from north to south, is part of an enormous tectonic fault that began to tear apart the earth's crust twenty to thirty million years ago. This geological wonderland runs from Lebanon's Bekaa Valley to the mouth of the Zambezi River in Mozambique, passing through a network of cracks across Djibouti, Ethiopia, Kenya and Tanzania – a distance of 6600km.

The gigantic fracture is at its most dramatic in East Africa, where the valley reaches up to 70km in width, and whose floor has sunk more than a kilometre beneath the surrounding plains in places. There are actually two distinct rift valleys in Tanzania: the western branch, which includes depressions occupied by Lake Tanganyika and Lake Nyasa; and the eastern Great Rift Valley, which is at its most spectacular west of Arusha, where it's marked by a long and almost unbroken ridge. In places, however, the exact limits of the fault are blurred by associated volcanic activity: mounts Kilimanjaro, Meru and Hanang are products of these cataclysms, as is the still-active Ol Doinyo Lengai.

Three major lakes fill depressions within the Great Rift Valley: Natron, Manyara and Eyasi. The southernmost is **Lake Eyasi**, at the base of the Ngorongoro Highlands. The surrounding woodland is home to one of Africa's last hunter-gatherer tribes, the **Hadzabe**, whose future looks as bleak as the lake itself. Increasing encroachment on their territory, the conversion of scrubland around their habitat into farmland and ranches, and insensitive tourism hyped around "Stone Age" images, may soon consign their way of life to oblivion.

Lake Manyara is situated at the foot of the highest and most spectacular section of the escarpment, and its northern extent is protected as a national park. The lake's water, though alkaline, is fresh enough for animals, including dense populations of plains game and large flocks of flamingos. **Mto wa Mbu**, the village serving as the base for visits here, has a popular cultural tourism programme that provides a good way of getting to know some of the dozens of tribes that have settled here, attracted – like the wildlife – by the year-round water supply.

Safari operators usually offer trips to Lake Manyara as an either/or choice with **Tarangire National Park**, southeast of the lake. But the two parks actually complement each other, both for wildlife and visually. Tarangire is the more open of the two, with lots of (partly seasonal) plains game and an immense variety of birds – over 550 species at the last count. It is also one of the best places in Africa to see elephants, especially in the dry season when animal densities in the park are second only to those of the Serengeti–Ngorongoro ecosystem.

Tarangire

Occupying four thousand square kilometres of pure Rift Valley wilderness southeast of Lake Manyara, **Tarangire National Park** and the adjacent **Burunge** and **Radilen** wildlife management areas possess a wild and unkempt beauty. Here, you'll find almost every animal species you could see on safari, with the exception of rhino, which were wiped out by poachers in the 1980s. Tarangire's signature attractions are **elephants** (head counts of several hundred a day are not unusual) and **baobabs** – weird, ungainly and hugely impressive trees with wonderful silhouettes that can live for over a thousand years.

The area's ecological importance stems from the **Tarangire River**, which loops through the park in an anticlockwise direction, emptying into the tsetse-fly-infested **Lake Burunge** just outside the park's western boundary. A bare string of isolated waterholes in the dry season, the river is in spate during the rains, and is the catalyst for an annual **wildlife migration** (see below). Many animals stay all year round however, including significant numbers of elephants, buffaloes, giraffes, zebras, ostriches and warthogs, and a full range of **antelopes**. Also present are **predators** – lions can usually be viewed lazing around by the river and, with luck, you might also spy a leopard. Cheetahs are rare, as the long grass doesn't favour their hunting technique, and you'd also be lucky to see hyenas, whether spotted or striped.

Tarangire National Park

Tarangire contains a range of different habitats, from grassland and woods in the north, to low hills, scrub and swampland further south. Cutting through these habitats is an evergreen corridor, the **Tarangire River**, which empties into Lake Burunge in the west. The river is the key to life here, and its northern extent – close to the park gate and *Tarangire Safari Lodge* – is the most popular area for game drives. In the dry season, when the bulk of the migration congregates around the river and its water pools, the area is phenomenal for game viewing. Fauna on the gently inclined grassland and woodland either side of the river is thinner, but the chance of spotting rarer animals like klipspringers and Bohor reedbuck, and rich birdlife, makes up for this, and the **baobab forests** in both areas are a big attraction.

With an extra day or two, you can venture farther afield. The shallow and alkaline **Lake Burunge** is an attractive destination, and usually has flocks of pink flamingos. South of here is **Gursi Swamp**, one of many marshes dominating the park's southern half and a paradise for birds. The **far south** is extremely remote, with access only guaranteed in dry weather.

TARANGIRE'S WILDLIFE MIGRATION

Albeit nowhere near as grand as Serengeti's migration, Tarangire is the centre of an annual **migration** that includes up to 3000 elephants, 25,000 wildebeest and 30,000 zebras, as well as such rare creatures as the fringe-eared oryx. In the dry season, from July to late October or early November, animals concentrate along the Tarangire River and its waterholes, before the onset of the short rains prompts wildebeest and zebra to head off north towards Lake Manyara, and east into the Simanjiro Plains of the Maasai Steppe. By April or May, when the long rains are at their height, the migration is also at its peak, with animals scattered over an area ten times larger than Tarangire, some even reaching Kenya's Amboseli National Park, 250km northeast on the northern side of Kilimanjaro.

When the rains come to an end, usually between mid-May and early June, the plains dry up and eland and oryx turn back towards Tarangire, followed by elephants, and then, by July, zebra and wildebeest. In August, the weather is hot and dry, so the bulk of the migrants are back in Tarangire, where they will stay a few months before the whole cycle begins anew.

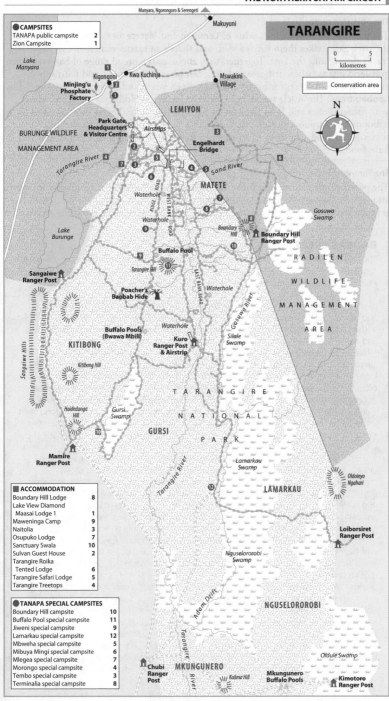

● CAMPSITES

TANAPA public campsite	2
Zion Campsite	1

TARANGIRE

Conservation area

■ ACCOMMODATION

Boundary Hill Lodge	8
Lake View Diamond Maasai Lodge	1
Maweninga Camp	9
Naitolia	3
Osupuko Lodge	7
Sanctuary Swala	10
Sulvan Guest House	2
Tarangire Roika Tented Lodge	6
Tarangire Safari Lodge	5
Tarangire Treetops	4

● TANAPA SPECIAL CAMPSITES

Boundary Hill campsite	10
Buffalo Pool special campsite	11
Jiweni special campsite	9
Lamarkau special campsite	12
Mbweha special campsite	5
Mibuya Mingi special campsite	6
Mlegea special campsite	7
Morongo special campsite	4
Tembo special campsite	3
Terminalia special campsite	8

The northern sector

The park's northern sector consists of **Lemiyon** and **Matete areas**. Their proximity to the park gate makes them easy to visit, and there's an extensive network of roads and tracks throughout the area. Together, they encompass a broad range of habitats, from grassland plains (where fringe-eared oryx can be seen), umbrella and flat-topped acacia woodland (great for birds) and more open woodland to the east, dominated by **baobab trees**. The acacia woodland is always good for wildlife viewing, providing year-round shelter and food, and there's abundant birdlife. Vervet monkeys and olive baboons are common in both areas, especially around picnic sites where they scavenge for food – be wary of **baboons**, which can be dangerous, especially if you have food in view.

The Tarangire River

The park's peerless attraction is the **Tarangire River**, which forms Lemiyon's southern and Matete's western boundary. Although good for wildlife all year round, the river is at its best in the dry season, when the migration is at home around the river's

7

BAOBAB TREES

The one thing that never fails to amaze Tarangire's visitors is its giant **baobab** trees. Known in Kiswahili as *mbuyu* (plural *mibuyu*) and popularly as the calabash tree, the baobab is one of Africa's most striking natural features. With its massive, smooth silver-grey trunk and thick, crooked branches, it's the grotesque and otherworldly appearance of the trees that impresses more than anything. The **trunk's circumference** grows to ten metres after only a century, and by the time the tree reaches old age, it may be several times more. Exact dating is difficult, as the tree leaves no rings in its often hollow trunks, but most live at least six hundred years, and one in South Africa has been carbon dated to 1700 years.

Needless to say, the baobab is supremely adapted to its semi-arid **habitat**, its range stretching right across Africa and eastwards to Australia, where it's known as the bottle tree. One of the secrets to its longevity is its fibrous wood, which is extremely porous and rots easily, often leaving a huge cavity in the trunk that fills with water during the rains. The immense water-carrying capacity of the trunks – anything from three hundred to a thousand litres – enables the tree to survive long spells of drought. For this reason the baobab has long been useful to humans, and the legends of Kenya's Kamba tribe (who migrated north from Kilimanjaro five centuries ago) say that they moved in search of the life-giving baobabs: the Ukambani Hills, where they settled, are full of them.

The tree's shape has given rise to several **legends**. Some say that baobabs used to walk around the countryside on their roots, until one day God got tired of their endless peregrinations and resolved to keep them forever rooted to the soil, replanting them upside down. On the Tanzanian coast, a pair of baobab saplings were traditionally planted at either end of the grave of an important person; in time they grew together to form one tree, enclosing the tomb within their roots. Baobabs were also, therefore, considered a propitious place to bury treasure, as the spirits of the ancestors would ensure their safekeeping.

The baobab has myriad other more **practical uses**. The gourd-like seed pods or calabashes, which grow up to 25cm long, form handy water containers and bailers for boats, and the seeds and fruit pulp ("monkey bread") are rich in protein and vitamin C, and effective against dysentery and circulatory disease. They're also a source of "cream of tartar" (found in baking powder). When soaked in water, the seeds make an invigorating drink (you can buy baobab seeds, *ubuyu*, at Arusha's market); and when roasted and ground, they taste similar to coffee. Young leaves are edible when boiled, and also have medicinal uses, and the bark, when pounded, yields a fibre suitable for making rope, paper and cloth, while glue can be made from the pollen. It's not just humans who benefit from the baobab though. Bees use the hollow trunks for hives, hornbills nest in their boughs, and elephants like to sharpen their tusks by rubbing them against the trees. In exceptionally dry seasons, they gouge deeper into the trunk to get at the water stored in the fibrous interior: the scars left by these activities are visible throughout Tarangire.

water pools. The section where the river flows from east to west has sandy cliffs along much of its northern bank, where there are several **viewpoints** and a picnic site – bring binoculars.

This east–west section of the river can be crossed at two points: across a concrete **causeway** in the west (dry season only) towards Lake Burunge, and over **Engelhardt Bridge** close to *Tarangire Safari Lodge*, which offers access to two south-running routes: Ridge Road down to Gursi Swamp, and West Bank Road which hugs the river. Following the east bank is another road, accessed from Matete, which heads down to Silale Swamp. Any of these riverside drives is ideal for getting close to wildlife. In the dry season, a number of **water pools** attract large numbers of thirsty zebra, wildebeest, elephant (who are responsible for creating a good many pools themselves by digging up the dry riverbed with their tusks), giraffe, eland, gazelle, impala, warthog and buffalo. Olive baboons are resident, and lions too are often found nearby. The bush on either side is ideal for hartebeest, lesser kudu and leopard, which usually rest up in the branches by day, their presence given away by little more than the flick of a tail. This part of the river, before it veers west, can be crossed along various dry-season causeways and small bridges.

There's a pleasant **picnic site** by the river south of Matete, about 6km north of the turning for *Tarangire Sopa Lodge*. The site, by a huge mango tree, gives a good view of the river, at a point where there's a popular mud wallow for elephants.

Ridge Road

A right fork just south of Engelhardt Bridge marks the start of **Ridge Road**, a superb 40km drive south through acacia woodland to Gursi Swamp, which in places offers beautiful vistas over much of the park and further afield. While wildlife is not as dense as around the river, there's still a decent selection, with mostly solitary elephants, giraffe, eland, warthog and buffalo. They're best seen at two sets of signposted **buffalo pools** along the way.

The other main attraction here is **Poacher's Hide**, its name possibly explaining the unusual jumpiness of the area's elephants. The hide is an enormous old baobab tree out of whose hollow trunk a small door has been carved, to resemble the dwellings of elves and sprites in children's books. The artificial doorway has led to lots of speculation about the original use of the hide: it seems likely that hunter-gatherers, possibly ancestors of Lake Eyasi's Hadzabe tribe (see box, p.328), used it as a shelter or for keeping honey beehives. The hide was certainly used by poachers in the 1970s and 1980s, hence its name – thick grass around the site, and a boulder that could be rolled across the entrance, completed the disguise. It's now used by animals – hyena cubs, bats and bat-eared foxes have all been seen inside, so take care.

The swamps

In the dry season, access to the **swamps** of central and southern Tarangire is possible. The swamps, which feed the Tarangire River, are among the richest areas in Tanzania for **birdlife**, especially water birds from November to May. During the dry season as the swamps begin to dry, the receding waterholes and remaining patches of marshland also offer superb game viewing, including large buffalo herds up to a thousand strong, and elephants longing for mud baths. The easiest to visit are Gursi Swamp, at the end of Ridge Road close to *Swala Camp*, and Silale Swamp at the end of the East Bank Road on the park's eastern border.

A game track runs all the way around **Gursi Swamp** and much of the grassland on its periphery is studded with tall termite mounds. Bushy-tailed ground squirrels are common, as are giraffes in the woodland. **Silale Swamp**, which should be accessible all year round, is perhaps better for birdlife; and lions, preying on herds of zebra and wildebeest, are often seen on the western side in October. The fringing woods are said to contain huge tree-climbing pythons.

At its southern end, Silale merges into the enormous **Lamarkau Swamp** (whose name comes from *il armarkau*, Maasai for "hippo"), which itself merges into **Nguselororobi Swamp** (Maasai for "cold plains"). Both areas, together with Ngahari Swamp and Oldule Swamp in the park's southeastern extremity, are exceedingly remote and virtually unvisited.

Radilen Wildlife Management Area

Entering Radilen costs $10 a day, $15 if you stay overnight, plus $4 per vehicle, payable at road barriers • The main approach is along a track from the Arusha highway, which starts 3km west of Makuyuni (the village at the junction of the road to Mto wa Mbu & Katatu). The turning is signposted for Naitolia School, but the track itself is badly signposted

In 1999, villagers in the northeastern region of Tarangire were granted the title deeds to their lands, and created Tanzania's first community-managed conservation area, the 970-square-kilometre **Radilen Wildlife Management Area**. The communities here earn income from various lodges and camps, one of which (*Boundary Hill*) is half-owned by the villagers. The concept's success has led to similar conservation areas being set up elsewhere, including Burunge Wildlife Management Area, on Tarangire's west side (see below).

Although Radilen lacks the year-round wildlife interest of the national park, it straddles the migratory route, so sees large numbers of animals passing through from December to March – at this time of year, wildlife viewing can be better here than inside the park. The migration returns to Radilen in May–June, but long grass at that time hinders visibility. Radilen is also home to a sizeable permanent population of elephants, and the area's camps and lodges offer **guided bush walks** and **night game-drives** in addition to game drives. To visit the area, you'll either need to come on an organized safari, or stay overnight at one of the lodges or camps.

Lake Burunge and Burunge Wildlife Management Area

Entering Burunge costs $10 a day, $15 if you stay overnight, plus $4 per vehicle, payable at road barriers • Access is from a signposted road on the right just before the Tarangire National Park's northern entrance gate

The Tarangire River empties into **Lake Burunge**, a small soda lake just outside the park's western boundary, which is home to flocks of flamingos from July to November. The

---

BIRDWATCHING IN TARANGIRE

With its wide variety of habitats and food sources, **birdwatching** in and around Tarangire is a major draw, with over 550 species recorded to date, the highest count of any Tanzanian park, and about a third of all Tanzania's species. In the swampy floodplains in the south and east, Tarangire also contains some of earth's most important breeding grounds for **Eurasian migrants**. Wherever you are, you'll rarely be left in silence: birdsong starts well before dawn, and continues deep into the night.

It's impossible to give a full list of what's around, but to give an idea, the **woodlands** are particularly good for hoopoes and hornbills, brown parrots and the white-bellied go-away-bird (named after its curious call), as well as for game birds such as helmeted guinea fowl, yellow-necked spurfowl and crested francolin. Other commonly sighted birds include yellow-collared lovebirds and lilac-breasted rollers, barbets and mousebirds, swifts, striped swallows and starlings, bee-eaters, hammerkops, owls, plovers and cordon bleus. There are also four **bustard species**, including the kori, the world's heaviest flying bird, albeit usually seen on the ground. High above, especially close to hills, soar bateleur eagles, their name – "tumbler" in French – aptly describing their aerobatic skills. Over fifty other species of **raptors** (birds of prey) have been recorded, from steppe eagles (migrants from Russia) and giants such as lappet-faced vultures, to the tiny pygmy falcon.

The **best months** for birdwatching are from September or October to April or May, when the winter migrants are present, though access – especially to the swamp areas – can become impossible at the height of the long rains from March to May. A recommended company for **specialist birding safaris** is The East African Safari & Touring Company in Arusha (see p.289), whose trips are based at *Naitolia Camp* or *Boundary Hill Lodge*, both in Radilen Wildlife Management Area.

lake is surprisingly large, and makes a pretty picture with the Great Rift Valley's western escarpment in the background. There's no outlet, so salts and other minerals washed in by the river have turned the lake inhospitably saline for all bur flamingos, although during the rains the water is fresh enough to serve as a watering point for animals, including elephants and lions. The lake's shallowness (barely 2m) means that its extent fluctuates widely. It tends to dry up completely at the end of the dry season, leaving only a shimmer of encrusted salt on its surface.

The lake is in the **Burunge Wildlife Management Area**, a community-run conservation area, similar to Radilen, but with less enthralling wildlife. It has and plenty of lodges and camps to stay in, though it still allows hunting in some areas. The road from the north – the last 3km of which are impassable in the rains – crosses the Tarangire River south of the Tarangire National Park's northern gate. It's not the most spectacular game-viewing area, but you may catch glimpses of lesser kudu or eland, steinbok in undergrowth, and small herds of shy and rare fringe-eared oryx. Closer to the lake are plains of tussock grass and clumps of fan palms, hemmed in by acacia woodland and scattered baobabs, and weirdly imposing cactus-like "trees" – **candelabra euphorbia**. Their sap is extremely corrosive, so the trees are usually left well alone by wildlife: the exceptions were the rhinos, which sadly were poached to extinction in the park in the 1980s.

The plains are best for wildlife at either end of the migration, when they fill up with large herds of wildebeest and zebra. But the main species to leave a mark, literally, are **tsetse flies**, clouds of them, especially in the vicinity of wildebeest.

7

ESSENTIALS

TARANGIRE

Tarangire National Park entrance fees The main national park entrance gate (daily 6.30am–6.30pm) is 7km south of the Babati Highway, and the national park headquarters (daily 7.30am–5.30pm; ☎ 0689 062248 or ☎ 0767 536139, ⊛ tanzaniaparks.com/tarangire.html) lie 1km beyond the gate. National park entry fees, payable at the gates on the access roads, are $45 per person, plus Tsh20,000 per vehicle (both for 24hrs); Visa or MasterCard are accepted, but not cash.

Information Tarangire Visitor Centre (daily 8am–4.30pm), close to the park headquarters, has loads of information, a viewing platform built around a baobab tree, and an artificial waterhole to attract wildlife. TANAPA's colourful guidebook can be bought here or in bookshops in Arusha, Dar and Stone Town ($10). The best map is Giovanni Tombazzi's beautiful hand-painted version, with two plans, one each for the dry and rainy seasons; ensure you get the one titled "New", as the road network on the old one is obsolete.

ARRIVAL AND DEPARTURE

By organized safari Arusha's safari operators usually offer Tarangire as an optional extra after Ngorongoro and/or Serengeti. Day-trips are possible, but you'll spend at least two hours on the road in either direction. Particularly good value is an overnight trip offered by the East African Safari & Touring Company (see p.289) for $200 per person, which includes a night at *Naitolia* camp, a five-hour guided walk and night game drive; the minor catch is that you have to make your own way from Arusha to Makuyuni, at the junction of the road to Ngorongoro (several daladalas, minivans or buses an hour), where they'll pick you up. Additional nights cost $150, and game drives into the national park are $80 per person, including park fees.

By car 4WDs can be hired in Arusha (see p.288): the first 104km from Arusha to the junction at Minjing'u (also called Kigongoni or Kibaoni – "signboards") is fast tarmac; the remaining 7km are all-weather gravel. Special permission from the park gate or headquarters is required to enter or leave through other gates (marked on our map as ranger

posts). The most useful of these is Boundary Hill in the northeast for access to and from Radilen Wildlife Management Area, but you'll need to have paid the entrance fee at the main gate first. Hiring an official guide on arrival ($20) is recommended but not essential if you have a good map. Self-drive in the adjacent wildlife management areas is difficult: there are no decent maps, and hardly anything is signposted.

By plane Passengers should prebook with a lodge or safari camp, to pick you up, as scheduled flights use Kuro airstrip in the centre of the park. The airlines are Air Excel (☎ 027 254 8429, ⊛ airexcelonline.com) and, requiring at least two passengers, Coastal Aviation (☎ 0752 627825, ⊛ coastal.co.tz). Both fly a circular route between Arusha ($120) and the Serengeti ($300–380), with Coastal flying on to Dar ($380), Ruaha ($390) and Zanzibar ($370).

Destinations Arusha (2 daily; 15min); Dar (1 daily; 5hr); Manyara (2 daily; 15min); Ndutu (2 daily; 2hr 45min); Ruaha (1 daily; 1hr 20min); Serengeti (2 daily; 3hr–4hr 40min); Zanzibar (1 daily; 4hr 20min).

TOURS AND ACTIVITIES

Balloon flights For a bird's eye view of Tarangire, Adventures Aloft (☎027 254 3300 or ☎0685 250153, ⓦmadahotels.com) offers early morning balloon flights for $450 per person, including a pre-dawn pick-up from lodges and camps inside the park.

Bush walks A bush walk is at times a heart-racing way to get a feel for the wild, and see the many details you'd miss from a car, such as the territorial markings of dikdiks. Walks are offered by some of the expensive camps in the national park, and – guided by Maasai – by the camps and lodges in the adjacent wildlife management areas.

Night game drives Spotlight night-time game drives are offered by the camps and lodges in Radilen Wildlife Management Area, giving you the chance of seeing otherwise elusive animals such as leopards and fringe-eared oryx. Strangely, they're quite unfazed by the lights.

ACCOMMODATION

There are **lodges and tented camps** in both the park and in the wildlife management areas. The cheapest overnight accommodation inside the park is **camping**; there are also a few campsites outside the park close to Minjing'u on the highway at the junction with the park's access road, where you should be able to arrange a safari if you have a day or two to spare. Minjing'u also has some surprisingly decent **guesthouses** used by safari drivers (no running water). For **food** most safari lodges and tented camps will pack you a picnic or a lunchbox, or you're welcome for a proper lunch at *Tarangire Safari Lodge* ($20), which has a great location. Minjing'u has basic *hotelis* and bars, and there are more along the park's access road, where you'll also find shady picnic spots operated by women's groups selling drinks and souvenirs.

TARANGIRE NATIONAL PARK

★**Maweninga Camp** 32km from the park gate ☎0784 228883 (Arusha) or ☎0752 994733, ⓦmaweninga -camp.com. On top of a kopje with views of Lake Burunge, 10km west and great sunsets, this French-owned place is staffed mostly by Maasai and has relatively few frills, but is a comfortable, stylish and personal base. Rooms are in sixteen well-equipped en-suite tents on polished wooden decks, all perched right on the kopje's edge, with marvellous views from their verandas. The cosy lounge and dining room also have views, but its hilltop location means there's no wildlife in the immediate vicinity other than hyraxes. Solar-powered electricity and hot water. FB €450

Sanctuary Swala Close to Gursi Swamp, 67km inside the park ☎027 250 9817 (Arusha), ⓦsanctuaryretreats .com. Sheltered in an acacia grove, the twelve luxurious en-suite tents here are stuffed with period furniture and each has a terrace overlooking a waterhole frequented by waterbuck, *swala* (impala), lions, elephants and leopards. Optional activities (included in the game package) are night game drives and walking safaris. No children under 12. Closed April–May. FB $1248, game package $1622

TANAPA public campsite 4km south of the park gate; pay at the park gate. The park's main campsite has decent enough facilities (plenty of shade, few tsetse flies, flush toilets and cold showers), but minimal wildlife interest. Firewood collection is forbidden, so bring gas cans, or buy charcoal at Minjing'u before entering the park. Per person $30

TANAPA special campsites Various locations; book in advance via the park headquarters (see p.319). Deep in the park are several "special" campsites. None has facilities of any kind, but they are often close to wildlife – an unnerving experience, for which the park may insist you also hire an armed ranger ($20). Per person $50

★**Tarangire Safari Lodge** High above the Tarangire River, 10km inside the park ☎027 254 4752 (Arusha) or ☎0784 202777, ⓦtarangiresafarilodge.com. The cheapest lodge in the park, and a long-standing favourite, primarily on account of its superb location, which allows wonderful wildlife viewing around the river below (binoculars recommended). The forty rooms and permanent tents are fine, and have verandas facing a lawn, often browsed by dikdiks at night. There's also a large swimming pool, a reasonably priced restaurant for hearty farmhouse-style meals (and affordable wines), and equally well-priced activities, including 1–2hr bush walks ($45–60 per person), night game drives ($70–100 per person) and game drives in an open vehicle (from $100 per vehicle for half a day). Accessible to wheelchairs. Wi-fi in the lounge. HB $360

RADILEN WILDLIFE MANAGEMENT AREA

★**Boundary Hill Lodge** 47km from the highway ☎0787 293727, ⓦtanzanianhorizons.info. Perched high on the rocky hillside, this is ruggedly romantic ecofriendly (relying on rainwater, solar panels and wind turbines) and 50 percent owned by the Maasai village of Lolkisale. Its eight spacious and very comfortable brick rooms (including a family room for the same price as a double) are partly built into the hillside and have spectacular views over the Silale and Gosuwa swamps (including from the toilet and the outdoor bathtub in the honeymoon suite; $500 a night). Activities, free if staying two nights, are bush walks guided by a Maasai *moran* ($10 per person), game drives ($80 per person

and night game drives with spotlights ($40 per person). FB $400

★**Naitolia** 18km from the highway ☏0787 293727, ⓦtanzanianhorizons.info. Located in baobab- and acacia-studded woodland, this is an intimate and informal place with friendly staff, and just three secluded stone-and-canvas rooms with spectacular views of the Lemiyon plains. All have flush toilets and bucket showers but no electricity other than solar lighting and battery charging. Activities include bush walks, sundowners on a nearby hill, night game drives, fly camping amid baobabs and in a (dry) sand river, and incredible birding (450 species and counting). Terrific value for money. FB (including activities if staying two nights) $280

Tarangire Treetops Lodge 37km from the highway ☏027 250 0630 (Arusha), ⓦelewanacollection.com. The ultimate in bush chic, but at prices that will leave you seeing reeling (and for which you might reasonably expect a little more exclusivity: the place houses up to forty guests). The accommodation is in twenty quirkily romantic tree-house tents with two beds, stone bathrooms, electricity, and sweeping 270-degree views from their balconies. The dining room is built close to a small swimming pool and waterhole used by elephants. Wi-fi in public areas. FB $1490, game package $1690

BURUNGE WILDLIFE MANAGEMENT AREA

★**Osupuko Lodge** 5.5km from the park gate, north side of the Tarangire River ☏0754 657737, ⓦosupukolodges.com. Tanzanian owned and run, with twelve spacious modern bungalows, each fitted with two showers (one outdoors, with views), electricity, fans and two verandas, with nice views over the park, including from the swimming pool and restaurant. The food is good, and the wines include some decent Tanzanian vintages, too. The place is famed as much for its super friendly staff as for its proximity to wildlife, including elephants just passing through. A raft of activities are on offer, including bush cycling, and "guided" star gazing, birding or "footprint walks" (at dawn), visits to Maasai bomas and community development projects, and occasional dances at night. Bush walks are included in the price, you'll need your own vehicle for game drives, including at night, or $300 to hire theirs for the day. Wi-fi. FB $360

★**Tarangire Roika Tented Lodge** 6km from the park gate, north side of the Tarangire River ☏027 250 9994 or ☏0754 001 444, ⓦtarangireroikatentedlodge.com. With lots of wood and thatch around its 21 tented rooms (all with private balconies, and amusing animal-shaped bathtubs at the back), this Maasai-run place doesn't pretend to be fancy, but the elephants that sneak in to drink from the swimming pool don't care (July–Feb, especially Aug), and nor should you: the staff are consistently welcoming, it's just a 20min drive from the park gate, lions and hyenas will serenade you at night, and there are plenty of activities, including bush meals and riverside sundowners, bush walks and boma visits, night game drives, and a couple of bizarre treats: fishing for tilapia in their fish ponds, and treasure hunts! Dodgy wi-fi. HB $340

MINJING'U AND AROUND

Minjing'u is the settlement at the junction of the 7km access road that leads to the park gate. There's no wildlife interest in the immediate vicinity, so the main reason to stay here is for a cheap night, and – for those coming by bus – to arrange a safari at the Zion Campsite.

Lake View Diamond Maasai Lodge 1.9km east of Minjing'u, then 500m north ☏0755 906607 or ☏0788 379555, ⓦlodgetarangire.com. This once plain campsite has some small and very dark rooms in flat-topped concrete boxes that resemble tembe homes, which are massively overpriced. Camping is much better value, and there is indeed a lake view (of Lake Manyara) in the distance, which you can enjoy from its breezy, open-sided bar. Lunch and dinner can be arranged; all prices are negotiable. Camping per pitch $10, rooms (BB, double) $100

Sulvan Guest House 100m along the park's access road from Minjing'u. The best of Minjing'u's safari driver lodgings, this guesthouse is clean, friendly and safe, and serves good cheap food too. En-suite rooms cost Tsh5000 extra. BB Tsh10,000

Zion Campsite 1km along the park's access road from Minjing'u ☏0754 460539 or ☏0754 318414. A dusty but tree-shaded patch, with clean toilets and showers (hot water mornings and evenings), and a kitchen. There are drinks, but no food – you'll find several cheap hotelis back up the road. They can arrange safaris but will need time to do so: as the place almost always has people staying, you might be able to share a safari with someone. Per person $10

Mto wa Mbu

Turning north at Makuyuni, the highway skirts the eastern edge of Lake Manyara's flood plain for 31km to **MTO WA MBU** ("River of Mosquitoes"), a small but lively town that is the main base for visiting Lake Manyara. It was just a village when, in the 1950s, the colonial government began an ambitious irrigation project aimed at controlling Lake Manyara's cyclical floods and turning "unproductive" swampland into farmland. The project was a big success, attracting farmers from all around, and in the

1960s Mto wa Mbu was declared a collective **Ujamaa village** as part of Tanzania's ultimately disastrous experiment in "African socialism". The legacy of *Ujamaa* is evident in the town's extraordinary **ethnic diversity**: it's home to almost fifty tribes, including Hehe from Iringa; Gogo, Gorowa, Mbugwe, Nyamwezi and Rangi from central Tanzania; Barbaig, Hadzabe and Maasai from the local region; Ha from Kigoma on the shore of Lake Tanganyika; and the Il Larusa, Chagga, Iraqw and Meru from the north and northeast. You get to know more about them via the town's excellent cultural tourism programme (see below).

Central market
South side of the highway • Sunrise–sunset

Given Mto wa Mbu's diversity, the town's markets are among the liveliest and most colourful in the country. The **central market** is a mishmash of shops and stalls where you'll find pretty much anything that's produced locally, including many of the town's estimated eighty varieties of **bananas**. One corner of the market, the so-called "Maasai Central Market", is a tourist trap flogging the usual trinkets such as Maasai beadwork jewellery and tartan *shuka* cloth, but an enjoyable one at that.

Animal auction and monthly market
3km east of Mto wa Mbu, just before the road to Lake Natron • Animal auction Thurs sunrise–sunset • Monthly market on the 22nd of each month, sunrise–sunset

An "authentic" Maasai experience can be had at the weekly roadside **animal auction**, 5km east of town, or at the **monthly market** (*mnada*) on the same site, which attracts buyers and herders from as far away as the Zanaki tribe of the Mara Region. Some of these herders continue to Arusha, and a handful even make it to Dar es Salaam – an epic journey of over 900km.

ARRIVAL AND DEPARTURE   MTO WA MBU

By bus There's no bus stand in town: buses and other vehicles stop outside the *Red Banana Café* on the highway. At least three buses leave Mto wa Mbu in the morning (the last around 10am), along the 113km sealed road to Arusha, turning back from Arusha in the afternoon. "Noahs" (minivans) cover the same route, and also run from Makuyuni, close to Tarangire National Park, and Karatu. Long-distance buses from Dar es Salaam to Karatu pass through – the safest, relatively speaking, is Dar Express; avoid Sai Baba, which has had countless fatal crashes.

Destinations Arusha (3–4 daily plus Noahs; 2hr 30min–3hr); Dar (2 daily; 11hr 30min–12hr); Engaruka (1 daily; 2hr); Karatu (hourly Noahs; 30min); Makuyuni (hourly Noahs; 30min).

By car Vehicles for safaris, with driver included, can be hired at *Twiga Campsite & Lodge* (see p.324), *Panorama Safari Camp* (see p.328), and through the cultural tourism programme (see below). Costs, excluding park fees, average $150 per vehicle per day for Manyara, and $200 for Ngorongoro.

TOURS AND SERVICES

Internet access Wireless internet access is available at the central lodge/campsites, and is free at *Sunbright Campsite* if you take a meal or drinks.

Money Strangely, for such a busy place, Mto wa Mbu has no ATMs that accept foreign credit cards – the closest machines are in Karatu.

CULTURAL TOURISM
Mto wa Mbu's ethnic diversity is best experienced through its successful cultural tourism programme, based at *Red Banana Café* on the highway, next to *Scorpion Pub* (daily 6am–8pm; ☎ 0784 606654 or ☎ 0767 606644, ⓦ tanzaniaculturaltourism.go.tz/mtowambu.htm). The various guided tours on offer are good for getting to

know a wide variety of tribes, as all include visits to farms, local artisans, Maasai *bomas*, and small-scale development projects. Tours last up to a day, and most cost $35 per person for cycling, and $20 per person for walks, including a traditional meal prepared by a women's group.

Farming tour Starting at the market, the farming tour covers a number of *shambas* north of town, where you'll meet farmers and see banana beer being brewed by Chagga, who moved here from Kilimanjaro, and taste the result.

Lake trips A visit to the papyrus-fringed Lake Miwaleni, 5km north of town at the foot of escarpment, together with a waterfall, is accessed by trails along small streams. There also are trips to Lake Manyara by bike (without entering the national park, but $10 per person is levied at government-run roadblocks to enter the Jangwani Wildlife Corridor), to view the game as well as some enormous baobabs.

Forest hikes The most adventurous option is the Selela Forest Hike, on the flank of the escarpment some 25km towards Lake Natron, for a clamber up the scarp to Upper Kitote village along trails opened by elephants ($45 per person excluding transport there and back).

ACCOMMODATION

Mto wa Mbu has accommodation to suit all budgets, though be wary of places that attempt to sell you significantly more expensive full-board options when bed and breakfast or bed-only is also available. If you prefer to stay out of town, there are several decent options on top of the escarpment, 4km west of Mto wa Mbu, which boast great views of Lake Manyara (see pp.327–328)

Camp Vision Lodge South of the highway (walk 50m west along from Double 'M', then turn left and go down two blocks) 0765 378645 or 0783 941814. The thirteen cell-like rooms here are perfectly fine (with box nets too), as are the showers, and it's safe, including for cars. The shared squat toilets have seen better days, though you can opt for en-suite rooms for an extra Tsh7000. **Tsh8000**

Chotikungu Lodge North of the highway behind Red Banana Café 0758 381022. The most welcoming of several guesthouses in this area, it's scruffy but exceptionally cheap, and adequate if you're used to such places. The "singles", sharing bathrooms, have a double bed; the "doubles" have two beds, and are en suite with hot water (Tsh12,000–15,000); the slightly more expensive ones have TVs. **Tsh6000**

Fanaka Campsite 1.25km east of the bus stop along the highway, then 500m north 0769 564170 or 0787 569099, fanakasafaricamps.co.tz. With an unmissable two-story gazebo at its entrance, this is good value, both for camping on the slightly formal lawns (with spotless bathrooms) or in proper rooms. The latter, some bigger than others, come with TVs, fans, box nets and hot showers; breakfast is $20 extra per room. There's also a swimming pool, a decent if unexciting restaurant ($10 for three courses), and a lounge in the gazebo. Free wi-fi for guests. Camping per person **$10** or **$20** in their tents, rooms **$40**

Migunga Tented Camp 2km east of the bus stop along the highway, then 1.5km south 027 250 6315 or 0754 324193 (Arusha), moivaro.com. Sitting pretty in a forest of yellow-bark acacia trees, this sophisticated yet unpretentious Dutch-run hideaway is the best of four campsites in the area, and also has nineteen en-suite tents and three bungalows, all with balconies facing a central lawn, where you can pitch your own tent. There's a pleasant open-sided bar and dining room, and activities ($15–20 per person) include cycling safaris,

nature walks and cultural tours. Camping per person **$15**, rooms HB **$318**

Njake Jambo Lodge & Campsite 1.3km east of the bus stop on the highway 0755 278187, njaketours@yahoo.com. Rivalling *Twiga* as the largest and busiest in town, this campsite is bordered by half a dozen two-storey brick houses split into smart, en-suite rooms, all large, with big beds or smaller twins, adequate nets and cable TV. Rooms on upper floors are brighter, and it's good value if you take a room without meals. There's also a swimming pool, and a bar. The meals are overpriced at more than $20, but there's a cheap pizza place next door. Camping per person **$10**, rooms BB **$60**, FB **$145**

★ Sunbright Campsite 1.65km east of the bus stop along the highway, then 250m north 0787 081111 or 027 250 6708, sunbrighthotels.com. Cheerful rustic-style place with loads more character than the more central campsite-lodges. It's not luxurious by any stretch, but comfortable, and has some charming touches, like the sunken campfire. Apart from camping, there are seven colourful if dark rooms, and twelve unadorned en-suite tents under thatched roofs, plus a swimming pool, a good poolside restaurant, free wi-fi, and enthusiastic guides to accompany you for birding. If a tent appeals, go for the more expensive "deluxe" ones, which are much larger. Camping per person **$10**, rooms and tents (BB double) **$70**

Twiga Campsite & Lodge 1.2km east of the bus stop on the highway 0783 555333 or 0716 239511, twigacampsitelodge.com. Dozens of en-suite twins and triples with hot water in the mornings and evenings, fans and box nets; the more expensive rooms are the same but with TVs. There's a swimming pool, bar and restaurant (order early to get what you want; $10 for three courses), and expensive wi-fi ($6/hr). The campsite is popular with overland trucks, and camping equipment is available to rent (tent $10, sleeping bag $5, mattress $5). They can also arrange safaris. Camping per person **$10**, rooms (BB) **$50**

EATING AND DRINKING

Rembo One block south of the market; turn south at Oryx petrol station and then left. Despite its dissolute

appearance, this is one of the better local restaurants, rustling up tasty and filling meals for under Tsh3000. Like

most of Mto wa Mbu's restaurants, it doubles as a bar and gets lively in the evenings. Daily 7am–midnight.
Double 'M' North side of the highway just west of Red Banana. Open throughout the day and for much of the night, this is an extremely popular nightspot, whether for a drink, or a meal, with dishes such as *nyama choma*

(Tsh8000/kg for beef, Tsh7000 for goat). Daily 24hrs
Sunbright Campsite 1.65km east of the bus stop along the highway, then 250m north. The town's best restaurant, with a short but appealing menu ($10 a meal), which always includes dishes from all over Africa, not just Tanzania, such as a Moroccan *tajine*. Daily 8am–8pm.

Lake Manyara National Park

Nestling at the foot of the Great Rift Valley's 600m-high western escarpment, Lake Manyara is a shallow soda lake whose northwestern section is protected within the **Lake Manyara National Park**. Despite its small size, the park contains a wide range of **habitats** including evergreen groundwater forest fed by springs, a swampy fan delta crowning the top of the lake, acacia woodland scattered with baobab trees, a small grassy plain and, of course, the lake itself. Together, they provide an oasis for wildlife, and the presence of year-round water makes the lake part of the same migratory system as Tarangire (see p.314). The result is a wide variety of **animals**, including elephants, great flocks of pink flamingo, large hippo pods, and much-hyped "tree-climbing lions". For many visitors, however, the park's great highlight is its particularly impressive **birdlife**.

The **best time to visit** for viewing big mammals is June/July to Sept/Oct, and Jan–Feb. For birds, Nov–May is best, but try to avoid the park from March to May, when heavy rains can limit road access to the far north. A day should be sufficient to see most of the park's sights. For a bird's-eye view of the lot, take the road from Mto wa Mbu up to the top of the Rift Valley escarpment (en route to Ngorongoro), and you'll get increasingly breathtaking views of Lake Manyara and the green expanse of vegetation around its shore. There's a **viewpoint** on top, as well as a number of lodges and campsites (see pp.327–328).

The wildlife

Manyara is perhaps most memorable for its **elephants**, which number around three hundred – down from 640 in the 1960s. Other impressive denizens include **buffalo**, sometimes in large herds, which feed on sedge by the lakeshore, and two hundred **hippos**, seen in water pools in the northern fan delta. **Antelope** include impala, bushbuck and waterbuck, and agile klipspringers on the rocky escarpment wall. Other plains game include zebra, giraffe, mongoose and warthog, together with their predators: leopards and, famously, **tree-climbing lions**, which are sometimes seen resting up in the boughs of acacia trees south of the groundwater forest – your best bet for spotting them is between June and August. The reason for their arboreal prowess is a mystery, though it's possibly an attempt to avoid the unwelcome attention of tsetse flies. **Primates** are represented by blue monkeys and vervet monkeys in the forest, and numerous baboon troops.

The vervets are preyed on by crested hawk eagles, one of Manyara's over 380 bird species. The shallow lakeshore is especially favoured by **water birds**, including pelicans, storks, herons, ibis, jacanas, egrets, plovers and lots of ducks and geese. But the undoubted avian stars are the vast, spectacular flocks of pink **flamingos**, attracted by the profusion of algae in the lake's shallow, alkaline waters.

The groundwater forest

Much of the park is covered by evergreen **groundwater forest**, which starts just outside Mto wa Mbu as you head west towards the park gate. It's a soothingly cool, refreshing habitat, which looks and feels like rainforest, but is fed by water from mineral springs seeping through the porous volcanic soil. Its thick tangle of bush and trees includes tall mahogany, croton and sausage trees, tamarind, wild date palms and strangling fig trees

7

– spotting wildlife here is harder than in the savanna, but it's all the more dramatic when an animal suddenly appears out of the vegetation.

This habitat is home to blue **monkeys**, vervet monkeys and baboons, who crash around in the branches (especially at the picnic site by the park gate), plus **elephants**, who use the larger trees as back-scrubbers. As for the **birdlife**, ground birds are most easily seen, including two species of guinea fowl, and the large silvery-cheeked hornbill, which lives in the canopy but is often seen on the ground. Also look out for **forest plants** such as orchids, which benefit from the shade of the trees.

The fan delta and hippo pools

About 4km southwest of the park gate along the main track is a signposted left turn towards a loop road around **Mahali pa Nyati** – the Place of Buffaloes – which is a good place for spotting those rather cantankerous and temperamental beasts. They are invariably accompanied by ox-peckers and buff-backed herons feeding on insects disturbed by the passing of their hosts. South of the buffalo circuit is another loop leading to the mouth of the Mto wa Mbu River, and a series of **hippo pools**.

The acacia woodland

To the south and east of the groundwater forest is more open **woodland**, dominated by umbrella acacias and dotted here and there by ancient baobab trees. It's a good habitat for all sorts of big game, especially elephant, giraffe and buffalo, and is good for spotting birdlife too, including various species of plover and kingfishers, larks and wagtails.

The Msasa and Ndala rivers

South of the groundwater forest, the park's main track crosses a series of small rivers, sometimes by bridge, other times by causeways that can become impassable if the rains hit hard. The main watercourse in the park's northern section is the **Msasa River**. This area is good for seeing solitary old male buffaloes, and if you're going to see **lions in trees**, it'll be here. There's a signposted picnic site under a big tree with benches, tables, a lake view and often uncomfortably close sightings of buffalo. There are two more picnic sites near the **Ndala River**, 9km south of the Msasa River, one of which has good lake views. The presence of buffalo, often in large herds, means tsetse flies start to be a nuisance south of the Msasa River.

The hot springs

Along the lake's western shore, flamingos can be seen close to a series of picturesque but pungently sulphurous **hot springs**, which are heated by geothermal activity associated with the Rift Valley's ongoing expansion. There are two main groups: the smaller but most accessible are **Maji Moto Ndogo**, 22km south of the park gate, which keep to a very pleasant 33°C and get covered whenever the lake level is high. Just over 17km further south, past the patch of grassland formed by the modest delta of the Endabash River, are the bigger and more scalding **Maji Moto Kubwa** springs, whose temperature averages 76°C – hot enough to give you a nasty burn and melt the soles of your shoes if you wander too close. They're at their most impressive when the lake level is low, and then especially in the rains when the water erupts in a series of highly pressurized flumes. Even when the lake level is high, however, there are some small springs closer to the road, which have remarkably beautiful colours and patterns formed by the heat- and sulphur-loving algal blooms, lichens and assorted moulds growing in and around the shallow pools.

ESSENTIALS   **LAKE MANYARA NATIONAL PARK**

Entrance fees Entrance fees are payable (by Visa or MasterCard, but not cash) at the park gate, 2km west of | Mto wa Mbu, just off the highway. Fees are $45 per person plus Tsh20,000 per vehicle, both valid 24hrs. The park headquarters are by the park gate (daily 6.30am–5.30pm ☎ 027 253 9112, ☎ 0689 062294 or ☎ 0767 536137, ⓦ tanzaniaparks.com/manyara.html).

Information The best source of information is the TANAPA guidebook to Manyara, available in Arusha ($10). An accurate map is published by Harms-Ic-Verlag in association with TANAPA, not that you really need one; more attractive is the hand-painted map by Giovanni Tombazzi.

ARRIVAL AND DEPARTURE

By organized safari Safaris can be arranged locally in Mto wa Mbu (see p.323), and needn't involve hiring a vehicle, as bush walks are also possible (see below). Coming from Arusha (see pp.288–289 for recommended companies), the park is best combined with one or two other parks over several days.

By car For self-drive, 4WD is recommended, but 2WD will get you to most places inside the park in dry weather.

By plane Lake Manyara airstrip is on top of the escarpment, 6km from the park gate, 7.5km from Mto wa Mbu. Airlines flying here are: Air Excel (AE; ⓦ airexcelonline.com); Auric Air (AA; ⓦ auricair.com); Coastal Aviation (CA; ⓦ coastal .co.tz); Regional Air (RA; ⓦ regionaltanzania.com); and Safari Airlink (SA; ⓦ flysal.com). The quickest airlines are listed below.

Destinations Arusha (AE CA RA SA: 8 daily; 20–25min); Dar (CA AE: 3 daily; 3hr–4hr 35min); Kilimanjaro (SA AE CA: 4 daily; 55min–2hr 45min); Mwanza (CA: 1 daily; 3hr); Ndutu (RA CA AE AA SA: 6 daily; 25min–1hr 45min); Pangani (SA: 1 daily; 8hr 10min); Ruaha (SA: 1 daily; 1hr 10min); Saadani (SA: 1 daily; 8hr 20min); Selous (CA: 1 daily; 4hr); Serengeti (RA AA CA AE SA: 7 daily; 35min–2hr 20min); Zanzibar (AE: 1 daily; 4hr).

TOURS AND ACTIVITIES

Bush walks Walking safaris are a nice change from being stuck in a car, but bear in mind that you won't be able to venture as far. Walks last three to four hours on average, and cost $20 for the obligatory ranger, in additional to park entry fees. You can arrange walks directly through the park headquarters, but it's easier to let Mto wa Mbu's cultural tourism programme handle things (see p.323).

Night game drives For night game drives, the park charges an additional $50 per person on top of the normal entry fee. Even if you have already paid to enter the park during the day, you are supposed to pay the fee again to re-enter, though in practice this is rarely enforced. Without your own vehicle, three-hour nocturnal safaris are offered by Wayo Africa (ⓦ wayoafrica.com), for whom Mto wa Mbu's cultural tourism programme (see p.323) acts as a go-between. The cost is $155 to $180 per person, depending on group size, and includes park fees.

ACCOMMODATION AND EATING

Accommodation inside the national park is limited to park-run campsites and *bandas*, plus an obscenely expensive tented camp. There's much more accommodation just outside the park, either on the escarpment above it, or in Mto wa Mbu (see p.324). Meals at lodges on the escarpment average $20–30, but the restaurant at the *Panorama Safari Camp* (see p.328) is cheaper, and way more characterful, and is open to non-residents.

INSIDE THE PARK

TANAPA bandas Just inside the park gate; book through the park headquarters (see above). A complex of ten brick cottages which, although basic, are comfortable, and have hot showers, proper toilets and electricity but no nets. There's no food, but firewood is supplied free of charge, and there's a kitchen and dining room. Per person **$30**

TANAPA public campsites Just inside the park gate; bookings not required; pay at the park gate. Three sites close to the *bandas*, each occupying a lovely forest clearing, all with toilets and cold showers. Although camping in Mto wa Mbu is much cheaper, the beauty and intimacy of these sites can't be matched. Don't bother with the three "special" campsites further into the park ($50), which are pricier and nothing special. Per person **$30**

ON THE ESCARPMENT

Kirurumu Manyara Lodge On the escarpment, 6km northeast of the highway ☎ 027 250 2417 (Arusha), ⓦ kirurumu.net. Twenty-two large, mostly twin-bed, en-suite tents on the ridge, some with lake views from their shady verandas. The lodge grounds are aflutter with birds, and the excellent restaurant serves produce from its organic garden. Ethno-botanical walks accompanied by Maasai warriors are offered, and fly camping in a nearby forest can be arranged. Good value compared with the other luxury options. FB **$346**

Lake Manyara Serena Safari Lodge On the escarpment, 2km northeast of the highway past the airstrip ☎ 027 253 9160 (Arusha), ⓦ serenahotels.com. The poshest of the escarpment lodges, whose painfully formal service makes it hard to remember you're on safari. Only a few of the 67 two-storey rondavels have lake views,

7

LAKE EYASI AND THE HADZABE

Occupying a shallow trough in the shadow of Ngorongoro's Mount Oldeani **Lake Eyasi** is another of the Rift Valley's soda lakes. In the dry woodland around its edges live the **Hadzabe tribe**. Numbering between five hundred and 2500, depending on how you count, the Hadzabe are Tanzania's last hunter-gatherers, a status they shared with the Sandawe further south until the latter were forced to settle forty years ago. Sadly, the Hadzabe appear to be heading the same way: much of their land has been taken by commercial plantations and ranches, which also form effective barriers to the seasonal wildlife migrations on which the hunting part of the Hadzabe lifestyle depends, while the unwelcome attentions of outsiders – notably tourists – is rapidly destroying their culture.

Short of convincing the Tanzanian government to protect Hadzabe land and its wildlife routes (most unlikely given the government's previous attempts to forcibly "civilize" the Hadzabe), the best thing you can do is to help **preserve their culture**. In the absence of any kind of tourism that directly benefits and is controlled by them, this means leaving them well alone.

7

but the vista from the swimming pool goes on, and on, and on… The gardens are not wild but planted with mostly indigenous species. FB $660

Lake Manyara Wildlife Lodge On the escarpment, 3km southeast of the highway ☎027 254 4595 or ☎0754 254600 (Arusha), ⒲hotelsandlodges-tanzania .com. A 1970s concrete hulk with magnificent views over the lake from most of its one hundred bedrooms. There's also a swimming pool, but it's rather bland for the price. FB $550

Njake Manyara View Lodge On the escarpment, just off the highway 100m beyond the turning for Panorama Safari Camp ☎027 250 1329, ⒠njaketours @yahoo.com. This is often empty, which is a shame, as it's well priced for its quirky mixture of cottages (not all with views though), ranging from colonial-style chalets, some built of wood, to a pair of fake baobab trees made of concrete, each containing two comfy guest rooms (great views). There's also a swimming pool (with view), and a massive thatched dining-cum-reception area

(meals $20 per person). BB $150, HB $200

★**Panorama Safari Camp** On the escarpment, 500m north of the highway beside the mobile-phone masts ☎0765 379641 or ☎0784 118514, ⒲panoramasafari .com. Gorgeously sited, this friendly, Hungarian-owned campsite has a series of individual pitches scattered around, some with vertiginous views from the escarpment edge, though most have their views obscured by trees. Visitors without tents can stay in one theirs, or sleep in "African igloos", made of mud covered in cement, containing one or two beds – there are plans to add bathrooms. The shared bathrooms, with piping hot showers, are squeaky clean. You can self-cater (they sell charcoal and have a kitchen), or eat at the funky, open-sided bar/restaurant/lounge, where meals are always fresh and feature plenty of fruit and veg, for a bargain $10. Free wi-fi, good gift shop, and car hire can be arranged ($200 per day including driver and fuel). Bookings advisable. Camping per person $10, ready-erected tents for two $20, "igloos" for two $45

Ngorongoro and around

One of Tanzania's best-known wildlife refuges is **Ngorongoro Conservation Area**, which together with the adjoining Serengeti National Park forms an immensely rich ecosystem. Ngorongoro's highlight is an enormous volcanic crater, providing one of Africa's most stunning backdrops for viewing a glut of wildlife, especially lion, elephant and highly endangered black rhino. Unsurprisingly, Ngorongoro is Tanzania's most visited wildlife attraction, with some 450,000 tourists a year. For some, the large number of visitors spoils the experience of being in a true wilderness – and the authorities are now tackling this with a massive increase in the entrance fees. Nonetheless, for all the tourists, the hype and the expense, Ngorongoro – designated a World Heritage Site in 1979 – is still a place that enchants, and few people leave disappointed.

There's plenty of upmarket **accommodation** inside the conservation area, as well as campsites, and a wide spread of hotels in **Karatu town**, 15km before its eastern gate.

Karatu

The dusty town of **KARATU** – periodically swept by red twisters in spite of the sealed road – is the main supply base for the Ngorongoro Conservation Area, and an obvious place to stay if you can't afford Ngorongoro's lodges and don't want to camp. Capital of a densely populated district, the town enjoys a fresher climate than Mto wa Mbu, and a lively **cultural tourism programme** through which you can get to learn more about the local Iraqw tribe. The **best day to visit** the town is on the 7th or 25th of each month, when a big market and livestock auction (*mnada*) attracts thousands of Maasai and Barbaig cattle herders, and Iraqw farmers.

ARRIVAL AND DEPARTURE

KARATU

By bus Buses leave Arusha around 2–3pm for the 3–4hr journey to Karatu along a good tarmac road. Buses back to Arusha leave Karatu at daybreak, after which time you can catch a Noah (minivans are gradually replacing the ancient Peugeot saloons). Dar Express is probably the safest bus company from Dar.

Destinations Arusha (3 daily plus Noahs; 4hr); Dar (2 daily; 12–13hr); Mto wa Mbu (hourly Noahs; 30min).

7

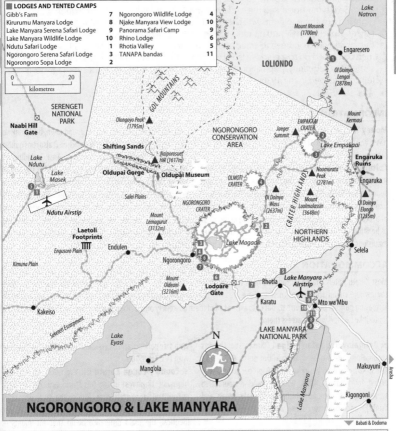

■ LODGES AND TENTED CAMPS

Gibb's Farm	7	Ngorongoro Wildlife Lodge	4
Kirurumu Manyara Lodge	8	Njake Manyara View Lodge	10
Lake Manyara Serena Safari Lodge	9	Panorama Safari Camp	9
Lake Manyara Wildlife Lodge	10	Rhino Lodge	6
Ndutu Safari Lodge	1	Rhotia Valley	5
Ngorongoro Serena Safari Lodge	3	TANAPA bandas	11
Ngorongoro Sopa Lodge	2		

NGORONGORO & LAKE MANYARA

● CAMPSITES

Empakaai Crater 1 special campsite	2	Nyati special campsite	7	Tembo A special campsite	9
Empakaai Crater 2 special campsite	3	Simba A special campsite	6	Tembo B special campsite	9
Lake Ndutu special campsites	5	Simba B special campsite	6	Waterfall Camp	1
Nanokanoka special campsite	4	TANAPA public campsites	8		

THE IRAQW

Karatu's main tribes are the cattle-herding Barbaig (see p.227) and the agricultural Iraqw. The history of the two-hundred-thousand-strong **Iraqw**, who occupy much of the area between Karatu and Mbulu town in the south, is fascinating, though the theory that they originally came from Mesopotamia (Iraq, no less) is unlikely. More likely is the link between the Iraqw and Ethiopia: their languages are closely related, and there's also physical resemblance, particularly their facial features, which are finer than those of their neighbours.

Exactly when the Iraqw arrived in Tanzania is not known, but a number of clues are offered by their agricultural practices – the use of sophisticated terracing to limit soil erosion, complex irrigation techniques, crop rotation and manure from stall-fed cattle – and provide uncanny parallels to the ruined irrigation channels, terraces and cattle pens of Engaruka (see p.352), at the foot of the Great Rift Valley's escarpment.

Iraqw **legend** makes no mention of Engaruka but does talk of a place called **Ma'angwatay**, which may have been their name for it. At the time, the Iraqw lived under a chief called **Haymu Tipe**, whose only son, Gemakw, was kidnapped by a group of young Iraqw warriors and hidden in the forest. Finally locating him, Haymu Tipe was given a curious ultimatum: unless he brought the warriors an enemy to fight, his son would be killed. So Haymu Tipe asked the cattle-herding Barbaig, who occupied the Ngorongoro highlands, to come to fight, which they did. It seems that the Iraqw lost the battle, as Haymu Tipe, his family and his remaining men fled to a place called Guser-Twalay, where Gemakw – who had been released as agreed – became ill and died. Haymu Tipe and his men continued on to a place called Qawirang in a forest west of Lake Manyara, where they settled. Subsequently, population pressure led to further migrations; the first Iraqw to settle in Karatu arrived in the 1930s.

INFORMATION

Money You can change money at NBC Bank, which also has a Visa/MasterCard ATM, as does Exim; both are on the highway.

Cultural tourism The office of Ganako Karatu cultural tourism programme is on the highway beside Miriam supermarket (daily 9am–5pm; ☎0767 612980, ✉kcecho .org or ⓦtanzaniaculturaltourism.go.tz/ganako.htm). Part of a locally run non-profit organization working in the areas of health, environmental education and culture, it arranges excursions to coffee plantations (fine Arabica has long been cultivated here), markets, walks around town, brick-making visits and lavish traditional Iraqw lunches. It also runs guided hikes inside Ngorongoro Conservation Area, including an elephant cave and waterfall, and a full-day to the top of Mlima Nyoka (Snake Hill), plus homestays and specialized activities (birding and botanical). Tours take anything from a couple of hours to a full day and prices are unlikely to be more than $30 per person for a full day, excluding motorized transport. They can also arrange 4WD rental: prices average $200 per day, including driver and fuel.

ACCOMMODATION

Most Karatu hotels charge outrageous rates to tourists, but for every car full of safari-goers there's a driver who needs somewhere cheap and decent to stay. There are a number of guesthouses two streets south of the highway, plus an increasing number of rural retreats out of town, not all of them obscenely priced, though you'll need your own vehicle or a motorbike taxi (*pikipiki*) to access them.

★**Bougainvillea Safari Lodge** 1.2Km west of the bus stand along the highway, then 200m north ☎027 253 4083, ⓦbougainvillealodge.net. A proper lodge, well priced for what it offers, with a grand restaurant, a swimming pool (around which you can take meals and drinks), and 32 cosy stone-walled bungalows with fireplaces. BB $174, HB $210

★**Candelabra Guest House** Two streets south of the highway (take the turning for Crater Rim View Inn) ☎0756 233032. The best of several good choices in this area, this guesthouse is a bargain. It's clean, welcoming, with safe parking, and its en-suite rooms (Tsh12,000) come with TVs. Tsh8,000

★**Country Lodge Karatu** Off the north side of the highway, 1km west of the bus stand ☎027 253 4622, ⓦcountrylodgekaratu.com. Run by the same people as the adjacent *Bougainvillea Safari Lodge*, this is almost identical, the main difference being that the rooms – which are a touch more rustic – are semi-detached rather than stand-alone, and the swimming pool also has a section for children. BB $160, HB $195

Gibb's Farm 5km off the highway northeast of town

☎0782 534397 or ☎027 253 4040, ⊛gibbsfarm.com. This working farm – surrounded by dry forest and coffee plantations – is by far the nicest place to stay around Ngorongoro, despite (or perhaps because of) the slightly formal colonial atmosphere. The best rooms are in the 1920s farmhouse, while other rooms occupy garden bungalows, and the food is top-notch. Guided walks are included and safaris can be arranged. HB **$850**

Karatu Lutheran Hotel 200m north of the highway at the west end of town ☎027 253 4230 or ☎0787 458856, ⊛karatuhotel.com. A friendly and predictably pious church-run hostel primarily used for conferences. Its rooms – all en-suite, and with TV – are in a curved one-storey block set amid pretty gardens. Also has a restaurant, and tours can be arranged. Nothing special, but well priced by Karatu's standards. Safe parking. BB **$25**

Octagon Lodge 1.2km south of the highway from the west end of town ☎0784 650324 or ☎0765 473564, ⊛octagonlodge.com. Run by an Irish–Tanzanian couple, this place has twelve bright rooms in individual raised wooden chalets, resembling garden sheds: all have verandas facing the garden and its resident crowned cranes and guinea fowl. There are also cottage suites for four

people, a nice Irish-themed bar and good, fresh food. Camping per person **$15**, ready-erected tents **$30**, chalets (HB) **$150**

★**Rhotia Valley** 10km northeast of Karatu by road: 5km east along the highway, then (signposted) along 5km of rough road ☎0784 446579, ⊛rhotiavalley.com. A stylish yet unpretentious Dutch-family-run place, on the boundary with Ngorongoro. Twenty percent of its profits fund the neighbouring children's home, and the sixty-odd staff are all local, and very welcoming. The grounds are a delight: a mixture of natural vegetation run wild, full of flowers and birds, and a colourful herb and vegetable garden that supplies the restaurant. The seventeen tented rooms (including two for families) are fresh, and pitched on wooden platforms under separate roofs. All have hot water, satellite TV, and verandas with views over farmland, forest or garden. Given that most of the ingredients are grown here, meals are always a delight, including breakfast – they bake their own bread, and milk their own cows. There's also a swimming pool (with a shallow section for children), village walks guided by local Iraqw, and the option of forest walks from the rim of Ngorongoro Crater back here. FB **$410**

EATING AND DRINKING

Country Lodge Karatu Off the north side of the highway, 1km west of the bus stand. Drinks and meals are served by the pool. The soups are especially tasty, and there are plenty of fresh salads, plus Italian favourites too. Full meals cost $16–20. The restaurant in the adjacent *Bougainvillea Safari Lodge* is similar. Daily 6.30am–10pm.

★**Gibb's Farm** 5km off the highway northeast of town ☎0782 534397, ⊛gibbsfarm.com. Something of a time warp back to the days of the British Empire – and pleasingly so. With nouvelle cuisine presentation, farm-grown

ingredients and some game meat, such as eland. Meals here are always an experience, served with flair; for example sorbet is served in a croquant cup as a starter (lunch $30; dinner $40). Digest it all with a guided walk around the coffee farm, or to some waterfalls. Book ahead. Daily noon–2pm & 7–9pm.

Paradise Garden North side of the highway. Good cheap meals, mainly rice with stews, chicken or *nyama choma* for around Tsh4000. You can eat either at tables on a lawn or in funny little conical *bandas*. There's also a bar. Daily 8am–8pm or later.

THE KARATU–DAREDA ROAD

For a fascinating diversion from the Northern Safari circus, take the slow but in places extremely beautiful, unsurfaced road due south of Karatu through the heart of Iraqw country. It passes through the town of **Mbulu** and the smaller market town of **Dongobesh**, then descends the Rift Valley's **Maldabow escarpment**, with fantastic views of Lake Balangida and Mount Hanang, ending at **Dareda** (or Ndareda), on the asphalt highway between Babati and Singida. The road is easy to follow and, in your own car (high clearance advisable), takes about four hours in good conditions. If the road hasn't been graded recently, or if it's been raining heavily, it may take a few hours longer, though the trickiest section – the steep escarpment descent above Dareda – is now sealed.

The route can also be done **by bus**. The quickest way is to catch a bus from Karatu to Babati or Singida, making sure it goes via Mbulu (otherwise, you're likely to find yourself on the tarmac Arusha–Babati highway). If you prefer to do it in stages, note that Mbulu has plenty of guesthouses, and Dongobesh has at least three, and there are more or less hourly buses along each section of the route.

Ngorongoro Conservation Area

"The eighth wonder of the world" is the brochures' clarion call, and for once they're not far wrong. The spectacular 8288-square-kilometre **Ngorongoro Conservation Area** occupies the highlands between the Great Rift Valley and the Serengeti Plains. It's the product of the volcanic upheavals that accompanied the formation of the Rift Valley, and its varied habitats virtually guarantee sightings of "the big five" – elephant, lion, leopard, rhino and buffalo. For animals, this place is a haven; for tourists, it's something close to heaven.

Coming from the east, the magic begins the instant you pass through Lodoare Gate. The road begins to climb up through the tall and liana-festooned Oldeani Forest, giving way to an unforgettable view of **Ngorongoro Crater**, an ever-changing patchwork of green and yellow hues streaked with shadows and mist. At its centre Lake Magadi reflects the silvery sky, while on the western horizon, there's the seemingly endless shimmer of the Serengeti Plains. The 19km-wide crater is Ngorongoro's incomparable highlight, a vast, unbroken caldera left behind when an enormous volcano collapsed. Its grasslands, swamps, glades, lakes and forests contain vast numbers of herbivores, together with Africa's highest density of predators. **Game viewing**, needless to say, is phenomenal, as is the abundance of photo opportunities, the crater's deep, bluish-purple sides providing a spectacular backdrop to any shot. The crater also contains a few highly endangered **black rhino**, which despite their disastrously reduced population (now about twenty) are easily seen. **Birdlife** is pretty decent, too, and includes ostriches, Verreaux's eagles, Egyptian vultures, kori bustards and lesser flamingos, the latter feeding on soda lakes occupying Ngorongoro and Empakaai craters, and at Lake Ndutu on the border with Serengeti.

Although the crater is often all that tourists see of Ngorongoro, there's much more besides. In the west, the rolling hills give way to the expansive grassland of the **Salei Plains**, which receive a good part of the Serengeti's annual wildlife migration between December and April. Both hyena and cheetah are frequently seen here, though in the dry season the plains resemble a desert. Right on the edge of the plains is a remarkable geological fissure, **Oldupai Gorge**, famous among paleontologists as the site of important hominid finds dating back millions of years. To the northeast, close to the edge of the Great Rift Valley's escarpment, are two smaller craters, **Olmoti and Empakaai**, which are also rich in wildlife yet see very few visitors. The craters form part of the so-called **Crater Highlands**, which can be visited on foot if accompanied by an armed ranger – an exciting if hair-raising prospect. For those with more time, and sturdy legs, it's also possible to walk across the highlands from Ngorongoro to Lake Natron via Ol Doinyo Lengai volcano, a journey that can take anything from two to seven days (see p.334).

Ngorongoro Crater

A crater fee of $300 per vehicle gives you up to six hours in the crater • Self-drivers must hire an official guide, and have a fully equipped 4WD (with jack, towrope, shovel and bushknife) • 25kph speed limit • Visitors must be out of the crater by 5.30pm

Some 2.5 million years ago, the reservoir of magma under an enormous volcano towering over the western flank of the Great Rift Valley emptied itself in an enormous explosion, leaving a vacuum that caused the mountain to implode under its own weight. In its wake, it left an enormous 600-metre deep crater (caldera), its 19-kilometre diameter now making it the world's largest unbroken and unflooded caldera. This is **Ngorongoro Crater**, one of Tanzania's wonders, covering approximately three hundred square kilometres and providing a natural amphitheatre for the wildlife spectacle on its floor. The crater contains 25,000 to 30,000 large mammals, which when viewed from the rim are a blur of pulsating specks arranged in fluid formations, while above the crater, eagles, buzzards, hawks and vultures circle.

The main feature on the crater floor is the shallow and alkaline **Lake Magadi**, whose extent varies according to the rains – flocks of flamingos feed here in the dry season. On the western shore is an enigmatic scattering of stone **burial mounds**, believed to have been left by the Datooga (Tatoga), ancestors of Barbaig cattle herders who occupied the crater until the Maasai pushed them out. At the lake's southern edge is **Lerai Forest**, a large patch of acacia woodland that takes its Maasai name from the dominant yellow-barked acacia, and is a good place for seeing waterbuck and flitting sunbirds. Swamp, thorn scrub and grassland fill the rest of the crater, and provide the bulk of the game viewing.

The majority of the animals are **herbivores**, supported by year-round supplies of water and fodder, and include vast herds of wildebeest (up to 14,000), zebra, buffalo, Grant's and Thomson's gazelle, eland, hartebeest and mountain reedbuck, warthog and hippo, and two of Africa's giants: elephants, of which a handful of bulls are always present, and a small population of **black rhino**. Once rhinos where common across all of eastern and southern Africa, but poaching in the 1970s and 1980s took a terrible toll on this magnificent creature, decimating the population from 108 in the 1960s to only fourteen in 1995. There are now 26.

Apart from rhino, the big draw is the transfixing sight of Africa's densest population of **predators** in action. Lions are very common and easily seen (best in the dry season), as are hyenas and jackals. Cheetahs are also sometimes present, as are leopards, which require some patience to spot, as they rest up in trees or thick bush by day.

Olmoti and Empakaai craters
North of Ngorongoro Crater • No extra entry fees

North of Ngorongoro Crater are two smaller craters, Olmoti and Empakaai. The shallow and grassy **Olmoti Crater**, accessed from Nanokanoka village (there's a special

---

NGORONGORO'S ECOLOGY: A PRECARIOUS BALANCE

Ngorongoro is a wilderness, but one that has also long been inhabited by humans, originally by hunter-gatherers collectively known as **Dorobo**, and later by cattle herders, including the ancestors of the Barbaig (see p.227) and then the Maasai (see pp.336–337). As with the Serengeti, humans were and are very much part of Ngorongoro's delicate ecological balance, a balance that has become increasingly precarious since the end of the nineteenth century, when Europe began to colonize East Africa.

The first *mzungu* to set eyes on Ngorongoro and its famous crater was the German explorer **Dr Oscar Baumann**, who in March 1892 reported a magnificent abundance of game, and promptly went on to bag three rhinos. So began a long history of European involvement, first for hunting, then for conservation, and which, for all their efforts and theories, has witnessed a massive decline in animal numbers.

Originally heavily exploiting the area for hunting, the British administration soon realized that their activities were having a detrimental effect on Ngorongoro's wildlife, and in 1921 Ngorongoro became a **game reserve**. Seven years later, locals were prohibited from hunting and cultivating in the crater, although – hypocritically – Europeans continued to do as they wished until the end of the 1930s, when trophy hunting was finally banned. In 1951, Ngorongoro became part of Serengeti National Park, and in 1958 the Maasai – under formidable pressure – formally renounced their claim to Serengeti. The following year, they were evicted and moved into Ngorongoro, which was declared a multiple land use area. This special status still allows Maasai to settle and graze their cattle in coexistence with wildlife, but this admirable idea conceals a more disturbing reality.

Although the **law** states that in cases of human-wildlife conflict in Ngorongoro, Maasai rights are to take precedence, this has rarely been the case, and relations between the authorities and the Maasai have at times been extremely bitter. Settlement in the crater itself was banned in 1974, and cultivation, which the Maasai increasingly had to adopt, was prohibited throughout Ngorongoro in 1975, and only periodically allowed since. Livestock too has been excluded from the crater since the early 1990s, denying the Maasai a critical dry-season pasture for their cattle, and making it progressively harder for them to scrape a living from their diminishing resources. Having lost water and pasture rights to the crater (and eighty percent of the land they controlled until a century ago), the Maasai have also been forbidden from hunting or cultivating. An estimated forty percent of Ngorongoro's Maasai are considered destitute, owning less than two livestock units per household.

7

CRATER HIGHLANDS TREKS

The **Crater Highlands** occupy the eastern section of Ngorongoro Conservation Area, roughly between Ngorongoro Crater and the Rift Valley. Much of the area is lushly forested, and includes several volcanic peaks, including the active Ol Doinyo Lengai volcano just outside the conservation area (see p.351).

The area is best experienced with an armed ranger on a **Crater Highlands trek,** which can be arranged via the NCAA office in Arusha (see p.287), Karatu's better hotels, or any safari company. Treks can be as short as half a day, or as long as a week, giving you ample time to get to Lake Natron, and perhaps climb Ol Doinyo Lengai along the way, while Olmoti and Empakaai craters can also be worked into the itinerary. **Costs** vary according to the level of service and back-up: count on anything from $200–500 a day. Upmarket operators offer something close to bush luxury, where a full camp attended by plenty of staff is set up ahead of your arrival, including mess tents, furniture, chemical toilets and ingenious bucket showers. Cheaper, more adventurous and definitely more "authentic" are humbler trips where the gear (dome tents, usually) is carried by donkey, which will also carry you if you're tired. These trips are often guided by Maasai warriors, who make up for their sometimes limited knowledge of English with tremendous practical botanical know-how and an astounding ability to spot all sorts of wildlife.

---

campsite there), contains several antelope species, and there are waterfalls nearby on the Munge River. Accompanied by an armed ranger (the post is in the village), the crater rim and its fringing forest can be explored on foot, taking anything from two to seven hours.

Northeast of here is the stunningly beautiful, 6km-wide **Empakaai Crater**, much of which is filled with a forest-fringed soda lake. This is better for wildlife than Olmoti, and resident species include bushbuck, reedbuck and waterbuck, buffalo, monkeys and an abundance of birds, including flamingos. You can walk along the rim (again, if accompanied by an armed ranger – the post is about 5km southeast) and into the crater itself (at least 7hr). There are two special campsites on the rim.

Oldupai Gorge

30km west of Ngorongoro Crater, 7km north of the road to Serengeti • $30 entrance fee includes a guided tour (tip expected), and gives access to Oldupai Museum and the Shifting Sands

Gouged from the edge of the Salei Plains, **Oldupai (or Olduvai) Gorge** is a steep-sided, 48km-long ravine with depths reaching 150m in places. Furrowed out of the volcanic land by the capricious Oldupai River, the eroded rock strata on either side of the gorge have exposed the **fossilized remains** of animals and over fifty hominids dating back almost two million years – an archeological trove of inestimable importance for understanding the origins of humankind.

Oldupai Gorge can be seen on foot or by vehicle, and even if old bones and stones don't appeal, the gorge itself is a pleasant diversion off the road to Serengeti, and there's also a range of fast-moving black sand dunes to explore.

Brief history

The fossils were first noted in 1911 by **Professor Kattwinkel**, a German butterfly collector, who found them by chance and took the fossilized remains of a three-toed horse back to Berlin's Museum für Naturkunde. Two decades later, Kattwinkel's findings aroused the curiosity of Kenyan-born British anthropologist, **Louis Leakey**, and in 1931 he began excavating at Oldupai.

For almost thirty years, Leakey and his wife Mary found only stone tools, the oldest belonging to the so-called **Oldowan industry** (1.2 to 1.8 million years ago). Spurred on by the belief that the remains of the hominids that had created the tools could not be far behind, they persevered, and their patience was finally rewarded in 1959 by the discovery of two large human-like teeth and a piece of skull. Four hundred additional fragments were eventually found, which were painstakingly reassembled to form the

1.75-million-year-old skull of *Australopithecus boisei* ("southern ape"), nicknamed the **Nutcracker Man** on account of his powerful jaws. The tool-maker had been found, and the discovery – at the time, the oldest known – provoked a sea change in paleontological circles, especially as the skull's size and dentition displayed uncanny similarities with modern man. The unavoidable conclusion was that the Leakeys had unearthed a direct ancestor of modern man, and that the much vaunted "missing link" had been found.

The theory was accepted until disproved by much older finds from Ethiopia, and from Laetoli, south of Oldupai (see below), and since then the Nutcracker Man has been consigned to history as an evolutionary dead end. His importance remains, however, in showing that hominid evolution was not a simple linear progression. The find sparked a flurry of **further excavations** at Oldupai, which showed conclusively that two other hominid species, almost certainly our ancestors, lived contemporaneously with the Nutcracker Man – *Homo habilis* ("handy man") and *Homo erectus* ("upright man"). Over the years, various claims have been made for one place or another being the "cradle of mankind", but what is certain is that the incredible journey into our prehistory first began to make sense at Oldupai.

Oldupai Museum

On the right before the entrance to Oldupai Gorge • Daily 8am–4.30pm

Next to the entrance to the gorge, small but fascinating **Oldupai Museum** documents the finds excavated in the region. Despite its modest size, the museum packs in a bewildering amount of information, with three rooms full of well-documented bones, tools and skilful reproductions of skulls, including that of Nutcracker Man (see p.91).

The Shifting Sands

9km beyond the entrance to Oldupai Gorge

Providing an appropriate metaphor for Oldupai's immense sweep though time are the **Shifting Sands**, beyond the northern edge of the gorge, which are a range of elegant black sand dunes forever being pushed eastward by the wind (an estimated 17m a year). Taking a guide is obligatory as you have to pass through the gorge to get there, and the authorities also discourage folk from clambering over the dunes, which destroys their fragile plant cover and hastens their onward advance.

Laetoli

54km west of Ngorongoro Crater (24km beyond Endulen village) • $20 entry

Tanzania's most astonishing prehistoric find occurred at **Laetoli** (or Garusi), 40km south of Oldupai, which offered up its first fossils in 1938. Its most spectacular discoveries came in the 1970s, including thirteen jaw fragments dating back 3.6 million years. They belonged to a species called *Australopithecus afarensis*, named after Ethiopia's Afar desert where, in 1974, the world got to know "Lucy" – a half-complete bipedal female skeleton, which the Ethiopian expedition members called Dinquenesh ("you are amazing").

Back at Laetoli, in 1979, archeologists discovered a trail of **fossilized footprints** that had been left in wet volcanic ash by two adults and a child some 3.75 million years ago. This proved that hominids were walking (and running) upright way before anyone had imagined, and that Lucy was indeed a member of our long-long ancestors. Further research suggested that *Australopithecus afarensis* stood fully erect, was about 100–150cm tall, and weighed up to 50kg. Its skull, although only fractionally larger than that of a modern chimpanzee, had dentition similar to that in modern humans.

After their discovery, the footprints were reburied beneath protective layers, until 2010, when they were re-excavated and given a temporary roof. They can now be visited, and there are plans to erect a museum on the site or nearby – possibly in the shape of a foot.

THE MAASAI

In the popular imagination, the **Maasai warrior**, with his red robe, spear and braided ochre-smeared hair, is *the* archetypal African, and a disproportionate amount of attention has been lavished on them, ever since the explorer Joseph Thomson published his best seller *Through Maasailand* in 1885. In those days, the Maasai were seen as perfect "**noble savages**", but their story is much more complex.

SOME HISTORY

What we know of their distant history is little more than conjecture – some say that they are one of the lost tribes of Israel and others that they came from North Africa. Still others believe that they are the living remnants of Egyptian civilization, primarily, it seems, on account of their warriors' braided hairstyles. Linguistically, the Maasai are among the southernmost of the Nilotic-speaking peoples, a loosely related group that came from the north, presumably from the Nile Valley in Sudan. It's thought that they left this area sometime between the fourteenth and sixteenth centuries, migrating southwards with their cattle herds along the fertile grasslands of the Rift Valley. The Maasai eventually entered what is now Kenya to the west of Lake Turkana, and quickly spread south into northern Tanzania, whose seasonal grasslands were ideal for their cattle. They reached their present extent around the eighteenth century, at which time they were the most powerful and feared tribe in East Africa. Their tight social organization, offensive warfare, deadly cattle raids, and mobility as semi-nomadic cattle herders ensured that they could go where they pleased, and could take what they wanted. Their **military prowess** and regimentation meant that they were rarely defeated and as a result their history before the arrival of the British was one of ceaseless expansion at the expense of others. Their combined Kenyan and Tanzanian territory in the seventeenth century has been estimated at 200,000 square kilometres.

The Maasai territory today is less than a quarter of what it was before the Europeans arrived, and they have been progressively confined to smaller and smaller regions. The British took much of their land away to serve as farms and ranches for settlers, and in recent decades the land expropriations have continued, this time to form the wildlife preserves of Serengeti, Tarangire, Mkomazi and part of Ngorongoro, to which the Serengeti Maasai were relocated when they were evicted.

THE MAASAI TODAY, AND IN THE FUTURE

Politically and economically, the Maasai remain marginalized from the Tanzanian mainstream, having refused to abandon their pastoralist way of life, or their traditions, despite repeated attempts by both colonial and post-Independence governments, and missionaries, to cajole or force them to settle. Many men persevere with the status of **warriorhood**, though modern Tanzania makes few concessions to it. Arrested for hunting lions, and prevented from building

ARRIVAL AND DEPARTURE

By organized safari Pretty much every tour operator in Tanzania offers safaris to Ngorongoro, and the sealed road from Arusha to Lodoare Gate means most safari vehicles cover the 160km in less than three hours.

By car Self-drive is possible as everything is signposted, but you won't be allowed into the crater without an officially licensed guide or driver-guide; they can be hired at the park gate for $20 a day. Open-topped vehicles are not admitted. Cars can be rented in Karatu (see p.330) – if you're adept at bargaining and have enough people to fill a car, it's cheaper than an organized safari.

By bus It's not possible to get around Ngorongoro by public transport, but the Ngorongoro Conservation Area Authority (NCAA) runs a bus from Arusha (Mon–Fri at

NGORONGORO CONSERVATION AREA

10am; returning in the afternoon) to its headquarters close to the crater, where you can pick up a ranger for walks, and possibly a vehicle, but only if you've arranged things in advance with their office in Arusha (see p.287).

By plane There's an airstrip on the crater rim, but scheduled flights use Ndutu on the border with Serengeti, 90km northwest of the crater. There's also an airstrip at Manyara, 55km southeast, near Mto wa Mbu (see p.327). The main airlines are: Air Excel (AE; ✆airexcelonline.com); Auric Air (AA; ✆auricair.com); Coastal Aviation (CA; ✆coastal.co.tz); Regional Air (RA; ✆regionaltanzania .com); and Safari Airlink (SA; ✆flysal.com). The following is for flights to and from Ndutu; the quickest airlines are listed first.

Destinations Arusha (CA AA AE SA: 5 daily; 50min–2hr

manyattas (cattle enclosures) for the *eunoto* transition in which they pass into elderhood, the warriors (*morani*) have kept most of the superficial marks of the warrior without being able to live the life. The ensemble of a red or purple cloth *shuka* tied over one shoulder, together with spear, sword, club and braided hair, is still widely seen, and after circumcision, in their early days as warriors, you can meet young men out in the bush, hunting for birds to add to their elaborate, taxidermic headdresses.

But the Maasai **lifestyle** is changing: education, MPs and elections, new laws and new projects, jobs and cash are all having mixed results. Their traditional staple dish of curdled milk and cow's blood is rapidly being replaced by cornmeal *ugali*. Many Maasai have taken work in the lodges and tented camps while others end up as security guards in Arusha and Dar es Salaam. A main source of income for those who remain is provided by the **tourist industry**. Maasai dancing is *the* entertainment, while necklaces, gourds, spears, shields, *rungus* (clubs, also known as knobkerries), busts and even life-sized wooden warriors are the stock-in-trade of the curio and souvenir shops.

For the Maasai themselves, the rewards are fairly scant. **Cattle** are still at the heart of their society but they are assailed on all sides by a climate of opposition to the old lifestyle. Sporadically urged to grow crops, go to school, build permanent houses and generally settle down, they face an additional dilemma in squaring these edicts with the demands of the tourist industry for traditional authenticity.

For the majority, who still live semi-nomadic lives among a growing tangle of constraints, **the future** would seem to hold little promise. However, the creation of community-run conservation areas outside the parks and reserves looks promising, generating income from annual land rents paid by tourist lodges and tented camps, and often a percentage of profits or overnight receipts.

VISITING MAASAI

Visitors can meet the red-robed Maasai in **cultural bomas** – "traditional" Maasai villages set up in various roadside locations in Ngorongoro Conservation Area expressly for tourists (entrance fees are negotiable, plus a $20 per vehicle levied by the Conservation Area authorities). The experience can feel uncomfortably staged and voyeuristic at times, but for many it's the only time they'll be able to meet one of Africa's traditional tribes, and of course the money is welcomed by local communities. A better way to meet Maasai, however, is via Tanzania's community-led **cultural tourism programmes**, several of which are run by Maasai around Engaruka (see p.353) and Arusha (see pp.303–307). In addition, the Crater Highlands treks (see p.334) from Ngorongoro to Lake Natron are usually guided in part by Maasai, and may include overnights in genuine, non-tourist-oriented *bomas*. For **more information**, see ⓦbluegecko .org/kenya/tribes/maasai, a comprehensive resource about Maasai culture, including their marvellously hypnotic singing.

10min); Dar (AE SA: 2 daily 4hr 35min–5hr 25min); Kilimanjaro (CA SA AE: 4 daily; 1hr 10min–2hr 45min); Mafia (SA: 1 daily; 6hr 30min); Manyara (CA AA AE SA: 5 daily; 25min–45min); Mwanza (CA: 1 daily; 2hr 40min);

Pangani (SA: 1 daily; 6hr 10min); Ruaha (SA CA: 2 daily; 2hr 20min–3hr); Saadani (SA: 1 daily; 6hr 20min); Serengeti (CA AA AE RA SA: 6 daily; 15min–1hr 45min); Zanzibar (CA AE: 2 daily; 3hr 10min–4hr).

ESSENTIALS

Park headquarters The Ngorongoro Conservation Area Authority (NCAA) headquarters are on the west side of the crater rim (daily 6.30am–6.30pm; ⓦngorongorocrater .org).

Entrance fees The main gates are Lodoare in the east, and Naabi Hill in the west (daily 6am–6pm). Entry fees are $60 per person and Tsh20,000 for a vehicle, both for 24hrs, plus additional fees for entering individual sights within the Conservation Area (see sights above). Cash is currently not accepted for entry fees (check ⓦngorongorocrater.org

for any changes), so payment is convoluted. First, you need to verify the total cost of entry at either the Conservation Area's information office in Arusha (see p.287) or at Lodoare gate. You then need to go to a bank in Arusha or Karatu to deposit the money in their account, and get a receipt. You then show the receipt to staff at the office or gate, who will give you a electronic payment card in return, which gives you access.

Information There's a very useful tourist information centre at Lodoare Gate where you can pick up a guidebook published by Ngorongoro Conservation Unit ($10), which contains a wealth of information about the region, its history, geology and inhabitants, as well as a number of other booklets covering geology, birdlife, wildlife, trees and plants, and prehistory. The most detailed and accurate map is Harms-IC-Verlag's. Not as detailed but more visually attractive is the painted dry-season/wet-season map by Giovanni Tombazzi.

ACCOMMODATION AND EATING

Apart from an often-packed public **campsite**, the only accommodation on the crater rim is pricey neo-colonial-style tented **camps** (not all of them with views), and some large **lodges**. There are more campsites and another lodge elsewhere in the conservation area, as well as much cheaper **hotels** in and around Karatu (see pp.330–331). Day-visitors can take **lunch** at some of the lodges: *Rhino Lodge* serves an excellent and affordable meal for $25, but for a crater view, *Ngorongoro Wildlife Lodge* is unmatched ($30), although its cuisine is distinctly average. *Ngorongoro Serena Safari Lodge* may also oblige ($40–60).

LODGES

★**Ndutu Safari Lodge** Next to Lake Ndutu on the border with Serengeti ☎ 0736 501045 or ☎ 0736 501046, ⏴ ndutu.com. A welcoming and friendly place well off the beaten track, with 32 comfortable bungalows, the best at the front facing the lake, which becomes a starkly beautiful salt-pan in the dry season – wonderful at sunrise. With no fences, wildlife can come and go: the migration is concentrated in this area between Dec and March. There's an open-sided bar, a lounge and dining room with superb food (perhaps explaining the nocturnal visits by resident genets). Evening meals can also be taken around a campfire within earshot of roaring lions. HB $̄453

Ngorongoro Serena Safari Lodge On the crater rim ☎ 027 253 9160 (Arusha), ⏴ serenahotels.com. The usual high standards of comfort from this chain make this a stylish but impersonal place. Most of the 75 rooms have verandas overlooking the crater, as do the restaurant and a terrace. The strange architecture, all brown, beige and pebble-dashed, camouflages the lodge reasonably well from a distance. FB $̄870

Ngorongoro Sopa Lodge On the crater rim ☎ 027 250 0630 (Arusha), ⏴ sopalodges.com. The only hotel on the eastern rim, so perfect for sunsets, but also the largest and least personal abode, with ninety mostly twin-bed rooms. The external architecture is an eyesore, but the views are fantastic from the public areas, the balconies of most of the rooms and the swimming pool. FB $̄650

Ngorongoro Wildlife Lodge On the crater rim ☎ 027 254 4595 or ☎ 0754 254600 (Arusha), ⏴ hotelsand lodges-tanzania.com. Another architectural mess, this place – nicknamed the "ski lodge" – was government-owned for years: now privately run, it has raised its rates rather more than its standards. On the positive side, the views are superb, whether from the 78 bedrooms (just four with balconies) or the lounge. FB $̄610

★**Rhino Lodge** Just south of the crater rim, 15km from Lodoare Gate ☎ 0785 500005 or ☎ 0762 359055, ⏴ ngorongoro.cc. This is not on the crater rim, so its views are of distant forest-covered hills, and you do get to see wildlife, sometimes even elephants, waltzing through the hotel's ground. The architecture is plain in the manner of a colonial farmstead, and both service and food are top-notch. The 24 rooms, in two L-shaped wings, are simple, but appealing, and have especially welcome fireplaces (you're 2270m above sea level). HB $̄243

CAMPING

Public campsite (Simba A) Southwest rim of Ngorongoro Crater; pay at the entrance gate. Ngorongoro's only public campsite has toilets and showers, and for most of the year is packed, noisy and often filthy. Nonetheless, the crater views are jaw-dropping, there's electricity (good for charging your camera) and the Woodstock/Glastonbury feel appeals to many, despite the discomforts. Reservations not required. Per person $̄40

Special campsites Various locations; ask about availability and book at Ngorongoro's office in Arusha (see p.287). Ngorongoro's "special" campsites are mostly in very scenic locations, but have no facilities at all, and can get block-booked by safari companies months or even years in advance. They are all recommended except *Nyati*, near Ngorongoro Crater, which lacks a view. The rest are: *Simba A* and *Simba B*, 1km apart, and both with good views; *Nanokanoka*, near Olmoti Crater and Nanokanoka village; two sites next to *Empakaai Crater*, perfect for descending into it; and three sites on the wooded northeastern rim of Ngorongoro Crater, *Tembo A*, *Tembo B* and *Lemala*, all of which occasionally see elephants. The seven special campsites around *Lake Ndutu* in the west often get very crowded. Per person $̄60

Serengeti National Park

Bordering Ngorongoro in the east, Kenya's Maasai Mara Game Reserve in the north, and reaching to within 8km of Lake Victoria in the west, the **Serengeti** is one of the world's most famous wildlife areas. This vast wilderness is home to Tanzania's oldest and largest national park, and one of the world's best-known wildlife sanctuaries, the 14,763-square-kilometre **Serengeti National Park**. Protected since 1929, and declared a national park in 1951, the Serengeti is also – together with Ngorongoro – a UNESCO World Heritage Site and International Biosphere Reserve. And with good reason – the Serengeti lies at the heart of the world's largest and most impressive **wildlife migration** (see box, p.340), at the peak of which it contains the highest concentration of mammals on earth.

Serengeti takes its name from the flat **grassland plains** that cover the eastern section of the park next to Ngorongoro, which the Maasai called *siringet*, meaning "endless plain". Along with the Kalahari, these plains are the Western imagination's archetypal African landscape, and the highlight of many a visit, certainly when the migration is in full swing. Even outside the migration, there's plenty to see, including large clans of hyenas and thriving lion prides, and a series of weathered granite outcrops called **kopjes** (pronounced kop-yees; from the Afrikaans for "little head"), one of which contains rock paintings, and another a mysterious "rock gong".

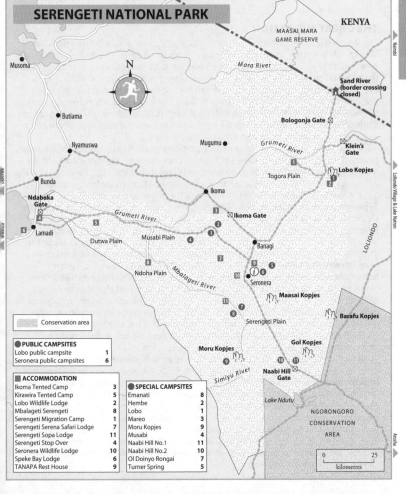

SERENGETI NATIONAL PARK

Kisumu

KENYA

MAASAI MARA GAME RESERVE

Musoma

N

Mara River

Sand River (border crossing closed)

Butiama

Bologonja Gate ⊠

Nyamuswa

Mugumu ●

Grumeti River

Klein's Gate ⊠

Lobo Kopjes

Togora Plain

Bunda

Ikoma ●

Ndabaka Gate ⊠

Grumeti River

Ikoma Gate ⊠

Lamadi

Dutwa Plain

Musabi Plain

Banagi

LOLIONDO

Mbalageti River

Seronera

Ndoha Plain

Maasai Kopjes

Barafu Kopjes

Conservation area

Serengeti Plain

Moru Kopjes

Gol Kopjes

Simiyu River

Naabi Hill Gate ⊠

Lake Ndutu

NGORONGORO CONSERVATION AREA

● PUBLIC CAMPSITES	
Lobo public campsite	1
Seronera public campsites	6

■ ACCOMMODATION			● SPECIAL CAMPSITES	
Ikoma Tented Camp	3		Emanati	8
Kirawira Tented Camp	5		Hembe	2
Lobo Wildlife Lodge	2		Lobo	1
Mbalageti Serengeti	8		Mareo	3
Serengeti Migration Camp	1		Moru Kopjes	9
Serengeti Serena Safari Lodge	7		Musabi	4
Serengeti Sopa Lodge	11		Naabi Hill No.1	11
Serengeti Stop Over	4		Naabi Hill No.2	10
Seronera Wildlife Lodge	10		Ol Doinyo Rongai	7
Speke Bay Lodge	6		Turner Spring	5
TANAPA Rest House	9			

0   25
kilometres

There's more to Serengeti than the plains though, which cover only one third of the park. In the hilly centre, around **Seronera** – where a good deal of the park's accommodation is located, along with an excellent visitors' centre – a series of lightly wooded valleys provide excellent year-round game viewing, while in the **north**, along a 40km-wide corridor connecting with Kenya's Maasai Mara Game Reserve, rolling hills and thorny acacia woodland dominate. To the west, another corridor of land runs along the **Grumeti River** to within 8km of Lake Victoria. The river's flanking evergreen forests are another special habitat, providing a home for primates as well as lurking leopards, while the river itself and its swamps are as perfect for water birds as they are for crocodiles preying on thirsty wildlife, a sight as enthralling as it is gruesome when the migration is passing through.

The Serengeti Plains

The undulating, semi-arid **Serengeti Plains** are the cornerstone of Serengeti's ecosystem. For a bird's-eye view, walk up the kopje behind **Naabi Hill Gate**; this

THE GREAT MIGRATION

The Serengeti owes its hallowed place in our imagination to the annual 800km **migration** of over 2.5 million animals, the largest mammalian migration on earth. A continuous, milling and unsettled mass, including almost two million wildebeest and close to a million other animals, the migration offers visitors one of nature's most staggering displays, one in which the ever-vigilant predators – lions, cheetahs, African hunting dogs and spotted hyenas – play a vital part. The river crossings are the biggest obstacle, namely the Grumeti in Serengeti, and the Mara along the border with Kenya in the north, and both can be the scene of true carnage as the panicked herds struggle across the raging flows in a writhing mass of bodies while the weak, injured or careless are picked off by crocodiles and lions.

The migration's ceaseless movement is prompted by a seasonal search for fresh water and pasture dictated by the rains. It moves in a roughly clockwise direction, concentrating in the national park from **April to June**, towards the end of the long rains, before leaving behind the withering plains of the Serengeti and journeying northward towards the fresh moisture and grass of Kenya's Maasai Mara Game Reserve, which the migration reaches in August. By **September and October**, the bulk of the migration is concentrated in Maasai Mara. By **late October and early November**, the Mara's grasslands are approaching exhaustion, so the migration turns back towards northern and eastern Serengeti, following the fresh grass brought by the short rains. In this period, the migration is widely spread out, and a large part of it circles through Loliondo and into Ngorongoro, beyond the Serengeti's eastern border. From **December to March**, the migration settles in the Serengeti Plains and western Ngorongoro, where it remains until the onset of the long rains. The wildebeest take advantage of this temporary pause to give birth (especially from late Jan to mid-March), accounting for half a million calves annually. The timing of this mass birthing provides security in numbers: predators will eat their fill, but within a few months, the surviving calves are much stronger and able to outrun their pursuers; nonetheless, the hazards of the migration are such that only one in three calves makes it back the following year. By April, the migration is once more concentrated inside Serengeti, and the whole cycle starts again.

The exact time and location of the migration varies annually, depending on the rains and other factors, so coinciding with it cannot be guaranteed. Nonetheless, as a general rule, the **best months** for seeing the migration in the Serengeti are from December to July, especially February and March in the plains when the wildebeest herds are dotted with new-born, and April to June when animal concentrations are at their highest. June is also the best time for catching the migration's perilous crossing of the Grumeti River, while the spectacular Mara River crossing, best seen from Kenya but also in northern Serengeti, is at its most awesome (and gruesome) in July and August. Taking into account the weather, the dry months of June and July, and usually also January, are probably the best time to visit, with the bulk of tourists coming in Dec–Feb and July–Aug.

viewpoint and picnic site is ideal for observing the **migration** (see box, p.340) between January and April, especially February and March, when literally hundreds of thousands of wildebeest, zebra and gazelle munch their way across the grasslands below. The popularity of the plains with wildlife appears to owe something to the alkaline nature of the soil, whose volcanic ash was laid down during the eruptions of Ngorongoro's Crater Highlands, and is therefore rich in **minerals** – something accentuated by the annual cycle of rain and evaporation, which sucks minerals to the surface. The main ones are calcium, potassium carbonate and sodium carbonate, which recent studies have shown are an essential component of many animals' diets, especially when lactating, and which explains why eighty percent of Serengeti's wildebeest give birth on these plains.

Even when the migration moves out of the area, and the plains turn into a dry and dusty shimmer of straw, there's still plenty of resident **wildlife** around, including lion prides, unusually large clans of hyenas (up to eighty strong), plus hartebeest, topi, warthog and ostrich. **Birdlife** is richest during the rains; through you'll see secretary birds and kori bustards throughout the year. Another bird worth looking for is the **black-throated honey guide**, which has a remarkable symbiotic relationship with the ratel (honey badger). The honey guide, as its name suggests, leads the ratel to wild beehives in trees, which the ratel – seemingly immune to the stings – pulls down and breaks open. The ratel eats the honey, and the honey guide treats itself to beeswax.

Moru Kopjes

The flat plains are broken in several places by isolated and much-eroded granite "islands" called **kopjes**. Also known as inselbergs ("island hills"), the kopjes were created millions of years ago when volcanic bubbles broached the surface and solidified, and were subsequently eroded by rains and floods, carving out the singularly beautiful and sensuous forms you see today. Rainwater run-off from the kopjes and permanent water pools caught in rocky clefts make them particularly good for spotting wildlife in the dry season, when **lions** like to lie in wait for other animals coming to feed or drink – for this reason, take care when walking around kopjes.

Humans, too, have long been attracted to kopjes, both hunter-gatherers such as the Dorobo, who were evicted in 1955, and seasonal "migrants" such as Maasai cattle herders. The Maasai, evicted in 1959, left their mark – literally – in a rock shelter on one of the **Moru Kopjes** 32km south of Seronera. Here, a natural rock shelter is daubed with **rock paintings** (in red, white and black) of Maasai shields identical to ceremonial shields still used today. The paintings, accompanied by drawings of elephants and less distinct animal and human forms, were left by young Maasai warriors (*morani*) for whom the site was the location of an *orpul* meat-feasting – as you can tell from soot lining the shelter's ceiling. According to Maasai custom, junior warriors were prohibited from eating meat, at least in public, so they'd steal a cow and bring it here. As with all rock art, the paintings are perishable (see p.221).

The rock gongs

Another thoroughly enigmatic kopje, 1km away, contains **rock gongs**, which are an ensemble of three loose boulders. One in particular – a large lemon-shaped wedge – bears dozens of circular depressions, created by people repeatedly striking the rock with stones to produce weirdly reverbative and metallic sounds (the sound differs depending where you strike the rock). Although rock gongs are nowadays played only by tourists, the wedge-shaped one was certainly used as a instrument way before the Maasai arrived a couple of centuries ago (they lack any musical tradition involving percussive instruments) and similar gong rocks have been found as far south as Zimbabwe. However, as little is known of the now vanished hunter-gatherers who presumably made and used the gongs, their exact age and purpose remain a mystery. Incidentally, time spent poking around the boulders may turn up a surprise – in 1992, a species of **tree frog** hitherto unknown to science was discovered in one of the rock gong's depressions.

Seronera

The central part of Serengeti is **Seronera**, which comprises the wooded valleys and savanna of the Grumeti River's main tributaries. There are a large number of drivable circuits in the area, which your driver or guide should know well, and the wildlife is representative of most of Serengeti's species. For many, the highlight is Seronera's famous **black-maned lions** – the cause of many sleepless nights at the campsites. **Leopards** also abound, though you'll need some luck, as they chill out by day in the leafy branches of yellow-barked acacias close to the rivers. The migration usually moves up to Seronera from the plains in April, before continuing on north and west.

Seronera Visitor Centre
1.5km south of Seronera village • Daily 8am–4.30pm

A great place to head after an early-morning game drive is the brilliantly designed **Seronera Visitor Centre**. It's a real pleasure, combining permanent exhibits, displays and wildlife video screenings at lunchtime (if the generator's working), with a humorous **information trail** around a nearby kopje. There's also a shop with drinks and snacks and a picnic site where semi-tame rock hyraxes and birds, including hoopoes and adorable Fischer's lovebirds, eye up your lunch. The centre's **gift shop** should have a booklet containing the information presented on the trail, and also a leaflet with a map and detailed descriptions of the various game drives around Seronera. The staff can usually fill you in on recent predator sightings and road conditions, and a number of park wardens are based here to answer more detailed queries.

The trails

A quick rundown of the **main trails** follows. Most have numbered road junctions corresponding to those on the leaflet available from the visitor centre (see p.342). The **Seronera River Circuit** (junctions 1–26) starts at Seronera Hippo Pool and follows the

---

THE SERENGETI'S WILDLIFE

Wildlife, of course, is why people come to Serengeti, and the figures are flabbergasting. Of the five million animals to be found during the migration (double the resident population) there are wildebeest, which numbered almost two million at the last count, gazelle, both Grant's and Thomson's, which are estimated at around half a million, and some three hundred thousand zebra. But even when the migration is up in Maasai Mara, or spread out across Ngorongoro and Loliondo, the park contains substantial populations of **plains game**, including buffalo, giraffe and warthog, and a wide range of antelopes, including dikdik, bushbuck, waterbuck and mountain reedbuck, eland and impala, plus the rarer oryx and topi. Some two thousand elephants, too, are present, though they are largely migratory and can easily be missed.

But all this is to forget perhaps the most memorable of Serengeti's animals, its **predators**, who thrive off the regal banquet on offer. Indeed, apart from Ngorongoro, Serengeti is probably the best place in Tanzania to see predators in action. Foremost are nearly eight thousand much-maligned spotted hyenas, which live in clans of up to eighty individuals. Also very visible are the park's three thousand or so lions, whose males have characteristic black manes. Other predators include cheetahs, which have been the subject of ongoing research since 1975, leopards and bat-eared foxes. **Scavengers**, apart from hyenas (which also hunt) include both golden and side-striped jackals and vultures. There are six species of vulture, representing a fraction of Serengeti's 520 **bird species** (including Eurasian winter migrants) – the country's second-highest count after Tarangire National Park. Keen birders can expect to see several hundred species in a two- or three-day safari, including many of the park's 34 raptors.

river, and offers sightings of lions, leopards, crocodiles and waterbuck, as well as hippos, giraffes, vervet monkeys, baboons and many birds. The circuit can be combined with the **Kopjes Circuit** (junctions 52–62; enter at junction 18 on the east bank of the Seronera River), which goes anti-clockwise around Maasai, Loliondo and Boma Kopjes. Climbing on the rocks is forbidden. **The Hills Circuit** (junctions 27–29) cuts through grassland to the wooded foothills of the Makori and Makoma Hills west of the Seronera Valley, and is good for hyena, zebra, ostrich, warthog, gazelle, topi and hartebeest. A drive along this circuit is best combined with the **Songore River Circuit** (junctions 30–34), which loops into the plains south of the Seronera River. Thomson and Grant's gazelle, topi, hartebeest and ostrich are frequent, as are cheetah during the dry season. Lastly, the **Wandamu River Circuit** (junctions 40–49) covers similar habitats to the Seronera River Circuit, and hugs the banks of the Wandamu River, especially popular with buffaloes.

The Western Corridor

The **Western Corridor** is the unlovely name given to the forty-kilometre-wide strip that reaches out from Seronera to within 8km of Lake Victoria. The forests and swamps of the **Grumeti River** mark the northern boundary, while to the south is an area of grassland flanked by low wooded hills. The area receives the annual migration between May and July, after which time the bulk of the herds head on north over the Grumeti River towards Maasai Mara. This is the best time to visit the area, especially if the river is in flood, when the crossing is extremely perilous. At first hesitant, the herds surge headlong with a lemming-like instinct into the raging waters, while crocodiles and lions lie in wait for those injured in the effort, too weak for the strong currents or who get stuck in the muddy quagmire at the river's edges. You can find the crossings just by looking for vultures circling overhead.

A small part of the migration forgoes the pleasures of the river crossing to stay behind in the grasslands in the western part of the corridor, which also contains substantial populations of **non-migratory animals**, including some wildebeest and zebra, and smaller populations of giraffe and buffalo, hartebeest, waterbuck, eland, topi, impala and Thomson's gazelle. Hippo are present in large numbers, and in the dry season can always be seen at **Retima Hippo Pool**, 20km north of Seronera. Given the abundance of food, predators flourish, too: **leopards** in the lush tangled forests and thickets beside the river, and **crocodiles** – especially around Kirawira in the west – for whom the migration's river crossing provides a Bacchanalian feast. A speciality of the forest is a population of **black-and-white colobus monkeys**, though you'll need time and patience to track them down. The forests are also rich in **birdlife**, especially during the European winter. With luck, you might see the rare olive-green bulbul.

Northern Serengeti

The patches of acacia woodland at Seronera begin to dominate the rolling hills of the **northern Serengeti**. The area contains at least 28 acacia species, each adapted to a particular ecological niche, and the change in species is often startlingly abrupt, with one completely replacing another within a distance of sometimes only a few dozen metres. The undulating nature of the landscape makes it easy to spot animals from a distance and, further north, especially around **Lobo Kopjes**, higher ground provides fantastic views of the migration in the grasslands to the east (the best months are July–September when it heads north, and November and December when it turns back). Elephants, buffalos, zebras, gazelles and warthogs can be seen all year. There's a game-drive circuit to the east of *Lobo Wildlife Lodge*, whose waterholes attract a variety of wildlife, although the natural spring mentioned on older maps has now been capped by a pump.

ESSENTIALS

SERENGETI NATIONAL PARK

Park headquarters The park's administrative headquarters are just outside Ikoma Gate, and handle bookings for the park-run *bandas* and special campsites (daily 7.30am–5.30pm, ☎0689 062243 or ☎0767 536125, ⓦtanzaniaparks.com/serengeti.html and ⓦserengeti.org).

Entrance fees Park entry fees, valid for 24 hours, are $60 per person and Tsh20,000 for a vehicle, payable at the entrance gates by Visa or MasterCard, but not cash.

Information There are useful visitor centres at Seronera (see p.342), *Lobo Wildlife Lodge* (see p.346) and Naabi Hill

Gate near Ngorongoro, which has a viewpoint over the plains. Maps and guidebooks can be bought at the park gates, in Arusha, Dar and Stone Town (Zanzibar), and at the park's lodges. The best guidebook is the full-colour, pocket-size edition published by TANAPA. Driving off the main routes is only allowed with a professional guide or driver-guide, so a decent map isn't that important. A nice one is Giovanni Tombazzi's hand-painted version. For Seronera, the park gates dispense A4 leaflets showing routes and junction markers.

ARRIVAL AND DEPARTURE

Serengeti's eastern entrance, shared with Ngorongoro Conservation Area, is Naabi Hill Gate, 17km inside Serengeti, 45km southeast of Seronera Visitor Centre and approximately 300km from Arusha. The western entrance, 145km from Seronera, is Ndabaka Gate, next to the Mwanza–Musoma Highway. Two other, less used, gates are Ikoma Gate north of Seronera, and Klein's Gate in the northeast, for access to Loliondo and the wild road to Lake Natron (see pp.347–349). There's no border crossing from the park into Kenya.

By organized safari Most visitors come on an organized safari from Arusha (pp.288–289) or Mwanza (see p.364), either by road or, for upmarket packages, by light aircraft, or in a rented 4WD.

By car Renting a 4WD, in Arusha, Karatu, Mto wa Mbu or Mwanza, gives you more flexibility than a standard safari, and works out pretty cheap if you can fill all the seats. Self-drive is possible, but restricts your movements to the main roads, so it's better to rent a vehicle with a driver (who usually doubles as a wildlife guide), or hire an official guide at the park gate ($20 per day). If you run short on fuel, you can top up at Seronera village.

By plane Half a dozen Serengeti airstrips are served by scheduled flights; which one you use depends on where you stay. If you pre-book with a lodge or tented camp, they'll pick you up from the airstrip. The airlines are: Air Excel (AE; ⓦairexcelonline.com); Auric Air (AA; ⓦauricair.com);

Coastal Aviation (CA; ⓦcoastal.co.tz); Regional Air (RA; ⓦregionaltanzania.com); and Safari Airlink (SA; ⓦflysal .com). Airlines with the quickest flights are listed first:

Destinations Arusha (AA AE CA RA SA: 7 daily; 1hr 5min–2hr 30min); Dar (AE CA SA: 3–4 daily; 3hr 30min–4hr 45min); Kilimanjaro (CA AE SA: 4 daily; 1hr 25min–2hr 45min); Mafia (CA SA: 2 daily; 4hr 45min–7hr 30min); Manyara (AA CA RA AE SA: 7 daily; 35min–1hr 45min); Mwanza (CA: 1 daily; 1hr 35min–2hr 20min); Ndutu (CA AA RA AE SA: 6 daily; 20min–1hr 30min); Pangani (CA SA: 2 daily; 4hr 20min–7hr 25min); Pemba (CA: 1 daily; 4hr 20min–5hr 20min); Ruaha (SA CA: 2 daily; 2hr 40min–4hr 15min); Rubondo (CA: 1 daily; 2hr 10min–3hr 5min); Saadani (SA: 1 daily; 6hr 40min–7hr 35min); Selous (CA: 1 daily; 4hr 40min–5hr 40min); Zanzibar (AE CA: 2–3 daily; 3hr–4hr 10min).

TOURS AND ACTIVITIES

Balloon safaris Watching the wildebeest migration from a hot-air balloon is the ultimate in bush chic. The balloons accommodate twelve to sixteen passengers, and cost $550 for the sixty- to ninety-minute flight, including a champagne breakfast. The inflation and lift-off at dawn is a spectacular affair, and the landing is often interesting, to say the least, as the basket may be dragged along before finally coming to rest. You get picked up from your lodge or campsite well before dawn (sometimes as early as

4.30am). Flights can be arranged at lodges and tented camps on arrival, but are best booked in advance. Adventures Aloft ☎027 254 3300 or ☎0685 250153, ⓦmadahotels.com) have launch sites in northern Serengeti, while Serengeti Balloons (☎027 254 8077 or ☎0784 308494, ⓦballoonsafaris.com) have launch sites in central Serengeti (Seronera; year-round), southern Serengeti (Ndutu; end-Dec to end-March), and the western corridor (Kirawira; June–Oct).

ACCOMMODATION AND EATING

Seronera is the busiest area for tourists, with heavy safari vehicle traffic, while the northern Serengeti is much quieter. The most likely months for the migration are given in each **lodge** or **camp** review, though it might still be an hour's drive away, even if you come at the right time, as the migration's location depends on the rains. Book early, particularly if your choice is likely to be close to the migration. Places outside the park's western boundary, including some on the

shore of Lake Victoria, are cheaper, but – with the exception of those just outside Ikoma Gate – see next to no plains game. You're welcome to drop in for **lunch** at some of the lodges – *Lobo Wildlife Lodge, Serengeti Sopa Lodge* and *Seronera Wildlife Lodge* are particularly recommended, not so much for their cuisine, which is buffet style ($30 per person), but for the amazing views. Much cheaper meals can be had a several *hotelis* near the Visitor Centre in Seronera, mainly used by park staff.

Kirawira Tented Camp Kirawira Hills, 100km west of Seronera ☎ 027 253 9160 (Arusha), ⊛ serenahotels .com. On a hilltop overlooking the savanna in the western corridor, this provides a 1920s "white hunter"-style experience, and pampers you silly with its valets, luxurious double tents kitted out with period furnishings, and refined dining, complete with bone china and starched napkins. Modern creature comforts include a plunge pool, and even wi-fi. Given that you could be sharing the experience with up to fifty other people, it's massively overpriced. Migration close by May–June. FB **$1845**

★**Lobo Wildlife Lodge** Lobo Kopjes, 76km north of Seronera ☎ 027 254 4595 or ☎ 0754 254600 (Arusha), ⊛ hotelsandlodges-tanzania.com. Don't expect tip-top standards, but do come for the fabulous location, around the crest of a high kopje, with awesome views of a vast game-filled plain from each of its 75 rooms, as well as from its swimming pool and two terraces (one for sunrise, the other sunset). There are plenty of animals close by, too, including large lion prides, hyraxes and baboons that use the lodge as a short cut to their favourite sunbathing boulders. Migration close by Oct–Nov, less so July–Sept. FB **$550**

Mbalageti Serengeti Mwamyeni Hill, 90km west of Seronera ☎ 028 262 2387 (Mwanza), ⊛ mbalageti .com. Among the Serengeti's most affordable options, offering a combination of small but comfy lodge rooms, and much better and well-spaced "tented chalets" (safari tents pitched on wooden platforms, with plumbed in bathrooms at the back), which have great over the plains from their decks. Even better views, and plenty of wildlife (including elephants attracted by the nearby Mbalageti River), can be seen from the opened-sided lounge, dining and swimming pool area. The only niggles are the mostly package tour clientele (so evening buffets rather than à la carte), and the need to prebook the obligatory Maasai guard to escort you to and from your room or tent (no fences). Wi-fi in the main building. Migration close by May–July. FB lodge room **$420**, tented chalet **$610**

Serengeti Migration Camp Ndassiata Hills, 80km north of Seronera ☎ 027 250 0630 (Arusha), ⊛ elewanacollection.com. Built into a kopje overlooking the Grumeti River, this has 21 super-luxurious tents, an open-sided bar, and small pool. A floodlit waterhole attracts wildlife including hippos, but it's pricey for a place that's popular with tour groups. Migration close by July–Aug, sometimes also Nov. Closed April–May. FB **$1490**,

game package **$1690**

Serengeti Serena Safari Lodge Mbingwe Hill, 24km northwest of Seronera ☎ 027 253 9160 (Arusha), ⊛ serenahotels.com. An architecturally inventive and unobtrusive lodge tucked into a thick stand of acacias. Rooms are in 22 two-storey thatched rondavels, that are topped with spikes, in the style of traditional huts, but also resemble WWI German helmets. The best views are from the upper floors of the rondavels lower down the hill. Facilities include a kidney-shaped swimming pool, two rooms for disabled guests, and optional bush dinners, and service is attentive without being over the top. Migration close by April–May, stragglers until July. FB **$855**

Serengeti Sopa Lodge Nyarboro Hills, 46km southwest of Seronera ☎ 027 250 0630 (Arusha), ⊛ sopalodges .com. Occupying a ridge, this is an architectural blot, but things perk up considerably inside where warm ochre tones and chunky armchairs with big cushions dominate public areas. The 79 rooms are large and have balconies with sweeping views, and there's a pool on a panoramic terrace. Migration close by March–May. FB **$650**

Seronera Wildlife Lodge Seronera ☎ 027 254 4595 or ☎ 0754 254600 (Arusha), ⊛ hotelsandlodges-tanzania .com. This breezy place has aged well and still looks good, though the 75 rooms are a little basic. The best, and with better views, are at the back. Migration close by April–July. FB **$610**

TANAPA Rest House 1km from Seronera village and the Visitor Centre; book through the park headquarters. This park-run place has three en-suite twin rooms, but lacks any "in the wild" feeling. Still, it benefits from the proximity of Seronera village, which has three *hotelis* dishing up cheap meals, bars and shops selling everything from chocolate to champagne. Migration close by April–July. Per person **$30**

OUTSIDE THE PARK

Ikoma Tented Camp 3km outside Ikoma Gate ☎ 027 250 6315 or ☎ 0754 324193 (Arusha), ⊛ moivaro.com. In a great location on the edge of the western migratory routes (May–July & Nov–Jan), this place has sixteen large and comfortable en-suite tents in a relaxed and friendly atmosphere. The camp offers reasonably priced excursions on foot (outside the park), including bush walks ($20 per person) and night game-drives ($40 per person). Camping per person **$20**, FB **$433**

Serengeti Stop Over On the highway 2km south of

Ndabaka Gate ☎028 262 2273 or ☎0784 422359, ⓦserengetistopover.com. A pleasant if largely shadeless place within walking distance of Lake Victoria (no swimming due to bilharzia). Apart from camping (those without tents can rent them for $10; hot showers), there are ten small well-tended *bandas*, each with two beds, big nets and good showers in their bathrooms, and meals are available ($4–10). They can also organize locally run cultural tourism activities among the Sukuma, including visits to traditional healers, dances and fishing trips. Safaris into the park can be arranged ($180 per vehicle per day, plus park fees). Camping per person $̄13, *bandas* (BB) $̄60

Speke Bay Lodge 13km south of Ndabaka Gate; the turning is 6km south of Lamadi ☎028 262 1237, ⓦspekebay.com. A great place to start or end a Serengeti safari, right on the shore on Lake Victoria (no swimming thanks to bilharzia, and crocs) on a lightly wooded plot that's fantastic for birding (some twitchers claim to have spotted over one hundred species here). Accommodation is in one of twelve too closely spaced and very basic tents, or, better, in eight attractive thatch-roofed circular bungalows on the shore with sideways views of the lake and sunset from their verandas. Also on offer are guided canoe trips, mountain biking, and fishing. Wi-fi is poor. BB tents $̄200, rooms $̄350

CAMPING

The most atmospheric (and nerve-jangling) way of overnighting is to camp at one of several **public campsites**. More remote are a scatter of **special campsites**, which have no facilities whatsoever ($50 per person). Reservations for special campsites are handled by the park headquarters (see p.344), or by TANAPA headquarters in Arusha (see p.287), though they are very difficult to book in advance as safari companies use them for their luxury tented camps – you may strike lucky if you enquire at the park gate on arrival. If you're self-driving, the car hire company should be able to find out what's available, and may even book it for you.

Lobo public campsite Lobo Kopjes, 76km north of Seronera, 300m northeast of Lobo Wildlife Lodge; pay at the park gates. Located at the foot of a kopje, with fantastic views over the plains to the east. There are decent bathrooms, but the showers are cold, and nights are chilly at 1800m above sea level. You can pop over to *Lobo Wildlife Lodge*, on top of the next kopje 300m southwest, for lunch or drinks. Per person $̄30

Seronera public campsites 6–7km northeast of Seronera Visitor Centre by road; pay at the park gates. Five campsites in two clusters: *Dikdik* and *Pimbi* in the west, *Nyani*, *Ngiri* and *Tumbili* in the east. Each has its own bathroom with good showers, and a fenced-off kitchen and dining *banda*, but the campsites themselves are not fenced so wildlife including lions comes and goes freely, although the last reported lion attack on humans here was in 1965. Exceptionally (driving is normally forbidden after 7pm), campers are allowed to drive to *Seronera Wildlife Lodge* for dinner ($30), but have to be back by 10pm. Per person $̄30

Loliondo

Bounded by the Serengeti, Ngorongoro, Lake Natron and the Kenyan border, **Loliondo** is a wild, remote, desolate and subtly beautiful region. Even in the dry season, the leafless trees and bushes are full of colour, from the blue or yellow bark of the acacias, through violet and rusty orange bushes, and the mauve and green of thorn trees. The area is especially good for **wildlife** in November and December when a good part of the annual migration heads down from Maasai Mara – as a consequence, it has long been favoured by trophy hunters.

Almost all of Loliondo is classified as a "**Game Controlled Area**", whose hunting concession has been held by a Dubai-based corporation since 1992. In 2009, a law was passed banning livestock and farming inside Game Controlled Areas, which meant that the land rights of Loliondo's villagers and herders were effectively voided. Following a series of violent incidents involving local communities, the hunting company, and police, in 2013 the Tanzanian government decided to evict all villagers from Loliondo – estimated at between 20,000 and 48,000 Maasai. This prompted an international outcry, including a petition with 1.7 million signatures against the decision, and the government climbed down. In late 2014, evictions were once again mooted, prompting Tanzanian President Kikwete to announce that the government had no intention, "ever", "to evict the Masai people from their ancestral land".

Wasso

Some 70km southeast of Serengeti's Klein's Gate (around a two-hour drive), the first major settlement in Loliondo is **Wasso**: its entrance is marked by a government building on the left with a flag, and a transmitter on the right, beyond which is a small river crossing. The road here from the Serengeti is easy to follow for the most part and passes through impressively craggy hills, heavily wooded save for clearings made by Maasai for their cattle and limited agriculture. Along the way you'll pass many Maasai who are not accustomed to tourists, so make a point of always obtaining (or paying for) permission before taking photos.

Loliondo Village

Some 6km beyond Wasso, the settlement of **Loliondo Village** is an oasis of lush vegetation amid desolate terrain. Before the sealed road from Kenya to Tanzania via Namanga was built, it was a major stop on the Great North Road from Nairobi to Arusha, which ultimately went on to Cape Town in South Africa. A handful of Europeans settled here early on, and the village still has an old colonial feeling to it, both in the style of its buildings, and because of the wide main road which was planted long ago with beautiful purple-flowered jacaranda trees. The village has a post office, a branch of NMB bank (ATM for Tanzanian cards only), and fuel, and its high altitude gives it a pleasantly breezy and cool climate, though it can be quite nippy at night.

ARRIVAL AND ACCOMMODATION   LOLIONDO VILLAGE

By bus Loliondo village has a Sunday bus service from Arusha (at least 12hr), run by Loliondo Bus or Coast Line. Buy your ticket at Arusha's bus stand days before as the buses are always full; ask on the north side of.

By car There are currently two road tolls between Loliondo village and Klein's Gate in The Serengeti ($25 and $20 per person), and four between Loliondo village and Mto wa Mbu (totalling $45, plus $20 per vehicle). From Wasso, turn left at the junction beyond the river crossing, and it's 6km to Loliondo.

Simon Kamakia's Oloolera Maasai Campsite Loliondo Village ☏ 0786 562617. Run by the affable octogenarian Simon Kamakia, this is a beautiful and extremely welcoming place to stay, and you don't need a tent, as you can borrow one for an extra $10 or so. The site is grassy, and surrounded by fever trees and candelabra euphorbia. You're provided with a guard at night, whether you want one or not, and food can be arranged. Camping per person **$10**

Sonjo village

Some 60km southeast of Wasso, **Sonjo village** is a large cluster of round thatched huts in the lee of an escarpment, and the main settlement of the agricultural **Sonjo tribe**.

DRIVING THE ECO TRAIL

Those with their own vehicles can tackle an adventurous drive from the Serengeti's Klein's Gate, across **Loliondo** district along an extremely dusty road to **Lake Natron**, and south from there, along an equally dusty road, past **Ol Doinyo Lengai volcano** and the enigmatic **ruins of Engaruka**, to the tarmac highway 3.5km east of Mto wa Mbu (see p.352). The entire route can just about be done in a day if you leave early, but it's better to spend a night beside Lake Natron. The road is extremely lightly travelled – you won't see more than a handful of other vehicles – but it is expensive, as a series of six **road tolls** along the way charge a total of $90 per person (non-residents) plus $20 per car (though some have reported $150 being charged for foreign-plated vehicles). The section between Klein's Gate and Wasso crosses a zone of black cotton soil, which can make it **impassable in the rains**, while some of the hairpins down the Nguruman Escarpment to Lake Natron can be washed away, but in dry weather the road is passable, if sometimes uncomfortable.

The Sonjo, who supplement their subsistence agriculture by hunting, may be one of the peoples responsible for having constructed the now-ruined villages and intricate irrigation complex at Engaruka, 100km to the south (see p.352), and have similar stone bases for building houses on. They settled in their present location at least three hundred years ago, but their more distant origins remain unknown, and academics can't agree on whether their language – quite distinct from Maasai – is Bantu or Cushitic, though it's probably a bit of both. There's no accommodation, and you'll need to obtain permission before taking pictures.

ARRIVAL AND DEPARTURE   **SONJO VILLAGE**

By car Turn right after the river crossing in Wasso, along a decently graded road which passes Wasso airfield after 2km, then bear left at all road forks. Some 15km from Wasso, a right fork heads on down to Ngorongoro Conservation Area, while the left one continues south/southeast for 8km before turning east into a valley. Follow this until the road turns south again: there's a beautiful viewpoint near the top, some 5km north of Sonjo Village.

Mount Mosonik and Seventeen Corners

From the north side of Sonjo village, the road veers east, starting a long, straight and very dusty drive due east to the edge of the Nguruman Escarpment. The low craggy mountain that gradually appears to the southeast is **Mount Mosonik**, rising on the southwestern side of Lake Natron. The road here is extremely sandy in places, and a 4WD is helpful even in dry weather. Along the way, there are fantastic candelabra euphorbia trees to admire, as well as bizarre giant aloe, which resemble palm trees with upturned fronds. With luck, you'll also see ostrich.

At the edge of the escarpment, the road – now a narrow rocky trail barely wider than a 4WD – twists down a frightening stretch known as **Seventeen Corners**. Some sections get washed away in the rains, so check on the road's condition at the army post before Sonjo (or at Engaresero if you're coming from the lake). Once down, the road heads south across a weird and extremely beautiful moonscape pitted with craters and gullies, before skirting the lake to arrive at Engaresero, an hour's drive from Seventeen Corners.

Lake Natron

To desert rats, the land around **Lake Natron** – a vast, shallow soda lake bordering Kenya in Tanzania's far north – is something of a dream: hellishly hot, dry, desolate and bizarrely beautiful, especially with the grandiose peak of Ol Doinyo Lengai rising at its southern end. This volcano is the cause of the lake's extreme alkalinity, which forms a pinkish-white crust of soda crystals across much of its surface in the dry season, cracked into a polygonal patchwork.

Covering over 1300 square kilometres, the lake, like the smaller Lake Magadi just over the border in Kenya, lacks any outlet, and receives only 400mm of rain a year, part of it falling as "phantom rain", meaning that the raindrops evaporate before hitting the surface. The amount lost by **evaporation** is eight times that; the shortfall is made up by volcanic springs and temporary streams, whose waters leach through Ol Doinyo Lengai's caustic lava flows before reaching the lake. The concentration of salt, sodium carbonate (soda, or natron) and magnesite in the lake water is highly corrosive and the surrounding land isn't much more hospitable.

Not surprisingly, the lake isn't the most conducive to life, the big exception being a flourishing population of sometimes several hundred thousand **lesser flamingos**, who feed on the lake's microscopic diatom algae, and who have made the lake the most important flamingo breeding ground in the world. At times, literally millions of birds paint the horizon with a shimmering line of pink, and the lake is protected as an Important Wetland Area under the international RAMSAR.

Engaresero

Some 56km north of Engaruka and 124km from Mto wa Mbu, **Engaresero** (also called Ngara Sero or Natron Village) near Lake Natron's southwestern shore is the only settlement of any size beside the lake. It has all the charm of a frontier outpost, which of course it is, and there isn't much to do here other than laze around the small **pool** at *Lake Natron Tented Camp* (see below), which is open to non-residents for $10 a day, or visit the **waterfalls** ($25 per guide), a 25-minute walk upstream from *Waterfalls Campsite*. Engaresero is, however, the only base for visiting Natron's **lakeshore**, 4km away across scorching grey sand (the level of the lake varies). As you approach the edge, soda and salt crystals appear, concealing a foul-smelling slurry of mud, which can burn your skin.

The hot springs

To visit the **hot springs** on Lake Natron's eastern shore needs a 4WD and a driver experienced on loose sand. Take care not to drive too close to the shore, where you're likely to get bogged down. The soda flats in the southeastern corner are used by **flamingos** to mate and nest between August and October; the nests, which you can see from a distance, are made from mud and resemble miniature volcanoes – rather fittingly, given the location. Flamingos can usually also be seen in Moniki area, roughly 10km north of Engaresero village. Other birds you might see include pelicans, ibis, ducks and geese, together with eagles and plovers. **Terrestrial wildlife** is also present, especially close to the springs, albeit in small numbers, and includes zebra, wildebeest, gazelle, ostrich, golden jackal, and – more rarely – fringe-eared oryx, lesser kudu and gerenuk.

The Nguruman Escarpment

The **Nguruman Escarpment**, within walking distance of Engaresero, contains a number of attractions, including a volcanic implosion crater, ravines containing nesting sites for Ruppell's griffon vultures, and several waterfalls along **Engaresero Gorge**. Swimming is possible, though women are expected to cover up while bathing – wear shorts and a T-shirt. Walks further up the escarpment can be arranged at the campsites, they can also fix up visits to a Maasai *boma*.

ARRIVAL AND INFORMATION   LAKE NATRON

By organized safari The East African Safari & Touring Company (see p.289) is one of few safari companies to run trips through this area. The lake can also be visited at the end of a Crater Highlands trek from Ngorongoro (see p.334).
By bus Engaresero is served by the Sunday bus service from Arusha (see p.348). Other than this, public transport to Engaresero is irregular, and usually takes the form of Land Rover pick-ups from Mto wa Mbu (5–6hr in good conditions). Mto wa Mbu's cultural tourism programme staff can point you in the right direction.
By car Ngorongoro District Council's toll gate is 6km south

of Engaresero, and charges $15 per person and $20 per car, per day. There are two more tolls to the south ($25 per person total), and three along the road to Loliondo (totalling $50 per person). The drive up from Mto wa Mbu can take as little as four or five hours, but the road is often impassable in the rains, and extremely dusty in the dry season. Locals either walk or wait around, sometimes for a day or three, for a lift on one of the very few private vehicles that make it up here, usually carrying supplies for Engaresero's poorly stocked stores. Note that there is no petrol or diesel in Engaresero.

ACCOMMODATION

In addition to the following camps, temporary campsites spring up from time to time, usually run by Arusha-based safari companies. There are also a couple of basic guesthouses in Engaresero, the cleanest being *Kidemi Guest House*. Engaresero has a couple of bars, of which *Magogo* is the best – they both also serve food, provided you're not in a hurry.

Lake Natron Tented Camp 1km west of Engaresero ☎ 027 250 6315 (Arusha), ⓦ moivaro.com. It's a surprise to find such affordable luxury in dusty Engaresero. The nine

permanent, en-suite tents are stylish and comfortable and have electricity, but there are also four much cheaper rooms in Maasai-style *bandas*, and a campsite. Facilities include a bar

and good simple food, internet access, a swimming pool, and walks guided by locals to the lake, the village, and to a waterfall: the three walks together cost $25 per person. The camp can also arrange transport here from Mto wa Mbu. Camping per person $10, rooms (HB) *bandas* $70, tents $343
Waterfalls Campsite In a ravine beside the Engaresero River, 2km from Engaresero. Despite the lack

of shade, this grassy site is recommended both for its great location (there are rock pools in the adjacent river where you can take a dip), and for the warm welcome – it's run by the very charming Mama Lulu. Drinks and meals are available, and there's a full range of guided walks, but you need your own tent. Per person $15

Ol Doinyo Lengai

Rising up at the south end of Lake Natron is East Africa's only active volcano, **Ol Doinyo Lengai**, whose Maasai name means "The Mountain of God". Despite its active status, very little is known about the mountain other than that it tends to erupt explosively every twenty to forty years, and manages smaller **eruptions** every decade or so. The last significant eruption was in 2007, continuing into 2008, so you should be safe for the next few years.

7

For **geologists**, the special thing about Ol Doinyo Lengai is that it is one of few volcanoes worldwide to emit sodium carbonate and potassium, whose run-off accounts for the extremely alkaline and corrosive swill of neighbouring Lake Natron. For **photographers**, Ol Doinyo Lengai's perfectly conical shape is a delight, while the lava flows on the summit can be every bit as terrifying and awe-inspiring as you might imagine. **Climbers** are also in for a treat, despite the volcano's summit (2889m) being but a pimple compared to the majesty of its giant but dormant brothers to the east – Meru and Kilimanjaro. Admittedly, any pleasure gained by climbing the mountain (which can be done without any special equipment) is distinctly masochistic: the searing sun, the notoriously prickly vegetation and rough surface, reported sightings of spitting cobras near the summit (and leopard tracks), and the almost 45-degree slope. But as a reward for your travails, there's the weird, wonderful, eggily pungent and positively perilous sight and sound of **lava flows** bubbling at 510°C on top. There are two summit craters: the southern one is dormant or extinct and almost filled to the brim with ash, but the northern one, over 200m deep, remains active (occasionally lobbing lava bombs into the sky) and should be treated with **extreme caution**, particularly given the highly fluid and potentially explosive nature of natrocarbonatite lava.

Climbing Ol Doinyo Lengai

The summit is 17km south of Engaresero; the trails starts 10km south of Engaresero • Accessible on a Crater Highlands trek from Ngorongoro (see p.334), directly from Engaresero (see p.350), or with one of Arusha's safari operators (see pp.288–289), but do check that they have their own experienced guides, and adequate back-up (vehicles rather than donkeys, and HF radio for emergencies) • No entrance fee other than the $15 per person toll, levied 6km south of Engaresero • ⓦ oldoinyolengai.pbworks.com is a useful website dedicated to the mountain, with lots of up-to-date practical info, photos and links

Climbing Ol Doinyo Lengai must be done with a **guide** who knows the mountain and its caprices. The climb starts about 10km south of Engaresero village, and takes at least seven hours: four hours up and three back down. If you don't have a vehicle and don't fancy walking from Engaresero to the start of the trail, you'll have to wait until a vehicle is available. The ride shouldn't cost more than a few thousand shillings. The ascent is steep and mostly on loose and uncompacted soil, and there's no shade, so set off before dawn to arrive at the summit by mid-morning. It's possible to camp on the summit – the inactive southern crater makes a distinctly safer campsite than the active northern one.

With your own vehicle, you also could try searching out one of several **volcanic cones** and craters on the eastern side of the mountain, the biggest of which is called Shimo la Mungu ("God's Hole").

Engaruka

The most intriguing of northern Tanzania's attractions is a complex of stone ruins at **ENGARUKA**, at the foot of the Great Rift Valley's western escarpment north of Mto wa Mbu. One of Africa's most enigmatic archeological sites, the ruins are of a city about which little is known other than that it was founded around six hundred years ago and abandoned in the eighteenth century. Today, most of Engaruka's inhabitants are Maasai, who are thought to have arrived roughly two hundred years ago, once the settlement had already been deserted.

As well as the ruins, there are two Engarukas – a dusty spread of huts at **Engaruka Chini** along the road from Mto wa Mbu to Lake Natron, and the bustling Maasai market centre of **Engaruka Juu**, spreading 2–4km west of here along the way to the ruins.

Engaruka ruins

The entrance is 1.5km west of Engaruka Juu • No formal hours, but usually daily 8am–6pm • Tsh10,000 is paid at the gate • Guides are optional but recommended, and will expect $10–15 per group: they can be arranged through the cultural tourism programme (see p.353) • John Sutton's *Engaruka: An Irrigation Agricultural Community in Northern Tanzania before the Maasai* can be consulted at *Jerusalem Campsite*, and is sold at the Arusha Declaration Museum (see p.285)

The **Engaruka ruins** comprise at least seven villages and a complex irrigation system of stone-walled canals, furrows and dams extending 9km along the escarpment base. The initial residents are thought to be the **Iraqw** (see p.330), who now live around Karatu, since they use a similar system of self-contained agriculture, and Iraqw history recounts their last major migration to be about the same time as Engaruka was deserted, following a battle and defeat by Barbaig cattle herders. Another present-day tribe that has been linked to Engaruka is the **Sonjo**, who now live west of Lake Natron (see p.348); their oral history also recounts a migration at the time Engaruka was abandoned, and their traditional method of building houses on **raised stone platforms** is identical to the remains at Engaruka. The reason for the site being abandoned was due possibly to conflict with the Barbaig, or possibly being the settlement's success at irrigation lead to a vastly increased human population, which became too much for its limited water supplies.

Two curious features of Engaruka are its cairns and stone circles. The **cairns**, up to 5m long and 2m high, appear to be little other than places where rocks and stones cleared from fields were gathered, although their carefully arranged square or angular faces suggest something rather more useful, or spiritual, than just a heap of stones. A human skeleton was found under one cairn but, other than that, excavations have yielded few clues as to their real purpose. More readily explained are the large **stone circles**, especially south of the river, which measure up to 10m in diameter and functioned as cattle pens.

ARRIVAL AND TOURS   ENGARUKA

By car Engaruka is roughly 55km north of Mto wa Mbu along the dusty but usually well-graded road to Lake Natron, which starts 3km east of Mto wa Mbu. After 50km, you'll reach the nondescript roadstead of Engaruka Chini, where a left turn brings you to after 3km to the village proper, Engaruka Juu, and, 2km further on, to the first of the ruins. Two road tolls are levied, one at Selela village half way along ($15 per person), the other at Engaruka itself ($10 per person). From Engaresero, the road has tricky sections of loose sand, and may be impassable during the rains, as there are no bridges over the normally dry streams that drop down from the escarpment. The only toll along

this section is the one at Engaruka.

By public transport You can get to Engaruka from Engaresero (2–4hrs depending on the state of the road), Mto wa Mbu (roughly 2hrs) and Arusha (4–5hrs), but timings and frequencies on all three routes are as wild as the scenery, so check on the latest at the camp in Engaresero (see p.351), at Mto wa Mbu's cultural tourism programme (see p.323), or at Arusha's tourist office (see p.287). From Mto wa Mbu, you'll join the locals in extremely packed Land Rover pick ups, of which there are several a day. From Arusha, there should be two buses, one leaving between 6am and 8am, the other between midday and 1pm.

Cultural tourism Engaruka is a fascinating area, whose Maasai inhabitants are far more "traditional" in their way of life than their cousins inside the adjacent Ngorongoro Conservation Area. The region has set up a cultural tourism programme, but its tours and visits have not really got going so far: for the latest, ask at the cultural tourism office in Arusha (see p.287), or consult Ⓦ tanzaniaculturaltourism .go.tz/engaruka.htm.

ACCOMMODATION

Jerusalem Campsite 6.5km west of the main road, beyond Engaruka Juu in the grounds of Engaruka Primary School. This campsite has no electricity but it's close to the escarpment, and has good views to the east. Despite being signposted, it's awkward to find: turn left just beyond *Mlezi Guest House*, cross the river immediately, and take the right fork on the opposite bank; the campsite is 4km on along a rough track. You're best bringing your own food. Per person Tsh10,000

Mlezi Guest House 2.5km west of the main road at Engaruka Juu. This very basic, and not overly clean, guesthouse is the only accommodation in Engaruka other than camping: its rooms share squat toilets and bucket showers, with no electricity. Tsh10,000

7

Lake Victoria and north-western Tanzania

FISHING BOATS, MUSOMA, LAKE VICTORIA

Lake Victoria and northwestern Tanzania

Dominating Tanzania's northwest is Lake Victoria (Lake Nyanza), filling a shallow depression between the Western and Eastern Rift Valleys. Covering an area of 69,484 square kilometres, and with a shoreline of 3220km, the lake is Africa's largest, and the world's second-largest freshwater lake. It's also the Nile's primary source, providing it with a steady, year-round flow. The lake region is densely inhabited by farmers and cattle herders, and also by people living in the major cities on its shores, including Kampala and Jinja in Uganda, Kisumu in Kenya, and Mwanza, Bukoba and Musoma in Tanzania, each with their own character and even charm.

The biggest of Tanzania's lakeside cities – at times frenetic, but rarely intimidating – is **Mwanza**, serving as the interface between the lake and its southern hinterland, which is home to Tanzania's largest tribe, the Sukuma – and to enough gold- and gemstone mining operations to have financed a building boom. Much smaller, but no less enjoyable, is the port of **Musoma**, perched at the end of a crooked peninsula on the lake's eastern side, which has some lovely beaches. Close by is the town of **Butiama**, home of Tanzania's much-revered founding father, Julius Nyerere, in whose memory a museum is dedicated, and whose son coordinates the area's **cultural tourism** programme. There's more cultural tourism over on the lake's west side, where the laid-back port town of **Bukoba** is a great base for exploring the little-visited northern reaches of Kagera Region, home to the Haya, whose culture resembles that of the Hutu and Tutsi of neighbouring Rwanda, but without the conflict. Several islands also warrant exploration, notably **Rubondo** in the southwest, famous for its rich birdlife, swamp-loving sitatunga antelopes, and some introduced elephants and chimpanzees; and agricultural **Ukerewe**, easy reachable from Mwanza or Serengeti, which also has cultural tourism programmes.

Mwanza Region

Mwanza Region, on the south side of Lake Victoria, is dominated by the port city of **Mwanza**. The region, much of it undulating plains scattered with large granite outcrops called *kopjes*, is home to the **Sukuma**, cattle herders by tradition, though many are now subsistence farmers. Mwanza is a handy base for a number of nearby attractions, including the **Sukuma Museum** and the island of **Ukerewe**, and also serves as a potential base for visiting Serengeti National Park, whose western border is barely 5km from the lakeshore.

SUKUMA DANCERS

Highlights

① Lake Victoria The world's second-largest freshwater lake is also the fabled source of the Nile, an enigma that baffled Europeans until Speke, heeding the advice of an Arab slaver, stumbled upon it in 1858. **See p.356**

② Sukuma Museum At Bujora near Mwanza, this is a great place for getting to know the Sukuma, Tanzania's largest tribe, and seeing their annual dance competitions. **See p.362**

③ Ukerewe Island Lake Victoria's largest island has a long and complicated history of tribal conquests and intrigues, but is rarely visited by tourists (part of the attraction), despite being just three hours from Mwanza by ferry. **See p.367**

④ Bukoba A pleasant port town connected to Mwanza by ferry and by road to Uganda and Rwanda. A lovely beach, laid-back feel and lots of cultural activities are the reasons to linger. **See p.374**

⑤ Rubondo Island Sitting in the lake's southwestern corner, its difficult (or expensive) access is compensated for by a host of endangered animals and breeding bird colonies. **See p.379**

HIGHLIGHTS ARE MARKED ON THE MAP ON P.358

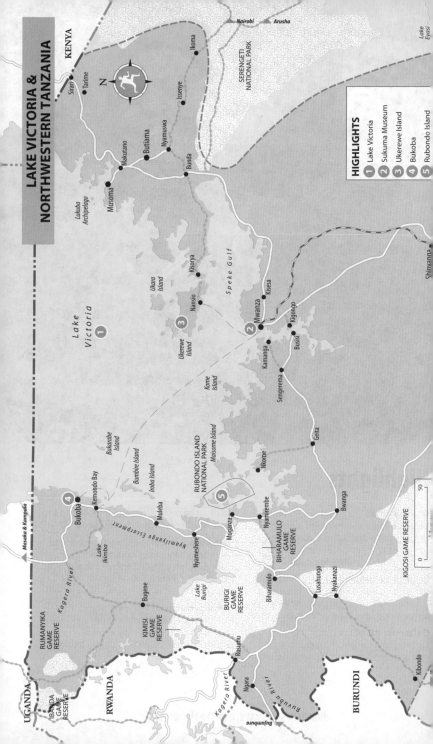

LAKE VICTORIA & NORTHWESTERN TANZANIA

HIGHLIGHTS

1. Lake Victoria
2. Sukuma Museum
3. Ukerewe Island
4. Bukoba
5. Rubondo Island

HEALTH HAZARDS ON LAKE VICTORIA

Lake Victoria presents a few potential health hazards. **Bilharzia**-carrying snails flourish in the reeds around the lake's fringes, and although you'll see local kids and fishermen in the water, the risk of contracting the disease is real. Similarly, while **crocodile and hippo** attacks are rare on the Tanzanian side of the lake, take local advice seriously. The steamy shore is also a fertile breeding ground for malarial **mosquitoes** – check bed nets carefully, and remember those pills. Note that **tap water** needs purifying for drinking (this may have been done for you in Mwanza, as its tap water reeks of chlorine).

Mwanza and around

Handsomely located amid rolling lakeside hills on Mwanza Gulf, in the southeast corner of Lake Victoria, the lively and friendly city of **MWANZA** is Tanzania's second-largest metropolis, one of Africa's fastest-growing cities (by twelve percent a year), and the country's busiest inland port, handling most of Tanzania's trade with Uganda. The city was founded in 1892 as a cotton-trading centre; nowadays, fishing, trade, some light industry and receipts from the region's **gold and diamond mines** are the city's economic mainstay.

Mwanza's inhabitants, the majority of them economic migrants, number around two million, seventy to eighty percent of whom live in slums on and around the hills on the city's outskirts. For a long time, population growth far outstripped the development of the city's infrastructure, but these days Mwanza is the recipient of sizeable investments, from the government and, notably, the Chinese, both of which dream of turning Mwanza into the principal conduit for East African trade. This explains the gargantuan shopping complex nearing completion 2km north of the city centre, which is intended to function as a showcase for all of East Africa.

None of this sounds especially enticing to tourists, but Mwanza is an enjoyable place, and even has a smattering of **beach hotels** to its name, although, as with the rest of the lake, swimming in its waters is not recommended.

Bismarck Rock

The lakeshore is Mwanza's main attraction. Heading south from the clock tower or ferry port you'll see the city's most photographed landmark, **Bismarck Rock**, a weathered granite *kopje* just offshore, whose profile, the Germans reckoned, resembled that of their nineteenth-century Chancellor. Although kids are fond of swimming around it, it's not recommended owing to the city's lack of sewage treatment, and the same applies to the adjacent beach, whose spruced up lawn behind it is a popular afternoon picnic site.

Capri Point

For the best views of the lake, get to the top of the boulder-strewn **Capri Point** peninsula south of the centre. This is the city's most affluent district, home to millionaires who have grown fat off diamonds, gold and the export of Nile perch. To get to the top, walk along Station Road and turn right before *Tilapia Hotel*. Take the first left, then right – ascending all the time. You should pass an enormous yellow mansion on your left (the road here is surfaced). Keep going straight up until the drivable road stops. From here, a footpath wends along the edge of the summit, giving fantastic views of Mwanza Creek, Lake Victoria and dozens of islands. You can also get there from Bismarck Rock by following the paved path around, then turning off and up to your right.

Saanane National Park

Saanane Island, between Capri Point and Bugando Hill • Park headquarters on Station Rd, before *Tilapia Hotel* • Daily 8am–5pm • ☎ 028 250 1205 or ☎ 0689 062276, ⓦ tanzaniaparks.com/saanane.html or ⓦ facebook.com/saananepark • $30 per person plus $35/group for the boat there and back

It's hard to understand the rationale behind the creation of Tanzania's newest, and tiniest, national park – **Saanane** – which is an island covering just 0.7 square

MWANZA

ACCOMMODATION

G.J. Hotel	9
Gold Crest Hotel	4
Isamo Hotel	12
JB Belmont Hotel	7
Lake Hotel	5
Malaika Beach Resort	2
Millenium Square Hotel	15
MS Hotel	10
New Mwanza Hotel	3
Rehema Hotel	8
Ryan's Bay Hotel	11
Tilapia Hotel	13
Waga Hill Lodge	14
Yun Long`	6

DRINKING & NIGHTLIFE

Gold Crest Hotel	2
JB Belmont Hotel	4
Royal Pub	5
Tilapia Hotel	6
Villa Park Resort & Club	1
Yun Long	3

SHOPPING

Imalaseko Supermarket	1

EATING

Food Square	3
Gold Crest Hotel	5
JB Belmont Hotel	7
Kuleana Pizzeria	4
Mid City Cafeteria	8
Ryan's Bay Hotel	10
Salma Cone	2
Surve Inn	9
Tilapia Hotel	11
Tunza Resort	1
Yun Long	6

N

Port & Ferries to Bukoba & Nansio

Ferries to Kamanga

Bismarck Rock

Lake Victoria

CAPRI POINT

Bank of Tanzania Training Institute

Hotel Under Construction

Train Station

Ryan's Bay Hotel

Nyamagana Stadium

Police

CCM House

Clock Tower

CRDB Bank

Fasjet

Mwanza Hotel

NMB Bank

Library

Fish Monument

Mirongo Hill

Serengeti Expedition

NBC Bank

Mirongo River

Central Market

Mwaloni Daladala Stand

Former Bus Stand

Fortes Safaris

Uhuru Monument

Pamba Secondary School

Barclays Bank

Aga Khan Medical Centre

Bugando Hill (Slum)

MAKONGORO RD

CUSTOM RD

REGIONAL DRIVE

BANTU STREET

UHURU STREET

BANDA STREET

LIBERTY STREET

NKOMO STREET

NYERERE ROAD

POST STREET

COURT ST

KENYATTA RD

KARUTA STREET

NYAMAGANA STREET

UHURU STREET

RWEGASORE STREET

TEMBO ROAD

LUMUMBA STREET

LIBERTY STREET

NYERERE ROAD

NYERERE ROAD

MATI MIRERU ROAD

WURZBURG ROAD

HOSSIM STREET

KENYATTA RD

STATION ROAD

CAPRI RD

1 (2.5km), Kirumba Mwaloni (3km), Airport (8km), 1 (8km), 1 & 2 (6km)

1 (2.5km), Kirumba Mwaloni (3km), Airport (8km)

metres 0 — 200

8

kilometres. In the 1960s, Saanane served as a quarantine station during the creation of Rubondo Island National Park (see p.379). Once that was done, it became a weekend picnic site, and a zoo, the latter encapsulating all that was most dismal and depressing about those places, as exemplified by a thoroughly depressed caged chimpanzee who endured decades of taunts from visitors. Now a national park, the zoo is gone, as is the old chimp; in their place, the island has been populated with very limited numbers of plains game including four zebra and some impala. TANAPA is planning all sorts of other activities here, from rock climbing and team-building seminars, to sports fishing, and even a venue for weddings.

Central market

Most of Mwanza's burgeoning population lives on the outskirts, in unplanned slums spread all over various boulder-strewn hills and outcrops, the most famous of which is Bugando Hill, crowned by the Government hospital. The area at the hill's base, stretching westwards towards the city centre, is a hive of activity, reaching a crescendo in the **market area** around the main daladala stand. Nearby, just north of the Uhuru Monument on both sides of a footbridge straddling the foul Mirongo River, are several **Maasai herbalists**, who apart from providing locally esteemed medicinal concoctions also sell cowrie-shell necklaces and other trinkets you won't easily find elsewhere.

Kenyatta Road

Kenyatta Road has a couple of roundabout monuments. At the junction with Station Road is the so-called **fish monument**, which is a life-size (ie giant) sculpture of a Nile perch, realistically painted, pointing skywards, its mouth letting forth a gush of water, and with which visiting Tanzanians love to have their pictures taken. Close to the ferry ports, a plaque next to the **clock-tower roundabout** at the west end of Nyerere Road commemorates the "discovery" of Lake Victoria and hence the source of the Nile in 1858

8

LAKE VICTORIA'S TROUBLED WATERS

Just over a century ago, Lake Victoria was one of the richest freshwater ecosystems on earth, with an estimated five hundred species of fish, including many brilliantly coloured cichlids. Today, only two hundred remain, the rest having vanished in the biggest **mass extinction of vertebrates** since the demise of the dinosaurs, while the lake itself is being systematically polluted, starved of oxygen and invaded by water hyacinth – all of which offers a bleak prospect for the forty million people who depend on it for survival.

The alarming collapse of Lake Victoria's ecosystem can be traced back to the arrival of the railways in colonial times and the subsequent development of lakeside cities, which began to place unsustainable pressure on the lake's resources. The Europeans also started commercial fishing, which by the 1950s had reduced catches of the two main edible species of tilapia to uneconomic levels. In a bid to find an alternative, moves were made to introduce non-native **Nile perch** (mbuta) into the lake. It was hoped that its size (up to 250kg) and carnivorous habits would convert smaller and commercially worthless cichlids into profitable protein. Scientists, who correctly predicted ecological disaster, fiercely opposed the proposal. Nonetheless, Nile perch found their way into the lake, having either been surreptitiously introduced, or having swum in along the Victoria Nile from Lake Kyoga in central Uganda. From a commercial point of view, the arrival of Nile perch was an enormous success, fuelling a lucrative export trade to Europe and Asia, which continues to this day (and explains why only few local restaurants offer it on their menus). Ecologically, however, the Nile perch was catastrophic: Lake Victoria's cichlid populations, which once constituted eighty percent of the lake's fish, are now estimated at less than one percent – the Nile perch have literally eaten their way through the lake's native species.

The whole sorry mess is the subject of *Darwin's Nightmare* (◍darwinsnightmare.com), a pessimistic documentary by Austrian director Hubert Sauper, which parallels the lake's ecological catastrophe with the dire social consequences of globalization in Mwanza.

by the English explorer Speke, who first saw the lake "from Isamilo Hill one mile from this point" (see p.515). The adjacent traffic island contains a small **memorial** to the men who died in the two world wars; the British as soldiers and the Africans as conscripted porters.

Sukuma Museum (Bujora Cultural Centre)

At Kisesa: 16km towards Musoma, then 1.5km (signposted) off the highway • Mon–Sat 9am–5pm, Sun 11am–5pm • Tsh15,000 entry, includes guided tour • ☎ 0754 637513, ⓦ sukumamuseum.org or ⓦ mwanza-guide.com/bujora.htm • Catch a daladala to Kisesa (Tsh500), then walk; taxis from Mwanza charge up to Tsh40,000

The **Sukuma Museum** is a good target for a day-trip from Mwanza. It covers the culture and traditions of Tanzania's largest tribe, the Sukuma, in great detail. The museum is in the compound of the **Bujora Catholic Mission**, founded in 1952 by a Canadian missionary, Father David Clement. Clement's open-minded approach saw Sukuma music, dance and history introduced into the mission's religious services, and is also reflected in the mission's **church**. Modelled along Sukuma lines, the church has a round peaked roof resembling a traditional Sukuma house, and is decorated inside with symbols of chiefly power: the altar is in the shape of a royal throne, and the tabernacle resembles a chief's house (*ikulu*), complete with a shield and crossed spears on the door.

The entrance to the **museum** is marked by a monument depicting a painted royal drum placed on a bas-relief map of Tanzania. The exhibits, covering every aspect of Sukuma life from the humdrum to the ritual, sacred and chiefly, are contained in a number of startlingly designed and colourfully painted pavilions. The Dance Society Pavilion has a wealth of information on the competing Bagika and Bagalu dance societies, while Sukuma history is presented in the Royal Pavilion, designed in the form

8

THE SUKUMA

The lake's southern and eastern hinterland, strewn with impressively eroded granite boulders, is the land of the seven-million-strong **Sukuma**, Tanzania's largest tribe. Their long-horned Ankole cattle – startlingly different from the short-horned Maasai race – provide the first inkling that central Africa is near. But the region is far from being a rural Nirvana: the area is notorious for its modern **witch-slaying** tradition – usually poor old ladies with red eyes caused by one too many years of hunkering over smoky kitchen fires. Fear of witchcraft is part of the problem, but so is greed for land: an old lady's soil, once inherited, may yield more than just crops: **diamonds** have been mined in the region since the 1920s, and the region's **gold reserves** – currently exploited by foreign mining corporations – are also staggering.

While the slayings are the most notorious facet of Sukuma superstition, the age-old Sukuma belief in magic is also more cheerfully expressed through **dance competitions**. Held in June and July, and sometimes also in August after the harvest that follows the long rains, they're particularly exuberant examples of a successful synthesis between old and new. The two oldest **dance societies** (*wigashe*), both of which perform annually at Bujora, are the Bagika and Bagalu, which were founded in the mid-nineteenth century by **rival healers** (good witches, if you like), Ngika and Gumha. As the two could not agree which of them had the most powerful medicine (*dawa*), a dance contest was organized to decide the issue.

The format, which remains unchanged, is for two competing dance societies to perform at the same time, with the crowd being free to move between the two – the better the medicine, the bigger the crowd. Obviously, good preparation is the key to success, and nothing is more important than **good luck medicine** (*samba*). This is dispensed by each dance society's healer (*nfumu*), and is intended to make the dancers, especially the dance leader (*mlingi*), appealing to the crowd. Given that crowd size is the key to success, each passing year sees new and innovative dance routines, costumes, tricks and props such as dancing on stilts, the use of articulated wooden puppets, fire breathing, and – an endearing favourite – the *Bugobugobo* **snake dance**, a hugely theatrical affair starring live pythons, which is a speciality of the Ngika Society.

The dance contests are best experienced at Bujora's two-week **Bulabo festival** following the Christian festival of Corpus Christi (usually early or mid-June). Alternatively, the Sukuma Museum can arrange dances at any time of year. There are some great photos of the event at ⓦ philip.greenspun.com/sukuma.

of a royal throne and containing a mass of genealogy, as well as royal drums, fly whisks, headdresses and other objects donated by the descendants of former chiefs.

Performances of **traditional drumming and dancing** can be arranged with a day's notice (Tsh130,000), and you can take lessons in traditional arts.

ARRIVAL AND DEPARTURE

BY PLANE

Mwanza Airport is 8km north of town. There are daladalas (marked "Airport") heading there from all over, including the bus stands (throughout the day, roughly four an hour, taking 20min). Taxis charge Tsh15,000. With the exception of flights to and from Dar on low-cost airline Fastjet (if bought well in advance), plane tickets are expensive: at least $320 to or from Arusha (Coastal Aviation), or $170 for Rubondo Island (Auric Air).

Airlines Companies flying from Mwanza are: **AA** (Auric Air: Mwanza Airport ☎0783 233334); **AT** (Air Tanzania: Kenyatta Rd ☎028 250 1059); **CA** (Coastal Aviation: Mwanza Airport ☎028 256 0441); **FJ** (FastJet: *New Mwanza Hotel*, Kenyatta Road ☎0756 754 0543); **PA** (Precisionair: Kenyatta Rd ☎028 250 0819).

Destinations Arusha (CA: daily; 3hr 15min); Bukoba (AA, PA: 2 daily; 45min); Dar (AT, CA, PA: 3–4 daily; 1hr 30min–2hr 15min); Entebbe (AA: 2 weekly; 1hr); Kigali (CA: daily; 1hr); Kilimanjaro (PA: 6 weekly; 1hr 20min); Manyara (CA: daily; 2hr 45min); Ngorongoro (CA: daily; 2hr 40min); Rubondo (CA: 2 weekly; 30min); Serengeti (CA: daily; 1hr 55min).

BY TRAIN

Mwanza station on Station Rd (☎028 250 2781 or ☎0754 460907) is the terminus of the Central Railway Line's northern branch from Tabora, but through-tickets can be bought to or from any station between Mwanza and Dar. The service is extremely unreliable, sometimes not running for weeks or even months, so if the ride is critical to your plans, ring them up to check the schedule. In 2014, trains left Dar at 5pm on Tues and Fri, and set off back from Mwanza at 6pm on Thurs and Sun. There's no first class to Tabora: a second-class sleeper costs Tsh22,700 (Tsh54,800 all the way to Dar), and third-class seating Tsh11,800. For sleepers, buy your ticket as early as possible to be sure of a bunk.

Destinations Dar (2 weekly; 37hr); Dodoma (2 weekly; 24hr 10min); Morogoro (2 weekly; 31hr 35min); Tabora (2 weekly; 10hr).

BY BUS

Mwanza has two bus stands, both outside the centre: services from Musoma, Butiama and Kenya terminate at

MWANZA

Buzuruga, 5km along the Musoma road (any daladala marked Kisesa or Kishiri passes by). All other buses finish at Nyegezi, 9km south along the Shinyanga road (daladalas marked Buhongwa pass by; taxis charge no less than Tsh15,000). To get to the city centre from either, catch a daladala marked "Airport", which can drop you at the clock-tower roundabout, and can also get you to within 1.5km of two beach hotels (see p.365). Both bus stands are chaotic affairs, and ticket touts are impossible to avoid (some of them even official, donning orange bibs), so get your ticket a day or two before, unencumbered by bags – ideally after having consulted the bus timetables at the tourist office (see below). Their list includes journey times: faster trips mean more dangerous driving.

Destinations Arusha (4 daily; 10–11hr); Biharamulo (2 daily; 4–5hr); Bukoba (2 daily; 6–7hr); Bunda (hourly; 2hr); Dar (11 daily; 13–15hr); Dodoma (3 daily; 9hr); Kigoma (2 daily; 12hr); Morogoro (3 daily; 11–12hr); Moshi (4 daily; 11–13hr); Musoma (hourly; 3–4hr); Nairobi (6 daily; 14–15hr); Singida (2 daily; 6–7hr); Sirari (hourly; 4hr); Tabora (4 daily; 6hr).

BY CAR

The road to Biharamulo (at the junction for Bukoba and Kigoma), via the gold-mining town of Geita, starts at Kamanga on the west side of Mwanza Gulf, accessed by vehicle ferry from the end of Posta St (hourly; Mon–Sat 7am–6pm, Sun 7am–5pm; 30min; Tsh6500 per vehicle plus Tsh1000 per passenger). There's another roll-on roll-off ferry 30km south of Mwanza connecting Busisi to Kigongo (every hour or two; daily 8am–9pm; same prices). Despite the welter of people and hawkers greeting passengers, there's not much hassle, but keep an eye on your bags.

BY FERRY

Mwanza's ferry port is at the end of Customs Rd just off the clock-tower roundabout (☎028 250 3081 or ☎028 250 0491, ⓦmscl.go.tz). There are daily ferries to Nansio on Ukerewe Island (see p.368), and the overnight MV *Victoria* to Bukoba (see p.377; currently 9pm Tues, Thurs and Sun). Destinations Bukoba (3 weekly; 10hr); Nansio (1–2 daily; 3hr).

INFORMATION

Tourist information The tourist board has an excellent tourist information office on Posta St, outside *New Mwanza Hotel* (Mon–Fri 8am–4pm, Sat 8.30am–1pm; ☎028 250

0818). It stocks reams of brochures, has transport timetables and lists of hotels (with prices), and information about cultural tourism in the lake zone. Also useful if

8

SAFARIS FROM MWANZA

Mwanza is sometimes touted as an alternative to Arusha for **Northern Circuit safaris**, on account of being closer to Serengeti. Strictly speaking, that's true, but the prime game viewing area of Seronera is about halfway between the two cities, and the other wildlife magnets – Ngorongoro, Manyara and Tarangire – are considerably closer to Arusha. Whichever way it's spun, a safari from Mwanza isn't cheaper than from Arusha, as prices are based on similarly inflated car rental rates: something like $170/day plus $1.20/km over 100km, with driver, which amounts to over $500 per person in a group of four for a two-night/three-day camping safari, park fees included, or twice that if staying in lodges.

The following **safari and car rental companies** are licensed and well reputed: Fortes Safaris, Lumumba Rd ☎028 250 1804, ⓦfortessafaris.com; Masumin, Kenyatta Rd (100m south of Rwagasore Rd) ☎028 250 0192, ⓦmasuminsafaris.com; and Serengeti Expedition, Nyerere Rd ☎028 254 2222, ⓦserengetiexpedition.com.

---

sometimes outdated is ⓦmwanza-guide.com.

Cultural tourism There are two cultural tourism programmes near Mwanza, both at Kisesa along the Musoma highway: the fledgling Sukumaland Destinations, at the Sukuma Museum (see p.362; ☎0754 637513, ⓔrichard_bulluma@yahoo.co.uk), and the more established Kisesa Eco & Cultural Tourism, signposted 1km south of the highway (Tsh2000 by *pikipiki*) from Kisesa daladala stand (☎0655 349348 or ☎0765 349348, ⓔkisesaculturalprogramme@gmail.com). Both offer a variety of loosely defined and similarly loosely priced options, the best being boat trips (for fishing, or exploring desert islands), canoeing and village tours to meet some of the healers and rain-makers of the Sukuma. Mwanza's tourist office has more information, and prices.

Getting around The city centre is small enough to walk around in. Taxis can be found everywhere: a short ride costs Tsh3000–4000. Daladalas, useful for the beach near the airport, and for getting to the bus stands, can be caught at the clock-tower roundabout.

ACCOMMODATION

The main concentration of lower-mid-range hotels is on and off Rwagasore Rd, but that area is noisy thanks to a ranting preacher's full-on sound system by day, and, at night, live bands on the rooftop of *JB Belmont Hotel* (the calls to prayer from the area's mosques, in contrast, are bewitchingly beautiful). More peaceful are a couple of beach hotels close to the airport north of the city, and – unless a disco pops up in the meantime – the lakeshore *Yun Long* in the centre itself. Many of Mwanza's hotels charge per room rather than per person, so "single" often means a double bed, and "double" means twin-bed. You can **camp** at *Tunza Resort* north of town.

IN TOWN

G.J. Hotel Rwagasore Rd ☎028 254 2061 or ☎0688 857191, ⓔgjhoteltours@yahoo.com. Best value of half a dozen hotels on this road, on six floors (with lift access from the second-floor reception upwards only), and currently free of other large buildings around it. Rooms are bright and even breezy, and all have shared balconies, fridge, TV and a/c. Restaurant and bar downstairs, and safe parking. One bed <u>Tsh30,000</u>, two beds <u>Tsh50,000</u>

Gold Crest Hotel Cnr Posta St and Kenyatta Rd ☎028 250 6058, ⓦgoldcresthotel.com. A swanky ten-storey hotel that's completely eclipsed the *New Mwanza* opposite. The rooms are large and comfortable, and have wi-fi. Good restaurant and café, and a wonderful rooftop bar complete with swimming pool (see p.366). Safe parking. BB <u>$125</u>, lake view <u>$145</u>

Isamo Hotel Rwagasore Rd ☎028 254 1616 or ☎0787 657399, ⓦisamohotel.com. Friendly and smart, a six-storey hotel (with no lift), with big well-kept rooms, all with satellite TV and fridge, some with a/c, and – still rare at the cheaper end of things – wi-fi. BB one bed <u>Tsh25,000</u>, two beds <u>Tsh40,000</u>

★JB Belmont Hotel Kenyatta Rd ☎028 250 5057 or ☎0689 602193, ⓦjbbelmonthotel.net. Similar to the *Gold Crest*, which it pips with better service and slightly cheaper rates, it's also one of only few hotels that doesn't equate conferences with bland and boring facilities. The guest rooms are on the seventh and eigth floors. Choose between lake view or "rock view", both fascinating. The main difference between standard and deluxe rooms is size; all are carpeted, and have a heap of mod cons, including flat-screen TV and wi-fi. The rooftop lounge, where you can also eat, is superb, and has a swimming pool, and rooms appear to be soundproofed against the live bands that perform there most nights of the week. Safe parking. BB <u>$100</u>, lake view <u>$120</u>

Lake Hotel Station Rd ☎028 250 0658. A funny old place near the train station accessed through a dark and sprawling yet genteel bar popular with elderly gents. There are forty-eight en-suite rooms ("singles", twins and triples), and they're pretty simple but good value if you don't mind the noise (upstairs is quieter). Cheap food at the bar. BB one bed T̲s̲h̲1̲5̲,̲0̲0̲0̲, two beds T̲s̲h̲2̲0̲,̲0̲0̲0̲

MS Hotel Off Karuta St ☎ 028 250 2001. Formerly the *Christmas Tree Hotel*, this is a reliable and well-priced choice. All thirty rooms have cable TV, fan, double bed and good bathroom with hot water; a handful of rooms (the best on the third floor) have views of the lake and Saanane Island. There's also a modest restaurant. BB T̲s̲h̲2̲0̲,̲0̲0̲0̲

New Mwanza Hotel Posta Rd ☎ 028 250 1070, ⓦ newmwanzahotel.com. Mwanza's oldest but least attractive tourist class hotel, trailing far behind its fresher rivals, and now mainly used for conferences. The rooms are OK and have wi-fi, some even have lake views, but you'll have to be OK with the noise from its discos and live bands (usually on Fri night). The swimming pool is indoors; there's also a casino and ground floor restaurant. BB T̲s̲h̲1̲2̲0̲,̲0̲0̲0̲

★**Rehema Hotel** Off Karuta St ☎ 0768 870438 or ☎ 0789 146871. A reliable budget choice with friendly staff, boasting small but spotless rooms, complete with TV, box nets, fan, and bathrooms with strong showers, but do check things work before settling in. T̲s̲h̲1̲5̲,̲0̲0̲0̲

Ryan's Bay Hotel Station Rd ☎ 028 254 1702 or ☎ 0784 699393, ⓦ ryansbay.com. Central Mwanza's newest lakeshore hotel. Its buildings, ranging from two to five storeys, are elegantly modern, and the lake views from the balconies of all fifty rooms are reason enough to stay. There's also a decent restaurant and bar, wi-fi throughout, a swimming pool (no lake views) and safe parking. BB $̲1̲4̲5̲

Tilapia Hotel Station Rd ☎ 028 250 0517 or ☎ 0784 700500, ⓦ hoteltilapia.com. This classic colonial-era hotel is tiring but remains popular with expats (hence the upmarket hookers in the bars), especially on account of its lakeshore location, but don't expect everything to be perfect. The spacious rooms come with cable TV, big beds, fans and a/c, and wi-fi; the better ones are higher up and have lake views. More atmospheric but noisier, and not unacquainted with the aforementioned ladies, are rooms on the *African Queen* houseboat (not Bogart's, mind). Several restaurants and a swimming pool complete the offering. BB $̲1̲2̲0̲

★**Yun Long** Nasser Drive, beyond Bismarck Rock ☎ 0752 243895 or ☎ 0754 243895. In a beautiful position right on the lakeshore are fifteen guestrooms (twins and doubles) in a long but low wing, all of them with lake-view verandas, and therefore very well priced. They're nicely decorated, all with TV and wi-fi. With a similarly beautiful location is the elegant bar and good if expensive restaurant. Safe parking. BB $̲6̲0̲, camping (planned) per person $̲1̲5̲

OUT OF TOWN

At the two beach hotels north of town, swimming in the lake is at your own risk. There's no public transport to either: daladalas drop you at one of two signposted access roads, the first is best for *Tunza*, the second for *Malaika*, both leaving you with a 1.5km walk, but you can catch a *pikipiki* at the first junction. Taxis from town charge T̲s̲h̲1̲5̲,̲0̲0̲0̲–̲2̲0̲,̲0̲0̲0̲.

Malaika Beach Resort 9km north of Mwanza ☎ 0686 735658 or ☎ 0689 603616, ⓦ malaikabeachresort .com. A Kenyan-style beach resort with manicured lawns and pompous afro-neoclassical decor. The main building, a huge round affair, contains the restaurant, coffee shop and some "premium" rooms (doublespeak for standard); other rooms are in closely spaced two-storey blocks at the back. Some of the "premium" rooms have lake views, as do the "executive," but not "deluxe". Unfortunately, conferences give it a thoroughly impersonal flavour, even allowing for the beachfront location, which comes with a fenced-in children's playground and beach bar. There's also a swimming pool and wi-fi. BB $̲1̲2̲0̲

Millenium Square Hotel Facing Nyegezi bus stand, 9km south of town ☎ 028 255 0420, ⓦ millenium squarehotel.co.tz. A pleasant modern choice if you're arriving late by bus, or leaving early, with a/c, wi-fi and a road-facing terrace for meals and drinks. BB $̲3̲0̲

★**Tunza Resort** 8km north of Mwanza ☎ 0689 305051, ☎ tunzabeach.com. Wonderfully quirky, starting with a broken-winged pink Cessna stuck on a pole by the entrance. The beach is lovely, as are the rooms, in a series of clean, comfortable and charming rustic *bandas* scattered around tropical gardens, all with lake views, big beds with huge walk-in nets, and – a nice touch – kettles and coffee. Add on a funky bar, good food (including weekend barbecues), and full English breakfast, and you have Mwanza's best choice for a proper holiday. Camping per person $10. BB $̲6̲5̲

★**Wag Hill Lodge** On the west side of Mwanza Gulf; accessed by boat from Mwanza Yacht Club ☎ 0754 917974, ⓦ waghill.com. Up above the western shore of Mwanza Gulf in a protected patch of indigenous forest, this romantic, friendly (and ecofriendly) lodge enjoys a glorious location teeming with birds. There are just five bungalows, secluded and cosy, and all built from natural materials, with balcony views of both forest and lake. There's also a swimming pool, fine food and a fire in the evenings. Rates include nature walks, kayaking, and fishing equipment. FB $̲4̲1̲3̲

EATING

Most mid-range hotels have decent if unmemorable restaurants, but you'll need to go upmarket to sample the lake's Nile perch. At night, Uhuru St is a good place for **street food**, with numerous stalls dishing up meat (goat is best), fish and bananas grilled on smoky *jiko* stoves. Also good for grills, even famous for them, is the pavement outside *Sizzlers* on Kenyatta Rd near Posta St (evenings only).

Food Square Bantu St. Good cheap eats, on two floors, with great *pilau* and other full meals (rice/*ugali* with fish/chicken; around Tsh4000), plus goatmeat *supu*, snacks and fresh juices. No alcohol. Mon–Sat 7am–5pm.

★ **Gold Crest Hotel** Cnr Kenyatta Rd and Posta St. The service here is slow, so, if your stomach's grumbling, tuck into the weekday Swahili lunch buffet (Tsh15,000), served in the first floor restaurant. More atmospheric is the rooftop *Summit Bar* on the eighth floor, whose à la carte includes pizzas (Tsh7000 vegetarian), burgers (Tsh12,000), grilled pork chops (Tsh17,000), salads and the like, and *nyama choma* (Tsh21,000/kg). Use of the swimming pool for non-guests costs Tsh10,000. Daily 9am–12.30am; buffet Mon–Fri noon–3pm.

★ **JB Belmont** Kenyatta Rd. Identical in almost every respect to the *Gold Crest*, with Tsh15,000 lunchtime buffets downstairs, and, much nicer, the rooftop "Ambassador's Lounge", above the 9th floor, with amazing views. The swimming pool there is smaller than *Gold Crest's*, but the furnishings are comfier, and it has a more open, eagle's nest kind of feeling. TVs screen sports, and there's a live band Wed–Sun nights, when they also have *nyama choma*. À la carte includes burgers from Tsh11,000 upwards, tilapia for Tsh15,000, steaks Tsh16,000, and a mixed grilled for Tsh25,000. Food 24hrs; buffet Mon–Fri midday–3pm.

★ **Kuleana Pizzeria** Posta St ☎ 028 250 0955. Semi-outdoors, this cheerfully decorated place is as popular with locals as travellers. The food – strictly vegetarian – is delicious, once the sullen waitresses finally get round to you: large pizzas for Tsh11,000, sandwiches, and a good range of cakes, biscuits and fresh bread. Daily 9am–7pm.

Mid City Cafeteria Karuta St. A plain local eatery with a handful of very tasty stews cooked up each day (even for breakfast), including liver, with nothing more than Tsh3500. They also have snacks, and good juice. No alcohol. Daily 7am–6pm.

Ryan's Bay Hotel Station Rd. You can't use the swimming pool here unless staying overnight, but you can savour the views from the open-sided first-floor restaurant, whose menu includes a handful of Goan specialities in amid a clutter of continental, Italian and Chinese. A Goan

fish curry, cooked in coconut sauce, goes for Tsh16,000, and evenings are famous for chicken tikka masala (Tsh17,000, with naan). Daily 11am–10pm.

Salma Cone Bantu St. A street-corner cafeteria, selling snacks such as samosas, cakes and buns, ice creams and good juices, sometimes including sugar cane, and plates of freshly cut fruit (Tsh2000). No alcohol. Daily 8.30am–11pm.

Surve Inn Lumumba Rd. Calm and clean, with just two tables (more at the back on Fri), especially good for breakfast, with great *katlesi* (minced meat wrapped in mashed potato, and fried), samosas, juices, and even espresso. No alcohol. Mon–Fri 8am–3.30pm.

Tilapia Hotel Station Rd ☎ 0784 700500. The breezy lakeside location and swimming pool (Tsh10,000) are the *Tilapia's* major draws, but the food – eaten in one of four restaurants – can also be excellent, although there's an element of luck involved. The vast menu covers all bases, from Tanzanian, Italian, Chinese, Indian, Japanese, Thai, Teppanyaki, Lebanese, junk food faves and even a handful of English classics like shepherd's pie. A plate featuring meat or fish (say, grilled tilapia, but also burgers) averages Tsh17,000; vegetarians will pay around Tsh12,000. Daily 7am–10pm.

★ **Tunza Resort** 8km north of Mwanza ☎ 0689 305051. The lush beachside location is the thing here, but also attracting punters – including lesser-spotted red-necked *wazungu* – is the lovely bar, and surprisingly affordable Sun barbecue lunch (beef *mishkaki* Tsh1000, chicken Tsh5000). À la carte is also well-priced, and includes possibly Mwanza's cheapest Nile perch (in coconut curry), as well as English-style fish and chips (both Tsh12,000). Also on offer are speedboat rides, at $60/hr for up to four people. Entry at weekends costs Tsh3000. Daily 11am–11pm.

Yun Long Nasser Drive, beyond Bismarck Rock ☎ 0752 243895 or ☎ 0754 243895. With its delightful lakeside terrace offering unmatched views, this Chinese restaurant is Mwanza's most attractive eating venue, but expensive, at around Tsh20,000 a plate, including rice. Daily 9am–midnight.

DRINKING AND NIGHTLIFE

Mwanza doesn't shy away from making a noise. Traditionally, the nocturnal focus is Kirumba suburb, 3km north of the city, but there's also more central nightlife.

Gold Crest Hotel Cnr Kenyatta Rd and Posta St. Two choices here: *Club Rockbottom* in the basement, swanky, even pretentious, and featuring the ickiest, stickiest Bongo Flava, and theme nights (usually Fri or Sat; Tsh15,000 entry most nights). More relaxing, and open by day, is the wonderfully sited *Summit Bar* on the roof. Daily: Summit Bar 9am–12.30am; Rockbottom 9pm–sunrise.

★ **JB Belmont** Kenyatta Rd. Head to the breezy rooftop

"Ambassador's Lounge" for fantastic views, or – the bane of many a light sleeper elsewhere – for its live band on Wed–Sun nights (from around 9pm), not that it's the best music you'll ever hear. Daily 10am–3am.

Royal Pub Off Karuta St. This once-classic beer garden no longer has a garden (too many tables), but remains popular throughout the day, with mellow music to boot, unless the commander of the remote has taken a fancy to something on one of the TVs. Food is available: very good in the morning (*supu*, and plates of freshly cut fruit), average at lunchtime (less than Tsh4500 for full meals), and terrible at night (carbonized, no veg). Daily 7am–midnight.

Tilapia Hotel Station Rd. The well-stocked bar here has great views over the inlet to Bugando Hill and Saanane Island, and is the main weekend hangout for the well-to-do. There's also a big TV screen for sports. Pay as you go or risk being overcharged. Daily 10am–late.

Villa Park Resort & Club 2.5km north of town at Kitangiri, near CCM Kirumba stadium ☎0787 799344, ⊛facebook.com/villaparkresortandclub. Mwanza's most happening nightspot, particularly for its live music on Fri, but don't expect to be let in wearing rags. A taxi shouldn't be more than Tsh7000. Daily 24hr.

Yun Long Nasser Drive, beyond Bismarck Rock. A lovely place for a lakeside drink, and good service, too. There's also a thatched rondavel at the back containing pool tables. Daily 9am–midnight.

DIRECTORY

Health Bugando Hospital, top of Würzburg Rd ☎028 250 0513, is government-run. Better for non-emergencies is the Aga Khan Hospital Medical Centre, cnr Würzburg and Miti Mirefu rds ☎028 250 2474. The FDS Pharmacy, *New Mwanza Hotel* building, Posta St, is reasonably well stocked.

Internet access Corner Internet Café, cnr Kenyatta and Posta sts (Mon–Fri 8am–6pm, Sat 8am–4pm). A growing number of hotels also offer wi-fi.

Money There are banks with ATMs all over town, including several on Kenyatta Rd; you can change cash at the forex in *New Mwanza Hotel* (also open Sun).

Police Customs Rd outside the ferry port.

Supermarkets Mwanza's supermarkets are expensive. Imalaseko, CCM Building by the clock tower, is convenient (Mon–Sat 9am–5.30pm, Sun 10am–2pm); there are several minimarkets along Nyerere Rd from there.

Swimming pools The best hotel pools open to non-guests (all charging Tsh10,000, and open during daylight only) are at *Tilapia Hotel*, and on the rooftops of the *JB Belmont* and *Gold Crest*.

Travel agents Fourways Travel Service, cnr Station Rd and Kenyatta Rd ☎028 250 1853, ⊛fourwaystravel.net.

Ukerewe

Lake Victoria's largest island is **UKEREWE**, north of Mwanza and separated from it by Speke Gulf. Nicknamed "UK", and originally called Ukerebe, this densely populated island of low wooded hills, craggy outcrops, granite boulders and almost Arcadian subsistence farms is the district capital of an archipelago comprising around forty islands and islets. Ukerewe itself is actually an artificial island – tired of attacks by militaristic tribes such as the Maasai, a nineteenth-century king ordered the excavation of a narrow channel across the marshy isthmus that connected it to the mainland (Maasai didn't swim). In time, erosion, and the widening of the channel by the British to create a faster steamer route between Mwanza and Kisumu in Kenya, made Ukerewe an island.

Despite its proximity to Mwanza, Musoma and the Serengeti, Ukerewe and its archipelago is among Tanzania's least-known areas, but, with the road between Bunda and Kisorya due to be paved, this may not be the case for much longer. Don't come expecting anything physically exceptional – there are few sights apart from the views – but if you indulge in a spot of **cultural tourism**, you will hear a lot of fascinating and often chilling tales relating to Ukerewe's turbulent and sometimes bloody past, full of invasions, imperious kings, skulduggery and magic.

Nansio

The town of **Nansio** contains Ukerewe's only guest rooms. The town has changed immensely since the arrival of electricity, scarcely ten years ago, when it shared the honours with Kilwa for Tanzania's most somnolent town. It's positively barking these days, but tourists are still rare enough to excite local children, who get beside themselves if you respond to their cheery "good morning teacher" or "shikamoo". At the beach facing *Monarch Beach Resort*, gaggles of kids happily spend hours messing about in the water: while it's tempting to jump in, too, bilharzia is present (to which locals may have some immunity, but not you). If you come in November, you might coincide with **boat races** – the cultural tourism outfits should have the dates.

8

Bukindo Palace

8km north of Nansio, 2km beyond Bukindo village • Tsh5000/group paid to the village • Catch a shared taxi from Nansio to Bugolora

Built in 1928 after plans by an Italian architect named Tonerro, the semi-ruined **Bukindo Palace** is a grand, colonial-style two-storey construction, surrounded on both levels by a wide balcony. It served as the palace of **Chief Gabriel Ruhumbika** (who died in 1938) and then of his son, **Chief Rukumbuzya**, who was the last king of Ukerewe; after his death in 1981, the palace was abandoned by the family, most of whom emigrated to Canada. The palace sits a few hundred metres to the right of the road in a stand of trees, but isn't signposted, so ask for Kasale Victor Mazura Rukumbuzya, who owns the place, and is the grandson of the last king of Ukerewe.

Handebezyo Museum

13km northwest of Nansio at Halwego • Tsh5000/group paid to the village • Catch the first daladala from Nansio to Rubya and get off at Mahande, leaving you with a pleasant 3km walk

First of all, **Handebezyo Museum** is not actually a museum, but a glorified picnic site, perched atop one of several boulder-strewn hills in the centre of the island, all named after 1960s African leaders. The misnomer comes from a small **cave** at the base of the highest hill, which, in the time of the Ukerewe kings (*watemi*), was placed under royal guard so that people could deposit their valuables for safekeeping – frequently necessary given the endless wars and invasions to which the island was subjected. As a store of old objects, someone evidently thought "museum" was an apt description. Concrete steps lead up to the top, which, at 172m above the lake surface, is Ukerewe's highest point, giving sweeping views over much of the island and the lake.

Rubya forest and Bwiru beach

18km west of Nansio • $10 permit for entering the forest reserve • Access is best by bicycle; there are two daily daladalas from Nansio, but unless you're camping at Rubya, the 11.30am run is your only option, giving you three hours at Rubya before catching the 4pm daladala back to Nansio

On Ukerewe's western side is **Bwiru beach**, said to be free of bilharzia, so if you want to swim, this is the place. In the same area is **Rubya forest**, which has two halves – a sustainable "production reserve" of commercial trees that was established in the 1950s, and first exploited in the 1980s, and a nature reserve, which has been left in its natural state, and is home to birds and vervet monkeys.

Ukara Island

North of Ukerewe, accessed by ferry (1hr) from Bugolora to Bwisya • Tsh20,000–30,000/group is paid to villagers • Catch a shared taxi from Nansio to Bugolora, then the ferry (Tsh800) • The Dancing Stone is reached by *pikipiki* from Bwisya (Tsh4000)

As its name suggests, **Ukara Island** is home to the Kara tribe. Like Ukerewe, it's heavily populated, has an isolated rural ambience (it's off the beaten track even for Ukerewe), some great beaches and a clutch of distant legends. The most vivid of these concerns the so-called **Dancing Stone of Butimba**, on the western shore, which is a boulder balanced on top of another, a visit to which gets you a lengthy explanation from an old man, who will regale you with the tale of two brothers, a betrayal, and – as with so many legends on these islands – a good dose of magic (how else to explain the stone "footprint" nearby?), before coaxing the stone into movement...

ARRIVAL AND DEPARTURE UKEREWE

By ferry from Mwanza The quickest and most enjoyable approach to Ukerewe is by ferry from Mwanza, taking about 3hr. The government-operated MV *Clarias* leaves Mwanza from the end of Customs Rd (Mon–Sat 9am, Sun 10am; Tsh5000), heading back from Nansio at 2pm. It doesn't take vehicles. The alternatives, which do take cars, are the MV *Nyehunge* and MV *Samar*, which are based at Kirumba Mwaloni, 3km north of the main ferry port in Mwanza, and in Nansio dock 50m west of the port. They have less reliable hours than the MV *Clarias*, but usually leave Nansio at 7.30am, and Mwanza at 9am (Tsh6000 inside, Tsh7000 on top, which is preferable).

ORIENTATION

Nansio's streets are named, but lack street signs, and there are few obvious landmarks. Arriving on the ferry from Mwanza, walk up the paved street 300m to the first four-way intersection (the "**first junction**" of our directions). A right here takes you to *La Bima*, and, eventually, to Rugezi and the ferry to Kisorya. A left at the junction (Nakatunguru Rd) takes you to several signposted hotels, including *Monarch Beach Resort*. Continuing straight ahead at the junction (Posta Rd) takes you past the market and bank, both on the left, to the bus stand, on your right, about 1km beyond.

By road and ferry from Bunda Bunda, on the highway between Mwanza and Musoma close to the Serengeti's Ndabaka Gate, is the start of a 83km road – due to be paved – west to Kisorya, a short ferry ride from Rugezi on Ukewere Island. The ferry takes about 20min (Tsh6500 for a car with driver, Tsh400 per passenger or pedestrian, Tsh2000 per cow). The schedule hasn't changed in years: it leaves Kisorya at 9.30am, 11.30am, 1.30pm, 3.30pm and 6pm, and heads back from Rugezi at 8.30am (Tuesday 8am), 10.30am, 12.30pm, 2.30pm and 5pm. The ferry is met on either side by public transport, including overcrowded and very badly driven shared taxis from Rugezi to Nansio (be thankful the ride takes just 10min). Buses run the whole way from Bunda to Nansio, currently taking 4hr including the ferry crossing. Bunda's bus stand is 1km west of the highway.

INFORMATION

Cultural tourism Nansio is the base for several competing cultural tourism "enterprises". Most are one-man operations (no women, alas), whose locations and contacts change frequently. If you can't reach them directly, any of the main hotels can put you in touch. Prices vary but shouldn't be more than Tsh30,000 for the guide, plus other costs, which amount to Tsh40,000–65,000 for a full day including lunch and transport by bicycle or shared taxi. For homestays, add Tsh15,000 per person plus additional meals. For fishing excursions, count on Tsh50,000/group for a half day, plus fuel and guide. Each of the outfits has its own style: for enthusiasm and encyclopedic knowledge of Ukerewe's turbulent history and culture, we'd recommend Tumaini Tours (Yohana Tumaini Ladislaus; office facing the ferry port's ticket office, ☎ 0714 466820, ✉ tumainitours@yahoo.com, 🌐 tumainitours.wordpress.com). Other outfits include: Ukerewe Cultural Tourism Program, favoured by the tourist board in Mwanza (☎ 0686 987045 or ☎ 0759 313731, 🌐 ukerewuculturaltourism.com), and Ukerewe Island Tours (Paschal Phares, ☎ 0763 480134, 🌐 ukereweislandtours .wordpress.com). Other than the attractions reviewed here, you can also go hippo-spotting, birding, fishing or sailing, take a crash course in local cooking techniques, traditional story telling, and music and dance.

Internet access There are three internet cafés at the first junction walking up from Nansio's port.

Money Change money before you come: no one accepts dollars (not even the bank, NMB, whose ATM is for Tanzanian cards only).

Transport Bicycles are the best way around (no more than Tsh15,000/day through a hotel or cultural tourism enterprise), as public transport is scant: more common than *Hiace* minivan daladalas are extremely packed shared taxis, called *mchomoko*. Normal taxis (ie just for you) are expensive even without price gouging, so consider a *pikipiki* motorbike taxi, who you should ask to ride slowly.

ACCOMMODATION

Holiday Motel 1km north of the first junction, one street back on the left before the bus stand ☎ 0783 386079. The location isn't special but the rooms are fine, seven of them "single" (ie doubles), with large beds and box nets, TV and clean bathrooms. There's also a nice quiet bar at the back, and affordable food for which pre-ordering is recommended: half a chicken for Tsh6000, beef Tsh5000 and grilled or fried tilapia for Tsh7500. Safe parking. BB **Tsh25,000**

La Bima 100m east of the first junction ☎ 028 251 5044. Hidden behind an enjoyable bar and restaurant are sixteen presentable rooms (no single rates), each with net, fan and TV, some with sofas, others with two beds. All have bathrooms (with hot water and squat toilets), some better than others. Safe parking. BB **Tsh15,000–20,000**

Monarch Beach Resort 500m west of the first junction, then 100m left (signposted opposite TANESCO) ☎ 0754 873138, ✉ ellymaganga@yahoo .com. Nansio's best lodging, both for its huge rooms (with TV, a/c and good bathrooms), and the delightful location, with a beautiful beach on the other side of a dusty road. Also has a restaurant and beach bar. BB **Tsh20,000**

Ua la Jangwani 600m west of the first junction, then 100m left on the following the Monarch Beach junction ☎ 0769 651262. Useful if you want somewhere really cheap but still decent: this has twenty rooms, with huge beds and big nets, TV, clean showers and squat toilets. **Tsh8000**

8

EATING AND DRINKING

Not so long ago, Nansio's restaurants could be counted on the fingers of one hand. No more – apart from the restaurants reviewed here, there's a growing number of tiny eateries (**mgahawa**) where you can eat tasty and wholesome meals for as little as Tsh2000 – there's an excellent unnamed one along the road to port, facing Tumaini Tours. A tasty local speciality is **red ugali**, made from sorghum (*mtama*) and/or cassava (*muhogo*). You can find **street food** along the road running west from the first junction.

Afro Beach Beside the ferry port. A big bar right next to the port with plenty of tables outside, including some at the water's edge. Daily 11am–10pm.

Fruit Juice Bar 20m north of the first junction. Three streetside tables and lots of fresh juices are reason enough to come here. Daily 7am–6pm.

La Bima 100m east of the first junction. A lively, welcoming and thoroughly African-style bar dominated by a two-storey thatched lounge by the entrance. Apart from snacks and the usual bar food (*chipsi mayai, nyama choma*), there's also a menu, most of which is not available (and which takes time if it is), so order early for things like curries, stews, spaghetti (all Tsh5000), or fish (tilapia fillet Tsh6000, whole Tsh10,000). Daily 5am–10pm.

Monarch Beach Resort 500m west of the first junction, then 100m left (signposted opposite TANESCO). Filling meals for around Tsh9000 (included stewed or fried tilapia), which take up to an hour to prepare. The dining room is nothing special, but who cares when there are tables under thatched shelters on the beach, where there's also a bar. Daily 11am–8pm or later.

Mara Region

8

The eastern shore of the Tanzanian portion of Lake Victoria is part of **Mara Region**, named after the **Mara River**, which rises to the north of Kenya's Maasai Mara Game Reserve. The river is famed as the scene of the carnage that results every year when massive herds of wildebeest and zebra attempt to cross the river on their great migration (see p.340), providing a feast for countless crocs and other carnivores. By the time the river approaches the lake, however, it has become one of the most sedate and beautiful in East Africa, creating a labyrinthine network of lazy waterways bounded by papyrus and reeds. While there's not an awful lot to do in the region, the area's natural beauty makes any journey a pleasure in itself.

Musoma

Mwanza's expansion has been at the expense of **MUSOMA**, a small port town located on a peninsula in Mara Bay, 120km south of Kenya. It's charming, laidback, and free of hassle. Other than informally arranged **boat trips** to various isles for fishing and birdwatching there aren't any sights as such, but a walk to the end of the peninsula is always fun, both for the views (and the bar and beaches at the end), and for the local **birdlife**, especially waders and raptors (which can be found around the papyrus beds that fringe the beaches), kingfishers, and all sorts of wonderful, garishly coloured birds. There are also a couple of small **markets**: one by the lakeshore to the east of town close to where fishing boats are repaired, the other a more generic affair next to the bus stand in the centre.

Unfortunately, **swimming** – although popular with local children – is not safe, as the papyrus and reed beds at the waterline are inhabited by freshwater snails, vectors for bilharzia-infected blood flukes.

ARRIVAL AND DEPARTURE

MUSOMA

By bus Most bus companies have offices at the centrally located bus stand, which is an orderly affair. There are also some bus company offices in town: Mohamed Trans (probably the safest for long distance routes) is on Kivukoni St. There's transport to Mwanza every half-hour or so from 6am to around 3pm and frequent daladalas to Tarime and on to Sirari on the Kenyan border, where you can catch a *matatu* (daladala) to Migori or Kisii, or a bus to Kisumu. For Arusha, the usual route is via Mwanza, Nzega, Singida and Babati. Quicker but very expensive for *wazungu* is straight through the Serengeti and Ngorongoro, incurring $120 in entry fees on top of the

Tsh35,000 fare. Operating this route (on different days) are Serengeti Liners and Coast Line, both with offices on Kivukoni St, and Kimotco, all leaving at 5am.
Destinations Arusha via Serengeti (4–6 weekly; 9–11hr); Butiama (every 2hr; 1hr 30min); Mwanza (hourly; 3–4hr);
Shinyanga (daily; 10–11hr); Sirari (hourly; 2hr); Tarime (hourly; 2hr).
By plane The airport is 500m west of the town centre; at the time of writing there were no scheduled flights (they had been operated by Precisionair from Dar).

ACCOMMODATION

Musoma's best digs are on the beaches north of town, where you can also camp. Couples can share a "single" wherever a "double" means a two beds.

Afrilux Hotel Afrilux Rd ☎028 262 0031, ⓦafriluxhotel.22web.org. At four storeys, this is Musoma's highest building, and biggest hotel, with 23 rooms, all en suite, most with cable TV, and those on the upper floors with good views of Mara Bay, but even so it's overpriced. There's also a bar and restaurant. Safe parking. BB **Tsh80,000**
Lukuba Island Lodge Lukuba archipelago, 13km

offshore ☎027 254 8840 (Arusha) or ☎0784 402344 (direct), ⓦanasasafari.com. If you have the money, this island getaway is very relaxing indeed, with the benefit of minimal risk of bilharzia should you wish to cool off in the lake itself, although there's a small swimming pool as well. Sleep in one of ten charming stone-walled lake-facing bungalows, sandy beaches to hand. The price includes boat trips and nature walks (birds, and the

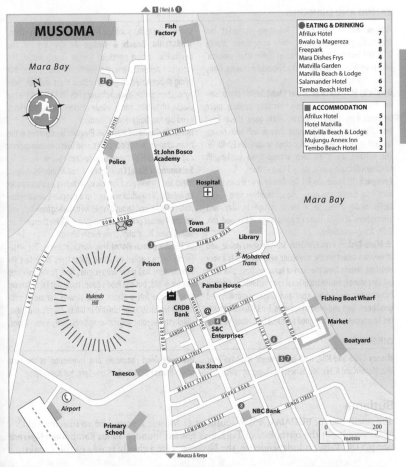

MUSOMA

Mara Bay

Mara Bay

EATING & DRINKING
Afrilux Hotel	7
Bwalo la Magereza	3
Freepark	8
Mara Dishes Frys	4
Matvilla Garden	5
Matvilla Beach & Lodge	1
Salamander Hotel	6
Tembo Beach Hotel	2

ACCOMMODATION
Afrilux Hotel	5
Hotel Matvilla	4
Matvilla Beach & Lodge	1
Mujungu Annex Inn	3
Tembo Beach Hotel	2

Fish Factory

St John Bosco Academy

Police

Hospital

LAKESIDE DRIVE

LIMA STREET

BOMA ROAD

Town Council

Library

DIAMOND ROAD

Prison

★ Mohamed Trans

KIVUKONI STREET

Pamba House

LAKESIDE DRIVE

NYERERE ROAD

Mukendo Hill

CRDB Bank

MUKENDO ROAD

GANDHI STREET

GANDHI STREET ROAD

S&C Enterprises

KUSAGA STREET

AFRILUX ROAD

KAWABE ROAD

Fishing Boat Wharf

Market

Boatyard

Tanesco

Bus Stand

MARKET STREET

UHURU ROAD

IRINGO STREET

Airport

Primary School

LUMUMBA STREET

NBC Bank

0	200
	metres

▲ ■ (1km) & ❶

▼ Mwanza & Kenya

8

otherwise rare spotted-necked otter), but not fishing or the boat transfer (45min by speedboat) from Musoma. All-inclusive **$737**

Hotel Matvilla Gandhi St ☏0769 659955, ⓦmatvillahotel.com. Friendly staff and smart accommodation, built above a strip of shops in the centre of town. All rooms are en suite and come with cable TV, hot water and box nets. BB **Tsh40,000**

★**Matvilla Beach & Lodge** At the top of the peninsula, 1.2km north of Tembo Beach Hotel ☏0769 614167, ⓦmatvillabeach.co.tz. Facing a couple of swoonsome beaches in a small north-facing bay, and with a third off the parking lot facing west, this trumps all others for location, thanks to picturesque guano-dashed boulders and islets a few metres offshore, and plentiful birdlife. The eleven rooms are in round cottages constructed on and around the boulders separating the two main beaches, with frilly cushions, stone floors, fan, fridge, big round nets,

TV, modern bathrooms and a sitting room. The "doubles" (twins) are larger, and have better bathrooms. Food and drinks available. BB "single" **Tsh40,000**, "double" **Tsh60,000**

Mujungu Annex Inn Diamond Rd ☏028 262 0017, ⓔmujungu2002@yahoo.com. Best of the cheaper central options: well kept, clean, calm and obligingly run. All 22 rooms are en suite, with hot water, fans, TV, big beds and box nets; more expensive rooms have fridges. Safe parking. BB **Tsh15,000–20,000**

Tembo Beach Hotel Off Lakeside Drive, 1km north of town ☏028 262 2887 or ☏0713 264287, ⓔtembobeach@yahoo.com. Sitting pretty on the beach facing west (wonderful sunsets), this is primarily used for camping by overland tourist trucks (per person $10), but also has seven en-suite rooms in a two-storey block, all with views of the beach and bay. There's also a restaurant and bar. No single rates. BB **$30**

EATING AND DRINKING

Afrilux Hotel Afrilux Rd. Relatively upmarket but reasonably priced restaurant, whose huge menu (mostly Tsh8000) includes pizza and Indian dishes (the "semsem" beef is with sesame). There's shady outdoor seating. Daily 7am–11pm.

Bwalo la Magereza (Prisons Club) Beside the prison off Mukendo Rd. A friendly, partially outdoor place frequented by prison wardens, with good cheap food (including *rost* platters of meat, liver or fish with beans, spinach and other veg, plus rice, chips or *ugali*, for Tsh4000). The inmates are often seen around town working in (unchained) chain gangs. Daily 11am–10pm.

Freepark Off Mukendo Rd. The first of several bars lining a little cul-de-sac, this one – like some others here – with tables under trees, so a lovely refuge by day, and atmospheric at night. There's a good range of bar food, too. Daily 7am–midnight.

★**Mara Dishes Frys** Kivukoni St. With seats inside, and at wooden tables on the streetside veranda, this is a very welcome respite from the land of *kuku na chipsi*: pick from big vats of inexpensive traditional food including a savoury brown *ugali* made from corn and cassava, *matoke*, and good bean, liver and even tripe stews. Tsh3500 will get you fed handsomely. Equally good for breakfast, when you can

sample *ulezi* millet porridge. No alcohol. Daily 6am–8pm.

★**Matvilla Beach & Lodge** At the top of the peninsula, 1.2km north of Tembo Beach Hotel. The location's delicious, and the food's not bad: simple but filling dishes based on grilled or fried meat and fish, with *ugali*, chips or rice: *nyama choma* costs Tsh12,000/kg, a big tilapia Tsh10,000, and a whole chicken Tsh16,000. Has a good bar too. Daily noon–10pm.

Matvilla Garden Gandhi St. Pleasant beer garden in the heart of town, with pool tables, cold beers, *nyama choma*, *chipsi mayai* and all the rest. Daily 7am–10pm.

Salamander Hotel Cnr Market St and Afrilux Rd. A basic, cheap and friendly place for snacks, including an unusual take on *kababu* (a meatball wrapped in a pancake), and combo-plates of tasty food (around Tsh3000) including fresh fish, and chicken – which, prior to becoming a meal, have the run of the dining room. No alcohol. Daily 6am–10pm.

★**Tembo Beach Hotel** 1km north of town. The west-facing beach backed by lilting palm trees is perfect for sundowners, and there are recliners, too. You're welcome just for drinks, but the food's good, though it takes forever to arrive. The fish is tilapia: fried, stewed, curried or with masala for Tsh5000, or Tsh6000 in fillets. There's also meat, spaghetti and some vegetarian options. Daily 8am–10pm.

DIRECTORY

Money CRDB and NBC, both on Mukendo Rd, have 24hr Visa/MasterCard ATMs. NBC is best for changing cash.

Internet Good computers and connection at the post office, Boma Rd (Mon–Fri 8am–5pm, Sat 8am–1pm).

Butiama

The small town of **BUTIAMA**, 45km southeast of Musoma, would be an unremarkable place were it not the birthplace of Tanzania's revered founder, **Julius Kambarage Nyerere** (see p.518). Prior to Independence, the Nyereres were a chiefly family of the Zanaki tribe. Their homestead, on a hilltop just north of Butiama, includes Nyerere's mausoleum, other family graves, a few granaries, and an interesting museum, and is also the base for a **cultural tourism** programme coordinated by one of the former president's sons.

The Mwalimu Julius K. Nyerere Memorial Museum

The museum is signposted along the highway from Busoma, but not as you approach – it's off on the left at Mwitongo, 1km before Butiama • Daily 7.30am–6.30pm • Tsh6500

Nyerere's life is commemorated by the **Mwalimu Julius K. Nyerere Memorial Museum**, which opened in 1999, just before his death. There is a mixture of personal items such as clothing, shoes, his favourite (and very battered) radio, presents from official tours and archival material documenting his presidency, including plenty of photos, an *Ujamaa*-style Makonde carving (see p.73) depicting the founding members of TANU who had spearheaded the drive for Independence, and ceremonial stools and other honorific presents given to Nyerere by traditional leaders following the routing of Idi Amin's invading army in the 1978–79 Kagera War (which also ended the Ugandan despot's bloody rule). Close by is Nyerere's **mausoleum**, a modest structure that was paid for by another great statesman, Nelson Mandela.

ARRIVAL AND INFORMATION   **BUTIAMA**

By daladala There are hourly daladalas from Musoma to Butiama, taking about 40min. The other approach, useful if coming from Mwanza or the Serengeti, starts at Bunda and goes via Nyamuswa: it's currently being paved, and will likely see regular public transport once complete.

Cultural tourism Butiama's cultural tourism programme is coordinated by the affable, modest and very energetic Madaraka Nyerere. Ask for him at the museum (☏0755 570795 or ☏0682 640033, ⓦtanzaniaculturaltourism .go.tz/butiama.htm). The programme offers a tour of the Nyerere homestead and mausoleum, and a variety of hikes and bicycle rides, which can be combined over several days with nights spent in local homes. Good targets include hot springs in the territory of the Ngoreme tribe, where an

elder will entertain you with traditional tales; a Zanaki healer reputed to cure infertility; a hike up Chamuriyo Hill for views, and to see caves used by German troops during World War I; birding in the Mara delta; and several sites with rock art, including on a boulder supporting one of the buildings in the Nyerere homestead. You can also visit weekly markets and community development projects, and basically get to know the Zanaki and their neighbours. For multi-day cycling trips, try the little travelled road to Ikoma, outside the Serengeti's Western Corridor, where almost every village contains a different tribe. Costs are not fixed, but very reasonable: for example, $5 per person for a guide for a few hours, plus transport, whatever you use or consume, village or consultation fees, and so on.

ACCOMMODATION

JKN Hotel Mwitongo, 1km north of Butiama centre ☏0755 570795, ✉madaraka.nyerere@gmail.com. Butiama has a few simple places at which to stay and eat, but

the best base for indulging in cultural tourism is here, right next to the Nyerere compound, which has thirteen decent rooms arranged around a raised courtyard. BB **Tsh30,000**

Kagera Region

The thickly forested hills, raincloud-filled skies, vibrant red laterite soil, and beehive-shaped grass houses (*mushonge*) of **Kagera Region**, in Tanzania's far northwest, provide a welcome, beautiful and truly tropical contrast to the unremitting scrub of central Tanzania. Sharing its borders with Uganda, Burundi and Rwanda, the region marks a political boundary, but also a natural one – the transition from East African bushland to the lusher vegetation of central Africa. The difference can also be heard: the Haya (see p.374) are among the few major tribes in Tanzania who still speak their own language in everyday conversation, in addition to Kiswahili.

The region is best explored from **Bukoba**, an attractive and lively port town connected to Mwanza by passenger ferry, and from where a couple of tour companies offer dozens

THE HAYA

Properly called Bahaya, the **Haya** of Tanzania's northwestern Kagera Region number around three million. Their history is complex, mirroring that of Rwanda and Burundi, but without the final tragedy of their neighbours. The Haya have two distinct ethnic elements: the Iru and the Hima.

The region's original inhabitants, whose descendants constitute the Haya's present-day **Iru clan**, were Bantu-speaking farmers and fishermen who excelled in iron and steel production. Kagera's earliest iron-working dates from around 500 BC, and excavations have revealed 1500-year-old forges that were capable of producing a higher grade of steel than that produced in eighteenth-century Europe, and using a fraction of the fuel. The art of metallurgy naturally led to a concentration of wealth and power, but the **kingdoms** for which Haya later became famous were founded by aristocratic cattle-herding northern immigrants in the fifteenth or sixteenth century, **the Hima**. Imposing a rigidly hierarchical social structure upon the Iru, the Hima feudal kingdoms effectively oppressed the Iru in much the same manner as the Tutsi dominated the Hutu in neighbouring Burundi and Rwanda.

Although the German and British colonial powers tacitly favoured the Hima, rising tensions between the two groups were defused after Tanzanian Independence. President Nyerere's emphasis on equality and togetherness across all tribes, and his **abolition of traditional chiefdoms** and kingdoms, brought an abrupt but peaceful end to the social divisions that had threatened to go the same way as Burundi and Rwanda. For more on Haya culture, especially music and epic poetry, see the excellent and wide-ranging *The Last of the Bards: The Story of Habibu Selemani of Tanzania (c.1929–93)* by M.M. Mulokozi, available for free at ⓦ jstor.org/stable/3819926.

of trips in northern Kagera, including to prehistoric rock paintings, millennial iron-working sites, waterfalls and ruined palaces that were part of eight traditional kingdoms. With more time, there's also the little-visited **Rubondo Island National Park** in the lake's southwest corner to explore – a wonderland if birds are your thing. The park's isolation, and hence inaccessibility to poachers, has also made it a preferred place for relocating species endangered elsewhere, including chimpanzees, black rhinos and elephants.

Bukoba

Tanzania's only major town on Lake Victoria's western shore is **BUKOBA**, a small but upbeat and enjoyable place. Most tourists here are passing to or from Uganda, but it's worth hunkering down for a while: the surrounding region contains a feast of attractions, while the gorgeous lakeshore location, backed by boulder-strewn and thickly vegetated hills, and plentiful birdlife in the surrounding swamps (indeed, hadada ibis can be seen throughout town), makes it a pleasant destination in its own right.

The market

Market St • Daily sunrise to sunset

Daily life centres on the bus stand and the lively and compact **market** to its east, in the middle of town. The market's a good place to buy Robusta coffee, and sample some of dozens of varieties of bananas that are now the region's major cash crop.

Mater Misericordiae Cathedral

Cnr Barongo St and Samuel Luangisa Rd • Mass daily 6.30am, plus 8am and 10am Sun

Bukoba is stuffed with places of worship, principally Christian but also Muslim: legacies of Bukoba's slave-trading and colonial past, and, more recently, as a major base for aid agencies and NGOs working not just in Kagera (where HIV is the main scourge) but in neighbouring Rwanda. The grandest temple, and Bukoba's tallest building by far, is the Catholic **Mater Misericordiae Cathedral**, whose slender spire is supported by four enormous concrete arcs. Inside is the tomb of Laurian Rugambwa, Africa's first Cardinal.

Kagera Museum

North of the airport • Daily 9.30am–6pm • $2 or Tsh3000

The small but reasonably absorbing **Kagera Museum** contains a collection of Haya artefacts, and an extensive photographic display of the region's wildlife. The easiest way to reach it is from the beach; walk along the sand past the end of the airport then take a sharp

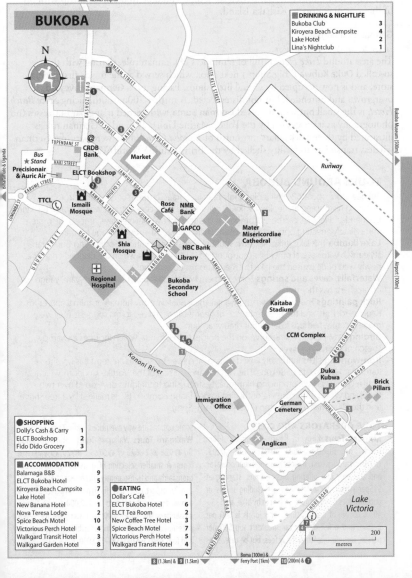

BUKOBA

▲ Kashozi Hospital

N

DRINKING & NIGHTLIFE
Bukoba Club	3
Kiroyera Beach Campsite	4
Lake Hotel	2
Lina's Nightclub	1

ZAMZAM STREET
KITE KETE STREET
KASHOZI ROAD
FUPI STREET
MARKET STREET
ARUSHA STREET
TUPENDANE ST
HAKI STREET
Bus Stand
★ Precisionair & Auric Air
KARUME STREET
ELCT Bookshop
KAWAWA STREET
MIGEVO ST
TAMMURI ROAD
CRDB Bank
Market
Ismaili Mosque
TTCL
UHURU STREET
UGANDA ROAD
SOKONI STREET
GUINEA ROAD
Shia Mosque
BAKOBEO STREET
Regional Hospital
Rose Café
NMB Bank
GAPCO
NBC Bank
Library
Bukoba Secondary School
SAMUEL LWANGISA ROAD
Mater Misericordiae Cathedral
MIEMBENI ROAD
Runway
Kaitaba Stadium
CCM Complex
ALEODROME ROAD
GHANA ROAD
Duka Kubwa
Brick Pillars
Kanoni River
Immigration Office
German Cemetery
SHORE ROAD
Anglican
CUSTOM'S ROAD
KANAZI ROAD
Lake Victoria
Boma (100m) &
Ferry Port (1km)

Bukoba Museum (500m) ►
Airport (100m) ►

◄ Nshamuliro & Uganda
LUMUMBA ST

SHOPPING
Dolly's Cash & Carry	1
ELCT Bookshop	2
Fido Dido Grocery	3

ACCOMMODATION
Balamaga B&B	9
ELCT Bukoba Hotel	5
Kiroyera Beach Campsite	7
Lake Hotel	6
New Banana Hotel	1
Nova Teresa Lodge	2
Spice Beach Motel	10
Victorious Perch Hotel	4
Walkgard Transit Hotel	3
Walkgard Garden Hotel	8

EATING
Dollar's Café	1
ELCT Bukoba Hotel	6
ELCT Tea Room	2
New Coffee Tree Hotel	3
Spice Beach Motel	7
Victorious Perch Hotel	5
Walkgard Transit Hotel	4

0   200
metres

8

8 (1.3km) & 9 (1.5km) ▼   10 (200m) & ⑦

turn left, following the road running alongside the airport's fence; the museum is 300m along the road.

The lakeshore

Bukoba's **lakeshore** is a very pretty place, with Musira Island a few kilometres offshore, and a sandy beach backed, in the north, by a wide grassy area (popular for impromptu football matches), and, in the centre – around the mouth of the Kanoni River which is actually more of a stream – by freshwater swamps full of papyrus and reeds, and therefore birds. According to locals, **swimming** is safe, but the swamps could be a breeding ground for bilharzia. Better, for a dip, would be to take a boat trip with one of the tour operators to Kishaka Island.

German buildings

Various sites along Shore and Aerodrome rds

The area around *Lake Hotel* is full of reminders of German rule, starting with the so-called **Duka Kubwa** ("Big Shop") next door, which served as the town's first general store, and is now occupied by several little shops. Facing it is a **German graveyard**, overgrown and untended, but not disrespected. A further 700m south, facing *Spice Beach Hotel*, is the small but well preserved **German Boma**, with serried triangular buttresses (no photography as it's occupied by the Police Marine Unit). The end of German rule is illustrated by three **brick pillars** just north of *Bukoba Club*, which were part of a German wireless transmissions facility shelled by the British during World War I.

8

TOURS AROUND BUKOBA

Bukoba's tour operators offer a pleasingly bewildering assortment of excursions in Kagera, featuring history and archeology, wildlife, culture and even cooking, and well as gorilla tracking in Uganda. Itineraries can be customized and extended over several days. Among the more immediately arresting options, many of which incur modest entry or village fees, are:

Lake Ikimba This lake, 40km southwest of Bukoba, shares a curious Sodom and Gomorrah-style myth with several other lakes surrounding Lake Victoria, in which the disobedience of a newly wed bride caused the lake to emerge from a cooking pot.

Waterfalls, caves and springs Some of them hot: the steep but climbable Nyamilyango escarpment has them all.

Rock paintings The best known at Bwanjai: there are few if any human or animal figures in Kagera's rock art, and the predominance of geometric or stylized forms suggests they were made recently, perhaps just five hundred years ago.

Birding At Minziro Forest Reserve, on the border with Uganda, which includes a swampy stretch of the Kagera River.

Iron-working sites Intimately linked with royal power, these sites are most easily visited at Katukura, 12km south of Bukoba. This was the ancient seat of the Maruku kingdom, which until recently was still producing high-quality steel using techniques developed over two thousand years before. The site of the first forge, dating from 500 BC, is marked by a tree shrine, and there's a small museum too (Tues–Sun 9am–5pm).

TOUR OPERATORS AND COSTS

Kiroyera Tours Kiroyera Beach Campsite, 400m south of Bukoba Club ☎028 222 0203, ⓦ kiroyeratours.com. Bukoba's original tour operator, and the only one offering bicycle tours, starting at $15per person for a few hours, excluding meals or entrance fees. Longer tours, on foot or by bike, are $35–40. A couple of hours' fishing with locals is $60 per person, and a full day by car shouldn't top $90 per person, including lunch and any fees, but be careful, as some options are way overpriced. Daily 7am–6pm.

Walkgard Tours Walkgard Transit Hotel, Uganda Rd ☎028 222 0626 or ☎0785 240229, ⓦ walkgard .com. A smaller selection of tours than *Kiroyera*, but more fairly and transparently priced: essentially the real cost (transport, entry fees, food) plus ten percent. Use of a boat for four hour costs Tsh120,000 (up to fifteen passengers) or Tsh150,000 (a faster one for seven passengers); use of a vehicle, including driver-guide and fuel, costs Tsh100,000–150,000. Daily 8am–8pm.

MWANZA–BUKOBA ON THE MV VICTORIA

The most relaxing and enjoyable way to travel between Bukoba and Mwanza is on the **MV Victoria** (built in Scotland in 1959–60, and reassembled on Lake Victoria in 1961), sailing from Mwanza at 9pm on Tues, Thurs and Sun, stopping en route (still at night) at Kemondo, arriving in Bukoba at around 7am. The ferry heads back to Mwanza (loaded with more bananas than you've ever dreamed of) at 9.30pm on Mon, Wed and Fri. As it sails at night in either direction, you won't see much more than the bobbing lights of fishermen, but dawn and sunrise is always nice.

Fares are the same for Tanzanians and tourists: in 2014, Tsh36,000 first-class (two berths per cabin), Tsh24,500 second-class (six berths), or Tsh17,500 for a seat in third-class, which can be hot, smelly, noisy and stuffy, so not recommended if you want to arrive fresh (buy tickets for first and second class in advance if you can). The ferry has two sets of restaurants and bars: one for first and second class, the other for third.

Musira (Musila) Island

No more than 30min by boat • Boats to the island leave from the lake end of the airport runway (Tsh1500, for locals at least), but it's easier – and you get to see more – on an organized tour (see p.376), costing upwards of Tsh30,000 per person, plus a variable "community fee" on arrival (usually Tsh3000)

Facing Bukoba is the strangely angular rocky island of **Musira**, which to some looks like a shoe. It was used as place of exile in pre-colonial times, and the caves in its cliffs served as tombs for witchdoctors. It's now home to a permanent fishing community, some of whose houses are traditional conical *mushonge*, thatched from their tops right down to the ground. You can hike up to the top for fabulous views.

ARRIVAL AND INFORMATION
BUKOBA

By plane Two airlines currently fly to Bukoba, both from Mwanza (45min; connections from there to elsewhere): Auric Air, with several flights a day by light aircraft; and Precisionair, operating larger turbo-props. Tickets for both are sold at a shared office on Karume St (☎0752 853476). The airport is near the lakeshore at the end of Aerodrome Rd. There are rarely any taxis there (no more Tsh4000 into town if there are), but it's a short and pleasant enough walk in.

By bus The bus stand is at the northwest end of town. Companies and schedules are very sketchy, and buses not always safely driven – a problem given northwest Tanzania's fast new tarmac, especially for Arusha, as the main company (Osaka) is infamously fast – Kimotco should be a little slower if less comfortable. Things look up for Dar (so also Nzega, Singida, Dodoma and Morogoro), with both Sumry and Mohamed Trans enjoying reasonable reputations. For Kigoma (a good part of the road to which remains unsealed), the only company is Visram Bus, leaving Bukoba at 6am on Mon, Wed, Fri and Sat.

Destinations Arusha (2 daily; 13–15hr); Biharamulo (6–7 daily plus daladalas; 2–3hr); Dar (4–5 daily; 15–18hr); Dodoma (4–5 daily; 10–13hr); Kampala (1 daily; 6hr); Kigoma (4 weekly; 13hr); Mwanza (2 daily; 6–7hr); Nzega, for Tabora (6–7 daily; 5–6hr); Uganda border (hourly daladalas; 1hr 30min).

By ferry The overnight MV *Victoria* sails three times a week between Bukoba and Mwanza (see box, above), taking ten hours. Bukoba's port, and the ticket office, is 1.5km south of *Lake Hotel*. Daladalas and taxis (Tsh5000) coincide with sailings; unless you're uncomfortable carrying valuables, you can walk into town by turning right (north) at the makeshift market and transport stand outside the port gate to follow the lakeshore road, which becomes a narrow footpath, widening once more at the *Spice Beach Hotel*. A paved road runs a short distance inland.

Information Bukoba's tour operators (see p.376) also serve as unofficial tourist information offices. For an overview of the town and its region, see ⓦ kagera.org.

ACCOMMODATION

★**Balamaga B&B** Balamaga Hill, 2km south of town ☎0787 757289, ⓦbalamagabb.com. Run by a Dutch–Tanzanian couple, it's the gorgeous gardens that set this place apart – filled with tropical plants and with views over the lake. There are just four rooms, two en suite, all with box nets and cable TV. Order meals in advance. <u>Tsh85,000</u>

ELCT Bukoba Hotel Airport Rd ☎028 222 3121 or ☎0754 415404, ⓦelctbukobahotel.com. Run by the Lutheran Church and used primarily for conferences, this is a predictably dull yet clean, secure and well-run choice, redeemed by its spacious lawns, mature trees and good restaurant. The 22 rooms range from doubles with shared bathrooms to en-suite twins and suites, all with TV, a/c

8

and box nets. Wi-fi planned. Safe parking. BB double $40, twin $45

Kiroyera Beach Campsite On the beach, 400m south of Bukoba Club ☎028 222 0203 or ☎0756 823250, ⊚kiroyeratours.co.tz. It's a beautiful location alright, and the three two-bed *mushonges* (reed huts resembling tropical igloos, one of them en suite) are sweet from the outside, but basic and unkempt inside, and thus overpriced. At weekends, the place gets absolutely packed with people coming for the beach and bar, so it's hardly private, either, or – for campers (Tsh8000 Per person, Tsh15,000 in their tents) – possibly even safe. *Mushonge* Tsh40,000

Lake Hotel Shore Rd ☎028 222 1024 or ☎0754 767964. A colonial survivor going to seed in gardens near the lakeshore. The rooms are huge, with box nets and washbasin, and better ones are en suite, but none have lake views (the ones that did have views, above the main building, are derelict). There's also a basic restaurant (meals around Tsh9000, and *nyama choma*) and a bar. The downside is the sometimes extremely loud music from the adjacent *Bukoba Club* Fri–Sun nights. BB Tsh10,000, en suite Tsh20,000

New Banana Hotel Zamzam St ☎028 222 0892. Usefully located for early morning bus journeys (the hotel's club-wielding *askari* will escort you for a modest tip), this has slightly tatty but still good-value rooms with decent beds, just about adequate box nets, cable TV, table and chair, and showers with hot water, but no fans. Safe parking. BB Tsh20,000

Nova Teresa Lodge Miembeni Rd ☎0753 923711. There used to be several really cheap yet good guesthouses along this cul-de-sac, in the shadow of the cathedral, but most have now gone, making this ever so slightly dissolute one the best. Its ten rooms are en suite, some with TV, and there's a bar. Tsh15,000

Spice Beach Motel On the beach, 700m south of Bukoba Club ☎0767 431036. In a colonial building near a patch of kopjes and boulders facing Musira Island, the beachside location makes it easier to forgive the shabby condition of its seven rooms. All are en suite (single, double or twin), and have box nets, cable TV, a/c and hot water for the showers. There's also a bar and restaurant. BB Tsh20,000

Victorious Perch Hotel Uganda Rd ☎028 222 0115 or ☎0756 189475, ⊚victoriousperchhotel.com. An efficiently run three-storey affair, with perfectly adequate but unmemorable rooms. The attached restaurant has good food, but you may need to endure synthesized Gospel music from a TV. Get a room at the back to lessen the impact of *Lina's Nightclub*, opposite. BB double Tsh50,000, twin-bed Tsh65,000

Walkgard Garden Hotel Balamaga Hill, 2km south of town ☎028 222 0935, ⊚walkgard.com. Occupying a high bluff overlooking the lake and port, this architectural mishmash has 42 bland but well-equipped rooms (no wi-fi, however). The restaurant is reasonable, and there's a swimming pool. BB double $45, twin-bed $50

Walkgard Transit Hotel Uganda Rd ☎028 222 0626, ⊚walkgard.com. A two-storey business-style option that's very good value if you can pay in shillings. All thirteen rooms have TV, wi-fi and hot water, and some also have balconies, but for a/c you'll need a suite. BB double Tsh35,000, suite Tsh60,000

EATING

Most of Bukoba's restaurants close when their supply of food is finished, so find a place early, or order even earlier. Bukoba's cuisine resolves around **bananas**, of which there are many varieties, including super-sweet finger-length ones, and giant **gonja** (also sweet, and squidgy when grilled, making it the perfect companion for *nyama choma*). **Ebitoke** (or *matoke*) is a savoury banana stew that locals dream about when they're away. The local **banana beer** is called *olubisi*; distilled, it becomes *nkonyagi* ("Cognac").

Dollar's Café Market St. An calm cafeteria whose very limited choice usually includes gorgeously aromatic *pilau* (Tsh3000). They also have snacks like samosas and *kababu*, and milky spiced tea. No alcohol. Daily 7am–6pm or a little later.

ELCT Bukoba Hotel Airport Rd. A great menu featuring plenty of local favourites (mostly Tsh8,000 a plate), including grilled tilapia, but order early to sample their *ebitoke*. No alcohol. Daily 6.30am–10pm.

★**ELCT Tea Room** Market St. The Lutheran Church's refectory attracts a flock of hungry diners attracted by truly excellent food, including subtly spiced Swahili-style stews (with cardamom or cinnamon), deliciously gloopy *ebitoke* and variants on ugali, all at around Tsh5000 a plate. They also sell real juices, and are good for breakfast, when you'll find pancakes. No alcohol. Mon–Sat 7am–5pm.

New Coffee Tree Hotel Samuel Luangisa Rd, by the stadium. A full plate here costs around Tsh6000, be it pasta or curried fish, but – as elsewhere – order early for better odds on success. Also has a pool table, and a beer "garden" at the side serving *nyama choma*. Daily noon–8pm.

Spice Beach Motel On the beach, 700m south of Bukoba Club. A breezy shoreline location with parasols facing the beach. Good *nyama choma* all day, plus basic cooked meals like rice with fish (Tsh10,000) "to order", meaning discuss the options with the cook, then wait, and wait some more. Daily: food noon–9pm, bar closes at midnight.

Victorious Perch Hotel Uganda Rd. Here's a novelty: fish, beef or chicken cooked "Haya House" style with peanut butter, beans and bananas (Tsh12,000). Almost everything else – including Chinese, Indian and Italian – costs Tsh10,000. Eat inside or outside, but be patient. Daily 11am–10pm.

Walkgard Transit Hotel Uganda Rd. Currently enjoying the services of a real Indian chef, this naturally recommends the subcontinent's cuisine, but they also have *ebitoke*, with meat or fish and beans (Tsh9000), and are happy to stoop to pasta, even burgers. Daily noon–10pm or later.

DRINKING AND NIGHTLIFE

Bukoba Club Shore Rd. Within staggering distance of the lakeshore, this isn't fenced so has tables spread far and wide over the grass, and hosts frequent but extremely loud events like promotions and weddings. There's the usual bar food (*nyama choma* and friends; Tsh10,000/kg), and proper meals. Daily noon–late.

★**Kiroyera Beach Campsite** On the beach, 400m south of Bukoba Club. Brilliantly located, with its toes in the sandy beach, and packed with locals at weekends, families included (the adjoining playground was donated by the Rotary Club), this has a cluster of thatched shelters just back from the beach, and but you can also take your

drinks on the beach itself. They sometimes have campfires, but you might wait up to three hours for food. Daily noon–11pm.

Lake Hotel Shore Rd. A hedge has blocked the lake views, but this classic colonial pile is still a nice place for a drink, either on the lawn (where you can marvel at its pretty but decrepit architecture), or inside a pub-like bar. Daily 11am–midnight.

Lina's Nightclub Uganda Rd. Bukoba's best nightspot, with live bands and a disco (Fri–Sun; Tsh3000 entry) that's packed till the wee small hours most weekends. Daily noon–late.

DIRECTORY

Bookshop ELCT Bookshop, cnr Kawawa and Market sts, has a good book on Haya proverbs, and also sells beads, necklaces, basketry and carvings (Mon–Fri 9am–5pm, Sat 10am–2pm).

Health The regional hospital (*Hospitali ya Mkoa*) is on Uganda Rd ☎028 222 0927. The best pharmacy is MK, facing *Rosé Café* on Samuel Luangisa Rd ☎028 222 0582; also open Sun.

Internet New Bukoba Cyber Centre, cnr Kashozi and

Jamhuri rds (Mon–Sat 8.30am–6.30pm); *ELCT Bukoba Hotel* also has a couple of terminals (daily 7am–10pm).

Money 24hr Visa/MasterCard ATMs at NBC, cnr Barongo St and Jamhuri Rd, and CRDB, Kashozi Rd.

Supermarkets Fido Dido Grocery, Jamhuri Rd (daily 9am–1pm & 3–8pm); Dolly's Cash & Carry, cnr Kashozi Rd and Arusha St (daily 9.30am–1pm & 3–9.30pm).

Swimming pool *Walkgard Garden Hotel* charges Tsh4000 for day guests.

Rubondo Island National Park

Tucked in to the lake's southwestern corner, **Rubondo Island National Park** is one of Tanzania's least-visited and best-preserved wildlife areas. It covers 457 square kilometres, little more than half of which is land, and includes eleven minor islets in addition to Rubondo Island itself. Most of the main island is scattered with the granite outcrops so characteristic of the lake region, and covered by moist evergreen forest – butterfly paradise. The rest is grassland, open *miombo* woodland, sandy beaches and papyrus swamps. The variety of habitats favours a diversity of plant and animal species, something that is especially evident in **birdlife** – close to four hundred species have been recorded so far. Among the more easily identifiable birds are hammerkops, cormorants, Goliath herons, saddle-billed storks, egrets and sacred ibises, kingfishers, geese, darters, bee-eaters, flycatchers, parrots, cuckoos, sunbirds and birds of prey, including martial eagles and the world's highest density of African fish eagles. A particular highlight is an unnamed islet to the east, which serves as a breeding ground for tens of thousands of birds.

In addition to the park's birdlife, a number of **endangered mammals** have been introduced, since the island's isolation makes it inherently safer from poachers. While attempts to introduce black rhinos and roan antelopes haven't met with much success, the introduced populations of elephants, chimpanzees, black-and-white colobus monkeys, suni antelopes and African grey parrots are flourishing and – with the exception of the elephants – can be seen with relative ease. The forest-dwelling

chimpanzees descend from a population of seventeen individuals rescued from smugglers and introduced in the late 1960s – most had been kept in cramped cages, some for as long as nine years. It speaks for the adaptability of chimps (like humans) that these ragged survivors apparently had few problems in establishing themselves on Rubondo, and their population now numbers around forty.

Of the native species, the undoubted stars (together with the birds) are the amphibious **sitatunga antelopes**, an unusual species with splayed and elongated hooves, though unless you catch a glimpse of one straying into the forest, you probably won't see them in all their glory, as they spend much of their lives partly submerged in the marshes and reed beds along the shore. Other frequently seen animals include vervet monkeys, bushbucks, large numbers of hippos and crocodiles, and a number of small predators including genets, spotted-necked otters and marsh mongooses.

The **best time to visit** depends on how important clear skies are to you: the best weather is in the dry season from June to the end of September or October, but butterflies and flowers – most spectacularly forest orchids, fireball lilies and red coral trees – are at their showiest during the rains (October to November and March to May), at which time migratory birds are abundant.

ESSENTIALS
RUBONDO ISLAND NATIONAL PARK

Park headquarters The park headquarters are at Kageye, halfway up the island's eastern side (daily 7.30am–5.30pm; ☎0767 536123 or ☎0689 062340, ✉sitatunga@tanzaniaparks.com).

Entrance fees $30 per person for 24hrs (payable by Visa or MasterCard only). Guides are obligatory for walks ($20 per group, plus $20–25 per person).

Tours The park can be explored on foot, by boat, or – if

staying at *Rubondo Island Camp* – by car. There are several walking trails from the park headquarters, including crocodile and sitatunga habitats. Short boat excursions cost $20 per person; for longer trips, boat rental costs fuel plus forty percent.

Information The park's official page is ⓦtanzaniaparks.com/rubondo.html.

ARRIVAL AND DEPARTURE

BY PLANE
The easiest approach is by light aircraft, but Auric Air (from Mwanza or Bukoba, $170 from either; 30min) and Coastal Aviation (from the Serengeti, upwards of $300; 1hr 30min–2hr30min) only land here "on inducement" (if there are enough passengers to make it profitable).

BY ROAD AND BOAT
There are two approaches by road, both feasible by public transport, and both requiring a boat ride at the end. Whichever you choose, let the park staff know you're coming beforehand, so they can pick you up, and you can be sure of finding a *banda*. While you can cut costs by arranging a ride with local fishermen at Nkome or Kasenda, the park's boat is safer.

From Mwanza Aim for Nkome, 60km north Geita along an unsurfaced but graded road. Geita is on the paved Mwanza–Bukoba highway, and has hourly buses from Mwanza until midday. From Geita, catch a connecting daladala to Nkome; the combined trip takes about four

hours. The park boat goes from Nkome to the headquarters at Kageye (90min; $185/boat).

From Bukoba The national park's launch (25min; $100/boat) picks you up at Kasenda village, 7km off the recently opened Nyameshere–Bwanga highway, which is now used by all buses from Bukoba to either Geita or Mwanza; most leave at 6am. These will get you as far as Muganza, 4.5km off the highway (160km or 2.5–3hr from Bukoba), from where there are motorbike taxis to Kasenda. The boat takes you to Mlaga, on Rubondo's west side, 6km from the park headquarters. Drivers can safely leave their car, by arrangement, at Muganza's church.

ON A TOUR
Surprisingly, few if any Mwanza-based safari operators offer Rubondo as an option. Bukoba's tour operators do (see p.376): Kiroyera Tours are overpriced; much more affordable are Walkgard Tours, whose staff tally up the real costs, and add on ten percent.

ACCOMMODATION

Visitors have three choices for accommodation: a campsite (closed at the time of writing), park-run *bandas* and a hyper-expensive tented lodge.

Rubondo Island Camp 2km from the park headquarters, on the east side ☎ 027 250 4118 (Arusha), ⊕ rubondo.asiliaafrica.com. You'd better hope for a clear night if staying here, otherwise the only stars you'll see are when receiving the bill. Stay in one of eight large but rather basic cottages, each overlooking the lake between the forest and the shore, around which there's plenty of wildlife, including hippo. There's also a swimming pool, and a nice open-sided lounge. Activities include game drives, boating (in dhows, too), forest hikes and chimp tracking (success not guaranteed). No children under 6. FB $2120

★ **TANAPA bandas** 2km from the park headquarters, on the east side (book via the park heasdquarters). Six simple yet comfortable rooms, all en suite with hot showers. Shelters outside give breezy lake views. Come with the food you'll need for the duration (drinks can be bought at the park's shop): there are cooking facilities nearby (or you can hire a cook), and evening meals can be taken around a campfire. Per person $35

TANAPA campsite (closed at the time of writing) 6km from the park headquarters, at Mlaga on the west side (book via the park heasdquarters). The superb but potentially dangerous lakeside position offers unnervingly close contact with grazing hippos at night (never position yourself between them and water). Per person $30

8

Lake Tanganyika and western Tanzania

HIPPOS AT KATAVI NATIONAL PARK

9

Lake Tanganyika and western Tanzania

Occupying a deep gash in the Rift Valley between Tanzania's semi-arid central plateau and the tropical forests of eastern Congo, Lake Tanganyika is bordered by Tanzania to the east, Burundi to the north, Congo to the west, and Zambia to the south. In the nineteenth century the lake's hinterland was a major source of slaves, and many of today's settlements began life as slaving depots. The biggest of these – and the main base for the few tourists venturing this far west – is Kigoma, an enjoyable lakeside town at the end of the 1254km railroad from Dar es Salaam. Apart from the lake itself, Kigoma's main attraction – a modest one at that – is Ujiji, a former slave-trading centre where Stanley and Dr Livingstone famously met.

Kigoma is also a convenient base for visiting the **chimpanzees** of Gombe Stream and Mahale national parks, neither of them accessible by road: Gombe is reached by boat, as is Mahale, which also has an airstrip. South of Mahale are a string of delightful **lakeside ports**, the most interesting of which are also accessible by road: a good thing, too, as these days the hundred-year-old **ferry** MV *Liemba*, connecting Kigoma with Mpulungu in Zambia, spends as much time being repaired as it does sailing. Heading away from the lake, the Central Line **railway** strikes out east across a seemingly interminable stretch of *miombo* woodland to arrive at the bustling but otherwise unremarkable town of **Tabora**, where the slave route from Lake Victoria (also shadowed by a railway line) joined the one from Lake Tanganyika. A railway branch, and a new tarmac road, runs from Tabora to Mpanda, beyond which lies the little-visited **Katavi National Park** – though much of it is swampy and infested by tsetse flies, it's extremely rich in wildlife, especially hippo, buffalo, crocodiles and birds.

Western Tanzania's lack of tourists is explained by its historically diabolical **roads**, but this is changing fast: ongoing road construction is likely to see asphalt all the way from Tabora to Kigoma, with possible connections also from the Lake Victoria area. Even the road from Kigoma to Mpanda, which was among Tanzania's most brutal, is now almost genteel, at least in the dry season: the stretch as far as Uvinza is paved, and other sections have been vastly improved, so although the daily bus is packed, its seven-hour journey is a vast improvement to the two-day trip in the back of a truck of a few years ago.

Lake Tanganyika

Occupying the southern end of the Western Rift Valley, **Lake Tanganyika** is the **world's longest freshwater lake**, measuring 677km from north to south. It is fed by the Malagarasi and Kalambo rivers on the Tanzanian side, and the turbulent Ruzizi River from Lake Kivu on the border of Burundi and Congo. The lake's maximum recorded

MV *LIEMBA* ON LAKE TANGANYIKA

Highlights

❶ **MV Liemba** Lake Tanganyika, the world's second deepest, is best viewed from the former German troopship MV *Liemba*: constructed before World War I, it's the world's oldest ferry still in service (if only just!) **See p.387**

❷ **Ujiji** Today a large fishing village, nineteenth-century Ujiji lay at the start of a 1200-kilometre slave route to Zanzibar, via the Indian Ocean port of Bagamoyo, and was where Stanley uttered the immortal words: "Dr Livingstone, I presume?" **See p.389**

❸ **Gombe Stream National Park** Tucked into the northeast corner of Lake Tanganyika close to

Burundi, Gombe is home to the most famous chimpanzees on the planet, studied by Jane Goodall and her successors since 1960. **See p.393**

❹ **Mahale Mountains National Park** Tanzania's other chimpanzee paradise, more challenging to reach than Gombe, but just as rewarding. **See p.398**

❺ **Katavi National Park** A remote wilderness whose pools of mud are home to thousands of hippo pods jostling for elbow room with crocodiles. **See p.409**

HIGHLIGHTS ARE MARKED ON THE MAP ON P.386

9

depth of 1436m (358m below sea level) also makes it the world's **second-deepest** lake after Siberia's Lake Baikal, and, at 32,900 square kilometres, Africa's **second-largest** (Lake Victoria is bigger). Lake Tanganyika is also one of the **world's oldest** lakes, having been formed around twenty million years ago during the tectonic upheavals that created the Rift Valley. Its great age, size, freshness, ecological isolation and geological and climatological stability have fostered the evolution of a remarkably diverse fauna. Animals that can be spotted here include various species of crabs, molluscs and

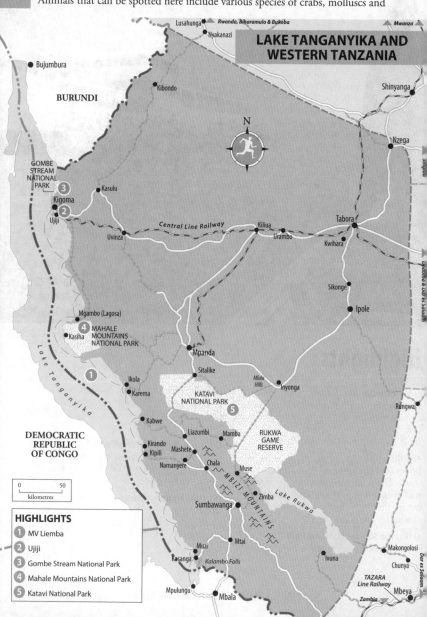

LAKE TANGANYIKA AND WESTERN TANZANIA

HIGHLIGHTS

1. MV Liemba
2. Ujiji
3. Gombe Stream National Park
4. Mahale Mountains National Park
5. Katavi National Park

THE MV LIEMBA

A much-loved feature of Lake Tanganyika is the **MV Liemba**, which has been ferrying passengers and cargo up and down the lake for over eighty years. Originally named the **Graf von Götzen**, after a former governor of German East Africa, the 1300-tonne steamship was constructed in Germany in 1913, then cut apart, shipped to Dar es Salaam, and, in the early stages of World War I, transported to Kigoma along the newly completed Central Line railway, where she was reassembled for use as an armed troop transport. In June 1916 the ship was bombed by Belgian aircraft, escaping with light damage, but when the British took control of the railway the following month, the Germans **scuttled** it at the mouth of the Malagarasi River south of Kigoma, after having carefully swathed it in grease to ward off corrosion. The *Graf von Götzen* remained submerged for eight years until, following an unsuccessful effort by the Belgians in 1921, the British finally salvaged the vessel in 1924 and rechristened it *Liemba*, after the lake's original name.

Any journey on the MV *Liemba* (or the lake's other ferry, the MV *Mwongozo*) is a memorable one – gorgeous sunsets over Congo's eastern highlands, and the frenetic activity that erupts in the port villages along the way whenever the ferry arrives. At most ports, the ferry drops anchor offshore, and passengers, luggage and cargo are carried to and from it in small lighters, invariably eliciting a chaotic scramble as people jostle to get on or off.

crustaceans, hippos and crocodiles, and over 250 species of fish, most of which are small, brightly coloured **cichlids**.

Swimming in Lake Tanganyika is less hazardous than in Lake Victoria, but you should seek local advice about crocodiles, hippos and water cobras. Bilharzia, too, is present along parts of the shoreline, so don't enter the water if there's shoreline vegetation nearby. Lastly, remember that many lakeshore settlements, including Kigoma, have sizeable Muslim populations, so women should avoid wearing swimming costumes when in view of locals.

Kigoma

Tucked into the southeastern corner of Kigoma Bay at the end of the Central Line railway, the bustling harbour town of **KIGOMA** is Lake Tanganyika's busiest port, handling most of Burundi's foreign trade and, over the last few decades, refugees fleeing central Africa's interminable conflicts. At present, both Burundi and eastern Congo enjoy relative peace, so the UN refugee camps that line the road north to Lake Victoria are gradually being wound up. The town itself is attractive, with a number of **colonial buildings**, a few beautiful **beaches** on which to escape the strength-sapping heat and humidity, and a tropical vegetation that provides a welcome contrast to the monotonous *miombo* woodland further east. For tourists, Kigoma serves primarily as the base for visiting **Gombe Stream** and **Mahale Mountains** national parks, both renowned for their chimpanzees, and for excursions to nearby **Ujiji**, scene of Stanley's famous meeting with Livingstone in 1871.

Brief history

In the nineteenth century, slaves were captured from as far west as the Congo Basin, and transported across Lake Tanganyika to a number of transit centres, of which **Ujiji** was the most infamous. **Kigoma** was just a small fishing village until towards the end of the nineteenth century when its sheltered location inside Kigoma Bay began to give it the edge over Ujiji. The town really took off in February 1914, when the 1254-kilometre **Central Line Railway** from Dar es Salaam finally reached the lake, establishing a reliable and rapid connection between the Indian Ocean and Lake Tanganyika, which has ensured Kigoma's livelihood to this day. The Germans (who built the railway and were the colonial power at the time) had little time to enjoy the fruits of their labour, however, since World War I broke out, and in 1916 they were ejected by troops from the Belgian Congo.

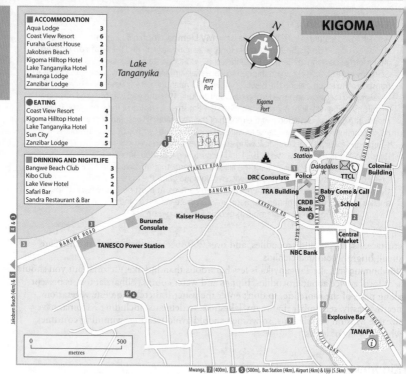

Mwanga, **7** (400m), **8**, **5** (500m), Bus Station (4km), Airport (4km) & Ujiji (5.5km)

Kigoma's indigenous population are the **Ha tribe**, who number over a million people spread out throughout the Kasulu and Kibondo districts to the north. They call themselves Muha, and their country Buha which, before the arrival of the Germans, comprised six independent chiefdoms organized into elaborate hierarchies of sub-chiefs and headmen, similar to that of the Haya in the north (see p.374) and the Nyamwezi in the east (see p.406). Following three centuries of commerce and intermarriage with Burundi's **Tutsi**, the two tribes share a good part of their language, and their reverence of cattle – the distinctive Ankole longhorn breed, common in Burundi and Rwanda, can be seen here and in Kagera region, where the Haya have similarly close ties with the Rwandan Tutsi.

The lake beaches

Jakobsen Beach Daily 8am–6.30pm • Entrance Tsh5000 • Daladalas marked "Katonga" drop you at a signposted junction 1.5km away; taxis charge Tsh10,000; a *bajaj* costs Tsh3000 • **Bangwe Beach Club** Daily 8am–9pm • Free • Daladalas can drop you at the entrance

The best place for swimming is **Jakobsen Beach**, which occupies a couple of sheltered coves below a wooded headland, 7km southwest of town off the Bangwe Road. With no reeds and little risk of bilharzia (the water is regularly tested), it has a selection of watersports equipment to rent, including sailing (a full day costs Tsh50,000), kayaks (Tsh25,000 a day), and snorkelling gear (Tsh10,000 a day). You can camp here or stay overnight in self-catering cottages (see p.391), though there is no food available, nor drinks other than sodas and water. Two kilometres (a thirty minute-walk) southwest of town, **Bangwe Beach Club** has food and drink (and possibly bilharzia), but no watersports – it's an ideal place to spend a lazy afternoon watching crows and dhows and, at night, the twinkling lights of *dagaa* fishermen offshore.

Kibirizi

9

3km north of town • Catch a daladala or taxi, or walk up from the railway station, turn left on to Kilezya Rd, and bear left at the fork 1.5km further on (through the oil terminal)

Kibirizi is the best place to see how **dagaa** – the lake's main commercial catch – is dried. These diminutive fish, 2–10cm in length, live in immense shoals near the surface, and are caught at night using pressure lamps mounted on wooden boats. The fishermen beat on the sides of the boat to panic the fish into tight shoals, which are then scooped up in nets. The flotilla leaves Kibirizi late in the afternoon in pairs, the lead boat towing the other to conserve fuel, and you can see their lights bobbing up and down from the coast at night; the season peaks in the second half of September. The fish are spread out the following morning to dry, either on gravel or over a suspended wire mesh.

Ujiji

7km southeast of Kigoma railway station • Daladalas leave from the square facing the railway station – ask to be dropped at the junction of Livingstone St

The relaxed atmosphere of **Ujiji** belies its terrible past as the place from where tens of thousands of shackled slaves began their gruelling 1200-kilometre march towards the Indian Ocean. The journey – to Bagamoyo, Saadani or Pangani – took anything from three to six months, and many died along the way, perishing either from exhaustion or being shot when they became too ill to move or tried to escape. During the fifty years that Zanzibar controlled the route, it is believed that **over a million people** (mostly from eastern Congo) were enslaved. These days, Ujiji has few visible reminders of its infamous past other than its distinctive Swahili-styled houses (more typical of the Indian Ocean coast), and a profusion of mango trees, said to have grown from stones discarded by slaves.

The Livingstone Memorial

Livingstone St, Ujiji • Daily 8am–5.30pm • Tsh20,000, including guide • Walk 1km from the junction along Livingstone St – the Memorial is on the right, 400m before the harbour • A return taxi from Kigoma costs Tsh15,000

The first Europeans to visit Ujiji were Burton and Speke, who arrived in February 1858 during their search for the source of the Nile (see p.515), though the town is more famous as the location of Henry Morton Stanley's legendary meeting with David Livingstone in 1871. The alleged site of their encounter – and the now-legendary exclamation "Dr Livingstone, I presume?" – is marked by the **Livingstone Memorial**, a curved stone wall with a brass plaque, next to a mango tree said to have been grafted from a descendant of the tree under which the duo met. A small **museum** here contains bad copies of contemporary prints depicting the encounter, and a couple of offbeat, larger-than-life sculptures of Livingstone and Stanley raising their hats to each other, but precious little else.

ARRIVAL AND DEPARTURE

KIGOMA

By plane Kigoma airport is 5km east of town, 3km east of Mwanza. Schedules change frequently: currently flying are Air Tanzania (AT; CRDB Bank Building, Lumumba Ave; ☎0784 737507, ⊛airtanzania.co.tz), Auric Air (AA; no office in Kigoma ☎0783 233334 in Mwanza, ⊛auricair .com) and Precisionair (PA; various agents on Lumumba Ave; ⊛precisionairtz.com).
Destinations Dar (AT & PA; 8 weekly; 3hr); Mpanda (AA; 3 weekly; 55min); Mwanza (AA; 3 weekly; 3hr); Tabora (AT; 2 weekly; 1hr).

By train Trains to and from Dar via Tabora, Dodoma and Morogoro leave Dar on Tues & Fri (at 5pm), and Kigoma on Thurs & Sun (at 5pm). Buy your ticket in advance from the ticket office at Kigoma station (Thurs & Sun 8am–noon & 2–6pm; Mon–Wed, Fri & Sat 8am–noon & 2–4.30pm) to

be sure of a first or second class bunk. Fares to Dar are Tsh75,550 (first class sleeper), Tsh55,400 (second class sleeper) and Tsh27,700 (third class seating).
Destinations Dar (3 weekly; 39hr); Dodoma (3 weekly; 24hr 10min); Morogoro (3 weekly; 31hr 35min); Tabora (3 weekly; 12hr).

By bus All buses leave from Kigoma's new bus stand – large, paved, and mostly deserted – 2.5km northeast of the centre, but 5km by road (turn left at Kasulu junction in Mwanga). Buy tickets the morning before, or earlier. All buses leave at 6am, when there are no daladalas, so book a taxi or *bajaj* the day before, or find a *pikipiki* in the morning along Ujiji Rd. Arriving in Kigoma, stay on the bus, as it should continue to the ticket office in Mwanga, 2km from the centre. For Burundi, there are sometimes direct buses, but it's quicker to

9

LIVINGSTONE...

Missionary-turned-explorer David Livingstone made his name with a bestseller, *Missionary Travels and Researches in South Africa*, but lasting fame came from his serialized journals – graphic and impassioned tirades against the horrors of the slave trade, particularly the massacre of hundreds of market women at Nyangwe in Congo by Arab slavers:

Shot after shot continued to be fired on the helpless and perishing. Some of the long line of heads disappeared quietly; while other poor creatures threw their arms high, as if appealing to the great Father above, and sank.

Livingstone's words obliged the British Government to blockade Zanzibar, forcing a reluctant Sultan Barghash to close Stone Town's slave market, thus hastening the end of the slave trade, and ultimately of slavery, in East Africa.

Born on March 19, 1813, near Glasgow in Scotland, the introspective **Livingstone** travelled to Cape Town in 1841 under the auspices of the London Missionary Society, where he married a missionary's daughter and set to work as a preacher and doctor. On his early expeditions he crossed the Kalahari Desert and explored Lake Nyasa, but his most famous discovery, in November 1855, was that of Mosi oa Tunya (the "Smoke that Thunders"), which he dutifully renamed **Victoria Falls**. His fourth major expedition (1858–64) covered the area between the Lower Zambezi River and Lake Nyasa.

After a brief sojourn in Britain, he returned to Africa in 1866, having been commissioned by the Royal Geographical Society to explore the area between Lake Nyasa and Lake Tanganyika and to solve the riddle of the Nile's source. So began the five-year odyssey that was to end with the famous **encounter with Stanley**. At the time of the meeting, Livingstone was suffering from dysentery, fever and foot ulcers, but within two weeks had recovered sufficiently to explore the northern shores of Lake Tanganyika with Stanley, before returning to Kazeh near Tabora, where Stanley headed to the coast.

Livingstone stayed behind awaiting supplies, and then set off in August 1872 on his fifth and final expedition, during which he again fell ill with dysentery and died at **Chitambo** village close to Lake Bangweulu (Zambia) in May 1873. He was buried as a national hero at Westminster Abbey on April 18, 1874.

...AND STANLEY

Among Livingstone's pallbearers was the Welshman **Henry Morton Stanley**. Twenty-eight years Livingstone's junior, Stanley had spent nine years in a workhouse as a child before taking a job on a ship from Liverpool to New Orleans at the age of 17. Eleven years later, while working for the *New York Herald*, he was commissioned to cover the inauguration of the Suez Canal and then, perchance, to "find" Livingstone, of whom there had been no news for five years.

Stanley's sizeable expedition set off from Zanzibar, and 236 days later, on November 10, 1871, having buried eighteen porters and guards, his two European companions, both his horses, all 27 donkeys and his watchdog, Stanley arrived in Ujiji, having been told that a white man was there. "I would have run to him," wrote Stanley, "only I was a coward in the presence of such a mob – would have embraced him, but that I did not know how he would receive me; so I did what moral cowardice and false pride suggested was the best thing – walked deliberately to him, took off my hat, and said: 'Dr Livingstone, I presume?'"

After the meeting, Stanley abandoned journalism and dedicated himself to exploring Africa. He was knighted in 1899, and died in London on May 10, 1904. His summation of Livingstone: "He is not an angel, but he approaches to that being as near as the nature of a living man will allow."

catch a daladala to the border, deal with formalities there, and catch another bus once you're through.

Destinations Arusha (NBS; supposedly 2 daily; 18–20hr); Bukoba (Visram Bus; 4 weekly on Wed, Thurs, Fri & Sun; 13hr); Bujumbura (mostly daily; 5–6hr); Burundi border (frequent daladalas; 1hr (Adventure Connection and Saratoga Line 2 daily; 27hr including an overnight stop); Mpanda (Adventure Connection; 1 daily;

7hr); Mwanza (NSL and Adventure Connection; 2 daily; 12hr); Tabora (NBS; 2 daily; 12hr).

By car Seek local advice about security, as all roads out of Kigoma have witnessed bandit attacks in the past, and isolated attacks are still reported in more remote areas close to the border with Burundi. So long as Burundi remains relatively peaceful, serious incidents on main roads are unlikely, but if things are risky, you'll be offered an armed escort at police roadblocks, for which a generous tip is expected.

By ferry The safest, most comfortable, most memorable, but least reliable conveyance southwards, as far as Mpulungu in Zambia, is the iconic MV *Liemba* ferry (see p.387), which is prone to ever-lengthier spells of repair, sometimes lasting months. Sadly, the same applies to the MV *Mwongozo*, which used to cover for the MV *Liemba* whenever it was being patched up. In theory, though, one or the other leaves Kigoma every other Wednesday at 4pm, and heads back from Zambia at 4pm on Friday. Accessing the harbour office in Kigoma requires politeness and patience, but it should have the latest information (Mon–Fri 7.30am–4.30pm; ☎0764 001992 or ☎028 280 2811, ✉bm.kigoma@mscl.go.tz or ✉info@mscl.go.tz, 🌐mscl.go.tz). Non-Tanzanians must buy tickets in dollars cash – the prices below are for first- and second-class bunks; third class is in seating, and not much cheaper.

Destinations Karema (19hr; $55/$45); Kasanga (38hr; $100/$90); Kipili (28hr; $70); Mgambo (Lagosa), for Mahale (10hr; $40/$35); Mpulungu (42hr; $105/$95).

By lake taxi Open-topped lake taxis ("kigoma-kigoma") leave from Kibirizi, 3km north of Kigoma. Their unpleasant reputation is due not so much to sinkings (frequent enough), or discomfort (packed, with no shade, water or toilets), but because they've been easy targets for bandits in the past (pirates, really), particularly in the vicinity of Burundi, though going as far as Gombe is fine. If you want to venture into Burundi, note that it's about nine hours from Kigoma to the border including loading and unloading along the way, and a further twelve hours from there to Rumonge. Heading south, it's possible to hop the entire length of the lake using a string of lake taxis, but you'll need a solid sense of adventure, be prepared to rough it (there are only few guesthouses along the way), and have oodles of time, not just for the rides, but the waits in between – rough weather can mean three- or four-day waits for the next boat in the chain. The total cost to Kipili, say, is at least Tsh50,000 for the taxis, plus whatever you need for food, drink and overnights.

INFORMATION

TANAPA Visitor Information Centre If you're planning to visit either Gombe or Mahale national parks, TANAPA's Visitor Information Centre, 600m up Lubengera St from the market (also signposted off Ujiji Rd; ☎028 280 4009, ✉gonapachimps@yahoo.com; daily 7am–6.30pm), is knowledgeable about the practicalities of getting to both parks, and handles bookings for the parks' own boat service, campsites and rest houses.

GETTING AROUND

By daladala The daladala terminal is an orderly affair at the top of Lumumba Ave, near the train station. Daladalas running along Bangwe Rd, to the southwest, are marked "Katonga".

By taxi, bajaj and motorbike Taxis can be rented at the airport, at the top of Lumumba Ave by the train station, and at the bus stand; short journeys cost Tsh4000. *Bajaj* can be found all over town, and are half the price. Motorbikes (called *pikipiki* or *bodaboda*) are even more numerous, and cost even less, but you may want to ask them to ride slowly.

ACCOMMODATION

The best budget options are up in Mwanga, 2km along Ujiji Rd, but it's worth spending a bit more to be close to the lake. In cheaper digs, "singles" can be shared by couples, as "double" here means two beds. Water supplies are erratic, so shower when you get the chance. You can camp safely at *Jakobsen Beach*.

Aqua Lodge 1.4km along Bangwe Rd; no sign – it's on the right just before the TANESCO power plant ☎0769 348958. Run by the Catholic Brothers of Charity, this has enormous en-suite rooms facing the orange-sand beach, with huge beds and adequately sized nets, ceiling fans and writing desk. The lake-view veranda are screened off against mosquitoes, but who cares when the beach is five metres away. There's wi-fi near the entrance, and a restaurant is planned. In the meantime, there's a basic tea room nearby for lunch, and *Bangwe Beach Club* is just up the road. Double T̲s̲h̲2̲0̲,̲0̲0̲0̲, twin-bed T̲s̲h̲2̲5̲,̲0̲0̲0̲

★**Coast View Resort** 1.5km along Bangwe Rd, then left (signposted) for 1km ☎028 280 3434 or ☎0713 491570, 🌐coastviewhotel.co.tz. Perched on a hillside in a pleasant garden planted with palms and other ornamental trees, this modern but understated place has fourteen spacious and very good value rooms, smart, comfortable, and with a/c, flat-screen TV and wi-fi. None have lake views, though the gazebo over the bar and the excellent restaurant offer vistas of the lake, including great sunsets over Kigoma Bay. BB T̲s̲h̲3̲0̲,̲0̲0̲0̲

Furaha Guest House Burton Rd ☎028 280 3665. A safe and acceptable but very basic budget choice close to the train station. All rooms have fans and nets, saggy beds, and clean squat toilets (either sharing or en suite), plus one "special" en-suite room with a Western-style toilet. T̲s̲h̲5̲0̲0̲0̲, en suite T̲s̲h̲8̲0̲0̲0̲

★**Jakobsen Beach** 6.5km southwest of town (5km down Bangwe Rd, then signposted) ☎0789 231215 or ☎0768 119449, 🌐kigomabeach.com. In a lovely location on a couple of small private beaches in adjacent sheltered coves, the accommodation here consists of two campsites on the edge of the beach, plus walk-in tents under thatched roofs that share bathrooms, some cottages and a guesthouse, all on

9

the wooded headland behind. All are well maintained, and the tents and cottages are charming (the guesthouse less so). It's all self-catering – there are cooking facilities, and the basics (dry pasta, tins) are sold at a small shop, but drinks are limited to water and sodas. Apart from admiring local wildlife (including zebra, duiker and vervet monkeys), you can go snorkelling, sailing or kayaking, and their transfers to Gombe ($210 return for the boat) are cheaper than the competition. No wi-fi. Camping per person Tsh15,000, tents per person Tsh25,000, cottages and guesthouse per person Tsh40,000

★**Kigoma Hilltop Hotel** 3km southwest of town, off Bangwe Rd ☎0732 978879 or ☎0737 206420, ⓦmbalimbali.com. On a wooded headland high above the shore, most of it enclosed by an electric fence (there are resident zebras, as well as monkeys), this is Kigoma's poshest hotel. Its thirty rooms – in chalets strung across the headland – offer lake views from their balconies, the best ones (facing west rather than north) from the more expensive suites. The rooms are large and comfortable, all with TV, a/c and – a welcome change from Gideon Bibles – a Qur'an at your bedside. The restaurant and swimming pool both have stunning views, there's a sandy beach a 15min walk away, and a gym. Also offers overpriced boat trips, but no snorkelling. Wi-fi in the main building. BB standard

("executive") Tsh140, suites Tsh225

Lake Tanganyika Hotel West of the ferry port, signposted off Bangwe Rd ☎028 280 3052, ⓦlaketanganyikahotel.com. On a lawn beside the reedy lakeshore (no swimming), this was once a rambling colonial hotel, but has been completely rebuilt as a series of ugly a/c bungalows, some two-storey, most with partial sea views (good sunsets), and all with wi-fi. The restaurant and bar are in an equally graceless building fronted by a neoclassical facade. There's a lakeside swimming pool, but overall it's quite charmless, even for a package tour type place. BB $105

Mwanga Lodge 1.6 km along Ujiji Rd, Mwanga ☎0752 926906. One of the better budget guesthouses, with good-sized nets, clean squat toilets, and acceptable bathrooms, both shared and en suite (the latter cost an extra Tsh3000). Tsh10,000

Zanzibar Lodge 1.7km along Ujiji Rd, Mwanga ☎0755 440575. Run by the same people as *Mwanga Lodge*, this tacks on a restaurant and glimpses of the lake from some upper-floor rooms, but there's a nightclub next door, so for a peaceful sleep *Mwanga Lodge* is better. The singles are among the cheapest in town (Tsh5000); en-suite doubles cost Tsh13,000. Tsh10,000

EATING

The local delicacies are **migebuka**, which looks like a thin mackerel and tastes similar, and diminutive **dagaa** a freshwater sardine, which is best roasted in palm oil (*mawese*, imparting a nutty taste) and served with dark *ugali* made from cassava. **Street food**, especially fried cassava, roasted maize cobs and seasonal fruit, is best along Lumumba Ave between the daladala stand and the train station. There are also plenty of dirt-cheap grilled meat and *chipsi mayai* places around the daladala stand and market. Mwanga, two kilometres along Ujiji Rd, is especially good in the evenings, with dozens of stands serving fried *dagaa* and tasty *mishkaki* (goat-meat skewers). Many bars also sell food.

Coast View Resort 1.5km along Bangwe Rd, then left (signposted) for 1km. It's a bit of a hike to get here, but worth it for a meal in the lake-view gazebo. The menu showcases Tanzania's best, all fresh (for which be patient): try the *mtori* banana stew (with beans, peanuts or meat), or *matoke* (mashed banana stew, served with curried fish, chicken, beef or vegetables), both under Tsh10,000. Daily noon–8pm.

Kigoma Hilltop Hotel 3km southwest of town, off Bangwe Rd ☎0732 978879 or ☎0737 206420. The fabulous 180 degree view from up on high is the reason to lunch here, as is the swimming pool (Tsh10,000), but ring beforehand, as they've been awkward about letting in day-guests in the past. Lunches are light, and almost everything costs Tsh15,000: grilled aubergine with cheese, say, or more unusual grilled fish, such as *kuhe* (yellow belly). Daily noon–3pm & 6–10pm.

Lake Tanganyika Hotel West of the ferry port,

signposted off Bangwe Rd. Central Kigoma's swishest abode has missed a trick by not having tables outside – you eat inside in an elegantly minimalist but bland a/c dining room. The food is average, and therefore pricey at Tsh18,000 for almost anything (try the fish), and with the exception of the soups (ginger and carrot, say; Tsh4000), the vegetarian selection is poor. Daily 7am–10pm.

Sun City Lumumba Ave. A tranquil, jauntily painted and deservedly popular place with tables on a street-view terrace. It's as good for breakfast (samosas, juices, aromatic cinnamon-laced tea), as it is for lunch, including *pilau*, beans or *migebuka*, and nothing costs over Tsh5000. Daily 9am–9pm.

Zanzibar Lodge 1.7km along Ujiji Rd, Mwanga. The offering here is limited to rice or *ugali* with chicken or fish. The former can be tough, but the latter is often excellent, including *migebuka* and *dagaa*, and it's very cheap at just Tsh3500 a plate. No alcohol. Daily 7am–9pm.

DRINKING AND NIGHTLIFE

Kigoma's location explains the local predilection for **Congolese music**, where the big stars – currently Fally Ipupa, and the indefatigable Koffi Olomidé – are yet to be knocked off their perches by the unrelenting advance of Bongo Flava. Central Kigoma is deserted at night, so don't walk around – catch a cab.

Bangwe Beach Club 1.8km along Bangwe Rd. Next to the prison, and with its toes in the sand, this is great place to chill out, and gives the inmates next door something to dance to at weekends, with a live band on Saturdays (from 4pm; Tsh2000) and a disco on Sundays (3–9pm; Tsh1000). Food is the inescapable *nyama choma* (goat or beef), *chipsi mayai*, grilled bananas and *ugali*. Daily 8am–9pm.

Kibo Club 750m up Ujiji Rd, then turn right opposite the *Explosive Bar*. Kigoma's main disco (entry Tsh4000) is at its busiest at weekends, and has all the spinning lights and strobes you could want, with music loud enough to obliterate conversation. If it's not to your liking, there are a number of other popular nightspots nearby, including *Safari Bar* on Ujiji Rd, just before *Explosive Bar*, which

currently favours modern taarab music (discos Tues & Wed). Daily 8pm–4am.

Lake View Hotel Lumumba Ave. This started off as a hotel, then a restaurant, and is now just a bar, albeit one with a pleasant shady terrace, and it vies with the *Sandra* for the attentions of local tipplers. No lake view, incidentally. Daily 10am–10pm.

Sandra Restaurant & Bar Stanley Rd. A local bar surrounded by a scrubby garden on three sides, conveniently close to the ferry port and train station, and also serving up good *nyama choma* and fried bananas (Tsh4500). It's particularly popular on Sun, when there's a live band in the evening. Daily 10am–midnight.

DIRECTORY

Consulates Burundi, Bangwe Rd ☎028 280 2865, ✉consbdi2010@hotmail.com; Democratic Republic of Congo, corner of Bangwe and Kaya roads ☎028 280 2401.

Health Kigoma's hospitals are in Mwanga; the best is the Baptist Hospital, 1km from Kasulu junction: turn left at the junction then first right (☎028 280 2241).

Immigration Exit formalities for Zambia are completed on the ferry. Tanzanian immigration is on Ujiji Rd in Mwanga, 100m beyond Maweni Hospital on the left.

Internet access Baby Come & Call, Lumumba Ave (daily 8am–6pm).

Money The banks are on Lumumba Ave: NBC and CRDB both have 24hr Visa/MasterCard ATMs, and also change cash.

Police Bangwe Rd, near the Tanzania Revenue Authority (TRA) building, and in the train station.

Swimming pool *Kigoma Hilltop Hotel* charges Tsh10,000 (daily 9am–6pm), and has a spectacular lake view.

Gombe Stream National Park

Just 16km north of Kigoma, **Gombe Stream National Park** is one of Tanzania's most inspiring parks, and the smallest after Saanane. Its 52 square kilometres cover a narrow strip of hilly country rising from Lake Tanganyika to the eastern ridge of the Western Rift Valley, and is sliced lengthways by thirteen wild river valleys. The variations in altitude and the variety of habitats make for a good mix of wildlife and flora, including more than 230 **bird species** – a modest count by Tanzanian standards, but containing many types found nowhere in the country. However, it's the **primates** that are the real draw – Gombe's ecosystem is a primate paradise, home to olive baboons and red colobus, redtail and blue monkeys. The redtails and blue monkeys are unusual in that, despite their striking physical differences, they have only recently diverged as separate species, and hybrids occur, usually with the redtail's white nose and the blue monkey's dark tail and larger size. In any other park, these would be a major highlight, but at Gombe they're just supporting acts for the real stars: the park's **chimpanzees**.

Naturally, **chimp tracking** in the evergreen riverine forests is reason enough to visit, but there are other rewarding activities, too, including **hikes** through the forest to the crest of the Rift Valley ridge, or along the lake shore, where **snorkelling** is possible. Also offered are **night walks**, which are especially exciting during a full moon, when you can dispense with a torch in your hunt for nocturnal porcupine and bushbuck, genet, white-tailed mongoose, hairy bush pigs, palm civet cats, or the slow-moving giant rat – up to 90cm from tail to snout. The park is explored on foot: nothing too strenuous, but it helps to be reasonably fit.

The shore

You can walk along the **beach** without a guide. The temporary camps along the way are occupied by *dagaa* fishermen during the dry seasons for about ten days a month, either side of the new moon, when catches are best, and it's their bobbing lanterns that you

9

TANZANIA'S CHIMPANZEES

We owe much of our knowledge of chimpanzees (see p.30) to two ground-breaking studies in Tanzania, one at Gombe Stream National Park, the other at Mahale Mountains National Park. Both studies continue to this day.

At Gombe, the trailblazer was **Jane Goodall**, who began her research in June 1960, having been encouraged by the Kenyan palaeontologist Louis Leakey, who believed that by observing the behaviour of great apes we could reconstruct something of the early life of mankind (Leakey's other protégées were Dian Fossey, tasked to study Rwanda's gorillas, and Birutè Galdikas, for Borneo's orangutans). Chimp research at Mahale, which started in 1961, was spearheaded by Junichiro Itani from Japan's **Kyoto University**.

The first major discovery, made by Goodall in November 1960, was **tool use** in chimpanzees (which was previously considered a uniquely human trait), when she observed a chimp "fishing" for termites by inserting a stick into their mound, and withdrawing it to lick it clean of insects. Goodall also discovered that chimpanzees are omnivorous, not vegetarian, as had previously been thought: indeed, their success rate at **hunting** – primarily of red colobus monkeys, young bush pigs and bushbuck – is far higher than specialized predators such as lions. The secret to their success is **cooperation**, as chimps working together can block their prey's escape routes.

Another surprising discovery, this one from Mahale, was the chimps' deliberate use of **medicinal plants**, specifically *Aspilia mossambicensis*, which contains a natural vermicide. The chimps eat the leaves in the morning before moving on to other foods. That alone doesn't prove anything, but the *method* of eating them does: using their lips, the chimps carefully pull one of the rough and hairy leaves from the plant into their mouths, and, using their tongue, fold it up like an accordion, and swallow without chewing. The chimps have learned that doing so not only kills intestinal worms, but physically removes them, too.

Another fascinating area of research concerns what might be termed **cultural differences** between the geographically separate Mahale and Gombe populations, as their social behaviour, use of tools and diet differ markedly – for example, Gombe's chimps eat termites by probing the mounds with sticks, but they don't eat tree ants, whereas Mahale's chimps catch tree ants in the same way, but leave the termites alone. Gestures such as "handshakes" and vocalizations also differ, and some researchers consider them languages and dialects.

A thread that's common to both populations is their all-too-human fondness for aggression, including **warfare**. In a series of raids between 1974 and 1977, the males of Gombe's Kasekela community exterminated those of the Kahama community, with whom they had formerly been allied. The males also attacked strange females, and in three cases the stranger's child was killed and later eaten. It may be that these behavioural extremes are related to **environmental pressures**, certainly in Gombe: hemmed in by humans on three sides and by the lake on the fourth, forest habitat suitable for chimpanzees is limited – and shrinking. As a sign that all is not well, the feeding station has been abandoned due to the increasingly aggressive behaviour of the chimpanzees.

Recommended **books** include the lavishly illustrated *40 Years at Gombe* (1999) by Stewart, Chabori and Chang, and numerous works by Jane Goodall, including: *In the Shadow of Man* (1971); *The Chimpanzees of Gombe: Patterns of Behaviour* (1986); *Through a Window: My Thirty Years with the Chimpanzees of Gombe* (1991); and *Reason for Hope* (2002). The Jane Goodall Institute **website** (🌐janegoodall.org) has a series short but informative pieces about all aspects of chimpanzee life, habitat and research, including videos. For a good essay on chimpanzee communication, see 🌐www2.nau.edu/gaud/bio301/content/chmplng.htm; for general information about the Mahale study, see 🌐jinrui.zool.kyoto-u.ac.jp/ChimpHome/mahaleE.html.

see at night. In parts, the forest reaches down to the beach, but there's little other permanent vegetation along the shore. As a result, hippos and crocodiles are rare if not completely absent; seek advice from park staff before **swimming**, and also about bilharzia. If you're given the all-clear, head to the river mouths or the rocky shore just north of Mitumba beach, where a mask and snorkel will reveal many beautifully coloured cichlid fish. In deeper water you may see the harmless Lake Tanganyika jellyfish, a tiny (2cm diameter) semi-transparent pulsating disc. Many beach strollers here are spooked by the sight of harmless **Nile monitor lizards**, which look like little crocodiles, but these skittish fellows are very shy and will dash off into the water when approached. Gombe's most common primate, the stocky and thick-furred **olive baboon**, is generally the only mammal seen by day on the shore, where they scavenge for fish and occasionally swim and play in the water – keep your distance.

The lack of mud flats, weeds or perches means there's little **birdlife**, but palm-nut vultures can sometimes be seen over the lake angling for fish. At the reed beds at the mouths of streams, pied kingfishers, African pied wagtails and common sandpipers are frequently seen; giant kingfishers are less common, and fish eagles comparatively rare. Winter migrants include white-winged black terns, hobbies and the lesser black-backed gull.

Evergreen riverine forest

The narrow **evergreen riverine forests** are the undoubted highlight of Gombe's habitats, and not just for the chimpanzees. They were originally part of the great forests of Central and West Africa, but became isolated by climatic change during the last eight thousand years, and more recently from each other by human activity. The nearest forest is straight up the Kakombe Valley from Kasekela: a high, tangled canopy of trees and vines. As you walk along, crushed undergrowth marks the hasty retreats beaten by chimpanzees and monkeys. The walk ends at the twenty-metre **Kakombe waterfall**.

Forest birdlife is melodious but difficult to see, usually no more than a brief flash of colour disappearing into the undergrowth or up into the canopy. The more easily seen birds are crimson-winged turacos: the mainly green Livingstone's; and Ross's with its blue body, yellow face and red crest – both have raucous calls. Of the four species of fruit-eating barbets, the only one you're likely to see is the tiny yellow-rumped tinkerbird, which has black-and-white facial stripes, a yellow rump and a monotonous "tink, tink, tink" call. More pleasant to the ear are the flute-like calls of the tropical boubou, a black-and-white shrike that duets in dense foliage. The African broadbill gives itself away by periodically flying up from its perch to do a somersault, emitting a small screech. The ground-feeding Peter's twinspot is an attractive finch with a red face and a white-spotted black belly. Winter migrants include various species of cuckoo, Eurasian swifts, bee-eaters and rollers, and four species of flycatcher. With luck, you might also spot the pennant-winged nightjar, or one of two species of warbler (icterine and willow).

Dry woodland and upper ridges

The drier valleys and higher slopes, especially in the south of the park, are neither as rich nor as interesting as the forest, and are even bleak in the dry season – the result of fires that devastated large areas of semi-deciduous woodland and thorn-scrub. Even so, a hike to the top of the escarpment (700m above the lake) is rewarded with sweeping views, and possibly the sight of soaring **crowned eagles** circling the forests in search of imprudent monkeys. There are several routes to the top, all of them steep; leave early in the morning, and don't expect to be back until around nightfall.

ESSENTIALS   GOMBE STREAM NATIONAL PARK

Park headquarters The park headquarters are at Kasekela, 24km north of Kigoma (☎0689 062303 or ☎0767 536426, ✉chimps@tanzaniaparks.com).

Entrance fees Entrance fees must be paid by Visa or MasterCard but not cash at Kasekela or at the information centre in Kigoma (see p.391), and are $100 for 24hrs, plus $20 per group for the obligatory ranger on hikes other than along the beach. Short boat excursions cost $20 per person.

Chimp tracking Gombe's chimpanzee population has dwindled from 150 in the 1960s to around a hundred today, due to poaching and diseases, including infectious pneumonia that killed almost a third of the main study community in the 1980s. Chimp tracers at Gombe and Mahale are therefore subject to a lot of rules, which you can consult online at ⓦmahalepark.org/information.html. The most important is not to come if you are ill, to avoid transmitting a disease to which the chimps may have no immunity. Chimp tracking groups are limited to six people each, including the ranger, and are allowed a maximum of one hour with the chimps over a three-hour period following the first sighting. Children under 12 are not allowed, nor is flash photography.

9

When to visit Photography is best in the dry season (July to mid-Oct and mid-Dec to Jan), but the chimps are easier to see in the rains (roughly Feb–June and mid-Oct to mid-Dec), when the vegetation on the higher slopes is at its greenest and most beautiful. There are occasional windy thunderstorms during April and May and from August to September.

Equipment Your shoes need good grip in wet conditions. Recommended optional equipment, which you may or may not be able to rent locally, include a torch (or mobile phone, which serves the same purpose) for walks along the beach at night, snorkelling equipment and binoculars.

Safety Gombe's baboons and chimps are completely unfazed by humans, and therefore extremely dangerous if teased or tempted. The golden rules are to put all food and valuables out of sight, keep tents and rooms closed, never eat or drink outdoors (they've developed a fondness for sodas), and never stare at a baboon. If threatened by one, look away, turn your back, and move away slowly. Should a baboon snatch something from you, don't resist but alert park staff, who'll try to get it back.

ARRIVAL AND INFORMATION

The park can only be reached by boat, usually from Kibirizi, 3km north of Kigoma. It takes thirty minutes by speed boat, and up to three hours in a lake taxi.

On organized safari Upmarket trips to Gombe, by plane to Kigoma and by boat from there, are offered by some safari operators in Arusha, Mwanza and Dar, but it's cheaper and just as simple to arrange things directly with *Gombe Forest Lodge*'s operator, Mbali Mbali (⚙ mbalimbali .com), based at *Kigoma Hilltop Hotel* (see p.392), who charge their own clients substantially less for the boat ride there and back.

By private boat Independent visits are easily arranged through TANAPA's Visitor Information Centre in Kigoma (see "Information", above), where staff can also book chimp tracking slots (rarely necessary), park-run accommodation, and the boat there and back. They currently charge $300 return per boat (for up to eight passengers), which is cheaper than boats booked through *Aqua Lodge* or *Kigoma Hilltop Hotel*, both in Kigoma, but more expensive than *Jakobsen Beach*'s $210 (see p.391), though *Jakobsen*

Beach's boat is for its own guests only.

By lake taxi The cheapest option (no more than Tsh8000 for tourists) is a *kigoma-kigoma* lake taxi. These overcrowded wooden boats powered by single outboard engines offer limited if any shade from the sun, and are potentially dangerous (you must be able to swim), but pleasingly adventurous. They leave Kibirizi, 3km north of Kigoma, at around 1pm. Returning to Kibirizi, the national park staff can help you find a boat at around 5–6pm.

Information The best source of information is the TANAPA Visitor Information Centre in Kigoma (see p.391), for brochures, practical advice, and booking boat transfers and accommodation. TANAPA's *Gombe* guidebook can be brought up in Arusha, Dar and Stone Town. The official website is the brief ⚙ tanzaniaparks .com/gombe.html; for the latest on Gombe's chimps, see ⚙ gombechimpanzees.org.

ACCOMMODATION AND EATING

Overnights are limited to an expensive lodge in the north, and a couple of rest houses and a campsite at Kasekela, near the park headquarters. **Meals** are available at *Kasekela Rest House*, though they are expensive at $15 each – but you're welcome to use the kitchen for self-catering. Basics foodstuffs can be bought at Kasekela, including beers, and fish from fishermen on the beach, though you'll need to bring everything else from Kigoma, and keep it concealed in sealed containers to avoid showdowns with baboons.

Gombe Forest Lodge Mitumba, 3.5km north of Kasekela; book through Mbali Mbali at Kigoma Hilltop Hotel in Kigoma ☎ 0732 978879 or ☎ 0737 206420, ⚙ mbalimbali.com. On a wide sandy beach at the mouth of the Mitumba stream in the north, this is a rather plain camp consisting of seven spacious en-suite tents, all but one twin-bedded, on wooden platforms under mango trees. Detracting from the romantic setting is the wire mesh covering the dining *banda*, installed after one too many raids by baboons. That said, evening sundowners and dinner can be taken around a campfire. Other features include a

small library, shop, bar and lounge. Rates include park fees, chimp trekking and snorkelling. The transfer from Kigoma costs $350 return per boat. Closed March–April. FB **$1250**

★ **Jane Goodall Memorial Rest House** Kasekela; book through TANAPA Visitor Information Centre (see p.391). More basic but way more atmospheric than *Kasekela Rest House*, this is a simple but comfortable green ply-board building with two bedrooms that was built some forty years ago for Dr Goodall's son. The veranda, complete with a set of old sofas and settees, is screened with chicken wire to keep out baboons and chimps. Per person **$20**

9

Kasekela Campsite Kasekela; book through TANAPA Visitor Information Centre (see p.391). This is a small pitch on the beach with space for three tents, but it's periodically closed whenever the baboons get too brazen. Per person $\underline{\$30}$

Kasekela Rest House Kasekela; book through TANAPA Visitor Information Centre (see p.391). Six clean twin-bed rooms in an ugly two-storey concrete block near the beach, which also houses a canteen. There's electricity mornings and evenings. Per person $\underline{\$30}$

Mahale Mountains National Park

Some 120km south of Kigoma, on a wide peninsula jutting out into Lake Tanganyika, the 1613-square-kilometre **Mahale Mountains National Park** is one of the country's least accessible parks (no road access), and – no coincidence – is also one of the world's last strongholds for wild **chimpanzees**, numbering well over one thousand individuals. Several communities have become habituated to humans, and can be visited – a heart-stopping and memorable experience.

Like Gombe, Mahale's habitats are a blend of eastern and central African biomes (biogeographical zones), and include forest, mountain, savanna, *miombo* woodland and lake environments – a diversity that has resulted in exceptionally rich **birdlife**, and **butterflies**, including over thirty species of fast-flying charaxes that feed on animal dung. Other **mammals** include seven other species of primate, plus elephants, buffalo, lion and leopard, giraffe, antelopes (including the rare roan and sable) and, equally rare, the brush-tailed porcupine – though sightings of these are not at all guaranteed.

The lakeshore

The **lakeshore**, with its reeds, swamps, grassland and sandy beaches is good for birds, including nesting speckled mouse-birds in the stands of oil palms around Kasiha. Large game is rare on the shore, although antelopes come here to drink and African hunting dogs are also seen from time to time. **Swimming and snorkelling** used to be a highlight, but the crocodiles got a little too hungry for comfort – entering the water at the lakeshore is currently not advisable.

The gallery forests

Mahale's richest habitat is its lowland **gallery forest** in the northwest, where the mountains rise from close to the shoreline, ascending to around 1300m. Apart from the famous chimpanzees and the leopards, the forest – like Gombe's – contains several animal and plant species more typical of western than eastern Africa, including the brush-tailed porcupine, the red-legged sun squirrel, the giant forest squirrel and the bushy-tailed mongoose. Forest birds to look out for are the crested guinea fowl and Ross's turaco – the latter is evasive, despite its vivid colour, as it spends all its time in the forest canopy.

The mountains

The misty **mountains** themselves are also home to a small population of black-and-white colobus monkeys. Their range is restricted to the belt of bamboo and montane forest above 2000m on Mount Nkungwe. Above 2300m the forests give way to grassland. One- or two-night camping hikes up and down **Mount Nkungwe** (2462m; almost 1700m above lake-level) are possible, but must be arranged in advance with the park authorities or the tented camps; longer trips can be arranged to explore the drier **eastern slopes** of the mountains, which are covered by *miombo* woodland, acacia and "terminalia" savanna (characterized by termite mounds). Plains game is abundant, and includes elephant, giraffe, zebra, buffalo and warthog, together with rare roan antelopes and their predators – lion, spotted hyena and the endangered African hunting dog.

ARRIVAL AND DEPARTURE   **MAHALE MOUNTAINS NATIONAL PARK**

On organized safari Organized safaris are pointless at the "budget" end (it's simple enough, and cheaper, to arrange things yourself in Kigoma or Karema). Flying safaris can be booked through mid- to upper-range safari companies in

9

MAHALE'S FIRST CONSERVATIONISTS: THE BATONGWE AND HOLOHOLO

The Mahale Mountains are the traditional home of the **Batongwe** and **Holoholo** (the latter also known as Horohoro or Kalanga) tribes. Following the establishment of the Mahale Mountains Wildlife Research Centre in 1979, however, all human habitation was demolished to make way for the national park (created in 1985), despite the fact that the Batongwe and Holoholo's lifestyles were highly adapted to the local environment. The Batongwe lived in compact communities of around forty people and practised sustainable shifting cultivation over a cycle of thirty to fifty years, giving ample time for forest regeneration. They did little or no commercial hunting, and fished with nets whose mesh size was no smaller than 12cm, while some parts of the land, considered the sacred abodes of guardian spirits, were left untouched. So while proponents of "high-cost, low-impact tourism" stretch moral boundaries to justify $2350 a night, the real guardians of the Mahale Mountains, the Batongwe and Holoholo, who lived in near-perfect symbiosis with their environment, have been excluded from their ancestral land, and their traditional livelihoods.

Arusha (see pp.288–289), Mwanza (see p.364) and Dar (p.103).

By plane Excepting charters, flights are currently limited to "on inducement" extensions of Auric Air's scheduled Mwanza–Kigoma–Mpanda–Mwanza route (Mon, Thurs & Sat; ⓦ auricair.com), and Safari Aviation's twice-weekly service to and from Ruaha National Park via Katavi National Park (Mon & Thurs; ⓦ safariaviation.info). The airstrip is 4.5km northeast of the park headquarters. If you're staying at the park-run *bandas* or rest house, let them know beforehand so you can be picked up: transfer pricing is whimsical, but no less than $50 one way.

By ferry The MV *Liemba* (see p.391), even if you coincide with it, is not very useful for Mahale, as it drops anchor off Mgambo (also called Lagosa), 20km northeast of the park headquarters, before midnight (in both directions), so you'll need to arrange a pick-up with the park beforehand via their office in Kigoma (see p.391) – which costs over $200 one-way. If you arrive in Mgambo without having contacted the authorities, you'll need to rent a local boat for the trip to the park headquarters at Bilenge, and on to the *bandas*. You might strike lucky at night, but it's safer to wait for sunrise before setting off.

By private boat A speedboat takes about five hours from Kigoma to the park headquarters, and a normal motorboat up to fourteen. Hiring a boat is bitterly expensive unless you can muster a large enough group, with costs starting at $640 per boat one-way if arranged at TANAPA's Visitor Information Centre in Kigoma (see above), for a boat seating five passengers. You can slash the cost to a "mere" $240 one-way if you catch the daily daladala to Sigunga, 150km south of Kigoma by road, where TANAPA's boat can pick you up.

By lake taxi The cheapest approach to Mahale, but potentially dangerous and uncomfortable, is to catch a *kigoma-kigoma* lake taxi all the way from Ujiji to Kalilani, 1.5km on the beach from the park headquarters. The boats leave Ujiji at nightfall on Mon, Fri and Sat, taking 24 hours (Tsh30,000) – staff at TANAPA's office in Kigoma (see p.391) should know the latest, and may even have a spare seat on one of their boats. Alternatively, find a lake taxi in Karema in the south (see p.400), for a six-hour ride.

ESSENTIALS

Park headquarters The park headquarters are at Bilenge, 130km south of Kigoma (ⓣ 0689 062326 or ⓣ 0767 536127, ⓔ sokwe@tanzaniaparks.com).

Entrance fees Entry costs $80 for 24hr; the obligatory guide/armed ranger costs $20 per walk, more if you're fly-camping and he stays overnight.

Information If you're coming from Kigoma, visit TANAPA's Visitor Information Centre (see p.391), whose staff are knowledgeable about all practicalities, and can book park-run accommodation, and the boat there and back. TANAPA's guidebook *Gombe* has a good section on Mahale, and is available in Arusha, Dar and Stone Town. A good coffee-table book is *Mahale: A Photographic Encounter with Chimpanzees* by Angelika Hofer et al (Sterling, 2000). The official websites are ⓦ tanzaniaparks.com/mahale.html and, much more detailed if rather out-of-date, ⓦ mahalepark.org.

Chimp tracking Despite their number, Mahale's chimps can be difficult to see, so be patient. Rules and regulations are the same as for Gombe (see "Chimp tracking", p.395).

When to visit The park is best visited during the dry season (May to mid-Oct).

ACCOMMODATION

Accommodation in Mahale is either basic and comparatively cheap (though don't forget the park fees), or pampered and expensive. The park-run rest house is at Bilenge; other accommodation is a thirty-minute boat ride south, close to Kasiha, where the chimp treks start.

9

Bilenge Rest House (TANAPA Rest House) Bilenge, 300m north of the park headquarters; book via one of the TANAPA offices (see p.399). This former guesthouse, 60m from the shore, has nice lake views, and eight good en-suite twin-bed rooms, plus a kitchen – you can buy the basics, including drinks, at the park headquarters, where there's also a canteen. Per person $\overline{\underline{\$30}}$

Greystoke Mahale 12km south of the park headquarters ⓦ nomad-tanzania.com. A shockingly pricey French-run set-up in an idyllic location on a small sandy bay backed by palm trees and forested slopes. The guides are good, as are the meals, and the six two-storey thatched *bandas* decorated with furniture fashioned from driftwood and old dhows are exquisite. All in all, satisfyingly pretentious glamour in the wild. The rates include chimp tracking, forest walks, dhow trips (in search of hippo or to the nearby village), fishing and even alcohol. Closed Mar–May. No children under six. All-inclusive double $\overline{\underline{\$2350}}$

Kungwe Beach Lodge 11km south of the park headquarters ☎0732 978879 or ☎0737 206420, ⓦ mbalimbali.com. One of Mbali Mbali's better properties, with ten bright twin-bed tents on wooden platforms and with plumbed-in bathrooms, perched at the back of two beaches between the Kasiha and Sinsiba streams. There's an attractive reception area on the beach with seats fashioned from wooden canoes split into two, beach loungers, and evening campfires. Chimp trekking, boat rides, forest walks and canoeing are included, but park fees are extra. Closed March to mid-May. All-inclusive double $\overline{\underline{\$1430}}$

TANAPA Bandas (Mango Tree Bandas) 9.5km south of the park headquarters; book via one of the TANAPA offices (see p.399). Five simple, modern but not unpleasant self-catering cottages set in woods, each containing two en-suite twin-bedded rooms, but lacking electricity and running water. Kitchen facilities are available, and a cook should you want one, but you'll need to bring all your food from Kigoma or, for basics and drinks, near the park headquarters in Bilenge. Per person $\overline{\underline{\$30}}$

TANAPA Campsites Various locations; pay at one of the TANAPA offices (see p.399). The main public campsite, long-drop toilets and water, is close to the park headquarters at Bilenge, from where you'll need to catch a boat to Kasiha and back when chimp tracking. Fly camping is possible elsewhere, but has to be arranged with the park headquarters. Bring enough food for the duration. Per person $\overline{\underline{\$30}}$

Karema

Some 275km south of Kigoma by ferry, the lakeshore town of **KAREMA** (also spelled and pronounced **Kalema**) is an attractive and relaxing place, with nice beaches, an intriguing history, and daily transport to Mpanda, inland. Because of its sparse population, the slave trade bypassed Karema and it became an appealing tranquil base for the Belgian **Association Internationale du Congo**, a supposedly humanitarian society that in reality was a front for the colonization and exploitation of Congo. The Association's **Fort Léopold** at Karema was named after the Belgian King Léopold II, whose brutal rule over the "Congo Free State" was to become notorious.

When the Berlin Conference of 1884/85 granted Congo to Belgium and Tanganyika to Germany, Belgium had no further claim to Karema, so it was given to the **Society of the Missionaries of Africa**, better known as the **White Fathers** (after the colour of their gowns). The Belgian fort, of which little remains today, was converted into a mission, and the adjacent village established by four or five hundred freed slaves. The mission included a clinic founded by Adrien Atiman (see p.401), a school (which is still there, albeit now in mostly modern buildings), and a church, which still retains its Italianate tower built in 1890 (the spire is modern). There's also a scattered of German ruins, identified by their brickwork door and window frames.

ARRIVAL AND DEPARTURE   KAREMA

By ferry In theory, the ferry from Kigoma (see p.391) drops anchor off Karema around midday on Thurs, and on Sat heading back north – though don't expect punctuality. **By road** The 120km of road between Karema is Mpanda is unpaved but graded. A daily bus (4–5hr; Tsh8000) leaves Karema at 6am, and heads back from Mpanda when full, usually between noon and 2pm; if road conditions are bad, the route is served by a couple of Land Rovers.

ACCOMMODATION

Accommodation in Karema is limited to a couple of basic guesthouses between the mission and the shore: *Mzazi Hauwi* (☎0782 894933; Tsh5000 with shared bathroom; Tsh7000 for an en-suite twin) and *Juliana Guest House* (Tsh5000 with shared bathroom). The toilets at both places are squat-style. There's also a resthouse in the Catholic Mission, but it's not always open to tourists.

DR JOSEPH ADRIEN ATIMAN

Karema was the adoptive home of a remarkable doctor named **Joseph Adrien Atiman** (1866–1956). Modest, cheerful, and extremely competent, he was born at Tindirma near Timbuktu (Mali). As a child, he was **enslaved** by the Tuareg, and transported across the Sahara to the slave market at Metlili in Algeria, where, in 1876, he was purchased and freed by missionaries of the **White Fathers**. Following schooling in Algiers, he was baptized by the Order's founder, Cardinal Lavigerie, and went on to study medicine in Malta. His studies complete, he returned to Africa in 1888. Except for a two-year stint in southern Zambia, he spent 67 years at Karema working as a medical catechist (doctor), where he successfully combined western with traditional medicine. Atiman's clinic still operates, and his grave, at the mission, can be seen.

For further reading, The Catholic Bookshop in Sumbawanga (see p.413) sells the highly recommended *A History of the White Fathers in Western Tanzania* by Piet van der Pas (Peter Simchile), published in 2010.

Kipili

There are several good reasons to visit **KIPILI**, including its lovely beach, the ruins of a gorgeous nineteenth-century church, one of Lake Tanganyika's best hotels, and some fantastic **scuba diving** (for those with PADI Open Water certification) and **snorkelling**. On the north side of a small but perfectly formed cove, Kipili village is a friendly place, within easy reach of both Mpanda and Sumbawanga: English-speakers are not unusual here, so it's easy enough to make new friends.

White Fathers' Mission

2.5km northwest of Kipili • Follow the signs for Lake Shore Lodge (west along the bay for 1km, then north up the hill; ignore the left turn for the lodge but continue straight for another 600m) • If the new port is finally completed, it's 450m up the road from there on the right

Constructed between 1890 and 1895, the picturesque, now ruined, **White Fathers' Mission** was one of Tanzania's first churches, and is arguably its most beautiful, especially in the evening, when the colours are truly divine. It was built by freed Congolese slaves for the Society of the Missionaries of Africa in the elegant Italianate style favoured by the White Fathers, and the extensive brickwork, including a beautiful series of arches, is largely intact, as is the imposing facade. Despite having lost its roof, the fact that almost all of it is still standing – in a zone known for earthquakes, and a climate hostile to the longevity of sub-par bricks – is testament to the skill and industry of those early pioneers.

ARRIVAL AND DEPARTURE   KIPILI

By ferry The ferry from Kigoma, 360km north, arrives in Kipili between Thurs 9pm and Fri 3am. Coming from the south, it should arrive at 8–9am on Sat. Lighters greeting the ferry drop you just west of the village, but once the new port is completed, it'll dock 3km northwest of the village.

By car The road to Kipili starts at Chala, 60km north of Sumbawanga on the Mpanda highway. The asphalt continues as far as Namanyere, 26km west, from where a (currently) unpaved road winds across the mountains to

Kipili, 64km further on. Driving from Mpanda, turn off the highway at Mashete for an unpaved but fast 16km to Namanyere.

By bus There's no direct bus to Kipili from Mpanda or Sumbawanga, but they do get close – buses for Kirando (daily) pass through Katongolo, 6km east of Kipili, where *Lake Shore Lodge* can pick you up ($20/car), or jump on the back of a *pikipiki*. Alternatively, catch a Sumry bus to Namanyere and wait there for a daladala or pick-up to Kipili.

ACCOMMODATION, EATING AND DRINKING

★**Lake Shore Lodge** 2.5km northwest of Kipili (signposted) 📞0684 540792 or 📞0783 993166, 🌐lakeshoretz.com. Owner-managed by a South African couple, the lake's best shoreline hotel is stylish in the "rustic chic" tradition and offers fabulous views over the lake and a quartet of islands just offshore, from all rooms, the lounge and dining area. The waterfront beach chalets are

expensive, but bright and airy, constructed of wood, thatch and stone, and fronted by verandas kitted out with hammocks and deckchairs. The cheapest rooms – sharing bathrooms – are "lawn bandas", 50m or more from the beach and, for those on a budget, there are also four camping pitches behind the chalets, under a mango tree. The food is a three-course extravaganza featuring only

9

local ingredients, which you can eat under the stars beside the beach. Activities include – for $25–35 – snorkelling, sundowner cruises or kayaking in search of hippos, crocs and birds, plus mountain biking ($15/day), quad biking and scuba diving ($75 including equipment and boat; accredited divers only). Longer trips include kayak safaris (in April and May; nights under canvas), and safaris to Katavi and Mahale national parks. Guests of *St Bernhard House* are welcome for meals ($20–25), drinks and activities. Closed Feb. Camping per person **$14**, HB lawn banda **$200**, beach chalet **$450**, honeymoon suite **$500**

St Bernhard House 1km west of the village on the

lakeshore; ask for "Nyumba ya ndugu" – House of the brothers ☎ 025 280 2287. No relation to Kipili's historic Catholic mission, this basic beachfront retreat was founded in 1998 by Benedictine monks, and welcomes anyone seeking a bit of peace and quiet. The rooms, in a brick wing, are tatty but adequate, each with small beds with nets, table, chair and sink, but no running water. Electricity is provided in the evening, and meals can be arranged – usually rice with fish or *ugali* (Tsh3500). They also have beer, and can arrange fishing trips with locals (hook and line, lit by kerosene lamps at night… quite an adventure). **Tsh15,000**

Kasanga

The last Tanzanian town before Zambia, **KASANGA** was originally a slaving port, and from 1888 a German outpost called Bismarckburg. It was captured by the British in 1915, but not before the Germans managed to escape by placing fake wooden artillery around the Boma (fortress) – this delayed the British long enough for them to slip away on dhows. The German Boma still exists, up the hill behind the port, but is on military land and cannot be visited. The town, 2km south of its port, spent most of the twentieth century as a forgotten backwater, and is still little more than a large village, though may change with the completion of the tarmac road from Sumbawanga, and the expansion of the port to handle trade with Congo. Other than getting on or off the MV *Liemba* and visiting the beach, the main reason for stopping here is to see the impressive **Kalambo Falls**.

Kalambo Falls

On the Zambian border 6km east of the lake • From Kasanga, drive 12km along the tarred road towards Sumbawanga, then turn right along an unpaved road for 15km to just before Kalambo Falls village, also called Kapozi, where a 2km track takes you to the falls • Daily pick-ups leave Kasanga at 6am for Kalambo Falls village, and there are also three buses a week • Liemba Beach Resort charges $100 per vehicle there and back, and also offers access by boat from the lake ($270 per boat there and back)

Dropping down into the Rift Valley, the breathtaking 215-metre **Kalambo Falls** are Africa's second-highest, almost twice the height of the Victoria Falls. Varying in width from three to fifteen metres (the latter in February and March), the falls – which are a breeding ground for giant **marabou storks** – cascade into the Kalambo River canyon, on the other side of which is Zambia. Aside from the natural beauty, it's an important archeological site where prehistoric artefacts have been found, including **three-hundred-thousand-year-old stone tools** from the Acheulian period, as well as some of the world's oldest evidence for the use of wood in construction, dating back sixty thousand years. Excavations of early Iron Age villages and campsites have also revealed a wealth of earthenware pottery – mainly globular pots and shallow bowls – the earliest of which were made 1600–1700 years ago.

ARRIVAL AND DEPARTURE

KASANGA

By ferry The ferry from Kigoma (see p.391) supposedly arrives at Kasanga between midnight and dawn on Friday, but frequently accumulates lengthy delays en route. An immigration officer boards the ferry to complete exit formalities.

By road The road all the way from Sumbawanga is currently being paved. At present, the main bus company is Hekima Coach, leaving Kasanga at 5am or 6am, and turning back in Sumbawanga at midday. The ride takes four hours.

ACCOMMODATION

Katebarry Lodge 500m from Kasanga port ☎ 0754 984545, ✉ kiyayaphoto@gmail.com. Run by a keen photographer, this new simple resort has eight rooms,

some en suite (Tsh20,000 extra), in thatch-roofed *bandas* set in a green garden, as is the *makuti*-thatched restaurant and lounge. If lounging around on the beach gets tiring, you can go boating with locals (no snorkelling equipment, however), or hire a car or bicycle for the ride to Kalambo Falls (negotiable rates). Performances of traditional music of the local Langu tribe can also be arranged. Tsh40,000

★ **Liemba Beach Resort** 5km north of Kasanga by road, 1km south of Muzi ✆ 0764 377534, ✉ oscarmangwangwa @yahoo.com. Between a low headland just south of Muzi and a lovely stretch of beach that's safe for swimming, this relaxed, locally run place is used to tourists (there's even a swimming pool), knowledgeable about the area, and will meet the ferry at Kasanga. If you're coming by bus, let them know beforehand if you want a lift. Stay in one of five permanent "cabin tents" (safari tents on platforms under thatched shelters) at the back of the beach, or in three secluded brick bungalows with thatched roofs, sleeping up to

six, with hot water in their bathrooms, and electricity from a generator. Meals are consistently good (Tsh10,000 each), and the bar is made from an old dhow. Among the activities on offer are excursions, by car or boat, to the Kalambo Falls. BB tents Tsh30,000, bungalows Tsh95,000

Mwenya Guesthouse Muzi, 5.5km north of Kasanga port. The best of the area's budget options, with shared bathrooms, mosquito nets (essential), a bar and a TV. It's located in Muzi, a tranquil and friendly fishing village, which is the main reason, other than the low cost, for staying here, as you'll quickly get to know the locals – a welcoming bunch. Meals are available in a handful of cheap restaurants (*mgahawa*). It's a 90min walk from Kasanga, from where there are occasional vehicles, but catching a lake taxi is more fun. Tsh7000

Inland from Lake Tanganyika

Lake Tanganyika's hinterland is geographically and ecologically varied. In the north, due east of Kigoma, tangled **miombo woodland** infested by tsetse flies dominates: the flies, and the swampy Malagarasi River, have ensured that the area is scarcely inhabited by humans, and the most you'll see of it is from a passing bus or train. The transport hub is **Tabora**, in the heartland of the Nyamwezi tribe, who in the nineteenth century controlled much of the logistics, and the central sections, of two of East Africa's most important **slave and ivory caravan routes**. Following the abolition of slavery, the town retained its importance thanks to the Central Line railway, and it looks set to prosper still further, thanks to spanking new asphalt roads in all directions.

South of Tabora, a couple of lonely roads and a railway wend down to **Mpanda**, also accessible via a much improved road from Kigoma. Of little intrinsic interest in itself, Mpanda makes a handy base for visiting Karema or Kipili on Lake Tanganyika, and **Katavi National Park**, half an hour's drive south. Home to enormous congregations of hippos and crocodiles, Katavi marks the end of the dusty *miombo* woodland, which gives way to open rolling hills as you approach the burgeoning highland town of **Sumbawanga**, in the lee of the little-visited Mbizi Mountains. Sumbawanga is an alternative starting point for visiting Katavi and Kipili, and is unavoidable if you're heading to Kasanga and the Kalambo Falls, on the border with Zambia, or on to Mbeya and the southern highlands (see chapter 10).

Tabora

Popularly called Unyamwezi, after its dominant tribe, the Tabora region occupies much of Tanzania's tsetse-fly-infested central plateau. In the nineteenth century, it straddled two of East Africa's most lucrative ivory and slave caravan routes to the coast: from Lake Victoria in the north, and Lake Tanganyika in the west. The routes converged on **Kazeh** ("Kingdom"), corresponding roughly to present-day **TABORA**. There's little left of Kazeh these days, but its hot and dusty successor is a prosperous town of 230,000 people, whose importance as a trading centre stems from the Central Line **railway**, which follows the old caravan routes, and provides easy access to and from Dar, Kigoma and Mwanza, as well as, via a branch line, to Mpanda in the southwest. Aside from the **Livingstone Memorial Museum** and a handful of German buildings and, there's little to see in Tabora, but it's a friendly place, whose shady, tree-lined streets provide a welcome respite from the blistering *miombo* woodland that stretches for hundreds of kilometres around.

9

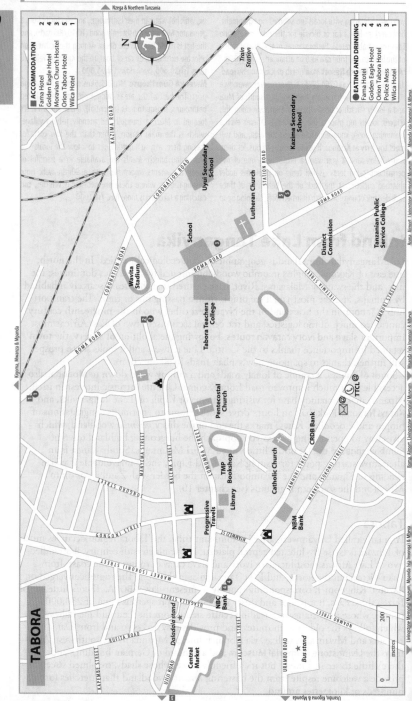

TABORA

Nzega & Noethern Tanzania

■ ACCOMMODATION	
Fama Hotel	2
Golden Eagle Hotel	4
Moravian Church Hostel	3
Orion Tabora Hotel	5
Wilca Hotel	1

● EATING AND DRINKING	
Fama Hotel	2
Golden Eagle Hotel	4
Orion Tabora Hotel	5
Police Mess	3
Wilca Hotel	1

Train Station

Kazima Secondary School

Uyui Secondary School

Lutheran Church

KAZIMA ROAD

CORONATION ROAD

BOMA ROAD

STATION ROAD

School

District Commission

Tanzanian Public Service College

Wavita Stadium

Tabora Teachers College

CORONATION ROAD

BOMA ROAD

JAMHURI STREET

ITETEMIA STREET

Pentecostal Church

MANYEMA STREET

BALEWA STREET

SONGORO STREET

LUMUMBA STREET

NYAMWEZI ST

TMP Bookshop

Library

Progressive Travels

Catholic Church

CRDB Bank

NBM Bank

JAMHURI STREET

MARKET (SOKONI) STREET

@

TTCL

GONGONI STREET

MARKET (SOKONI) STREET

NBC Bank

Daladala stand

UGALLA STREET

Central Market

KAPEMBE STREET

RUFIYA ROAD

UJIJI ROAD

SALAMINI STREET

URAMBO ROAD

Bus stand

NOAMBO STREET

0   200

metres

N

Kigoma, Mwanza & Mpanda

Roma Airport, Livinstone Memorial Museum ► Mpanda (via Inyonga) & Mbeya

Boma Airport, Livingstone Memorial Museum ► Mpanda (via Inyonga) & Mbeya

Livingstone Memorial Museum, Mpanda (via Inyonga) & Mbeya

Urambo, Kigoma & Mpanda

Brief history

9

The history of Tabora and its forerunner Kazeh is very much the history of the million-strong **Nyamwezi tribe**, who by the mid-1700s had opened up several major ivory-carrying routes to the coast. A century later, with the Zanzibar-dominated **slave trade** eclipsing ivory, the Nyamwezi became, along with Arabs and Swahili, one of the main organizers of slave hunts, as far as Congo, on the other side of Lake Tanganyika. By the 1850s, under the rule of chiefs Swetu I and Saidi Fundikira I, both Tabora and Kazeh were well established, and over the following decade an estimated half a million porters passed through the twin towns every year. The towns – and the Nyamwezi – grew rich on the taxes levied on caravans, as well as from their own caravans. Their increasing power was typified by the establishment of a short-lived but extremely powerful new state established by **Chief Mirambo** (see box, p.406), which successfully challenged Zanzibari hegemony over the slaving routes in the 1870s.

During the **German conquest** of Tanganyika, an outpost and then a fort (the still-existing Boma) were built in Tabora, surviving an armed rebellion in 1891 led by Chief Isike "Mwana Kiyungi" of Unyanyembe. The German victory made a considerable impression on lesser chiefs, who took to sending envoys to Tabora for help in local conflicts. In signing treaties with the Germans, they effectively handed over their land to the colonists, and with the Nyamwezi "pacified", the Germans set about developing Tabora itself. The **Central Line railway** (*Mittelland Bahn*) from Dar reached Tabora in 1912, but German efforts to open up the territory were in vain: they were ejected from Tabora in September 1916, after a fierce ten-day battle with Belgian troops from the Congo commanded by Colonel Tombeur. The British took control of Tabora after the war, and in 1928 gave the go-ahead for a branch line to Mwanza on to Lake Victoria, thereby assuring the prosperity of both towns.

Central Tabora

An aimless wander about Tabora is a pleasant affair, thanks to its plentiful mango and flame trees, and a variety of colonial architecture. The mango trees are thought to have been unwittingly introduced by slaves who discarded the stones during their painful trek to the coast. Colonial relics include the **train station**, with its steep central gable and lime-green roof, and the imposingly robust **German Boma** (or fort) at the south end of Boma Road, overlooking a small valley to the east. It's occupied by the military, so a visit (and photography) is out of the question.

The lively **central market** is also worth a look, with distinct areas set aside for anything from bicycle parts and tyre recyclers to a huge section dedicated to the diminutive dried *dagaa* fish which is brought in by rail from Kigoma. Prized locally is dark brown **honey** – one of few natural gifts from an otherwise unproductive and unforgiving region. For *kangas* (the colourful wraps worn by Tanzanian women), try any of the shops on Balewa Street off Market Street.

Livingstone Memorial Museum (Tembe la Livingstone)

8.5km southwest of Tabora · Daily 8am–4pm, but ring beforehand to check the caretaker's about · Tsh10,000 · ☎ 0784 506024 · From Tabora, catch a daladala for Kwihara and get off after 6km at the junction for "Livingstone" – the museum is 2.5km northwest of the junction · Taxis charge from Tsh15,000 return

All that remains of Kazeh is a handful of crumbling earth houses, a few mango trees and coconut palms, and the quirky **Livingstone Memorial Museum** – *Tembe la Livingstone*, or Livingstone's House. Livingstone and Stanley arrived in Kazeh on February 18, 1872, following their famous meeting in Ujiji. While Stanley went back to the coast, Livingstone stayed on awaiting supplies until August 25, when he left Kazeh for the interior on what proved to be his final journey.

The museum occupies a traditional earthen flat-roofed house (a *tembe*) with a beautiful Swahili-style carved doorframe, and is a 1957 reconstruction of the house that Livingstone stayed in, which at the time belonged to Sheikh Sayd bin Salim,

9

CHIEF MIRAMBO

It was only in the nineteenth century that the Nyamwezi tribe coalesced into a unified state, **Unyanyembe**, which was largely built on the wealth they accrued from the ivory trade. The appearance of wealthy Nyamwezi traders in the coastal ports aroused the avarice of the Zanzibari sultanate, which from the 1850s onwards launched increasingly confident incursions along Nyamwezi caravan routes, dealing in both ivory and slaves. As a result, the balance of power between hundreds of central Tanzanian clans and tribes broke down, and a new generation of leaders rose to prominence.

One of these was **Chief Mirambo-ya-Banhu**, who by 1871 had managed, mainly through conquest, to establish a rival state to Unyanyembe called **Unyamwezi**, which at its zenith between 1876 and 1881 extended into northwest Tanzania and Congo. Mirambo controlled the western caravan route from Tabora to Ujiji, as well as another caravan route heading up the western shore of Lake Victoria towards Uganda's Buganda empire. Not without reason did Stanley dub him "this black Bonaparte"; like Napoleon, Mirambo's rule was very much a product of his character. "He is tall, large chested and a fine specimen of a well-made man. As quiet as a lamb in conversation, he's rather harmless looking than otherwise, but in war the skulls which line the road to his gates reveal too terribly the ardour which animates him," effused Stanley in 1876.

Mirambo's success was manifold. Geographically, his empire blocked the Arab trade routes to Lake Tanganyika. Militarily, the vast wealth that the Nyamwezi had gained from the ivory and slave trades enabled the purchase of firearms and the hiring of *Ruga-Ruga* mercenaries from the Ngoni tribe (originally from southern Africa), all of which means that Mirambo's empire was engaged in **incessant warfare**, be it against Arabs or neighbouring chiefs. To consolidate his power, Mirambo reappointed governors of captured territories as agents and consuls, and even made an alliance with Sultan Barghash of Zanzibar.

The fact that the empire was held together largely by war, and the force of Mirambo's personality, meant that it quickly disintegrated following his death in 1884, paving the way for the arrival of the Germans a few years later. Nowadays, Mirambo is considered something of a national hero, not so much for his empire-building skills as for the fact that he managed to trump the Arabs over so many years.

governor of Tabora's "Arabs" (Zanzibaris). One room houses a mildly diverting display of memorabilia, including a lock of Livingstone's hair, and a piece of the mango tree beneath which Stanley and Livingstone allegedly met at Ujiji. Another room contains photocopies of pages from Livingstone's journals, reproductions of hand-drawn maps, and copies of contemporary US newspapers. The other, empty, rooms bear labels: Donkeys, Kitchen, Askaris, Bombay. The latter refers to Saidi Mbarak Mombay, the leader of Stanley's "exceedingly fine-looking body of men" during his quest for Livingstone – he'd previously worked for Burton, Speke and Grant.

During the expedition, Stanley was also accompanied by **John William Shaw**, who fell ill repeatedly and finally died in Kazeh in 1871. During their journey, Stanley and Shaw had travelled for a time with an Arab army, thinking it would offer safe passage further west; unfortunately for them it was routed by Chief Mirambo at Wilyankuru. Stanley blamed Shaw for the defeat, calling him "base and mean" in his memoirs, though the phrase is surely more applicable to the heartless Stanley himself, as amply evidenced by his own writings (see *How I Found Livingstone* at ⊛gutenberg.org /etext/5157). Shaw's grave lies 100m from the museum under a coconut tree, but the iron headstone is housed in the museum for safekeeping.

ARRIVAL AND DEPARTURE   TABORA

By plane Tabora airport is 5km southeast of town. At present, only Air Tanzania flies here (⊛airtanzania.co.tz) from Kigoma and Dar on Mon & Thurs, and back on Tues & Sat. Its agent is Progressive Travels, Lumumba St (☎026 260 4401 or ☎0784 273080).

Destinations Dar (2 weekly; 2hr); Kigoma (2 weekly: 1hr). **By train** The train station is at the east end of Station Rd (tickets on sale daily 8am–noon & 2–4.30pm, and two hours before departure). Trains leave Tabora around 8am for Dar (Mon & Fri), at 9pm for Kigoma (Wed & Sat) and Mpanda

(Mon, Wed & Sat), and at 9.30pm for Mwanza (Wed & Sat). Trains from Dar should pull in just after sunset; ones from Mwanza, Kigoma and Mpanda should arrive around sunrise. **Destinations** Dar (3 weekly; 26hr); Dodoma (3 weekly; 11hr); Kigoma (3 weekly; 12hr); Morogoro (3 weekly; 19hr); Mpanda (3 weekly; 14hr); Mwanza (3 weekly; 11hr).
By bus The bus stand is on the west side of town at the start of the road to Urambo and Kigoma. Most buses are fully booked the day before, so buy your ticket as soon as you can. The usual departure time is 6am, but you can find buses to Mwanza until 10am. There are two routes to Mbeya in southern Tanzania: via Mpanda and Sumbawanga (with an overnight in one of those

towns), or direct via Sikonge and Chunya, which used to be a bone-crunching dry-season-only ride but is currently being upgraded, and perilously fast in places. The safest companies on the Mwanza route are probably Mohamed Trans and NBS, but check with locals first, as during the research for this edition, there were fatal bus crashes on all four roads out of Tabora, three of which involved an AM Coach.
Destinations Arusha (2–4 daily; 12hr); Dar (2–3 daily; 16hr); Dodoma (1–2 daily plus buses for Dar; 8hr); Kigoma (1 daily; 12hr); Mbeya (1 daily; 18hr); Mpanda (2–3 daily; 8hr); Mwanza (6–7 daily; 5–6hr); Singida (2 daily plus buses for Arusha; 6hr).

ACCOMMODATION

There are many cheap guesthouses spread out around the junction of Boma Rd and Manyema St. "Single" rooms (those with one bed) can be shared by couples, except at the *Moravian Church Hostel* and *Orion Tabora Hotel*. Tabora's tap water is often highly discoloured, but drinkable if purified.

Fama Hotel North off Lumumba St ☎ 026 260 4657. A lovely little place tucked away in a quiet corner with a few shady Indian almond (*mkungu*) trees. The thirteen rooms are tatty but clean, the restaurant is good, and there's also safe parking. BB Tsh20,000
★**Golden Eagle Hotel** Cnr of Market and Jamhuri st ☎ 026 260 4623. Close to the bus stand and accessed through a parking lot, this promises little, but is excellent inside: it's friendly, and attuned to the tastes of passing tourists (how can you a fault a place with a rooftop bar and pool table?) There's also an oft-excellent restaurant. All the rooms have TV, box nets, fans and hot water; en-suite rooms coast an extra Tsh8000. BB Tsh12,000
Moravian Church Hostel Cnr of Kapembe and Mwanza st ☎ 0787 401613 or ☎ 0754 653157. The best-value budget option in town. The clean, cool rooms have

mosquito nets and washbasins, or you can opt for en suite for an extra Tsh4000. Food is available if ordered well in advance. Tsh8000
★**Orion Tabora Hotel** Station Rd ☎ 0767 610560, ✉ oriontbrhotel@yahoo.com. This charming colonial hunting lodge has been renovated and expanded, but still retains its charm. Rooms have big beds with giant mosquito nets, fan (no a/c), digital TV, and balconies facing the gardens. There's also a restaurant and two bars (live music Fri, discos Wed & Sat), free wi-fi and safe parking. BB Tsh80,000
Wilca Hotel Boma Rd ☎ 026 260 4106 or ☎ 0754 695451. This has ten en-suite rooms in a calm and peaceful atmosphere around a leafy courtyard, all with large double beds, nets on request (rooms are usually sprayed), ceiling fans, hot running water, and satellite TV. There are also a bar, restaurant and safe parking. BB Tsh20,000

EATING AND DRINKING

Tabora's good for food, and isn't bad for nightlife, either, especially live music: Nyanyembe Stars are worth seeking out, as are the famous and eminently danceable Tabora Sound Band (formerly Tabora Jazz; also known by its "Sensema Malunde" dance style), both of them performing several times a week at various venues. Gigs are advertised on posters and banners all over town.

Fama Hotel North off Lumumba St. The pleasantly calm bar here (even the TV volume is kept down) also serves up some superb food for under Tsh4000 – the *maini* (ox liver) in particular is delicious. Daily noon–8pm.
Golden Eagle Hotel Cnr of Market and Jamhuri sts. Friendly service and great for Indian food, especially *thalis* (Tsh6000 for the vegetarian) and chicken samosas. It also has a well-stocked rooftop bar. Daily 10am–9pm.
★**Orion Tabora Hotel** Station Rd. This renovated old hotel serves good food and has an extremely well-stocked bar. The food is accomplished, with local dishes (under Tsh10,000) featuring cassava leaves (*kisamvu*), and pumpkin leaves (*msusa*), Tabora cheese and grilled fish from either Lake Victoria or Lake Tanganyika. There's

also a selection of Indian and Chinese dishes. Tabora Sound Band plays here on Fri (9pm–3am; Tsh5000), and there are free discos Wed & Sat. Food served daily noon–10pm.
Police Mess Boma Rd. This 24-hour outdoor bar dishes up good food (oxtail soup, *mtori* banana stew and *nyama choma*), and hosts live bands every so often, usually on a Saturday, including Nyanyembe Stars. Open 24hr.
Wilca Hotel Boma Rd. A calm place with a wide choice of well-prepared food, which you eat in the garden outside. Dishes are all around Tsh6000 – the roast chicken is especially good, as is other grilled meat, and there are also a few cheap vegetarian dishes. You're also welcome just for drinks. Daily 11am–2.30pm & 6–8pm.

9

DIRECTORY

Bookshops TMP Bookshop, Lumumba St (Mon–Fri 8-30am–4pm, Sat 8.30am–2pm) stocks some interesting books of Tanzanian proverbs (*methali*).
Health District Hospital, Kitete St ☏ 026 260 3269.
Internet access Posta Internet Café, at the post office,

Jamhuri St (Mon–Fri 8am–5pm, Sat 8am–1pm).
Money NBC Bank, cnr of Market and Lumumba streets, is the most efficient for changing cash, and also has a Visa/MasterCard ATM.

Mpanda

Sprawling over several kilometres at the end of the Central Line's southern branch, 360km southwest from Tabora and 380km from Kigoma, the fast-growing town of **MPANDA** is capital of the recently formed Katavi Region. It's not worth a visit in itself, but is a likely stop for travellers between Kigoma or Tabora in the north, and Sumbawanga and Mbeya in the south. It also serves as a springboard for **Katavi National Park**, 35km away, and for visiting Karema and Kipili on Lake Tanganyika. Newspapers still arrive two or three days late, but the once-isolated Mpanda now has good transport connections: apart from the railway, it sports a new airport, and all three access roads are being asphalted – those from Tabora and Sumbawanga are almost complete, and work has begun on the historically atrocious road from Kigoma.

ARRIVAL AND DEPARTURE   MPANDA

Mpanda has few obvious sights, but a useful landmark is the Super City roundabout on the Kigoma–Sumbawanga road on the south side of town, 50m north of *Super City Hotel* (which all the locals know). From the roundabout, a paved avenue heads northeast and eventually becomes the road to Tabora.

By bus The bus stand is 750m northeast of the Super City roundabout – walk 500m up the avenue from the roundabout and take the last street on the right (before the avenue veers left); the bus stand is 200m along, on the left. The bus to Sumbawanga (240km) traverses Katavi National Park (no park fees if you stay on the bus), and the most reliable service here is Sumry (☏ 0756 896222 or ☏ 0784 563323), which you can catch as late as 2pm – though to reach Mbeya in a day, you'll need the 6am bus. The Tabora route also offers a choice of companies – ask around for the safest (slowest) bus, as the newly paved sections are dangerously fast.
Destinations Karema (1 daily; 4–5hr); Kigoma (1 daily; 7hr); Mamba (1 daily; 3–5hr); Mbeya (1–2 daily; 11hr); Sumbawanga (4–5 daily; 4hr); Tabora (2–3 daily; 8hr).

By train The train station is 1km west of the Super City roundabout. To get from the station into town, follow the stream of passengers back along the rail tracks and turn left after 800m onto the main road: Super City roundabout is 250m along. There are three trains a week leaving Tabora at 9pm (Mon, Wed & Sat; 14hr), supposedly arriving the following morning at around 11am, though delays are frequent. The train back to Tabora leaves at 4pm on Tues, Thurs & Sat. Fares are Tsh27,500 in first class, Tsh21,200 in second, and Tsh11,100 in third.
By plane The airport is 1.5km southeast of town. It features on the Mwanza–Kigoma–Mpanda–Mwanza route operated by Auric Air (☏ 0783 233334, ⊕ auricair.com), which currently runs on Mon, Thurs & Sat, taking 2hrs to Mwanza.

ACCOMMODATION AND EATING

There are plenty of half-decent hotels scattered about, but running water is erratic at all of them. If you fancy a night out, find a reliable local to accompany you, as there are next to no taxis.

New Dubai Lodge 200m east of Super City roundabout ☏ 0758 010265, ✉ newdubai@hotmail.com. The best of Mpanda's guesthouses, secure, well run and friendly, its ten en-suite rooms kitted out with ceiling fan and TV. There's safe parking, and an internet café next door. **Tsh20,000**
South Lodge 500m east of Super City roundabout, 50m north of the bus stand ☏ 0763 951910. Nothing special, and somewhat overpriced, but handy for early buses, and decent enough, with small but clean en-suite rooms all with TV and fridge. **Tsh20,000**

Super City Hotel 50m south of the roundabout. Overnighting here is no longer recommended (there are excruciatingly loud discos most nights, fittings are cheap and usually broken, and there have been reports of laptops being stolen from locked bedrooms here), but the restaurant and bar are still decent: you'll pay around Tsh5000 for a stew with rice/chips/ugali (the liver is good), which you can eat at tables out in front. They also serve *chipsi mayai* and *nyama choma*. Daily noon–10pm.

Katavi National Park

Some 35km south of Mpanda and 143km north of Sumbawanga, **Katavi National Park** covers 4471 square kilometres, making it Tanzania's fourth-largest protected wildlife area. The scenery isn't that spectacular, but **dry-season wildlife viewing** is, when vast quantities of game are concentrated around rapidly receding water sources. Three species in particular offer stunning photo opportunities: the park is home to one of Africa's most extensive **buffalo** herds, estimated at around sixty thousand, while several thousand **crocodiles** and **hippo** are packed into a handful of muddy lake-swamps. **Other wildlife** you're likely to see includes elephant, giraffe, zebra, lion, gazelle, large herds of roan and sable antelopes, topi, eland and – in reed beds near swamps – the southern reedbuck. **Birders** are in for a treat, too, with over four hundred species recorded, including eagles, hawks, marabou storks and palm-nut vultures.

The park takes its name from a semi-legendary ancestor of the Pimbwe, Fipa and Bende tribes, **Katabi**. A famed hunter in his time, his spirit is said to reside near Lake Katavi, in a small clearing around two tamarind trees, and the vast hippo pods in the lakes are said to be Katabi's herds. The site remains sacred, and locals still come here to leave offerings, seeking Katabi's intercession with God in worldly matters like asking for rain.

The grasslands

The park's main attraction is its **seasonally flooded grasslands**, around Lake Katavi, in the central Katisunga Plains, and north of the Nsaginia River northeast of Lake Chada. In the dry season, the grasslands support vast herds of buffalo and plains game, and when they're flooded attract waterbirds in their thousands. With exceptional luck, you

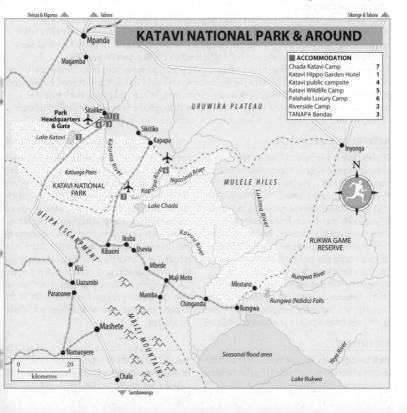

KATAVI NATIONAL PARK & AROUND

ACCOMMODATION	
Chada Katavi Camp	7
Katavi Hippo Garden Hotel	1
Katavi public campsite	4
Katavi Wildlife Camp	5
Palahala Luxury Camp	6
Riverside Camp	2
TANAPA Bandas	3

9

may see the shy and rare puku antelope (*Kobus vardoni*), about which very little is known – it's also found in Mahale, the Kilombero Valley and in isolated pockets across southern Africa. The **thickets and short grasses** around the edges of the flood plains are inhabited by leopard (difficult to spot), lion and elephant, and various antelope species, including roan and sable, southern reedbuck, eland and topi.

The lakes

The park's **lakes** – the palm-fringed Lake Katavi, and Lake Chada at the confluence of the Kavuu and Nsaginia rivers in the centre of the park – are nowadays little more than seasonal flood plains. Their gradual disappearance is due to river-borne silt deposits from the arid badlands between Mpanda and the park – a vivid example of the environmentally damaging consequences of concentrating human settlement in marginally productive areas, the result both of Nyerere's failed *Ujamaa* programme and of evicting people from the park. Nonetheless, both lakes retain some extraordinary wildlife viewing, most famously in the form of enormous herds of buffalo, birds in flocks of biblical proportions, and – most amazing in the dry season – literally thousands of hippos squashed together in the park's few remaining **mud pools**. At the edges of these glorious mud baths, and along riverbanks, large crocodiles also seek shelter from the dry-season sun by burrowing out nests, often stacked one atop the other. The hippos are best seen at Lake Chada, particularly at the pool close to Nzinge Ranger Post, while buffaloes, pelicans and marabou storks yanking out catfish from the mud are best seen from the observation hut overlooking Lake Katavi.

The rest of the park

With your own transport, you can visit the permanent streams, small cascades and year-round springs of the cooler and wetter escarpment in the forested **Mulele Hills** (also spelled Mlala or Mlele), at the eastern boundary of the park beside Rukwa Game Reserve. Alternatively, in the far southeast you might head to the **Rungwa (Ndido) Falls** on the Rungwa River, a thundering hundred-metre drop into a hippo- and croc-filled pool. If you get this far down, instead of retracing your steps you could follow the dirt road outside the park west from Rungwa village to Kibaoni, where a right turn takes you back into the park. Roughly 40km west of Rungwa you'll pass through the booming agricultural town of **Maji Moto** ("hot water"), just before which there are – no surprise – hot springs.

ARRIVAL AND DEPARTURE   KATAVI NATIONAL PARK

By plane Auric Air will stop off at Katavi "on inducement" on its regular Mwanza–Kigoma–Mpanda–Mwanza routing if there are two or more or you (Mon, Thurs & Sat; $320 from Mwanza; ⊛auricair.com), while Safari Airlink flies here on its Ruaha–Katavi–Mahale–Katavi–Ruaha routing (Mon & Thurs; $500 from Ruaha; ⊛safariaviation.info), with connections to and from Dar, Selous, Pangani and Zanzibar. There are several airstrips in the park: just west of Sitalike, in the middle of the park between the Katisunga Plains and Lake Chada, and in the north at Palahala.

By car With a 4WD, the park's your oyster. You can rent one easily in Sumbawanga from the tourist information centre (see p.412), or in Sitalike at *Riverside Camp* or *Katavi Hippo Garden Hotel*. Prices depend on your bargaining skills and

how much terrain you'll cover, but it probably won't be less than $200 a day, including driver and fuel but excluding park fees. The park headquarters used to rent vehicles, and it's worth asking if that's resumed. They also provide optional guides ($20 for a few hours), whose services are recommended to winkle out as much wildlife as possible.

By bus Catch a bus (approx hourly until mid-afternoon) from Mpanda (30min) or Sumbawanga (3hr 30min), as far as Sitalike, just outside the park's northern boundary. The bus from Sumbawanga passes straight through the park, and should give you fleeting glimpses of antelopes, at least. You can then arrange your safari at one of the riverside hotels just south of Sitalike, or at the park headquarters.

ESSENTIALS

Park headquarters The park headquarters are 500m south of Sitalike village – turn right 180m after the bridge and its guardian hippos (☎025 282 0352, ☎0689 062314

or ☎0767 536128, ⊛katavi@tanzaniaparks.com).

Entrance fees Entry fees are $30 per person and Tsh20,000 per vehicle, and are valid for 24hrs. Fees are paid at the park headquarters, or at ranger posts near the airstrips, and Visa or MasterCard are accepted, but not cash. There's no fee for just passing along the Mpanda–Sumbawanga road, or for staying at the riverside hotels at Sitalike, just outside the park.

When to visit Animal concentrations, and their visibility, are best once the dry season has set in, meaning July or August to October. The park is at its least appealing during and shortly after the rains (especially the long rains, Mar–May), when part of the park's internal road network gets flooded, most of the plains game migrates outside the park (or into hillier and less accessible terrain), and the place is even more infested than usual with tsetse flies (which, at least, don't carry sleeping sickness).

Information The best sources of information are the official websites: ⓦ katavipark.org and ⓦ tanzaniaparks .com/katavi.html; ⓦ friendsofkatavi.org is also useful if brief.

Walking safaris Parts of the park can be explored on foot if escorted by an armed ranger ($20 per group plus $20–25 per person depending on the duration, on top of entrance fees), and walking safaris are offered as a standard activity by the park's upmarket lodges and camps. If you're staying elsewhere, walks are best arranged in advance: if you just turn up at the headquarters, you may need to offer a little extra to make it worth the ranger's while, and it helps if you have a car. Without a car, you're limited to a half day's walk, coolest in the morning, west from the gate along the meandering Katuma River (part of which is outside the park), and back through *miombo* woodland on the south side of the airstrip.

Night game drives Along with Lake Manyara, Katavi is the only national park allowing nocturnal game drives. These are bookable at the park headquarters ($50 per person): reserve ahead to avoid disappointment.

ACCOMMODATION

Those with full wallets can opt for one of a quartet of upmarket places, three of them reviewed below, whose rates all include game drives and bush walks. Poorer folk will have to settle for Sitalike in the north – which, if you stay by the river, could be one of the more memorable places you'll ever stay, thanks to yawning hippo pods that are so close you can see their tonsils. Sitalike village itself, a ragged roadstead starting 500m north of the river, has plenty of shops, bars and restaurants.

INSIDE THE PARK

Chada Katavi Camp On a wooded rise northwest of the Chada flood plain ⓦ nomad-tanzania.com. A classic colonial-era safari in a remote wilderness, far from the crowds, this camp is comfortable rather than luxurious, and doesn't go overboard on the Edwardian chintz. Despite the Heminwayesque gloss, it's still just a bunch of tents (six, to be precise), where the quality of service, food and guides for game drives and bush walks is top-notch. No children under 12. Closed Mar–May. Game package $1550

Katavi Wildlife Camp Katisunga Plains, at the mouth of the Katuma River ☎ 0713 237422 or ☎ 0754 237422, ⓦ kataviwildlifecamp.com. Run by Foxes Safari Camps, this is similar to *Chada Katavi* in feel, but less fancy and more rustic, and strikes a good balance between comfort and a classic "in the bush" experience. This is thanks in part to a spectacular location on the edge of the vast Katisunga Plains, where the six tented rooms (more planned) have sweeping views. Pitched on polished wooden decks, they have lots of windows (screened with white nets), so are bright, and come with hammock-draped verandas. The lounge, bar and dining area are in a rustic two-storey construction, and meals are reliably good. Most guests fly in from Ruaha, where Foxes have another camp. Aug–Sept. Closed Mar–May. Game package $1090

Palahala Luxury Camp Kapapa River, northern Katavi ☎ 027 250 8773 (Arusha), ⓦ tanzaniafirelightsafaris .com. Wild, rustic and welcoming, and with an almost jungly riverside location jumping with monkeys and birds, this is an upmarket take on *Katavi Hippo Garden* and *Riverside Camp*, outside the park, with just as many

heaving hippos, even more crocodiles, and even elephants drinking on the opposite bank – and all can be seen from your own veranda. The eight permanent tents, pitched on platforms and with plumbed in bathrooms, are large and relatively bright, despite the surrounding vegetation, thanks to an unusual octagonal design. The downside to such lushness is more mosquitoes and tsetse flies. Closed mid-April to mid-May. Game package $1340

TANAPA bandas 2km south of Sitalike; book via the park headquarters, or TANAPA in Arusha (see p.287). Six simple, angular cement cottages – not unbecoming – set in woodland, through which wildlife often comes ambling (no fences). The rooms are spacious, airy and comfortable, and you're free to use the kitchen at the park headquarters, a ten-minute walk away. Per person $30

TANAPA campsites Various locations; book at the park headquarters. Katavi's public campsite is at Sitalike near the park headquarters and the staff houses: although it is only just inside the park, it sees a good deal wildlife. It also has toilets, showers and a cooking area. Wilder, and requiring your own vehicle, are a number of "special" campsites with variable locations deeper in park, which however tend to be booked by safari companies. They have no facilities whatsoever, so you'll need to be self-sufficient. Basic supplies can be bought in Sitalike. Public campsite $30 per person, special campsites per person $50

OUTSIDE THE PARK

★**Katavi Hippo Garden Hotel** South end of Sitalike, on the north bank of the Katuma River. The extraordinary location, rather than the quality of the rooms, is the reason

9

for our recommendation here – though it has been closed for a couple of lengthy spells of late. If it is open, chose a room in one of the cottages closest to the river, barely 25m from several resident hippo pods. The place is also frequented by very pretty giraffes, and occasionally even elephants. There are 45 rooms, all en suite and clean, despite being run down, and the staff are friendly. There's also a restaurant with drinks, and you're welcome to camp. Camping per person Tsh10,000, rooms BB Tsh40,000

★**Riverside Camp** South end of Sitalike, on the north bank of the Katuma River ☎0784 754740. Just before *Katavi Hippo Garden*, and in similarly thrilling proximity to the river's pink-skinned buck-toothed wallowers, winsome giraffes and admirable birdlife. It's currently the better of the two in its of rooms and standards, and is also a little cheaper, but the water runs cold (hot is in buckets), and there's only electricity in the evenings. The staff are welcoming and knowledgeable about the park, and the campsite is on grass – a rare luxury. Camping per person Tsh10,000, rooms Tsh30,000

Sumbawanga

The capital of Rukwa region is **SUMBAWANGA**, in the lee of the Mbizi Mountains, whose breezes lend the town a refreshing climate – chilly at night, and just right by day. The town's main attraction is the cosy **market** off Mpanda Rd – just the place for cheap seasonal fruit and vegetables, *dagaa* fish from Lake Tanganyika and the traditional assortment of imported plastic and aluminium household goods from China and Taiwan. There's really nothing else to see in town, so unless you've got the patience and the stamina to arrange a hike in the Mbizi Mountains or down to Lake Rukwa, most people just stay a night before heading on towards Mpanda, Katavi National Park, Mbeya or Kasanga on the shore of Lake Tanganyika.

ARRIVAL AND INFORMATION

By bus Sumbawanga's bus stand is full of pushy touts, as the new asphalt roads have vastly increased competition to many destinations. Most companies have just one or two small buses that leave when full, though the larger companies have schedules. Of these, the safest reputation lies with Sumry (office on Baruti St on the south side of the stand; ☎0784 418139 or ☎0767 370054), while the worst is Air Bus. For Mbeya and Mpanda, buses leave as late as 2pm, but you'll arrive at night. For Kasanga on Lake Tanganyika, Hekima Coach heads off at around midday.
Destinations Kasanga (1 daily; 4hr); Mbeya (7–8 daily; 7hr); Mpanda (4–5 daily; 4hr).
Tourist office Bethlehem Tourism Information Centre,

Mpanda Rd (Mon–Sat 7.30am–10pm, Sun noon–7pm; ☎0784 704343 or ☎0753 807593, ✉charlesnkuba450 @hotmail.com) is Sumbawanga's unofficial but very helpful tourist office, which also serves as a travel agency. Staff can answer most queries about Lake Tanganyika and Katavi, and offer well-priced tours there, as well as shorter excursions closer to home, such as a two-hour walk out of town to meet villagers ($10 the guide), and various half-day hikes ($20 for the guide, plus transport; bicycle hire costs Tsh2000/hr or Tsh5000/day). Although there's nothing organized at present, it's worth asking them about them about trips to the nearby Mbizi Mountains and the alkaline Lake Rukwa, both completely off the beaten track.

ACCOMMODATION

Holland Hotel Rainer St ☎0786 553753 or ☎025 280 2786, ✉rlukarah@yahoo.com. Sumbawanga's best lodgings, albeit functional rather than memorable, with nice fresh double rooms on three floors, and better value for couples than the *Moravian Conference Centre*. All rooms have cable TV, big round nets, free coffee and Ethernet. Bathrooms are okay but have buckets. Safe parking. BB Tsh35,000

Mfugaji Guest House Nkuruma St ☎0766 341586 or ☎0762 680083. Simple, with squat toilets, but surprisingly fresh, and the best of the really cheap hotels south of the bus stand, in part because it's well kept, but also because it's far enough away from the area's noisy nightlife a few hundred metres east. All rooms (some en suite) have cable TV, and there's hot water. No breakfast,

but you do get fresh milk for free. Tsh10,000
Moravian Conference Centre Nyerere Rd ☎025 280 2853. Large, clean and very quiet (it's in a calm part of town), with dozens of rooms priced a little over the odds but well kept and therefore still reasonable value: all have cable TV. The cheapest, on the second floor, share bathrooms; the en-suite rooms include breakfast and cost an extra Tsh10,000. There's also a decent restaurant. Tsh15,000

Tanzanite Lodge Nyerere Rd, next to the CCM Building ☎025 280 2772. Easy to find, modern, reliable, efficiently run and friendly, but dull. This has thirteen en-suite rooms, all with box nets and cable TV, and there's a good little restaurant at the front. Safe parking. BB Tsh20,000

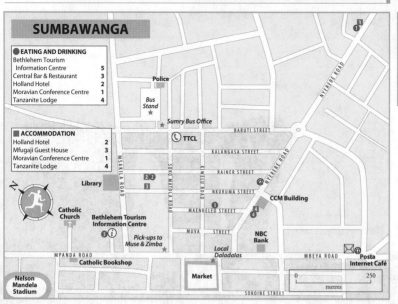

EATING AND DRINKING

The main concentration of restaurants is on Maendeleo St, where competition keeps standards fairly high. The nocturnal focus is Kalangasa St, particularly its eastern section, where you'll find lots of bars and even a few clubs.

Bethlehem Tourism Information Centre Mpanda Rd. Simple but filling meals for next to nothing, with a choice of meat stew, roast chicken (or *supu*), fish or liver with *ugali* or rice, plus beans and greens. Fish dishes cost Tsh2500, meat up to Tsh4000. Mon–Sat 6am–7pm.

Central Bar & Restaurant Maendeleo St. Friendly local restaurant with cheap breakfasts (great savoury *supus*) and lunches (under Tsh4000). The attached bar is great for an afternoon drink, its TV tuned to Discovery Channel and CNN. Daily 7am–11pm.

Holland Hotel Rainer St. Pricier than the others, but good, and with unusual specialities, such as *dagaa* with coconut sauce served with cassava *ugali* (Tsh7000; ask for

samaki wa kupaka). Meat dishes cost up to Tsh12,000, and there's also a selection of Chinese dishes. Daily 7am–11pm.

Moravian Conference Centre Nyerere Rd. Reliable and sometimes excellent meals, including liver fried with onion served with *ugali*, plus all sorts of burgers and pizzas. Most mains cost Tsh6500. No alcohol. Daily 7.30am–10pm.

Tanzanite Lodge Nyerere Rd, next to the CCM Building. A clean and bright dining room, often serving a mini buffet at lunchtimes, as well as a menu offering mostly Tanzanian dishes for Tsh5000. It's a good place to try fish from Lake Tanganyika and Lake Nyasa. No alcohol. Daily noon–8.30pm.

DIRECTORY

Bookshop The Catholic Bookshop, Mpanda Rd (Mon–Fri 8.30am–4pm, Sat 8.30am–2pm), stocks the excellent *A History of the White Fathers in Western Tanzania*.

Internet access *City Internet Café*, Nyerere Rd (daily

8am–8pm); *Posta Internet Café*, at the post office, Mbeya Rd (Mon–Fri 8am–4.30pm, Sat 9am–1pm).

Money NBC, Mpanda Rd, has a 24-hour Visa/MasterCard ATM.

Southern Tanzania

ISIMILA

Southern Tanzania

10

Little visited but often wildly beautiful, southern Tanzania is an enchanting and surprisingly easy place to explore, whether it's mountains you hanker for, or ancient forests, wildlife and birds, culture, or merely magnificent scenery. Coming from central Tanzania, first stop is Iringa town, a pleasant base from which to explore the bird-filled forests of the western Udzungwa Mountains, a number of historical sites related to the struggle against German conquest, and the huge if fragile wilderness of Ruaha National Park – equal to the northern circuit for wildlife, but with only a fraction of the crowds. Ruaha, together with the western Udzungwa Mountains, is also prime bird-viewing territory, with over seven hundred species recorded between them.

Southern Tanzania's other main base, and its biggest town, is **Mbeya**, whose colonial core is refreshingly genteel. It's surrounded by the evergreen **southern highlands**, product of tectonic upheavals that also wrenched apart the Rift Valley. The mountains are a giant's playground of forested peaks, crater lakes, hot springs, flower-strewn plateaux, and even a dormant volcano, Mount Rungwe. All in all perfect hiking terrain, with good access thanks to **cultural tourism** programmes in Mbeya and the agricultural town of Tukuyu – Tanzania's wettest place. To the east, the land levels off on to the **Kitulo Plateau**, declared a national park to protect over fifty species of rare orchids, which put on delirious displays during the rains. But flowers aren't the park's only rarity: it's also home to **kipunji**, an entirely new species and genera of monkey that was only discovered in 2003.

Beyond the southern highlands, the land drops down to **Lake Nyasa**, which fills a deep trough at the junction of the eastern and western branches of the Rift Valley. Flanked by the soaring Livingstone Mountains, it's a stunningly picturesque stretch of water – a ferry ride here makes a short but most memorable journey. In contrast to the lake's Malawian shoreline, however, tourism on the Tanzanian side is virtually non-existent: the main beach, at Matema in the north, has just three modest hotels, while the southern town (and sands) of Mbamba Bay is about as far as you can get from mainstream Tanzania without tripping over the border into Mozambique.

Iringa and around

The main base for visiting Ruaha National Park is the quietly prosperous, laidback rural town of **IRINGA**, some 500km southwest of Dar, and perched on an escarpment amid jagged hills and cracked granite boulders. It's a refreshing place to settle into for a few days, not just because of its altitude (1600m above sea level), but also because there are a number

ELEPHANTS IN RUAHA NATIONAL PARK

Highlights

❶ **Neema Crafts Centre, Iringa** An uplifting arts and crafts project for disabled people, where you're most welcome to muck in, too. **See p.419**

❷ **Kalenga** The historic seat of the Hehe tribe who, under Chief Mkwawa, famously resisted the Germans in the 1890s. A museum tended by his descendants contains his skull. **See p.421**

❸ **Isimila** Spectacular series of gullies near Iringa, resembling a miniature Grand Canyon, and site of numerous finds of prehistoric stone tools and fossils. **See p.421**

❹ **Ruaha National Park** Tanzania's best-kept secret, Ruaha contains most of the Northern Safari Circuit's wildlife but few of the crowds. **See p.425**

❺ **The southern highlands** Hike or bike from Mbeya and Tukuyu to waterfalls, crater lakes or, a lava-stone bridge, or up the forested peaks. **See pp.430–441**

❻ **Kitulo National Park** Known as God's Garden, this highland plateau contains an immense diversity of flowers, especially orchids. It's best experienced during the rains. **See p.436**

❼ **Lake Nyasa** The most beautiful of the Rift Valley lakes, best seen from the weekly ferry between Itungi Port and Mbamba Bay. **See pp.441–446**

HIGHLIGHTS ARE MARKED ON THE MAP ON P.418

of possible excursions in the vicinity, including to a Stone Age site at **Isimila**, set amid a natural "forest" of bizarrely shaped sandstone pillars, and a **Mkwawa Museum** in nearby Kalenga, which houses the skull of the Hehe tribe's most famous nineteenth-century leader, Chief Mkwawa.

Iringa market

Between Jamhuri and Jamat sts • Daily 7am–6pm

Iringa's rural essence is best sampled by rummaging around the **market**, a colourful,

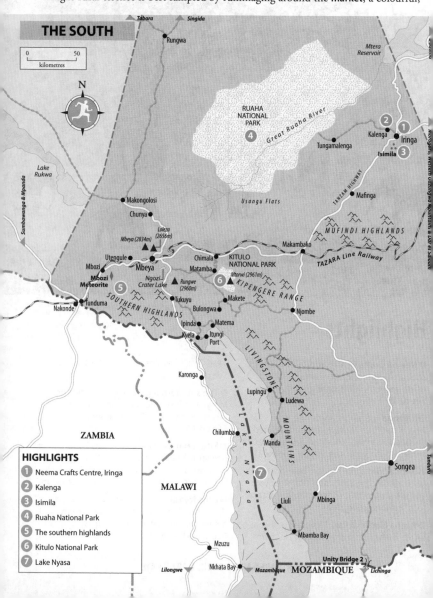

THE SOUTH

0   50
kilometres

N

HIGHLIGHTS

1. Neema Crafts Centre, Iringa
2. Kalenga
3. Isimila
4. Ruaha National Park
5. The southern highlands
6. Kitulo National Park
7. Lake Nyasa

ZAMBIA

MALAWI

MOZAMBIQUE

Tabora   *Singida*

Rungwa

Mtera Reservoir

RUAHA NATIONAL PARK ④

Great Ruaha River

Tungamalenga

② Kalenga ① Iringa ③

Isimila

Lake Rukwa

Makongolosi

Chunya

Usangu Flats

Mafinga

TANZAM HIGHWAY

MUFINDI HIGHLANDS

Loleza (2656m)
Mbeya (2834m) ▲ ▲

Utengule

Mbozi   Mbeya

Mbozi Meteorite ⑤

Ngozi Crater Lake
▲ *Rungwe (2960m)*

Chimala   KITULO NATIONAL PARK
Matamba   ⑥ ▲ *Mtorwi (2961m)*

Makambako

TAZARA Line Railway

KIPENGERE RANGE

SOUTHERN HIGHLANDS

Tunduma   Tukuyu
Nakonde

Bulongwa   Makete

Ipinda   Matema
Kyela   Itungi Port

Karonga

Njombe

LIVINGSTONE

Lupingu   Ludewa

MOUNTAINS

Chilumba   Manda

⑦

Songea

Mzuzu

Liuli   Mbinga

Mbamba Bay

Unity Bridge 2

Lilongwe   Nkhata Bay   *Mozambique*   MOZAMBIQUE   *Lichinga*

Sumbawanga & Mpanda

Morogoro, western Usangwa mountains & Dar es Salaam

Tunduru

Lake Nyasa

vibrant and hustler-free shambles built in 1940. Among the many specialities on offer are beautifully woven (and sometimes aromatic) baskets made from reeds or sisal, pumice stones and honey, bath sponges and loofahs imported from the coast, and even cow bells. There's also a riotous selection of *kanga* wraps, *kibatari* oil lamps, pungent dried fish from Mtera Reservoir (along the road to Dodoma), and pottery from various places, including – if you're lucky – the gorgeous cream-and-red ware from Lake Nyasa's Kisi tribe. For medicinal herbs and tree bark, have a mooch down the alleyway on the west side of Uhuru Park, where several Maasai sit behind their wares, together with others making and selling beaded jewellery, or plaiting people's hair. On the south side of the market, next to the police station, the **Maji Maji Memorial** honours African soldiers who died while in the service of Germany during the uprising (see p.517).

The Jamatkhana

Jamat St • Entry should be possible for genuinely interested non-Muslims – ask at the entrance

Iringa's compact colonial quarter occupies the streets west of the market. The most impressive building here is the gorgeous Ismaïli mosque – the **Jamatkhana**. It's an amazingly elegant structure, its two-tiered ornamental facade reminiscent of the Old Dispensary in Zanzibar's Stone Town, but with a tall clocktower that lends it an almost Bavarian vibe – the clock inside is the original, and still works. The mosque was built in 1932, to a design based on the Ismaïli mosque in Dar es Salaam, built two years earlier.

Iringa war cemetery

Old Dodoma Rd • Daily 6am–6pm in theory, though the gate is usually locked; if it is, you can get the combination by calling ☎ 005 20 260 4301 (a Kenyan number) Mon–Fri 8.30am–12.30pm & 1.30–4.30pm • ⓦ cwgc.org/find-a-cemetery/cemetery/12105 /Iringa20Cemetery

Iringa's **War Cemetery**, tended by the Commonwealth War Graves Commission, contains the remains of soldiers and porters who died in World War I, not just during the capture of Iringa in September 1916, but from other battles too: Iringa was the site of a major hospital, and after the war many graves were exhumed and reburied here. There are 131 "British" graves, mostly colonial-era South Africans and Rhodesians, and sixteen Germans, as well as the graves of Europeans who died in the 1960s and 1970s.

Neema Crafts Centre

Hakimu St • Mon–Sat 8.30am–5pm, workshops closed Sat afternoon • ☎ 0783 760945, ⓦ neemacrafts.com

A short walk southwest of the cemetery, **Neema Crafts Centre** is a vocational handicrafts training project for disabled youths. Established in 2003 with three young deaf people and one volunteer, it now employs more than a hundred people – with an impressively positive impact not just on their lives, but on local attitudes towards disabled people as well. You're welcome to tour the **workshops** (an industrious hive), or have a dabble yourself: weaving on wooden looms, printing using batiks, recycling glass to make jewellery, preparing solar panels, poking around with pottery, or making paper from a murky vat of elephant dung. A **shop** sells the project's output, ranging from the said dung paper to cards and lamps made from maize or pineapple leaves, paintings, collages, screen prints, candles, jewellery, patchworks and wall-hangings. The first floor has a restaurant and coffee shop (p.424), a gallery and events space: cinema on Saturday nights with a buffet dinner, pizza and games nights on Fridays, and regular live music events, including *ngoma*. There's also a book exchange, and a physiotherapist for hour-long **massages** (Tsh35,000; weekday afternoons).

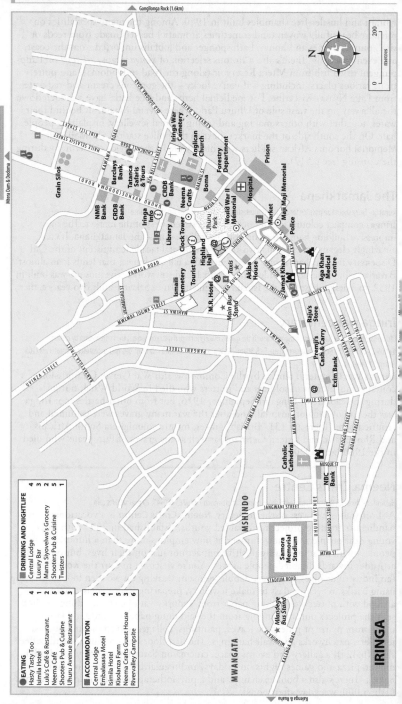

▲ Gangilonga Rock (1.6km)

Iringa War Cemetery

Anglican Church

Forestry Department

Prison

Grain Silos

Barclays Bank

Tatanca Safaris & Tours

CRDB Bank

Boma

Neema Crafts

World War II Memorial

Hospital

Maji Maji Memorial

NMB Bank

CRDB Bank

Iringa Info

Uhuru Park

Market

Police

Library

Clock Tower

Highland Hall

Taxis

Akiba House

Jamat Khana

Aga Khan Medical Centre

Tourist Board

Ismaili Cemetery

M.R. Hotel

Main Bus Stand

Raju's Store

Premji's Cash & Carry

Exim Bank

Catholic Cathedral

MOSQUE ST

NBC Bank

Samora Memorial Stadium

Mlandege Bus Stand

STREETS: KENYATTA DRIVE, OLD DODOMA ROAD, CHURCHILL ROAD, BIBI TITI STREET, HAILE SELASSIE STREET, KAWAWA ROAD, UHURU AVENUE (DODOMA ROAD), 6TH BELLA STREET, MKWAWA ST, MAKUNGANYA ST, KITWANA ST, PAWAGA ROAD, MWEMBE TOGWA STREET, UHEMBULISO ST, MAHIWA ST, SOKO MUU ST, SUKOMI ST, MUMIANI ST, MISITINI ST, NASSER ST, PANGANI STREET, MKWAWA ST, LIWALE STREET, MLANGENEMA STREET, MWANGATA, UVINZA STREET, BANKANYULASA STREET, MAREMA STREET, MKONJIA STREET, KILANI/NJILI ST, MAPAGORO STREET, RUAHA STREET, MWAWA STREET, UHURU AVENUE, MSHINDO STREET, JANGWANI STREET, MTWA ST, STADIUM ROAD, MLOWOKA ST, KALENGA ROAD

MSHINDO

MWANGATA

MWEMBE TOGWA STREET

◀ Mtera Dam & Dodoma

◀ Kalenga & Ruaha

Gangilonga Rock (1.6km) ▲

IRINGA

10

0 — 200 metres

N

Gangilonga Rock

2km northeast of the town centre • Walk east along Kawawa Rd, or northeast along Kenyatta Rd; after the junction of the two roads, the road heads east for 300m, then turns north; after 500m, take the second right; the road turns southeast, then north – after 900m you'll see a small trail on your left, which takes you the remaining 100m to the rock

A large, orange-streaked (and graffiti-scrawled) boulder nestling in a vale between two peaks, **Gangilonga Rock** is where Chief Mkwawa, the Hehe tribe's celebrated leader, is said to have come to meditate. The rock's name means "talking stone", alluding to a legend that the rock gave advice when asked – perhaps inspired by the whistling sound which cracks in the boulder emit when the wind blows in the right direction. Either way, it's a nice walk (45min each way) which rewards you with stunning views over Iringa and great sunsets, though as there have been a few isolated muggings you should get a local to accompany you – ask at your hotel, or at *Hasty Tasty Too*.

Isimila

20km southwest of Iringa, 1km off the Tanzam highway • Daily 9am–4pm • Tsh20,000 entry (possibly negotiable), includes guided tour and entrance to a small museum • All southbound buses and daladalas from Iringa pass by; taxis charge Tsh35,000 return, including waiting time

ISIMILA is one of Africa's richest Stone Age sites. Since 1958, excavations here have uncovered thousands of stone tools dating from the **Acheulian period**, some sixty thousand years ago. The tools, most of which have been left in situ, cover much of the area – you're allowed to handle but not remove them. Pear-shaped hand-axes and cleavers are the most common; there are also cutters, hammers, picks and scrapers, and spherical balls whose use has never been fully explained. At the time the tools were made part of the site was occupied by a shallow lake, attracting both wildlife and hunters. The **fossil remains** of various animals hint at an environment not too different from today: elephants and antelopes, and various extinct mammals, including a giant hog, a short-necked giraffe and a weird species of hippo, which appears to have been even more boggle-eyed than its modern form.

None of the exhibits frankly would merit the extortionate entrance fee were it not for the scenery – the site is riddled with a series of miniature canyons carved out by the seasonal Isimila River. This has left a series of bizarre pink and orange **sandstone needles**, which are extremely photogenic, as are the resident rock hyraxes.

Mkwawa Memorial Museum

Kalenga, 13km from Iringa towards Ruaha National Park • Daily 9am–4pm • Tsh20,000 entry, possibly negotiable • Hourly daladalas from Mlandege bus stand on the west side of Iringa; taxis charge up to Tsh25,000 for the return journey

The historic village of Kalenga was the headquarters of Chief Mkwawa (see p.423) until German troops drove him out in 1894. The history of the struggle is recorded at the **Mkwawa Memorial Museum**, signposted 1.5km from the village. Tended by the warrior's descendants, the museum contains an assortment of clubs, spears and shields, as well as the shotgun with which Mkwawa committed suicide. The chief exhibit though is Chief Mkwawa's **skull**, which was returned to the Hehe in 1954 after a 56-year exile in Germany. Outside the museum are the tombs of Mkwawa's descendants, including his son and grandson, both of them also chiefs. Five hundred metres away is the tomb of **Erich Maas**, a German commando sent to infiltrate the fort and capture Mkwawa; he was subsequently discovered by Mkwawa, at whose hands he met his fate.

ARRIVAL AND DEPARTURE   IRINGA AND AROUND

By bus Iringa is 3km west of the Tanzam highway. The bus stand is in the centre of town, but buses en route to other destinations may only stop at Ipogoro on the highway, from where a taxi into town costs Tsh5000, or a daladala Tsh400. As ever, keep an eye on your bags, and use taxis at night unless you're in a group. The Tanzam highway is terrifyingly fast in places, so be careful which bus company you choose: Sumry has a relatively safe reputation (office at

10

CHIEF MKWAWA OF THE HEHE

In the latter half of the nineteenth century, the Tanzanian interior was in a state of chaotic flux. Incursions by **Arab slave traders** from the coast had disrupted the balance of power between clans and tribes, while the militaristic **Ngoni tribe's invasion** in the south had triggered mass migrations. This uncertain climate provided ideal soil on which opportunistic leaders such as Chief Mirambo of the Nyamwezi (see p.406) could plant their personal kingdoms.

Another who emerged triumphantly was a Hehe chief named Mtwa Mkwawa Mwamnyika ("Conqueror of Many Lands"), better known as **Chief Mkwawa**. Born near Kalenga in 1855, Mkwawa's ambitious character was well suited to his time. By 1889 he had become undisputed leader of the Hehe, whom he made the region's dominant tribe by uniting – though force or diplomacy – more than one hundred clans and smaller tribes. It was not just numbers, but regimented **military organization** that formed the basis of Hehe power, and which gave Mkwawa the ability to stem the hitherto inexorable southward advance of the Maasai. Mkwawa also began to threaten Arab control over the lucrative slave- and ivory-carrying caravan routes that passed through his territory, though declining Arab power meant that it was not against the sultans of Zanzibar that the showdown eventually came, but against the **German colonial war machine**.

At first, Mkwawa tried to secure treaties with the Germans, but when they refused (on fair terms, that is), the Hehe turned their arms against the newcomers. On August 17, 1891, a year after the Germans had placed a garrison in Iringa, Mkwawa's troops ambushed a German expeditionary force led by Lieutenant Emil von Zelewski in the **Lugalo Hills** east of Iringa, killing nearly five hundred soldiers and capturing a vast quantity of firearms and munitions. Only two German officers and fifteen men escaped.

Mkwawa was no fool, and anticipated German revenge by building a thirteen-kilometre, four-metre-high wall around his palace and military base at **Kalenga**. The Germans took time to reorganize, and it wasn't until October 1894 that they made their move, establishing themselves on a hill overlooking Kalenga, now the site of **Tosamaganga**, from where they began a two-day bombardment (the name *tosamaganga* means to "throw stones"). On October 30, the Germans under **Tom von Prince** stormed and took Kalenga with relative ease. The extent of Mkwawa's wealth can be gauged by the fact that it took four hundred porters to cart his ivory away. The Germans also found thirty thousand pounds of gunpowder, which they used to level the town. For Mkwawa, the loss of Kalenga was a double tragedy, since his mother – who had been told that her son had been captured – committed suicide.

In fact, Mkwawa had escaped into the forests west of Kalenga, from where he waged a four-year **guerrilla war** against the Germans. He was finally cornered in 1898, having been betrayed by informers attracted by a five-thousand-rupee reward. Rather than surrender, he shot his bodyguard, and then himself. The Germans, arriving on the scene shortly after, placed another shot into Mkwawa's head just to be sure, then severed it. The chief's headless body was buried at Mlambalasi, 12km south of the road to Ruaha National Park, while his **skull** was sent to Berlin and then to the Bremen Anthropological Museum. There it remained until 1954, when it was finally returned – it's now the star exhibit in Kalenga's museum.

Mkwawa's death marked the end of a decade of armed resistance to German rule across Tanganyika, but the ensuing peace was short-lived: the Maji Maji Uprising was only seven years away. For more on Chief Mkwawa and the Hehe, see ⓦ mkwawa.com.

---

the central bus stand; ☎ 0713 838483 or ☎ 0715 605060) and covers all routes from Iringa. B.M. Bus is fine for Morogoro.

Destinations Arusha (1–2 daily; 12hr); Dar (7 daily; 6–7hr); Dodoma (4–6 daily; 4–5hr); Kalenga (hourly daladalas; 20min); Mbeya (hourly; 5–6hr); Morogoro (hourly; 4–5hr); Moshi (1–2 daily; 11hr); Songea (hourly Coasters; 8hr); Tungamalenga (1 daily; 3hr).

INFORMATION AND TOURS

Tourist information Iringa's official tourist board office, in the NSSF Building, Pawaga Rd (Mon–Fri 8am–4pm, Sat 8.30am–1pm; ☎ 0737 177288, ✉ ttbiringa @tanzaniatourism.go.tz), keeps lists of hotels and tour companies, plus transport schedules for much of southern Tanzania, and has plenty of brochures. Much less formal are the staff of *Neema Café* (see p.424), and Shaffin Haji, the charming owner of *Hasty Tasty Too* restaurant (see p.423). Opposite the restaurant on Uhuru Ave, Iringa Info (Mon–Sat 9am–5pm, Sun 9am–2pm; ☎ 026 270 1988) is run by Warthog Adventures and *Rivervalley Campsite* (see below), and is very knowledgeable on birding and the western Udzungwa Mountains.

Tours Iringa's tour operators can arrange safaris to Ruaha National Park, and offer a range of other excursions, including trips to see rock art, and birding in the western Udzungwa Mountains. Tatanca Safaris & Tours, Uhuru Ave close to Ben Bella St (☎ 026 270 0610 or ☎ 0766 338334, ⓦ tatancasafaris.co.tz), and Warthog Adventures, at Iringa Info, Uhuru Ave (☎ 026 270 1988, ⓦ warthogadventures .com), are both recommended.

ACCOMMODATION

10

TOWN CENTRE

Central Lodge Uhuru Ave ☎ 0769 305315, ⓦ centrallodgeiringa.blogspot.com. A very pleasant, almost rural alternative to the gloomy central guesthouses, with seven large en-suite rooms, some twins, with big beds and box nets, plus functional plumbing (warm if not hot water) and TVs. The best thing though is the lovely garden-bar at the back. Safe parking. BB T̲s̲h̲3̲0̲,̲0̲0̲0̲

Embalasasa Motel Uhuru Ave ☎ 026 270 2948. With many of Iringa's "budget" places priced well over the odds, this dark and clunky old place looks like good value, with en-suite rooms on several floors, all with huge beds and box nets, and TV. There are also some some suites, and a basic bar and restaurant downstairs. BB T̲s̲h̲2̲0̲,̲0̲0̲0̲

Isimila Hotel Uhuru Ave ☎ 026 270 1194, ⊖ isimilahotel@yahoo.com. Friendly and calm with 48 en-suite rooms including suites, in several big and quite likeable 1970s blocks surrounded by cypress and bottlebrush trees. Some rooms have been renovated, but even the older ones are comfortable despite being a little forlorn. There's also a restaurant, bar and safe parking. Loud on Friday and Saturday nights (to 4am), thanks to a disco in the street behind. BB double $̲2̲5̲, twin $̲3̲0̲

★ **Neema Crafts Guest House** Neema Crafts, Hakimu St ☎ 0683 380492, ⓦ neemacrafts.com. Far and away Iringa's best-value accommodation, above Neema Crafts' colourfully painted workshops (see p.419), with ten en-suite rooms, mostly doubles and twins but also with a three-bed dorm and family rooms (with views). Wi-fi throughout, and there's an internet café, next door. All profits go straight back into the project. 10pm curfew. BB dorm per person T̲s̲h̲1̲8̲,̲0̲0̲0̲; room T̲s̲h̲4̲5̲,̲0̲0̲0̲

OUT OF TOWN

★ **Kisolanza Farm (The Old Farm House)** 54km southwest of Iringa along the highway (51km from Ipogoro) ☎ 0754 306144, ⓦ kisolanza.com. This delightful colonial-era farm is a stopover for overland tourist trucks, which have their own campsite. There's another campsite, and a wide selection of attractive rooms, including rustic chalets sharing bathrooms, en-suite cottages with log fires, and, top of the line, a couple of luxurious "farm cottages" with their own gardens. There's also a bar (in an authentic-looking tribal house) whose many treats include hot chocolate Amarula and cakes, and a restaurant ably showing off the farm's produce, which you can also buy from their shop. Camping per person $̲7̲, chalets and cheaper cottages BB $̲4̲0̲, luxury farm cottages HB $̲1̲4̲0̲

★ **Rivervalley Campsite** 14km east of town: 12.5km towards Morogoro then 1.5km south ☎ 0782 507017, ⓦ rivervalleycampsites.com. Set beside the Little Ruaha River, this lovely British-run hideaway has a campsite, six chalets in Hansel and Gretel style (two with kitchens), nine tented *bandas* sharing toilets, and eight "tents with beds". Good food available, often as evening buffets if there are enough people around, but the main attraction is a welter of activities, including several kilometres of walking trails, swimming in the river, village tours, mountain biking, horseriding, visits to Lugalo, Isimila and Kalenga, safaris to Ruaha National Park, and hikes in and around the western Udzungwa Mountains. A taxi from town costs Tsh30,000. Book the chalets well in advance. Camping per person $10, bandas and chalets (BB) $̲5̲0̲–̲6̲0̲

EATING

Annex Staff Inn Lodge Uhuru Ave. Busy local eatery with a nice streetside terrace behind a shady vine, making it a lovely hideaway for lunch as well as dinner. The liver stew is excellent. No smoking or alcohol. Daily 7am–10pm.

★ **Hasty Tasty Too** Uhuru Ave ☎ 026 270 2061. Long established, geared up for tourists, and happy to cater for peculiar tastes or particular diets. The cooked breakfasts (from Tsh4500) are uncommonly good, and full meals (around Tsh8000, or Tsh6000 for a light lunch) are tasty, too: try the *quesadillas* (chapati rolls filled with beans, cheese, onion and avocado, fried and sliced). The freshly brewed Arabica is good (especially with cardamom). Also sells juices, chocolates, jam and cakes. Mon–Sat 7.30am–8pm, Sun 10am–2pm.

Isimila Hotel Uhuru Ave. The second-floor restaurant here is usually empty and has a limited choice (Tanzanian staples, meaning rice or chips with everything), but the food – especially stews – can be excellent (around Tsh6000). Don't come if you're in a rush. Daily midday–8pm.

★ **Lulu's Café & Restaurant** Churchill Rd. Like *Hasty Tasty Too*, a favourite with travellers and expats, and affordable – try the Greek salad with salty, tangy home-made feta (Tsh3000), or meat balls with mashed potato (Tsh5000). As well as other Greek dishes, it also serves some Chinese, plus snacks, real juices and coffee, ice cream

10

and toasts. Good cheap breakfasts too. No alcohol. Mon–Sat 9am–3pm & 6.30–9pm.

★**Neema Café** Neema Crafts, Hakimu St ☎0683 380492, ⊚neemacrafts.com. Above the workshops, this is a reasonably priced gallery and coffee shop rolled into one, whose profits are ploughed back into the project. The foodie limelight shines brightest on its snacks, including bacon and avocado paninis, plus fabulous carrot cake; the chocolate cake isn't bad either, especially when served hot with home-made ice cream. And where else can you slurp a baobab shake? Top marks also for the coffee: a special Arabica roast from Utengule (Mbeya). There's also wi-fi. On

Friday evenings, there's an Indian buffet (Tsh10,000). No alcohol. Mon–Sat 9am–6.30pm plus Fri to 10pm.

Shooters Pub & Cuisine Miomboni St. Meaty dishes with a touch of Indian and Chinese served up in a bright dining room beside the bar. Main courses around Tsh8000. Be prepared to wait. Tues–Thurs 2–11pm, Fri–Sun noon–midnight.

Uhuru Avenue Restaurant Ben Bella St. Popular with locals, this restaurant serves tasty full meals (*ugali* or rice with beans and meat, Tsh3000), plus snacks, and some unusual juices, including avocado. Has a few tables outside, too. Mon–Sat midday–8pm.

DRINKING AND NIGHTLIFE

The main venue for visiting bands from Dar is Highland Hall on Uhuru Avenue, opposite the post office. There are loads of bars and "groceries" throughout town, especially along Mahiwa Street north of the bus stand, but few are particularly salubrious, or enticing. Below are a selection of the more attractive, even genteel, options.

Central Lodge Uhuru Ave. A calm, dignified bar set in an enchanting Alice in Wonderland-style garden behind Iringa Info, where the shady magnolia trees, yellow-bark fever trees and bougainvillea bushes make for a blissful setting. Line your stomach with the usual bar food (*mishkaki, chipsi mayai, nyama choma*), or proper meals. Daily 11am–10pm.

Luxury Bar Mwembe Togwa St. The most appetizing of the many local bars in this area, friendly, with colourful murals, European football on the TVs (attracting crowds of several hundred), and usually live bands on Fri. There is a handful of tables on a veranda outside, and excellent grilled chicken in the evenings. Daily 11am–late.

Mama Siyovelwa's Grocery Kawawa Rd/Old Dodoma Rd. A nice chilled-out garden bar, that has seating beneath

thatched shelters and big trees. Food is available, including their renowned pork roasts. Daily midday–10pm or later.

Shooters Pub & Cuisine Miomboni St. Iringa's only upmarket bar is also the nocturnal hub for expats, with a TV (mostly international football), a pool table, and a restaurant. You can also sit out on a very narrow balcony overlooking the street. Tues–Thurs 2–11pm, Fri–Sun noon–midnight.

Twisters Haile Selassie St. Once a dark and sleepy bar, this has blossomed into a major nightspot on Fri and Sat night (Tsh5000 entry), when there are either live bands (including rap) or, more usually, discos. There's also a pool table. Keep an eye on your stuff, and use a taxi. Daily noon–midnight: Fri & Sat discos 9pm–4am.

BIRDING IN THE WESTERN UDZUNGWA MOUNTAINS

A hundred kilometres east of Iringa rise the first peaks of the **Udzungwa Mountains**. The thick, primate-rich forest on the eastern side of the mountains is accessed from Mang'ula (see p.213), though the western flanks have less vegetation so are best for **birds** – more than three hundred bird species have been recorded here so far, including the Udzungwa partridge, rufous-winged and Moreau's sunbirds, dappled mountain robins, spot-throats, Nduk eagle owls and Iringa akalats, all of them endemic and braggably rare. The best months for birding are September to early December. Apart from birds, there are several rivers along whose banks you may see bush pigs, duikers and monkeys.

ORGANIZED TOURS

Getting around the western side of the mountains independently is difficult: much of the area is part of Udzungwa Mountains National Park, the **entry fees** for which can only be paid at Mang'ula, 250km from Iringa, so most visitors stray no further than the forest and nature reserves adjoining the park. The entry fees for these (supposedly $10 per person per day, though you may be charged $30 per person) are paid at the Forestry Department in Iringa, on the corner of Mkoa St and Old Dodoma Rd (Mon–Fri 8am–5pm; ☎026 270 2246). There's next to no public transport into the mountains, nor much accommodation, so your best option is to go with one of Iringa's **tour operators**. The most knowledgeable, for western Udzungwa, is Warthog Adventures (see p.423), which is affiliated with *Rivervalley Campsite*, being the closest decent accommodation, and also maintains several informal campsites in the mountains themselves.

DIRECTORY

Banks Most banks, all with ATMs, are on Uhuru Ave; the exception is Exim, at the west end of Jamat St. You can change cash at Iringa Bureau de Change, 2nd floor, Akiba House, Soko Kuu St (Mon–Fri 8am–6pm, Sat 9am–3pm).

Internet access *Neema Café*, Neema Crafts Centre, Hakimu St (daily 10am–6.30pm); *M.R. Hotel*, Mwembe Togwa St (daily 8.30am–10pm); and the post office, Uhuru Ave (Mon–Fri 8am–8.30pm, Sat 9am–6pm, Sun 11am–6pm) all have internet access.

Supermarkets Fresh milk and yoghurt is sold at the petrol station at the junction of Uhuru Ave and Miomboni Street. The main minimarkets, Premji's and Raju's, are on Jamat St (both Mon–Sat 9am–5.30pm, Sun 10am–2pm).

10

The Mufindi Highlands

South of Iringa, the **Mufindi Highlands** are exceptionally scenic, with bright green tea estates, scattered lakes and forests, and dramatic views from peaks and ridges over the Kilombero Valley to the east. The forests are especially rich in **birdlife**, with rare species including blue swallows, the Uhehe fiscal, short-tailed pipit, mountain marsh whydah, and Iringa akalat.

ARRIVAL AND DEPARTURE   THE MUFINDI HIGHLANDS

By car The only real way to see this area is by car. Access is via one of two settlements on the Tanzam highway: Mafinga itself (also called "John's Corner"), 90km southwest of Iringa, and Nyororo ("James' Corner"), 40km further on.

ACCOMMODATION

Mufindi Highland Lodge 40km southeast of Mafinga ☎ 0713 237422 or ☎ 0754 237422, ⬡ mufindi highlandlodge.com. Other than local guesthouses, this is the only accommodation option. Located on an eight-square-kilometre estate, the main building is a rustic two-storey granite-and-timber affair containing bar, dining room, TV lounge, snooker room and large veranda with great views of the surrounding forests. The bedrooms are in twelve en-suite log cabins; room rates include guided forest walks, birding, mountain biking, horseriding, a cultural tour to local villages and fishing for rainbow trout – so are excellent value for money. Two nights at least are recommended. The easiest way to get here is for the lodge to pick you up at Mafinga ($50 per person); if you're driving, turn off the highway at Mafinga and head south into the hills until Sawala, then turn left along the road to Lupeme Tea Estate and follow the signs for 15km. FB $̶3̶0̶0̶

Ruaha National Park

At over 20,000 square kilometres, **RUAHA NATIONAL PARK** is Tanzania's largest protected area after Selous, but one of the least visited, with barely a hundred tourists on any one day. The park is home to more than 1650 plant species, plus a wealth of wildlife, including most of the species you're likely to see in the northern parks except for black rhinos. The natural **biodiversity** here stems from the Great Ruaha River and the park's location, straddling the Rift Valley and the biological transition between eastern and southern African biomes. The humble **tsetse fly** is also to thank, since its presence has kept herders out of the region – the sleeping sickness that it spreads (see p.58) affects livestock and people, but not wildlife.

The **dry season** (June to October, sometimes extending to mid-November), particularly towards the end, is best for viewing big animals, which concentrate around receding waterholes in the sand rivers. The **rains** start for real in December, after which resurgent vegetation makes the big game harder to see, but birding at that time is a delight. The rains are heaviest in January and continue until mid-May, but by the end of March the park is waterlogged, including the airstrips, so most hotels close in April and May.

10

The wildlife

Ruaha is noted for its **antelopes**, being one of only a few areas where you can see both greater and lesser kudu, and the elusive sable and roan antelopes. Other denizens include zebra, the shy bushbuck, Grant's gazelle, eland, giraffe, impala, reedbuck, Defassa waterbuck, Liechtenstein's hartebeest, klipspringer, Kirk's dikdik, mongooses (slender, banded and dwarf) and, near water, large herds of buffalo. You'll also find **predators** out in force, including lions, leopards, cheetahs, jackals, crocodiles and several packs of highly endangered African hunting dogs. The park is also the southernmost range of the striped hyena. **Nocturnal animals**, which may be glimpsed in the early morning or late evening, include the aardwolf, ratel, lesser galago (bushbaby), porcupine and bats.

Ruaha's **birdlife** is equally rich and colourful, with 529 species recorded to date, many of them migrants (especially mid-Nov to March). Two species to look out for are the rare sooty falcon, which breeds in the Sahara and the Middle East, and Eleonora's falcon, which breeds further north in the Mediterranean. Other raptors include the African hawk, Pel's fishing owl and eagles: bateleur, martial, long-crested and snake.

The park was once home to numerous **black rhino**, which were, tragically, poached into oblivion during the 1980s. Ruaha's **elephants** almost suffered the same fate in the 1980s – their population recovered well, but a resurgence in poaching since 2009 has slashed their numbers by a third in little over five years. An aerial census in 2013 counted just over twenty thousand elephants, which is still enough to guarantee sightings of them, especially in the dry season, but the poachers shows no sign of relenting.

The Great Ruaha River and Msembe area

Most safari-goers limit themselves to the park's low-lying southeastern section around the **Great Ruaha River** near the park entrance and lodges. This area boasts a network of several hundred kilometres of drivable trails, with road junctions marked by **numbered**

signposts, corresponding to the park's guidebooks – provided the signs haven't been trashed by elephants looking for back scrubbers. The area is representative of most of Ruaha's habitats, including *miombo* woodland plateau and isolated hills in the west; undulating plains; acacia and baobab bushland; palm-fringed swamps; grassland; evergreen forest around the main rivers; seasonal "sand rivers", whose water pools draw wildlife in the dry season; and, of course, the Great Ruaha River itself.

The **tracks** along the river downstream from Msembe are good for a broad range of wildlife, including elephants, lions, leopards and most of the park's ungulates. Hippos and crocodiles also put in an appearance, but you'll need luck to see sable antelopes, cheetahs or hunting dogs. There's a **picnic site** in a grove of acacia trees by junction R24, where you can leave your car. Once done, head back to Msembe along the south bank of the **Mwagusi Sand River**: elephants and plains game are frequent visitors to its dry-season waterholes, as are predators – easily camouflaged in the flanking vegetation.

Msembe area itself has a web of tracks: the highlights include a **hippo pool** close to junction R8, which also has crocodiles, and Kimiramatonge Hill to the north, where you might see klipspringers. Msembe's dominant tree species here is the tall *Acacia albida*, ecologically important for its role in preventing soil erosion. Unfortunately, most of the tree cover disappeared in the wake of the catastrophic poaching in the 1980s: the presence of the park headquarters led elephants to associate Msembe with safety, but their resulting high numbers ending up trashing the acacias. Things haven't been helped since by the drying of the Great Ruaha River, which has increased pressure on areas surrounding the remaining waterholes.

Ruaha Escarpment and beyond

In dry weather, you can extend your exploration westwards. From junction W8, a trail hugs the base of the **Ruaha Escarpment**. After some 10km you reach Mwayembe Spring, a popular salt lick spot for elephant and buffalo. In the surrounding swamp, you might spot the rare Bohor reedbuck. The road continues along the escarpment base to the **Mdonya Sand River**, just below Mdonya Gorge. Returning to Msembe along the river's south bank, keep an eye out for eland, black-backed jackals, and – in the evergreen riverine forest – birds. Another good long drive follows the north bank of the Great Ruaha River from Msembe to its confluence with the (usually dry) **Jongomero River**, whose flanking trees are likely haunts for **leopards**. With more time, but in dry weather only, you can tackle the 95km drive northwest to the **Mzombe River**. Up the escarpment, the road passes through undulating woodland where you should see small groups of elephants, and perhaps also sable antelope or Liechtenstein's hartebeest. There are some **walking trails** at Mpululu by the Mzombe River, on the border with Rungwa Game Reserve. The river is dry from July to September, when hippos congregate in pools. Walkers need to be accompanied by a park ranger or guide.

THE GREAT RUAHA RIVER – NOT SO GREAT?

Tour brochures paint Ruaha in idyllic shades of unspoilt wilderness, abounding in wildlife, and indeed it is. But behind the gloss, trouble stirs. Since 1993, the **Great Ruaha River**, the park's lifeblood, has, with few exceptions (2014 was one of them, following exceptionally good rains), dried up entirely during the dry season, each time for longer periods. The cause is unsustainable water use in its catchment area northeast of Mbeya, but the culprits are many and varied: overgrazing of the swampy Usangu flats by an estimated 1.5 million cattle belonging to migrant Sukuma cattle herders (who were evicted in 2008); vast commercial rice paddies with little official oversight; a million or so subsistence farmers; and forest clearance. An NGO-led attempt to reduce water wastage in Usangu came to nothing, as did the government's forcible eviction of the herders, and of many villagers. Although the national park was enlarged to include a large part of Usangu, including the sponge-like **Ihefu wetland**, the river isn't getting any wetter.

10

10

ESSENTIALS

RUAHA NATIONAL PARK

Entrance fees The park headquarters are at Msembe, 9km beyond the Ruaha River bridge, 17.5km beyond the park gate (daily 7.30am–5.30pm; ☏0689 062338 or ☏0767 536129, ⊚ tanzaniaparks.com/ruaha.html). Entrance fees for 24hr are $30 per person, plus Tsh20,000 per vehicle, and are paid at the park gate, 18km from Tungamalenga; Visa or MasterCard accepted, but not cash.
Information The rangers at the park gate can answer most questions, while TANAPA's guidebooks can be bought at the gate, the lodges, or in bookshops in Arusha, Dar and Stone Town. The older monochrome booklet describes game drives in scientific detail; the full-colour edition is a more attractive souvenir, and is essential for self-driving, as it corresponds to the junction numbers you'll see when driving around.

ARRIVAL AND DEPARTURE

By public transport Buses from Iringa only go as far as Tungamalenga, 18km short of the gate. Buses to Tungamalenga leave Iringa's Mlandege bus stand between midday and 2pm, and take three hours (Tsh6000) to cover the 90km.
By organized safari The camps and hotels between Tungamalenga and the park gate (see below) all have 4WD vehicles and can arrange safaris into the park, currently costing $200–250 for a full day including driver and fuel, to which add park fees and lunch. Alternatively, a safari arranged through a tour company in Iringa (see p.423) costs upwards of $180 per person per day all-inclusive. Less appealing, unless you're also planning to visit Mikumi or Selous, is a safari from Dar es Salaam (see p.103 for operators), as you'll be spending most of your first and last day along the Tanzam highway.

By plane Most upmarket visitors come on all-inclusive flying safaris, which can also be arranged through the park's camps and lodges, or via Coastal Aviation or Safari Airlink, associated with *Mdonya Old River Camp* and *Ruaha River Lodge*. Flying to Ruaha is expensive: $290 from Selous or $330 from Dar, up to $675 to Mahale. The airlines are Auric Air (AA: ☏0783 233334, ⊚ auricair.com), Coastal Aviation (CA: ☏0752 627825, ⊚ coastal.co.tz) and Safari Airlink (SA: ☏0777 723274, ⊚ flysal.com). In the following, airlines with quicker flights are listed first.
Destinations Arusha (CA SA: 2 daily; 1hr 20min–2hr 30min); Dar (CA, SA, AA: 3–4 daily; 1hr 30min–2hr 30min); Katavi (SA: Mon & Thurs; 2hr 10min); Mafia (CA: daily; 3hr 45min); Mahale (SA: Mon & Thurs; 3hr); Mikumi (SA: daily; 1hr); Pemba (CA: daily; 3hr 20min); Selous (CA, SA: 2 daily; 1hr 20min–2hr); Zanzibar (CA: 3 daily; 1hr 50min–3hr).

ACCOMMODATION

The luxury tented camps and lodges inside the park are often neo-colonial in feel and searingly expensive (even more so if you plump for the "fly camping" offered by *Jongomero Camp* and *Ruaha River Lodge*, which gets you champagne breakfasts and personal butlers as well as the delights of bucket showers and dome tents), but their "game packages" do include game drives and sometimes bush walks. If you're coming by road, you should be able to get cheaper "drive in" rates – full board without game drives, as you won't need their vehicles. None of the lodges or camps are fenced, so there's always a chance of seeing (or at least hearing) wildlife pass through. The park authority (TANAPA) maintains more sanely priced accommodation in the form of *bandas* and a campsite near the park headquarters, and there's also some affordable accommodation outside the park, some of it excellent. All accommodation is best reserved in advance. The prices quoted below exclude park fees.

IN THE PARK

Jongomero Camp 63km southwest of Msembe ☏022 212 8485 (in Dar), ⊚ selous.com. Gloriously isolated and expensive, this slick, chic camp occupies a grove of acacias on the north bank of the usually dry Jongomero River. The eight spacious tents are on raised platforms beneath thatched roofs, each with a veranda for wildlife viewing. There's also a swimming pool with uninterrupted river views. No children under 8. Closed mid-March to end-May. Game package <u>$1600</u>, fly camping (minimum two nights) <u>$2220</u>
Mdonya Old River Camp 40km west of Msembe

BUSH WALKS AT RUAHA

A great way of getting to experience Ruaha between June and November is on a **bush walk**, accompanied by an armed ranger. Clients at the park's lodges have priority, but it may also be possible to arrange a walk through lodges and camps outside the park – you'll need a vehicle to pick up the ranger and reach the walking zone, though. The nominal cost is $20 per ranger, plus park entry fees.

☎ 022 260 1747 (in Dar), ⓦ mdonya.com. Set amid large sycamore figs and acacias beside Mdonya Sand River, this decidedly plain camp offers isolation, intimacy and wildlife walking through, rather than creature comforts. The twelve green tents have private verandas and alfresco showers, and a resident genet entertains guests at night. Children under 6 discouraged. Closed April & May. FB $\underline{\$720}$, game package $\underline{\$830}$

★**Msembe bandas and cottages** Near the park headquarters, Msembe; book through the park headquarters (see p.423). There are three types of accommodation here: a modern guesthouse, which is mainly intended for big groups; cottages (also called new *bandas*), with en-suite rooms that can sleep up to five; and, cheapest but with the best location right by the river, plain *bandas* (or old *bandas*), whose rooms have two small beds each, and share bathrooms (hot showers, western toilets) some forty metres away. There's a kitchen and dining area (with a functional fridge): basic provisions may be available at the park headquarters, but it's best to bring what you'll need with you; firewood can be provided. Prices are per person. *Bandas* $\underline{\$20}$, guesthouse $\underline{\$30}$, cottages $\underline{\$50}$

Msembe public campsite Near the park headquarters, Msembe; pay at the park gate. Apart from "special" campsites, which tend to be block-booked by upmarket safari companies, camping inside the park is limited to a shadeless site along the Great Ruaha. There are pit latrines but no other facilities, though you can use the showers at the nearby *bandas*. Per person $\underline{\$30}$

Mwagusi Safari Camp 9km north of Msembe, book through UK office on ☎ 0182 261 5721, ⓦ mwagusicamp.com. Established in 1987, this sits in prime game-viewing territory on the banks of the Mwagusi Sand River, especially popular with buffalo. The thirteen comfortable *bandas*, almost entirely built of natural materials, are actually large tents pitched beneath thatched roofs, with bathrooms at the back, and a private veranda with a hammock overlooking the river. The excellent meals are taken in a stylish building decorated with branches and skulls, or on the sandy river bed, and the wildlife guides are superb (there's a school for them here, too). Children under 6 discouraged. Game package $\underline{\$1150}$

★**Ruaha River Lodge** 18km southwest of Msembe ☎ 0713 237422, ⓦ ruahariverlodge.com. Built on and around a granite outcrop overlooking rapids where hippos and crocodiles gather, this is another fine place for wildlife (seen from armchairs on your private veranda, no less). The rooms are in twenty large riverside stone-and-thatch cottages clumped into two areas, and facilities include bars and a split-level restaurant with glorious views, lounges, evening campfires and a library. FB $\underline{\$480}$, game package $\underline{\$700}$, fly camping (minimum two nights) $\underline{\$1050}$

OUTSIDE THE PARK

★**Chogela Camp Site** 1km west of Tungamalenga ☎ 0782 032025, ⓦ facebook.com/chogelasafaricamp. This is a gem no matter your budget: in a shady acacia grove along the Tungamalenga River bristling with birdsong, the owner (Chogela) and the staff are exceptionally welcoming, helpful and enthusiastic. Primarily a campsite, they also provide beds in simple dome tents under thatched shelters; the shared bathrooms are clean and western-style, and hot water can be provided. Self-caterers have a kitchen and a small store, but invariably delicious meals can be provided (including cardamom-laced pancakes), so you might as well go full-board. With close ties to Tungamalenga village and local Maasai, cultural tourism is high on the list of attractions ($10–20 per person for guided village walks, visits to Maasai *bomas*, or to a waterfall; more info on ⓦ ruahaculturaltours.com) – the tours are open to non-residents too – and their wildlife safaris aren't bad either, as the guides are very knowledgeable (even for birding) – a vehicle costs $250 for a day, to which add park fees. Night game drives outside the park cost $25 per person. Camping per person $\underline{\$10}$, their tents (double) BB $\underline{\$60}$, FB $\underline{\$100}$

★**Ruaha Hilltop Lodge** 4km from Tungamalenga (1.5km west of the road) ☎ 026 270 1806 or ☎ 0784 726709, ⓦ ruahahilltoplodge.com. On a scrubby hill with unforgettable views over the bush, this is an exceptionally welcoming, affordable and romantic Tanzanian-run place, with fifteen beautifully decorated en-suite cottages complete with solar-heated water, electricity and verandas with 180° views – a brick-and-thatch building lower down contains the bar and a consistently excellent restaurant. They have a great reputation for their driver-guides, with full-day game drives inside the park costing $200 for the vehicle, plus park fees. A three- to four-hour bush walk costs $20 per person, plus $40 per group for the ranger. FB $\underline{\$160}$

Tandala Tented Camp 13km from Tungamalenga (8km from the park gate) ☎ 0755 680220 or ☎ 0757 183420, ⓦ tandalacamp.com. It may be outside the park, but the wildlife here is unparalleled – the camp is located on both sides of the Mdekwa Sand River, whose waterholes attract game, and its swimming pool is also popular with elephants tired of the muddy river water. There are eleven comfortable en-suite tents on raised wooden platforms, each with a large veranda, plus a thatched bar and restaurant featuring Mediterranean cuisine, and candlelit dinners around a campfire. Activities include safaris (they're licensed), bush walks, visits to a Maasai village and hot-water springs, and nocturnal game drives. Part of the profits benefit Mbomipa village, which can also be visited. FB $\underline{\$470}$, including activities $\underline{\$630}$

10

The southern highlands

Geologically, the **southern highlands** are a fascinating area, having been formed by the violent plate-tectonic activity that also created the Rift Valley and its lakes, including Nyasa just to the south. The volcanic soil and heavy rainfall lends itself perfectly to agriculture, including coffee, bananas, rice and – uniquely for Tanzania – cocoa. Despite the high human population density, a few isolated patches of **primary forest** have survived, providing one of the highlights for visitors, along with impressive waterfalls, crater lakes and hot springs. Needless to say, the highlands are ideal for **hiking** – at its most spectacular in **Kitulo National Park**, over two and a half kilometres above sea level, and famed for orchids as well as a recently discovered species of monkey. Two good bases for exploring the region are Southern Tanzania's main town, **Mbeya**, and agricultural **Tukuyu**, in the lee of the currently sleepy Mount Rungwe volcano: both towns have **cultural tourism** programmes which can arrange everything for you.

Mbeya and around

The regional capital of **MBEYA**, 1700m above sea level, is tucked into a fold between the Mbeya Range and Panda Hills, 140km north of Lake Nyasa. Founded in 1927 as a supply town during a gold rush at Lupa, in the north, Mbeya's importance was assured by its position on the Great North Road (now the Tanzam highway), which runs for

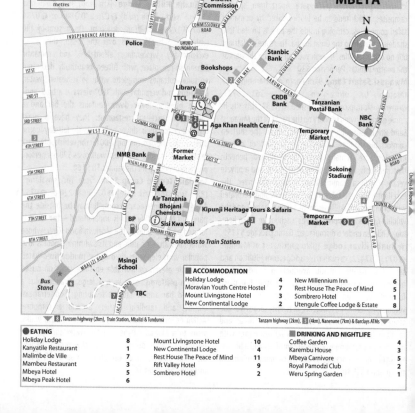

MBEYA

■ ACCOMMODATION			
Holiday Lodge	4	New Millennium Inn	6
Moravian Youth Centre Hostel	7	Rest House The Peace of Mind	5
Mount Livingstone Hotel	3	Sombrero Hotel	1
New Continental Lodge	2	Utengule Coffee Lodge & Estate	8

● EATING				■ DRINKING AND NIGHTLIFE	
Holiday Lodge	8	Mount Livingstone Hotel	10	Coffee Garden	4
Kanyatile Restaurant	1	New Continental Lodge	4	Karembu House	3
Malimbe de Ville	7	Rest House The Peace of Mind	11	Mbeya Carnivore	5
Mambeu Restaurant	3	Rift Valley Hotel	9	Royal Pamodzi Club	2
Mbeya Hotel	5	Sombrero Hotel	2	Weru Spring Garden	1
Mbeya Peak Hotel	6				

over five thousand kilometres from Nairobi to Cape Town and the construction of the TAZARA railway into Zambia in the 1960s. There's not much to see in the town itself, but it has a refreshing climate, and its superb **cultural tourism programme** Sisi kwa Sisi (see p.433) offers a wide range of activities in the vicinity, including hikes up **Loleza and Mbeya peaks**, which dominate Mbeya's northern skyline, and excursions to **crater lakes**, waterfalls, and even a giant **meteorite**.

Central market

West and north sides of Sokoine Stadium • Daily 7am–6pm, but not all stalls open on Sun

10

Most of Mbeya's four hundred thousand inhabitants live in crowded suburbs south of town, leaving the old colonial centre eerily quiet, especially after the original **central market** burned down in 2011. Pending its reconstruction (not guaranteed), the stall holders currently occupy a series of new buildings beside the stadium. It's a good place to admire and buy the beautiful cream-and-ochre Kisi pots from Ikombe (near Matema) on Lake Nyasa.

Loleza peak

5km northwest of Mbeya • Sisi kwa Sisi (see p.433) charges $20 per person for a guided hike

The closest of the Mbeya Range's two highest points is the 2656-metre **Loleza Peak** (also called Kaluwe), which is covered in beautiful flowers during the rains (at its best from Nov/Dec–May). Provided you're reasonably fit, you should be able to tackle the steep three- to four-hour climb up (plus two hours back down), which starts from Hospital Hill, off Independence Avenue. Much of the walk follows a ridge flanked on either side by forest lower down, though the summit itself is topped by an array of transmitters.

Mbeya Peak

10km northwest of Mbeya, 7.5km northeast of Utengule • Sisi kwa Sisi (see p.433) charges $40 per person for a guided hike, plus $20 per group for a taxi to and from Iziwa at the start of the climb

The highest and wildest point in the immediately vicinity of Mbeya (and with no transmitters) is the 2834-metre **Mbeya Peak**, 6km west of Loleza Peak. The easiest access to the peak is from **Iziwa** village, 8km northwest of Mbeya on a drivable dirt road. From Iziwa, it's a 6km walk to the summit – the first 2km head up through farmland and forest to a ridge, which turns west and gradually rises up to the peak.

Alternatively, a multiplicity of trails head off from **Utengule** in southwest, which can be as short as 10km (passing through eucalyptus plantations en route), or as long as 14km, via much wilder terrain further north, which includes some scree. The route can be combined with the one from Iziwa, and it's also possible, and not difficult but seldom done, to tackle the 6km **traverse** along the ridge between Loleza and Mbeya peaks.

Mbozi Meteorite

70km west of Mbeya, 13km south off the Tunduma Rd • Tsh5000 • Sisi kwa Sisi in Mbeya (see p.433) charges $30 per person for a guide, plus transport and admission • Catch a Coaster for Tunduma but get off at the signposted junction (on your left) just after Malenje, 4km before Mbozi town; bicycles can be rented at the junction (Tsh10,000) to cover the remaining 13km due south off the highway

Weighing in at a cool sixteen tons, **Mbozi Meteorite** is the seventh largest known in the world. The meteorite is a fragment of interplanetary matter that was large enough to avoid being completely burned up when entering earth's atmosphere, and small enough not to explode; of the estimated five hundred meteorites that fall to earth each year, only thirty percent strike land, and less than ten are reported and recorded. Mbozi has been known for centuries by locals, who call it **Kimwondo**, but the absence of legends recounting its sudden and undoubtedly fiery arrival suggest that it fell to earth long before the present inhabitants arrived, a thousand years ago. The meteorite was officially discovered in 1930. At the time only the top was visible. It was excavated, leaving a pillar of soil underneath, which was reinforced with concrete to serve as a plinth. The irregular notches on the pointed end were caused by souvenir hunters hacking out chunks – no easy task given the strength of the nickel-iron from which it's made. Most meteorites consist of silicates or stony-irons, so Mbozi is uncommon in that it's composed mainly of iron (90.45 percent) and nickel (8.69 percent), with negligible amounts of copper, sulphur and phosphorus.

Ngozi Crater Lake

Some 40km southeast of Mbeya • Tsh5000, plus Tsh3000 per vehicle • Guided tours are offered by Sisi kwa Sisi in Mbeya (see p.433) for $25 per person, and Rungwe Tea & Tours in Tukuyu (see p.440) for Tsh13,500 plus transport • Catch a bus from Mbeya or Tukuyu to Mchangani (also called "Mbeya Moja"), at the signposted junction of a rough road heading 4km west to the base of Ngozi mountain; from here, it's an hour's strenuous walk up the forested crater rim

10

Up in the Poroto Mountains, the two-kilometre-wide **Ngozi Crater Lake** (marked as Poroto Crater Lake on some maps) is the most popular destination for day-trippers from both Mbeya and Tukuyu. In the local Kisafwa language, Ngozi (or Ngosi) means "very big", referring to the lake rather than the 2620-metre Mount Ngozi in whose crater it resides. The lakeshore is tricky to reach (it's 200m below the crater rim along a steep and potentially dangerous footpath); the walk there is really the attraction, winding uphill through tropical rainforest, stands of giant bamboo and wild banana plants. Among the forest denizens are black-and-white colobus monkeys, colourful birds and vocal tree frogs. Local legend speaks of the lake's magical powers, and of a **lake monster** that has the ability to change the colour of the water. Though quaint, the tale should urge caution, as such stories are usually grounded in real-life perils, probably, in this case, volcanically induced currents. Note also that locals don't swim in the lake.

ARRIVAL AND DEPARTURE

MBEYA AND AROUND

By plane Mbeya's airport is at Songwe, 22km along the road west to Tunduma. Budget airline Fastjet (ⓦ fastjet .com) flies here twice a day from Dar (1hr 20min), while Air Tanzania (Lupa Way; ☏ 0689 737206 or ☏ 0788 008568, ⓦ airtanzania.co.tz) flies once a day from Dar; prices average Tsh100,000–150,000, but Fastjet tickets can be as cheap as Tsh50,000, if bought in advance. A taxi from the airport into town costs Tsh30,000; alternatively, walk down to the highway and flag down any daladala heading east (Tsh400 to Mbalizi, and another Tsh400 from there into the town centre).
By bus Mbeya's main bus stand is 8km east of town at Nanenane, on the Tanzam highway, but most buses continue on to the central bus stand on Mbalizi Rd. Most long distance buses leave Mbeya's central stand at 5–7am, so buy your ticket in advance from the ticket offices here. Mbeya is notorious for fake ticket salesmen, so never buy tickets from touts. For journeys by Coaster minibus (shorter trips, and to Njombe along the road to Songea),

catch a daladala to Nanenane (Tsh400) and take the first Coaster for your destination. Driving standards for both buses and Coasters can be poor, especially along the Tanzam highway. Reputations vary, so enquire about the safest, which are usually also the slowest. At the time of writing, the best bus operators were Sumry (old but relatively slow buses to Dar and Sumbawanga), Super Feo (for Songea), Chaula Bus and Nganga (both for Iringa), and B.M. Bus (Morogoro). Companies with consistently perilous reputations include Happy Nation, Hood and Mchape (which operate Coasters).
Destinations Arusha (2 daily; 16–18hr); Dar (10 daily; 11–12hr); Iringa (hourly; 5–6hr); Kyela (hourly; 2hr 30min–3hr); Mikumi (hourly; 8–9hr); Morogoro (hourly; 11–12hr); Mpanda (1–2 daily; 11hr); Njombe (hourly; 4hr 30min); Songea (3–4 daily; 8–9hr); Sumbawanga (7–8 daily; 7hr); Tabora (1 daily; 18hr); Tukuyu (hourly; 1hr 30min); Tunduma (hourly; 1hr 30min–2hr).

SAFETY IN MBEYA

Mbeya's population includes a sizeable contingent of mostly unemployed migrants from Zambia, Malawi and Congo, who have given the town a somewhat unsavoury reputation. That said, the old colonial part – where you'll likely be staying – is a very laidback sort of place once you've extricated yourself from the hustlers at the **bus and train stations**. Although some of the characters are genuine, unwary travellers do get tripped up, so stay cool, and keep a close eye on your bags while you get your bearings. If you're being followed, jump in a cab rather than walk the short stretch into town: **taxis** can be found inside the bus stand – make sure you get one with white number plates.

By day, **walking around** is quite safe so long as your valuables are not visible, but you should take taxis at night, and in the morning until around 7.30am, after sunrise. This applies especially to Jacaranda Road, for the *Moravian Youth Centre Hostel*, and Jamatikhana Road.

By train Mbeya station is on the Tanzam highway, 5km southwest of the centre (tickets Mon–Fri 8am–12.30pm & 2–4pm, Sat 8am–12.30pm, Sun 8–11am; ☎0754 686810, ⓦtazarasite.com) – a daladala from here into town costs Tsh400, a taxi Tsh8000. Mbeya is the last major stop on the Tanzanian section of the TAZARA line (change at the border if continuing into Zambia), with two trains a week to Dar (Wed at 5.25pm for the Express, Sat at 9.38pm for the Ordinary), both with useful timings for Mang'ula (Udzungwa Mountains National Park) and Kisaki (Selous Game Reserve).
Destinations Dar (2 weekly; 22hr–25hr); Kisaki (2 weekly; 17hr 30min–20hr); Mang'ula (2 weekly; 15–17hr 30min).

TOURS AND ACTIVITIES

10

Sisi kwa Sisi Mbeya's ever-helpful cultural tourism programme, Sisi kwa Sisi, is on Mbalizi Rd, 300m uphill from the bus stand (Mon–Sat 8am–1pm & 2–4pm; ☎0754 463471 or ☎0784 333269, ⓦsisi-kwa-sisi.com or ⓦtanzaniaculturaltourism.go.tz/mbeya.htm). It offers a wide range of day-trips and hikes for $25–30 per person, including public transport, but excluding any entrance fees and meals. It also runs highly recommended, longer, off-the-beaten track tours such as a five- to ten-day hike across the southern highlands via Kitulo National Park down to Lake Nyasa. Some trips include a modest "village development fee", which pays for dispensaries and school books. In addition to organizing tours, the programme rents out bicycles and tents ($10 for either). Be wary of people on the street or at the bus stand telling you they're with Sisi kwa Sisi: some are scammers, others are thieves.
Kipunji Heritage Tours & Safaris For more formal trips, including Southern Circuit safaris, Kipunji, on Lupa Way (☎025 250 4036 or ☎0687 264 4374, ⓦkipunjiheritage -tours.org) is a recommended and licensed tour operator.

ACCOMMODATION

Mbeya's cheapest **guesthouses** are a sorry lot, often dirty or insecure. If you get a bad vibe, or if your door key looks like it'd open every second door in town, heed your instinct and look elsewhere. Sisi kwa Sisi can point you to reliable places. In spite of the altitude, **mosquitoes** abound, so check nets or window screens before signing in. Mbeya's **tap water** should be sterilized for drinking.

Holiday Lodge Jamatikhana Rd ☎025 250 2821. A calm and friendly place with over thirty big and bright en-suite rooms in a three-storey block, all with cable TV and adequately sized mosquito nets. There are also some very cheap singles (Tsh8000) sharing bathrooms behind the reception, which are slightly shabby but clean and have excellent beds. The included breakfast is pathetic, but meals in the restaurant (see p.434) are good, and cheap. Safe parking. BB Tsh17,000
Moravian Youth Centre Hostel Jacaranda Rd ☎025 250 3263. The main backpackers' choice, in a very calm location amid pleasant gardens. It has nineteen small but decent rooms, six of them en-suite "singles" (which can be shared by couples who can prove they're married), with the remaining rooms sharing clean bathrooms and squat toilets. Food occasionally available. BB Tsh12,000
Mount Livingstone Hotel Off Jamatikhana Rd ☎025 250 3332, ⓦtwiga.ch/tz/mtlivingstone.htm. A modern but somewhat gloomy fifty-room hotel aimed at tourists and conferences, but unmissable for lovers of kitsch – check out the fake satin bed covers adorned with pink appliqué hearts and flowers, plus matching flip-flops! All the rooms have parquet floors, cable TV and fridge, but you'll need to ask for mosquito nets. There's also a bar, internet access and safe parking. BB double Tsh65,000, twin Tsh75,000
New Continental Lodge North St ☎0759 825157. A reasonable, central option accessed through its bar and restaurant, but with only six rooms, either twin-bed or double. The cheapest share bathrooms (hot showers and Western toilets); the best have narrow balconies overlooking the street, and all have flat screen TVs. No access after midnight. BB Tsh30,000
New Millennium Inn Mbalizi Rd ☎0754 885265. A secure, comfortable and affordable option facing the bus stand, with thirty small but clean rooms (no twins) with or without bathrooms, all with cable TV. Safe parking. Shared bathrooms Tsh15,000, en suite Tsh20,000
★ **Rest House The Peace of Mind** Jamatikhana Rd ☎025 250 0498 or ☎0754 277410, ⓔpeaceofm13 @gmail.com. A wonderfully imaginative and hugely enjoyable set-up with 21 rooms (only one of them twin-bedded) in a three-storey building painted in dazzling lime green and shocking pink. Everything inside is more tasteful, especially the third-floor "culture" floor, whose rooms are stuffed with traditional art and superior trinkets. All rooms have good views, feature lots of marble and wood, and are very well equipped, with cable TV, a/c and wi-fi. The cheapest rooms share bathrooms; the most expensive – a bargain at Tsh60,000 – are beautiful suites. There's also a good restaurant and classy bar downstairs, and even a swimming pool. Safe parking. BB Tsh40,000
Sombrero Hotel Post St ☎025 250 2979 or ☎025 250 0663, ⓔhotelsombrero@yahoo.com. Efficient, friendly and accommodating, and with twenty spotless rooms on several floors, including two suites, all with good bathrooms (hot water), wall-to-wall carpet and most but not all with cable TV. The upper front rooms have great views of Loleza Peak. BB double Tsh30,000, twin Tsh40,000

10

★**Utengule Coffee Lodge & Estate** 20km northwest of Mbeya: the turning is at Mbalizi, 11km along the Tunduma road ☏0753 020901 or ☏0786 481902, ⓦriftvalley-zanzibar.com. Set in lovely gardens to the west of Mbeya Peak, this extremely pleasant hotel is part of a working coffee estate that produces some of Tanzania's most delicate Arabica. It has sixteen large and beautifully decorated rooms and bungalows, all spacious and comfortable. The suites cost around $30 more than standard rooms and are a delight, especially the two-floor "Executive King-size", whose top floor has a wooden floor and ceiling. The farmhouse-style cooking is superb, there's a swimming pool, and an interesting tour of the coffee production process. It's also a good base for climbing Mbeya Peak. Camping per person $̲10̲, rooms $̲88̲, cottage (for families) $̲140̲

EATING

Mbeya's subtly aromatic **rice** is prized throughout the country, though its large-scale cultivation is partly to blame for the drying up of the Great Ruaha River. The local Arabica **coffee**, best known under the Utengule brand, isn't bad either, while its bottled "Rungwe" **mineral water** makes a very welcome change from the usual filtered stuff.

Holiday Lodge Jamatikhana Rd. Decent meals in a plain dining room: rice with liver, *filigisi* (chicken gizzards), or deep fried *dagaa* (freshwater sardines) costs Tsh3500, with other meat and fish dishes touching Tsh6000. No alcohol. Daily 7am–10pm daily.

Kanyatile Restaurant Cnr Lupa Way and Maktaba St. A very popular local place for stews (Tsh3400), bites, or just a cup of milky *chai*, and with several tables on a streetside veranda. Daily 7.30am–9pm.

Malimbe de Ville Lupa Way. A fast-food joint billing itself as a pizza parlour (Tsh12,000), but cheaper for traditional "bites" (*kababu*, *sambusa* and so on), burgers (from Tsh3000) and proper meals (most Tsh6000), including *pilau*, stews and fish. Also serves good juices. Has a couple of tables outside, facing the street. No alcohol. Daily 6.30am–10pm.

Mambeu Restaurant Cnr Mbalizi Rd and Sisimba St. This characterful and very basic place does good snacks, such as *sambusas*, and very cheap meals (Tsh2500–3500), including an excellent liver and banana (*mtori*) stews. Daily 7.30am–9pm.

Mbeya Hotel Karume Ave. A wide selection of well-priced, mostly Indian cuisine, including prawns, with most mains costing Tsh10,000 and soups no more than Tsh3500. The place is falling apart a bit, but remains charming in a 1970s Tanzanian way. It also has a well-stocked bar, popular whenever there's English football on the telly. If the weather's fine, eat outside in one of several extremely battered brick *bandas*. The lounge area has wi-fi. Daily 6.30am–10pm.

Mbeya Peak Hotel Acacia St. A small and very shady garden bar with *bandas* for daytime drinks or meals, including tangy *supu* for a late breakfast, plus succulent *nyama choma* (grilled meat) with grilled bananas (Tsh5000/kg). Daily 7am–11pm.

Mount Livingstone Hotel Off Jamatikhana Rd. The massive à la carte menu here (main courses from Tsh10,000) boasts almost a hundred dishes from all over the world, from Chinese and Italian to *bourguignon* fondues, pizzas, lasagna (Tsh12,500) and seafood paellas (Tsh19,500). Amazingly, most of it is usually available, and tasty too. It caters for vegetarians with dishes like stuffed aubergine, and the desserts can be inspired, including apricot or banana fritters. Daily 6am–10.30am & 11.30am–midnight.

New Continental Lodge North St. Unrivalled for its cheap, traditional Tanzanian food, with especially good breakfasts (great *supu*, nice crispy snacks, as well as juice). In the smoky courtyard at the back, it serves up the best *nyama choma* in town, succulent, and best enjoyed with grilled bananas. Full meals no more than Tsh4000. Daily 6.30am–10pm.

Rest House The Peace of Mind Jamatikhana Rd. In a pub-like interior, big portions are the thing, starting with its English-style breakfast (Tsh10,000). The menu is as quirky as the decor, featuring a pleasing array of freshly cooked Tanzanian dishes (including several kinds of fish from Lake Nyasa and Lake Tanganyika), a touch of Indian and Chinese, and some Italian dishes, including pasta and pizzas. Most main courses cost Tsh10,000–15,000. Daily 6am–10pm (food), 11.30am–midnight (drinks).

Rift Valley Hotel Cnr of Jamatikhana and Lumumba rds. This 1970s hotel has very run-down rooms, but the restaurant is fine, with a simple menu (meat, pork, fish, pasta, curries) on which almost everything costs a mysteriously precise Tsh8600. Daily 7am–9pm.

Sombrero Restaurant North St. One of the town's better lunch spots (under Tsh8000), with good pasta and curries – the kidney stew is a especially good – plus fresh juices and milkshakes. If you give them enough time, they're also happy to make dishes not on the menu, including vegetarian. Daily 6.30am–9pm.

DRINKING AND NIGHTLIFE

Mbeya is considered Tanzania's second city on the **rap** scene, but unfortunately anyone who makes it big promptly absconds to Dar. It might be worth asking around though, to see if you can catch some live rap. Wherever you're going out at night, always takes a taxi.

10

Coffee Garden South end of Karume Ave, facing the stadium. A forlorn but pleasant spot for an afternoon drink with *nyama choma*, it has plenty of tables along its long grassy plot, plus swings, slides and a roundabout for kids. The coffee is instant, though. Mon–Fri 7am–7pm, Sat–Sun 7am–10pm.

Karembu House 4th St. A great place to get to know people, this local bar is always busy, with a TV for European football, a popular dartboard and plenty of friendly punters. Daily 8am–midnight or later.

Mbeya Carnivore Tanzam highway, junction with Karume Rd. A popular disco and bar that's lively at weekends. Plays all kinds of music, from Congolese and Tanzanian dance to Bongo Flava, pure hip-hop and reggae. Also serves food and occasionally hosts live bands. Daily 24hrs.

Royal Pamodzi Club Lupa Way. Dark, loud and rather rough round the edges, this is Mbeya's main uptown disco, playing a wide range of music. Fri–Sun 8pm–late.

Weru Spring Garden Umoja Rd, 250m north of the roundabout. A very pleasant and relaxing outdoor bar and restaurant beside a small stream overgrown with datura trees and bamboo. There are tables on a lawn, and in open-sided *makuti*-thatched buildings. Also has a great children's playground, and very cheap food (meals from Tsh2000). Daily 8am–10pm (food served from midday onwards).

DIRECTORY

Football Prisons FC and popular newcomers Mbeya City Council FC ("Mbeya City", 2011) are both in the Tanzanian Premier League, and play at Sokoine Stadium. Tickets at the gate cost Tsh5000.

Health The Aga Khan Health Centre, on the corner of North St and Post St, is the first port of call for consultations (☎025 250 2896). Mbeya Regional Hospital is on Hospital Hill north of town (☎025 250 2985). Bhojani Chemists, Lupa Way (Mon–Sat 8am–8pm, Sun 10am–2pm) is a good pharmacy.

Immigration Behind the District Commissioner's Office, off Karume Ave (☎025 250 3664).

Internet access Mnasi, beside *New Continental Lodge* (Mon–Sat 8am–6pm), and at the post office, Lupa Way (Mon–Fri 7.30am–7pm, Sat 8am–4pm).

Money All Mbeya's banks have ATMs. The quickest place to change cash is Stanbic on Karume Ave, though it charges a $20 commission. You'll pay less at NBC down the road, but will need patience.

Swimming pool The *Rest House The Peace of Mind* lets non-guests use their pool for Tsh10,000 (daily sunrise–sunset).

Kitulo National Park

The **Kipengere Mountain Range**, comprising much of the region between Mbeya and Njombe, contains areas of immense ecological importance, notably the remote grasslands of a highland plateau protected as **Kitulo National Park**. Comprising 135 square kilometres of the plateau's northern sector, and twice as much montane forest on its western and southwestern flanks (412 square kilometres in all), the park promises more than just a taste of paradise for botanists, birdwatchers and hikers alike.

Known locally as *Bustani ya Mungu* ("God's Garden"), the plateau – which lies around 2600m above sea level – contains great numbers of endemic wild flowers,

---

OVERLAND INTO ZAMBIA OR MALAWI

Crossing over to Tanzania's neighbours can be quite a hassle thanks to clouds of hustlers and hucksters, and sometimes corrupt officials on the other side – be patient and polite and you'll eventually get through. Pickpockets and bag snatchers abound, so keep a close eye on your belongings, and avoid money-changers, too, many of whom are just con-artists. If you must change money on the street, keep it small. **Visas** can be bought on arrival, though you're unlikely to need one: EU, US, Canadian and most other Commonwealth nationals are currently exempt.

There are usually one or two through **buses** each day from Mbeya into Zambia and Malawi, but these can be held up for hours at the border, so it's much quicker to take transport as far as the border, walk through passport control, then catch onward transport on the other side. Be sure to make an early start as immigration closes at 6pm.

For **Zambia**, the crossing is at Tunduma, 114km along the Tanzam highway. Neither it, nor its Zambian counterpart, Nakonde, are pleasant places to hang around in, and are infamous for thieves, so be wary. The gentle approach to **Malawi** is by ferry (see p.445); otherwise, catch a Coaster from Mbeya to the border at Songwe River Bridge (hourly; 2hr–2hr 30min). If, as occasionally happens, the vehicle doesn't actually go to the border as promised, you'll be dumped at a junction 5km away, from where you can catch a *pikipiki* (motorbike) or a *bajaj*.

THE KIPUNJI MONKEY

Although heavily degraded by illegal logging, the forest fringing the Kitulo Plateau gave rise to a startling discovery in December 2003 – the hitherto unknown **Kipunji monkey** (*Rungwecebus kipunji*). Not just a new species, it turned out to be an entirely new genera, more closely related genetically to baboons than to the slender mangabeys it resembles. By coincidence, in early 2004 – before the announcement of the discovery – the monkey turned up again, 400km away in the western Udzungwa Mountains. Hopefully it will stick around, though the total population is estimated at just over 1100, ranking it as critically endangered on the IUCN's Red List. See ⓦ wcs.org for the full story: tap Kipunji into the search box.

10

including over fifty species of **orchids**. Their protection was the primary impetus behind the park's creation in 2002, as a growing illegal trade with Zambia – where orchids were traditionally a famine food but had become more of a staple – was threatening their extinction: at the start of the millennium, an estimated four million orchids were being smuggled out of southern Tanzania each year.

Unusually for a national park, the **best time to visit** is during the rains (more or less continuous from November to May), when the plateau erupts in a glorious show of colour, contrasting beautifully with the lingering morning mists, ominous storm clouds and deep, enveloping silence.

The wildlife

The park's flora attracts **insects** aplenty – notably moths and butterflies – which in turn provide food for frogs, chameleons and lizards. Kitulo is also home to breeding colonies of rare **birds**, including the pallid harrier, Njombe cisticola, Denham's bustard, blue swallow and Kipengere seed-eater. There are few large **mammals**, although some may be reintroduced: the plateau's grasslands owe their existence to the grazing habits of large herbivores, whether indigenous eland, impala and montane reedbuck, or the cattle that replaced them in the 1980s. A small population of reedbuck remain, and the fringing forests contain a unique subspecies of black-and-white colobus monkey, the threatened Abbot's duiker, and the wondrous **kipunji monkey** (see above), which was only discovered by modern science in 2003.

Hiking trails

The park has at least seven distinct **hiking trails** – the park headquarters gives out sketch maps of them. The shortest takes about three hours; the longest eight or more, and some can be combined if you have a tent and are self-sufficient. A twenty-kilometre hike from Matamba village up to **Matamba Ridge** overlooking the plateau, is recommended, but only for the fit, as it's a strenuous up-and-down affair. Once at the ridge, you can either follow it eastwards, or descend beyond the 2750-metre Matamba Pass into the flower-bedecked **Numbe Valley**, which slopes down along the ridge towards **Numbe Juniper Forest**. Many of the trees here reach a height of more than 50m, making them amongst the world's tallest of their kind. Further east, **Mount Mtorwi**, at 2961m, pips Mount Rungwe by a metre to claim the status of southern Tanzania's highest peak. Lastly, when leaving the park, consider walking down to Matema on Lake Nyasa (see p.442) – it's a three- to five-day hike, but can be reduced to a single day if you start at Bulongwa: some of the park guides can provide information about the route.

ESSENTIALS   **KITULO NATIONAL PARK**

Park headquarters The park headquarters are at Matamba, an hour's drive outside the park's northeastern boundary (daily 7.30am–5.30pm; ☏ 0689 062322 or ☏ 0767 536130, ⓦ tanzaniaparks.com/kitulo.html)

Entrance fees Park entry fees are $30 for 24 hours, plus

$30 for camping, and can be paid at the park headquarters if coming from the Tanzam highway, or at a park gate if approaching from the west. Official guides (optional but highly recommended) cost $20 a day.

10

ARRIVAL AND DEPARTURE

BY GUIDED TOUR

Two new access roads have opened over the last few years, and more alterations are planned in the park itself, so practicalities are likely to continue changing. Sisi kwa Sisi in Mbeya (see p.433) can provide information about the latest developments and can also arrange the whole trip for you for a very reasonable $30 per group plus park fees and transport. Tours are also offered by Rungwe Tea & Tours in Tukuyu (see p.440) and *Utengule Coffee Lodge & Estate* west of Mbeya (see p.434).

national park!), 9km east of Chimala, which takes a more leisurely 32km to reach Matamba.

From the west The alternative, and now favoured, approach (less grinding of gears, and a better road surface) is along a soon-to-be-paved road from Mbeya to Njombe via Isyonje, which passes straight through the park. Isyonje is 35km from Mbeya; the turning for Matamba and the park headquarters is 28km beyond Isyonje; a new park gate lies 8.5km from the turning; and the park headquarters are 15km beyond the gate.

BY CAR

From the north There are two access roads from the Tanzam Highway, north of the park. The original road, for which a 4WD is essential, starts just west of Chimala, 73km east of Mbeya, and passes an eye-popping 57 hairpins in its first nine kilometres, before levelling off as it nears Matamba. The road is extremely muddy in the rains. Much more comfortable is a new road from Ruaha (not the

BY BUS

You can catch any Coaster minibus from Mbeya heading to Makambako and ask to be dropped at "*njia panda ya Matamba*" (the junction for Matamba; Tsh4000). From the junction, Land Rovers (Tsh5000) and a battered bus (1pm) head up to Matamba. Buses also run along the Mbeya–Njombe road (includes buses ending at Bulongwa), but there's nothing yet from the junction to the park gate or up to Matamba.

ACCOMMODATION AND EATING

There are, as yet, next to no facilities in the park itself: the long-promised park-run campsites and *bandas* have yet to materialize, but that leaves you free to **camp wild** ($30 per person) – do wrap up, though, as it's chilly at night, and often freezes in June and July. For those without canvas, Matamba (2170m above sea level) has some surprisingly good guesthouses, and cheap restaurants too.

FEMA Matamba ☎0768 331723. Run by the Lutheran Church, this guesthouse has comfortable en-suite rooms, usually with hot water. Food can be arranged, too, though the religious atmosphere may not appeal to everyone. <u>Tsh20,000</u>

Mama Izengo Hotel Matamba ☎0752 294775, ✉solomonsopeter@gmail.com. This is one of Matamba's cheapest guesthouses, but absolutely fine, with good en-suite rooms in a modern building, and food available. It's positively luxurious for the price. <u>Tsh6000</u>

Tukuyu and around

The ride south from Mbeya to Lake Nyasa is one of Tanzania's most scenic, wending up through the lush foothills of Rungwe volcano before sinking into the swampy tropical forests hugging Lake Nyasa's northern shoreline. Close to the highest point of the road, 71km southeast of Mbeya, is the rural town of **TUKUYU**. Founded just over a century ago by the Germans as a replacement for the mosquito-ridden lakeshore town of Matema (Langenburg), Neu Langenburg – as they called Tukuyu – became an administrative headquarters. The **German Boma**, whose ramparts have been incorporated into today's municipal buildings, date from this time. Tukuyu could scarcely be more different from prosperous Mbeya. There's none of the latter's cosmopolitan feeling, and the atmosphere is decidedly small town (or big village). Yet Tukuyu is an attractive and refreshing place to spend some time, with wonderful views over the lushly vegetated hillocks and valleys far below, many of them extensively cultivated with tea, banana groves and sweet potatoes.

The main reason for staying is to visit various natural attractions in the surrounding area, which are accessible both under your own steam and, better, through one of two cultural tourism outfits, one in Tukuyu itself, the other based at a campsite a few kilometres to the north. Foremost among the local sights are the dormant volcanic mass of **Mount Rungwe** (which can be climbed in a day, just), associated **crater lakes** in the Poroto Mountains to the west, waterfalls and a natural lava-stone bridge over a river. The **best months** to visit, also coinciding with the traditional drumming season following the year's main harvest, are September and October, as for much of the rest of the year it rains … and rains. With annual precipitation sloshing around the 3m mark, Tukuyu is Tanzania's wettest town.

Mount Rungwe

The forest reserves around Mount Rungwe require a $10 per person per day permit, and $30 for camping, though tour operators will arrange this for you • Guided hikes are offered by *Bongo Camping* and Rungwe Tea & Tours in Tukuyu (see p.440); both charge around Tsh20,000 per person per day, excluding forest permit. Sisi kwa Sisi in Mbeya (see p.433) charges $30 excluding transport but including the permit

A climb to the 2960-metre summit of **Mount Rungwe**, 14km north of Tukuyu, is an enticing prospect, passing through wild and varied scenery. The summit itself gives breathtaking views of the Nyasa Trough to the south and the Kitulo Plateau to the east. Formed 2.5 million years ago, the volcano – which comprises at least ten craters and domes – dominates the skyline for miles around. Its last eruption was two centuries ago, but **earthquakes** still occur, frequently rendering thousands homeless. Part of the mountain's forested eastern flanks have been incorporated into Kitulo National Park (see p.436). The **best time to visit** is September or October, when there's ever so slightly less chance of rain.

Routes to the summit

There are two approaches to the summit, both passing from montane forest (around 1500m) to high-altitude bushland and heath. It's fine to take one route up and the other down; whichever route you take, you'll need a **guide**. Two days are recommended, with the night spent camping on the way up.

The **Syukula route** approaches from Syukula village in the southeast, 11km north of Tukuyu; catch the 7am daladala to Kikota, from where it's a ninety-minute walk east to Rungwe village, then another hour's walk east. The climb takes upwards of four to five hours to the southern crater summit rim, and two and a half hours back down. The last daladala to Tukuyu leaves Kikota no later than 7.30pm.

The **northeastern route** via Shiwaga Crater is the easier of the two, and arguably more scenic, but trickier to access initially. Catch a bus or a Coaster along the highway between Mbeya and Tukuyu as far as Isongole (also called "Number One", as it's the first big settlement south of the Tanzam highway), and wait for a truck heading east. Get off at Unyamwanga, 10km along, and head up from there.

The Kiwira River

20km west of Tukuyu • Tsh5000 admission fee • Catch any Coaster between Tukuyu and Mbeya and get off at Kyimo, 11km northwest of Tukuyu, where you can hire a bicycle for around Tsh10,000 • Sisi kwa Sisi in Mbeya (see p.433) charges $25 per person for a day-trip, including a tea and coffee tour, or $30 with a homestay; Rungwe Tea & Tours in Tukuyu (see p.440) charges Tsh18,000

The **Kiwira River** has three distinct attractions: God's Bridge and the Kijungu Falls, which can be visited together as a day-trip, and the Marasusa Falls, which have to be visited separately. **God's Bridge** (**Daraja la Mungu**) is a natural lava-stone archway over the river that was formed a few hundred years ago during one of Mount Rungwe's eruptions, when river water cooled a lip of lava before it could collapse. Three kilometres northwest along the river are the **Kijungu Falls**, whose name, meaning "cooking pot", alludes to the impressive pothole in which the river disappears before reappearing downstream. Further upstream are the impressively thunderous **Marasusa Falls**.

Kaporogwe Falls

25km south of Tukuyu • Tsh5000 admission fee • Take a bus or Coaster from Mbeya or Tukuyu to Ushirika, 10km south of Tukuyu, then rent a bicycle at the junction (no more than Tsh10,000) and cycle along a 12–15km dirt road west of the highway • Sisi kwa Sisi in Mbeya (see p.433) offers guided excursions for $30 per person, while Rungwe Tea & Tours (see p.440) charges Tsh15,000 for a round trip from Tukuyu by bicycle (5hrs in all)

The 25-metre **Kaporogwe Falls** (also called Kala Falls) on the Kala River, a tributary of the Kiwira, are a good target for a day-trip. As well as swimming, you can walk between the tumbling torrent and enter the cave behind it, where you can see a concrete wall behind which Germans are said to have hidden during World War I. The discovery of **stone tools** above the waterfall – knives, scrapers, picks and core axes from

10

the "Kiwira Industry" – indicate that the place was intensively occupied during the Stone Age. It was later abandoned, possibly when it became covered by pumice and volcanic debris from one of Mount Rungwe's eruptions.

Masoko Crater Lake

17km southeast of Tukuyu along the unsurfaced road to Ipinda • Tsh5000 admission fee • Any pick-up from Tukuyu to Ipinda or Matema passes by; get off when you see the lake on your right; the last reliable public transport passes by 4pm • A full-day excursion with Rungwe Tea & Tours in Tukuyu (see p.440), including hot water springs, costs Tsh18,000, or Tsh20,000 including camping

10

An attractive by-product of Mount Rungwe's volcanic rumblings is **Masoko Crater Lake** (also called Kisiba Crater Lake), 15km southeast of Tukuyu along the unsurfaced road to Ipinda and Matema. It's easy to find, being right next to the road (on the right coming from Tukuyu). The stone building on Masoko's crater rim housed the German Fifth Field Garrison before and during World War I, and was afterwards occupied by British troops, who later turned it into a courthouse (*mahakama*). Legend has it that before the Germans were routed by the British, they buried treasure here – or, more precisely, dumped it in the lake. This theory is borne out by the fact that old German and Austro–Hungarian coins are periodically washed up on the shore, encouraging intrepid locals to dive in for more (the coins are sold to tourists for under Tsh5000, though these days you're more likely to be offered coins from the British colonial period).

ARRIVAL AND DEPARTURE   TUKUYU

By bus or daladala There are frequent Coasters to Tukuyu to and from Mbeya and Kyela (Tsh2500), the first at 6.30am, the last – unusually late for Tanzania – at 7pm. Dar–Kyela buses also pass through. The bus stand is in the town centre on the east side of the highway. Be wary of hangers on when you arrive: tourists have been robbed in the past by newly-made "friends", so insist on carrying your own bags if not catching a *bajaj*.
Destinations Ipinda (5–6 pick-ups daily; 3hr); Kyela (hourly; 1hr 30min); Matema (1 bus daily plus pick-ups; 4–8hr); Mbeya (hourly; 1hr–1hr 30min).

INFORMATION AND TOURS

Two excellent places in town offer information and cultural tourism, such as affordable trips to the attractions around Tukuyu, including tea plantation tours, hikes up Mount Rungwe, and excursions to various waterfalls, Masoko Crater Lake and the natural stone arch ("God's Bridge") over the Kiwira River. Their profits fund a variety of good causes, including schools. Both charge a bargain Tsh15,000–20,000 for a full day, a little more if you're cycling or camping, plus any entrance fees.

★**Bongo Camping** Kibisi village: 5.5km towards Mbeya, then 750m off on the right (signposted) ☎ 0732 951763 or ☎ 0783 402778, ⓦ bongocamping .com. Based at their campsite, this indefatigable NGO prioritizes education, but is also involved in music, theatre and even film projects. Particularly recommended for if you want to get to know people well over a longer period of time than a day or two.
★**Rungwe Tea & Tours** In town, near the Landmark Hotel roundabout ☎ 025 255 2489 or ☎ 0767 940100, ⓦ rungwetea.com. Established by the local tea growers' association (which supplies the English fair-trade market, among others), this is a professionally and ethically run tour operator, with very knowledgeable guides.

ACCOMMODATION, EATING AND DRINKING

Tukuyu has few mosquitoes and no malaria. The following hotels are the pick of the best, but you can find plenty more cheap and basic guesthouses. Except for *Bongo Camping*, the places below are east of the highway: turn right 50m north of the bus stand. Tukuyu's restaurants double as bars, serving meals until 8 or 9pm – most are pretty tawdry, and you may need a smattering of Kiswahili language to break the ice. The two local brews are *kimpuno* (made from millet) and *kyindi* (millet with maize).

★**Bongo Camping** Kibisi village: 5.5km towards Mbeya, then 750m off on the right (signposted) ☎ 0732 951763 or ☎ 0783 402778, ⓦ bongocamping.com or ⓦ facebook.com/BongoCamping. This is a really great place, non-profit-making, and your money goes straight to the local community. You can bring your own tent, or staff can provide one with a mattress, pitched on a lawn under avocado trees; the bathrooms have solar-heated water. The food is excellent (no more than Tsh3500), and there are various tours on offer, as well as plenty happening on site, too, whether impromptu rap sessions, Kiswahili lessons or even theatre. Camping per person Tsh6000, ready-erected

AGE VILLAGES OF THE NYAKYUSA

The **Nyakyusa** are the dominant ethnic group between Tukuyu and Lake Nyasa, numbering well over a million in Tanzania, and around four hundred thousand in Malawi, where they're called Ngonde (or Nkonde). A unique but now extinct feature of traditional Nyakyusa society was their **age villages**, brand-new villages established by boys between the ages of 11 and 13, to which they would later bring wives and start families of their own. The villages died on the death of their last founding member, after which the land was reallocated by the district chief. Age villages served both to preserve the privileges and land of the older generation, and also to spread population pressure on the land more evenly, thereby avoiding unsustainable agricultural use. However, with each generation the available land was repeatedly divided among the sons of each chief, until the system finally collapsed when the land plots became too small to subdivide (a problem that also afflicts the Chagga around Kilimanjaro).

10

tents per person Tsh8000

Landmark Hotel 300m east of the highway (turn right 50m north of the bus stand) ☏ 025 255 2400 or ☏ 0782 164160. A surprisingly fancy, modern, decently priced hotel containing the town's best rooms, all large and in good condition, with huge beds, cable TV and reliable hot showers. The more expensive rooms have balconies and views of Mount Rungwe. It has a nice garden, where you're welcome to camp (no fixed price), and a fine restaurant, offering a good choice of local and international dishes (including cheese to go with pasta; meals from Tsh5000), and even wine. The upstairs bar has great views. Safe parking, and an internet café across the street. BB $30

Langboss Lodge 1km east of the highway (continue past *Landmark Hotel*, follow the road around, and turn left

after 650m) ☏ 025 255 2080. Best of the budget places, even though it's beginning to fall apart. The more acceptable rooms are large en-suite doubles (it's worth paying the Tsh5000 extra); singles share grim bathrooms and are best avoided. The restaurant cooks filling meals for around Tsh3500, but you'll have to wait an hour. There's also a bar – quiet unless there's European football on the telly. Tsh10,000

Laxmi Garden Centre Bar & Restaurant 120m north of the *Landmark Hotel* roundabout. Downmarket but pleasant and cheerful, this is good for roast meat in the garden at the back, breakfast *supu*, and even fresh pork (*kiti moto*, meaning "hot chair"). Its bar is the town's liveliest, and gets packed at weekends and during its live music promotions, when you'll see a surprising number of prostitutes, too. Daily 8am–10pm or later.

Lake Nyasa

Straddling the border between Tanzania, Malawi and Mozambique is the 31,000-square-kilometre **Lake Nyasa**, East Africa's third largest lake, and probably its most beautiful. The first European to record it was a Portuguese, Gaspar Bocarro, in 1616, whose account only came to light after David Livingstone's "discovery" of the same lake in 1859. By that time, **Arab slavers** following caravan routes developed by the Yao tribe had been exploiting the region's human resources for over a century, making Nyasa a major source of slaves for Zanzibar. The lake is perhaps better known by its Malawian name, Lake Malawi, though it's best not to use this term while in Tanzania, owing to Malawi's aggressive moves to claim the entire lake as its own (unsurprisingly, it's all about oil).

Geologically, the lake is similar to Lake Tanganyika, having been formed in the same period of Rift Valley faulting some twenty million years ago. Like Lake Tanganyika, Nyasa is long and narrow, measuring 584km from north to south, but only 80km at its widest. It reaches a maximum depth of almost 700m at its north end, where the jagged and largely unexplored **Livingstone Mountains** rise precipitously to over two kilometres above the lake's level, providing an unforgettable backdrop to a **ferry ride**, either along the Tanzanian shore, or across to Malawi. Snorkellers are also in for a treat, as most of the lake's four hundred colourful **cichlid species** – piscine marvels of evolution – favour the rocky northeastern shoreline, accessible by boat, or dugout, from the village of **Matema**, which also has an alluring beach. Equally relaxing, and with a wonderful stretch of sand, too, is the diminutive and exceptionally friendly town of **Mbamba Bay**, near the Mozambican border, although facilities here are extremely limited.

Unfortunately the price of paradise at either place is having to put up with plagues of mosquitoes: cerebral **malaria** is a problem, so make sure you're adequately protected. The **best time to visit** is from September to November, when the weather is hot and dry, or June to August, which is cooler and sometimes windy but has fewer bugs.

Matema and around

Tucked into Lake Nyasa's northeastern corner, between the Lufilyo River, the almost sheer Livingstone Mountains and a magnificent beach, is the fishing village of **MATEMA**. There's superb snorkelling on the rocky shoreline just to the east, while the energetic can clamber up to a waterfall, or explore the thick forest and *shambas* inland. But don't

LAKE NYASA FERRIES

A ride on Lake Nyasa is one of Tanzania's great journeys, as much for the views and remote villages as for the unorthodox docking technique, which involves ramming the ship's prow into the beach and dropping a couple of ladders, a trick occasioned by the collapse, long ago, of every pier and jetty along the way (though some have finally been rebuilt). The ferries themselves – the *MV Songea* and the MV *Iringa* – are equally ramshackle these days, while their **schedules** often can't be relied upon. Both ships spend long spells under repair or awaiting spare parts – the MV *Songea* is currently out of action, and its route is being operated by the MV *Iringa*. Indeed, it's not uncommon for both ships to be out of action – contact Marine Services Ltd for the latest (☎0713 736681, ⟨w⟩mscl.go.tz).

In theory, the **MV Songea** sails every Thurs at 1pm from Itungi Port in the north, calling at a string of minor harbours before reaching Mbamba Bay in the south (see p.445) on Friday morning: the journey takes about twenty hours in all. The ferry turns around on Fri at 1pm, to arrive back in Itungi Port on Sat morning. The much smaller **MV Iringa** supposedly leaves Itungi Port on Tues at 11am for Manda, little more than halfway to Mbamba Bay; the journey takes about twelve hours. It heads back in the wee hours of Wed morning to arrive at Itungi Port at 4pm.

TICKETS

Tickets can only be bought at the ports. If you have the choice, go **first class** in a two-bunk cabin on the MV *Songea*, as **third class** (there's no second) is massively overcrowded, with many more passengers than seats or benches. If you do travel third class, get your ticket as soon as the office opens (three hours before departure) or you might be stuck in a steamy windowless dungeon below deck. Given that neither ferry is well maintained, it would be safer, in case of capsize, to remain on the upper deck in any case. Itungi Port to Mbamba Bay, in a first class bunk costs $30 for tourists, which is sometimes asked for in dollars cash, so have some US bank notes with you. Cheap meals and drinking water are available on both vessels.

PRINCIPAL PORTS

Itungi Port The port itself is silted up, so motorboats shuttle passengers to the ferry waiting offshore. There are no hotels in Itungi Port, but it can be reached by Coaster from Mbeya and Tukuyu in plenty of time to buy tickets.

Matema (see p.442) Three hours from Itungi Port.

Lupingu Five to seven hours from Itungi Port, and also accessible by bus and pick-up from Njombe via Ludewa (or Rudewa), where there are a couple of guesthouses. The settlement's name means "protected by a charm", and it certainly is charming – arriving ferries are greeted by swimming or wading women and children who have perfected the art of selling meals (fish and cassava) to passengers high up on deck via plastic jugs strapped to long poles: take the food from the jug, and put money in its place.

Manda There are plenty of guesthouses here, and a very rough road via Ludewa to the highway between Njombe and Songea.

Liuli With luck, you'll arrive here after dawn, to see some impressive boulders protruding from the lake. The profile of the one furthest from the shore as seen from Liuli inspired the Germans to call the place Sphinxhafen. There should be buses from here to Mbamba Bay, continuing on to Mbinga.

Mbamba Bay The end of the ferry line, with onward options across the lake to Nkhata Bay in Malawi (see p.445).

expect many mod cons: Matema lacks mains electricity or land line telephones, and a bank. It does however have a good hospital, run by the Lutheran Church, whose mission house resembles a Bavarian barn. Under colonial rule, Matema was briefly the regional headquarters, before mosquitoes pushed the Germans up to Tukuyu. The bay on which Matema sits is named after the imperial commissioner and former explorer **Hermann von Wissmann**, whose two side-to-side crossings of Africa spurred his country's colonizing drive. Matema is now inhabited mainly by the Nyakyusa tribe.

Matema market
At the east end of the village, beyond a river ford • Daily sunrise–sunset

10

The diminutive **Matema market** sells only the barest necessities, but the clearing at the end by the beach usually has towers of Kisi pots made in Ikombe village (see below) awaiting transport, which you should be able to buy. There are also a couple of people selling skewers of grilled goat meat, fish and bananas, and a simple restaurant, but other than that there's little else to the village other than the fun of either amusing or inadvertently terrifying the kids.

Matema Beach
The coarse grey sand of **Matema Beach** starts at Ipinda junction beside the hospital, a little over 2km west of the market. The water is apparently free of bilharzia, and crocodiles – which elsewhere have a habit of lunching on locals – are thankfully absent, but check locally before bathing. The walk to the mouth of the **Lufilyo River**, 4km west of the hotels along the beach via a small lagoon, is recommended, but take care along the river itself, which is definitely home to crocodiles as well as hippo, and may also carry bilharzia.

The Ipinda road
The walk along **the Ipinda road** passes through satisfyingly thick tropical vegetation positively awash with birdlife, and all sorts of strange fruit, including cocoa. Some of the vegetation is wild (look for vervet monkeys in the tall and bushy palms), but much is planted with banana and papaya plants, mango trees, stands of giant bamboo and sugar cane. Many of the houses in the clearings are built in traditional Nyakyusa fashion, using straight bamboo stalks lashed together for walls, and reeds for their pointed roofs. Look out too for the curious toadstool-like granaries made from woven reeds and topped by broad straw-thatch roofs.

The Livingstone Mountains
Guides can be arranged through any of Matema's hotels for $20 per person

Matema lies tantalizingly close to the northernmost spur of the **Livingstone Mountains**, which run most of the way along the Tanzanian side of the lake. The mountains' thick forests and steep slopes are sparsely inhabited, and the entire range is little explored. For a taste, there's a **waterfall** about three hours' walk from Matema, with a beautiful plunge pool deep enough for swimming in. The trail there is very steep in parts (so much so that ropes come in helpful), and you'll need a guide.

Ikombe village
Access to Ikombe is either on foot on a narrow path along the lakeshore, or by dugout from Matema, which takes just over an hour and costs Tsh10,000 to hire • Matema's hotels offer excursions for around $20 per person

A trip you can do by boat or on foot is to **Ikombe village**, a few kilometres southeast of Matema on a small peninsula backed by almost vertical mountains. Its inhabitants are from the Kisi tribe, famed in Tanzania for their prowess as fishermen, and for the women's skills as **potters**. Unlike other Tanzanian potters, the Kisi women use wheels – actually thick, ash-sprinkled plates – which help create the pots' characteristically rounded forms. When the pot is ready, it's smoothed with pebbles or maize cobs and rubbed with a greyish clay to give a creamy colour after firing. After a few days of

10

CANOEING AND SNORKELLING AROUND MATEMA

To mess about on the water, **dugouts** can be rented from locals, but for motorboats go through a hotel (around $25/hr, plus $2/litre of fuel). **Snorkelling** is best off the rocky eastern shore, where you'll see many of the lake's cichlids in the crystalline water. There are shoreline **caves** nearby but access depends on the water level, the best time being towards the end of the dry season (Oct and Nov), when the lake is lower. Snorkelling equipment can be rented at *Matema Lake Shore Resort* and *Blue Canoe Safari Camp*.

---

drying, the pots are decorated with red ochre and sometimes incised with motifs. The final firing is done in a shallow depression in the ground lined with dry banana leaves. The resulting pottery is ideal for cooking or storing cool liquids. The **best time to visit** is on Friday to coincide with the weekly market.

ARRIVAL AND DEPARTURE

MATEMA AND AROUND

By road There are two practical approaches by road from Mbeya or Tukuyu to Matema. The first is via the scruffy town of Kyela, 54km south of Tukuyu along a paved road, followed by 40km of mostly well-graded road. The second rougher but more scenic route, ducks and swerves as it plunges down from Tukuyu towards the lake, passing Masoko Crater Lake (65km) along the way. The two roads join at Ipinda, 22km before from Matema.

By bus/Coaster Kyela is easily reached by bus or Coaster from Mbeya, which run throughout the day from 6.30am to 7pm (2hr 30min–3hr). From Kyela, a motley assortment of buses and pick-ups set off at sporadic intervals for Matema (40km; usually 1hr 30min). You can also catch a

direct bus (currently Sumba Bus; 5hr), which leaves Mbeya at 12.30pm, and Matema at 6am. Approaching via Masoko Crater Lake, Coasters and pick-ups currently leave from the roundabout facing Tukuyu's *Landmark Hotel*, the first between 8am and 9am, though they may start leaving from the new bus stand, so ask there first. It takes about three hours from Tukuyu to Ipinda in dry weather, where you may have to change vehicles for the remaining 20km; in poor conditions, the whole journey can take almost a full day.

By ferry Matema is the first stop on the ferry ride down from Itungi Port: the ferry is the only practical way to get to or from Mbamba Bay (see p.442).

ACCOMMODATION AND EATING

Matema has three beach hotels: two of them are church-run; the other has a great backpacker vibe, and you can also camp here. All three are a fair distance west of the village. Food is available at all of them, but it's cheaper to eat in the village itself at the *mgahawa* by the market, where you can fill up for Tsh2000 a plate, or at a couple of stalls nearby.

★**Blue Canoe Safari Camp** 2.5km west of Ipinda junction ☎0783 575451, ⓦbluecanoelodge.com. A funky sun- and wind-powered place backed by over a thousand exotic fruit trees, this is one of the nicest places to stay in southern Tanzania on any budget. Founded by a veteran German overlander in 2008, and run in partnership with Tanzanians, it has a thoroughly green ethos, chilled-out vibe, and pretty stilted cottages in traditional style, made almost entirely of natural materials like bamboo. There's also a great bar, and tasty organic food, albeit not cheap at $20 per meal. It also offers a full range of activities, including birding by canoe ($15 per person), and snorkelling (also by canoe; $30 per person). Closes in May or June. Camping per person $7, rooms (BB) bamboo *banda* $35, beach bungalow BB $90

Matema Beach View Lutheran Centre 600m west of Ipinda junction ☎0684 991030 or ☎0767 552143, ⓦmatemabeachview.com. Idyllically located in the grounds of the historic mission with its school and hospital, this hotel has simple, well-maintained rooms and *bandas* (the

en-suite ones cost an extra Tsh10,000), three of them in the 1911 German mission house, and others right on the beach. There's a small shop, excellent meals to order (including pizza), soft drinks, and a generator until 10pm. BB **Tsh20,000**

Matema Lake Shore Resort 2km west of Ipinda junction ☎0782 179444, ⓦmec-tanzania.ch/matema. Run by a Swiss Evangelistic Church, this modern place has a wide variety of spotless rooms in one- and two-storey beach-front buildings (top-floor rooms have balconies), each with large box nets, and most of them en suite. There's also a communal kitchen, barbecue area, average meals (Tsh10,000) and even beers, plus snorkelling equipment and motorboats for hire. BB shared bathrooms **Tsh25,000**, en suite **Tsh50,000**

Unnamed guest house ("Nyumba ya Wageni") Lufilyo, 2km east of Matema Beach View Lutheran Centre. Matema's only locally run guesthouse, in the village proper near the market but on the beach, with a very welcoming vibe, clean rooms, and satellite TV in the bar. **Tsh15,000**

Mbamba Bay

MBAMBA BAY, the last Tanzanian port of call for the Lake Nyasa ferry (see p.442), is the nation's southernmost town, "town" being a generous term for such a dusty little place, where the streets are lined with racks for drying *dagaa* sardines, goats browse under baobabs, and locals sit pondering in the shade of mango trees. There's no running water, nor electricity other than that provided by generators, nor a bank, and the town can still find its road to the rest of the world (namely Mbinga, 70km inland) cut off during the rains.

This isolation is all part of Mbamba Bay's considerable charm, along with its laidback feeling, and its **beaches**: there's a nice one in the bay immediately north of the ferry landing, plus an immense 10km-long beach that begins 4km south of the centre. But it's the people who really make Mbamba Bay special – instead of running away in terror like some do in Matema, the children here are delighted whenever they elicit a "*Marahaba*" from visitors in reply to their chirpy "*Shikamoo*".

However, this may all change in light of the government's promise to pave the road here, combined with the numerous **projects** planned for this hitherto forgotten corner of the country, including coal, iron ore and nickel mines, oil and gas exploration in the lake itself (assuming Malawi and Tanzania can agree on who owns what, as Malawi claims the entire Tanzanian side of the lake), and a proposed 860km railway linking Mbamba Bay with Mtwara on the coast.

ARRIVAL AND DEPARTURE   MBAMBA BAY

By ferry (Tanzania) In theory, the MV *Songea* or MV *Iringa* (see p.442) dock here twenty hours after leaving Itungi Port. They're met by two or three Land Rover pickups headed to Mbinga and Songea; you'll need to rush to get a seat, but there's really no reason to dash away from Mbamba Bay so soon.

By ferry (Malawi) Following years of unreliable government-run ferry services to and from Malawi, a private company has launched the MV *Mwande*, an eighty-seat ferry that's basically a two barges supporting two tiers of seats, powered by two 300-horsepower outboards (w slsafaris.com). It sails from Nkhata Bay to Mbamba Bay every Friday at 6.30am, and turns back the same day at 1.30pm. The journey takes three hours, and costs $50. If you can't wait, cargo boats (5–6hr), which are just large wooden canoes with outboards, leave most nights around midnight (Tsh10,000). For any crossing to Malawi, visit the immigration officer at the police station behind the port to stamp your passport. You can change money unofficially in Mbamba Bay, and not always at rip-off rates. Nkhata Bay has proper banking facilities.

By bus or pick-up The only road into Mbamba Bay is from Songea via Mbinga. The 70km from Mbinga, across the spectacularly steep Matengo highlands, have yet to be surfaced, so may be impassable after unusually heavy rains. In fair weather, there's a daily bus from Songea around 6–6.30am, and from Mbamba Bay at around 10pm. Pick-ups – usually Land Rovers – cover both stages, and get packed to the seams.

Destinations Mbinga (1 daily plus pickups; 3hr); Songea (1 daily plus pick-ups; 5hr).

PRECIOUS, PRECOCIOUS, PRECARIOUS... LAKE NYASA'S CICHLIDS

Although eclipsed in absolute size and depth by Lake Tanganyika, Nyasa (simply meaning "lake" in Kiyao) trumps its big brother in its **biological diversity**. While Tanganyika boasts a hugely impressive two hundred **cichlid** species (fish belonging to the order of *Perciformes*, ranging in length from 2.5cm to almost a metre), Lake Nyasa contains over four hundred, representing no less than one-third of the world's known species, most of which exist only here – and in hobbyists' aquariums. Cichlids, both male and female, are devoted parents, and a good number are **mouthbrooders**, incubating eggs in their mouths and sometimes, once they hatch, keeping the fry safe, too, until they get big enough to fend for themselves. Other species, perhaps even all, can **change sex** if needed (and without the help of steroids), but the really remarkable thing is that the cichlids of Lake Nyasa and Lake Tanganyika, out of touch for millions of years, have **evolved in parallel**, with genetically different species sharing similar colour patterns, mouth adaptations or feeding techniques. For more about Nyasa's evolutionary marvels, see w malawicichlids.com.

ACCOMMODATION AND EATING

Mbamba Bay's cheapest guesthouses are signposted from the roundabout between the port and the bus stand, though they depend on the Malawi ferry for their survival, so tend to disappear whenever the ferry service is suspended. Basic *mgahawa* (tea rooms) are scattered around town and sell fish or beans with ugali or rice for as little as Tsh2000. Early in the year, more intrepid travellers might care to sample the local speciality, lake fly (*inzi*): enormous clouds of them float in on the wind and settle on trees, from where they're shaken into baskets, and subsequently fried.

10

Bio Camp Mbegele, 5.5km north of the port and bus stand (15min by pikipiki) ☎0768 053544 (SMS), ⓦ bushkomba.de. German owned, locally managed, on a beautiful and quiet beach, but pricey (bargaining is possible). Sleep in tiny dome tents with mattresses, pitched under large thatched roofs that almost touch the ground, and which shared clean ablutions; or in cute round brick bungalows with thatched roofs and their own western-style bathrooms. The restaurant (breakfast Tsh5000, lunch or dinner – mostly fish – Tsh8000) faces the beach, and there's also a *banda* on the beach itself for dining. People staying elsewhere are welcome so long as they buy drinks or meals. Snorkelling trips can be arranged to a couple of islands 6–7km away. Camping per person T̄sh15,000, BB tents S̄25, bungalows S̄50
Neema Lodge 2km south of town. Top marks for location,

right on the beach on the north side of the boulder-strewn headland south of town, but a little run down, often without electricity, and not always open. It has six en-suite doubles with mosquito nets. To get there, walk south along the road to Mbinga (it starts just west of the bus stand), turn right after 1km after the bridge, and follow the track. T̄sh12,000
St Benadeta Hotel 400m northeast of the bus stand (ask for "*Hotel ya Masista*") ☎0768 443238, ⓔ milingaf @gmail. com. Built and run by Catholic sisters, this two-storey construction 450m inland from the port is one of Mbamba Bay's grandest buildings, and opens year-round, regardless of whether the ferry is running. It has good en-suite rooms, eight of them with lake views from their verandas, and good food, too, which you can eat in the garden accompanied by statues of frolicking wildlife. BB T̄sh18,000

Njombe

East of Lake Nyasa, beyond the Livingstone Mountains, are the rolling hills of the Kipengere Range, a beautiful area with sweeping views over a huge expanse of land. Perched on a ridge at the eastern end of the range, midway between Mbeya and Songea, is the agricultural centre of **NJOMBE** – at 1900m above sea level, one of Tanzania's highest, coolest and breeziest towns. The fresh climate and expansive views are the main attractions, making it a likeable sort of place to break a journey. If you've got an hour to spare, there's a set of **waterfalls** beside the highway 800m north of the NBC bank, while the **market**, one street west of the highway at the end of Mlowezi and UWT streets, is a good place to buy naturally dyed woven baskets made from a reed-like grass called *milulu*; the baskets are at their freshest and most aromatic after the long rains.

ARRIVAL AND INFORMATION

NJOMBE

By bus or daladala Njombe's chaotic bus stand is on the west side of the Mbeya–Songea highway, which runs north–south through town. There are frequent Coasters from Makambako on the Tanzam Highway and from Songea, and fewer in number from Mbeya; Coasters can be caught in Njombe until mid-afternoon, as can buses passing through if they have empty seats.

Destinations Dar (5 daily; 9hr); Iringa (2 daily plus Coasters; 4hr); Mbeya (hourly Coasters; 4hr); Morogoro (1 daily; 7–8hr); Songea (hourly Coasters; 4hr).
Services The NBC bank, on the highway 1km north of the bus stand, has an ATM. There's internet access at Ngewe .com (daily 8am–8pm), beside *Wasia Hotel* one block east of the highway opposite the bus stand.

ACCOMMODATION, EATING AND DRINKING

★**Hillside (Chani) Hotel** 1.2km northwest of the bus stand (500m along the highway, then left along Mabatini Rd, taking the second right after New Magazeti Inn) ☎0655 834356 or ☎0768 834356, ⓔ chanihotel@yahoo.com. On one of the few remaining green patches around town, this is Njombe's best hotel – its twelve large and comfortable rooms (with more being built)

have wall-to-wall carpet, big comfortable beds, spotless bathrooms with hot water and cable TV. The restaurant is surprisingly elegant, and has tables on a veranda facing the garden. Most mains (mainly chicken) cost Tsh6000; try also the cream of peanut soup (Tsh2500). They sell alcohol, but it's not really a bar. Safe parking. BB T̄sh30,000
MG-Classic Lodge Mabatini Rd (500m north of the bus

stand, then left; it's 30m after *New Magazeti Inn*) ☎ 026 278 2241. Nothing special, but adequate: the large en-suite rooms have big beds with box nets, and cable TV. There's also a small bar, and a restaurant selling stews, fish or meat with rice or *ugali* for Tsh3500–5000. BB **Tsh18,000**

New Magazeti Inn Mabatini Rd (500m north of the

bus stand, then left one block) ☎ 026 278 2913. The best of the really cheap places, its somnolent atmosphere conceals some cheerful rooms decorated with woodcarvings and Tingatinga paintings; some are en suite (so-so squat toilets and showers). Also has a popular bar. **Tsh8000**

Songea

10

If you can ignore the often reckless driving, the long, swooping descent from Njombe to the large market town of **SONGEA** is gloriously exhilarating, passing through majestic granite scenery complete with rushing rivulets, misty moorlands and incredibly long views over the hills. Some 237km southeast of Njombe, Songea was until recently a scruffy tobacco-producing town at the junction of two very rough roads: one to Mbamba Bay on the lakeshore, the other east towards the Indian Ocean. But various ambitious infrastructure projects in the region, including a new border crossing into Mozambique, seem to have brought out the best in the town, making it an enjoyable place to break a journey, even if the local attractions are scant.

Maji Maji Memorial and Museum

1.8km north east of the bus stand • Daily 8am–7pm • Tsh6500

Songea's main attraction is the **Maji Maji Memorial and Museum**, dominating the memorial ground northeast of the centre. The ground is a large square lawn flanked on three sides by the cement busts of twelve Ngoni chiefs who were captured and executed by the Germans during the Maji Maji Uprising. At its centre stands the bulky statue of a soldier with a machine-gun in his hand, while facing the ground in a pagoda is a large cement statue of Nyerere looking uncharacteristically solemn. Though crudely fashioned, the busts are rendered poignant by garlands hung around their necks. Three of the chiefs are depicted with turbans, an unwitting reminder of the Arab-dominated slave trade in which the Ngoni also participated,

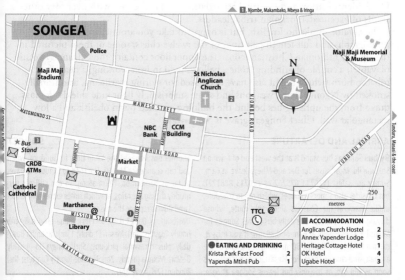

10

THE NGONI INVASIONS

Songea is the main town of the **Ngoni** tribe, who occupy much of southwestern Tanzania (they're also found in Malawi, and in scattered groups as far north as Lake Victoria). The Ngoni are relatively recent immigrants, having arrived only in the 1840s, at the end of a remarkable twenty-year, 3500-kilometre migration from KwaZulu-Natal in southern Africa.

At the beginning of the nineteenth century, the militaristic **Zulu empire** under King Shaka (or Chaka) began to make its presence felt, until by the 1830s many of southern Africa's people were on the move, fleeing either the Zulu armies, or the famine and drought that accompanied the conflict. Twelve major migrations out of South Africa occurred during this period, half of which resulted in the creation of new kingdoms elsewhere: the Basotho in Lesotho; Ndebele in Zimbabwe; Gaza in Mozambique; Kololo in Zambia; and the Ngoni in Malawi and Tanzania.

The Ngoni were led by **Zwangendaba**, a former Zulu commander who had fallen out of favour. Copying the regimented military organization and strategies of the Zulu, in 1822 Zwangendaba and the Ngoni crossed into southern Mozambique, and subsequently followed the course of the Zambezi into Zimbabwe, where in 1834 they destroyed the three-hundred-year-old Changamire empire of the Shona people. The following year, the Ngoni crossed the Zambezi and headed into Malawi, and by 1840 they had reached the Ufipa Plateau in southwestern Tanzania.

On Zwangendaba's death in 1845, the Ngoni split into several groups and continued their odyssey of conquest and migration. One group, known as the **Tuta**, headed north and settled between Lake Tanganyika and Unyamwezi, where they were welcomed by Chief Mirambo (see p.406), who took advantage of their military skills by hiring them as mercenaries for his own expansionist plans. Other groups went southwest to Malawi and eastern Zambia, while others headed east to set up independent states at Songea and Njombe in Tanzania, displacing the indigenous Ndendeule and Matengo tribes respectively, all the while waging war against other tribes, and among themselves. The ensuing chaos that enveloped southern Tanzania greatly eased the German conquest fifty years later, although the Germans themselves later met serious opposition from the Ngoni during the 1905–07 Maji Maji Uprising.

both as traders and captives. One of the busts represents **Chief Songea Luwafu Mbano**, from whom the town takes its name. As the most famous of the Ngoni resistance leaders, he was honoured by the Germans with decapitation rather than hanging – his cranium presumably lies in a German museum's storeroom, awaiting DNA identification and eventual repatriation – as is the case with over fifty other skulls of executed Tanzanian tribal leaders.

The curator speaks no English, but is happy to take you around. Inside are photographs and full-length paintings of the twelve chiefs, some of them pictured in the style of Ethiopian Christian icons. The **upper floor** contains three drums (two still playable), a couple of grinding stones, bellows used in iron-working, a beautiful tobacco horn (which might also have been used for storing marijuana, traditionally smoked by Ngoni elders), weapons and some surprisingly light hide shields. A **mass grave** from the uprising lies behind the building, marked by an obelisk and a low rectangular wall. Chief Songea's grave is 50m away.

ARRIVAL AND DEPARTURE   SONGEA

By bus Songea's bus stand is at the west end of town on Sokoine Rd. Most buses for Dar and Mbeya leave at 6am; Sumry are safest (☎0713 625262 or ☎0713 888122), but consider also Super Feo buses, which run to schedule, unlike many of the Coasters along this route, whose driving can be reckless. One daily bus leaves Songea for Mbamba Bay (usually at 6am or 6.30am); if you miss it, catch a Coaster to Mbinga, 80km along at the end of the asphalt, and change there. For Masasi, buy your ticket as soon as you can, as the only bus leaves Songea at 6am;

another bus leaves at the same time for Tunduru, where you can change for Masasi. The road to Tunduru is paved as far as Namtumbo, 71km along, so can still get very muddy during the rains, at which times extremely packed Land Rovers replace the buses.

Destinations Dar (3 daily; 9–11hr); Iringa (3–4 daily plus hourly Coasters; 8hr); Masasi (1 daily; 13hr); Mbamba Bay (1 daily plus occasional pick-ups; 5hr); Mbeya (3–4 daily; 8–9hr); Mbinga (hourly; 2hr); Njombe (hourly Coasters; 4hr); Tunduru (2 daily; 7–8hr).

ACCOMMODATION

There are dozens of cheap guesthouses scattered about: the older ones are often dire, but newer ones fare better. There are plenty of mosquitoes, so ensure your bed has a good net. Tap water is unsafe to drink.

Anglican Church Hostel Just off Njombe Rd by the church ☎025 260 0693. The most acceptable budget option, with clean cell-like rooms around a courtyard, including some with bathrooms. Food can be arranged. Tsh8000

Annex Yapender Lodge Deluxe St ☎0766 456360 or ☎0755 013079. The ten en-suite doubles at this calm, welcoming place are fine for the price, well kept, with good cold showers (hot water comes in buckets), screened windows, decent mosquito nets, and TVs. There's also a basic restaurant (no set menu; give them plenty of time), a small garden, and safe parking. BB Tsh16,000

★**Heritage Cottage Hotel** 2km along Njombe Rd ☎025 260 0888, ⓦheritage-cottage.com. A friendly place set in a huge garden complete with playground: the twelve motel-style rooms all come with satellite TV and even hot baths. There's a good bar and restaurant with great food (especially curries; from Tsh8000), but you'll have to wait at least an hour. Internet access. BB Tsh60,000

OK Hotel Deluxe St ☎025 260 2640. Dependable and welcoming, with 21 en-suite rooms, a little worn but clean, all with cable TV, fans, box net and writing desk. There's also a restaurant with four tables on a terrace outside (mostly Tsh7000–8000 for chicken or beef with rice, chips or *ugali*), and safe parking. BB Tsh18,000

Ugabe Hotel By the bus stand ☎0767 971899, ⓔugabehotel@gmail.com. A modern, if a little pricey, hotel with 38 rooms (no twins) on several floors, that is perfectly located for a 6am bus departure. The rooms are fine if small, and have cable TV, but the lack of windows or other ventilation in the bathrooms explains the often musty smell, and there are no nets (the place relies on fans, window screens and bug spray to keep out mosquitoes). Tsh25,000

EATING AND DRINKING

Krista Park Fast Food Deluxe St. Songea's best restaurant, with good pre-cooked snacks such as *sambusa* and *kababu*, and an ambitious menu for lunch and dinner, even prawns (Tsh8000) – in line with the rest of the town, chicken is considered a luxury (Tsh15,000). All meals include fruit salad and juice, which can be inventive – avocado with pineapple, say (Tsh1000 if not with a meal). They also sell very decent bread and cakes. The dining room is unmemorable, so try for one of the tables facing the street outside. Daily 7am–10pm.

Yapenda Mtini Pub Deluxe St. The town's most enjoyable bar: a large, *makuti*-thatched place built around a venerable old fig tree, with loads of seating outside. It gets really lively after sunset. It also has good music and boasts Songea's best goat meat *nyama choma*. There's a similar bar next door. Daily 6.30am–late.

DIRECTORY

Internet The post office on Sokoine Rd has reliable computers (Mon–Fri 7.30am–7pm, Sat 8am–4pm), or try Marthanet on Mission St (Mon–Sat 8am–6.30pm, Sun 9am–5pm).

Money NBC, on the corner of Jamhuri and Karume roads, is helpful and averagely efficient, with an ATM. There are more machines operated by CRDB facing the bus stand, but their location is too visible for comfort.

Shopping The market on the north side of Sokoine Rd (daily sunrise–sunset) is a good place for sampling or smelling the dried fish from Lake Nyasa, but for *kangas* and *kitenges*, rummage through the shops and stalls at the west end of Jamhuri Rd.

CROSSING INTO MOZAMBIQUE

Some 100km south of Songea (125km by road), there's a border crossing with Mozambique at the so-called **Unity Bridge 2**, 1km south of Kivikoni village. Note that this is not the original "Unity Bridge", further east (see p.183). As with all Mozambican crossings, you need to have obtained your **visa** at the embassy in Dar es Salaam (p.113) beforehand.

Minibuses to Kivikoni leave from the main road in Songea's Majengo area, 1km southwest of the bus stand across a maze of streets: cross over the main road from the bus stand to enter Makita Rd, take the first right (behind CRDB's ATMs), and turn left at the end. Then take the second right, which becomes Majengo's main road on the other side of some fields. Unhelpfully, the minibuses leave Songea between 11am and 2pm, and take about four hours. As the border closes at 6pm, and there's no guarantee of onward transport late in the afternoon, expect to spend the night in Kivikoni, which currently has just one extremely grotty guesthouse to its name. After dealing with border formalities the next morning (the border opens at 8am), you should find a vehicle on the Mozambican side for **Lichinga**, 200km beyond.

Zanzibar

WOMAN ON JAMBIANI BEACH

Zanzibar

The Zanzibar archipelago is one of Africa's most bewitching destinations, the name itself evoking palm-backed beaches, languid tropical waters and colourful coral reefs. But the islands are more than just the backdrop for dedicated beach bumming. Their history is a visitors' book of peoples from around the Indian Ocean and even the Mediterranean, each of which left their mark, whether in the form of ruined palaces, fortresses or citadels, or Zanzibar's famous cuisine, or some very strange but enjoyable cultural events, including Pemba's Portuguese-style bullfights, and Makunduchi's raucous celebration of the Persian New Year.

11

Unguja is the archipelago's main island, and the one with the best beaches. The historical **Stone Town**, part of the capital Zanzibar Town, is an alluring Arabian-style labyrinth densely packed with mansions, palaces and bazaars, most of them constructed on the back of the nineteenth-century **slave trade**, which Zanzibar controlled. Unguja's sister island of **Pemba**, 48km to the north, is quite a contrast. With few beaches to write home about, tourist facilities are extremely limited, so the main reason for coming is for **scuba diving**. History buffs can poke around a host of medieval ruins dating from the height of the Swahili trading civilization, while nature lovers have **Ngezi Forest**, an incredibly dense tangle that's home to unique birds, and the giant Pemba fruit bat.

Stone Town

The greedy spider at the heart of East Africa's slave trade was **STONE TOWN**, the historical part of Zanzibar's capital, Zanzibar Town. Known locally as Mji Mkongwe ("Old Town"), it resembles the medinas of North Africa and Arabia, with its maze of narrow twisting streets, bustling bazaars and grand Arabian and Indian mansions. In spite of its quasi-medieval appearance (ably helped along by a most inimical climate as far as wood, masonry and roofs are concerned), the town is relatively sprightly, most of it no older than 160 years. Wandering about aimlessly here is a pleasure in itself, but there are also specific places to aim for, including the harrowing cells of Africa's last slave market, two cathedrals linked to the slave trade's abolition, and – along the waterfront – two majestic palaces (now museums) and a brooding Omani fortress.

Stone Town's showpiece is its grandiose **waterfront**, a series of monumental buildings between the port and Shangani in the southwest. This is the Stone Town that the sultans wanted you to see, and admire. Yet barely a hundred metres behind the palaces and their facades is another world entirely: the souk-like labyrinth of **central Stone Town**. Positively dripping in atmosphere, it's a bewildering warren of narrow alleyways and dead-ends, decaying mansions and colourful shops – an architectural trove, hugely

Highlights

❶ Stone Town Africa meets the Orient – a place where the line between reality and imagination can easily fade away. **See p.452**

❷ Scuba diving Whether you're an experienced diver or a novice, Unguja and Pemba offer unforgettable underwater experiences. **See pp.462–463**

❸ Spice tours See, touch, smell and taste Zanzibar's famous spices, learn about their myriad uses, and finish with a slap-up meal. **See p.464**

❹ Seafood Tuck into crab claws, stewed octopus, or the classic Zanzibari fish dish with coconut milk sauce, at any of Stone Town's myriad restaurants, or on *The Rock*, perched on its very own coral islet. **See p.467 & P.489**

❺ Chumbe Island Surrounding this coral island are some of the world's finest snorkelling reefs: a perfect day-trip, and you can stay overnight too. **See p.473**

❻ Jozani Forest A soothingly cool tangle of vegetation that contains troops of endangered red colobus monkeys. **See p.476**

❼ Safari Blue A great day out from Fumba in the southwest, this excursion combines a dhow cruise, sailing in outriggers, snorkelling, and lunch on an uninhabited isle. **See p.476**

❽ Beaches Get intimate with the sweetness of doing nothing on a picture-perfect beach. Our favourites: Jambiani, Bwejuu, Matemwe and Kendwa. **See p.480, p.486, p.492 & p.497**

HIGHLIGHTS ARE MARKED ON THE MAP ON P.454

photogenic, and very much lived in, which just adds to its charm. The eastern side of the old town is bounded by Creek Road – a real creek until the British drained it – beyond which lies Ng'ambo, literally "the other side", where the majority of Zanzibar Town's inhabitants live.

Equally beguiling are several attractions within day-tripping distance, including Zanzibar's famous **spice tours**, a handful of reef-fringed **islands** for often magical

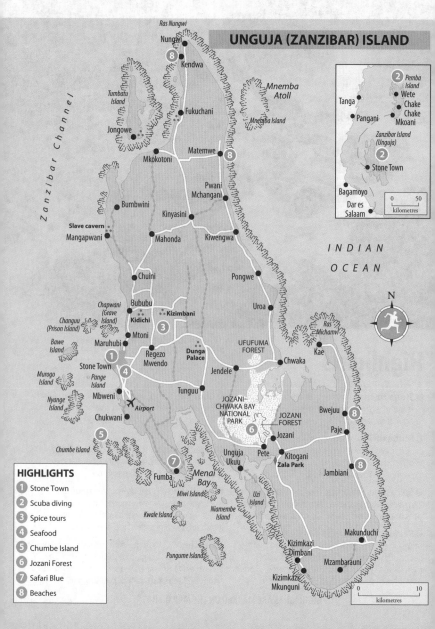

UNGUJA (ZANZIBAR) ISLAND

Ras Nungwi
Nungwi
8
Kendwa
Tumbatu Island
Fukuchani
Mnemba Atoll
Mnemba Island
Jongowe
Matemwe
8
Mkokotoni
Z a n z i b a r   C h a n n e l
Bumbwini
Pwani Mchangani
Slave cavern
Kinyasini
Kiwengwa
Mangapwani
Mahonda
Chuini
Pongwe
INDIAN
OCEAN
Chapwani (Grave Island)
Bububu
Uroa
Kizimbani
Changuu (Prison Island)
Kidichi
3
Bawe Island
Mtoni
Maruhubi
Ras Michamvi
Murogo Island
Stone Town
1
Regezo Mwendo
Dunga Palace
UFUFUMA FOREST
Kae
4
Pange Island
Chwaka
Nyange Island
Mbweni
Jendele
Airport
Tunguu
JOZANI–CHWAKA BAY NATIONAL PARK
Chukwani
JOZANI FOREST
Bwejuu
8
5
6
Paje
Chumbe Island
Unguja Ukuu
Pete
Jozani
Kitogani
Zala Park
7
Fumba
Menai Bay
Jambiani
8
Miwi Island
Uzi Island
Kwale Island
Niamembe Island
Makunduchi
Pungume Island
Kizimkazi Dimbani
Mzambarauni
Kizimkazi Mkunguni

N

Pemba Island
2
Tanga
Wete
Chake Chake
Pangani
Mkoani
Zanzibar Island (Unguja)
2
Stone Town
Bagamoyo
Dar es Salaam
0   50
kilometres

0   10
kilometres

HIGHLIGHTS

1 Stone Town
2 Scuba diving
3 Spice tours
4 Seafood
5 Chumbe Island
6 Jozani Forest
7 Safari Blue
8 Beaches

RESPONSIBLE TOURISM IN ZANZIBAR

Tourism is Tanzania's second-biggest foreign exchange earner. If well managed, it can boost local economies and even preserve cultural traditions that might otherwise be swept away. But unbridled tourism can wreak havoc on local communities and cause irreversible environmental damage.

Unfortunately, Zanzibar is a case a point. Some coastal villages there have been all but bought out by all-inclusive package **holiday resorts**. Although land prices are now in the millions of dollars, the first resorts managed to buy up vast acreages for a pittance. Cocooned within tall walls, often topped with shards of broken glass, razor wire or electrified wires, these newcomers rarely contribute much to the local economy, and some of them even import the most basic foodstuffs. Others take the lion's share of already stretched **water resources**, and the bulk of the profits rarely get anywhere close to Tanzania, as most of the big hotels are foreign-owned. We can blame the entrepreneurs, corrupt politicians and bureaucrats, but individual tourists are also responsible. Circa 1995, it was unheard of for kids in Zanzibar to demand "presents" of tourists. Now, you're as likely to be greeted with a chorus of "Give me money!" as you are the traditional "Jambo!". Zanzibar's age-old **tolerance** is also being pushed to the brink. In Stone Town, you'll see female tourists wearing little more than bikinis, which is astonishingly disrespectful given that almost all the locals are Muslim. It's perhaps no coincidence that the rise of mass-market tourism has coincided with the increased adoption of veils, and even full-on burkas. As a tourist, then, do please take your responsibilities seriously.

snorkelling, **ruined palaces** and baths, and a former Anglican mission whose **botanical garden** is a superb spot for birding.

Along the waterfront

Lining the **waterfront** is a wonderful strip of monumental yet delicate buildings through which the Busaïdi sultanate expressed its ever-burgeoning wealth and power. The approach by ferry, or any trip to the islands off Stone Town, gives you the best view. The main sights can easily be browsed in an hour, but to spend any time inside either of the museums, or bargain-hunting in the Old Fort, plan on half a day. Lastly, although you'll see kids happily leaping into the sea, the water here is polluted, dangerously so during the rains.

The Old Dispensary

Mizingani Rd • Daily 9am–5pm • Free entry

Facing the ferry terminal is the **Old Dispensary**, a grand four-storey building which, in spite of the port robbing it of its waterfront location, is one of East Africa's finest and most beautiful landmarks. Opened as a charitable health centre, its sumptuous design and decor is reminiscent of British colonial architecture in India – no coincidence, given that it was constructed by craftsmen brought in from India by the dispensary's patron, **Sir Tharia Topan**. An Ismaïli businessman, Topan's wealth accrued from multiple functions as head of customs, financial adviser to the sultan, and banker to the most infamous of slave traders, Tippu Tip. Left to fall into ruin after the 1964 Revolution, the building was restored by the Aga Khan Trust for Culture in the 1990s, and you're welcome to look around – though these days it's mostly occupied by offices.

The Palace Museum

Mizingani Rd • Daily 9am–6pm; Ramadan daily 8am–2.30pm • $5 or Tsh7000

A large, whitewashed, three-storey building facing the ocean, the **Palace Museum** (*Makumbusho ya Kasri*) occupies the former residence of Zanzibar's last sultan, Jamshid bin Abdullah. It contains some of the possessions that the Sultan and his family left behind in the wake of the 1964 Revolution, though the really valuable items were either salvaged before his escape, or otherwise vanished. The museum's main draw is a

11

STONE TOWN

Blue Mosque, Livingstone House, Bububu, Mtoni & north ▲

● TOUR COMPANIES

Eco-Culture Tours	4
Fisherman Tours & Travel	8
Mitu's Spice Tour	1
The Original Dhow Safaris	7
Sama Tours	3
Tabasam Tours & Travel	5
Zanzibar Different	6
ZanTours	2

■ ACCOMMODATION

Abuso Inn	18
Africa House Hotel	25
Beit-al-Amaan	27
Beyt al Salaam	19
Chavda Hotel	22
Dhow Palace Hotel	23
Emerson on Hurumzi	4
Emerson on Hurumzi	12
Flamingo Guest House	26
Funguni Palace Hotel	2
Hotel Kiponda	10
Jafferji House & Spa	16
Jambo Guest House	24
Karibu Inn	17
Kholle House	7
Kokoni's Hotel	9
Malindi Guest House	6
Malindi Lodge	8
Mizingani Seafront Hotel	3
Princess Salme Inn	2
Rumaisa Hotel	21
St Monica's Lodge	15
Tembo House Hotel	13
The Swahili House	5
Warere Town House	14
Zanzibar Coffee House	11
Zanzibar Palace Hotel	2
Zanzibar Serena Inn	20

● EATING

6 Degrees South	19
Amore Mio	17
Bahari Restaurant	9
Café Miwa	13
Dolphin Café	14
Emerson on Hurumzi	4
Forodhani Gardens	3
Le Spices Rendez-Vous	20
Livingstone's Beach Restaurant	8
Luis Yoghurt Parlour & Restaurant	12
Lukmaan Restaurant	16
Mercury's	2
Mistress of Spices Lounge	11
Monsoon Restaurant	5
New Radha Vegetarian Restaurant	10
Old Fort Restaurant	6
Pagoda Chinese Restaurant	18
Passing Show Hotel	1
Sambusa Two Tables	21
Stone Town Café	15
Zanzibar Coffee House	7

● DRINKING & LIVE MUSIC

6 Degrees South	7
Africa House Hotel	8
Culture Music Club	9
Dhow Countries Music Academy	4
Komba Disco	1
Livingstone's Beach Restaurant	6
Mercury's	3
Ngome Kongwe	5
Zanzibar Pub	2

● SHOPPING

Abeid Curio Shop	8
Fahani Zanzibar	3
Kwality Supermarket	9
Lookmanji Arts & Antiques	4
Memories of Zanzibar	7
MOTO & DADA Shop	5
Zanzibar Curio Shop	2
Zanzibar Gallery	6
Zenji Café & Boutique	1

FUNGUNI

MCHANGANI

MBUYUNI

DHOW HARBOUR

ZANZIBAR PORT

Fish Market

MALINDI

Police

Mnara Mosque

Bharmal Building

Khoja Charitable House

Petrol Station

Nungwi stand (northbound daladalas)

KOKONI

DARAJANI

KIPONDA

Ismaili Mosque

Old Dispensary

FERRY TERMINAL

The "Big Tree"

Old Customs House

Palace Museum

Shiva Shakti Hindu Temple

HURUMZI

House of Wonders

Ngome Kongwe (Old Fort)

FORODHANI GARDENS

MLANDEGE STREET

11

11

MICHENZANI ROUNDABOUT

Airport & Fumba

NGAMBO

VIKOKOTONI

KISIWANDUI

KARUME ROAD

Central Market

Darajani Daladala Terminus

JAMHURI GARDENS

MCHAMBAWIMA

MCHANGANI STREET

Shamshuddin Supermarket

Anglican Cathedral

MKUNAZINI

NEW MKUNAZINI ROAD

Haile Selassie School

Airport & Fumba

MNAZI MMOJA GROUNDS

THARIA STREET

Slave Market

Khalifa Hall

CREEK ROAD

Beit al-Amani

Hamamni Persian Baths

MKUNAZINI STREET

KIIFECHENI STREET

HAMAMINI STREET

SOKOMUHOGO

SOKOMUHOGO STREET

KIBOKONI

HEALTH OFFICE ROAD

Mrembo Spa

JAWS CORNER

CATHEDRAL STREET

FORODHANI

NBC

GIZENGA STREET

Shangani Post Office

Catholic Cathedral

BAGHANI

BAGHANI STREET

PYAMWEMBE STREET

VUGA ROAD

VICTORIA STREET

Victoria Hall & gardens

Milestone

VUGA

Mnazi Mmoja Hospital

KENYATTA ROAD

SHANGANI STREET

Doric Archway

High Court

TUUNDA ROAD

State House

SHANGANI

SHANGANI STREET

Tippu Tip's House

Africa House Hotel

KENYATTA ROAD

SUICHALLEY

KELELE SQUARE

Mambo Msiige

Zanzibar Serena Inn

N

0   200
metres

room dedicated to **Princess Salme** (see p.474), whose elopement in 1866 with a German merchant caused such uproar that she was ostracized by her family for the rest of her life. There are a few photos, an impressively heavy and richly embroidered costume, and ample descriptions written in Gothic script.

The ground floor covers the Sultanate's dealings with foreigners: boxed international trade treaties, and gifts from foreign powers, including paintings of the Austro–Hungarian Emperor Franz-Josef I and his wife, Elizabeth of Austria, assassinated by Anarchists in 1898. Look out for what's probably the very first **photograph** of Stone Town, a blurred daguerreotype waterfront panorama taken from the French Captain Guillain's ship in 1846 or 1847 (it's the original, too, partly devoured by bugs and fungi). On the third floor, you can check out a display of the **Sultan's furniture**: as well as predictable ebony heavyweights, there's a surprisingly proletarian five-piece suite in battered Formica, "much favoured in the Fifties", according to the caption.

Beit al-Ajaib: The House of Wonders

11

Mizingani Rd • Currently closed, but likely to be daily 9am–6pm on reopening • $5 or Tsh7000

With its colonnaded facade and imposing clock-tower, the Beit al-Ajaib – the **House of Wonders** – is Zanzibar's most distinctive landmark. The present building, housing the Zanzibar National Museum, was built as a palace in 1883. The culmination of Sultan Barghash's extravagant building spree, it was for a long time East Africa's tallest structure, and was also the first to have running water, electric light, and an electric lift (long since broken); inside, the rooms have heavy ornamental doors whose gilded Qur'anic inscriptions were ostentatious statements of the sultanate's vast wealth. The building's entrance is flanked by two **Portuguese cannons** captured by the Persians at the siege of Hormuz in 1622, which marked the beginning of the end of Portuguese hegemony over East Africa. The cannons didn't help the Portuguese, but may have worked magic in protecting the House of Wonders during the **British bombardment** of August 27, 1896, when two adjoining palaces were reduced to rubble.

In December 2012, part of the building's balcony and roof collapsed, following years of neglect, and the museum has been closed to the public ever since. As yet, no date has been given for its reopening, but when it does the following are likely to be highlights: a replica of a **sewn dhow**, a *jahazi la mtepe*, constructed in Zanzibar in 2003–4, with a display chronicling its construction, other forms of boat-building, traditional navigation, and the evolution of the monsoon-driven dhow trade; and a smashed-up 1950s **Ford Zephyr** automobile, once driven by President Karume. Other exhibits cover most aspects of **Zanzibari life, culture and history**, with good photographs and detailed information in both Kiswahili and English. Artefacts from the museum's collection that are likely to be on display include a collection of kangas; Dr David Livingstone's medicine chest; a thoughtful display on traditional Swahili music; plus exhibits on food and cooking; and a fascinating section about **traditional healing**, which includes a *pini* (charm) containing herbs and, so it is said, a dog's nose.

Ngome Kongwe (the Old Fort)

Forodhani St, facing Forodhani Gardens • Daily 9am–10pm or later • Free entry except on evenings when performances are held

Ngome Kongwe (also called the Old Fort or Omani Fort) comprises four heavy coral ragstone walls with squat cylindrical towers and castellated defences, and makes for a calm and surprisingly hustler-free place to sit for an hour or two. The fort dates back to the expulsion of the Portuguese in 1698. The victorious Omanis were quick to consolidate their gains, completing the fort just three years later. It now houses craft shops, an open-air amphitheatre (concerts are announced on a sign outside), the *Old Fort Restaurant* (see p.469), and – in the gate house – a tourist information desk (see p.464).

Forodhani Gardens

Forodhani St • open access

The formal **Forodhani Gardens** were the original site of the two cannons outside the House of Wonders, part of a battery of guns which gave their name ("*mizingani*" meaning cannons) to the shore-front road. The name "*forodhani*" – meaning a ship's cargo or a reloading place – alludes to the **slave trade**, when slaves would be landed here before being taken to the market further south in what's now Kelele Square. Despite the *papasi*, the gardens are a pleasant place to relax, but are best after sunset for the magical **street-food market** (see pp.468–469).

Shangani

A footbridge from the Forodhani Gardens leads to the Zanzibar Orphanage, under which the road tunnels to emerge in **Shangani** district. This, the westernmost point of Stone Town, was where, in the mid-nineteenth century, Seyyid Saïd gave Europeans land for building their embassies, consulates and missions. Nowadays, Shangani is where you'll find most of the **upmarket hotels**, **restaurants** and **bars**, and – of course – a good many *papasi*.

Kelele Square

Nowadays perfectly peaceful, **Kelele Square** – its name means "shouting", "noisy" or "tumultuous" – hints at a terrible past, when it was used as Zanzibar's main **slave market** until the 1860s. The first building on your right is **Mambo Msiige** (not open to visitors), which means "Inimitable Thing". The name apparently derives from the extravagance of its construction, for which thousands of eggs were used to strengthen the mortar, together with – according to legend – live slaves, who were entombed in the walls. The room at the very top, visibly not part of the original structure, is said to have been built for the explorer Henry Morton Stanley.

The **Zanzibar Serena Inn**, next door, occupies a nineteenth-century **telegraph office** that was once connected directly to Aden (Yemen) by underwater cable. The building has been overly restored and is now rather anodyne but – provided you don't look too scruffy – you can have a look around the hotel including a room on the first floor, beside the *Terrace Restaurant*, which contains old phones and relays.

Tippu Tip's House

Suicide Alley, south of Kelele Square, Shangani • It's a private home, but the residents will show tourists around, for which a tip is expected

South of Kelele Square along the bizarrely named Suicide Alley (a mystery in itself) is **Tippu Tip's House**, whose door is one of Stone Town's most elaborate – look for the dandy set of black and white steps. In the middle of the nineteenth century, mainland

---

STAYING SAFE IN STONE TOWN

Bag-snatching from tourists is reported frequently enough, but a dash of common sense is all you need: mainly, don't go wandering around with valuables you'd hate to lose. Although it doesn't feel like it, walking around the maze-like old town at night is usually perfectly safe. Where you should **be wary** at night is in areas immediately surrounding the labyrinth, especially if you're alone. On the west side, this includes Mizingani Road and the section between Kelele Square and Suicide Alley. On the east side, beware of the market area on Creek Road. Also, don't walk around Stone Town between 6pm and 8pm during **Ramadan**, when the streets clear as people descend on the mosques and then return home for dinner, leaving plenty of room for the less scrupulous to target unsuspecting tourists.

As for Stone Town's many loveable **papasi** (the Zanzibari name for hustlers, literally 'ticks'), they're a complete pain to shake off but are usually just an annoyance rather than anything more serious.

Tanzania was in considerable turmoil, with the warlike Maasai and Ngoni pushing in from the north and south respectively, and slave traders pushing from the east. Of the latter, the most successful, and infamous, was Hamed bin Muhammed al-Murjebi, better known – on account of a facial twitch – as Tippu Tip (a bird with characteristic blinking eyes). By the late 1860s, Tippu Tip was leading **slave caravans** of more than four thousand men, and over the years became king-maker among many of the chiefdoms the caravan routes passed through, including Upper Congo, of which he was the de facto ruler. The house is currently occupied by various families, evidently undaunted by the popular belief that the house is haunted by the spirits of slaves.

Vuga

South of Shangani, beyond the edge of the old town's labyrinth, is grassy **Vuga**, which was the administrative district. Walking down to the end of Kenyatta Road you reach a Doric archway, which marks the start of Vuga district: home to several "Saracenic" buildings designed by J.H. Sinclair, all of them characterized by a blend of Arabian-style Orientalism and classical (European) proportions. The sweetest of these, at the south end of Kaunda Road and Creek Road, is the **Beit al-Amani** ("House of Peace"). Originally a museum, it's currently shuttered, but even seeing it from the outside is worth the walk: a squat but elegant hexagonal construction topped by a Byzantine-style dome. It's the most Islamic of Sinclair's works, dubbed "Sinclair's mosque" by his detractors, and the "House of Ghosts" by locals, for whom the concept of a museum was a strange novelty.

Central Stone Town

Away from the waterfront, Stone Town is a spaghetti-like tangle of twisted alleyways dotted with mildew-cloaked mansions and mosques, and getting lost is unavoidable – and a pleasure. If you really get stuck, any local will help you out, or just keep walking along the busiest street – you should eventually emerge onto one of the roads bounding the old town. The **main commercial areas**, containing a clutter of shops and stalls in the manner of Arabian souks, are along and off Hurumzi and Gizenga streets, and Changa Bazaar, where you'll find dozens of antique dealers, craft shops, fabric and jewellery stores. The main streets running north to south – Sokomuhogo and Tharia/Mkunazini – are less hectic and have fewer souvenir shops, so provide a more leisurely introduction to life in the old town.

The slave market

Off New Mkunazini Rd, Mkunazini • The cells are visitable on a guided tour, which includes the Anglican Cathedral • Daily 9am–6pm • $5 or Tsh7000

The Anglican Cathedral occupies the site of Africa's last **slave market**, closed in 1873 by a reluctant Sultan Barghash under pressure from the British. Stone Town's original slave market had been at Kelele Square in Shangani, but it's here in Mkunazini, where the market shifted in the 1860s, that the appalling cruelty of the trade hits home. Next to the cathedral, in the basement of the former mission hospital (now part of *St Monica's Lodge*), are the **slave chambers**: tiny, dingy cells that each housed up to seventy-five people each. The only furnishings were a pit in the centre serving as a toilet, and a low platform around the sides. There were no windows. One of the cells is now lit by artificial light; the other has been left unlit save for two slits at one end that hardly make a dent in the gloom. You can lunch in *St Monica's Lodge* restaurant.

The Anglican Cathedral

Off New Mkunazini Rd, Mkunazini • Daily 9am–6pm • Free for worshippers, access otherwise is on the guided tour of slave market

The juxtaposition of the cells with the imposing **Anglican Cathedral Church of Christ** might appear grimly ironic but, in the spirit of Christian evangelism, replacing the inhumanity of the slave trade with the salvation of God made perfect sense. The foundation stone was laid on Christmas Day, 1873, the year the market closed, on land donated by a wealthy Indian merchant. The project was funded by the Oxford-based Universities' Mission in Central Africa, and construction proceeded under the supervision of **Bishop Edward Steere**, third Anglican bishop of Zanzibar.

The cathedral's design follows a basilican plan, blending Victorian neo-Gothic with Arabesque details. The unusual barrel-vaulted roof was completed in 1879, and the spire was added in 1890. A devastatingly poignant **sculpture** by Clara Sornas in the cathedral courtyard shows five bleak figures placed in a rectangular pit, shackled by a chain brought from Bagamoyo.

The cathedral's **interior** also abounds with reminders of slavery. A red circle in the floor beside the altar marks the position of a post to which slaves were tied and whipped to show their strength and resilience before being sold, while behind the altar is the grave of Bishop Steere. The small crucifix on a pillar beside the chancel is said to have been fashioned from a branch of the tree under which David Livingstone's heart was buried. Livingstone is also remembered in a stained-glass window, as are British sailors who died on anti-slaving patrols. The cathedral organ, imported from Ipswich in England, can be heard on Sundays.

Hamamni Persian Baths

Off Kajificheni St, Sokomuhogo • Daily 9am–6pm; ask for the caretaker across the road to let you in • $3

The contrast between the slave market's misery and the slave-financed luxuries of the Persian-style **Hamamni Persian Baths**, 250m to the west, come as something of a shock. Commissioned in the early 1870s by Sultan Barghash, the Hamamni baths (from the Arabic word for baths, *hammam*) were open to the public, with the proceeds benefiting a charitable trust (*wakf*). The baths, which are surprisingly plain, ceased functioning in the 1920s, and despite partial restoration in 1978, remain bone dry. The guided **tour** included in the entrance fee isn't up to much, but the thick walls and stone floors provide a welcome respite from the midday heat.

The Catholic Cathedral of Saint Joseph

Cathedral St, Baghani • Generally only open for Sunday Mass (at 7am, 9am & 4.30pm)

The towers of the **Catholic Cathedral of Saint Joseph** can be seen from pretty much every rooftop in Stone Town, but the cathedral isn't all that easy to locate on foot. The easiest approach is down Gizenga Street from Kenyatta Road, turning right immediately after the Gallery Bookshop. The cathedral lacks the historical significance of the Anglican Cathedral, but the Catholic Church was also committed to the anti-slavery movement, its main memorial being Bagamoyo's Freedom Village on the mainland. The cathedral's foundation stone was laid in July 1896, and the first Mass was celebrated on Christmas Day, 1898, two years before completion. The design is loosely based on the Romano–Byzantine style of Notre Dame de la Garde in Marseilles, while the interior is painted with deteriorated frescoes depicting scenes from the Old Testament.

> ### MREMBO SPA
>
> There are dozens of **health spas** scattered around Stone Town – particularly recommended is the German–Zanzibari family-run **Mrembo Spa** on Cathedral St, just west of Jaws Corner (daily 10am–6pm; ☎ 0777 430117, ⓦ mrembospa.com or ⓦ facebook.com/mrembo.spa). The spa's design, essentially a traditional home, is a delight, and staff use only natural ingredients in their scrubs and lotions. They're particularly knowledgeable, too, about the history of beauty treatments on Zanzibar, and have a shop selling Fairtrade handicrafts as well as Taarab CDs. Men are welcome, but should you want to preserve an aura of machismo, you can always talk football at the barbershop opposite while your better half gets revived.

Hurumzi House

Emerson on Hurumzi hotel, 236 Hurumzi St, Hurumzi • The hotel will let you look around when they are quiet, provided you don't look scruffy • Free • ☎ 024 223 2784, ⓦ facebook.com/emersononhurumzi

Running a short distance west–east from behind the House of Wonders is **Hurumzi Street**, a great place for rummaging around souvenir and antique shops. Near the end on the right, an unassuming sign marks the entrance to the beautifully restored and opulent **Hurumzi House**, now the *Emerson on Hurumzi* hotel (see p.465). The house was constructed by Tharia Topan, the wealthy Indian businessman who was also responsible for the Old Dispensary, and served as both the sultanate's customs house and Topan's private residence. Topan's good relations with Sultan Barghash allowed him to make it the second-highest building in Stone Town, after the House of Wonders. Its name comes from its use by the British after 1883 to buy the freedom of slaves, to ease the pain of Arab slave-owners after the abolition of slavery; "*hurumzi*" means "free men" (literally "those shown mercy"). The conversion into the present hotel has been gloriously done, and it's well worth looking around; its rooftop restaurant (see p.467) is also the best place to see the colourful tower of the **Shiva Shakti Hindu Temple** across the road.

Khoja Charitable House

Just off Dega St, Kiponda • Private housing, so ask if you want to be shown around

Northeast of Hurumzi towards Malawi Road, **Khoja Charitable House** is a treat for architecture fans. The huge carved door and door frame is a mind-bogglingly intricate

---

SCUBA DIVING OFF ZANZIBAR

Nourished by the warm South Equatorial Current, Zanzibar's fringing **reefs** abound with colourful and often heart-stopping marine life, much of it within a short boat ride of a beach. For a general introduction to diving and snorkelling, see p.67.

SNORKELLING

Snorkelling is the cheap way of getting face to face with the marvels dwelling beneath the surface, and can be arranged at most beaches, either through hotels or dive centres, or informally with fishermen. In most places you need a boat to get out to the best reefs, although much of Unguja's east coast – which is tidal – has reefs within walking or wading distance; you'll need to take care with incoming tides, however. Among East Africa's best snorkelling reefs – out of bounds to scuba divers, too – are those around **Chumbe Island** near Stone Town (see p.473). Other great reefs include **Mnemba Atoll** off Matemwe, and off **Misali Island** (see p.502) in Pemba. If you arrange things through a fisherman, you'll pay upwards of $15 for him and his *ngalawa* outrigger. He may also have snorkelling equipment; if not, the cost of renting a mask, snorkel and flippers averages $5–10 a day (or you can buy equipment in shops near Stone Town's Central Market; around $30). Going through a scuba diving company, you'll pay $25–50 per trip if hitching a ride with divers, for which you should get at least an hour on each of two reefs, and possibly lunch too.

DIVE SITES

There are good diving reefs almost everywhere around Zanzibar. The reefs **off Stone Town** are cheapest to access, and even though visibility averages a modest ten metres, there's a good range of corals and critters, and plenty of safe locations for first-timers. Experts have a couple of wrecks, including the *Great Northern*, a cable layer that foundered on the last day of 1902.

The barrier reef off Unguja's **southeast coast**, between Ras Michamvi and Jambiani, is dominated by supremely photogenic soft corals. The shallow and sheltered coral gardens inside the lagoon offer ideal conditions for beginners (and night divers). In the very south diving is a relatively new thing: best are the sea mounts inside Menai Bay, which attract all sorts of large pelagics including sailfish and dolphins.

Off Unguja's **northeast coast** is one of Zanzibar's big diving attractions: the heart-shaped **Mnemba Atoll**, which has a huge range of reefs with something for all tastes (and abilities), a

and beautiful work of art, and easily Zanzibar's fanciest. The door's inscription explains that it was founded in 1892 for use as a *musafarkhana* (a temporary rest house) for Khoja immigrants from India, most of whom arrived in the 1870s. Nowadays it serves as low-income housing, so ask if you want to take a photo.

ARRIVAL AND DEPARTURE — STONE TOWN

BY PLANE

Zanzibar International Airport Abeid Amani Karume International Airport (Zanzibar's international Airport) is 7km south of town. The exchange bureau in the arrival hall changes cash at decent rates; the closest ATM is in town. When leaving, check whether departure tax and safety levy is included in the ticket. If not (Precisionair is the main culprit), make sure you have the right amount in cash: $8 plus $1 for domestic flights, or $40 plus $8 for international.

Airport transport You can catch daladalas into town from the traffic island just beyond the airport car park, which drop you at the Darajani terminal on Creek Rd (Tsh500); going back to the airport, catch daladala #350 or #505 (both marked "U/Ndege") from Darajani. Taxis are shameless in overcharging tourists: Tsh18,000 is the "normal" tourist fare (about $10), fifty percent more than

what locals pay. Transfers organized by hotels or tour operators can be even more expensive, or free – check beforehand.

Airlines Few airlines have offices in Zanzibar, but flights can be booked online (see p.48) or through a travel agent (see p.472). The short hop from Dar costs $80; Arusha costs around $275. The airlines codes below refer to: AA (Auric Air: ☎0783 233334 in Mwanza, ⊛auricair.com); AE (Air Excel: ☎027 254 8429 in Arusha, ⊛airexcelonline.com); CA (Coastal Aviation: ☎0752 627825 in Dar, ⊛coastal.co.tz); PA (Precisionair: Muzammil Centre, Mlandege St, Stone Town ☎024 223 5126, ⊛precisionairtz.com); RA (Regional Air: ☎027 250 2541 in Arusha, ⊛regionaltanzania.com); SA (Safari AirLink: ☎0777 723274 in Dar, ⊛flysal.com); TA (Tropical Air: Creek Rd, beside Bharmal Building, Stone Town ☎024 223 2511, ⊛tropicalair.co.tz); ZA (ZanAir: off Malawi

11

---

wide variety of corals and fish life, plus reasonable odds on biggies, including turtles. If you're going to be diving exclusively at Mnemba, consider basing yourself at Matemwe, as trips from elsewhere attract surcharges of up to $60 a day.

Pemba's spectacular underwater realm – comprising almost half of Tanzania's reefs – is among the world's best diving destinations, particularly if you're experienced (the currents that make drift dives so exhilarating are also why novices might be better off learning the ropes on Unguja). The caverns, drop-offs, swim-throughs and immense coral gardens shelter a cornucopia of marine life, including an abundance of large open-water species. Other than drift dives, another highlight is **Misali Island** (see p.502), whose reefs have exceptional visibility, pristine corals, and the chance of spotting sharks, manta rays and turtles.

DIVE CENTRES

Scuba diving can only be done through a **dive centre**. The ones below are PADI-accredited and have solid safety reputations. **Costs** average $500–600 for a four- or five-day Open Water diving course (excluding accommodation); already qualified divers pay $100–120 a day for two dives, including lunch. The only centre with **Nitrox** facilities (for those with suitable experience) is Nungwi's East Africa Diving.

Fumba Blue World Diving, *Fumba Beach Lodge* ☎0777 860504, ⊛fumbabeachlodge.com.

Kendwa Scuba Do, *Sunset Bungalows* ☎0777 417157, ⊛scuba-do-zanzibar.com; Zanzibar Watersports, *Kendwa Rocks* ☎0773 235030, ⊛zanzibarwatersports.com.

Kiwengwa One Ocean, *Bluebay Beach Resort* ☎0777 414332, *Meliá Hotel* ☎0774 164816, ⊛zanzibarone ocean.com.

Matemwe One Ocean, *Matemwe Beach Village* ☎0777 473128, ⊛zanzibaroneocean.com.

Michamvi Peninsula Rising Sun Dive Centre, *Breezes Beach Club* ☎0774 440883, ⊛risingsun -zanzibar.com.

Nungwi East Africa Diving, *Jambo Bungalows* ☎0777 416425, ⊛diving-zanzibar.com; Scuba Do, *My Blue Hotel* ☎0777 15040, ⊛scuba-do-zanzibar.com.

Paje Buccaneer Diving, *Arabian Nights Hotel* ☎0777 853403, ⊛buccaneerdiving.com.

Pemba Swahili Divers, *Kervan Saray Beach*, Ras Kigomasha ☎0773 176737, ⊛swahilidivers.com.

Pwani Mchangani One Ocean, *Ocean Paradise Resort* ☎0777 453892; *Neptune Pwani Hotel* ☎0779 557087, ⊛zanzibaroneocean.com.

Stone Town One Ocean, Kenyatta Rd, just before *Livingstone's Beach Hotel* ☎024 223 8374, ⊛zanzibaroneocean.com.

Rd, behind *Passing Show Hotel*, Stone Town ☎024 223 3670, ⓦzanair.com).

Destinations Arusha (all airlines: hourly; 1hr 10min–2hr 30min); Dar (all airlines: hourly; 20–25min); Kilimanjaro (AE PA: 2 daily; 1hr 30min–2hr 30min); Kilwa (CA: 1 daily; 2hr 15min); Lake Manyara (AE: 1 daily; 4hr); Mafia (CA TA: 3 daily; 1hr 35min–1hr 50min); Ngorongoro (CA AE: 2 daily; 3hr 10min–4hr); Pangani (SA CA: 2 daily; 20min); Pemba (CA TA ZA: 4 daily; 30–40min); Ruaha National Park (CA: 3 daily; 1hr 50min–3hr); Saadani (CA SA ZA: 3 daily; 15min); Serengeti (AE CA: 2–3 daily; 3hr–4hr 10min); Tanga (AA CA: 3 daily; 1hr 5min); Tarangire (CA: 1 daily; 4hr 20min).

BY FERRY

The port Stone Town is accessed by ferries from Dar (5–9 daily; 2–5hr) and Pemba (at least 2 weekly; 6hr), which arrive at the port at the north end of town. Tourists are expected to clear immigration inside the port, a farcical procedure given that Zanzibar is part of Tanzania, but one that local officials take seriously. Your Tanzanian visa is also valid for Zanzibar. A valid yellow fever certificate will almost certainly be demanded, irrespective of where you have come from (see p.56). Taxis from the harbour entrance

shouldn't charge more than Tsh8000 for a ride around town. If walking, stick to one of the main roads flanking Stone Town before diving into the maze.

Tickets Tickets for most ferries can be bought inside the port; buy in advance to be sure of a seat, and to minimize hassle from *papasi*. The offices are open until 6pm, but tickets for night ferries can be bought until departure time. If you're being trailed by a *papasi*, ensure it's you and not him who does the talking when buying. Alternatively, buy your ticket from one of the offices outside the port on Mizingani and Malawi roads. If you're heading to Pemba, ask about the ticket options as soon as you can: Azam Marine currently sails there twice-weekly (Wed & Sat at 9am), but schedules for Pemba are historically extremely fluid.

Fares Tourist fares ("non-residents") are priced in dollars and include $5 port tax; you can pay the shilling equivalent, but exchange rates are poor. Don't try to get the cheaper "resident" fares, or you'll run into trouble with the ticket inspector. The best kept vessels, run by Azam Marine (also called Kilimanjaro Ferries or Coastal Fast Ferries; ☎024 2231655, ⓦazammarine.com), are not that much more expensive than the others ($35 to/from Dar or Pemba, as opposed to $30, including harbour tax).

INFORMATION

Tourist information There's no official tourist information centre, but there is an unofficial help desk in the gatehouse of the Old Fort (daily 9am–5pm), which has a few brochures. Printed practical information is

limited to the free *Swahili Coast* (also at ⓦswahilicoast .com), a glossy listings booklet with good articles and tide tables; pick it up at hotels, restaurants or tour operators.

GETTING AROUND

On foot The best way of exploring Stone Town is on foot. Distances are short, and in any case most of the streets are too narrow for cars.

By daladala Useful daladala routes are noted throughout this chapter, with most rides costing Tsh2000–3000. The main place to catch them in Stone Town is Darajani terminal, being two places on Creek Road: opposite the Central Market for vehicles heading south and east, and just north of the market for vehicles heading north. The other terminals, out of town but accessible by daladala from Darajani, are Mwembe Ladu, 2km east along Gulioni Road, and Mwana Kwerekwe, 5km southeast.

By minibus The easy way to reach Paje, Jambiani, Bwejuu,

Nungwi or Kendwa from Stone Town is on a beach transfer minibus for tourists, which will deposit you directly outside your chosen hotel. Most tour operators and all budget hotels in Stone Town can fix you up with a seat. The fare is negotiable, but never less than the $10.

By car or motorbike Car or motorbike rental (roughly $30/day and $40–70/day respectively) can be organized through tour operators and hotels, which will also arrange a temporary $10 permit from the police. Alternatively, the following rental companies are reliable: Kibabu Cars (☎0772 755788 or ☎0689 500020, ⓦkibabucars.com) and Zanzibar Car Hire, Kenyatta Rd, Shangani (☎024 223 5485, ⓦzanzibarcarhire.com). Any hotel should be able to rent you a bicycle for $10/day.

TOURS

Eco+Culture Tours Hurumzi St ☎024 223 3731, ⓦecoculture-zanzibar.org. A good range of options, often with a cultural spin. Their spice tour is particularly good, as is their unique tour of Unguja Ukuu and Menai Bay in the south ($45–80 per person). Mon–Sat 8am–5pm.

Fisherman Tours & Travel Vuga St ☎024 223 8790, ⓦfishermantours.com. Long established and efficient,

offering full-day cultural tours of Nungwi or Mangapwani in addition to the usual excursions. Mon–Sat 8am–5pm.

Mitu's Spice Tour Funguni Rd, Malindi ✉mituspicetour@yahoo.com, ⓦmituspicetourzanzibar .blogspot.com. Self-proclaimed inventor of spice tours, Mitu's is also the cheapest operator for spice tours ($15 per person on a shared tour, including lunch, and swimming at

Mangapwani) as well as for other standard trips, such as Jozani Forest ($25 per person), Prison Island ($20 per person) and city tours ($10). Mon–Sat 8am–5pm.

The Original Dhow Safaris Mbweni, but bookable at the *Zanzibar Serena Inn* ☎ 0772 007090, ⊛ dhowsafaris .net. Dhow cruises on one of three specially designed *jahazis*: trips include Changuu Island, snorkelling, and picnic lunch on a sandbank (daily 9.30am–4.30pm; $90 per person), and a two-hour sunset cruise (4.30–6.30pm; $50 per person), with drinks taken to the sound of live Taarab. Mon–Sat 8am–5pm.

Sama Tours Gizenga St ☎ 024 223 3543 or ☎ 0777 430385, ⊛ samatours.com. Knowledgeable, unhurried, and one of few operators whose quoted prices include meals and entrance fees. Their unique offering is a six-hour

cultural tour of Vijijini suburb south of Stone Town ($35–50 per person). Mon–Sat 8am–5pm.

Tabasam Tours & Travel Old Dispensary, first floor, room 13 ☎ 024 223 0322, ⊛ tabasamzanzibar.com. A well-connected, calm and professional travel agent, whose reliability is worth the slight premium. Staff can arrange more complicated trips further afield, including Pemba for scuba diving. Mon–Sat 8am–5pm.

Zanzibar Different Mrembo Spa, Cathedral St ☎ 0777 430117 or ☎ 024 223 0004, ⊛ zanzibardifferent.com. Pioneers of the Princess Salme Spice Tour (see p.474), this company runs plenty of themed tours, including architecture, art, music workshops, tours for children (painting, music), and the preparation of traditional beauty products. All can be tailored to your preferences. Mon–Sat 8am–5pm.

ACCOMMODATION

There's plenty of accommodation in and around Stone Town, but, as throughout Zanzibar, it's almost impossible to find a free double room for under $40 in high season. At all times hotels can be extremely damp and stuffy, so go for rooms as high as possible to catch a breeze, or for ones with balconies. Almost all hotels have wi-fi, even the cheapest.

CENTRAL AND NORTHERN STONE TOWN

The heart of Stone Town, especially Hurumzi, Kiponda and Kokoni districts, is the most picturesque part of the city, and the easiest area to get lost in. Most of the hotels here are at least five minutes from the nearest drivable road, but can be accessed by motorbike.

★ **Emerson on Hurumzi** Hurumzi St, Hurumzi ☎ 024 223 2784, ⊛ facebook.com/emersononhurumzi. Set in Tharia Topan's magnificent Hurumzi House (see p.462), this is East Africa's most atmospheric hotel. Each of the sixteen rooms (accessed by steep staircases) has its own quirks, from the "Ballroom", dominated by a giant chandelier, and the "North" and "South" rooms with open-air bathtubs shielded from the street by wooden latticework screens, to the "Keep", "Pavilion" and "Tour" suites, which have open-sided, turret-top gazebos fitted with day beds. Most rooms have unobtrusive a/c and fans. Restaurant on top. Closed mid-April to end-May. BB **$190**

★ **Hotel Kiponda** Nyumba ya Moto St, Kiponda ☎ 024 223 3052, ⊛ kiponda.com. Quiet and comfortable, with fifteen rooms, including singles and triples. The walls are thick, so the interior stays cool. Rooms vary greatly in size and price (the priciest cost double the cheaper ones); most have box nets, some have a/c, and all have ceiling fans. On top is a rooftop café and bar. BB **$40**

★ **Kholle House** Off Mizingani Rd, behind the Old Dispensary, Kiponi ☎ 0772 161033, ⊛ khollehouse .com. This is just what a boutique hotel should be – achingly elegant, and not at all pretentious. Built as a palace in 1860 for Princess Kholle, it's been beautifully restored to house ten uniquely designed rooms, most with terraces, including some spectacular suites with fantastic views from their balconies ($220). There are

polished floors throughout, plus plenty of Arabian styling, exposed mangrove pole rafters, carved woodwork, and tasteful antiques. All the rooms have a/c and fans, and there's a lovely swimming pool, too, and a rooftop tea house. BB **$130**

Kokoni's Hotel Kokoni ☎ 024 223 0239, ⊜ kokonishotel@hotmail.com. This lovely four-storey mansion towers over one side of a sweet little square. Its rooms have high ceilings; most contain nothing more than beds and box nets, but a handful have TVs, and two have bathrooms. BB **$30**

Mizingani Seafront Hotel Mizingani Rd, close to Big Tree, Kiponda ☎ 024 223 5396, ⊛ mizinganiseafront .com. Fronted by a quartet of cannons, this classic four-storey building (with lift access) is a beauty, with a wonderfully intricate facade made of wood and stained glass, which provides some of the rooms with balconies. All the rooms are large and surprisingly light and airy, and furnished with four-poster beds plus a scatter of antiques or reproductions. There's also a/c, and a small swimming pool in a courtyard. BB **$115**, suite with sea view **$156**

★ **St Monica's Lodge** Off New Mkunazini Rd by the Anglican Cathedral, Mkunazini ☎ 024 223 0773, ⊛ zanzibarhostel.com. Run by the Anglican Church, this hostel has recently been renovated, though lingering ghosts remain: one of the two buildings sits astride the former slave market's cells. En-suite rooms ($15 extra) have a/c; others have fans, and some share wooden verandas. Plain but with a good restaurant (daily 1–3pm). No alcohol or smoking. BB **$35**

The Swahili House South of Kiponda St, Mchambawima ☎ 0778 919525, ⊛ theswahilihouse .com. A five-storey building with 22 swanky rooms around

11

an internal courtyard; some have exterior balconies, others fancy stand-alone bathtubs, but the main attraction is the rooftop restaurant and bar, complete with jacuzzi. Wi-fi in reception only. BB $170

★**Zanzibar Coffee House** Tharia St, Mchambawima ☏024 223 9319, 🌐riftvalley-zanzibar.com. In a building dating from 1885, this guesthouse has just eight rooms above a café (see p.468), each with its own character, all with a/c, and very good value for money. The cheapest have external (but private) bathrooms. The staff are great, and the rooftop's a delight: there's also a cosy lounge with a wrap-around balcony. Closed May. BB $95

★**Zanzibar Palace Hotel** Off Nyumba ya Moto St, Kiponda ☏024 223 2230 or ☏0773 079222, 🌐zanzibarpalacehotel.com. A magnificently renovated four-storey townhouse heavy on spangly fabrics, gilded furniture, fancy mirror frames and Persian rugs. Splash out on a "deluxe" room or, even better, a (gigantic) suite – they are all different, all plush, all charming, and all with a/c, fans, and TVs. Some have balconies, others massive bathtubs in the middle of the room, and one of the suites has a private roof terrace with sun loungers and views. Also has a fine restaurant and bar downstairs. BB $225

WESTERN STONE TOWN

The west end of Stone Town, comprising the districts of Shangani, Baghani and Forodhani, has plenty of restaurants, souvenir shops and internet cafés, and is where the bulk of Stone Town's more opulent palaces and mansions are located, many of them now hotels. Most are on or just off one of three main thoroughfares – Shangani St, Forodhani St and Kenyatta Rd – so are easy to find.

Abuso Inn Above Wings restaurant, off Shangani St, Shangani ☏024 223 5886, 🌐facebook.com/pages /Abuso-Inn/281407878587933. Unassuming, homely and calm. Unusually for Stone Town, the rooms are mostly large and well ventilated, and many catch the evening sun. The beds are big, and all rooms have a/c, fans and box nets. Buffet breakfast on the roof. BB $80

Africa House Hotel Suicide Alley, Shangani ☏024 223 3127, 🌐africahousehotel.co.tz. A grand old grand colonial pile, once the English Club, housing fourteen elegant rooms with a/c and cable TV, including some with full-on sea views. The decor makes ample use of antiques, Persian carpets, old photographs, gilded mirrors, and golden tassels and brocades. Facilities include two restaurants, and the famous *Sunset Bar*. BB $170, sea views $190

Beyt al Salaam Kelele Square, Shangani ☏0774 444111, 🌐beytalsalaam.com. Occupying a gorgeous three-storey nineteenth-century building, this has just ten wooden-floored rooms, stylishly decked out in draperies and comfy antiques, with the more expensive "Sultan" rooms having bathtubs in their bedrooms ($75 extra). All

have a/c, and the two on top have sea views over Kelele Square. Closed May. BB $225

Chavda Hotel Baghani St, Baghani ☏0777 878900, 🌐chavdahotel.co.tz. Several conjoined former mansions enclosing an airy courtyard, all adorned with imported Indian fittings, reproduction furniture and China vases. The sixteen rooms, on three floors, come with all mod cons. The more expensive twin-bed rooms ($130) have balconies, and there's a good rooftop restaurant. BB $120

Dhow Palace Hotel Kenyatta Rd, Shangani ☏024 223 3012, 🌐dhowpalace-hotel.com. A beautiful and tranquil 1870s mansion, preserving much of its Arabian flair. Service is smart and efficient, and the 28 spacious rooms are good value, featuring a/c, cable TV, box nets, a smattering of antiques, and blue-tiled sunken baths. Some have balconies; on the inside, these open on the swimming pool. There's also an attractive rooftop restaurant. Closed April & May. BB $120

Jafferji House & Spa Gizenga St, Forodhani ☏0777 589518, 🌐jafferjihouse.net. An elegant blend of Zanzibari, Arabian and Moroccan styles, with ten suites stuffed with antiques collected by renowned Zanzibari photographer Javed Jafferji; you'll find his photos scattered about, too. Each room has its own style and colour scheme, including some wonderfully earthy reds. Along with the antiques are modern touches like throw cushions and, unobtrusively positioned, flat screen TVs. The restaurant downstairs is the *Mistress of Spices Lounge* (see p.469). No smoking except in the courtyard. BB from $200

Karibu Inn Off Forodhani St, Forodhani ☏024 223 3058, ✉karibuinnhotel@yahoo.com. Partly renovated but still rather shabby, this guesthouse is friendly and – compared with the rest of Zanzibar – something of a bargain. The en-suite rooms are scattered over four half-storeys, some on the ground floor, and can be stuffy when the weather's sultry. There are also three dorms (BB $15 per person), each with a/c (not always functional) and bathroom. BB $40

Tembo House Hotel Shangani St, Shangani ☏024 223 3005, 🌐tembohotel.com. Built as the American Embassy in the 1830s, this is now a busy package-tour hotel, thankfully not overshadowed by its uninspiring modern wing. Although it's not as stylish as other sea-front options, and has variable standards, the beachfront location and swimming pool are undeniable draws. Choose a room with an ocean view ($140) or, better still, a sea-facing balcony. Sunbathers have a rooftop terrace. The hotel's *Bahari Restaurant* is right by the beach (see p.468): it doesn't serve alcohol, but the neighbouring *Livingstone's Beach Restaurant* and bar (see p.470) does. BB $130

Zanzibar Serena Inn Kelele Square, Shangani ☏024 223 3587, 🌐serenahotels.com. In common with other properties in the Aga Khan's *Serena* chain, service here is faultless, standards solidly five-star, and the rooms – all sea-facing – come with all mod cons. There are several bars and restaurants, and a large shoreline swimming pool. BB $590

SOUTHERN STONE TOWN AND VUGA

The southern part of the old town contains a number of budget hotels that are easily reached from Vuga Road. Vuga is the broad, leafy district which spreads south of the old town, so the handful of hotels here should benefit from better ventilation.

★**Beit-al-Amaan** Victoria St, Vuga ☎0777 414364, ✉beit2000@hotmail.com. This "House of Peace" occupies a two-storey townhouse, and is the business for comfort and (authentic) Zanzibari style. The six large rooms and its common areas are decorated with colourful Swahili artwork, seashells, Persian carpets and all sorts of antiques. All but the huge downstairs room have private bathrooms, and there's a kitchen on top. BB $95

Flamingo Guest House Mkunazini St, Kibokoni ☎024 223 2850. Cheapest of Stone Town's guesthouses, and not at all bad so long as the drains aren't blocked. All six rooms have box nets and fans: the en suites cost $10 extra. BB $20

Jambo Guest House Off Mkunazini St, Sokomuhogo ☎024 223 3779 or ☎0777 496571, ✉info@jamboguest .com. Ever-popular with backpackers, this guesthouse has friendly staff and a shady garden restaurant opposite. The eight rooms, six with a/c, are large and clean if bare, and share bathrooms (there's hot water). BB $40

MALINDI AND FUNGUNI

Just north of the old town, Malindi district is not the most atmospheric of areas, but it's well placed if you're arriving by ferry, though you should ask someone to escort you back to your hotel at night. The southern boundary of the area is marked by Malawi Road, which is good for cheap eats.

Funguni Palace Hotel Funguni Rd, off the top of Mizingani Rd ☎0777 411842, ⓦfungunipalace.com.

This is clean no-frills place has thirteen en-suite rooms, simply furnished with *semadari* beds, box nets, a/c and cable TV, and there's also a roof-top restaurant. Free airport transfer. BB $50

Malindi Guest House Funguni Rd, off the top of Mizingani Rd ☎0777 458584 or ☎024 223 0165, ⓦmalindiguesthouse.com. Wonderful decor throughout, including an old piano: the rooms are well kept with nets and fans, and most have bathrooms, though some of the beds are a bit short. The rooftop restaurant has varying standards. BB $75

Malindi Lodge Malawi Rd ☎0777 952007. Best avoided in the rains when it gets invaded by mosquitoes, this is a good budget choice at other times. The welcome is friendly, and the rooms are ragged but adequate with aging a/c units. The best rooms are at the corner and have street views and breezes. Rates are negotiable. BB $35, en suite $40

Princess Salme Inn Just off Mizingani Rd ☎0777 435303, ⓦprincesssalmeinn.com. The friendliest accommodation in this area, with twelve clean rooms: the en-suite ones cost $67, and there are good showers throughout. The second-floor rooms, arranged around a sunny courtyard, are the best, if a little cramped. In really hot weather you'll appreciate one of the rooms with a/c. BB $45

Rumaisa Hotel Bwawani Rd, Funguni ☎024 223 9024 or ☎0777 410695, ⓦrumaisahotel.blogspot.com. Away from the action, this small hotel has seven decent en-suite rooms, all with balconies, a/c, fan TV and wi-fi. It also boasts Zanzibar's only 3D HD digital cinema. BB $55

Warere Town House Off Mizingani Rd ☎024 223 3835, ⓦwarere.com. A simple, decent and welcoming option, with ten smallish en-suite rooms on three floors, all with *semadari* beds, a/c and cable TV. The best are the ones with balconies at the front ($70); for the others, you'll definitely need the a/c (check it works and isn't too noisy), as they can otherwise be very stuffy. Breakfast is taken on the roof. They Staff organize affordable excursions. BB $55

EATING

Stone Town is Tanzania's culinary apotheosis, offering an embarrassment of choice when it comes to eating out, from the famous nightly food market in the Forodhani Gardens to dozens of sophisticated or romantic establishments, including several right by the shore, and others on rooftops in the old town. Most menus feature **Zanzibari cuisine**, a subtle combination of the island's spices and coconuts with all manner of seafood. Those with more conservative tastes can choose from pasta, pizza, Indian and Chinese, or even burgers and chips. Eating out during **Ramadan** can be expensive, as restaurants not attached to hotels are banned from opening during the day. There are some exceptions, but most restaurants are covered with cloth screens during Ramadan, lending a furtive aspect to dining.

CENTRAL AND NORTHERN STONE TOWN

Emerson on Hurumzi 236 Hurumzi St, Hurumzi ☎024 223 2784. Stone Town's original rooftop restaurant, and still one of the more enticing venues, with giant pillows, Persian rugs, inspirational views, and a great atmosphere on Sat, when you can hear live Taarab. A three-course meal

costs Tsh40,000, excluding drinks. Reservations recommended. Closed mid-April to end-May. Sundowners from 6pm, dinner 7–11pm.

★**Lukmaan Restaurant** New Mkunazini Rd, Mkunazani ⓦlukmaan.blogspot.com. A great restaurant for affordable, tasty and authentic Zanzibari cuisine, as a

11

STREET FOOD

As well as at the Forodhani Gardens (see p.459 & below), **street food** can be found around the market on Creek Road, at the daladala stand opposite, and along Malawi Road at night. All these places have coffee sellers in the morning, but the best place for a **traditional coffee** is a *baraza* in the old town, where the beans are roasted, ground and brewed on the stone benches (*barazas*) that line the streets – a tiny cup of piping Arabica costs a negligible Tsh100. You can also try the **spiced tea** called *zamzam*, named after a sacred well in Mecca, accompanied by a diamond-shaped chunk of **kashata** – sugared cashews, peanuts or coconut. One of the liveliest *barazas* is *Jaws Corner*, at the corner of Sokomuhogo and Baghani streets. Its name derives from the film once shown on its TV.

result of which it's always packed with locals. A wide selection of dishes is prepared daily and presented in heated vats (a generous plateful costs around Tsh5000): point out what you fancy, pay at the counter, and you're away. Try the *pilau* or the octopus curry, both fabulous. They also have snacks. Closed Ramadan daytime. Daily 7am–9pm.

★**Mercury's** North end of Mizingani Rd near the Big Tree, Kiponda ☎024 223 3076. Named after Zanzibar's most famous son, the rock star Freddie Mercury, this stylish yet informal bar and restaurant has a beautiful oceanside setting, especially striking at sunset (there are plenty of tables on wooden decking over the beach). The fun menu includes both classic Zanzibari dishes and international favourites, with plenty of fresh salads and pasta, consistently excellent thin-crust pizzas, and subtly seasoned seafood. Desserts are hearty: chocolate cake, mango crumble or sticky almond *halua* goo, and you can finish with a *shisha* pipe. There's live music Fri–Sun (see p.470). Closed during Ramadan. Daily 10am–10pm.

★**Zanzibar Coffee House** Tharia St, Mchambawima ☎024 223 9319, ⍟riftvalley-zanzibar.com. Owned by the Utengule Coffee Estate near Mbeya, this relaxed and relaxing café is sophisticated without being suffocating, and serves excellent Arabica, some of which is roasted round the back. You can also try a cup of Zanzibar's very own Liberica strain. Accompanying the coffee are all manner of treats, savoury or sweet, all very reasonably priced at around Tsh4500. Decamp to the rooftop for views over town. Closed May. Daily 8–6pm.

WESTERN STONE TOWN

6 Degrees South Shangani St, one block north of *Africa House Hotel*, Shangani ☎0779 666050, ⍟facebook.com/6DegreesSouthZanzibar. A popular upmarket grill house and bar, even a tad pretentious (check out the mock-neoclassical facade), with three dining areas, including on the roof, all with sea views. It serves a good selection of Zanzibari dishes, including *urojo*, a lime and tumeric soup accompanying goat meat *mishkaki* (Tsh12,500), and the classic fish in coconut sauce (Tsh16,000). International dishes are a deal more expensive, starting at Tsh20,000 for a burger, and up to

Tsh40,000 for something more fancy. There's also a café with snacks and fresh pastries. Daily 8am–11pm.

Amore Mio Shangani St, Shangani ☎0776 211071, ⍟facebook.com/amoremio.zanzibar. Right by the ocean under a billowing awning, the sea view is the main reason for dining here, but the food too can be excellent: full meals cost up to Tsh20,000, including pasta, pizza and a wicked aubergine lasagne (*Malanzane alla Parmigiana*). The snacks are good, too, with real coffee, milk shakes, decent ice cream, fresh pastries (the doughnuts are a delight), juices and salads. Closed in May. Daily 10am–10pm.

Bahari Restaurant Tembo House Hotel, Shangani, Shangani ☎024 223 3005, ⍟tembohotel.com. The menu flirts briefly with most styles, and is one of few to feature a proper Tanzanian breakfast ($12 buffet, complete with cassava leaf porridge), but the best thing about it is the location – there's a lovely row of tables right beside the beach beneath Indian almond trees. If you're lucky you might be able to use the hotel swimming pool, too. No alcohol. Closed Ramadan daytimes. Daily 6.30am–10pm.

Café Miwa First floor, Shangani Post Office, Kenyatta Rd, Shangani ☎0778 933144, ⍟cafemiwa.com. Perfectly located for the passing tourist trade, this place, above the old post office (and with a streetview terrace), serves some of the island's best coffee. Dishes include burgers, wraps, fresh salads and inventive sandwiches, as well as cakes, smoothies, shakes and juice blends. There's also reliable wi-fi. Daily 10am–10pm.

Dolphin Café Kenyatta Rd, Shangani ☎024 223 9096, ⍟facebook.com/dolphincafezanzibar. An attractive place with exposed roof rafters that serves up consistently good snacks such as *sharwarma* and samosas, plus pizzas and even sushi, plus a lunchtime Swahili buffet (Tsh15,000). Also has fresh juices, smoothies and ice cream, and plenty of flavours for shisha pipes. Fast wi-fi. No alcohol. Closed Ramadan daytimes. Daily 8am–midnight.

★**Forodhani Gardens** Forodhani St. Stone Town's most atmospheric venue is the waterfront Forodhani Gardens – by day, you can settle down at several cafés, while after 5pm or so, the stalls of its famous open-air street food market combine a magical twilight atmosphere with a variety and quality of seafood to put many a five-star hotel to shame (including crab claws, grilled shrimp skewers, and octopus). That said, in low season, do check seafood before ordering, as it's not always fresh. Don't miss out the sugar cane juice, either – freshly pressed through wailing mangles. Snacks average Tsh2000–4000; Tsh10,000 should leave you well and truly stuffed, though you will have to bargain to avoid getting ripped off. Daily 7am–9pm.

★**Livingstone's Beach Restaurant** North end of Kenyatta Rd, Shangani ☏0779 548730, ⓦfacebook .com/pages/Livingstones-Beach-Restaurant/ 108047199259693. Right on the beach, this occupies the former British Consulate, where David Livingstone's body was laid out in 1874 before being transported to London. While primarily an upmarket bar, it also serves very good international food (Tsh20,000–30,000 for most main courses) – the prawns are particularly good. Also has proper coffee, and tables right on the beach (lit by candles at night). Daily 10am–2am.

Luis Yoghurt Parlour & Restaurant Gizenga St, beside Gallery Bookshop, Baghani ☏0765 759579. A quiet little place run by a friendly Goan woman with the kitchen equivalent of green fingers (try the octopus). Good for vegetarians, too, with the *thali* featuring several types of lentils and curried beans (Tsh12,000). Mon–Sat 10am–3pm & 6–9pm.

Mistress of Spices Lounge Jafferji House & Spa, Gizenga St, Forodhani ⓦ0774 078441, ⓦjafferjihouse .net. The enchanting decor of the ground floor dining room delves straight into the nineteenth century – it's not too pretentious and is one of the few Stone Town restaurants where eating inside is more atmospheric than outdoors. The rooftop is good too, though, with lots of carved wood, and the House of Wonders framing the sea view. The menu is strong on Swahili flavours and spices, and it's a place to savour the subtleties of coconut sauce with seafood or meat. Full meals costs around $20, excluding drinks. Staff also run cooking classes. No alcohol. Daily 7am–9pm.

★**Monsoon Restaurant** Forodhani Gardens ☏0777 410410, ⓦmonsoon-zanzibar.com. Top of the range in everything but price, this is one of Zanzibar's most romantic restaurants, whether you eat outside (not during Ramadan) under a canopy of palm trees and bougainvillea, or inside, on cushions or woven rugs in a pillared dining room. The Oriental charm is especially pervasive on Wed and Fri (7–10pm), when the delightful Matona Group explore the rhythmic and melodic synergies of Africa, Asia and Arabia; there's more earthy traditional *ngoma* on Sat. The inspired menu makes good use of fruits and spices (passion fruit with shellfish), and there are good vegetarian options such as stuffed aubergine. All main courses (Tsh12,000–24,000) are accompanied by side dishes you won't find elsewhere, such as pumpkin cooked in creamy

coconut. To finish, ice cream, anything with dates, or sticky *halua* should do the trick. Good wine list, and good snacks throughout the day, as well as drinks. Reservations advisable. Daily 11am–10pm (drinks until midnight).

New Radha Vegetarian Restaurant Off Forodhani St beside Karibu Inn, Forodhani ☏024 223 4808. Forget about the rather grotty setting and concentrate on the food: excellent Indian vegetarian cuisine, from the blow-out all you can eat *thali* (Tsh10,000), through cauliflower *tikka masala* (most mains, including rice and chapatti, cost under Tsh12,000) to snacks such as samosas, spring rolls, lentil or chickpea cakes, and perfumed sweets. Closed during Ramadan. Mon–Sat 8am–9.30pm.

Old Fort Restaurant Ngome Kongwe (Old Fort), Forodhani St ☏0777 878737 or ☏0777 416736. A relaxed place for lunch, with outdoor tables beside the amphitheatre. It tends to change tenants – and menus – every couple of years, but for now, it serves up a good if slightly pricey selection of Asian–Swahili fusion cuisine. Try the barracuda "*coco poa*" in coconut masala, or red snapper in green curry (both Tsh15,000). Also has snacks, milkshakes, coffee, booze, and a pool table. Closed Ramadan daytimes. Daily 8am–8pm.

Pagoda Chinese Restaurant Suicide Alley, facing Africa House Hotel, Shangani ☏024 223 4688. This has been around for ages, and offers the usual wide selection. Cheap by local standards (under Tsh15,000 for most mains, and even the duck costs less than Tsh20,000), with a good lunchtime special for Tsh9000. No pork. Daily 11.30am–2.30pm & 6–11pm.

★**Stone Town Café** Kenyatta Rd, Baghani ⓦstonetowncafe.com. A great place for a light meal or snack, or even an all-day breakfast, albeit of the healthy variety. Except for salads, it's well priced, and the menu includes divine cakes, real coffee (cappuccino, espresso or cardamom-laced), falafel, grilled kingfish with olive tapenade or fillet steak with anchovy garlic, both of these costing a very reasonable Tsh12,000. To finish, how about sticky date pudding? No alcohol. Closed Ramadan daytimes. Daily 8am–10pm.

SOUTHERN STONE TOWN AND VUGA

Le Spices Rendez-Vous Kenyatta Rd, Vuga ☏0777 410707. With an attractive terracotta-tiled interior, this is justly famed for its superb (and generously portioned) north Indian cuisine; main courses from Tsh15,000. Good for vegetarians too. Closed for a month after Easter. Tues–Sun 11.30am–3pm & 6.30–11pm.

★**Sambusa Two Tables** Victoria St, just off Kaunda Rd, Vuga ☏0777 088409. An unusual place, situated on the first-floor veranda of a private home, complete with pillows and rugs to lounge on. The food just keeps on coming (samosas, fishcakes, marinated aubergine and superb octopus), and costs $15 for the lot. No alcohol.

11

Reservations advisable. Closed Ramadan daytimes. Daily noon–2pm & 6–8pm.

MALINDI

★**Passing Show Hotel** Malawi Rd, Malindi. A typical Tanzanian restaurant, with linoleum-topped tables, metal-legged furniture and TV in the corner, but the crowd of diners that make it so difficult to find a table at lunchtime provides a clue about the excellent, cheap and generously portioned food. The *pilau*, *biriani* and stews are outstanding, including fish or cashew nuts in coconut sauce, and few dishes cost over Tsh5000. It's best for lunch when there's more choice, and for breakfast. No alcohol. Closed during Ramadan. Daily 7am–9pm.

DRINKING, NIGHTLIFE AND ENTERTAINMENT

Tourism has brought with it an ever-growing number of bars and nightclubs, which sit somewhat uncomfortably in this Muslim town – part of the reason why police have the whimsical habit of bringing an abrupt end to proceedings after midnight (should this happen, be polite and just go home). As for entertainment, ignoring tourist-oriented bands performing medleys of old pop, love songs and reggae, Stone Town's live-music scene is a modest affair, the big exceptions being its annual festivals (see below).

BARS

6 Degrees South Shangani St, one block north of Africa House Hotel, Shangani ☎0779 666050, ⓦfacebook.com/6DegreesSouthZanzibar. Currently the in-spot among tourists and wealthier locals, this grill, wine and sports bar has three sea-view terraces, good food and a huge range of drinks, including wines (from Tsh33,000 a bottle). The main party nights, up on the roof, are Fri and Sat (from 6pm, Tsh10,000 admission after 9.30pm), but you might find DJs on other nights too (for which entry is usually Tsh5000 after 10pm). Sun afternoon is brunch, with live Taarab. Also has shisha pipes. Daily 10am–1pm.

Africa House Hotel Suicide Alley, Shangani. Ever since colonial times, this has been the favoured haunt of expats, tourists and mainlanders, drawn to the first-floor *Sunset Bar* terrace, now under a voluptuous draped awning, to watch the sun set behind the ocean. Just as inspiring is the Persian-style interior, where you lounge around on embroidered cushions and rugs amid a scatter of samovars and low carved tables. There's also a good snack menu and all-day breakfast, while darts, a pool table and *shisha* pipes are available. Friday evenings feature a cheesy but cheery band playing tourist favourites (including the execrable "Jambo Bwana"). Daily 10am–10pm.

Komba Disco Bwawani Hotel, Funguni. Adjacent to the clunky 1970s monolith is Zanzibar's main disco, ever popular, and currently featuring only the sassiest, most saccharine Bongo Flava, with nary a *mzungu* in sight. No smoking. Closed during Ramadan. Fri & Sat from 8pm.

★**Livingstone's Beach Restaurant** North end of Kenyatta Rd. A nicely laid-back and very well-stocked bar and restaurant (see p.469) popular with tourists and expats. It's an especially lovely afternoon refuge, whose main draw is its decked seafront terrace (great sunsets, but you can't eat or drink there during Ramadan), partly shaded by Indian almond trees and palms. Also has tables on the beach itself, and good musical taste. Free wi-fi. Daily until midnight or later.

★**Mercury's** Mizingani Rd. This beachside venue is the place for sunsets, and can be packed whenever there's live music (see below). The bar is very well stocked, with a ton of unique cocktails (try the "Zanzibarbarian" for a scent of cloves, or "Obama's Dawa", a take on the Brazilian *caipirinha*). Good coffee, and *shisha* pipes. Especially recommended for live music on Fri and Sun after 7pm, often *taarab* or *kidumbak*, though Saturday's musical menu is a sop to tourists. Closed during Ramadan. Daily 10am–10pm, often closing much later.

Zanzibar Pub The Old Dispensary, Mizingani Rd. On the second floor of Tharia Topan's most exquisite architectural creation is a dinky little bar and restaurant, with local prices, mostly local clientele, and partial sea views from over the customs sheds in front. Daily, supposedly 24hrs.

LIVE MUSIC

Culture Music Club Vuga Rd, Vuga. The headquarters of Zanzibar's best-loved Taarab orchestra, who practise here most afternoons (visitors are welcome to come along and listen).

STONE TOWN'S ANNUAL FESTIVALS

"The greatest cultural festival in East Africa" trumpets the brochure, and that's no exaggeration. Established in 1997, the **Zanzibar International Film Festival** (ⓦziff.or.tz) is a firm fixture on the African cultural calendar, and provides as good a reason as any to try to get to Zanzibar in July, even if you're not into celluloid: the festival also features musicians and acrobats from around the western Indian Ocean. The other big date is the four-day **Sauti za Busara festival** (ⓦbusaramusic.org) in February, covering everything from Taarab, Bongo Flava and mainland jazz bands to West Africa's biggest stars, and even Sufi dervishes.

Dhow Countries Music Academy Old Customs House, Mizingani Rd ☎0777 416529, ⓦzanzibarmusic.org. If anyone knows about upcoming events, venues and the latest vibes, it's this lot. They also host concerts on the third Wednesday of each month (8pm; Tsh4000), themed around a certain style or instrument, and run music courses. Mon–Fri 9am–7pm, Sat 9am–5pm.

Ngome Kongwe (Old Fort) Forodhani St. In the dry seasons (June–Sept & Dec–Feb), the fort's open-air amphitheatre hosts evening concerts and performances. Exactly what's on, and entrance fees (if any) change from season to season; a sign outside the fort announces the next one.

SHOPPING

Stone Town is shopaholic's paradise, with hundreds of stores selling a huge variety of souvenirs, and prices can be reasonable, too, if you're into bargaining. **Locally made items** to look out for include jewellery, modern and antique silverwork, and wooden Zanzibari chests with brass hasps, staples and straps, and secret compartments. Also typically Zanzibari are woven palm-weave *mkeka* (mats) and *mkoba* (baskets), and the woven men's *barghashia* hats (named after Sultan Barghash), which cost up to Tsh100,000 for the finest handmade ones. Unfortunately, the **spices** for which Zanzibar is famous usually come powdered and pre-packaged, and are nothing you can't buy back home. Rather better are **aromatic oils**, which use coconut oil as a neutral base, and all manner of scented soaps, scrubs, incense, and even spicy bubble bath. **Clothing and fabrics** are another speciality, especially colourful cotton *kangas* (see p.74) and *kitenges*. The biggest concentration of **souvenir and craft shops** is along Gizenga Street, Changa Bazaar and Hurumzi Street, all close to each other in the north of the old town, where you'll also find several henna "tattoo" parlours and chest-makers.

11

ANTIQUES AND SOUVENIRS

Abeid Curio Shop Cathedral St, facing the cathedral ☎024 223 3832. The best of several antique shops along this street – anything from Zanzibari chests, silverwork and clocks to gramophones, furniture, beds, coins and British colonial kitsch. Mon–Sat Mon–Fri 9am–5.30pm.

Lookmanji Arts & Antiques Off Forodhani St, under Archipelago Café & Restaurant ☎0783 772177. A large selection of arts and antiques covering most bases, especially good for woodcarvings, masks and batiks. Mon–Fri 9am–noon & 2–6pm, Sun 9am–1pm.

Memories of Zanzibar Kenyatta Rd, opposite Shangani Post Office ☎024 223 9376, ⓦmemories-zanzibar.com. Tons of stuff here: reproduction maps, banana-leaf collages, batiks, rugs, some very luxurious Indian fabrics, masks, loads of jewellery, and some wicked metal sculptures from the Wonder Welders workshop in Dar es Salaam. Also stocks books and CDs. Daily 9am–6pm, but closed Sat & Sun March–May.

Zanzibar Curio Shop Changa Bazaar ☎024 223 2077. A glorified junk shop, packed to the rafters with fascinating stuff from old marine compasses and Omani astrolabes to gramophones and novelty tin models from British times (the best stuff is upstairs). The owners know the value of their stock, so don't expect to find a hidden treasure going for a song. Daily 9am–6pm.

Zanzibar Gallery Cnr Kenyatta Rd and Gizenga St ☎024 223 2721, ⓦzanzibargallery.net. Zanzibar's best bookshop also doubles as a souvenir shop, selling everything from clothes to pickles, reproductions of ancient maps, Indian fabrics, masks, studded wooden chests, *bao* games and scented toiletries. Among the books are those of the shop's owner, renowned photographer Javed Jafferji. Daily 9am–6pm (9am–2pm in low season).

ARTS AND CRAFTS

Fahari Zanzibar Kenyatta Rd ☎0714 541537, ⓦfahari-zanzibar.com. A women's crafts cooperative, whose workshops are on site, making and selling elegant bags (leather, woven or fabric), purses, jewellery and other accessories. Most items are priced $50–100 (some of the bags can take a good while to make), but there's also a good choice of cheaper items, such as scented soaps wrapped in plaited palm weave ($5), and a trio of pumice stones strung on a coconut rope ($3). Daily 9am–5.30pm.

MOTO & DADA Shop 416 Hurumzi St ☎0777 466304, ⓦmotozanzibar.wordpress.com. The main outlet for a community crafts project based at Pete, near Jozani Forest (see p.478), this sells a wild selection of naturally made items, mostly woven palm leaf (*ukili*) or colourful *kikoi* fabric, including bags, baskets and hats, plus a temptingly unusual selection of jams, including baobab with carrot, or lemongrass. Daily 9.30am–6pm.

Zenji Cafe & Boutique Zenji Hotel, Malawi Rd ☎0777 247243, ⓦzenjicafeboutique.com. Two good things rolled into one: a nice café (good coffee, cakes, ice cream, and light lunches, plus wi-fi), and an admirably ethical crafts shop that only sources from Tanzanian self-help groups. Particularly unique is the output from their own "Chako" project – jewellery, lamps and wineglasses made entirely from recycled bottles and paper. Daily 7am–8pm.

SUPERMARKET

Kwality Supermarket Mlandege St, Ngambo. Zanzibar's first proper supermarket sells a full array of expensive goodies, including international produce and imported brands. Mon–Sat 9am–8pm, Sun 9am–2pm.

DIRECTORY

Hospitals and clinics The government-run Mnazi Mmoja Hospital, Kaunda Rd (☎ 024 223 1071), isn't brilliantly equipped but has good (Cuban) paediatricians. Staff also do blood tests, as do a number of clinics, whose reputations vary according to the doctor in charge; any expat will be able to recommend a reliable one.

Internet access Almost all hotels now have wi-fi. Usefully located internet cafés include *Shangani Internet Café*, Kenyatta Rd (daily 8.30am–9pm), and *Palace Restaurant & Inter Café*, between *Zanzibar Palace Hotel* and *Hotel Kiponda* (daily 9am–9pm).

Language courses KIU is based in Dar but runs some courses here, usually at 657 Kokoni St – the best time to catch them is 8.30am–noon (☎ 0777 422499 or ☎ 0773 030546, ⓦ swahilicourses.com).

Money NBC bank, Forodhani St, is slow, but has the best rates for changing cash, minimal commission, and an ATM.

There are more banks and machines along Kenyatta Rd. Rates at foreign exchange bureaux are bad but the service is quick: try New Malindi Bureau de Change, Malawi Rd (Mon–Sat 8am–4pm, Sun 8am–3pm). Note that there are no ATMs elsewhere on the island (though there are on Pemba), so if plastic is your only source of money, hit the machines here before heading off to a beach.

Pharmacies The main pharmacies are in the streets around the market, including Fahud Pharmacy, Creek Rd, just north of the market (daily 8am–midnight; ☎ 024 223 5669 or ☎ 0777 428888).

Police Corner of Malawi and Creek roads, Malindi ☎ 024 223 0771 or ☎ 024 223 0772.

Travel agents The following are reliable: Tabasam Tours & Travel, Kenyatta Rd (☎ 024 223 0322, ⓦ tabasamzanzibar .com), and ZanTours, behind *Passing Show Hotel* off Malawi Rd, Malindi (☎ 024 223 3116, ⓦ zantours.com).

Around Stone Town

There is no shortage of attractions to see around Stone Town, including **Mbweni**'s impressive botanical garden, the **Maruhubi and Mtoni ruins**, and the slave chamber at **Mangapwani**. Most of these can be easily and quite cheaply visited on day-trips run by local tour companies (see p.464–465). Some may also be included on the virtually obligatory **Spice tours** (from $15 per person), which centre on guided walks around a farm where you're shown herbs, spices and other crops; they also usually take in the ruined nineteenth-century Kidichi Persian Baths and finish with a slap-up meal.

Also popular are boat trips to islands and reefs just offshore. Other than beach lounging, **snorkelling** is the main activity: it's very good off **Changuu Island** (which also has giant tortoises), and almost miraculous off **Chumbe Island**, which also offers **scuba diving** (see pp.462–463).

Changuu Island

A trip to **CHANGUU (Prison Island)**, a 700m-long strip 5km northwest of Stone Town, makes a great excursion. Once a transit camp for slaves, the imposing building on the island's northeastern side was erected by the British in the 1890s to serve as a prison, but was only ever used as a **yellow-fever quarantine camp**. As even that use was limited, the island became a popular weekend retreat for the well-to-do. Snorkelling on the surrounding reefs is always fun, and the island's **coral rag forest** is home to duiker antelopes, bats, butterflies and weavers, but Changuu's long-lasting attraction is its fenced-in colony of over a hundred **Aldabra giant tortoises** (*changuu*), descended from four individuals imported from the Seychelles in 1919. Weighing over 200kg, the biggest – which can live to one hundred years – are second in size only to Galapagos tortoises, and like their cousins were contemporaries of dinosaurs. Tsh1000 buys you a bowl of spinach and quality bonding time, but watch out for sharp beaks.

ARRIVAL AND DEPARTURE   CHANGUU ISLAND

By boat Tour operators (see pp.464–465) and hotels can arrange excursions here for $30–40 per person for half a

day, including snorkelling. Boats take half an hour each way, giving you two or three hours to explore. Trips can be extended to a full day, perhaps in combination with snorkelling off Bawe Island. Arranging things yourself isn't necessarily cheaper: if you want to try, talk to the boatmen hanging around the "Big Tree" on Mizingani Road. A fair price for the ride there and back would be $35 for the boat, plus $6 per person for entrance fees.

ACCOMMODATION AND EATING

Meals and drinks are available at the restaurant within the original prison building (see below), with seafood costing upwards of $12. Alternatively, you can get refreshments at *Mathews Restaurant* on the island's eastern tip: it's a beautifully restored nineteenth-century holiday home built over an arcade, with a broad patio up front overlooking the sea.

Changuu Private Island Paradise ☎ 0773 333241 or ☎ 027 254 4595 (Arusha), ⊚ privateislands-zanzibar .com. This comprises a number of buildings and facilities scattered around the diminutive island, notable not only for their location, but the attractive interior decor. The original prison, enclosing a courtyard, is now a restaurant and bar. There's also a swimming pool and a floodlit tennis court. No children under 12. HB **$440**

Chumbe Island

11

The shallow reefs around **CHUMBE ISLAND**, south of Stone Town, enclose some of the finest coral gardens on earth, as aptly described by the island's name, which means a creature, or a being. Coral growth and diversity are among East Africa's highest, with more than two hundred species of stone corals (around ninety percent of all East African species), plus over four hundred kinds of fish, including blue-spotted stingrays, moray eels, dolphins, and – if you're lucky – turtles or batfish. Needless to say, the **snorkelling** is superb, but it's not just marine life that makes Chumbe special. The island's pristine **coral rag forest** contains a surprisingly rich variety of flora and fauna, whose survival is largely the result of human settlement having been limited to temporary fishermen's camps and the keeper of the lighthouse (built in 1904; its 132 steps can be climbed). The forest, which can be explored along **nature trails**, is one of the last natural habitats for two rare species: the arboreal **coconut crab**, and **Ader's duiker**. At low tide, you can explore mangroves, or poke around rock pools for starfish, crabs and other shellfish. On the bleak and rocky eastern side of the island, look out for 15,000-year-old **fossilized giant clams**.

ARRIVAL AND DEPARTURE   CHUMBE ISLAND

By boat Chumbe is visitable on a day-trip, or by staying at its lodge. The daily boat leaves from the beach in front of the *Mbweni Ruins*, 7km south of Stone Town, at 10am, taking half an hour for the 8km crossing. The return trip costs $90 per person, which includes snorkelling (and snorkelling guide), and lunch on a beautiful sea-view terrace. Visitor numbers are strictly limited, so day-trips must be booked exactly two days before – contact the lodge, or let a tour operator do it for you.

ACCOMMODATION

★**Chumbe Island Eco-Lodge** ☎ 024 223 1040 or ☎ 0777 413232, ⊚ chumbeisland.com. Intimate and justifiably expensive, this is a haven for snorkellers or romancers, with just seven split-level *bandas* overlooking the ocean. All have casuarina poles for walls and palm fronds for roofs, with a large living room, handmade furniture and hammock. The ecotourism tag is genuine: rainwater is filtered and stored under the floors, hot water and electricity are solar powered (no TVs), ventilation is via cleverly designed roofs, toilets create no waste, and profits fund environmental activities. Great food (including vegetarian). There's no real beach, but with so much other beauty around you'll hardly miss it. The price includes everything except alcohol. Closed mid-April to mid-June. FB **$560**

Mbweni

Some 7km south of Stone Town, **MBWENI** tells part of the story of the fight against the slave trade. At its heart is a seven-acre Anglican mission established by the Oxford-based **Universities' Mission to Central Africa** in 1871. Four years later it became a colony for freed slaves. The chapel and school are in ruins, but its church – St John's – still stands, and services are held every Sunday at 9am. In its graveyard are the remains of Caroline Thackeray, the school's first headmistress and cousin of novelist William Makepeace Thackeray. Mbweni's highlight though is its cascaded **botanical garden**, founded by the Scottish physician **Sir John Kirk** during his lengthy stint as Britain's first Consul General (1866–87). A botanist by profession (in which capacity he had accompanied Livingstone up the Zambezi), Kirk was a major authority on East African flora, and introduced many of the 650 species found in the garden, including sausage trees, Madagascan periwinkle, devil's backbone and over 150 palms. This variety has in turn attracted a wide range of birds: sixty at the last count.

ARRIVAL AND DEPARTURE MBWENI

By taxi Getting to Mbweni is easiest by taxi: expect to pay around Tsh15,000 for the return trip.

By daladala Catch the #505 daladala from Darajani terminal in Stone Town and get off at Mazizini police station beside the signposted junction for Mbweni. Follow that road and turn right after 800m. The ruins are 900m along.

The Maruhubi and Mtoni ruins

The shoreline north of Stone Town was favoured by Zanzibar's sultans for their palaces, though all but one of them burned down many moons ago. The only one remaining is used by the government and therefore inaccessible, but the **ruins** of two of them, at **Maruhubi** and **Mtoni**, can be easily visited.

Maruhubi palace
3km north of Stone Town • $2

The ruins of **MARUHUBI PALACE**, built by Sultan Barghash in 1882 to house his harem of ninety-nine concubines and one wife, nestle in a grove of mango trees and coconut palms. Dark legend tells of concubines being killed if they did not satisfy the sultan's wishes, and of others being put to death after fulfilling the carnal desires of visiting dignitaries. The palace was gutted in 1899 and the marble from its Persian-style baths stolen, leaving only the bath-house foundations, an overgrown collection of massive coral stone pillars, and a small aqueduct that carried water from a nearby spring to cisterns.

Mtoni palace
4km north of Stone Town, just beyond the *Mtoni Marine* hotel • $5

One kilometre north of Maruhubi, the older and more atmospheric ruins of **MTONI PALACE** are quite substantial, and include an impressive colonnaded courtyard. The palace was built by Sultan Seyyid Saïd between 1828 and 1832, and levelled by fire in 1914. At one time, it housed the sultan's three wives, forty-two children and hundreds of concubines, while the gardens contained a menagerie of wildlife, including ostriches, flamingos and gazelles. The palace was home to **Princess Salme**, a daughter of Seyyid Saïd, whose elopement with a German merchant in 1866 caused a colossal scandal. In her autobiography, *Memoirs of an Arabian Princess*, she beautifully evokes the opulence of life here in the 1850s and 1860s, when she was a child.

ARRIVAL AND DEPARTURE THE MARUHUBI AND MTONI RUINS

By daladala Both Maruhubi and Mtoni are on the #502 daladala route from Stone Town's Darajani terminal.

On a tour Mtoni Palace can be visited on a standard Spice Tour: the best is the Princess Salme Spice Tour, run by Zanzibar Different (see p.465) for $70–90 per person. It includes a tour of the ruins, a boat ride to Bububu for a "coffee ceremony" in a beautiful Omani house (with an enchanting Alice in Wonderland-style garden), where Salme is said to have spent her last night before eloping, plus a Salme-themed spice tour that ends with lunch prepared by a local family. Tour operators (see pp.464–465) and staff at the *Mtoni Marine* hotel can also organize a candlelit "dinner and concert" inside the ruins, to the sound of a live *Taarab* orchestra. There are no fixed days for this, but the event is held frequently in high season, provided there are enough diners; prices start at $45 per person, including transport to and from Stone Town, and a guided tour of the ruins and of Kidichi Persian Baths.

ACCOMMODATION

Mtoni Marine Mtoni, 4km north of Stone Town ☎024 225 0140, ⓦmtoni.com. An elegant and well-priced beach resort nestled in palm tree-studded gardens. The rooms here are very good – the "Palm Court" rooms have a private veranda and sea views ($180), and there are also family apartments sleeping four ($240). The beach here is in two parts, one between mangroves and a jetty, the other, more open, fronted by the restaurant: the water is OK for swimming though the sand can feel a little slimy. Amenities include three restaurants, a sports bar, a spa, a swimming pool, children's playground and various activities (at extra cost), including dhow cruises. BB **$120**

Mangapwani

Just under 25km north of Stone Town • Slave chamber $2, though you may be asked for considerably more

The fishing village of **MANGAPWANI** has a lovely stretch of beach and a couple of caves in the coral ragstone facing the sea. Its name means "Arabian Shore", possibly alluding to one of the caves, a man-made chamber used for hiding slaves after the trade with Oman was outlawed in 1845. The cave had even more use after the slave trade with the African mainland was banned in 1873, when black-market prices took off.

The dank and claustrophobic **slave chamber** is one of the most shocking of Zanzibar's sights and, like the cells beneath the former slave market in Stone Town, conveys the full horror of the slave trade. It consists of two rectangular cells hewn out of the soft coral rock, accessed along a deep and narrow passage and sealed by a heavy door, which was originally covered with coral ragstone, all of which served to hide slaves from the prying eyes of British Navy cruisers on anti-slavery patrols.

Two kilometres south is a **coral cavern**, this one natural, and of interest for its spiritual importance to locals. The cavern, which contains a small pool of fresh water, was discovered in the early 1800s by a plantation slave-boy when one of the goats he was herding fell into the void. Like other caves in Zanzibar and on the mainland, it contains offerings to ancestors left by locals seeking their intercession in mortal affairs – a good example of the syncretic nature of rural Zanzibari Islam, which blends orthodox teachings with popular beliefs – much to the anguish of urbane imams.

ARRIVAL AND DEPARTURE   MANGAPWANI

By daladala To reach Mangapwani by public transport, catch a #102 ("Bumbwini") daladala from Stone Town's Darajani terminal. Some daladalas turn left off the main road into the village and continue towards the coast, which is preferable if you don't fancy walking. If you're dropped on the main road, which is more likely, walk northwest through Mangapwani village. The turning for the coral cavern is 600m along on the left – it lies 1km south of there along a narrow track. For the slave chamber, ignore the turning and continue on to the coast. Just before the shore (roughly 1.5km from the main road, or 1km beyond the coral cavern turning), the road veers north – the slave chamber is 500m further on.

On a tour Mangapwani can be included on a spice tour (see pp.464–465) if the entire group agrees.

EATING AND ACTIVITIES

Mangapwani Serena Beach Club If all you want is an easy day-trip, consider taking lunch at the stunningly situated *Mangapwani Serena Beach Club*, halfway between the coral cavern and slave chamber, and right on the shore over a private beach. For $50, paid at the *Zanzibar Serena Inn* (see p.466), you get transport from Stone Town, a slap-up seafood buffet, and a good half-day on the beach, plus – at extra cost – snorkelling, canoeing and dhow trips. They may even have a dhow heading there from Stone Town, which will cost $60 for the package.

Southern Unguja

Beautiful beaches, romantic hotels, snorkelling, scuba diving, an ancient mosque, a ruined palace, the **Jozani-Chwaka Bay National Park** comprising primeval forest, mangroves, monkeys, dhow trips, dolphins – **southern Unguja** has it all. And despite the proliferation of hotels, most of the area retains a local and untrammelled kind of feeling, where you're as likely to share the sand with fishermen and women harvesting seaweed as you are with fellow tourists.

The best **beaches** hug the southeastern shore, from **Kae** in the north to **Jambiani** in the south. In general, the hotels in this area are small-scale bungalow "resorts", and pretty good value considering their location. In keeping with Zanzibar's proud culinary tradition, restaurants can be truly excellent, whether inside hotels, or run independently. As with the northeast coast, the ocean recedes by a kilometre or more at low tide, so **swimming** straight from the shore is only possible in two six-hour windows each day. Most hotels can fix you up with a dhow or outrigger for snorkelling, and there is also a handful of reliable **dive centres** (see p.462). On Unguja's southern tip, **Kizimkazi** is the other main place for tourists, not on account of its beaches (most of which disappear at high tide), but for its **dolphin tours**, and for snorkelling or scuba diving in the Menai Bay Conservation Area. Also part of the conservation area is **Fumba Peninsula** to the west, which has just one (very fine) hotel and a dive centre, and is the base for Zanzibar's best day-trip, the so-called "**Safari Blue**" dhow excursion.

Menai Bay and Fumba Peninsula

The innumerable mangrove-lined inlets, hidden beaches, coral atolls and sandbanks around **Fumba Peninsula** are protected within the **Menai Bay Conservation Area**. Although the tip of the peninsula lies barely 18km south of Stone Town, the creation of the conservation area in 1997 has successfully limited hotel development here to just one lodge on the entire peninsula.

ARRIVAL AND DEPARTURE · MENAI BAY AND FUMBA PENINSULA

On a tour Menai Bay is most easily explored on the full-day Safari Blue excursion (🌐 safariblue.net) from Fumba on the west side of the bay. The tour kicks off with a dhow trip to a sandbank for guided snorkelling, beach lounging and snacks, before cruising to Kwale Island for dolphin-watching, a sumptuous seafood lunch and tropical-fruit tasting. The trip also includes a nose around a mangrove-lined lagoon, the chance to climb an ancient baobab tree, and *ngalawa* (outrigger) sailing. Safari Blue's success has spawned a number of imitators, but there's little difference in cost between these and the real thing, and to guarantee quality, safety and ethics (the project employs seventy local villagers and supports a bunch of worthy projects), we'd recommend you settle for the original. Excursions leave Fumba daily except Fridays and cost $55 per person, or $80–100 including transport from Stone Town.

ACCOMMODATION

Fumba Beach Lodge ☎ 0778 919525 or ☎ 027 2506315 (Arusha), 🌐 fumbabeachlodge.com or 🌐 moivaro.com. A welcoming Dutch-run place with an impressive 2km of coastline containing three sandy coves accessed via steps. The twenty rooms, most with sea views, are spacious, breezy and nicely decked out in a fresh and colourful blend of Scandinavian and Swahili styles. For something really special, the suites ($465) come complete with outdoor shower and rooftop terrace, while the "Baobab suite" ($505) is built around a tree and boasts a double bath with a view. Amenities include a cliff-top infinity pool, a bar built into an old dhow and excellent food, plus therapeutic massages, windsurfing, kayaking, scuba diving, snorkelling and picnic trips. They can arrange transport here from Stone Town ($45 per vehicle each way). HB sea view **$365**

Jozani and around

The road to the beaches south and east of Stone Town skirts the magnificent **Jozani Forest**, famous for its red colobus monkeys, and a popular excursion from both Stone Town and the beach resorts. For a closer look at the forest's other denizens, two nearby places also warrant a visit: **Zala Park**, for its reptiles and dikdik antelopes, and the **Zanzibar Butterfly Centre**, a local breeding project. The nearby **MOTO Handicraft Museum and Workshop** is also worth a visit to watch high quality handicrafts being made.

Jozani–Chwaka Bay National Park

38km southeast of Stone Town • Daily 7.30am–5pm • $10, including entrance to the mangrove boardwalk and a guide (tip expected) some guides may try to charge for each thing separately – feel free to refuse • The park information centre at the entrance gate also has a gift shop and snack bar

A popular stop on the way to the beaches further south and east is the fifty-square-kilometre **JOZANI–CHWAKA BAY NATIONAL PARK**. At its heart is **Jozani Forest**, a thick, tangled jungle famous for its red colobus monkeys (sightings of which are almost guaranteed), as well as blue or Sykes' monkeys, bush pigs, diminutive Ader's duiker and suni antelopes, elephant shrews, chameleons and a fluttering multitude of birds and butterflies. Several **nature trails**, from easy hour-long strolls to half-day hikes, allow you to explore the forest at your own pace: the trails are described in leaflets available at the park information centre. The national park also encompasses other ecologically connected areas, including the mangroves and intertidal zones of Chwaka Bay to the north. Similar environments can be seen along the short **Pete–Jozani mangrove boardwalk**, which starts and finishes in a car park 1km south of the park entrance. Mangrove **birdlife** is rich if characteristically elusive: lucky twitchers might spot purple-banded or olive sunbirds, kingfishers or blue-cheeked bee-eaters. The best **time to visit** is early morning when there are fewer people, wildlife is more active and the light, filtered through the lush vegetation, is deliciously soothing. It quietens down again in the evening, when conditions are superb for photography.

Zanzibar Butterfly Centre

1km west of the Jozani Park entrance • Daily 9am–5pm • Tsh10,000 or $6 • ⓦ zanzibarbutterflies.com

The **Zanzibar Butterfly Centre** (ZBC) is home to more than a dozen of the fifty-odd species of butterfly native to Jozani. They live in some five hundred square metres of tropical garden enclosed by netting, which you're free to walk around in: a tour of the centre will take around forty minutes. The centre's primary purpose is to reduce pressure on the forest's natural resources by providing an alternative source of income for villagers living on the fringes, in this case through the farming and selling of pupae to collectors internationally – the gold chrysalises, in particular, are quite something.

Zala Park

5.5km south of Jozani along the road to Kizimkazi • Daily 8.30am–5.30pm • Tsh5000 entry, including guided tour • ☎ 0777 850816, ⓦ zalapark.com

Another local scheme worth visiting is **Zala Park** (the Zanzibar Land Animals Park), founded by a schoolteacher in 1994 to educate his pupils on environmental matters. Basically a nicely overgrown garden, it contains a small zoo where various reptiles and amphibians reside. Some of the animals can be handled, like chameleons and tortoises, others, not so much… like pythons. The park is also home to some diminutive dikdik antelopes as part of a breeding experiment, and village tours can be arranged if you contact them in advance.

MOTO Handicraft Museum and Workshop

3km west of the Jozani park entrance, facing Pete School, Pete village • Daily 9am–5.30pm • Guided tour $50–60 per group (enquire in advance for groups larger than four people), excluding transport to and from Pete (Tsh2000 by daladala) • ☎ 0773 031178, ⓦ gomotozanzibar.wordpress.com.

Women are the lifeblood of Zanzibar society, yet traditionally have had very little financial independence. Changing this for the better is the superb **MOTO Handicraft Museum and Workshop**, which currently employs over a hundred villagers (most but not all women) from Pete, near Jozani Forest, in the production of high quality handicrafts. A tour around their workshops takes two or three hours, and includes hands-on activities such as plaiting *ukili* (palm fronds), screen printing and batik making, and ends up with a fabulous lunch taken with local families. A shop here sells the project's produce, which can also be bought at MOTO & DADA Shop in Stone Town (see p.471).

ARRIVAL AND DEPARTURE   **JOZANI AND AROUND**

By daladala Most people visit Jozani on a half-day excursion from Stone Town (see p.464) or when returning from a dolphin tour at Kizimkazi (see below), but it can be more cheaply reached by public transport: daladalas (Tsh2000) from Stone Town's Darajani terminal to Bwejuu (#324), Jambiani (#309) and – most frequently – Makunduchi (#310) pass Pete village and the park gate throughout the day. For Zala Park, catch one going to Kizimkazi (#326), which also passes Pete and Jozani. The last daladala back to Stone Town leaves around sunset, but it's wise to get to the road by 5pm.

Kizimkazi

Almost at the southern tip of Unguja, 53km from Stone Town, **KIZIMKAZI** is best known to tourists for its **dolphin tours** (see box below), and to historians for being one of the oldest continuously inhabited settlements on Zanzibar, one that served for a time as capital of the island's traditional rulers, the Wawinyi Wakuu, before the Omani conquest in the eighteenth century. It's also home to East Africa's oldest standing **mosque** (1107 AD), which – exceptionally – can be visited by non-Muslims. Kizimkazi is actually two places. **Kizimkazi Dimbani** is the village itself, set behind a lovely sheltered bay in which dozens of outrigger canoes bob up and down at their moorings. Three kilometres to the south is **Kizimkazi Mkunguni** (also called Kizimkazi Mtendeni), which has a string of hotels and a couple of ancient **baobab trees**, the older and larger of which is thought to be over six hundred years old, and was used as a transmissions mast during World War II.

Dolphin tours aside, tourism has never quite taken off in Kizimkazi, because its **beaches**, especially Kizimkazi Mkunguni's, are strongly tidal and disappear

11

KIZIMKAZI DOLPHIN TOURS

Menai Bay is home to resident pods of bottlenose and Indo-Pacific humpback, and **swimming with dolphins** is, for many visitors, a dream come true. However, the effects of hundreds of suncream-smothered tourists leaping into the water each day to "play and swim with the dolphins" (as the brochures put it) are still subject to ongoing research, so think twice before taking part. If you do decide to go, try and adhere to the following **guidelines**: encourage your skipper not to chase the pods; as you enter the water, do so away from the dolphins and with as little disturbance as possible; when in the water, stay close to the boat; avoid sudden movements; allow the dolphins to come to you; and do not under any pretext attempt to touch them. Obviously, sightings of dolphins are not guaranteed, but in general the **best months** are August to December.

Zanzibar's classic **dolphin tour** lasts just two or three hours, and leaves from Kizimkazi, whose former fishermen have turned the experience into a veritable industry. Taking an **organized trip** through a tour operator (see pp.464–465) or via most hotels in Stone Town or southeastern Unguja is the easiest way to go about things. Prices start at $35–40 per person from Stone Town excluding lunch. Lunch can add $5–15 depending on what and where you eat. If you combine the tour with a visit to Jozani Forest (see p.478), add $10 to cover the park entry fee. Note that most of the trips are shared with up to a dozen other people no matter what you're paying; the only real difference is that the more expensive excursions have smaller group sizes, road transport by Land Cruiser rather than minibus, and boats made of fibreglass rather than wood.

Arranging things independently involves spending the night before or after in Kizimkazi, and has the advantage of being able to set off early morning or late afternoon, avoiding rush hour. It also lets you extend the trip to a full day, including, for instance, snorkelling around **Pungume Island**, 13km offshore. To avoid Kizimkazi's often offensively pushy touts, arrange things through a hotel as early as possible: *Karamba Resort* (see p.480) is reasonably priced, and staff can also arrange other trips in Menai Bay, too. The main cost is boat rental, generally $35–50 (per boat) for a few hours, plus entry fee ($5 per person), snorkelling equipment ($5–10) and, optionally, lunch. Check beforehand that the boat has adequate shade.

completely when the water is in. The shoreline behind is also rocky, and backed by bushy vegetation that is a fertile breeding ground for mosquitoes. The prettiest beach is the bay in Kizimkazi Dimbani, although it's in full view of the village, and fishermen mending nets or making rope. Locals are used to seeing tourists in swimsuits, though, and indeed local kids messing about tend to wear nothing at all, so don't feel awkward.

ARRIVAL AND INFORMATION

By daladala The #326 daladala runs throughout the day from Stone Town's Darajani terminal to Kizimkazi (approx 2hr).

Guided walks To get to know the place better, any hotel can arrange a guided village walk; the $5 fee benefits the local school.

ACCOMMODATION

Kizimkazi has plenty of hotels and resorts, most of them huddled shoulder-to-shoulder in a row of narrow plots. However the cheaper ones – which here means under $300 a double – rarely stay open for more than a couple of years (*Karamba Resort* is one of the few exceptions), while the others are frankly overpriced.

★**Karamba Resort** Kizimkazi Dimbani ☎0773 166406, ⓦkarambaresort.com. This Spanish-run hotel (not really a resort) on the northern headland flanking the bay and backed by gardens is the best mid-range option, thanks in part to glorious views from each of the twenty large and bright rooms (two per bungalow), their verandas, and – in the more expensive rooms – from large open-air baths. There's a swimming pool, and a large bar and restaurant which is popular with day-trippers, but quiet at night. Other facilities include a children's playground and aromatic massages combinable with yoga, Reiki or reflexology for a spiritual pep. Closed April & May. BB $140

Unguja Lodge Kizimkazi Mkunguni, 500m north of the baobabs ☎0774 477477, ⓦungujalodge.com. The best of Kizimkazi's upmarket hotels, this is small, personable and very stylish in a rustic way. Set in lush gardens behind a narrow beach, it has just twelve large, two-storey villas cleverly designed with soft, rounded forms, all with terraces, sea views and plenty of privacy. Some also have a/c, but really cool are the ones with private plunge pools. Other facilities include a swimming pool, wi-fi, fine dining, and various excursions in the area. HB $524, sea view $556

EATING AND DRINKING

★**Karamba Resort** Kizimkazi Dimbani. Large but still sophisticated, this gets packed for lunch and has a great reputation for seafood, featuring sushi and sashimi. The pasta is unusually good, as are – unsurprisingly for a

Spanish-run place – the tapas and paella. They also cater well for vegetarians. Seafood costs upwards of $18; other mains are around $12. Daily 7am–10pm.

Jambiani

The long beach at **JAMBIANI**, starting around 2km south of Paje and continuing unbroken for 7km, possesses a wild and windy beauty, and is quite the best place in Zanzibar to enjoy the pleasures of both **beach and village life** without feeling hampered about where you can swim, or how you dress (on the beach, that is; obviously, cover up

KIZIMKAZI CULTURAL MUSIC FESTIVAL

If you're around at the end of December, it's well worth trying to coincide with the two-day **Kizimkazi Cultural Music Festival** (ⓦkizinoor.org). Set up on a shoestring budget in 2008, the festival has got bigger and better each year, and garners an impressive line-up of Tanzanian musicians, covering all musical styles from Bongo Flava and reggae to traditional *ngoma*, taarab, and *kidumbak*. You can also try your hand at heaps of activities including coir rope making, henna and batik painting, and learning to play local instruments. The festival's base is Kizi-Noor Cultural Centre in Kizimkazi Mkunguni, 1.5km south of Kizimkazi's famous pair of ancient baobab trees. A full-blown cultural centre is currently under construction to host the festival, with some reasonably priced accommodation planned.

THE MWAKA KOGWA FESTIVAL

The nebulous town of **Makunduchi**, in Unguja's southeastern corner, is a strange place indeed, not least for its faceless blocks of Soviet-style flats built in the early 1970s by East German "Friendship Brigades". Despite the visibly crumbling "veneer" of socialist modernity, it's a very traditional sort of place, something best experienced during the exuberant **Mwaka Kogwa Festival**. Held in the third or fourth week of July, the four-day shindig was introduced by Zoroastrian immigrants from Shiraz (now Iran) over a millennium ago to celebrate the Persian New Year (Nairuzi). Although the dates no longer coincide, they do align with the end of the harvest after the long rains and the traditional resumption of dhow traffic, and so as a celebration of new beginnings the festival has survived.

The proceedings begin with houses being swept clean, and a **ritual bath** in the sea (*mwaka kogwa* means "washing the year"). By mid-morning, most of Makunduchi's inhabitants descend on the centre of town, where a medicine man (*mganga*) erects a **thatched hut** accompanied by the singing of women. A group of elders enter the hut, upon which the *mganga* sets it alight. The men's subsequent "escape" gives a fine opportunity to the more theatrically inclined; the smoke that issues at this moment indicates the direction in which the fortunes of the following year will blow, and it's perhaps no coincidence that the Kiswahili word for the year's end, *kibunzi*, also means a divining board.

The burning of the hut is followed by the settling of old grievances in the form of not entirely **mock fights** between two groups of men, one from the north of Makunduchi, the other from the south, who, after taunting each other in the best football hooligan style (and chanting pleas to spirits), indulge in a fine display of unbridled machismo by flailing each other with banana stems, a dusty chaotic brawl spurred on by raucous insults from the ever-vocal women. Tourists of a masochistic bent are welcome to join in: when you've had enough flagellation, just hold your hand up to surrender.

With the new year thus cleansed of past squabbles, the following three days consist of much merrymaking, dancing and even drinking (albeit behind cloth screens). During this time, women dress in their finest *kangas*, and young girls in the frilly Edwardian-style frocks so typical of Africa. All wear lots of kohl around their eyes, vibrant lipstick and garishly painted cheeks, and have their hands and feet painted with henna arabesques. The undercurrent is desire: children born of illicit Mwaka Kogwa couplings, far from being scorned, are highly regarded socially.

The celebrations over, the bottles are stashed away, the veils rise once more and life resumes its normal course.

PRACTICALITIES

Outsiders are welcome to join the celebrations; in fact, it's considered bad luck to be without at least one guest over this period, so you might also be invited to **stay with locals**. A good thing too, as Makunduchi has just one hotel, and that's reserved for all-inclusive Italian package tours. Any Stone Town tour operator should be able to arrange a **trip** to coincide with Mwaka Kogwa, but book well in advance, as the dates tend to overlap with the equally popular Zanzibar International Film Festival (see p.470).

11

when in the village). The beach's name derives from the Arabic word *jambiya*, meaning a dagger with a broad curved blade, an example of which was reputedly found on the beach by early settlers. The **barrier reef** lies several kilometres out, so the lagoon in between is a mix of sandbanks, coral reefs and shallow water, great for **snorkelling**, and for poking around pools at low tide. The beach, as along much of the east coast, is very tidal, so swimming is only possible at high tide unless you fancy a long walk.

The beach is one thing that makes Jambiani special; the other is its strong **sense of community**. Unlike Nungwi and Kiwengwa in northern Unguja, Jambiani's villagers have full access to the shore, so you'll be sharing the sands with fishermen and their butterfly-like *ngalawa* outriggers, women collecting seaweed, and lots of children: sailing toy dhows made from sandals, plastic bottles or bits of wood with plastic bags for sails is a particular favourite.

ARRIVAL AND INFORMATION

JAMBIANI

By minibus The beach transfer tourist minibuses (see p.464) take an hour to cover the 56km from Stone Town, and will drop you at your chosen hotel. Returning to Stone Town, the tourist minibuses leave around 10am.

By daladala Daladalas – #309 from Stone Town (Tsh2000) – can take up to two hours. There are several a day (the last leaving no later than 3–4pm), but timings are unpredictable, so enquire the day before on Creek Road, and be prepared to

head out to Mwana Kwerekwe, 5km southeast of town, to catch it. Returning to Stone Town, daladalas only leave when full: the first around 6am, the last no later than 3.30pm.

By taxi If you are good at haggling, you should be able to talk a taxi driver into taking you from Stone Town to Jambiani for $40, though $50 is more likely, or $65 from the airport. Transport organized through Jambiani's hotels costs about the same.

TOURS AND SERVICES

INFORMATION AND TOURS

Bike rental The minimarket/post office on Jambiani's former main road rents out bicycles, as do a handful of other places on the same street.

Internet access Most of the town's lodges and more touristy restaurant/bars now have wi-fi. Networked computers can be found at *Visitor's Inn*, at Beedrake & Hasu Secretarial Centre beside *Casa del Mar Hotel*, and at the Zanzibar Action Project just south of *Blue Oyster Hotel*.

Jambiani Cultural Village Tour This modest community-run project, based at Jambiani School (open most days, no fixed times; ☎ 0777 469118), was set up by Eco+Culture Tours in Stone Town (see p.464) to offer tourists the chance to explore various aspects of local life and culture: the profits fund healthcare, a nursery and

various educational projects. On a typical walk you'll be briefed on Jambiani's history before touring a farm, visiting a traditional herbalist (*mganga*), and seeing a seaweed farm. There's also the option of visiting a sacred limestone cave (*kumbi*), which may have been used to hide slaves after the abolition of the slave trade; it's a four-hour walk there and back, so cycling is best. Expect to pay around Tsh20,000 per person for a three-hour tour, or Eco+Culture Tours charges $50 per person in a group of four, or $85 per person for a couple, for a day-trip from Stone Town.

Shops and post office Jambiani's former main road, a sandy strip halfway between the shore and the new tarmac, has a number of modest shops, including a combined post office and minimarket (daily 6am–10pm).

ACCOMMODATION

Jambiani's hotels (see map, p.484) were once almost all budget level, but are rapidly moving upmarket. The result is that any decent *and* cheap budget place is unlikely to survive for more than a couple of years before the landowner sells it to foreign developers. The distances given in the reviews below are from Jambiani School.

Al Hapa Bungalows 1km south ☎ 0773 048894 or ☎ 0777 485842, ⊛ alhapazanzibar.com. A Swedish–Zanzibar run place, with clean and comfortable bungalows just a few sandy strides back from the beach, plus four rooms in a two-storey house that resembles a tower. All have balconies and sea views. The restaurant and bar occupy much of the beach above the high-tide line, and the low price attracts a youthful crowd, which is all part of the fun. BB **$65**

Bahari View Lodge 3.2km north ☎ 0784 419232 (Arusha), ⊛ bahari-view-lodge.com. An unpretentious bungalow resort, blessed with an extraordinary beautiful, powdery soft beach. There are twelve comfortable but mundane bungalows, and a good raft of amenities, including a restaurant and beach bar, massages, hammocks hung from trees, wi-fi, and a freeform swimming pool with sea view. BB **$180**, HB **$230**

Blue Oyster Hotel 800m north ☎ 024 224 0163, ⊛ blueoysterhotel.com. German-run, this is an architecturally inelegant two-storey affair, but very good value, with friendly and efficient staff, and clean, well-maintained rooms, the cheapest of which share bathrooms. There's also a very good beachside restaurant and bar, and excursions can be arranged. BB **$110**, sea view **$130**

Casa del Mar Hotel 500m north ☎ 0777 455446, ⊛ casa-delmar-zanzibar.com. A tasteful mid-range choice on the beach, with twelve rooms in two well-maintained, thatch-roofed two-storey buildings, all with sea views, and nicely decked out in rustic style. The suites on top ($118), reached via steep ladders, each have a living room complete with king-size futon. The restaurant has a great reputation, but doesn't sell alcohol (you can bring your own). Also has a swimming pool, and a boat for snorkelling excursions. Closed April–May. BB **$96**

Jambiani Guesthouse 600m south ☎ anne @zanzibar-guesthouse.com, ⊛ zanzibar-guesthouse .com. Danish-owned but locally run, this calls itself a kind of youth hostel, but is really just a small basic holiday house right on the beach: you can rent the whole house (sleeping 7–10 people) for $150–200. There are just five rooms, one with its own bathroom, and a shared lounge. BB **$50**

Pakachi Beach Hotel 3.4km north ☎ 0773 621086, ⊛ pakachi.com. Snug on a low headland a few steps above the beach but beside a dismal German-owned resort, this Tanzanian–Norwegian place has a chilled-out Rastafarian vibe, and good ties with the local community. There are just three rooms, plus a bungalow ($120), a family house ($140), and a funky *banda* built almost entirely of natural material; all are en suite and with *semadari* beds. The bar and very mellow restaurant have good views. BB $\overline{$60}$

★**Red Monkey Lodge** 2.2km south ☎ 0777 713366, ⓦ redmonkeylodge.com. Named after the denizens of a small patch of forest inland from here, this is a nicely chilled out and quirky place that has close ties to the local community (you can even stay for free if you have skills that might come in handy to them). It's on a small breezy plot at the south end of the beach, and has nine bungalows, with twelve rooms in all – they are all simple but comfortable, and with touches of Oriental style. The restaurant and bar both have unimpeded sea views, there are sunbeds and

parasols on the beach itself, and a kiteboarding centre too, and they also offer keenly priced scuba diving packages ($750 per person for Open Water certification, including seven nights here). BB $\overline{$100}$

Shehe Bungalows 1.4km south ☎ 0779 041645, ⓦ shehebungalows.co.uk. Despite the sometimes surly staff, this is a decent budget choice thanks to its great location right on the beach. There are three sets of rooms (25 in all), all with box nets, fans and bathrooms. The best ones, large but a little faded, are in a row of bungalows on the north side, behind a narrow garden – all have sea views ($55). There's also a first-floor restaurant and bar, and massages can be arranged. BB $\overline{$35}$

EATING AND DRINKING

There are lots of restaurants to choose from, and not just in the hotels, so prices are keen. In the village itself several *hotelis* sell fairly basic meals (mainly rice or *pilau* with grilled fish, but also beans). The locally-run restaurants right on the beach, often built with little more than palm fronds, are an ever-changing lot. At their prime they can be truly excellent, but give them at least an hour or two to prepare your meal – or, for something special, drop by the day before to discuss the options.

Al Hapa Bungalows 1km south ☎ 0773 048894 or ☎ 0777 485842. Right on the beach, the bar here is one of Jambiani's most popular, which lends it an attractively youthful vibe. Daily noon–10pm.

Blue Oyster Hotel 800m north ☎ 024 224 0163. The restaurant here is a breezy first-floor terrace with great views, and serves a good range of snacks, pizzas and full meals, the latter making subtle use of the island's spices. Around Tsh15,000 a plate, or Tsh8000 for snacks. Daily 10am–10pm.

★**Kim's Restaurant** 900m north, near Blue Oyster Hotel ☎ 0777 457733. Among the best of the locally run places, this is decorated with shells and serves tasty and unusual traditional meals for under Tsh8000. For starters, you could try fish cakes, succulent fried octopus or spicy fish soup. Main courses include the classic coconut-crusted fish with mango chutney, or baby octopus grilled with ginger and chilli, and for dessert try *kaimati* (flour, sugar and

coconut), or pumpkin stewed in sweet coconut milk. Daily, but variable hours – drop by beforehand to fix a time.

Red Monkey Lodge 2.2km south ☎ 0777 713366, ⓦ facebook.com/redmonkeylodge. The location is one draw, seriously good seafood the other, either grilled or – if booked in advance – as part of a Swahili buffet. The menu is limited to light lunches and snacks; full-on meals are four-course spreads which change daily. Special diets or requests are catered for given advance notice. On Mon nights, you'll likely be serenaded by local musicians, and staff also host other special events; see their Facebook page for details. Daily 8am–10pm or later.

Shehe Bungalows 1.4km south ☎ 0779 041645. The first-floor open-front bar enjoys a fantastic view over the beach and lagoon. The limited choice of dishes must be ordered well in advance, and range from average to excellent depending on who's cooking. Around Tsh10,000 a plate. Daily 11am–8pm or later.

Paje

The beach at **PAJE**, 51km east of Stone Town, is beautiful with white sands backed by swaying palms, and the sea more often than not imbued with heart-lifting shades of turquoise. Over the years, it has become a major centre for **kite surfing** and, for the most part, Paje's hotels are integrated with the local community, with whom you'll likely be sharing the beach. Among them are several hundred women seaweed farmers, whom you're welcome to join for a few hours. Women needn't feel awkward about donning swimming costumes on the **beach**, but should cover their legs and shoulders when in the village itself.

Seaweed Center

1km north of the junction in from Stone Town, 200m before *Ndame Beach Lodge* • Mon–Sat 9am–4pm • Tsh10,000 or $7 for a guided tour • ☎ 0777 107248, ⓦ seaweedcenter.com

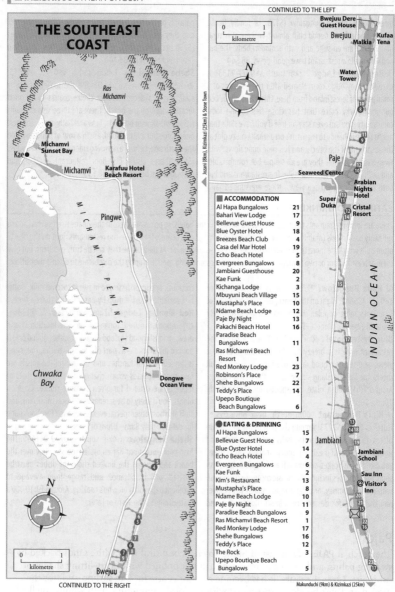

CONTINUED TO THE LEFT

THE SOUTHEAST COAST

Bwejuu Dere Guest House

Bwejuu

Kufaa Tena

Malkia

Water Tower

Ras Michamvi

N

Michamvi Sunset Bay

Kae

Michamvi

Karafuu Hotel Beach Resort

Paje

Seaweed Center

Arabian Nights Hotel

Super Duka

Cristal Resort

Pingwe

MICHAMVI PENINSULA

Chwaka Bay

DONGWE

Dongwe Ocean View

■ ACCOMMODATION

Al Hapa Bungalows	21
Bahari View Lodge	17
Bellevue Guest House	9
Blue Oyster Hotel	18
Breezes Beach Club	4
Casa del Mar Hotel	19
Echo Beach Hotel	5
Evergreen Bungalows	8
Jambiani Guesthouse	20
Kae Funk	2
Kichanga Lodge	3
Mbuyuni Beach Village	15
Mustapha's Place	10
Ndame Beach Lodge	12
Paje By Night	13
Pakachi Beach Hotel	16
Paradise Beach Bungalows	11
Ras Michamvi Beach Resort	1
Red Monkey Lodge	23
Robinson's Place	7
Shehe Bungalows	22
Teddy's Place	14
Upepo Boutique Beach Bungalows	6

● EATING & DRINKING

Al Hapa Bungalows	15
Bellevue Guest House	7
Blue Oyster Hotel	14
Echo Beach Hotel	4
Evergreen Bungalows	6
Kae Funk	2
Kim's Restaurant	13
Mustapha's Place	8
Ndame Beach Lodge	10
Paje By Night	11
Paradise Beach Bungalows	9
Ras Michamvi Beach Resort	1
Red Monkey Lodge	17
Shehe Bungalows	16
Teddy's Place	12
The Rock	3
Upepo Boutique Beach Bungalows	5

INDIAN OCEAN

Jambiani

Jambiani School

Sau Inn @ Visitor's Inn

Jozani (8km), Kizimkazi (25km) & Stone Town

Makunduchi (9km) & Kizimkazi (25km)

Bwejuu

CONTINUED TO THE RIGHT

The art of seaweed farming was introduced to Paje by an NGO over two decades ago, as a means of providing additional income for local women. The project was a great success, and seaweed farms (those mysterious fields of poles sticking out of the water) are a common sight throughout Zanzibar, which now accounts for three percent of global production. Paje's **Seaweed Center** was founded in 2011 to turn the raw material into seaweed products, which you can watch being made, then sample or buy. All sorts of artistically presented beauty products (soaps and creams, scented with cloves among other spices), and a very refreshing as well as hyper-healthy juice can be bought here.

The **tour** of the "factory" and adjacent herb garden is guided by enthusiastic-women: meals can be provided by prior arrangement. The **shop** also stocks non-seaweed-related products of no less quality, including clove honey from Pemba.

ARRIVAL AND DEPARTURE PAJE

By minibus The beach transfer minibus from Stone Town (see p.464) costs no more than $10.

By daladala Paje is easy to reach by public transport, with several #209 daladalas a day leaving from Stone Town's Darajani terminal (Tsh3000); daladala #324 to Bwejuu also passes by. Daladalas run from dawn to around 4pm, taking no more than ninety minutes. The last daladala leaves Paje for Stone Town no later than 4.30pm.

By taxi A taxi from Stone Town costs $35–40, or up to $60 from the airport.

ACTIVITIES

Cycling Bicycles can be hired locally for as little as $5 a day from *Paradise Beach Bungalows*. Forget the highway and head along the beach instead: except at high tide, it's ridable all the way from Jambiani in the south to Dongwe in the north.

Kite surfing Paje's has three kite surfing centres, all of which quote their prices in Euro, though you can pay in dollars or shillings. Paje by Kite (ⓦpajebykite.com), at *Paje by Night* hotel, is the cheapest, charging €60 for an hour's tuition, or €300 for between six and ten hours. The others are Zanzibar Kite Paradise (ⓦzanzibarkiteparadise.com) and Kite Centre Zanzibar (ⓦkitecentrezanzibar.com). The main seasons (depending on the wind) are mid-June to mid-Oct and mid-Dec to mid-Mar.

Scuba diving Paje's highly recommended dive centre is Buccaneer Diving, based at the *Arabian Nights Hotel* (☎0777 853403, ⓦbuccaneerdiving.com), close to *Paje by Night*.

ACCOMMODATION

Paje has a few great and affordable hotels, plus some big resorts – many are decidedly average, even the upmarket ones, but the good ones, of which there are several, are quite gloriously brilliant. Distances below are from the junction of the road in from Stone Town.

Mbuyuni Beach Village 2.6km south of the junction ☎0773 659989, ⓦmbuyuni.com. Halfway to Jambiani in an area known as Mwanawanu, this is far from central Paje, and it's unsafe to walk back here at night, but if you're looking to strand yourself in a secluded yet affordable hideaway, this could be it. Set in tropical gardens are ten large, attractively designed and stylishly equipped thatch-roofed bungalows, all with big beds and decent bathrooms. There's a reasonably priced restaurant facing the beach (mainly seafood), and frequent bonfires on the beach itself, where there are also hammocks and sun loungers. Very good value. BB $55, HB $80

Ndame Beach Lodge 700m northeast of the junction ☎0777 886611, ⓦndamezanzibar.com. A well-priced, sixty-bed Swedish-run resort set in a grove of coconut palms behind a lovely stretch of beach. The rooms, in one or two-storey chalets (only a few have sea views), are small and not terribly inspiring but comfortable, and very cheap for families ($128 in high season). There's also a bar, gift shop, coconut-rope loungers and parasols on the beach, plus a good seafood restaurant. BB $98

★**Paje By Night** 500m southeast of the junction ☎0777 000589, ⓦpajebynight.net. First off, the bad news: this is not on the beach, but 100m behind it (and *Kitete Beach Bungalows*), so has no sea views. The rest is all good news, starting with its excellent bar and sublime restaurant (see below), together with a friendly, funky and laid-back atmosphere, and, rare for Italian-run places on Zanzibar, healthy community relations. Rooms are in 24 simple but well-kept rooms in colourfully painted rows, some with a/c. There's also a couple of quirky two-floor "jungle bungalows" ($125) with rooftop terraces, and some psychedelic "concept rooms" ($125) – fancy sleeping in a room of purple spirals? A range of personalized tours can be arranged with locals, including village walks, birding, time with fishermen, even Uzi Island on the south coast. Also has a swimming pool, nice craft shop, and hammocks slung all over the place. Rates include wi-fi (or use of a laptop). Closed mid-April to end-May. BB $100

★**Paradise Beach Bungalows** 1km north of the junction ☎0777 414129 or ☎0785 340516, ⓦnakama .main.jp/paradisebeachbungalows. Run by a Japanese–Zanzibari team, this is a peaceful and very likeable no-frills place snuggled in a grove of coconut palms right on the beach, and famed for its exquisite but affordable food. Its thirteen Swahili-styled bedrooms, all en suite (ten have sea views, including three with rooftop terraces), are large and comfortable, and have hot water and electricity. Facilities include a bar, a good library, cultural tours and dhow trips, and Swahili cooking courses (see below). Bicycles and snorkelling equipment are available, and a huge range of affordable excursions and activities can be arranged, including half a day spent fishing with locals from a dhow ($20). BB $80

★**Teddy's Place** 1km south of the junction, next to *Cristal Resort* ☎0773 096306, ⊕teddys-place.com. Possibly the best budget lodging on the island, with a scatter of cool beach *bandas* made almost entirely out of thatch, palm weave and coconut wood, including their carved wooden doors: the only modern accessories are ceiling fans, bed linen, mosquito nets and lightbulbs – even the floor is sand. Bathrooms are shared. There's chilled music, good food, and weekly parties at its beach bar. BB: dorms per person $19, *banda* (double) $42, bungalow $50

EATING AND DRINKING

Most of Paje's bars and restaurants are in its hotels, but in high season, at least, you'll often find impromptu chill-out parties on the beach: just look for a campfire, but heed local advice about safety if walking around unaccompanied at night – it is not unknown for tourists to be mugged. For something deliciously different, *Paradise Beach Bungalows* can arrange a four-hour Swahili **cooking course** with local women. It's actually more of a demonstration, including the art of making coconut milk (and getting to grips with a "goat", *mbuzi* also being the word for a coconut grater). All great fun, and just $10 per person, including the resulting meal.

Ndame Beach Lodge 700m northeast of the junction ☎0777 886611. Often excellent, this restaurant serves Italian or Swahili dishes ($10–15 for a main course, $25 for a three-course dinner), including octopus and potato salad with basil and garlic, pasta with crab sauce, pizzas, mixed fish grills and grilled prawns with spinach. The sea view is delightful, as is the sensation of eating with your toes in the sand. Also has wi-fi. Daily 7am–10pm.

★**Paje By Night** 500m southeast of the junction ☎0777 000589. Among Zanzibar's best bars, with good music, a laid-back atmosphere, and plenty of chatter about kite surfing. The food is good too, with vegetarian options and many home-grown ingredients: the wood-fired pizzas please even the pickiest Italians, and where else could you sample home-made ravioli stuffed with fish and almonds? The wines (mainly South African and Spanish) are cheap for Zanzibar, starting at Tsh20,000 a bottle. Diners are welcome to use the swimming pool. Discos on Friday. Food daily 10am–10.30pm; drinks 10am–2am.

★**Paradise Beach Bungalows** 1km north of the junction ☎0777 414129 or ☎0785 340516. An unusual and successful blend of Swahili and Japanese cuisine, with a daily changing menu: it's incredibly good value at around Tsh7000 for most dishes, with the exception of sushi and sashimi (nonetheless a bargain at Tsh15,000) and lobster (Tsh30,000). The Japanese dishes are especially recommended, including a classic take on chicken teriyaki seasoned with Coca-Cola. There's also a small bar, and – for that extra thrill – a table in a tree house. Book ahead if you're not staying overnight. Daily 11am–3pm & 6–9pm.

★**Teddy's Place** 1km south of the junction, next to *Cristal Resort* ☎0773 096306. Good food, a lively vibe and cool music make this beachfront hotel a great place to hang out. Fridays feature a seafood barbecue, and Sat is party night, with a DJ from 9pm onwards. Full meals average $12–25. There's also a shisha lounge. Daily 7am–midnight.

Bwejuu

The village of **BWEJUU** is 3km north of Paje, and shares the same beach, which continues northwards for another 4km until veers into Dongwe. For most of the year, the beach is a peach, backed by slender coconut palms and dozens of modest bungalow hotels, but be aware that around Christmas it can be covered in seaweed. There are some excellent **snorkelling** spots within walking or wading distance at low tide, and **kite surfing** can be arranged through one of the Paje-based centres (your hotel can help set things up).

Bwejuu village is home to two women's self-help groups, both of which are worth supporting. **Kufaa Tena & Women's Voice Project** on the north side of the village, just before the collapsing *Bwejuu Dere Guest House*, make and sell woven baskets and colourful bags, and offer henna painting and massages. You're welcome to watch the women at work at the lively **Malkia**, opposite *Palm Beach Inn* down the same road, who make and sell fine handmade clothes, and also offer internet access.

ARRIVAL AND DEPARTURE   BWEJUU

By daladala Bwejuu is served by roughly hourly daladalas (#324 or #340) from Creek Road in Stone Town, the first leaving at around 9am, the last at 2pm. The ride takes just over an hour and costs Tsh2000, but to reach the hotels at the north end of Bwejuu, the only daladala at present is a single daily run from Stone Town to Kae (ask for Michamvi) in the afternoon. Leaving Bwejuu, the first daladala (coming from Kae) passes through around 6am, and the last leaves Bwejuu at 4pm.

By taxi A taxi from Stone Town, or a transfer arranged through a hotel, costs $35–40 (per vehicle).

By minibus Beach transfer minibuses from Stone Town (see p.464) charge no less than $10.

By bicycle Most hotels have bicycles for their guests, either free or for a nominal sum.

ACCOMMODATION

Bwejuu's accommodation (see map, p.484) is mostly in small bungalow "resorts", and generally reasonably priced. All have wi-fi except *Robinson's*. Distances below are given from the water tower at the junction of the asphalt road and the unsurfaced road into the village itself.

Bellevue Guest House 2.4km north ☎0777 209576, ⓦbellevuezanzibar.com. A small, friendly, Dutch-run place on a low ridge 100m back from the shore, with good views, though not being on the beach (there's a private villa in front) is a drawback. It has six rooms (four standard, plus two with hot water and other minor treats), all with huge beds, box nets, fans and good bathrooms, and the restaurant and bar have an excellent reputation. The management also runs a kite surfing centre. BB **$75**

Evergreen Bungalows 2.6km north ☎0686 919081, ⓦevergreen-bungalows.com. German-run, the beach-front plot is the thing here, though the seven rustic beach bungalows are also impressive, using plenty of driftwood, wonky beams, bamboo and mangrove poles. All have vaulted lofts (accessed by steep staircases) that serve as separate guest rooms, so there are fourteen rooms, all with box nets over their big beds. There's a well-priced restaurant, and various excursions on offer. BB **$70**

Mustapha's Place 800m south ☎0772 099422 or ☎024 224 0069, ⓦmustaphasplace.com. Heavy on the reggae and Rasta culture, this nicely chilled-out and lovingly decorated place has several coral-walled bungalows set in an amazing garden a couple of minutes from the beach, each with its own style, some sharing bathrooms, others on two levels, and all decorated with colourful wildlife murals and fabrics; the en-suite rooms cost $50. Also has Bwejuu's best bar, a health spa, and a

decent if slow restaurant. Staff offer a range of locally-run trips, whether cultural or ecological. BB **$30**

★**Robinson's Place** 3km north ☎0777 413479, ⓦrobinsonsplace.net. Set in an almost jungly beach garden, this is a small, whimsical, unpretentious and highly recommended place run by a charming Zanzibari–British family, who have resisted the temptation to move into "boutique hotel" territory. It's also properly ecofriendly: electricity is limited to wind-powered battery chargers; lighting is by kerosene lamps; and all produce is sourced locally. There are only six rooms (twelve guests), so book well ahead. All are eclectic in design, though the best is at the top of a two-storey Robinson Crusoe-style house by the beach. Meals, drinks and siestas are taken in a cool beach *banda*, a circular take on the traditional Swahili coffee *barazas* in soft and colourful adobe-like forms. Meals are limited to a sumptuous breakfast and dinner (overnight guests only; around Tsh15,000). BB **$60**

Upepo Boutique Beach Bungalows 3.5km north ☎0784 619579, ⓦzanzibarhotelbeach.com. A sleepy, small and warmly welcoming place on a sandy plot studded with coconut palms and backed by tropical gardens. There are three bungalows (one with a full-on sea view), a couple of two-storey houses (upper floor is best), and a very fine seaside restaurant and a bar. BB **$70**

EATING AND DRINKING

Most of Bwejuu's restaurants are attached to its hotels. For your own supplies, there is a handful of basic shops (*dukas*) in the village.

★**Bellevue Guest House** 2.4km north ☎0777 209576. A nicely rounded menu covering most bases but concentrating on seafood (including, unusual elsewhere, some smoked) and Zanzibari classics, like fish or chicken in coconut, and curried rice. Main courses start at Tsh15,000, but it's worth spending a little more for something fancy, such as crab in its shell. Proper coffee, either straight or laced with ginger or spice, and how about passion fruit mousse for dessert? Also functions as a pleasantly shady bar, and has barbecue nights if busy at the weekend. No beach. Daily 8am–9pm.

Evergreen Bungalows 2.6km north ☎0686 919081. Eat by the beach, or take a drink on a swing. Choose from a modest selection of dishes announced on a blackboard: nothing fancy, but all tasty, and, at around Tsh11,000 for seafood, very reasonably priced. Daily 8am–9pm.

Mustapha's Place 800m south ☎0772 099422. The restaurant is fine, but it's the bar – popular with backpackers for years – that's worth a special visit, particularly if reggae's your thing. It's also as good a place as any in which to learn African drumming, or the finer points of playing *bao*. No beach. Daily 11am–10pm or later.

11

Upepo Boutique Beach Bungalows 3.5km north ☎0784 619579. The beachside restaurant here has a fine reputation, with, as you might guess, ultra fresh seafood being the speciality (Tsh12000–18,000), but there's also pasta, sandwiches and various vegetarian options, including coconut milk-based curries. Finish with a chocolate pancake. Good bar, complete with sangria. Daily 8am–9pm or later.

Michamvi Peninsula

North of Bwejuu, the **MICHAMVI PENINSULA** is flanked to the east by especially dreamy beaches. The peninsula is sparsely inhabited, and has three distinct areas for tourists. First up from Bwejuu is **Dongwe**. Dusty and rather dull when seen from land, its beautiful sandy beaches are hidden behind the walls of the beach resorts have attracted a number of wilfully expensive hotels, most of them dealing with pre-booked package tours. More personal are a couple of hotels perched atop the headland of **Ras Michamvi** at the peninsula's northern tip, which have lovely sandy coves down below, and superb views. At the end of the road, looking west over Chwaka Bay, is **Kae**, whose superb beach has attracted a number of hotels, some eclectic, others bland. Wherever you stay on Michamvi, interaction with locals is limited, and you're also limited in your choice of restaurants and bars, as the ones in all-inclusive resorts (mostly in and around Dongwe) do not admit day-trippers. That said, if you just want sand and sea, and are content with the activities offered by your chosen hotel, you'll have a wonderful time.

ARRIVAL AND DEPARTURE

MICHAMVI PENINSULA

By daladala The only daladala venturing as far as Kae leaves Stone Town's Darajani terminal no later than 3.30pm, and takes about two hours (Tsh3000). Confusingly, the vehicle is marked "Bwejuu" (#324), so be sure to ask whether it goes to Kae (or, if that should draw a blank stare, Michamvi). In the opposite direction, the vehicle leaves Kae at around 5am. Tourist beach transfer minibuses don't cover this area.

ACCOMMODATION

Breezes Beach Club Dongwe ☎0774 440883, ⓦbreezes-zanzibar.com. The oldest of the big beach resorts, impersonal, but stuffed with amenities including a huge swimming pool, health spa, fitness centre, floodlit tennis court, several restaurants and bars, evening entertainment, the Rising Sun Dive Centre (see p.463), other water sports, and a great beach. The rooms, seventy of them, are in a series of bland two-storey blocks. HB **$320**

Echo Beach Hotel Dongwe ☎0773 593260, ⓦechobeachhotel.com. A calm, intimate, romantic, and unfailingly friendly British-run hideaway, with nine spacious rooms in bungalows sweetly decorated in Afro-Arabian style, all with a/c, and sea-view terraces. Other than the superb restaurant, there's not a mass of things to do (there is a small pool though, and a jacuzzi), but you can always drop in to *Breezes Beach Club* next door to arrange something. HB **$390**

★**Kae Funk** Kae ☎0773 600859, ⓦkaefunk.com. This started off as a backpacker's bar, and is now a welcome mid-range addition to Kae's hotels. It's also by far the jolliest, built largely out of driftwood, old boats and other assorted junk. The beach itself is spectacular, and the accommodation – in ten outwardly rustic *bandas* – is surprisingly elegant, very comfortable, and great value for money. The bar, which spills down to the beach, is a delight, but don't come here looking for peace and quiet – the music goes on until midnight, or 3am on Wed.

Snorkelling, dhow sailing and padding in *ngalawa* canoes can be arranged on site, other watersports through the nearby *Michamvi Sunset Bay* resort. BB **$90**, deluxe **$120**

★**Kichanga Lodge** Ras Michamvi (turning is 2km east of Pingwe) ☎0777 835515, ⓦkichanga.com. Set on a high grassy bluff, this beautifully designed and elegant lodge has a distinctly rustic style, making able use of coir rope, palm weave and driftwood, and those silky-smooth cement floors typical of Zanzibar, which are a pleasure to walk on barefoot. Guest rooms are in a scatter of well-spaced bungalows and villas. The best is the utterly gorgeous honeymoon suite, and the equally stylish "Villa" bungalows at the front, with astounding sea views. All make nice use of fabrics, and have terraces with rope beds and hammocks. Other than soaking up the atmosphere, the main on-site activity is yoga. BB garden view **$220**, sea view **$260**

★**Ras Michamvi Beach Resort** Ras Michamvi ☎0657 432020 or ☎0777 413434, ⓦrasmichamvi.com. The awkward gate security – similar to *Kichanga's* – comes as a surprise for a locally owned place, but once in you get to enjoy one of the most spectacular hotel locations on the island. Like *Kichanga*, it's set on a high bluff at the peninsula's very tip, giving 180-degree sea views. There are fifteen rooms in bungalows connected by shaded wooden walkways. All are large, and come with a/c, box nets, fans and tiled bathrooms. The swimming pool is a beauty if not quite "infinity" (there's a

11

little wall around it that stops it merging visually with the ocean). Three rooms are suitable for guests with disabilities, but unfortunately the two secluded beaches are accessed via long flights of stairs. Other facilities include a restaurant, well-equipped open-air gym, internet access and snorkelling trips. HB garden view $214, sea view $229

EATING AND DRINKING

Echo Beach Hotel Dongwe ☎ 0773 593260. This has long enjoyed a solid reputation for five-star dining: beautifully laid-out tables, toes-in-the-sand beach chic, knock-out views and refined cuisine. The seafood garners heaps of praise (it's the perfect place for a classic French Bouillabaisse, say), and there's plenty of it, but you'll also find British favourites such as lamb with mint sauce. Fine wines too. Expect to pay over $40 for a full meal with drinks. Daily 7.30am–10pm.

★**Kae Funk** Kae ☎ 0773 600859, ⓦ facebook.com /pages/Kae-Funky-Zanzibar/132287396809495. A supremely chilled out two-storey bar built out of old boats, logs that drifted ashore, and lots of mangrove poles and thatch. There are plenty of hammock-like swings, a garden at the side, a huge selection of drinks, good meals for under $10, and a party every Wed that goes on until 3am. Other events are announced on their Facebook page. Open 24hr.

Ras Michamvi Beach Resort Ras Michamvi ☎ 0657 432020 or ☎ 0777 413434. Don't mind the Maasai guards at the gate – the restaurant here is open to all, and though the menu is modest, that means everything on it should be available. The real reason for taking lunch here though is the fantastic view. Meals or snacks cost $10–14; three-course dinners go for $20–25. Reservations required. Daily 11am–9.30pm.

★**The Rock** Kijiweni Beach, 900m south of Karafuu Hotel Beach Resort, Pingwe ☎ 0776 591360, ⓦ therockrestaurantzanzibar.com. You won't believe this place unless you see it: perched atop a tiny coral outcrop just off the beach, which at high tide becomes an island that you have to wade out to before clambering up a wonky ladder (though at low tide, you can simply walk out). It was set up many years ago by a charmingly dreamy villager, and, depending on the tide, required the waiter to swim out to fishermen on the reef to collect your order. No more: it's a proper restaurant now, even a pretentious one, and priced accordingly (main courses from $30). The seafood is always fresh, of course, but quality and portion sizes vary – but it's the unique location you're paying for, and that will always recommend it. Good wine list. Daily 11am–10pm.

Northern Unguja

The beaches of **northern Unguja** were the first to be discovered by foreign beach bums, when – back in the bell-bottomed 1970s – a handful of hippy escapees started calling at Zanzibar on their cosmic journey to Kathmandu. Even today, with the bulk of the island's visitors sunning themselves in the north, hotel development has been surprisingly unobtrusive (the big bad exception being Kiwengwa in the northeast), and by and large the place still lives up to the old mantra of "peace and love", a refrain you'll hear a fair amount from dreadlocked Rasta-lookalike beach boys.

The northernmost beaches of **Nungwi** and **Kendwa** (the only ones covered by beach transfer minibuses from Stone Town) are the ones to head for if you're looking for nightlife; more sedate are **Matemwe** and **Pongwe** in the east. At all four places you can arrange **snorkelling** (for which you don't necessarily need a boat; there are shallow intertidal reefs within wading distance), as well as **scuba diving** (see pp.462–463) and dhow cruises. The bigger resort-style hotels have other watersports, too.

As with southern Unguja, at **low tide** the ocean recedes considerably; the exceptions, allowing swimming at all times of day, are Kendwa and Pongwe. Note that all these beaches can be adorned by pungent **seaweed** (sometimes laced with sea urchins) between December and February, though most hotels clear their beaches. If all that beach lounging gets tedious, an excursion to **Kiwengwa-Pongwe Forest Reserve** is a refreshing change, and even has bat-filled caves to explore.

Pongwe

Following the abolition of the slave trade by a reluctant Sultan Barghash in 1873, a number of places along the then extremely remote northeastern coastline, especially Chwaka Bay and Pongwe, were used as illegal **slaving ports**, continuing the trade with the Seychelles and other French Indian Ocean possessions until the beginning of the twentieth century. Still retaining a somewhat isolated feel is the tiny fishing village of **PONGWE**, 46km from Stone Town. There's nothing much to it, but the **beach** – with unbelievably clear water and lots of swaying palm trees – is the stuff of dreams.

ARRIVAL AND DEPARTURE PONGWE

By daladala Getting here by daladala can be awkward, as they don't run every day, so enquire the day before: the #209 leaves Stone Town's Darajani terminal, usually at 7am, while the #233 from Mwembe Ladu leaves at variable times (both cost Tsh2000). Incidentally, don't confuse Pongwe with Mwera Pongwe (daladala #225), which is another place entirely.

ACCOMMODATION

The following are right on the swoonsome beach. The sections in front of *Pongwe Beach Hotel* and *Santa Maria Coral Park* are swimmable at all tides; the others can be swum at high tide only.

Pongwe Beach Hotel 700m north of the village ☎ 0784 336181, ⓦ pongwe.com. A favourite of honeymooners, this tourist enclave offers next to no contact with locals thanks to its walled cocoon. Scattered around the mature gardens inside are sixteen spacious if somewhat basic thatched bungalows, with carved wooden doors and *semadari* beds, and fans but no a/c, plus four suites with private plunge pools ($345). There's also a bar, a fancy restaurant doling out generous portions (and candlelit dining on the beach if you wish), a huge freeform infinity swimming pool, a pleasant lounge area, and various pricey tours and activities. HB garden view **$280**, sea view **$300**

Queen of Sheba Beach Lodge 300m north of the village ⓦ santamaria-zanzibar.com. Architecturally similar to *Seasons Lodge* in its use of coral ragstone for building, with seven bungalows, all beside the shore, plus a similarly situated restaurant and bar, and swimming pool. The German–Zanzibar couple behind it give it quite a local flavour, and there's a boat for snorkelling. HB **$170**

Santa Maria Coral Park 400m south of the village ⓦ santamaria-zanzibar.com. Owned by the same people as the *Queen of Sheba*, this is on the other side of the village in delightful grounds, all soft white sand with lots of weird, wonderful and wild indigenous plants including tall, swaying coconut palms and bizarre screw palms. The rooms are more basic than in the other hotels as they were originally part of a budget resort, but they're comfortable, and have been smartened up with thatched roofs. All have verandas, and there's a brilliant two-storey cottage (perfect for families) with a sea view from its top balcony (the only room with a view). There's also a breezy beach bar complete with a rocking rope swing, and a restaurant. Day-trippers are welcome for meals or drinks. BB **$80**

Seasons Lodge Zanzibar 500m north of the village ☎ 0776 107225, ⓦ seasonszanzibar.com. Irish–Ugandan owned, and less formal but also less classy than the next door *Pongwe Beach Hotel*. It does have more space, however, with ten bright and breezy rooms, and the beach is nice, while the restaurant and lounge are spectacularly located just above the shore. BB **$240**

Kiwengwa and Pwani Mchangani

As Zanzibar's main package-holiday destination, **KIWENGWA** is dominated by enormous all-inclusive resorts catering almost entirely to Italians, and as the beach is similar to that in far more intimate Matemwe, further north, there's frankly little to recommend Kiwengwa, although there are a couple of hotels worth considering, and those are reviewed below.

Kiwengwa is actually rather difficult to pin down, seeing as it sprawls along almost 10km of coastline. The middle bit is called **Kijangwani** (not that many people know the name), and the package-hotel strip fizzles out a couple of kilometres before **PWANI MCHANGANI** (also called Kwa Pangaa), before picking up again on the other side.

Kiwengwa-Pongwe Forest

2km west of Kiwengwa • Daily 7.30am–5pm • $10 • Walk west from Kiwengwa along the tarmac 1.7km beyond the junction for Pwani Mchangani, and turn south just after Mwanza village on to a rough track; the visitor centre is 750m along • Daladala #117 runs along the main road – ask to be dropped at Mchekeni

In 2009, the 33-square-kilometre **Kiwengwa-Pongwe Forest Reserve** was set up by the Kiwengwa Ecotourism Project (ⓦ tms.utu.fi/kiwa), with the aim of getting locals – especially women – to benefit from tourism. The reserve, much of which is **coral rag forest** (which takes longer than most forests to recover from logging and land clearance), encloses some of the most biodiverse terrestrial habitat on the islands. **Animals** you might see include red colobus monkeys, Sykes' and blue monkeys, Ader's duikers and – among forty-seven bird species – the delightfully gaudy Fischer's turaco.

In the interests of preservation, visitors are restricted to three **nature trails** (200m, 400m and 2km), a small farm, and the bat-filled **Mchekeni caves**, Zanzibar's largest coral caverns: basically big gaps in what used to be coral reefs when sea levels were higher. Historically, the caves were regarded by locals with considerable unease, as they were home to all manner of malevolent spirits, as well as wild pigs and leopards (now extinct on Zanzibar), which were kept as symbols of spiritual power by witchdoctors.

ARRIVAL AND DEPARTURE
KIWENGWA AND PWANI MCHANGANI

By daladala Kiwengwa is covered by frequent #117 daladalas from Stone Town (Tsh2000), finishing at Kiwengwa village south of the main hotel strip; daladala drivers should be happy to divert to your hotel for a tip of Tsh2000–5000. Daladalas to Pwani Mchangani, 8km north of Kiwengwa, are far less frequent; enquire about them the day before. Both routes start on Creek Road in Stone Town, just north of the Central Market.

ACCOMMODATION

Ocean Paradise Resort Kijangwani ☎0774 440990, ⓦ oceanparadisezanzibar.com. Best of the big five-star resorts on this stretch of coast, very stylish and making good use of local materials in both its rooms and common areas. Facilities include Zanzibar's largest swimming pool, tons of watersports including scuba diving, run by One Ocean (see p.463), the inevitable "spa", and tennis courts, ocean-view restaurant, various bars and a disco. Rooms must be booked in advance. HB $280

★ **Shooting Star Lodge** Kijangwani ☎0777 414166, ⓦ shootingstarlodge.com. Perched on a clifftop halfway between Kiwengwa and Pwani Mchangani, this intimate lodge boasts wonderful sea views (the beach is down a steep flight of steps), and is one of the northeast coast's most romantic options. The fifteen rooms are attractively furnished, but even better are two turret-like villas, each with two floors, private swimming pool, and a bath on top ($575). All guests have use of a small but lovely infinity pool (the horizon just goes on and on). So long as the lodge isn't jam-packed, day-trippers can also use the pool if they buy lunch. The food is exquisite, and at night you can enjoy a seafood dinner on the beach in the light of candles and torches. There's also a beauty spa, and other activities can be arranged through the nearby *Bluebay Beach Resort*. HB garden view $250, sea view $350

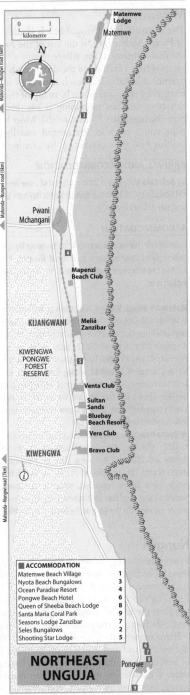

11

ACCOMMODATION

NORTHEAST UNGUJA

Matemwe

The beautiful palm-fringed beach south of the fishing village of **MATEMWE**, 6km north of Pwani Mchangani, is the last of the main northeast-coast destinations, and one of the more intimate. The village retains a tangible sense of community, and is one of few places where you'll share the dusty roads with cows, chickens and goats, and gaggles of irrepressible kids. The beach itself is an utter delight, broad and white, though it's fringed by two dozen hotels, many of them mid-size resorts. As with most other east-coast beaches, **swimming** at low tide is impossible unless you fancy a long walk over the coral flats (with sandals). Most hotels have kayaks and can organize sailing trips, which can also be arranged, usually for less, directly with locals. Other than just chilling out, the main reason for coming is superb **diving and snorkelling**.

ARRIVAL AND ACCOMMODATION   MATEMWE

By daladala Matemwe is 50km northeast of Stone Town. #118 daladalas (Tsh2000) run throughout the day from the west side of Creek Road.

By taxi Few if any beach transfer minibuses (see p.464) go to Matemwe, and a taxi costs $30–40, though you'll need to bargain.

ACCOMMODATION

Matemwe has plenty of accommodation to choose from, much of it pricey "boutique" hotels or package-tour sprawls. The smaller places fill up quickly, so book ahead. The asphalt road ends at the shore, with most of Matemwe's hotels spreading out over two kilometres north from there, finishing just before the village itself. The "junction" referred to below is from the asphalt road.

Matemwe Beach Village 1km north of the junction ⓦ matemwebeach.com. Located amid palm trees on a large beachside plot, this place needs an overhaul, but for the price is still quite reasonable. The suites ($300) are best, especially #1 and #5 which have sea views. There's a cosy bar and a superb restaurant serving international and Zanzibari cuisine, plus a swimming pool, and a branch of One Ocean (see p.463) for diving and watersports. In brief, a lovely place to chill out, but don't come expecting resort-style standards or facilities. HB $̲2̲2̲0̲

★**Nyota Beach Bungalows** 800m east of the junction ☎ 0777 484303, ⓦ nyotabeachbungalows.com. A dreamy and affordable Italian-run place on a beautiful stretch of sand. The ten rooms, all en suite, are darkish but comfy; some are in bungalows, others in two-storey houses; all have small fans and box nets, but only one has a proper sea view. On the edge of the beach is a charming

Robinson Crusoe-esque bar-cum-restaurant on two floors, all wood and palm weave, complete with a swing. The menu offers a wide choice of mostly Swahili dishes, plus a few Italian faves; the basics are around $10. Other facilities, at extra cost, are snorkelling off Mnemba, and bicycle and boat rental. BB $̲7̲5̲

★**Seles Bungalows** 900m north of the junction ☎ 0776 931690, ⓦ selesbungalows.com. If only more hotels were like this. Small, charming, laid-back, unpretentious, homely, tasteful and bursting with character: the lopsided but lovely two-storey bar/restaurant/lounge is made from mangrove poles, palm leaves, driftwood, thatch and an old dhow. The rooms, two per cottage, are simple but great value and have big draped nets. Good food too (catch of the day), and staff are happy to serve breakfast in bed. BB $̲9̲0̲

Nungwi

From humble beginnings as a fishing village and dhow-making centre known only to a handful of hippies, **NUNGWI** – being the village and beaches either side of Unguja's northernmost point, Ras Nungwi – has become, in little more than a decade, Zanzibar's second most popular beach resort after Kiwengwa. There's plenty on offer, not least the island's liveliest nightlife, dozens of seafood restaurants, plus snorkelling, scuba diving, a turtle pool, village tours and sunset dhow cruises.

There are actually three, very different, Nungwis: the village itself, which sits a short distance inland and is practically invisible from the shore, and the two main stretches of beach, where almost all the hotels, bars and restaurants are located. The **eastern shore** is quite calm, with no facilities outside of its few hotels, which makes it a nice retreat for smoochy couples, and its beach – at the foot of a very low headland – is attractively wild. The **western shore** is a different story, having been overrun by a flurry of uncontrolled development, and it's infested with tourists and associated hangers-on, including an army of often very pushy touts, as well as a surprising number of wannabe gigolos (there's evidently a market). The western beach used to be bliss, but as many hotels and their walls have encroached on it, erosion is now a problem, something that a series of ill-conceived breakwaters is only worsening. As such, western Nungwi is great if you're in party mood, but for a perfect stretch of sand, look elsewhere.

For a long time, locals managed to shrug off the tourist invasion, but these days there's a palpable sense of bitterness in the air, which you might feel when walking around the village: one too many years of tourists sauntering around the village in swimwear, and the ever-increasing number of walls around resorts that are blocking access to the coast.

The dhow builders and fish market

In spite of the tourist trade, Nungwi itself remains a traditional fishing village, whose history of seafaring and dhow building is a source of pride. The **dhow builders** use the stretch of beach beyond the *DoubleTree* resort – the craftsmen are used to inquisitive tourists, but ask before taking photos. Nearby, at the back of the beach, is a cluster of wooden structures that become the daily **fish market** whenever the fishermen return (depends on the tides). Moored just offshore here are dozens of *ngalawa* outriggers.

Mnarani Aquarium

Ras Nungwi • Daily 9am–6pm • $5

At the northernmost tip of Unguja, Ras Nungwi, stands a lighthouse built in 1886, which is out of bounds. Just before the lighthouse, **Mnarani Aquarium** is a natural 60m by 20m pond of usually murky water that's surrounded by porous coral ragstone into which seawater seeps at high tide (the water is clearest two hours before). Housing a number of hawksbill and green turtles (*ng'amba* and *kasakasa* respectively), this started out in 1993 as little more than a money-making scheme for locals, but over time has accrued more noble aims, these days tagging and releasing excess turtles: the pool rarely contains more than twenty, and the average sojourn of an individual before being released is about three years. The turtles, both species of which are endangered, are brought in by fishermen who occasionally catch them in their nets. There's a walkway over the pond from where you can feed seaweed to the denizens, and for an extra $5 you can jump in and swim around with them; the water, whose level varies according to the tide, also contains grey mullet and trevally.

ARRIVAL AND DEPARTURE | NUNGWI

By daladala Nungwi is 59km from Stone Town. #116 daladalas run here throughout the day (roughly 2hr; Tsh2000) from the west side of Creek Road, north of the Central Market, and drop you at the end of the tarmac, just short of the village centre.

By minibus Most tourists come on shared minibuses (see p.464), which cost $10, and are bookable at Stone Town's hotels. Most leave at 8am; in high season, they may also leave at 3pm, and they will drop you at your chosen hotel.

ACTIVITIES AND TOURS

The following activities can be arranged at most hotels, dive centres, and through the tour kiosk outside the aquarium. If arranged on the beach, prices should be a deal less than those quoted by hotels, but you'll need to bargain. Note that if you need cash to pay for activities, you'll have to get it in advance as Nungwi has no banks, nor an ATM machine.

Cycling Bicycles can be rented from locals and hotels for around $10 a day.

Dhow cruises A two- to three-hour dhow cruise is a magnificent way of whiling away a lazy afternoon, ideally catching the sunset shortly before you return. You have two

options: a boat just for you (around $40–50), or cheaper, and better for those in a party mood, shared excursions ($20 per person, or $30 with drinks), which may include a drink or two. The usual route is down the coast to well beyond Kendwa, then back.

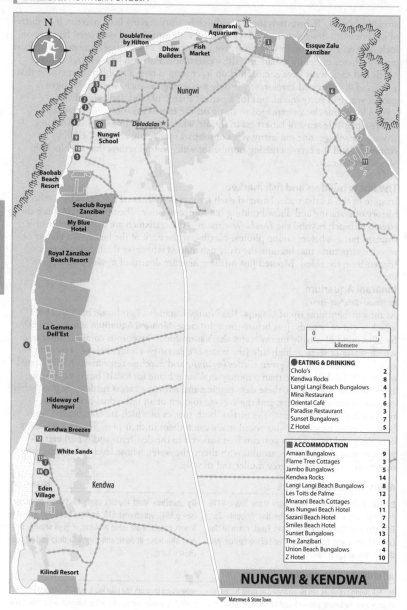

Matemwe & Stone Town

EATING & DRINKING

Cholo's	2
Kendwa Rocks	8
Langi Langi Beach Bungalows	4
Mina Restaurant	1
Oriental Café	6
Paradise Restaurant	3
Sunset Bungalows	7
Z Hotel	5

ACCOMMODATION

Amaan Bungalows	9
Flame Tree Cottages	3
Jambo Bungalows	5
Kendwa Rocks	14
Langi Langi Beach Bungalows	8
Les Toits de Palme	12
Mnarani Beach Cottages	1
Ras Nungwi Beach Hotel	11
Sazani Beach Hotel	7
Smiles Beach Hotel	2
Sunset Bungalows	13
The Zanzibari	6
Union Beach Bungalows	4
Z Hotel	10

NUNGWI & KENDWA

Kite surfing Kiteboarding Zanzibar (☎0779 720259, ⓦkiteboardingzanzibar.com) is based at *Sazani Beach Hotel* on the eastern shore. Equipment hire costs $60 for half a day; a three-hour introductory course, which can be in a group, costs $165; an hour's private tuition is $90.

Snorkelling and diving Any hotel can arrange a snorkelling trip or equipment to rent ($5 a day is fair, but $10 is the norm), but for longer trips – where safety is a concern – it would be better to go through one of the dive centres (see p.463). A day-trip snorkelling off Mnemba Atoll, off the eastern shore, costs upwards of $60 per person.

Village tour The "Nungwi Cultural Village Tour", bookable at a hut outside the aquarium, is a two-and-a-half-hour walk that includes the aquarium and dhow builders, plus an old mosque, medicinal trees and plants, markets, basket-weavers, and a visit to a supposedly haunted saltwater well, much used for washing in the morning (spirits are evidently late risers).

Watersports Windsurfing, kayaking (both from $30/hour) and waterskiing (from $70 for 15min) can be arranged through most hotels or at the tour kiosk.

ACCOMMODATION

Nungwi has over three dozen hotels: a mixture of whitewashed bungalow resorts with standard-issue *makuti* thatch roofs, and an increasing number of brash and architecturally trite all-inclusive resorts that cater mainly for Italian package tours. Almost all are overpriced even by Zanzibar's standards, but there are still plenty of more decent places to choose from. Most hotels have wi-fi internet access, and the presence or absence of watersports shouldn't be a factor when choosing a hotel, as activities can be arranged anywhere, though location is important: hotels on the east side are calm and quiet, those on the west are in the thick of action, so can be noisy. If you're staying on the east side, be aware that the beach east of the lighthouse is unsafe to walk at night.

WEST SIDE

Amaan Bungalows ☎0775 044719, ⓦocean.co.tz. Nungwi's oldest hotel, once a collection of shacks, has undergone several dramatic face lifts over the years. The latest has endowed it with a swimming pool and renovated the rooms to a high standard. The best are in a wooden terrace partly *over* the sea, whose stilted supports get wet feet at high tide. The hotel's restaurant is average at best, however. BB $80, sea view $160

Flame Tree Cottages ☎024 224 0100 or ☎0752 526366, ⓦflametreecottages.com. A short distance beyond the busiest part of northwest Nungwi, this is a very calm, walled-in collection of bungalows run by a Zanzibari–Scottish couple, with a homely feel. The beach wall keeps out Nungwi's ever-burgeoning army of touts, though of course it also means you're less likely to meet locals. The twelve one-storey cottages and the two-storey honeymoon suite are simple and comfortable, with a/c, fans, fridge, a kitchen, and a breakfast terrace. The beachside restaurant varies from average to good. Village tours can be arranged with the staff. BB $170

Jambo Brothers Bungalows ☎0773 109343 or ☎0777 473901, ⓔjambobungalows@yahoo.com. A fairly reliable budget mainstay with a nice stretch of beach nearby. It's still quite basic and not everything works, but usually clean, and has partial sea views from most of its rooms (two per bungalow). The staff are helpful, and on the whole the restaurant is acceptable. In short: no complaints for the price (which is negotiable). BB $30–40

★**Langi Langi Beach Bungalows** ☎024 224 0470 or ☎0773 911000, ⓦlangilangizanzibar.com. The Arabian design, both outside and in, is sophisticated and somehow Mediterranean, and sets a good vibe for this calm, elegant, friendly and effectively run hotel. Rooms at the back, hidden amid lush gardens, are in semi-detached bungalows and are very well equipped (including a/c); those at the front – with arched doorways, exposed roof pillars, and a smattering of antiques – are more expensive suites ($200), some with spectacular sea views (and balconies too), others overlooking the swimming pool. The

open-sided restaurant also has great views, and is among Nungwi's best and most consistent. BB $140

Smiles Beach Hotel West side ☎0773 444105 or ☎0774 444334, ⓦsmilesbeachhotel.com. An amusing foray into kitsch, with four two-storey Toytown houses with red tin roofs and external spiral staircases facing sea (the beach lies beyond an unsightly seawall, as with other hotels in the area). The sixteen rooms, including triples, have a/c, sea-view balconies, satellite TV and spotless bathrooms. There's a restaurant by the ocean, a boat for snorkelling or sunset cruises, and the staff are helpful. Closed April & May. BB $140

Union Beach Bungalows ☎0777 354927, ⓦfacebook.com/unionbeachbungalows. For anywhere else this, too, is cheap so outrageously overpriced, but it's cheap for Nungwi and, although a little run-down, is a welcoming place. The rooms, all twin-bed, are in five semi-detached cottages beside the shore, fringed by an ugly scatter of rocks. There's also a small restaurant (no alcohol). BB $60

Z Hotel ☎0774 266266, ⓦthezhotel.com. Nungwi's oldest "boutique" hotel, a graceless four-storey block dumped on the edge of a once beautiful coral rise – all in the best tradition of contemporary designs, meaning a complete eyesore. The love-it-or-loathe-it theme continues inside, where you can look forward to designer accoutrements in the manner of Philippe Starck, together with the latest mod cons, including cable TV delivered via wall-mounted plasma screens – to be fair the hotel hits the mark for its intended market, and it's cheap for the standards offered. There's an infinity swimming pool on a deck in front, a nicely positioned restaurant (see p.497) with sea views, and a tapas and cocktail bar. Closed mid-April to end-May. HB garden view $220, sea view $250

EAST SIDE

Mnarani Beach Cottages ☎0713 334062, ⓦmnarani-beach-cottages.com. There's always a warm welcome at this small, intimate and efficiently run mini-resort on the quieter eastern flank of the peninsula, set beside a wonderful cove (accessed via steps) in lush gardens full of plants and

11

trees. The standard rooms are twelve smallish, bright orange *makuti*-thatched cottages with a/c, eight of which have sea views – and are good value. Larger and more fancifully decorated "superior" rooms ($400) and family apartments are also available. There are sun loungers and hammocks on the beach, a bar nestled among coconut palms, a curvaceous swimming pool, and an average-to-good seafood restaurant – dine on a terrace or, at night, on the beach. Snorkelling equipment is available, and there is a dhow for cruises and fishing. BB **$160**

Ras Nungwi Beach Hotel ☎ 024 223 3767 or ☎ 0777 417316, ⓦ rasnungwi.com. An unusually pretty 32-room resort set on a palm-dotted outcrop beside a lovely stretch of sand on the east coast. Prices depend on room size and proximity to the beach – in this bracket, you might as well cough up the extra for a sea-view chalet ($450). All rooms have a/c, fans and balconies, and are attractively decorated. The hotel also boasts a swimming pool, several bars and restaurants (occasional live music, and seafood buffets twice a week), a spa (massages), and plenty of watersports,

including windsurfing. Closed April–May. BB **$360**

Sazani Beach Hotel East side ☎ 0776 668681, ⓦ sazanibeach.com. A small, relaxed place on a lovely east-coast beach, miles from the western tourist hub. It has just ten well-equipped, en-suite rooms (they call them "snuggeries") in the colourful gardens, most with sea views from their verandas. There's also a good beachside bar and restaurant. BB **$130**

★**The Zanzibari** ☎ 0772 222919, ⓦ thezanzibari .com. An airy boutique hotel with just eight rooms on the headland, and vegetation between them and the sea. The style of the rooms is somewhat Mediterranean (spacious, elegant and uncluttered, with plenty of whitewash and rustic furniture), but the two-floor "Frangipane suites" ($575) are quite spectacular, with superb sea views and stupendous bathrooms. Also has an infinity swimming pool, a bar, restaurant and two lounges constructed entirely out of bits of old dhows (including an unfurled sail). Genuine ecological ethos, too. Garden view **$363**, sea view **$398**

EATING AND DRINKING

The string of **restaurants and bars** along the west side of the cape is one of Nungwi's main attractions, where competition has succeeded, in some cases, to keep standards high. Overall, they're quite similar, both in price (Tsh15,000–20,000 for a main course) and menus (pizzas, pasta and lots of seafood), though ones right on the shore can be lackadaisical about service and quality, since their location guarantees passing trade. Better than menu items, in many cases, are the daily specials chalked up on boards by the beach. If you're on a tight budget, there are a few **local eat houses** (*mgahawa*) in the village behind the shore, particularly around and to the east of the school. Nungwi's **nightlife** is Zanzibar's liveliest, with plenty of bars to choose from along the western cape, impromptu moonlit drumming sessions on the beach, and **full-moon beach parties** at *Cholo's*.

WEST SIDE

★**Cholo's** ☎ 0777 505434, ⓦ facebook.com/pages /Cholos-Bar/147383858786054. This *Mad Max*-style Rasta refuge is right on the beach, and easily Nungwi's weirdest and funkiest joint, constructed almost entirely from flotsam. The seats are canoes, the bar is a dhow's prow, there's a motorbike up in a tree (don't ask), hammocks slung all over the place, and a cool chill-out zone perched on stilts above the bar. The food is also generally good, including grilled shrimp and lobster (upwards of Tsh20,000), and so long as you're in synch with the music (more techno than reggae), you should have a blast. Upcoming events are announced on their Facebook page. Daily 10am–3pm.

★**Langi Langi Beach Bungalows** ☎ 024 224 0470 or ☎ 0773 911000. The elegant *Marhaba Café & Restaurant* here is perched on a deck over the edge of the beach (it's on stilts), and decorated with Arabian reproduction antiques, old prints and octagonal Ottoman-style marble-topped coffee tables. The views are wonderful, and the seafood is consistently excellent (try *pilau* with octopus and coconut curry; Tsh18,000) and comes in big portions; they also cater for pizza fanatics. The service is efficient and there's proper

coffee, fresh juices and decadent desserts. No alcohol, but you can bring your own (there's a store nearby). Book ahead for dinner. Daily noon–3pm & 6.30–9.30pm.

Mina Restaurant, next to Jambo Brothers Bungalows. A shack may not promise much in the way of culinary delights, but this one's the perfect antidote to the often overworked (and always pricey) fare in more touristy places. The speciality is *pilau*, served, as is traditional, with beans, vegetables, and either fish or beef, all for just Tsh3000. Daily 8am–8pm or later.

★**Paradise Restaurant** Paradise Beach Bungalows ☎ 0773 203786. This enjoys a wonderfully romantic view from its wooden terrace, and has plenty of tables with unobstructed sea views. Both the service and the food are generally excellent, whether full meals (a wide variety of barbecued fish, also lemongrass-laced seafood), lighter bites such as pizzas (wood-fired), snacks or real coffee. Particularly good is the grilled seafood platter, which includes lobster, crayfish, crab, calamari, octopus and fish (Tsh40,000; enough for two people). The sea-view terrace, looking both north and west, is smaller than at other places, so come early for a table right at the edge. It also functions as a bar, with a preference for Tanzanian sounds.

Closed in May. Daily 7.30am–10pm.

Z Hotel 0774 266266. Pretentious, certainly, but the restaurant and bar here are beautifully sited on a wooden deck extending over the beach. Both meals and drinks are expensive (over Tsh20,000 for main courses), but worth it for the delicious views. Also does great cappuccino, and the bar has huge comfy sofas and even swings. Daily 7am–10pm.

Kendwa

Nungwi's little sister, just 3km to the south, has come of age. A decade or so ago, **KENDWA** was cheap, cheerful, calm and very cool. The beach is still exceptional – a wide and blindingly white stretch suitable for swimming at all tides, or just lounging around in a hammock with cocktail to hand. And cheerful it is, too, but cheap no more, nor always calm – the beach parties, especially around full moon, have seen to that. Nonetheless, despite a rash of new hotels and a train of beach boys, souvenir salesmen and gigolos, it is definitely the place to head for if Nungwi feels too brash. For now, there are few noisy watersports to disturb you, but there's plenty to do on or under the water, not least **scuba diving**, for which Scuba Do (see p.463) at *Sunset Bungalows* comes highly recommended. For **dhow cruises**, ask around, as the operators (or the fishermen's contacts) change constantly. The big *jahazi* dhow that you might see on the beach belongs to *Kendwa Rocks*, and is used in high season for cruises and evening sundowners.

ARRIVAL AND INFORMATION

KENDWA

By minibus Kendwa lies west of the asphalt road to Nungwi. Daily beach transfer tourist minibuses ($10) leave Stone Town at 8am, turning back around 10.30am.

By daladala The #116 Nungwi daladala leaves from the west side of Creek Road (every half hour or so from 6am to 6pm; Tsh2000; around 2hr); get off at the signposted junction for Kendwa and walk the remaining 1.5km. To get here from Nungwi, 2–3km to the north, catch a daladala back down to the junction. Alternatively, ask around for a boat: there's nothing formal, but you shouldn't pay more than Tsh6000 if sharing with others, or Tsh30,000 per boat.

On foot Walking to or from Nungwi along the beach is possible, but avoid a rising or high tide, or you risk getting stuck between the coral cliffs and the sea.

ACCOMMODATION

The majority of Kendwa's hotels deal only with prebooked all-inclusive packages, and don't accept walk-ins. The following are pretty much the only exceptions. Despite a few bumps along the way, all three have been fairly reliable over the years.

Kendwa Rocks 0774 415475 or 0777 415528, kendwarocks.com. A huge selection of rooms at this bungalow resort, including Kendwa's cheapest, those being very basic palm-thatch *bandas* right at the back ($60). Costing almost twice as much are eight large coconut-wood cabins on stilts in a sandy clearing behind the beach, most of them containing two guest rooms; all have lots of varnished wood, rattan furniture, woven mats and partial sea views. At the back of the beach are several two- and three-storey buildings containing all sorts of other rooms, some extremely stylish and decked out in fake antiques. Bar and restaurant on the beach. BB **$100**

Les Toits de Palme 0777 418548, lestoitsdepalme .com. Just ten rooms: six in three bungalows up on the hill, and four in individual and very cute rustic *bandas* on the beach made of wood, palm wave, thatch and old ropes, all with fans and private bathrooms. Good food and beach bar, too. BB **$70**

★ **Sunset Bungalows** 0777 413818, sunsetkendwa.com. This is a bargain, especially the eighteen large, modern apartments right at the back, which are in excellent shape. Occupying a series of two-storey buildings, these are very well kitted out, including a/c, and have distant sea views from their verandas. The beach comes right up to the edge of the coral bluff, forming a kind of (dry) sandy inlet scattered with trees. Lining this are six small and relatively basic beach *bandas* decorated with colourful *kangas*; each has two guest rooms, but no sea views as they're side-on, and the beach bar and restaurant sit between them and the ocean. BB **$100**

EATING AND DRINKING

All Kendwa's hotels have their own **beach bars**, **restaurants** and musical tastes; you're welcome at most of them, even the all-inclusives. Menus and prices are very similar across the board, with fishy main courses starting at Tsh15,000. Much cheaper is an unnamed local restaurant, just south of the small shops on the rocky road leading to the hotels: here you can eat your fill for Tsh5000. On the Saturday closest to a full moon, *Kendwa Rocks* hosts its famous **full-moon beach party** (Tsh10,000, redeemable against drinks), which kicks off a few hours after sunset with acrobats, and continues well into the night. *Kendwa Rocks* also offers a distinctly provocative evening "booze cruise" in a converted *jahazi* dhow, for $25.

Kendwa Rocks This *makuti*-thatched bar and restaurant, the bar itself constructed from *mitumbwi* dugouts, is plush in appearance, but the quality of the cooking is variable – ask other tourists for their opinion before splashing out. When it's good, it's excellent, and has plenty of vegetarian choices, such as spinach lasagne. BBQ buffets are held on the beach whenever it's busy. Free wi-fi. Meals daily 7am–9pm; drinks til midnight or later

Oriental Café La Gemma Dell'Est ⓦ lagemmadellest .diamonds-resorts.com. This massive all-inclusive resort is an architectural blight, but the theatrical Ottoman-style restaurant, bar and lounge propped up at the end of its wooden jetty – right over the water – are perfectly placed, as long as your table faces out to sea. Particularly nice at sunset, whether in the company of a shisha pipe, a cup of tea or a beer. For a full meal, expect to pay at least $40. Daily 6.30am–10pm.

Sunset Bungalows On the beach and with a youthful vibe, the restaurant here has a well-rounded menu – à la carte, plus specials chalked up on a blackboard – with delights such as grilled calamari in ginger sauce, and no fewer than seven lobster dishes, including kebabs. Carnivores have a good choice, too, but don't expect the steak – something of a novelty on Zanzibar – to be anything like tender. The vegetarian selection is poor other than some surprisingly decent pizzas (Tsh12,000). It lets itself down, though, with instant coffee and (sometimes) juice from a bottle rather than freshly pressed. Meals daily 7am–9pm; drinks til midnight or later.

Pemba

The island of **Pemba**, 48km northeast of Unguja, is Zanzibar's forgotten half, traditionally conservative, religious and superstitious, and far removed from the Zanzibari mainstream. Measuring 67km from north to south and 22km from east to west, Pemba's highest point is no more than 100m above sea level, yet with its low hills gouged by gullies and entered by snaking mangrove-lined creeks, the island presents a lush and fertile profile compared with Unguja, and aptly fits the name given it by the Arab geographer Yakut ibn Abdallah al-Rumi (1179–1229), who called it *Jazirat al-Khadhra*, the Green Island – which holiday brochures have since changed to "Emerald Island".

Not that you'll find that many holiday brochures for Pemba: the island – and its tourism potential – has long been ignored by Zanzibar's Unguja-based government, with the result that Pemba sits at the bottom of a raft of Tanzanian statistics: per capita income is Tanzania's lowest, child mortality among the country's highest, and the infrastructure, although improving, is still paltry. Not surprisingly, Pemba is a stronghold of Zanzibar's opposition party, the **Civic United Front** (**CUF**) (see p.522), support for which has only deepened Pemba's marginalization. There are some positive signs however: thanks to the power-sharing accord on Zanzibar, the 2010 elections were the island's first that were not marred by violence or police repression. Pemba is also now connected to the national power grid, ending decades of reliance on unreliable generators.

Pemba has three main towns: the capital **Chake Chake** in the centre, **Mkoani**, the main port, in the south, and the livelier dhow harbour of **Wete** in the north. There's not an awful lot to do in any of them, but they do contain most of Pemba's accommodation and are good bases for exploring further afield. Rewarding stops include the primeval **Ngezi Forest** in the north; a scatter of tumbledown **ruins** that tell the story of much of the Swahili coast; a handful of deserted beaches (they are difficult to access, which is part of their charm); beautiful offshore islets; and great **scuba diving** – which is really the main reason to come. Despite these attractions, there are rarely more than a few dozen tourists on the island at any one time, and facilities are extremely limited, so you should **book ahead** for beachside accommodation and diving.

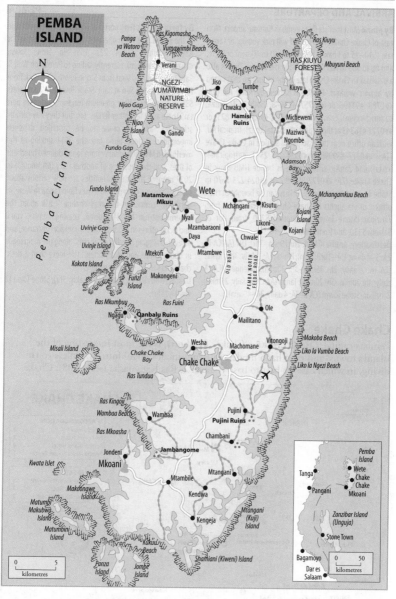

PEMBA ISLAND

Pemba's **climate** is wetter than Unguja's. The **long rains** (*masika*), during which it can pour constantly for weeks, fall between April and June, with May often completely washed out, as well as windy. The **short rains** (*vuli*), generally brief bursts early in the morning and again in the afternoon, supposedly fall between mid-October and end-November, but September can be very wet, too, as can December. Unless you're diving, the rains aren't an ideal time to be around. Nor is **Ramadan** (dates on p.79), when eating out by day is quite impossible.

ARRIVAL AND DEPARTURE — PEMBA

By plane Most tourists fly to Pemba's Karume airport, 6km east of Chake Chake. Hotels staff will pick you up, or take a taxi ($10–15 to Chake Chake, $35–40 to Mkoani or Wete, and up to $80 to Ras Kigomasha in the north). There's also a daladala to Chake Chake late in the afternoon that's used by airport workers. Pemba is served by Auric Air (AA: Ⓣ0783 491496 or Ⓣ0757 466648, both in Mwanza, Ⓦauricair.com); Coastal Aviation (CA: Ⓣ0752 627825, or Ⓣ0777 418343 at the airport, Ⓦcoastal.co.tz); Tropical Air, with an office near the Esso petrol station in Chake Chake (TA: Ⓣ0777 859996 or Ⓣ024 223 2511, Ⓦtropicalair.co.tz); and ZanAir, whose office is beside NMB Bank in Chake Chake (ZA: Ⓣ0777 859996, or Ⓣ024 223 3670 in Stone Town, Ⓦzanair.com). Tickets can be bought at their offices, or via agents in Chake Chake. Average fares from Zanzibar (Stone Town) are around $100, from Dar es Salaam $130, and from Tanga $70–90.

Destinations Arusha (CA ZA: 2hr 15min–3hr); Dar (AA CA TA ZA: 3–4 daily; 1hr–1hr 30min); Kilwa (CA: 1 daily; 3hr); Mafia (CA TA: 2 daily; 2hr 35min–3hr 30min); Serengeti (CA: 1 daily; 4hr 20min–5hr 20min); Tanga (AA CA: 2 daily; 25min); Zanzibar (Stone Town) (CA TA ZA: 4 daily; 30–40min).

By ferry Pemba's ferry port is at Mkoani, on the south side of the island. The main operator, with fast catamarans, is Azam Marine (Ⓣ024 223 1655 in Stone Town, Ⓦazammarine.com), currently sailing to Pemba on Wed & Sat (7am from Dar, 9am from Stone Town), and back from Pemba on Thurs & Sun at 8am. Stone Town to Mkoani costs $35 in economy, $40 in premium (on top), including port tax. There are a few other ferries, too, but they have erratic schedules, and are prone to be cancelled or even impounded. A good thing too: the 2011 sinking of the overloaded MV *Spice Islander* from Tanga claimed hundreds of lives, and the capsizing of another ferry (off Unguja) in 2012 ensured that the authorities are now serious about safety. There are currently no ferries from Tanga to Wete, in northern Pemba, but this may change – ask about the government-run MV *Maendeleo*. Leaving Pemba, you'll find ticket offices in sheds by the Mkoani port entrance, and an ever-changing handful of "agents" along the main roads in Chake Chake and Wete, often little more than a desk, chair and someone with a mobile.

Destinations Dar es Salaam (2 weekly; 5hr); Stone Town (2 weekly; 3hr).

Chake Chake

Pemba's capital, **CHAKE CHAKE** ("Chake" for short), is the most interesting of the island's towns, and even has a modest museum in an Omani fortress. Unless you're diving, in which case it's best to base yourself at Ras Kigomasha (see p.508), Chake

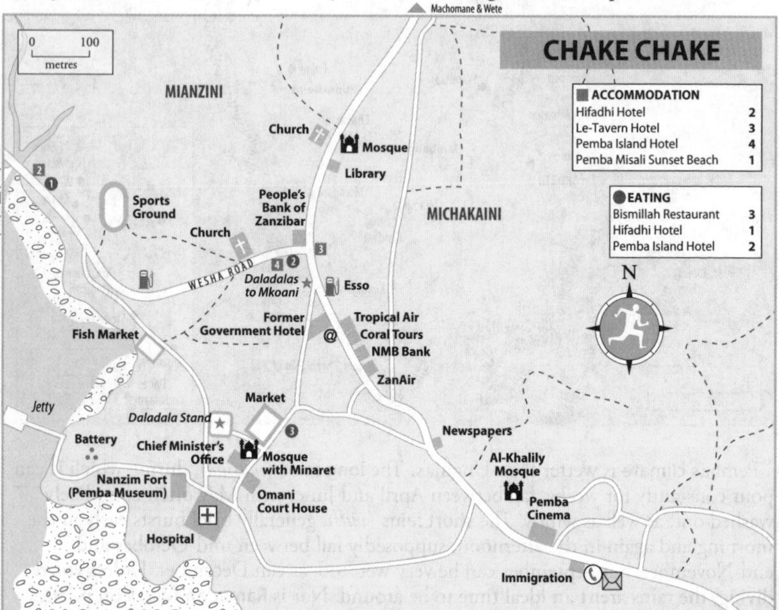
Machomane & Wete
CHAKE CHAKE
0 100
metres
ACCOMMODATION
Hifadhi Hotel 2
Le-Tavern Hotel 3
Pemba Island Hotel 4
Pemba Misali Sunset Beach 1
EATING
Bismillah Restaurant 3
Hifadhi Hotel 1
Pemba Island Hotel 2
N
MIANZINI
MICHAKAINI
Wesha (6km) & 1 (7km)
Church
Mosque
Library
Sports Ground
People's Bank of Zanzibar
Church
WESHA ROAD
Daladalas to Mkoani
Esso
Former Government Hotel
Tropical Air
Coral Tours
NMB Bank
ZanAir
Fish Market
Jetty
Market
Daladala Stand
Battery
Chief Minister's Office
Mosque with Minaret
Newspapers
Al-Khalily Mosque
Nanzim Fort (Pemba Museum)
Omani Court House
Pemba Cinema
Hospital
Immigration
Karume Airport (5km) & Mkoani

Chake is the most useful base for exploring the island, as there are daladalas from here to most destinations, plus a couple of affordable tour companies. A special treat, especially for snorkellers, is **Misali Island** – an unspoilt gem of a place said to be the spot where Captain Kidd buried his loot. Another good excursion is to **Pujini**, for its medieval tyrant's ruined citadel. Chake Chake has a nicely relaxed atmosphere, and people are genuinely pleased – and curious – to see tourists looking around.

The market
Daily 7am–6pm

The town's liveliest spot is its **market** where, aside from herbs and spices, you can buy aromatic essential oils, and tasty, if expensive, clove honey. Also on offer are colourfully painted straw plate-covers that look like hats, and aromatic **halua** – a sticky boiled goo (think Turkish Delight) inherited from the Omanis. It's at its busiest on Mondays and Fridays.

Chief Minister's Office and Omani Court House
Following the narrow road south of the market brings you to the **Chief Minister's Office**, a bizarre, pale blue building dominated by a round tower studded with protruding hollow cylinders, that perhaps aptly resemble the suckers on octopus tentacles. Opposite is the glorious colonial-era **Omani Court House**, with an impressive carved door and a clock tower that only tells the time twice a day.

Nanzim Fort and Pemba Museum
Museum Mon–Fri 8.30am–4.30pm, Sat & Sun 9am–4pm • $3 • Continue along the same street as the Ormani Court House, then turn right at the junction

The diminutive **Nanzim Fort** was built in the eighteenth century by the Omanis, incorporating the foundations of a Portuguese fortress built in 1594 (the square towers are the clue, as Omanis preferred round ones). Much of the fort was demolished in the early 1900s, and what remains houses the charming **Pemba Museum**. It has just three small rooms, but the displays – in English and Kiswahili – are very well done, and cover archaeology, seafaring, and the role of Zanzibar's rulers in relation to Pemba.

11

ARRIVAL AND TOURS   **CHAKE CHAKE**

By daladala Arriving by daladala #606 from Wete (Tsh1000) or #603 from Mkoani (Tsh1000), you'll be dropped either at the junction by the Esso petrol station, or at the stand behind the market.

Tour operators There are hardly any tourists in Chake Chake, so it's rare for its tour operators to survive for more than a few years. The main one is Coral Tours on the main road, just north of NMB Bank (Mon–Sat 8am–5pm; ☏ 0777 437397, ✉ tours_travelpemba@yahoo.com). *Hifadhi Hotel* can also arrange tours and is more reliable, but pricier. Both operators can rent out bikes, cars and motorbikes – expect to pay around $15 a day for a guide, $10 a day for a bicycle, and $25–30 for a 125cc motorbike, excluding fuel, or $120 for car with driver-guide for a full day.

ACCOMMODATION

Hifadhi Hotel Wesha Rd ☏ 024 254 2775 or ☏ 0777 245777, ⊕ hifadhihotel.com. The town's best accommodation, a modern blue-glass business-class affair down by the mangrove swamp, complete with a swimming pool at the back. There are two types of room, both a/c: most of the "standard" ones are at the back; the "del uxe" rooms at

---

PEMBA CINEMA

For something completely different, try an evening out at the four-hundred-seat **Pemba Cinema** on the main road south. Mind-bogglingly dilapidated, it's not just Zanzibar's but Tanzania's only surviving original (pre-multiplex) cinema, built around 1930. It still manages to get hold of real celluloid, with Bollywood films on weekday evenings (at 6pm), and American B-movies at weekends. Be patient while the projectionist changes reels, as he needs to manually rewind the first reel before popping on the second. All in all, a great night out for a mere Tsh600.

the front overlook the mangroves. All have four-poster beds and box nets, fans as well as a/c, furniture made from stripy coconut wood, satellite TV and wi-fi. There's a good restaurant, reliable wi-fi, and they are happy to arrange tours. BB $110

Le-Tavern Hotel Main road, facing Wesha Rd ☎0777 429057 or ☎024 245 2660. This modern two-storey place was once a reasonable option, and friendly if you can surmount the language barrier, but the rooms are badly kept, and it's only really worth considering if you can't afford anywhere else. Breakfast is taken on the roof. BB shared bathroom $30, en suite $40

Pemba Island Hotel Wesha Rd ☎0777 490041 or ☎024 245 2215, ✉pembaislandhotel@yahoo.com. A clean, modern four-storey building with fifteen en-suite rooms (smallish mosquito nets), fans, a/c, fridge and satellite TV; twin-bed rooms cost $10 more and have better bathrooms. There's also a rooftop restaurant (see below); no alcohol. BB $50

Pemba Misali Sunset Beach West of Chake Chake, 7.5km along Wesha Rd ☎0786 497673, �🌐pembamisalibeach.com. Run by the same people as Nungwi's *Amaan Bungalows* (see p.495), this is an affordable beach hotel, if not brilliantly located: it's 300m from a oil depot, and still well within the mangrove forest, so the beach is silty. That said, it catches the sunset, and most of the rooms – in a tightly spaced row of bungalows containing two rooms each – face the beach. There's also a swimming pool, bar, restaurant, wi-fi, and even an ATM, so it's perfectly fine for a no-frills stay by the water. BB garden view $120, sea view $150

EATING AND DRINKING

Most of Chake Chake's restaurants are attached to hotels, and charge touristy prices (around Tsh12,000 a plate for the basics). For cheaper eats, explore the area around the market, or try the street-food stalls on the main road just north of the People's Bank of Zanzibar. Busiest at night, this is where you can find everything from *chipsi mayai* and grilled goat meat to superb seafood, including succulent octopus stew, bite-sized fish cakes, grilled squid and fish, and various juices: try tamarind (*ukwaju*) or the rather wonderful *bungo*, halfway between a mango and a peach. To finish off, track down a coffee vendor, where for Tsh200 or less you'll be handed a tiny porcelain cup filled with scaldingly hot and bitter coffee. None of the restaurants serve alcohol, and there are no bars in town.

Bismillah Restaurant Facing the market. The only real cheapie, a simple *mgahawa* that dishes up meals in the "rice with fish, chicken with chips" tradition, at Tsh5000 a plate. Order early for a little more choice. Daily 8am–6pm or later.

Hifadhi Hotel Wesha Rd. Chake Chake's plushest place, with a large, if rather soulless a/c dining room. But what matters is the food, and it's good, including a tempting selection of vegetarian options, such as vegetable *pilau* with pickles, or vegetable curry (Tsh10,000). Officially, in Ramadan it's only open to overnight guests, but they'll likely make an exception for tourists. Daily 7am–10pm.

Pemba Island Hotel Wesha Rd ☎0777 490041 or ☎024 245 2215. The third-floor restaurant has good views and a typical Swahili menu (mains Tsh6000–10,000), including octopus with coconut sauce and chicken *pilau*. Daily lunch and dinner; pre-ordering advisable.

DIRECTORY

Health Mkoani's hospital (☎024 245 6075 or ☎024 245 6011) is way better than Chake Chake's. For diagnostic tests, the Public Health Laboratory in Machomane (☎024 245 2473) is reliable.

Internet access Adult Training Centre, on the main road facing Tropical Air (daily 7.30am–4pm; Tsh1000 per hr).

Money Chake's banks – NMB and the People's Bank of Zanzibar on the main road, and Barclays in the former *Government Hotel* – all change cash without much fuss. Barclays' ATM is the only one that accepts international plastic, though there's no guarantee it's filled with money!

Misali Island

17km west of Chake Chake • $5 per person payable on arrival • Organized tours cost around $40 from Mkoani, or $55–70 from Chake Chake • Camping and alcohol prohibited

The island of **MISALI** is a reef that emerged from the ocean some fifteen thousand years ago. It's one of Pemba's highlights, offering idyllic beaches, nature trails for spotting flying foxes (fruit bats), good snorkelling and superb diving. It also has a touch of historical romance, as the legendary pirate **Captain Kidd** is said to have used the island as a hideaway, and to have buried booty here.

A more evident treasure is Misali's rich **ecosystem**, which boasts 42 types of coral, over three hundred species of fish, a rare subspecies of vervet monkey, endangered colonies of flying foxes, nesting sites for green and hawksbill turtles, and a large, if rarely seen, population of nocturnal **coconut crabs**. The island, part of a conservation area, is uninhabited except for rangers and passing fishermen. Its sanctity, and its name, are explained by the legend of a **prophet** named Hadhara (meaning "knowledge" or "culture"), who appeared before Misali's fishermen and asked them for a prayer mat (*msala*). There was none, so Hadhara declared that since the island pointed towards Mecca, it would be his prayer mat.

The island's **visitor centre**, on Baobab Beach where the boats pull up, has good displays on ecology and wildlife plus information sheets that you can take with you while snorkelling or walking the trails

The reef

The shallow reef around Misali is good for snorkelling, though the current can be trying for weaker swimmers and you should stay close to the shore as currents further out can be dangerously strong; ask the folks at the visitor centre for advice. For confident swimmers, a **submerged coral mountain** off the western shore is an extraordinary place; the mountain, one of four in the area, peaks at 3–5m below sea level, and you'll need a boat to get there. More accessible is the shallow reef flanking Baobab Beach, which starts a mere 10–40m from the shore. The shallower part features **conical sponges**, traditionally collected by fishermen for use as hats; further out, the reef is cut by sandy gullies and teems with life.

Nature trails

A series of nature trails has been established around the island; pick up one of the information sheets from the visitor centre. The **Mangrove Trail** can be followed on foot at low tide or in combination with snorkelling. The **Intertidal Trail** (low tide only) starts at Turtle Beach on the west side of the island, and includes a small isle connected by causeway that is popular with nesting sea birds. Mangroves and low-tide pools also feature. Another trail takes you past one of Misali's three **sacred caves**, believed by locals to be the abode of benevolent spirits. Each cave has a specially appointed traditional guardian (healer), and people leave offerings to the spirits, or to Allah, to seek intercession in worldly matters. The caves' sacred nature means that tourists should not enter if scantily dressed.

There's also a trail from Baobab Beach to Turtle Beach and to Mpapaini, whose caves contain roosts of **Pemban flying foxes**, an endangered species of bat. Go with a guide to avoid disturbing them. If you can get to Misali very early in the morning (leave before sunrise), you stand a slim chance of spotting a rare and shy subspecies of **Pemba vervet monkey**; your best bet is on the western beaches where they hunt for ghost crabs.

The Pujini ruins

10km southeast of Chake Chake • Free • A taxi from Chake Chake costs $40 return, but the ruins are not signposted, so make sure the driver knows the place; coming from Chake Chake, turn right 1km before the airport and continue south for 4km

The **PUJINI RUINS** are the remains of a citadel dating from the heyday of the **Diba tribe** – possibly Persian descendants – who ruled eastern Pemba from the fifteenth to seventeenth centuries. The citadel was built by the tyrant Muhammad bin Abdulrahman, a merchant and pirate whose nickname, **Mkama Ndume**, means "grasper of men". The ruins (also known by his name) are defensively located on a hilltop and are now mostly rubble, but the presence of old tamarind and baobab trees makes them singularly photogenic. A **mosque** is the best-preserved building, but also noteworthy is a **well** half-filled with rubble, in the enclosure's northeastern corner. Legend has it that Mkama Ndume had two jealous wives; to prevent them meeting at the well, he had a dividing wall built inside it. One of the wives would use a bucket and rope while the other descended by a staircase – still visible – to reach the water. More likely though is that the small chamber at the foot of the staircase was a shrine to spirits (*majini*).

Carved out of the soft limestone, it contains a lamp niche and a small plaster relief of a **siwa horn**. Long, heavy and frequently ornate, they were made from ivory, brass or wood and were symbols of sovereignty and authority all along the Swahili coast and on the Arabian Peninsula – the House of Wonders in Stone Town (see p.458) has a few examples. Another **staircase** leads up to the battlements, beyond which what looks like a dried moat was actually a canal that enabled dhows to be pulled inland for loading and offloading.

Mkoani

Pemba's main port, **MKOANI**, is where ferries from Stone Town and Dar dock, in spite of which the town is complete wasteland when it comes to facilities: it has just one guesthouse, doubling as a restaurant, and virtually nothing else of use to travellers other than the island's best equipped hospital. Still, the market on the beach south of the ferry jetty is worth a peek before you move on and the locals are an unfailingly friendly bunch. A pleasant way to while away a few hours is to take a **boat trip** (see below) or to walk up the coast to a lovely sandspit at **Ras Mkoasha**, 4km north from town: just follow the road past the *Zanzibar Ocean Panorama*.

ARRIVAL AND TOURS
MKOANI

By ferry The ferry port (see p.500) is 1km west of the town centre, which sits on top of a hill.

By daladala There are frequent daladalas (#603) to Chake Chake (Tsh1500) from along the road between the port and the town centre.

Boat trips and snorkelling There are several good destinations within an hour's sail of Mkoani, including Makoongwe Island, 3km offshore, with a roost of rare Pemba flying foxes, and minuscule Kwata Islet, 7km west of Mkoani, which is practically all beach and has decent snorkelling and a patch of mangroves nearby. Mkoani's *Zanzibar Ocean Panorama* can arrange affordable boat trips to each island for $25 per person (minimum two). They also offer snorkelling at Misali Island (see p.502) for $40 per person including entrance fee, and snorkelling over a shallow wreck at Panza Point in the south for $60. Also possible are high-tide mangrove tours by dugout canoe ($10 per person) for birding and swimming, and sailing in *ngalawa* outriggers ($15 per person). All these trips require a day or two to arrange.

ACCOMMODATION AND EATING

Mkoani has only one guesthouse, which doubles as the town's best restaurant, but it's worth asking whether *Jondeni Guest House*, 100m beyond, has reopened. Otherwise, eating out is limited to a couple of food stalls by the market and a couple more in front of the former *Government Hotel*, on the main road 600m east from the port, for *mishkaki*, grilled or fried fish, and octopus.

BULLFIGHTING, PEMBA-STYLE

The village of **Kengeja** in Pemba's deep south would be unremarkable were it not for the curious spectacle of **bullfighting** (*Mchezo wa ngombe*), which takes place in the dry months of December to February, especially February. The fights are a hangover from the Portuguese presence, and, like the Portuguese *touradas*, don't result in the death of the animals.

The evening before a fight, villagers hold a dance called *umund* and visit graves to receive help from their ancestors and request the arrival of the rains. In the fights themselves, the bulls – initially tethered – are provoked by jostling crowds and pipe music until, sufficiently enraged, they are released, the crowd scatters and the "matador" takes over. Completely unarmed, he goads the bull with a white cloth. His skill lying in artfully dodging the bull's charges, while the pleasure for the crowd lies in observing the deft movements of the fighter (or seeing him scamper up the nearest tree whenever things get hairy).

Tickets for seats in the gender-segregated grandstands cost a few hundred shillings; it's free to join the crowds around the arena. **To get there**, catch a #215 daladala from Mkoani marked "Mwambe". From Chake Chake, take a #603 daladala towards Mkoani but get off at Mtambile junction and change there for a #215. There's no accommodation in the village.

★**Zanzibar Ocean Panorama** 750m north of the port ☎024 245 6166, ⓦzanzibaroceanpanorama.com. Set on a high grassy bluff overlooking the sea, this is great value for the inspiring sea views from the garden at the back, and is well worth the trip from backpackers. There are just four rooms, including a dorm ($20 per person) – in a couple of whitewashed brick houses. All are comfortable and clean, and have *semadari*

beds, big nets, a/c, fan, fridge and a scatter of furniture, plus a hammock on their terraces. Good views from the garden and restaurant at the back, which also has recliners. The food is excellent, and ample ($20 for a platter of grilled tuna, crab and clams, plus starter and dessert; or around $10 for spiced octopus in coconut with mashed potatoes). Staff can organize affordable boat and snorkelling excursions. BB **$50**

Wete

North of Chake Chake, the land is flatter but just as lush, with extensive patches of forest surviving between cultivated areas. Rice is the staple crop here, although cloves are also grown – as your nostrils will tell you. The main town is the likeable dhow port of **WETE**, which has several good guesthouses and serves as a base for a series of attractions in the area, including **Ngezi Forest**; beautiful beaches at **Ras Kigomasha** in the far north, where you'll find Pemba's best beach hotels, both with **scuba diving** centres; and several scatters of medieval **ruins**. For souvenirs, try the nameless but sweetly scented shop beside *Pemba Crown Hotel*, which is filled with herbs and spices, aromatic oils, honey, and pottery incense burners.

ARRIVAL AND TOURS WETE

By daladala There are two roads from Chake Chake to Wete: the old and more direct one (30km; daladala #606 with the number painted in red) to the west, whose surface has all but vanished, and the fast Pemba North Feeder Road (35km; daladala #606, with the number painted in blue), which starts 7km north of Chake Chake at Melitano junction. Daladalas charge Tsh1500 from Chake, and drop off beside the market in the centre of Wete.

Tours Excursions in northern Pemba, including spice tours, can be arranged at Wete's hotels, the most experienced being either of the *Sharook* hotels, or *Pemba Crown Inn*. The standard cost for visiting Ngezi Forest is $40 per vehicle plus entrance fees, or $35 per person. Wete's speciality, though, is a trip to Fundo Island by *mashua* dhow; you can either camp for the night or stay with a family for around $70–80 per person.

ACCOMMODATION

Hill View Inn On the way in from Chake Chake, behind the Soviet-style apartment blocks ☎0776 338366. A grey two-storey house with nine rooms, most with *semadari* beds; five have their own bathrooms ($30). All have box nets and ceiling fans, and the management are friendly and happy to arrange tours. To get there, follow the track from the main road between blocks #1 and #4 (the numbers are painted on the side). BB **$20**

Pemba Crown Hotel Bomani St, in the centre ☎024 245 4191 or ☎0773 336867, ⓦpembacrown.com. Centrally located and very good value modern four-storey hotel, with eleven rooms on its top two floors, all with decent bathrooms, a/c, fans, TV, round nets, hot water and balconies. The staff are friendly and helpful, and there's internet access. BB **$40**

Sharook Guesthouse In the centre ☎0777 431012 or ☎024 245 4386, ⓦpembaliving.com. Run by the

ever-welcoming and helpful Sharook family, this calm place feels like you're staying in their home, and is well used to tourists. Its four rooms are large and have fans and round nets, and three also have bathrooms… complete with toilet seats and paper (a rarity elsewhere). There's satellite TV in the communal sitting room, an internet café around the corner, and a wide choice of reliable tours on offer. BB **$30**

★**Sharook Riviera Grand Lodge** 150m west of Sharook Guesthouse ☎0777 431012 or ☎024 245 4386, ⓦpembaliving.com. Also run by the Sharook family, this is an elegant and modern three-storey affair in a lovely setting backed by mature trees and with a banana grove in front. All eight rooms are large, tiled and well equipped (hot water, fans, a/c and wi-fi), and all but one – a dorm – are en suite. The west-facing rooms on the second floor have sea views, as does the rooftop restaurant. BB **$50**

EATING AND DRINKING

Apart from the following restaurants, try the **street food** stalls around the market and daladala stand, and along the main road near the post office. Wete's unusual speciality is winkles, of which there are at least two kinds: *kombe*, having black-and-white shells, and *chaza*, with reddish ones. Grilled, they're a superb accompaniment to a filling and spicy soup based on tomatoes, potatoes and sliver-thin sticks of fried cassava. There's also goat meat *mishkaki* (which goes well with

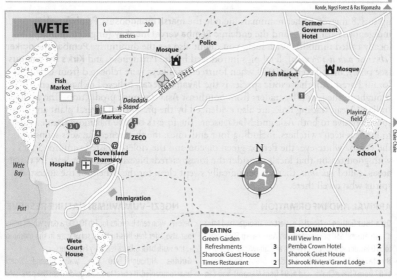

WETE

EATING
Green Garden	
Refreshments	3
Sharook Guest House	1
Times Restaurant	2

ACCOMMODATION
Hill View Inn	1
Pemba Crown Hotel	2
Sharook Guest House	4
Sharook Riviera Grand Lodge	3

11

shellfish), and it's all very cheap indeed: a full bowl of soup with a skewer of meat or shells costs just Tsh500, the same as a glass of freshly pressed sugar cane juice. As with Mkoani, there are no bars in town, nor restaurants selling alcohol.

Green Garden Refreshments Bomani St. This is the best of several basic restaurants along the main road that provide cheap meals, open air, *chipsi mayai* and *mishkak,i* etc; simple meals cost Tsh2500–3500. Mon–Sat 8am–5pm.

★**Sharook Riviera Grand Lodge** 150m west of Sharook Guesthouse ☎ 0777 431012 or ☎ 024 245 4386. Order a few hours in advance for a good range of very well-prepared local dishes starting at Tsh10,000. There's a very

tasty sea view, too, from this rooftop restaurant, where you also get to admire flying foxes as they skim overhead. Big portions. Daily, any time (drop in beforehand).

Times Restaurant Bomani St, near Pemba Crown Hotel. Popular for its a/c and free newspapers, this has a bit more choice than the average local eatery, including barbecued meat (Tsh6500), tandoori prawns, and even pizzas. It also sells snacks. Daily 8am–5pm.

DIRECTORY

Health Wete Hospital (☎ 024 245 4001) between the centre and the port is in reasonable shape, and Clove Island Pharmacy opposite *Garden Restaurant* is well stocked.
Internet access Available at *Pemba Crown Hotel*, at Benjamin Mkapa Teacher Training College, 100m further

along Bomani St, and beside Sharook Guesthouse; all charge Tsh2000 per hr.
Money As in Mkoani, there's no bank, so change money before coming or in Chake Chake (see p.502).

Ngezi–Vumawimbi Nature Reserve (Ngezi Forest)

20km north of Wete, on the road between Konde and Ras Kigomasha • Daily 7.30am–4pm • $5 plus tips, or $10 for birdwatching (including a park guide) • $2 per person to just pass through

Until the introduction of cloves in the nineteenth century, sixty percent of Pemba was covered by indigenous forest. Nowadays, the only sizeable remnants are small patches at Ras Kiuyu and Msitu Mkuu in the northeast, and **NGEZI FOREST**, being one-third of the 29-square-kilometre Ngezi–Vumawimbi Nature Reserve straddling the neck of Ras Kigomasha peninsula in the northwest.

Wilder, junglier, darker and more brooding than Jozani Forest on Unguja, Ngezi is an ecological island towered over by 40m-tall mvule teak trees festooned with necklaces of lianas and vines. The major attraction for naturalists is the chance of spotting the endemic **Pemba flying fox**, actually a species of fruit-eating bat (*popo*) with a wingspan up to 1.8 metres. Other mammals include the **marsh mongoose** – Pemba's only indigenous carnivore – and the endemic **Pemba vervet monkey** (or green monkey, locally called tumbili). With luck, you might also see the diminutive **Pemba blue duiker** (*chesi* or *paa wa Pemba*), feral pigs introduced by the Portuguese, and **Kirk's red colobus** (see p.30), introduced in 1970 when fourteen monkeys were relocated from Unguja's Jozani Forest. Another exotic species is the **Javan civet cat**, believed to have been brought to the island by traders from Southeast Asia for musk production. The ancient Indian Ocean trading links are also evidenced by the presence of several plant and tree species native to both Asia and Madagascar. The forest's **birdlife** has more than enough to interest keen twitchers, including four endemics: the threatened Russet's scops owl, the Pemba white-eye, the Pemba green pigeon and the violet-breasted sunbird. So it's with good reason that locals consider the forest sacred: Ngezi contains at least six **ritual areas**, called *mizimu*, that are periodically swept clean for the benefit of the ancestral spirits who dwell there.

ARRIVAL AND INFORMATION   NGEZI–VUMAWIMBI NATURE RESERVE

On a tour Getting to Ngezi is easiest on an organized tour: it costs around $50 per person from Wete (see p.506), or up to $70 including a couple of hours at Vumawimbi Beach.

By daladala Coming by daladala (#601 from Wete, #602 from Chake Chake, and #604 from Mkoani), you can get as far as the scruffy market town of Konde, 4km east of the reserve. Daladala drivers should be happy to take you straight to the gate for an extra few thousand shillings.

By bicycle It's a 36-kilometre round-trip bike ride from Wete, or less if you base yourself at *Kervan Saray Beach* (see

below), who rent bicycles for Tsh10,000 a day; which rents out also offer free lifts to the reserve gate in the morning – the walk back takes a leisurely two hours.

Guides Although you can walk around Ngezi unaccompanied, it's best to take a guide from the park gate ($5 per person), both for their knowledge and for security, as there have been muggings in the past. With advance notice, you could also go looking for flying foxes, or scout for scops owls. There are a few interesting leaflets posted on the walls inside the park office by the gate, but nothing to take away.

Ras Kigomasha

Passing through Ngezi, the forest ends as suddenly as it began, giving way to scrub, patches of cultivation, a rubber plantation started by the Chinese, and a couple of fabulous and virtually deserted beaches on either side of Pemba's northernmost point, **Ras Kigomasha** ("ras" means "head"). The beach on the west side is known as **Panga ya Watoro**, curiously meaning "the knife of the refugees". To the east, **Vumawimbi** ("roaring surf") is a gently curving, four-kilometre-long bay.

ARRIVAL AND DEPARTURE   RAS KIGOMASHA

By daladala Daladalas (#601 from Wete, #602 from Chake Chake, and #604 from Mkoani) only go as far as Konde, but your hotel should be able to pick you up from there.

By car If you're driving, be aware that the road through Ngezi Forest gets very muddy during and after the rains, often requiring 4WD, high clearance and ample mud-driving skills, though the road is rarely blocked completely.

ACCOMMODATION

★**Kervan Saray Beach** Ras Kigomasha, 10km from Konde ☎0773 176 737, ⓦkervansaraybeach.com. Set just back from the beach on the west coast, this is the base for Swahili Divers (see p.463), and is great value even for non-divers. With just twelve rooms, it's intimate and the dorm is a bargain (FB $55 per person). The other rooms are in huge stand-alone cottages, while the bungalows (FB $275) are very stylishly decked out, with their enormous beds on cement pedestals. Apart from diving and snorkelling ($25 if sharing a boat with divers), you can go

kayaking around the mangroves of Njao Gap (initial access is by motorboat), and staff are happy to give lifts to Ngezi Forest in the morning. No wi-fi, but you can use a computer if needed. FB **$150**

★**The Manta Resort** Ras Kigomasha, 14km from Konde ☎0776 718852, ⓦthemantaresort.com. Near the top of the island, this relaxed and unpretentious place sits on a coral bluff above the magical Panga ya Watoro beach; it's particularly recommended for scuba divers, as they have their own dive centre (Dive 360 Pemba).

Although the standard accommodation is overpriced even by Zanzibar's standards (the cheapest room with a sea view costs $745), it stands out on account of its floating plexiglass-walled underwater bedroom, something like an inverted fish tank (an eye-watering $1500 a night, full board). As gimmicks go, this is a marvellous one: the water around it is lit by spotlight at night, so you get to sleep (and wake up) with the fishes without getting wet. There's a delightful thatched restaurant overlooking the beach, an equally lovely beach bar, a swimming pool (also with views), and a host of activities, including a spa, nature and bird walks, fishing from inflatable kayaks, and road and sea excursions. No children under 7, or under 12 in the underwater room. FB $495

Hamisi ruins

8km east of Konde • Open access • Free

Several medieval ruins lie off the road east of Konde. The most impressive, and easiest to find, are the sixteenth-century **Hamisi ruins** (also known as the Haruni or Chwaka ruins). Tradition has it that the fortified town and palace was the seat of Harun bin Ali, a son of Muhammad bin Abdulrahman (see p.503). Tyranny appears to have been a family trait, as hinted at by Harun's nickname, Mvunja Pau: *mvunja* means destroyer, and *pau* is the pole that takes the weight of a thatched roof.

11

The first building you see is a small **mosque**, much of it reduced to blocks of collapsed masonry. The *mihrab* remains more or less intact, in spite of a tree root growing into it. The mosque was built for Harun's wife and gets its nickname of Msikiti Chooko ("Mosque of the Green Bean") from the ground beans or peas that were blended with the mortar to strengthen it. Some 100m southeast of the mosque are the remains of a particularly large **tomb**, surmounted by a ten-sided pillar bearing curious upside-down shield-like indents on one side. On the other side of the pillar is an incised eight-petalled floral motif, oddly off-centre. The tomb is said to be that of Harun.

Fifty metres south of here is a large **Friday mosque** that appears to be raised by a metre or so above the ground, a false impression caused by the amount of rubble covering the original floor. Its mihrab is in almost perfect condition; the five circular depressions on either side of it originally held Chinese porcelain bowls, and people still leave offerings there.

SAUTI ZA BUSARA MUSIC FESTIVAL, ZANZIBAR

Contexts

History

Tanzania's history is the intertwining of two tales: that of the coast (including Zanzibar and Mafia), and that of the hinterland (Tanganyika). Tanganyika's written history started just five hundred years ago, and little is known of earlier times other than the rough direction of mass migrations, and what little can be gleaned from archeological records. In contrast, the coast's turbulent and often brutal history is well recorded, as the western Indian Ocean's monsoon winds and currents brought it within reach of sailors from Persia and Arabia, India and the Far East, ancient Greece, Egypt and Rome, Phoenicia, Assyria and Sumeria.

The first lasting link between Tanganyika and Zanzibar was the Zanzibari-controlled ivory and slave trade, which drew its raw materials – people and elephant tusks – from the mainland. The second link was the unification of Tanganyika and Zanzibar in 1964 to create the present **United Republic of Tanzania**. A marriage of convenience, some say, and indeed the two parties have shown little affection for one another over the course of their union. In spite of this, Tanzania continues to be held up as an example of mutual cooperation between different peoples and cultures, showing that ethnic conflict ignited by artificial national boundaries imposed by the Europeans can be overcome.

The people of Tanzania

Mainland Tanzania has been inhabited since the dawn of mankind. Some 3.75 million years ago, a family of hominids with chimpanzee-like faces strode across an area of wet volcanic ash in **Laetoli** in Ngorongoro. At the time of their discovery in the 1970s, the fossilized footprints of these three *Australopithecus afarensis* provided the first absolute proof that our ancestors were walking upright way before anyone had imagined. Fossilized hominid remains and stone tools found at **Oldupai Gorge** nearby trace the evolution of man from those first faltering steps to the genesis of *Homo sapiens*.

Tanzania's "modern" historical record starts with a modest collection of 70,000-year-old **ostrich shell beads** unearthed in the Serengeti, which are among the **earliest man-made items** intended for something other than just survival. More beautiful, and visitable, are Tanzania's **rock paintings**, especially in the Irangi Hills. The most recent were left barely a hundred years ago, but the oldest may be a mind-boggling 30,000 years old. Given that they're all outdoors (not in caves), the thousands of paintings are miraculously well preserved, and depict a land of wild animals and everyday domestic life not so different from today.

The artists were **hunter-gatherers**, living off wild game, honey, berries, fruits, nuts and roots; most of these cultures disappeared long ago, having been either assimilated or annihilated by more powerful newcomers. Two exceptions were the **Hadzabe and**

3,750,000 BC	1,750,000 BC	70,000 BC	30,000 BC
Australopithecus afarensis walking upright at Laetoli, Ngorongoro	*Homo habilis* and *Homo erectus* living at Oldupai Gorge, Ngorongoro	Ostrich shell beads, possibly decorative, made in the Serengeti	Rock paintings daubed on rock shelters at Kolo, central Tanzania

Sandawe tribes of central Tanzania. The Sandawe abandoned their ancient way of life in the 1950s, but the Hadzabe persist, albeit under immense adverse pressure (including ill-managed tourism) that looks set to extinguish their culture within the next decade. Interestingly, both tribes speak languages characterized by clicks, similar to those spoken by southern Africa's hunter-gatherers (the "San" or "Bushmen"), who also had a strong tradition of rock painting. The similarities point to the existence of a loosely linked and widely dispersed hunter-gathering culture across much of sub-Saharan Africa, before the arrival of the Bantu turned their world upside-down.

The Bantu

Cameroon is considered to be the cradle of the ethno-linguistic group known as the **Bantu**. Nowadays spread over much of sub-Saharan Africa, the Bantu are primarily an agricultural people, and have been for thousands of years. Their success at agriculture ultimately led to overpopulation, so starting the first of several waves of **Bantu migrations** in search of fresh land. The first to reach Tanzania arrived as early as 1000 BC, with the last coming just a few centuries ago. Over time the migrants split into myriad distinct tribes, each developing their own cultures, belief systems and languages. Elements common to most Bantu societies, apart from linguistic roots, are their agricultural way of life, monotheism, and knowledge of **iron working**. Excavations in Ufipa in southwestern Tanzania, and Kagera, west of Lake Victoria, have shown that, until the European method of mass-produced steel was perfected, Tanzania's deceptively simple furnaces produced the world's highest-quality steel, fired at temperatures that were unthinkable in eighteenth-century Europe. Nowadays, Bantu-speakers comprise all but a handful of Tanzania's 129 officially recognized tribes.

The Nilotes

Tanzania's second-largest and most traditional ethno-linguistic group are the so-called **Nilotes**, or Nilotic-speakers, and include the country's most famous tribe, the Maasai. As the academic label suggests, their origins lie in the Upper Nile valley of southern or central Sudan, from where their ancestors began fanning out, both south and west, as early as two thousand years ago. Indeed, there are compelling similarities between present-day tribes and ancient Egypt's and Sudan's "Black Pharaohs": physical traits, hairstyles, the reliance on cattle, the belief in a unique God, social structure, even language. Some theorists posit that the Nilotes are in fact one of Israel's "lost tribes", seemingly borne out by the existence of traditional Jewish communities in Ethiopia and Uganda.

Cattle define all Nilotic tribes, providing everything from daily sustenance (blood and milk rather than meat) to clothing and shelter, and social standing. The semi-arid nature of Nilotic terrain, however, exposed them to frequent droughts, something that has become acutely problematic in recent decades. Aggressive **territorial expansion** was the way to minimize the blows of nature, as typified by the hierarchical, quasi-militaristic form of traditional Nilotic society. The first Nilotes to enter Tanzania were presumably ancestors of central Tanzania's **Gogo** (who are now mixed with Bantu), followed by the **Barbaig**, both of whom were pushed south by the arrival of the **Maasai** some three hundred years ago. In the modern world, the nomadic lifestyle is increasingly untenable, especially as the best grazing lands – now national parks – are

2000 BC	1000 BC	500 BC	500 BC–200 AD
Sumerians trading with East Africa	The first of several Bantu migrations reaches Lake Victoria	The oldest surviving iron forges, Kagera Region	Ancient Egyptians, Greeks and Romans trading with Rhapta

closed to herders. As such, some Nilotes have done the unthinkable by becoming farmers, but Nilotic traditions are amazingly resilient, as you'll be able to see at one of several cultural tourism programmes around Arusha.

Empires of the monsoon

The first non-Africans to visit Tanzania, sometime before 2000 BC, were **Sumerian traders** from Mesopotamia, followed a millennium later by the **Phoenicians**, who used Zanzibar as a stopover en route to Sofala in Mozambique, to trade in gold. The earliest coins found in Zanzibar are over two thousand years old, and come from ancient Parthia (northeast Iran), Sassania (Iran/Iraq), Greece and Rome. Egyptian coins and a dagger have also been found, as have Roman glass beads, all proving that trading connections between East Africa and the **Mediterranean** were strong. At that time it would appear that Zanzibar and the coast were controlled by Sabaeans from the kingdom of Sheba (modern Yemen), who brought weapons, wine and wheat to exchange for ivory and other East African goods.

The sailors were carried by the **monsoon**'s winds and currents, which blow south for half the year, and north for the other. This obliged sailors to stay a while before the monsoon switched direction, and in due course **trading towns** sprouted along the coastline. The second-century *Periplus of the Erythraean Sea*, which calls the coast Azania, mentions one such place called **Rhapta**, which scholars tentatively identify with Pangani or an as yet unknown location in the Rufiji Delta. Also mentioned, two days' sail away, is the island of **Menouthias**, probably Pemba.

The Swahili

In later centuries, the East African coast became part of a vast trading network that included China, Malaysia and Indonesia. Malay and Indonesian influence lasted from the sixth century to at least the twelfth, and the **Indonesians** are believed to have introduced coconuts, bananas, and possibly the Polynesian-style *ngalawa* outriggers still used today. Chinese presence is seen in numerous finds of coins and porcelain, and in written accounts.

The first outsiders who can be positively identified as establishing a permanent presence in East Africa were the **Persians**: by the end of the first millennium AD, they ruled a series of city-states from Somalia in the north to Mozambique in the south. According to legend, they arrived in 975 AD after the king of Shiraz dreamt that a **giant iron rat** destroyed the foundations of his palace. Taking it as a bad omen, the king set sail with his six sons in seven dhows. Separated in a storm, each went on to found a city, including Kizimkazi in Zanzibar, and Kilwa on the mainland. Whatever the truth of the tale, Persian traders were certainly well acquainted with the East African coast, which they called Zang-I-Bar ("the sea of the blacks"), hence the name Zanzibar.

The Persians were not averse to marrying Africans, and in so doing gave rise to East Africa's "Shirazi" culture. Later, intermarriage with Arabs created the **Swahili** (from the Arabic word *sahel*, meaning "coast"), whose birth coincided with an upsurge in Indian Ocean trade. **Gold** and **ivory** were the main African exports, though slaves, turtle shell, leopard skin, rhinoceros horn, indigo and timber also found ready markets. The Swahili civilization reached its peak in the fourteenth and fifteenth centuries, when its

975 AD	1498	1500–1750	1505
According to legend, a Shirazi king and his six sons found East Africa's city-states, including Kilwa	First contact with Europeans, when Vasco da Gama stops at Tongoni, en route to India	Arrival of cattle-herding Nilotes from the north, including Maasai	Kilwa is sacked by the Portuguese

city-states – especially **Kilwa** – controlled the flow of gold from the port of Sofala in Mozambique, itself controlling mines in what is now Zimbabwe, and which some scholars say were the original King Solomon's Mines.

The main legacy of Swahili civilization is its language, **Kiswahili**; essentially it is a Bantu tongue enriched with thousands of words borrowed from Persian and Arabic, and nowadays also Portuguese, Hindi, English and German. Over the centuries Kiswahili spread inland along trade routes, and is now the lingua franca of eastern Africa, and the official language of Tanzania and Kenya.

The Portuguese

The growth and prosperity of the Swahili came to an abrupt end following the arrival of the **Portuguese**. The first to visit was Vasco da Gama in 1498, en route to "discovering" the ocean route to India, which would circumvent the need to trade across a series of Arab middlemen in the Middle East. Although Portuguese involvement in East Africa was initially limited to its use as a staging post, the riches of the Swahili trade quickly kindled an avaricious interest. In 1503, part of Unguja Island (Zanzibar Island) was sacked by the Portuguese captain **Ruy Lourenço Ravasco**, who exacted an annual tribute in gold from Unguja's traditional rulers, the Mwinyi Mkuu. Kilwa Kisiwani on the mainland – East Africa's most prosperous city – was sacked two years later, and within a decade the Portuguese had conquered most of the Swahili coast. However, the Portuguese presence disrupted the ancient trading network so badly that the entire region fell into decline, and formerly prosperous cities were abandoned and crumbled away.

The collapse of the trading network deterred further Portuguese interest other than maintaining a number of harbours to act as stepping stones along the route to India. This lack of attention, and increasingly stretched military resources, opened the door to a new power: **Oman**. In 1606 Pemba was taken by Omanis based in Malindi, Kenya, and in 1622 the Portuguese suffered a monumental defeat at the **Battle of Hormuz**. The defeat signalled the *de facto* ascendancy of Omani power in the region, although the Portuguese held on to Unguja until 1652, when the Omani sultanate sent a fleet at the behest of the Mwinyi Mkuu. The last Portuguese stronghold in East Africa north of Mozambique, Mombasa's Fort Jesus, fell to the new rulers in 1698.

Zanzibar and the slave trade

Having ejected the Portuguese, Oman was swift to assert its control over East Africa. The only real threat to their sovereignty was from a rival Omani dynasty, the Mazrui family, based in Mombasa. The Mazruis seized Pemba in 1744, but were unsuccessful in their attempt to take Unguja eleven years later. In spite of the rivalry, Zanzibar's trade flourished, the key to its wealth being **slavery**, demand for which rocketed after the establishment of sugar and clove plantations in European-owned Indian Ocean territories.

The spiralling prices for slaves, and ivory, gave Zanzibar considerable economic independence from Oman. The pivotal figure was Seyyid bin Sultan bin Ahmad bin Saïd al-Busaïdi (ruled 1804–56), **Seyyid Saïd** for short, who at the age of 15 assassinated his cousin to become the sole ruler of the Omani empire. The sultan recognized the importance of Zanzibar and East Africa, and spent most of his reign developing and consolidating it, encouraging merchants to emigrate from Oman, and

1513	1652	1698	1700s
As Muslim traders abandon Kilwa, so do the Portuguese	The Portuguese are ejected from Zanzibar by Oman	The Portuguese lose Mombasa, their last stronghold north of Mozambique	Slaves begin to replace ivory as East Africa's main export

continuing incursions on the African mainland. In 1811 he opened Stone Town's notorious **slave market**, which during the following sixty years traded over a million lives. Shrewd diplomacy with the British – who were increasingly pushing for the trade's abolition – allowed Seyyid Saïd to wrest Mombasa from the Mazrui family in 1827. The sultan also cultivated trading relationships beyond the Indian Ocean: the United States opened their consulate in Stone Town in 1837, and European nations swiftly followed.

In 1841, with the entire East African coast now under his control, and backed by the Western powers, Seyyid Saïd took the unusual step of moving the **Omani capital** from Muscat to Zanzibar, beginning a short-lived but immensely prosperous golden age, bankrolled not just by ivory and slaves, but **cloves** – a shrewd introduction by Seyyid Saïd as Zanzibar accounted for four-fifths of the global output.

Explorers and colonizers

Seyyid Saïd was succeeded by **Sultan Majid**, and after a brief power struggle between him and his brother, the Omani empire was split into two: the Arabian half centred on Muscat, and the vastly more prosperous African one centred on Zanzibar and headed by Majid.

The African half's control of the mainland trade routes made it, and the mainland port of Bagamoyo, logical bases for the European exploration of the "dark continent".

THE RIDDLE OF THE NILE

Africa's Great Lakes – Victoria (Nyanza), Tanganyika and Nyasa – remained virtually unknown outside Africa until the second half of the nineteenth century, when they suddenly became the centre of attention amid the scramble to pinpoint the **the source of the Nile**. This was no mere academic exercise, for whoever controlled the Nile, controlled Egypt.

Yet it was a riddle that had bamboozled geographers and travellers alike since ancient times, when **Herodotus**, the "Father of History", had wrongly stated that West Africa's Niger was a branch of the Nile. Pliny the Elder compounded the confusion with his belief that the Nile had its head in a "mountain of lower Mauritania, not far from the [Atlantic] Ocean", while early Arab geographers didn't help matters by calling the Niger *al-Nil al-Kebir*, meaning the Great Nile.

In February 1858, the English explorers **John Hanning Speke** and **Richard Francis Burton** became the first white men to set eyes on Lake Tanganyika. The impetuous Burton instinctively believed Lake Tanganyika to be the Nile's source, but Speke argued – correctly, it turned out – that the lake lay too low. Leaving behind a grumbling and poorly Burton, Speke headed north, having been told of Lake Victoria by an Arab slave trader. As soon as he reached the shore, where Mwanza is now, in August 1858, Speke was convinced that the quest was finally over.

To verify his theory, Speke returned to the lake in October 1861, accompanied by the Scottish explorer **James Augustus Grant**, and, after circling half the lake, sailed down the Nile in 1863 all the way to Cairo. "The Nile is settled," he wrote in a telegram from Khartoum to the Royal Geographic Society. Many people remained sceptical of Speke's claim, however, while Burton himself continued to insist that Lake Tanganyika was the true source of the Nile. In the end, it took a circumnavigation of Lake Victoria by Stanley in 1875 to prove Speke right. Sadly, Speke didn't live to enjoy his triumph, having died in a hunting accident in 1864.

1811	1841	1842	1848
Stone Town's slave market opened	Sultan Seyyid Saïd shifts the Omani capital to Stone Town, Zanzibar	Kilwa captured by Zanzibar	German missionary Krapf sets eyes on Kilimanjaro

The first Europeans known to have travelled through Tanzania were the German missionaries **Johann Ludwig Krapf** and **Johannes Rebmann**, who in the 1840s tried to convert several tribes to Christianity, without much success. In 1848, Krapf – who considered Africans "the fallen man, steeped in sin, living in darkness and [the] shadow of death" – moved inland to try his luck elsewhere, and became the first European to describe Mount Kilimanjaro (to the incredulity of bigwigs back home, who ridiculed the idea of a snow-capped mountain on the Equator). Hot on his heels came a train of other **explorers** and missionaries, among them such Victorian heroes as Sir Richard Francis Burton, James Augustus Grant, Joseph Thomson, Samuel White Baker and John Hanning Speke. Many of them set out to locate **the source of the Nile** (see p.515), a riddle that had baffled Europeans since Herodotus in the fifth century BC. The search for the Nile's source was not just an academic exercise or vain glory seeking: whoever controlled the Nile's headwaters would control Egypt and (from 1869) the Suez Canal.

The "riddle of the Nile" was finally solved by **John Hanning Speke**, who reached Lake Victoria in 1858, and went on to sail down the great river. The most famous explorers to have graced East Africa though are a duo whose names have become inseparable: the journalist-turned-adventurer **Henry Morton Stanley**, and the missionary-turned-explorer **David Livingstone**. Their famous "Dr Livingstone, I presume?" encounter took place in 1871 at Ujiji, on the eastern shore of Lake Tanganyika (see p.390).

Although Livingstone was careful about how he went around preaching the gospel of the Lord, he was an exception among a motley bunch of missionaries who believed that Africans were primitive and inferior and therefore in need of "civilizing". But with competition heating up between European powers for new markets and natural resources, the supposedly backward nature of the Africans and the handy excuse of wanting to stamp out the slave trade (in which Europeans had freely participated) gave them the perfect excuse to begin the conquest of the continent by force. The **partition of Africa** was rendered official in a series of conferences and treaties in the 1880s, and in 1890 Germany took nominal control of Tanganyika, while Britain grabbed Kenya, Uganda and Zanzibar.

The German conquest of Tanganyika

The mid-1880s were a time of considerable turmoil throughout Tanganyika, with arrival of the militaristic **Ngoni tribe** in the south (see p.448), the expansion of the equally warlike Maasai in the north (see pp.336–337), and increasingly bloody incursions by Zanzibari slavers right across the country from east to west. For most tribes, this period was a disaster, but a handful managed to take advantage of the situation, most famously the **Nyamwezi**. Under the wily leadership of **Chief Mirambo** (see p.406), they took military control of portions of the trade routes, which they used to exact tributes from passing caravans. The tributes financed the purchase of arms, with which Mirambo constructed a short-lived empire between central Tanganyika and what's now Burundi, Rwanda and Uganda.

This turbulent state of affairs should have eased the **German conquest** of Tanganyika, but their problems began the instant they arrived. In 1888, coastal slave traders – who were none too appreciative of Germany's intention to wrest away control of the caravan routes, and levy taxes – rose up in arms. Led initially by a slaver named

1858	1871	1873	1876–81
English explorer Speke reaches Lake Victoria and the source of the Nile	Stanley meets Livingstone at Ujiji, Lake Tanganyika	Abolition of the slave trade	Chief Mirambo controls the caravan routes to lakes Victoria and Tanganyika

Abushiri ibn Salim al-Harthi – who gave the uprising its name, the **Abushiri War** (see p.121) – the conflict dragged on for over a year before the Germans finally crushed resistance. Having "pacified" the coast, German troops headed inland. Central Tanganyika was an easy conquest as Mirambo's empire had crumbled following the chief's death in 1884, but further south the Hehe tribe, under **Chief Mkwawa** (see p.422), were a formidable adversary, which they proved in 1891 by annihilating an attacking German force. Hehe resistance only ended in 1898 with Mkwawa's suicide, but his death signalled a mere lull in armed resistance. In 1905, frustrated by harsh German rule, a vast swathe of central and southern Tanganyika rose up once more in what became known as the **Maji Maji Uprising** (see p.447). Using scorched-earth and terror tactics, the German army (the *Schutztruppe*) took two years to crush the uprising, after which colonization proper began.

Work included the construction of a railway from Dar es Salaam to Kigoma port on Lake Tanganyika, following almost exactly the route of the most infamous of nineteenth-century slave roads. The railway arrived in Kigoma in February 1914, just before **World War I**. Although the war's main focus was Europe, the German troops posted in Tanganyika, ably led by Paul von Lettow-Vorbeck – chief architect also of the genocide perpetrated against Namibia's Herero tribe in 1904–08 – began a guerrilla-style conflict against the British based in Kenya and Zanzibar, and Belgians in Burundi and Rwanda. Lettow-Vorbeck's purpose was not to defeat the numerically superior Allied forces, but to tie down resources that might have been more productively used back in Europe. The strategy worked, and Lettow-Vorbeck's force remained undefeated until 1918, when the Armistice brought an end to the slaughter and forced his surrender.

The British Protectorate of Zanzibar

Sultan Majid's successor, **Sultan Barghash** (ruled 1870–88), inherited vast wealth, but also an empire on its last legs. Barghash must have felt particularly ill-starred: his accession coincided with a devastating **cholera epidemic** that killed ten thousand people in Stone Town alone, and in April 1872, a **cyclone** destroyed all but one ship in Stone Town's harbour (around three hundred in all), and levelled 85 percent of Unguja's clove plantations. These disasters were compounded in 1873 when the British, backed by their all-powerful navy, forced the **abolition of the slave trade** between the mainland and Zanzibar (slavery itself only ended in 1897). Meanwhile, European plans for **the partition of Africa** proceeded at full clip, and Zanzibar's mainland possessions – with the exception of a six-kilometre coastal strip – were taken from it in 1886. Barghash was succeeded in 1888 by his son, Khalifa bin Saïd, but when he too died, just two years later, Zanzibar was declared a **British Protectorate**. The sultanate was allowed to continue in ceremonial capacity, but the real shots were called by the British – quite literally, in August 1896. Two hours after the passing of Sultan Hamad bin Thuwaini bin Saïd, the palace complex in Stone Town was seized by Khalid, a son of Barghash, who, urged on by 2500 supporters, proclaimed himself sultan. The British, who preferred Thuwaini's cousin, Hamud ibn Mohammed, issued an ultimatum that Khalid ignored. At precisely 9.02am on August 27, the **shortest war in history** began when three British warships opened fire on the palace complex. By 9.40am the British had reduced two palaces to rubble, killed five hundred people and forced the surrender of Khalid, who took refuge in the German consulate from where he fled into exile.

1888–90	1890	1891–98	1897
Abushiri War against European presence	Partition of Africa: Germany gets Tanganyika, Zanzibar becomes a British Protectorate	Chief Mkwawa resists German rule	Abolition of slavery

The road to Independence

At the end of World War I, the British were given control of Tanganyika, though the administration remained separate from that of Zanzibar, which was nominally still a sultanate. **British rule** in Tanganyika (1919–61) was relatively benign, and merely picked up where the Germans left off: Dar es Salaam was expanded, as were agricultural towns such as Arusha and Morogoro, and the railway was extended to Mwanza on Lake Victoria. The five-decade British Protectorate over Zanzibar was similarly uneventful, the highlight being the installation of a much-needed sewerage system for Stone Town.

World War II was a major turning point in the history of Tanzania, and Africa. Many East African had been conscripted as soldiers and porters for the British and expected something in return – self-rule, or even independence. Opposition to colonial rule sprang up right across the continent, and with the new world order now dominated by the United States and the Soviet Union change was inevitable. In Tanganyika, the independence movement was headed by **TANU** (the Tanganyika African National Union), founded as the Tanganyika African Association in 1929. From 1954 onwards, TANU was led by **Julius Kambarage Nyerere**, a mild-mannered schoolteacher from Butiama close to Lake Victoria, and graduate of Edinburgh University. Professing a peaceful path to change inspired by Mahatma Gandhi, Nyerere's open-minded and down-to-earth style won TANU widespread support, and the grudging respect of the British, who, faced with the inevitability of independence, saw in Nyerere a figure they could trust. Following a string of rigged legislative elections, in August 1960 mounting tension finally forced free elections for 71 seats of the Tanganyika Legislative Council. TANU won all but one, Nyerere became chief minister, and in that capacity led the move towards **Tanganyikan Independence**, which was proclaimed on December 9, 1961.

BABA WA TAIFA: JULIUS NYERERE

Tanzania's first and still much-loved president, **Julius Kambarage Nyerere**, was born in 1922 to a chief of the small Zanaki tribe in Mwitongo village, near Butiama close to the eastern shore of Lake Victoria. Nyerere was educated at Tabora Secondary School in central Tanzania and at Uganda's celebrated Makerere College, before going on to study history and economics at Edinburgh University. One of Tanganyika's first university graduates, he returned to Tanganyika in 1952 where he became leader of TANU, and succeeded in securing Tanzania's peaceful transition to Independence in 1961 (in contrast to neighbouring Kenya, whose road to freedom was long and bloody). Nyerere's unpretentious, softly spoken and light-hearted style (and wonderful smile) perfectly complemented his political vision of tolerance, courtesy, modesty and non-violence, words that could equally be applied to the nation as a whole. Although Nyerere's economic legacy – the decade-long **Ujamaa** experiment (see p.520) – was utterly disastrous, the one unassailable achievement over his 24-year tenure as president was as nation builder. From 129 different tribes, he forged a cohesive state completely free of the divisive tribalism that has plunged many other African countries into chaos. As a result, Nyerere is affectionately known to Tanzanians as **Mwalimu** ("Teacher") and **Baba wa Taifa** ("Father of the Nation").

Nyerere died of leukaemia on October 14, 1999 (now a national holiday), and is buried in the family graveyard close to the museum in Butiama (see p.373). He ranks with Nelson Mandela as one of the twentieth century's great African statesmen.

1905–06	1918–18	1919–61
Maji Maji Uprising	A small German force under von Lettow-Vorbeck ties down Allied troops in a cat-and-mouse chase throughout East Africa	British rule over Tanganyika

Zanzibari Independence – and revolution

In Zanzibar the situation was more complicated, as there were effectively **two colonial overlords**: the British, who wielded political, judicial and military power, and the Omanis, who owned most of the island's resources, and whose sultans remained heads of state, in name at least.

The first rumblings of **discontent** came in 1948, when African dockers and trade unionists publicly protested against British and Arab domination. Britain eventually allowed the formation of political parties to dispute elections held in 1957. Africans were represented by the **Afro-Shirazi Party** (**ASP**), while the Arab minority supported the Zanzibar Nationalist Party (ZNP). Between 1959 and 1961 a series of increasingly rigged elections gave the ZNP, in coalition with the Zanzibar and Pemba People's Party (ZPPP), disproportionate representation in the council, with the ASP consistently denied its rightful share. Heedless of the rising tension, the British instituted limited self-government in June 1963, and the following month another round of elections was held, which again saw the ASP lose, despite having polled 54 percent of the vote. Nonetheless, Britain went ahead with plans for independence, and on December 10, 1963, the **Sultanate of Zanzibar** came into being.

African resentment of the Arabs, who made up just twenty percent of the isles' population, was barely contained, and on January 12, 1964, four weeks after Independence, **John Okello**, a Ugandan migrant labourer and self-styled "Field Marshal", led six hundred armed supporters in a bloody **revolution**. In one night of terror, some twelve thousand Arabs and Indians were massacred, and all but one percent of Stone Town's non-African inhabitants fled the country. Among them was Zanzibar's last sultan, Jamshid ibn Abdullah, who ended up exiled in England. Okello was merely the spark; the real power was wielded by the ASP leader, Sheikh Abeid Amani Karume, who declared himself Prime Minister of the Revolutionary Council of the **People's Republic of Zanzibar and Pemba**.

The United Republic of Tanzania

As President of Tanganyika, Nyerere's first moves were to promote a sense of national consciousness: Kiswahili was made the official language and was to be taught in every school, while tribal chiefdoms – a potential source of conflict – were abolished. Elections in 1962 overwhelmingly returned Nyerere as President, who in 1963 consolidated his power by declaring Tanganyika a **one-party state**.

The chaos of the Zanzibari Revolution coincided with the height of the **Cold War**, and came shortly after Nyerere had survived an army mutiny, for which he had recourse to the British marines. Feeling threatened by the possibility of extremists taking power in Zanzibar, Nyerere sought to defuse the threat through an **Act of Union** between Tanganyika and Zanzibar, which would give him the power to intervene militarily on the isles. Karume, for his part, was in a quandary, as the exodus of Arabs and Indians devastated Zanzibar's economy, and few international organizations were willing to help a left-wing regime that had come to power through such violent means. The solution was to accept Nyerere's overtures for the Union, which was signed on April 26, 1964, bringing into existence the present **United Republic of Tanzania**. Nyerere became Union president and Karume one of two vice-presidents. Zanzibar retained political

1922	1929	1954	Dec 9, 1961
Julius Kambarage Nyerere is born	Tanganyika African Association (later TANU) is founded	Nyerere takes leadership of TANU	Tanganyikan Independence; Nyerere first President

and economic autonomy, including its own president and parliament, and also gained fifty of the 169 seats in the Tanzanian National Assembly. In spite of these concessions, Karume came to view the Union as a mainland plot to take over the islands, and even now – almost five decades down the road – few people on either side are happy with the marriage.

Ujamaa

As first President of the Union, Nyerere faced huge **challenges**. Tanzania was one of the poorest countries on earth, with just twelve doctors and 120 university graduates to its name. Life expectancy was 35 years, and 85 percent of the adult population was illiterate. The outside world was willing to help, but the inevitable strings would compromise Tanzania's independence. Instead, in February 1967, at the height of an extended drought, Nyerere delivered a speech that became known as the **Arusha Declaration**, in which he laid out his vision of self-reliant, non-Marxist "African socialism": "The development of a country is brought about by people, not by money. Money, and the wealth it represents, is the result and not the basis of development... The biggest requirement is hard work. Let us go to the villages and talk to our people and see whether or not it is possible for them to work harder."

In practice, those noble ideals translated into "villagization": the resettlement of rural households, which accounted for over ninety percent of the population, into collective **Ujamaa villages** – *Ujamaa* being the Kiswahili word for brotherhood or familyhood, meaning "togetherness". Until 1972 resettlement was voluntary, and around twenty percent of the population shifted. This, however, wasn't enough, so **forcible resettlement** started and by 1977 over thirteen million people, or about eighty percent of the population, resided in some eight thousand *Ujamaa* villages.

Unfortunately, the policy was an **economic disaster**. Vast areas of formerly productive land were left untended and the communal system proved to be more fertile for corruption and embezzlement than for agriculture. Yet the policy did have its successes: access to clean water, health care and schools was vastly improved, and by the 1980s adult **literacy** had soared to over ninety percent. Equally important, throwing everyone together in the same, sinking, boat forged a strong and peaceful sense of **national identity** that completely transcended tribal lines, and created a nation of people justifiably proud of their friendly relations with each other, and with outsiders. Tanzania is one of the few African countries wholly unaffected by ethnic or religious conflict, and is unique in having a population that takes pride in both its tribal and national identity.

Depression, collapse and conciliation

By the mid-1970s, Tanzania was in a terrible state. On the mainland, *Ujamaa* bequeathed a **wrecked economy**, and the one-party system and opposition to forced relocation meant that by 1979 Tanzania's jails contained more political prisoners than in apartheid South Africa. Over on Zanzibar, Karume, who had courted the USSR, Cuba and China for help in establishing state-run plantations, had brought about similar ruin but without any sense of unity: the isles remained, and still remain, bitterly divided, the most obvious political gulf mirroring geography, with pro-government Unguja Island and pro-opposition Pemba Island. Karume became increasingly

1963	Dece 10, 1963	Jan 12, 1964
Tanganyika becomes a one-party state	Zanzibari Independence, as a Sultanate	Revolution in Zanzibar, end of Sultanate

paranoid and dictatorial. He deported Asians whom he believed were "plotting" to take over the economy, elections were banned, arbitrary arrests and human-rights abuses became commonplace, and there were even allegations that Karume was behind the murder of leading politicians and businessmen. In April 1972, following two previous attempts on his life, an **assassin's bullet** finally found its mark.

Big changes came in 1977. The economic failure of *Ujamaa* was glaringly apparent, and the same year the **East African Community** between Tanzania, Kenya and Uganda, founded in 1967, was buried when rock-bottom relations with capitalist Kenya closed the border between the two countries. With both sides of the Union increasingly isolated, closer ties seemed to be the way forward. In February 1977, Zanzibar's ASP – under Karume's more moderate successor, Aboud Jumbe – merged with TANU to form the **CCM** (Chama Cha Mapinduzi – The Revolutionary Party), which remains in power today. Nyerere became chairman, and Jumbe vice-chairman.

The Kagera War and the road to change

While relations with Kenya were sour, things were worse with **Idi Amin**'s brutal dictatorship in Uganda. Matters came to a head in October 1978, when Uganda invaded Tanzania's northwestern **Kagera Region**. Tanzania barely had an army worth the name, so it took a few months to train up a force of some fifty thousand men, who responded, assisted by armed Ugandan exiles, with a counter-attack in January 1979. Much to the surprise of seasoned military observers, they completely routed the supposedly better-trained, US-backed Ugandan army, and pushed on to Uganda's capital, Kampala, driving Idi Amin into exile. The war, although brief, was something that Tanzania could ill afford, and the estimated $500-million cost ensured further economic misery back home.

As Tanzania sank deeper into **debt** and finally resorted to international donors for aid, Nyerere found himself increasingly at odds with his socialist ideals. Far from being self-reliant, Tanzania was more dependent than ever. The economy had collapsed, agriculture barely sufficed, and the country was saddled with a crippling debt. In 1985, with the donors demanding economic reforms, **Nyerere resigned**. It was time for change.

The multi-party era

The 1985 elections ushered in a Union government headed by the pragmatic **Ali Hassan Mwinyi**, whose ten-year tenure was characterized by the wholesale desertion of Nyerere's socialist policies. Instead, IMF-imposed capitalist reforms were the order of the day. A condition of donor support was the scrapping of the one-party political system, so since 1995 Tanzania has been a **multi-party democracy**, with elections held every five years. On the mainland people vote for the Union parliament and presidency; on Zanzibar, there are two additional polls, one for Zanzibar's separate executive, and the other for the Zanzibari president. On the mainland, the electoral process has been smooth and, despite media bias in the run-ups, has given little reason to doubt the results, with the ruling CCM and their presidential candidates romping home every time (Benjamin Mkapa in 1995 and 2000, Jakaya Kikwete in 2005 and 2010). A **booming economy**, and a hopelessly divided mainland opposition, should ensure that CCM's winning streak will continue at the next vote, scheduled for end-2015.

April 26, 1964	Feb 1967	April 1972	1978–79
Union of Tanganyika and Zanzibar creates Tanzania	Arusha Declaration launches *Ujamaa* experiment in "African socialism"	Assassination of Zanzibar's President Karume	Kagera War ends Ugandan Amin's dictator Idi bloody reign

Zanzibar's troubles

Things could not have been more different on **Zanzibar**, whose experience of multi-party politics has been marred by bitterly disputed elections, condemnation from international observers, withdrawal of foreign aid, outbursts of violence, political repression, an increase in Islamic fundamentalism, and a whole lot of bad blood between the CCM and their formidable foes, the **Civic United Front** (**CUF**). As heir to the ZNP and ZPPP, CUF favours looser ties with the mainland, even secession, and at one time rather foolishly vaunted the imposition of Islamic sharia law, which lost it the support of Western nations, and most Tanzanian mainlanders.

In 1995, CCM was declared victorious by the slenderest of margins, with 26 seats to CUF's 24. **Salmin Amour** was duly reinaugurated as Zanzibari president, responding to his critics with police harassment and arbitrary arrests, causing around ten thousand CUF supporters to flee and the European Union to cut off aid. As had become habitual with Zanzibar's embattled leaders, Amour claimed that the isles' troubles were being orchestrated by an external "plot", and only after four years of bitter wrangles did CCM and CUF agree to a Commonwealth-brokered reconciliation, known as **Muafaka** – "the Accord". For a while, *Muafaka* gave a glimmer of hope, but the 2000 elections – which saw Karume's son, **Amani Karume,** elected president – were just as divisive, as were the elections in 2005.

The 2010 elections, however, surprised everyone. The result was exceedingly close (the CCM's Ali Mohamed Shein clinched the presidency by just 3500 votes), but, impelled by President Kikwete, the feuding sides quickly agreed on **power-sharing**, in which CUF's leader, Seif Sharif Hamad, became Zanzibar's vice-president. The deal avoided the violence that had plagued previous elections, and – especially in the context of rising Islamic extremism – it is to be hoped that a similar arrangement is put in place after the 2015 elections, continuing to defuse half a century's worth of tensions and distrust.

Economic resurrection

President Kikwete's stars have been felicitous. Despite endemic and deepening corruption, his rule will be remembered for an extraordinary revival in Tanzania's economic fortunes. Since 2008, the economy has been **booming**, and is growing faster by the year, currently at just over seven percent per annum. Part of that is thanks to **China** – the first country to forgive Tanzania's historic debt, and also the principal funder behind a series of ambitious infrastructural projects, including the asphalting of the nation's previously lamentable main roads (most of which are now paved), plans for giant ports, new rail lines and the incessant development of natural resources – including natural gas, due on line in 2020. Ten years ago, to opine that Tanzania might surpass Kenya as East Africa's economic powerhouse would have been a bad joke; now, it's a question of when.

Change can be seen everywhere, and is nowhere more remarkable than in Dar es Salaam, which, in little over a decade, has morphed from a slumbering and quaint seaside city to a jungle of ever-taller high-rises, some of which are well and truly skyscrapers. There's good reason to think that this will continue for some time to come, as China's interest in Tanzania is not just for Tanzania itself, but for its strategic role as a conduit for trade throughout eastern and central Africa.

1980s–1990s	1985–95	1995
Tanzania's economy is in tatters	President Mwinyi ushers in market reforms	Multi-party democracy replaces one-party state; election violence on Zanzibar (also in 2000 and 2005)

Macro-economics and global politics are not the only changes. Tanzania is on track with achieving most of its **Millennium Development Goals**, so, even though 36 percent of the population still lives below the poverty line (considerably less than in Kenya), universal primary education has hiked up the literacy rate among 15–24 year olds to eighty percent, and, possibly related, reduced HIV infection rates among the same age group to two percent, compared with eight percent for 30–49 year olds. Child and natal mortality rates have also halved in the last decade. Of course, the gap between rich and poor is getting wider, and corruption is booming too, but so long as the real purchasing power of common folk – the *wananchi* – manages to keep up with or outpace inflation, there's every reason to believe that Tanzania's transformation from moribund basket case to regional powerhouse can bring benefits for everyone.

1995–2005	Oct 14, 1999	2001	2005–2015
President Mkapa continues market reforms	Death of Julius Nyerere	East African Union resurrected	President Kikwete presides over an unprecedented economic boom

Books

There's woefully little published about Tanzania other than superficial coffee-table tomes waxing lyrically about wildlife or the Maasai. Locally produced books are mostly in Kiswahili, a notable exception being the output of Zanzibar's Gallery Publications (⟨w⟩gallery-publications.net). A handful of other English-language works trickle onto the market each year, mostly self-published collections of fables and proverbs – snap them up wherever you can, as specific titles are often impossible to obtain elsewhere.

Tanzanian **bookshops** are mentioned in the "Listings" sections trailing our town accounts; the best ones are in Arusha, Dar and Stone Town. Gift shops in larger beach hotels and safari lodges usually stock small selections of more touristy titles. Many of the books reviewed below can be bought **online** (try Amazon or ⟨w⟩africabookcentre .com). Books marked ★ are particularly recommended.

TRAVEL AND GENERAL ACCOUNTS

★ **Peter Matthiessen** *The Tree Where Man Was Born* (Harvill, UK/NAL-Dutton, US). Wanderings and musings of the Zen-thinking polymath in Kenya and northern Tanzania. Enthralling for its detail on nature, society, culture and prehistory, this beautifully written book is a gentle, appetizing introduction to the land and its people.

★ **George Monbiot** *No Man's Land* (Picador, UK). A journey through Kenya and Tanzania providing shocking expos of Maasai dispossession and a major criticism of the wildlife conservation movement.

Shiva Naipaul *North of South* (Penguin, UK). A fine but caustic account of Naipaul's travels in Kenya, Tanganyika and Zambia. Always readable and sometimes hilarious, the insights make up for the occasionally angst-ridden social commentary and some passages that widely miss the mark.

COFFEE-TABLE BOOKS

Mitsuaki Iwago *Serengeti* (Thames and Hudson, UK/ Chronicle, US). Simply the best volume of wildlife photography ever assembled.

Javed Jafferji *Images of Zanzibar* (Gallery, Zanzibar). Superb photos by Zanzibar's leading photographer.

★ **Javed Jafferji & Graham Mercer** *Tanzania: African*

Eden (Gallery, Zanzibar). A brochure in book form but stunningly beautiful, with many photos taken from the air.

Javed Jafferji & Gemma Pitcher *Safari Living*; *Zanzibar Style*; *Recipes from the Bush*; and *Zanzibar Style: Recipes* (all Gallery, Zanzibar). Four volumes of stylish eye-candy that should find favour with homemakers.

HISTORY

Little of non-academic nature has been written about the history of mainland Tanzania; most of what's available covers Zanzibar and the Swahili coast. Nineteenth-century works, including those reviewed below, are almost all in the public domain, and can be found online.

Heinrich Brode *Tippu Tip & the Story of his Career* (Gallery, Zanzibar). The semi-autobiographical story of East Africa's most notorious slave trader.

★ **Richard Hall** *Empires of the Monsoon* (HarperCollins, UK). A majestic sweep across the history of the western Indian Ocean.

Christopher Hibbert *Africa Explored: Europeans in the Dark Continent 1769–1889* (Penguin, UK). An entertaining read, devoted in large part to the "discovery" of East and Central Africa.

★ **John Iliffe** *A Modern History of Tanganyika*; *Africans:*

the History of a Continent (both Cambridge UP, UK). The former is the definitive textbook for mainland Tanzania; the latter gives a general overview.

★ **I.N. Kimambo & A.J. Temu** (eds) *A History of Tanzania* (Kapsel, Tanzania). A comprehensive round-up from various authors, and the only one widely available in Tanzania. Ends at *Ujamaa* (1967).

Alan Moorehead *The White Nile* (Penguin, UK/Harper Perennial, US). A riveting Anglo-centric account of the search for the Nile's source, good for a quick portrayal of nineteenth-century explorers' attitudes.

Thomas Pakenham The Scramble for Africa (Abacus, UK/Harper Perennial, US). Elegantly written and exhaustive treatment of a nasty subject; it can seem a bit Eurocentric, but what do you expect from a book about the world's biggest land grab?

Kevin Patience Zanzibar: Slavery and the Royal Navy; Zanzibar and The Bububu Railway; Zanzibar and the Loss of HMS Pegasus; Zanzibar and the Shortest War in History; Königsberg – A German East African Raider (all self-published, ⓦ zanzibar.net/zanzibar/zanzibar_books). Short, informative and well-researched reads. Most are available in Zanzibar or Dar.

Emily Ruete Memoirs of an Arabian Princess from Zanzibar (Gallery, Zanzibar). The extraordinary (true) tale of Princess Salme, who eloped in the 1860s with a German merchant.

Abdul Sheriff Slaves, Spices and Ivory in Zanzibar (James Currey, UK/Ohio University, US). Covers the immensely profitable eighteenth- and nineteenth-century slave trade. Abdul Sheriff is also editor of Zanzibar under Colonial Rule (James Currey, UK) and Historical Zanzibar – Romance of the Ages (HSP, UK).

Gideon S. Were & Derek A. Wilson East Africa through a Thousand Years (Evans Brothers, Kenya/UK). An authoritative round up, including the cultures and traditions of several tribes.

EXPLORERS' ACCOUNTS

Richard Francis Burton The Lake Regions of Central Africa (Narrative Press, US); Zanzibar; City, Island and Coast (Adamant Media, US); and other titles. Entertaining but extremely bigoted accounts of the explorer's adventures, also amusing for the jealous scorn he heaped on his estranged companion, Speke, who really did discover the source of the Nile.

★**Martin Dugard** Into Africa: The Epic Adventures of Stanley and Livingstone (Broadway, US). A compelling, blow-by-blow retelling of the explorers' travels before and after their famous meeting, relying heavily on their own accounts.

Henry Morton Stanley Autobiography of… (Narrative Press, US). Typical self-aggrandizement by the famous, and famously bombastic, explorer. His best-seller, How I Found Livingstone (Epaulet, US), needs no explanation.

Joseph Thomson Through Masai Land (Rediscovery Books). This 1885 blockbuster was the originator of "Maasai-itis". To his credit, Thomson was one of few explorers to prefer the power of friendly relations to that of the gun.

TANZANIA'S PEOPLE

Aside from glossy and usually superficial coffee-table splashes on the Maasai, decent material on any of Tanzania's tribes is difficult to come by, and there's no general overview.

James de Vere Allen Swahili Origins (Nkuki na Nyota, Tanzania). Masterful treatment of a potentially thorny question: exactly who are the Swahili?

★**Jakob Janssen Dannholz** Lute – The Curse and the Blessing (private publication, Germany). Written almost a century ago by a German missionary, this is still the best work on Pare culture and society, both for content, and in its approachable and non-judgemental style. Available in Mbaga, Tanzania.

Gregory H. Maddox (ed) The Gogo: History, Customs and Traditions (M.E. Sharpe, UK/US). Covers most facets of central Tanzania's Gogo tribe, including very detailed histories of separate clans, and song transcriptions.

★**Sarah Mirza & Margaret Strobel** Three Swahili Women (Indiana UP, UK/US). Born between 1890 and 1920 into different social backgrounds, these biographies of three women document enormous changes from the most important of neglected viewpoints.

★**Gervase Tatah Mlola** The Ways of the Tribe (E&D Vision Publishing, Tanzania). Written by a former cultural tourism programme cxoordinator, this is a colourful, very readable and nicely illustrated introduction to the cultures of fourteen northern Tanzanian tribes, with their history, culture and traditions.

David Read Barefoot over the Serengeti (self-published, Kenya). No colonial rose-tint here – the author tells of his early Kenyan childhood and later upbringing in northern Tanzania with his Maasai friend, all in a refreshingly matter-of-fact way, making it a useful resource for Maasai culture, too.

Frans Wijsen & Ralph Tanner Seeking a Good Life (Paulines, Kenya). Religion and society among the Sukuma of northern Tanzania, with a Christian undertone.

THE ARTS

Anon Tribute to George Lilanga (East African Movies, Tanzania). Gorgeously illustrated tome collecting many works by one of Tanzania's leading Tingatinga painters.

★**Busara Promotions** Busara: Promoting East African Music – the First Five Years (Gallery, Zanzibar). Clunky title, great content: reflecting the diversity of the annual Sauti za Busara festival, this is a collection of intelligent and enthusiastic articles, interviews and bios, with great pictures too.

Manfred Ewel & Anne Outwater (eds) From Ritual to Modern Art: Tradition and Modernity in Tanzanian Sculpture (Mkuki na Nyota, Tanzania). Authoritative and scholarly essays on all aspects of Tanzanian sculpture, illustrated in black and white.

★**Yves Goscinny** (ed) *East African Biennale* (Tanzanian Publishers, Tanzania); and *Art in Tanzania* (East African Movies, Tanzania). Gloriously illustrated catalogues for the East African Biennale (formerly "Art in Tanzania"): fantastic and inspiring stuff, from Tingatinga to the brilliant woodcarvings of Bagamoyo's artists.

Uwe Rau & Mwalim A. Mwalim *The Doors of Zanzibar* (Gallery, Zanzibar/HSP, UK). Glossy treatment of those beautiful old carved doors and frames.

★**Ali Saleh, Fiona McGain & Kawthar Buwayhid** *Bi Kidude: Tales of a Living Legend* (Gallery, Zanzibar). Brilliant, intense and loving hagiography of the great Zanzibari singer, compiled from various interviews.

FICTION

Tanzanian novels in English are rare animals indeed, as most popular fiction is written in Kiswahili and books go out of print quickly. The same applies to poetry and folk tales. Strangely, you're more likely to find Tanzanian fiction in Nairobi's bookshops.

A.M. Hokororo *Salma's Spirit* (Nkuki na Nyota, Tanzania). Boy meets girl, except the girl has been dead for three years … An interesting window into the Tanzanian conception of life after death, and witchcraft.

★**Aniceti Kitereza** *Mr Myombekere and His Wife Bugonoka, Their Son Ntulanalwo and Daughter Bulihwali* (Nkuki na Nyota, Tanzania). First published in 1945, this epic novel from Lake Victoria's Ukerewe Island tells the story of a couple's deepening devotion to one another despite the social stigma of infertility. Superbly translated by Gabriel Ruhumbika, a descendant of Kitereza, the descriptions of local life remain as fresh as ever.

Shaaban Robert (tr. Clement Ndulute) *The Poetry of Shaaban Robert* (Dar es Salaam UP, Tanzania). The only English translation of works by Tanzania's foremost poet and writer, with the Kiswahili original on facing pages: a great tool if you're learning the language.

ORAL TRADITIONS AND PROVERBS

Oral traditions (orature) are one of the jewels of Africa, encapsulating every aspect of myth, morals and reality with ogres, strange worlds and lots of talking animals symbolizing virtues and vices – hare is cunning, hyena greedy and stupid, elephant powerful but gullible, and lion

a show-off. Anthologies of transcribed stories are extremely thin on the ground, so buy what you can.

George Bateman *Zanzibar Tales: Told by the Natives of East Africa* (Gallery, Zanzibar). A delightful collection of fables and legends first published in 1908.

★**A.C. Hollis** *Masai Myths, Tales and Riddles* (Dover, US). Collected and translated over a century ago, this is a very welcome reprint of a superb work. Time has done little to dampen Hollis's evident enthusiasm and respect.

★**Naomi Kipury** *Oral literature of the Maasai* (East African Educational Publishers, Kenya). A lovely selection of transcribed narratives, proverbs, songs and poetry.

Jan Knappert *Myths & Legends of the Swahili* (East African Educational Publishers, Tanzania). An entertaining selection of tales similar to stories told across the Muslim world, with strong echoes of the *Arabian Nights*.

★**Joseph M. Mbele** *Matengo Folktales* (Infinity Publishing US). Ably translated tales from Lake Nyasa featuring that lovable trickster the hare, and ever-hungry monsters.

Amir A. Mohamed *Zanzibar Ghost Stories* (Good Luck Zanzibar). Weird and wonderful tales from the isles.

O. Mtuweta H. Tesha *Famous Chagga Stories* (Twenty First Century Enterprises, Tanzania). A short but sweet collection from Tanzania's most prosperous tribe.

GUIDEBOOKS AND FIELD GUIDES

Helpful guidebooks to individual national parks are published by TANAPA in Tanzania, and can be bought locally, and at the park gates. There's also a series of guidebooks for Ngorongoro published by the Ngorongoro Conservation Area Authority.

MAMMALS

★**Richard Estes & Daniel Otte** *The Safari Companion: A Guide to Watching African Mammals* (Chelsea Green Pub Co, UK). Reliable, beautifully illustrated by Otte, and especially detailed on social behaviour, this is one you'll love consulting on safari. Even more detailed but impractical in the field is Estes' *The Behavior Guide to African Mammals* (California UP, US).

David Hosking & Martin Withers *Wildlife of Kenya, Tanzania and Uganda* (Collins, UK). A handy pocket guide for first-timers, with colour photos, is readily available in Tanzania. Covers 475 species, including birds and reptiles.

★**Jonathan Kingdon** *The Kingdon Field Guide to African*

Mammals (Princeton UP, US). Probably the most respected guide, illustrated with drawings and paintings (most of them good), and covering all of continental Africa. It's not too handy on safari, however: for that, get the condensed *Kingdon Pocket Guide to African Mammals* (also Princeton).

Chris & Tilde Stuart *Field Guide to the Mammals of Southern Africa* (Struik, South Africa). Comprehensive coverage, with hundreds of distribution maps and photos, and a decent selection of smaller mammals, too, including bats.

BIRDS

Ber van Perlo *Birds of Eastern Africa* (Princeton, US) Lightweight, compact and comprehensive, but with small illustrations and little in the way of descriptive text.

★ **Terry Stevenson & John Fanshawe** *Birds of East Africa* (Helm, UK). Pick of the bunch for ease of use in the field, with distribution maps in the text itself.

Dale Zimmerman, David Pearson & Donald Turner *A Field Guide to the Birds of Kenya and Northern Tanzania* (Helm, UK). A hefty book with unmatched coverage so long as you're not straying beyond the northern circuit.

SCUBA DIVING AND SNORKELLING

Helmut Debelius *Indian Ocean Reef Guide* (IKAN, Germany). Debelius is a prolific and highly regarded author of marine guides. This catch-all, ranging from East Africa to Thailand, includes over one thousand (superb) photos. Also worth getting are Debelius' and Rudie Kuiter's more specialist IKAN publications, including the weirdly enchanting *Nudibranchs of the World*.

★ **Anton Koornhof** *The Dive Sites of Kenya and Tanzania* (New Holland, UK). A slim and dated but recommended practical guide, especially useful for first-timers, and snorkellers as well.

★ **Matthew Richmond** (ed) *A Field Guide to the Seashores of Eastern Africa and the Western Indian Ocean Islands*. The underwater bible, covering the most common species together with geology, biology, tides, even local culture and fishing techniques. Too big to take with you, though.

Music

With almost 130 tribes, and an open attitude to foreign influences, Tanzania presents a rich musical panorama. On the coast, Arabia and India express themselves through the eclectic blend that is Swahili Taarab, while on the mainland Cuban rhythms underlie the brassy sounds of Dar es Salaam's ever-popular dance bands. The other major musical current, and a huge commercial hit across East Africa, is Bongo Flava, Tanzania's remarkably successful rap scene. The other genre of note, musically often far more sophisticated than the others but now sadly disappearing, is *ngoma* – the catch-all for countless flavours of traditional tribal music.

Traditional music

Music, songs and dance played, and in parts still play, a vital role in traditional culture, not least in providing a sense of continuity from the past to the present, as can be seen in the Kiswahili name for traditional music, **ngoma ya kiasili** – "music of the ancestors". Traditional music is also a cohesive force: *ngomas* involve everyone present, whether as singers, dancers, instrumentalists, or in combination. Often drum-based, *ngoma* (which also means drum) tends to keep to its roots, giving each tribe's output a distinctive quality. The **lyrics**, typically poetry making full use of riddles, proverbs and metaphors, change according to the occasion, and are used to transmit all kinds of information, from family histories and advice to youngsters, to informing newlyweds of the pains and joys of married life, and perhaps seeking the intervention of spirits to bring rain to parched and dusty lands.

Unfortunately, traditional music is **disappearing** as rapidly as the cultures from which it sprung, so it's only in particularly remote areas (untouched by missionaries) where you're likely to come across really traditional music, or festivities. Nonetheless, even the most "developed" tribes, such as the Chagga, still have a soft spot for *ngoma* for events including weddings and baptisms, meaning that so as long you're reasonably adventurous and inquisitive in your travels, you should be able to witness something more authentic than the medleys performed in tourist hotels. Two **traditional festivals** at which music is a constant companion are **Mwaka Kogwa** at Makunduchi on Zanzibar (p.481), which celebrates the Persian New Year, and the Sukuma tribe's often comical **Bulabo festival** at Bujora near Mwanza (see p.362), which is rooted in a nineteenth-century squabble between rival witchdoctors. In southern Tanzania, there's also a fun neo-traditional festival designed to keep the old music alive, Mtwara's **MaKuYa Festival**, held every August (p.178).

If you can't coincide with these festivals, and don't have time to hunt down the real thing, there is one easy way of at least getting to *hear* traditional music. Though the *Ujamaa* period of the 1960s and 1970s destroyed a good deal of the old ways, it also limited airtime for non-Tanzanian music, with the result that sound engineers from Radio Tanzania Dar es Salaam (now the Tanzania Broadcasting Company) set off to record traditional music. The result is a priceless **archive** housed at their headquarters in Dar (see p.112), of which over a hundred recordings – covering almost as many tribes – are for sale.

Technique and meaning

"Call and refrain" is Tanzania's predominant traditional musical style, where a soloist is responded to by a chorus, but far more interesting – often brilliantly so – is the

hypnotic quality characteristic of the musical traditions of Nilotic cattle-herding tribes, and among the more traditional of the Bantu-speakers.

Among the semi-nomadic Nilotes, **multipart polyphony** is the main theme, where each singer or player performs only part of a rhythm (which they're free to embellish, with some restrictions), and which, combined, create a complex overlay of different rhythms, giving rise to what's been dubbed "micropolyphony" (which does funny things to your head) and would be impossible to achieve were there fewer performers, or were everyone playing or singing the same thing. The vibrant, growling throat singing of **Maasai warriors** (*morani*) is a perfect illustration, and were the complexity of the whole not enough, the buzzing of vocal chords is quite entrancing to the singers themselves. The songs are usually competitive, expressed through the singers leaping as high as they can, or bragging about killing a lion or rustling cattle. The **Gogo** (who are actually half Bantu) are equally genial with polyrhythms, more instrumental than vocal, blending orchestras of *marimba ya mkono* "thumb pianos" with single-stringed *zeze* fiddles and sensuously caressing voices to mesmerizing effect (for more on their music, see p.219).

Some Bantu-speaking tribes also possess extraordinary musical talents, including the matrilineal **Luguru**, whose ever so subtle transitions between voices and flutes are simply mind-bending. On the east side of Lake Victoria, lyres are the favoured instruments. The **Kuria** tribe, straddling the Kenyan border, play the *litungu* (or *iritungu*), Africa's largest and weirdest-sounding lyre, whose deep, resonant buzzing provides the hypnotic impetus. Their neighbours, the **Luo**, play the smaller but no less gratifying *nyatiti*, an eight-stringed affair whose resonator the performer also taps using a ring on his toe. In southern Tanzania there are several more excellent musical traditions. The **Makonde** are famed for their insistent drumming (by all-women groups, too), which accompanies the unique *sindimba* stilt dance and other dances using masks – such masquerades are almost completely absent elsewhere in Tanzania. The other big musical area is Lake Nyasa, especially Mbamba Bay, where the **Nyasa** (or Nyanja) compete in a series of musical contests (*mashindano*) held in the "dance season" that follows the harvest after the long rains. The music is quite unlike anything else in Tanzania, with weirdly rasping pipes accompanied by big drums.

All wonderful stuff, but there's a serious purpose to these trance-inducing sounds. **Strident rhythms** in the agricultural work songs of the Luo and Kuria, for instance, keep fatigue at bay, while the intended effects of the ethereal rhythms and intricate harmonies of ritual dances can transport not just the living into a mental limbo, but the spirits of the deceased, too. An astonishing shifting of senses and dimensions can be conjured up at funerals to enable the living to bid farewell to the recently departed, or at initiation time for young men of warrior age, enabling them to come into direct contact with their proud ancestors. The concept underlying all these ideas is **continuity**, the idea that a person is never completely "dead" until forgotten by the living – a crucial concept for understanding the origin and development of many traditional African societies.

Popular music

The heart of Tanzania's live music scene is Dar es Salaam, where dozens of **dance bands** as well as **Modern Taarab** orchestras perform in an ever-changing rota in bars and clubs in the suburbs; some of these bands also tour other towns and cities. As might be expected, **Kwaya** (meaning "choir") can be heard every Sunday in church. To catch other genres, your best bet would be to coincide with a **festival**. Of the contemporary ones, the best, attracting an extraordinary variety and quality of performers from around the Indian Ocean as well as Africa, is Zanzibar's **Sauti za Busara**, held in February (p.470). Also boasting big names is the **Zanzibar International Film Festival**, in July (p.470).

Dance bands

For most people, Tanzania's most enjoyable music is *muziki wa dansi* or *muziki wa jazzi* – **dance music**. It's the longest-established form of popular music in the country, having started in the 1930s when gramophone records were becoming all the rage. **Latin rhythms**, as filtered through the lens of Congo's enormously successful Afro-Cuban dance bands, have had an incredibly pervasive influence on the scene ever since its inception, and styles such as rumba, cha-cha-cha, salsa, soukous, kwasa kwasa, ndombolo and mayemu are recognized everywhere.

The Congolese style reached its apogee in the 1970s, after a number of musicians fled their war-torn country to establish a flurry of extremely popular bands in East Africa. Greatest of the lot, gathering the cream of Congo's expatriate musicians, was Tanzania's **Maquis du Zaïre**, which later became **Orchestre Maquis Original**. But after the death of their charismatic lead singer and saxophonist Chinyama Chiaza, in 1985, the band began to disintegrate. Many of its musicians went off to form their own bands, of which there's only one survivor, **Kilimanjaro Band**, whose arrangements include rhythms borrowed from traditional Tanzanian *ngomas*. Although the Congolese period was dominated by big bands (no relation to US or European "Big Bands"), an individual immigrant that made it big was **Remmy Ongala**, much admired for his powerful political and social lyrics, and driving guitar riffs.

These days, dance band line-ups commonly include several electric guitars and basses, drums, synthesizers, a brass section, a lead singer (usually also a guitarist), and female dancers whose stage antics may leave little to the imagination. Band sizes can be large – anything up to thirty members – a necessity given the almost nightly performances, and all-too-frequent defections of musicians to rival bands. Most bands are known by at least two names: their proper name, and their **mtindo**, or dance style.

Contemporary dance bands

A throwback to traditional *ngomas* and their competing dance societies was the habit of Tanzanian dance bands to come in **rival pairs**. In the early 1980s, Orchestra Safari Sound sparred with Maquis, and at the start of this millennium African Stars was pitted against African Revolution. But the most endearing rivalry was between Dar es Salaam's longest-established bands. The oldest, nicknamed *Baba wa Muzuki* ("Father of Music"), is **Msondo Ngoma**, founded in 1964 as NUTA Jazz (the initials of the trade union that funded them), and subsequently called JUWATA Jazz and OTTU Jazz. Until around 2010, Msondo's output was dominated by supremely fluid guitar licks and rough, brassy horns, and was the most danceable live music to be heard in Dar, but since the death of its older members, the band has moved into the mushier recesses of *Bongo Flava*, much to the anguish of older fans. Still true to the cherished jazz band style though are Msondo's eternal rivals, **DDC Mlimani Park Orchestra** ("Sikinde"), who have been going strong since 1978 when a number of Msondo's musicians defected. Their style is tight, upbeat, cohesive rhythms, blissful harmonies, and famously poetic lyrics.

Also popular, and just as danceable as DDC Mlimani (if not as melodic), are a handful of brash Congolese-style bands complete with raunchy, butt-swivelling dancing girls: **FM Academia** (also known as "Wazee wa Ngwasuma" or, by detractors, as "Wazee ya Bling Bling"); **Akudo Impact** ("Vijana wa Masauti" or "Pekecha Pekecha"); **Twanga Peteta** (African Stars); and **Diamond Musica International** (also called Vijana Classic, formerly Diamond Sound and Vijana Jazz), who you're more likely to see on tour than the others. All play heady, noisy blends of whatever rhythms and styles are currently making waves in Kinshasa.

Taarab and Kidumbak

Taarab is the quintessential music of the Swahili coast, from Somalia in the north to Mozambique in the south. It's actually barely a century old, but has roots stretching way back to pre-Islamic Arabia, Persia and India – a quixotic synthesis easily discernible in its sound. The soloist – in Zanzibar usually female – sings with a high-pitched and distinctly Arabian nasal twang, and is accompanied by an orchestra of up to fifty musicians, often dressed in full European-style dinner suits (the word "*taarab*" derives from the Arabic for "civilized"). The main instruments are cellos and violins (*fidla*), Arabic lutes (*udi*), the Egyptian *qanun* (a 72-string trapezoid zither), reed clarinets (*zumari*; picture a snake-charmer's pipe), and sometimes drums (*ngoma*). Contemporary Taarab orchestras also feature accordions (*kodian*), trumpets (*tarumbeta*), electric guitars and synthesizers, with the latter replacing almost all instruments in so-called **Modern Taarab** groups, lending them a distinctly "Sonic the Hedgehog goes to Bollywood" kind of sound. No coincidence, as Modern Taarab is heavily influenced by Indian movie scores.

The cost of hiring a full Taarab orchestra means it's usually only performed at weddings and other large **social gatherings**, when the poetic lyrics – composed in Kiswahili and laced with Arabic – come into their own. Dealing with love, jealousy and relationships, they're often specially composed, and some songs, called *mipasho*, are specifically requested by one person to criticize or upbraid another. Although the "accused" is never named, his or her identity is easily guessed by the parties involved. Taarab is danced almost entirely by women, who shuffle along in a conga while shaking their bottoms in a rippling movement called *kukata kiuno*, meaning "to cut the waist" – it looks lazy, but drives men crazy.

The more traditional Taarab orchestras are in Stone Town, the main ones being **Malindi Taarab** ("Ikhwani Safaa"), founded in 1905, and **Culture Music Club** ("Mila na Utamaduni"), the largest and most successful, who began life in the Afro-Shirazi Party in the years before Independence. In Dar es Salaam, synthesizer-heavy "**Modern Taarab**" orchestras are all the rage, the main exponents of which are Jahazi Modern Taarab, Zanzibar Stars Modern Taarab and East African Melody.

The cheaper alternative to a Taarab orchestra is the more percussive and dance-friendly **Kidumbak**, unkindly dubbed Kitaarab ("small Taarab") by some, on account of its traditional role as a proving ground for musicians. The usual Kidumbak ensemble consists of just four or five musicians, and includes drums (*dumbak*), and a peculiar bass made from a tea chest, both instruments giving a far more African flavour than

---

THE DOYENNES OF TAARAB

Over the century or so that Taarab has been around, two Zanzibari stars have stood out from the firmament. The first was the hugely influential **Siti Bint Saad**, Zanzibar's first female Taarab singer and also the first to perform in Kiswahili rather than Arabic. In so doing, she did more than anyone else to popularize Taarab across the social spectrum, reaching the peak of her fame in the 1930s and 1940s, when her voice became synonymous with Swahili culture.

Equally beloved, and only recently departed after a career spanning well over eight decades (!), is and was the all-drinking, all-smoking and all-conquering **Bi Kidude** (real name Fatuma Binti Baraka), who began her career in the 1920s under the tutelage of Siti Bint Saad, and continued performing right up to her death in 2013. Like her mentor, Bi Kidude was not afraid to broach controversial topics in her songs, including the abuse of women, and as her fame grew, she did away with the veil that she and Siti Bint Saad had been obliged to wear for public performances. Old age did absolutely nothing to temper her independence, or her verve: she experimented with jazz/dance fusion, graciously collaborated with various Bongo Flava stars, and popularized drum-based *Unyago* (which she played in "hobby horse" style), whose **sexually explicit** lyrics were traditionally reserved for getting girls up to speed at their initiation ceremonies. With her deep, bluesy and mesmerizing (if not exactly pretty) voice, the "little granny", her nickname, was a true giant among African musicians.

The current queen of Taarab, performing since 1990, is **Khadija Kopa**: while the sound is close to Modern Taarab, the lyrics – invariably socially engaged and conversational – are very much in the tradition, and include complaints, critiques, tales of problems not always resolved, and even self-parody, all of which endear her to a legion of fans.

"pure" Taarab. **Makame Faki**, also known as "Sauti ya Zege" (gravel voice), is the main exponent, and performs regularly in Stone Town.

Rap and Bongo Flava

Tanzanian rap and hip-hop have taken the country, and East Africa, by storm. The most popular genre, propelled by ample airtime, is a fusion of rap and R&B known as **Bongo Flava** (*bongo*, meaning "brains", being the nickname for Dar es Salaam and, nowadays, Tanzania). Bongo Flava's massive success single-handedly revived Tanzania's recording industry, and created a film industry, but the commercial focus is often quite obvious, not least when songs are penned in English, and there are also rather a lot of proponents merely mimicking what's on MTV, rarely straying beyond mushy love songs or equally vapid "ghetto" posturing (the current big star, Diamond Platinum, being a fine example). At its best, though, Bongo Flava can be mind-bendingly inventive in its use of samples and computer-generated riffs, and equally inspired in the rhythms of their raps. The most popular acts change on a quasi-monthly basis: you can listen to the latest, and a heap more besides, on the internet: see p.534 for websites. Of the more established acts, ones worth listening to include **Mwana FA** (or Mwanafalsafa, "Philosopher"), for lush backing tracks, and who's more socially committed than his Gangsta style suggests; the similarly "hard" **Fid Q**, with witty lyrics and a musically more eclectic offering than most; the slick, R&B-leaning **Chid Benz**; the cheerfully upbeat **"Sir" Juma Nature**; and, rapping since 1994 (then as "Nigga J" as part of Hard Blasters), **Professor Jay**, who sits comfortably in the rapidly narrowing no man's land between Bongo Flava and purer hip-hop (see below).

If you're into the history of Bongo Flava, the "granddaddies" were Hard Blasters (1989 to mid-1990s), **Kwanza Unit** (early 1990s), **Mr II** (aka Sugu or 2Proud), and, for Bongo Flava's R&B roots, **Afro Reign** circa 1995/96.

All boys so far, but the few girls in Bongo Flava aren't to be outdone, although, as you might guess, the sexy, sassy, soul diva stereotypes hang thick – essentially Tanzanian takes on Mariah Carey. The doyenne is the raunchy **Lady Jaydee**, who favours R&B but whose broad musical palette has seen her collaborate with many other Bongo Flava stars as well as jazz bands, *ngoma* groups, and even Zanzibar's then-nonagenarian wonder Bi Kidude. Currently popular are **Mwasiti**, with clean vocals, a feel-good sound, and who frequently collaborates with male stars; and **Linah Sanga**, smooth and upbeat, chatty lyrics, and a lot of fun.

Far less commercial and more likely to be performed in Kiswahili is **hip-hop**, whose lyrics typically broach thorny social issues such as poverty, AIDS, politics and identity. Sometimes performing with no backing at all, some hip-hop artists have experimented with traditional music crossovers, with some inspiring results. Worth seeking out are the gravelly voiced **Kikosi cha Mizinga**, some great crossover riffs from **Watengwa**, and **X-Plastaz**'s Maasai rap.

Reggae

While popular, **reggae** is woefully under-represented, historically because of government crackdowns on "subversive" ganja-smoking types, and nowadays as it's simply been eclipsed by Bongo Flava. The official distrust of reggae started in Nyerere's time. The story goes that during the celebrations for Zimbabwe's Independence in 1980, Nyerere refused to shake hands with Bob Marley. Come evening, Marley's rendition of *Africa Unite* was persuasion enough, and Nyerere got on stage to make amends, to huge applause. The government gave up hassling Rastas in 1995. **Jhikoman** is the most active performer; also well regarded is **Roots & Culture**, founded in 1983 by Jah Kimbute. **Ras Nas** is the other star.

Kwaya

With its roots steeped in American gospel and European hymns, **Kwaya** ("choir") is perhaps the least Tanzanian of the popular music styles, though if the blaring wattage from mobile tape vendors is any indication, *Kwaya* cassettes far outsell any other genre. The best make superb use of traditional *ngoma* rhythms, vocal power and instruments; the worst, which sadly is a lot of them, use quite awful synthesized loops – no fun if you're stuck on a bus blasting it out. Each *Kwaya* belongs to a church; Sunday Mass is the time and place for catching it live, with luck peppered with fiery admonitions from a crazed preacher.

Discography

Not to toot our own horn, but one of the best compilations for a bit of everything is the *Rough Guide to the Music of Tanzania* (World Music Network). It, and the following CDs, are found easily enough on the internet (ⓦsternsmusic.com has a particularly good selection, most with playable clips), but keep looking while you're in Tanzania, as most recordings – especially on tape – never make it out of the country. A great place to start is the Tanzania Broadcasting Company in Dar es Salaam (see p.112), which has several hundred different cassettes of dance band classics and traditional *ngoma*.

TRADITIONAL MUSIC

Gogo Hukwe Zawose, *Chibite* (RealWorld); Master Musicians of Tanzania, *Mateso* (Triple Earth); *Chants des Wagogo et des Kuria* (Inedit); *Musiques rituelles Gogo* (VDE-Gallo).
Maasai *Rhythm of the Maasai* (ⓦcdbaby.com/cd/maasaipeople).
Sukuma *Tanzania: Music of the Farmer Composers of Sukumaland* (Multicultural Media).
Various tribes *East Africa: Ceremonial & Folk Music* (Nonesuch); *Tanzania Instruments 1950* (Sharp Wood); *Tanzania Vocals 1950* (Sharp Wood).
Zanzibar Imani Ngoma Troupe: *BAPE, Songs and Dances from Zanzibar* (Felmay).

DANCE MUSIC

African Revolution *Maisha Kitendawili* (ASET).
African Stars (Twanga Pepeta) *Mtaa wa Kwanza* (ASET); *Password* (ASET).
Bana Maquis *Leila* (Dakar Sound).
DDC Mlimani Park Orchestra *Sikinde* (World Music Network); *Sungi* (Popular African Music).
FM Academia *Dunia Kigeugeu* (Ujamaa Records).
Mbaraka Mwinshehe/Morogoro Jazz Band *Masimango* (Dizim).
Msondo Ngoma (OTTU Jazz Band) *Piga Ua* (Ujamaa Records); *The Best of Msondo Ngoma* (Ujamaa Records).
Remmy Ongala & Orchestre Super Matimila *Songs for the Poor Man* (Real World/Womad); *The Kershaw Sessions* (Strange Roots); *Sema* (Womad Select).
Various artists *Dada Kidawa, Sister Kidawa – Classic Tanzanian Hits from the 1960s* (Original Music); *The Tanzania Sound* (Original Music); and *Musiki wa Dansi: Afropop Hits from Tanzania* (World Music Network/Africassette).

TAARAB AND KIDUMBAK

Bi Kidude *Zanzibar* (RetroAfric); *Machozi ya Huba: Bi Kidude, Zanzibar 2003* (HeartBeat Records, Zanzibar); *Zanzibara 4: The Diva of Zanzibari* (Buda).
Culture Musical Club *Taarab 1 & 4: The Music of Zanzibar* (Globestyle); *Spices of Zanzibar* (Network Medien); *Bashraf: Taarab Instrumentals from Zanzibar* (Dizim); *Waridi, Scents of Zanzibar* (Jahazi Media/EMI).
Ikhwani Safaa *Taarab 2: The Music of Zanzibar* (Globestyle); *Zanzibara 1: A Hundred Years of Taarab in Zanzibar* (Buda).
Makame Faki Various Zanzibar-published CDs, and, with Kidumbak Kalcha group, *Ng'ambo – The Other Side of Zanzibar* (Dizim).
Various artists *Music from Tanzania and Zanzibar* (3 vols, Caprice); *Poetry and Languid Charm* (Topic/BLSA); *Soul & Rhythm: Zanzibar* (2 CDs, Jahazi Media/EMI); *Zanzibar: Music of Celebration* (Topic).

BONGO FLAVA AND HIP-HOP

Kwanza Unit *Kwanzanians* (Madunia/RAHH).
Lady Jaydee *Machozi* (Benchmark); *Binti* (Smooth Vibes); *Moto* (Smooth Vibes).
Mr II *Bongo Flava* (Kwetu Entertainment); *Sugu* (Social Misfit).
Mwanafalsafa *Unanitega* (Mawingu Records).
Professor Jay *Machozi, Jasho na Damu* (GMC); *Mapinduzi Halisi* (GMC).

X-Plastaz *Maasai Hip Hop* (OutHere Records).
Ray C *Na Wewe Milele...* (GMC Wasanii).

Various artists *Bongo Flava* – Swahili rap from Tanzania (OutHere Records).

ONLINE RESOURCES

Ⓦ **africanhiphop.com** News and reviews of rap and hip-hop across the continent, plus two-hour webcasts (and archive).

Ⓦ **afropop.org** Lots of good features on Tanzanian music.

Ⓦ **bluegecko.org/kenya** Principally Kenya, this site includes dozens of traditional recordings from the Luo, Maasai, Kuria, Makonde and Digo.

Ⓦ **bongoradio.com** Chicago-based Tanzanian internet radio station.

Ⓦ **busaramusic.org** Organizers of Zanzibar's foot-hopping Sauti za Busara festival. Click through to the database for performer bios.

Ⓦ **eastafricantube.com** Heaps of music and video clips, mainly Bongo Flava, making this *the* place to get attuned to the latest.

Ⓦ **natari.com** An amazing resource from a cassette fanatic, with many sound clips (mostly from the heyday of the dance bands), and some tapes for sale, too.

Ⓦ **the-real-africa.com** Hundreds of contemporary videos from Tanzania, plus thousands from elsewhere around Africa.

Ⓦ **tzhiphop.com** Loads of articles, videos and playable playlists they call "joints".

Kiswahili

Kiswahili is the glue that binds Tanzania together. It's essentially a Bantu tongue, enriched by thousands of loan words, primarily Persian and Arabic, but also Hindi, Portuguese, German and English. English is widely spoken in touristic areas, but elsewhere you'll need to learn the basics. Don't worry about getting things wrong: people will be delighted (and no doubt amused) to hear you try.

A recommended **book** is the *Rough Guide Swahili Phrasebook*. There's also an excellent **online dictionary** at ⓦkamusi.org; ⓦtranslate.google.com is handier for quick translations. For **language courses** and tuition, see this book's Index.

Pronunciation

Kiswahili is **pronounced exactly as it's written**, with the stress nearly always on the penultimate syllable. Where an apostrophe precedes a vowel (eg *ng'ombe*, cattle), the vowel is accentuated, something like a gulp.

A as in appetite
AO sounds like "ow!"
B as in bedbug
CH as in China, but often sounds like "dj"
D as in dunderhead
DH like a cross between dhow and thou
DJ as in ginger
E between the "e" in bed and "i" in bid
F as in fan
G as in guide
GH at the back of the throat, like a growl; nearly an "r"
H as in harmless
I as in happy
J as in jug
K as in kiosk
KH as in a growling loch
L as in lullaby; often pronounced "r"
M as in munch; preceding a consonant, it's one

syllable, eg *mnazi* (coconut), "mna-zi"
N as in nonsense; preceding a consonant, it gives a nasal quality
NG as in bang
O as in orange
P as in paper
Q same as K
R as in rough, or rolled; often pronounced "l"
S as in silly
T as in Tanzania!
TH as in thanks
U has no English equivalent; it's the "ou" in a properly pronounced French *vous*
V as in victory
W as in wobbly
Y as in you
Z as in Zanzibar!

WORDS AND PHRASES

GREETINGS AND GENERAL CONVERSATION

Tourists are greeted with Jambo or, more correctly, Hujambo (**"Things"**). If you don't speak Kiswahili, the reply is also Jambo, but if you want to make an effort, reply with Sijambo and continue with one of the following:

News?	Habari?
Your news?	Habari gani?
What news?	Habari yako?
Good morning	Habari za asubuhi
How's work?	Habari za kazi?
How was the trip?	Habari za safari?
How's the day?	Habari za leo?

Reply with:
good/very good	Mzuri/Mzuri sana
clean or pure	Safi
not bad	Sibaya

I show my respect Shikamoo or Shikamooni (when greeting several). Said to elders on the mainland, usually qualified by a title, eg Shikamoo, bibi, for an old woman (reply with Marahaba)

Peace	Salaam, Salamu or Salama
Reply with	Salaam, Salamu or Salama

Good morning	Subalkheri
/ good evening	/Masalkheri (used in Zanzibar)
What's up?	Vipi? or Mambo? or Mambo Vipi?
Reply with	Poa, Bomba, Fresh or Gado

Hello?! (said on knocking or entering) Hodi?! **reply with welcome** Karibu or Karibuni **if replying to several**

What is your name?	Jina lako nini?
My name is…	Jina langu…
Where are you from?	Unatoka wapi?
I am from…	Ninatoka…
May I take your picture?	Ninakwenda kupiga picha?

TITLES

Use the following freely in greetings, and don't be afraid of calling an old lady you've never met before "grandmother" – it's a compliment.

friend	rafiki
child	mtoto, *pl* watoto
mother/father	mama/baba (also an older person)
sister/brother	dada/kaka (also someone your age)
grandmother	bibi/babu (also an elderly
/ grandfather	person)
mister	bwana (lit. "master")
relative	ndugu (also figurative)
sir	mzee, *pl* wazee (respectful)
teacher	mwalimu (also anyone intelligent)

NATIONALITIES

Australia; Australian	Australia; Mwaustralia, *pl* Waaustralia
Canada; Canadian	Kanada; Mkanada, *pl* Wakanada
England; English	Uingereza; Mwingereza, *pl* Waingereza
Europe; European	Ulaya; mzungu, *pl* wazungu
Ireland; Irish	Ayalandi; Mwayalandi, *pl* Waayalandi
New Zealand; New Zealander	Nyuzilandi; Mnyuzilandi, *pl* Wanyuzilandi
Scotland; Scottish	Uskoti; Mskoti, *pl* Waskoti

KISWAHILI PROVERBS

The ability to pepper conversation with appropriate **proverbs** (*methali*) is much admired in Africa, and Tanzania is no exception, the pithier sayings even finding their way onto *kangas* worn by women, to express sentiments that might be taboo if spoken aloud. You might find some of the following useful yourself.

Asifuye mvuwa imemnyea He who praises rain has been rained on.
Atangaye na jua hujuwa He who wanders around by day a lot, learns a lot.
Fadhila ya punda ni mateke The gratitude of a donkey is a kick.
Fumbo mfumbe mjinga mwerevu huligangua Put a riddle to a fool, a clever person will solve it.
Haba na haba, hujaza kibaba Little and little, fills the measure.
Haraka haraka haina baraka Hurry hurry has no blessings.
Heri kufa macho kuliko kufa moyo Better to lose your eyes than your heart.
Heri kujikwa kidole kuliko ulimi Better to stumble with toe than tongue.
Kila ndege huruka na mbawa zake Every bird flies with its own wings.
Kizuri chajiuza kibaya chajitembeza A good thing sells itself, a bad one advertises itself.
Maji ya kifufu ni bahari ya chungu Water in a coconut shell is like an ocean to an ant.
Mchumia juani, hilla kivulini He who earns his living in the sun, eats in the shade.
Mgeni ni kuku mweupe A stranger is like a white fowl (noticeable)
Mjinga akierevuka mwerevu yupo mashakani When a fool becomes enlightened, the wise man is in trouble.
Moyo wa kupenda hauna subira A heart deep in love has no patience.
Mwenye pupa hadiriki kula tamu A hasty person misses the sweet things.
Nazi mbovu harabu ya nzima A rotten coconut in a heap spoils its neighbours.
Penye nia ipo njia Where there's a will there's a way.
Ukipenda boga penda na ua lake If you love a pumpkin also love its flower.
Ulimi unauma kuliko meno The tongue hurts more than the teeth.
Usisa firie Nyota ya Mwenzio Don't set sail using somebody else's star.

South Africa; South African	Afrika Kusini; Mwafrika Kusini, pl Waafrika Kusini
United States; American	Marekani; Mmarekani, pl Wamarekani
Wales; Welsh	Welisi; Mwelisi, pl Wawelisi

BASIC WORDS AND PHRASES

please	tafadhali
thank you	asante (asanteni when speaking to several), or ushukuru, or, on Zanzibar, shukrani
yes/no	ndio/la (or hapana as an adverb)
none, there isn't	hakuna or hamna
maybe	labda
here/there	hapa/hapo
this or these	hii
my or mine	yangu for friend(s) or family (eg mama yangu, my mother); langu (pl yangu) for possessions (eg jina langu, my name); changu (pl vyangu) for objects (eg kitanda changu, my bed; vitabu vyangu, my books)
Really?	Kweli?
bad luck	bahati mbaya
I'm sorry (to sympathize)	pole (usually pole sana I'm very sorry)
I'm sorry (to apologize)	samahani
Excuse me (make room)	samahani kidogo
And the same to you	Na wewe pia
God willing	Mungu akipenda or (Muslim) Inshallah
OK	sawa or sawasawa
No problem	Hakuna matata, Hamna shida, or Wasiwasi
good, pretty, tasty, excellent	zuri
bad	baya
big/small	kubwa/dogo
a lot/a little	ingi/akali
fast/slow	epesi/pole
difficult/easy	zito/epesi
clean	safi

FAREWELLS

Goodbye	Kwaheri ("with blessings"; Kwaherini speaking to several)
Good night	Usiku mwema (when leaving)
Sleep well	Lala salama
Come back again	Rudi tena
We shall meet again	Tutaonana

LANGUAGE DIFFICULTIES

I don't understand	Sifahamu
Sorry, I don't understand Kiswahili	Samahani, sifahamu Kiswahili
My Kiswahili is very bad	Kiswahili changu ni kibaya sana
Could you repeat that?	Sema tena?
Do you speak English?	Unasema Kiingereza?
How do you say… in Kiswahili?	Unasemaje kwa Kiswahili…?

GETTING AROUND

car or vehicle or passenger vehicle	gari/gari ya abiria/
bus/taxi/daladala	basi/teksi/daladala/ bajaj/treni
bicycle	baiskeli
motorbike	pikipiki, bodaboda or motobaiki
driver/mechanic/petrol/oil	dereva/fundi/petroli/ mafuta
boat/ferry/passenger boat	boti/meli/meli ya abiria
dhow	jahazi (large), mashua (smaller), ngalawa (outrigger)
canoe	mtumbwi
plane	ndege
on foot	kwa miguu
bus stop/taxi rank	kituo cha basi/kituo cha teksi
train station	stesheni
port/crossing place (for a ferry)	bandari/kivuko
airport	uwanja wa ndege (lit. "stadium of birds")
Where is the bus station?	Kiko wapi kituo cha basi?
Where are you going?	Unaenda wapi?
Is this the bus to…	Hii ni basi kwenda…
When is the first/last/ next bus to…	Basi la kwanza/mwisho/ jingine la kwenda… saangapi?
When will we arrive?	Tutafika saa ngapi?
ticket	tikiti
I'd like one ticket to…	Naomba tiketi moja ya kwenda…
one-way/return	kwenda tu/kwenda na kurudi

DIRECTIONS

Where is…?	Iko wapi…?
Where does this road go?	Njia hii inakwenda wapi?
the junction for…	njia panda ya…
left/right	kushoto/kulia
up/down	juu/chini
north/east/south/west	kaskazini/mashariki/ kusini/magharibi
signpost/signposts	kibao/kibaoni
straight ahead	moja kwa moja
keep going	twende tu
just there	palepale
wait (or be patient)	subiri
road/streetway or path	barabara/mtaa/njia
roundabout	kiplefti ("keep left", from old English road signs!)
Can I walk?	Naweza kwenda kwa miguu?
slowly/carefully	pole pole/taratibu
quickly	haraka
Stop!	Simama!
How many kilometres?	Kilometa ngapi?
I'm going to…	Ninaenda…
Let's go!	Twende!
I want to get off here	Nataka kushuka hapa
The car has broken down	Gari imevunjika
Safe journey	Safari njema

NUMBERS, TIME AND DATES

¼	robo
½	nusu
1	moja
2	mbili
3	tatu
4	nne
5	tano
6	sita
7	saba
8	nane
9	tisa
10	kumi
11	kumi na moja
12	kumi na mbili
20	ishirini
21	ishirini na moja
30	thelathini
40	arbaini
50	hamsini
60	sitini
70	sabaini
80	themanini
90	tisini
100	mia or mia moja
121	mia moja na ishirini na moja
200	mia mbili
1000	elfu or elfu moja
2000	elfu mbili
1,000,000	milioni

TIME

hour(s)/minutes	saa/dakika
What time?/	Saa ngapi?/Saa ngapi
What time is it now?	sasa hivi?
ten o'clock	saa kumi
ten o'clock exactly	saa kumi kamili
quarter past ten	saa kumi na robo
quarter to ten	saa kumi kasa robo
half past ten	saa kumi na nusu
dawn/morning/midday	alfajiri/asubuhi/adhuhuri
afternoon/evening/night	mchana/jioni/usiku
now/right now	sasa/sasa hivi
not yet/later	bado/baadaye

DAYS AND WEEKS

every day/every week	kila siku/kila wiki
Which day?	Siku gani?
today/tomorrow/	leo/kesho/
in two days	kesho kutwa
yesterday/several days ago	jana/majuzi
Monday	Jumatatu
Tuesday	Jumanne
Wednesday	Jumatano
Thursday	Alhamisi
Friday	Ijumaa
Saturday	Jumamosi
Sunday	Jumapili

MONTHS

this month/this year	mwezi huu/mwaka huu
January	Januari
February	Februari
March	Machi
April	Aprili
May	Mei
June	Juni
July	Julai
August	Agosti
September	Septemba
October	Oktoba
November	Novemba
December	Desemba

ACCOMMODATION

hotel	hotel, nyumba ya wageni, nyumba ya kulala, or gesti
campsite	uwanja wa kambi
Where can I stay?	Naweza kukaa wapi?

Can I stay here?	Naweza kukaa hapa?
reception	mapokezi
room	chumba, pl vyumba
bedroom	chumba cha kulala
room with bathroom	chumba selfu, chumba kwa bafu or chumba self containa
room sharing bathroom	chumba siselfu
I'd like to see a room	Napenda kuona chumba
I want a room for two/three nights	Nataka kukaa kwa usiku mbili/tatu
Where's the bathroom /toilet?	Bafu/choo kiko wapi?
hot water/cold water	maji moto/maji baridi
bed	kitanda, pl vitanda; two beds vitanda viwili
bedsheet/pillow	shiti/mto
towel	taulo
mosquito net	chandarua
table and chair	kiti na meza
television	televisheni
candle	mshumaa
key	funguo or msingi
laundry	ufuaji
firewood	kuni

SECURITY

security guard	askari
danger	hatari (seen on signs)
guard dog	mbwa mkali
thief	mwizi
police/officer	polisi/afisa

HEALTH

I'm ill	Mimi ni mgonjwa
doctor/dentist/hospital	daktari/daktari wa meno /hospitali
pharmacy	duka la madawa (or dispensari)
pain/fever/nausea /headache	umivo or umo/homa/ kichefuchefu/maumivu ya kichwa
medicine	dawa (Western: dawa baridi; traditional: dawa kali)
pills	vidonge
I'm allergic to...	Nina mzio wa...
mosquito repellent	dawa ya mbu
razor/soap/toothpaste	sembe/sabuni/dawa ya meno

SHOPPING

money/shilling/dollar	pesa/shilingi/dola
credit card/travellers'	kadi ya benki/hundi
cheques	ya msafiri
bank	benki
shop	duka (eg duka la vitabu, bookshop)
receipt	risiti
bag	mfuko
What is this?	Nini hii?
Do you have...	Kuna...
May I have/I want/ Give me...	Naomba/Nataka/ Nipe...
I don't want...	Sitaki...
I don't want to do business	Sitaki biashara
What's the price?	Pesa ngapi?, Bei gani? or Shilingi ngapi? (pronounced "shilingapi")
That's very expensive/cheap	Ni ghali/rahisi sana
Do you have something cheaper?	Una chochote kilicho rahisi zaidi?
Do you accept dollars?	Mnakubali dola?
Can you reduce the price?	Utapunguza tena kidogo?
OK, that's fine	Haya, sawa

ANIMALS (WANYAMA)

aardvark	mhanga, pl wahanga
aardwolf	fisi mdogo, pl fisi wadogo
baboon	nyani
bat	popo, pl mapopo
bat-eared fox	mbweha masikio
bee	nyuki
bird	ndege
blue monkey	nyabu
buffalo	nyati or mbogo
bushbaby (galago)	komba
bushbuck	kulungu or mbawala
bush pig	nguruwe mwitu
butterfly	kipepeo, pl vipepeo
cane rat	ndezi
caracal	simba mangu
cat	paka
cow, cattle	ng'ombe or gombe, pl magombe
chameleon	kinyonga, pl vinyonga
cheetah	duma
chicken	kuku (kuku kisasa is battery farmed; kuku kienyeji is free-range)
chimpanzee	sokwe
civet	fungo
colobus monkey	mbega
crocodile	mamba
dikdik	digidigi or dika
dog	mbwa

dog (wild, or African hunting)	mbwa mwitu
dolphin	pomboo, *pl* mapomboo
donkey, ass	punda
duck	bata, *pl* mabata
dugong (manatee)	nguva
duiker	nysa (common), mindi (Abbot's), funo or kiduku (red; *pl* viduku), paa (blue)
eland	mpofu or mbungu
elephant	tembo or ndovu
elephant shrew	sengi
fish	samaki
frog	chura, *pl* vyura
gazelle	swala granti (Grant's), tomi (Thomson's)
genet	kanu
gerenuk	swala twiga
giraffe	twiga
goat	mbuzi
Guinea fowl	kanga
hare	sungura
hartebeest	kongoni
hippopotamus	kiboko, *pl* viboko
horse	farasi
hyena	fisi madoa (spotted), fisi miraba (striped)
impala	swala pala
insect	dudu, *pl* madudu
jackal	bweha
klipspringer	mbuzi mawe
kudu	tandala mkubwa (greater), tandala mdogo (lesser)
leopard	chui
lion	simba
lizard or gecko	mjusi, *pl* mijusi
mongoose	nguchiro
monkey	tumbili
monitor lizard	kenge
oribi	kasia, *pl* makasia
oryx	choroa
ostrich	mbuni
otter	fisi maji
pangolin	kakakuona
pig	nguruwe
porcupine	nungu or nungunungu
rat	panya
ratel (honey badger)	nyegere
reedbuck	tohe
rhinoceros	kifaru, *pl* vifaru
roan antelope	kirongo, *pl* virongo
rock hyrax	pimbi or wibari
sable antelope	palahala
safari ant	siafu
serval	mondo
shark	papa
sheep	kondoo
snake	nyoka
spring hare	kamendegere
squirrel	kindi or chindi
steinbok, grysbok	dondoo or dondoro
topi	nyamera
tortoise	kobe, *pl* makobe
tree hyrax	pelele or perere
turtle	kasa kikoshi (Olive Ridley), kasa mwamba (Hawksbill), kasa uziwa (Green)
vervet monkey	ngedere
warthog	ngiri or gwasi, *pl* magwasi
waterbuck	kuro
whale	nyangumi
wild dog	mbwa mwitu
wildebeest	nyumbu
zebra	punda milia

EATING AND DRINKING

food	chakula
restaurant	hoteli (mgahawa is a very basic one)
street food vendor	mama lisha ("feeding lady"; also baba lisha)
breakfast/lunch/dinner	chakula cha asubuhi/ chakula cha mchana/ chakula cha jioni
table/chair	meza/kiti
knife/fork/spoon	kisu/uma/kijiko
plate	sahani
glass/cup/bottle/sachet	bilauri (or glasi)/kikombe/ chupa/kiroba
a piece of…	kipande cha…
half (portion)	nusu
mixture	mchanganyiko (or nusu nusu for half-half)
enough!	tosha! or basi!
roast/boiled/stewed/ fried/mashed	kuchoma/kuchemsha/ rosti/kukaanga /kuponda
Is there any…?	Iko…? or Kuna…?
I am hungry	Ninasikia njaa
I am thirsty	Nina kiu
Do you serve food?	Kuna huduma ya chakula?
I don't eat meat	Mimi sili nyama
hot/cold	moto/baridi

Enjoy your meal!	Karibu chakula! or Kufurahia chakula!	**Cheers!**	Maisha marefu! ("Long life!"); Maisha mazuri! ("Life is good!"); Afya! ("Health!")
Good food!	Chakula kizuri! or Chakula kitamu!		
		I'd like the bill	Lete bili tafadhali

MENU READER

Except in basic places whose menus are chalked up on blackboards (if they have more than one dish), menus tend to have English translations, or are simple couplets (rice/chips/*ugali*/chapati/*pilau* with beef/goat/fish/prawns/beans): once you learn the words for the basic staples, you're on your way. Particularly notable dishes are mentioned in Basics (see pp.53–54) but there are some things that aren't immediately obvious.

BASICS

achali/kachumbari/ kiungo cha embe	pickle/pickled onion/ mango relish
adesi or **dengu**	lentils
chumvi	salt
haradali/kechap	mustard/ketchup
jibini or **chisi**	cheese
korosho/karanga	cashew/peanuts
mafuta	oil
maharage or **kunde**	beans
mahindi	corn (maize)
mayai…	eggs
… ya kuvuruga/kukaanga /kuchemsha	scrambled/fried/boiled
mkate	bread
mtama	millet
muhogo	cassava
pilipili manga	pepper
pilipili or **pilipili hoho shelisheli**	chilli breadfruit
siki	vinegar
sukari	sugar
wali	rice

MEAT (NYAMA)

figo	kidney
firigisi	gizzards
kiti moto	pork
maini	liver
nyama ya …	Used to describe the type of meat
…bata	…duck
…bata mzinga	…goose
…kondoo	…mutton
…kuku	…chicken
…mbuzi	…goat
…ng'ombe	…beef
…nguruwe	…pork
steki	steak
ulimi	tongue
utumbo	tripe

FISH (SAMAKI) AND SEAFOOD

changu	bream
chewa	rock cod
kaa	crab
kamba	prawns
kamba mtii (or kamba kochi)	lobster
kolekole or **nguru**	kingfish
pweza/ngisi	octopus/squid
sangara	Nile perch

VEGETABLES (MBOGA)

biringani	aubergine (eggplant)
boga	pumpkin
kabichi	cabbage
karoti	carrots
kisamvu	cassava leaves
matembere or **mabamia**	okra (gumbo)
mbaazi or **pizi**	peas
mchicha	spinach
nyanya	tomatoes
nyanya chungu	"bitter tomato", an aubergine used in stews
pilipili mboga	sweet pepper
pombo	green leaves (generic)
saladi	salad
tango	cucumber
uyoga	mushrooms
viazi	potatoes
viazi vitamu	sweet potatoes
vitunguu	onions

HERBS AND SPICES (VIUNGO VYA CHAKULA)

giligilani	coriander
hiliki	cardamom
jira	cumin
karafuu	cloves
kungumanga	nutmeg
manjano	turmeric
mchaichai	lemon grass
mdalasini	cinnamon

mrehani	sweet basil
simsim	sesame
tangawizi	ginger

FRUIT (TUNDA, **PL** MATUNDA)

dafu	coconut for drinking
embe	mango
fenesi	jackfruit
limao	lemon
machungwa	orange
mchekwa, mtopetope or mtomoko	custard apple
mishmishi	apricot
mua	sugar cane
nanasi	pineapple
nazi	coconut
ndimu	lime
ndizi	banana
papai	papaya (pawpaw)
pasheni	passion fruit
pea	avocado
pera	guava
shokishoki	lychee
stafeli	soursop
tende	dates
tikiti maji	watermelon
tunda la kizungu (or tofaa)	apple
ukwaju	tamarind
zabibu	grapes

DRINKS (KINYWAJI, PL VINYWAJI)

barafu	ice
bia (also pombe, busa)	beer
buli la chai/kahawa	pot of tea/coffee
chai	tea
chai rangi/maziwa/masala/ tagawizi	black tea/milky/spiced/ ginger
juisi/juisi ya matunda	juice/fruit juice
kahawa	coffee
kokoa iliyo moto	hot chocolate
maji/maji ya kunywa	water/drinking water
maziwa	milk
mtindi or maziwa mgando	fermented milk (yoghurt, buttermilk)
tuwi	coconut milk
yenye barafu/yasiyokuwa barafu	with ice/without ice

DISHES AND SNACKS

andazi	doughnut (rarely sweet)
ashikrimu	ice cream

biriani	highly spiced dish of meat and rice
biskuti	biscuits
chipsi	chips
chipsi mayai	chip omelette
chop	several possibilities, all with an oily deep-fried batter: hard-boiled egg (egg chop), a short cylinder of meat and other stuff, or even a rib of mutton or chicken leg (chicken lollipop)
halua	an aromatic, super-sticky, super-sweet glob of cooked wheat gluten
kababu	fried meatball
katlesi or kachori	minced meat wrapped in mashed potato
keki	cake (eg keki ya matunda, fruit cake)
kitumbua	deep-fried rice cake
kiwanda	omelette
mahindi	maize cob
mantabali	"Zanzibari pizza", suppos- edly stuffed chapati but can be almost anything
matoke	banana stew
mchuzi	stew, sauce or curry
mishkaki or mishikaki	a little skewer of grilled meat, usually beef or goat
mtori	a light banana soup (Moshi and westwards)
nyama choma	char-grilled meat (goat is best), traditionally accompanied by grilled bananas (*ndizi*) and chilli
pilau	rice spiced with cardamom, cinnamon, cloves and pepper, and whatever else comes to hand
pweza na nazi	octopus simmered in coconut sauce – a Zanzibari favourite
sambusa	samosa (triangle of pastry, usually stuffed with minced meat, onion and pepper, sometimes just potato)

supu
literally soup, in local places this is a spicy broth (usually goat or beef, supu ya mbuzi/ ng'ombe) served with lemon and chilli, and eaten at breakfast along with chapatis. Supu ya makongoro is with animal hooves, supu ya

utumbo is with intestines

ugali
Tanzania's staple, a stodgy cornmeal polenta usually served with a small bowl of stewed fish, meat or vegetables

uji
porridge; traditionally made from finger millet (*uji wa ulezi*)

Glossary

Afrika ya Mashariki East Africa
askari security guard or soldier
banda, *pl* **mabanda** any kind of hut, usually rectangular and with a sloping thatched roof
bao a chess-like board game
baraza stone bench, a sitting or meeting place
boma semi-permanent settlement formed around protective cattle corrals, especially Maasai; also German-era colonial headquarters
boriti mangrove poles used in building
buibui the black cover-all cloak and veil of Muslim women
chai a bribe (literally "tea")
choo toilet (gents **wanaume**, ladies **wanawake**)
chuo kikuu university
imamu Imam, a mosque's prayer-leader
fly catcher tourist tout (called *papasi* on Zanzibar)
jengo, *pl* **majenjo** building
kabila, *pl* **makabila** tribe
kanga or **khanga** printed cotton sheet incorporating a proverb, worn by women
kanisa church
kanzu man's long robe (Muslim areas)
kaskazi northeast monsoon (Dec–March)
kitabu book
kitenge, *pl* **vitenge** double-paned cotton cloth
kofia man's embroidered cap (Muslim areas)
kopje a low, eroded granite outcrop, a feature of the Serengeti
korongo ditch or ravine
kusi southwest monsoon (June–Sept)

makuti palm-leaf thatch, used for roofing
malaya prostitute (easily confused with *malaika*, angel…)
mbuga black cotton soil, impassable by motor vehicles in rains
mgahawa small restaurant
mihrab prayer niche set in a mosque's *qibla*, the wall facing Mecca
msikiti mosque
mtaa ward or neighbourhood; street
Mungu God
murram red clay and gravel road
mzungu, *pl* **wazungu** European or white person
ngoma dance, drum, music, celebration (*ngoma ya kiasili* traditional music)
panga machete or knife
posta post office
rondavel round hut or cottage, often thatched
safari any journey
semadari traditional Zanzibari four-poster bed
serikali government
shamba farm
shisha water pipe
shuka red robe worn by Maasai men
shule school (mainland)
simu telephone
skuli school (Zanzibar)
soko, soko kuu market, main market
tembe flat-roofed hut, common in central Tanzania
ubalozi embassy, consulate
utalii tourism

Small print and index

A ROUGH GUIDE TO ROUGH GUIDES

Published in 1982, the first Rough Guide – to Greece – was a student scheme that became a publishing phenomenon. Mark Ellingham, a recent graduate in English from Bristol University, had been travelling in Greece the previous summer and couldn't find the right guidebook. With a small group of friends he wrote his own guide, combining a highly contemporary, journalistic style with a thoroughly practical approach to travellers' needs.

The immediate success of the book spawned a series that rapidly covered dozens of destinations. And, in addition to impecunious backpackers, Rough Guides soon acquired a much broader readership that relished the guides' wit and inquisitiveness as much as their enthusiastic, critical approach and value-for-money ethos.

These days, Rough Guides include recommendations from budget to luxury and cover more than 120 destinations around the globe, as well as producing an ever-growing range of ebooks.

Visit **roughguides.com** to find all our latest books, read articles, get inspired and share travel tips with the Rough Guides community.

ABOUT THE AUTHOR

Africa was love at first sight for Jens Finke… an unplanned bicycle ride that saw him huff and puff (and sometimes walk) across the Sahara in 1988, en route from Manchester to The Gambia. His book, *Chasing the Lizard's Tail*, describes the journey. Apart from a scatter of other Rough Guides, he's also the author of the Traditional Music & Cultures of Kenya website at www.bluegecko.org. When not examining long-drops for a living, he can be found under a virtual mountain of digital manuscripts and incunabula relating to portolan charts of Africa.

Rough Guide credits

Editors: Eleanor Aldridge and Amanda Tomlin
Layout: Ankur Guha
Cartography: Swati Handoo
Picture editors: Raffaella Morini and Michelle Bhatia
Proofreader: Susannah Wight
Managing editor: Keith Drew
Assistant editor: Payal Sharotri
Production: Nicole Landau

Cover design: Nicole Newman, Dan May, Roger Mapp and Ankur Guha
Editorial assistant: Rebecca Hallett
Senior pre-press designer: Dan May
Programme manager: Gareth Lowe
Publisher: Joanna Kirby
Publishing director: Georgina Dee

Publishing information

This fourth edition published July 2015 by
Rough Guides Ltd,
80 Strand, London WC2R 0RL
11, Community Centre, Panchsheel Park,
New Delhi 110017, India
Distributed by Penguin Random House
Penguin Books Ltd,
80 Strand, London WC2R 0RL
Penguin Group (USA)
345 Hudson Street, NY 10014, USA
Penguin Group (Australia)
250 Camberwell Road, Camberwell,
Victoria 3124, Australia
Penguin Group (NZ)
67 Apollo Drive, Mairangi Bay, Auckland 1310,
New Zealand
Penguin Group (South Africa)
Block D, Rosebank Office Park, 181 Jan Smuts Avenue,
Parktown North, Gauteng, South Africa 2193
Rough Guides is represented in Canada by Tourmaline
Editions Inc. 662 King Street West, Suite 304, Toronto,
Ontario M5V 1M7
Printed in Singapore

© Rough Guides, 2015
Maps © Rough Guides
No part of this book may be reproduced in any form
without permission from the publisher except for the
quotation of brief passages in reviews.
560pp includes index
A catalogue record for this book is available from the
British Library
ISBN: 978-1-40935-486-4
The publishers and authors have done their best to ensure
the accuracy and currency of all the information in
The Rough Guide to Tanzania, however, they can accept
no responsibility for any loss, injury, or inconvenience
sustained by any traveller as a result of information or
advice contained in the guide.
1 3 5 7 9 8 6 4 2

Help us update

We've gone to a lot of effort to ensure that the fourth edition of **The Rough Guide to Tanzania** is accurate and up-to-date. However, things change – places get "discovered", opening hours are notoriously fickle, restaurants and rooms raise prices or lower standards. If you feel we've got it wrong or left something out, we'd like to know, and if you can remember the address, the price, the hours, the phone number, so much the better.

Please send your comments with the subject line "**Rough Guide Tanzania Update**" to ✉ mail @uk.roughguides.com. We'll credit all contributions and send a copy of the next edition (or any other Rough Guide if you prefer) for the very best emails.

Find more travel information, connect with fellow travellers and plan your trip on ⊕ roughguides.com.

Acknowledgements

Many people have helped me out with this edition, for which I'm grateful. Especial thanks go to Amiri Saidi Sheghembe, Berrums Mwaijengo, Charles Nkuba, Gloria Munhambo, Hyasintha and Bona and the kids, the indefatigable Innocent, Joas Kahembe, Madaraka Nyerere, Michelle Bragg, Simon King, Wilfred Mirambo, and Yohana Tumaini Ladislaus, all in Tanzania; also my editors Eleanor Aldridge and Amanda Tomlin; and, back home, Maria Helena Moura Pinheiro.

Readers' updates

Thanks to all the readers who have taken the time to write in with comments and suggestions (and apologies if we've inadvertently omitted or misspelt anyone's name):

Elizabeth Arend, Richard Blindell, Siska D'hoore, Martin Lind, Karoli Nyalali, Tarun Mistry, Suzanne Swift, Alice Rayner, Jose Rocha, Brecht De Vos, Stacey Wilkinson

Photo credits

p.1 Getty Images/Tore Thiis Fjeld/Flickr RF
p.2 Alamy Images/PhotoStock-Israel
p.4 Getty Images/Altrendo
p.5 Getty Images/Christophe Paquignon
p.9 Corbis/Nick Ledger/AI (b); Getty Images/Daniel Hayduk/AFP (t)
p. 10 Alamy Images/Michele Burgess (t); Robert Harding Picture Library (b)
p. 12 Getty Images/Moment Open
p.13 Corbis/Olivier Goujon/Robert Harding World Imagery (t); Corbis/Tom Brakefield (b); Latitude/LOOK (c)
p.14 Corbis/Amyn Nasser (t); Corbis/Erich Schmidt/imageBROKER (b)
p.15 Alamy Images/Eyal Bartov (bl); Alamy Images/Ulrich Doering (tr); Getty Images/Farley Baricuatro (www.colloidfarl.blogspot.com)/Flickr RF (tl); Getty Images/Flickr Vision/BOAZ ROTTEM (br)
p.16 Alamy Images/Chris Whiteman (t); Corbis/167/Jason Edwards/National Geographic RF/Ocean (c); Corbis/Nigel Pavitt/JAI (b)
p.17 Corbis/Franz-Marc Frei (t); Getty Images/Michele D'Amico supersky77/Flickr Open (b)
p.18 Corbis/Winfried Wisniewski
p.21 naturepl.com/Andy Rouse (tr); naturepl.com/Anup Shah (tl, c, r); naturepl.com/Ole Jorgen Liodden (bl)
p.23 Corbis/James Hager/Robert Harding World Imagery (bl); Getty Images/Joe McDonald (cra); naturepl.com/Charlie Summers (clb); naturepl.com/Laurent Geslin (cla); naturepl.com/Nick Garbutt; naturepl.com/Ole Jorgen Liodden (tl); naturepl.com/Christophe Courteau (crb); naturepl.com/Peter Blackwell (br); naturepl.com/Jabruson (tr)
p.25 naturepl.com/Andy Rouse (t); naturepl.com/Anup Shah (c, bl, br)
p.27 Alamy Images/Images of Africa Photobank (bc); Getty Images/Manoj Shah (clb); Getty Images/Roger de la Harpe (cr); Getty Images/Sue Flood (tr); naturepl.com/Andy Rouse (cla); naturepl.com/Anup Shah (tl, br, bl); Visuals Unlimited (cra)
p.29 naturepl.com/Tony Heald (cla, bl, br); naturepl.com/T.J. Rich (tl); naturepl.com/Peter Blackwell (cra); naturepl.com/Richard Du Toit (crb); naturepl.com/Paul Hobson (tr)
p.31 Getty Images/Martin Harvey (tr); naturepl.com/Ann & Steve Toon (br); naturepl.com/Bernard Castelein (bl, c); naturepl.com/Anup Shah (cla, tl, cr)
p.33 naturepl.com/Anup Shah (br); naturepl.com/Roland Seitre (cl); naturepl.com/Pete Oxford (tr); naturepl.com/Rod Williams (tl); naturepl.com/Nick Garbutt (cr); Robert Harding Picture Library/Ronald Wittek (bl)
p. 35 Corbis/David A. Northcott (b, cr); Corbis/First Light/Thomas Kitchin Victoria Hurst (cl); Corbis/Photononstop/Frederic Soreau (tl); Corbis/Nature Picture Library/Michael D. Kern (tr)
p.37 Alamy Images/Nick Biemans (br); Corbis/George D. Lepp (cra, clb); Corbis/Michal Bednarek/incamerastock (tl); naturepl.com/Charlie Summers (cla); naturepl.com/Guy Edwardes (tr); naturepl.com/Edwin Giesbers (ca); Robert Harding Picture Library/Annie Katz (bl)

p. 39 Corbis/167/Kelley Miller/Ocean (cr); Getty Images/Nigel Pavitt (c); Robert Harding Picture Library/Ann & Steve Toon (tr); Robert Harding Picture Library/James Hager (tl); Robert Harding Picture Library/Uwe Skrzypczak (cl); Robert Harding Picture Library/Okapia (bl); Robert Harding Picture Library/Ignacio Palacios (cb); TipsImages/Reinhard Dirscherl (br)
p.41 Corbis/Stephen Frink (cla, tl, tr, bl); Getty Images/Gerard Soury (br); Kristen Elsby/esthet photography (cb). Robert Harding Picture Library/imageBROKER (cra)
p.42 Getty Images/Nigel Pavitt/AWL Images
pp.82–83 Alamy Images/Charles O. Cecil
p.85 Corbis/A3534/_Michael Hanschke/dpa
pp.114–115 Dreamstime.com/Alextara
p.117 Corbis/Nigel Pavitt/JAI
pp.148–149 4Corners/Aldo Pavan/SIME
p.151 ADEA/MaKuYa
p.179 Corbis/Gideon Mendel (b); Corbis/Nigel Pavitt/JAI (t)
pp.188–189 AWL Images/Will Gray
p.191 Corbis/Nigel Pavitt/JAI
p.209 Getty Images/Rieger Bertrand/Hemis.fr
pp.230–231 Dreamstime.com/Svetlana485
p.233 Corbis/Nigel Pavitt/JAI
p.255 Alamy Images/Bert Hoferichter (br); Getty Images/Johnathan Ampersand Esper/Aurora Creative (t)
pp.276–277 Alamy Images/Kuttig-Travel-2
p.279 Alamy Images/Sabena Jane Blackbird
pp.308–309 AWL Images/Ivan Vdovin
p.311 Alamy Images/imageBROKER
p.320 Dreamstime.com/Moizhusein (b)
p.321 Corbis/Gerry Ellis/Minden Pictures (t)
p.345 Alamy Images/Ulrich Doering
pp.354–355 Getty Images/Danita Delimont/Gallo Images
p.357 Alamy Images/MJ Photography
pp.382–383 Alamy Images/John Warburton-Lee Photography
p.385 Corbis/Olivier Goujon/Robert Harding World Imagery
p.397 Alamy Images/Sue Cunningham Photographic (t, bl); Corbis/Ingo Arndt/Minden Pictures (br)
pp.414–415 Dreamstime.com/Blossfeldia
p.417 Getty Images/Nigel Pavitt/AWL Images
p.435 Alamy Images/Maciej Dakowicz (b); Getty Images/Nigel Pavitt/AWL Images (t)
pp.450–451 Getty Images/Federic Soreau/Photononstop
p.453 Corbis/Bob Krist
p.477 Corbis/Nigel Pavitt/JAI (tr); Getty Images/Michael Heffernan (tl)
pp.505–506 Alamy Images/age fotostock Spain, S.L.
p.505 Getty Images/Nigel Pavitt/AWL Images
p.510 Corbis/Mandy Glinsbockel/Demotix

Front cover & spine Herd of Blue Wildebeest © SuperStock/Uwe Skrzypczakimageb
Back cover A Maasai at Lake Natron © Corbis/Franck Guiziou (t); Dhow, Zanzibar © AWL Images/Paul Harris (br); Ol Doinyo Lengai © Corbis/Nigel Pavitt/JAI (bl)

Index

Maps are marked in **grey**

Map symbols

The symbols below are used on maps throughout the book

Main road		Place of interest		Mountain range		Mosque
Minor road		Museum		Mountain peak		Hindu temple
Motorway		Lighthouse		Cave		Sikh temple
Pedestrianised road		Viewpont		Swamps		Christian Cemetery
Steps		Statue		Crater		Muslim Cemetery
Unpaved road		Campsite		Gorge		Park
Railway		Bridge		Hill		Beach
Footpath		Ruins		Waterfall		Mangrove swamp
Ferry		Fountain		Reef		Coral reef
International airport		Mountain refuge		Spring		Coconut plantation
Domestic airport		Ranger station		Beach (regional)		Mango tree
Parking		Gate		Arch		
Toilets		Swimming pool		Dam		
Post office		Golfcourse		Building		
Information centre		Fuel		Church		
Telephone office		Hospital		Market		
Internet access		Bus stop		Stadium		

Listings key

- Accommodation
- Eating and drinking
- Nightlife
- Shopping

Tanzanian Horizons is a collection of small, unique lodges and camps in Northern Tanzania.

The emphasis is on experiencing the Tanzanian wilderness without the crowds.
Each camp and lodge is located in an area of exceptional natural beauty and wildlife experiences,
whether it is elephants tearing trees apart outside your room at Boundary Hill,
or flamingos and pelicans on the lake shore at Ol Tukai.
Walking in the acacia and boabab forests of Naitolia tracking giraffe,
or a night drive looking for porcupines,
bat eared foxes and the elusive nocturnal cats.

Tanzanian Horizons

Tanzanian Horizons

Each lodge and camp has been designed with the emphasis on the environment and how we and
your visitors can experience the beauty of Tanzania, without leaving any impact.

In fact Boundary Hill Lodge is the only lodge in Tanzania that has been recognized as an eco-lodge.
Whereas other lodges have been given "star" ratings by the Ministry of Tourism,
Boundary Hill was recognized as unique, and a new rating system for eco-lodges is now being
developed.

Why not let your clients and guests experience what we think are some of the
most unique and finest wildlife lodges and camps in Tanzania.

www.tanzanianhorizons.com
info@tanzanianhorizons.com

tanzanian horizons
camps and lodges